HOW TO PREPARE FOR THE SCHOLASTIC APTITUDE TEST

SAT*

FOURTEENTH EDITION

D0473821

SAMUEL C. BROWNSTEIN
Formerly Chairman Science Department
George W. Wingate High School, Brooklyn, N.Y.

MITCHEL WEINER
Formerly Member, Department of English
James Madison High School, Brooklyn, N.Y.

SHARON WEINER GREEN
Instructor in English
Merritt College, Oakland, California

* "Scholastic Aptitude Test" and "SAT" are registered trademarks of the College Entrance Examination Board. This book was prepared by Barron's Educational Series, Inc., which is solely responsible for its contents. It is not endorsed by any other organization.

BARRON'S

New York • London • Toronto • Sydney

The SAT questions on pages 11–20 (40 verbal questions, 30 math questions, 6 TSWE questions) were selected from *10 SATs, 5 SATs,* and *Taking the SAT.* College Entrance Examination Board, 1986. Reprinted by permission of Educational Testing Service, the copyright owner of the sample questions.

Permission to reprint the SAT material does not constitute review or endorsemesnt by Educational Testing service or the Collegè Board of this publication as a whole or of any other testing information it may contain.

The authors gratefully acknowledge the following copyright holders for permission to reprint material used in reading passages:
Page 34: From *Black Boy* by Richard Wright. Copyright 1937, 1942, 1944, 1945, by Richard Wright, Reprinted by permission of Harper & Row Publishers, Inc.

Page 50: Passage from *Civilization* by Kenneth Clark. © 1969 Harper & Row, Publishers, Inc. Reprinted with permission.

Page 140: *Sculpture/Inuit,* © 1971. Reproduced with permission of the Canadian Eskimo Arts Council.

Pages 143–44: From *Silent Spring* by Rachel Carson. Copyright 1962 by Rachel L. Carson. Reprinted by permission of Houghton Mifflin Company.

Page 144: From ''Introduction' by Leal, Antonio Castro, to *Twenty Centuries of Mexican Art,* Museum of Modern Art, 1940. Reprinted with permission.

Pages 147–48: Ladislas Segy ''African Sculpture'' Dover Publications, New York 1958.

Pages 153–54: From *Asians in America: Filipinos, Koreans, and East Indians* by H. Brett Melendy, © 1977. Reprinted with permission by G.K. Hall & Co., Boston.

Page 411: From *Song from the Earth: American Indian Painting* by Jamake Highwater. Copyright © 1976 by Jamake Highwater. By permission of Little, Brown and Company. A New York Graphic Society Book.

Page 474: From *From Slavery to Freedom: A History of Negro Americans,* by John Hope Franklin, © 1947 by Alfred A. Knopf, Inc. Reprinted by permission of the publisher.

Page 515: From *The Hunger of Memory* by Ricardo Rodriguez. Copyright © 1983 by Ricardo Rodriguez. Reprinted by permission of David R. Godine, Publishers, Boston.

Page 531: William Faulkner, ''A Rose for Emily,'' © 1930 and renewed 1958 by William Faulkner. Reprinted from *Collected Stories of William Faulkner* by William Faulkner, by permission of Random House, Inc.

Page 563: From *The Indian in America* by Wilcomb E. Washburn, copyright © 1975 by Wilcomb E. Washburn. Reprinted by permission of Harper & Row Publishers, Inc.

Pages 630–31: Excerpted from ''Learning by Instinct,'' by James L. Gould and Peter Marler, *Scientific American,* January 1987. Copyright © 1987 by Scientific American, Inc. All rights reserved.

Page 675: Excerpted from ''Hot Spots on the Earth's Surface,'' by Kevin C. Burke and J. Tuzo Wilson, *Scientific American,* August 1976. Copyright © 1976 by Scientific American, Inc. All rights reserved.

All inquiries should be addressed to:
Barron's Educational Series, Inc.
250 Wireless Boulevard
Hauppauge, NY 11788

Library of Congress Catalog Card No. 87-18845

Cloth International Standard Book No. 0-8120-5908-5
Paper International Standard Book No. 0-8120-3844-4

Library of Congress Cataloging-in-Publication Data

Brownstein, Samuel C.
  How to prepare for the scholastic aptitude test: SAT.

  1. Scholastic aptitude test—Study guides. I. Weiner, Mitchel. II. Green, Sharon. III. Title.
LB2353.57.B765 1987   378'.1664   87-18845
ISBN 0-8120-3844-4

PRINTED IN THE UNITED STATES OF AMERICA

789   100   98765432

Contents

PART ONE

Organize Your Study Plan

PART TWO

Pinpoint Your Trouble Spots

PART THREE

Tactics, Strategies, Practice

Verbal

Mathematics

TSWE

PART FOUR

Test Yourself

PART FIVE

Organize Your Admissions Game Plan

Preface

Welcome to the Fourteenth Edition of *Barron's How to Prepare for the SAT.* More than thirty years ago the appearance of the First Edition of this book marked the opening of a long-term campaign to give *all* students—not just those able to afford the fees of private preparatory schools—a better chance to gain admission to the nation's most prestigious universities. Based on the authors' experience as founders of New York's College Entrance Tutoring Service, this book provided a wealth of comprehensive review materials and updated study techniques for all those who sought that better chance.

Today's Fourteenth Edition contains the best features of that ground-breaking First Edition and much, much more.

It takes you step by step through dozens of verbal and mathematical questions from actual published SATs, showing you how to solve them and how to avoid going wrong.

It offers you dozens of clear-cut Testing Tactics (illustrated with questions from current SATs) and shows you how to use them to attack every question type you will find on the SAT.

It pinpoints specific sources of SAT reading passages, naming authors and books and magazines, and provides a college-level reading list that can guide you to these works and more.

It gives you the *newly-revised* 320-word High-Frequency Word List, 320 words from *abstract* to *zealot* that have been shown by computer analysis to occur and reoccur on actual published SATs, plus Barron's 3,500 Basic Word List, your best chance to acquaint yourself with the whole range of college-level vocabulary you will face on the SAT.

No other book offers you as much. No other book analyzes as many actual SAT questions.

This Fourteenth Edition is a sign of Barron's ongoing commitment to make this publication America's outstanding SAT study guide. It has benefited greatly from the research that went into developing our award-winning *Computer Study Program for the SAT.* Even more, it has benefited from the dedicated labors of the editorial staff of Barron's, and in particular from the work of Judy Makover, to whom the authors give their sincere thanks.

TIMETABLE FOR THE SAT*   Total Time: 3 Hours

9:00 to 9:30	Section 1	**Verbal**	15 Antonym Questions 10 Analogy Questions	10 Sentence Completion Questions 10 Reading Comprehension Questions
9:30 to 10:00	Section 2	**Mathematics**	25 Standard Multiple-Choice Questions	
10:00 to 10:05			Break	
10:05 to 10:35	Section 3	**Test of Standard Written English**	35 Usage Questions 15 Sentence Correction Questions	
10:35 to 11:05	Section 4	**Verbal**	10 Antonym Questions 10 Analogy Questions	5 Sentence Completion Questions 15 Reading Comprehension Questions
11:05 to 11:10			Break	
11:10 to 11:40	Section 5	**Mathematics**	15 Standard Multiple-Choice Questions 20 Quantitative Comparison Questions	
11:40 to 12:10	Section 6	**Verbal** (40 or 45 Questions) or **Mathematics** (25 or 35 Questions) or **Test of Standard Written English** (50 Questions)		

*Actual times will vary in accordance with the time the proctor takes to complete the preliminary work and begin the actual test. Format and timing are subject to change.

SAT TEST DATES

Test Dates		Registration Deadlines	
National	**New York State**	**Regular**	**Late**
*October 10,1987		September 18, 1987	September 30, 1987
November 7, 1987	November 7, 1987	October 2, 1987	October 14, 1987
December 5, 1987	December 5, 1987	October 30, 1987	November 11, 1987
January 23, 1988	January 23, 1988	December 18, 1987	December 30, 1987
March 19, 1988	March 19, 1988	February 12, 1988	February 24, 1988
May 7, 1988	May 7, 1988	April 1, 1988	April 13, 1988
June 4, 1988	June 4, 1988	April 29, 1988	May 11, 1988

*Only in California, Florida, Georgia, Illinois, North Carolina, South Carolina, and Texas.

PART ONE

Organize Your Study Plan

1 What You Need to Know About the SAT

- An Overview of the SAT
- Commonly Asked Questions About the SAT

An Overview of the SAT

The SAT is a multiple-choice examination designed to measure your ability to do college work. There are six sections on the test: two verbal sections, two mathematics sections, one Test of Standard Written English (TSWE) section, and one experimental section that may have either verbal, mathematics, or TSWE questions. The verbal sections measure the extent of your vocabulary, your reading comprehension (how well you understand what you read), and your ability to think clearly. The mathematics sections measure your ability to use and reason with numbers or mathematical concepts. The TSWE tests your ability to recognize standard written English, the kind of language you will find in your college textbooks and that you will be expected to use in writing papers for college courses. Only the two math sections and the two verbal sections count toward your SAT score. You're given thirty minutes to answer the questions in each section; you may not go back to a section once the time is up for that section. In Chapter 2 you'll find a detailed description of the test that will include information on each type of verbal, mathematics, and TSWE question, as well as general test-taking strategies.

Standardized tests like the SAT are required for admission to most colleges. These tests are designed to predict how well a student will perform in college. College admissions officers rely on them to compare candidates from different secondary schools where courses and grading standards may vary widely.

Commonly Asked Questions About the SAT

How Does the SAT Differ from Other School Tests?

Most tests secondary school students take are achievement tests. They attempt to find out how much the student learned, usually in a specific subject, and how well he or she can apply that information. Without emphasis on memorized information, the SAT measures verbal and mathematical reasoning ability that you've developed both in and out of school.

How Can I Determine Which Is the Experimental Section?

Don't waste time in the examination room trying to identify which is the experimental section. Do your best on all six sections. Some claim that most often the last section is the experimental part. Others claim that the section with unusual questions is the one that does not count. If you do encounter a series of questions that seem strange, do your best. Either these won't count, in which case you have no reason to worry about them, or they will count, in which case they probably will seem just as strange and troublesome to everyone taking the test with you.

3

Is It Wise to Leave Troublesome Questions Unanswered?

Not if you can eliminate even one of the answer choices. Some tests give credit for correct answers and do not penalize guesses. The SAT gives one point for each correct answer and deducts a fraction of a point for each wrong answer. No deduction is made for answers left blank. Since only a fraction of a point is deducted for a wrong answer, you should guess if you can narrow down the choices.

Should I Make an Educated Guess?

Once again, sure, if you're a good guesser. At times you may have a strong feeling that a certain choice is correct, but you have difficulty proving or explaining your choice. On a test where a penalty is imposed for wrong answers, you may hesitate to answer the question. The best advice is for you to find out whether you are a good guesser. Use the practice exercises and model tests in this book as a chance to analyze your guessing skills. The next chapter will show you how. Remember, though, that you should guess when you can eliminate at least one of the choices.

Is It Advisable to Begin by Doing All the Easy Questions First?

Yes, but don't get hung up on a question just because you think it should be an easy one for you. Usually, the earlier questions of each type, except for reading comprehension questions, are easier. Most tests begin with "warm-up" questions. That is fair for all. But what is easy for one person may be hard for another, so it is good advice not to get bogged down with any one question. Remember, all questions carry the same point value. After a reasonable length of time, give up. Leave it blank. Just make sure the answer sheet correctly reflects your omission, and check to make certain that the subsequent answers are placed in the proper spot.

How Important Is Scrap Work on the SAT?

Your scrap work, including your doodling, is done directly in the question booklet and is strictly to help you. Don't hesitate to mark key words or phrases in the verbal sections. Do any necessary mathematics calculations on or near the problem. Since scrap work is not subject to inspection, keep it down to a minimum to save time. Be careful not to do any scrap work or leave any stray markings on your answer sheet. The machine that scores the test may mistake a stray mark for a second answer and give you no credit for a question.

You should also circle any questions you want to come back to in your test booklet. And be sure to cross out answer choices you are sure are wrong,

so that you don't have to spend time considering them again.

How Much High School Mathematics Is Required for the SAT?

The purpose of the SAT is not to find out how much mathematics you know. The test attempts to discover your ability to understand and to reason with mathematical symbols, to solve problems, and to interpret data. No advanced mathematics is required. The subject matter covered includes the mathematics studied by most college-bound students. It includes basic arithmetic, elementary algebra, and plane geometry. Since these questions are designed to test thinking power rather than recall of complicated formulas, you should expect to solve most problems by close inspection, insight, and reasoning rather than by complicated computational work.

You do have to know certain facts, formulas, and concepts in arithmetic, algebra, and geometry, so use Chapter 12 to review.

When and Where Is the Test Given?

The SAT is given seven times a year in high schools throughout the country. Your high school guidance office will have information about the exact test dates and should be able to provide you with a registration form. If a registration form is not available at your school, request one by mail from College Board ATP, CN 6200, Princeton, NJ 08541-6200. You should also request two very helpful booklets published by Educational Testing Service (ETS), which develops and administers the SAT for the College Board: *Taking the SAT* and the *Registration Bulletin* for the SAT and Achievement Tests. Both are free and should be available from your high school guidance office.

How Are SAT Scores Reported?

The raw score, the number of correct answers minus a fraction of a point for each wrong answer, is converted to a score on a scale of 200 to 800. With no correct answers at all, a student would still have a score of 200, and a student could have a score of 800 even with unanswered or incorrectly answered questions. Separate scores (from 200 to 800) are given for the verbal and the mathematical sections. The score given in the TSWE (from 20 to 60+) does not affect the other two.

You'll receive your score report in the mail about five to six weeks after the test date.

How Important Are SAT Scores?

Most colleges will hesitate to officially announce any cut-off points for SAT scores. They feel that announcing such scores would discourage otherwise potential candidates for admission. Most schools consider far more than these scores when making their admissions decisions. You should bear in mind, however, that a poor score on the examination, even if accompanied by a fairly good high school record, may make a college think twice about accepting you. On the other hand, a good college entrance examination score with an accompanying mediocre high school record is not uncommon. Since the scores are a sign you have good potential, admissions officers may spend some time going over the reasons your grades were only so-so.

The results of college entrance examinations are important because they are a scientific way of comparing all candidates in regard to their abilities to do college work. A high school record alone cannot be a yardstick of academic promise. Marking standards differ among high schools. Class standing in a small high school is not as significant as it is in a large city school. The standing in a specialized school is of little significance except for those at the very top. Entrance examinations afford equal opportunity to every one of you.

2 A Description of the Test

- ■ **SAT Test Format**
- ■ **The Verbal Sections**
- ■ **The Mathematics Sections**
- ■ **The TSWE Section**
- ■ **Tactics and Strategies**
- ■ **Guessing**
- ■ **Sample SAT Questions**

In Chapter 1 you learned that the SAT is a multiple-choice test, that it has six sections, and that it tests verbal ability, mathematics ability, and the ability to recognize standard written English. There are three other very important general points you should be aware of:

- ■ All of the questions are multiple-choice questions. That means that you have to recognize and choose a correct answer from the five (or four) choices given; you don't have to write an answer yourself.

- ■ Each question is worth the same number of points. Whether it was easy or difficult, whether it took you 10 seconds or 2 minutes to answer, you get the same number of points for each question answered correctly.

- ■ In each group of questions, the questions go from easy to more difficult. This means that the first analogy question in a group will probably be easier than the fifth analogy question in that group, and so on. (An exception to this is the reading comprehension questions, which are not ordered by level of difficulty.)

Keep these three points in mind as you learn more about what's on the test, and the tactics and strategies that will help you maximize your test score.

SAT Test Format

The following six sections are on the test. You will be given 30 minutes to complete each of them.

40-question verbal section

45-question verbal section

25-question math section

35-question math section

50-question TSWE section

an experimental section (which can be any one of the five sections described above)

These sections always appear on the SAT, but the order varies. The organization within each section does not vary; they will always be organized as outlined below:

40-Question Verbal Section
1–10 antonym questions

11–15 sentence completion questions

16–25 analogy questions

26–40 reading comprehension questions

45-Question Verbal Section
1–15 antonym questions

16–20 sentence completion questions

21–30 reading comprehension questions

31–35 sentence completion questions

36–45 analogy questions

or

1–15 antonym questions

16–25 sentence completion questions

26–35 reading comprehension questions

36–45 analogy questions

25-Question Math Section
1–25 standard multiple-choice questions

35-Question Math Section
  1–7 standard multiple-choice questions

  8–27 quantitative comparison questions

  28–35 standard multiple-choice questions

50-Question TSWE Section
  1–25 usage questions

  26–40 sentence correction questions

  41–50 usage questions

The Verbal Sections

The two verbal sections contain four types of questions: antonyms, analogies, sentence completions, and reading comprehension questions. Your college success will be closely bound up with your verbal abilities—especially your ability to understand what you read. This often means your ability to understand the words you read: your vocabulary. In fact, the more you study actual SAT verbal questions, the more you realize that the key to doing well on the verbal sections of the SAT is a strong working vocabulary of college-level words.

As in all SAT sections, the questions in the verbal sections progress from easy to difficult within each group of the same type of question. In other words, the first antonym question will probably be easier than the last antonym question; the first analogy questions will probably be easier than the last analogy question, and the first sentence completion question will probably be easier than the last sentence completion question. Reading comprehension questions, however, are not arranged in order of difficulty. They are arranged according to the logic and organization of the passage they are based on. The passages, however, are usually ordered from easy to difficult within the section.

Although the amount of time spent on each type of question varies with the individual, in general, antonyms take the least time, then analogies, then sentence completions, and, finally, reading comprehension. Since reading comprehension questions take much longer to answer (you have to spend time reading the passage before you can tackle the questions), you should do these questions last.

Antonym Questions

The antonym questions are always the first group of questions in a verbal section. They are the most straightforward vocabulary questions on the test. You are given a word and must choose, from the five choices that follow it, the best antonym (opposite). The vocabulary in this section includes words that you have probably seen in your reading, although you may never have used or even heard them in everyday conversations.

See Chapter 5 for antonym testing tactics and practice exercises.

Analogy Questions

Analogy questions test your understanding of the relationships among words and ideas. You are given one pair of words and must choose another pair that is related in the same way. Many relationships are possible. The two terms in the pair can be synonyms; one term can be a cause, the other the effect; one can be a tool, the other the worker who uses the tool.

Analogies are the questions that people seem to think of most often when they think about the SAT. They may well be the most difficult kind of question on the test, but they aren't impossible, and at least some of them will be fairly easy. The testing tactics and practice exercises in Chapter 6 will help you handle analogy questions.

Sentence Completion Questions

The sentence completion questions ask you to choose the best way to complete a sentence from which one or two words have been omitted. These questions test a combination of reading comprehension skills and vocabulary. You must be able to recognize the logic, style, and tone of the sentence, so that you will be able to choose the answer that makes sense in this context. You must also be able to recognize the way words are normally used. The sentences cover a wide variety of topics of the sort you have probably encountered in your general reading. However, this is not a test of your general knowledge. You may feel more comfortable if you are familiar with the topic the sentence is discussing, but you should be able to handle any of the sentences using your understanding of the English language.

The testing tactics and practice exercises in Chapter 7 will help you handle sentence completion questions.

Reading Comprehension Questions

Reading comprehension questions test your ability to understand and interpret what you read. This is probably the most important ability you will need in college and afterward. It's the ability you are using right now, when you are reading about the SAT.

As we already noted, reading comprehension questions take more time than any other questions on the test because you have to read a passage before you can answer them. Therefore, you should do the reading comprehension questions last. Make sure, though, that when you're working on a 45-question verbal section, where the reading comprehension questions will be in the middle of the section (they'll generally be questions 21–30), you take care to mark your answer sheet correctly, putting the answer to question 31, the first of the second group of sentence completion questions, in the space for question 31 and not in the space for question 21.

There will be several reading passages on the SAT. The 40-question verbal section will have 4 passages; the 45-question section will have 2 passages. The passages will be taken from the following categories: narrative, science, the humanities, and social studies. There will also be what the test-makers call an "argumentative" passage, one that presents a topic from a definite point of view. Although the passages may be about any subject matter, you do not need to know anything about the subject discussed in the passage in order to answer the questions on that passage. The purpose of the questions is to test your reading ability, not your knowledge of history, science, literature, or art. It is true, however, that you might feel more comfortable reading a passage on a topic with which you are familiar. You should, therefore, skim the passages in each section before you start working on the reading comprehension questions, and then start with the questions on the passage with which you feel most comfortable.

See Chapter 8 for reading comprehension tactics and practice exercises that will help you handle these questions.

The Mathematics Sections

The two mathematics sections have a total of 60 questions, including 20 quantitative comparison questions. These questions assume that you have had, and remember, arithmetic, elementary algebra, and geometry. You do not need to know any more advanced mathematics. You will be asked to use graphic, spatial, numerical, and symbolic techniques in a variety of problems. The questions are intended to show how well you understand elementary mathematics, how well you can apply your knowledge to solve problems, and how good your mathematical instincts are—how well you can use nonroutine ways of thinking. What do we mean by "mathematical instincts" or "nonroutine ways of thinking"? In one sense, you need some insight to spot the right approach for solving any mathematical question. More important, on the SAT, is the ability to see which answer must be correct, or at least which answers are impossible, without actually solving the problem. This is basically the ability to apply mathematical rules and principles that you already know. For example, imagine that you are asked to multiply $27,654 \times 3,042$. You should see right away that the

answer will have to end in 8. When the multiplicand ends in a 4 and the multiplier ends in a 2, then the product must end with an 8. This is a typical illustration of saving time with insight rather than doing lengthy, time-consuming computation, which, incidentally, may lead to computational errors. So not only is it a time-saver, it may also be an error-saver.

Standard Multiple-Choice Questions

The standard multiple-choice questions are found on both math sections. Each question has 5 answer choices. Some of these questions are like the math questions you've had in your textbooks; others are not. Whether they are similar to math problems you've had before or not, they will only cover math concepts that you have learned in school. So, if a question seems unusual to you, keep in mind that you probably know the necessary facts, formulas, and concepts to work it out.

The testing tactics and practice exercises in Chapter 10 will help you handle these questions.

Quantitative Comparison Questions

You may never have seen questions like these before, so they require some explanation. You will be given two quantities. Sometimes you will also be given information about one or both of them. Then you must decide whether one of the quantities is greater than the other, or whether they are equal. Sometimes there will not be enough information for you to be able to make a decision.

These questions reflect the contemporary emphasis on inequalities in school mathematics courses. In general, these questions require less time than the other mathematics questions, since they require less reading and, usually, less computation. These are the only questions on the SAT that have only four answer choices.

The testing tactics and practice exercise in Chapter 11 will help you handle these questions.

The Test of Standard Written English Section

The Test of Standard Written English (TSWE) is not really part of the SAT. It is graded separately and is intended to help colleges place students in composition courses. The 30-minute section has 50 questions. Of these, 35 are usage questions and 15 are sentence correction questions. You do not have to write anything yourself on this test, but you are expected to recognize the grammatical forms and usage that are considered acceptable in formal written English.

Usage Questions

In the usage questions, four words or groups of words will be underlined in each sentence. You do not have to correct the sentence. All you need to do is find the error, if there is one.

Chapter 13 contains additional information about usage questions, including appropriate testing tactics and practice exercises.

Sentence Correction Questions

With sentence correction questions you have to do more than just spot the error. You have to find the correction as well. These questions give you sentences in which one section is underlined. The answer choices repeat the underlined section and give you four other versions of the same section. You must decide which version is best. Since these questions can deal with large sections of a sentence, many of them cover errors in the structure or logic of a sentence.

Chapter 13 contains additional information about sentence correction questions, including appropriate testing tactics and practice exercises.

Tactics and Strategies

The easiest way to answer a question correctly is to know the answer. If you know what all the words mean in an antonym question, you won't have any trouble choosing the right answer. If you know exactly how to solve a mathematics question and don't make any mistakes in arithmetic, you won't have any trouble choosing the right answer. However, some sensible strategies will help you maximize your score.

The tactics and strategies in this chapter apply to all sections of the test. In Part Three of this book, you'll find tactics and strategies that apply specifically to each type of question.

Tactic 1

Know what to expect. By the time you have finished with this preparation program, you will be familiar with all the kinds of questions that are going to appear on the SAT. You should also be aware of how long it is going to take. There are six sections on the test. Each one is half-an-hour long, and there is supposed to be a five-minute break between sections. If you are scheduled to start the SAT at 9 a.m., do not make a dentist appointment for noon. You can't possibly get there on time, and you'll just spend the last two sections of the test worrying about it.

Tactic 2

Memorize the directions for each type of question. These don't change. The test

time you would spend reading the directions can be better spent answering the questions.

Tactic 3

Don't get bogged down on any one question. By the time you get to the actual SAT, you should have a fair idea of how much time to spend on each question. If a question is taking too long, leave it and go on to the next question. This is no time to try to show the world that you can stick to a job no matter how long it takes. All the machine that grades the test will notice is that you didn't have any correct answers.

Tactic 4

On the other hand, don't rush. Since your score will depend on how many *correct* answers you give *within a definite period* of time, speed and accuracy are both important. You will be better off answering 75 percent of the questions carefully and accurately than answering 100 percent of the questions hastily and inaccurately. Make sure you are answering *the question asked* and not one it may have reminded you of or the one you thought was going to be asked. Underline key words like "not" and "except" to make sure that you do not end up trying to answer the exact opposite of the question asked.

Tactic 5

First answer all the easy questions; *then* tackle the hard ones if you have time. (Circle any questions that you're not sure of. Then if you have time at the end of the test, you will be able to locate them quickly.) The questions in each segment of the test get harder as you go along (except the reading comprehension questions). But each new segment starts with easy questions. So don't get bogged down on a difficult antonym question when only three questions away the easy sentence completion questions begin.

Tactic 6

Eliminate as many wrong answers as you can. Deciding between two choices is easier than deciding among five. Even if you have to guess, every answer you eliminate improves your chances of guessing correctly.

Tactic 7

Change answers only if you have a reason for doing so. It's usually best not to change based on a hunch or a whim.

Tactic 8

Remember that you don't have to answer every question to do well. According to the College Board, "many students who receive average or slightly above-average scores answer only 40–60 percent of the questions correctly."

Tactic 9

Remember that you are allowed to write in the test book. You can write anything you want in the test book. You can and should do your mathematics computations in the booklet. There is absolutely no need to try to do them in your head. And if it helps you to doodle while you think, then doodle away. What is written in the test booklet does not matter to anyone.

Tactic 10

Be careful not to make any stray marks on the answer sheet. This test is graded by a machine, and a machine cannot tell the difference between an accidental mark and a filled-in answer. When the machine sees two marks, it calls the answer wrong.

Tactic 11

Check frequently to make sure you are answering the questions in the right spots. No machine is going to notice that you made a mistake early in the test, answered question 4 in the space for question 5, and all your following answers are the right answers, but in the wrong place.

Tactic 12

Get a good night's sleep. The best way to prepare for any test you ever take is to get a good night's sleep before the test so you are well rested and alert.

Tactic 13

Allow plenty of time for getting to the test site. Taking a test is pressure enough. You don't need the extra tension that comes from worrying about whether you will get there on time.

Tactic 14

Bring four sharpened number 2 pencils to the test. The College Board tells you to bring two sharpened number 2 pencils to the test, but bring four. They don't weigh much, and this might be the one day in the decade when two pencil points decide to break. And bring full-size pencils, not little stubs. They are easier to write with, and you might as well be comfortable.

Tactic 15

Wear comfortable clothes. This is a test, not a fashion show. And bring a sweater. The test room may be hot, or it may be cold. You can't change the room, but you can put on a sweater.

Tactic 16

Bring an accurate watch. The room in which you take the test may not have a clock, and some proctors are not very good about posting the time on the blackboard. Each time you begin a test section, write down in your booklet the time by your watch. That way you will always know how much time you have left.

Guessing

Since wrong answers count against you on the SAT, you may think that you should never guess if you aren't sure of the right answer to a question. But even if you guessed wrong four times for every time you guessed right, you would still come out even. A wrong answer costs you only $\frac{1}{4}$ of a point ($\frac{1}{3}$ on the quantitative comparison questions). The most usual advice is to guess if you can eliminate one or two of the answers. You have a better chance of hitting the right answer when you make this sort of "educated guess." To find out whether this advice works for you, test yourself. Use the chart at the end of this section to see how guessing would affect your score.

First, take part of any test that you have not taken before. You don't have to take an entire test section, but you should take at least 25 questions. Answer only those questions to which you definitely know the answer. See what your score is.

Next, retake the same test section. Do not change any of your original answers, but whenever you can make an educated guess on one of the questions you originally passed, do so. See what your score is now. Finally, take the same test section one last time, this time guessing blindly to answer all the remaining questions. Don't forget to subtract $\frac{1}{4}$ point for wrong answers ($\frac{1}{3}$ point on quantitative comparison questions).

Compare your scores from the three different approaches to the test. For most people, the second score will be the best one. But you may be different. Maybe you are such a poor guesser that you should never guess at all. Or maybe you are such a good guesser that you should try every question you hit.

SHOULD YOU GUESS?

	Number Right	Number Wrong	Total
No guesses			
Educated guesses			
Blind guesses			

Sample SAT Questions*

The purpose of this section is to familiarize you with the kinds of questions that appear on the SAT by reprinting questions from recent SATs with the permission of Educational Testing Service. Knowing what to expect when you take the examination is an important step in preparing for the test and succeeding in it.

Verbal Section
Antonym Questions

Each question below consists of a word in capital letters, followed by five lettered words or phrases. Choose the word or phrase that is most nearly opposite in meaning to the word in capital letters. Since some of the questions require you to distinguish fine shades of meaning, consider all the choices before deciding which is best.

Example:

GOOD: (A) sour (B) bad (C) red
(D) hot (E) ugly   Ⓐ ● Ⓒ Ⓓ Ⓔ

1. LICENSED: (A) unnoticed (B) unwritten
   (C) unstable (D) not formally authorized
   (E) not properly trained

2. OBSTINATE: (A) intermittent (B) yielding
   (C) uncertain (D) careless (E) despairing

3. INANIMATE: (A) somber (B) valiant
   (C) supportive (D) hidden (E) alive

4. UNDERMINE: (A) entangle (B) parch
   (C) overwork (D) enter (E) support

5. DOCUMENT: (A) edit (B) withhold
   (C) reproduce in full (D) write for pay
   (E) leave unsupported

---

6. RESERVE: (A) compassion   (B) irascibility
   (C) incoherence   (D) lack of restraint   (E) lack
   of strength

7. DISPUTE: (A) dispose   (B) answer
   (C) qualify   (D) befriend   (E) concede

8. ADVOCACY: (A) disrepute   (B) opposition
   (C) ascendancy   (D) justice
   (E) unconsciousness

9. QUALIFIED: (A) underlying   (B) disregarded
   (C) unrestricted   (D) predetermined
   (E) rehabilitated

10. NEOLOGISM:
    (A) nameless article
    (B) foreign object
    (C) exaggerated movement
    (D) impoverished condition
    (E) obsolete expression

Sentence Completion Questions

Each sentence below has one or two blanks, each blank indicating that something has been omitted. Beneath the sentence are five lettered words or sets of words. Choose the word or set of words that best fits the meaning of the sentence as a whole.

Example:

Although its publicity has been ----, the film itself is intelligent, well-acted, handsomely produced, and altogether ----.

(A) tasteless..respectable (B) extensive..moderate
 (C) sophisticated..amateur (D) risqué..crude
  (E) perfect..spectacular

● Ⓑ Ⓒ Ⓓ Ⓔ

11. Medieval kingdoms did not become constitutional republics overnight; on the contrary, the change was ----.

    (A) unpopular   (B) unexpected
     (C) advantageous   (D) sufficient   (E) gradual

12. Chameleons, since they move quickly and adopt the color of their surroundings, are so difficult to ---- that even a careful observer can ---- their presence.

    (A) eradicate..notice   (B) detect..overlook
     (C) ignore..misjudge   (D) discern..recognize
      (E) miss..deduce

13. The instructor added the restriction that all projects had to be ----: no student could research an area that had been investigated previously by anyone else.

    (A) acceptable   (B) useful   (C) extensive
     (D) authoritative   (E) original

14. Physical laws do not, of course, in themselves force bodies to behave in a certain way, but merely ---- how, as a matter of fact, they do behave.

    (A) determine   (B) preclude   (C) counteract
     (D) describe   (E) commend

15. The discussions were often ----, degenerating at times into name-calling contests.

    (A) lofty   (B) auspicious   (C) acrimonious
     (D) lethargic   (E) pragmatic

16. Of all the phases of filmmaking, screenwriting is the most ----; it is a rare instance when only one person is responsible for a script.

    (A) prolific   (B) collaborative   (C) substantive
     (D) impassioned   (E) illustrious

17. In comparative anatomy, all methods of analysis, save direct observation, are beset with ---- which require great ---- if reliable conclusions are to be drawn.

    (A) analogies..duplication
    (B) problems..supposition
    (C) premises..inducement
    (D) pitfalls..circumspection
    (E) judgments..prerogative

18. Ms. Wilton urged patience and ---- in dealing with the protesters rather than the unyielding attitude the administration had adopted.

    (A) obstinacy   (B) desperation   (C) arrogance
     (D) compromise   (E) retaliation

19. Public education is regarded in America as the pathway to social salvation, a ---- for secular difficulties.

    (A) panacea   (B) scapegoat   (C) prototype
     (D) criterion   (E) fountainhead

20. His habitual ---- had seemingly left its imprint on both his physique and speech, the one lean, the other ----.

    (A) puritanism..indecent
    (B) duplicity..guileless
    (C) frugality..laconic
    (D) debauchery..bombastic
    (E) loquacity..refined

Analogy Questions

Each question below consists of a related pair of words or phrases, followed by five lettered pairs of words or phrases. Select the lettered pair that best expresses a relationship similar to that expressed in the original pair.

Example:

YAWN : BOREDOM :: (A) dream : sleep
(B) anger : madness (C) smile : amusement
(D) face : expression (E) impatience : rebellion

Ⓐ Ⓑ ● Ⓓ Ⓔ

21. RACQUET : TENNIS :: (A) springboard : diver
(B) horse : polo (C) glove : boxing
(D) club : golf (E) gun : hunting

22. SYNCHRONIZE : MOVEMENTS ::
(A) sublimate : goals
(B) realize : dreams
(C) prolong : intervals
(D) remit : payments
(E) harmonize : voices

23. SCALPEL : SURGEON :: (A) razor : barber
(B) weed : gardener (C) recipe : chef
(D) medicine : patient (E) compass : engineer

24. THIMBLE : FINGER :: (A) armor : body
(B) crown : head (C) torso : waist
(D) earring : ear (E) stocking : leg

25. ENDURE : SURVIVOR :: (A) condemn : culprit
(B) applaud : performer (C) evade : guardian
(D) excel : imitator (E) compete : rival

26. INTERLOPER : INTRUSION ::
(A) witness : interrogation
(B) actor : intermission
(C) recluse : interference
(D) mediator : intercession
(E) orator : interruption

27. MOUNTAIN : RANGE :: (A) lake : ocean
(B) glacier : snow (C) island : archipelago
(D) sand : dune (E) surf : beach

28. INTROSPECTIVE : SELF ::
(A) pompous : thoughts
(B) conceited : others
(C) miserly : accomplishments
(D) impetuous : decisions
(E) scrupulous : principles

29. INCITE : SEDITIONIST :: (A) parade : heckler
(B) assault : victor (C) abdicate : autocrat
(D) arbitrate : mediator (E) donate : financier

30. HUSBAND : RESOURCES ::
(A) conserve : energy
(B) spend : salary
(C) predict : hurricane
(D) analyze : statement
(E) revise : story

Reading Comprehension Questions

Each passage below is followed by questions based on its content. Answer all questions following a passage on the basis of what is stated or implied in that passage.

Lois Mailou Jones is one example of an answer to the charge that there are no Black or female American artists to include in art history textbooks and classes. Beginning her formal art education at the School of the Museum of Fine Arts in Boston, Lois Jones found herself strongly attracted to design rather than fine arts. After teaching for a while, she went to Paris to study, on the advice of the sculptor Meta Warrick Fuller.

It was in Paris that she first felt free to paint. Following her return to this country in 1938, Jones had an exhibit at the Vose Gallery in Boston, a major breakthrough for a Black artist at that time. Her work during this period consisted of excellent impressionist scenes of Paris. It was not until the early 1940's, after she met the Black aesthetician Alain Locke, that she began to paint works like *Mob Victim,* which explicitly dealt with her own background as a Black American. Later, in the fifties, she went often to Haiti, which had yet another influence on her style. Then a sabbatical leave in Africa again changed her imagery. Indeed, the scope of this distinguished artist's career so well spans the development of twentieth-century art that her work could be a textbook in itself.

31. The passage primarily focuses on the

(A) influence of Lois Jones on other artists
(B) recognition given to Lois Jones for her work
(C) experiences that influenced the work of Lois Jones
(D) obstacles that Lois Jones surmounted in her career
(E) techniques that characterize the work of Lois Jones

32. Which of the following best summarizes the relationship of the first sentence to the rest of the passage?

    (A) Assertion followed by supporting evidence
    (B) Challenge followed by debate pro and con
    (C) Prediction followed by analysis
    (D) Specific instance followed by generalizations
    (E) Objective reporting followed by personal reminiscences

33. It can be inferred from the passage that Alain Locke encouraged Lois Jones to

    (A) exhibit her work at recognized galleries
    (B) use her experiences as a Black American in her work
    (C) incorporate Haitian imagery in her work
    (D) work in art media other than painting
    (E) continue her studies abroad

"Imagine. Forty days in the boats!" cried Mrs. Perrot. Everything over the river was still and blank.

Line
(5) "The French behaved well this time at least," Dawson remarked.

"They've only brought in the dying," the doctor retorted. "They could hardly have done less."

Dawson exclaimed and struck at his hand.

(10) "Come inside," Mrs. Perrot said. "The windows are netted." The stale air was heavy with the coming rains.

"There are some cases of fever," said the doctor, "but most are just exhaustion—the worst

(15) disease. It's what most of us die of in the end."

Mrs. Perrot turned a knob; music from the London Orpheum filtered in. Dawson shifted uncomfortably; the Wurlitzer organ moaned and boomed. It seemed to him outrageously

(20) immodest.

Wilson came in to a welcome from Mrs. Perrot. "A surprise to see *you*, Major Dawson."

"Hardly, Wilson," Mr. Perrot injected. "I told you he'd be here." Dawson looked across at

(25) Wilson and saw him blush at Perrot's betrayal, saw too that his eyes gave the lie to his youth.

"Well," sneered Perrot, "any scandals from the big city?" Like a Huguenot imagining Rome, he built up a picture of frivolity, viciousness, and

(30) corruption. "We bush-folk live quietly."

Mrs. Perrot's mouth stiffened in the effort to ignore her husband in his familiar part. She pretended to listen to the old Viennese melodies.

"None," Dawson answered, watching Mrs.

(35) Perrot with pity. "People are too busy with the war."

"So many files to turn over," said Perrot. "Growing rice down here would teach them what work is."

34. The evidence in the passage suggests that the story most likely takes place

    (A) on a boat during a tropical storm
    (B) at a hospital during a wartime blackout
    (C) in a small town in France
    (D) near a rice plantation in the tropics
    (E) among a group of people en route to a large Asian city

35. The tone of the doctor's remarks (lines 6-7, 13-15) indicates that he is basically

    (A) unselfish   (B) magnanimous   (C) indifferent
    (D) rich in patience   (E) without illusions

36. Perrot betrays Wilson by revealing that

    (A) Dawson's presence should be no surprise to Wilson
    (B) Perrot's wife had expected Wilson's arrival
    (C) Wilson has ignored the plight of the victims
    (D) Wilson has been involved in a scandal in the city
    (E) Wilson has lied about his age

Prostaglandins are short-lived hormonelike substances made by most cells in the body after injury or shock. They are responsible for a number of physiological reactions. Prostaglandins have been shown to influence blood pressure, muscle contraction, and blood coagulation and are involved in producing pain, fever, and inflammation. When released from platelets—minute discs in the blood—a prostaglandin derivative called thromboxane makes the platelets clump together and thus initiates clotting.

In 1971, John Vane, a British researcher, discovered that aspirin interferes with the synthesis of prostaglandins. Scientists now know that aspirin relieves pain by inactivating cyclooxygenase, an enzyme that aids in initiating the synthesis of prostaglandins. When scientists realized that aspirin can also interfere with clotting, they began to wonder whether it could help prevent heart attacks and strokes, which are often caused by blood clots that block arteries in the chest or neck. Studies now indicate that low daily doses of aspirin can cut the risk of a second heart attack by about twenty percent and the risk of a second stroke by nearly half. It seems logical to assume that if the drug can prevent second heart attacks, it can also ward off an attack the first time around. Therefore, many doctors recommend an aspirin tablet every other day to inhibit excessive platelet clumping among people who have high blood pressure or other symptoms that increase the risk of heart attacks.

37. According to the passage, prostaglandins play a role in all of the following EXCEPT the

    (A) clotting of blood
    (B) sensation of pain
    (C) contraction of muscles
    (D) manufacture of platelets
    (E) inflammation of tissue

38. The passage suggests that which of the following would be most likely to initiate the production of prostaglandins?

   (A) Taking an aspirin
   (B) Spraining an ankle
   (C) Climbing stairs
   (D) Flexing a muscle
   (E) Running a fever

39. It can be inferred from the passage that when the production of prostaglandins is impeded, which of the following occur(s)?

   I. Blood coagulation is slowed.
   II. Pain is reduced.
   III. Inflammation increases.

   (A) I only   (B) II only   (C) I and II only
   (D) II and III only   (E) I, II, and III

40. It can be inferred from the passage that aspirin helps prevent heart attacks by

   (A) interfering with the production of thromboxane
   (B) lowering blood pressure
   (C) easing muscular contractions
   (D) initiating the production of cyclooxygenase
   (E) widening the arteries

Mathematics Section

Standard Multiple-Choice Questions

The following information is for your reference in solving some of the problems.

Circle of radius r: Area $= \pi r^2$; Circumference $= 2\pi r$
   The number of degrees of arc in a circle is 360.
The measure in degrees of a straight angle is 180.

Definitions of symbols:

$=$ is equal to $\leq$ is less than or equal to
$\neq$ is unequal to $\geq$ is greater than or equal to
$<$ is less than $\parallel$ is parallel to
$>$ is greater than $\perp$ is perpendicular to

Triangle: The sum of the measures in degrees of the angles of a triangle is 180.

If $\angle CDA$ is a right angle, then

   (1) area of $\triangle ABC = \dfrac{AB \times CD}{2}$

   (2) $AC^2 = AD^2 + DC^2$

Note: Figures that accompany problems in this test are intended to provide information useful in solving the problems. They are drawn as accurately as possible EXCEPT when it is stated in a specific problem that its figure is not drawn to scale. All figures lie in a plane unless otherwise indicated. All numbers used are real numbers.

---

1. A gymnast competed in a meet and received the following scores for three events: 9.5 for bars, 8.7 for balance beam, and 8.8 for floor routine. What is the average (arithmetic mean) of these three scores?

   (A) 8.9 (B) 9.0 (C) 9.1 (D) 9.2 (E) 9.3

2. If $\dfrac{(20 + 50) + (30 + N)}{2} = 70$, then $N =$

   (A) 30 (B) 40 (C) 50 (D) 60 (E) 70

3. If the first and last digits are interchanged in each of the following numbers, which will yield the number with the *least* value?

   (A) 4,321   (B) 3,241   (C) 2,431   (D) 4,231
   (E) 3,421

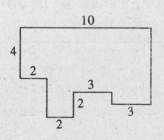

Note: Figure not drawn to scale.

4. What is the perimeter of the figure above?

   (A) 15 (B) 20 (C) 26 (D) 32
   (E) It cannot be determined from the information given.

Questions 5-6 refer to the following definition:

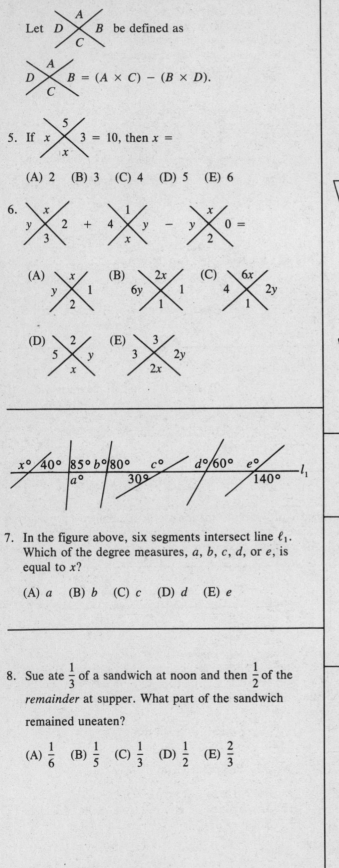

Let $D \diagdown\diagup B$ be defined as (with A top, C bottom)

$D \diagdown\diagup B = (A \times C) - (B \times D)$.

5. If $x \times 3 = 10$, then $x =$ (with 5 top, x bottom)

(A) 2 (B) 3 (C) 4 (D) 5 (E) 6

6. $y \diagdown\diagup 2 + 4 \diagdown\diagup y - y \diagdown\diagup 0 =$

(A) $y \diagdown\diagup 1$ (B) $6y \diagdown\diagup 1$ (C) $4 \diagdown\diagup 2y$

(D) $5 \diagdown\diagup y$ (E) $3 \diagdown\diagup 2y$

$x^\circ \diagup 40^\circ \diagdown 85^\circ b^\circ \diagup 80^\circ \quad c^\circ \diagup d^\circ \diagup 60^\circ \quad e^\circ \diagup$
$a^\circ \quad 30^\circ \quad 140^\circ \quad l_1$

7. In the figure above, six segments intersect line ℓ_1. Which of the degree measures, a, b, c, d, or e, is equal to x?

(A) a (B) b (C) c (D) d (E) e

8. Sue ate $\frac{1}{3}$ of a sandwich at noon and then $\frac{1}{2}$ of the *remainder* at supper. What part of the sandwich remained uneaten?

(A) $\frac{1}{6}$ (B) $\frac{1}{5}$ (C) $\frac{1}{3}$ (D) $\frac{1}{2}$ (E) $\frac{2}{3}$

Topless Container

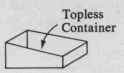

9. The container above has a rectangular base with sides that are perpendicular to the base. If a cut is made along each of the four vertical edges and the sides folded out flat, which of the following patterns results?

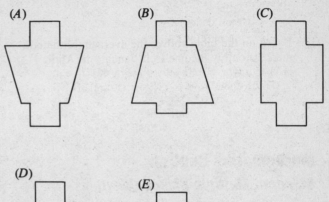

(A) (B) (C)

(D) (E)

10. If $40 \cdot 20{,}000 = 8 \cdot 10^x$, then $x =$

(A) 4 (B) 5 (C) 6 (D) 7 (E) 8

11. If $\lfloor x \rfloor$ is defined by the equation $\lfloor x \rfloor = \frac{\sqrt{x}}{2}$ for all whole numbers x, which of the following equals 5?

(A) $\lfloor 10 \rfloor$ (B) $\lfloor 20 \rfloor$ (C) $\lfloor 25 \rfloor$

(D) $\lfloor 50 \rfloor$ (E) $\lfloor 100 \rfloor$

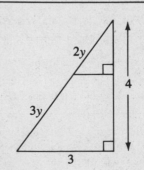

12. In the figure above, $y =$

(A) 1 (B) 2 (C) 3 (D) 4 (E) 5

INCOME FOR THE EXCEL COMPANY

January to April, 1980

January	+ $4,700,000
February	− $4,000,000
March	+ $5,300,000
April	+ $2,000,000

13. Based on the table above, the average (arithmetic mean) monthly income from January to April, inclusive, for the Excel Company was

(A) $2,000,000 (B) $3,000,000 (C) $3,500,000
(D) $4,000,000 (E) $4,100,000

14. At Central High School, the math club has 15 members and the chess club has 12 members. If a total of 13 students belong to only one of the two clubs, how many students belong to both clubs?

(A) 2 (B) 6 (C) 7 (D) 12 (E) 14

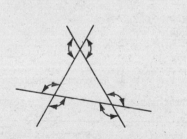

15. Three lines intersect as shown in the figure above. What is the sum of the degree measures of the marked angles?

(A) 360° (B) 540° (C) 720° (D) 900°
(E) It cannot be determined from the information given.

16. If $\begin{array}{cc} a & b \\ c & d \end{array}$ is defined to equal $ab - cd$

and $\begin{array}{cc} a & b \\ c & d \end{array}$ $+ y = 0$, then $y =$

(A) $ab - cd$ (B) $ac - bd$ (C) $ad - bc$
(D) $bc - ad$ (E) $cd - ab$

17. If it takes 10 people 12 hours to do a certain job, how many hours would it take 6 people, working at the same rate, to do $\frac{1}{4}$ of the same job?

(A) 6 (B) 5 (C) $4\frac{1}{2}$ (D) 4 (E) $3\frac{3}{4}$

Questions 18-19 refer to the operation represented by ∇ and defined by the equation $x \nabla y = x + y + xy$ for all numbers x and y, for example,
$(-6) \nabla (2) = (-6) + (2) + (-12) = -16$.

18. $\left(-\frac{1}{2}\right) \nabla 3 =$

(A) -5 (B) $-\frac{3}{2}$ (C) 1 (D) 4 (E) 5

19. If $8 \nabla k = 3$, then $k =$

(A) -5 (B) $-\frac{5}{9}$ (C) $\frac{3}{8}$ (D) $\frac{5}{9}$ (E) 5

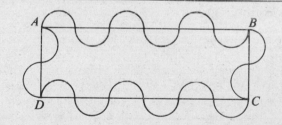

20. In the figure above, $ABCD$ is a rectangle and the curved path is made up of 16 semicircles of equal diameter. If the total length of this curved path is 32π, then the *area* of rectangle $ABCD$ is

(A) 24 (B) 32 (C) 48 (D) 64 (E) 192

Quantitative Comparison Questions

Questions 21–30 each consist of two quantities, one in Column A and one in Column B. You are to compare the two quantities and on the answer sheet blacken space

A   if the quantity in Column A is greater;
B   if the quantity in Column B is greater;
C   if the two quantities are equal;
D   If the relationship cannot be determined from the information given.

AN E RESPONSE WILL NOT BE SCORED.

Notes:

1.   In certain questions, information concerning one or both of the quantities to be compared is centered above the two columns.
2.   In a given question, a symbol that appears in both columns represents the same thing in Column A as it does in Column B.
3.   Letters such as x, n, and k stand for real numbers.

EXAMPLES

	Column A	Column B	Answers
E1.	2×6	$2 + 6$	●ⒷⒸⒹⒺ
E2.	$180 - x$	y	ⒶⒷ●ⒹⒺ
E3.	$p - q$	$q - p$	ⒶⒷⒸ●Ⓔ

For E2: $x°$ / $y°$

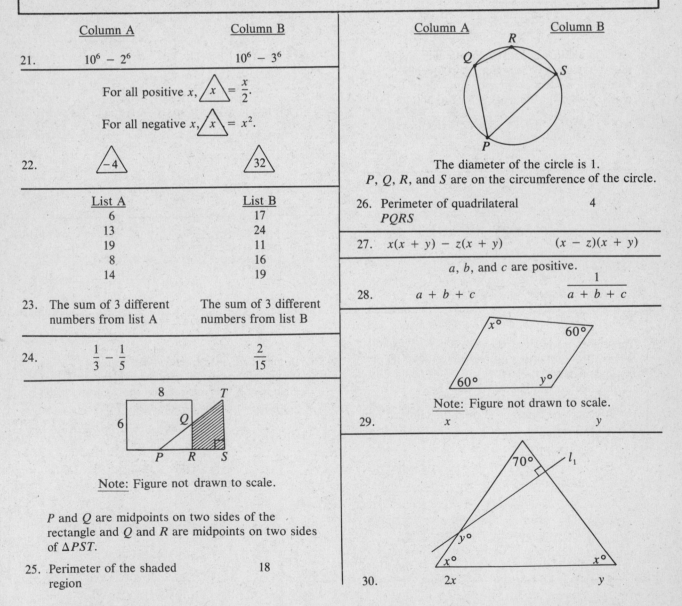

Column A   Column B

21. $10^6 - 2^6$ $10^6 - 3^6$

For all positive x, $\boxed{x} = \dfrac{x}{2}$.

For all negative x, $\boxed{x} = x^2$.

22. $\boxed{-4}$ $\boxed{32}$

List A	List B
6	17
13	24
19	11
8	16
14	19

23.   The sum of 3 different numbers from list A   The sum of 3 different numbers from list B

24. $\dfrac{1}{3} - \dfrac{1}{5}$ $\dfrac{2}{15}$

Note: Figure not drawn to scale.

P and Q are midpoints on two sides of the rectangle and Q and R are midpoints on two sides of $\triangle PST$.

25.   Perimeter of the shaded region   18

Column A   Column B

The diameter of the circle is 1.
P, Q, R, and S are on the circumference of the circle.

26.   Perimeter of quadrilateral $PQRS$ 4

27. $x(x + y) - z(x + y)$ $(x - z)(x + y)$

a, b, and c are positive.

28. $a + b + c$ $\dfrac{1}{a + b + c}$

Note: Figure not drawn to scale.

29. x y

30. $2x$ y

TSWE
Usage Questions

Directions: The following sentences contain problems in grammar, usage, diction (choice of words), and idiom.

Some sentences are correct.

No sentence contains more than one error.

You will find that the error, if there is one, is underlined and lettered. Assume that elements of the sentence that are not underlined are correct and cannot be changed. In choosing answers, follow the requirements of standard written English.

If there is an error, select the one underlined part that must be changed to make the sentence correct and blacken the corresponding space on your answer sheet.

If there is no error, blacken answer space Ⓔ.

EXAMPLE:

The region has a climate so severe that plants
                                A

growing there rarely had been more than twelve
      B   C

inches high. No error
      D   E

SAMPLE ANSWER

Ⓐ Ⓑ ● Ⓓ Ⓔ

1. Whenever we hear of a natural disaster, even in a
      A   B
distant part of the world, you feel sympathy for the
                          C   D
people affected. No error
                  E

2. The leading roles in the widely acclaimed play, a
                              A
modern version of an Irish folktale, were performed
   B   C
by Jessica and he. No error
            D   E

3. The energy question, along with several other issues,
                                   A
are going to be discussed at the next meeting of the
 B   C   D
state legislature. No error
                   E

Sentence Correction Questions

Directions: In each of the following sentences, some part or all of the sentence is underlined. Below each sentence you will find five ways of phrasing the underlined part. Select the answer that produces the most effective sentence, one that is clear and exact, without awkwardness or ambiguity, and blacken the corresponding space on your answer sheet. In choosing answers, follow the requirements of standard written English. Choose the answer that best expresses the meaning of the original sentence.

Answer (A) is always the same as the underlined part. Choose answer (A) if you think the original sentence needs no revision.

EXAMPLE:

Laura Ingalls Wilder published her first book
and she was sixty-five years old then.

(A) and she was sixty-five years old then
(B) when she was sixty-five years old
(C) at age sixty-five years old
(D) upon reaching sixty-five years
(E) at the time when she was sixty-five

SAMPLE ANSWER

Ⓐ ● Ⓒ Ⓓ Ⓔ

4. Many memos were issued by the director of the agency that had an insulting tone, according to the staff members.
   (A) Many memos were issued by the director of the agency that
   (B) Many memos were issued by the director of the agency who
   (C) The issuance of many memos by the director of the agency which
   (D) The director of the agency issued many memos that
   (E) The director of the agency, who issued many memos that

5. Consumers are beginning to take notice of electric cars because they are quiet, cause no air pollution, and gasoline is not used.
   (A) cause no air pollution, and gasoline is not used
   (B) air pollution is not caused, and gasoline is not used
   (C) cause no air pollution, and use no gasoline
   (D) causing no air pollution and using no gasoline
   (E) air pollution is not caused, and no gasoline is used

6. Light reaching earth from the most distant stars originated billions of years ago.
   (A) reaching earth from the most distant stars
   (B) which reaching earth from the most distant stars
   (C) from the most distant stars reaching earth
   (D) that is from the most distant stars and reaches earth
   (E) reaching earth which is from stars that are most distant

Answer Key

Verbal Sections

1.	D	9.	C	17.	D	25.	E	33.	B
2.	B	10.	E	18.	D	26.	D	34.	D
3.	E	11.	E	19.	A	27.	C	35.	E
4.	E	12.	B	20.	C	28.	E	36.	A
5.	E	13.	E	21.	D	29.	D	37.	D
6.	D	14.	D	22.	E	30.	A	38.	B
7.	E	15.	C	23.	A	31.	C	39.	C
8.	B	16.	B	24.	A	32.	A	40.	A

Mathematics Sections

1.	B	7.	E	13.	A	19.	B	25.	C
2.	B	8.	C	14.	C	20.	E	26.	B
3.	D	9.	D	15.	C	21.	A	27.	C
4.	E	10.	B	16.	E	22.	C	28.	D
5.	D	11.	E	17.	B	23.	D	29.	D
6.	B	12.	A	18.	C	24.	C	30.	B

TSWE

1. C
2. D
3. B
4. D
5. C
6. A

3 Three Sensible Study Programs

- ■ The Two-Day Crash Program
- ■ The Two-Week Concentrated Program
- ■ The Comprehensive Study Program

Chapter 2 showed you what to expect on the SAT. Now it's time to start planning how you're going to prepare for the test. Your method of preparation will depend on how much time you have between now and the test date. But no matter how little time you have to prepare for the SAT, it can be put to good use if you use it efficiently. To help you organize your SAT preparation, we offer three plans for different amounts of time—two days, two weeks, and ten or more weeks. Choose the one that's best for you, depending on how much time you have available. But please remember that these are suggestions, not requirements. If you need to spend more or less time on any part of the program, do just that. The program is intended to help you, not limit you.

The Two-Day Crash Program

It's Wednesday and you are taking the SAT on Saturday, and you are starting to panic. You just became acquainted with this "bible" for preparing for the SAT. Follow this crash program. It's not the ideal way to prepare, but intensive preparation with this book is better than walking in cold.

Day 1

Do the sample SAT Questions (in Chapter 2.) Make sure you know how to do each type. Take the Diagnostic SAT in Chapter 4. Score your test. Study the answer explanations for all questions you missed or omitted, so you understand where you went wrong.

Day 2

Study the tactics for handling verbal and mathematics questions at the beginning of Chapters 5–11, paying particular attention to the types of questions that gave you trouble. Make sure you known the directions for the different types of questions that will appear on the SAT. Review the general test-taking strategies in Chapter 2. Spend as much time as you can learning the words on the High Frequency Word List in Chapter 9, and reviewing the information in Important Facts and Formulas in Chapter 10 and Principles Involving Inequalities in Chapter 11.

The Two-Week Concentrated Program

This is the program to follow when you haven't waited until the *very* last minute, but you've waited long enough that time is getting tight. Concentrate on the areas that give you trouble. Don't spend your time reviewing material you already know well. Do as many of the exercises as you can in your problem areas.

Session	Topic	Activity
1.	The SAT	Do the Sample SAT Questions in Chapter 2. Check your answers.
2.	The Trial Run and Self-Evaluation	Under simulated test conditions, take the Diagnostic SAT in Chapter 4. Score and evaluate the results of your diagnostic test. Make a list of your weak areas to use later in doing practice exercises. Carefully study the answer explanations for the questions you missed.
3.	Vocabulary Building, Antonyms, Analogies	Study the High-Frequency Word List in Chapter 9. Study the tactics and do the exercises in Chapters 5 and 6. Check your answers. Study the answer explanations for questions you missed.
4.	Reviewing Arithmetic and Algebra	Study the tactics in Chapter 10 and the review material in Chapter 12. Do the exercises. Concentrate on areas of weakness discovered in the Diagnostic SAT. Study the answer explanations for questions you missed.
5.	Vocabulary Building, Sentence Completion	Study the Basic Word Parts in Chapter 9. Study the tactics for handling sentence completion questions in Chapter 7. Do the exercises, and compare your answers with the correct ones.
6.	Plane Geometry	Review geometric facts (Chapter 12). Do the geometry exercises, and study the correct answers.
7.	Reading Comprehension	Study the tactics in Chapter 8. Do the first two reading comprehension exercises. Check your answers. Study the answer explanations for questions you missed.
8.	Solving Verbal Problems	Do the verbal problems in Chapter 12: Fractions (pages 348–49), Percent (pages 355–56), Average (page 358), Motion (pages 360–61), Ratio and Proportion (pages 364–66), Mixture and Solution (pages 367–68), and Work (pages 369–71).
9.	Reading Comprehension	Finish the exercises in Chapter 8. Check your answers. Study the answer explanations for the questions you missed.
10.	Quantitative Comparison	Study the tactics in Chapter 11. Do the exercises. Study the answer explanations for the questions you missed.
11.	TSWE	Study the tactics in Chapter 13. Do the exercises. Check your answers. Study the answer explanations for questions you missed.
12.	Getting Ready	Establish test conditions and take Model SAT Test 1. Score your results. Study the answer explanations for questions you missed.

Session	Topic	Activity
13–14.	Final Dress Rehearsal	Complete as many of the model SATs in Chapter 14 as you can in the time you have left. Score your results. Study the answer explanations for questions you missed.

NOTE: Sessions 4 through 11 need not be followed in this sequence.

The Comprehensive Study Program

This is the plan to use when you have ten weeks or more to study for the SAT. It allows you to work slowly and steadily, building on what you have already learned, which is the best way to prepare for this or any other test.

The study program includes 15 math sessions and 15 verbal/TSWE sessions. Together, the 30 sessions total approximately 30 hours of work (this does not include the time you'll need to take the Diagnostic SAT in the next chapter and the six model SATs in Chapter 14). The sessions are keyed to specific review material and practice exercises in the verbal, mathematical, and standard written English parts of this book.

The verbal section covers antonym, sentence completion, analogy, and reading comprehension questions, as well as the usage and sentence correction questions on the TSWE section of the SAT. Each session will require 30 to 60 minutes of your time, though this will vary according to individual needs.

The math section of this study program covers the material expected of a high school senior. Each session will require approximately 90 minutes of your time, though, again, this will vary. You may find that you can complete several sessions in that time, and you may find sessions on which you need to spend more time.

Take the Diagnostic SAT before you begin this study program. Use the Self-Evaluation section to discover which topics and/or types of questions are troublesome for you. Adjust the study program, if necessary, so that you can concentrate on the areas that give you trouble.

Work out a suitable time schedule and carefully follow it until you have completed the study program. In planning your schedule, find time to work on vocabulary in addition to working with the topics covered in the study program given here (see the separate plans for vocabulary study on page 163). After you finish your review, take the six model SATs in Chapter 14. Each test will provide you with valuable test-taking experience. Though you may decide to work on these tests section by section rather than as a complete test, you should make time to take at least one or two of the three-hour tests in one sitting, under test conditions.

VERBAL AND TSWE

Session	Topic	Activity
1.	Antonyms	Study the tactics in Chapter 5. Do Antonym Exercise A and check your answers. Study the answer explanations for questions you missed.
2.	Analogies	Study the tactics in Chapter 6. Do questions 1–25 in Exercise A. Check your answers. Study the answer explanations for questions you missed.
3.	Sentence Completion	Study the tactics in Chapter 7. Do questions 1–25 in Exercise A. Check your answers.

Session	Topic	Activity
4.	Reading Comprehension	Study the tactics in Chapter 8.
5.	Reading Comprehension	Do Exercise A in Chapter 8. Check your answers. Study the answer explanations for questions you missed.
6.	Antonyms	Do Exercise B in Chapter 5. Check your answers. Study the answer explanations for questions you missed.
7.	Analogies	Do questions 26–50 in Exercise A (Chapter 6). Check your answers.
8.	Sentence Completion	Do questions 26–50 in Exercise A (Chapter 7). Check your answers.
9.	Reading Comprehension	Do Exercise B in Chapter 8. Check your answers. Study the answer explanations for the questions you missed.
10.	Analogies	Do questions 1–25 in Exercise B (Chapter 7). Check your answers. Study the answer explanations for questions you missed.
11.	Sentence Completion	Do Exercise B in Chapter 7. Check your answers. Study the answer explanations for questions you missed.
12.	Reading Comprehension	Do Exercise C in Chapter 8. Check your answers. Study the answer explanations for the questions you missed.
13.	Analogies	Do questions 26–50 in Exercise B (Chapter 7). Check your answers. Study the answer explanations for the questions you missed.
14.	Reading Comprehension	Do Exercise D in Chapter 8. Check your answers. Study the answer explanations for questions you missed.
15.	TSWE	Study the tactics in Chapter 13. Do the Practice Exercise. Check your answers. Study the answer explanations for questions you missed.

MATHEMATICS

Session	Topic	Activity
1.	Arithmetic and Algebra	Study pages 327–30. Do the Practice Exercises on pages 336–37.
2.	Algebra	Study pages 330–34. Do the Practice Exercises on pages 338–39.
3.	Using Algebra	Study solving problems by equations on pages 334–35. Do the Practice Exercises on pages 337–38.
4.	Fractions	Study the definitions and basic operations on pages 341–44, and do the Practice Exercises on pages 345–48.
5.	Fractions	Study the sections on solving fractional equations and problems involving fractions on pages 344–45, and do the Practice Exercises on pages 348–49.
6.	Decimals and Percentages	Study the sections on decimals and percents on pages 351–55, and do the Practice Exercises on pages 353 and 355–56.
7.	Problems Involving Averages, Motion Problems	Study the definitions, formulas, and verbal problems on pages 357–59, and do the Practice Exercises on pages 358 and 360–61.
8.	Ratio and Proportion Problems	Study the definitions, principles, and verbal problems on pages 362–64, and do the Practice Exercises on pages 364–67.
9.	Mixture and Solution Problems, Work Problems	Study the section on mixture and solution problems on page 367 and the section on work problems on page 369. Do the Practice Exercises on pages 367–68 and 369–71.
10.	Reviewing Geometry	Study the definitions and formulas, and the applications of definitions and formulas on pages 371–76. Do the Practice Exercises on pages 376–81.
11.	Coordinate Geometry, Interpreting Data	Study the definitions and applications on pages 381–82 and 383–84, and do the Practice Exercises on pages 382–83 and 384–88.
12.	Standard Multiple-Choice Questions	Study the tactics in Chapter 10, and do Mathematics Exercise A. Check your answers. Study the answer explanations for any questions you missed.
13.	Quantitative Comparison Questions	Study the tactics in Chapter 11, and do questions 1–71 in the Practice Exercise. Check your answers. Study the answer explanations for questions you missed.
14.	Standard Multiple-Choice Questions	Do Mathematics Exercise B (Chapter 10). Check your answers. Study the answer explanations for any questions you missed.
15.	Quantitative Comparison Questions	Do questions 72–142 in the Practice Exercise (Chapter 11). Check your answers. Study the answer explanations for any questions you missed.

PART TWO

Pinpoint Your Trouble Spots

4 A Diagnostic SAT

- **Diagnostic Test**
- **Answer Key**
- **Self-Evaluation**
- **Answer Explanations**

This chapter contains a diagnostic SAT. Like the actual SAT which you'll be taking soon, it has 6 sections: 2 verbal, 2 math, 1 TSWE, and 1 experimental (which in this case is another verbal section). Each section has the same number and type of questions as you'll find on the actual SAT. And each section should be completed in 30 minutes. At the end of the test are answer keys, self-evaluation charts, and answer explanations.

The diagnostic test in this chapter is a multipurpose tool. First, it is a tool to help you identify your problem areas and skills. Take the test, evaluate your results following our charts, and you will discover your strengths and weaknesses. You will know what to study.

Second, this test is a tool to help you design a study plan that's right for you. Use the information you get from this test to tailor one of our study plans in the preceding chapter to fit your particular needs. If you

find you need extra time on a certain topic, build that time in. You are in charge of your study program—make it work for you.

Third, this test is your introduction to the format and content of the actual SAT. There is nothing like working your way through actual SAT-type questions for three hours to teach you how much stamina you need and how much speed.

Finally, this test is your chance to learn how to profit from your mistakes. It will expose you to the sorts of "traps" the test-makers set for you and the sorts of "shortcuts" we recommend you take. Read the answer explanations for every question you miss. You'll be amazed to see how much you'll learn.

You are about to take a Diagnostic Test that can change the way you do on the SAT. You have three hours to get through the six sections. Make every minute pay.

Answer Sheet–Diagnostic Test

Start with number 1 for each new section. If a section has fewer than 50 questions, leave the extra spaces blank.

Section 1

1. Ⓐ Ⓑ Ⓒ Ⓓ Ⓔ	11. Ⓐ Ⓑ Ⓒ Ⓓ Ⓔ	21. Ⓐ Ⓑ Ⓒ Ⓓ Ⓔ	31. Ⓐ Ⓑ Ⓒ Ⓓ Ⓔ	41. Ⓐ Ⓑ Ⓒ Ⓓ Ⓔ
2. Ⓐ Ⓑ Ⓒ Ⓓ Ⓔ	12. Ⓐ Ⓑ Ⓒ Ⓓ Ⓔ	22. Ⓐ Ⓑ Ⓒ Ⓓ Ⓔ	32. Ⓐ Ⓑ Ⓒ Ⓓ Ⓔ	42. Ⓐ Ⓑ Ⓒ Ⓓ Ⓔ
3. Ⓐ Ⓑ Ⓒ Ⓓ Ⓔ	13. Ⓐ Ⓑ Ⓒ Ⓓ Ⓔ	23. Ⓐ Ⓑ Ⓒ Ⓓ Ⓔ	33. Ⓐ Ⓑ Ⓒ Ⓓ Ⓔ	43. Ⓐ Ⓑ Ⓒ Ⓓ Ⓔ
4. Ⓐ Ⓑ Ⓒ Ⓓ Ⓔ	14. Ⓐ Ⓑ Ⓒ Ⓓ Ⓔ	24. Ⓐ Ⓑ Ⓒ Ⓓ Ⓔ	34. Ⓐ Ⓑ Ⓒ Ⓓ Ⓔ	44. Ⓐ Ⓑ Ⓒ Ⓓ Ⓔ
5. Ⓐ Ⓑ Ⓒ Ⓓ Ⓔ	15. Ⓐ Ⓑ Ⓒ Ⓓ Ⓔ	25. Ⓐ Ⓑ Ⓒ Ⓓ Ⓔ	35. Ⓐ Ⓑ Ⓒ Ⓓ Ⓔ	45. Ⓐ Ⓑ Ⓒ Ⓓ Ⓔ
6. Ⓐ Ⓑ Ⓒ Ⓓ Ⓔ	16. Ⓐ Ⓑ Ⓒ Ⓓ Ⓔ	26. Ⓐ Ⓑ Ⓒ Ⓓ Ⓔ	36. Ⓐ Ⓑ Ⓒ Ⓓ Ⓔ	46. Ⓐ Ⓑ Ⓒ Ⓓ Ⓔ
7. Ⓐ Ⓑ Ⓒ Ⓓ Ⓔ	17. Ⓐ Ⓑ Ⓒ Ⓓ Ⓔ	27. Ⓐ Ⓑ Ⓒ Ⓓ Ⓔ	37. Ⓐ Ⓑ Ⓒ Ⓓ Ⓔ	47. Ⓐ Ⓑ Ⓒ Ⓓ Ⓔ
8. Ⓐ Ⓑ Ⓒ Ⓓ Ⓔ	18. Ⓐ Ⓑ Ⓒ Ⓓ Ⓔ	28. Ⓐ Ⓑ Ⓒ Ⓓ Ⓔ	38. Ⓐ Ⓑ Ⓒ Ⓓ Ⓔ	48. Ⓐ Ⓑ Ⓒ Ⓓ Ⓔ
9. Ⓐ Ⓑ Ⓒ Ⓓ Ⓔ	19. Ⓐ Ⓑ Ⓒ Ⓓ Ⓔ	29. Ⓐ Ⓑ Ⓒ Ⓓ Ⓔ	39. Ⓐ Ⓑ Ⓒ Ⓓ Ⓔ	49. Ⓐ Ⓑ Ⓒ Ⓓ Ⓔ
10. Ⓐ Ⓑ Ⓒ Ⓓ Ⓔ	20. Ⓐ Ⓑ Ⓒ Ⓓ Ⓔ	30. Ⓐ Ⓑ Ⓒ Ⓓ Ⓔ	40. Ⓐ Ⓑ Ⓒ Ⓓ Ⓔ	50. Ⓐ Ⓑ Ⓒ Ⓓ Ⓔ

Section 2

1. Ⓐ Ⓑ Ⓒ Ⓓ Ⓔ	11. Ⓐ Ⓑ Ⓒ Ⓓ Ⓔ	21. Ⓐ Ⓑ Ⓒ Ⓓ Ⓔ	31. Ⓐ Ⓑ Ⓒ Ⓓ Ⓔ	41. Ⓐ Ⓑ Ⓒ Ⓓ Ⓔ
2. Ⓐ Ⓑ Ⓒ Ⓓ Ⓔ	12. Ⓐ Ⓑ Ⓒ Ⓓ Ⓔ	22. Ⓐ Ⓑ Ⓒ Ⓓ Ⓔ	32. Ⓐ Ⓑ Ⓒ Ⓓ Ⓔ	42. Ⓐ Ⓑ Ⓒ Ⓓ Ⓔ
3. Ⓐ Ⓑ Ⓒ Ⓓ Ⓔ	13. Ⓐ Ⓑ Ⓒ Ⓓ Ⓔ	23. Ⓐ Ⓑ Ⓒ Ⓓ Ⓔ	33. Ⓐ Ⓑ Ⓒ Ⓓ Ⓔ	43. Ⓐ Ⓑ Ⓒ Ⓓ Ⓔ
4. Ⓐ Ⓑ Ⓒ Ⓓ Ⓔ	14. Ⓐ Ⓑ Ⓒ Ⓓ Ⓔ	24. Ⓐ Ⓑ Ⓒ Ⓓ Ⓔ	34. Ⓐ Ⓑ Ⓒ Ⓓ Ⓔ	44. Ⓐ Ⓑ Ⓒ Ⓓ Ⓔ
5. Ⓐ Ⓑ Ⓒ Ⓓ Ⓔ	15. Ⓐ Ⓑ Ⓒ Ⓓ Ⓔ	25. Ⓐ Ⓑ Ⓒ Ⓓ Ⓔ	35. Ⓐ Ⓑ Ⓒ Ⓓ Ⓔ	45. Ⓐ Ⓑ Ⓒ Ⓓ Ⓔ
6. Ⓐ Ⓑ Ⓒ Ⓓ Ⓔ	16. Ⓐ Ⓑ Ⓒ Ⓓ Ⓔ	26. Ⓐ Ⓑ Ⓒ Ⓓ Ⓔ	36. Ⓐ Ⓑ Ⓒ Ⓓ Ⓔ	46. Ⓐ Ⓑ Ⓒ Ⓓ Ⓔ
7. Ⓐ Ⓑ Ⓒ Ⓓ Ⓔ	17. Ⓐ Ⓑ Ⓒ Ⓓ Ⓔ	27. Ⓐ Ⓑ Ⓒ Ⓓ Ⓔ	37. Ⓐ Ⓑ Ⓒ Ⓓ Ⓔ	47. Ⓐ Ⓑ Ⓒ Ⓓ Ⓔ
8. Ⓐ Ⓑ Ⓒ Ⓓ Ⓔ	18. Ⓐ Ⓑ Ⓒ Ⓓ Ⓔ	28. Ⓐ Ⓑ Ⓒ Ⓓ Ⓔ	38. Ⓐ Ⓑ Ⓒ Ⓓ Ⓔ	48. Ⓐ Ⓑ Ⓒ Ⓓ Ⓔ
9. Ⓐ Ⓑ Ⓒ Ⓓ Ⓔ	19. Ⓐ Ⓑ Ⓒ Ⓓ Ⓔ	29. Ⓐ Ⓑ Ⓒ Ⓓ Ⓔ	39. Ⓐ Ⓑ Ⓒ Ⓓ Ⓔ	49. Ⓐ Ⓑ Ⓒ Ⓓ Ⓔ
10. Ⓐ Ⓑ Ⓒ Ⓓ Ⓔ	20. Ⓐ Ⓑ Ⓒ Ⓓ Ⓔ	30. Ⓐ Ⓑ Ⓒ Ⓓ Ⓔ	40. Ⓐ Ⓑ Ⓒ Ⓓ Ⓔ	50. Ⓐ Ⓑ Ⓒ Ⓓ Ⓔ

Section 3

1. Ⓐ Ⓑ Ⓒ Ⓓ Ⓔ	11. Ⓐ Ⓑ Ⓒ Ⓓ Ⓔ	21. Ⓐ Ⓑ Ⓒ Ⓓ Ⓔ	31. Ⓐ Ⓑ Ⓒ Ⓓ Ⓔ	41. Ⓐ Ⓑ Ⓒ Ⓓ Ⓔ
2. Ⓐ Ⓑ Ⓒ Ⓓ Ⓔ	12. Ⓐ Ⓑ Ⓒ Ⓓ Ⓔ	22. Ⓐ Ⓑ Ⓒ Ⓓ Ⓔ	32. Ⓐ Ⓑ Ⓒ Ⓓ Ⓔ	42. Ⓐ Ⓑ Ⓒ Ⓓ Ⓔ
3. Ⓐ Ⓑ Ⓒ Ⓓ Ⓔ	13. Ⓐ Ⓑ Ⓒ Ⓓ Ⓔ	23. Ⓐ Ⓑ Ⓒ Ⓓ Ⓔ	33. Ⓐ Ⓑ Ⓒ Ⓓ Ⓔ	43. Ⓐ Ⓑ Ⓒ Ⓓ Ⓔ
4. Ⓐ Ⓑ Ⓒ Ⓓ Ⓔ	14. Ⓐ Ⓑ Ⓒ Ⓓ Ⓔ	24. Ⓐ Ⓑ Ⓒ Ⓓ Ⓔ	34. Ⓐ Ⓑ Ⓒ Ⓓ Ⓔ	44. Ⓐ Ⓑ Ⓒ Ⓓ Ⓔ
5. Ⓐ Ⓑ Ⓒ Ⓓ Ⓔ	15. Ⓐ Ⓑ Ⓒ Ⓓ Ⓔ	25. Ⓐ Ⓑ Ⓒ Ⓓ Ⓔ	35. Ⓐ Ⓑ Ⓒ Ⓓ Ⓔ	45. Ⓐ Ⓑ Ⓒ Ⓓ Ⓔ
6. Ⓐ Ⓑ Ⓒ Ⓓ Ⓔ	16. Ⓐ Ⓑ Ⓒ Ⓓ Ⓔ	26. Ⓐ Ⓑ Ⓒ Ⓓ Ⓔ	36. Ⓐ Ⓑ Ⓒ Ⓓ Ⓔ	46. Ⓐ Ⓑ Ⓒ Ⓓ Ⓔ
7. Ⓐ Ⓑ Ⓒ Ⓓ Ⓔ	17. Ⓐ Ⓑ Ⓒ Ⓓ Ⓔ	27. Ⓐ Ⓑ Ⓒ Ⓓ Ⓔ	37. Ⓐ Ⓑ Ⓒ Ⓓ Ⓔ	47. Ⓐ Ⓑ Ⓒ Ⓓ Ⓔ
8. Ⓐ Ⓑ Ⓒ Ⓓ Ⓔ	18. Ⓐ Ⓑ Ⓒ Ⓓ Ⓔ	28. Ⓐ Ⓑ Ⓒ Ⓓ Ⓔ	38. Ⓐ Ⓑ Ⓒ Ⓓ Ⓔ	48. Ⓐ Ⓑ Ⓒ Ⓓ Ⓔ
9. Ⓐ Ⓑ Ⓒ Ⓓ Ⓔ	19. Ⓐ Ⓑ Ⓒ Ⓓ Ⓔ	29. Ⓐ Ⓑ Ⓒ Ⓓ Ⓔ	39. Ⓐ Ⓑ Ⓒ Ⓓ Ⓔ	49. Ⓐ Ⓑ Ⓒ Ⓓ Ⓔ
10. Ⓐ Ⓑ Ⓒ Ⓓ Ⓔ	20. Ⓐ Ⓑ Ⓒ Ⓓ Ⓔ	30. Ⓐ Ⓑ Ⓒ Ⓓ Ⓔ	40. Ⓐ Ⓑ Ⓒ Ⓓ Ⓔ	50. Ⓐ Ⓑ Ⓒ Ⓓ Ⓔ

Start with number 1 for each new section. If a section has fewer than 50 questions, leave the extra spaces blank.

Section 4

1. Ⓐ Ⓑ Ⓒ Ⓓ Ⓔ   11. Ⓐ Ⓑ Ⓒ Ⓓ Ⓔ   21. Ⓐ Ⓑ Ⓒ Ⓓ Ⓔ   31. Ⓐ Ⓑ Ⓒ Ⓓ Ⓔ   41. Ⓐ Ⓑ Ⓒ Ⓓ Ⓔ
2. Ⓐ Ⓑ Ⓒ Ⓓ Ⓔ   12. Ⓐ Ⓑ Ⓒ Ⓓ Ⓔ   22. Ⓐ Ⓑ Ⓒ Ⓓ Ⓔ   32. Ⓐ Ⓑ Ⓒ Ⓓ Ⓔ   42. Ⓐ Ⓑ Ⓒ Ⓓ Ⓔ
3. Ⓐ Ⓑ Ⓒ Ⓓ Ⓔ   13. Ⓐ Ⓑ Ⓒ Ⓓ Ⓔ   23. Ⓐ Ⓑ Ⓒ Ⓓ Ⓔ   33. Ⓐ Ⓑ Ⓒ Ⓓ Ⓔ   43. Ⓐ Ⓑ Ⓒ Ⓓ Ⓔ
4. Ⓐ Ⓑ Ⓒ Ⓓ Ⓔ   14. Ⓐ Ⓑ Ⓒ Ⓓ Ⓔ   24. Ⓐ Ⓑ Ⓒ Ⓓ Ⓔ   34. Ⓐ Ⓑ Ⓒ Ⓓ Ⓔ   44. Ⓐ Ⓑ Ⓒ Ⓓ Ⓔ
5. Ⓐ Ⓑ Ⓒ Ⓓ Ⓔ   15. Ⓐ Ⓑ Ⓒ Ⓓ Ⓔ   25. Ⓐ Ⓑ Ⓒ Ⓓ Ⓔ   35. Ⓐ Ⓑ Ⓒ Ⓓ Ⓔ   45. Ⓐ Ⓑ Ⓒ Ⓓ Ⓔ
6. Ⓐ Ⓑ Ⓒ Ⓓ Ⓔ   16. Ⓐ Ⓑ Ⓒ Ⓓ Ⓔ   26. Ⓐ Ⓑ Ⓒ Ⓓ Ⓔ   36. Ⓐ Ⓑ Ⓒ Ⓓ Ⓔ   46. Ⓐ Ⓑ Ⓒ Ⓓ Ⓔ
7. Ⓐ Ⓑ Ⓒ Ⓓ Ⓔ   17. Ⓐ Ⓑ Ⓒ Ⓓ Ⓔ   27. Ⓐ Ⓑ Ⓒ Ⓓ Ⓔ   37. Ⓐ Ⓑ Ⓒ Ⓓ Ⓔ   47. Ⓐ Ⓑ Ⓒ Ⓓ Ⓔ
8. Ⓐ Ⓑ Ⓒ Ⓓ Ⓔ   18. Ⓐ Ⓑ Ⓒ Ⓓ Ⓔ   28. Ⓐ Ⓑ Ⓒ Ⓓ Ⓔ   38. Ⓐ Ⓑ Ⓒ Ⓓ Ⓔ   48. Ⓐ Ⓑ Ⓒ Ⓓ Ⓔ
9. Ⓐ Ⓑ Ⓒ Ⓓ Ⓔ   19. Ⓐ Ⓑ Ⓒ Ⓓ Ⓔ   29. Ⓐ Ⓑ Ⓒ Ⓓ Ⓔ   39. Ⓐ Ⓑ Ⓒ Ⓓ Ⓔ   49. Ⓐ Ⓑ Ⓒ Ⓓ Ⓔ
10. Ⓐ Ⓑ Ⓒ Ⓓ Ⓔ   20. Ⓐ Ⓑ Ⓒ Ⓓ Ⓔ   30. Ⓐ Ⓑ Ⓒ Ⓓ Ⓔ   40. Ⓐ Ⓑ Ⓒ Ⓓ Ⓔ   50. Ⓐ Ⓑ Ⓒ Ⓓ Ⓔ

Section 5

1. Ⓐ Ⓑ Ⓒ Ⓓ Ⓔ   11. Ⓐ Ⓑ Ⓒ Ⓓ Ⓔ   21. Ⓐ Ⓑ Ⓒ Ⓓ Ⓔ   31. Ⓐ Ⓑ Ⓒ Ⓓ Ⓔ   41. Ⓐ Ⓑ Ⓒ Ⓓ Ⓔ
2. Ⓐ Ⓑ Ⓒ Ⓓ Ⓔ   12. Ⓐ Ⓑ Ⓒ Ⓓ Ⓔ   22. Ⓐ Ⓑ Ⓒ Ⓓ Ⓔ   32. Ⓐ Ⓑ Ⓒ Ⓓ Ⓔ   42. Ⓐ Ⓑ Ⓒ Ⓓ Ⓔ
3. Ⓐ Ⓑ Ⓒ Ⓓ Ⓔ   13. Ⓐ Ⓑ Ⓒ Ⓓ Ⓔ   23. Ⓐ Ⓑ Ⓒ Ⓓ Ⓔ   33. Ⓐ Ⓑ Ⓒ Ⓓ Ⓔ   43. Ⓐ Ⓑ Ⓒ Ⓓ Ⓔ
4. Ⓐ Ⓑ Ⓒ Ⓓ Ⓔ   14. Ⓐ Ⓑ Ⓒ Ⓓ Ⓔ   24. Ⓐ Ⓑ Ⓒ Ⓓ Ⓔ   34. Ⓐ Ⓑ Ⓒ Ⓓ Ⓔ   44. Ⓐ Ⓑ Ⓒ Ⓓ Ⓔ
5. Ⓐ Ⓑ Ⓒ Ⓓ Ⓔ   15. Ⓐ Ⓑ Ⓒ Ⓓ Ⓔ   25. Ⓐ Ⓑ Ⓒ Ⓓ Ⓔ   35. Ⓐ Ⓑ Ⓒ Ⓓ Ⓔ   45. Ⓐ Ⓑ Ⓒ Ⓓ Ⓔ
6. Ⓐ Ⓑ Ⓒ Ⓓ Ⓔ   16. Ⓐ Ⓑ Ⓒ Ⓓ Ⓔ   26. Ⓐ Ⓑ Ⓒ Ⓓ Ⓔ   36. Ⓐ Ⓑ Ⓒ Ⓓ Ⓔ   46. Ⓐ Ⓑ Ⓒ Ⓓ Ⓔ
7. Ⓐ Ⓑ Ⓒ Ⓓ Ⓔ   17. Ⓐ Ⓑ Ⓒ Ⓓ Ⓔ   27. Ⓐ Ⓑ Ⓒ Ⓓ Ⓔ   37. Ⓐ Ⓑ Ⓒ Ⓓ Ⓔ   47. Ⓐ Ⓑ Ⓒ Ⓓ Ⓔ
8. Ⓐ Ⓑ Ⓒ Ⓓ Ⓔ   18. Ⓐ Ⓑ Ⓒ Ⓓ Ⓔ   28. Ⓐ Ⓑ Ⓒ Ⓓ Ⓔ   38. Ⓐ Ⓑ Ⓒ Ⓓ Ⓔ   48. Ⓐ Ⓑ Ⓒ Ⓓ Ⓔ
9. Ⓐ Ⓑ Ⓒ Ⓓ Ⓔ   19. Ⓐ Ⓑ Ⓒ Ⓓ Ⓔ   29. Ⓐ Ⓑ Ⓒ Ⓓ Ⓔ   39. Ⓐ Ⓑ Ⓒ Ⓓ Ⓔ   49. Ⓐ Ⓑ Ⓒ Ⓓ Ⓔ
10. Ⓐ Ⓑ Ⓒ Ⓓ Ⓔ   20. Ⓐ Ⓑ Ⓒ Ⓓ Ⓔ   30. Ⓐ Ⓑ Ⓒ Ⓓ Ⓔ   40. Ⓐ Ⓑ Ⓒ Ⓓ Ⓔ   50. Ⓐ Ⓑ Ⓒ Ⓓ Ⓔ

Section 6

1. Ⓐ Ⓑ Ⓒ Ⓓ Ⓔ   11. Ⓐ Ⓑ Ⓒ Ⓓ Ⓔ   21. Ⓐ Ⓑ Ⓒ Ⓓ Ⓔ   31. Ⓐ Ⓑ Ⓒ Ⓓ Ⓔ   41. Ⓐ Ⓑ Ⓒ Ⓓ Ⓔ
2. Ⓐ Ⓑ Ⓒ Ⓓ Ⓔ   12. Ⓐ Ⓑ Ⓒ Ⓓ Ⓔ   22. Ⓐ Ⓑ Ⓒ Ⓓ Ⓔ   32. Ⓐ Ⓑ Ⓒ Ⓓ Ⓔ   42. Ⓐ Ⓑ Ⓒ Ⓓ Ⓔ
3. Ⓐ Ⓑ Ⓒ Ⓓ Ⓔ   13. Ⓐ Ⓑ Ⓒ Ⓓ Ⓔ   23. Ⓐ Ⓑ Ⓒ Ⓓ Ⓔ   33. Ⓐ Ⓑ Ⓒ Ⓓ Ⓔ   43. Ⓐ Ⓑ Ⓒ Ⓓ Ⓔ
4. Ⓐ Ⓑ Ⓒ Ⓓ Ⓔ   14. Ⓐ Ⓑ Ⓒ Ⓓ Ⓔ   24. Ⓐ Ⓑ Ⓒ Ⓓ Ⓔ   34. Ⓐ Ⓑ Ⓒ Ⓓ Ⓔ   44. Ⓐ Ⓑ Ⓒ Ⓓ Ⓔ
5. Ⓐ Ⓑ Ⓒ Ⓓ Ⓔ   15. Ⓐ Ⓑ Ⓒ Ⓓ Ⓔ   25. Ⓐ Ⓑ Ⓒ Ⓓ Ⓔ   35. Ⓐ Ⓑ Ⓒ Ⓓ Ⓔ   45. Ⓐ Ⓑ Ⓒ Ⓓ Ⓔ
6. Ⓐ Ⓑ Ⓒ Ⓓ Ⓔ   16. Ⓐ Ⓑ Ⓒ Ⓓ Ⓔ   26. Ⓐ Ⓑ Ⓒ Ⓓ Ⓔ   36. Ⓐ Ⓑ Ⓒ Ⓓ Ⓔ   46. Ⓐ Ⓑ Ⓒ Ⓓ Ⓔ
7. Ⓐ Ⓑ Ⓒ Ⓓ Ⓔ   17. Ⓐ Ⓑ Ⓒ Ⓓ Ⓔ   27. Ⓐ Ⓑ Ⓒ Ⓓ Ⓔ   37. Ⓐ Ⓑ Ⓒ Ⓓ Ⓔ   47. Ⓐ Ⓑ Ⓒ Ⓓ Ⓔ
8. Ⓐ Ⓑ Ⓒ Ⓓ Ⓔ   18. Ⓐ Ⓑ Ⓒ Ⓓ Ⓔ   28. Ⓐ Ⓑ Ⓒ Ⓓ Ⓔ   38. Ⓐ Ⓑ Ⓒ Ⓓ Ⓔ   48. Ⓐ Ⓑ Ⓒ Ⓓ Ⓔ
9. Ⓐ Ⓑ Ⓒ Ⓓ Ⓔ   19. Ⓐ Ⓑ Ⓒ Ⓓ Ⓔ   29. Ⓐ Ⓑ Ⓒ Ⓓ Ⓔ   39. Ⓐ Ⓑ Ⓒ Ⓓ Ⓔ   49. Ⓐ Ⓑ Ⓒ Ⓓ Ⓔ
10. Ⓐ Ⓑ Ⓒ Ⓓ Ⓔ   20. Ⓐ Ⓑ Ⓒ Ⓓ Ⓔ   30. Ⓐ Ⓑ Ⓒ Ⓓ Ⓔ   40. Ⓐ Ⓑ Ⓒ Ⓓ Ⓔ   50. Ⓐ Ⓑ Ⓒ Ⓓ Ⓔ

Remove answer sheet by cutting on dotted line

SECTION 1 Time—30 minutes 45 Questions

For each question in this section, choose the best answer and blacken the corresponding space on the answer sheet.

Each question below consists of a word in capital letters, followed by five lettered words or phrases. Choose the word or phrase that is most nearly <u>opposite</u> in meaning to the word in capital letters. Since some of the questions require you to distinguish fine shades of meaning, consider all the choices before deciding which is best.

Example:

   GOOD: (A) sour   (B) bad   (C) red
   (D) hot   (E) ugly

   Ⓐ ● Ⓒ Ⓓ Ⓔ

---

1. RESOLVE: (A) remove   (B) waver
   (C) diversify   (D) elect   (E) lubricate

2. AUTHENTIC: (A) gracious   (B) intellectual
   (C) incomprehensible   (D) counterfeit
   (E) unwritten

3. CRAMPED: (A) domestic   (B) spacious
   (C) remodeled   (D) lighthearted   (E) erratic

4. ALLEVIATE: (A) aggravate   (B) darken
   (C) mystify   (D) scatter   (E) inter

5. DISENGAGE: (A) forget   (B) attach
   (C) remain nearby   (D) circulate openly
   (E) repent

6. ADVERSARY: (A) informer   (B) laughingstock
   (C) ancestor   (D) malefactor   (E) proponent

7. HUBBUB: (A) central position   (B) lack of time
   (C) disinterest   (D) modesty   (E) quiet

8. MUTABLE: (A) impervious   (B) natural
   (C) reluctant   (D) permanent   (E) mortal

9. HAMPER: (A) sanitize   (B) further   (C) soften
   (D) renovate   (E) corroborate

10. PLACATE: (A) anticipate   (B) exaggerate
    (C) neglect   (D) delude   (E) exasperate

11. INTREPID: (A) cowardly   (B) aware
    (C) proper   (D) external   (E) sociable

12. RIFLE: (A) leave undisturbed   (B) facilitate
    (C) extricate   (D) remain indifferent
    (E) disarm

13. PULCHRITUDE: (A) magnificence
    (B) ignorance   (C) ugliness   (D) lassitude
    (E) punctuality

14. HACKNEYED: (A) driven   (B) novel
    (C) startled   (D) dominant   (E) rational

15. INNOCUOUS: (A) guilty   (B) blasphemous
    (C) blatant   (D) hallowed   (E) harmful

Each sentence below has one or two blanks, each blank indicating that something has been omitted. Beneath the sentence are five lettered words or sets of words. Choose the word or set of words that <u>best</u> fits the meaning of the sentence as a whole.

Example:

Although its publicity has been ----, the film itself is intelligent, well-acted, handsomely produced, and altogether ----.

(A) tasteless..respectable   (B) extensive..moderate
   (C) sophisticated..amateur   (D) risqué..crude
   (E) perfect..spectacular

   ● Ⓑ Ⓒ Ⓓ Ⓔ

---

16. The officers of the corporation pledged there would be no ----; nothing would be held against the strikers.

    (A) truce   (B) retaliations   (C) reservations
    (D) scabs   (E) favoritism

17. Having published over three hundred books in less than fifty years, science fiction writer Isaac Asimov may well be the most ---- author of our day.

    (A) fastidious   (B) insecure   (C) outmoded
    (D) prolific   (E) indigenous

18. In a time of fiscal crisis, such a ---- expenditure of public funds must be ----.

    (A) rapid..hastened
    (B) proper..vindicated
    (C) lavish..justified
    (D) judicious..condemned
    (E) righteous..criticized

GO ON TO THE NEXT PAGE →

1   1   1   1   1   1   1   1   1   1   1   1

19. Because his time was limited, John decided to read the ---- novel *War and Peace* in ---- edition.

(A) wordy..an unedited
(B) lengthy..an abridged
(C) famous..a modern
(D) romantic..an autographed
(E) popular..a complete

20. In giving a speech, the speaker's goal is to communicate ideas clearly and ----, so that the audience will be in no ---- about the meaning of the speech.

(A) effectively..haste
(B) indirectly..distress
(C) vigorously..discomfort
(D) unambiguously..confusion
(E) tactfully..suspense

Each passage below is followed by questions based on its content. Answer all questions following a passage on the basis of what is <u>stated</u> or <u>implied</u> in that passage.

That night in my rented room, while letting the hot water run over my can of pork and beans in the sink, I opened Mencken's *A Book of*
Line *Prejudices* and began to read. I was jarred and
(5) shocked by the style, the clear, clean, sweeping sentences. Why did he write like that? And how did one write like that? I pictured the man as a raging demon, slashing with his pen, consumed with hate, denouncing everything American,
(10) extolling everything European, laughing at the weaknesses of people, mocking God, authority. What was this? I stood up, trying to realize what reality lay behind the meaning of the words. Yes, this man was fighting, fighting with words. He
(15) was using words as a weapon, using them as one would use a club. Could words be weapons? Well, yes, for here they were. Then, maybe, perhaps a Negro could use them as a weapon? No. It frightened me. I read on, and what
(20) amazed me was not what he said, but how on earth anybody had the courage to say it.
      What strange world was this? I concluded the book with the conviction that I had somehow overlooked something terribly important in life. I
(25) had once tried to write, had once reveled in feeling, had let my crude imagination roam, but the impulse to dream had been slowly beaten out of me by experience. Now it surged up again and I hungered for books, new ways of looking and
(30) seeing. It was not a matter of believing or disbelieving what I read, but of feeling something new, of being affected by something that made the look of the world different.
      As dawn broke I ate my pork and beans, feel-
(35) ing dopey, sleepy. I went to work, but the mood of the book would not die; it lingered, coloring everything I saw, heard, did. I now felt that I knew what the white men were feeling. Merely because I had read a book that had spoken of
(40) how they lived and thought, I identified myself with that book. I felt vaguely guilty. Would I, filled with bookish notions, act in a manner that

would make the whites dislike me?
      I forged more notes and my trips to the library
(45) became frequent. Reading grew into a passion. My first serious novel was Sinclair Lewis's *Main Street*. It made me see my boss, Mr. Gerald, and identify him as an American type. I would smile when I saw him lugging his golf bags into the
(50) office. I had always felt a vast distance separating me from the boss, and now I felt closer to him, though still distant. I felt now that I knew him, that I could feel the very limits of his narrow life. This had happened because I had
(55) read a novel about a mythical man called George F. Babbitt. But I could not conquer my sense of guilt, my feeling that the white men around me knew that I was changing, that I had begun to regard them differently.

21. The speaker's initial reaction to Mencken's prose can best be described as one of

(A) wrath   (B) disbelief   (C) remorse
(D) laughter   (E) disdain

22. To the speaker, Mencken appeared to be all of the following EXCEPT

(A) intrepid   (B) articulate   (C) satiric
(D) reverent   (E) opinionated

GO ON TO THE NEXT PAGE

1   1   1 1 1 1 1 1 1 1 1 1   1

23. The passage as a whole is best characterized as

(A) an impassioned argument in favor of increased literacy for blacks
(B) a description of a youth's gradual introduction to racial prejudice
(C) a comparison of the respective merits of Mencken's and Lewis's literary styles
(D) an analysis of the impact of ordinary life on art
(E) a portrait of a youth's response to expanding intellectual horizons

24. The speaker's attitude in lines 28–30 is best described as one of

(A) dreamy indifference   (B) sullen resentment
 (C) impatient ardor   (D) wistful anxiety
  (E) quiet resolve

25. It can be inferred from the passage that the speaker smiled when he saw Mr. Gerald carrying the golf clubs out of a sense of

(A) relief   (B) duty   (C) recognition
 (D) disbelief   (E) levity

There are some terrible robbers in the pond world, and, in our aquarium, we may witness all the cruelties of an embittered struggle for exis-
Line tence enacted before our very eyes. If you have
(5) introduced to your aquarium a mixed catch, you will soon see an example of such conflicts, for, amongst the new arrivals, there will probably be a larva of the water-beetle Dytiscus. Considering their relative size, the voracity and cunning with
(10) which these animals destroy their prey eclipse the methods of even such notorious robbers as tigers, lions, wolves, or killer whales. These are all as lambs compared with the Dytiscus larva.

It is a slim, streamlined insect, rather more
(15) than two inches long. Its six legs are equipped with stout fringes of bristles which form broad oar-like blades that propel the animal quickly and surely through the water. The wide, flat head bears an enormous, pincer-shaped pair of jaws
(20) which are hollow and serve not only as syringes for injecting poison, but also as orifices of ingestion. The animal lies in ambush on some waterplant; suddenly it shoots at lightning speed towards its prey, darts underneath it, then
(25) quickly jerks up its head and grabs the victim in its jaws. "Prey," for these creatures, is all that moves or that smells of "animal" in any way. It has often happened to me that, while standing quietly in the water of a pond, I have been
(30) "eaten" by a Dytiscus larva. Even for man, an

injection of the poisonous digestive juice of this insect is extremely painful.

These beetle larvae are among the few animals which digest "out of doors." The glandular
(35) secretion that they inject, through their hollow forceps, into their prey, dissolves the entire inside of the latter into a liquid soup, which is then sucked in through the same channel by the attacker. Even large victims, such as fat tadpoles
(40) or dragon-fly larvae, which have been bitten by a Dytiscus larva, stiffen after a few defensive moments, and their inside, which, as in most water animals, is more or less transparent, becomes opaque as though fixed by formalin.
(45) The animal swells up first, then gradually shrinks to a limp bundle of skin which hangs from the deadly jaws, and is finally allowed to drop. In the confines of an aquarium, a few large Dytiscus larvae will, within days, eat all living things over
(50) quarter of an inch long. What happens then? They will eat each other, if they have not already done so; this depends less on who is bigger and stronger than upon who succeeds in seizing the other first. I have often seen two nearly equal
(55) sized Dytiscus larvae each seize the other simultaneously and both die a quick death by inner dissolution. Very few animals, even when threatened with starvation, will attack an equal sized animal of their own species with the
(60) intention of devouring it. I only know this to be definitely true of rats and a few related rodents; that wolves do the same thing, I am much inclined to doubt, on the strength of some observations of which I shall speak later. But
(65) Dytiscus larvae devour animals of their own breed and size, even when other nourishment is at hand, and that is done, as far as I know, by no other animal.

26. The author suggests that the presence of Dytiscus larvae in an aquarium would be of particular interest to naturalists studying

(A) means of exterminating water-beetle larvae
(B) predatory patterns within a closed environment
(C) genetic characteristics of a mixed catch
(D) the effect of captivity on aquatic life
(E) the social behavior of dragon-fly larvae

GO ON TO THE NEXT PAGE

1   1   1   1   1   1   1   1   1   1   1

27. The passage mentions all of the following facts about Dytiscus larvae EXCEPT that they

(A) secrete digestive juices
(B) attack their fellow larvae
(C) are attracted to motion
(D) provide food for amphibians
(E) have ravenous appetites

28. The author implies that in subsequent passages he will discuss

(A) the likelihood of cannibalism among wolves
(B) the metamorphosis of dragon-fly larvae into dragon-flies
(C) antidotes to cases of Dytiscus poisoning
(D) the digestive processes of killer whales
(E) the elimination of Dytiscus larvae from aquariums

29. By digesting "out of doors" (line 34), the author is referring to the Dytiscus larva's

(A) preference for open-water ponds over confined spaces
(B) metabolic elimination of waste matter
(C) amphibious method of locomotion
(D) extreme voraciousness of appetite
(E) external conversion of food into absorbable form

30. According to the author, which of the following is (are) true of the victim of a Dytiscus larva?

   I. Its interior increases in opacity.
  II. It shrivels as it is drained of nourishment.
 III. It is beheaded by the larva's jaws.

(A) I only   (B) II only   (C) III only
(D) I and II only   (E) II and III only

Select the word or set of words that best completes each of the following sentences.

31. He remained ---- and in full command of the situation in spite of the hysteria and panic all around him.

(A) impervious   (B) imperturbable
(C) imperious   (D) frenetic   (E) lackadaisical

32. Puzzling over the ---- failure of her laboratory experiment, the physics major seemed more ---- than was usual for someone of her normally gregarious disposition.

(A) violent..exhilarated
(B) monetary..extravagant
(C) temporary..sociable
(D) unexpected..withdrawn
(E) thorough..composed

33. The voters never thought that the candidate would resort to ---- to win; he seemed to be ---- man.

(A) charm..an amazing
(B) bombast..a pompous
(C) innuendo..a devious
(D) subterfuge..an honest
(E) argument..a controversial

34. As the increasingly popular leader of America's second largest tribe, Cherokee Chief Wilma Mankiller not only has ---- the myth that only males could be leaders in American Indian government, but also has gained the ---- of other tribal leaders.

(A) shattered..respect
(B) perpetuated..affection
(C) exaggerated..cooperation
(D) confirmed..loyalty
(E) defied..distrust

35. Although he had spent many hours at the computer trying to solve the problem, he was the first to admit that the final solution was ---- and not the ---- of his labor.

(A) trivial..cause
(B) incomplete..intent
(C) adequate..concern
(D) worthwhile..fault
(E) fortuitous..result

Each question below consists of a related pair of words or phrases, followed by five lettered pairs of words or phrases. Select the lettered pair that best expresses a relationship similar to that expressed in the original pair.

Example:

   YAWN : BOREDOM ::   (A) dream : sleep
   (B) anger : madness   (C) smile : amusement
    (D) face : expression   (E) impatience : rebellion

Ⓐ Ⓑ ● Ⓓ Ⓔ

36. QUARRY : MARBLE ::   (A) metal : silver
    (B) ore : gold   (C) mine : coal   (D) prey : rabbit
     (E) necklace : diamonds

37. CHAIRMAN : GAVEL ::   (A) conductor : baton
    (B) violinist : bow   (C) orator : dais
     (D) teacher : blackboard   (E) pianist : keys

GO ON TO THE NEXT PAGE

1   1 1 1 1 1 1 1 1 1 1

38. CONSTITUTION:PREAMBLE ::
   (A) prelude:overture
   (B) legislation:introduction
   (C) opera:intermezzo
   (D) book:preface
   (E) play:epilogue

39. JOY:ECSTASY :: (A) rain:drought
   (B) breeze:hurricane   (C) river:creek
   (D) deluge:flood   (E) jazz:opera

40. DEPTH:FISSURE :: (A) breadth:scope
   (B) height:peak   (C) velocity:road
   (D) weight:diet   (E) length:duration

41. BLATANT:OBTRUSIVENESS ::
   (A) cynical:anger
   (B) weary:hopelessness
   (C) erudite:ignorance
   (D) lavish:extravagance
   (E) arrogant:humility

42. EMACIATED:GAUNT ::
   (A) liberated:gigantic
   (B) dwarfed:tall
   (C) overweight:haggard
   (D) eaten:distinguished
   (E) obese:corpulent

43. BLIND:SIGHT :: (A) diabetic:sugar
   (B) indigent:tact   (C) amnesiac:memory
   (D) benevolent:charity   (E) misanthropic:hate

44. STRIDENT:VOICE :: (A) muted:music
   (B) smooth:texture   (C) acrid:taste
   (D) fragrant:odor   (E) tuned:instrument

45. GAMBIT:CHESS :: (A) pass:poker
   (B) jump:checkers   (C) fumble:football
   (D) queen:pawn   (E) finesse:bridge

IF YOU FINISH BEFORE TIME IS CALLED, YOU MAY CHECK YOUR WORK ON THIS SECTION ONLY. DO NOT WORK ON ANY OTHER SECTION IN THE TEST.   **S T O P**

2   2   2   2   2   2   2   2   2   2   2

SECTION 2   Time—30 minutes   In this section, solve each problem, using any available space on
                    25 Questions   the page for scratchwork. Then decide which is the best of the
                                      choices given and blacken the corresponding space on the answer
                                      sheet.

The following information is for your reference in solving some of the problems.

Circle of radius r: Area $= \pi r^2$; Circumference $= 2\pi r$
  The number of degrees of arc in a circle is 360.
The measure in degrees of a straight angle is 180.

Definitions of symbols:
$=$ is equal to $\leqq$ is less than or equal to
$\neq$ is unequal to $\geqq$ is greater than or equal to
$<$ is less than $\parallel$ is parallel to
$>$ is greater than $\perp$ is perpendicular to

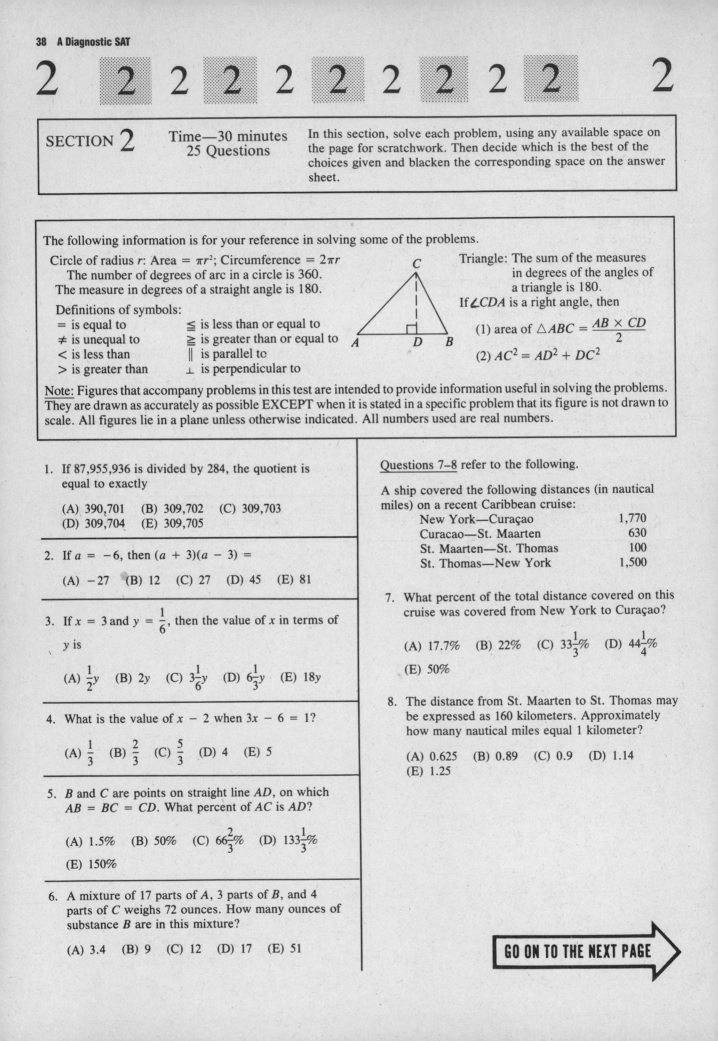

Triangle: The sum of the measures
  in degrees of the angles of
  a triangle is 180.
If $\angle CDA$ is a right angle, then

(1) area of $\triangle ABC = \dfrac{AB \times CD}{2}$

(2) $AC^2 = AD^2 + DC^2$

Note: Figures that accompany problems in this test are intended to provide information useful in solving the problems.
They are drawn as accurately as possible EXCEPT when it is stated in a specific problem that its figure is not drawn to
scale. All figures lie in a plane unless otherwise indicated. All numbers used are real numbers.

1. If 87,955,936 is divided by 284, the quotient is
    equal to exactly

    (A) 390,701   (B) 309,702   (C) 309,703
    (D) 309,704   (E) 309,705

2. If $a = -6$, then $(a + 3)(a - 3) =$

    (A) -27 (B) 12   (C) 27   (D) 45   (E) 81

3. If $x = 3$ and $y = \dfrac{1}{6}$, then the value of x in terms of

    y is

    (A) $\dfrac{1}{2}y$ (B) $2y$ (C) $3\dfrac{1}{6}y$ (D) $6\dfrac{1}{3}y$ (E) $18y$

4. What is the value of $x - 2$ when $3x - 6 = 1$?

    (A) $\dfrac{1}{3}$ (B) $\dfrac{2}{3}$ (C) $\dfrac{5}{3}$ (D) 4   (E) 5

5. B and C are points on straight line AD, on which
    $AB = BC = CD$. What percent of AC is AD?

    (A) 1.5%   (B) 50%   (C) $66\dfrac{2}{3}\%$ (D) $133\dfrac{1}{3}\%$

    (E) 150%

6. A mixture of 17 parts of A, 3 parts of B, and 4
    parts of C weighs 72 ounces. How many ounces of
    substance B are in this mixture?

    (A) 3.4   (B) 9   (C) 12   (D) 17   (E) 51

Questions 7–8 refer to the following.

A ship covered the following distances (in nautical
miles) on a recent Caribbean cruise:

New York—Curaçao	1,770
Curacao—St. Maarten	630
St. Maarten—St. Thomas	100
St. Thomas—New York	1,500

7. What percent of the total distance covered on this
    cruise was covered from New York to Curaçao?

    (A) 17.7%   (B) 22%   (C) $33\dfrac{1}{3}\%$ (D) $44\dfrac{1}{4}\%$

    (E) 50%

8. The distance from St. Maarten to St. Thomas may
    be expressed as 160 kilometers. Approximately
    how many nautical miles equal 1 kilometer?

    (A) 0.625   (B) 0.89   (C) 0.9   (D) 1.14
    (E) 1.25

GO ON TO THE NEXT PAGE

2   2 2 2 2 2 2 2 2 2   2

9. In the figure above, the area of each circle is 9π. What is the area of the shaded part?

(A) $36 - 9\pi$ (B) $36 - 36\pi$ (C) $36\pi - 144$
(D) $144 - 9\pi$ (E) $144 - 36\pi$

10. After purchasing a square sheet of plywood (area = 169 square feet), I found that I must cut off 2 feet from one of its edges in order to fit it onto the side of a wall. What is the area, in square feet, of this wall?

(A) 117   (B) 121   (C) 143   (D) 165   (E) 167

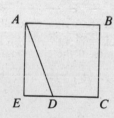

11. In the figure above, the area of square $ABCE = x^2$ and $DC = y$. What is the area of triangle AED?

(A) $\dfrac{x^2 - xy}{2}$ (B) $\dfrac{y(x - y)}{2}$ (C) $x^2 - xy$
(D) $y^2 - xy$ (E) $xy - x^2$

12. If n and p are both odd numbers, which of the following numbers MUST be an even number?

(A) $n + p$ (B) np (C) $np + 2$
(D) $n + p + 1$ (E) $2n + p$

13. Of the 30,000 tickets for the state football championship game, $\dfrac{1}{4}$ were sold at $3.00, $\dfrac{1}{3}$ were sold at $2.50, and the rest were sold at $1.25. How many were sold at $1.25?

(A) 5,000   (B) 7,500   (C) 10,000   (D) 12,500
(E) 25,000

14. The average weight of 3 boys is 53 pounds. Not one of these boys weighs less than 51 pounds. What is the maximum weight, in pounds, of any one boy?

(A) 53   (B) 55   (C) 57   (D) 59   (E) 61

15. If $a < b$ and $c < d$, then

(A) $c + a < d + b$
(B) $c + a > d + b$
(C) $c = b$
(D) $a = b$
(E) $ac = bd$

16. Mark can row downstream on the Saco River for 5 miles in 2 hours. It takes him 4 hours to return to his original destination. What is Mark's average rate of speed, in miles per hour, for the round trip?

(A) $\dfrac{5}{6}$ (B) $1\dfrac{2}{3}$ (C) $1\dfrac{7}{8}$ (D) 3   (E) $3\dfrac{3}{4}$

17. If (triangle with x, y, z) is defined to equal $\dfrac{xy}{z}$,

and (triangle with x, y, z) $- \dfrac{1}{A} = 0$,

then $A =$

(A) $\dfrac{xy}{z}$ (B) $\dfrac{xz}{y}$ (C) $\dfrac{z}{xy}$ (D) $\dfrac{yz}{x}$ (E) $\dfrac{x}{yz}$

18. Point A (1, 0) is joined to B (5, 0) and is joined to C (3, 4). Which of the following is true?

(A) $CA = CB$ (B) $AB = BC$ (C) $AC = AB$
(D) $AC > BC$ (E) $AC < BC$

GO ON TO THE NEXT PAGE

Questions 19–22 refer to the following table.

PAYROLL OF THE ABC MANUFACTURING
COMPANY

Rank	Number of Employees	Wages Paid (in thousands)
Office Managers	5	$ 110
Factory Supervisors	25	$ 350
Assembly Workers	500	$ 600
TOTAL	530	$1060

19. The wages paid to managers make up what percent (to the nearest percent) of the total payroll?

(A) 5   (B) 9   (C) 10   (D) 11   (E) 42

20. The average wage for all employees is

(A) $1,200   (B) $2,000   (C) $18,000
(D) $20,000   (E) $22,000

21. The ratio of the average salary of a manager to the average salary of an assembly worker is

(A) 3:55   (B) 11:60   (C) 11:6   (D) 60:11
(E) 55:3

22. If four of the managers are paid wages of x dollars each, then the remaining manager is paid

(A) $22,000   (B) $(110,000 − x)

(C) $\left(\dfrac{110,000 − x}{4}\right)$ (D) $(110,000 − 4x)$

(E) $(22,000 − x)$

23. The base of an isosceles triangle is 16 units, and each side is 10 units. What is the area of this triangle in square units?

(A) 24   (B) 36   (C) 48   (D) 50   (E) 100

24. If the area of rectangle R with altitude 4 feet is equal to the area of square S, which has a perimeter of 24 feet, then the perimeter of rectangle R, in feet, is

(A) 9   (B) 16   (C) 24   (D) 26   (E) 36

25. There are 20 members on a football squad. In electing a captain and a cocaptain, how many different outcomes of the election are possible?

(A) 20   (B) 39   (C) 190   (D) 380   (E) 760

IF YOU FINISH BEFORE TIME IS CALLED, YOU MAY CHECK YOUR WORK ON
THIS SECTION ONLY. DO NOT WORK ON ANY OTHER SECTION IN THE TEST.   S T O P

3 3 3 3 3 3 3 3 3 3 3

SECTION 3   Time—30 minutes   The questions in this section measure skills that are important to
50 Questions   writing well. In particular, they test your ability to recognize and
use language that is clear, effective, and correct according to the
requirements of standard written English, the kind of English
found in most college textbooks.

Directions: The following sentences contain problems in grammar, usage, diction (choice of words), and idiom.

Some sentences are correct.
No sentence contains more than one error.

You will find that the error, if there is one, is underlined and lettered. Assume that elements of the sentence that are not
underlined are correct and cannot be changed. In choosing answers, follow the requirements of standard written
English.

If there is an error, select the <u>one underlined part</u> that must be changed to make the sentence correct
and blacken the corresponding space on your answer sheet.

If there is no error, blacken answer space Ⓔ.

EXAMPLE: SAMPLE ANSWER

The region has a climate <u>so severe that plants</u>   Ⓐ Ⓑ ● Ⓓ Ⓔ
                              A
<u>growing there</u> rarely <u>had been</u> more than twelve
        B   C
inches <u>high.</u> <u>No error</u>
         D   E

---

1. <u>In order to</u> conserve valuable gasoline, motorists
      A
<u>had ought to</u> check their speedometers <u>while</u>
        B   C
driving along the highways <u>since it is</u> very easy to
                                    D
exceed 55 miles per hour while driving on open

roads. <u>No error</u>
            E

2. The book <u>must be</u> old, <u>for</u> its cover <u>is torn</u> <u>bad</u>.
              A   B   C   D
<u>No error</u>
   E

3. <u>Not one</u> of the children <u>has ever sang</u> <u>in public</u>
      A   B   C
<u>before.</u> <u>No error</u>
   D   E

4. Neither you nor <u>I</u> can realize the <u>affect</u> his
                    A   B
behavior <u>will have</u> on his chances <u>for promotion</u>.
              C   D
<u>No error</u>
   E

5. The <u>apparently</u> <u>obvious solution to</u> the problem
          A   B
<u>was overlooked</u> by <u>many of</u> the contestants.
        C   D
<u>No error</u>
   E

6. <u>After</u> he <u>had drank</u> the warm milk, he began
      A   B
<u>to feel sleepy</u> and <u>finally decided</u> to go to bed.
        C   D
<u>No error</u>
   E

7. <u>Without hardly</u> a moment's delay, the computer
          A
began <u>to print out</u> the <u>answer to</u> the problem.
        B   C   D
<u>No error</u>
   E

GO ON TO THE NEXT PAGE

8. After <u>conferring with</u> John Brown and Mary Smith,
         A
   I <u>have decided</u> that she is <u>better qualified</u> than <u>him</u>
        B   C   D
   to edit the school newspaper. <u>No error</u>
                                        E

9. <u>Of</u> the two candidates for this <u>newly formed</u>
   A   B
   government position, Ms. Rivera is the

   <u>most qualified</u> <u>because of</u> her experience in the
        C   D
   field. <u>No error</u>
              E

10. Diligence and honesty, <u>as well as</u> <u>being intelligent</u>,
                              A   B
    <u>are</u> qualities which I look for <u>when</u> I interview
    C   D
    applicants. <u>No error</u>
                    E

11. <u>Dashing across</u> the campus, John <u>tried to</u> overtake
        A   B
    the instructor <u>who</u> <u>had forgotten</u> his briefcase.
                     C   D
    <u>No error</u>
        E

12. Neither the earthquake <u>or</u> the <u>subsequent</u> fire
                             A   B
    <u>was able</u> to destroy the <u>spirit of</u> the city dwellers.
     C   D
    <u>No error</u>
        E

13. I <u>might of passed</u> if I <u>had done</u> my homework, <u>but</u>
        A   B   C
    I <u>had to go</u> to work. <u>No error</u>
        D   E

14. Writing a <u>beautiful sonnet</u> is <u>as much</u> an
                  A   B
    achievement as <u>to finish</u> a <u>400-page novel</u>.
                      C   D
    <u>No error</u>
        E

15. The <u>impatient customer</u> had <u>scarcely enough</u>
            A   B
    money <u>to pay</u> the clerk <u>at</u> the checkout counter.
             C   D
    <u>No error</u>
        E

16. The <u>principal</u> of equal justice <u>for all</u> is <u>one</u> of the
            A   B   C
    cornerstones of our democratic <u>way of life</u>.
                                       D
    <u>No error</u>
        E

17. Neither the players <u>nor</u> the trainer <u>were</u> in the
                          A   B
    locker room <u>when</u> the thief <u>broke in</u> the door.
                   C   D
    <u>No error</u>
        E

18. <u>If</u> anyone <u>calls</u> while we are in conference, tell
    A   B
    <u>them</u> I will <u>return the call</u> after the meeting.
       C   D
    <u>No error</u>
        E

19. <u>Either</u> of the two boys who <u>sing</u> in the chorus
        A   B
    <u>are now</u> <u>capable of</u> taking the job of understudy to
       C   D
    the star. <u>No error</u>
                  E

20. We have <u>come to the conclusion</u> that we can end
                    A
    hostilities in <u>that area</u> of the world by providing
                      B
    food to both sides, bringing the opposing forces to

    the <u>negotiation table</u>, and <u>to guarantee</u> financial aid
            C   D
    to both sides once peace is established. <u>No error</u>
                                                  E

21. Numerous <u>collections of</u> short stories include
                  A
    works by Isaac Bashevis Singer who, <u>despite living</u>
                                            B
    in the United States over fifty years, <u>continues</u>
                                               C
    <u>to write</u> primarily in Yiddish. <u>No error</u>
       D   E

22. Public television <u>has succeeded</u> <u>admirably</u> in
                      A   B
    raising money for <u>its</u> future programs through
                      C
    marathon <u>fund-raising projects</u>. <u>No error</u>
                      D   E

23. <u>By the time</u> the bank guard closed the doors, a riot
    A
    <u>had erupted</u> <u>due to</u> the long lines and <u>shortage of</u>
       B   C   D
    tellers. <u>No error</u>
             E

24. The <u>ancient concept</u> which <u>states that</u> the sun
           A   B
    <u>revolves around</u> the earth <u>is questioned by</u>
       C   D
    Copernicus. <u>No error</u>
                E

25. <u>If</u> the by-stander had not been <u>familiar with</u> first-
    A   B
    aid techniques, the young diver <u>which</u> had the bad
                                     C
    fall <u>might have been</u> paralyzed. <u>No error</u>
         D   E

Directions: In each of the following sentences, some part or all of the sentence is underlined. Below each sentence you will find five ways of phrasing the underlined part. Select the answer that produces the most effective sentence, one that is clear and exact, without awkwardness or ambiguity, and blacken the corresponding space on your answer sheet. In choosing answers, follow the requirements of standard written English. Choose the answer that best expresses the meaning of the original sentence.

Answer (A) is always the same as the underlined part. Choose answer (A) if you think the original sentence needs no revision.

EXAMPLE:
Laura Ingalls Wilder published her first book
<u>and she was sixty-five years old then.</u>

(A) and she was sixty-five years old then
(B) when she was sixty-five years old
(C) at age sixty-five years old
(D) upon reaching sixty-five years
(E) at the time when she was sixty-five

SAMPLE ANSWER

(A) ● (C) (D) (E)

---

26. <u>If he was to decide to go to college,</u> I, for one, would recommend that he plan to go to Yale.

(A) If he was to decide to go to college
(B) If he were to decide to go to college
(C) Had he decided to go to college
(D) In the event that he decides to go to college
(E) Supposing he was to decide to go to college

27. <u>Except for you and I, everyone brought</u> a present to the party.

(A) Except for you and I, everyone brought
(B) With the exception of you and I, everyone brought
(C) Except for you and I, everyone had brought
(D) Except for you and me, everyone brought
(E) Except for you and me, everyone had brought

28. <u>Had I realized how close</u> I was to failing, I would not have gone to the party.

(A) Had I realized how close
(B) If I would have realized how close
(C) Had I had realized how close
(D) When I realized how close
(E) If I realized how close

GO ON TO THE NEXT PAGE

29. <u>Being a realist</u>, I could not accept his statement that supernatural beings had caused the disturbance.

    (A) Being a realist
    (B) Due to the fact that I am a realist
    (C) Being that I am a realist
    (D) Being as I am a realist
    (E) Realist that I am

30. Having finished the marathon in record-breaking time, <u>the city awarded him its Citizen's Out-standing Performance Medal</u>.

    (A) the city awarded him its Citizen's Outstanding Performance Medal
    (B) the city awarded the Citizen's Outstanding Performance Medal to him
    (C) he was awarded the Citizen's Outstanding Performance Medal by the city
    (D) the Citizen's Outstanding Performance Medal was awarded to him
    (E) he was awarded by the city with the Citizen's Outstanding Performance Medal

31. <u>The football team's winning its first game of the season</u> excited the student body.

    (A) The football team's winning its first game of the season
    (B) The football team having won its first game of the season
    (C) Having won its first game of the season, the football team
    (D) Winning its first game of the season, the football team
    (E) The football team winning its first game of the season

32. Anyone interested in the use of computers can learn much <u>if you have access to</u> a Radio Shack TRS-80 or a Pet Microcomputer.

    (A) if you have access to
    (B) if he or she has access to
    (C) if access is available to
    (D) by access to
    (E) from access to

33. I have <u>to make dinner, wash the dishes, do my homework, and then relaxing</u>.

    (A) to make dinner, wash the dishes, do my homework, and then relaxing
    (B) to make dinner, washing the dishes, my homework, and then relax
    (C) to make dinner, wash the dishes, doing my homework and then relaxing
    (D) to prepare dinner, wash the dishes, do my homework, and then relaxing
    (E) to make dinner, wash the dishes, do my homework, and then relax

34. The climax <u>occurs when he asks who's</u> in the closet.

    (A) occurs when he asks who's
    (B) is when he asks who's
    (C) occurs when he is asking who's
    (D) is when he is asking who's
    (E) occurs when he asked who's

35. Setting up correct bookkeeping procedures <u>is important to any new business, it helps</u> to obtain the services of a good accountant.

    (A) is important to any new business, it helps
    (B) are important to any new business, it
    (C) is important to any new business, therefore, try
    (D) is important to any new business; it helps
    (E) are important to any new business, so try

36. The grocer <u>hadn't hardly any of those kind</u> of canned goods.

    (A) hadn't hardly any of those kind
    (B) hadn't hardly any of those kinds
    (C) had hardly any of those kind
    (D) had hardly any of those kinds
    (E) had scarcely any of those kind

37. <u>Having stole the money, the police searched the thief</u>.

    (A) Having stole the money, the police searched the thief.
    (B) Having stolen the money, the thief was searched by the police.
    (C) Having stolen the money, the police searched the thief.
    (D) Having stole the money, the thief was searched by the police.
    (E) Being that he stole the money, the police searched the thief.

38. <u>No student had ought to be put into a situation where</u> he or she must choose between loyalty to friends and duty to class.

    (A) No student had ought to be put into a situation where
    (B) No student had ought to be put into a situation in which
    (C) No student should be put into a situation where
    (D) No student ought to be put into a situation in which
    (E) No student ought to be put into a situation where

GO ON TO THE NEXT PAGE

3   3 3 3 3 3 3 3 3 3 3   3

39. Juan broke his <u>hip, he has not been able to run</u>
<u>and possibly never will be able to run</u> the mile
again.

  (A) hip, he has not been able to run and possibly
      never will be able to run
  (B) hip; he has not been able to run and possibly
      never will be able to run
  (C) hip; he has not and possibly never will be able
      to run
  (D) hip, he has not been and possibly never would
      be able to run
  (E) hip; he has not and possibly will never be able
      to run

40. I came late to class <u>today; the reason being that</u>
the bus broke down.

  (A) today; the reason being that
  (B) today, the reason being that
  (C) today because
  (D) today;
  (E) today; since

Note: The remaining questions are like those at the beginning of the section.

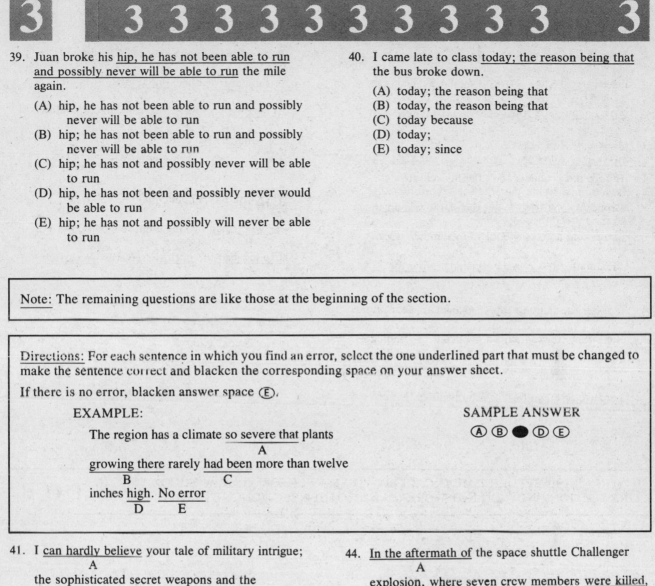

Directions: For each sentence in which you find an error, select the one underlined part that must be changed to make the sentence correct and blacken the corresponding space on your answer sheet.

If there is no error, blacken answer space Ⓔ.

    EXAMPLE:

      The region has a climate <u>so severe that</u> plants
                      A

      <u>growing there</u> rarely <u>had been</u> more than twelve
         B   C

      inches <u>high</u>. <u>No error</u>
          D   E

SAMPLE ANSWER
Ⓐ Ⓑ ● Ⓓ Ⓔ

---

41. I <u>can hardly believe</u> your tale of military intrigue;
       A

the sophisticated secret weapons and the

<u>increasing violent</u> actions <u>that</u> were exhibited by
   B   C

just one man <u>seem</u> incredible. <u>No error</u>
        D   E

42. The animals <u>who</u> were chosen <u>to represent</u> the
         A   B

Democratic and Republican parties, the donkey

and the elephant, <u>were created</u> by the
             C

<u>renowned cartoonist</u> Thomas Nast. <u>No error</u>
    D   E

43. I <u>should like</u> you and <u>he</u> to supply the
     A   B

<u>necessary data</u> for the annual statement which
    C

must be prepared <u>in advance of</u> the spring meeting.
              D

<u>No error</u>
  E

44. <u>In the aftermath of</u> the space shuttle Challenger
    A

explosion, <u>where</u> seven crew members <u>were killed</u>,
        B   C

the NASA program underwent a

<u>massive examination</u> of priorities. <u>No error</u>
    D   E

45. Twenty-five <u>restless five-year-olds</u> <u>were throwing</u>
          A   B

paper clips, were drawing at the blackboard, and

<u>called to</u> one another <u>while their</u> teacher went
  C   D

searching for milk and cookies. <u>No error</u>
                E

GO ON TO THE NEXT PAGE

46. Recent medical breakthroughs, including the

    <u>discovery of</u> a vaccine to slow the AIDs virus,
       A

    <u>have encouraged</u> researchers; <u>and</u> a cure is still
        B   C

    <u>eluding</u> them. <u>No error</u>
      D   E

47. <u>Before</u> the producer took the musical to
     A

    Broadway, he <u>tried to get</u> the show with all <u>their</u>
                B   C

    actors and actresses booked in summer stock

    theaters for <u>last-minute revisions</u>. <u>No error</u>
                 D   E

48. Neither the mid-life career change applicant <u>nor</u>
                               A

    the young, inexperienced applicant <u>are finding</u> it
                              B

    easy <u>to begin</u> a career in data processing
        C

    <u>because of</u> a shortage of job openings. <u>No error</u>
      D   E

49. Even <u>after</u> you have endured a cold winter
        A

    in sub-zero weather, <u>one finds</u> <u>it</u> possible
                    B   C

    <u>to become acclimated</u> to tropical temperatures in
            D

    the summer. <u>No error</u>
            E

50. <u>When</u> you buy a condominium, you will have
     A

    <u>less work than</u> owning a house entails, but you
      B

    <u>have not had</u> the <u>intrinsic</u> rewards. <u>No error</u>
      C   D   E

IF YOU FINISH BEFORE TIME IS CALLED, YOU MAY CHECK YOUR WORK ON
THIS SECTION ONLY. DO NOT WORK ON ANY OTHER SECTION IN THE TEST.

S T O P

4   4 4 4 4 4 4 4 4 4 4 4   4

SECTION 4   Time—30 minutes   For each question in this section, choose the best answer and
40 Questions   blacken the corresponding space on the answer sheet.

Each question below consists of a word in capital letters, followed by five lettered words or phrases. Choose the word or phrase that is most nearly opposite in meaning to the word in capital letters. Since some of the questions require you to distinguish fine shades of meaning, consider all the choices before deciding which is best.

Example:

GOOD: (A) sour   (B) bad   (C) red
(D) hot   (E) ugly

Ⓐ ● Ⓒ Ⓓ Ⓔ

1. PROPER: (A) unsuitable   (B) not secure
(C) exact   (D) out of focus   (E) unstable

2. INTENTIONAL: (A) final   (B) accidental
(C) suggestive   (D) aggressive   (E) typical

3. PAMPER: (A) work diligently
(B) treat harshly   (C) protect carefully
(D) educate in depth   (E) remove from sight

4. NAIVE: (A) devoted   (B) urbane
(C) ingenious   (D) hostile   (E) foreign

5. ATROPHY: (A) incite   (B) prize   (C) flourish
(D) refuse   (E) maintain

6. ASTUTE: (A) enigmatic   (B) absurd
(C) emaciated   (D) elaborate   (E) propitious

7. APPLICATION: (A) lack of industry
(B) loss of standing   (C) improbability
(D) prohibition   (E) promotion

8. ALTRUISM: (A) antipathy   (B) chauvinism
(C) selfishness   (D) seriousness   (E) empathy

9. COMPLAISANCE: (A) distastefulness
(B) egotism   (C) irrelevance   (D) suspicion
(E) recalcitrance

10. TENDER: (A) avoid   (B) retract   (C) deride
(D) constrict   (E) sympathize

Each sentence below has one or two blanks, each blank indicating that something has been omitted. Beneath the sentence are five lettered words or sets of words. Choose the word or set of words that best fits the meaning of the sentence as a whole.

Example:

Although its publicity has been ----, the film itself is intelligent, well-acted, handsomely produced, and altogether ----.

(A) tasteless..respectable   (B) extensive..moderate
(C) sophisticated..amateur   (D) risqué..crude
(E) perfect..spectacular

● Ⓓ Ⓒ Ⓓ Ⓔ

11. Hoping to compensate for their relative lack of numbers, the rebels sought to overcome the ---- of strength of the government forces by engaging in guerilla tactics and hit and run methods of warfare.

(A) diversion   (B) illusion   (C) diminution
(D) superiority   (E) absence

12. No summary of the behavior of animals toward reflected images is given, but not much else that is ---- seems missing from this comprehensive yet compact study of mirrors and mankind.

(A) redundant   (B) contemplative   (C) relevant
(D) peripheral   (E) disputable

13. Dr. Charles Drew's technique for preserving and storing blood plasma for emergency use proved so ---- that it became the ---- for the present bloodbank system used by the American Red Cross.

(A) irrelevant..inspiration
(B) urgent..pattern
(C) effective..model
(D) innocuous..excuse
(E) complex..blueprint

GO ON TO THE NEXT PAGE

14. The likenesses of language around the Mediterranean were sufficiently marked to ---- ease of movement both of men and ideas: it took relatively few alterations to make a Spanish song intelligible in Italy, and an Italian trader could, without much difficulty, make himself at home in France.

   (A) eliminate   (B) facilitate   (C) hinder
   (D) clarify   (E) aggravate

15. Much of the clown's success may be attributed to the contrast between the ---- manner he adopts and the general ---- that characterizes the circus.

   (A) giddy..sobriety
   (B) lugubrious..hilarity
   (C) gaudy..clamor
   (D) joyful..hysteria
   (E) frenetic..excitement

Each question below consists of a related pair of words or phrases, followed by five lettered pairs of words or phrases. Select the lettered pair that best expresses a relationship similar to that expressed in the original pair.

Example:

YAWN : BOREDOM ::   (A) dream : sleep
(B) anger : madness   (C) smile : amusement
   (D) face : expression   (E) impatience : rebellion

Ⓐ Ⓑ ● Ⓓ Ⓔ

---

16. PLAY : ACTS ::   (A) opera : arias
   (B) novel : chapters   (C) poem : rhymes
   (D) essay : topics   (E) game : athletes

17. GEOLOGY : SCIENCE ::
   (A) biology : laboratory
   (B) astronomy : galaxy
   (C) fashion : style
   (D) fir : tree
   (E) theory : practice

18. PLANE : SMOOTH ::   (A) boat : sink
   (B) arc : circle   (C) cheese : grate
   (D) axe : sharpen   (E) wrench : twist

19. FUNDS : EMBEZZLED ::   (A) loot : buried
   (B) writings : plagiarized   (C) ransom : demanded
   (D) money : deposited   (E) truth : exaggerated

20. UNCOUTH : GRACELESSNESS ::
   (A) petulant : agreement
   (B) avaricious : greed
   (C) indifferent : concern
   (D) malicious : dishonesty
   (E) reticent : shamelessness

21. TOURNIQUET : BLEEDING ::
   (A) resuscitation : drowning
   (B) fatigue : sunshine
   (C) red light : traffic
   (D) panacea : coughing
   (E) microbe : disease

22. ELEVATOR : SHAFT ::
   (A) electricity : outlet
   (B) water : conduit
   (C) escalator : step
   (D) railroad : train
   (E) skyscraper : foundation

23. PARSIMONY : FRUGALITY ::   (A) agony : pain
   (B) steam : water   (C) anger : wrath
   (D) warmth : flame   (E) pleasure : gloom

24. EMACIATED : OBESITY ::
   (A) penurious : wealth
   (B) calorific : heat
   (C) affluent : health
   (D) honest : truth
   (E) careless : knowledge

25. TACITURNITY : LACONIC ::
   (A) improvisation : unrehearsed
   (B) verbosity : pithy
   (C) silence : golden
   (D) ballet : clumsy
   (E) vacation : leisurely

GO ON TO THE NEXT PAGE

4 4 4 4 4 4 4 4 4 4 4 4

Each passage below is followed by questions based on its content. Answer all questions following a passage on the basis of what is <u>stated</u> or <u>implied</u> in that passage.

Before taking up the subject of primitivism in United States painting, we must first consider whether there actually is such a thing as United States painting. Perhaps the U.S. art form merely belongs to the sum total of Western or, more precisely, European painting. The mere fact that there are painters in the United States does not necessarily imply the existence of a distinctive U.S. art form.

We believe, however, that U.S. painting has a native and singular flavor that sets it apart. True enough, some painters like Whistler, Sargent, and Mary Cassatt belong to the English or French school, but they are the exceptions. Almost all U.S. artists have developed on their own. They have been self-taught artists who have perfected their talents to a greater or lesser degree. Those who felt the imperious need to visit Europe did so when they had already achieved maturity. For them the Old World influence served more to improve their techniques than to modify their already existing styles. For some artists, for example Grant Wood, a European tour stimulated awareness of their own national roots, and convinced them that their true place was in their own country and in their own setting.

Many factors point to the existence of a vernacular, homegrown U.S. school, similar to the European schools, but with a special stamp of its own. By way of introduction a brief review of the pioneer painters who came to the New World is in order.

26. The title below that best expresses the ideas of this passage is

(A) An Indigenous Art Form in America
(B) Europe's Influence on American Painters
(C) Grant Wood's Experience
(D) American Pioneer Painters
(E) Self-taught American Artists

27. The author's attitude regarding America's self-taught artists is one of

(A) great indignation
(B) measured admiration
(C) deliberate indifference
(D) active suspicion
(E) amused irritation

28. In the paragraph following this passage, we may expect a discussion of

(A) primitivism and American Indian art
(B) English and French influence on Sargent
(C) Grant Wood's independence
(D) the founding fathers of American art
(E) a vernacular American school

29. The author maintains that Whistler, Sargent, and Mary Cassatt are exceptions because

(A) they developed on their own in isolation
(B) their styles were influenced by their European contacts
(C) they became aware of their national roots
(D) they were self-taught originals
(E) they were immature when they visited Europe

30. The author's primary purpose in this passage is to

(A) compare the English and French schools to their American counterpart
(B) affirm the existence of a uniquely American painting style
(C) assert the superiority of Old World technical training
(D) set forth a new definition of Western art
(E) explore the influence of primitivism on American painters

There was a stumbling rush for the cover of the fortification proper; and there the last possible line of defense was established instinctively and in a moment. Officers and men dropped on their knees behind the low bank of earth and continued an irregular deliberate fire, each discharging his piece as fast as he could load and aim. The garrison was not sufficient to form a continuous rank along even this single front, and on such portions of the works as were protected by the ditch, the soldiers were scattered almost as sparsely as sentinels. Nothing saved the place from being carried by an assault except the fact that the assailants were unprovided with scaling ladders. The adventurous fellows who had flanked the palisade rushed to the gate, and gave entrance to a torrent of tall, lank men in butternut or dirty gray clothing, their bronzed faces flushed with the excitement of supposed victory, and their yells of exultation drowning for a minute the sharp outcries of the wounded and the rattle of the musketry. But the human billow was met by such a fatal discharge that it could not come over the rampart.

GO ON TO THE NEXT PAGE

The foremost dead fell across it, and the mass reeled backward. Unfortunately for the attack, the exterior slope was full of small knolls and gullies, besides being cumbered with rude shanties, of four or five feet in height made of bits of board, and shelter tents, which had served as the quarters of the garrison. Behind these covers, scores if not hundreds sought refuge and could not be induced to leave them for a second charge.

31. The major subject of the passage is

(A) the garrison's overthrow at the hands of the enemy
(B) the use of strategy by the defenders
(C) the hardships of the life of the common soldier
(D) the battle to take the rampart
(E) the courage of the attacking officers

32. In the passage, the final defense line is portrayed most specifically as

(A) ineffectual   (B) abandoned   (C) orderly
(D) exultant   (E) spontaneous

33. According to the passage, which of the following can be inferred about sentinels?

(A) They are provided with scaling ladders.
(B) They fight alongside regular soldiers.
(C) They are stationed widely apart.
(D) They are usually officers.
(E) They form a continuous rank with guards.

34. According to the passage, the attackers were most hindered in their attack by

(A) the terrain
(B) the presence of the wounded
(C) lack of ammunition
(D) their presupposition of victory
(E) the ineptitude of their leaders

35. The passage indicates that many of the attackers

(A) surrendered to the garrison
(B) were hampered by inferior training
(C) refused to make another assault
(D) were overwhelmed by superior numbers
(E) were scattered sparsely around the fortification

I am in the Gothic world, the world of chivalry, courtesy and romance; a world in which serious things were done with a sense of play—where even war and theology could become a sort of game; and when architecture reached a point of extravagance unequalled in history. After all the great unifying convictions that inspired the medieval world, High Gothic art can look fantastic and luxurious—what Marxists call conspicuous waste. And yet these

centuries produced some of the greatest spirits in the history of man, amongst them St.Francis of Assisi and Dante. Behind all the fantasy of the Gothic imagination there remained, on two different planes, a sharp sense of reality. Medieval man could see things very clearly, but he believed that these appearances should be considered as nothing more than symbols or tokens of an ideal order, which was the only true reality.

The fantasy strikes us first, and last; and one can see it in the room in the Cluny Museum in Paris hung with a series of tapestries known as *The Lady with the Unicorn*, one of the most seductive examples of the Gothic spirit. It is poetical, fanciful and profane. Its ostensible subject is the four senses. But its real subject is the power of love which can enlist and subdue all the forces of nature, including those two emblems of lust and ferocity, the unicorn and the lion. They kneel before this embodiment of chastity, and hold up the corners of her cloak. These wild animals have become, in the heraldic sense, her supporters. And all round this allegorical scene is what the medieval philosophers used to call *natura naturans*—nature naturing—trees, flowers, leaves galore, birds, monkeys, and those rather obvious symbols of nature, rabbits. There is even nature domesticated, a little dog, sitting on a cushion. It is an image of worldly happiness at its most refined, what the French call the *douceur de vivre*, which is often confused with civilization.

We have come a long way from the powerful conviction that induced medieval knights and ladies to draw carts of stone up the hill for the building of Chartres Cathedral. And yet the notion of ideal love, and the irresistible power of gentleness and beauty, which is emblematically conveyed by the homage of these two fierce beasts, can be traced back for three centuries, to days long before these tapestries were conceived.

36. The author distinguishes the Medieval imagination from the Gothic on the basis of the latter's

(A) heraldic sense
(B) respect for tradition
(C) elaborateness of fancy
(D) philosophical unity
(E) firm belief

GO ON TO THE NEXT PAGE

4 4 4 4 4 4 4 4 4 4 4 4

37. The author thinks of the unicorn tapestries as exemplifying the essence of the Gothic imagination because
    (A) their allegorical nature derives from medieval sources
    (B) their use as wall hangings expresses the realistic practicality of the Gothic mind
    (C) they demonstrate the wastefulness and extravagance of the period
    (D) they combine worldly and spiritual elements in a celebration of love
    (E) they confuse the notion of civilization with worldly happiness

---

It is sometimes said that detective stories are read by respectable law-abiding citizens in order to gratify in fantasy the violent or murderous wishes they dare not, or are ashamed to, translate into action. This may be true for the readers of thrillers (which I rarely enjoy), but it is quite false for the reader of detective stories. On the contrary, the magical satisfaction the latter provide (which makes them escape literature not works of art) is the illusion of being dissociated from the murderer.

The magic formula is an innocence which is discovered to contain guilt; then a suspicion of being the guilty one; and finally a real innocence from which the guilty other has been expelled, a cure effected, not by me or my neighbors, but by the miraculous intervention of a genius from outside who removes guilt by giving knowledge of guilt. (The detective story subscribes, in fact, to the Socratic daydream: "Sin is ignorance.")

If one thinks of a work of art which deals with murder, *Crime and Punishment* for example, its effect on the reader is to compel an identification with the murderer which he would prefer not to recognize. The identification of fantasy is always an attempt to avoid one's own suffering: the identification of art is a compelled sharing in the suffering of another. Kafka's *The Trial* is another instructive example of the difference between a work of art and the detective story. In the latter it is certain that a crime has been committed and, temporarily, uncertain to whom guilt should be attached; as soon as this is known, the innocence of everyone else is certain. (Should it turn out that after all no crime has been committed, then all would be innocent.) In *The Trial*, on the other hand, it

is the guilt that is certain and the crime that is uncertain; the aim of the hero's investigation is, not to prove his innocence (which would be impossible for he knows he is guilty), but to discover what, if anything, he has done to make himself guilty. K, the hero, is, in fact, a portrait of the kind of person who reads detective stories for escape.

The fantasy, then, which the detective story addict indulges is the fantasy of being restored to the Garden of Eden, to a state of innocence, where he may know love as love and not as the law. The driving force behind this daydream is the feeling of guilt, the cause of which is unknown to the dreamer. The fantasy of escape is the same, whether one explains the guilt in Christian, Freudian, or any other terms. One's way of trying to face the reality, on the other hand, will, of course, depend very much on one's creed.

38. The author asserts that readers of detective fiction can most accurately be described as
    (A) believers in the creed of art for art's sake
    (B) people bent on satisfying an unconscious thirst for blood
    (C) dreamers unable to face the monotony of everyday reality
    (D) persons seeking momentary release from a vague sense of guilt
    (E) idealists drawn to the comforts of organized religion

39. The author cites the example of Kafka's *The Trial* to do which of the following?
    (A) Dramatize the plot of a typical detective story
    (B) Analyze its distinctive qualities as a work of art
    (C) Refute a common opinion about readers of detective fiction
    (D) Demonstrate the genius of the outside investigator
    (E) Discredit a theory about Kafka's narrative

40. It can be inferred from the passage that the author's attitude toward detective fiction is one of
    (A) fastidious distaste
    (B) open skepticism
    (C) profound veneration
    (D) aloof indifference
    (E) genuine appreciation

IF YOU FINISH BEFORE TIME IS CALLED, YOU MAY CHECK YOUR WORK ON THIS SECTION ONLY. DO NOT WORK ON ANY OTHER SECTION IN THE TEST.   S T O P

5

SECTION 5   Time—30 minutes
35 Questions

In this section, solve each problem, using any available space on the page for scratchwork. Then decide which is the best of the choices given and blacken the corresponding space on the answer sheet.

The following information is for your reference in solving some of the problems.

Circle of radius r: Area $= \pi r^2$; Circumference $= 2\pi r$
  The number of degrees of arc in a circle is 360.
The measure in degrees of a straight angle is 180.

Definitions of symbols:
$=$ is equal to $\leqq$ is less than or equal to
$\neq$ is unequal to $\geqq$ is greater than or equal to
$<$ is less than $\parallel$ is parallel to
$>$ is greater than $\perp$ is perpendicular to

Triangle: The sum of the measures in degrees of the angles of a triangle is 180.
If $\angle CDA$ is a right angle, then

(1) area of $\triangle ABC = \dfrac{AB \times CD}{2}$

(2) $AC^2 = AD^2 + DC^2$

Note: Figures that accompany problems in this test are intended to provide information useful in solving the problems. They are drawn as accurately as possible EXCEPT when it is stated in a specific problem that its figure is not drawn to scale. All figures lie in a plane unless otherwise indicated. All numbers used are real numbers.

---

1. If $9x - 5 = 3y$, then $\dfrac{9x - 5}{3} =$

    (A) $\dfrac{y}{3}$ (B) $\dfrac{3}{y}$ (C) y (D) $3y$ (E) $y + 3$

2. A class has b number of boys and g number of girls. The ratio of girls to boys is

    (A) bg (B) $\dfrac{b}{g}$ (C) $\dfrac{b}{b+g}$ (D) $\dfrac{g}{b}$ (E) $\dfrac{g}{b+g}$

3. $\sqrt{\dfrac{1}{16} + \dfrac{1}{9}} =$

    (A) $\dfrac{1}{7}$ (B) $\dfrac{2}{7}$ (C) $\dfrac{25}{144}$ (D) $\dfrac{5}{12}$ (E) $\dfrac{7}{12}$

4. $\dfrac{a + b}{b} =$

    (A) a (B) $\dfrac{a}{b} + b$ (C) $\dfrac{a}{b} + 1$ (D) $a^2 + 1$

    (E) $\dfrac{a + b}{a}$

5. How many kilometers are there in 12 miles?
    (1 kilometer $= \dfrac{5}{8}$ mile.)

    (A) 7.2   (B) 7.5   (C) 19.2   (D) 19.5   (E) 22.3

6. Having installed a new gas tank in my car, the attendant took $1\dfrac{3}{4}$ minutes to completely fill my gas tank. What part of the tank would have been filled if he had stopped after a full minute?

    (A) $\dfrac{2}{7}$ (B) $\dfrac{3}{7}$ (C) $\dfrac{4}{7}$ (D) $\dfrac{3}{4}$ (E) $\dfrac{5}{7}$

7. If I can purchase 2 items for c cents, at the same rate, how many items will I receive for x cents?

    (A) $\dfrac{c}{2x}$ (B) $\dfrac{2c}{x}$ (C) $\dfrac{cx}{2}$ (D) $2cx$ (E) $\dfrac{2x}{c}$

GO ON TO THE NEXT PAGE

5

Questions 8–27 each consist of two quantities, one in Column A and one in Column B. You are to compare the two quantities and on the answer sheet blacken space

A   if the quantity in Column A is greater;
B   if the quantity in Column B is greater;
C   if the two quantities are equal;
D   If the relationship cannot be determined from the information given.

AN E RESPONSE WILL NOT BE SCORED.

EXAMPLES			Answers
	Column A	Column B	
E1.	2×6	$2 + 6$	●Ⓑ©Ⓓ©
E2.	$x°\ /\ y°$		
	$180 - x$	y	ⒶⒷ●ⒹⒺ
E3.	$p - q$	$q - p$	ⒶⒷ©●Ⓔ

Notes:

1.   In certain questions, information concerning one or both of the quantities to be compared is centered above the two columns.
2.   In a given question, a symbol that appears in both columns represents the same thing in Column A as it does in Column B.
3.   Letters such as x, n, and k stand for real numbers.

Column A   Column B

$(a)(b) = 0$

8. a b

$xy = 5$
$x^2 + y^2 = 7$

9. $(x + y)^2$ 17

---

10. $\sqrt{0.3}$ 0.49

---

11.   One half of 1%   0.05

Column A   Column B

$x = 2, y = 3, z = 7$

12. $x(y + z)$ $xz + y$

AGFC and *BEDC* are rectangles.

13.   Perimeter of *AGFC*   Perimeter of shaded region

GO ON TO THE NEXT PAGE

5

SUMMARY DIRECTIONS FOR COMPARISON QUESTIONS

Answer: A   if the quantity in Column A is greater;
              B   if the quantity in Column B is greater;
              C   if the two quantities are equal;
              D   if the relationship cannot be determined from the information given.

AN E RESPONSE WILL NOT BE SCORED.

	Column A	Column B
	$x > 0$	
14.	$2x^2$	$(2x)^2$

Basketball Player	Points Scored in Game
A	20
B	8
C	22
D	14
E	2

	Column A	Column B
15.	Average score of all players	Points scored by player D

AB and CD are parallel lines.

	Column A	Column B
16.	Area of triangle PCD	Area of triangle RCD

	Column A	Column B
17.	x	y

$$5x = 729$$
$$3y = 729$$

	Column A	Column B
18.	x	y

	Column A	Column B

Nineteen years from now, Mark will be 3 times as old as Philip is now. Michael is 3 years younger than Mark.

19.	Michael's age now	Philip's age now

$$1 < a < 5$$
$$1 < b < 5$$

20.	$b - a$	$a - b$
21.	$3\frac{1}{2}\%$	$\dfrac{35}{1000}$

$$\frac{1}{A} = \frac{1}{x} + \frac{1}{y}$$

22.	A	$\dfrac{xy}{x + y}$

$$x < -1$$

23.	x	$\dfrac{1}{x}$

$$a > 1$$
$$b > 1$$

24.	$\dfrac{a^2 - b^2}{(a - b)^2}$	$\dfrac{a + b}{a - b}$
25.	120	$\sqrt{1440}$
26.	3 feet 5 inches	1.5 yards

$$\frac{x}{y} = 1$$

27.	x^2	y^2

GO ON TO THE NEXT PAGE →

5

Solve each of the remaining problems in this section using any available space for scratchwork. Then decide which is the best of the choices given and blacken the corresponding space on the answer sheet.

28. Which of the following statements is (are) always true?
    I. A root of a negative number may be a real number.
    II. The positive square root of a number is smaller than the number.
    III. A binomial multiplied by a binomial yields a trinomial.

    (A) I only
    (B) II only
    (C) III only
    (D) II and III
    (E) All are true.

29. The radius of the pool in Shelter Rock Park is twice the radius of the pool in Martin's backyard. The area of the pool in the park is how many times the area of Martin's pool?

    (A) $\frac{1}{4}$ (B) $\frac{1}{2}$ (C) 2   (D) 4   (E) 8

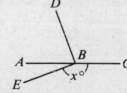

30. In the figure above, $BD \perp BE$ and $\angle DBA = 70$. What is the value of x?

    (A) 20   (B) 110   (C) 120   (D) 160   (E) 290

31. Of a group of 80 applicants for a civil service examination, 20 persons failed to appear for the first part of the test. What percent of the total applicants did appear for this part of the test?

    (A) 4   (B) 16   (C) 25   (D) 60   (E) 75

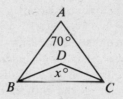

32. In isosceles triangle ABC above, BD and CD are the bisectors of the base angles. The vertex angle has a measure of 70°. What is the value of x?

    (A) 35   (B) 70   (C) 100   (D) 125   (E) 155

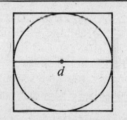

33. In the figure above, how much paper (in terms of π) is wasted if the largest possible circle with a diameter of d is cut out of the square?

    (A) $d - \pi d^2$ (B) $\frac{d^2\pi}{4}$ (C) $\frac{\pi d^2}{4} - d^2$

    (D) $\frac{4d^2 - \pi d^2}{4}$ (E) $\frac{16d^2 - \pi d^2}{4}$

34. If $\begin{array}{|cc|} w & x \\ y & z \end{array}$ is defined to equal $wy - xz$,

    and $\begin{array}{|cc|} w & x \\ y & z \end{array} - K = 0$, then $K =$

    (A) $wy - wz$ (B) $xz + wy$ (C) $-xz$
    (D) $xz - wy$ (E) $wy - xz$

35. Seven pounds of pears costs as much as 10 pounds of apples and 1 pound of oranges. Seven pounds of oranges costs as much as 1 pound of pears and 2 pounds of apples. How many pounds of apples can be purchased for the amount of money required to purchase 12 pounds of pears?

    (A) 8   (B) 14   (C) 16   (D) 18   (E) 24

IF YOU FINISH BEFORE TIME IS CALLED, YOU MAY CHECK YOUR WORK ON THIS SECTION ONLY. DO NOT WORK ON ANY OTHER SECTION IN THE TEST.

S T O P

6   6   6   6   6   6   6   6   6   6   6

SECTION 6   Time—30 minutes   For each question in this section, choose the best answer and
45 Questions   blacken the corresponding space on the answer sheet.

Each question below consists of a word in capital letters, followed by five lettered words or phrases. Choose the word or phrase that is most nearly opposite in meaning to the word in capital letters. Since some of the questions require you to distinguish fine shades of meaning, consider all the choices before deciding which is best.

Example:

GOOD: (A) sour   (B) bad   (C) red
(D) hot   (E) ugly   Ⓐ ● Ⓒ Ⓓ Ⓔ

1. FLOURISH: (A) darken   (B) waste away
   (C) beckon   (D) endure   (E) bring back

2. TOLERATE: (A) refuse to bear
   (B) act wrongly   (C) take seriously
   (D) use foolishly   (E) shout angrily

3. ENHANCE: (A) retreat   (B) loathe
   (C) detract   (D) pursue   (E) convert

4. SPIRITED: (A) remote   (B) unanimated
   (C) unimaginative   (D) insincere   (E) awkward

5. HEFTY: (A) frail   (B) liquid   (C) feminine
   (D) quick   (E) undisturbed

6. PURIFY: (A) resolve   (B) desire   (C) pollute
   (D) discriminate   (E) agitate

7. SAGE: (A) upright   (B) foolish   (C) cheerful
   (D) deliberate   (E) unconcerned

8. ENACT: (A) improvise   (B) defy   (C) suffer
   (D) externalize   (E) repeal

9. DISMANTLE: (A) reassure   (B) kindle
   (C) equip   (D) impede   (E) suppose

10. CLEMENCY: (A) stupidity   (B) filth   (C) lack
    of money   (D) lack of mercy   (E) slowness

11. MITIGATE: (A) disarm   (B) worsen
    (C) predict   (D) initiate   (E) compensate

12. SURREPTITIOUS: (A) sugary (B) monotonous
    (C) rash   (D) open   (E) wholesome

13. CORPULENCE: (A) energetic nature
    (B) spiritual bent   (C) juvenile behavior
    (D) untidiness   (E) slenderness

14. METICULOUS: (A) careless   (B) shapeless
    (C) transient   (D) intrepid   (E) dogmatic

15. PROCLIVITY:
    (A) fear of interference
    (B) contradiction in terms
    (C) lack of inclination
    (D) need for reassurance
    (E) position of strength

Each sentence below has one or two blanks, each blank indicating that something has been omitted. Beneath the sentence are five lettered words or sets of words. Choose the word or set of words that best fits the meaning of the sentence as a whole.

Example:

Although its publicity has been ----, the film itself is intelligent, well-acted, handsomely produced, and altogether ----.

(A) tasteless..respectable (B) extensive..moderate
(C) sophisticated..amateur (D) risqué..crude
(E) perfect..spectacular
   ● Ⓑ Ⓒ Ⓓ Ⓔ

16. Despite the ---- of the materials with which he worked, many of Tiffany's glass masterpieces have survived for over seventy years.

(A) beauty   (B) translucence   (C) abundance
(D) majesty   (E) fragility

17. Although similar to mice in many physical characteristics, voles may be ---- mice by the shortness of their tails.

(A) distinguished from   (B) classified with
(C) related to   (D) categorized as
(E) enumerated with

18. Because he saw no ---- to the task assigned him, he worked at it in a very ---- way.

(A) function..systematic
(B) method..dutiful
(C) purpose..diligent
(D) end..rigid
(E) point..perfunctory

GO ON TO THE NEXT PAGE →

6   6   6   6   6   6   6   6   6   6   6

19. The herb Chinese parsley is an example of what
we mean by an acquired taste: Westerners who
originally ---- it eventually come to ---- its flavor in
Oriental foods.

(A) relish..enjoy
(B) dislike..welcome
(C) savor..abhor
(D) ignore..detest
(E) discern..recognize

20. Although the doctor's words were ----, the
patient's family hoped against hope for a ---- of the
disease.

(A) discouraging..resurgence
(B) disheartening..remission
(C) inaudible..report
(D) reassuring..transfusion
(E) authoritative..diagnosis

Each passage below is followed by questions based on its content. Answer all questions following a passage on the
basis of what is <u>stated</u> or <u>implied</u> in that passage.

To the world when it was half a thousand
years younger, the outlines of all things seemed
more clearly marked than to us. The contrast
Line between suffering and joy, between adversity and
(5) happiness, appeared more striking. All experience had yet to the minds of men the directness
and absoluteness of the pleasure and pain of
child-life. Every event, every action, was still
embodied in expressive and solemn forms, which
(10) raised them to the dignity of a ritual. For it was
not merely the great facts of birth, marriage, and
death which, by their sacredness, were raised to
the rank of mysteries; incidents of less importance, like a journey, a task, a visit, were equally
(15) attended by a thousand formalities: benedictions,
ceremonies, formulae.

Calamities and indigence were more afflicting
than at present; it was more difficult to guard
against them, and to find solace. Illness and
(20) health presented a more striking contrast; the
cold and darkness of winter were more real evils.
Honors and riches were relished with greater
avidity and contrasted more vividly with surrounding misery. We, at the present day, can
(25) hardly understand the keenness with which a fur
coat, a good fire on the hearth, a soft bed, a glass
of wine, were formerly enjoyed.

Then, again, all things in life were of a proud
or cruel publicity. Lepers sounded their rattles
(30) and went about in processions, beggars exhibited
their deformity and their misery in churches.
Every order and estate, every rank and profession, was distinguished by its costume. The great
lords never moved about without a glorious dis-
(35) play of arms and liveries, exciting fear and envy.
Executions and other public acts of justice,
hawking, marriages and funerals, were all
announced by cries and processions, songs and
music. The lover wore the colors of his lady;
(40) companions the emblem of their confraternity;
parties and servants the badges or blazon of their
lords. Between town and country, too, the con-

trast was very marked. A medieval town did not
lose itself in extensive suburbs of factories and
(45) villas; girded by its walls, it stood forth as a compact whole, bristling with innumerable turrets.
However tall and threatening the houses of
noblemen or merchants might be, in the aspect of
the town the lofty mass of the churches always
(50) remained dominant.

The contrast between silence and sound,
darkness and light, like that between summer and
winter, was more strongly marked than it is in
our lives. The modern town hardly knows silence
(55) or darkness in their purity, nor the effect of a
solitary light or a single distant cry.

All things presenting themselves to the mind
in violent contrasts and impressive forms, lent a
tone of excitement and of passion to everyday
(60) life and tended to produce the perpetual
oscillation between despair and distracted joy,
between cruelty and pious tenderness which
characterizes life in the Middle Ages.

21. The author's main purpose in this passage is best
defined as an attempt to show how

(A) extremes of feeling and experience marked the
Middle Ages
(B) the styles of the very poor and the very rich
complemented each other
(C) twentieth century standards of behavior
cannot be applied to the Middle Ages
(D) the Middle Ages developed out of the Dark
Ages
(E) the medieval spirit languished five hundred
years ago

GO ON TO THE NEXT PAGE

6   6   6   6   6   6   6   6   6   6   6   6

22. According to the passage, surrounding an activity with formalities makes it

(A) less important
(B) more dignified
(C) less expensive
(D) more indirect
(E) less solemn

23. To the author, the Middle Ages seem to be all of the following EXCEPT

(A) harsh and bleak
(B) festive and joyful
(C) dignified and ceremonious
(D) passionate and turbulent
(E) routine and boring

24. According to the passage, well above the typical medieval town there towered

(A) houses of worship
(B) manufacturing establishments
(C) the mansions of the aristocracy
(D) great mercantile houses
(E) walled suburbs

25. The author's use of the term "formulae" (line 16) could best be interpreted to mean which of the following?

(A) set forms of words for rituals
(B) mathematical rules or principles
(C) chemical symbols
(D) nourishment for infants
(E) prescriptions for drugs

It is a most miserable thing to feel ashamed of home. There may be black ingratitude in the thing, and the punishment may be retributive and well deserved; but, that it is a miserable thing, I can testify.

Home had never been a very pleasant place to me, because of my sister's temper. But Joe had sanctified it and I believed in it. I had believed in the best parlor as a most elegant salon; I had believed in the front door, as a mysterious portal of the Temple of State whose solemn opening was attended with a sacrifice of roast fowls; I had believed in the kitchen as a chaste though not magnificent apartment; I had believed in the forge as the glowing road to manhood. Now, it was all coarse and common, and I would not have had Miss Havisham and Estella see it on any account.

Once, it had seemed to me that when I should at last roll up my shirt sleeves and go into the forge, Joe's 'prentice, I should be distinguished and happy. Now the reality was in my hold, I only felt that I was dusty with the dust of small coal, and that I had a weight upon my daily remembrance to which the anvil was a feather. There have been occasions in my later life (I suppose as in most lives) when I have felt for a time as

if a thick curtain had fallen on all its interest and romance, to shut me out from anything save dull endurance any more. Never has that curtain dropped so heavy and blank, as when my way in life lay stretched out straight before me through the newly-entered road of apprenticeship to Joe.

I remember that at a later period of my "time," I used to stand about the churchyard on Sunday evenings, when night was falling, comparing my own perspective with the windy marsh view, and making out some likeness between them by thinking how flat and low both were, and how on both there came an unknown way and a dark mist and then the sea. I was quite as dejected on the first working-day of my apprenticeship as in that after time; but I am glad to know that I never breathed a murmur to Joe while my indentures lasted. It is about the only thing I *am* glad to know of myself in that connection.

For, though it includes what I proceed to add, all the merit of what I proceed to add was Joe's. It was not because I was faithful, but because Joe was faithful, that I never ran away and went for a soldier or a sailor. It was not because I had a strong sense of the virtue of industry, but because Joe had a strong sense of the virtue of industry, that I worked with tolerable zeal against the grain. It is not possible to know how far the influence of any amiable honest-hearted duty-going man flies out into the world; but it is very possible to know how it has touched one's self in going by, and I know right well that any good that intermixed itself with my apprenticeship came of plain contented Joe, and not of restless aspiring discontented me.

26. The passage as a whole is best described as

(A) an analysis of the reasons behind a change in attitude
(B) an account of a young man's reflections on his emotional state
(C) a description of a young man's awakening to the harsh conditions of working class life
(D) a defense of a young man's longings for romance and glamor
(E) a criticism of young people's ingratitude to their elders

27. It may be inferred from the passage that the young man has been apprenticed to a

(A) cook   (B) forger   (C) coal miner
 (D) blacksmith   (E) grave digger

GO ON TO THE NEXT PAGE

DISCOVER
BARRON'S
BOOK NOTES

CHOOSE YOUR FREE* COPY FROM THESE 101 TITLES:

BOOK #	TITLE
3400-7	THE AENEID
3401-5	ALL QUIET ON THE WESTERN FRONT
3500-3	ALL THE KING'S MEN
3402-3	ANIMAL FARM
3501-1	ANNA KARENINA
3502-X	AS I LAY DYING
3503-8	AS YOU LIKE IT
3504-6	BABBIT
3403-1	BEOWULF
3404-X	BILLY BUDD & TYPEE
3405-8	BRAVE NEW WORLD
3505-4	CANDIDE
3406-6	CANTERBURY TALES
3506-2	CATCH-22
3407-4	THE CATCHER IN THE RYE
3409-0	CRIME AND PUNISHMENT
3408-2	THE CRUCIBLE
3507-0	CRY, THE BELOVED COUNTRY
3508-9	DAISY MILLER & TURN OF THE SCREW
3509-7	DAVID COPPERFIELD
3410-4	DEATH OF A SALESMAN
3411-2	THE DIVINE COMEDY: THE INFERNO
3510-0	DOCTOR FAUSTUS
3511-9	A DOLL'S HOUSE & HEDDA GABLER
3512-7	DON QUIXOTE
3513-5	ETHAN FROME
3412-0	A FAREWELL TO ARMS
3514-3	FAUST: PARTS I AND II
3515-1	FOR WHOM THE BELL TOLLS
3516-X	THE GLASS MENAGERIE & A STREETCAR NAMED DESIRE
3517-8	THE GOOD EARTH
3413-9	THE GRAPES OF WRATH
3414-7	GREAT EXPECTATIONS
3415-5	THE GREAT GATSBY

BOOK #	TITLE
3416-3	GULLIVER'S TRAVELS
3417-1	HAMLET
3518-6	HARD TIMES
3418-X	HEART OF DARKNESS & THE SECRET SHARER
3419-8	HENRY IV, PART I
3519-4	THE HOUSE OF THE SEVEN GABLES
3420-1	HUCKLEBERRY FINN
3421-X	THE ILIAD
3520-8	INVISIBLE MAN
3422-8	JANE EYRE
3423-6	JULIUS CAESAR
3424-4	THE JUNGLE
3425-2	KING LEAR
3521-6	LIGHT IN AUGUST
3522-4	LORD JIM
3426-0	LORD OF THE FLIES
3523-2	THE LORD OF THE RINGS & THE HOBBIT
3427-9	MACBETH
3524-0	MADAME BOVARY
3525-9	THE MAYOR OF CASTERBRIDGE
3526-7	THE MERCHANT OF VENICE
3527-5	A MIDSUMMER NIGHT'S DREAM
3428-7	MOBY-DICK
3528-3	MY ANTONIA
3529-1	NATIVE SON
3530-5	NEW TESTAMENT
3449-X	1984
3429-5	THE ODYSSEY
3430-9	OEDIPUS TRILOGY
3431-7	OF MICE AND MEN
3432-5	THE OLD MAN AND THE SEA
3531-3	OLD TESTAMENT
3532-1	OLIVER TWIST
3433-3	ONE FLEW OVER THE CUCKOO'S NEST

BOOK #	TITLE
3434-1	OTHELLO
3533-X	OUR TOWN
3435-X	PARADISE LOST
3534-8	THE PEARL
3535-6	PORTRAIT OF THE ARTIST AS A YOUNG MAN
3437-6	PRIDE AND PREJUDICE
3536-4	THE PRINCE
3438-4	THE RED BADGE OF COURAGE
3436-8	THE REPUBLIC
3439-2	RETURN OF THE NATIVE
3537-2	RICHARD III
3440-6	ROMEO AND JULIET
3442-2	THE SCARLET LETTER
3441-4	A SEPARATE PEACE
3538-0	SILAS MARNER
3539-9	SLAUGHTERHOUSE-5
3540-2	SONS AND LOVERS
3541-0	THE SOUND AND THE FURY
3542-9	STEPPENWOLF & SIDDHARTHA
3543-7	THE STRANGER
3443-0	THE SUN ALSO RISES
3444-9	A TALE OF TWO CITIES
3544-5	THE TAMING OF THE SHREW
3545-3	THE TEMPEST
3445-7	TESS OF THE D'URBERVILLES
3446-5	TO KILL A MOCKINGBIRD
3546-1	TOM JONES
3547-X	TOM SAWYER
3548-8	TWELFTH NIGHT
3600-X	UNCLE TOM'S CABIN
3447-3	WALDEN
3549-6	WHO'S AFRAID OF VIRGINIA WOOLF?
3448-1	WUTHERING HEIGHTS

ACCLAIMED BY TEACHERS AND STUDENTS

▟▛ Very well written…BARRON'S BOOK NOTES give more explanations of what is going on, and they are easier to understand. BARRON'S BOOK NOTES will be very helpful to students. ▟▛

—Denise Sheridan, *student*

▟▛ I enjoyed reading the BOOK NOTES very much. As a student, I found them very clear and easy to read…[They] make reading the book much more enjoyable. ▟▛

—Roseanne Rizzuto, *student*

▟▛ The quality of the writing in BOOK NOTES is first-rate. Our students will find that it is an excellent supplement to the assigned literature. ▟▛

—Mark Weyne, Principal, *Wantagh High School, New York*

▟▛ I have never encountered a clearer explanation of a text at this level of difficulty [*Plato's Republic*]…It is a magnificent effort. Well done! …should be enormously successful. ▟▛

—Frank O'Hare, Professor of English, *Ohio State University*

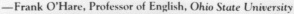

6 6 6 6 6 6 6 6 6 6 6 6

28. In the passage, Joe is portrayed most specifically as

(A) distinguished   (B) virtuous
(C) independent   (D) homely   (E) coarse

29. According to the passage, the narrator gives himself a measure of credit for

(A) working diligently despite his unhappiness
(B) abandoning his hope of a military career
(C) keeping his menial position secret from Miss Havisham
(D) concealing his despondency from Joe
(E) surrendering his childish beliefs

30. The passage suggests that the narrator's increasing discontent with his home during his apprenticeship was caused by

(A) a new awareness on his part of how his home would appear to others
(B) the increasing heaviness of the labor involved
(C) the unwillingness of Joe to curb his sister's temper
(D) the narrator's lack of an industrious character
(E) a combination of simple ingratitude and sinfulness

Select the word or set of words that best completes each of the following sentences.

---

31. We were distressed by these inexplicable ---- from his generally ---- taste.

(A) departures..execrable
(B) lapses..flawless
(C) deviations..questionable
(D) results..faulty
(E) variations..unusual

32. Because they did not accept his basic ----, they were ---- by his argument.

(A) assumption..convinced
(B) motivation..confused
(C) bias..impressed
(D) premise..unconvinced
(E) supposition..justified

33. Pain is the body's early warning system: loss of ---- in the extremities leaves a person ---- injuring himself unwittingly.

(A) agony..incapable of
(B) sensation..vulnerable to
(C) consciousness..desirous of
(D) feeling..habituated to
(E) movement..prone to

34. She was ---- her accomplishments and properly unwilling to ---- them before her friends.

(A) excited by..parade
(B) immodest about..discuss
(C) deprecatory about..flaunt
(D) uncertain of..concede
(E) unaware of..conceal

35. Despite their ---- of Twain's *Huckleberry Finn* for its stereotyped portrait of the slave Jim, even the novel's ---- agreed it was a masterpiece of American prose.

(A) admiration..critics
(B) denunciation..supporters
(C) criticism..detractors
(D) defense..censors
(E) praise..advocates

Each question below consists of a related pair of words or phrases, followed by five lettered pairs of words or phrases. Select the lettered pair that best expresses a relationship similar to that expressed in the original pair.

Example:

YAWN : BOREDOM :: (A) dream : sleep
(B) anger : madness   (C) smile : amusement
(D) face : expression   (E) impatience : rebellion

Ⓐ Ⓑ ● Ⓓ Ⓔ

---

36. SIGNATURE : PORTRAIT ::
(A) title · novel
(B) negative : photograph
(C) autograph : celebrity
(D) postscript : letter
(E) byline : article

37. BREEZE : TORNADO :: (A) ice : floe
(B) trickle : gusher   (C) conflagration : flame
(D) river : stream   (E) eruption : volcano

38. ARCHIVES : RECORDS :: (A) catalog : shelves
(B) aviary : birds   (C) thread : spindle
(D) clothes : shoes   (E) pedestal : statue

39. ENVELOP : SURROUND :: (A) efface : confront
(B) house : dislodge   (C) loiter : linger
(D) distend : struggle   (E) ascend : agree

GO ON TO THE NEXT PAGE ➡

6   6   6   6   6   6   6   6   6   6   6

40. INDIFFERENT:CONCERN ::
   (A) intrepid:bravery
   (B) arrogant:modesty
   (C) unbigoted:tolerance
   (D) unnatural:emotion
   (E) variable:change

41. DILETTANTE:DABBLE ::   (A) coquette:flirt
   (B) gymnast:exercise   (C) soldier:drill
    (D) embezzler:steal   (E) benefactor:donate

42. BARREN:FECUND ::
   (A) dry:parched
   (B) naked:sinful
   (C) hackneyed:original
   (D) incessant:continuous
   (E) impetuous:rash

43. SLANDER:DEFAMATORY ::
   (A) fraud:notorious
   (B) tenet:devotional
   (C) elegy:sorrowful
   (D) edict:temporary
   (E) exhortation:cautionary

44. SLOUGH:SKIN ::   (A) shed:hair
   (B) polish:teeth   (C) shade:eyes
    (D) tear:ligaments   (E) remove:tonsils

45. HYPERBOLIC:EXAGGERATED ::
   (A) metabolic:restrained
   (B) choleric:fitful
   (C) capricious:whimsical
   (D) idiomatic:impersonal
   (E) melancholy:bemused

IF YOU FINISH BEFORE TIME IS CALLED, YOU MAY CHECK YOUR WORK ON
THIS SECTION ONLY. DO NOT WORK ON ANY OTHER SECTION IN THE TEST   **S T O P**

Answer Key

Note: The answers to the math sections are keyed to the corresponding review areas in Chapter 12. The numbers in parentheses after each answer refer to

topics as listed below. (Note that to review for number 16, Quantitative Comparison, study Chapter 11.)

1. Fundamental Operations
2. Algebraic Operations
3. Using Algebra
4. Roots and Radicals
5. Inequalities
6. Fractions
7. Decimals
8. Percent
9. Averages
10. Motion
11. Ratio and Proportion
12. Mixtures and Solutions
13. Work
14. Coordinate Geometry
15. Geometry
16. Quantitative Comparison
17. Data Interpretation

Section 1   Verbal

1. B	10. E	19. B	28. A	37. A
2. D	11. A	20. D	29. E	38. D
3. B	12. A	21. B	30. D	39. B
4. A	13. C	22. D	31. B	40. B
5. B	14. B	23. E	32. D	41. D
6. E	15. E	24. C	33. D	42. E
7. E	16. B	25. C	34. A	43. C
8. D	17. D	26. B	35. E	44. C
9. B	18. C	27. D	36. C	45. E

Section 2   Math

1. D (1)	6. B (6)	11. A (15)	16. B (10)	21. E (11, 17)
2. C (2)	7. D (8, 17)	12. A (1, 3)	17. C (2)	22. D (3, 17)
3. E (2)	8. A (11, 17)	13. D (6)	18. A (14)	23. C (15)
4. A (2)	9. E (15)	14. C (9)	19. C (8, 17)	24. D (15)
5. E (8)	10. C (15)	15. A (5)	20. B (9, 17)	25. D (1)

Section 3   Test Of Standard Written English

1. B	11. E	21. E	31. A	41. B
2. D	12. A	22. E	32. B	42. A
3. B	13. A	23. C	33. E	43. B
4. B	14. C	24. D	34. A	44. B
5. E	15. E	25. C	35. D	45. C
6. B	16. A	26. B	36. D	46. C
7. A	17. B	27. D	37. B	47. C
8. D	18. C	28. A	38. D	48. B
9. C	19. C	29. A	39. B	49. B
10. B	20. D	30. C	40. C	50. C

Section 4   Verbal

1. A	9. E	17. D	25. A	33. C
2. B	10. B	18. E	26. A	34. A
3. B	11. D	19. B	27. B	35. C
4. B	12. C	20. B	28. D	36. C
5. C	13. C	21. C	29. B	37. D
6. B	14. B	22. B	30. B	38. D
7. A	15. B	23. A	31. D	39. B
8. C	16. B	24. A	32. E	40. E

Section 5 Math

1.	C (2)	8.	D (2, 16)	15.	B (9, 16)	22.	C (2, 16)	29.	D (15)
2.	D (11)	9.	C (2, 16)	16.	C (15, 16)	23.	B (6, 16)	30.	D (15)
3.	D (4)	10.	A (4, 7, 16)	17.	A (15, 16)	24.	C (2, 16)	31.	E (8)
4.	C (2, 6)	11.	B (7, 8, 16)	18.	B (2, 16)	25.	A (4, 16)	32.	D (15)
5.	C (11)	12.	A (2, 16)	19.	D (3, 16)	26.	B (1, 16)	33.	D (15)
6.	C (6, 11)	13.	C (15, 16)	20.	D (2, 16)	27.	C (4, 16)	34.	E (2)
7.	E (3, 11)	14.	B (2, 4, 16)	21.	C (6, 8, 16)	28.	A (2, 4)	35.	D (3)

Section 6 Verbal

1.	B	10.	D	19.	B	28.	B	37.	B
2.	A	11.	B	20.	B	29.	D	38.	B
3.	C	12.	D	21.	A	30.	A	39.	C
4.	B	13.	E	22.	B	31.	B	40.	B
5.	A	14.	A	23.	E	32.	D	41.	A
6.	C	15.	C	24.	A	33.	B	42.	C
7.	B	16.	E	25.	A	34.	C	43.	C
8.	E	17.	A	26.	B	35.	C	44.	A
9.	C	18.	E	27.	D	36.	E	45.	C

Self-Evaluation

Now that you have completed the Diagnostic Test, evaluate your performance. Identify your strengths and weaknesses, and then plan a practical study program based on what you have discovered. Follow these steps to evaluate your work on the Diagnostic Test. (Note: You'll find the charts referred to in steps 1–5 on the next four pages.)

■ **STEP 1**   Use the Answer Key to check your answers for each section.

■ **STEP 2**   For each section, count the number of correct and incorrect answers (remember that you don't count omitted answers), and enter the numbers on the appropriate lines of the chart "Calculate Your Raw Score." Then do the indicated calculations to get your Raw Verbal Score, your Raw TSWE Score, and your Raw Math Score.

■ **STEP 3**   Consult the chart "Evaluate Your Performance" to see how well you did.

■ **STEP 4**   To pinpoint the specific areas in which you need to improve, circle the numbers of the questions that you either left blank or got wrong on the "Identify Your Weaknesses" charts. This will tell you where to concentrate your efforts to get the most out of your study time. The chart for the math sections gives you page references for review and practice by skill areas. The charts for the verbal and TSWE sections refer you to the appropriate chapters to study for each question type.

■ **STEP 5**   Do the review and practice indicated on the charts wherever you had a concentration of circles.

Important: Remember that, in addition to evaluating your scores, you should read all of the answer explanations for questions you answered incorrectly, questions you omitted, and questions you answered correctly but found difficult. Reviewing the answer explanations will help you understand concepts and strategies, and may point out short-cuts.

Calculate Your Raw Score

Verbal

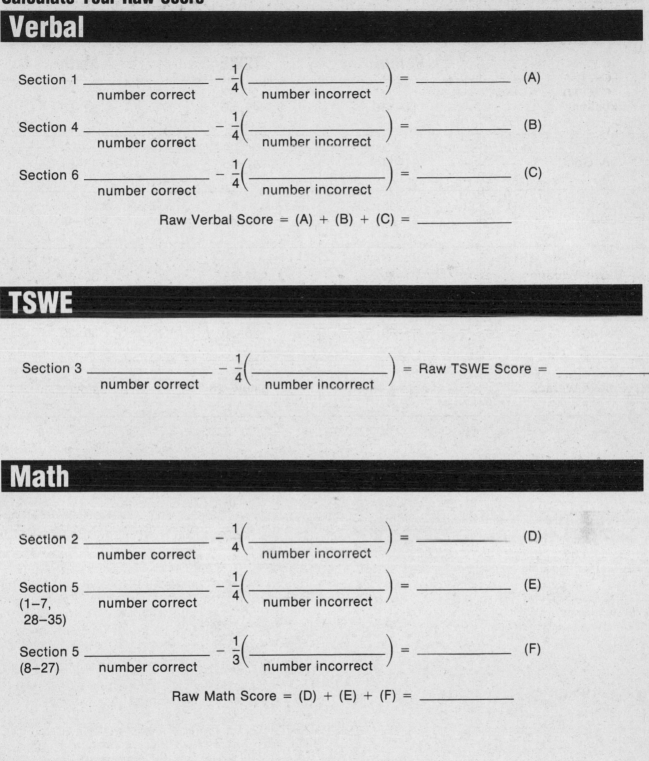

Section 1 _____ − $\frac{1}{4}$(_____) = _____ (A)
number correct   number incorrect

Section 4 _____ − $\frac{1}{4}$(_____) = _____ (B)
number correct   number incorrect

Section 6 _____ − $\frac{1}{4}$(_____) = _____ (C)
number correct   number incorrect

Raw Verbal Score = (A) + (B) + (C) = _____

TSWE

Section 3 _____ − $\frac{1}{4}$(_____) = Raw TSWE Score = _____
number correct   number incorrect

Math

Section 2 _____ − $\frac{1}{4}$(_____) = _____ (D)
number correct   number incorrect

Section 5 _____ − $\frac{1}{4}$(_____) = _____ (E)
(1–7,   number correct   number incorrect
28–35)

Section 5 _____ − $\frac{1}{3}$(_____) = _____ (F)
(8–27)   number correct   number incorrect

Raw Math Score = (D) + (E) + (F) = _____

Evaluate Your Performance

Verbal, TSWE, Math

	Verbal	TSWE	Math
Excellent	111–130	46–50	52–60
Very Good	91–110	41–45	45–51
Good	81–90	36–40	36–44
Above Average	61–80	31–35	30–35
Average	45–60	26–30	20–29
Below Average	below 45	below 26	below 20

Identify Your Weaknesses

Verbal

Question Type	Question Numbers			Chapter to Study
	Section 1	**Section 4**	**Section 6**	
Antonym	1, 2, 3, 4, 5, 6, 7, 8, 9, 10, 11, 12, 13, 14, 15	1, 2, 3, 4, 5, 6, 7, 8, 9, 10	1, 2, 3, 4, 5, 6, 7, 8, 9, 10, 11, 12, 13, 14, 15	Chapter 5
Analogy	36, 37, 38, 39, 40, 41, 42, 43, 44, 45	16, 17, 18, 19, 20, 21, 22, 23, 24, 25	36, 37, 38, 39, 40, 41, 42, 43, 44, 45	Chapter 6
Sentence Completion	16, 17, 18, 19, 20, 31, 32, 33, 34, 35	11, 12, 13, 14, 15	16, 17, 18, 19, 20, 31, 32, 33, 34, 35	Chapter 7
Reading Comprehension	21, 22, 23, 24, 25, 26, 27, 28, 29, 30	26, 27, 28, 29, 30, 31, 32, 33, 34, 35, 36, 37, 38, 39, 40	21, 22, 23, 24, 25, 26, 27, 28, 29, 30	Chapter 8

TSWE

Question Type	Question Numbers	Chapter to Study
Usage	1, 2, 3, 4, 5, 6, 7, 8, 9, 10, 11, 12, 13, 14, 15, 16, 17, 18, 19, 20, 21, 22, 23, 24, 25, 41, 42, 43, 44, 45, 46, 47, 48, 49, 50	Chapter 13
Sentence Correction	26, 27, 28, 29, 30, 31, 32, 33, 34, 35, 36, 37, 38, 39, 40	Chapter 13

Identify Your Weaknesses

Math

Skill Area	Question Numbers		Pages to Study
	Section 2	Section 5	
Fundamental Operations	1, 12, 25	26	328–29
Algebraic Operations	2, 3, 4	1, 4, 8, 9, 12, 14, 18, 20, 22, 24, 28, 34	329–34
Using Algebra	12, 22	7, 19, 35	334–35
Fractions	6, 13	4, 6, 21, 23	341–45
Decimals and Percents	5, 7, 19	10, 11, 21, 31	351–55
Verbal Problems	14, 16, 17, 20	15	357–58
Ratio and Proportion	8, 21	2, 5, 6, 7	362–64
Geometry	9, 10, 11, 23, 24	13, 16, 17, 29, 30, 32, 33	371–76
Coordinate Geometry	18		381–82
Inequalities	15		335–36
Quantitative Comparison		8, 9, 10, 11, 12, 13, 14, 15, 16, 17, 18, 19, 20, 21, 22, 23, 24, 25, 26, 27	309–13
Roots and Radicals	4	3, 10, 14, 25, 27, 28	332–33

Answer Explanations

Section 1   Verbal

1. B.   To *resolve* is to decide, to come to a decision. Its opposite is to hesitate or *waver*.
Context Clue: Think of "resolving to join the Peace Corps."

2. D.   *Authentic* means genuine or real. Its opposite is *counterfeit*.
Context Clue: Think of "an authentic painting by Van Gogh."

3. B.   *Cramped* means confined or restricted. Its opposite is *spacious*.
Context Clue: Think of "cramped quarters."

4. A.   To *alleviate* something is to lessen or lighten it; to make it better. Its opposite is to *aggravate* or make worse.
Context Clue: Think of "taking medicine to alleviate the pain."

5. B.   To *disengage* is to unfasten or release. Its opposite is to *attach*.
Context Clue: Think of "disengaging your hand" from somebody's grasp.

6. E.   An *adversary* is an enemy or opponent. Its opposite is a supporter or *proponent*.
Context Clue: Think of "a dangerous adversary."

7. E.   *Hubbub* means noise, a loud uproar. Its opposite is *quiet*.
Context Clue: Think of "the hubbub of many voices."

8. D.   *Mutable* means changeable. Its opposite is *permanent*.
Context Clue: Think of "mutable luck."
Word Parts Clue: *Mut-* means change.

9. B.   To *hamper* is to hinder or to get in the way. Its opposite is to *further* or encourage.
Remember, look at the answer choices to determine the main word's part of speech. *Hamper* here is not a noun (laundry hamper, picnic hamper) but a verb.
Context Clue: Think of "hampering all progress."

10. E.   To *placate* is to soothe, to try to calm someone down. Its opposite is to *exasperate* or irritate someone.
Context Clue: "Angry parents can be hard to placate."

11. A.   *Intrepid* means brave. Its opposite is *cowardly*.
Context Clue: Think of "intrepid James Bond."
Word Parts Clue: *In-* means not. *Trep-* means fear. Someone *intrepid* does not fear.

12. A.   To *rifle* is to ransack or rummage through things (in order to steal). Its opposite is to *leave undisturbed*.
Remember, look at the answer choices to determine the main word's part of speech. As you can tell from looking at the first answer choice, *rifle* here is a verb, not a noun.
Context Clue: Think of someone "rifling through a desk."

13. C.   *Pulchritude* means beauty; its opposite is *ugliness*. There's no short cut for knowing this word.
Context Clue: Think of "the pulchritude of a beauty queen."

14. B.   *Hackneyed* means worn out and tired, lacking in freshness or originality. Its opposite is *novel* or fresh.
Context Clue: Think of "a hackneyed phrase."

15. E.   *Innocuous* means harmless. Its opposite is *harmful*.
Context Clue: "Watch out for that drink—it looks innocuous, but it packs a punch!"

16. B.   The management will not hold anything against the strikers; they will take no *retaliations* or revenge. Note how the second clause of the sentence serves to clarify or define the missing word.

(Definition)

17. D.   Anyone who has produced over three hundred books in a single lifetime is an enormously productive or *prolific* writer. Writers are often described as prolific, but few, if any, are as prolific as Asimov.
Beware Eye-Catchers: Choice A is incorrect. *Fastidious* means painstakingly careful; it has nothing to do with writing fast.

(Examples)

18. C.   In a time of financial crisis, one worries about spending money. Any expenditure of the public's money must be *justified* (proved desirable); a *lavish* or extravagant expenditure of funds definitely should be.

(Argument Pattern)

19. B. Time limitations would cause problems for you if you were reading a *lengthy* book. To save time, you might want to read it in an *abridged* or shortened form.

Remember to watch for signal words that link one part of the sentence to another. The use of "because" in the opening clause is a cause signal.

(Cause and Effect Signal)

20. D. Speakers wish to communicate *unambiguously* in order that there may be no *confusion* about their meaning.

Remember to watch for signal words that link one part of the sentence to another. The presence of *and* linking two items in a series indicates that the missing word may be a synonym or near-synonym for the other linked word. In this case, *unambiguously* is a synonym for *clearly*. Similarly, the use of "so that" in the second clause signals cause and effect.

(Argument Pattern)

21. B. The author describes himself as "jarred and shocked" (line 4–5). He asks himself, "What strange world was this?" His initial reaction to Mencken's prose is one of disbelief.

Choice A is incorrect. Mencken rages; the speaker does not.

Choice C is incorrect. It is unsupported by the passage.

Choices D and E are incorrect. Again, these terms apply to Mencken, not to the speaker.

(Specific Details)

22. D. The speaker does *not* portray Mencken as reverent or respectful of religious belief. Instead, he says that Mencken mocks God.

Choice A is incorrect. The speaker portrays Mencken as intrepid (brave); he wonders where Mencken gets his courage.

Choice B is incorrect. The speaker portrays Mencken as articulate (verbally expressive); he says Mencken writes clear, clean sentences.

Choice C is incorrect. The speaker portrays Mencken as satiric (mocking); he says Mencken makes fun of people's weaknesses.

Choice E is incorrect. The speaker portrays Mencken as opinionated (stubborn about his opinions; prejudiced). Mencken's book, after all, is *A Book of Prejudices*.

Remember, when asked about specific details in the passage, spot key words in the question and scan the passage to find them (or their synonyms).

(Specific Details)

23. E. Phrases like "feeling something new, being affected by something that made the look of the world different" and "filled with bookish notions" reflect the speaker's response to the new books he reads. You have here a portrait of a youth's response to his expanding intellectual horizons.

Choice A is incorrect. The speaker is not arguing in favor of a cause; he is recounting an episode from his life.

Choice B is incorrect. The speaker was aware of racial prejudice long before he read Mencken.

Choice C is incorrect. The passage is not about Mencken's and Lewis's styles; it is about their effect in opening up the world to the speaker.

Choice D is incorrect. The passage is more about the impact of art on life than about the impact of life on art.

Remember, when asked to find the main idea, be sure to check the opening and summary sentences of each paragraph.

(Main Idea)

24. C. The speaker feels a hunger for books that surges up in him. In other words, he is filled with *impatient ardor* or eagerness.

Choice A is incorrect. The speaker has his dreams, but he is involved rather than indifferent.

Choices B and D are incorrect. There is nothing in the lines to suggest them.

Choice E is incorrect. The speaker is determined, but his resolve is active and eager rather than quiet.

Remember, when asked to determine the author's attitude or tone, look for words that convey emotion or paint pictures.

(Attitude/Tone)

25. C. The speaker is able to identify Mr. Gerald as an American type. He feels closer to Mr. Gerald, familiar with the limits of his life. This suggests that he smiles out of a sense of recognition.

Choices A, B, D, and E are incorrect. There is nothing in the passage to suggest them.

Remember, when asked to make inferences, base your answers on what the passage implies, not what it states directly.

(Inference)

26. B. The opening paragraph states that the introduction of the Dytiscus larvae to the aquarium will result in a struggle for existence in which the larvae will destroy their prey. The larvae, thus, are predators (hunters of prey). This suggests that their presence would

be of particular interest to naturalists studying predatory patterns at work within a closed environment such as an aquarium.

(Inference)

27. D. Though the passage mentions amphibians—tadpoles—and food, it states that the tadpoles provide food for the larvae, not vice versa. The passage nowhere states that the larvae are a source of food for amphibians.
Choice A is incorrect. The passage states that the larvae secrete digestive juices; it mentions secretion in line 35.
Choice B is incorrect. The passage states that the larvae attack one another: they seize and devour their own breed (lines 51–57).
Choice C is incorrect. The passage states that the larvae are attracted to motion: prey for them "is all that moves."
Choice E is incorrect. The passage states that the larvae have ravenous appetites: their "voracity" is unique.
Remember, when asked about specific details in the passage, spot key words in the question and scan the passage to find them (or their synonyms).

(Specific Details)

28. A. In line 64 the author mentions some "observations of which I shall speak later." These observations deal with whether wolves try to devour other wolves. Thus, the author intends to discuss the likelihood of cannibalism among wolves.
In answering questions about what may be discussed in subsequent sections of the text, pay particular attention to words that are similar in meaning to subsequent: *following, succeeding, successive, later*.

(Inference)

29. E. Digesting "out of doors" refers to the larva's external conversion of food into absorbable form.
Look at the sentence beginning in line 34. Break down the process step by step. The larva injects a secretion into the victim. The secretion dissolves the victim's insides. That is the start of the digestive process. It takes place inside the victim's body; in other words, *outside* the larva's body—"out of doors." Only then does the larva begin to suck up the dissolved juices of his prey.
Remember, when asked to give the meaning of an unfamiliar word, look for nearby context clues.

(Word from Context)

30. D. Choice D is incorrect. You can arrive at it by the process of elimination.
Statement I is true. The inside of the victim "becomes opaque" (line 44); it increases in opacity. Therefore, you can eliminate Choices B, C, and E.
Statement II is also true. As it is drained, the victim's body shrivels or "shrinks to a limp bundle of skin." Therefore, you can eliminate Choice A.
Only Choice D is left. It is the correct answer.
Statement III has to be untrue. The victim's head must stay on; otherwise, the dissolving interior would leak out.

(Specific Details)

31. B. The subject remained calm and in full command in spite of the panic. In other words, he was *imperturbable*, not capable of being agitated or perturbed.
Note how the phrase *in spite of* signals the contrast between the subject's calm and the surrounding hysteria. Similarly, note how other signal words link one part of the sentence to another. The presence of *and* linking two items in a series indicates that the missing word may be a synonym or near-synonym for the linked phrase "in full command."

(Contrast Pattern)

32. D. To puzzle over something is to exercise your mind going over and over it. The physics major is absorbed in trying to figure out the *unexpected* failure of her experiment. Thus, although she is normally *gregarious* (sociable), because of her involvement she seems *withdrawn* (unresponsive socially).
Note how the use of "more . . . than usual" indicates a contrast between her normally sociable and presently unsociable states. In addition, note how the opening phrase set off by the comma serves to clarify in what way she is withdrawn.

(Definition)

33. D. To resort to something is to turn to it, often as a last resort. Because the voters thought he was an *honest* man, they thought the candidate would tell the truth. They did not think he would resort to *subterfuge* or evasion.
Note how the contrast is implicit in the juxtaposition of the two clauses.

(Contrast Pattern)

34. A. Wilma Mankiller has both *shattered* a myth of male supremacy and gained the *respect* of her fellow leaders.

Note how the use of the "not only . . . but also . . ." structure links the two sentence elements and indicates that both support the same thought. This is an example of parallel structure.

(Support Signal)

35. E.   Despite his hard work trying to solve the problem, the solution was not the *result* or *outcome* of his labor. Instead, it was *fortuitous* or accidental.
Remember to watch for signal words that link one part of the sentence to another. The use of the "was . . . and not . . ." structure sets up a contrast. The missing words must be antonyms or near-antonyms.

(Contrast Pattern)

36. C.   A *quarry* is a place from which one extracts or digs *marble*. A *mine* is a place from which one extracts or digs *coal*.

(Defining Characteristic)

37. A.   A *chairman* uses a *gavel* to conduct meetings. A *conductor* uses a *baton* to conduct musical performances.
Remember, if more than one answer appears to fit the relationship in your sentence, look for a narrower approach. "A chairman uses a gavel" is too broad a framework; it could fit Choices B, C, D, and E, as well as Choice A.

(Worker and Tool)

38. D.   A *constitution* is introduced by a *preamble*. A *book* is introduced by a *preface*.

(Part to Whole)

39. B.   *Ecstasy* is an extreme form of *joy*; a *hurricane* is an extreme form of a wind or *breeze*.

(Degree of Intensity)

40. B.   A *fissure* (cleft) is a geographical feature measured in terms of its *depth*; a *peak* is a geographical feature measured in terms of its *height*.

(Defining Characteristic)

41. D.   Something *blatant* (obtrusive; brazenly obvious) is characterized by *obtrusiveness* (conspicuousness). Something *lavish* (prodigal; excessive) is characterized by *extravagance*.

(Synonym Variant)

42. E.   *Emaciated* (lean, haggard) and *gaunt* are synonyms. *Obese* or fat and *corpulent* are also synonyms.

(Synonyms)

43. C.   A *blind* person suffers from a loss of *sight*. Similarly, an *amnesiac* suffers from a loss of *memory*.

(Antonym Variant)

44. C.   Neither a *strident* (unpleasantly grating) *voice* nor an *acrid* (bitterly sharp) *taste* appeals to the senses.

(Defining Characteristic)

45. E.   A *gambit* is a move in *chess* by which the player attempts to gain an advantage. A *finesse* is a move in *bridge* by which the player attempts to gain an advantage.
Remember, if more than one answer appears to fit the relationship in your sentence, look for a narrower approach. "A gambit is a move in chess" is too broad a framework; it could fit both Choices B and E.

(Defining Characteristic)

Section 2   Math

1. D.   Time does not permit actually doing the long division. Also, bear in mind this is not an arithmetic test. Observe that the dividend ends with a 6 and the divisor ends with a 4. Only one choice ends in a 4.

2. C. $(a + 3)(a - 3) = a^2 - 9$
Substitute value of a:
$(-6)(-6) - 9 = +36 - 9 = 27$
The time-consuming method is to substitute the values given and multiply: $(-6 + 3)(-6 - 3)$, which equals $(-3)(-9)$ or $+27$. In choice (B) algebraic addition is done incorrectly and multiplication is not done. In (A) the signed number properties, $(+)(+) = +$, $(-)(-) = +$, and $(-)(+) = -$, are not observed. Choices (D) and (E) fail to add algebraically.

3. E. $$y = \frac{1}{6}$$
$$6y = 1$$
$$18y = 3$$
Since $x = 3$ (given)
then $x = 18y$ (things equal to the same thing are equal to each other)

4. A. $3x - 6 = 1$
Then $x - 2 = \frac{1}{3}$ (division by 3)

5. E. $\frac{AD}{AC} = \frac{3 \text{ of the equal units}}{2 \text{ of the equal units}} = 1\frac{1}{2}$ or 150%.

6. B. Substance B makes up $\frac{3}{24}$ or $\frac{1}{8}$ of the total

mixture. $\frac{1}{8}$ of 72 oz. equals 9 oz.

7. D. The total distance covered during the cruise was 4,000 nautical miles. To change to a percent, first change to a fraction with denominator of 100. The part covered from New York to Curaçao was

$\frac{1770}{4000} = \frac{44.25}{100} = 44.25\%$

8. A. Let x = number of nautical miles in 1 kilometer. Set up a proportion:

$\dfrac{\text{nautical mile}}{\text{kilometer}} = \dfrac{100}{160} = \dfrac{x}{1} = \dfrac{5}{8} = 0.625$

9. E. Since the area of each circle = 9π, the radius of each circle = 3 and the diameter of each circle = 6. Each side of the square = 2 diameters or 12. The area of the square = 144. The shaded area constitutes the area of the square minus the area of the 4 circles (4 times 9π).

10. C.

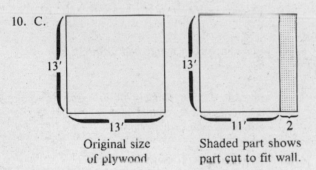

Original size
of plywood

Shaded part shows
part cut to fit wall.

Area of wall = (13')(11') or 143 sq. ft.

11. A. Since the area of the square = x^2, each side = x. ED, the base of triangle AED, = $x - y$ since $EC = x$ and $DC = y$. Area of triangle AED = $\frac{1}{2}(AE)(ED)$ or $\frac{1}{2}(x)(x - y)$ or $\dfrac{x^2 - xy}{2}$

12. A. Odd numbers are of the form $2x + 1$, where x is an integer. Thus, if $n = 2x + 1$ and $p = 2k + 1$, then $n + p = 2x + 1 + 2k + 1 = 2x + 2k + 2$, which is even. Using $n = 3$ and $p = 5$, each of the other choices gives an odd number. In general, if a problem involves odd or even numbers, try using the fact that odd

numbers are of the form $2x + 1$ and even numbers of the form $2y$, where x and y are integers.

13. D. The time-consuming method would calculate the number sold at \$3 $\left(\frac{1}{4} \text{ of } 30,000\right)$, add the number sold at \$2.50 $\left(\frac{1}{3} \text{ of } 30,000\right)$, and subtract the sum from 30,000. The suggested method first alerts you to the fact that you may disregard the prices in your computation, for the problem could have referred to color of tickets. Of the tickets in the upper price ranges, $\frac{1}{4} + \frac{1}{3}$ or $\frac{7}{12}$ were sold, so that the rest, or $\frac{5}{12}$ of 30,000 or 12,500, were sold at \$1.25.

14. C. Since the average weight of the 3 boys is 53 lb., the total weight of the 3 is 159 lb. Since we are looking for the maximum weight for one boy, we should assume the minimum weight for the other two. Choices (A) and (B) fail to do so. Assume that two boys each weigh 51 lb. for a total of 102 lbs., leaving 57 lb. for the third boy. Choice (D) leaves 100 lb. to be divided between the other two; this is impossible since each must have a minimum weight of 51 lb. Choice (E) is incorrect for the same line of reasoning.

15. (A) Recall the basic principles of inequalities. Choice (A) is correct since, if two inequalities are of the same type (both greater or both less), adding the respective sides gives the same type of inequality. Choice (B) is incorrect since inequalities are reversed if you multiply or divide by a negative number. Choices (C), (D), and (E) are not consistent with the given information.

16. B. Do not compute the rates. Mark traveled 10 miles in 6 hr. Substitute in the formula:

Rate (in miles per hour) = $\dfrac{\text{Distance (in miles)}}{\text{Time (in hours)}}$

Choice (C) is incorrect. The rate going may not be averaged with the rate returning, since the time spent returning was twice as much as the time spent at the faster rate going downstream. Choice (E) gives the sum of the rates.

17. C. Solve for A:

$\dfrac{xy}{z} - \dfrac{1}{A} = 0$

$\dfrac{xy}{z} = \dfrac{1}{A}$ (by addition)

$\dfrac{z}{xy} = A$ (reciprocals of equals are equal)

18. A.   Observe that an isosceles
         triangle is formed.

19. C.   The total payroll = $1,060,000, and the wages
         paid to managers = $110,000.
         $$\frac{110,000}{1,060,000} = \frac{11}{106} = 0.10 \text{ (rounding to the}$$
         nearest hundredth) or 10%.

20. B.   The average wage is $1,060,000 divided by
         530, or $2,000.

21. E.   The average salary of a manager is $\dfrac{\$110,000}{5}$ or
         $22,000. The average salary of an assembly
         worker is $600,000 divided by 500, or $1,200.
         So the ratio is 220:12 or 55:3.

22. D.   All five managers together earn $110,000.
         Since each one of four makes x dollars, the
         remaining manager is paid $(110,000 − 4x)$.

23. C.   Since the triangle is isosceles,
         altitude AH will bisect BC.
         Therefore, $BH = 8$. Right
         triangle ABH is a 3-4-5
         triangle with hypotenuse
         $AB = 10 = 2(5)$ and leg
         $BH = 8 = 2(4)$; thus leg
         $AH = 2(3) = 6$. The area of
         $$\triangle ABC = \frac{1}{2}(16)(6) = 48$$
         units. Do not assume that
         there is a right angle at
         A and that the area can
         be obtained by using $\dfrac{1}{2}$
         the product of 10×10,
         which yields incorrect choice (D).

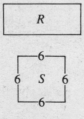

24. D   Since the perimeter of the
         square is 24, each side is
         6 and its area is 36. Since
         the area of R is also 36
         and its altitude is 4, its
         base is 9; note that this is
         incorrect choice (A). The
         perimeter of R is $(2)(4) +$
         $(2)(9)$ or 26 feet. Choice
         (E) gives the area of R. Choice (B) fails to
         consider R a rectangle. Choice (C) assumes
         that the base of R equals the side of the
         square.

25. D.   Any one of the 20 members on the squad may
         be elected captain. Since the elected captain
         may not also be cocaptain, that leaves any one
         of the remaining 19 squad members as a
         possible cocaptain. Therefore there are
         (20)(19), or 380, different outcomes of this
         election. Choice (A) fails to account for the
         fact that one election can occur in 20 different
         ways and is followed by a second election that
         can occur in 20 − 1 or 19 different ways.

Section 3   Test of Standard Written English

1. B.   Error in diction. Change *had ought* to *ought*.

2. D.   Misuse of adjective for adverb. Change *bad* to
         badly.

3. B.   Error in tense. Change *has sang* to *has sung*.

4. B.   Error in diction. Change *affect* to *effect*.

5. E.   Sentence is correct.

6. B.   Error in verb. Change *had drank* to *had
         drunk*.

7. A.   Error in diction. Since *without hardly* is a
         double negative, change *without hardly* to
         either *without* or *with hardly*.

8. D.   Error in case. Change *him* to *he*.

9. C.   Incorrect use of the superlative. Change *most*
         to *more*.

10. B.   Lack of parallel structure. Change *being
         intelligent* to *intelligence*.

11. E.   Sentence is correct.

12. A.   Error in diction. Change *or* to *nor*.

13. A.   Error in diction. Change *might of* to *might
         have*.

14. C.   Lack of parallel structure. Change *to finish* to
         finishing.

15. E.   Sentence is correct.

16. A.   Error in diction. Change *principal* to *principle*.

17. B.   Error in agreement. Change *were* to *was*.

18. C. Error in agreement. Change *them* to *him* or *her*.

19. C. Error in agreement. Change *are* to *is*.

20. D. Lack of parallel structure. Change *to guarantee* to *guaranteeing*.

21. E. Sentence is correct.

22. E. Sentence is correct.

23. C. Error in diction. Change *due to* to *as a result of*.

24. D. Error in tense. Change *is questioned by* to *was questioned by*.

25. C. Misuse of relative pronoun. Change *which* (that refers to things) to *who* (that refers to people).

26. B. This corrects the misuse of the subjunctive.

27. D. This corrects the error in the case of the pronoun. Choice E corrects the error in case but introduces an error in tense.

28. A. The clause is correct.

29. A. Sentence is correct.

30. C. This corrects the dangling participle.

31. A. Sentence is correct.

32. B. This corrects the unnecessary switch in the pronouns, *anyone–you*.

33. E. This corrects the error in parallel structure.

34. A. Sentence is correct.

35. D. The run-on sentence is corrected by the use of a semicolon.

36. D. This corrects the double negative *hadn't hardly* and the misuse of *those* with *kind*.

37. B. This corrects the dangling participle and the misuse of *stole* for *stolen*.

38. D. This corrects the error in diction and in the use of adjective and adverbial clauses.

39. B. In Choice B, the run-on sentence is corrected by the use of a semicolon, and the omission of the past participle *been* is also corrected.

40. C. Choice C expresses the author's meaning directly and concisely. All other choices are either indirect or ungrammatical.

41. B. Error in using an adjective in place of an adverb. Change *increasing* to *increasingly*.

42. A. Misuse of relative pronoun. Change *who* (that refers to people) to *which* (that refers to things).

43. B. Error in case. Change *he* to *him*.

44. B. Incorrect introduction to noun clause. Change *where* to *in which* to modify *explosion*.

45. C. Lack of parallel structure. Change *called* to *were calling*.

46. C. Incorrect coordinating conjunction. Change *and* to *but*.

47. C. Error in agreement. Change *their* to *its*.

48. B. Error in agreement. Change *are finding* to *is finding*.

49. B. Unnecessary switch in pronouns. Change *one* to *you*.

50. C. Error in tense. Change *have not had* to *will not have*.

Section 4   Verbal

1. A. *Proper* (appropriate or fitting) is the opposite of *unsuitable*.
Context Clue: "Eat a proper breakfast."

2. B. *Intentional* means deliberate, done on purpose. Its opposite is *accidental*.
Context Clue: Think of "an intentional walk" in baseball.

3. B. To *pamper* is to treat indulgently or kindly; to coddle. Its opposite is to *treat harshly*.
Context Clue: Think of "pampering the baby of the family."

4. B. *Naive* means unsophisticated, artless. Its opposite is sophisticated, artful, worldly, or *urbane*.
Context Clue: Think of "a naively innocent remark."

5. C. To *atrophy* is to waste away. Its opposite is to *flourish* or thrive.
Context Clue: "Unused muscles *atrophy*."

6. B.   Something *astute* is keenly perceptive or ingenious. Its opposite is foolish or *absurd*.
Context Clue: Think of "an *astute* investor," "an *astute* advertising campaign."

7. A.   *Application* means honest effort, hard work. Its opposite is *lack of industry* (lack of hard work).
Remember, consider secondary meanings of the capitalized words as well as their primary meanings. This sense of application has to do with applying oneself (making an effort), not with applying for a job.
Context Clue: Think of "application to your studies."

8. C.   *Altruism* means unselfish concern for others. It is the opposite of *selfishness* (concern only for one's own interests or person).
Context Clue: Think of "a generous act of altruism."
Word Parts Clue: *Altr* or *alter* means other. Altruism is concern for others.

9. E.   *Complaisance* means the quality of being obliging in manner, aiming to please. Its opposite is *recalcitrance* (stubbornness, the quality of being hard to deal with or manage).
Context Clue: Think of "the complaisance of a smiling host."

10. B.   To *tender* something is to offer it or present it for acceptance. Its opposite is to *retract* or withdraw.
Remember, look at the answer choices to determine the main word's part of speech. From looking at the first answer choice you can tell you are dealing with the unfamiliar verb tender, not the extremely familiar adjective tender.
Context Clue: Think of having "to tender your resignation."

11. D.   The rebels tried to overcome the greatness or *superiority* of strength of the government forces.
Remember, before you look at the choices, read the sentence and think of a word that makes sense.
Likely Words: abundance, superiority.

(Contrast Pattern)

12. C.   A comprehensive or thorough study would not be missing *relevant* or important material.
Remember to watch for signal words that link one part of the sentence to another. The use of "but" in the second clause sets up a contrast.

(Contrast Signal)

13. C.   Because Dr. Drew's method proved *effective*, it became a *model* for other systems.
Remember to watch for signal words that link one part of the sentence to another. The "so . . . that" structure signals cause and effect.

(Cause and Effect Signal)

14. B.   The fact that the languages of the Mediterranean area were markedly (strikingly) alike eased or *facilitated* the movement of people and ideas from country to country.
Note how the specific examples in the second part of the sentence clarify the idea stated in the first part.

(Examples)

15. B.   A *lugubrious* (exaggeratedly gloomy) appearance may create laughter because it is so inappropriate in the *hilarity* (noisy gaiety) of the circus.
The clown's success stems from a contrast. The missing words must be antonyms or near-antonyms. You can immediately eliminate Choices C, D, and E as non-antonym pairs. In addition, you can eliminate Choice A; *sobriety* or seriousness is an inappropriate term for describing circus life.

(Contrast Pattern)

16. B.   A *play* is made up of *acts*. A *novel* is made up of *chapters*.

(Part to Whole)

17. D.   *Geology* is an example of a *science*. A *fir* tree is an example of a *tree*.

(Class and Member)

18. E.   A *plane* is a tool used to *smooth* objects; a *wrench* is a tool used to *twist* objects.
Remember to watch out for errors stemming from grammatical or logical reversals. Choice D is incorrect. An axe is sharpened. It does not sharpen; it hews or chops.

(Tool and Action)

19. B.   *Funds* that are *embezzled* are appropriated fraudulently. Similarly, *writings* that are *plagiarized* are appropriated fraudulently.

(Defining Characteristic)

20. B.   *Uncouth* is a synonym for *graceless*. Therefore, gracelessness is the quality of being uncouth. Similarly, *avaricious* is a synonym for *greedy*. Therefore, greed is the quality of being *avaricious*.

(Synonym Variant)

21. C.   A *tourniquet* stops *bleeding*, or the flow of blood. A *red light* stops *traffic*, or the flow of vehicles.

(Function)

22. B.   An *elevator* moves through a *shaft*. *Water* moves through a *conduit* (a pipe or channel for fluids).
Beware Eye-Catchers: Choice C is incorrect. Just because elevators and escalators have similar functions, don't expect that the relationship between elevator and shaft is similar to the relationship between escalator and step.

(Location)

23. A.   *Parsimony* (stinginess) is extreme thrift or *frugality*. *Agony* is extreme suffering or *pain*.

(Degree of Intensity)

24. A.   Someone emaciated (extremely thin) is the opposite of someone obese (extremely fat). Someone *emaciated* does not exhibit *obesity*. Similarly, someone penurious (extremely poor) is the opposite of someone wealthy. Someone *penurious* lacks *wealth*.

(Antonym Variant)

25. A.   Laconic (brief, curt in speech) is similar in meaning to taciturn (disinclined to talk). Thus, someone *laconic* reflects *taciturnity*. Similarly, unrehearsed is similar in meaning to improvised (composed and performed without preparation). Something *unrehearsed* therefore reflects *improvisation*.

(Synonym Variant)

26. A.   Phrases such as "a distinctive U.S. art form" and "a vernacular, homegrown U.S. school" emphasize that in this section the author is discussing an indigenous or native American art form.
Choices B, C, D, and E are incorrect. They are far too specific to cover the passage as a whole.
Remember, when asked to choose a title, watch out for choices that are too specific or too broad.

(Main Idea/Title)

27. B.   In speaking of "the special stamp" of the American school, the author indicates a measured admiration for these painters.
Remember, when asked to determine the author's attitude or tone, look for words that convey value judgments.

(Attitude/Tone)

28. D.   The last sentence of the passage indicates that the author is immediately about to discuss "pioneer painters who came to the New World," or the founding fathers of American art, artists who migrated to America and began an artistic tradition here.
Choice A is incorrect. Although the author indicates he intends to discuss primitivism eventually, the last line indicates that before he can take up this topic he must discuss the immigrant European artists and their art.
Choices B, C, and E are incorrect. Nothing in the passage indicates the author is about to discuss any of them.

(Specific Details)

29. B.   The author maintains that most American artists "developed on their own." Whistler, Sargent, and Mary Cassatt are exceptions to this general rule; they were affected by their European visit.
Remember, when asked about specific details in the passage, spot key words in the question and scan the passage to find them (or their synonyms). In this case, look for the three painters' names.

(Specific Details)

30. B.   The opening sentences of the three paragraphs support Choice B. The author is affirming or asserting that there is a distinctive or unique American style.
Choice A is incorrect. The author mentions the English and French schools only in passing.
Choice C is incorrect. The author appears to prefer the "native and singular flavor" of American art.
Choice D is incorrect. It is unsupported by the passage.
Choice E is incorrect. The first sentence indicates that the author will discuss primitivism in a later passage, not in the present one.
Remember, when asked to find the main idea, be sure to check the opening and summary sentences of each paragraph.

(Main Idea)

31. D.   The entire passage describes the battle in detail.
Choice A is incorrect. The garrison was not overthrown by the attackers; instead, the attackers were repelled.
Choice B is incorrect. The defenders used no strategy; they just fired at will.
Choice C is incorrect. The passage depicts a specific attack, not general hardships.

Choice E is incorrect. The attackers were both courageous and cowardly.

(Main Idea)

32. E.   The opening sentence states "the last possible line of defense was established instinctively and in a moment." In other words, its formation was spontaneous.
Choice A is incorrect. The defense line was effectual; it drove off the attackers.
Choice B is incorrect. The defense line was not abandoned; the defenders stayed in place.
Choice C is incorrect. The defense line was not orderly; the defenders were scattered here and there.
Choice D is incorrect. Not the defenders, but the attackers were exultant, excited by the hope of victory.
Remember, when asked about specific details in the passage, spot key words in the question and scan the passage to find them (or their synonyms).

(Specific Details)

33. C.   The statement in the third sentence that "the soldiers were scattered almost as sparsely as sentinels" implies that sentinels are usually stationed widely apart.

(Inference)

34. A.   The reference to knolls and gullies in the next to last sentence describes the terrain (a tract of land considered with reference to its physical attributes). Choices B, C, D, and E are incorrect. Nothing in the passage supports them.

(Specific Details)

35. C.   The last sentence describing the attackers who cannot be induced to leave cover supports Choice C. The attackers refused to make another assault.
Choices A and B are incorrect. No mention is made of surrender or poor training.
Choices D and E are incorrect. The defenders, not the attackers, were faced with superior numbers ("the human billow") and were scattered along the works (the breastworks, or improvised fortification).

(Specific Details)

36. C.   In the opening paragraph the writer speaks of the Gothic world in terms of play and extravagance, of the fantastic and the luxurious. In other words, he speaks of it in terms of its *elaborateness of fancy* or fantasy.
Choices A and B are incorrect. They are unsupported by the passage.

Choices D and E are incorrect. They are attributes of the Medieval imagination, not of the Gothic.

37. D.   The tapestries combine worldly elements (mythological beasts that symbolize lust and ferocity, wild creatures that symbolize fertility) with spiritual ones (the lady who embodies chastity) to express "the power of love."
Choice A is incorrect. It is unsupported by the passage.
Choice B is incorrect. Though the Gothic imagination has a "sharp sense of reality," it is more inclined to be playful than to be practical.
Choice C is incorrect. Nothing in the passage suggests that wall hangings are wasteful.
Choice E is incorrect. It is unsupported by the passage.

(Specific Details)

38. D.   In the closing paragraph the author states that readers of detective fiction indulge in a fantasy of escape or release that is prompted by a "feeling of guilt, the cause of which is unknown to the dreamer." Thus, they are *seeking release from a vague sense of guilt.*
Choice A is incorrect. Nothing in the passage supports it.
Choice B is incorrect. The author denies that readers of detective fiction are bent on satisfying "violent or murderous wishes."
Choice C is incorrect. Although the author depicts readers of detective fiction as dreamers, he depicts them as dreamers impelled by a sense of guilt, not by a sense of boredom.
Choice E is incorrect. Nothing in the passage supports it.

(Specific Details)

39. B.   Kafka's *The Trial* is cited as an "instructive example of the difference between a work of art and the detective story." The author then goes on to analyze *The Trial* to point out its qualities as a work of art that distinguish it from mere detective fiction.
Choice A is incorrect. *The Trial* is a work of art, not a detective story.
Choice C is incorrect. The author is not discussing readers of detective fiction in the third paragraph.
Choice D is incorrect. The outside investigator, the genius who removes guilt by giving knowledge of guilt, is a figure out of the detective story; he has no place in the work of art. Although K investigates his situation, he is trapped inside it; he is no genius from outside.
Choice E is incorrect. There is nothing in the passage to support it.

40. E. The author explicitly disassociates himself from the readers of thrillers (which he rarely enjoys). However, he associates himself with the readers of detective fiction ("me and my neighbors"), those who are caught up in the mystery, but, unlike the outside investigator, unable to solve it. This suggests he is a fan of detective fiction, one who views it with *genuine appreciation*.

Choices A, B, C, and D are incorrect. Nothing in the passage suggests them.

(Inference)

Section 5   Math

1. C. $\dfrac{9x-5}{3} = \dfrac{3y}{3}$ (division by 3)

$$\dfrac{9x-5}{3} = y$$

2. D. Ratio is a comparison of two quantities by division in correct order. Unlike correct choice (D), (B) gives the ratio of boys to girls. Choice (C) gives the part of the number of boys in the entire class, and (E) gives the part of the number of girls in the entire class. This question does not ask for that information. Recall Testing Tactic: KNOW WHAT THE QUESTION IS ASKING.

3. D. $\sqrt{\dfrac{1}{16} + \dfrac{1}{9}} = \sqrt{\dfrac{25}{144}}$ or $\dfrac{5}{12}$

The trap in this question is to think that

$\sqrt{\dfrac{1}{16} + \dfrac{1}{9}} = \dfrac{1}{4} + \dfrac{1}{3}$ or $\dfrac{7}{12}$,

leading to incorrect choice (E). Here $\dfrac{1}{16}$ and $\dfrac{1}{9}$ are *terms*, and terms may not be removed from under a radical sign by taking their square roots; only factors of the expression under the radical sign may be removed in this way.

4 C. The fraction $\dfrac{a+b}{b}$ may be written as $\dfrac{a}{b} + \dfrac{b}{b}$.

Since $\dfrac{b}{b} = 1$, the correct choice is (C).

5. C. Conversion problems involve proportions. One kilometer $= \dfrac{5}{8}$ mile. Let $x =$ number of kilometers in 12 miles. Then

$\dfrac{\text{kilometers}}{\text{miles}} = \dfrac{1}{\frac{5}{8}} = \dfrac{x}{12}$

$$\dfrac{5}{8}x = 12$$

$$\left(\dfrac{8}{5}\right)\dfrac{5}{8}x = 12\left(\dfrac{8}{5}\right)$$

$$x = \dfrac{96}{5} = 19\dfrac{1}{5} \text{ or}$$

$$19.2 \text{ km}$$

Note that incorrect choices (A) and (B) fail to keep the correct order of kilometers:miles. Those who choose (D) evidently perform the operations and then, when the numeral 5 appears as a remainder of the division of 96 by 5, carelessly choose 19.5 as their answer.

6. C. Since the tank was completely filled in $1\dfrac{3}{4}$ min., it would be proportionately less full in 1 min.

$\dfrac{\text{time (in minutes)}}{\text{part filled}} = \dfrac{1\frac{3}{4}}{1} = \dfrac{1}{x}$

$$\dfrac{7}{4}x = 1$$

$$x = \dfrac{4}{7}$$

Choice (B) gives the part not filled in 1 min. Choice (D) gives the time not used to completely fill the tank.

7. E. The time-consuming method is to find the cost of one item, $\left(\dfrac{c}{2}\right)$¢, and divide the amount of money available (x¢) by the cost of one item. The quick method sets up a proportion:

$\dfrac{\text{number of items purchased}}{\text{cost (in cents)}} = \dfrac{2}{c} = \dfrac{?}{x}$

$$(c)(?) = 2x \text{ and } ? = \dfrac{2x}{c}$$

8. D. Both a and b, or either a or b, may be equal to zero.

9. C. $(x+y)^2 = x^2 + 2xy + y^2$
Substitute $xy = 5$ and $x^2 + y^2 = 7$.
$2xy = 10$
$x^2 + 2xy + y^2 = 10 + 7 = 17$

10. A. $\sqrt{0.3} = \sqrt{0.30} = 0.5+; 0.5+ > 0.49.$

11. B. $1\% = 0.01$ and $\dfrac{1}{2}\% = 0.005; 0.05 > 0.005.$

12. A.   Substitute values given:

$$x(y + z) = 2(3 + 7) \text{ or } 20$$
$$xz + y = (2)(7) + 3 \text{ or } 17$$

13. C.   Notice that the perimeter of the shaded region is the same as the perimeter of $AGFC$, except that $BC + CD$ is replaced by $BE + ED$. But since $BEDC$ is a rectangle, $BC = ED$ and $CD = BE$, so the replacement leaves the total perimeter unchanged.

14. B.   Since x is positive, $2x^2 = (2)(x)(x)$ and $(2x)^2 = 4x^2$ or $(4)(x)(x)$.

15. B.   The team scored a total of 66 points in this game. The average for all players is therefore $66 \div 5$, or $13\frac{1}{5}$ points. Player D scored 14 points, which is better than the average for the entire team.

16. C.   Both triangles have a common base (CD). Both triangles have equal altitudes since perpendiculars between parallel lines are equal.

17. A. $2x = 3y$, since $AB = AC$
$x = \dfrac{3}{2y}$ or $x = 1\frac{1}{2}$ times y

18. B.   Things equal to the same thing are equal to each other. Therefore $5x = 3y$ and $x = \dfrac{3}{5}y$.

19. D.   Let x = Mark's age now.
Let y = Philip's age now.
Let z = Michael's age now.
From the first sentence we may write the equation $x + 19 = 3y$, and from the second sentence the equation $x = z + 3$. With three unknowns we must have three different equations in order to solve the unknowns.

20. D.   It is possible for a and b each to have any value between 1 and 5. Therefore a may be greater than b, smaller than b, or even equal to b, so there are many possibilities for values of $b - a$ and $a - b$.

21. C. $3\frac{1}{2}\% = 3.5\% = \dfrac{3.5}{100}$ or $\dfrac{35}{1000}$

22. C. $\dfrac{1}{A} = \dfrac{1}{x} + \dfrac{1}{y}$
$\dfrac{1}{A} = \dfrac{x + y}{xy}$
$A = \dfrac{xy}{x + y}$ (reciprocals of equals are equal)

23. B.   Since x has a value less than -1, arbitrarily let $x = -5$.
$\dfrac{1}{-5} = 1 \div -5$ or -0.2
$-0.2 > -5.0$

24. C. $\dfrac{a^2 - b^2}{(a - b)^2} = \dfrac{(a + b)(a - b)}{(a - b)(a - b)} = \dfrac{a + b}{a - b}$

25. A. $\sqrt{1440}$ is a two-digit number ($37+$). Do not work the computation out, or even bother to estimate. Note that $120^2 = 14400$, so $120 > \sqrt{1440}$.

26. B.   1 yard = 3 feet
0.5 or $\frac{1}{2}$ yd. = 1 ft. 6 in.
1.5 or $1\frac{1}{2}$ yd. = 4 ft. 6 in.

27. C. $x = y$
Therefore $x^2 = y^2$

28. A.   I is true, e.g., $\sqrt[3]{-8} = -2$.
II is false; $\sqrt{\dfrac{1}{4}}$ is not smaller than $\dfrac{1}{4}$: $\sqrt{\dfrac{1}{4}} = \dfrac{1}{2}$; $\dfrac{1}{2}$ is larger than $\dfrac{1}{4}$.
III is false; $(A - B)(A + B) = A^2 - B^2$.

29. D.   This problem tests your ability to apply the formula used to find areas of circles. Since the area of a circle is πr^2, any change in r will affect the area by that quantity squared. Since we are concerned with area, we are evidently concerned with the area of the empty pool or its floor. Since the radius is doubled, the area will be 4 times as much. Some of the incorrect choices reflect confusion regarding the effect on the circumference by changes in radius. Since the formula for circumference is $C = \pi d$ or $2\pi r$, any change in radius or diameter will affect the circumference in the same numerical way.

30. D.   Since $\angle DBE$ is a right angle, $\angle ABE$ is the complement of $\angle DBA$ and has a measure of $90° - 70°$ or $20°$. Since ABC is a straight line, $x = 180° - 20°$ or $160°$.

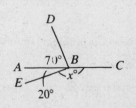

31. E. Sixty out of 80 applicants *did* appear.

$$\frac{60}{80} = \frac{3}{4} = 75\%$$

Choice (C) does not answer the question. It gives the percent of the total applicants that failed to appear. Choices (A) and (D) result from guessing by dividing or subtracting the numerals given. Choice (B) evidently tries multiplication and then rounds off zeros to change to percent.

32. D. Since the measure of $\angle A = 70$, $m\angle ABC + m\angle ACB = 110$, or the measure of each angle $= 55$, and each bisected angle (DBC and DCB) has a measure of $\frac{55}{2}$ degrees.

In triangle DBC,
$m\angle BDC + m\angle DCB + m\angle DBC = 180$ degrees.
Since $m\angle DBC + m\angle DCB = 55$,
$x = 180 - 55$ or 125.

33. D. The paper wasted is the difference between the area of the square and the area of the circle. Note that choice (B) gives the area of the circle only, and that (C) gives the difference of the circle from the square. Since we are cutting the largest possible circle, the diameter must equal the side of the square. The area of the square is d^2, the radius of the circle is $\frac{d}{2}$, and the area

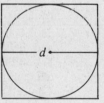

of the circle is $\pi \left(\frac{d}{2}\right)^2$ or $\frac{\pi d^2}{4}$. The correct solution is

$$d^2 - \left(\frac{d}{2}\right)^2 \pi$$

$$\frac{d^2}{1} - \frac{\pi d^2}{4}$$

$$\frac{4d^2}{4} - \frac{\pi d^2}{4}$$

$$\frac{4d^2 - \pi d^2}{4}$$

34. E. Substitute: $wy - xz - K = 0$
$\qquad\qquad wy - xz = K$ (adding K)

35. D. Let $A = $ cost of 1 lb. of apples.
$\qquad P = $ cost of 1 lb. of pears.
$\qquad R = $ cost of 1 lb. of oranges.

Then $7P = 10A + R$ (1)
$\qquad 7R = P + 2A$ (2)
$\qquad R = 7P - 10A$ (3) from (1)
$\qquad R = \dfrac{P + 2A}{7}$ (4) from (2)

$$\frac{7P - 10A}{1} = \frac{P + 2A}{7} \qquad (5) \quad R = R$$

$49P - 70A = P + 2A$ (6) (product of means equals product of extremes)

$\qquad 48P = 72A$ (7)
$\qquad 12P = 18A$ (8)

Section 6   Verbal

1. B. To *flourish* is to flower or to increase in prosperity. Its opposite is to *waste away* or *decay*.
Context Clue: Think of "a flourishing community."

2. A. To *tolerate* something is to endure or bear it. The opposite of *tolerate* is to *refuse to bear*.
Context Clue: "How can she tolerate such behavior?"

3. C. To *enhance* something is to advance or increase it. Its opposite is to *detract*.
Context Clue: Think of "enhancing your self-image."

4. B. *Spirited* means lively, full of spirit. Its opposite is *unanimated*, lacking life.
Context Clue: Think of "a spirited performance."

5. A. *Hefty* means big and burly. Its opposite is *frail* (slight; delicate).
Context Clue: Think of "a hefty truck driver."

6. C. *Purify* means to cleanse or make pure. Its opposite is *pollute*.
Context Clue: Think of "purifying the atmosphere."

7. B. *Sage* means perceptive and wise. Its opposite is *foolish*.
Context Clue: Think of "sage advice."

8. E. To *enact* is to make something into law. The opposite of enact is *repeal*. When you repeal a law, you revoke it or take it back.
Context Clue: "The Senate enacts legislation."

9. C.   To *dismantle* is to remove coverings or equipment. The opposite of dismantle is *equip*.
Context Clue: Think of "dismantling the sound system after a concert."

10. D.   *Clemency* is leniency or mercy. The opposite of *clemency* is a *lack of mercy*.
Context Clue: "The prisoner asked the judge for clemency."

11. B.   To *mitigate* is to lessen in intensity or make less severe; its opposite is to *worsen*.
Context Clue: Think of "mitigating the pain."

12. D.   *Surreptitious* means secret; done by stealth. Its opposite is *open* or *aboveboard*.
Context Clue: "He glanced surreptitiously at his classmate's paper."

13. E.   *Corpulence* is largeness or bulkiness of body; excessive fatness. Its opposite is *slenderness*.
Context Clue: Think of "fighting a tendency to corpulence."

14. A.   *Meticulous* means painstaking; very careful. Its opposite is sloppy or *careless*.
Context Clue: "She did a meticulous job."

15. C.   A *proclivity* is a leaning toward or inclination to something. Its opposite is *lack of inclination*.
Context Clue: Think of "a proclivity for driving fast cars."

16. E.   Tiffany's works of art have survived in spite of their *fragility* (tendency to break).
Remember to watch for signal words that link one part of the sentence to another. The use of "despite" in the opening phrase sets up a contrast. *Despite* signals you that Tiffany's glass works were unlikely candidates to survive for several decades.

(Contrast Signal)

17. A.   Voles are similar to mice; however, they are also different from them, and may be *distinguished from* them.
Note how the use of "although" in the opening phrase sets up the basic contrast here.

(Contrast Signal)

18. E.   Feeling that a job was *pointless* might well lead you to perform it in a *perfunctory* (indifferent or mechanical) manner.
Remember, watch for signal words that link one part of the sentence to another. The use of "because" in the opening clause is a cause signal.

(Cause and Effect Signal)

19. B.   To acquire a taste for something, you must originally not have that taste or even *dislike* it; you acquire the taste by growing to like or *welcome* it.
Note how the second clause of the sentence serves to clarify what is meant by the term "acquired taste."

(Examples)

20. B.   The doctor's words are *disheartening* (discouraging); logically, the family should lose hope. Instead, they cling to the hope of a *remission* (lessening of the symptoms of a disease).
Note how the use of "although" sets up the contrast.

(Contrast Signal)

21. A.   The opening paragraph, with its talk of clearly marked outlines and contrasts "between suffering and joy," and the concluding sentence, with its mentions of "violent contrasts" and "the perpetual oscillation between despair and joy" emphasize the author's main idea: the Middle Ages were marked by extremes.
Choice B is incorrect. Though the author depicts aspects of the lives of the very rich and the very poor, he does not stress the notion that their styles complemented one another.
Choice C is incorrect. The author's concern is for the Middle Ages, not for the twentieth century.
Choices D and E are incorrect. They are unsupported by the text.
Remember, when asked to find the main idea, be sure to check the opening and summary sentences of each paragraph.

(Main Idea)

22. B.   The cloaking of minor activities (journeys, visits, etc.) with forms (line 9) "raised them to the dignity of a ritual"; in other words, the forms (fixed or formal ways of doing things) made the acts more dignified.
Choices A, C, D, and E are incorrect. They are not supported by the passage.
Remember, when asked about specific details in the passage, spot key words in the question and scan the passage to find them (or their synonyms).
Key Word: formalities.

(Specific Details)

23. E.   In cataloging the extremes of medieval life, the author in no way suggests the Middle Ages were *boring*.
Choice A is incorrect. The author suggests the

Middle Ages were harsh and bleak; he
portrays them as cold and miserable.
Choice B is incorrect. The author portrays the
Middle Ages as festive and joyful; he says
they were filled with vivid pleasures and
proud celebrations.
Choice C is incorrect. The author portrays the
Middle Ages as filled with ceremony and
ritual.
Choice D is incorrect. The author portrays the
Middle Ages as passionate and turbulent; he
mentions the "tone of excitement and of
passion" in everyday life.

(Specific Details)

24. A. The last sentence of the third paragraph states
that the lofty churches, the houses of worship,
towered above the town. The churches always
"remained dominant."
When asked about specific details, spot the
key words in the question and scan the
passage to find them (or their variants).
Key Words: above, towered.

(Specific Details)

25. A. The linking of "formulae" with "ceremonies"
(formal series of acts) and "benedictions"
(words of blessing) suggests that these
formulae are most likely *set forms of words
for rituals*.
Note how the use of the colon suggests that
all three words that follow are examples of
"formalities."

(Word from Context)

26. B. The opening lines indicate that the narrator is
reflecting on his feelings. Throughout the
passage he uses words like "miserable,"
"ashamed," and "discontented" to describe
his emotional state.
Choice A is incorrect. The narrator does not
analyze or dissect a change in attitude; he
describes a continuing attitude.
Choice C is incorrect. The passage gives an
example of emotional self-awareness, not of
political consciousness.
Choice D is incorrect. The narrator condemns
rather than defends the longings that brought
him discontentment.
Choice E is incorrect. The narrator criticizes
himself, not young people in general.

(Main Idea)

27. D. The references to the forge and the anvil
support Choice D. None of the other choices
are suggested by the passage.
Remember, when asked to make inferences,
base your answers on what the passage
implies, not what it states directly.

(Inference)

28. B. Note the adjectives used to describe Joe:
"faithful," "industrious," "kind." These are
virtues, and Joe is fundamentally virtuous.
Choice A is incorrect. Joe is plain and hard-
working, not eminent and distinguished.
Choice C is incorrect. The passage portrays
not Joe but the narrator as desiring to be
independent.
Choice D is incorrect. It is unsupported by the
passage.
Choice E is incorrect. The narrator thinks his
life is coarse; he thinks Joe is virtuous.

(Specific Details)

29. D. In the last two sentences of the fourth
paragraph the narrator manages to say
something good about his youthful self: "I am
glad to know I never breathed a murmur to
Joe." He gives himself credit for concealing
his despondency.
Choices A and B are incorrect. The narrator
gives Joe all the credit for his having worked
industriously and for his not having run away
to become a soldier.
Choices C and E are incorrect. They are
unsupported by the passage.

(Specific Details)

30. A. Choice A is supported by the last sentence of
the second paragraph in which the narrator
states he "would not have had Miss Havisham
and Estella see (his home) on any account."
Choices B and C are incorrect. Nothing in the
passage suggests either might be the case.
Choice D is incorrect. Though the narrator
may not show himself as hard-working,
nothing in the passage suggests laziness led to
his discontent.
Choice E is incorrect. Nothing in the passage
suggests that sinfulness has prompted his
discontent. In addition, although ingratitude
may play a part in his discontent, shame of his
background plays a part far greater.

(Inference)

31. B. For us to be distressed by his *lapses*, his usual
taste must be extremely good or even *flawless*
so that the lapses or deviations would be bad.

(Examples)

32. D. An argument is *unconvincing* if you don't
agree to all its *premises*.
Remember, watch for signal words that link
one part of the sentence to another. The use
of "Because" in the opening clause is a cause
signal.

(Cause and Effect Signal)

33. B.   Pain is a *sensation*. Losing the ability to feel pain would leave the body *vulnerable*, or defenseless, lacking its usual warnings against impending bodily harm.
Note how the second clause serves to clarify or explain what is meant by pain's being an "early warning system."

(Definition)

34. C.   If she *deprecated* her accomplishments (diminished them or saw nothing praiseworthy in them), she would show her unwillingness to boast about them or *flaunt* them.
Note the use of *properly* to describe her unwillingness to do something. This suggests that the second missing word would have negative associations.

(Definition)

35. C.   A stereotyped or oversimplified portrait of a slave would lead sensitive readers to *criticize* it for dismissing the issue of slavery so casually. Thus, they normally would be *detractors* of the novel. However, *Huckleberry Finn* is such a fine work that even its critics acknowledge its greatness.
Signal words are helpful here. *Despite* in the first clause implies a contrast, and *even* in the second clause implies that the subjects somewhat reluctantly agree that the novel is a masterpiece.

(Contrast Signal)

36. E.   A *signature* on a *portrait* establishes who painted it. A *byline* on an *article* establishes who wrote it.

(Function)

37. B.   Just as a *breeze* is a less intense wind than a *tornado* (violent windstorm), a *trickle* is a less intense outpouring of liquid than a *gusher*.

(Degree of Intensity)

38. B.   *Records* are kept in *archives*; *birds* are kept in an *aviary* (bird house).

(Location)

39. C.   *Envelop* and *surround* are synonyms; *loiter* and *linger* (hang back) are synonyms also.

(Synonyms)

40. B.   Someone *indifferent* is uncaring or unconcerned; he is lacking in *concern*. Someone *arrogant* is proud and immodest; he is lacking in *modesty*.

(Antonym Variant)

41. A.   A *dilletante* is not serious about his art; he merely *dabbles*. A *coquette* is not serious about her affairs of the heart; she merely *flirts*.

(Definition)

42. C.   *Barren* (unable to produce offspring; infertile) and *fecund* (fertile) are antonyms, as are *hackneyed* (trite) and *original*.

(Antonyms)

43. C.   *Slander* is by its nature *defamatory* (injurious to one's reputation); an *elegy* (poem or song of mourning) is by nature *sorrowful*.

(Defining Characteristic)

44. A.   A snake *sloughs* or casts off its dead *skin*; people and animals *shed* their unneeded *hair*.

(Function)

45. C.   *Hyperbolic* and *exaggerated* are synonyms. So are *capricious* (unpredictable; fanciful) and *whimsical*.

(Synonyms)

PART THREE

Tactics, Strategies, Practice

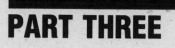

PART THREE

Verbal

Tactics, strategies, practice

5 The Antonym Question

- ■ **Testing Tactics**
- ■ **Long-Range Strategies**
- ■ **Practice Exercises**
- ■ **Answer Key**
- ■ **Answer Explanations**

Antonym questions are the most straightforward vocabulary questions on the test. You are given a word and must choose, from the five choices that follow it, the best antonym or opposite. The vocabulary in antonym questions includes words that you have probably seen in your reading, although you may never have used or even heard them in everyday conversation.

Here are the directions for antonym questions. Learn them now. They won't change. The test time you would spend reading the directions can be better spent answering questions.

> Each question below consists of a word in capital letters, followed by five lettered words or phrases. Choose the word or phrase that is most nearly opposite in meaning to the word in capital letters. Since some of the questions require you to distinguish fine shades of meaning, consider all the choices before deciding which is best.
>
> Example:
>
> GOOD: (A) sour   (B) bad   (C) red
> (D) hot   (E) ugly   Ⓐ ● Ⓒ Ⓓ Ⓔ

You won't see anything quite this easy on the SAT, but this question illustrates a point you should remember. The question asks for the best answer, not a possible answer. Now you may think of sour things as bad or ugly things as bad, but neither of these is as clear an antonym for *good* as *bad* is. And you don't get any partial credit for a close answer.

Testing Tactics

Think of a Context for the Capitalized Word.

Take a quick look at the word in capital letters. If you don't recollect its meaning right away, try to think of a phrase or sentence in which you have heard it used. The context may help you come up with the word's meaning. For example:

> MAGNIFY: (A) forgive   (B) comprehend
> (C) extract   (D) diminish   (E) electrify

The term "magnifying glass" should immediately come to mind. A magnifying glass enlarges things. The opposite of enlarging something is to make it smaller or *diminish* it. The answer is D.

Similarly, take the word *confiscate*.

> CONFISCATE: (A) correct   (B) distribute
> (C) hasten   (D) organize   (E) shatter

Think of the sentence "The police confiscated the gang's weapons." From the context you realize that to *confiscate* weapons is to seize or commandeer them. Once you feel sure of the capitalized word's meaning, you are on firmer ground when you look for its antonym. The opposite of seizing weapons is giving them out or distributing them. *Distribute*, Choice B is correct.

Before You Look at the Choices, Think of Antonyms for the Capitalized Word.

Suppose your word is *industrious* (hard-working). What opposites come to your mind? You might come up with *lazy, idle, slothful, inactive*—all words that mean lacking industry and energy.

Now look at the choices.

> INDUSTRIOUS: (A) stupid   (B) harsh
> (C) indolent   (D) complex   (E) inexpensive

Lazy, idle, and *slothful* are all synonyms for *indolent*. The correct answer is Choice C.

This tactic will help you even when you have to deal with unfamiliar words among your answer choices. Suppose you do not know the meaning of the word *indolent*. You know that one antonym for your key word *industrious* is *lazy*. Therefore, you know that you are looking for a word that means the same thing as *lazy*. At this point you can go through the answer choices eliminating answers that don't work. Does *stupid* mean the same thing as *lazy*? No, smart people can be lazy, too. Does *harsh* mean the same

thing as *lazy*? No, *harsh* means cruel or rough. Does *indolent* mean the same thing as *lazy*? You don't know; you should check the other choices and then come back. Does *complex* mean the same thing as *lazy*? No, *complex* means complicated or intricate. Does *inexpensive* mean the same thing as *lazy*? No. So what is left? *Indolent*. The correct answer is Choice C.

Now think of antonyms for the capitalized word in this example.

> DEBASE: (A) recall   (B) import   (C) found
> (D) participate in   (E) enhance

To *debase* something is to lower or lessen it in value. In thinking of possible antonyms for *debase*, you may have come up with words like *elevate, augment*, or *exalt*, words signifying raising something or increasing it in value. *Elevate, augment*, and *exalt* are all synonyms for *enhance*. The correct answer is Choice E.

Read All the Choices Before You Decide Which Is Best.

On the SAT you are working under time pressure. You may be tempted to mark down the first answer that feels right and ignore the other choices given. Don't do it. Consider each answer. Only in this way can you be sure to distinguish between two possible answers and come up with the best answer for the question.

Words have shades of meaning. In matching a word with its opposite, you must pay attention to these shades of meaning. Try this example from an actual SAT to see how it works.

> OBSTINATE: (A) intermittent   (B) yielding
> (C) uncertain   (D) careless   (E) despairing

Obstinate means stubborn or pig-headed. Commonly, when you think of someone obstinate, you think of someone who has made up his mind, the sort of person who is sure he's right. An obstinate person is *certain* his opinion is correct. However, this does not mean that the *best* antonym for obstinate is *uncertain*.

The key thing about someone obstinate is not that he is certain but that he won't give in. You can argue with him all day and he will not yield. Thus, the true opposite of someone obstinate is not someone simply uncertain or wavering. It is someone who readily gives in or yields. The correct answer is *yielding*, Choice B.

Here is a second SAT question to examine, one similar in content but on a slightly more difficult vocabulary level.

> DISPUTE: (A) dispose (B) answer
> (C) qualify (D) befriend (E) concede

To *dispute* is to argue or debate. There is a common phrase, to *answer an argument*, that sometimes occurs in connection with disputes or debates. ("They disputed for hours, but neither could answer the other's argument.") However, *answer* is not a good antonym for *dispute*. One who disputes a point continues to argue about it. One who does not dispute a point *concedes* it or yields.

Look at the Answer Choices to Determine the Main Word's Part of Speech.

Look at the capitalized word. What part of speech is it? Words often exist in several forms. You may think of *run* as a verb, for example, but in the phrases "a run in her stocking" and "hit a home run" *run* is a noun.

The SAT plays on this confusion in testing your verbal ability. When you look at a particular capitalized word, you may not know whether you are dealing with a noun, a verb, or an adjective. *Harbor*, for example, is a very common noun; in "to harbor a fugitive," to give refuge to a runaway, it is a much less common verb.

If you suspect that a capitalized word may have more than one part of speech, don't worry. Just look at the first answer choice and see what part of speech it is. That part of speech will be the capitalized word's part of speech.

In SAT Antonym Questions, all the answer choices belong to the same part of speech.

Here's an example where you'll need to look at the answer choices to determine the main word's part of speech.

> CONTRACT: (A) weaken (B) resist
> (C) dilate (D) specify (E) resemble

Are you dealing with *contract* ('kon-ˌtrakt) the noun or *contract* (kun-'trakt) the verb?

A quick look at the answers assures you that they are all verbs. (The *-en* and *-ify* word endings are common verb endings.) *Contract* means to shrink or lessen. Its opposite is to expand or *dilate*. The correct answer is Choice C.

Now try an example from an actual SAT.

> DOCUMENT: (A) edit (B) withhold
> (C) reproduce in full (D) write for pay
> (E) leave unsupported

Are you dealing with *document* the common noun or *document* the somewhat less common verb?

A quick look at the first answer choice reveals that it is a verb. (The copy editor *edits* the manuscript.) One definition of the verb *document* is to support with documentary evidence, as in *documenting a case* or *documenting your expenses* for your boss. Thus, its opposite is *leave unsupported*, Choice E.

Note, by the way, how many of the incorrect answers have to do with aspects of writing. The SAT-makers often supply wrong answers that are not actual antonyms of the capitalized word but that relate to it in some manner.

Watch Out for Errors Caused by Eye-Catchers.

When you look at answer choices, do you find that certain ones seem to leap right off the page? For instance, when you were looking for an antonym for *document* just now, did the words having to do with writing catch your eye? These words are eye-catchers. They look good—but not if you take a second look.

Try these next SAT antonym questions to see just how an eye-catcher works. First, an easy one.

> LICENSED: (A) unnoticed (B) unwritten
> (C) unstable (D) not formally authorized
> (E) not properly trained

To be *licensed* is to be permitted to do something, to be *authorized*. Obviously, the best antonym for *licensed* is Choice D, *not formally authorized*. Most students who take the test will get it right. However, some won't. Some will pick Choice E, *not properly trained*.

To most high school students, the license that counts is the driver's license. Students pay a great deal of attention to every aspect of getting a license, and that includes *drivers' training*. Someone who fails the driving test is *unlicensed*; someone who fails the test must *not* have been *properly trained*.

You've just seen an example of how someone can be fooled by an eye-catcher, an answer choice set up to tempt the unwary into guessing wrong. Eye-catchers are words that somehow remind you of the capitalized word. They're related in a way; they feel as if they belong in the same set of words, the same *semantic field*.

Here's a more difficult SAT example. See if you can spot the eye-catcher.

UNDERMINE: (A) entangle   (B) parch
(C) overwork   (D) enter   (E) support

What's the opposite of *under*? *Over*. What's the opposite of *undermine*? No, it's not *overwork*. Be suspicious of answers that come too easily. To *undermine* means to weaken something or cause it to collapse by removing its underlying supports. The opposite of to *undermine* is Choice E, to *support*.

Here's another SAT antonym question. Once again, see if you can spot the eye-catcher.

ADVOCACY: (A) disrepute   (B) opposition
(C) ascendancy   (D) justice
(E) unconsciousness

Advocacy has to do with pleading or arguing for a cause, advocating or supporting it. Susan B. Anthony, for example, was noted for her *advocacy* of women's rights. The antonym of *advocacy* is *opposition*, Choice B.

Where is the eye-catcher in this question? *Advocacy* may remind you of *justice*. (*Advocate* is another word for lawyer, after all.) Don't let it catch you. Watch out for those easy-looking answer choices that leap right off the page.

Tactic 6

Consider Secondary Meanings of the Capitalized Word as Well as Its Primary Meaning.

If none of the answer choices seems right to you, take another look at the capitalized word. It may have more than one meaning. The SAT often constructs questions that make use of secondary, less well-known meanings of deceptively familiar words. Take, for example, this typical SAT question.

RESERVE: (A) compassion   (B) irascibility
(C) incoherence   (D) lack of restraint
(E) lack of strength

Here, *reserve* does *not* mean set apart or kept back, like books on reserve at the library or money in reserve in a savings bank. Instead *reserve* means formality and self-restraint in manner: "His natural reserve made people think he was stand-offish." By definition, the best antonym for this meaning of *reserve* is Choice D, *lack of restraint*.

Try a second, more difficult SAT question involving the secondary meaning of a deceptively familiar word.

QUALIFIED: (A) underlying   (B) disregarded
(C) unrestricted   (D) predetermined
(E) rehabilitated

Qualified most commonly means having the accomplishments that qualify or fit you for a particular office or task. "She was a *qualified* accountant," for example. Its opposite would be *unqualified* or unfit. However, none of the answer choices has this meaning. Obviously, some other meaning of *qualified* must be involved.

Here is a different context for *qualified*: "Unsure about the project, the Mayor gave it only a *qualified* endorsement." In this case, *qualified* means limited or modified in some way. The Mayor does not give the project unlimited or *unrestricted* support; he gives it *qualified* support. The best antonym for *qualified* is *unrestricted*, Choice C.

Notice how the word *conviction* is used in this next example.

CONVICTION: (A) crime   (B) veto
(C) dearth   (D) argument   (E) uncertainty

The most familiar context for the word *conviction* is a legal one. The District Attorney is out to get a *conviction* to prove someone guilty of a crime. However, a *conviction* is also a strong persuasion or belief. Its antonyms are doubt, lack of belief—in other words, *uncertainty*. Choice E is the best answer.

Break Down Unfamiliar Words into Recognizable Parts.

When you come upon a totally unfamiliar word, don't give up. Break it down and see if you recognize any of its parts. Pay particular attention to prefixes—word parts added to the beginning of a word—and to roots, the building blocks of the language.

More than half of the words in the English language derive from Latin and Greek. Students who attend prep schools and study Latin or Greek have a built-in advantage when they take standard vocabulary tests. Knowing Latin and Greek word parts helps them figure out the meanings of new words they come across.

Without spending three or four years studying Latin in high school, you still can profit from the word-parts approach. See how it works.

> CIRCUMSPECT: (A) disregarded (B) rash
> (C) unclear (D) idle (E) roundabout

You may not have seen *circumspect* before, but you've seen other words beginning with *circum-*: *circumstance, circumference*. Take circumference. What is a circumference? The distance around a circle. *Circum-* means *around*. To circumnavigate the globe, you sail around it.

What about the other part, *-spect*? Think of spectacles or spectator. *-Spect* means *look*. And when you look around before you cross the street, you're being cautious or careful—in other words, *circumspect*.

At this point, you know the meaning of the capitalized word. What answer is most nearly opposite to it in meaning? Choice B, *rash* or careless.

Now try a fairly easy example from a recently published SAT.

> INANIMATE: (A) somber (B) valiant
> (C) supportive (D) hidden (E) alive

In- means not. *Anim-* means spirit, breath, or soul. Something that does *not breathe* lacks consciousness or life. The opposite of *inanimate* is Choice E, *alive*.

Here is another SAT antonym, one of the hardest you're likely to see.

> NEOLOGISM:
> (A) nameless article
> (B) foreign object
> (C) exaggerated movement
> (D) impoverished condition
> (E) obsolete expression

Neo- means new. *Log-* means word or speech. A *neologism* must have to do with a new sort of word or speech. Similarly, the opposite of *neologism* must have to with a sort of word or speech that's old. Only one answer seems possible: Choice E, *obsolete expression. Obsolete* means out of date; an *expression* is a word or phrase. Choice E is correct.

If you find this word part approach appealing, try to spend some time working with the Basic Word Parts List in Chapter 9.

Long-Range Strategies

"Build Your Vocabulary," Chapter 9, contains a thorough description of strategies you can use to increase your word power, as well as a program to help you work your way through our entire Basic Word List. In addition, it contains an expanded Word Parts List—prefixes, suffixes, and roots—invaluable for both short-term and long-term SAT study programs.

One special feature in Chapter 9 is our revised High-Frequency SAT Word List, 320 words which computer analysis has shown turn up again and again on actual published SAT tests. Master these words: no matter what words turn up on your particular SAT test, these words *will* turn up in your college textbooks and your general reading. They are words every educated reader should know.

Work with the Word List
Flash Cards

Use our word lists as a guide in making flash cards. Scan a list looking for words you don't quite know—not words you are totally unfamiliar with, but words you are on the brink of knowing. Look for words you have heard or seen before but can't use in a sentence or define. Effort you put into mastering such "borderline" words will pay off—soon!

Be brief—but include all the information you need. On one side write the word. On the other side write *concise* definitions—two or three words at most—for each major meaning of the word you want to learn. Include an antonym, too: the synonym-antonym associations can help you remember both words. To fix the word in your mind, use it in a short phrase. Then write that phrase down.

Sample Flash Card

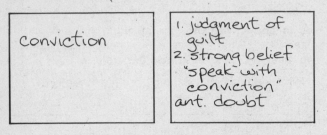

Carry a few of your flash cards with you every day. Look them over whenever you have a spare moment or two. Work in short bursts. Try going through five flash cards at a time, shuffling through them rapidly so that you can build up your rapid sight recognition of the words for the test. You want these words and their antonyms to spring to your mind instantaneously, so that you can speed through the antonym section of the SAT.

Test your memory: don't look at the back of the card unless you must. Go through your five cards several times a day. Then, when you have mastered two or three of the cards and have them down pat, set those cards aside and add a couple of new ones to your working pile. That way you will always be working with a limited group, but you won't be wasting time reviewing words you already recognize on sight.

Never try to master a whole stack of flash cards in one long cram session. It won't work.

Dictionary Drill

Use the Basic Word List as you would a specialized dictionary. You will find in it thousands of college-level words and their meanings, plus illustrative sentences to give you a sense of just how these words are used. Often the Word List does *not* include a word's most common definiton; instead, it contains unusual definitions of familiar words, definitions that are not commonly known but that you need to know.

Consider, for example, the word *intimate*. As an adjective it is familiar: an intimate friend, a close personal friend. As a verb, however, its meaning is less familiar. "Jim *intimated* he had something more to say to her after her little brother left." Here *intimate* means to hint or suggest. This is the meaning you will find in the Word List.

Beyond the Word List

Learn to consult an unabridged dictionary when you need to find out just how a word is used (and how it differs in usage from other similar words). At the end of the entry for *obese*, for example, you will find this direction:

syn see FAT

If you then turn to the entry for *fat*, glancing down the lengthy entry you will eventually come to:

syn FLESHY, STOUT, CORPULENT, OBESE, CHUBBY, ROTUND, PORTLY, PLUMP . . .

By reading the usage note that follows, you will learn the exact shades of meaning conveyed by each of these similar, but very different, words.

A word of warning. Some unabridged dictionaries arrange their definitions chronologically, giving the oldest definition of a word first. Others give a word's commonest definition first. The way a word was used in Shakespeare's time is often *not* the way it is most commonly used today. Look at your dictionary's introduction to see which approach it takes.

Memory Tricks

Remembering words takes work. It also takes wit. You can spend hours memorizing dictionary definitions and get no place. You can also capitalize on your native intelligence to think up mnemonic devices—memory tricks—to help you remember new words.

Consider the word *hovel*. A hovel is a dirty, mean house. How can you remember that? *Hovel* rhymes with shovel. You need to shovel out the hovel to live in it. Rhymes can help you remember what words mean.

Now consider the word *hover*. To hover is to hang fluttering in the air or to wait around. Can rhyme help you here? *Hover* rhymes with cover. That doesn't seem to work. However, take another look at *hover*. Cut off the letter *h* and you're left with the word *over*. If a helicopter hovers over an accident, it hangs in the air.

Try the hidden word trick with a less familiar word than *hover*. Take the world *credulous*. Credulous means gullible or easily fooled. A credulous person will give money to someone who wants to sell him the Brooklyn Bridge. Now look closely at *credulous*. What little word is hidden within it? The hidden word is red. What happens when a person finds out he's been taken for a fool? Often, the poor fool turns red. Credulous, red in the face. There's your memory trick.

Practice Exercises

The two exercises that follow will give you practice in handling antonym questions. Each 50-question exercise should take you about 25 to 30 minutes. When you've completed an exercise, check your answers against the answer key. Then read the an-swer explanations for any questions you either answered incorrectly or omitted. Going over the answer explanations will help you build your vocabulary, which is an important part of preparing for the verbal sections of the SAT.

Antonym Exercise A

Each question below consists of a word in capital letters, followed by five lettered words or phrases. Choose the word or phrase that is most nearly <u>opposite</u> in meaning to the word in capital letters. Since some of the questions require you to distinguish fine shades of meaning, consider all the choices before deciding which is best.

Example:

GOOD: (A) sour   (B) bad   (C) red
(D) hot   (E) ugly   Ⓐ ● Ⓒ Ⓓ Ⓔ

1. SCUFF: (A) polish   (B) stimulate
   (C) lengthen   (D) enclose   (E) regulate

2. ACQUIT: (A) install   (B) slow down
   (C) convict   (D) give back   (E) evade

3. PENALIZE: (A) exhibit   (B) observe
   (C) inherit   (D) enlighten   (E) reward

4. HOSPITALITY: (A) loss of health
   (B) concern for self   (C) clear proof
   (D) lack of welcome   (E) fresh venture

5. LOOSE: (A) determine   (B) disconcert
   (C) obscure   (D) confine   (E) provide

6. SYNTHETIC: (A) cosmetic   (B) affable
   (C) plastic   (D) apathetic   (E) natural

7. INFINITESIMAL: (A) everlasting (B) colossal
   (C) peripheral   (D) major   (E) telescopic

8. ACCUMULATE: (A) respect   (B) define
   (C) mature   (D) estimate   (E) squander

9. MISFORTUNE: (A) desire for power
   (B) gloom   (C) good luck
   (D) lack of speed   (E) solitude

10. REPROACH: (A) intend   (B) praise
    (C) expand   (D) project   (E) clarify

11. CONTEND: (A) provide food
    (B) set in place   (C) cease to struggle
    (D) branch out   (E) show interest

12. INSIGNIFICANCE: (A) genuineness
    (B) experience   (C) mercy   (D) carefulness
    (E) importance

13. ESTEEM: (A) scorn   (B) persist
    (C) cause harm   (D) change in nature
    (E) subdue

14. HEED: (A) control   (B) guarantee   (C) imitate
    (D) ignore   (E) unify

15. APPROPRIATE: (A) obvious   (B) unsuitable
    (C) similar   (D) admirable   (E) inexpensive

16. ABOMINATE: (A) love   (B) despair
    (C) abate   (D) implore   (E) attach

17. IRASCIBLE: (A) dominant   (B) silent
    (C) skeptical   (D) crafty   (E) good-natured

18. ENERGIZE: (A) alleviate   (B) make weary
    (C) promote   (D) decrease in value
    (E) despise

19. RALLY: (A) weaken   (B) dignify
    (C) transform   (D) proclaim   (E) sustain

20. OBSEQUIOUS: (A) obsolete   (B) mournful
    (C) supercilious   (D) improper   (E) sympathetic

21. AMENABLE: (A) genuine   (B) intractable
    (C) indifferent   (D) reckless   (E) correct

22. ALTRUISM: (A) honesty   (B) tolerance
    (C) sarcasm   (D) thievery   (E) selfishness

23. DISCORD: (A) simplicity   (B) amity
    (C) irritation   (D) gentility   (E) activity

24. VIGILANT: (A) hopeful   (B) unwary
    (C) uncertain   (D) lifeless   (E) unambitious

25. INGENUOUS: (A) clever   (B) sacred
    (C) hypothetical   (D) valid   (E) certain

26. ALLEVIATE: (A) allow   (B) aggravate
    (C) instigate   (D) belittle   (E) refuse

27. OBSOLETE: (A) acute   (B) unforgiven
    (C) free   (D) renovated   (E) temporary

28. BLASÉ: (A) different   (B) awed   (C) afraid
    (D) cultured   (E) unanswerable

29. PLACATE: (A) nettle   (B) modify
    (C) saturate   (D) reply   (E) retaliate

30. HUSBANDRY: (A) munificence   (B) greed
    (C) malignancy   (D) matrimony
    (E) widowhood

31. ZEALOT:
    (A) heretic
    (B) hypocrite
    (C) person who is careless
    (D) person who is rich
    (E) person who is indifferent

32. JOCUND: (A) rotund   (B) flattering
    (C) judicial   (D) irregular   (E) melancholy

33. DILETTANTE: (A) loyal supporter
    (B) professional   (C) late arrival   (D) superior
    (E) advanced beginner

34. AMORPHOUS:
    (A) lacking in virtue
    (B) translucent
    (C) organic
    (D) appreciative of beauty
    (E) having definite form

35. AUDACITY: (A) swiftness   (B) cowardice
    (C) conciseness   (D) patricide   (E) pugnacity

36. CIRCUITOUS: (A) weak-willed   (B) direct
    (C) rotund   (D) high-minded   (E) radical

37. ABHOR: (A) deter   (B) absolve   (C) accuse
    (D) bedizen   (E) adore

38. FLAMBOYANT: (A) tasteless   (B) impersonal
    (C) plain   (D) unconvincing   (E) terse

39. PERFUNCTORY: (A) thorough   (B) individual
    (C) anxious   (D) irate   (E) sinister

40. PENURY: (A) custom   (B) power
    (C) numismatics   (D) affluence   (E) crime

41. FURTIVE: (A) sated   (B) facile   (C) overt
    (D) nostalgic   (E) lethargic

42. DECOROUS: (A) unadorned   (B) homely
    (C) indecisive   (D) improper   (E) childish

43. PROPENSITY: (A) disinclination (B) transience
    (C) probity   (D) intelligence   (E) fascination

44. TRACTABLE: (A) varied   (B) incapable
    (C) weary   (D) forward   (E) recalcitrant

45. ADROIT: (A) bungling (B) antique (C) jovial
    (D) affirmative   (E) entire

46. EXPUNGE: (A) promote   (B) predict
    (C) unite   (D) insert   (E) assign

47. ALTERCATION: (A) adjustment   (B) repair
    (C) amity   (D) reaction   (E) viewpoint

48. SUMPTUOUS: (A) swampy   (B) irritable
    (C) meager   (D) fanciful   (E) eloquent

49. RETICENCE: (A) brazenness   (B) elegance
    (C) retention   (D) remoteness   (E) magnitude

50. ADVERSITY: (A) diversity   (B) ease
    (C) indifference   (D) agency   (E) agreement

Antonym Exercise B

Each question below consists of a word in capital letters, followed by five lettered words or phrases. Choose the word or phrase that is most nearly <u>opposite</u> in meaning to the word in capital letters. Since some of the questions require you to distinguish fine shades of meaning, consider all the choices before deciding which is best.

Example:

  GOOD: (A) sour   (B) bad   (C) red
  (D) hot   (E) ugly   Ⓐ ● Ⓒ Ⓓ Ⓔ

1. INDULGE: (A) observe secretly
    (B) restrain oneself   (C) exhale
     (D) divert   (E) outweigh

2. OUTPUT:
    (A) lack of production
    (B) absence of talent
    (C) return from exile
    (D) unexpected reward
    (E) inner harmony

3. DEFINITE: (A) radical   (B) unavoidable
    (C) boring   (D) practical   (E) vague

4. WITHER: (A) equal   (B) pierce   (C) flourish
    (D) hasten   (E) assist

5. PRECEDE: (A) follow   (B) deviate   (C) fail
    (D) initiate   (E) summarize

6. STURDY: (A) mutual   (B) delicate
    (C) prompt   (D) meticulous   (E) kind-hearted

7. MANIFEST: (A) obstruct   (B) detest   (C) alter
    (D) manipulate   (E) conceal

8. CHERISH: (A) contemplate   (B) reconcile
    (C) perish   (D) disdain   (E) modify

9. RECOVERY: (A) loss   (B) repose
    (C) exploration   (D) confession   (E) guarantee

10. SUPPRESS: (A) abandon   (B) forget
    (C) disclose   (D) work diligently
     (E) convince wholly

11. ALIGHT: (A) stimulate   (B) burden   (C) injure
    (D) quench   (E) mount

12. CONCAVE: (A) central   (B) solid   (C) convex
    (D) complex   (E) intermittent

13. PROLONG: (A) insure   (B) decrease in speed
    (C) hesitate   (D) reduce in duration
     (E) alter in extent

14. VEX: (A) grow smaller   (B) make denser
    (C) soothe   (D) discuss   (E) predict

15. SUMMIT: (A) novel thought
    (B) lowest point   (C) departure
    (D) introduction   (E) extended account

16. DISPARITY: (A) similarity   (B) aspersion
    (C) allusion   (D) equanimity   (E) permanence

17. ESTRANGED: (A) reconciled   (B) smug
    (C) foreign   (D) frightened   (E) embarrassed

18. SUBSERVIENT:
    (A) complacent   (B) omnipresent   (C) partial
    (D) haughty   (E) miserly

19. FUMBLE: (A) perform faithfully
    (B) handle skillfully   (C) stroll
    (D) accept   (E) alter suddenly

20. REBUKE: (A) assign   (B) mature   (C) expand
    (D) commend   (E) falsify

21. PLACID: (A) serious   (B) tardy   (C) copious
    (D) derelict   (E) ruffled

22. WANE: (A) enlarge   (B) endorse   (C) soothe
    (D) enforce   (E) regret

23. FRUGALITY: (A) extravagance   (B) apathy
    (C) timeliness   (D) anxiety   (E) ire

24. INDIGENCE: (A) nativity   (B) tolerance
    (C) gossip   (D) wealth   (E) altruism

25. HAGGARD: (A) robust   (B) irascible
    (C) wise   (D) sluggish   (E) witty

26. IMMUTABLE: (A) forgetful   (B) victorious
    (C) changeable   (D) showy   (E) unprejudiced

27. MOLLIFY: (A) loosen   (B) irritate
    (C) applaud   (D) flatter   (E) discourage

28. TACIT: (A) explicit   (B) quick   (C) frigid
    (D) indifferent   (E) gloomy

29. RELINQUISH: (A) afford   (B) follow
    (C) scorn   (D) claim   (E) qualify

30. IMPECCABLE: (A) impervious   (B) faulty
    (C) devious   (D) naive   (E) irate

31. INANE: (A) lifeless   (B) clever   (C) hopeful
    (D) faithless   (E) futile

32. COMMODIOUS: (A) equipped   (B) formidable
    (C) unequal   (D) cramped   (E) distant

33. ANIMOSITY: (A) unanimity   (B) intensity
    (C) failure   (D) alacrity   (E) amity

34. DUPLICITY: (A) complexity   (B) miserliness
    (C) calm   (D) candor   (E) originality

35. ILLICIT: (A) apathetic   (B) private   (C) weary
    (D) angry   (E) lawful

36. DEPRECATE: (A) predict   (B) approve
    (C) increase   (D) immigrate   (E) exile

37. CORROBORATION: (A) provocation
    (B) arrest   (C) invalidation   (D) contamination
    (E) alias

38. SURMISE: (A) be uneasy   (B) have qualms
    (C) make ready   (D) be certain   (E) rest

39. CHASTISE: (A) reward   (B) pursue
    (C) precede   (D) stop   (E) prolong

40. AVARICIOUS: (A) altruistic   (B) mandatory
    (C) wicked   (D) renowned   (E) eager

41. MOROSE: (A) cheerful   (B) mortal
    (C) benevolent   (D) questioning   (E) fortuitous

42. ADAMANT: (A) yielding   (B) primitive
    (C) elementary   (D) essential   (E) inefficient

43. EPHEMERAL: (A) central   (B) deciduous
    (C) lethal   (D) everlasting   (E) tactile

44. LANGUID: (A) pusillanimous   (B) sickly
    (C) humid   (D) vigorous   (E) temperate

45. AMELIORATE: (A) repeat   (B) coarsen
    (C) aggravate   (D) improvise   (E) conserve

46. ASSUAGE: (A) meet   (B) abolish
    (C) separate   (D) irritate   (E) demonstrate

47. DEARTH: (A) seriousness   (B) brevity
    (C) abundance   (D) brightness   (E) mourning

48. EXEMPLARY: (A) deplorable   (B) imitative
    (C) definite   (D) condoning   (E) additional

49. CAPRICIOUS: (A) haughty   (B) consistent
    (C) infinite   (D) honest   (E) hypocritical

50. OBFUSCATE: (A) clarify   (B) magnify
    (C) intensify   (D) belittle   (E) resist

Answer Key
Antonym Exercise A

1.	A	11.	C	21.	B	31.	E	41.	C
2.	C	12.	E	22.	E	32.	E	42.	D
3.	E	13.	A	23.	B	33.	B	43.	A
4.	D	14.	D	24.	B	34.	E	44.	E
5.	D	15.	B	25.	A	35.	B	45.	A
6.	E	16.	A	26.	B	36.	B	46.	D
7.	B	17.	E	27.	D	37.	E	47.	C
8.	E	18.	B	28.	B	38.	C	48.	C
9.	C	19.	A	29.	A	39.	A	49.	A
10.	B	20.	C	30.	A	40.	D	50.	B

Antonym Exercise B

1.	B	11.	E	21.	E	31.	B	41.	A
2.	A	12.	C	22.	A	32.	D	42.	A
3.	E	13.	D	23.	A	33.	E	43.	D
4.	C	14.	C	24.	D	34.	D	44.	D
5.	A	15.	B	25.	A	35.	E	45.	C
6.	B	16.	A	26.	C	36.	B	46.	D
7.	E	17.	A	27.	B	37.	C	47.	C
8.	D	18.	D	28.	A	38.	D	48.	A
9.	A	19.	B	29.	D	39.	A	49.	B
10.	C	20.	D	30.	B	40.	A	50.	A

Answer Explanations
Antonym Exercise A

1. A. The opposite of *scuff* (to roughen) is *polish* (to smooth).

2. C. The opposite of *acquit* (to free from, or find innocent of, a charge) is *convict* (to find guilty of a charge).

3. E. The opposite of *penalize* (to impose a hardship) is *reward*.

4. D. The opposite of *hospitality* (a pleasant welcome) is *lack of welcome*.

5. D. The opposite of *loose* (to free from restriction) is *confine* (to restrict).

6. E. The opposite of *synthetic* (artificial) is *natural*.

7. B. The opposite of *infinitesimal* (very small) is *colossal* (huge).

8. E. The opposite of *accumulate* (to gather) is *squander* (to scatter).

9. C. The opposite of *misfortune* (bad luck) is *good luck*.

10. B. The opposite of *reproach* (blame) is *praise*.

11. C. The opposite of *contend* (to struggle to achieve) is *cease to struggle*.

12. E. The opposite of *insignificance* (lack of meaning or importance) is *importance*.

13. A. The opposite of *esteem* (to appreciate or regard highly) is *scorn* (to despise or regard as worthless).

14. D. The opposite of *heed* (to notice) is *ignore*.

15. B. The opposite of *appropriate* (suitable or fitting) is *unsuitable*.

16. A. The opposite of *abominate* (to hate) is *love*.

17. E. The opposite of *irascible* (irritable or easily angered) is *good-natured*.

18. B. The opposite of *energize* (to make active or forceful) is *make weary*.

19. A. The opposite of *rally* (to regain strength) is *weaken*.

20. C. The opposite of *obsequious* (slavishly attentive or flattering) is *supercilious* (arrogant).

21. B. The opposite of *amenable* (easily managed) is *intractable* (unruly).

22. E. The opposite of *altruism* (generosity) is *selfishness*.

23. B.   The opposite of *discord* (conflict) is *amity* (friendly relations).

24. B.   The opposite of *vigilant* (alert and attentive) is *unwary* (not alert).

25. A.   The opposite of *ingenuous* (naive) is *clever*.

26. B.   The opposite of *alleviate* (to relieve) is *aggravate* (to worsen).

27. D.   The opposite of *obsolete* (outmoded) is *renovated* (renewed).

28. B.   The opposite of *blasé* (bored, unimpressed) is *awed* (admiring or showing solemn wonder).

29. A.   The opposite of *placate* (to pacify or soothe) is *nettle* (to annoy).

30. A.   The opposite of *husbandry* (thriftiness) is *munificence* (generosity).

31. E.   The opposite of *zealot* (a fanatic, or person who has excessive enthusiasm) is a *person who is indifferent*.

32. E.   The opposite of *jocund* (merry) is *melancholy*.

33. B.   The opposite of *dilettante* (amateur) is *professional*.

34. E.   The opposite of *amorphous* (shapeless) is *having a definite form*.

35. B.   The opposite of *audacity* (boldness) is *cowardice*.

36. B.   The opposite of *circuitous* (roundabout) is *direct*.

37. E.   The opposite of *abhor* (to detest or hate) is *adore*.

38. C.   The opposite of *flamboyant* (ornate) is *plain*.

39. A.   The opposite of *perfunctory* (superficial or not thorough) is *thorough*.

40. D.   The opposite of *penury* (extreme poverty) is *affluence* (wealth).

41. C.   The opposite of *furtive* (stealthy) is *overt* (open to view).

42. D.   The opposite of *decorous* (proper) is *improper*.

43. A.   The opposite of *propensity* (natural inclination) is *disinclination*.

44. E.   The opposite of *tractable* (docile or obedient) is *recalcitrant* (obstinately stubborn).

45. A.   The opposite of *adroit* (skillful) is *bungling* (clumsy).

46. D.   The opposite of *expunge* (to cancel or remove) is *insert*.

47. C.   The opposite of *altercation* (quarrel) is *amity* (friendly relationship).

48. C.   The opposite of *sumptuous* (lavish) is *meager* (sparse).

49. A.   The opposite of *reticence* (reserve) is *brazenness* (defiant boldness).

50. B.   The opposite of *adversity* (poverty or misfortune) is *ease*.

Antonym Exercise B

1. B.   The opposite of *indulge* (to yield to) is *restrain oneself*.

2. A.   The opposite of *output* (the process or product of production) is *lack of production*.

3. E.   The opposite of *definite* (certain) is *vague* (not precise).

4. C.   The opposite of *wither* (to shrivel or lose freshness) is *flourish* (to prosper or grow well).

5. A.   The opposite of *precede* (to lead or go ahead of) is *follow*.

6. B.   The opposite of *sturdy* (strongly built) is *delicate*.

7. E.   The opposite of *manifest* (to show or make clear) is *conceal*.

8. D.   The opposite of *cherish* (to treat with affection and appreciation) is *disdain* (to treat with scorn or contempt).

9. A.   The opposite of *recovery* (the act of regaining) is *loss*.

10. C.   The opposite of *suppress* (to conceal) is *disclose* (to reveal).

11. E.   The opposite of *alight* (to descend) is *mount* (to ascend).

12. C.   The opposite of *concave* (hollow, curving inward) is *convex* (curving outward).

13. D.   The opposite of *prolong* (to increase in duration) is to *reduce in duration*.

14. C.   The opposite of *vex* (annoy) is *soothe*.

15. B.   The opposite of *summit* (highest point) is *lowest point*.

16. A.   The opposite of *disparity* (difference) is *similarity*.

17. A.   The opposite of *estranged* (separated) is *reconciled* (brought together or made friendly after a quarrel).

18. D.   The opposite of *subservient* (slavishly attentive) is *haughty* (arrogant).

19. B.   The opposite of *fumble* (to handle clumsily) is to *handle skillfully*.

20. D.   The opposite of *rebuke* (to criticize) is *commend* (to compliment).

21. E.   The opposite of *placid* (calm) is *ruffled* (upset or irritated).

22. A.   The opposite of *wane* (to grow gradually smaller) is *enlarge*.

23. A.   The opposite of *frugality* (thrift) is *extravagance* (excess or waste).

24. D.   The opposite of *indigence* (poverty) is *wealth*.

25. A.   The opposite of *haggard* (wasted away and gaunt) is *robust* (healthy).

26. C.   The opposite of *immutable* (unchangeable) is *changeable*.

27. B.   The opposite of *mollify* (to soothe) is *irritate*.

28. A.   The opposite of *tacit* (understood, not put into words) is *explicit* (definite, openly stated).

29. D.   The opposite of *relinquish* (to abandon) is *claim* (to demand as one's own).

30. B.   The opposite of *impeccable* (faultless) is *faulty*.

31. B.   The opposite of *inane* (silly) is *clever*.

32. D.   The opposite of *commodious* (spacious) is *cramped*.

33. E.   The opposite of *animosity* (active enmity or hostility) is *amity* (friendship).

34. D.   The opposite of *duplicity* (double-dealing) is *candor* (honesty).

35. E.   The opposite of *illicit* (unlawful) is *lawful*.

36. B.   The opposite of *deprecate* (to disapprove regretfully) is *approve*.

37. C.   The opposite of *corroboration* (confirmation) is *invalidation* (nullification).

38. D.   The opposite of *surmise* (to guess) is *be certain*.

39. A.   The opposite of *chastise* (to punish) is *reward*.

40. A.   The opposite of *avaricious* (greedy for wealth) is *altruistic* (generous).

41. A.   The opposite of *morose* (ill-humored or sullen) is *cheerful*.

42. A.   The opposite of *adamant* (inflexible) is *yielding* (flexible).

43. D.   The opposite of *ephemeral* (short-lived) is *everlasting*.

44. D.   The opposite of *languid* (sluggish or weary) is *vigorous*.

45. C.   The opposite of *ameliorate* (to improve) is *aggravate* (to make worse).

46. D.   The opposite of *assuage* (to ease or lessen [as pain]) is *irritate*.

47. C.   The opposite of *dearth* (scarcity) is *abundance*.

48. A.   The opposite of *exemplary* (outstanding) is *deplorable* (wretched).

49. B.   The opposite of *capricious* (fickle or unpredictable) is *consistent*.

50. A.   The opposite of *obfuscate* (to confuse) is *clarify*.

6 The Analogy Question

- ■ Testing Tactics
- ■ Long-Range Strategies
- ■ Practice Exercises
- ■ Answer Key
- ■ Answer Explanations

Analogy questions ask you to determine the relationship in a pair of words and then recognize a similar or parallel relationship in a different pair of words. You are given one pair of words and must choose from the five pairs given as answer choices another pair that is related in the same way. The relationship between the words in the original pair will always be a specific, precise one; the same is true for the relationship between the words in the correct answer pair.

Here are the directions for the analogy questions. Learn them now. They won't change. The test time you would spend reading the directions can be better spent answering questions.

Each question below consists of a related pair of words or phrases, followed by five lettered pairs of words or phrases. Select the lettered pair that best expresses a relationship similar to that expressed in the original pair.

Example:

YAWN : BOREDOM :: (A) dream : sleep
(B) anger : madness   (C) smile : amusement
 (D) face : expression   (E) impatience : rebellion

Ⓐ Ⓑ ● Ⓓ Ⓔ

Just as a yawn is a physical sign of boredom, a smile is a physical sign of amusement. To put it another way, a yawn *signifies* boredom, a smile *signifies* amusement. Choice E is correct. Choice D is not. A face merely *shows* expression; it does not *signify* expression. Analogies can be tricky.

Note how an SAT analogy question is set up. First you have the two capitalized words linked by a symbol. Take a look at a few examples.

ACTOR : STAGE

An actor is related to a stage. How? An actor works or performs on a stage.

SCRIBBLE : WRITE

Scribble is related to write. How? To scribble is to write hastily, even carelessly.

DOG : POODLE

Dog is related to poodle. How? A poodle is a kind of dog. Notice the wording of the last sentence. You could equally have said "One kind of dog is a poodle" and maintained the word order of the analogy. However, it sometimes is easier to express a relationship if you reverse the order of the words.

Some of the analogies on the SAT are as clearcut as the ones above. Others are far more complex. In some questions, for example, you are asked to carry an analogy from a concrete example to a more abstract or less tangible one.

SURGEON : SCALPEL :: satirist : words

A surgeon *literally* uses a scalpel to make an incision, to cut. A satirist (a writer of literary satire) uses words to cut and ridicule the pride and folly of his subjects. As you can see, answering such questions correctly involves more than knowing single meanings of words. You'll find practice exercises containing both straightforward and tricky analogies at the end of this chapter.

Analogy questions are a bit like riddles; they're a kind of word game. At first analogies may seem a stumbling block to you, but once you master our tactics for solving them, you may even find them fun.

Testing Tactics

1 Before You Look at the Choices, Try to State the Relationship Between the Capitalized Words in a Good Sentence.

In answering an analogy question, your first step is to determine the exact nature of the relationship that exists between the two capitalized words. *Before you look at the answer pairs*, make up a sentence that shows how these capitalized words are related. Then test the possible answers by seeing how well they fit in your sentence.

Take, for example, this analogy question.

CONSTELLATION:STARS :: (A) prison:bars
(B) assembly:speaker   (C) troupe:actors
(D) mountain:peak   (E) flock:shepherds

A *constellation* is made up of *stars*. A *troupe* (not *troop* but *troupe*) is made up of *actors* (and actresses, of course). Choice C is correct.

Don't let Choice E fool you: a flock is made up of sheep, not of shepherds.

Now try stating the relationship between the capitalized words in this next example.

COMPOSER:SYMPHONY ::
(A) porter:terminal   (B) writer:plagiarism
(C) coach:team   (D) painter:mural
(E) doctor:stethoscope

A *composer* creates a *symphony*. You therefore are looking for a relationship between a worker and a work he or she has created. You can easily eliminate Choices A and E: a porter works *at* a terminal; a doctor works *with* a stethoscope. You can also eliminate Choice C: no coach literally *creates* a team in the same way that a composer creates a symphony.

Writers and painters, however, both create works of art. Which answer is better, B or D? If you know the meanings of *plagiarism* and *mural*, the question is easy. What if you don't?

If you do not know the definitions of *plagiarism* and *mural*, think of a context for them. Someone is "accused of plagiarism." From this you can infer that plagiarism is a crime (passing off someone else's work as your own), not a created work. A mural is a picture painted on a wall. The correct answer is Choice D.

2 If More Than One Answer Fits the Relationship in Your Sentence, Look for a Narrower Approach.

When you try to express the relationship between the two capitalized words in sentence form, make sure you include enough details to particularize your analogy. Otherwise, more than one answer may fit the relationship, and you will have to go back to the original pair and analyze it more.

Consider this actual analogy from a recent SAT.

RACQUET:TENNIS :: (A) springboard:diver
(B) horse:polo   (C) glove:boxing
(D) club:golf   (E) gun:hunting

Suppose your original sentence is "A racquet is a piece of equipment one uses in tennis." That sentence is too broad. It could equally well fit Choices C, D, and E.

Go back to the original pair of words for more details. How does one use a racquet in tennis? "In tennis one uses a racquet to strike the ball." Similarly, "in golf one uses a club to strike the ball." Choice D is best.

Your sentence should reflect the relationship between the two capitalized words *exactly*. If it doesn't, try again.

Here is another actual SAT question to examine.

THIMBLE:FINGER :: (A) armor:body
(B) crown:head   (C) torso:waist
(D) earring:ear   (E) stocking:leg

Suppose your original sentence was "One wears a thimble on one's finger." Again, that framework is too broad: it could accommodate Choices A, B, D, and E. By definition, a thimble is a small hard cap that you wear over your finger to protect your finger from needles or pins. Because thimbles are defined as being intended for protection, the SAT-makers consider the correct answer to be Choice A. "Armor is a covering that you wear on your body to protect your body from weapons."

If you're not entirely happy with this answer, you're not alone. Some people would argue in favor of Choice B, maintaining that a crown fits on top of a head in the same way that a thimble fits on top of a finger. The SAT would mark them wrong. *In answering analogy questions on the SAT, pay special attention to how a dictionary would define the words involved.*

Watch Out for Errors Stemming from Reversals.

In an analogy you have two capitalized words that relate in a set way. In setting up the answer choices, the SAT-makers will often tempt you with pairs of words that relate in a grammatically opposite way. See how it works in two examples from published SATs.

ENDURE:SURVIVOR :: (A) condemn:culprit
(B) applaud:performer (C) evade:guardian
(D) excel:imitator (E) compete:rival

At first glance several of these answers may seem to work. "A survivor is someone who endures." "A culprit is someone who is condemned." The relationship looks promising, but it's not correct. Ask yourself *who is doing what to whom?* In the original pair, the survivor is doing something; the survivor is enduring. In Choice A, the culprit is *not* the person doing something; the culprit is the person to whom something is being done. The culprit is the object of the verb condemn, not the verb's subject. The original grammatical relationship is reversed.

The correct answer to this question is Choice E. By

definition, a survivor is a person who endures. In the same way, by definition, a rival is a person who competes.

INTERLOPER:INTRUSION ::
(A) witness:interrogation
(B) actor:intermission
(C) recluse:interference
(D) mediator:intercession
(E) orator:interruption

Again, ask yourself who is doing what to whom. An interloper is a person who butts in or thrusts himself into the business of others. An interloper commits an intrusion; he or she intrudes. A witness, on the other hand, is not the person who conducts the interrogation. A witness is the person who is being interrogated. You can eliminate Choice A and any other answer choices in which the original relationship is reversed. In this case, Choice D is correct. The mediator or go-between is the person who acts, trying to reconcile quarreling parties by means of intercession.

Be Guided by the Parts of Speech.

Grammatical information can help you recognize analogy types and spot the use of unfamiliar or secondary meanings of words. In SAT analogy questions, the relationship between the parts of speech of the capitalized words and the parts of speech of the answer choices is consistent. If your capitalized words are a noun and a verb, each one of your answer pairs will be a noun and a verb. If they are an adjective and a noun, each one of your answer pairs will be an adjective and a noun. If you can recognize the parts of speech in a single answer pair, you know the parts of speech of every other answer pair, and of the original pair as well.

See how this tactic works in a somewhat difficult question from a recently published SAT.

HUSBAND:RESOURCES ::
(A) conserve:energy (B) spend:salary
(C) predict:hurricane (D) analyze:statement
(E) revise:story

At first glance, *husband* and *resources* seem only vaguely related. After all, a husband is a married man; he may have resources, or he may not. However, take a look at the answer pairs. *Conserve, spend*, they're verbs, not nouns. *Husband* must be a verb as well.

You now know you're dealing with an unfamiliar meaning of *husband*. However, you also know that husbanding is an action that has something to do with *resources* or assets. Typically, you do one of two things with resources or assets: save them or expend them. You've just narrowed things down to a decision between Choice A, *conserve*:*energy*, and Choice B, *spend*:*salary*. Choice B, however, is an eye-catcher: it's set up to remind you that "husbands" earn a *salary*. The correct answer is Choice A. To husband resources is to use them economically, conserving them as much as you can. This is comparable to conserving energy.

Tactic 5

Familiarize Yourself with Common Analogy Types.

Analogies tend to fall into certain basic types. Do not go overboard and try to memorize these types. Just try to get a feel for them, so that you'll be able to recognize how each pair of words is linked.

Common Analogy Types

Definition

REFUGE : SHELTER
A *refuge* (place of asylum) by definition *shelters*.

NOMAD : WANDER
A *nomad* by definition *wanders*.

HAGGLER : BARGAIN
A *haggler*, a person who argues over prices, by definition *bargains*.

Defining Characteristic

TIGER : CARNIVOROUS
A *tiger* is defined as a *carnivorous* or meat-eating animal.

ENTOMOLOGIST : INSECTS
An *entomologist* is defined as a person who studies *insects*.

HIVE : BEE
A *hive* is defined as a home for *bees*.

Class and Member

RODENT : SQUIRREL
A *squirrel* is a kind of *rodent*.

SOFA : FURNITURE
A *sofa* belongs to the category known as *furniture*.

SONNET : POEM
A *sonnet* is a kind of *poem*.

Antonyms

Antonyms are words that are opposite in meaning. Both words belong to the same part of speech.

CONCERNED : INDIFFERENT
Indifferent means *unconcerned*.

WAX : WANE
Wax, to grow larger, and *wane*, to dwindle, are opposites.

ANARCHY : ORDER
Anarchy is the opposite of *order*.

Antonym Variants

In an Antonym Variant, the words are not strictly antonyms; however, their meanings are opposed. Take the adjective *nervous*. A strict antonym for the adjective *nervous* would be the adjective *poised*. However, where an Antonym would put the adjective *poised*, an Antonym Variant puts the noun *poise*. It looks like this:

NERVOUS : POISE
Nervous means lacking in *poise*.

WICKED : VIRTUE
Something *wicked* lacks *virtue*. It is the opposite of virtuous.

WILLFUL : OBEDIENCE
Willful means lacking in *obedience*. It is the opposite of obedient.

Synonyms

Synonyms are words that have the same meaning. Both words belong to the same part of speech.

MAGNIFICENT : GRANDIOSE
Grandiose means *magnificent*.

NARRATE : TELL
To *narrate* is to *tell*.

EDIFICE : BUILDING
An *edifice* is a *building*.

Synonym Variants

In a Synonym Variant, the words are not strictly synonyms; however, their meanings are similar. For example, take the adjective *willful*. A strict synonym for the adjective *willful* would be the adjective *unruly*. However, where a Synonym would put the adjective *unruly*, a Synonym Variant would put the noun *unruliness*. It looks like this:

WILLFUL : UNRULINESS
Willful means exhibiting *unruliness*.

VERBOSE : WORDINESS
Someone *verbose* is wordy; he or she exhibits *wordiness*.

FRIENDLY : AMICABILITY
Someone *friendly* is amicable; he or she shows *amicability*.

Degree of Intensity

LUKEWARM : BOILING
Lukewarm is less extreme than *boiling*.

FLURRY : BLIZZARD
A *flurry* or shower of snow is less extreme than a *blizzard*.

ANNOYED : FURIOUS
To be *annoyed* is less intense an emotion than to be *furious*.

Part to Whole

ISLAND : ARCHIPELAGO
Many *islands* make up an *archipelago*.

LETTER : ALPHABET
The English *alphabet* is made up of 26 *letters*.

FINGER : HAND
The *finger* is part of the *hand*.

Function

ASYLUM : REFUGE
An *asylum* provides *refuge* or protection.

FEET : MARCH
A function of *feet* is to *march*.

LULL : STORM
A *lull* temporarily interrupts a *storm*.

Manner

MUMBLE : SPEAK
To *mumble* is to *speak* indistinctly, that is, to speak in an indistinct manner.

STRUT : WALK
To *strut* is to *walk* proudly, that is, to walk in a proud manner.

STRAINED : WIT
Wit that is *strained* is forced in manner.

Worker and Article Created

POET : SONNET
A *poet* creates a *sonnet*.

ARCHITECT : BLUEPRINT
An *architect* designs a *blueprint*.

MASON : WALL
A *mason* builds a *wall*.

Worker and Tool

PAINTER : BRUSH
A *painter* uses a *brush*.

GOLFER : CLUB
A *golfer* uses a *club* to strike the ball.

CARPENTER : VISE
A *carpenter* uses a *vise* to hold the object being worked on.

Worker and Action

ACROBAT : CARTWHEEL
An *acrobat* performs a *cartwheel*.

FINANCIER : INVEST
A *financier* invests.

TENOR : ARIA
A *tenor* sings an *aria*.

Worker and Workplace

TEACHER : CLASSROOM
A *teacher* works in a *classroom*.

SCULPTOR : STUDIO
A *sculptor* works in a *studio*.

DRUGGIST : PHARMACY
A *druggist* works in a *pharmacy*.

Tool and Object It Acts Upon

KNIFE : BREAD
A *knife* cuts *bread*.

PEN : PAPER
A *pen* writes on *paper*.

RAKE : LEAVES
A *rake* gathers *leaves*.

Tool and Its Action

SAW : CUT
A *saw* is a tool used to *cut* wood.

CROWBAR : PRY
A *crowbar* is a tool used to *pry* things apart.

SIEVE : SIFT
A *sieve* is a tool used to strain or *sift*.

Action and Its Significance

HUG : AFFECTION
A *hug* is a sign of *affection*.

NOD : ASSENT
A *nod* signifies *assent* or agreement.

WINCE : PAIN
A *wince* is a sign that one feels *pain*.

Less Common Analogy Types

Cause and Effect

VIRUS : INFLUENZA
A *virus* causes *influenza*.

Time Sequence

FIRST : LAST
First and *last* mark the beginning and end of a sequence.

Spatial Sequence

ATTIC : BASEMENT
The *attic* is the highest point in the house; the *basement*, the lowest point.

Gender

DOE : STAG
A *doe* is a female deer; a *stag*, a male deer.

Age

COLT : STALLION
A *colt* is a young *stallion*.

Symbol and Abstraction It Represents

DOVE : PEACE
A *dove* is the symbol of *peace*.

Long-Range Strategies

The vocabulary in the analogy section differs slightly from the vocabulary tested in the antonym section. Somewhat fewer words come from Latin. Fewer words are abstract; more are concrete.

You need to know the names of everyday objects and parts of objects, names which the testmakers assume are in your everyday vocabulary but which nonetheless may be unfamiliar to you. You need to know that hawks have talons and trout have gills, that a group of islands is called an archipelago and a group of lions is called a pride. You need to know that calipers measure and that augers bore, that painters paint murals and that poets write odes.

How can you build up the sort of wide-ranging, concrete vocabulary you need to see the variety of relationships possible between words? The words are there; they're yours for the taking.

Words for the Taking

To meet new words, branch out in your reading. Try magazines in fields you haven't pursued before. Geology, geography, natural history, astronomy, art—terms from these disciplines appear again and again. Branch out in your viewing as well. You can watch *National Geographic* specials and other documentaries on television and build your vocabulary by attaching the names of objects to the things themselves: people need pictures as well as words.

Unabridged dictionaries often provide pictures of everyday objects: color plates of insects and flowers, birds and fish; line drawings of tools and machines. Picture dictionaries also exist. There is even a splendid visual glossary entitled *What's What*, consisting of hundreds of illustrations of everyday objects—from paper clips to passenger ships—carefully labeled to identify every part.

Learn by Doing

As you expand your vocabulary, try constructing some analogies using your new words. Go through the list of analogy types, modeling your analogies on the samples given. You should have no difficulty constructing innumerable synonyms and antonyms. Challenge yourself. Try to construct analogies where the relationship is one of cause and effect or one of a part to the whole. The better able you are to create good analogies of your own, the better able you will be to analyze the analogies of others.

Practice Exercises

Use the two exercises that follow to practice handling analogy questions. When you've completed an exercise, check your answers against the answer key. Then, read the answer explanations for any questions you either answered incorrectly or omitted.

The answer explanations will show you how to state the relationship in each analogy in a good sentence; they'll provide definitions for words you might not have known; and they'll point out the analogy type for each question. So, if you missed a question because you didn't know the meaning of a word, you'll learn the meaning of that word. If you missed a question because you didn't understand the relationship between the two words, you'll see what that relationship was.

Analogy Exercise A

Each question below consists of a related pair of words or phrases, followed by five lettered pairs of words or phrases. Select the lettered pair that best expresses a relationship similar to that expressed in the original pair.

Example:

YAWN : BOREDOM :: (A) dream : sleep
(B) anger : madness   (C) smile : amusement
   (D) face : expression   (E) impatience : rebellion

Ⓐ Ⓑ ● Ⓓ Ⓔ

1. FISH:TROUT :: (A) ocean:wave
(B) mammal:whale   (C) bird:aviary
(D) antenna:insect   (E) stag:doe

2. FISH:SCALES :: (A) plane:wings
(B) bird:feathers   (C) cat:claws
(D) snake:fangs   (E) song:notes

3. FISH:SCHOOL :: (A) book:education
(B) team:practice   (C) dog:sled   (D) bear:lair
(E) lion:pride

4. CLOCK:TIME :: (A) watch:wrist
(B) odometer:speed   (C) hourglass:sand
(D) yardstick:distance   (E) radio:sound

5. DOCTOR:DISEASE ::
(A) moron:imbecility
(B) pediatrician:senility
(C) psychiatrist:maladjustment
(D) broker:stocks
(E) charlatan:truth

6. SCISSORS:SEVER .. (A) scales:average
(B) barrel:roll   (C) eraser:smudge
(D) millstone:grind   (E) match:strike

7. HONE:SHARP :: (A) polish:shiny
(B) whet:blunt   (C) memorize:minor
(D) erode:moist   (E) varnish:sticky

8. PATRON:SUPPORT ::
(A) spouse:divorce
(B) restaurant:management
(C) counselor:advice
(D) host:hostility
(E) artist:imitation

9. DIMMED:LIGHT :: (A) bleached:texture
(B) muffled:sound   (C) measured:weight
(D) fragrant:smell   (E) garish:color

10. STETHOSCOPE:PHYSICIAN ::
(A) kaleidoscope:mortician
(B) microscope:astronomer
(C) plot:author
(D) studio:sculptor
(E) transit:surveyor

11. DAUNTLESS:COURAGE ::
(A) ruthless:compassion
(B) affable:suspicion
(C) unruffled:composure
(D) energetic:indifference
(E) dutiful:sympathy

12. CUMULONIMBUS:CLOUD ::
(A) grasshopper:insect
(B) rainbow:shower
(C) twilight:dusk
(D) omnibus:road
(E) bough:tree

13. OCEAN:BAY :: (A) archipelago:atoll
(B) island:inlet   (C) headland:promontory
(D) continent:peninsula   (E) comet:galaxy

14. INTREPID:VALOR :: (A) clever:ingenuity
(B) boisterous:grief   (C) timorous:haste
(D) frivolous:fervor   (E) derelict:duty

15. LEOPARD:CARNIVOROUS ::
(A) tiger:ominous
(B) cat:feline
(C) cow:herbivorous
(D) quadruped:four-legged
(E) crab:crustacean

16. VACCINE:PREVENT :: (A) wound:heal
(B) victim:attend   (C) antidote:counteract
(D) diagnosis:cure   (E) antiseptic:infect

17. ANARCHY:GOVERNMENT ::
(A) penury:wealth
(B) chaos:disorder
(C) monarchy:republic
(D) verbosity:words
(E) ethics:philosophy

18. CIRCUITOUS:DIRECTNESS ::
(A) cautious:duplicity
(B) religious:faith
(C) faulty:impropriety
(D) inexact:accuracy
(E) sentimental:hypocrisy

19. IMPECUNIOUS:MONEY ..
(A) generous:charity
(B) impeccable:flaws
(C) honest:integrity
(D) bankrupt:industry
(E) mendacious:dreams

20. DELUGE:SHOWER :: (A) ecstasy:joy
(B) sophistication:naivete   (C) opinion:notion
(D) breeze:air   (E) inception:termination

21. ROBIN:NEST :: (A) animal:cave
(B) horse:stall   (C) alligator:swamp
(D) clam:shell   (E) rabbit:burrow

22. SILO:STORAGE :: (A) sanctuary:refuge
(B) oasis:mirage   (C) restaurant:corkage
(D) fine:damage   (E) butcher:carnage

23. TIRADE:ABUSIVE :: (A) diatribe:familial
(B) satire:pungent   (C) panegyric:laudatory
(D) eulogy:regretful   (E) elegy:religious

24. PRICK:STAB :: (A) point:thrust
(B) lend:borrow   (C) sip:gulp   (D) thread:sew
(E) push:shove

25. INTEREST:FASCINATE :: (A) vex:enrage
(B) vindicate:condemn   (C) regret:rue
(D) appall:bother   (E) weary:fatigue

26. INDUSTRIOUS:ASSIDUOUS ::
(A) affluent:impecunious
(B) mendacious:beggarly
(C) fortuitous:fortunate
(D) impoverished:poor
(E) impartial:biased

27. INDUSTRY:BEAVER ::
(A) ferocity:lion
(B) cowardice:tiger
(C) indolence:wolf
(D) forgetfulness:elephant
(E) pride:peacock

28. KANGAROO:MARSUPIAL :: (A) rose:hybrid
(B) antelope:gazelle   (C) bee:drone
(D) quail:bevy   (E) mushroom:fungus

29. HELMET:HEAD :: (A) insignia:office
(B) amulet:shoulder   (C) sceptre:crown
(D) gauntlet:hand   (E) planet:sun

30. VENISON:DEER :: (A) bison:cattle
(B) mutton:sheep   (C) mallard:duck
(D) antler:stag   (E) fawn:doe

31. SOLDIER:REGIMENT :: (A) colonel:martinet
(B) dancer:balletomane   (C) singer:chorus
(D) trooper:rifle   (E) student:professor

32. LIGHT YEAR:DISTANCE ::
(A) decibel:sound
(B) black hole:proximity
(C) meteor:intensity
(D) microphone:volume
(E) heat wave:brightness

33. DEBATER:LARYNGITIS ::
(A) actor:stage fright
(B) pedestrian:sprained ankle
(C) doctor:tonsilitis
(D) writer:thesis
(E) swimmer:aquacade

34. TEAM:ATHLETES ::
(A) games:series
(B) alliance:nations
(C) delegates:alternates
(D) congregation:preachers
(E) term:holidays

35. ENTREPRENEUR:PROFITS ::
(A) laborer:wages
(B) manager:employees
(C) moonlighter:debts
(D) arbitrator:complaints
(E) financier:mortgages

36. ANATHEMA:CURSE ::
(A) benediction:song
(B) admonition:reproach
(C) supposition:proof
(D) exhortation:flattery
(E) homage:disrespect

37. GUSTATORY:TASTE :: (A) kinesthetic:sight
(B) olfactory:smell   (C) hortatory:hearing
(D) myopic:vision   (E) palpable:touch

38. STUBBORN:MULISH :: (A) coy:kittenish
(B) fierce:doglike   (C) contrite:lionhearted
(D) devoted:sheepish   (E) glib:fishy

39. RUSE:DECEIVE :: (A) policy:change
(B) argument:persuade   (C) subterfuge:revenge
(D) strategy:gamble   (E) denial:confuse

40. DRAB:COLOR :: (A) resonant:sound
(B) insipid:flavor   (C) pungent:smell
(D) pert:liveliness   (E) dismal:size

41. RATTLE:COMPOSE :: (A) disperse:collect
(B) brush:touch   (C) spatter:spill
(D) crash:collide   (E) clatter:knock

42. LARIAT:COWBOY :: (A) rink:skater
(B) apron:chef   (C) oasis:nomad
(D) chariot:charioteer   (E) snare:trapper

43. PREAMBLE:CONSTITUTION ::
(A) amendment:bill
(B) prologue:play
(C) episode:serial
(D) by-line:article
(E) premonition:omen

44. DISBAND:ARMY :: (A) convene:assembly
(B) muster:platoon   (C) dissolve:corporation
(D) abandon:navy   (E) countermand:order

45. DETRITUS:GLACIER :: (A) thaw:snowfall
(B) snow:ice cap   (C) silt:river
(D) range:mountain   (E) foliage:tree

46. DECREPIT:RENOVATION ::
(A) enervated:invigoration
(B) languid:confrontation
(C) pallid:purification
(D) gullible:vehemence
(E) tearful:reconciliation

47. SILO:CORN :: (A) acre:wheat
(B) reservoir:water   (C) mill:grain
(D) paddy:rice   (E) furrow:seed

48. STATIC:MOVEMENT ::
(A) humdrum:excitement
(B) chronic:timeliness
(C) ecstatic:decay
(D) diligent:industry
(E) prestigious:wealth

49. SIDEREAL:STARS ::
    (A) ethereal:planets
    (B) central:earth
    (C) chimerical:matter
    (D) horticultural:plants
    (E) supernatural:heavens

50. DESCRY:DISTANT :: (A) mourn:lost
    (B) whisper:muted   (C) discern:subtle
     (D) destroy:flagrant   (E) entrap:hostile

Analogy Exercise B

Each question below consists of a related pair of words
or phrases, followed by five lettered pairs of words or
phrases. Select the lettered pair that best expresses a
relationship similar to that expressed in the original
pair.

Example:

YAWN : BOREDOM :: (A) dream : sleep
 (B) anger : madness   (C) smile : amusement
  (D) face : expression   (E) impatience : rebellion

                          Ⓐ Ⓑ ● Ⓓ Ⓔ

1. TELLER:BANK :: (A) artist:museum
   (B) cashier:check   (C) waiter:restaurant
    (D) borrower:loan   (E) mourner:funeral

2. INNING:BASEBALL :: (A) round:boxing
   (B) puck:hockey   (C) touchdown:football
    (D) serve:tennis   (E) outing:hiking

3. DEGREE:TEMPERATURE :: (A) ounce:weight
   (B) fathom:volume   (C) mass:energy
    (D) time:length   (E) light:heat

4. PICK:GUITAR :: (A) peg:ukelele
   (B) string:banjo   (C) pipe:organ
    (D) bow:violin   (E) head:tambourine

5. FRAGILE:BREAK :: (A) vital:destroy
   (B) hostile:invite   (C) vivid:grow
    (D) flexible:bend   (E) fertile:smell

6. SPOKE:WHEEL :: (A) square:circle
   (B) balance:lever   (C) door:latch
    (D) book:shelf   (E) rung:ladder

7. VESSEL:FLEET :: (A) wolf:pack
   (B) forest:clearing   (C) vehicle:truck
    (D) carriage:horse   (E) squadron:rank

8. PICADOR:BULL :: (A) heckler:speaker
   (B) executioner:victim   (C) shepherd:sheep
    (D) singer:song   (E) matador:cow

9. CORPULENCE:STOUT ::
   (A) baldness:hirsute
   (B) erudition:learned
   (C) gauntness:beautiful
   (D) steadfastness:mercurial
   (E) competence:strict

10. ASYLUM:SHELTER ::
    (A) harbor:concealment
    (B) palisade:display
    (C) stronghold:defense
    (D) hospice:exile
    (E) cloister:storage

11. MOTION PICTURE:SCENARIO ::
    (A) drama:setting
    (B) play:plot
    (C) theater:program
    (D) ballet:pirouette
    (E) recital:review

12. MILDEW:DANKNESS ::
    (A) gangrene:infection
    (B) dew:sunshine
    (C) dawn:darkness
    (D) canker:blossom
    (E) rust:hardness

13. CALLOW:MATURITY ::
    (A) fallow:productivity
    (B) crusty:incivility
    (C) eager:anxiety
    (D) spoiled:common sense
    (E) callous:growth

14. ENIGMA:PUZZLING ::
    (A) dilemma:compelling
    (B) labyrinth:disorienting
    (C) sphinx:massive
    (D) riddle:humorous
    (E) maze:extensive

15. KERNEL:CORN :: (A) neck:bottle
    (B) eye:storm   (C) grain:wheat
     (D) stem:carrot   (E) nose:bouquet

16. FLABBY:FIRMNESS ::
    (A) definite:accuracy
    (B) tired:fatigue
    (C) solvent:wealth
    (D) defiant:strength
    (E) humble:arrogance

17. ARCHIPELAGO:ISLAND ::
    (A) peninsula:strait
    (B) cluster:star
    (C) border:nation
    (D) nucleus:atom
    (E) skyscraper:building

18. HOBBLE:WALK :: (A) gallop:run
(B) stammer:speak   (C) stumble:fall
(D) sniff:smell   (E) amble:stroll

19. EXUBERANT:DOWNCAST ::
(A) exiled:overthrown
(B) extravagant:lavish
(C) effusive:undemonstrative
(D) parsimonious:eager
(E) formidable:dismal

20. MINISTER:SERMON ::
(A) politician:promises
(B) heckler:interruptions
(C) doctor:diagnosis
(D) lecturer:speech
(E) curator:museum

21. HOBNOB:COMPANIONS ::
(A) conspire:plotters
(B) kowtow:servants
(C) blackmail:police
(D) kidnap:victims
(E) quarrel:friends

22. GOURMET:DELICACY ::
(A) clairvoyant:seance
(B) connoisseur:masterpiece
(C) socialite:seclusion
(D) commoner:aristocracy
(E) chef:scullery

23. INADVERTENT:THOUGHT ::
(A) gauche:grace
(B) clandestine:secrecy
(C) lugubrious:gloom
(D) wealthy:money
(E) curious:opinion

24. GAGGLE:GEESE :: (A) coop:chickens
(B) muzzle:dogs   (C) gill:fish   (D) swarm:bees
(E) waddle:ducks

25. UNICORN:CHASTITY ::
(A) sea serpent:invulnerability
(B) centaur:mortality
(C) sphinx:mystery
(D) dragon:swiftness
(E) phoenix:loyalty

26. UNEMPLOYED:WORKER ::
(A) unknown:artist
(B) fallow:field
(C) renovated:house
(D) observant:spectator
(E) unconscious:sleeper

27. DISCONSOLATE:GRIEF ::
(A) fatuous:weight
(B) incurable:disease
(C) explicit:statement
(D) perfunctory:sympathy
(E) solitary:confinement

28. CATCALL:DERISION ::
(A) wolf whistle:admiration
(B) horselaugh:dismay
(C) snort:approval
(D) mutter:indifference
(E) sputter:sympathy

29. CRACK:CIPHER :: (A) break:platter
(B) divide:number   (C) strike:hammer
(D) unriddle:mystery   (E) detonate:revolver

30. PAN:CAMERA :: (A) ban:book
(B) tune:radio   (C) charge:battery
(D) filter:lens   (E) rotate:periscope

31. HAIR:SCALP :: (A) dimple:cheek
(B) elbow:knee   (C) tooth:gum
(D) beard:moustache   (E) waist:torso

32. BUSTLE:MOVE :: (A) hum:sing
(B) shuffle:walk (C) lope:run (D) glide:dance
(E) chatter:talk

33. TOLERANCE:BIGOTRY ::
(A) prodigality:ribaldry
(B) magnanimity:parsimony
(C) exigency:urgency
(D) emulation:rivalry
(E) patience:conformity

34. BUNGLER:COMPETENCE ::
(A) beggar:influence
(B) jester:wit
(C) meddler:patience
(D) grumbler:satisfaction
(E) cobbler:leather

35. ABHOR:DISLIKE :: (A) calcify:petrify
(B) torture:discomfort   (C) rebuke:ridicule
(D) admire:disdain   (E) magnify:enlarge

36. BULLY:BLUSTER ::
(A) coward:rant
(B) charlatan:snivel
(C) cutthroat:mutter
(D) stool pigeon:squeal
(E) blackguard:cringe

37. CARESS:AFFECTION ::
(A) curtsy:respect
(B) salute:admiration
(C) handshake:indifference
(D) wink:suspicion
(E) wave:agitation

38. FOOLHARDY:CAUTION ::
(A) hardhearted:fear
(B) careworn:anxiety
(C) high-strung:tension
(D) thick-skinned:sensitivity
(E) spendthrift:resource

39. VERTEX:CONE :: (A) perimeter:rectangle
(B) whirlpool:pond   (C) pod:seed
(D) peak:mountain   (E) step:staircase

40. GEOLOGIST:FELDSPAR ::
    (A) meteorologist:orbit
    (B) botanist:zinnia
    (C) architect:monolith
    (D) cosmetologist:space
    (E) philanthropist:stamp

41. FELON:PENITENTIARY ::
    (A) perjurer:perjury
    (B) conniver:constabulary
    (C) malefactor:sanctuary
    (D) juvenile delinquent:reformatory
    (E) hedonist:confessional

42. TRAVELER:ITINERARY ::
    (A) tourist:vacation
    (B) lecturer:outline
    (C) pedestrian:routine
    (D) explorer:safari
    (E) soldier:furlough

43. AERIE:EAGLE :: (A) hawk:falcon
    (B) viper:reptile   (C) venom:rattlesnake
    (D) lair:wolf   (E) fang:adder

44. IMPROMPTU:REHEARSAL ::
    (A) practiced:technique
    (B) makeshift:whim
    (C) offhand:premeditation
    (D) glib:fluency
    (E) numerical:calculation

45. EVANESCENT:VANISH ::
    (A) volatile:vaporize
    (B) incandescent:flee
    (C) ethereal:drift
    (D) celestial:disappear
    (E) transient:gravitate

46. ELISION:SYLLABLES ::
    (A) contraction:letters
    (B) thesis:ideas
    (C) diagnosis:symptoms
    (D) almanac:facts
    (E) abacus:numbers

47. STICKLER:INSIST ::
    (A) mumbler:enunciate
    (B) trickster:risk
    (C) haggler:concede
    (D) laggard:outlast
    (E) braggart:boast

48. PLUMAGE:BIRD :: (A) foliage:horse
    (B) fleece:sheep   (C) forage:cattle
    (D) hive:bee   (E) carnage:beast

49. TRUNCATE:PYRAMID ::
    (A) excavate:ruin
    (B) ignite:fire
    (C) consecrate:church
    (D) erect:statue
    (E) behead:man

50. ABOLITIONIST:SLAVERY ::
    (A) capitalist:commerce
    (B) militarist:war
    (C) pugilist:victory
    (D) conservationist:wildlife
    (E) prohibitionist:liquor

Answer Key
Analogy Exercise A

1.	B	11.	C	21.	E	31.	C	41.	A
2.	B	12.	A	22.	A	32.	A	42.	E
3.	E	13.	D	23.	C	33.	B	43.	B
4.	D	14.	A	24.	C	34.	B	44.	C
5.	C	15.	C	25.	A	35.	A	45.	C
6.	D	16.	C	26.	D	36.	B	46.	A
7.	A	17.	A	27.	E	37.	B	47.	B
8.	C	18.	D	28.	E	38.	A	48.	A
9.	B	19.	B	29.	D	39.	B	49.	D
10.	E	20.	A	30.	B	40.	B	50.	C

Analogy Exercise B

1.	C	11.	B	21.	A	31.	C	41.	D
2.	A	12.	A	22.	B	32.	E	42.	B
3.	A	13.	A	23.	A	33.	B	43.	D
4.	D	14.	B	24.	D	34.	D	44.	C
5.	D	15.	C	25.	C	35.	B	45.	A
6.	E	16.	E	26.	B	36.	D	46.	A
7.	A	17.	B	27.	B	37.	A	47.	E
8.	A	18.	B	28.	A	38.	D	48.	B
9.	B	19.	C	29.	D	39.	D	49.	E
10.	C	20.	D	30.	E	40.	B	50.	E

Answer Explanations

Analogy Exercise A

1. B. A *trout* is a kind of *fish*. A *whale* is a kind of *mammal*.

    (Class and Member)

2. B. The body of a *fish* is covered with *scales*. The body of a *bird* is covered with *feathers*.

    (Defining Characteristic)

3. E. A *school* is a group of *fish*. A *pride* is a group of *lions*.

    (Part to Whole)

4. D. A *clock* measures *time*. A *yardstick* measures *distance*.

    (Function)

5. C. A *doctor* attempts to treat a *disease*. A *psychiatrist* attempts to treat a *maladjustment*.

    (Function)

6. D. *Scissors* by definition cut or *sever*. A *millstone* by definition *grinds*.

    (Tool and Action)

7. A. One *hones* or sharpens something to make it sharp. One *polishes* something to make it *shiny*.

    (Cause and Effect)

8. C. A *patron* by definition provides patronage or support. A *counselor* by definition provides *advice*.

    (Defining Characteristic)

9. B. *Light* that is *dimmed* is lessened in brightness. *Sound* that is *muffled* is lessened in volume.

    (Manner)

10. E. A *stethoscope* is the tool of a *physician*. A *transit* (measuring instrument) is the tool of a *surveyor*.

    (Worker and Tool)

11. C. Someone *dauntless* (unable to be frightened) possesses *courage*. Someone *unruffled* (not flustered) possesses *composure* (poise).

    (Synonym Variant)

12. A. A *cumulonimbus* is a kind of *cloud*. A *grasshopper* is a kind of *insect*.

    (Class and Member)

13. D. A *bay* is an inlet, part of an *ocean* or sea that projects out into the land. A *peninsula* is a point of land, part of a *continent* that projects out into the water.

    (Part to Whole)

14. A. Someone *intrepid* (brave) shows *valor* (bravery). Someone *clever* shows *ingenuity* (cleverness).

    (Synonym Variant)

15. C. A *leopard* is a *carnivorous* (meat-eating) animal. A *cow* is a *herbivorous* (grass-eating) animal.

    (Defining Characteristic)

16. C. A *vaccine's* purpose is to *prevent* the harmful development of disease-causing microorganisms. An *antidote's* purpose is to *counteract* the harmful effects of poison.

    (Function)

17. A. *Anarchy* is the absence of *government*. *Penury* (poverty) is the absence of *wealth*.

    (Antonyms)

18. D. Something *circuitous* (roundabout) is lacking in *directness*. Something *inexact* (inaccurate) is lacking in *accuracy*.

(Antonym Variant)

19. B. *Impecunious* (impoverished) means without *money*. *Impeccable* (flawless) means without *flaws*.

(Antonym Variant)

20. A. A *deluge* (flood; drenching rainburst) is more intense than a *shower*. *Ecstasy* (rapture) is more intense than *joy*.

(Degree of Intensity)

21. E. A *robin* constructs a *nest* to live in. A *rabbit* digs out a *burrow* to live in.

(Defining Characteristic)

22. A. The function of a *silo* is to provide *storage* space. The function of a *sanctuary* is to provide *refuge* or shelter.

(Function)

23. C. A *tirade* (bitter, condemnatory speech) is by definition *abusive*. A *panegyric* (speech of praise) is by definition *laudatory*.

(Defining Characteristic)

24. C. To *prick* someone is not as extreme as to *stab* him. To *sip* something is not as extreme as to *gulp* it.

(Degree of Intensity)

25. A. To *fascinate* (interest strongly) is more intense than merely to *interest*. To *enrage* (anger deeply) is more intense than merely to *vex* (annoy).

(Degree of Intensity)

26. D. *Industrious* (hard-working) and *assiduous* are synonyms. *Impoverished* and *poor* are synonyms also.

(Synonyms)

27. E. The *beaver* is a symbol of *industry* ("busy as a beaver"). The *peacock* is a symbol of *pride* ("proud as a peacock").

(Symbol and Abstraction It Represents)

28. E. A *kangaroo* is a kind of *marsupial*. A *mushroom* is a kind of *fungus*.

(Class and Member)

29. D. A *helmet* protects the *head*. A *gauntlet* (armored glove) protects the *hand*.

(Function)

30. B. *Venison* is the meat of a deer. *Mutton* is the meat of a *sheep*.

(Defining Characteristic)

31. C. A *soldier* is part of a *regiment* (military unit). A *singer* is part of a *chorus*.

(Part to Whole)

32. A. A *light year* is a measure of *distance*. A *decibel* is a measure of *sound*.

(Function)

33. B. *Laryngitis* is a physical ailment that could prevent a *debater* (public speaker) from functioning. A *sprained ankle* is a physical ailment that could prevent a *pedestrian* (walker) from functioning.

(Function)

34. B. A *team* is made up of *athletes*. An *alliance* is made up of *nations*.

(Part to Whole)

35. A. An *entrepreneur* (organizer of a business) works for *profits*. A *laborer* works for *wages*.

(Person and Objective)

36. B. An *anathema* is a *curse*. An *admonition* is a *reproach* or scolding.

(Synonyms)

37. B. *Gustatory* by definition means related to the sense of *taste*. *Olfactory* by definition means related to the sense of *smell*.

(Defining Characteristic)

38. A. *Stubborn* and *mulish* are synonyms. *Coy* (flirtatious; artfully shy) and *kittenish* are synonyms.

(Synonyms)

39. B. The purpose of a *ruse* (trick or stratagem) is to *deceive*. The purpose of an *argument* is to *persuade*.

(Function)

40. B. *Drab* (dull, colorless) means lacking in *color*. *Insipid* (bland) means lacking in *flavor*.

(Antonym Variant)

41. A.   To *rattle* or fluster is the opposite of to *compose* or calm. To *disperse* or scatter is the opposite of to gather or *collect*.

(Antonyms)

42. E.   A *lariat* or lasso is a tool a *cowboy* uses to catch animals. Similarly, a *snare* is a tool a *trapper* uses to catch animals.

(Worker and Tool)

43. B.   A *preamble* or preface introduces a *constitution*. A *prologue* or introduction introduces a *play*.

(Part to Whole)

44. C.   To break up an *army* is to *disband* it. To break up a *corporation* is to *dissolve* it.

(Function)

45. C.   *Detritus* is disintegrated debris found deposited in the path of a *glacier*. *Silt* is disintegrated rock particles found deposited in the path of a *river*.

(Defining Characteristic)

46. A.   Something *decrepit* (worn out; broken down) needs *renovation*. Someone *enervated* (exhausted; tired out) needs *invigoration*.

(Antonym Variant)

47. B.   A *silo* is built to store or hold *corn* or grain. A *reservoir* is built to store or hold *water*.

(Function)

48. A.   Something *static* (unmoving) lacks *movement*. Something *humdrum* (dull) lacks *excitement*.

(Antonym Variant)

49. D.   *Sidereal* means pertaining to the *stars*. *Horticultural* means pertaining to the cultivation of *plants*.

(Defining Characteristic)

50. C.   To *descry* something is to make out or see something that is *distant*. To *discern* something is to make out or see something that is *subtle*.

(Defining Characteristic)

Analogy Exercise B

1. C.   A *teller* works in a *bank*. A *waiter* works in a *restaurant*.

(Worker and Workplace)

2. A.   An *inning* is a division of a *baseball* game. A *round* is a division of a *boxing* match.

(Part to Whole)

3. A.   A *degree* is a measure of *temperature*. An *ounce* is a measure of *weight*.

(Function)

4. D.   A *pick* is a device used to pluck or sound the strings of a *guitar*. A *bow* is an instrument used to play or sound the strings of a *violin*.

(Function)

5. D.   Something *fragile* or delicate is able to *break*. Something *flexible* is able to *bend*.

(Definition)

6. E.   A *spoke* is part of a *wheel*. A *rung* is part of a *ladder*.

(Part to Whole)

7. A.   A *fleet* is made up of *vessels*. A *pack* is made up of *wolves*.

(Part to Whole)

8. A.   A *picador* physically jabs at a *bull* to annoy it. A *heckler* verbally jabs at a *speaker* to annoy him.

(Function)

9. B.   *Corpulence* (fatness) is the state of being *stout*. *Erudition* (scholarliness) is the state of being knowledgeable or *learned*.

(Synonym Variant)

10. C.   An *asylum* provides refuge or *shelter*. A *stronghold* or fortress provides *defense*.

(Function)

11. B.   A *scenario* is the story line of a *motion picture*. A *plot* is the story line of a *play*.

(Defining Characteristic)

12. A.   *Dankness* or dampness leads to *mildew* (spreading discoloration, as of fabric). *Infection* leads to *gangrene* (spreading tissue rot).

(Cause and Effect)

13. A.   A *callow* (immature) person is lacking in *maturity*. A *fallow* (uncultivated) field is lacking in *productivity*.

(Antonym Variant)

14. B. An *enigma* or puzzle is by definition *puzzling*. A *labyrinth* or maze is by definition *disorienting*.

(Defining Characteristic)

15. C. A *kernel* is a seed of *corn*. A *grain* is a seed of *wheat*.

(Defining Characteristic)

16. E. *Flabby* means lacking *firmness*. *Humble* means lacking *arrogance*; modest.

(Antonym Variant)

17. B. An *archipelago* is a group of *islands*. A *cluster* is a group of *stars*.

(Part to Whole)

18. B. To *hobble* is to *walk* laboriously and with difficulty. To *stammer* is to *speak* laboriously and with difficulty.

(Manner)

19. C. *Exuberant* or extremely high-spirited is the opposite of *downcast*. *Effusive* or emotionally unrestrained is the opposite of *undemonstrative*.

(Antonyms)

20. D. A *sermon* is a religious discourse delivered by a *minister*. A *speech* is a formal discourse delivered by a *lecturer*.

(Defining Characteristic)

21. A. *Companions* by definition socialize or *hobnob* with one another. *Plotters* by definition conspire or scheme with one another.

(Definition)

22. B. A *gourmet* is an appreciator and judge of food *delicacies*. A *connoisseur* is an appreciator and judge of *masterpieces* of art.

(Defining Characteristic)

23. A. Something *inadvertent* or unintentional is lacking in *thought*. Something *gauche* or clumsy is lacking in *grace*.

(Antonym Variant)

24. D. A *gaggle* is a group of *geese*. A *swarm* is a group of *bees*.

(Part to Whole)

25. C. A *unicorn* is a mythological creature that symbolizes or represents *chastity* (purity). A *sphinx* is a mythological creature that symbolizes or represents *mystery*.

(Symbol and Abstraction It Represents)

26. B. A *worker* that is *unemployed* by definition is not being productive. A *field* that is *fallow* (uncultivated) by definition is not being productive.

(Function)

27. B. A *grief* that is *disconsolate* is not able to be eased or consoled. A *disease* that is *incurable* is not able to be cured.

(Manner)

28. A. A *catcall* expresses *derision* or disapproval. A *wolf whistle* expresses *admiration*.

(Action and Its Significance)

29. D. To *crack* a *cipher* (code) is to solve or decode it. To *unriddle* a *mystery* is to puzzle it out or solve it.

(Function)

30. E. To *pan* a *camera* is to rotate it to get a comprehensive view. To *rotate* a *periscope* is to turn it to get a comprehensive view.

(Function)

31. C. *Hair* grows from the *scalp*. A *tooth* grows from the *gum*.

(Defining Characteristic)

32. E. To *bustle* is to *move* in a hurried manner, with more fuss than productivity. To *chatter* is to *talk* in a hurried manner, with more sound than sense.

(Manner)

33. B. *Tolerance* is the opposite of prejudice or bigotry. *Magnanimity* (greatness of spirit; generosity) is the opposite of *parsimony* or stinginess.

(Antonyms)

34. D. A *bungler* (fumbler; person who botches things) lacks *competence* or skill. A *grumbler* (complainer) lacks contentment or *satisfaction*.

(Antonym Variant)

35. B. To *abhor* (greatly hate) someone is more intense than to *dislike* him. To *torture* someone is more intense than merely to *discomfort* or disturb him.

(Degree of Intensity)

36. D.   A *bully* by definition is someone who *blusters* or storms around uttering threats. A *stool pigeon* (informer or tattletale) by definition is someone who *squeals*.

(Definition)

37. A.   A *caress* or embrace is a sign of *affection*. A *curtsy* is a sign of politeness or *respect*.

(Action and Its Significance)

38. D.   Someone *foolhardy* (rash, unthinking) lacks *caution*. Someone *thick-skinned* lacks *sensitivity*.

(Antonym Variant)

39. D.   The *vertex* is defined as the top part of a *cone*. A *peak* is defined as the top part of a *mountain*.

(Part to Whole)

40. B.   A *geologist* studies rocks; *feldspar* is a kind of rock. A *botanist* studies plants; a *zinnia* is a kind of plant.

(Defining Characteristic)

41. D.   A *felon* (major offender) is confined in a *penitentiary*. A *juvenile delinquent* (youthful offender) is confined in a *reformatory*.

(Function)

42. B.   A *traveler* follows an *itinerary* (plan of a journey). A *lecturer* follows an *outline* (lecture plan).

(Defining Characteristic)

43. D.   An *aerie* is the resting place of an *eagle*. A *lair* is the resting place of a *wolf*.

(Function)

44. C.   Something *impromptu* or improvised is performed without *rehearsal*. Something *offhand* is said or done without *premeditation* or advance thought.

(Antonym Variant)

45. A.   Something *evanescent* tends to *vanish* or disappear. Something *volatile* tends to *vaporize* or evaporate.

(Definition)

46. A.   *Elision* is the omission of *syllables* from spoken words. *Contraction* is the omission of *letters* from written words.

(Defining Characteristic)

47. E.   A *stickler* (person who insists on something) by definition *insists*. A *braggart* (boaster) by definition *boasts*.

(Definition)

48. B.   A *bird's plumage* is its feathery outer covering. A *sheep's fleece* is its wooly outer covering.

(Defining Characteristic)

49. E.   To *truncate* a *pyramid* is to cut its top off. To *behead* a *man* is to cut his head off.

(Function)

50. E.   An *abolitionist* is a person who seeks to put an end to the practice of *slavery*. A *prohibitionist* is a person who seeks to put an end to the use of hard *liquor*.

(Defining Characteristic)

7 The Sentence Completion Question

- ■ **Testing Tactics**
- ■ **Long-Range Strategies**
- ■ **Practice Exercises**
- ■ **Answer Key**

The sentence completion questions ask you to choose the best way to complete a sentence from which one or two words have been omitted. These questions test a combination of reading comprehension skills and vocabulary. You must be able to recognize the logic, style, and tone of the sentence, so that you will be able to choose the answer that makes sense in this context. You must also be able to recognize the way words are normally used. Once you understand the implications of the sentence, you should be able to choose the answer that will make the sentence clear, logical, and stylistically consistent.

The sentences cover a wide variety of topics of the sort you have probably encountered in your general reading. However, this is not a test of your general knowledge. You may feel more comfortable if you are familiar with the topic the sentence is discussing, but you should be able to handle any of the sentences using your understanding of the English language.

Here are the directions for the sentence completion questions just as they will appear on the actual SAT when you take it. Learn them now. They won't change, and the test time you would spend reading the directions can be better spent answering questions.

Each sentence below has one or two blanks, each blank indicating that something has been omitted. Beneath the sentence are five lettered words or sets of words. Choose the word or set of words that best fits the meaning of the sentence as a whole.

Example:

Although its publicity has been ----, the film itself is intelligent, well-acted, handsomely produced, and altogether ----.

(A) tasteless..respectable (B) extensive..moderate
(C) sophisticated..amateur (D) risqué..crude
(E) perfect..spectacular

● Ⓑ Ⓒ Ⓓ Ⓔ

The word *although* is a signal word: it suggests that the film's publicity contrasts with the film itself. The main clause describes the film in positive, even glowing terms: "intelligent, well-acted, handsomely produced." The film is well done. Therefore, the film's publicity must be poorly done.

You are looking for two words more or less opposite in meaning. The first, describing the publicity, must be negative; the second, summing up the film as intelligent, well-acted, etc., must be positive.

A quick glance at the first words in each of the answer choices reveals two negative terms: (A) *tasteless*, and (D) *risqué*. Since *crude*, the second half of Choice D, is not positive, it is an unlikely word to describe this ''intelligent, well-acted . . .'' film. Eliminate Choice D; Choice A is correct.

Now that you know what to expect on sentence completion questions, work through the following tactics and learn to spot the signals that will help you fill in the blanks. Then do the practice exercises at the end of the chapter.

Testing Tactics

Before You Look at the Choices, Read the Sentence and Think of a Word That Makes Sense.

Your problem here is to find a word that best completes the sentence's thought. Before you look at the answer choices, see if you can come up with a word that makes logical sense in this context. Then look at all five choices supplied by the SAT-makers. If the word you thought of is one of your five choices, select it as your answer. If the word you thought of is *not* one of your five choices, look for a synonym of that word. Select the synonym as your answer.

See how the process works in two examples from recent SATs.

> The instructor added the restriction that all projects had to be ----; no student could research an area that had been investigated previously by anyone else.

Note how the part of the sentence following the semicolon (the second clause, in technical terms) is being used to define or clarify what the instructor means by the rule. What words does this suggest to you? *Original*, certainly, or *uncopied*. Either of these words could complete the sentence's thought.

Here are the five choices provided by the SAT:

> (A) acceptable   (B) useful   (C) extensive
> (D) authoritative   (E) original

The answer clearly is *original*, Choice E.

See how the same principle works in a harder question from a different SAT.

> Of all the phases of filmmaking, screenwriting is the most ----; it is a rare instance when only one person is responsible for a script.

If more than one person works on a script, what does this suggest to you? Screenwriting is not a solo operation; it is *cooperative*.

Now turn to the answers, looking for *cooperative* or a synonym.

> (A) prolific   (B) collaborative   (C) substantive
> (D) impassioned   (E) illustrious

Choice B, *collaborative*, should jump right out at you. To collaborate is to work together, to cooperate. The correct answer is Choice B.

Look At All the Possible Answers Before You Make Your Final Choice.

You are looking for the word that *best* fits the meaning of the sentence as a whole. In order to be sure you have not been hasty in making your decision, substitute all the answer choices for the missing word. Don't spend a lot of time doing this, but do try them all. That way you can satisfy yourself that you have come up with the answer that best fits.

Take, for example, this typical SAT question.

> Physical laws do not, of course, in themselves force bodies to behave in a certain way, but merely ---- how, as a matter of fact, they do behave.
>
> (A) determine   (B) preclude   (C) counteract
> (D) describe   (E) commend

A hasty reader might be content with Choice A, *determine*, but *determine* doesn't really work. However, there are reasons for its appeal.

Determine can be a synonym for *find out* or *discover*. It's a word you may have come across in science classes in discussions about experiments. "By flying a kite during a lightning storm, Benjamin Franklin tried to *determine* just how lightning worked."

Because you have seen *determine* previously in a scientific context, you may be tempted to select it as your answer without thinking the sentence through. But you must take the time to think the

sentence through, to figure out what it is talking about. Here it's talking about physical laws. But do physical laws discover or find out things about how bodies behave? No. *People* discover things about how bodies behave. Then to describe what they have discovered, people write down physical laws. The correct answer for this question is Choice D, *describe*.

In a sense, *determine* is an eye-catcher. To avoid being caught by such eye-catchers among the answer choices, make sure you think through the sentence carefully and consider every answer choice.

Tactic 3: In Double-Blank Sentences, Go Through the Answers, Testing the *First* Word in Each Choice (and Eliminating Those That Don't Fit).

In a sentence completion question with two blanks, read through the entire sentence. Then insert the first word of each answer pair in the sentence's first blank. Ask yourself whether this particular word makes sense in this blank. If the initial word of an answer pair makes no sense in the sentence, you can eliminate that answer pair.

Try this example from an actual SAT to see how this tactic works.

> Chameleons, since they move quickly and adopt the color of their surroundings, are so difficult to ---- that even a careful observer can ---- their presence.
>
> (A) eradicate..notice   (B) detect..overlook
>   (C) ignore..misjudge   (D) discern..recognize
>   (E) miss..deduce

If you test the first word in each choice, you can eliminate several choices. Chameleons change color to blend in with their surroundings. Therefore, they would be hard to see; in other words, not difficult but easy to ignore or miss. You can definitely eliminate Choices C and E.

Having eliminated Choices C and E, turn to the second blank. *Even* intensifies the meaning of the phrase "a careful observer." They are so hard to see that an *extremely* careful observer can miss them. In other words, they are so hard to *detect* that even someone who looks closely can *overlook* them. The correct answer is Choice B.

Remember, in double-blank sentences, the right answer must correctly fill *both* blanks. A wrong answer choice often includes one correct and one incorrect answer. Always test the second word.

Tactic 4: Use Your Knowledge of Word Parts and Context Clues to Get at the Meanings of Unfamiliar Words.

If a word used by the author is unfamiliar, or if an answer choice is unknown to you, look at its context in the sentence to see whether the context provides a clue to the meaning of the word. Often authors will use an unfamiliar word and then immediately define it within the same sentence. For example:

> The discussions were often ----, degenerating at times into name-calling contests.
>
> (A) lofty   (B) auspicious   (C) acrimonious
>   (D) lethargic   (E) pragmatic

Looking at the five answer choices, you may feel unequipped to try to tackle the sentence at all. However, the phrase that immediately follows the blank ("degenerating . . . into name-calling contests"—the group of words set off by the comma) is there to explain and clarify that missing word. The two groups of words are juxtaposed—set beside one another—to make their relationship clear. The missing word has something to do with name-calling; the discussions have turned nasty and mean.

Now that you know the missing word's general meaning, go through the answer choices to see which one makes sense. *Lofty* means elevated or on a high plane. These talks were on a much lower level; you can eliminate Choice A. *Auspicious* (as in "an auspicious occasion") means favorable, promising success; you can eliminate Choice B. *Acrimonious* means bitter or stinging; Choice C seems likely, but check the other answers anyway. *Lethargic* means sluggish, drowsy; you can eliminate Choice D. *Pragmatic* means practical, realistic; you can

eliminate Choice E. The correct answer is *acrimonious*, Choice C.

Note that your knowledge of word parts could have helped you arrive at the correct answer here. *Acri-* means sharp, sour, or bitter—think of "an acrid taste." Break down unfamiliar words like *acrimonious* into their recognizable parts.

Watch for Signal Words That Link One Part of the Sentence to Another.

Writers use transitions to link their ideas logically. These transitions or signal words are clues that can help you figure out what the sentence actually means.

Contrast Signals

Look for words or phrases that indicate a contrast between one idea and another. In such cases an antonym or near-antonym for another word in the sentence should provide the correct answer.

Signal Words

although	instead of
but	nevertheless
despite	on the contrary
even though	on the other hand
however	rather than
in contrast	still
in spite of	yet

See how a contrast signal works in an easy question from a recent SAT.

> Medieval kingdoms did not become constitutional republics overnight; on the contrary, the change was ----.
>
> (A) unpopular   (B) unexpected
>   (C) advantageous   (D) sufficient   (E) gradual

On the contrary sets up a contrast between a hypothetical change and the actual one. Instead of happening *overnight*, it takes time; it is *gradual*. The correct answer is Choice E, *gradual*.

Support Signals

Look for words or phrases that indicate that the omitted portion of the sentence supports or continues a thought developed elsewhere in the sentence. In such cases, a synonym or near-synonym for another word in the sentence should provide the correct answer.

Signal Words

additionally	furthermore
also	in addition
and	likewise
besides	moreover

See how *and* works as a support signal in the following SAT question.

> Ms. Wilton urged patience and ---- in dealing with the protesters rather than the unyielding attitude the administration had adopted.
>
> (A) obstinacy   (B) desperation   (C) arrogance
>   (D) compromise   (E) retaliation

The presence of *and* linking two items in a series indicates that the missing word may be a synonym or near-synonym for the other linked word. In this case, *compromise* (agreement reached by mutual concessions) is similar in meaning to *patience*. The correct answer is Choice D.

Note, by the way, that the missing word, like *patience*, must be a word with positive associations. Therefore, you can eliminate any word with negative ones. Choices A, B, C, and E all have negative associations. Only Choice D can be correct.

Cause and Effect Signals

Look for words or phrases that indicate that one thing causes another.

Signal Words

accordingly	in order to
because	so...that
consequently	therefore
for	thus
hence	when...then

See how a cause and effect signal works in a question from a recent SAT.

> Because even the briefest period of idleness bored and exasperated her, she worked ---- at some project or activity.
>
> (A) constantly   (B) reluctantly
>   (C) occasionally   (D) cynically   (E) languidly

Because sets up a relationship of cause and effect. What is the effect of her being bothered by "even the briefest" period of inactivity? She chooses to work nonstop or *constantly*. The correct answer is Choice A.

Long-Range Strategies

Although you certainly will wish to consult "Build Your Vocabulary," Chapter 9, and work on the vocabulary development methods there, answering sentence completion questions involves more than recognizing individual words. You need to know idiomatic expressions—groups of words always used together—those used so frequently in formal prose that they seem to be clichés. Similarly, you need to know the typical patterns that writers follow in developing their thoughts.

Idiomatic Expressions and Clichés

In their general tips for answering sentence completion questions, the SAT-makers say, "Don't select an answer simply because it is a popular cliché or 'sounds good.'" The key word here is *simply*. If an answer is a popular cliché, it may well be right. *Don't* disregard an answer just because it's a cliché.

If you look at the answers to the sentence completion questions in *10 SATs* and *5 SATs*, the College Board's own publications, you will swiftly discover a high proportion of the correct answers are, in fact, clichés—set phrases an experienced reader will find extremely familiar. Consider, for example, phrases such as *avert disaster, cavalier treatment, render unnecessary, overt acts*. The more formal prose you read, the more you will encounter set phrases such as these.

Sentence Patterns
Definitions

In a definition, the author restates a word or phrase to clarify its meaning. The author commonly will set the definition beside the word being defined, juxtaposing them. Commas, hyphens, and parentheses are used to signal definitions.

1. The *rebec*, a medieval stringed instrument played with a bow, has only three strings.
2. *Paleontologists*—students of fossil remains—explore the earth's history.
3. Most mammals are *quadrupeds* (four-footed animals).

Definitions also follow forms of the verb "to be" and other connecting verbs.

1. A *stoic* **is** a person who is indifferent to pleasure or pain.
2. A three-pronged spear **is called** a *trident*.

Often an unfamiliar word in one clause of a sentence will be defined in the sentence's other clause.

1. That Barbie doll is a *lethal* weapon; your daughter nearly killed me with it!
2. The early morning dew had frozen, and everything was covered with a thin coat of *rime*.

Examples

By presenting specific, concrete examples, an author makes a general, abstract word come to life.

1. Crates of coins, paintings by Rubens and Renoir, diamond tiaras and rings of rubies and gold—I never realized the extent of President Marcos' *affluence* until I read the accounts of what he brought with him from the Philippines.
2. Cowards, we use *euphemisms* when we cannot bear the truth, calling our dead "the dear departed," as if they have just left the room.
3. I'm impressed by Trudy's business *acumen*: she buys sound but aging houses, renovates them relatively inexpensively, and then rents them out for fabulous sums.

Comparisons

Just as concrete examples make abstract words come to life, in the same way the use of a familiar object in a comparison can bring home the meaning of an unfamiliar word or phrase.

1. Some *circumstantial evidence* is very strong, as when you find a trout in the milk. — Thoreau.
2. Our impact on this world is as *evanescent* as a skywriter's impact on the sky.

Contrasts

You can learn a great deal about what something *is* if you come to terms with what it *is not*. Notice the signal words at work in the sentences that follow.

1. **Although** America's total Vietnamese population is *minuscule*, the number of Vietnamese students attending major American universities is surprisingly high.
2. Marriage has many pains, **but** *celibacy* has no pleasures. — Johnson.
3. **In place of** *complacency*, I give you unrest; in place of sameness I give you variety.

Often a writer contrasts two ideas without using a signal word. The contrast is implicit in the juxtaposition of the two clauses.

1. The *optimist* proclaims that we live in the best of all possible worlds; the *pessimist* fears this is true. — Cabell.

2. Lord, make me an instrument of Your peace.
Where there is hatred, let me sow love;
Where there is injury, pardon;
Where there is doubt, faith;
Where there is despair, hope;
Where there is darkness, light; and
Where there is sadness, joy. — St. Francis

Arguments

Sentences which present arguments often follow the pattern of cause and effect. You must try to fol-low the author's reasoning as you work towards his or her conclusion.

1. When *tillage* begins, other arts follow. The farmers, **therefore**, are the founders of human civilization. — Webster.

2. A man ought to read just as *inclination* leads him; **for** what he reads as a task will do him little good. — Johnson.

Practice Exercises

Use the following practice exercises as a warm-up before you go on to the model tests. Check your answers against the answer key. For every answer you get incorrect, follow this procedure:

1. Review the unfamiliar words. Check them out in the Basic Word List in Chapter 9, or look them up in your dictionary. Again, remember that these are SAT-level words. Make use of this chance to go over what they mean.

2. Once you know the meaning of the words, see if you can spot signal words or context clues that might have helped you get the answer right. Note any word parts that you can find in the unfamiliar words.

3. Go over your guessing tactics. If you eliminated any answer choices, see whether you were correct in eliminating them. Remember, if you *can* eliminate one or two answer choices, you *should* guess. Even if you get a particular question wrong, in the long run, if you use the process of elimination correctly, you'll come out ahead of the game.

Sentence Completion Exercise A

Each sentence below has one or two blanks, each blank indicating that something has been omitted. Beneath the sentence are five lettered words or sets of words. Choose the word or set of words that best fits the meaning of the sentence as a whole.

Example:

Although its publicity has been ----, the film itself is intelligent, well-acted, handsomely produced, and altogether ----.

(A) tasteless..respectable (B) extensive..moderate
(C) sophisticated..amateur (D) risqué..crude
(E) perfect..spectacular

● Ⓑ Ⓒ Ⓓ Ⓔ

1. The selection committee for the exhibit was amazed to see such fine work done by a mere ----.

(A) connoisseur   (B) artist   (C) amateur
(D) entrepreneur   (E) exhibitionist

2. The teacher suspected cheating as soon as he noticed the pupil's ---- glances at his classmate's paper.

(A) futile   (B) sporadic   (C) furtive   (D) cold
(E) inconsequential

3. Known for his commitment to numerous worthy causes, the philanthropist deserved ---- for his ----.

(A) recognition..folly
(B) blame..hypocrisy
(C) reward..modesty
(D) admonishment..wastefulness
(E) credit..altruism

4. If you listen carefully, you can hear this simple ---- throughout the entire score.

(A) metaphor   (B) paean   (C) banality
(D) motif   (E) trilogy

5. Either the surfing at Maui is ----, or I went there on an off day.

(A) consistent   (B) thrilling   (C) invigorating
(D) overrated   (E) scenic

6. Your ---- remarks spoil the effect of your speech; try not to stray from your subject.

(A) innocuous   (B) digressive   (C) derogatory
(D) persistent   (E) enigmatic

7. We need both ornament and implement in our society; we need the artist and the ----.

(A) beautician   (B) writer   (C) politician
(D) artisan   (E) model

8. When such ---- remarks are circulated, we can only blame and despise those who produce them.

(A) adulatory   (B) chance   (C) rhetorical
(D) redundant   (E) reprehensible

9. The stereotypical image of masculinity assumes that weeping is ---- ''unmanly'' behavior, and not simply a human reaction which may be ---- by either sex.

(A) inexplicably..repented
(B) excessively..discerned
(C) essentially..defined
(D) inherently..adopted
(E) intentionally..exaggerated

10. We need more men and women of culture and enlightenment in our society; we have too many ---- among us.

(A) pedants   (B) philistines   (C) ascetics
(D) paragons´   (E) apologists

11. Courteously and ----, but persistently, the members of the special investigatory commission asked question after question of all the President's aides.

(A) intrusively   (B) belligerently   (C) urbanely
(D) remorselessly   (E) intermittently

12. Many educators argue that a ---- grouping of students would improve instruction because it would limit the range of student abilities in the classroom.

(A) heterogeneous   (B) systematic
(C) homogeneous   (D) sporadic
(E) fragmentary

13. As news of his indictment spread through the town, the citizens began to ---- him and to avoid meeting him.

(A) ostracize   (B) congratulate   (C) desecrate
(D) minimize   (E) harass

14. These sporadic raids seem to indicate that the enemy is waging a war of ---- rather than attacking us directly.

(A) retribution   (B) attrition   (C) conquest
(D) subversion   (E) words

15. There are too many ---- and not enough serious workers.

(A) sycophants   (B) kleptomaniacs   (C) novices
(D) dilettantes   (E) zealots

16. Unlike W. E. B. Dubois, who was ---- of the vocational emphasis in black education, Booker T. Washington favored ---- the limited funds available

for educating blacks to programs that prepared people for practical jobs.

(A) critical..restricting
(B) aware..confining
(C) suspicious..denying
(D) protective..allotting
(E) appreciative..allocating

17. Many elderly people are capable of working, but they are kept from gainful employment by the ---- of those employers who mistakenly believe that young people alone can give them adequate service.

(A) philosophy   (B) parsimony
(C) conservatism   (D) rationalizations
(E) short-sightedness

18. The college president made the ---- statement that no student athlete on academic probation, not even the top-scorer of the varsity team, would be allowed to participate in intercollegiate sports.

(A) impertinent   (B) uncontroversial
(C) opinionated   (D) categorical
(E) equivocal

19. The fire marshalls spend many hours seeking the cause of the ---- in which so many people were killed and so many others hospitalized with major burns.

(A) maelstrom   (B) labyrinth   (C) conflagration
(D) torpor   (E) carnage

20. If you come to the conference table with such an ---- attitude, we can not expect to reach any harmonious agreement.

(A) exemplary   (B) iridescent   (C) indolent
(D) obdurate   (E) unwonted

21. I can vouch for his honesty; I have always found him ---- and carefully observant of the truth.

(A) arbitrary   (B) plausible   (C) volatile
(D) veracious   (E) innocuous

22. This well-documented history is of importance because it carefully ---- the ---- accomplishments of Indian artists who are all too little known to the public at large.

(A) recognizes..negligible
(B) overlooks..purported
(C) scrutinizes..illusory
(D) distorts..noteworthy
(E) substantiates..considerable

23. Perhaps because he feels ---- by an excess of parental restrictions and rules, at adolescence the repressed child may break out dramatically.

(A) nurtured   (B) appeased   (C) confined
(D) fascinated   (E) liberated

24. Sue felt that Jack's ---- in the face of the compelling evidence which she had presented was an example of his ---- mind.

   (A) truculence..unbiased
   (B) skepticism..open
   (C) incredulity..closed
   (D) acquiescence..keen
   (E) reluctance..impartial

25. ---- his broker had told him that the stock was a ---- investment, he insisted on buying 100 shares.

   (A) Because..speculative
   (B) Although..precarious
   (C) Since..negligible
   (D) Although..formidable
   (E) Because..dwindling

26. The enemy soldiers were hot in pursuit; desperate, the fugitive sought ---- in the village church.

   (A) salvation   (B) sanctuary   (C) confirmation
   (D) therapy   (E) repudiation

27. She is an interesting ----, an infinitely shy person who, in apparent contradiction, possesses an enormously intuitive ---- for understanding people.

   (A) aberration..disdain
   (B) caricature..talent
   (C) specimen..loathing
   (D) phenomenon..disinclination
   (E) paradox..gift

28. We cannot pardon such ---- act of violence.

   (A) an expedient   (B) an egregious
   (C) a munificent   (D) a circumspect
   (E) an insipid

29. At the present time, we are suffering from ---- of stories about the war; try writing about another subject.

   (A) a calumny   (B) a dearth   (C) an insurgence
   (D) a plethora   (E) an inhibition

30. Because he was ----, he shunned human society.

   (A) a misanthrope   (B) an oligarch   (C) an anomaly
   (D) a stereotype   (E) a nonentity

31. The police feel that the ---- shown by the judges to first offenders unfortunately ---- many youngsters to embark on a life of crime.

   (A) understanding..condemns
   (B) clemency..encourages
   (C) harshness..predisposes
   (D) indifference..directs
   (E) intolerance..induces

32. He has the ---- distinction of being the only one in the class to fail the examination.

   (A) voluntary   (B) dubious   (C) exemplary
   (D) partial   (E) logical

33. It is wise to begin to treat a progressive disease while it is still in its ---- stage.

   (A) climactic   (B) clinical   (C) incipient
   (D) terminal   (E) pharmaceutical

34. Crowther maintained that the current revival was the most fatuous and ---- production of the entire theatrical season.

   (A) gripping   (B) inane   (C) prophetic
   (D) memorable   (E) salubrious

35. His olfactory sense was so highly developed that he was often called in to judge ----.

   (A) productivity   (B) colors   (C) litigation
   (D) perfume   (E) acoustics

36. Although I have always been confused by our ---- system, I ---- traveling on the subways occasionally.

   (A) mercantile..remember
   (B) monetary..deplore
   (C) social..ponder
   (D) transit..relish
   (E) revolutionary..prefer

37. In his address, the superintendent exhorted the teachers to discover and ---- each student's ---- talents.

   (A) suppress..unrecognized
   (B) develop..intrinsic
   (C) redirect..specious
   (D) belittle..dormant
   (E) justify..gratuitous

38. Micawber's habit of spending more than he earned left him in a state of perpetual ----, but he ---- hoping to see a more affluent day.

   (A) indigence..persevered in
   (B) confusion..compromised by
   (C) enervation..retaliated by
   (D) motion..responded by
   (E) opulence..insisted on

39. The ---- of such utopian notions is reflected by the quick disintegration of the idealistic community at Brooke Farm.

   (A) timeliness   (B) creativity
   (C) impracticability   (D) effervescence
   (E) vindication

40. We were amazed that a man who had been heretofore the most ---- of public speakers could, in a single speech, electrify an audience and bring them cheering to their feet.

   (A) enthralling   (B) accomplished
   (C) pedestrian   (D) auspicious   (E) masterful

41. Despite the mixture's ---- nature, we found that by lowering its temperature in the laboratory we could dramatically reduce its tendency to vaporize.

    (A) resilient   (B) volatile   (C) homogeneous
    (D) insipid   (E) acerbic

42. Surrounded by a host of besiegers and unable to ---- their supplies, the defenders of the castle feared their food would soon be ----.

    (A) replenish..exhausted
    (B) consume..hoarded
    (C) replace..obtainable
    (D) estimate..superfluous
    (E) deplete..rationed

43. Fitness experts claim that jogging is ----; once you begin to jog regularly, you may be unable to stop, because you are sure to love it more and more all the time.

    (A) exhausting   (B) illusive   (C) addictive
    (D) exotic   (E) overrated

44. Although newscasters often use the terms Chicano and Latino ----, students of Hispanic-American culture are profoundly aware of the ---- the two

    (A) interchangeably..dissimilarities between
    (B) indifferently..equivalence of
    (C) deprecatingly..controversies about
    (D) unerringly..significance of
    (E) confidently..origins of

45. She maintained that the proposed legislation was ---- because it simply established an affirmative action task force without making any appropriate provision to fund such a force.

    (A) inevitable   (B) inadequate   (C) prudent
    (D) necessary   (E) beneficial

46. The faculty senate warned that, if its recommendations were to go unheeded, the differences between the administration and the teaching staff would be ---- and eventually rendered irreconcilable.

    (A) rectified   (B) exacerbated   (C) imponderable
    (D) eradicated   (E) alienated

47. Hroswitha the nun, though hidden among the cloisters and ---- time, is now considered an important literary figure of the medieval period.

    (A) oppressed by   (B) fighting against
    (C) celebrated throughout   (D) elapsed from
    (E) obscured by

48. Famed athlete Bobby Orr was given his first pair of skates by a ---- Canadian woman who somehow "knew" he would use them to attain sporting greatness.

    (A) prosperous   (B) prescient   (C) notorious
    (D) skeptical   (E) fallible

49. Why is it that even the most ---- of students occasionally ---- a seemingly simple question, and finds herself unable to determine the correct answer?

    (A) conscientious..balks at
    (B) dogged..proposes
    (C) intuitive..resolves
    (D) erudite..overlooks
    (E) incompetent..stumbles over

50. She has sufficient tact to ---- the ordinary crises of diplomatic life; however, even her diplomacy is insufficient to enable her to ---- the current emergency.

    (A) negotiate..comprehend
    (B) survive..exaggerate
    (C) handle..weather
    (D) ignore..transform
    (E) aggravate..resolve

Sentence Completion Exercise B

Each sentence below has one or two blanks, each blank indicating that something has been omitted. Beneath the sentence are five lettered words or sets of words. Choose the word or set of words that best fits the meaning of the sentence as a whole.

Example:

Although its publicity has been ----, the film itself is intelligent, well-acted, handsomely produced, and altogether ----.

(A) tasteless..respectable   (B) extensive..moderate
(C) sophisticated..amateur   (D) risqué..crude
(E) perfect..spectacular

● Ⓑ © Ⓓ Ⓔ

1. Because he is so ----, we can never predict what course he will take at any moment.

    (A) incoherent   (B) superficial   (C) capricious
    (D) deleterious   (E) conventional

2. The bank teller's ---- of the funds was not discovered until the auditors examined the accounts.

    (A) extradition   (B) embezzlement
    (C) patronage   (D) subordination
    (E) verification

3. He was so convinced that people were driven by ---- motives that he believed there was no such thing as a purely unselfish act.

    (A) sentimental   (B) personal   (C) altruistic
    (D) ulterior   (E) intrinsic

4. Because he was ---- by nature, he preferred reading a book in the privacy of his own study to visiting a night club with friends.

    (A) an exhibitionist   (B) a hedonist
    (C) an adversary   (D) an egoist   (E) an introvert

5. Surprisingly enough, it is more difficult to write about the ---- than about the ---- and strange.

   (A) specific..foreign
   (B) abstract..prosaic
   (C) commonplace..exotic
   (D) simple..routine
   (E) ludicrous..dejected

6. The plot of this story is so ---- that I can predict the outcome.

   (A) intricate   (B) theoretical   (C) pivotal
   (D) trite   (E) fictitious

7. These regulations are so ---- that we feel we have lost all our privileges.

   (A) stringent   (B) aristocratic   (C) redundant
   (D) specious   (E) garish

8. She was pleased by the accolades she received; like everyone else, she enjoyed being ----.

   (A) entertained   (B) praised   (C) playful
   (D) vindicated   (E) charitable

9. Safire as a political commentator is patently never ----; he writes ---- editorials about every action the government takes.

   (A) content..deferential
   (B) querulous..biased
   (C) amazed..bemused
   (D) overawed..flattering
   (E) satisfied..peevish

10. We must overcome his ---- social change if we wish to win his support for this innovative program of home health care for the elderly.

    (A) tendency to   (B) endorsement of
    (C) antipathy to   (D) respect for
    (E) achievement of

11. The tapeworm is an example of ---- organism, one that lives within or on another creature, deriving some or all of its nutriment from its host.

    (A) a hospitable   (B) an exemplary
    (C) a parasitic   (D) an autonomous
    (E) a protozoan

12. He found himself in the ---- position of appearing to support a point of view which he abhorred.

    (A) obvious   (B) innocuous   (C) anomalous
    (D) enviable   (E) auspicious

13. The younger members of the company resented the domineering and ---- manner of the office manager.

    (A) urbane   (B) prudent   (C) convivial
    (D) imperious   (E) objective

14. In view of the fact that there are mitigating circumstances, we must consider this a ---- offense.

    (A) heinous   (B) venal   (C) criminal
    (D) propitious   (E) venial

15. I regret that my remarks seemed ----; I never intended to belittle you.

    (A) inadequate   (B) justified   (C) unassailable
    (D) disparaging   (E) shortsighted

16. A ---- glance pays ---- attention to details.

    (A) furtive..meticulous
    (B) cursory..little
    (C) cryptic..close
    (D) keen..scanty
    (E) fleeting..vigilant

17. The surgeons were worried about the possibility of finding ---- growth in the patient.

    (A) a benign   (B) a superficial   (C) an organic
    (D) an operable   (E) a malignant

18. The advocates of anarchy are ignoring the ---- such a form of government will bring with it.

    (A) chaos   (B) restrictions   (C) advantages
    (D) renewal   (E) compromises

19. Such an ---- act of hostility can only lead to war.

    (A) erratic   (B) occasional   (C) overt
    (D) isolated   (E) anticlimactic

20. When we saw black smoke billowing from the wing of the plane, we were certain that disaster was ----.

    (A) unlikely   (B) catastrophic   (C) imminent
    (D) undeserved   (E) averted

21. Upon realizing that his position was ----, the general ---- his men to retreat to a neighboring hill.

    (A) valuable..admonished
    (B) untenable..ordered
    (C) overrated..forbade
    (D) exposed..urged
    (E) salubrious..commanded

22. The seriousness of the drought could only be understood by those who had seen the ---- crops in the fields.

    (A) copious   (B) deluged   (C) wilted
    (D) bumper   (E) diversified

23. As ecologists recently ---- in studying the effects of naturally induced forest fires, some phenomena

that appear on the surface to be destructive often have a hidden ---- effect on balance.

(A) disproved..beneficial
(B) discovered..positive
(C) hypothesized..catastrophic
(D) disclosed..unecological
(E) determined..disastrous

24. The dispute became so ---- that we were afraid the adversaries would come to blows.

(A) ironic   (B) generalized   (C) didactic
(D) articulate   (E) acrimonious

25. With the rift between the two sides apparently widening, analysts said they considered the likelihood of a merger between the two corporations to be ----.

(A) deteriorating   (B) substantial
(C) coincidental   (D) legitimate   (E) plausible

26. Fossils may be set in stone, but their interpretation is not; a new find may necessitate the ---- of a traditional theory.

(A) ambiguity   (B) revision   (C) formulation
(D) validation   (E) assertion

27. In attempting to reconcile estranged spouses, counselors try to foster a spirit of ---- rather than one of stubborn implacability.

(A) disillusionment   (B) ambivalence
(C) compromise   (D) antagonism
(E) independence

28. Shakespeare's reference to clocks in "Julius Caesar" is an example of ----; that is, it is chronologically out of place.

(A) timeliness   (B) antiquarianism
(C) anachronism   (D) synchronization
(E) ignorance

29. A diligent scholar, she devoted herself ---- to the completion of the book.

(A) assiduously   (B) ingenuously
(C) theoretically   (D) voluminously
(E) sporadically

30. He was ---- success, painting not for the sake of fame or monetary reward, but for the sheer love of art.

(A) indifferent to   (B) destined for   (C) avid for
(D) jaded by   (E) enamored of

31. The thought of being trapped in a stalled elevator terrifies me; it brings out all my ---- fears of small, enclosed places.

(A) agoraphobic   (B) kleptomaniac
(C) hypochondriac   (D) therapeutic
(E) claustrophobic

32. When the news of his ---- the enemy became known, he was hanged in effigy.

(A) contempt for   (B) enmity toward
(C) collusion with   (D) conspiracy against
(E) interrogation by

33. At the height of the storm, the savages tried to ---- the angry gods by offering sacrifices.

(A) modify   (B) appall   (C) vilify
(D) propitiate   (E) instigate

34. You should ---- this paragraph in order to make your essay more ----.

(A) delete..succinct
(B) enlarge..redundant
(C) remove..discursive
(D) revise..abstruse
(E) excise..legible

35. Only the fear of immediate ---- prevents that country from launching an attack.

(A) reprisal   (B) surrender   (C) truce
(D) surveillance   (E) rebuke

36. His submissiveness of manner and general air of self-effacement made it ---- he would be ---- to take command of the firm.

(A) unlikely..selected
(B) implausible..hesitant
(C) clear..designated
(D) puzzling..disinclined
(E) probable..demoted

37. She was accused of plagiarism in a dispute over a short story, and, though ----, she never recovered from the accusation and the scandal.

(A) indicted   (B) verified   (C) exonerated
(D) retaliated   (E) convinced

38. The child needed physical therapy to ---- the rigidity that had tragically immobilized his legs.

(A) prescribe   (B) protract   (C) counteract
(D) accentuate   (E) restore

39. The members of the Better Government League vowed to ---- all traces of ---- between criminals and politicians.

(A) exterminate..controversy
(B) instigate..contact
(C) abhor..animosity
(D) eradicate..collusion
(E) impound..ties

40. Watching the hang gliders soar above the fields, I marveled at how they seemed to ---- gravity, hovering in the sky like rainbow-colored birds.

(A) release   (B) adorn   (C) defy   (D) emulate
(E) abet

41. Her novel published to universal acclaim, her literary gifts acknowledged by the chief figures of the Harlem Renaissance, her reputation as yet ---- by envious slights, Hurston clearly was at the ---- of her career.
    (A) undamaged..ebb
    (B) untarnished..zenith
    (C) untainted..extremity
    (D) blackened..mercy
    (E) unmarried..brink

42. In *Anne of Green Gables*, the heroine turns down a prestigious scholarship so that the young hero may receive it; once more, the woman ---- her own ---- to those of the man.
    (A) prefers..ambitions
    (B) sacrifices..losses
    (C) surrenders..talents
    (D) accommodates..beliefs
    (E) subordinates..interests

43. Having envisioned atomic weapons a decade before, Leo Szilard felt horror and guilt at the bombings of Hiroshima and Nagasaki, calling them "a flagrant ---- of our own moral standards."
    (A) violation   (B) exposition   (C) punishment
    (D) vindication   (E) agitation

44. From the lunch counter sit-ins and bus boycotts to the historic freedom march from Selma to Montgomery, this fine volume shows how ---- Americans from every walk of life fought ---- battle for "liberty and justice for all."
    (A) revolutionary..an unnecessary
    (B) typical..an ignoble
    (C) progressive..a vainglorious
    (D) ordinary..an inspiring
    (E) pugnacious..a dubious

45. Despite an affected ---- which convinced casual observers that he was indifferent about his painting

and enjoyed only frivolity, Warhol cared deeply about his art and labored at it ----.
    (A) nonchalance..diligently
    (B) empathy..methodically
    (C) fervor..secretly
    (D) gloom..intermittently
    (E) hysteria..sporadically

46. Cancer cells are normal cells run riot, growing and multiplying out of ----.
    (A) spite   (B) danger   (C) control   (D) apathy
    (E) range

47. Science progresses by building on what has come before; important findings thus form the basis of ---- experiments.
    (A) gradual   (B) subsequent   (C) ingenious
    (D) repetitive   (E) perfunctory

48. Harriman, Kennan, and Acheson were part of that inner ---- of the American diplomatic establishment whose distinguished legacy ---- U. S. foreign policy to this day.
    (A) circle..grieves
    (B) sanctum..absorbs
    (C) core..dominates
    (D) life..biases
    (E) coterie..exacerbates

49. Even if you do not ---- what I have to say, I would appreciate your listening to me with an open mind.
    (A) concur with   (B) reject   (C) clarify
    (D) deviate from   (E) anticipate

50. Paradoxically, Helen, who had been a strict mother to her children, proved ---- mistress to her cats.
    (A) a harsh   (B) an indolent   (C) an ambivalent
    (D) a cautious   (E) a lenient

Answer Key

Sentence Completion Exercise A

1.	C	9.	D	17.	E	25.	B	33.	C	41.	B	49.	A
2.	C	10.	B	18.	D	26.	B	34.	B	42.	A	50.	C
3.	E	11.	C	19.	C	27.	E	35.	D	43.	C		
4.	D	12.	C	20.	D	28.	B	36.	D	44.	A		
5.	D	13.	A	21.	D	29.	D	37.	B	45.	B		
6.	B	14.	B	22.	E	30.	A	38.	A	46.	B		
7.	D	15.	D	23.	C	31.	B	39.	C	47.	E		
8.	E	16.	A	24.	C	32.	B	40.	C	48.	B		

Sentence Completion Exercise B

1.	C	9.	E	17.	E	25.	A	33.	D	41.	B	49.	A
2.	B	10.	C	18.	A	26.	B	34.	A	42.	E	50.	E
3.	D	11.	C	19.	C	27.	C	35.	A	43.	A		
4.	E	12.	C	20.	C	28.	C	36.	A	44.	D		
5.	C	13.	D	21.	B	29.	A	37.	C	45.	A		
6.	D	14.	E	22.	C	30.	A	38.	C	46.	C		
7.	A	15.	D	23.	B	31.	E	39.	D	47.	B		
8.	B	16.	B	24.	E	32.	C	40.	C	48.	C		

8 The Reading Comprehension Question

- **Testing Tactics**
- **Long-Range Strategies**
- **Practice Exercises**
- **Answer Key**
- **Answer Explanations**

SAT reading comprehension questions test your ability to understand what you read—both content and technique. Each verbal section on the SAT will include two or more passages of different length, followed by two to five questions of assorted types. One passage on the test will be **narrative** (a passage from a novel, a short story, a biography, or a personal essay). One or more will deal with the **sciences** (including medicine, botany, zoology, chemistry, physics, geology, astronomy); with the **humanities** (including art, literature, music, philosophy, folklore); or with the **social sciences** (including history, economics, sociology, government). Some passages may be what the College Board calls **argumentative**; these passages present a definite point of view on a subject. One passage certainly will be **"ethnic"** in content: whether it is a history passage, a personal narrative, or a passage on music, art, or literature, it will deal with concerns of a particular minority group. Whatever the subject, the passage will contain all the information you'll need to answer the questions on it.

The verbal sections fall into two basic patterns.

40-question section

15 reading comprehension questions

4 reading passages (each 200–450 words)

Passages located at end of section

45-question section

10 reading comprehension questions

2 reading passages (each 500 words or more)

Passages located in middle of section

In a group of reading passages, the easiest passages generally come first. You should find the first passage of a group of four much easier than the last. However, the questions that come after each passage are not arranged in order of difficulty. They are arranged to suit the way the passage's content is organized; a question based on information found at the beginning of the passage will come before a question based on information at the passage's end. If you are stumped by a tough reading question, don't skip the other questions on that passage. A tough question may be just one question away from an easy one.

This chapter contains three recently-published SAT reading passages together with several types of questions about them. Some of the questions are factual, asking you about specific details in the passages. Others ask you to interpret the passages, to make judgments about them. Many of these questions are actual questions from the SAT. Others are new questions, created for this book, but based on the actual SAT passages. Tactics 1–3 tell you how to deal with SAT reading questions in general. Tactics 4–11 give you solid hints about how to answer each type of reading question, plus short lists of key words that occur and reoccur in major question types.

The directions for the reading comprehension section on the SAT are minimal. They are:

Each passage below is followed by questions based on its content. Answer all questions following a passage on the basis of what is <u>stated</u> or <u>implied</u> in that passage.

Testing Tactics

Save the Reading Comprehension Questions for Last.

To answer an antonym question takes you seconds; to answer a reading comprehension question, you have to spend minutes going over the passage before you ever get to the questions at all.

On the SAT, you get the same points for answering a "quick and easy" question correctly as you do for answering a time-consuming one. Each correct answer on the verbal section is worth roughly 10 points to you. The more questions you answer correctly, the higher your score will be. Therefore, it makes sense for you to tackle the quick-to-answer

questions—the antonyms, the analogies, the sentence completions—*first*. Get as many of them right as you can, and then settle down to answering the reading questions, knowing you've done everything possible to maximize your score.

One word of caution: Remember that in a 45-question verbal section, the reading questions typically occur in the *middle* of the section. If you plan to skip them and come back to them later, *be very careful in marking your answer sheet*. Check the numbering of your answer sheet often.

Tackle Passages with Familiar Subjects Before Passages with Unfamiliar Ones.

Just as it is common sense for you to tackle quick-to-answer questions before you tackle time-consuming ones, it is also common sense for you to tackle reading passages with familiar subjects before you tackle reading passages with unfamiliar ones. If you know very little about botany or are uninterested in it, you are all too likely to run into trouble reading a passage about plant life.

It is hard to concentrate when you read about something wholly unfamiliar to you. Give yourself a break. Concentrate on the reading passages that interest you or that deal with topics you are well-grounded in. There is nothing wrong in skipping questions. Just remember to check the numbering of your answer sheet. You should, of course, go back to the questions you skipped if you have time.

First Read the Passage; Then Read the Questions.

Students often ask whether it is better to read the passage first or the questions first. Those who want to read the questions before reading the passage think it will save time. Ninety-nine times out of a hundred they are wrong.

Reading the questions before you read the passage will not save you time. It will cost you time. If you read the questions first, when you turn to the passage you will have a number of question words and phrases dancing around in your head. These phrases won't focus you; they'll distract you. You will be so involved in trying to spot the places they occur in the passage that you'll be unable to concentrate on comprehending the passage as a whole. Why increase your anxiety and decrease your capac-

ity to think? First read the passage, using the following technique:

1. Read as rapidly as you can with understanding, but do not force yourself. Do not worry about the time element. If you worry about not finishing the test, you will begin to take short cuts and miss the correct answer in your haste. Remember, if you have followed Tactic 1 and answered the quick questions first, you've maximized your score and made the best use of your time.

2. As you read the opening sentences, try to anticipate what the passage will be about. Who or what is the author talking about?

3. As you continue reading, try to remember in what part of the passage the author makes major points. In that way, when you start looking for the phrase or sentence which will justify your choice of answer, you will be able to save time by going to that section of the passage immediately rather than having to reread the entire selection. (This is particularly important when the passages become longer than 250 words.)

4. Your first reading of the passage should give you a general impression of the theme of the passage and the location of its major subdivisions. In order to answer each question properly, *you must go back to the passage* to verify your choice of answer. Do not rely on memory, and, above all, do not rely on knowledge gained outside of the passage.

5. Underline sparingly, if at all. Underlining is great when you're reading a textbook chapter that you want to review at a later time. On the SAT, underlining is not so great. It slows you down. It also can confuse you. If you underline everything in sight, it will be harder for you to spot an important word or phrase. A * or √ in the margin is all the underlining you could possibly need.

If you have any serious reservations about this tactic, feel free to try alternate approaches doing some of the practice exercises at the end of this chapter. Compare the scores you get using each different approach. Reading is a highly individual skill. See what approach works best for you. The important thing is to know yourself and to feel comfortable with what you do.

Learn to Spot the Major Reading Question Types.

Just as it will help you to know the directions for the antonym, analogy, and sentence completion questions on the SAT, it will also help you to familiarize yourself with the major types of reading questions on the test.

If you can recognize just what a given question is asking for, you'll be better able to tell which particular reading tactic to apply.

Here are six categories of reading questions you are sure to face.

1. **Main Idea**   Questions that test your ability to find the central thought of a passage or to judge its significance often take the following form:

   The main point of the passage is to

   The passage is primarily concerned with

   The author's primary purpose in this passage is to

   The chief theme of the passage can best be described as

   Which of the following titles best describes the content of the passage?

   Which of the following statements best expresses the main idea of the passage?

2. **Finding Specific Details**   Questions that test your ability to understand what the author states *explicitly* are often worded:

   According to the author

   The author states all of the following EXCEPT

   According to the passage, which of the following is true of the

   According to the passage, the chief characteristic of the subject is

   Which of the following statements is (are) best supported by the passage?

   Which of the following is NOT cited in the passage as evidence of

3. **Drawing Inferences**   Questions that test your ability to go beyond the author's explicit statements and see what these statements imply may be worded:

   It can be inferred from the passage that

   The passage suggests that the author would support which of the following views?

   The author implies that

   The author apparently feels that

   According to the passage, it is likely that

   The passage is most likely directed toward an audience of

   Which of the following statements about . . . can be inferred from the passage?

4. **Tone/Attitude**   Questions that test your ability to sense an author's or character's emotional state often take the form:

   The author's attitude to the problem can best be described as

   Which of the following best describes the author's tone in the passage?

   The author's tone in the passage is that of a person attempting to

The author's presentation is marked by a tone of

The passage indicates that the author experiences a feeling of

5. **Determining the Meaning of Words from Their Context**   Questions that test your ability to work out the meaning of unfamiliar words from their context often are worded:

As it is used in the passage, the term . . . can best be described as

The phrase . . . is used in the passage to mean that

In the passage, the word . . . means

The author uses the phrase . . . to describe

6. **Technique**   Questions that test your ability to recognize a passage's method of organization or technique often are worded:

Which of the following best describes the development of this passage?

In presenting the argument, the author does all of the following EXCEPT

The relationship between the second paragraph and the first paragraph can best be described as

In the passage, the author makes the central point primarily by

The organization of the passage can best be described as

When Asked to Find the Main Idea, Be Sure to Check the Opening and Summary Sentences of Each Paragraph.

The opening and closing sentences of a paragraph are key sentences for you to read. They can serve as guideposts for you, pointing out the author's main idea.

Whenever you are asked to determine a passage's main idea, *always* check the opening and summary sentences of each paragraph. Authors typically provide readers with a sentence which expresses a paragraph's main idea succinctly. Although such *topic sentences* may appear anywhere in the paragraph, readers customarily look for them in the opening or closing sentences.

Notice the impact of words like *again, also, as well as, furthermore, moreover*, and *significantly* in the passage. These signal words may call your attention to the main idea.

Note that in SAT reading passages topic sentences are sometimes implied rather than stated directly. If you cannot find a topic sentence, ask yourself these questions:

1. Who or what is this passage about?

2. What aspect of this subject is the author talking about?

3. What is the author trying to get across about this aspect of the subject?

Read the following ethnic passage from a recent SAT and apply this tactic.

Lois Mailou Jones is one example of an answer to the charge that there are no Black or female American artists to include in art history textbooks and classes. Beginning her formal art education at the School of the Museum of Fine Arts in Boston, Lois Jones found herself strongly attracted to design rather than fine

arts. After teaching for a while, she went to Paris to study, on the advice of the sculptor Meta Warrick Fuller.

It was in Paris that she first felt free to paint. Following her return to this country in 1938, Jones had an exhibit at the Vose Gallery in Boston, a major breakthrough for a Black artist at that time. Her work during this period consisted of excellent impressionist scenes of Paris. It was not until the early 1940's, after she met the Black aesthetician Alain Locke, that she began to paint works like *Mob Victim*, which explicitly dealt with her own background as a Black American. Later, in the fifties, she went often to Haiti, which had yet another influence on her style. Then a sabbatical leave in Africa again changed her imagery. Indeed, the scope of this distinguished artist's career so well spans the development of twentieth-century art that her work could be a textbook in itself.

Now look at a question on this passage. It's a good example of a main idea question.

> The passage primarily focuses on the
>
> (A) influence of Lois Jones on other artists
> (B) recognition given to Lois Jones for her work
> (C) experiences that influenced the work of Lois Jones
> (D) obstacles that Lois Jones surmounted in her career
> (E) techniques that characterize the work of Lois Jones

Look at the opening and summary sentences of the two paragraphs that make up the passage: "Lois Mailou Jones is one example of . . . Black or female

American artists to include in art history textbooks and classes''; ''It was in Paris she first felt free to paint''; ''Indeed, the scope of (her) career so well spans the development of twentieth-century art.'' Note particularly the use of the signal word ''indeed'' to call your attention to the author's point. Lois Jones has had a vast range of experiences that have contributed to her work as an artist. The correct answer is Choice C.

Choice A is incorrect. The passage talks of influences on Lois Jones, not of Lois Jones's influence on others. Choice B is incorrect. The passage mentions recognition given to Jones only in passing. Choice D is incorrect. There is nothing in the passage to support it. Choice E is incorrect. The passage never deals with specific questions of craft or technique.

Certain words occur and reoccur in questions on a passage's purpose or main idea. You probably know most of these words, but if you're shaky about any of their meanings, look them up in a good dictionary and familiarize yourself with how they are used. It would be silly to miss an answer not because you misunderstood the passage's meaning but because you failed to recognize a common question word.

Important Words in Questions on Main Idea or Purpose

bolster (verb)	elaborate (verb)
delineate	exemplify
depict	illustrate
discredit	refute
document (verb)	speculate
endorse	verify

Familiarize Yourself with the Technical Terms Used to Describe a Passage's Organization.

Another part of understanding the author's point is understanding how the author organizes what he or she has to say. To do so, often you have to figure out how the opening sentence or paragraph is connected to the passage as a whole.

Try this SAT question on the author's technique, based on the previous passage about Lois Mailou Jones.

Which of the following best summarizes the relationship of the first sentence to the rest of the passage?

(A) Assertion followed by supporting evidence
(B) Challenge followed by debate pro and con
(C) Prediction followed by analysis
(D) Specific instance followed by generalizations
(E) Objective reporting followed by personal reminiscences

The correct answer is Choice A. The author makes an assertion (a positive statement) about Jones's importance and then proceeds to back it up with specific details from her career.

Choice B is incorrect. There is no debate for and against the author's thesis or point about Jones; the only details given support that point. Choice C is incorrect. The author does not predict or foretell something that is going to happen; the author asserts or states positively something that is an accomplished fact. Choice D is incorrect. The author's opening general assertion is followed by specific details to support it, not the reverse. Choice E is incorrect. The author shares no personal memories or reminiscences of Jones; the writing is objective throughout.

Important Words in Questions on Technique or Style

abstract	explanatory
analogy	expository
antithesis	generalization
argumentative	narrative
assertion	persuasive
cite	rhetorical
concrete	thesis
evidence	

When Asked to Choose a Title, Watch Out for Choices That Are Too Specific or Too Broad.

A paragraph has been defined as a group of sentences revolving around a central theme. An appropriate title for a paragraph, therefore, must include this central theme that each of the sentences in the paragraph is developing. It should be neither too broad nor too narrow in its scope; it should be specific and yet comprehensive enough to include all the essential ideas presented by the sentences. A good title for a passage of two or more paragraphs should include the thoughts of ALL the paragraphs.

This third question on the Jones passage is a title question. Note how it resembles questions on the passage's purpose or main idea.

Which of the following is the best title for the passage?

(A) Unsung Black Artists of America
(B) A Hard Row to Hoe: The Struggles of Lois Jones
(C) Locke and Jones: Two Black Artistic Pioneers
(D) African and Haitian Influences on Lois Mailou Jones
(E) The Making of an Artist: Lois Mailou Jones

When you are trying to select the best title for a passage, watch out for words that come straight out of the passage. They may not always be your best choice. Consider Choice C. Though the author mentions Alain Locke and suggests the importance of his influence in prompting Jones to use her experiences as a black American in her art, the passage as a whole is about Jones, not about Locke and Jones. Likewise, although the passage refers to African and Haitian influences in her imagery and style, the passage is about how Jones's experiences formed her as an artist, not about the specific influences on her style. Choice D is too narrow in scope to be a good title for this text.

Choice A has the opposite problem. As a title for this passage, *Unsung Black Artists of America* is far too broad. This passage concerns itself with a particular black artist whose fame deserves to be sung.

While Choice B limits itself to Jones, it too has a flaw. The passage clearly does not dwell on Jones's struggles; instead, it focuses on influences on her artistic growth.

Of the titles suggested, Choice E is best. The passage refers to the many and varied experiences that have made Jones an important figure in the world of art. Following her progress step by step, it portrays "the making of an artist."

Tactic 8

When Asked About Specific Details in the Passage, Spot Key Words in the Question and Scan the Passage to Find Them (or Their Synonyms).

In developing the main idea of a passage, a writer will make statements to support his or her point. To answer questions about such supporting details, you *must* find a word or group of words in the passage which supports your choice of answer. The words "according to the passage" or "according to the author" should focus your attention on what the passage explicitly states. Do not be misled into choosing an answer (even one that makes good sense) if you can not find it supported in the text.

Often detail questions ask about a particular phrase or line. In such instances, use the following technique:

1. Look for key words (nouns or verbs) in the answer choices.

2. Run your eye down the passage, looking for those key words or their synonyms. (This is called *scanning*. It is what you do when you look up someone's number in the phone book.)

3. When you find a key word or its synonym, reread the sentence to make sure the test-writer hasn't used the original wording to mislead you.

Read the following scientific passage from a recently published SAT and apply this tactic.

Prostaglandins are short-lived hormonelike substances made by most cells in the body after injury or shock. They are responsible for a number of physiological reactions. Prostaglandins have been shown to influence blood pressure, muscle contraction, and blood coagulation and are involved in producing pain, fever, and inflammation. When released from platelets—minute discs in the blood—a prostaglandin derivative called thromboxane makes the platelets clump together and thus initiates clotting.

In 1971, John Vane, a British researcher, discovered that aspirin interferes with the synthesis of prostaglandins. Scientists now know that aspirin relieves pain by inactivating cyclooxygenase, an enzyme that aids in initiating the synthesis of prostaglandins. When scientists realized that aspirin can also interfere with clotting, they began to wonder whether it could help prevent heart attacks and strokes, which are often caused by blood clots that block arteries in the chest and neck. Studies now indicate that low daily doses of aspirin can cut the risk of a second heart attack by about twenty percent and the risk of a second stroke by nearly half. It seems logical to assume that if the drug can prevent second heart attacks, it can also ward off an attack the first time around. Therefore, many doctors recommend an aspirin tablet every other day to people who have high blood pressure or other symptoms that increase the risk of heart attacks.

Now look at a question on a specific detail in the passage.

> According to the passage, prostaglandins play a role in all of the following EXCEPT the
>
> (A) clotting of blood
> (B) sensation of pain
> (C) contraction of muscles
> (D) manufacture of platelets
> (E) inflammation of tissue

Watch out for questions containing the word EXCEPT. To answer them, you must go through each answer choice in turn, checking to see if you can find it supported in the passage. If you can find support for it, then you must rule it out. When you find an answer choice *without* support in the passage, that's the answer you want.

The last two sentences in the first paragraph are the key to this question. These two sentences cite the physiological reactions caused by prostaglandins. Check each of the answer choices against the information in these sentences.

Choice A is incorrect. Prostaglandins influence "blood coagulation" or *clotting*. Note the use of *clotting*, a synonym for *coagulation*, rather than the passage's original wording.

Choice B is incorrect. Prostaglandins are involved in producing pain.

Choice C is incorrect. Prostaglandins influence muscle contraction.

Choice E is incorrect. Prostaglandins are involved in producing inflammation.

The correct answer is Choice D. While prostaglandins do have an influence on platelets, they play a role in causing platelets to clump or gather together, *not* in manufacturing them.

Important Words in Questions on Specific Detail

aesthetic	indicative
allusion	inherent
assumption	innate
attribute	innovative
divergent	misconception
fluctuate	phenomenon
hypothetical	preclude
incompatible	

Tactic 9

When Asked to Make Inferences, Base Your Answers on What the Passage Implies, Not What It States Directly.

In *Language in Thought and Action*, S. I. Hayakawa defines an inference as "a statement about the unknown made on the basis of the known."

Inference questions require you to use your own judgment. You must not take anything directly stated by the author as an inference. Instead, you must look for clues in the passage that you can use in coming up with your own conclusion. You should choose as your answer a statement which is a logical development of the information the author has provided.

Try this fairly easy SAT inference question, based on the previous passage about prostaglandins.

> The passage suggests that which of the following would be most likely to initiate the production of prostaglandins?
>
> (A) Taking an aspirin
> (B) Spraining an ankle
> (C) Climbing stairs
> (D) Flexing a muscle
> (E) Running a fever

The justification for Choice B as an answer comes in the opening sentence, which states that prosta-

glandins are produced in response to injury or shock. Choice B, *spraining an ankle*, is an example of an injury. As such, it is likely to initiate or set into motion the production of prostaglandins. None of the other choices is an example of an injury or shock. Thus, you can logically infer they are unlikely to start prostaglandin production going. Taking an aspirin, in fact, would interfere with or block prostaglandin production. Only Choice B is logical to suggest.

Now read this SAT fiction passage, taken from the novel *The Heart of the Matter* by Graham Greene.

"Imagine. Forty days in the boats!" cried Mrs. Perrot. Everything over the river was still and blank.
"The French behaved well this time at least,"
Line Dawson remarked.
(5) "They've only brought in the dying," the doctor retorted. "They could hardly have done less."
Dawson exclaimed and struck at his hand. "Come inside," Mrs. Perrot said, "The windows are netted." The stale air was heavy with the coming rains.
(10) "There are some cases of fever," said the doctor, "but most are just exhaustion—the worst disease. It's what most of us die of in the end."
Mrs. Perrot turned a knob; music from the London

Orpheum filtered in. Dawson shifted uncomfortably;
(15) the Wurlitzer organ moaned and boomed. It seemed to
him outrageously immodest.

Wilson came in to a welcome from Mrs. Perrot. "A
surprise to see *you*, Major Dawson."

"Hardly, Wilson," Mr. Perrot injected. "I told you
(20) he'd be here." Dawson looked across at Wilson and
saw him blush at Perrot's betrayal, saw too that his
eyes gave the lie to his youth.

"Well," sneered Perrot, "any scandals from the big
city?" Like a Huguenot imagining Rome, he built up a
(25) picture of frivolity, viciousness, and corruption. "We
bush-folk live quietly."

Mrs. Perrot's mouth stiffened in the effort to ignore
her husband in his familiar part. She pretended to listen
to the old Viennese melodies.
(30)   "None," Dawson answered, watching Mrs. Perrot
with pity. "People are too busy with the war."

"So many files to turn over," said Perrot. "Growing rice down here would teach them what work is."

The first question based on this SAT passage is an
inference question. Note the use of the terms "suggests" and "most likely." The passage never tells
you directly where the story takes place. You must
put two and two together and see what you get.

The evidence in the passage suggests that the
story most likely takes place

(A) on a boat during a tropical storm
(B) at a hospital during a wartime blackout
(C) in a small town in France
(D) near a rice plantation in the tropics
(E) among a group of people en route to a
     large Asian city

Go through the answer choices one by one.
Remember that in answering inference questions
you must go beyond the obvious, beyond what the

author explicitly states, to look for logical implications of what the author says.

The correct answer is Choice D, *near a rice plantation in the tropics*. Several lines in the passage suggest it: Perrot's reference to "bush-folk," people living in a tropical jungle or similar uncleared
wilderness; Perrot's comment about the work
involved in growing rice; the references to fever and
the coming rains.

Choice A is incorrect. The people rescued have
been in the boats for forty days. The story itself is
not set on a boat.

Choice B is incorrect. Although the presence of a
doctor and the talk of dying patients suggests a
hospital and Dawson's comment implies that people
elsewhere are concerned with a war, nothing in the
passage suggests that it is set in a wartime blackout. The windows are not covered or blacked out to
prevent light from getting out; instead, they are netted to prevent mosquitos from getting in. (Note how
Dawson exclaims and swats his hand; he has just
been bitten by a mosquito.)

Choice C is incorrect. Although the French are mentioned, nothing suggests that the story takes place
in France, a European country not noted for
uncleared wilderness or tropical rains.

Choice E is incorrect. Nothing in the passage suggests these people are en route elsewhere. In addition, Wilson could not logically pretend to be surprised by Dawson's presence if they were
companions on a tour.

Important Words in Inference Questions

criterion	likelihood
derive	overrated
excerpt	plausible
implication	suggestive
imply	tentative

When Asked to Determine Questions of Attitude, Mood, or Tone, Look for Words that Convey Emotion, Express Values, or Paint Pictures.

In determining the attitude, mood, or tone of an
author or character, examine the specific language
used. Is the author using adjectives to describe the
subject? If so, are they words like *fragrant, tranquil,
magnanimous*—words with positive connotations?
Or are they words like *fetid, ruffled, stingy*—words
with negative connotations?

When we speak, our tone of voice conveys our
mood—frustrated, cheerful, critical, gloomy, angry.
When we write, our images and descriptive phrases
get our feelings across.

The second SAT question on the Greene passage is
a tone question. Note that the question refers you to

specific lines in which a particular character speaks. Those lines are repeated here so that you can easily refer to them.

"They've only brought in the dying," the doctor retorted. "They could hardly have done less."

"There are some cases of fever," said the doctor, "but most are just exhaustion—the worst disease. It's what most of us die of in the end."

The tone of the doctor's remarks (lines 5–6, 10–12) indicates that he is basically

(A) unselfish
(B) magnanimous
(C) indifferent
(D) rich in patience
(E) without illusions

Note the doctor's use of "only" and "hardly," words with a negative sense. The doctor is deprecating or belittling what the French have done for the sufferers from the boats, the people who are dying from the exhaustion of their forty-day journey. The doctor is *retorting*: he is replying sharply to Dawson's positive remark about the French having behaved well. The doctor has judged the French. In his eyes, they have not behaved well.

Go through the answer choices one by one to see which choice comes closest to matching your sense of the doctor's tone.

Choice A is incorrect. Nothing in the passage specifically suggests selfishness or unselfishness on his part, merely irritability.

Choice B is incorrect. The doctor sounds irritable, critical, sharp-tempered. He feels resentment for the lack of care received by the victims. He does not sound like a magnanimous, forgiving man.

Choice C is incorrect. The doctor is not indifferent or uncaring. If he did not care, he would not be so sharp in challenging Dawson's innocent remark.

Choice D is also incorrect. The doctor is quick to counter Dawson, quick to criticize the French. Impatience, not patience, distinguishes him.

The correct answer is Choice E. The doctor is *without illusions*. Unlike Dawson, he cannot comfort himself with the illusion that things are going well. He has no illusions about life or death: most of us, he points out unsentimentally, die of exhaustion in the end.

When you are considering questions of attitude and tone, bear in mind the nature of the SAT. It is a standardized test aimed at a wide variety of test-takers—heavy metal fans, political activists, 4-H members, computer hacks, readers of *GQ*. It is taken by Native Americans and Cambodian refugees, evangelical Christians and Orthodox Jews, Buddhists and Hindus, Hispanics and blacks, New Yorkers and Nebraskans—a typically American mix.

The SAT-makers are very aware of this diversity. As members of their staff have told us, they are particularly concerned to avoid using material on the tests that might upset students (and possibly adversely affect their scores). For this reason, their goal is to be noncontroversial: to present material that won't offend *anyone*. Thus, in selecting potential reading passages, the SAT-makers tend to avoid subjects that are sensitive in favor of ones that are bland. In fact, if a passage doesn't start out bland, they revise it and cut out the spice. One SAT test, for example, includes Kenneth Clark's comment about the "sharp wits" of Romans, but cuts out his comment about their "hard heads." Another uses a passage from Mary McCarthy's prickly *Memories of a Catholic Girlhood*, but cuts out every reference to Catholic and Protestant interaction—and much of the humor, too.

How does this affect the sort of tone and attitude questions the SAT-makers ask? As you can see, the SAT-makers attempt to respect the feelings of minority group members. Thus, you can expect minority group members to be portrayed in SAT reading passages in a favorable light. If, for example, there had been an attitude question based on the Lois Mailou Jones passage, it might have been worded like this:

The author's attitude toward the artistic achievements mentioned in the passage can best be described as one of

(A) incredulity
(B) suspicion
(C) condescension
(D) indifference
(E) admiration

Admiration is the only possible choice.

Important Words in Questions on Attitude, Mood, and Tone

aloof	ironic
ambivalent	judicious
brusque	naive
cautionary	nostalgia
compassionate	objective
condescension	optimism
cynical	pedantic
defensive	pessimism
detachment	pomposity
didactic	prosaic
disdain	resigned (adjective)
disparaging	sarcasm
dispassionate	satirical
esteem	skeptical
flippant	trite
grudging	whimsical
hypocritical	

When Asked to Give the Meaning of an Unfamiliar Word, Look for Nearby Context Clues.

Every student who has ever looked into a dictionary is aware that many words have more than one meaning. A common question that appears on the SAT tests your ability to determine the correct meaning of a word from its context. Sometimes the word is a common one, and you must determine its exact meaning as used by the author. At other times, the word is uncommon. You can determine its meaning by a careful examination of the text.

As always, use your knowledge of context clues and word parts (Chapter 7) to help you discover the meanings of unfamiliar words.

One final question based on the Greene passage concerns an unfamiliar word. Here is the paragraph the word appeared in.

"Well," sneered Perrot, "any scandals from the big city?" Like a Huguenot imagining Rome, he built up a picture of frivolity, viciousness, and corruption. "We bush-folk live quietly."

A Huguenot, as used in the passage, is most likely

(A) a person dying of exhaustion
(B) a doctor angered by needless suffering
(C) an admirer of the Roman aristocracy
(D) a city-dweller scornful of country ways
(E) a puritan who suspects others of immorality

What is a Huguenot? It's certainly not an everyday word. You may never have encountered the term before you read this passage. But you can figure it out. A Huguenot is someone who, when he thinks of Rome, thinks of it in terms of vice and lack of seriousness. He disapproves of it for its wickedness and frivolity. Thus, he is a puritan of sorts, a person who condemns practices which he regards as impure or corrupt. The correct answer is Choice E.

Look at the words in the immediate vicinity of the word you are defining. They will give you a sense of the meaning of the unfamiliar word.

Long-Range Strategies

Are you a good reader? Do you read twenty-five or more books a year in addition to those books assigned in school? When you read light fiction, do you cover a page per minute? Do you read only light fiction, or have you begun to read "heavy" books—books on science, political theory, literary criticism, art? Do you browse regularly through magazines and newspapers?

Faced with the above questions, students frequently panic. Used to gathering information from television and radio rather than from books, they don't know how to get back on the track. But getting back on the track is easier than they think.

Read, Read, Read!

Just do it.

There is no substitute for extensive reading as a preparation for the SAT and for college work. The only way to obtain proficiency in reading is by reading books of all kinds. As you read, you will develop speed, stamina, and the ability to comprehend the printed page. But if you want to turn yourself into the kind of reader the colleges are looking for, you must develop the habit of reading—every day.

25 Books a Year

Suppose you're an average reader; you read an ordinary book at about 300 words a minute. In 20 minutes, how many words can you read? Six thousand, right?

In a week of reading 20 minutes per day, how many words can you read? Seven days, 42,000 words.

Now get out your calculator. In 52 weeks of reading 20 minutes per day, how many words can you read? That's 52 times 42,000, a grand total of 2,184,000 words!

Now here comes the hard part. Full-length books usually contain 60,000 to 100,000 words. Say the average book runs about 75,000 words. If reading 20 minutes a day you can read 2,184,000 words in a year, how many average, 75,000-word books can you read in a year?

The answer is a little over 29. Twenty-nine books in a year. So don't panic at the thought of reading 25 books a year. Anybody can find 20 minutes a day, and if you can do that, you can read *over* 25 books a year. The trick is always to have your book on hand, so that you don't have to waste time hunting around for it if you suddenly find yourself with some free time.

Schedule a set time for non-school reading. Make the 20-minute-a-day plan part of your life.

Speed Up Your Reading

If you have trouble getting through a typical verbal section in 30 minutes, you may want to work on ways to build up your reading speed.

One thing you should be aware of is that to build speed you have to practice with easy materials. Most slow readers are used to reading everything— technical material, sports columns, comics—at one slow, careful speed. To build up speed, you have to get your eyes and brain accustomed to moving rapidly, and that means working with passages that are easy for you. Given sufficiently easy material, there are all sorts of techniques that you can try: you can draw a line down the middle of a newspaper column, for example, and then, focusing your eyes on the line, try to get the meanings of the words on each side as you read straight down the column. It's a great exercise for your peripheral vision.

One major cause of slow reading is that sometimes you don't focus. Your eyes keep moving down the page, but your mind is out to lunch. Then bang! You wake up from your daydream and say, "Hey! What was I reading?" And your eyes jump back to an earlier spot on the page and you wind up rereading the whole thing.

Obviously regressing, going back and rereading words or whole passages you've already supposedly read, slows you down. Regressing is a habit, but like any other habit, you can break it.

One way to reduce regressions is to preview a passage before you read. A quick look at the introductory sentences of paragraphs, at titles and section headings, at words in italics and other key words, will give you an idea of what you're about to read. At that point, you have a sense of the material and you come to read the passage with some questions in mind—you read actively, not passively.

A second way to reduce regressions is to make it impossible to look back. Take a 3 × 5 card and use it like a shutter to cover what you've already read. That way you force yourself to keep going. You have to concentrate: you have no choice.

One last speed-reading technique you should be aware of is called clustering or phrase-reading. Have you ever watched somebody's eyes when he or she is busy reading? Do it sometime. You'll see the eyes move, then come to a stop, then dart back for a second, stop, then sweep forward again, stop, and so on. The stops last only a fraction of a second, but they're important: it's only when the eyes stop that you actually read. In that fraction-of-a-second stop, or fixation, your eyes *fix* on a word. If you're skilled at clustering, however, in that one stop your eyes fix on not one, but a group of words. Clustering, phrase-reading, prevents word-by-word reading. It speeds you up where word-by-word reading slows you down.

Here's how to practice clustering. First, find something easy to read. Don't start out with SAT tests. Divide up the passage into 3 or 4 word phrases. Next read it trying to see those 3 or 4 words in a single fixation. Then reread it at your normal speed to catch anything you've missed.

One final, crucial point: These pointers on how to build up your reading speed are long-range strategies. They are not specific tactics for how to go about dealing with the SAT test you're going to face next Saturday morning. The SAT is no time for you to try out new techniques you've heard of but have yet to master.

Upgrade What You Read

Challenge yourself. Don't limit your reading to light fiction and biography as so many high school students do. Branch out a bit. Go beyond *People* magazine. Try to develop an interest in as many fields as you can. Sample some of the quality magazines: *The New Yorker, Smithsonian, Scientific American, National Geographic, Newsweek, Time.* In these magazines you'll find articles on literature, music, science, philosophy, history, the arts—the whole range of fields touched on by the SAT. If you take time to acquaint yourself with the contents of these magazines, you won't find the subject matter of the reading passages on the examination so strange.

Selected Reading List for the SAT

The reading passages you will face on the SAT are excerpts from the sorts of books your college instructors will assign you in your freshman and sophomore years. You can get a head start on college (and on the SAT) by beginning to read college-level material now—today.

The following reading list is divided into seven sections:

1. Fiction

2. Personal Narrative

3. Ethnic (autobiography, biography, art, music, history)

4. Literary Criticism

5. Humanities (art, music, drama, dance)

6. Science (biology, chemistry, physics, mathematics, geology, astronomy)

7. Social Sciences (history, political science, archaeology, sociology)

A number of the books on this list have been the source of passages on the actual SAT.

Follow these steps in working through the list. Choose material from areas with which you feel unfamiliar. Do not worry if the first book you tackle seems difficult to you. Try working your way through a short section—the first chapter should be enough to give you a sense of what the author has to say. *Remember that this is college-level material*: it is bound to be challenging to you; be glad you're getting a chance at it so soon.

If you get stuck, work your way up to the level of the book, taking it step by step. If E. M. Forster's novel *A Room with a View* seems hard, try reading it after you've seen the award-winning movie of the same name. If an article in the Scientific American book *The Brain* seems hard, try reading it after you've read Isaac Asimov's popular *The Human Brain*. Get introductory books on your subject from the high school library or from the Young Adults section of the local public library. There isn't one of these books that's beyond you; you just need to fill in some background first.

(Note that books marked with an asterisk (*) have been the sources for reading passages used in published SAT tests; books marked "M" or "TV" have been made into excellent motion pictures or television shows.)

Fiction

James Agee, *A Death in the Family*
Kingsley Amis, *Lucky Jim*
Jane Austen, *Emma*
   Lady Susan
   *Pride and Prejudice** (M)
James Baldwin, *Go Tell It on the Mountain*
Charlotte Bronte, *Jane Eyre*
   Villette
Joseph Conrad, *The Heart of Darkness*
Charles Dickens, *Barnaby Rudge**
   Great Expectations (M)
   *Little Dorritt**
   Nicholas Nickleby (TV)
   *Our Mutual Friend**
Margaret Drabble, *A Summer Bird-Cage*
George Eliot, *Middlemarch**
Ralph Ellison, *The Invisible Man*
William Faulkner, *Collected Stories of William Faulkner*
   Intruder in the Dust
   Sartoris
F. Scott Fitzgerald, *Babylon Revisited*
   The Great Gatsby
E. M. Forster, *A Room with a View* (M)
Elizabeth Gaskell, *Cranford*
   *Sylvia's Lovers**
William Golding, *Lord of the Flies*
Graham Greene, *The Heart of the Matter**
   Our Man in Havana (M)
   The Power and the Glory
   The Third Man (M)

Thomas Hardy, *Far from the Madding Crowd*
   Jude the Obscure
Ernest Hemingway, *A Farewell to Arms*
   For Whom the Bell Tolls (M)
   The Nick Adams Stories, "The Last Good Country"*
   The Sun Also Rises
William Dean Howells, *A Modern Instance**
Henry James, *The American**
   Daisy Miller
   The Portrait of a Lady
   The Turn of the Screw
James Joyce, *Dubliners*, "Araby"*
Arthur Koestler, *Darkness at Noon*
D. H. Lawrence, *Sons and Lovers*
   Women in Love (M)
C. S. Lewis, *The Screwtape Letters*
Herman Melville, *Billy Budd*
   Moby Dick (M)
George Orwell, *Animal Farm* (M)
   1984 (M)
William Makepeace Thackeray, *Vanity Fair*
Anthony Trollope, *Barchester Towers* (TV)
   The Warden (TV)
Mark Twain, *The Adventures of Huckleberry Finn*
Robert Penn Warren, *All the King's Men* (M)
Evelyn Waugh, *Brideshead Revisited* (TV)
   Men at Arms
Mary Webb, *The House in Dormer Forest**
Virginia Woolf, *Orlando*
   To the Lighthouse

Personal Narrative

Pablo Casals, *Joys and Sorrows*
M. F. K. Fisher, *As They Were*
Janet Flanner, *Paris Journal/1944–1965*
Robert Graves, *Goodbye to All That*
Lillian Hellman, *An Unfinished Life*
C. S. Lewis, *A Grief Observed* (TV)
Mary McCarthy, *Memories of a Catholic Girlhood**
   How I Grew
George Orwell, *Such, Such Were the Joys*
Arthur Rubinstein, *My Young Years*
Gertrude Stein, *The Autobiography of Alice B. Toklas*
Gloria Steinem, *Outrageous Acts and Everyday Rebellions*

Ethnic

Maya Angelou, *I Know Why the Caged Bird Sings*
   The Heart of a Woman
James Baldwin, *The Fire Next Time*
   Nobody Knows My Name
   No Name in the Street
Vine Deloria, *Custer Died for Your Sins*
Frederick Douglass, *Narrative of the Life of an American Slave*
W. E. B. DuBois, *The Souls of Black Folk*
Ralph Ellison, *Going to the Territory*
John Hope Franklin, *From Slavery to Freedom*
Jamake Highwater, *Songs from the Earth: American Indian Painting*
   Words in the Blood: Contemporary Indian Writers
Nathan I. Huggins, *Black Odyssey*

Harlem Renaissance
Slave and Citizen: The Life of Frederick Douglass
Leroi Jones, *Blues People* (music)
Maxine Hong Kingston, *China Men*
The Woman Warrior
Samella Lewis, *Art: African American*
N. Scott Momaday, *The Way to Rainy Mountain*
H. Brett Melendy, *Asians in America*
William Peterson, *Japanese Americans*
Richard Pollenberg, *One Nation Divisible: Class, Race, Ethnicity in the U.S. Since 1938*
Alan Riding, *Our Distant Neighbors*
Richard Rodriguez, *The Hunger of Memory*
Lesley Byrd Simpson, *Many Mexicans*
Eileen Southern, *Music of Black Americans*
Stan Steiner, *La Raza: The Mexican Americans*
Wilcomb E. Washburn, *The Indian in America*
Richard Wright, *American Hunger**
Black Boy

Literary Criticism
Marchette Chute, *Geoffrey Chaucer of England*
John Ciardi, *How Does a Poem Mean*
E. M. Forster, *Aspects of the Novel*
Arnold Kettle, *An Introduction to the English Novel**
D. H. Lawrence, *Studies in Classic American Literature*
J. R. R. Tolkien, "Beowulf, the Monsters, & the Critics"*
Dorothy Van Ghent, *The English Novel*
Virginia Woolf, *The Second Common Reader*

Humanities
Sally Barnes, *Terpsichore in Sneakers* (dance)
Bruno Bettelheim, *The Uses of Enchantment*
Kenneth Clark, *Civilization** (TV)
Marcia Davenport, *Mozart*
John Gassner, *Masters of the Drama*
Harley Granville-Barker, *Prefaces to Shakespeare*
Joseph Kerman, *Contemplating Music*
Beaumont Newhall, *The History of Photography*
Marcia B. Siegal, *The Shapes of Change* (dance)
C. P. Snow, *The Two Cultures*
Walter Sorell, *Dance in Its Time*

Science
Isaac Asimov, *The Human Body*
The Human Brain
Eric T. Bell, *The Development of Mathematics*
Jeremy Bernstein, *Experiencing Science*
Science Observed
Jacob Bronowski, *The Ascent of Man*

N. P. Davis, *Lawrence and Oppenheimer*
Adrian Desmond, *The Hot-Blooded Dinosaurs*
Gerald Durrell, *My Family and Other Animals*
Fauna and Family
Richard Feynman, *Surely You're Joking, Mr. Feynman*
Karl von Frisch, *Animal Architecture*
George Gamow, *Mr. Tompkins* (series)
One, Two, Three . . . Infinity
Jane Goodall, *In the Shadow of Man*
Stephen Jay Gould, *Ever Since Darwin*
Arthur Koestler, *The Case of the Midwife Toad*
Aldo Leopold, *Sand County Almanac*
Konrad Lorenz, *King Solomon's Ring*
On Aggression
Jonathan Miller, *The Body in Question*
Scientific American Books, *The Biosphere*
The Brain
Energy and Power
Evolution
The Ocean
The Solar System
Volcanoes and the Earth's Interior
James Watson, *The Double Helix*
Gary Zukav, *The Dancing Wu Li Masters*

Social Sciences
Frederick Lewis Allen, *Only Yesterday*
Stephen Ambrose, *Rise to Globalism: U.S. Foreign Policy, 1938–1980*
Corelli Barnet, *The Desert Generals*
The Sword Bearers
Peter Berger, *Invitation to Sociology*
Fritjof Capra, *The Turning Point*
Vincent Cronin, *Napoleon*
Will and Ariel Durant, *The Story of Civilization*
Einhard and Notken the Stammerer, *Two Lives of Charlemagne*
J. Huizinga, *The Waning of the Middle Ages*
Joseph P. Lash, *Eleanor and Franklin* (TV)
Joe McGinniss, *The Selling of the President, 1968*
Paul MacKendrick, *The Mute Stones Speak*
Nancy Mitford, *Frederick the Great*
Edmund Morgan, *The Puritan Dilemma*
Johannes Nohl, *The Black Death*
Eileen Power, *Medieval People*
Josephine Tey, *The Daughter of Time*
Barbara Tuchman, *A Distant Mirror*
The Guns of August
T. H. White, *The Making of the President* (series)
Edmund Wilson, *To the Finland Station*
Michael Wood, *In Search of the Trojan War* (TV)

Practice Exercises

On the following pages you will find four reading exercises. Allow about 30 minutes for each group. The correct answers, as well as answer explanations, are given at the end of the chapter.

Practice the testing tactics you have learned as you work. Your reading score will improve.

Reading Comprehension Exercise A

Each passage below is followed by questions based on its content. Answer all questions following a passage on the basis of what is stated or implied in that passage.

The best Eskimo carvings of all ages seem to possess a powerful ability to reach across the great barriers of language and time and communicate directly with us. The more we look at these carvings, the more life we perceive hidden within them. We discover subtle living forms of the animal, human, and mystical world. These arctic carvings are not the cold sculptures of a frozen world. Instead, they reveal to us the passionate feelings of a vital people well aware of all the joys, terrors, tranquility, and wildness of life around them.

Eskimo carvers are people moved by dreams. In spite of all their new contacts with outsiders, they are still concerned with their own kind of mystical imagery. The most skillful carvers possess a bold confidence, a direct approach to their art that has a special freedom unsullied by any kind of formalized training.

Eskimo carvers have strong skilled hands, used to forcing hard materials with their simple tools. Their hunting life and the northern environment invigorates them. Bad weather often imposes a special kind of leisure, giving them time in which to perfect their carvings.

They are among the last of the hunting societies that have retained some part of the keen sense of observation that we have so long forgotten. The carvers are also butchers of meat, and therefore masters in the understanding of animal anatomy. Flesh and bones and sheaths of muscle seem to move in their works. They show us how to drive the caribou, how to hold a child, how to walk cautiously on thin ice. Through their eyes we understand the dangerous power of a polar bear. In the very best of Eskimo art we see vibrant animal and human forms that stand quietly or tensely, strongly radiating a sense of life. We can see, and even feel with our hands, the cold sleekness of seals, the hulking weight of walrus, the icy swiftness of trout, the flowing rhythm in a flight of geese. In their art we catch brief glimpses of a people who have long possessed a very different approach to the whole question of life and death.

In Eskimo art there is much evidence of humour which the carvers have in abundance. Some of the carvings are caricatures of themselves, of ourselves, and of situations, or records of ancient legends. Their laughter may be subtle, or broad and Chaucerian.

Perhaps no one can accurately define the right way or wrong way to create a carving. Each carver must follow his own way, in his own time. Technique in itself is meaningless unless it serves to express content. According to the Eskimo, the best carvings possess a sense of movement that seems to come from within the material itself, a feeling of tension, a living excitement.

1. The author is primarily concerned with
   (A) showing how Eskimo carvings achieve their effects
   (B) describing how Eskimo artists resist the influence of outsiders
   (C) discussing the significant characteristics of Eskimo art
   (D) explaining how Eskimo carvers use their strength to manipulate hard materials
   (E) interpreting the symbolism of Eskimo art

2. The author's attitude toward Eskimo art is one of
   (A) condescension   (B) awe   (C) admiration
     (D) regret   (E) bewilderment

3. With which of the following statements would the author most likely agree?
   (A) Formal training may often destroy an artist's originality.
   (B) Artists should learn their craft by studying the works of experts.
   (C) The content of a work of art is insignificant.
   (D) Caricatures have no place in serious art.
   (E) Eskimo art is interesting more as an expression of a life view than as a serious art form.

4. The author gives examples of the subjects of Eskimo carvings primarily to
   (A) show that they have no relevance to modern life
   (B) indicate the artist's lack of imagination
   (C) imply that other artists have imitated them
   (D) prove that the artists' limited experience of life has been a handicap
   (E) suggest the quality and variety of the work

5. According to the passage, Eskimo carvings have all the following characteristics EXCEPT
   (A) wit   (B) subtlety   (C) passion
     (D) formality   (E) terror

The whole atmosphere of the world in which we live is tinged by science, as is shown most immediately and strikingly by our modern conveniences and material resources. A little deeper thinking shows that the influence of science goes much farther and colors the entire mental outlook of modern civilized man on the world about him. Perhaps one of the most telling evidences of this is his growing freedom from superstition. Freedom from superstition is the result of the conviction that the world is not governed by caprice, but that it is a world of order and can be understood by man if he will only try hard enough and be clever enough. This conviction that the world is understandable is, doubtless, the most important single gift of science to civilization. The widespread acceptance of this view can be dated to the discovery by Newton of the universal sway of the law of gravitation; and for this reason Newton may be justly regarded as the most important single contributor to modern life.

6. Which of the following best expresses the author's purpose in writing this passage?

   (A) To give an opinion of the chief benefit of science
   (B) To enumerate the modern conveniences produced by science
   (C) To inform readers about important scientific principles
   (D) To describe Newton's discoveries
   (E) To persuade readers that science leads to civilization

7. According to the author, Newton's chief contribution was his

   (A) encouragement of intelligent inquiry
   (B) great book on the laws of gravity
   (C) understanding of a world based on order
   (D) early development of scientific methodology
   (E) many practical inventions that have given rise to modern conveniences

---

"But perhaps you are telling lies?" Raskolnikov put in.

"I rarely lie," answered Svidrigaïlov
Line thoughtfully, apparently not noticing the rudeness
(5)   of the question.

"And in the past, have you ever seen ghosts before?"

"Y-yes, I have seen them, but only once in my life, six years ago. I had a serf, Filka; just
(10) after his burial I called out forgetting 'Filka, my pipe!' He came in and went to the cupboard where my pipes were. I sat still and thought 'he is doing it out of revenge,' because we had a violent quarrel just before his death. 'How dare
(15) you come in with a hole in your elbow,' I said. 'Go away, you scamp!' He turned and went out, and never came again. I didn't tell Marfa Petrovna at the time. I wanted to have a service sung for him, but I was ashamed."
(20) "You should go to a doctor."

"I know I am not well, without your telling me, though I don't know what's wrong; I believe I am five times as strong as you are. I didn't ask you whether you believe that ghosts are seen, but
(25) whether you believe that they exist."

"No, I won't believe it!" Raskolnikov cried, with positive anger.

"What do people generally say?" muttered

Svidrigaïlov, as though speaking to himself,
(30) looking aside and bowing his head: "They say, 'You are ill, so what appears to you is only unreal fantasy.' But that's not strictly logical. I agree that ghosts only appear to the sick, but that only proves that they are unable to appear except
(35) to the sick, not that they don't exist."

"Nothing of the sort," Raskolnikov insisted irritably.

"No? You don't think so?" Svidrigaïlov went on, looking at him deliberately. "But what do
(40) you say to this argument (help me with it): ghosts are as it were shreds and fragments of other worlds, the beginning of them. A man in health has, of course, no reason to see them, because he is above all a man of this earth and is bound
(45) for the sake of completeness and order to live only in this life. But as soon as one is ill, as soon as the normal earthly order of the organism is broken, one begins to realise the possibility of another world; and the more seriously ill one is,
(50) the closer becomes one's contact with that other world, so that as soon as the man dies he steps straight into that world. I thought of that long ago. If you believe in a future life, you could believe in that, too."

8. The passage indicates that Raskolnikov thinks Svidrigaïlov's belief in ghosts is

   (A) justified by the experiences he relates
   (B) a symptom of some illness
   (C) totally inexplicable
   (D) the result of a dream
   (E) a fit subject for scientific experiment

9. Raskolnikov's anger (lines 26–27) suggests that

   (A) he is bored with Svidrigaïlov's conversation
   (B) he is eager to recount an experience of his own
   (C) he is unaccustomed to polite conversation
   (D) he has some personal distaste for the subject
   (E) Svidrigaïlov's theories would annoy anyone

10. According to Svidragaïlov, most people do not see ghosts because they

    (A) are unworthy of seeing them
    (B) are too concerned with worldly affairs
    (C) have been taught that ghosts do not exist
    (D) do not know anyone who has died
    (E) do not know how to summon ghosts

11. Which of the following definitions of "ghost" is closest to Svidrigaïlov's view as presented in the passage?

    (A) A ghost is a visitor from another world.
    (B) A ghost is a symbol of evil.
    (C) A ghost is a product of the imagination.
    (D) A ghost is a messenger of doom.
    (E) A ghost is a lost spirit.

The passage below was written by Samuel Taylor Coleridge.

During the first year that Mr. Wordsworth and I were neighbours, our conversations turned frequently on the two cardinal points of poetry,
Line the power of exciting the sympathy of the reader
(5) by a faithful adherence to the truth of nature, and the power of giving the interest of novelty by the modifying colours of imagination. The sudden charm, which accidents of light and shade, which moonlight or sunset diffused over a known and
(10) familiar landscape, appeared to represent the practicability of combining both. These are the poetry of nature. The thought suggested itself— (to which of us I do not recollect)—that a series of poems might be composed of two sorts. In the
(15) one, the incidents and agents were to be, in part at least, supernatural; and the excellence aimed at was to consist in the interesting of the affections by the dramatic truth of such emotions, as would naturally accompany such
(20) situations, supposing them real. And real in this sense they have been to every human being who, from whatever source of delusion, has at any time believed himself under supernatural agency. For the second class, subjects were to be chosen
(25) from ordinary life; the characters and incidents were to be such as will be found in every village and its vicinity, where there is a meditative and feeling mind to seek after them, or to notice them, when they present themselves.
(30)   In this idea originated the plan of the LYRICAL BALLADS; in which it was agreed, that my endeavours should be directed to persons and characters supernatural, or at least romantic; yet so as to transfer from our inward nature a human
(35) interest and a semblance of truth sufficient to procure for these shadows of imagination that willing suspension of disbelief for the moment, which constitutes poetic faith. Mr. Wordsworth, on the other hand, was to propose to himself as
(40) his object, to give the charm of novelty to things of every day, and to excite a feeling analogous to the supernatural, by awakening the mind's attention to the lethargy of custom, and directing it to the loveliness and the wonders of the world
(45) before us; an inexhaustible treasure, but for which, in consequence of the film of familiarity and selfish solicitude, we have eyes, yet see not, ears that hear not, and hearts that neither feel nor understand.

12. Which of the following is the best title for this passage?

(A) Suspension of Disbelief
(B) A Great Poetic Collaboration
(C) Adherence to Nature
(D) Two Great Minds
(E) Wordsworth and Coleridge

13. The two poets differed in their

(A) ideas of the two main points of poetry
(B) desire to write a book of poems
(C) choice of subject matter
(D) plans for the organization of *Lyrical Ballads*
(E) evaluation of the merits of their poems

14. From the author's discussion of the supernatural in lines 14–23, which of the following can be inferred?

(A) He believes that the supernatural is real.
(B) He does not believe that supernatural agencies exist.
(C) He thinks supernatural events have no place in poetry.
(D) He feels readers will doubt the truth of supernatural events.
(E) He thinks the supernatural is boring.

15. The last three lines of the passage can best be restated as

(A) beauty is in the eye of the beholder
(B) people spend too much time alone
(C) only a poet can appreciate nature
(D) familiarity breeds contempt
(E) out of sight, out of mind

In the warm enclosed waters of farm ponds, conditions are very likely to be lethal for fish when insecticides are applied in the vicinity. As many examples show, the poison is carried in by rains and runoff from surrounding lands. Sometimes the ponds receive not only contaminated runoff but also a direct dose as crop-dusting pilots neglect to shut off the duster in passing over a pond. Even without such complications, normal agricultural use subjects fish to far heavier concentrations of chemicals than would be required to kill them. In other words, a marked reduction in the poundages used would hardly alter the lethal situation, for applications of over 0.1 pound per acre to the pond itself are generally considered hazardous. And the poison, once introduced is hard to get rid of. One pond that had been treated with DDT to remove unwanted shiners remained so poisonous through repeated drainings and flushings that it killed 94 percent of the sunfish with which it was later stocked. Apparently the chemical remained in the mud of the pond bottom.

In some parts of the world the cultivation of fish in ponds provides an indispensable source of food. In such places the use of insecticides without regard for the effects on fish creates immediate problems. In Rhodesia, for example, the young of an important food fish, the Kafue bream, are killed by exposure to only 0.04 parts per million of DDT in shallow pools. Even smaller doses of many other insecticides would be lethal. The shallow waters in which these fish live are favorable mosquito-breeding places. The problem of

controlling mosquitoes and at the same time conserving
a fish important in the Central African diet has
obviously not been solved satisfactorily.

16. Which of the following would be the best title for
this passage?

(A) The Water of Farm Ponds
(B) The Effects of Insecticides on Fish
(C) The Uses of DDT
(D) The Cultivation of Fish as Food
(E) Saving African Food Supplies

17. The author's tone in this passage can best be
described as

(A) reportorial   (B) sarcastic   (C) angry
   (D) condemnatory   (E) mournful

18. According to the passage, which of the following
are responsible for the presence of insecticides in
ponds?

   I. The weather
   II. Human error
   III. Common farming methods

(A) I only   (B) III only   (C) I and II only
(D) I and III only   (E) I, II, and III

19. The author uses the case of the Rhodesian fish
primarily in order to

(A) show the harmful effects of killing fish
(B) prove that problems are the same everywhere
(C) evaluate African farming practices
(D) consider the problem of controlling
    mosquitoes
(E) contrast African and American insecticide use

20. In this passage, the author does all of the following
EXCEPT

(A) state a problem
(B) propose a solution
(C) give examples
(D) relate causes
(E) state effects

   When a new movement in Art attains a certain
vogue, it is advisable to find out what its
advocates are aiming at, for however farfetched
Line and unreasonable their tenets may seem today, it
 (5) is possible that in years to come they may be
regarded as normal. With regard to Futurist
poetry, however, the case is rather different; for
whatever Futurist poetry may be—even
admitting that the theory on which it is based
(10) may be right—it can hardly be classed as
Literature.
   This, in brief, is what the Futurist says: for a
century past conditions of life have been
continually speeding up, till now we live in a
(15) world of noise and violence and speed.

Consequently, our feelings, thoughts and
emotions have undergone a corresponding
change. This speeding up of life, says the
Futurist, requires a new form of expression. We
(20) must speed up our literature too, if we want to
interpret modern stress. We must pour out a
cataract of essential words, unhampered by
stops, or qualifying adjectives, or finite verbs.
Instead of describing sounds we must make up
(25) words that imitate them; we must use many sizes
of type and different colored inks on the same
page, and shorten or lengthen words at will.
   Certainly their descriptions of battles are
vividly chaotic. But it is a little disconcerting to
(30) read in the explanatory notes that a certain line
describes a fight between a Turkish and a
Bulgarian officer on a bridge over which they
both fall into the river—and then to find that the
line consists of the noise of their falling and the
(35) weights of the officers: "Pluff! Pluff! a hundred
and eighty-five kilograms."
   This, though it fulfils the laws and requirements of Futurist poetry, can hardly be classed
as Literature. All the same, no thinking man can
(40) refuse to accept their first proposition: that a
great change in our emotional life calls for a
change of expression. The whole question is
really this: have we essentially changed?

21. The main idea of this selection is best expressed as

(A) the Past versus the Future
(B) changes in modern life
(C) merits of the Futurist movement
(D) what constitutes literature
(E) an evaluation of Futurist poetry

22. When novel ideas appear, it is desirable, according
to the writer, to

(A) discover the goals of their adherents
(B) ignore them entirely
(C) follow the fashion of the moment
(D) regard them as normal until proven otherwise
(E) adopt them slowly

23. According to the passage, the Futurist poet uses
all of the following devices EXCEPT

(A) imitative sounds
(B) modifying adjectives
(C) inks of various hues
(D) stream of necessary words
(E) lengthened words

24. It can be inferred that the author quotes a Futurist
poem (lines 35–36) to

(A) emphasize the importance of good literature
(B) indicate that Futurists describe battles vividly
(C) show that it is in keeping with the speed of
    modern life
(D) suggest that it is not great poetry
(E) identify the source of poetic imagination

25. The last two sentences in the passage (lines 39–43) chiefly suggest which of the following?

    (A) A new type of writing is needed in the modern world.
    (B) Futurist theories are correct.
    (C) Traditional literature still expresses human emotions.

(D) When people change, they will be better able to appreciate poetry.
(E) No literature can fully express human emotions.

Reading Comprehension Exercise B

Each passage below is followed by questions based on its content. Answer all questions following a passage on the basis of what is <u>stated</u> or <u>implied</u> in that passage.

Great mural painting begins in Mexico after the Revolution. Having already given proof of his artistic ability in the delicate lines of pre-Spanish
Line reliefs and in the religious pictures of the colonial
(5) period, the Mexican was ready for the notable achievements of the mural painting of today. A wave of social fervor, of passionate convictions, and of beauty animates the forms of the great Mexican frescoes. On Mexican walls were
(10) written the life of the people and the history of the nation.
This painting was the perfect union of a strong art and a living thought. Diego Rivera drew the life and the history of the country with a richness
(15) of composition, a formal harmony, and a sense of mass and space that no one has surpassed in our time. José Clemente Orozco, penetrating yet deeper, painted with a generous cruelty and a rough tenderness the bold and broken symbols of
(20) contemporary wickedness, truth everlasting, and innate tragedy. With these men, there came a whole new generation of painters.
Mexican mural painting of the twentieth century is not only Mexico's greatest contribu-
(25) tion to the art of our time but one of the most vigorous and original contemporary esthetic manifestations.

1. The passage primarily concerns the
    (A) influence of Mexican art on the rest of the world
    (B) art of Mexican mural painting
    (C) paintings of Diego Rivera and José Clemente Orozco
    (D) life and history of the Mexican people
    (E) history of Mexican art

2. The word ''frescoes'' (line 9) means
    (A) beautiful paintings   (B) Mexican art
    (C) wall paintings   (D) convictions
    (E) modern art

3. The author's attitude toward the art of Diego Rivera and José Clemente Orozco is
    (A) sarcastic   (B) condescending
    (C) wondering   (D) exultant   (E) approving

4. Based on the information in the passage, an artist inspired by the Mexican muralists would most likely produce which of the following?
    (A) A painting of a bowl of fruit
    (B) An abstract pattern of stripes
    (C) A panorama of the history of a country
    (D) A portrait of a family
    (E) A realistic study of a landscape

5. With which of the following statements would the author most likely agree?
    (A) The subject matter of a painting is unimportant.
    (B) The twentieth-century muralists were the first great artists in Mexico.
    (C) Diego Rivera was a better artist than José Clemente Orozco.
    (D) Composition and harmony are important elements in painting.
    (E) Mural painting is Mexico's only contribution to the art of our time.

Geometry is a very old science. We are told by Herodotus, a Greek historian, that geometry had its origin in Egypt along the banks of the river Nile. The first record we have of its study is found in a manuscript written by Ahmes, an Egyptian scholar, about 1550 B.C. This manuscript is believed to be a copy of a treatise which dated back probably more than a thousand years, and describes the use of geometry at that time in a very crude form of surveying or measurement. In fact, geometry, which means ''earth measurement,'' received its name in this manner. This re-measuring of the land was necessary due to the annual overflow of the river Nile and the consequent destroying of the boundaries of farm lands.

This early geometry was very largely a list of rules or formulas for finding the areas of plane figures. Many of these rules were inaccurate, but, in the main, they were fairly satisfactory.

6. The title below that best expresses the ideas of this passage is
   (A) Plane Figures
   (B) Beginnings of Geometry
   (C) Manuscript of Ahmes
   (D) Surveying in Egypt
   (E) Importance of the Study of Geometry

7. According to the passage, in developing geometry the early Egyptians were primarily concerned with
   (A) discovering why formulas used in measuring were true
   (B) determining property boundaries
   (C) measuring the overflow of the Nile
   (D) generalizing formulas
   (E) constructing a logical system of geometry

8. It can be inferred that one of the most important factors in the development of geometry as a science was
   (A) Ahmes' treatise
   (B) the inaccuracy of the early rules and formulas
   (C) the annual flooding of the Nile Valley
   (D) the destruction of farm crops by the Nile
   (E) an ancient manuscript copied by Ahmes

The single business of Henry Thoreau, during forty-odd years of eager activity, was to discover an economy calculated to provide a satisfying life. His one concern, that gave to his ramblings in Concord fields a value of high adventure, was to explore the true meaning of wealth. As he understood the problem of economics, there were three possible solutions open to him: to exploit himself, to exploit his fellows, or to reduce the problem to its lowest denominator. The first was quite impossible—to imprison oneself in a treadmill when the morning called to great adventure. To exploit one's fellows seemed to Thoreau's sensitive social conscience an even greater infidelity. Freedom with abstinence seemed to him better than serfdom with material well-being, and he was content to move to Walden Pond and so set about the high business of living, "to front only the essential facts of life and to see what it had to teach." He did not advocate that other men should build cabins and live isolated. He had no wish to dogmatize concerning the best mode of living—each must settle that for himself. But that a satisfying life should be lived, he was vitally concerned. The story of his emancipation from the lower economics is the one romance of his life, and *Walden* is his great book. It is a book in praise of life rather than of Nature, a record of calculating economies that studied saving in order to spend more largely. But it is a book of social criticism as well, in spite of its explicit denial of such a purpose. In

considering the true nature of economy he concluded, with Ruskin, that the cost of a thing is the amount of life which is required in exchange for it, immediately or in the long run. In *Walden* Thoreau elaborated the text: "The only wealth is life."

9. The author's primary purpose in this passage is to
   (A) discuss and assess economic problems
   (B) describe Thoreau's philosophy of life
   (C) prove that *Walden* was Thoreau's greatest book
   (D) show how Thoreau was able to live in isolation
   (E) reevaluate life at Walden Pond

10. On the basis of the passage, Thoreau was all of the following EXCEPT
    (A) dogmatic   (B) liberated   (C) energetic
    (D) self-denying   (E) critical

11. It can be inferred that the author thinks of Thoreau's "emancipation from the lower economics" as a romance because it
    (A) wholly captured Thoreau's imagination
    (B) involved him in the love of a woman
    (C) entailed social criticism
    (D) was an adventure story
    (E) was embodied in Thoreau's greatest book

12. On the basis of the passage, it can be inferred that Thoreau believed the wealth of an individual is measured by
    (A) the money he or she makes
    (B) the experience he or she gains
    (C) the amount he or she saves
    (D) his or her good deeds
    (E) his or her social standing in the community

13. The author's tone in speaking of Thoreau is
    (A) ironic   (B) critical   (C) indifferent
    (D) admiring   (E) effusive

Newman promised himself to pay Mademoiselle Noémie another visit at the Louvre. He was curious about the progress of his
Line copies, but it must be added that he was still
(5) more curious about the progress of the young lady herself. He went one afternoon to the great museum, and wandered through several of the rooms in fruitless quest of her. He was bending his steps to the long hall of the Italian masters,
(10) when suddenly he found himself face to face with Valentin de Bellegarde. The young Frenchman greeted him with ardor, and assured him that he was a godsend. He himself was in the worst of humors and he wanted some one to contradict.
(15)   "In a bad humor among all these beautiful things?" said Newman. "I thought you were so fond of pictures, especially the old black ones. There are two or three here that ought to keep

you in spirits.''

(20)   ''Oh, to-day,'' answered Valentin, ''I am not in a mood for pictures, and the more beautiful they are the less I like them. Their great staring eyes and fixed positions irritate me. I feel as if I were at some big, dull party, in a room full of (25) people I shouldn't wish to speak to. What should I care for their beauty? It's a bore, and, worse still, it's a reproach. I have a great many *ennuis*; I feel vicious.''

''If the Louvre has so little comfort for you, (30) why in the world did you come here?'' Newman asked.

''That is one of my ennuis. I came to meet my cousin—a dreadful English cousin, a member of my mother's family—who is in Paris for a week (35) with her husband, and who wishes me to point out the 'principal beauties.' Imagine a woman who wears a green crape bonnet in December and has straps sticking out of the ankles of her interminable boots! My mother begged I would (40) do something to oblige them. I have undertaken to play *valet de place* this afternoon. They were to have met me here at two o'clock, and I have been waiting for them twenty minutes. Why doesn't she arrive? She has at least a pair of feet (45) to carry her. I don't know whether to be furious at their playing me false, or delighted to have escaped them.''

''I think in your place I would be furious,'' said Newman, ''because they may arrive yet, and (50) then your fury will still be of use to you. Whereas if you were delighted and they were afterwards to turn up, you might not know what to do with your delight.''

''You give me excellent advice, and I already (55) feel better. I will be furious; I will let them go to the deuce and I myself will go with you—unless by chance you too have a rendezvous.''

14. The passage indicates that Newman has gone to the Louvre in order to

(A) meet Valentin
(B) look at the paintings
(C) explore Paris
(D) keep an appointment
(E) see Mademoiselle Noémie

15. According to the passage, Valentin is unhappy about being at the Louvre because he

(A) hates the paintings of the Italian masters
(B) has accidentally met Newman in the long hall
(C) wishes to be at a party
(D) feels that beauty should be that of nature
(E) is supposed to guide his cousin through it

16. It can be inferred from the passage that in lines 23–27 Valentin is expressing his annoyance by

(A) walking out of the Louvre in a fit of temper
(B) making insulting remarks about a woman

(C) not accepting Newman's advice
(D) criticizing the paintings
(E) refusing to do as his mother wishes

17. With which of the following statements would Valentin most likely agree?

  I. Clothes make the man.
  II. Blood is thicker than water.
  III. Better late than never.

(A) I only   (B) II only   (C) III only
  (D) I and II only   (E) I, II, and III

18. Newman's role in the conversation is that of

(A) a heckler   (B) a gossiper   (C) a confidant
(D) an enemy   (E) a doubter

Both plants and animals of many sorts show remarkable changes in form, structure, growth habits, and even mode of reproduction in *Line* becoming adapted to different climatic (5) environments, types of food supply, or modes of living. This divergence in response to evolution is commonly expressed by altering the form and function of some part or parts of the organism, the original identity of which is clearly (10) discernible. For example, the creeping foot of the snail is seen in related marine pteropods to be modified into a flapping organ useful for swimming, and is changed into prehensile arms that bear suctorial disks in the squids and other (15) cephalopods. The limbs of various mammals are modified according to several different modes of life—for swift running (cursorial) as in the horse and antelope, for swinging in trees (arboreal) as in the monkeys, for digging (fossorial) as in the (20) moles and gophers, for flying (volant) as in the bats, for swimming (aquatic) as in the seals, whales and dolphins, and for other adaptations. The structures or organs that show the main change in connection with this adaptive (25) divergence are commonly identified readily as homologous, in spite of great alterations. Thus, the finger and wristbones of a bat and whale, for instance, have virtually nothing in common except that they are definitely equivalent elements (30) of the mammalian limb.

19. The best title for this passage is

(A) Adaptive Divergence
(B) Evolution
(C) Mammals and Other Animals
(D) Changes in Organs
(E) Our Changing Times

20. The word ''homologous'' (line 26) means

(A) having the same origin
(B) used for the same purpose
(C) identical
(D) dissimilar
(E) greatly altered

Music and literature, the two temporal arts,
contrive their pattern of sounds in time; or, in
other words, of sounds and pauses. Communi-
Line cation may be made in broken words, the busi-
(5) ness of life be carried on with substan-
tives alone; but that is not what we call literature; and the true business of the literary artist
is to plait or weave his meaning, involving
it around itself; so that each sentence, by
(10) successive phrases, shall first come into a kind of
knot, and then, after a moment of suspended
meaning, solve and clear itself. In every properly
constructed sentence there should be observed
this knot or hitch; so that (however delicately)
(15) we are led to foresee, to expect, and then to
welcome the successive phrases. The pleasure
may be heightened by an element of surprise, as,
very grossly, in the common figure of the
antithesis, or, with much greater subtlety, where
(20) an antithesis is first suggested and then deftly
evaded. Each phrase, besides, is to be comely in
itself; and between the implication and the
evolution of the sentence there should be a
satisfying equipoise of sound; for nothing more
(25) often disappoints the ear than a sentence
solemnly and sonorously prepared, and hastily
and weakly finished. Nor should the balance be
too striking and exact, for the one rule is to be
infinitely various; to interest, to disappoint, to
(30) surprise, and yet still to gratify; to be ever
changing, as it were, the stitch, and yet still to
give the effect of an ingenious neatness.

21. According to the author, great literature depends
on its

(A) clarity of thought

(B) subtleties of sound
(C) sense of logic
(D) preciseness of balance
(E) use of broad contrasts

22. The author calls music and literature "the two
temporal arts" because

(A) they are impermanent by nature
(B) they are both used in temples
(C) they are both based on antithesis
(D) they are composed of periods of sound and
silence
(E) they both depend on balance

23. The author implies that the function of the writer
is to

(A) communicate with the reader
(B) carry on the business of life
(C) move the reader to action
(D) present ideas attractively
(E) capture balance and antithesis

24. The author believes that antithesis (line 20) is a
means of securing

(A) surprise   (B) subtlety   (C) comeliness
(D) balance   (E) solemnity

25. According to the passage, writers should do all of
the following EXCEPT

(A) lead readers to anticipate what is coming next
(B) surprise readers
(C) disappoint readers
(D) construct sentences carefully
(E) balance sounds exactly

Reading Comprehension Exercise C

Each passage below is followed by questions based on its content. Answer all questions following a passage on the
basis of what is stated or implied in that passage.

When you first saw a piece of African art, it
impressed you as a unit; you did not see it as a
collection of shapes or forms. This, of course,
Line means that the shapes and volumes within the
(5) sculpture itself were coordinated so successfully
that the viewer was affected emotionally.

It is entirely valid to ask how, from a purely
artistic point of view, this unity was achieved.
And we must also inquire whether there is a
(10) recurrent pattern or rules or a plastic language
and vocabulary which is responsible for the
powerful communication of emotion which the
best African sculpture achieves. If there is such a
pattern or rules, are these rules applied
(15) consciously or instinctively to obtain so many
works of such high artistic quality?

It is obvious from the study of art history that

an intense and unified emotional experience, such
as the Christian credo of the Byzantine or 12th or
(20) 13th century Europe, when expressed in art
forms, gave great unity, coherence, and power to
art. But such an integrated feeling was only the
inspirational element for the artist, only the
starting point of the creative act. The expression
(25) of this emotion and its realization in the work
could be done only with discipline and thorough
knowledge of the craft. And the African sculptor
was a highly trained workman. He started his
apprenticeship with a master when a child, and
(30) he learned the tribal styles and the use of tools
and the nature of woods so thoroughly that his
carving became what Boas calls "motor action."
He carved automatically and instinctively.

The African carver followed his rules without

(35) thinking of them; indeed, they never seem to have been formulated in words. But such rules existed, for accident and coincidence can not explain the common plastic language of African sculpture. There is too great a consistency from *(40)* one work to another. Yet, although the African, with amazing insight into art, used these rules, I am certain that he was not conscious of them. This is the great mystery of such a traditional art: talent, or the ability certain people have, without *(45)* conscious effort, to follow the rules which later the analyst can discover only from the work of art which has already been created.

1. The author is primarily concerned with

   (A) discussing how African sculptors achieved their effects
   (B) listing the rules followed in African art
   (C) relating African art to the art of 12th or 13th century Europe
   (D) integrating emotion and realization
   (E) expressing the beauty of African art

2. According to the passage, one of the outstanding features of African sculpture is

   (A) its subject matter
   (B) the feelings it arouses
   (C) the training of the artists
   (D) its strangeness
   (E) its emphasis on movement

3. The word "plastic" in line 38 means

   (A) synthetic
   (B) linguistic
   (C) consistent
   (D) sculptural
   (E) repetitive

4. According to the information in the passage, an African carver can best be compared to a

   (A) chef following a recipe
   (B) fluent speaker of English who is just beginning to study French
   (C) batter who hits a homerun in his or her first baseball game
   (D) concert pianist performing a well-rehearsed concerto
   (E) writer who is grammatically expert but stylistically uncreative

5. Which of the following titles best summarizes the content of the passage?

   (A) The Apprenticeship of the African Sculptor
   (B) The History of African Sculpture
   (C) How African Art Achieves Unity
   (D) Analyzing African Art
   (E) The Unconscious Rules of African Art

One of the most urgent problems in teaching handwriting is presented by the left-handed child. The traditional policy has been to attempt to induce all children to write with their right hands. Parents and teachers alike have an antipathy to the child's using his left hand. On the other hand, psychologists have shown beyond a doubt that some persons are naturally left-handed and that it is much more difficult for them to do any skillful act with the right hand than with the left hand. Some believe, furthermore, that to compel a left-handed child to write with his right hand may make him nervous and may cause stammering. There seems to be some cases in which this is true, although in the vast majority of children who change over, no ill effects are noticed. In addition to these difficulties, left-handedness sometimes seems to cause mirror writing—writing from right to left—and reversals in reading, as reading "was" for "saw."

6. The title below that best expresses the ideas of this passage is

   (A) Nervous Aspects Connected with Handwriting
   (B) Teaching Handwriting
   (C) The Problems of the Left-handed Child
   (D) A Special Problem in Teaching Handwriting
   (E) Stammering, Mirror Writing and Reversals

7. The author implies that

   (A) parents should break children of left-handedness
   (B) left-handed children need special consideration
   (C) left-handed persons are inclined to stutter
   (D) left-handed persons are not more brilliant than right-handed ones
   (E) left-handed persons are less skillful than right-handed ones

8. According to the passage, the traditional policy in teaching handwriting has

   (A) dismayed the experts
   (B) resulted in failure to learn to write
   (C) aimed at mirror writing
   (D) made many children skillful with both hands
   (E) resulted in unsolved problems

'My father is not very well,' said Eleanor.

John Bold was very sorry—so sorry. He hoped it was nothing serious, and put on the unmeaningly solemn face which people usually use on such occasions.

'I especially want to speak to you about my father, Mr. Bold. Indeed, I am now here on purpose to do so. Papa is very unhappy, very unhappy indeed, about this affair of the hospital. You would pity him, Mr. Bold, if you could see how wretched it has made him.'

'Oh, Miss Harding!'

'Indeed you would—any one would pity him; but a friend, an old friend as you are—indeed you would. He is an altered man; his cheerfulness has all gone, and his sweet temper, and his kind happy tone of voice; you would hardly know him if you saw him, Mr. Bold, he is so much altered; and—and—if this goes on, he will die.' Here Eleanor had recourse to her handkerchief, and so also had her auditors; but she plucked up her courage, and went on with her tale. 'He will break his heart, and die. I am sure, Mr. Bold, it was not you who wrote those cruel things in the newspaper—'

John Bold eagerly protested that it was not, but his heart smote him as to his intimate alliance with Tom Towers.

'No, I am sure it was not; and papa has not for a moment thought so; you would not be so cruel—but it has nearly killed him. Papa cannot bear to think that people should so speak of him, and that everybody should hear him so spoken of. They have called him avaricious, and dishonest, and they say he is robbing the old men, and taking the money of the hospital for nothing.'

'I have never said so, Miss Harding. I—'

'No,' continued Eleanor, interrupting him, for she was now in the full flood tide of her eloquence; 'no, I am sure you have not; but others have said so; and if this goes on, if such things are written again, it will kill papa. Oh! Mr. Bold, if you only knew the state he is in! Now papa does not care much about money.'

Both her auditors, brother and sister, assented to this, and declared on their own knowledge that no man lived less addicted to filthy lucre than the warden.

9. According to the passage, Eleanor believes her father will die because

(A) he is suffering from a deadly disease
(B) he has told her so
(C) he is very depressed
(D) John Bold intends to kill him
(E) he plans to commit suicide

10. Of which of the following has Eleanor's father been accused?

  I. Greed
  II. Theft
  III. Blackmail

(A) I only   (B) II only   (C) III only
(D) I and II only   (E) I and III only

11. Eleanor believes all the following about her father EXCEPT that he

(A) has been greatly transformed
(B) is guilty of the charges against him
(C) cares what people think of him
(D) is pitiable in his anguish
(E) is greatly afflicted by his troubles

12. It can be inferred that John Bold

(A) had something to do with Eleanor's father's problems
(B) is indifferent to what Eleanor thinks about him
(C) lied about Eleanor's father for his own personal gain
(D) believes Eleanor's father is an evil person
(E) is one of the old men cheated by Eleanor's father

13. In the last line, the term "filthy lucre" means

(A) tobacco   (B) stealing   (C) extravagance
(D) money   (E) gambling

Our theory and practice in the area of sentencing have undergone a gradual but dramatic metamorphosis through the years. Primitive man believed that a crime created an imbalance which could be rectified only by punishing the wrongdoer. Thus, sentencing was initially vengeance-oriented. Gradually, emphasis began to be placed on the deterrent value of a sentence upon future wrongdoing.

Though deterrence is still an important consideration, increased emphasis on the possibility of reforming the offender—of returning him to the community a useful citizen—bars the harsh penalties once imposed and brings into play a new set of sentencing criteria. Today, each offender is viewed as a unique individual, and the sentencing judge seeks to know why he has committed the crime and what are the chances of a repetition of the offense. The judge's prime objective is not to punish but to treat.

This emphasis on treatment of the individual has created a host of new problems. In seeking to arrive at the best treatment for individual prisoners, judges must weigh an imposing array of factors. I believe that the primary aim of every sentence is the prevention of future crime. Little can be done to correct past damage, and a sentence will achieve its objective to the extent that it upholds general respect for the law, discourages those tempted to commit similar crimes, and leads to the rehabilitation of the offender, so that he will not run afoul of the law again. Where the offender is so hardened that rehabilitation is plainly impossible, the sentence may be designed to segregate the offender from society so that he will be unable to do any future harm. The balancing of these interacting, and often mutually antagonistic, factors requires more than a good heart and a sense of fair play on the judge's part, although these are certainly prerequisites. It requires the judge to know as much as he can about the prisoner before him. He should know the probable effects of sentences upon those who might commit similar crimes and how the prisoner is likely to react to imprisonment or probation. Because evaluation of these various factors may differ from judge to judge, the same offense will be treated differently by different judges.

The task of improving our sentencing techniques is so important to the nation's moral health that it deserves far more careful attention than it now receives from the bar and the general public. Some of those at the bar and many civic-minded individuals who usually lead even the judges in the fight for legal reform approach this subject with apathy or with erroneous preconceptions. For example, I have observed the sentiment shared by many that, after a judge has sentenced several hundred defendants, the whole process becomes one of callous routine. I have heard this feeling expressed even by attorneys who should know better.

14. The author's purpose in this passage is to
    (A) entertain readers by telling anecdotes about criminal sentencing
    (B) inform readers of sentencing practices in the past
    (C) convince judges of the need for harsher sentences
    (D) tell people not to commit crimes for which they might receive unfair sentences
    (E) persuade readers that it is important to improve sentencing techniques

15. The work "metamorphosis" in the first sentence means
    (A) restoration (B) interpretation (C) lethargy
    (D) change   (E) fault

16. A situation comparable to the ancient idea of sentencing would be
    (A) a lion stalking and killing a deer
    (B) a traffic officer putting a ticket on an illegally parked car
    (C) a child slapping a playmate who has slapped him or her
    (D) a customer returning defective merchandise
    (E) an owner scolding a pet that has tried to run away

17. The author would agree with each of the following statements EXCEPT
    (A) a judge should treat each offender as an individual
    (B) a judge should try to correct past damage
    (C) the problem of sentencing deserves study
    (D) a judge should refrain from imposing harsh penalties
    (E) a judge has to be a student of human nature

18. According to the passage, judges today should impose sentences for any of the following reasons EXCEPT
    (A) upholding respect for the law
    (B) segregating the offender
    (C) rehabilitating the offender
    (D) avenging the victim
    (E) discouraging others from committing crime

then burned. The heat they produce while burning is used to heat a known amount of water. The heat energy, or calories, contained in the plant material can then be calculated. It is also possible to tell how much energy is required to produce each calorie of food. Plants get some of their energy from the sun. However, farmers give plants that are grown for food additional energy in the form of fertilizers and other materials. In other words, the plants are given energy subsidies. In the past, energy subsidies to agricultural products were provided mainly through the labor of people and domesticated animals. Now, in our society, agriculture depends to a large extent on machines that use coal, petroleum, and natural gas, thus consuming energy sources from the past. Energy is also spent in packaging, preserving, and transporting agricultural products. It has therefore been calculated that each calorie of food we eat costs ten calories of subsidized energy.

19. Which of the following is the best title for the passage?
    (A) Getting the Most from Potential Energy
    (B) What Is a Calorie?
    (C) Conserving Energy
    (D) The Future of Energy Subsidies
    (E) Measuring Energy and Food Supplies

20. Which of the following comparisons most closely parallels the relationship between potential and kinetic energy described in the first paragraph?
    (A) A savings account to money spent on purchases
    (B) Computer memory to human intelligence
    (C) An atom to a molecule
    (D) A parasite to its host
    (E) A mountain to a valley

21. It can be inferred from the passage that the definition of energy subsidies for plants includes which of the following?
    I. Solar energy
    II. Human and animal labor
    III. Energy supplied by machines
    (A) III only   (B) I and II only
    (C) I and III only   (D) II and III only
    (E) I, II, and III

All living organisms possess energy. Energy that is not being used is known as potential energy. As the organism uses it, potential energy becomes transformed into kinetic energy. Kinetic energy can take many forms, including sound, light, and motion, but, in living organisms, all energy eventually is changed into heat. Energy is therefore measured in calories, one calorie being the amount of heat needed to warm a gram of water one degree Celsius.

It is thus possible to measure the potential energy of food supplies. Plants, for example, may be dried and

The great question that this paper will, but feebly, attempt to answer is: What is the creative process?

Line   Though much theory has accumulated, little is
(5)   really known about the power that lies at the bottom of poetic creation. It is true that great poets and artists produce beauty by employing all the powers of personality and by fusing emotions, reason and intuitions. But, what is the
(10)   magical synthesis that joins and arranges these complex parts into poetic unity?

John L. Lowes, in his justly famous *The Road to Xanadu*, developed one of the earliest and still generally acceptable answers to this tantalizing
(15) question. Imaginative creation, he concludes, is a complex process in which the conscious and unconscious minds "jointly operate." "There is . . . the deep well with its chaos of fortuitously blending images; but there is likewise the Vision
(20) which sees shining in and through the chaos, the potential lines of Form, and with the Vision the controlling Will, which gives to that potential beauty actuality."

The Deep Well is the unconscious mind that is
(25) peopled with the facts, ideas, feelings of conscious activity. The imaginative vision, an unconscious activity, shines through this land of chaos, of lights and shadows, silently seeking pattern and form. Finally, the conscious mind
(30) again, through Will, captures and embodies the idea in the final work of art. In this way is unity born out of chaos.

Though there can be no absolute certainty, there is general agreement that the periods in the
(35) development of a creative work parallel, to some extent, Lowes' theory of Well, Vision, Form and Will. There are at least three stages in the creative process: *preparation, inspiration, work.*

In a sense, the period of preparation is all of
(40) the writer's life. It is the Deep Well. It is especially a period of concentration which gives the unconscious mind an opportunity to communicate with the conscious mind. When remembrances of things past reach the conscious
(45) level of the writer's mind, he is ready to go on with the process. Part of this preparation involves learning a medium—learning a language,

learning how to write, learning literary forms. It is important to note here that form cannot be
(50) imposed upon the idea. Evidence, though sparse, shows that the idea gives birth to the form that can best convey it. It is the Vision, according to Lowes, "which sees shining in and through the chaos the potential lines of Form . . ."

22. According to the author, when remembrances of things past reach the conscious level, the poet has reached the stage called

(A) Well   (B) Vision   (C) Form   (D) Will
(E) Magical synthesis

23. According to the passage, which of the following statements is true?

(A) The form determines the subject matter.
(B) The idea determines the form.
(C) Vision makes beauty an actuality.
(D) A writer's period of preparation is spent at school.
(E) A writer is unconscious when he prepares his work.

24. In line 18, "fortuitously" means

(A) accidentally   (B) luckily   (C) thoroughly
(D) unconsciously   (E) potentially

25. The style and content of the passage indicate that it was most likely written by

(A) an artist or poet
(B) a critic or book reviewer
(C) a psychologist or psychoanalyst
(D) an English teacher
(E) a newspaper reporter

Reading Comprehension Exercise D

Each passage below is followed by questions based on its content. Answer all questions following a passage on the basis of what is stated or implied in that passage.

Solitude is a great chastener when once you accept it. It quietly eliminates all sorts of traits that were a part of you—among others, the desire to pose, to keep your best foot forever in evidence, to impress people as being something you would like to have them think you are even when you aren't. Some men I know are able to pose even in solitude; had they valets they no doubt would be heroes to them. But I find it the hardest kind of work myself, and as I am lazy I have stopped trying. To act without an audience is so tiresome and profitless that you gradually give it up and at last forget how to act at all. For you become more interested in making the acquaintance of yourself as you really are, which is a meeting that, in the haunts of men, rarely takes place. It is gratifying, for example, to discover that you prefer to be clean rather than dirty

even when there is no one but God to care which you are; just as it is amusing to note, however, that for scrupulous cleanliness you are not inclined to make superhuman sacrifices, although you used to believe you were. Clothes, you learn, with something of a shock, have for you no interest whatsoever. You learn to regard dress merely as covering, a precaution. For its color and its cut you care nothing.

1. Which of the following best expresses the main idea of the passage?

(A) Clothes make the man.
(B) No man is a hero to his valet.
(C) Seclusion permits self-discovery.
(D) One's own company is the best company.
(E) One should always live as one pleases.

2. The word "chastener" in the first sentence means

(A) discomfort
(B) means of discipline
(C) troublemaker
(D) misgiving
(E) method of saving time

3. The author points out that solitude primarily gives us the chance to

(A) learn our own peculiarities
(B) keep our best foot forward
(C) impress people
(D) dress as we would like
(E) be immaculately clean

4. In describing his self-discoveries, the author's tone can best be described as

(A) arrogant   (B) sullen   (C) self-mocking
(D) defeated   (E) abashed

The near-legendary history of the American West might have been quite different had the Mexican not brought cattle-raising to New Mexico and Texas. The Spanish style of herding cattle on open ranges was different from the style of other Europeans, particularly the English. The American *rancho* was possible because of the lack of enough water for normal agricultural practices, and because of the easy availability of large amounts of land. This land-extensive form of cattle-raising required different techniques and brought forth the *vaquero*, the cowboy (from the Spanish *vaca*, cow) who tended the widely-scattered herds of Spanish longhorn cattle. Because of the American penchant to be considered the inventors of nearly everything, the wide-open style of cattle-ranching was appropriated from the Mexican originators. As popular a folk-hero as the American cowboy is, he owes his development to the Spanish and the Mexicans, not to the English. It is quite probable, as McWilliams asserts, that "with the exception of the capital required to expand the industry, there seems to have been nothing the American rancher or cowboy contributed to the development of cattle-raising in the Southwest."

Other contributions of the Mexican cowboy were: the western-style saddle with a large, ornate horn; *chaparejos*, or chaps; *lazo*, lasso; *la reata*, lariat; the cinch; the halter; the *mecate*, or horsehair rope; chin strap for the hat; feed bag for the horse; ten-gallon hat (which comes from a mistranslation of a Spanish phrase "su sombrero galoneado" that really meant a "festooned" or "galooned" hat). Cowboy slang came from such words as: *juzgado*, hoosegow; *ranchero*, rancher; *estampida*, stampede; *calabozo*, calaboose; and *pinto* for a painted horse.

Just as the Mexican associations for the protection of the rights of sheepherders gave rise to the American Sheepmen's Associations, the Spanish system of branding range animals and registering these brands became standard practice among Anglo stockmen. The idea of brands originated in North Africa and was brought to Spain by the Moors, along with their stocky ponies. The Mexican brands are of great antiquity, having been copied from earlier Indian signs which include symbols of the sky—sun, moon and stars. Hernando Cortez is said to have been the first to use a brand on the continent.

5. Which of the following would be the best title for this passage?

(A) How to Herd Cattle
(B) The American Cowboy: A Romantic Figure
(C) Farming Practices in Europe and America
(D) Hispanic Contributions to Western Ranching
(E) Spanish Influence on American Culture

6. It can be inferred from the passage that American ranches developed in the West rather than the East because

(A) more Spanish-speaking people lived in the West
(B) there was more money available in the West
(C) people in the East were more bound by tradition
(D) many jobless men in the East wanted to become cowboys
(E) there was more unsettled land available in the West

7. The author gives examples of cowboy slang in order to

(A) arouse the reader's interest
(B) show that he is familiar with the subject
(C) prove that many cowboys lacked education
(D) point out the differences between America's East and West
(E) demonstrate how these terms originated

8. According to the author, which of the following did Mexicans contribute to ranching?

I. Money to buy ranches
II. Methods of handling animals
III. Items of riding equipment

(A) I only   (B) II only   (C) III only
(D) I and II only   (E) II and III only

9. Which of the following best describes the development of this passage?

(A) Major points, minor points
(B) Statement of problem, examples, proposed solution
(C) Introduction, positive factors, negative factors
(D) Cause, effects
(E) Comparison, contrast

I smiled: I thought to myself, Mr. Rochester *is* peculiar—he seems to forget that he pays me £30 per annum for receiving his orders.

"The smile is very well," said he, catching instantly the passing expression; "but speak too."

"I was thinking, sir, that very few masters would trouble themselves to inquire whether or not their paid subordinates were piqued and hurt by their orders."

"Paid subordinates! What, you are my paid subordinate, are you? Oh yes, I had forgotten the salary! Well then, on that mercenary ground, will you agree to let me browbeat you a little?"

"No, sir, not on that ground: but, on the ground that you did forget it, and that you care whether or not a dependent is comfortable in his dependency, I agree heartily."

"And will you consent to dispense with a great many conventional forms and phrases, without thinking that the omission arises from insolence?"

"I am sure, sir, I should never mistake informality for insolence: one I rather like, the other nothing free-born would submit to, even for a salary."

"Humbug! Most things free-born will submit to anything for a salary; therefore, keep to yourself, and don't venture on generalities of which you are intensely ignorant. However, I mentally shake hands with you for your answer, despite its inaccuracy; and as much for the manner in which it was said, as for the substance of the speech: the manner was frank and sincere; one does not often see such a manner: no, on the contrary, affectation, or coldness, or stupid, coarse-minded misapprehension of one's meaning are the usual rewards of candour. Not three in three thousand raw school-girl governesses would have answered me as you have just done. But I don't mean to flatter you: if you are cast in a different mould to the majority, it is no merit of yours: Nature did it. And then, after all, I go too fast in my conclusions: for what I yet know, you may be no better than the rest; you may have intolerable defects to counterbalance your few good points."

10. It can be inferred that Mr. Rochester is speaking to

(A) an enemy   (B) a friend   (C) a relative
(D) an employee   (E) a colleague

11. According to Mr. Rochester, most people would agree with which of the following?

(A) Honesty is the best policy.
(B) Virtue is its own reward.
(C) He who pays the piper calls the tune.
(D) A penny saved is a penny earned.
(E) Experience is the best teacher.

12. Which of the following does Mr. Rochester appear to value LEAST?

(A) honesty   (B) informality   (C) submissiveness
(D) openness   (E) generosity

13. Mr. Rochester's tone in the passage can best be described as

(A) sympathetic   (B) pompous   (C) humorous
(D) loving   (E) cynical

As the market for hay declined, other farmers looked west and saw that in the flat lands of the prairie country the farmers were growing rich by raising corn and hogs; and they said, without thought or wisdom or knowledge, "If they can do it, we can." And so they plowed the grass and meadowlands and even the pastures of that rolling, hilly country and planted corn. They planted the corn in rows, running more often than not up and down slopes and hills. Every time it rained, each furrow between the standing corn became a miniature gully carrying off the precious rainfall and bearing with it the good topsoil that remained and the fertilizer the farmer had bought out of his hard-earned income.

14. The title that best expresses the ideas of this passage is

(A) Waste of the Soil
(B) Rotating Crops
(C) Rainfall and the Corn Crop
(D) Why Farmers Become Discouraged
(E) The Reward of Courage

15. The author implies that corn was a less satisfactory crop in the more easterly section because the land in this section was less

(A) fertile   (B) moist   (C) flat
(D) thoroughly fertilized   (E) arid

16. We may infer from the passage that the farmers would have been wiser to

(A) irrigate the land
(B) add topsoil to the fields
(C) plow furrows across the slope
(D) use more fertilizer
(E) fill the gullies

17. The author's attitude toward the farmers could best be described as

(A) humorous   (B) critical   (C) indifferent
(D) callous   (E) philanthropic

India's river systems have played a dominant role. In the west, the Indus traverses the Punjab, the land of five rivers, from Himalayan snows
Line through an alluvial plain to the Arabian Sea, a
(5) course of 1,800 miles. Below the junction of the five rivers, in the land of Sind, human habitation has been possible only because of irrigation systems. Sind normally receives five inches of rain annually. The upper Indus Valley of Punjab
(10) receives eight to twelve inches of rain. Its natural ground cover is that of a dry tropical forest while its dry hilly districts have a desert ecology.

The Indus River Valley is separated from the Ganges River basin to the east by the extensive
(15) Thar Desert which stretches along the western border of present-day India. The highland corridor of eastern Punjab, known historically as

the cockpit of India, has always provided easy access to the Ganges for the Indus hills people.
(20) Conquerors, avoiding the Thar Desert, marched through the hills into the fertile and heavily populated Ganges River Valley. This flood plain, an area of over 300,000 square miles, is watered by the Ganges and its five large tributaries. The
(25) great Hindu empires thrived along the length of ''Mother Ganges,'' the sacred river, from the uplands around Delhi to the low lying cities of Calcutta and Dacca. The valley remains one of the world's most heavily populated regions. The
(30) upland region, the present Indian state of Uttar Pradesh, averages about twenty-five inches of rainfall annually while Bengal's range is forty to sixty inches.

To the south of the Ganges River basin is the
(35) Deccan plateau which extends southward to the Krishna River. Beyond this river is South India which has, more or less, remained apart from the north, and has maintained its own ancient culture. Along the western edge of the Deccan
(40) plateau, facing the Arabian Sea, an eroded mountain wall, some 600 miles long, has isolated the people of the interior from those of the coast. The survival of these inhabitants of the Deccan plateau and those of South India depends upon
(45) the July to October seasonal monsoon. During the monsoon, rain storms from the Arabian Sea cross over the peninsula to the Himalayas. Unlike the snow-fed rivers in Northern India, the rivers of the plateau and the south are dependent
(50) upon this rain. Any lasting drought brings famine and death.

18. Which of the following titles best expresses the ideas of this passage?

(A) Drought and Famine in India
(B) The Ganges: A Sacred River
(C) The Influence of Rainfall in India
(D) India: Its History and Geography
(E) Waterways of the Indian Subcontinent

19. The author's tone in this passage can best be described as

(A) scholarly (B) enthusiastic (C) sympathetic
  (D) biased (E) nostalgic

20. It can be inferred from the passage that one reason the great Hindu empires thrived was that they

(A) emphasized religion
(B) were irrigated by the Ganges River
(C) reached from Delhi to other cities
(D) had no enemies
(E) were great cultural centers

21. It can be inferred from the passage that

(A) the seasonal monsoon brings destruction and death
(B) the rain season in India lasts for one month
(C) it never rains in the Himalayas

(D) people in Southern India welcome the monsoon
(E) South India is underpopulated

In 1896 Henri Becquerel found that uranium salts emitted penetrating radiations similar to those which Roentgen had produced only a year earlier with a gas discharge tube. The tremendous importance of this discovery was not apparent until a few years later when Pierre and Marie Curie announced the isolation from a uranium mineral, pitchblende, of two substances many times more radioactive than uranium itself. These two substances were subsequently shown to be two new elements, polonium and radium. Elements which are naturally radioactive spontaneously emit radiations without the addition of any energy to them. Later we shall see that artificial radioactivity can be produced by adding energy to originally stable nuclei.

Rutherford and Soddy, investigating the phenomenon discovered by Becquerel, found that the empirical facts of radioactivity could be explained by assuming that radioactive atoms were not stable but disintegrated at characteristic rates to form new atoms of other elements. As soon as the radioactive emissions were experimentally identified and it was proved that alpha ''rays'' are actually helium ions, it became clear that the assumptions made by Rutherford and Soddy were correct. It was soon found that the disintegration product of radium is also naturally radioactive and investigations of decay products led to the identification of other radioelements ranging in atomic number from 92 (uranium) to 81 (thallium). These radioelements are now known to be intimately related to each other in the *radioactive series*.

During the early years of the Curie investigations uranium had only a limited industrial use, chiefly in the glass industry, and most of the material came from the Joachimstal mines in Czechoslovakia. As industrial uses for radioactive elements developed, uranium ore was found widely scattered throughout the world with extensive deposits in the Belgian Congo and in the Great Bear Lake region in Canada. The element is principally mined in the form of pitchblende, which may contain a high percentage of U_3O_8. The ore presents a brown-black appearance somewhat resembling pitch in luster. In the United States, deposits of another uranium ore, known as carnotite, are found in several Rocky Mountain states.

22. The title that best expresses the ideas of this passage is

(A) Scientists in the Atomic Age
(B) The Curies
(C) The Discovery of Radiation
(D) Pitchblende and Its Products
(E) Uranium and Radiation

23. According to the passage, uranium

(A) was discovered in 1896
(B) is used in the glass industry

(C) is found in pure form in the United States
(D) is more radioactive than polonium
(E) contains helium atoms

24. According to the passage atoms that are naturally radioactive

(A) disintegrate over time
(B) have energy added to the nuclei
(C) were discovered by Rutherford
(D) were discovered by Roentgen
(E) are mined in the Congo

25. It can be inferred that more uranium ore has been found because

(A) its radioactivity makes it easy to find
(B) its value makes people look for it
(C) it is contained in pitchblende and carnotite
(D) there is more of it now than in the past
(E) it has a brown-black appearance in its natural state

Answer Key

Reading Comprehension Exercise A

1.	C	6.	A	11.	A	16.	B	21.	E
2.	C	7.	C	12.	B	17.	A	22.	A
3.	A	8.	B	13.	C	18.	E	23.	B
4.	E	9.	D	14.	B	19.	A	24.	D
5.	D	10.	B	15.	D	20.	B	25.	C

Reading Comprehension Exercise B

1.	B	6.	B	11.	A	16.	B	21.	B
2.	C	7.	B	12.	B	17.	D	22.	D
3.	E	8.	C	13.	D	18.	C	23.	D
4.	C	9.	B	14.	E	19.	A	24.	A
5.	D	10.	A	15.	E	20.	A	25.	E

Reading Comprehension Exercise C

1.	A	6.	D	11.	B	16.	C	21.	D
2.	B	7.	B	12.	A	17.	B	22.	D
3.	D	8.	E	13.	D	18.	D	23.	B
4.	D	9.	C	14.	E	19.	E	24.	A
5.	E	10.	D	15.	D	20.	A	25.	C

Reading Comprehension Exercise D

1.	C	6.	E	11.	C	16.	C	21.	D
2.	B	7.	E	12.	C	17.	B	22.	E
3.	A	8.	E	13.	E	18.	E	23.	B
4.	C	9.	A	14.	A	19.	A	24.	A
5.	D	10.	D	15.	C	20.	B	25.	B

Answer Explanations

Reading Comprehension Exercise A

1. C. Each paragraph discusses some important feature of Eskimo art.

   (Main Idea)

2. C. The author's use of such terms as "powerful ability" (first paragraph), "masters in the understanding of animal anatomy" (third paragraph), and "living excitement" (last paragraph) indicates an admiration for the art.

   (Attitude/Tone)

3. A. Statement A agrees with the author's comment in the second paragraph that Eskimo art "has a special freedom unsullied by any kind of formalized training."

   (Inference)

4. E. Each example the author uses describes a type of Eskimo sculpture.

   (Inference)

5. D. The second paragraph notes the absence of "formalized training" in Eskimo art. The other characteristics are mentioned in the passage.

   (Specific Details)

6. A. The nature of what, in the author's view, is science's chief contribution to the world is discussed throughout the passage.

   (Main Idea)

7. C. According to the author, science's greatest gift is the "conviction that the world is understandable," which "can be dated" back to Newton.

   (Specific Details)

8. B. Raskolnikov tells Svidrigaïlov, "You should go to a doctor" (line 20). This indicates he thinks Svidrigaïlov is suffering from a delusion brought about by illness.

   (Specific Details)

9. D. Since nothing in the conversation accounts for Raskolnikov's anger, it is most likely that he has some personal reason for his feelings.

   (Inference)

10. B. In lines 42–46, Svidrigaïlov says many people are too worldly to see ghosts.

    (Specific Details)

11. A. In lines 40–42, Svidrigaïlov states that ghosts are "shreds and fragments of other worlds."

    (Specific Details)

12. B. The passage is not about Coleridge and Wordsworth as individuals; it is about them as collaborators on a specific project.

    (Main Idea/Title)

13. C. In the last paragraph, the author states that he was to write about supernatural or romantic subjects, while Wordsworth was to write about everyday life.

    (Specific Details)

14. B. Lines 21–23 suggest that a belief in the supernatural is caused by delusion.

    (Inference)

15. D. The author gives examples that can best be summed up by the saying *familiarity breeds contempt*.

    (Inference)

16. B. The topic discussed throughout the passage is best expressed in the title "The Effects of Insecticides on Fish."

    (Main Idea/Title)

17. A. The author states the effects of insecticides in a factual, unemotional, reportorial way.

    (Attitude/Tone)

18. E. All the factors are mentioned as responsible for the presence of insecticides.

    (Specific Details)

19. A. The author states, in the last paragraph, that the killing of food fish can pose problems. She uses the term "for example" when she cites the case of the African fish.

    (Technique)

20. B. Nowhere in the passage does the author suggest a solution to the situation she has described.

    (Technique)

21. E. Futurist poetry is discussed and evaluated throughout the passage.

    (Main Idea)

22. A. The first sentence of the passage gives this view of what to do when new ideas appear.

    (Specific Details)

23. B. In line 23, the author remarks on the absence of qualifying adjectives in Futurist poetry.

(Specific Details)

24. D. The author's general opinion of the poetry and the description of the quoted line as "disconcerting" show that the quotation is meant to prove the poetry's inferiority.

(Inference)

25. C. The author accepts the idea that a change in emotions calls for a change in literature; but he implies that emotions have not really changed. Therefore, it can be inferred that there is no need for a change in literature.

(Inference)

Reading Comprehension Exercise B

1. B. Each paragraph in the passage discusses some aspect of Mexican mural painting.

(Main Idea)

2. C. Because the passage discusses murals and even states that the paintings were done "on Mexican walls," it is obvious that the word *frescoes* is a synonym for *murals*, or wall paintings.

(Word from Context)

3. E. The author's remarks in the second paragraph about Orozco's style and subject matter indicate that his basic attitude is approving.

(Attitude/Tone)

4. C. The passage states twice (first and second paragraphs) that Mexican muralists painted the history of their country. An artist inspired by them would probably follow their example.

(Inference)

5. D. The author's comments in the second paragraph about Rivera's use of composition and harmony imply that he considers these elements important.

(Inference)

6. B. The *beginnings of geometry* is the topic that is discussed throughout the passage.

(Main Idea/Title)

7. B. The passage states that geometry means "earth measurement," and that the Egyptians used this science for remeasuring the boundaries of farmlands.

(Specific Details)

8. C. According to the passage, Egyptians developed geometry to remeasure land flooded by the Nile River. It follows that this annual flooding was an important reason for the development of geometry.

(Inference)

9. B. Almost every sentence in this passage discusses Thoreau's thoughts about life.

(Main Idea)

10. A. Toward the end of the passage, the author notes that Thoreau "had no wish to dogmatize" and that he believed each person should choose the way that was best for him or herself.

(Specific Details)

11. A. The author describes Thoreau as vitally concerned with his emancipation and calls it the one romance of Thoreau's life because it wholly absorbs him.

(Inference)

12. B. In the last line, Thoreau's philosophy is said to be, "The only wealth is life." From this we can infer that Thoreau believed wealth consists of the experience a person gains.

(Inference)

13. D. Phrases such as "eager activity" and "high adventure" demonstrate that the author is speaking of Thoreau in an admiring tone.

(Attitude/Tone)

14. E. The first sentence of the passage states that Newman's purpose is to see Mademoiselle Noémie.

(Specific Details)

15. E. In the fifth paragraph, Valentin explains that he has reluctantly decided to guide his cousin through the Louvre.

(Specific Details)

16. B. Valentin shows what a bad mood he is in when he insults his cousin.

(Inference)

17. D. Valentin's concern with fashionable clothing is evident from the disparaging remarks he makes about his cousin's clothes. On the other hand, he does respect family relationships, for he has agreed with his mother's request to show the cousin around. Thus, he would appear to agree with Statements I and II.

(Inference)

18. C. Newman advises Valentin how to feel, and, in the last paragraph, Valentin says, "You give me excellent advice."

(Specific Details)

19. A. The topic discussed throughout the passage is adaptive divergence, the changes undergone by plants and animals to adapt to different ways of life.

(Main Idea/Title)

20. A. The author illustrates the meaning of *homologous* by stating that the finger and wristbones of bats and whales are "equivalent elements" of the mammalian limb.

(Word from Context)

21. B. The entire passage is concerned with the sound of great literature.

(Main Idea)

22. D. The author states that music and literature "contrive their pattern of sounds in time."

(Specific Details)

23. D. The emphasis on the sound patterns of writing and on achieving effects suggests that the function of the writer is to present ideas attractively.

(Inference)

24. A. Lines 17–19 state that an element of *surprise* can be achieved by antithesis.

(Word from Context)

25. E. In lines 27–28, the author warns against using an exact balance.

(Specific Details)

Reading Comprehension Exercise C

1. A. Each paragraph of the passage discusses how African sculptors achieved their effects.

(Main Idea)

2. B. Both the first and second paragraphs mention the emotion aroused by African sculpture.

(Specific Details)

3. D. The passage discusses sculpture, so it can be inferred that "the common plastic language" means the common *sculptural* language.

(Word from Context)

4. D. We are told that the African sculptor was highly trained and followed the rules without

thinking of them. Similarly, a well-rehearsed pianist can perform a concerto without worrying too much about the notes. Both artists have become free to concentrate on mood or creativity.

(Inference)

5. E. Throughout the passage, the author discusses the rules of African art. He concludes that they were unconscious.

(Main Idea/Title)

6. D. Of the titles given, only "A Special Problem in Teaching Handwriting" fits the topic discussed throughout the passage.

(Main Idea/Title)

7. B. The discussion of the problems faced by left-handed children implies that such children need special consideration.

(Inference)

8. E. The author gives several examples of problems that may result when a left-handed child is forced to write with the right hand.

(Specific Details)

9. C. Eleanor says of her father (fifth paragraph), "He will break his heart, and die." This shows that she fears he will die because he is depressed.

(Specific Details)

10. D. Toward the end of the passage, Eleanor mentions that her father has been called *avaricious* (greedy) and has been accused of robbing old men.

(Specific Details)

11. B. Eleanor's impassioned speech and her statement that her father does not care about money indicate that she does not believe in his guilt.

(Specific Details)

12. A. From the way Eleanor talks to John Bold and from the fact that "his heart smote him as to his intimate alliance with Tom Towers," we can infer that he is somehow implicated in the father's problems.

(Inference)

13. D. Eleanor says that her father does not care about money, and her listeners agree that he does not care for filthy lucre. Therefore, *filthy lucre* must be a synonym for *money*.

(Word from Context)

14. E. The discussion of sentencing practices throughout the passage leads up to the statement in the last paragraph about the importance of improving sentence techniques.

(Main Idea)

15. D. The author explains the difference between primitive and later sentencing. Therefore, *metamorphosis* means *change*.

(Word from Context)

16. C. The author states that primitive sentencing was vengeance-oriented. A child's return of a playmate's slap is also motivated by the wish for revenge.

(Inference)

17. B. In the third paragraph, the author states, "Little can be done to correct past damage."

(Specific Details)

18. D. Every factor except revenge is discussed in the second and third paragraphs of the passage.

(Specific Details)

19. E. The measurement of energy and food supplies is discussed throughout the passage.

(Main Idea/Title)

20. A. Like money in a savings account, potential energy is not being used by its owner. Like money spent on purchases, kinetic energy is being used.

(Inference)

21. D. In the second paragraph, energy subsidies, including human and animal labor and energy supplied by machines, are differentiated from energy from the sun. We can therefore infer that solar energy is the main source of energy for plants, not a subsidy.

(Inference)

22. D. Lines 29–31 explain the relationship between consciousness and Will.

(Specific Details)

23. B. In line 51, the author says, "The idea gives birth to the form."

(Specific Details)

24. A. The "fortuitously blending images" the passage speaks of occur in the midst of *chaos*, which means "complete disorder and

confusion." In such an atmosphere, any blending must be accidental.

(Word from Context)

25. C. A stress on defining conscious and unconscious activities is characteristic of psychologists and psychoanalysts.

(Inference)

Reading Comprehension Exercise D

1. C. Throughout the passage, the author discusses the discoveries one can make through solitude or seclusion.

(Main Idea)

2. B. The examples the author gives in the second sentence make it clear that he regards solitude as a means of self-discipline.

(Word in Context)

3. A. The author states that in solitude "you become more interested in making the acquaintance of yourself as you really are."

(Specific Details)

4. C. The author calls himself "lazy" and finds his lack of scrupulous cleanliness "amusing." His tone is self-mocking.

(Attitude/Tone)

5. D. The topic discussed throughout this passage is Hispanic (Spanish and Mexican) contributions to Western ranching.

(Main Idea/Title)

6. E. The first paragraph notes that ranches can develop where large amounts of land are available. It can be inferred that more unsettled land was available in the West than in the East.

(Inference)

7. E. The use of only Mexican terms suggests that the author is using these examples of cowboy slang to demonstrate the origins of the words and prove how much Mexicans contributed.

(Inference)

8. E. The first paragraph tells of the adoption of Mexican methods of handling animals, and the second speaks of Mexican contributions to riding equipment. The quotation at the end of the first paragraph implies that the money for the ranching industry was provided by Americans.

(Inference)

9. A. The passage starts with the major Mexican contribution of the whole concept of ranching, goes on, in the second paragraph, to discuss lesser contributions of equipment and slang, and ends, in the third paragraph, with the relatively minor contribution of branding.

(Technique)

10. D. The person mentions that Mr. Rochester pays her a salary. Therefore, she must be an employee.

(Inference)

11. C. In the last paragraph, Mr. Rochester says that most people "will submit to anything for a salary." We can therefore infer that he believes that he who pays the piper calls the tune.

(Inference)

12. C. In the last paragraph, Mr. Rochester congratulates his listener for her frankness, which he contrasts with the servility of other employees. It can be inferred from this that the quality he values least is submissiveness.

(Inference)

13. E. Mr. Rochester's cynicism is shown by his negative comments about other people and in his distrust of even his listener's good points.

(Attitude/Tone)

14. A. The waste of the soil is the topic discussed throughout the passage.

(Main Idea/Title)

15. C. The author states that corn did well in the flat prairie lands. He goes on to describe what happened in other regions where corn was often planted on slopes and hills. From this we can infer that the crop failed because the land was less flat.

(Inference)

16. C. Because furrows that ran up and down carried off rain and topsoil, we can infer it would have been wiser to plow the furrows horizontally.

(Inference)

17. B. The author says the farmers were "without thought or wisdom or knowledge." His attitude is critical.

(Attitude/Tone)

18. E. The waterways of the Indian subcontinent are discussed throughout the passage.

(Main Idea/Title)

19. A. The author does not express or imply opinions about the topic. The tone is objective and scholarly.

(Attitude/Tone)

20. B. Lines 25–26 note that "the great Hindu empires thrived along the length of" the Ganges River. We may infer that they prospered because the river irrigated them.

(Inference)

21. D. The passage states (lines 43–45) that the survival of people in Southern India depends on the monsoon. It can therefore be inferred that they welcome it.

(Inference)

22. E. The topic discussed throughout the passage is uranium and radiation.

(Main Idea/Title)

23. B. The last paragraph states that uranium is used in the glass industry.

(Specific Details)

24. A. The second paragraph states that radioactive atoms disintegrate over time.

(Specific Details)

25. B. The third paragraph states that uranium ore was found throughout the world as industrial uses for it developed. From this we can infer that as its value increased, more people looked for and found uranium.

(Inference)

9 Build Your Vocabulary

- ■ SAT High-Frequency Word List
- ■ 3,500 Basic Word List
- ■ Basic Word Parts

The more you study actual SAT verbal questions, the more you realize one thing: *the key to doing well on the verbal part of the SAT is a strong working vocabulary of college-level words.* And the key to building that strong working vocabulary can be summed up in one word: READ.

Read widely, read deeply, read daily. If you do, your vocabulary will grow. If you don't it won't.

Reading widely, however, may not always help you remember the words you read. You may have the words in your passive vocabulary and be able to recognize them when you see them in a context and yet be unable to define them clearly or think of antonyms for them. In addition, unless you have already begun to upgrade your reading to the col-

lege level, reading widely also may not acquaint you most efficiently with college-level words.

What are college-level words? In going through the preceding four chapters, you have examined dozens of questions taken from recently-published SATs. Some of the words in these questions—*applaud* and *rival*—have been familiar to you; others—*recluse* and *interloper*—have not. Still others—*husband* and *reserve*—have looked familiar, but have turned out to be defined in unexpected ways. All these words belong in your college-level vocabulary; any of them may turn up when you take the SAT.

Use the vocabulary and word parts lists in this chapter to upgrade your vocabulary to a college level. They are all excellent vocabulary building tools.

The SAT High-Frequency Word List

No matter how little time you have before you take the SAT, you can familiarize yourself with the sort of vocabulary you will be facing on the test. First, look over the 320 words you will find on our SAT High-Frequency Word List. Each of these words, ranging from everyday words such as *abstract* and *complacent* to less commonly known ones such as *apathy* and *virtuoso*, has appeared (as answer choices or as question words) from three to twenty times on SATs published in the 1980s.

Next, proceed to master the words on the High-Frequency Word List. First, check off those words you think you know. Then, look up all 320 words and their definitions in our 3,500 Basic Word List. Pay particular attention to the words you thought you

knew. See whether any of them are defined in an unexpected way. If they are, make a special note of them. As you know from the preceding chapters, the SAT often stumps students with questions based on unfamiliar meanings of familiar-looking words.

Create flash cards for the words you want to master. Work up memory tricks to help yourself remember them. (Follow the methods described in Chapter 5.) Try using them on your parents and friends. Not only will going over these high-frequency words reassure you that you *do* know some SAT-type words, but also it may well help you on the actual day of the test. These words have turned up on recent tests: some of them may well turn up on the test you take.

SAT High-Frequency Word List

abstract
acquiesce
acuity
advocate
aesthetic
alienate
aloof
altruistic
amass
ambiguous
ambivalence
amend
amity
analogous
anarchist
anonymity
antagonistic
apathy
appease
apprehensive
arbitrary
arduous
arid
arrogance
articulate
ascetic
assessment
astute
asylum
augment
austerity
authoritarian
autocrat
banal
belittle
benefactor
benign
blithe
bolster
bombastic
braggart
brevity
candor
capricious
caustic
censorious
censure
chaotic
chimerical
coercion
collaborate
complacent
compliance
comprehensive
conciliatory
concise
conclusive

condescend
conformity
conscientious
contempt
contrite
conviction
copious
cordial
crescendo
cringe
criterion
cynical
daunt
decadence
deference
deliberate
delineate
denounce
depict
deplete
depravity
deprecate
derivative
despondent
detached
deterrent
detrimental
deviate
didactic
digression
diligence
discerning
discordant
discretion
discrimination
discursive
disdain
disinclination
dismantle
disparage
disparity
dispassionate
disperse
disputatious
dissemble
dissonance
distant
divergent
diverse
diversion
document
dogmatic
dubious
duplicity
eccentric
effervescence
elaboration

eloquence
elusive
emulate
endorse
enervation
engender
enhance
enigmatic
ephemeral
erratic
erroneous
erudite
esoteric
esteem
evasive
exacerbate
execute
exemplary
expedient
expedite
expertise
explicit
exploit (N)
expunge
extol
extraneous
extricate
facilitate
fallacious
fanaticism
fastidious
fervor
flagrant
fledgling
flippancy
foresight
frivolity
furtive
glutton
gravity
grudging
gullible
hamper
heckler
hilarity
hindrance
humility
hyperbole
hypocritical
hypothetical
illusory
immutable
impecunious
implication
imprudent
inadvertently
inane

incompatible
inconsequential
incorrigible
indifferent
indiscriminate
indolent
indulgent
inevitable
infamous
infer
inflated
inhibit
initiate
injurious
innate
innocuous
innovative
insipid
insolvent
insurgent
interminable
ironic
irresolute
judicious
laconic
languish
laudable
laudatory
legacy
lethargic
levity
listless
lofty
malicious
marred
methodical
meticulous
mire
miserly
mitigate
morose
muted
novelty
objective (A, N)
obscure (A, V)
obsolete
obstinate
opportunist
optimist
optional
opulence
overt
painstaking
partial
partisan
patronize
paucity

pedantic
perfunctory
peripheral
pessimism
petty
phenomena
pious
placate
plagiarize
plausible
ponderous
pragmatist
prattle
preclude
predecessor
prestige
prodigal
prodigious
profusion
prolific
provoke
prudent
qualified
rebuff
rebuttal
rectify
redundant
refute
relegate
remorse
renegade
reprehensible
reproach
repudiate
repulsion
rescind
reserve
resignation
resolution
restraint
reticence
reverent
rhetorical
sanction
sarcasm
satirical
saturate
scanty
scrupulous
seclusion
sequester
severity
shrewd
skeptic
sluggish
soporific
sporadic

squander	superficial	taciturn	unobtrusive	virtuoso
stagnant	supersede	tentative	unprecedented	virulent
stanza	surpass	thrifty	vacillation	volatile
steadfast	surreptitious	turbulence	venerate	voluminous
stoic	susceptible	tyranny	verbose	whimsical
stringent	swindler	undermine	viable	wither
subtlety	symmetry	uniformity	vilify	zealot

The 3,500 Basic Word List

The 3,500 Basic Word List begins on the following pages. *Do not let this list overwhelm you.* You do not need to memorize every word.

The more than 3,500 words in this list have been compiled from various sources. They have been taken from the standard literature read by high school students throughout the country and from the many tests taken by high school and college students. Ever since this book first appeared in 1954, countless students have reported that working with this list has been of immense value in the taking of all kinds of college entrance and scholarship tests. It has been used with profit by people preparing for civil service examinations, placement tests, and promotional examinations in many industrial fields. Above all, it has been used with profit by people studying for the SAT.

Even before the College Board began publishing its own SAT sample examinations, the Basic Word List was unique in its ability to reflect, and often predict, the actual vocabulary appearing on the SAT. Today, thanks to our ongoing research and computer analysis of published SAT materials, we believe our 3,500 Basic Word List is the best in the field.

For those of you who wish to work your way through the *entire* word list and feel the need for a plan, we recommend that you follow the procedure described below in order to use the lists and the exercises most profitably:

1. Allot a definite time each day for the study of a list.

2. Devote at least one hour to each list.

3. First go through the list looking at the flagged High-Frequency words and the short, simple-looking words (6 letters at most). Mark those you don't know. In studying, pay particular attention to them.

4. Go through the list again looking at the longer words. Pay particular attention to words with more than one meaning and familiar-looking words which have unusual definitions that come as a surprise to you. Study these secondary definitions.

5. List unusual words on index cards which you can shuffle and review from time to time. (Use the flash card technique described in Chapter 5.)

6. Use the illustrative sentences in the list as models and make up new sentences of your own.

7. Take the test which follows each list at least one day after studying the words. In this way, you will check your ability to remember what you have studied.

8. If you can answer correctly 12 of the 15 questions in the test, you may proceed to the next list; if you cannot answer this number, restudy the list.

9. Keep a record of your guesses and of your success as a guesser. (Use the chart in Chapter 2.)

For each word, the following is provided:

1. The word (printed in heavy type).

2. Its part of speech (abbreviated).

3. A brief definition.

4. A sentence illustrating the word's use.

5. Whenever appropriate, related words are provided, together with their parts of speech.

The word lists are arranged in strict alphabetical order. In each word list, High-Frequency Words are marked with a square bullet (■).

Basic Word List

Word List 1   abase-adroit

abase V. lower; humiliate. His refusal to *abase* himself in the eyes of his followers irritated the king, who wanted to humiliate him.

abash V. embarrass. He was not at all *abashed* by her open admiration.

abbreviate V. shorten. Because we were running out of time, the lecturer had to *abbreviate* her speech.

abdicate V. renounce; give up. When Edward VIII *abdicated* the British throne, he surprised the entire world.

aberration N. wandering or straying; in optics, failure of rays to focus. In designing a good lens for a camera, the problem of correcting chromatic and rectilinear *aberration* was a serious one. aberrant, ADJ. and N.

abettor N. encourager. She was accused of being an aider and *abettor* of the criminal. abet, V.

abeyance N. suspended action. The deal was held in *abeyance* until her arrival.

abhor V. detest; hate. She *abhorred* all forms of bigotry. abhorrence, N.

abjure V. renounce upon oath. He *abjured* his allegiance to the king. abjuration, N.

ablution N. washing. His daily *ablutions* were accompanied by loud noises that he humorously labeled "Opera in the Bath."

abnegation N. repudiation; self-sacrifice. No act of *abnegation* was more pronounced than his refusal of any rewards for his discovery.

abolish V. cancel; put an end to. The president of the college refused to *abolish* the physical education requirement. abolition, N.

abominate V. loathe; hate. Moses scolded the idol worshippers in the tribe because he *abominated* the custom. abominable, ADJ.

aboriginal ADJ., N. being the first of its kind in a region; primitive; native. Her studies of the primitive art forms of the *aboriginal* Indians were widely reported in the scientific journals. aborigines, N.

abortive ADJ. unsuccessful; fruitless. We had to abandon our *abortive* attempts.

abrade V. wear away by friction; erode. The skin of her leg was *abraded* by the sharp rocks. abrasion, N.

abridge V. condense or shorten. Because the publishers felt the public wanted a shorter version of *War and Peace,* they proceeded to *abridge* the novel.

abrogate V. abolish. He intended to *abrogate* the decree issued by his predecessor.

abscond V. depart secretly and hide. The teller *absconded* with the bonds and was not found.

absolve V. pardon (an offense). The father confessor *absolved* him of his sins. absolution, N.

abstemious ADJ. sparing in eating and drinking; temperate. The drunkards mocked him because of his *abstemious* habits.

abstinence N. restraint from eating or drinking. The doctor recommended total *abstinence* from salted foods. abstain, V.

■ **abstract** ADJ. theoretical; not concrete; nonrepresentational. To him, hunger was an *abstract* concept; he had never missed a meal.

abstruse ADJ. obscure; profound; difficult to understand. She read *abstruse* works in philosophy.

abusive ADJ. coarsely insulting; physically harmful. An *abusive* parent damages a child both mentally and physically.

abut V. border upon; adjoin. Where our estates *abut,* we must build a fence.

abysmal ADJ. bottomless. His arrogance is exceeded only by his *abysmal* ignorance.

accede V. agree. If I *accede* to this demand for blackmail, I am afraid that I will be the victim of future demands.

accelerate V. move faster. In our science class, we learn how falling bodies *accelerate.*

accessible ADJ. easy to approach; obtainable. We asked our guide whether the ruins were *accessible* on foot.

accessory N. additional object; useful but not essential thing. She bought an attractive handbag as an accessory for her dress. also ADJ.

acclimate V. adjust to climate. One of the difficulties of our present air age is the need of travelers to *acclimate* themselves to their new and often strange environments.

acclivity N. sharp upslope of a hill. The car could not go up the *acclivity* in high gear.

accolade N. award of merit. In Hollywood, an "Oscar" is the highest *accolade.*

accomplice N. partner in crime. Because he had provided the criminal with the lethal weapon, he was arrested as an *accomplice* in the murder.

accord N. agreement. She was in complete *accord* with the verdict.

accost V. approach and speak first to a person. When the two young men *accosted* me, I was frightened because I thought they were going to attack me.

accoutre V. equip. The fisherman was *accoutred* with the best that the sporting goods store could supply. accoutrements, N.

accretion N. growth; increase. The *accretion* of wealth marked the family's rise in power.

accrue V. come about by addition. You must pay the interest which has *accrued* on your debt as well as the principal sum. accrual, N.

acerbity N. bitterness of speech and temper. The meeting of the United Nations Assembly was marked with such *acerbity* that little hope of reaching any useful settlement of the problem could be held.

acetic ADJ. vinegary. The salad had an exceedingly *acetic* flavor.

acidulous ADJ. slightly sour; sharp, caustic. James was unpopular because of his sarcastic and *acidulous* remarks.

acknowledge V. recognize; admit. When pressed for an answer, she *acknowledged* the existence of another motive for the crime.

acme N. top; pinnacle. His success in this role marked his *acme* as an actor.

acoustics N. science of sound; quality that makes a room easy or hard to hear in. Carnegie Hall is liked by music lovers because of its fine *acoustics*.

■ **acquiesce** V. assent; agree passively. Although she appeared to *acquiesce* to her employer's suggestions, I could tell she had reservations about the changes he wanted made.

acquiescence N. submission; compliance. It is impossible to obtain their *acquiescence* to the proposal because it is abhorrent to their philosophy.

acquiescent ADJ. accepting passively. His *acquiescent* manner did not indicate the extent of his reluctance to join the group. acquiesce, V.

acquittal N. deliverance from a charge. His *acquittal* by the jury surprised those who had thought him guilty. acquit, V.

acrid ADJ. sharp; bitterly pungent. The *acrid* odor of burnt gunpowder filled the room after the pistol had been fired.

acrimonious ADJ. stinging; caustic. His tendency to utter *acrimonious* remarks alienated his audience. acrimony, N.

actuarial ADJ. calculating; pertaining to insurance statistics. According to recent *actuarial* tables, life expectancy is greater today than it was a century ago.

actuate V. motivate. I fail to understand what *actuated* you to reply to this letter so nastily.

■ **acuity** N. sharpness. In time his youthful *acuity* of vision failed him, and he needed glasses.

acumen N. mental keenness. His business *acumen* helped him to succeed where others had failed.

adage N. wise saying; proverb. There is much truth in the old *adage* about fools and their money.

adamant ADJ. hard; inflexible. He was *adamant* in his determination to punish the wrongdoer. adamancy, N.

adapt V. alter; modify. Some species of animals have become extinct because they could not *adapt* to a changing environment.

addiction N. compulsive, habitual need. His *addiction* to drugs caused his friends much grief.

addle ADJ. rotten; muddled; crazy. This *addle*-headed plan is so preposterous that it does not deserve any consideration. also V.

adduce V. present as evidence. When you *adduce* material of this nature, you must be sure of your sources.

adept ADJ. expert at. She was *adept* at the fine art of irritating people. also N.

adhere V. stick fast. I will *adhere* to this opinion until proof that I am wrong is presented. adhesion, N.

adjunct N. something attached to but holding an inferior position. I will entertain this concept as an *adjunct* to the main proposal.

adjuration N. solemn urging. Her *adjuration* to tell the truth did not change the witnesses' testimony.

adjure V. request solemnly. I must *adjure* you to consider this matter carefully as it is of utmost importance to all of us.

admonish V. warn; reprove. He *admonished* his listeners to change their wicked ways. admonition, N.

admonition N. warning. After repeated rejections of its *admonitions,* the country was forced to issue an ultimatum.

adorn V. decorate. Wall paintings and carved statues *adorned* the temple. adornment, N.

adroit ADJ. skillful. His *adroit* handling of the delicate situation pleased his employers.

Test

Word List 1   *Synonyms*

Each of the questions below consists of a word in capital letters, followed by five lettered words or phrases. Choose the lettered word or phrase that is most nearly similar in meaning to the word in capital letters and write the letter of your choice on your answer paper.

1. ABASE (A) incur (B) tax (C) ground floor
   (D) humility (E) humiliate
2. ABERRATION (A) deviation (B) abhorrence
   (C) dislike (D) absence (E) anecdote
3. ABETTOR (A) conception (B) one who wagers
   (C) encourager (D) evidence (E) protection
4. ABEYANCE (A) obedience (B) discussion
   (C) excitement (D) suspended action (E) editorial
5. ABJURE (A) discuss (B) renounce (C) run off
   secretly (D) perjure (E) project
6. ABLUTION (A) censure (B) forgiveness
   (C) mutiny (D) survival (E) washing
7. ABNEGATION (A) blackness (B) self-denial
   (C) selfishness (D) cause (E) effect
8. ABORIGINES (A) first designs (B) absolutions
   (C) finales (D) concepts (E) primitive inhabitants

9. ABORTIVE (A) unsuccessful (B) consuming (C) financing (D) familiar (E) fruitful

10. ABSTINENCE (A) restrained eating or drinking (B) vulgar display (C) deportment (D) reluctance (E) population

11. ABSTRUSE (A) profound (B) irrespective (C) suspended (D) protesting (E) not thorough

12. ABUT (A) stimulate (B) grasp (C) oppose (D) widen (E) adjoin

13. ABYSMAL (A) bottomless (B) eternal (C) meteoric (D) diabolic (E) internal

14. ACCEDE (A) fail (B) compromise (C) correct (D) consent (E) mollify

15. ACCLIVITY (A) index (B) report (C) upslope of a hill (D) character (E) negotiator

---

Word List 2   adulation-amend

adulation N. flattery; admiration. He thrived on the *adulation* of his henchmen.

adulterate V. make impure by mixing with baser substances. It is a crime to *adulterate* foods without informing the buyer.

adulterated ADJ. made impure or spoiled by the addition of inferior materials. The health authorities ordered the sale of the meat stopped because they found it *adulterated*.

advent N. arrival. Most Americans were unaware of the *advent* of the Nuclear Age until the news of Hiroshima reached them.

adventitious ADJ. accidental; casual. He found this *adventitious* meeting with his friend extremely fortunate.

adverse ADJ. unfavorable; hostile. *Adverse* circumstances compelled him to close his business.

adversity N. poverty; misfortune. We must learn to meet *adversity* gracefully.

advert V. refer to. Since you *advert* to this matter so frequently, you must regard it as important.

■ **advocate** V. urge; plead for. The abolitionists *advocated* freedom for the slaves. also N.

aegis N. shield; defense. Under the *aegis* of the Bill of Rights, we enjoy our most treasured freedoms.

aeon N. long period of time; an age. It has taken *aeons* for our civilization to develop.

■ **aesthetic** ADJ. artistic; dealing with or capable of appreciation of the beautiful. Because of his *aesthetic* nature, he was emotionally disturbed by ugly things. aesthete, N.

affable ADJ. courteous. Although he held a position of responsibility, he was an *affable* individual and could be reached by anyone with a complaint.

affected ADJ. artificial; pretended. His *affected* mannerisms irritated many of us who had known him before his promotion. affectation, N.

affidavit N. written statement made under oath. The court refused to accept his statement unless he presented it in the form of an *affidavit*.

affiliation N. joining; associating with. His *affiliation* with the political party was of short duration for he soon disagreed with his colleagues.

affinity N. kinship. She felt an *affinity* with all who suffered; their pains were her pains.

affirmation N. solemn pledge by one who refuses to take an oath. The Constitution of this country provides for oath or *affirmation* by officeholders.

affluence N. abundance; wealth. Foreigners are amazed by the *affluence* and luxury of the American way of life.

affray N. public brawl. He was badly mauled by the fighters in the *affray*.

agape ADJ. openmouthed. She stared, *agape*, at the many strange animals in the zoo.

agenda N. items of business at a meeting. We had so much difficulty agreeing upon an *agenda* that there was very little time for the meeting.

agglomeration N. collection; heap. It took weeks to assort the *agglomeration* of miscellaneous items she had collected on her trip.

aggrandize V. increase or intensify. The history of the past quarter century illustrates how a President may *aggrandize* his power to act aggressively in international affairs without considering the wishes of Congress.

aggregate ADJ. sum; total. The *aggregate* wealth of this country is staggering to the imagination. also V.

aghast ADJ. horrified. He was *aghast* at the nerve of the speaker who had insulted his host.

agility N. nimbleness. The *agility* of the acrobat amazed and thrilled the audience.

agitate V. stir up; disturb. Her fiery remarks *agitated* the already angry mob.

agitation N. strong feeling; excitement. We felt that he was responsible for the *agitation* of the mob because of the inflammatory report he had issued.

agnostic N. one who is skeptical of the existence or knowability of a god or any ultimate reality. The *agnostic* demanded proof before she would accept the statement of the minister. also ADJ.

agrarian ADJ. pertaining to land or its cultivation. The country is gradually losing its *agrarian* occupation and turning more and more to an industrial point of view.

alacrity N. cheerful promptness. He demonstrated his eagerness to serve by his *alacrity* in executing the orders of his master.

albeit CONJ. although. *Albeit* fair, she was not sought after.

alchemy N. medieval chemistry. The changing of baser metals into gold was the goal of the students of *alchemy*. alchemist, N.

alias N. an assumed name. John Smith's *alias* was Bob Jones. also ADV.

■ **alienate** V. make hostile; separate. Her attempts to *alienate* the two friends failed because they had complete faith in each other.

alimentary ADJ. supplying nourishment. The *alimentary* canal in our bodies is so named because digestion of foods occurs there.

alimony N. payment by a husband to his divorced wife. Mrs. Jones was awarded $200 monthly *alimony* by the court when she was divorced from her husband.

allay V. calm; pacify. The crew tried to *allay* the fears of the passengers by announcing that the fire had been controlled.

allege V. state without proof. It is *alleged* that she had worked for the enemy. allegation, N.

allegory N. story in which characters are used as symbols; fable. *Pilgrim's Progress* is an *allegory* of the temptations and victories of man's soul. allegorical, ADJ.

alleviate V. relieve. This should *alleviate* the pain; if it does not, we shall have to use stronger drugs.

alliteration N. repetition of beginning sound in poetry. "The furrow followed free" is an example of *alliteration*.

allocate V. assign. Even though the Red Cross had *allocated* a large sum for the relief of the sufferers of the disaster, many people perished.

alloy N. a mixture as of metals. *Alloys* of gold are used more frequently than the pure metal.

allude V. refer indirectly. Try not to *allude* to this matter in his presence because it annoys him to hear of it.

allure V. entice; attract. *Allured* by the song of the sirens, the helmsman steered the ship toward the reef. also N.

allusion N. indirect reference. The *allusions* to mythological characters in Milton's poems bewilder the reader who has not studied Latin.

alluvial ADJ. pertaining to soil deposits left by rivers, etc. The farmers found the *alluvial* deposits at the mouth of the river very fertile.

■ **aloof** ADJ. apart; reserved. Shy by nature, she remained *aloof* while all the rest conversed.

aloft ADV. upward. The sailor climbed *aloft* into the rigging.

altercation N. wordy quarrel. Throughout the entire *altercation,* not one sensible word was uttered.

■ **altruistic** ADJ. unselfishly generous; concerned for others. In providing tutorial assistance and college scholarships for hundreds of economically disadvantaged youths, Eugene Lang performed a truly *altruistic* deed. altruism, N.

amalgamate V. combine; unite in one body. The unions will attempt to *amalgamate* their groups into one national body.

■ **amass** V. collect. The miser's aim is to *amass* and hoard as much gold as possible.

amazon N. female warrior. Ever since the days of Greek mythology we refer to strong and aggressive women as *amazons.*

ambidextrous ADJ. capable of using either hand with equal ease. A switch-hitter in baseball should be naturally *ambidextrous.*

ambience N. environment; atmosphere. She went to the restaurant not for the food but for the *ambience.*

■ **ambiguous** ADJ. unclear or doubtful in meaning. His *ambiguous* instructions misled us; we did not know which road to take. ambiguity, N.

amble N. moving at an easy pace. When she first mounted the horse, she was afraid to urge the animal to go faster than a gentle *amble.* also V.

■ **ambivalence** N. the state of having contradictory or conflicting emotional attitudes. Torn between loving her parents one minute and hating them the next, she was confused by the *ambivalence* of her feelings. ambivalent, ADJ.

ambrosia N. food of the gods. *Ambrosia* was supposed to give immortality to any human who ate it.

ambulatory ADJ. able to walk. He was described as an *ambulatory* patient because he was not confined to his bed.

ameliorate V. improve. Many social workers have attempted to *ameliorate* the conditions of people living in the slums.

amenable ADJ. readily managed; willing to be led. He was *amenable* to any suggestions which came from those he looked up to; he resented advice from his inferiors.

■ **amend** V. correct; change, generally for the better. Hoping to *amend* his condition, he left Vietnam for the United States.

Test

Word List 2 *Antonyms*

Each of the questions below consists of a word in capital letters, followed by five lettered words or phrases. Choose the lettered word or phrase that is most nearly opposite in meaning to the word in capital letters and write the letter of your choice on your answer paper.

16. ADULATION (A) youth (B) purity (C) brightness (D) defense (E) criticism

17. ADVOCATE (A) define (B) oppose (C) remove (D) inspect (E) discern

18. AFFABLE (A) rude (B) ruddy (C) needy (D) useless (E) conscious

19. AFFECTED (A) weary (B) unfriendly (C) divine (D) unfeigned (E) slow

20. AFFLUENCE (A) poverty (B) fear (C) persuasion (D) consideration (E) neglect

21. AGILITY (A) awkwardness (B) solidity (C) temper (D) harmony (E) warmth

22. ALACRITY (A) slowness (B) plenty (C) filth (D) courtesy (E) despair

23. ALLEVIATE (A) endure (B) worsen (C) enlighten (D) maneuver (E) humiliate

24. ALLURE (A) hinder (B) repel (C) ignore (D) leave (E) wallow

25. ALOOF (A) triangular (B) gregarious (C) comparable (D) honorable (E) savory

26. AMALGAMATE (A) equip (B) separate (C) generate (D) materialize (E) repress

27. AMBIGUOUS (A) salvageable (B) corresponding (C) responsible (D) clear (E) auxiliary

28. AMBLE (A) befriend (B) hasten (C) steal (D) browse (E) prattle

29. AMBULATORY (A) convalescent (B) conservatory (C) bedridden (D) emergency (E) congenital

30. AMELIORATE (A) make slow (B) make sure (C) make young (D) make worse (E) make able

Word List 3   amenities-apothecary

amenities N. agreeable manners; courtesies. She observed the social *amenities*.

amiable ADJ. agreeable; lovable. His *amiable* disposition pleased all who had dealings with him.

amicable ADJ. friendly. The dispute was settled in an *amicable* manner with no harsh words.

amiss ADJ. wrong; faulty. Seeing her frown, he wondered if anything were *amiss*. also ADV.

■ **amity** N. friendship. Student exchange programs such as the Experiment in International Living were established to promote international *amity*.

amnesia N. loss of memory. Because she was suffering from *amnesia*, the police could not get the young girl to identify herself.

amnesty N. pardon. When his first child was born, the king granted *amnesty* to all in prison.

amoral ADJ. nonmoral. The *amoral* individual lacks a code of ethics; he should not be classified as immoral.

amorous ADJ. moved by sexual love; loving. Don Juan was known for his *amorous* adventures.

amorphous ADJ. shapeless. She was frightened by the *amorphous* mass which had floated in from the sea.

amortization N. act of reducing a debt through partial payments. Your monthly payments to the bank include provisions for taxes, interest on the principal, and *amortization* of the mortgage.

amphibian ADJ. able to live both on land and in water. Frogs are classified as *amphibian*. also N.

amphitheater N. oval building with tiers of seats. The spectators in the *amphitheater* cheered the gladiators.

ample ADJ. abundant. He had *ample* opportunity to dispose of his loot before the police caught up with him.

amplify V. enlarge. Her attempts to *amplify* her remarks were drowned out by the jeers of the audience.

amputate V. cut off part of body; prune. When the doctors decided to *amputate* his leg to prevent the spread of gangrene, he cried that he preferred death to incapacity.

amuck ADV. in a state of rage. The police had to be called in to restrain him after he ran *amuck* in the department store.

amulet N. charm; talisman. Around her neck she wore the *amulet* that the witch doctor had given her.

anachronism N. an error involving time in a story. The reference to clocks in *Julius Caesar* is an *anachronism*.

analgesic ADJ. causing insensitivity to pain. The *analgesic* qualities of this lotion will provide temporary relief.

■ **analogous** ADJ. comparable. She called our attention to the things that had been done in an *analogous* situation and recommended that we do the same.

analogy N. similarity; parallelism. Your *analogy* is not a good one because the two situations are not similar.

■ **anarchist** N. person who rebels against the established order. Only the total overthrow of all governmental regulations would satisfy the *anarchist*.

anarchy N. absence of governing body; state of disorder. The assassination of the leaders led to a period of *anarchy*.

anathema N. solemn curse. He heaped *anathema* upon his foe.

anathematize V. curse. The high priest *anathematized* the heretic.

ancillary ADJ. serving as an aid or accessory; auxiliary. In an *ancillary* capacity he was helpful; however, he could not be entrusted with leadership. also N.

andirons N. metal supports in a fireplace for cooking utensils or logs. She spent many hours in the department stores looking for a pair of ornamental *andirons* for her fireplace.

anemia N. condition in which blood lacks red corpuscles. The doctor ascribes her tiredness to *anemia*. anemic, ADJ.

anesthetic N. substance that removes sensation with or without loss of consciousness. His monotonous voice acted like an *anesthetic*; his audience was soon asleep. anesthesia, N.

angular ADJ. sharp-cornered; stiff in manner. His features, though *angular*, were curiously attractive.

animadversion N. critical remark. He resented the *animadversions* of his critics, particularly because he realized they were true.

animated ADJ. lively. Her *animated* expression indicated a keenness of intellect.

animosity N. active enmity. He incurred the *animosity* of the ruling class because he advocated limitations of their power.

animus N. hostile feeling or intent. The *animus* of the speaker became obvious to all when he began to indulge in sarcastic and insulting remarks.

annals N. records; history. In the *annals* of this period, we find no mention of democratic movements.

anneal V. reduce brittleness and improve toughness by heating and cooling. After the glass is *annealed,* it will be less subject to chipping and cracking.

annihilate V. destroy. The enemy in its revenge tried to *annihilate* the entire population.

annotate V. comment; make explanatory notes. In the appendix to the novel, the critic sought to *annotate* many of the more esoteric references.

annuity N. yearly allowance. The *annuity* he set up with the insurance company supplements his social security benefits so that he can live very comfortably without working.

annul V. make void. The parents of the eloped couple tried to *annul* the marriage.

anodyne N. drug that relieves pain; opiate. His pain was so great that no *anodyne* could relieve it.

anoint V. consecrate. The prophet Samuel *anointed* David with oil, crowning him king of Israel.

anomalous ADJ. abnormal; irregular. He was placed in the *anomalous* position of seeming to approve procedures which he despised.

anomaly N. irregularity. A bird that cannot fly is an *anomaly.*

■ **anonymity** N. state of being nameless; anonymousness. The donor of the gift asked the college not to mention him by name; the dean readily agreed to respect his *anonymity.*

anonymous ADJ. having no name. She tried to ascertain the identity of the writer of the *anonymous* letter.

antagonism N. active resistance. We shall have to overcome the *antagonism* of the natives before our plans for settling this area can succeed.

■ **antagonistic** ADJ. hostile; opposed. Despite his lawyers' best efforts to stop him, the angry prisoner continued to make *antagonistic* remarks to the judge.

antecede V. precede. The invention of the radiotelegraph *anteceded* the development of television by a quarter of a century.

antediluvian ADJ. antiquated; ancient. The *antediluvian* customs had apparently not changed for thousands of years. also N.

anthropoid ADJ. manlike. The gorilla is the strongest of the *anthropoid* animals. also N.

anthropologist N. a student of the history and science of mankind. *Anthropologists* have discovered several relics of prehistoric man in this area.

anthropomorphic ADJ. having human form or characteristics. Primitive religions often have deities with *anthropomorphic* characteristics.

anticlimax N. letdown in thought or emotion. After the fine performance in the first act, the rest of the play was an *anticlimax.* anticlimactic, ADJ.

antipathy N. aversion; dislike. His extreme *antipathy* to dispute caused him to avoid argumentative discussions with his friends.

antiseptic N. substance that prevents infection. It is advisable to apply an *antiseptic* to any wound, no matter how slight or insignificant. also ADJ.

antithesis N. contrast; direct opposite of or to. This tyranny was the *antithesis* of all that he had hoped for, and he fought it with all his strength.

apathetic ADJ. indifferent. He felt *apathetic* about the conditions he had observed and did not care to fight against them. apathy, N.

■ **apathy** N. lack of caring; indifference. A firm believer in democratic government, she could not understand the *apathy* of people who never bothered to vote.

ape V. imitate or mimic. He was suspended for a week because he had *aped* the principal in front of the whole school.

aperture N. opening; hole. She discovered a small *aperture* in the wall, through which the insects had entered the room.

apex N. tip; summit; climax. He was at the *apex* of his career.

aphasia N. loss of speech due to injury or illness. After the automobile accident, the victim had periods of *aphasia* when he could not speak at all or could only mumble incoherently.

aphorism N. pithy maxim. An *aphorism* differs from an adage in that it is more philosophical or scientific. aphoristic, ADJ.

apiary N. a place where bees are kept. Although he spent many hours daily in the *apiary,* he was very seldom stung by a bee.

aplomb N. poise. His nonchalance and *aplomb* in times of trouble always encouraged his followers.

apocalyptic ADJ. prophetic; pertaining to revelations. His *apocalyptic* remarks were dismissed by his audience as wild surmises.

apocryphal ADJ. not genuine; sham. Her *apocryphal* tears misled no one.

apogee N. highest point. When the moon in its orbit is furthest away from the earth, it is at its *apogee.*

apoplexy N. stroke; loss of consciousness followed by paralysis. He was crippled by an attack of *apoplexy.*

apostate N. one who abandons his religious faith or political beliefs. Because he switched from one party to another, his former friends shunned him as an *apostate.*

apothecary N. druggist. In the *apothecaries'* weight, twelve ounces equal one pound.

Test

Word List 3   *Antonyms*

Each of the questions below consists of a word in capital letters, followed by five lettered words or phrases. Choose the lettered word or phrase that is most nearly opposite in meaning to the word in capital letters and write the letter of your choice on your answer paper.

31. AMICABLE (A) penetrating (B) compensating (C) unfriendly (D) zig-zag (E) inescapable
32. AMORAL (A) unusual (B) unfriendly (C) ethical (D) suave (E) firm
33. AMORPHOUS (A) nauseous (B) obscene (C) providential (D) definite (E) happy
34. AMPLIFY (A) distract (B) infer (C) publicize (D) decrease (E) pioneer
35. ANALOGOUS (A) not comparable (B) not capable (C) not culpable (D) not corporeal (E) not congenial
36. ANATHEMATIZE (A) locate (B) deceive (C) regulate (D) radiate (E) bless

37. ANEMIC (A) pallid (B) cruel (C) red-blooded (D) ventilating (E) hazardous
38. ANIMATED (A) worthy (B) dull (C) humorous (D) lengthy (E) realistic
39. ANIMUS (A) pterodactyl (B) bastion (C) giraffe (D) grimace (E) favor
40. ANOMALY (A) desperation (B) requisition (C) registry (D) regularity (E) radiation
41. ANONYMOUS (A) desperate (B) signed (C) defined (D) expert (E) written
42. ANTEDILUVIAN (A) transported (B) subtle (C) isolated (D) celebrated (E) modern
43. ANTIPATHY (A) profundity (B) objection (C) willingness (D) abstention (E) fondness
44. ANTITHESIS (A) velocity (B) maxim (C) similarity (D) acceleration (E) reaction
45. APHASIA (A) volubility (B) necessity (C) pain (D) crack (E) prayer

---

Word List 4   apothegm-astigmatism

apothegm N. pithy, compact saying. Proverbs are *apothegms* that have become familiar sayings.

apotheosis N. deification; glorification. The *apotheosis* of a Roman emperor was designed to insure his eternal greatness.

appall V. dismay; shock. We were *appalled* by the horrifying conditions in the city's jails.

apparition N. ghost; phantom. Hamlet was uncertain about the identity of the *apparition* that had appeared and spoken to him.

■ **appease** V. pacify; soothe. We have discovered that, when we try to *appease* our enemies, we encourage them to make additional demands.

appellation N. name; title. He was amazed when the witches hailed him with his correct *appellation*.

append V. attach. I shall *append* this chart to my report.

apposite ADJ. appropriate; fitting. He was always able to find the *apposite* phrase, the correct expression for every occasion.

appraise V. estimate value of. It is difficult to *appraise* the value of old paintings; it is easier to call them priceless. appraisal, N.

apprehend V. arrest (a criminal); dread; perceive. The police will *apprehend* the culprit and convict him before long.

■ **apprehensive** ADJ. fearful; discerning. His *apprehensive* glances at the people who were walking in the street revealed his nervousness.

apprise V. inform. When he was *apprised* of the dangerous weather conditions, he decided to postpone his trip.

approbation N. approval. She looked for some sign of *approbation* from her parents.

appropriate V. acquire; take possession of for one's own use. The ranch owners *appropriated* the lands that had originally been set aside for the Indians' use.

appurtenances N. subordinate possessions. He bought the estate and all its *appurtenances*.

apropos PREP. with reference to; regarding. I find your remarks *apropos* of the present situation timely and pertinent. also ADJ. and ADV.

aptitude N. fitness; talent. The counselor gave him an *aptitude* test before advising him about the career he should follow.

aquiline ADJ. curved, hooked. He can be recognized by his *aquiline* nose, curved like the beak of the eagle.

arable ADJ. fit for plowing. The land was no longer *arable*; erosion had removed the valuable topsoil.

arbiter N. a person with power to decide a dispute; judge. As an *arbiter* in labor disputes, she has won the confidence of the workers and the employers.

■ **arbitrary** ADJ. fixed or definite; imperious; tyrannical; despotic. Any *arbitrary* action on your part will be resented by the members of the board whom you do not consult.

arcade N. a covered passageway, usually lined with shops. The *arcade* was popular with shoppers because it gave them protection from the summer sun and the winter rain.

arcane ADJ. secret; mysterious. What was *arcane* to us was clear to the psychologist.

archaeology N. study of artifacts and relics of early mankind. The professor of *archaeology* headed an expedition to the Gobi Desert in search of ancient ruins.

archaic ADJ. antiquated. "Methinks," "thee," and "thou" are *archaic* words which are no longer part of our normal vocabulary.

archetype N. prototype; primitive pattern. The Brooklyn Bridge was the *archetype* of the many spans that now connect Manhattan with Long Island and New Jersey.

archipelago N. group of closely located islands. When he looked at the map and saw the *archipelagoes* in the South Seas, he longed to visit them.

archives N. public records; place where public records are kept. These documents should be part of the *archives* so that historians may be able to evaluate them in the future.

ardor N. heat; passion; zeal. His *ardor* was contagious; soon everyone was eagerly working.

■ **arduous** ADJ. hard; strenuous. Her *arduous* efforts had sapped her energy.

argot N. slang. In the *argot* of the underworld, she "was taken for a ride."

aria N. operatic solo. At her Metropolitan Opera audition, Marian Anderson sang an *aria* from *Norma.*

■ **arid** ADJ. dry; barren. The cactus has adapted to survive in an *arid* environment.

aromatic ADJ. fragrant. Medieval sailing vessels brought *aromatic* herbs from China to Europe.

arraign V. charge in court; indict. After his indictment by the Grand Jury, the accused man was *arraigned* in the County Criminal Court.

arrant ADJ. thorough; complete; unmitigated. *"Arrant* knave," an epithet found in books dealing with the age of chivalry, is a term of condemnation.

array V. marshal; draw up in order. His actions were bound to *array* public sentiment against him. also N.

array V. clothe; adorn. She liked to watch her mother *array* herself in her finest clothes before going out for the evening. also N.

arrears N. being in debt. He was in *arrears* with his payments on the car.

■ **arrogance** N. pride; haughtiness. The *arrogance* of the nobility was resented by the middle class.

arrogate V. claim without reasonable grounds. I am afraid that the manner in which he *arrogates* power to himself indicates that he is willing to ignore Constitutional limitations.

arroyo N. gully. Until the heavy rains of the past spring, this *arroyo* had been a dry bed.

■ **articulate** ADJ. effective; distinct. Her *articulate* presentation of the advertising campaign impressed her employers. also V.

artifacts N. products of primitive culture. Archaeologists debated the significance of the *artifacts* discovered in the ruins of Asia Minor and came to no conclusion.

artifice N. deception; trickery. The Trojan War proved to the Greeks that cunning and *artifice* were often more effective than military might.

artisan N. a manually skilled worker. Artists and *artisans* alike are necessary to the development of a culture.

ascendancy N. controlling influence. President Marcos failed to maintain his *ascendancy* over the Philippines.

ascertain V. find out for certain. Please *ascertain* her present address.

■ **ascetic** ADJ. practicing self-denial; austere. The wealthy young man could not understand the *ascetic* life led by the monks. also N.

asceticism N. doctrine of self-denial. We find *asceticism* practiced in many monasteries.

ascribe V. refer; attribute; assign. I can *ascribe* no motive for her acts.

aseptic ADJ. preventing infection; having a cleansing effect. Hospitals succeeded in lowering the mortality rate as soon as they introduced *aseptic* conditions.

ashen ADJ. ash-colored. Her face was *ashen* with fear.

asinine ADJ. stupid. Your *asinine* remarks prove that you have not given this problem any serious consideration.

askance ADV. with a sideways or indirect look. Looking *askance* at her questioner, she displayed her scorn.

askew ADV. crookedly; slanted; at an angle. When he placed his hat *askew* upon his head, his observers laughed.

asperity N. sharpness (of temper). These remarks, spoken with *asperity,* stung the boys to whom they had been directed.

aspersion N. slanderous remark. Do not cast *aspersions* on her character.

aspirant N. seeker after position or status. Although I am an *aspirant* for public office, I am not willing to accept the dictates of the party bosses. also ADJ.

aspiration N. noble ambition. Man's *aspirations* should be as lofty as the stars.

assail V. assault. He was *assailed* with questions after his lecture.

assay V. analyze; evaluate. When they *assayed* the ore, they found that they had discovered a very rich vein. also N.

assent V. agree; accept. It gives me great pleasure to *assent* to your request.

■ **assessment** N. estimation. I would like to have your *assessment* of the situation in South Africa.

assiduous ADJ. diligent. He worked *assiduously* at this task for weeks before he felt satisfied with his results. assiduity, N.

assimilate V. absorb; cause to become homogeneous. The manner in which the United States was able to *assimilate* the hordes of immigrants during the nineteenth and the early part of the twentieth centuries will always be a source of pride.

assuage V. ease; lessen (pain). Your messages of cheer should *assuage* her suffering. assuagement, N.

asteroid N. small planet. *Asteroids* have become commonplace to the readers of interstellar travel stories in science fiction magazines.

astigmatism N. eye defect which prevents proper focus. As soon as his parents discovered that the boy suffered from *astigmatism,* they took him to the optometrist for corrective glasses.

Test

Word List 4   *Synonyms and Antonyms*

Each of the following questions consists of a word in capital letters, followed by five lettered words or phrases. Choose the lettered word or phrase which is most nearly similar or the opposite of the word in capital letters and write the letter of your choice on your answer paper.

46. APPEASE (A) agitate (B) qualify (C) display
    (D) predestine (E) interrupt
47. APPOSITE (A) inappropriate (B) diagonal
    (C) exponential (D) unobtrusive (E) discouraging
48. APPREHEND (A) obviate (B) set free (C) shiver
    (D) understand (E) contrast
49. APTITUDE (A) sarcasm (B) inversion (C) adulation
    (D) lack of talent (E) gluttony
50. AQUILINE (A) watery (B) hooked (C) refined
    (D) antique (E) rodentlike
51. ARCHAIC (A) youthful (B) cautious (C) antiquated
    (D) placated (E) buttressed

52. ARDOR (A) zeal (B) paint (C) proof (D) group
    (E) excitement
53. ARROGATE (A) swindle (B) balance (C) claim
    (D) perjure (E) effect
54. ARROYO (A) crevice (B) gully (C) value
    (D) food (E) fabric
55. ARTIFICE (A) spite (B) exception (C) anger
    (D) candor (E) loyalty
56. ARTISAN (A) educator (B) decider (C) sculptor
    (D) discourser (E) unskilled laborer
57. ASCERTAIN (A) amplify (B) master (C) discover
    (D) retain (E) explode
58. ASPERITY (A) anguish (B) absence (C) innuendo
    (D) good temper (E) snake
59. ASSUAGE (A) stuff (B) describe (C) wince
    (D) worsen (E) introduce
60. ASTEROID (A) Milky Way (B) radiance (C) large
    planet (D) rising moon (E) setting moon

Word List 5   astral-barb

astral ADJ. relating to the stars. She was amazed at the number of *astral* bodies the new telescope revealed.

astringent ADJ. binding; causing contraction. The *astringent* quality of the unsweetened lemon juice made swallowing difficult. also N.

astronomical ADJ. enormously large or extensive. The government seems willing to spend *astronomical* sums on weapons development.

■ **astute** ADJ. wise; shrewd. That was a very *astute* observation. I shall heed it.

asunder ADV. into parts; apart. Their points of view are poles *asunder*.

■ **asylum** N. place of refuge or shelter; protection. The refugees sought *asylum* from religious persecution in a new land.

atavism N. resemblance to remote ancestors rather than to parents; deformity returning after passage of two or more generations. The doctors ascribed the child's deformity to an *atavism*.

atelier N. workshop; studio. Stories of Bohemian life in Paris are full of tales of artists' starving or freezing in their *ateliers*.

atheistic ADJ. denying the existence of God. His *atheistic* remarks shocked the religious worshippers.

athwart PREP. across; in opposition. His tendency toward violence was *athwart* the philosophy of the peace movement. also ADV.

atone V. make amends for; pay for. He knew no way in which he could *atone* for his brutal crime.

atrocity N. brutal deed. In time of war, many *atrocities* are committed by invading armies.

atrophy N. wasting away. Polio victims need physiotherapy to prevent the *atrophy* of affected limbs. also V.

attenuate V. make thin; weaken. By withdrawing their forces, the generals hoped to *attenuate* the enemy lines.

attest V. testify, bear witness. Having served as a member of the Grand Jury, I can *attest* that our system of indicting individuals is in need of improvement.

attribute N. essential quality. His outstanding *attribute* was his kindness.

attribute V. ascribe; explain. I *attribute* her success in science to the encouragement she received from her parents.

attrition N. gradual wearing down. They decided to wage a war of *attrition* rather than to rely on an all-out attack.

atypical ADJ. not normal. You have taken an *atypical* case. It does not prove anything.

audacity N. boldness. Her *audacity* in this critical moment encouraged us.

audit N. examination of accounts. When the bank examiners arrived to hold their annual *audit,* they discovered the embezzlements of the chief cashier. also V.

■ **augment** V. increase. How can we hope to *augment* our forces when our allies are deserting us?

augury N. omen; prophecy. He interpreted the departure of the birds as an *augury* of evil. augur, V.

august ADJ. impressive; majestic. Visiting the palace at Versailles, she was impressed by the *august* surroundings in which she found herself.

aureole N. sun's corona; halo. Many medieval paintings depict saintly characters with *aureoles* around their heads.

auroral ADJ. pertaining to the aurora borealis. The *auroral* display was particularly spectacular that evening.

auscultation N. act of listening to the heart or lungs to discover abnormalities. The science of *auscultation* was enhanced with the development of the stethoscope.

auspicious ADJ. favoring success. With favorable weather conditions, it was an *auspicious* moment to set sail.

austere ADJ. strict, stern. His *austere* demeanor prevented us from engaging in our usual frivolous activities.

■ **austerity** N. sternness; severity; lack of luxuries. The *austerity* and dignity of the court were maintained by the new justices, who were a strict and solemn group.

authenticate V. prove genuine. An expert was needed to *authenticate* the original Van Gogh painting, distinguishing it from its imitation.

■ **authoritarian** ADJ. favoring or exercising total control; nondemocratic. The people had no control over their own destiny; they were forced to obey the dictates of the *authoritarian* regime. also N.

authoritative ADJ. having the weight of authority; dictatorial. We accepted her analysis of the situation as *authoritative*.

■ **autocrat** N. monarch with supreme power. He ran his office like an *autocrat*, giving no one else any authority. autocracy, N.

automaton N. mechanism which imitates actions of humans. Long before science fiction readers became aware of robots, writers were presenting stories of *automatons* who could outperform men.

autonomous ADJ. self-governing. This island is a colony; however, in most matters, it is *autonomous* and receives no orders from the mother country. autonomy, N.

autopsy N. examination of a dead body; post-mortem. The medical examiner ordered an *autopsy* to determine the cause of death. also V.

auxiliary ADJ. helper, additional or subsidiary. To prepare for the emergency, they built an *auxiliary* power station. also N.

avarice N. greediness for wealth. King Midas's *avarice* has been famous for centuries. avaricious, ADJ.

avatar N. incarnation. In Hindu mythology, the *avatar* of Vishnu is thoroughly detailed.

aver V. state confidently. I wish to *aver* that I am certain of success.

averse ADJ. reluctant. He was *averse* to revealing the sources of his information.

aversion N. firm dislike. Their mutual *aversion* was so great that they refused to speak to one another.

avert V. prevent; turn away. She *averted* her eyes from the dead cat on the highway.

aviary N. enclosure for birds. The *aviary* at the zoo held nearly 300 birds.

avid ADJ. greedy; eager for. He was *avid* for learning and read everything he could get. avidity, N.

avocation N. secondary or minor occupation. His hobby proved to be so fascinating and profitable that gradually he abandoned his regular occupation and concentrated on his *avocation*.

avow V. declare openly. I must *avow* that I am innocent.

avuncular ADJ. like an uncle. *Avuncular* pride did not prevent him from noticing his nephew's shortcomings.

awe N. solemn wonder. The tourists gazed with *awe* at the tremendous expanse of the Grand Canyon.

awry ADV. distorted; crooked. He held his head *awry*, giving the impression that he had caught cold in his neck during the night. also ADJ.

axiom N. self-evident truth requiring no proof. Before a student can begin to think along the lines of Euclidean geometry, he must accept certain principles or *axioms*.

azure ADJ. sky blue. *Azure* skies are indicative of good weather.

babble V. chatter idly. The little girl *babbled* about her doll. also N.

bacchanalian ADJ. drunken. Emperor Nero attended the *bacchanalian* orgy.

badger V. pester; annoy. She was forced to change her telephone number because she was *badgered* by obscene phone calls.

badinage N. teasing conversation. Her friends at work greeted the news of her engagement with cheerful *badinage*.

baffle V. frustrate; perplex. The new code *baffled* the enemy agents.

bagatelle N. trifle. Trying to reassure Roxanne about his wound, Cyrano claimed it was a mere *bagatelle*.

baleful ADJ. deadly; destructive. The drought was a *baleful* omen.

bait V. harass; tease. The soldiers *baited* the prisoners, terrorizing them.

balk V. foil. When the warden learned that several inmates were planning to escape, he took steps to *balk* their attempt.

balm N. something that relieves pain. Friendship is the finest *balm* for the pangs of disappointed love.

balmy ADJ. mild; fragrant. A *balmy* breeze refreshed us after the sultry blast.

■ **banal** ADJ. hackneyed; commonplace; trite. His frequent use of clichés made his essay seem *banal*. banality, N.

bandanna N. large, bright-colored handkerchief. She could be identified by the gaudy *bandanna* she wore as a head covering.

bandy V. discuss lightly; exchange blows or words. The President refused to *bandy* words with the reporters at the press conference.

bane N. cause of ruin. Lack of public transportation is the *bane* of urban life.

baneful ADJ. ruinous; poisonous. His *baneful* influence was feared by all.

bantering ADJ. good-natured ridiculing. They resented his *bantering* remarks because they thought he was being sarcastic.

barb N. sharp projection from fishhook, etc. The *barb* from the fishhook caught in his finger as he grabbed the fish. barbed, ADJ.

Test

Word List 5   *Synonyms*

Each of the questions below consists of a word in capital letters, followed by five lettered words or phrases. Choose the lettered word or phrase that is most nearly similar in meaning to the word in capital letters and write the letter of your choice on your answer paper.

61. ASTUTE (A) sheer (B) noisy (C) astral (D) unusual (E) clever

62. ATROCITY (A) endurance (B) fortitude (C) session (D) heinous act (E) hatred

63. ATROPHY (A) capture (B) waste away (C) govern (D) award prize (E) defeat

64. ATTENUATE (A) appear (B) be absent (C) weaken (D) testify (E) soothe

65. ATYPICAL (A) superfluous (B) fortitude (C) unusual (D) clashing (E) lovely

66. AUDACITY (A) boldness (B) asperity (C) strength (D) stature (E) anchorage

67. AUGMENT (A) make noble (B) anoint (C) increase (D) harvest (E) reach

68. AUXILIARY (A) righteous (B) prospective (C) assistant (D) archaic (E) mandatory

69. AVARICE (A) easiness (B) greed (C) statement (D) invoice (E) power

70. AVATAR (A) hedge (B) hypnosis (C) incarnation (D) perfume (E) disaster

71. AWRY (A) recommended (B) commiserating (C) startled (D) crooked (E) psychological

72. BALEFUL (A) doubtful (B) virtual (C) deadly (D) conventional (E) virtuous

73. BALMY (A) venturesome (B) dedicated (C) mild (D) fanatic (E) memorable

74. BANAL (A) philosophical (B) trite (C) dramatic (D) heedless (E) discussed

75. BANEFUL (A) intellectual (B) thankful (C) decisive (D) poisonous (E) remorseful

Word List 6   bard-bludgeon

bard N. poet. The ancient *bard* Homer sang of the fall of Troy.

baroque ADJ. highly ornate. They found the *baroque* architecture amusing.

barrage N. barrier laid down by artillery fire. The company was forced to retreat through the *barrage* of heavy cannons.

barrister N. counselor-at-law. Galsworthy started as a *barrister,* but, when he found the practice of law boring, turned to writing.

barterer N. trader. The *barterer* exchanged trinkets for the natives' furs.

bask V. luxuriate; take pleasure in warmth. *Basking* on the beach, she relaxed so completely that she fell asleep.

bassoon N. reed instrument of the woodwind family. In the orchestra, the *bassoon* is related to the oboe and the clarinet.

bastion N. fortress; defense. Once a *bastion* of democracy, under its new government the island became a dictatorship.

bate V. let down; restrain. Until it was time to open the presents, the children had to *bate* their curiosity. bated, ADJ.

bauble N. trinket; trifle. The child was delighted with the *bauble* she had won in the grab bag.

bawdy ADJ. indecent; obscene. She took offense at his *bawdy* remarks.

beatific ADJ. giving bliss; blissful. The *beatific* smile on the child's face made us very happy.

beatitude N. blessedness; state of bliss. Growing closer to God each day, the mystic achieved a state of indescribable *beatitude.*

bedizen V. dress with vulgar finery. The witch doctors were *bedizened* in all their gaudiest costumes.

bedraggle V. wet thoroughly. We were so *bedraggled* by the severe storm that we had to change into dry clothing. bedraggled, ADJ.

befuddle V. confuse thoroughly. His attempts to clarify the situation succeeded only in *befuddling* her further.

begrudge V. resent. I *begrudge* every minute I have to spend attending meetings.

beguile V. amuse; delude; cheat. He *beguiled* himself during the long hours by playing solitaire.

behemoth N. huge creature; monstrous animal. Sportscasters nicknamed the linebacker "The *Behemoth.*"

beholden ADJ. obligated; indebted. Since I do not wish to be *beholden* to anyone, I cannot accept this favor.

behoove V. suited to; incumbent upon. In this time of crisis, it *behooves* all of us to remain calm and await the instructions of our superiors.

belabor V. beat soundly; assail verbally. He was *belaboring* his opponent during the debate.

belated ADJ. delayed. He apologized for his *belated* note of condolence to the widow of his friend and explained that he had just learned of her husband's untimely death.

beleaguer V. besiege. As soon as the city was *beleaguered,* life became more subdued as the citizens began their long wait for outside assistance. beleaguered, ADJ.

■ **belittle** V. disparage; depreciate. Although I do not wish to *belittle* your contribution, I feel we must place it in its proper perspective.

bellicose ADJ. warlike. His *bellicose* disposition alienated his friends.

belligerent ADJ. quarrelsome. Whenever he had too much to drink, he became *belligerent* and tried to pick fights with strangers.

benediction N. blessing. The appearance of the sun after the many rainy days was like a *benediction.*

■ **benefactor** N. gift giver; patron. Scrooge later became Tiny Tim's *benefactor* and gave him gifts.

beneficiary N. person entitled to benefits or proceeds of an insurance policy or will. You may change your *beneficiary* as often as you wish.

benevolent ADJ. generous; charitable. His *benevolent* nature prevented him from refusing any beggar who accosted him.

benighted ADJ. overcome by darkness. In the *benighted* Middle Ages, intellectual curiosity was discouraged by the authorities.

■ **benign** ADJ. kindly; favorable; not malignant. The old man was well liked because of his *benign* attitude toward friend and stranger alike.

benignity N. state of being kind, benign, gracious. We have endowed our Creator with a *benignity* which permits forgiveness of our sins and transgressions.

benison N. blessing. Let us pray that the *benison* of peace once more shall prevail among the nations of the world.

berate V. scold strongly. He feared she would *berate* him for his forgetfulness.

bereavement N. state of being deprived of something valuable or beloved. His friends gathered to console him upon his sudden *bereavement.*

bereft ADJ. deprived of; lacking. The foolish gambler soon found himself *bereft* of funds.

berserk ADV. frenzied. Angered, he went *berserk* and began to wreck the room.

beset V. harass; trouble. Many problems *beset* the American public school system.

besmirch V. soil, defile. The scandalous remarks in the newspaper *besmirch* the reputations of every member of the society.

bestial ADJ. beastlike; brutal. We must suppress our *bestial* desires and work for peaceful and civilized ends.

bestow V. confer. He wished to *bestow* great honors upon the hero.

bête noire N. aversion; person or thing strongly disliked or avoided. Going to the opera was his personal *bête noire* because high-pitched sounds irritated him.

betroth V. become engaged to marry. The announcement that they had become *betrothed* surprised their friends who had not suspected any romance. betrothal, N.

bevy N. large group. The movie actor was surrounded by a *bevy* of starlets.

bicameral ADJ. two-chambered, as a legislative body. The United States Congress is a *bicameral* body.

bibulous ADJ. inclined to drink; affected by alcohol. We could not help laughing at his *bibulous* farewells.

bicker V. quarrel. The children *bickered* morning, noon, and night, exasperating their parents.

biennial ADJ. every two years. The group held *biennial* meetings instead of annual ones.

bifurcated ADJ. divided into two branches; forked. With a *bifurcated* branch and a piece of elastic rubber, he made a crude but effective slingshot.

bigotry N. stubborn intolerance. Brought up in a democratic atmosphere, the student was shocked by the *bigotry* and narrowness expressed by several of his classmates.

bilious ADJ. suffering from indigestion; irritable. His *bilious* temperament was apparent to all who heard him rant about his difficulties.

bilk V. swindle; cheat. The con man specialized in *bilking* insurance companies.

bivouac N. temporary encampment. While in *bivouac*, we spent the night in our sleeping bags under the stars. also V.

bizarre ADJ. fantastic; violently contrasting. The plot of the novel was too *bizarre* to be believed.

blanch V. bleach; whiten. Although age had *blanched* his hair, he was still vigorous and energetic.

bland ADJ. soothing; mild. She used a *bland* ointment for her sunburn.

blandishment N. flattery. Despite the salesperson's *blandishments,* the customer did not buy the outfit.

blasé ADJ. bored with pleasure or dissipation. Your *blasé* attitude gives your students an erroneous impression of the joys of scholarship.

blasphemous ADJ. profane; impious. The people in the room were shocked by his *blasphemous* language.

blatant ADJ. loudly offensive. I regard your remarks as *blatant* and ill-mannered. blatancy, N.

blazon V. decorate with an heraldic coat of arms. *Blazoned* on his shield were the two lambs and the lion, the traditional coat of arms of his family. also N.

bleak ADJ. cold; cheerless. The Aleutian Islands are *bleak* military outposts.

blighted ADJ. suffering from a disease; destroyed. The extent of the *blighted* areas could be seen only when viewed from the air.

■ **blithe** ADJ. gay; joyous. Shelley called the skylark a "*blithe* spirit" because of its happy song.

bloated ADJ. swollen or puffed as with water or air. Her *bloated* stomach came from drinking so much water.

bludgeon N. club; heavy-headed weapon. His walking stick served him as a *bludgeon* on many occasions. also V.

Test

Word List 6   *Antonyms*

Each of the questions below consists of a word in capital letters, followed by five lettered words or phrases. Choose the lettered word or phrase that is most nearly opposite in meaning to the word in capital letters and write the letter of your choice on your answer paper.

76. BAROQUE (A) polished (B) constant (C) transformed (D) simple (E) aglow
77. BEATIFIC (A) glorious (B) dreadful (C) theatrical (D) crooked (E) handsome
78. BELITTLE (A) disobey (B) forget (C) magnify (D) extol (E) envy
79. BELLICOSE (A) peaceful (B) navel (C) amusing (D) piecemeal (E) errant
80. BENIGN (A) tenfold (B) peaceful (C) blessed (D) wavering (E) malignant
81. BENISON (A) curse (B) bachelor (C) wedding (D) orgy (E) tragedy

82. BERATE (A) grant (B) praise (C) refer (D) purchase (E) deny
83. BESTIAL (A) animated (B) noble (C) zoological (D) clear (E) dusky
84. BIGOTRY (A) arrogance (B) approval (C) mourning (D) promptness (E) tolerance
85. BIZARRE (A) roomy (B) veiled (C) subdued (D) triumphant (E) outspoken
86. BLANCH (A) bleach (B) scatter (C) darken (D) analyze (E) subdivide
87. BLAND (A) caustic (B) meager (C) soft (D) uncooked (E) helpless
88. BLASÉ (A) fiery (B) clever (C) intriguing (D) slim (E) ardent
89. BLEAK (A) pale (B) sudden (C) dry (D) narrow (E) cheerful
90. BLITHE (A) spiritual (B) profuse (C) cheerless (D) hybrid (E) comfortable

Word List 7   blunder-canter

blunder N. error. The criminal's fatal *blunder* led to his capture. also V.

blurt V. utter impulsively. Before she could stop him, he *blurted* out the news.

bode V. foreshadow; portend. The gloomy skies and the sulphurous odors from the mineral springs seemed to *bode* evil to those who settled in the area.

bogus ADJ. counterfeit; not authentic. The police quickly found the distributors of the *bogus* twenty-dollar bills.

boisterous ADJ. violent; rough; noisy. The unruly crowd became even more *boisterous* when he tried to quiet them.

■ **bolster** V. support; prop up. I do not intend to *bolster* your hopes with false reports of outside assistance; the truth is that we must face the enemy alone. also N.

■ **bombastic** ADJ. pompous; using inflated language. The orator's *bombastic* manner left the audience unimpressed. bombast, N.

boorish ADJ. rude; clownish. Your *boorish* remarks to the driver of the other car were not warranted by the situation and served merely to enrage him.

bouillon N. clear beef soup. The cup of *bouillon* served by the stewards was welcomed by those who had been chilled by the cold ocean breezes.

bountiful ADJ. generous; showing bounty. She distributed gifts in a *bountiful* and gracious manner.

bourgeois N. middle class. The French Revolution was inspired by the *bourgeois*, who resented the aristocracy. also ADJ.

bowdlerize V. expurgate. After the film editors had *bowdlerized* the language in the script, the motion picture's rating was changed from "R" to "PG."

brackish ADJ. somewhat saline. He found the only wells in the area were *brackish*; drinking the water made him nauseated.

braggadocio N. boasting. He was disliked because his manner was always full of *braggadocio*.

■ **braggart** N. boaster. Modest by nature, she was no *braggart*, preferring to let her accomplishments speak for themselves.

bravado N. swagger; assumed air of defiance. The *bravado* of the young criminal disappeared when he was confronted by the victims of his brutal attack.

brazen ADJ. insolent. Her *brazen* contempt for authority angered the officials.

brazier N. open pan in which live coals are burned. On chilly nights, the room was warmed by coals burning in *braziers* set in the corners of the room.

breach N. breaking of contract or duty; fissure; gap. They found a *breach* in the enemy's fortifications and penetrated their lines. also V.

breadth N. width; extent. We were impressed by the *breadth* of her knowledge.

■ **brevity** N. conciseness. *Brevity* is essential when you send a telegram or cablegram; you are charged for every word.

brindled ADJ. tawny or grayish with streaks or spots. He was disappointed in the litter because the puppies were *brindled;* he had hoped for animals of a uniform color.

bristling ADJ. rising like bristles; showing irritation. The dog stood there, *bristling* with anger.

brittle ADJ. easily broken; difficult. My employer's *brittle* personality made it difficult for me to get along with her.

broach V. open up. He did not even try to *broach* the subject of poetry.

brocade N. rich, figured fabric. The sofa was covered with expensive *brocade.*

brochure N. pamphlet. This *brochure* on farming was issued by the Department of Agriculture.

brooch N. ornamental clasp. She treasured the *brooch* because it was an heirloom.

brusque ADJ. blunt; abrupt. She was offended by his *brusque* reply.

bucolic ADJ. rustic; pastoral. The meadow was the scene of *bucolic* gaiety.

buffoonery N. clowning. Jimmy Durante's *buffoonery* was hilarious.

bugaboo N. bugbear; object of baseless terror. If we become frightened by such *bugaboos,* we are no wiser than the birds who fear scarecrows.

bullion N. gold and silver in the form of bars. Much *bullion* is stored in the vaults at Fort Knox.

bulwark N. earthwork or other strong defense; person who defends. The navy is our principal *bulwark* against invasion.

bumptious ADJ. self-assertive. His classmates called him a show-off because of his *bumptious* airs.

bungle V. spoil by clumsy behavior. I was afraid you would *bungle* this assignment but I had no one else to send.

bureaucracy N. government by bureaus. Many people fear that the constant introduction of federal agencies will create a government by *bureaucracy.*

burgeon V. grow forth; send out buds. In the spring, the plants that *burgeon* are a promise of the beauty that is to come.

burlesque V. give an imitation that ridicules. In his caricature, he *burlesqued* the mannerisms of his adversary. also N.

burly ADJ. husky; muscular. The *burly* mover lifted the packing crate with ease.

burnish V. make shiny by rubbing; polish. The *burnished* metal reflected the lamplight.

buskin N. thick-soled half boot worn by actors of Greek tragedy. Wearing the *buskin* gave the Athenian tragic actor a larger-than-life appearance and enhanced the intensity of the play.

buttress N. support or prop. The huge cathedral walls were supported by flying *buttresses.* also V.

buxom ADJ. plump; vigorous; jolly. The soldiers remembered the *buxom* nurse who had always been so pleasant to them.

cabal N. small group of persons secretly united to promote their own interests. The *cabal* was defeated when their scheme was discovered.

cache N. hiding place. The detectives followed the suspect until he led them to the *cache* where he had stored his loot. also V.

cacophony N. discord. Some people seem to enjoy the *cacophony* of an orchestra that is tuning up.

cadaver N. corpse. In some states, it is illegal to dissect *cadavers.*

cadaverous ADJ. like a corpse; pale. By his *cadaverous* appearance, we could see how the disease had ravaged him.

cajole V. coax; wheedle. I will not be *cajoled* into granting you your wish.

calamity N. disaster; misery. As news of the *calamity* spread, offers of relief poured in to the stricken community.

caliber N. ability; capacity. A man of such *caliber* should not be assigned such menial tasks.

calligraphy N. beautiful writing; excellent penmanship. As we examine ancient manuscripts, we become impressed with the *calligraphy* of the scribes.

callous ADJ. hardened; unfeeling. He had worked in the hospital for so many years that he was *callous* to the suffering in the wards. callus, N.

callow ADJ. youthful; immature. In that youthful movement, the leaders were only a little less *callow* than their immature followers.

calorific ADJ. heat-producing. Coal is much more *calorific* than green wood.

calumniate V. slander. Shakespeare wrote that love and friendship were subject to envious and *calumniating* time.

calumny N. malicious misrepresentation; slander. He could endure his financial failure, but he could not bear the *calumny* that his foes heaped upon him.

camaraderie N. good-fellowship. What he loved best about his job was the sense of *camaraderie* he and his co-workers shared.

cameo N. shell or jewel carved in relief. Tourists are advised not to purchase *cameos* from the street peddlers of Rome who sell poor specimens of the carver's art.

canard N. unfounded rumor; exaggerated report. It is almost impossible to protect oneself from such a base *canard.*

■ **candor** N. frankness. The *candor* and simplicity of his speech impressed all; it was clear he held nothing back. candid, ADJ.

canine ADJ. related to dogs; dog-like. Some days the *canine* population of Berkeley seems almost to outnumber the human population.

canker N. any ulcerous sore; any evil. Poverty is a *canker* in the body politic; it must be cured.

canny ADJ. shrewd; thrifty. The *canny* Scotsman was more than a match for the swindlers.

cant N. jargon of thieves; pious phraseology. Many listeners were fooled by the *cant* and hypocrisy of his speech.

cantankerous ADJ. ill humored; irritable. Constantly complaining about his treatment and refusing to cooperate with the hospital staff, he was a *cantankerous* patient.

cantata N. story set to music, to be sung by a chorus. The choral society sang the new *cantata* composed by its leader.

canter N. slow gallop. Because the racehorse had outdistanced its competition so easily, the reporter wrote that the race was won in a *canter*. also V.

Test

Word List 7   *Synonyms*

Each of the questions below consists of a word in capital letters, followed by five lettered words or phrases. Choose the lettered word or phrase that is most nearly similar in meaning to the word in capital letters and write the letter of your choice on your answer paper.

91. BOISTEROUS (A) conflicting (B) noisy (C) testimonial (D) grateful (E) adolescent
92. BOMBASTIC (A) sensitive (B) pompous (C) rapid (D) sufficient (E) expensive
93. BOORISH (A) brave (B) oafish (C) romantic (D) speedy (E) dry
94. BOUILLON (A) insight (B) chowder (C) gold (D) clear soup (E) stew
95. BRACKISH (A) careful (B) salty (C) chosen (D) tough (E) wet
96. BRAGGADOCIO (A) weaponry (B) boasting (C) skirmish (D) encounter (E) position

97. BRAZEN (A) shameless (B) quick (C) modest (D) pleasant (E) melodramatic
98. BRINDLED (A) equine (B) pathetic (C) hasty (D) spotted (E) mild tasting
99. BROCHURE (A) opening (B) pamphlet (C) censor (D) bureau (E) pin
100. BUCOLIC (A) diseased (B) repulsive (C) rustic (D) twinkling (E) cold
101. BUXOM (A) voluminous (B) indecisive (C) convincing (D) plump (E) bookish
102. CACHE (A) lock (B) hiding place (C) tide (D) automobile (E) grappling hook
103. CACOPHONY (A) discord (B) dance (C) applause (D) type of telephone (E) rooster
104. CALLOW (A) youthful (B) holy (C) mild (D) colored (E) seated
105. CANDID (A) vague (B) outspoken (C) experienced (D) anxious (E) sallow

Word List 8   canto-champ

canto N. division of a long poem. Dante's poetic masterpiece *The Divine Comedy* is divided into *cantos*.

canvass V. determine votes, etc. After *canvassing* the sentiments of his constituents, the congressman was confident that he represented the majority opinion of his district. also N.

capacious ADJ. spacious. In the *capacious* areas of the railroad terminal, thousands of travelers lingered while waiting for their train.

caparison N, V. showy harness or ornamentation for a horse; put showy ornamentation on a horse. The audience admired the *caparison* of the horses as they made their entrance into the circus ring.

capillary ADJ. having a very fine bore. The changes in surface tension of liquids in *capillary* vessels is of special interest to physicists. also N.

capitulate V. surrender. The enemy was warned to *capitulate* or face annihilation.

caprice N. whim. Do not act on *caprice*. Study your problem.

■ **capricious** ADJ. fickle; incalculable. The storm was *capricious* and changed course constantly.

caption N. title; chapter heading; text under illustration. I find the *captions* which accompany these cartoons very clever and humorous. also V.

captious ADJ. faultfinding. His criticisms were always *captious* and frivolous, never offering constructive suggestions.

carafe N. glass water bottle; decanter. With each dinner, the patron receives a *carafe* of red or white wine.

carat N. unit of weight for precious stones; measure of fineness of gold. He gave her a three-*carat* diamond mounted in an eighteen-*carat* gold band.

carcinogenic ADJ. causing cancer. Many supposedly harmless substances have been revealed to be *carcinogenic*.

cardinal ADJ. chief. If you want to increase your word power, the *cardinal* rule of vocabulary-building is to read.

careen V. lurch; sway from side to side. The taxicab *careened* wildly as it rounded the corner.

caricature N. distortion; burlesque. The *caricatures* he drew always emphasized a personal weakness of the people he burlesqued. also V.

carillon N. a set of bells capable of being played. The *carillon* in the bell tower of the Coca Cola pavilion at the New York World's Fair provided musical entertainment every hour.

carmine N. rich red. *Carmine* in her lipstick made her lips appear black in the photographs.

carnage N. destruction of life. The *carnage* that can be caused by atomic warfare adds to the responsibilities of our statesmen.

carnal ADJ. fleshly. The public was more interested in *carnal* pleasures than in spiritual matters.

carnivorous ADJ. meat-eating. The lion is a *carnivorous* animal. carnivore, N.

carousal N. drunken revel. The party degenerated into an ugly *carousal*.

carping ADJ. finding fault. A *carping* critic disturbs sensitive people.

carrion N. rotting flesh of a dead body. Buzzards are nature's scavengers; they eat the *carrion* left behind by other predators.

carte blanche N. unlimited authority or freedom. Use your own discretion in this matter; I give you *carte blanche*.

cartographer N. map-maker. Though not a professional *cartographer*, Tolkien was able to construct a map of his fictional world.

caryatid N. sculptured column of a female figure. The *caryatids* supporting the entablature reminded the onlooker of the columns he had seen in the Acropolis at Athens.

cascade N. small waterfall. We could not appreciate the beauty of the many *cascades* as we made detours around each of them to avoid getting wet. also V.

caste N. one of the hereditary classes in Hindu society. The differences created by *caste* in India must be wiped out if true democracy is to prevail in that country.

castigate V. punish. The victim vowed to *castigate* the culprit personally.

casualty N. serious or fatal accident. The number of automotive *casualties* on this holiday weekend was high.

casuistry N. subtle or sophisticated reasoning resulting in minute distinctions. You are using *casuistry* to justify your obvious violation of decent behavior.

cataclysm N. deluge; upheaval. A *cataclysm* such as the French Revolution affects all countries. cataclysmic, ADJ.

catalyst N. agent which brings about a chemical change while it remains unaffected and unchanged. Many chemical reactions cannot take place without the presence of a *catalyst*.

catapult N. slingshot; a hurling machine. Airplanes are sometimes launched from battleships by *catapults*. also V.

cataract N. great waterfall; eye abnormality. She gazed with awe at the mighty *cataract* known as Niagara Falls.

catastrophe N. calamity. The Johnstown flood was a *catastrophe*.

catechism N. book for religious instruction; instruction by question and answer. He taught by engaging his pupils in a *catechism* until they gave him the correct answer.

catharsis N. purging or cleansing of any passage of the body. Aristotle maintained that tragedy created a *catharsis* by purging the soul of base concepts.

cathartic N. purgative. Some drugs act as laxatives when taken in small doses but act as *cathartics* when taken in much larger doses.

catholic ADJ. broadly sympathetic; liberal. He was extremely *catholic* in his taste and read everything he could find in the library.

caucus N. private meeting of members of a party to select officers or determine policy. At the opening of Congress, the members of the Democratic Party held a *caucus* to elect the Majority Leader of the House and the Party Whip.

■ **caustic** ADJ. burning; sarcastically biting. The critic's *caustic* remarks angered the hapless actors who were the subjects of his sarcasm.

cauterize V. burn with hot iron or caustic. In order to prevent infection, the doctor *cauterized* the wound.

cavalcade N. procession; parade. As described by Chaucer, the *cavalcade* of Canterbury pilgrims was a motley group.

cavil V. make frivolous objections. I respect your sensible criticisms, but I dislike the way you *cavil* about unimportant details. also N.

cede V. transfer; yield title to. I intend to *cede* this property to the city.

celerity N. speed; rapidity. Hamlet resented his mother's *celerity* in remarrying within a month after his father's death.

celestial ADJ. heavenly. She spoke of the *celestial* joys that awaited virtuous souls in the hereafter.

celibate ADJ. unmarried; abstaining from sexual intercourse. The perennial bachelor vowed to remain *celibate*. celibacy, N.

censor N. overseer of morals; person who reads to eliminate inappropriate remarks. Soldiers dislike having their mail read by a *censor* but understand the need for this precaution. also V.

■ **censorious** ADJ. critical. *Censorious* people delight in casting blame.

■ **censure** V. blame; criticize. He was *censured* for his inappropriate behavior. also N.

centaur N. mythical figure, half man and half horse. I was particularly impressed by the statue of the *centaur* in the Roman Hall of the museum.

centigrade ADJ. measure of temperature used widely in Europe. On the *centigrade* thermometer, the freezing point of water is zero degrees.

centrifugal ADJ. radiating; departing from the center. Many automatic drying machines remove excess moisture from clothing by *centrifugal* force.

centripetal ADJ. tending toward the center. Does *centripetal* force or the force of gravity bring orbiting bodies to the earth's surface?

centurion N. Roman army officer. Because he was in command of a company of one hundred soldiers, he was called a *centurion*.

cerebral ADJ. pertaining to the brain or intellect. The content of philosophical works is *cerebral* in nature and requires much thought.

cerebration N. thought. Mathematics problems sometimes require much *cerebration*.

ceremonious ADJ. marked by formality. Ordinary dress would be inappropriate at so *ceremonious* an affair.

cessation N. stopping. The workers threatened a *cessation* of all activities if their demands were not met. cease, V.

cession N. yielding to another; ceding. The *cession* of Alaska to the United States is discussed in this chapter.

chafe V. warm by rubbing; make sore by rubbing. The collar *chafed* his neck. also N.

chaff N. worthless products of an endeavor. When you separate the wheat from the chaff, be sure you throw out the *chaff*.

chaffing ADJ. bantering; joking. Sometimes his flippant and *chaffing* remarks annoy us.

chagrin N. vexation; disappointment. Her refusal to go with us filled us with *chagrin*.

chalice N. goblet; consecrated cup. In a small room adjoining the cathedral, many ornately decorated *chalices* made by the most famous European goldsmiths were on display.

chameleon N. lizard that changes color in different situations. Like the *chameleon,* he assumed the political thinking of every group he met.

champ V. chew noisily. His dining companions were amused by the way he *champed* his food.

Test

Word List 8 *Antonyms*

Each of the questions below consists of a word in capital letters, followed by five lettered words or phrases. Choose the lettered word or phrase that is most nearly opposite in meaning to the word in capital letters and write the letter of your choice on your answer paper.

106. CAPACIOUS (A) warlike (B) cordial (C) curious (D) not spacious (E) not capable
107. CAPRICIOUS (A) satisfied (B) insured (C) photographic (D) scattered (E) steadfast
108. CAPTIOUS (A) tolerant (B) capable (C) frivolous (D) winning (E) recollected
109. CARNAL (A) impressive (B) minute (C) spiritual (D) actual (E) private
110. CARNIVOROUS (A) gloomy (B) tangential (C) productive (D) weak (E) vegetarian
111. CAROUSAL (A) awakening (B) sobriety (C) acceleration (D) direction (E) production
112. CARPING (A) acquiescent (B) mean (C) limited (D) farming (E) racing
113. CARTE BLANCHE (A) capitalistic (B) investment (C) importance (D) restriction (E) current
114. CATHOLIC (A) religious (B) pacific (C) narrow (D) weighty (E) funny
115. CELERITY (A) assurance (B) state (C) acerbity (D) delay (E) infamy
116. CELIBATE (A) investing (B) married (C) retired (D) commodious (E) dubious
117. CENSURE (A) process (B) enclose (C) interest (D) praise (E) penetrate
118. CENTRIFUGAL (A) centripetal (B) ephemeral (C) lasting (D) barometric (E) algebraic
119. CESSATION (A) premium (B) gravity (C) beginning (D) composition (E) apathy
120. CHAFFING (A) achieving (B) serious (C) capitalistic (D) sneezing (E) expensive

Word List 9   champion-colander

champion V. support militantly. Martin Luther King, Jr., won the Nobel Peace Prize because he *championed* the oppressed in their struggle for equality.

■ **chaotic** ADJ. in utter disorder. He tried to bring order into the *chaotic* state of affairs. chaos, N.

charisma N. divine gift; great popular charm or appeal of a political leader. Political commentators have deplored the importance of a candidate's *charisma* in these days of television campaigning.

charlatan N. quack; pretender to knowledge. Because he was unable to substantiate his claim that he had found a cure for the dread disease, he was called a *charlatan* by his colleagues.

chary ADJ. cautiously watchful. She was *chary* of her favors because she had been hurt before.

chasm N. abyss. They could not see the bottom of the *chasm*.

chassis N. framework and working parts of an automobile. Examining the car after the accident, the owner discovered that the body had been ruined but that the *chassis* was unharmed.

chaste ADJ. pure. Her *chaste* and decorous garb was appropriately selected for the solemnity of the occasion. chastity, N.

chasten V. discipline; punish in order to correct. Whom God loves, God *chastens*.

chastise V. punish. I must *chastise* you for this offense.

chattel N. personal property. When he bought his furniture on the installment plan, he signed a *chattel* mortgage.

chauvinist N. blindly devoted patriot. A *chauvinist* cannot recognize any faults in his country, no matter how flagrant they may be.

checkered ADJ. marked by changes in fortune. During his *checkered* career he had lived in palatial mansions and in dreary boardinghouses.

cherubic ADJ. angelic; innocent-looking. With her cheerful smile and rosy cheeks, she was a particularly *cherubic* child.

chicanery N. trickery. Your deceitful tactics in this case are indications of *chicanery*.

chide V. scold. Grandma began to *chide* Steven for his lying.

■ **chimerical** ADJ. fantastic; highly imaginative. Poe's *chimerical* stories are sometimes too morbid for reading in bed. chimera, N.

chiropodist N. one who treats disorders of the feet. The *chiropodist* treated the ingrown nail on the boy's foot.

chivalrous ADJ. courteous; faithful; brave. *Chivalrous* behavior involves noble words and good deeds.

choleric ADJ. hot-tempered. His flushed, angry face indicated a *choleric* nature.

choreography N. art of dancing. Martha Graham introduced a form of *choreography* which seemed awkward and alien to those who had been brought up on classic ballet.

chronic ADJ. long established as a disease. The doctors were finally able to attribute his *chronic* headaches and nausea to traces of formaldehyde gas in his apartment.

churlish ADJ. boorish; rude. Dismayed by his *churlish* manners at the party, the girls vowed never to invite him again.

ciliated ADJ. having minute hairs. The paramecium is a *ciliated*, one-celled animal.

cipher N. nonentity; worthless person or thing. She claimed her ex-husband was a total *cipher* and wondered why she had ever married him.

circlet N. small ring; band. This tiny *circlet* is very costly because it is set with precious stones.

circuitous ADJ. roundabout. Because of the traffic congestion on the main highways, she took a *circuitous* route. circuit, N.

circumlocution N. indirect or roundabout expression. He was afraid to call a spade a spade and resorted to *circumlocutions* to avoid direct reference to his subject.

circumscribe V. limit; confine. Although I do not wish to *circumscribe* your activities, I must insist that you complete this assignment before you start anything else.

circumspect ADJ. prudent; cautious. Investigating before acting, she tried always to be *circumspect*.

circumvent V. outwit; baffle. In order to *circumvent* the enemy, we will make two preliminary attacks in other sections before starting our major campaign.

citadel N. fortress. The *citadel* overlooked the city like a protecting angel.

cite V. quote; commend. She could *cite* passages in the Bible from memory. citation, N.

clairvoyant ADJ., N. having foresight; fortuneteller. Cassandra's *clairvoyant* warning was not heeded by the Trojans. clairvoyance, N.

clamber V. climb by crawling. She *clambered* over the wall.

clamor N. noise. The *clamor* of the children at play outside made it impossible for her to take a nap. also V.

clandestine ADJ. secret. After avoiding their chaperon, the lovers had a *clandestine* meeting.

clangor N. loud, resounding noise. The blacksmith was accustomed to the *clangor* of hammers on steel.

clarion ADJ. shrill, trumpetlike sound. We woke to the *clarion* call of the bugle.

claustrophobia N. fear of being locked in. His fellow classmates laughed at his *claustrophobia* and often threatened to lock him in his room.

clavicle N. collarbone. Even though he wore shoulder pads, the football player broke his *clavicle* during a practice scrimmage.

cleave V. split asunder. The lightning *cleaves* the tree in two. cleavage, N.

cleft N. split. Erosion caused a *cleft* in the huge boulder. also ADJ.

clemency N. disposition to be lenient; mildness, as of the weather. The lawyer was pleased when the case was sent to Judge Smith's chambers because Smith was noted for her *clemency* toward first offenders.

cliché N. phrase dulled in meaning by repetition. High school compositions are often marred by such *clichés* as "strong as an ox."

clientele N. body of customers. The rock club attracted a young, stylish *clientele*.

climactic ADJ. relating to the highest point. When he reached the *climactic* portions of the book, he could not stop reading. climax, N.

clime N. region; climate. His doctor advised him to move to a milder *clime*.

clique N. small exclusive group. She charged that a *clique* had assumed control of school affairs.

cloister N. monastery or convent. The nuns lived in the *cloister*.

cloven ADJ. split. Popular legends maintain that the devil has *cloven* hooves.

coadjutor N. assistant; colleague. He was assigned as *coadjutor* of the bishop.

coalesce V. combine; fuse. The brooks *coalesce* into one large river.

cockade N. decoration worn on hat. Members of that brigade can be recognized by the green and white *cockade* in their helmets.

codicil N. supplement to the body of a will. This *codicil* was drawn up five years after the writing of the original will.

■ **coercion** N. use of force. They forced him to obey, but only under great *coercion.* coerce, V.

coddle V. to treat gently. Don't *coddle* the children so much; they need a taste of discipline.

coeval ADJ. living at the same time as; contemporary. *Coeval* with the dinosaur, the pterodactyl flourished during the Mesozoic era.

cog N. tooth projecting from a wheel. On steep slopes, *cog* railways are frequently used to prevent slipping.

cogent ADJ. convincing. She presented *cogent* arguments to the jury.

cogitate V. think over. *Cogitate* on this problem; the solution will come.

cognate ADJ. allied by blood; of the same or kindred nature. In the phrase "die a thousand deaths," the word "death" is a *cognate* object.

cognizance N. knowledge. During the election campaign, the two candidates were kept in full *cognizance* of the international situation.

cognomen N. family name. He asked the court to change his *cognomen* to a more American-sounding name.

cohere V. stick together. Solids have a greater tendency to *cohere* than liquids.

cohesion N. force which keeps parts together. In order to preserve our *cohesion,* we must not let minor differences interfere with our major purposes.

cohorts N. armed band. Caesar and his Roman *cohorts* conquered almost all of the known world.

coincident ADJ. occurring at the same time. Some people find the *coincident* events in Hardy's novels annoying.

colander N. utensil with perforated bottom used for straining. Before serving the spaghetti, place it in a *colander* to drain it.

Test

Word List 9   *Synonyms*

Each of the questions below consists of a word in capital letters, followed by five lettered words or phrases. Choose the lettered word or phrase that is most nearly similar in meaning to the word in capital letters and write the letter of your choice on your answer paper.

121. CHASTE (A) loyal (B) timid (C) curt (D) pure (E) outspoken

122. CHIDE (A) unite (B) fear (C) record (D) skid (E) scold

123. CHIMERICAL (A) developing (B) brief (C) distant (D) economical (E) fantastic

124. CHOLERIC (A) musical (B) episodic (C) hotheaded (D) global (E) seasonal

125. CHURLISH (A) marine (B) economical (C) impolite (D) compact (E) young

126. CILIATED (A) foolish (B) swift (C) early (D) constructed (E) hairy

127. CIRCUITOUS (A) indirect (B) complete (C) obvious (D) aware (E) tortured

128. CITE (A) galvanize (B) visualize (C) locate (D) quote (E) signal

129. CLANDESTINE (A) abortive (B) secret (C) tangible (D) doomed (E) approved

130. CLAUSTROPHOBIA (A) lack of confidence (B) fear of spiders (C) love of books (D) fear of grammar (E) fear of closed places

131. CLEFT (A) split (B) waterfall (C) assembly (D) parfait (E) surplus

132. CLICHÉ (A) increase (B) vehicle (C) morale (D) platitude (E) pique

133. COERCE (A) recover (B) total (C) force (D) license (E) ignore

134. COGNIZANCE (A) policy (B) knowledge (C) advance (D) omission (E) examination

135. COGNOMEN (A) family name (B) dwarf (C) suspicion (D) kind of railway (E) pseudopod

Word List 10   collaborate-congenital

■ **collaborate** V. work together. Two writers *collaborated* in preparing this book.

collage N. work of art put together from fragments. Scraps of cloth, paper doilies, and old photographs all went into her *collage.*

collate V. examine in order to verify authenticity; arrange in order. They *collated* the newly found manuscripts to determine their age.

collateral N. security given for loan. The sum you wish to borrow is so large that it must be secured by *collateral.*

collation N. a light meal. Tea sandwiches and cookies were offered at the *collation.*

collier N. worker in coal mine; ship carrying coal. The extended cold spell has prevented the *colliers* from delivering the coal to the docks as scheduled.

colloquial ADJ. pertaining to conversational or common speech. Your use of *colloquial* expressions in a formal essay such as the one you have presented spoils the effect you hope to achieve.

colloquy N. informal discussion. I enjoy our *colloquies,* but I sometimes wish that they could be made more formal and more searching.

collusion N. conspiring in a fraudulent scheme. The swindlers were found guilty of *collusion.*

colossal ADJ. huge. Radio City Music Hall has a *colossal* stage.

comatose ADJ. in a coma; extremely sleepy. The long-winded orator soon had his audience in a *comatose* state.

combustible ADJ. easily burned. After the recent outbreak of fires in private homes, the fire commissioner ordered that all *combustible* materials be kept in safe containers. also N.

comely ADJ. attractive; agreeable. I would rather have a poor and *comely* wife than a rich and homely one.

comestible N. something fit to be eaten. The roast turkey and other *comestibles,* the wines, and the excellent service made this Thanksgiving dinner particularly memorable.

comeuppance N. rebuke; deserts. After his earlier rudeness, we were delighted to see him get his *comeuppance.*

comity N. courtesy; civility. A spirit of *comity* should exist among nations.

commandeer V. to draft for military purposes; to take for public use. The policeman *commandeered* the first car that approached and ordered the driver to go to the nearest hospital.

commemorative ADJ. remembering; honoring. The new *commemorative* stamp honors the late Martin Luther King, Jr.

commensurate ADJ. equal in extent. Your reward will be *commensurate* with your effort.

commiserate V. feel or express pity or sympathy for. Her friends *commiserated* with the widow.

commodious ADJ. spacious and comfortable. After sleeping in small roadside cabins, they found their hotel suite *commodious.*

communal ADJ. held in common; of a group of people. When they were divorced, they had trouble dividing their *communal* property.

compact N. agreement; contract. The signers of the Mayflower *Compact* were establishing a form of government.

compact ADJ. tightly packed; firm; brief. His short, *compact* body was better suited to wrestling than to basketball.

compatible ADJ. harmonious; in harmony with. They were *compatible* neighbors, never quarreling over unimportant matters.

compendium N. brief comprehensive summary. This text can serve as a *compendium* of the tremendous amount of new material being developed in this field.

compensatory ADJ. making up for; repaying. Can a *compensatory* education program make up for the inadequate schooling he received in earlier years?

compilation N. listing of statistical information in tabular or book form. The *compilation* of available scholarships serves a very valuable purpose.

■ **complacent** ADJ. self-satisfied. There was a *complacent* look on his face as he examined his paintings. complacency, N.

complaisant ADJ. trying to please; obliging. The courtier obeyed the king's orders in a *complaisant* manner.

complement N. that which completes. A predicate *complement* completes the meaning of the subject. also V.

■ **compliance** N. readiness to yield; conformity in fulfilling requirements. The design for the new school had to be in *compliance* with the local building code.

compliant ADJ. yielding. He was *compliant* and ready to conform to the pattern set by his friends.

complicity N. participation; involvement. You cannot keep your *complicity* in this affair secret very long; you would be wise to admit your involvement immediately.

component N. element; ingredient. I wish all the *components* of my stereo system were working at the same time.

comport V. bear one's self; behave. He *comported* himself with great dignity.

composure N. mental calmness. Even the latest work crisis failed to shake her *composure.*

■ **comprehensive** ADJ. thorough; inclusive. This book provides a *comprehensive* review of verbal and math skills for the SAT.

compress V. close; squeeze; contract. She *compressed* the package under her arm.

compromise V. adjust; endanger the interests or reputation of. Your presence at the scene of the dispute *compromises* our claim to neutrality in this matter. also N.

compunction N. remorse. The judge was especially severe in his sentencing because he felt that the criminal had shown no *compunction* for his heinous crime.

compute V. reckon; calculate. He failed to *compute* the interest, so his bank balance was not accurate.

concatenate V. link as in a chain. It is difficult to understand how these events could *concatenate* as they did without outside assistance.

concave ADJ. hollow. The back-packers found partial shelter from the storm by huddling against the *concave* wall of the cliff.

conceit N. whimsical idea; extravagant metaphor. He was an entertaining companion, always expressing himself in amusing *conceits* and witty turns of phrase.

concentric ADJ. having a common center. The target was made of *concentric* circles.

conception N. beginning; forming of an idea. At the first *conception* of the work, he was consulted. conceive, V.

concession N. an act of yielding. Before they could reach an agreement, both sides had to make certain *concessions.*

conch N. large seashell. In this painting we see a Triton blowing on his *conch.*

■ **conciliatory** ADJ. reconciling; soothing. She was still angry despite his *conciliatory* words. conciliate, V.

■ **concise** ADJ. brief and compact. The essay was *concise* and explicit.

conclave N. private meeting. He was present at all the *conclaves* as an unofficial observer.

■ **conclusive** ADJ. decisive; ending all debate. When the stolen books turned up in John's locker, we finally had *conclusive* evidence of the identity of the mysterious thief.

concoct V. prepare by combining; make up in concert. How did the inventive chef ever *concoct* such a strange dish? concoction, N.

concomitant N. that which accompanies. Culture is not always a *concomitant* of wealth. also ADJ.

concordat N. agreement, usually between the papal authority and the secular. One of the most famous of the agreements between a Pope and an emperor was the *Concordat of Worms* in 1122.

concur V. agree. Did you *concur* with the decision of the court or did you find it unfair?

concurrent ADJ. happening at the same time. In America, the colonists were resisting the demands of the mother country; at the *concurrent* moment in France, the middle class was sowing the seeds of rebellion.

■ **condescend** V. bestow courtesies with a superior air. The king *condescended* to grant an audience to the friends of the condemned man. condescension, N.

condign ADJ. adequate; deservedly severe. The public approved the *condign* punishment for the crime.

condiments N. seasonings; spices. Spanish food is full of *condiments*.

condole V. express sympathetic sorrow. His friends gathered to *condole* with him over his loss. condolence, N.

condone V. overlook; forgive. We cannot *condone* your recent criminal cooperation with the gamblers.

conduit N. aqueduct; passageway for fluids. Water was brought to the army in the desert by an improvised *conduit* from the adjoining mountain.

confidant N. trusted friend. He had no *confidants* with whom he could discuss his problems at home.

confiscate V. seize; commandeer. The army *confiscated* all available supplies of uranium.

conflagration N. great fire. In the *conflagration* that followed the 1906 earthquake, much of San Francisco was destroyed.

confluence N. flowing together; crowd. They built the city at the *confluence* of two rivers.

■ **conformity** N. harmony; agreement. In *conformity* with our rules and regulations, I am calling a meeting of our organization.

confound V. confuse; puzzle. No mystery could *confound* Sherlock Holmes for long.

congeal V. freeze; coagulate. His blood *congealed* in his veins as he saw the dread monster rush toward him.

congenial ADJ. pleasant; friendly. My father loved to go out for a meal with *congenial* companions.

congenital ADJ. existing at birth. His *congenital* deformity disturbed his parents.

Test

Word List 10   *Synonyms and Antonyms*

Each of the following questions consists of a word in capital letters, followed by five lettered words or phrases. Choose the lettered word or phrase which is most nearly similar or the opposite of the word in capital letters and write the letter of your choice on your answer paper.

136. COLLATION (A) furor (B) emphasis (C) distillery (D) spree (E) lunch
137. COLLOQUIAL (A) burnt (B) polished (C) political (D) gifted (E) problematic
138. COLLOQUY (A) dialect (B) diversion (C) announcement (D) discussion (E) expansion
139. COMATOSE (A) cozy (B) restrained (C) alert (D) dumb (E) grim
140. COMBUSTIBLE (A) flammable (B) industrious (C) waterproof (D) specific (E) plastic
141. COMESTIBLE (A) vigorous (B) fit to be eaten (C) liquid (D) beautiful (E) circumvented

142. COMMISERATE (A) communicate (B) expand (C) repay (D) diminish (E) sympathize
143. COMMODIOUS (A) numerous (B) yielding (C) leisurely (D) limited (E) expensive
144. COMPLIANT (A) numerous (B) veracious (C) soft (D) adamant (E) livid
145. CONCILIATE (A) defend (B) activate (C) integrate (D) quarrel (E) react
146. CONCOCT (A) thrive (B) wonder (C) intrude (D) drink (E) invent
147. CONDONE (A) build (B) evaluate (C) pierce (D) infuriate (E) overlook
148. CONFISCATE (A) discuss (B) discover (C) seize (D) exist (E) convey
149. CONFORMITY (A) agreement (B) ambition (C) confinement (D) pride (E) restraint
150. CONGENITAL (A) slight (B) obscure (C) thorough (D) existing at birth (E) classified

Word List 11   conglomeration-countermand

conglomeration N. mass of material sticking together. In such a *conglomeration* of miscellaneous statistics, it was impossible to find a single area of analysis.

congruence N. correspondence of parts; harmonious relationship. The student demonstrated the *congruence* of the two triangles by using the hypotenuse-arm theorem.

conifer N. pine tree; cone-bearing tree. According to geologists, the *conifers* were the first plants to bear flowers.

conjecture N. surmise; guess. I will end all your *conjectures;* I admit I am guilty as charged. also V.

conjugal ADJ. pertaining to marriage. Their dreams of *conjugal* bliss were shattered as soon as their temperaments clashed.

conjure V. summon a devil; practice magic; imagine; invent. He *conjured* up an image of a reformed city and had the voters completely under his spell.

connivance N. pretense of ignorance of something wrong; assistance; permission to offend. With the *connivance* of his friends, he plotted to embarrass the teacher. connive, V.

connoisseur N. person competent to act as a judge of art, etc.; a lover of an art. She had developed into a *connoisseur* of fine china.

connotation N. suggested or implied meaning of an expression. Foreigners frequently are unaware of the *connotations* of the words they use.

connubial ADJ. pertaining to marriage or the matrimonial state. In his telegram, he wished the newlyweds a lifetime of *connubial* bliss.

consanguinity N. kinship. The lawsuit developed into a test of the *consanguinity* of the claimant to the estate.

■ **conscientious** ADJ. scrupulous; careful. A *conscientious* editor, she checked every definition for its accuracy.

consecrate V. dedicate; sanctify. We shall *consecrate* our lives to this noble purpose.

consensus N. general agreement. The *consensus* indicates that we are opposed to entering into this pact.

consequential ADJ. pompous; self-important. Convinced of his own importance, the actor strutted about the dressing room with a *consequential* air.

consonance N. harmony; agreement. Her agitation seemed out of *consonance* with her usual calm.

consort V. associate with. We frequently judge people by the company with whom they *consort.*

consort N. husband or wife. The search for a *consort* for the young Queen Victoria ended happily.

conspiracy N. treacherous plot. Brutus and Cassius joined in the *conspiracy* to kill Julius Caesar.

constituent N. supporter. The congressman received hundreds of letters from angry *constituents* after the Equal Rights Amendment failed to pass.

constraint N. compulsion; repression of feelings. There was a feeling of *constraint* in the room because no one dared to criticize the speaker. constrain, V.

construe V. explain; interpret. If I *construe* your remarks correctly, you disagree with the theory already advanced.

consummate ADJ. complete. I have never seen anyone who makes as many stupid errors as you do; you must be a *consummate* idiot. also V.

contagion N. infection. Fearing *contagion,* they took great steps to prevent the spread of the disease.

contaminate V. pollute. The sewage system of the city so *contaminated* the water that swimming was forbidden.

■ **contempt** N. scorn; disdain. I will not tolerate those who show *contempt* for the sincere efforts of this group. contemptuous, contemptible, ADJ.

contentious ADJ. quarrelsome. We heard loud and *contentious* noises in the next room.

contest V. dispute. The defeated candidate attempted to *contest* the election results.

context N. writings preceding and following the passage quoted. Because these lines are taken out of *context,* they do not convey the message the author intended.

contiguous ADJ. adjacent to; touching upon. The two countries are *contiguous* for a few miles; then they are separated by the gulf.

continence N. self-restraint; sexual chastity. She vowed to lead a life of *continence.* continent, ADJ.

contingent ADJ. conditional. The continuation of this contract is *contingent* on the quality of your first output. contingency, N.

contortions N. twistings; distortions As the effects of the opiate wore away, the *contortions* of the patient became more violent and demonstrated how much pain she was enduring.

contraband N, ADJ. illegal trade; smuggling. The Coast Guard tries to prevent traffic in *contraband* goods.

contravene V. contradict; infringe on. I will not attempt to *contravene* your argument for it does not affect the situation.

■ **contrite** ADJ. penitent. Her *contrite* tears did not influence the judge when he imposed sentence. contrition, N.

controvert V. oppose with arguments; contradict. To *controvert* your theory will require much time but it is essential that we disprove it.

contumacious ADJ. disobedient; resisting authority. The *contumacious* mob shouted defiantly at the police. contumacy, N.

contusion N. bruise. She was treated for *contusions* and abrasions.

conundrum N. riddle. During the long car ride, she invented *conundrums* to entertain the children.

convene V. assemble. Because much needed legislation had to be enacted, the governor ordered the legislature to *convene* in special session by January 15.

conventional ADJ. ordinary; typical. His *conventional* upbringing left him wholly unprepared for his wife's eccentric family.

converge V. come together. Marchers *converged* on Washington for the great Peace March.

conversant ADJ. familiar with. The lawyer is *conversant* with all the evidence.

converse N. opposite. The inevitable *converse* of peace is not war but annihilation.

convex ADJ. curving outward. He polished the *convex* lens of his telescope.

conveyance N. vehicle; transfer. During the transit strike, commuters used various kinds of *conveyances.*

■ **conviction** N. strongly held belief. Nothing could shake his *conviction* that she was innocent. (secondary meaning)

convivial ADJ. festive; gay; characterized by joviality. The *convivial* celebrators of the victory sang their college songs.

convoke V. call together. Congress was *convoked* at the outbreak of the emergency. convocation, N.

convoluted ADJ. coiled around; involved; intricate. His argument was so *convoluted* that few of us could follow it intelligently.

■ **copious** ADJ. plentiful. She had *copious* reasons for rejecting the proposal.

coquette N. flirt. Because she refused to give him an answer to his proposal of marriage, he called her a *coquette.* also V.

■ **cordial** ADJ. gracious; heartfelt. Our hosts greeted us at the airport with a *cordial* welcome and a hearty hug.

cordon N. extended line of men or fortifications to prevent access or egress. The police *cordon* was so tight that the criminals could not leave the area. also V.

cormorant N. greedy, rapacious bird. The *cormorants* spend their time eating the fish which they catch by diving. also ADJ.

cornice N. projecting molding on building (usually above columns). Because the *cornice* stones had been loosened by the storms, the police closed the building until repairs could be made.

corollary N. consequence; accompaniment. Brotherly love is a complex emotion, with sibling rivalry its natural *corollary.*

corporeal ADJ. bodily; material. He was not a churchgoer; he was interested only in *corporeal* matters.

corpulent ADJ. very fat. The *corpulent* man resolved to reduce. corpulence, N.

correlation N. mutual relationship. He sought to determine the *correlation* that existed between ability in algebra and ability to interpret reading exercises.

corroborate V. confirm. Unless we find a witness to *corroborate* your evidence, it will not stand up in court.

corrosive ADJ. eating away by chemicals or disease. Stainless steel is able to withstand the effects of *corrosive* chemicals.

corrugated ADJ. wrinkled; ridged. She wished she could smoothe away the wrinkles from his *corrugated* brow.

corsair N. pirate; pirate ship. The *corsairs,* preying on shipping in the Mediterranean, were often inspired by racial and religious hatreds as well as by the desire for money and booty.

cortege N. procession. The funeral *cortege* proceeded slowly down the avenue.

coruscate V. glitter; scintillate. His wit is the kind that *coruscates* and startles all his listeners.

cosmic ADJ. pertaining to the universe; vast. *Cosmic* rays derive their name from the fact that they bombard the earth's atmosphere from outer space. cosmos, N.

coterie N. group that meets socially; select circle. After his book had been published, he was invited to join the literary *coterie* that lunched daily at the hotel.

countenance V. approve; tolerate. He refused to *countenance* such rude behavior on their part.

countermand V. cancel; revoke. The general *countermanded* the orders issued in his absence.

Test

Word List 11   *Synonyms*

Each of the questions below consists of a word in capital letters, followed by five lettered words or phrases. Choose the lettered word or phrase that is most nearly similar in meaning to the word in capital letters and write the letter of your choice on your answer paper.

151. CONJECTURE (A) magic (B) guess (C) position (D) form (E) place

152. CONNOISSEUR (A) gourmand (B) lover of art (C) humidor (D) delinquent (E) interpreter

153. CONSANGUINITY (A) kinship (B) friendship (C) bloodletting (D) relief (E) understanding

154. CONSENSUS (A) general agreement (B) project (C) insignificance (D) sheaf (E) crevice

155. CONSTRUE (A) explain (B) promote (C) reserve (D) erect (E) block

156. CONTAMINATE (A) arrest (B) prepare (C) pollute (D) beam (E) inform

157. CONTENTIOUS (A) squealing (B) surprising (C) quarrelsome (D) smug (E) creative

158. CONTINENCE (A) humanity (B) research (C) embryology (D) bodies of land (E) self-restraint

159. CONTRABAND (A) purpose (B) rogue (C) rascality (D) difficulty (E) smuggling

160. CONTRITE (A) smart (B) penitent (C) restful (D) recognized (E) perspiring

161. CONTROVERT (A) turn over (B) contradict (C) mind (D) explain (E) swing

162. CONVENE (A) propose (B) restore (C) question (D) gather (E) motivate

163. CONVERSANT (A) ignorant (B) speaking (C) incorporated (D) familiar (E) pedantic

164. COPIOUS (A) plentiful (B) cheating (C) dishonorable (D) adventurous (E) inspired

165. CORPULENT (A) regenerate (B) obese (C) different (D) hungry (E) bloody

---

Word List 12 counterpart-decelerate

counterpart N. a thing that completes another; things very much alike. Night and day are *counterparts*.

coup N. highly successful action or sudden attack. As the news of his *coup* spread throughout Wall Street, his fellow brokers dropped by to congratulate him.

couple V. join; unite. The Flying Karamazovs *couple* expert juggling and amateur joking in their nightclub act.

courier N. messenger. The publisher sent a special *courier* to pick up the manuscript.

covenant N. agreement. We must comply with the terms of the *covenant*.

covert ADJ. secret; hidden; implied. She could understand the *covert* threat in the letter.

covetous ADJ. avaricious; eagerly desirous of. The child was *covetous* by nature and wanted to take the toys belonging to his classmates. covet, V.

cower V. shrink quivering, as from fear. The frightened child *cowered* in the corner of the room.

coy ADJ. shy; modest; coquettish. She was *coy* in her answers to his offer.

cozen V. cheat; hoodwink; swindle. He was the kind of individual who would *cozen* his friends in a cheap card game but remain eminently ethical in all his business dealings.

crabbed ADJ. sour; peevish. The *crabbed* old man was avoided by the children because he scolded them when they made noise.

crass ADJ. very unrefined; grossly insensible. The philosophers deplored the *crass* commercialism.

craven ADJ. cowardly. Her *craven* behavior in this critical period was criticized by her comrades.

credence N. belief. Do not place any *credence* in his promises.

credo N. creed. I believe we may best describe his *credo* by saying that it approximates the Golden Rule.

credulity N. belief on slight evidence. The witch doctor took advantage of the *credulity* of the superstitious natives. credulous, ADJ.

creed N. system of religious or ethical belief. In any loyal American's *creed*, love of democracy must be emphasized.

crepuscular ADJ. pertaining to twilight. Bats are *crepuscular* creatures since they begin their flights as soon as the sun begins to sink below the horizon.

■ **crescendo** N. increase in the volume or intensity, as in a musical passage; climax. The overture suddenly changed from a quiet pastoral theme to a *crescendo* featuring blaring trumpets and clashing cymbals.

crestfallen ADJ. dejected; dispirited. We were surprised at his reaction to the failure of his project; instead of being *crestfallen,* he was busily engaged in planning new activities.

crevice N. crack; fissure. The mountain climbers found footholds in the tiny *crevices* in the mountainside.

■ **cringe** V. shrink back, as if in fear. The dog *cringed,* expecting a blow.

■ **criterion** N. standard used in judging. What *criterion* did you use when you selected this essay as the prizewinner? criteria, PL.

crone N. hag. The toothless *crone* frightened us when she smiled.

crotchety ADJ. eccentric; whimsical. Although he was reputed to be a *crotchety* old gentleman, I found his ideas substantially sound and sensible.

cruet N. small glass bottle for vinegar, oil, etc. The waiter preparing the salad poured oil and vinegar from two *cruets* into the bowl.

crux N. crucial point. This is the *crux* of the entire problem.

crypt N. secret recess or vault, usually used for burial. Until recently, only bodies of rulers and leading statesmen were interred in this *crypt*.

cryptic ADJ. mysterious; hidden; secret. His *cryptic* remarks could not be interpreted.

cubicle N. small chamber used for sleeping. After his many hours of intensive study in the library, he retired to his *cubicle*.

cuisine N. style of cooking. French *cuisine* is noted for its use of sauces and wines.

cul-de-sac N. blind alley; trap. The soldiers were unaware that they were marching into a *cul-de-sac* when they entered the canyon.

culinary ADJ. relating to cooking. Many chefs attribute their *culinary* skill to the wise use of spices.

cull V. pick out; reject. Every month the farmer *culls* the nonlaying hens from his flock and sells them to the local butcher. also N.

culmination N. attainment of highest point. His inauguration as President of the United States marked the *culmination* of his political career.

culpable ADJ. deserving blame. Corrupt politicians who condone the activities of the gamblers are equally *culpable*.

culvert N. artificial channel for water. If we build a *culvert* under the road at this point, we will reduce the possibility of the road's being flooded during the rainy season.

cumbersome ADJ. heavy; hard to manage. He was burdened down with *cumbersome* parcels.

cupidity N. greed. The defeated people could not satisfy the *cupidity* of the conquerors, who demanded excessive tribute.

curator N. superintendent; manager. The members of the board of trustees of the museum expected the new *curator* to plan events and exhibitions which would make the museum more popular.

curmudgeon N. churlish, miserly individual. Although he was regarded by many as a *curmudgeon,* a few of us were aware of the many kindnesses and acts of charity which he secretly performed.

curry V. dress; treat leather; seek favor. The courtier *curried* favors of the king.

cursive ADJ. flowing, running. In normal writing we run our letters together in *cursive* form; in printing, we separate the letters.

cursory ADJ. casual; hastily done. A *cursory* examination of the ruins indicates the possibility of arson; a more extensive study should be undertaken.

curtail V. shorten; reduce. During the coal shortage, we must *curtail* our use of this vital commodity.

■ **cynical** ADJ. skeptical or distrustful of human motives. *Cynical* at all times, he was suspicious of all altruistic actions of others. cynic, N.

cynosure N. the object of general attention. As soon as the movie star entered the room, she became the *cynosure* of all eyes.

dais N. raised platform for guests of honor. When he approached the *dais,* he was greeted by cheers from the people who had come to honor him.

dally V. trifle with; procrastinate. Laertes told Ophelia that Hamlet could only *dally* with her affections.

dank ADJ. damp. The walls of the dungeon were *dank* and slimy.

dappled ADJ. spotted. The sunlight filtering through the screens created a *dappled* effect on the wall.

dastard N. coward. This sneak attack is the work of a *dastard.* dastardly, ADJ.

daub V. smear (as with paint). From the way he *daubed* his paint on the canvas, I could tell he knew nothing of oils. also N.

■ **daunt** V. intimidate. Your threats cannot *daunt* me.

dauntless ADJ. bold. Despite the dangerous nature of the undertaking, the *dauntless* soldier volunteered for the assignment.

dawdle V. loiter; waste time. Inasmuch as we must meet a deadline, do not *dawdle* over this work.

deadlock N. standstill; stalemate. The negotiations had reached a *deadlock.* also V.

deadpan ADJ. wooden; impersonal. We wanted to see how long he could maintain his *deadpan* expression.

dearth N. scarcity. The *dearth* of skilled labor compelled the employers to open trade schools.

debacle N. breaking up; downfall. This *debacle* in the government can only result in anarchy.

debase V. reduce to lower state. Do not *debase* yourself by becoming maudlin.

debauch V. corrupt; make intemperate. A vicious newspaper can *debauch* public ideals. debauchery, N.

debenture N. bond issued to secure a loan. The manager of the company urged that the company try to raise money by issuing *debentures* rather than by selling stock.

debilitate V. weaken; enfeeble. Overindulgence *debilitates* character as well as physical stamina.

debonair ADJ. friendly; aiming to please. The *debonair* youth was liked by all who met him, because of his cheerful and obliging manner.

debris N. rubble. A full year after the earthquake in Mexico City, they were still carting away the *debris.*

debutante N. young woman making formal entrance into society. As a *debutante,* she was often mentioned in the society columns of the newspapers.

■ **decadence** N. decay. The moral *decadence* of the people was reflected in the lewd literature of the period.

decant V. pour off gently. Be sure to *decant* this wine before serving it.

decapitate V. behead. They did not hang Lady Jane Grey; they *decapitated* her.

decelerate V. slow down. Seeing the emergency blinkers in the road ahead, he *decelerated* quickly.

Test

Word List 12   *Antonyms*

Each of the questions below consists of a word in capital letters, followed by five lettered words or phrases. Choose the lettered word or phrase that is most nearly opposite in meaning to the word in capital letters and write the letter of your choice on your answer paper.

166. COY (A) weak (B) airy (C) brazen (D) old (E) tiresome
167. COZEN (A) amuse (B) treat honestly (C) prate (D) shackle (E) vilify
168. CRAVEN (A) desirous (B) direct (C) bold (D) civilized (E) controlled
169. CRUX (A) affliction (B) spark (C) events (D) trivial point (E) belief
170. CRYPTIC (A) tomblike (B) futile (C) famous (D) candid (E) indifferent
171. CUPIDITY (A) anxiety (B) tragedy (C) generosity (D) entertainment (E) love
172. CURTAIL (A) mutter (B) lengthen (C) express (D) burden (E) shore
173. CYNICAL (A) trusting (B) effortless (C) conclusive (D) gallant (E) vertical
174. DANK (A) dry (B) guiltless (C) warm (D) babbling (E) reserved

175. DASTARD (A) illegitimacy (B) hero (C) presence (D) warmth (E) idol
176. DAUNTLESS (A) stolid (B) cowardly (C) irrelevant (D) peculiar (E) particular
177. DEARTH (A) life (B) abundance (C) brightness (D) terror (E) width
178. DEBACLE (A) progress (B) refusal (C) masque (D) cowardice (E) traffic
179. DEBILITATE (A) bedevil (B) repress (C) strengthen (D) animate (E) deaden
180. DEBONAIR (A) awkward (B) windy (C) balmy (D) strong (E) stormy

Word List 13   deciduous-dermatologist

deciduous ADJ. falling off as of leaves. The oak is a *deciduous* tree.

decimate V. kill, usually one out of ten. We do more to *decimate* our population in automobile accidents than we do in war.

decipher V. decode. I could not *decipher* the doctor's handwriting.

declivity N. downward slope. The children loved to ski down the *declivity*.

decollete ADJ. having a low-necked dress. Current fashion decrees that evening gowns be *decolleté* this season; bare shoulders are again the vogue.

decomposition N. decay. Despite the body's advanced state of *decomposition*, the police were able to identify the murdered man.

decorous ADJ. proper. Her *decorous* behavior was praised by her teachers. decorum, N.

decoy N. lure or bait. The wild ducks were not fooled by the *decoy*. also V.

decrepit ADJ. worn out by age. The *decrepit* car blocked traffic on the highway.

decrepitude N. state of collapse caused by illness or old age. I was unprepared for the state of *decrepitude* in which I had found my old friend; he seemed to have aged twenty years in six months.

decry V. disparage. Do not attempt to increase your stature by *decrying* the efforts of your opponents.

deducible ADJ. derived by reasoning. If we accept your premise, your conclusions are easily *deducible*.

defalcate V. misuse money held in trust. Legislation was passed to punish brokers who *defalcated* their clients' funds.

defamation N. harming a person's reputation. Such *defamation* of character may result in a slander suit.

default N. failure to do. As a result of her husband's failure to appear in court, she was granted a divorce by *default*. also V.

defeatist ADJ. attitude of one who is ready to accept defeat as a natural outcome. If you maintain your *defeatist* attitude, you will never succeed. also N.

defection N. desertion. The children, who had made him an idol, were hurt most by his *defection* from our cause.

■ **deference** N. courteous regard for another's wish. In *deference* to his desires, the employers granted him a holiday.

defile V. pollute; profane. The hoodlums *defiled* the church with their scurrilous writing.

definitive ADJ. final; complete. Carl Sandburg's *Abraham Lincoln* may be regarded as the *definitive* work on the life of the Great Emancipator.

deflect V. turn aside. His life was saved when his cigarette case *deflected* the bullet.

defray V. pay the costs of. Her employer offered to *defray* the costs of her postgraduate education.

deft ADJ. neat; skillful. The *deft* waiter uncorked the champagne without spilling a drop.

defunct ADJ. dead; no longer in use or existence. The lawyers sought to examine the books of the *defunct* corporation.

degraded ADJ. lowered in rank; debased. The *degraded* wretch spoke only of his past glories and honors.

deify V. turn into a god; idolize. Admire the rock star all you want; just don't *deify* him.

deign V. condescend. He felt that he would debase himself if he *deigned* to answer his critics.

delete V. erase; strike out. If you *delete* this paragraph, the composition will have more appeal.

deleterious ADJ. harmful. Workers in nuclear research must avoid the *deleterious* effects of radioactive substances.

■ **deliberate** V. consider; ponder. Offered the new job, she asked for time to *deliberate* before she told them her decision.

■ **delineate** N. portray. He is a powerful storyteller, but he is weakest when he attempts to *delineate* character. delineation, N.

deliquescent ADJ. capable of absorbing moisture from the air and becoming liquid. Since this powder is extremely *deliquescent*, it must be kept in a hermetically sealed container until it is used.

delirium N. mental disorder marked by confusion. The drunkard in his *delirium* saw strange animals.

delude V. deceive. Do not *delude* yourself into believing that he will relent.

deluge N. flood; rush. When we advertised the position, we received a *deluge* of applications.

delusion N. false belief; hallucination. This scheme is a snare and a *delusion*.

delusive ADJ. deceptive; raising vain hopes. Do not raise your hopes on the basis of his *delusive* promises.

delve V. dig; investigate. *Delving* into old books and manuscripts is part of a researcher's job.

demagogue N. person who appeals to people's prejudice; false leader of people. He was accused of being a *demagogue* because he made promises which aroused futile hopes in his listeners.

demean V. degrade; humiliate. He felt that he would *demean* himself if he replied to the scurrilous letter.

demeanor N. behavior; bearing. His sober *demeanor* quieted the noisy revelers.

demented ADJ. insane. She became increasingly more *demented* and had to be hospitalized.

demesne N. domain; land over which a person has full sovereignty. The lord of the manor proudly surveyed his *demesne*.

demise N. death. Upon the *demise* of the dictator, a bitter dispute about succession to power developed.

demolition N. destruction. One of the major aims of the air force was the complete *demolition* of all means of transportation by bombing of rail lines and terminals.

demoniac ADJ. fiendish. The Spanish Inquisition devised many *demoniac* means of torture. demon, N.

demotic ADJ. pertaining to the people. He lamented the passing of aristocratic society and maintained that a *demotic* society would lower the nation's standards.

demur V. delay; object. To *demur* at this time will only worsen the already serious situation; now is the time for action.

demure ADJ. grave; serious; coy. She was *demure* and reserved.

denigrate V. blacken. All attempts to *denigrate* the character of our late President have failed; the people still love him and cherish his memory.

denizen N. inhabitant of. Ghosts are *denizens* of the land of the dead who return to earth.

denotation N. meaning; distinguishing by name. A dictionary will always give us the *denotation* of a word; frequently, it will also give us its connotation.

denouement N. outcome; final development of the plot of a play. The play was childishly written; the *denouement* was obvious to sophisticated theatergoers as early as the middle of the first act.

■ **denounce** V. condemn; criticize. The reform candidate *denounced* the corrupt city officers for having betrayed the public's trust. denunciation, N.

■ **depict** V. portray. In this book, the author *depicts* the slave owners as kind and benevolent masters.

depilate V. remove hair. Many women *depilate* their legs with a razor; some use a cream.

■ **deplete** V. reduce; exhaust. We must wait until we *deplete* our present inventory before we order replacements.

deplore V. regret. Although I *deplore* the vulgarity of your language, I defend your right to express yourself freely.

deploy V. move troops so that the battle line is extended at the expense of depth. The general ordered the battalion to *deploy* in order to meet the offensive of the enemy.

depose V. dethrone; remove from office. The army attempted to *depose* the king and set up a military government.

deposition N. testimony under oath. He made his *deposition* in the judge's chamber.

■ **depravity** N. corruption; wickedness. The *depravity* of the tyrant's behavior shocked all.

■ **deprecate** V. disapprove regretfully. I must *deprecate* your attitude and hope that you will change your mind.

deprecatory ADJ. disapproving. Your *deprecatory* criticism has offended the author.

depreciate V. lessen in value. If you neglect this property, it will *depreciate*.

depredation N. plundering. After the *depredations* of the invaders, the people were penniless.

deranged ADJ. insane. He had to be institutionalized because he was mentally *deranged*.

derelict ADJ. abandoned. The *derelict* craft was a menace to navigation. also N.

deride V. scoff at. The people *derided* his grandiose schemes.

derision N. ridicule. They greeted his proposal with *derision* and refused to consider it seriously.

■ **derivative** ADJ. unoriginal; derived from another source. Although her early poetry was clearly *derivative* in nature, the critics thought she had promise and eventually would find her own voice.

dermatologist N. one who studies the skin and its diseases. I advise you to consult a *dermatologist* about your acne.

Test

Word List 13   *Synonyms*

Each of the questions below consists of a word in capital letters, followed by five lettered words or phrases. Choose the lettered word or phrase that is most nearly similar in meaning to the word in capital letters and write the letter of your choice on your answer paper.

181. DECIMATE (A) kill (B) disgrace (C) search (D) collide (E) deride

182. DECLIVITY (A) trap (B) quadrangle (C) quarter (D) activity (E) downward slope

183. DECOLLETÉ (A) flavored (B) demure (C) flowery (D) low-necked (E) sweet

184. DECREPIT (A) momentary (B) emotional (C) suppressed (D) worn out (E) unexpected

185. DECREPITUDE (A) feebleness (B) disease (C) coolness (D) melee (E) crowd

186. DEFALCATE (A) abscond (B) elope (C) observe (D) panic (E) invest
187. DEFECTION (A) determination (B) desertion (C) invitation (D) affection (E) reservation
188. DEFILE (A) manicure (B) ride (C) pollute (D) assemble (E) order
189. DEGRADED (A) surprised (B) lowered (C) ascended (D) learned (E) prejudged
190. DELETERIOUS (A) delaying (B) experimental (C) harmful (D) graduating (E) glorious

191. DELUGE (A) confusion (B) deception (C) flood (D) mountain (E) weapon
192. DENIGRATE (A) refuse (B) blacken (C) terrify (D) admit (E) review
193. DENOUEMENT (A) action (B) scenery (C) resort (D) character (E) solution
194. DEPRAVITY (A) wickedness (B) sadness (C) heaviness (D) tidiness (E) seriousness
195. DERANGED (A) insane (B) announced (C) neighborly (D) alphabetical (E) surrounded

---

Word List 14   derogatory-disgruntle

derogatory ADJ. expressing a low opinion. I resent your *derogatory* remarks.

descant V. discuss fully. He was willing to *descant* upon any topic of conversation, even when he knew very little about the subject under discussion. also N.

descry V. catch sight of. In the distance, we could barely *descry* the enemy vessels.

desecrate V. profane; violate the sanctity of. The soldiers *desecrated* the temple.

desiccate V. dry up. A tour of this smokehouse will give you an idea of how the pioneers used to *desiccate* food in order to preserve it.

desideratum N. that which is desired. Our first *desideratum* must be the establishment of peace; we can then attempt to remove the causes of the present conflict.

desolate V. rob of joy; lay waste to; forsake. The bandits *desolated* the countryside, burning farms and carrying off the harvest.

despicable ADJ. contemptible. Your *despicable* remarks call for no reply.

despise V. scorn. I *despise* your attempts at a reconciliation at this time and refuse to meet you.

despoil V. plunder. If you do not yield, I am afraid the enemy will *despoil* the countryside.

■ **despondent** ADJ. depressed; gloomy. To the dismay of his parents, he became more and more *despondent* every day. despondency, N.

despotism N. tyranny. The people rebelled against the *despotism* of the king.

destitute ADJ. extremely poor. The illness left the family *destitute*.

desuetude N. disused condition. The machinery in the idle factory was in a state of *desuetude*.

desultory ADJ. aimless; jumping around. The animals' *desultory* behavior indicated that they had no awareness of their predicament.

■ **detached** ADJ. emotionally removed; calm and objective; indifferent. A psychoanalyst must maintain a *detached* point of view and stay uninvolved with her patients' personal lives. detachment, N. (secondary meaning)

detergent N. cleansing agent. Many new *detergents* have replaced soap.

determinate ADJ. having a fixed order of procedure; invariable. At the royal wedding, the procession of the nobles followed a *determinate* order of precedence.

■ **deterrent** N. something that discourages; hindrance. Does the threat of capital punishment serve as a *deterrent* to potential killers?

detonation N. explosion. The *detonation* of the bomb could be heard miles away.

detraction N. slandering; aspersion. He is offended by your frequent *detractions* of his ability as a leader.

■ **detrimental** ADJ. harmful; damaging. Your acceptance of her support will ultimately prove *detrimental* rather than helpful to your cause. detriment, N.

■ **deviate** V. turn away from. Do not *deviate* from the truth; you must face the facts.

devious ADJ. going astray; erratic. Your *devious* behavior in this matter puzzles me since you are usually direct and straightforward.

devoid ADJ. lacking. He was *devoid* of any personal desire for gain in his endeavor to secure improvement in the community.

devolve V. deputize; pass to others. It *devolved* upon us, the survivors, to arrange peace terms with the enemy.

devotee N. enthusiastic follower. A *devotee* of the opera, he bought season tickets every year.

devout ADJ. pious. The *devout* man prayed daily.

dexterous ADJ. skillful. The magician was so *dexterous* that we could not follow him as he performed his tricks.

diabolical ADJ. devilish. This scheme is so *diabolical* that I must reject it.

diadem N. crown. The king's *diadem* was on display at the museum.

dialectic N. art of debate. I am not skilled in *dialectic* and, therefore, cannot answer your arguments as forcefully as I wish.

diaphanous ADJ. sheer; transparent. They saw the burglar clearly through the *diaphanous* curtain.

diatribe N. bitter scolding; invective. During the lengthy *diatribe* delivered by his opponent he remained calm and self-controlled.

dichotomy N. branching into two parts. The *dichotomy* of our legislative system provides us with many safeguards.

dictum N. authoritative and weighty statement. She repeated the statement as though it were the *dictum* of the most expert worker in the group.

■ **didactic** ADJ. teaching; instructional. The *didactic* qualities of his poetry overshadow its literary qualities; the lesson he teaches is more memorable than the lines.

diffidence N. shyness. You must overcome your *diffidence* if you intend to become a salesperson.

diffusion N. wordiness; spreading in all directions like a gas. Your composition suffers from a *diffusion* of ideas; try to be more compact. diffuse, ADJ. and V.

■ **digression** N. wandering away from the subject. His book was marred by his many *digressions*. digress, V.

dilapidated ADJ. ruined because of neglect. We felt that the *dilapidated* building needed several coats of paint. dilapidation, N.

dilate V. expand. In the dark, the pupils of your eyes *dilate*.

dilatory ADJ. delaying. Your *dilatory* tactics may compel me to cancel the contract.

dilemma N. problem; choice of two unsatisfactory alternatives. In this *dilemma,* he knew no one to whom he could turn for advice.

dilettante N. aimless follower of the arts; amateur; dabbler. He was not serious in his painting; he was rather a *dilettante.*

■ **diligence** N. steadiness of effort; persistent hard work. Her employers were greatly impressed by her *diligence* and offered her a partnership in the firm.

dilute V. make less concentrated; reduce in strength. She preferred her coffee *diluted* with milk.

diminution N. lessening; reduction in size. The blockaders hoped to achieve victory as soon as the *diminution* of the enemy's supplies became serious.

dint N. means; effort. By *dint* of much hard work, the volunteers were able to place the raging forest fire under control.

dipsomaniac N. one who has a strong craving for intoxicating liquor. The picture *The Lost Weekend* was an excellent portrayal of the struggles of the *dipsomaniac.*

dire ADJ. disastrous. People ignored her *dire* predictions of an approaching depression.

dirge N. lament with music. The funeral *dirge* stirred us to tears.

disabuse V. correct a false impression; undeceive. I will attempt to *disabuse* you of your impression of my client's guilt; I know he is innocent.

disapprobation N. disapproval; condemnation. The conservative father viewed his daughter's radical boyfriend with *disapprobation*.

disarray N. a disorderly or untidy state. After the New Year's party, the once orderly house was in total *disarray*.

disavowal N. denial; disclaiming. His *disavowal* of his part in the conspiracy was not believed by the jury.

disburse V. pay out. When you *disburse* money on the company's behalf, be sure to get a receipt.

discernible ADJ. distinguishable; perceivable. The ships in the harbor were not *discernible* in the fog.

■ **discerning** ADJ. mentally quick and observant; having insight. Because he was considered the most *discerning* member of the firm, he was assigned the most difficult cases. discern, V.

disclaim V. disown; renounce claim to. If I grant you this privilege, will you *disclaim* all other rights?

discomfit V. put to rout; defeat; disconcert. This ruse will *discomfit* the enemy. discomfiture, N.

disconcert V. confuse; upset; embarrass. The lawyer was *disconcerted* by the evidence produced by her adversary.

disconsolate ADJ. sad. The death of his wife left him *disconsolate.*

■ **discordant** ADJ. inharmonious; conflicting. She tried to unite the *discordant* factions.

discount V. disregard. Be prepared to *discount* what he has to say about his ex-wife.

discrepancy N. lack of consistency; difference. The police noticed some *discrepancies* in his description of the crime and did not believe him.

discrete ADJ. separate; unconnected. The universe is composed of *discrete* bodies.

■ **discretion** N. prudence; ability to adjust actions to circumstances. Use your *discretion* in this matter and do not discuss it with anyone. discreet, ADJ.

■ **discrimination** N. ability to see differences; prejudice. They feared he lacked sufficient *discrimination* to judge complex works of modern art. (secondary meaning) discriminating, ADJ.

■ **discursive** ADJ. digressing; rambling. They were annoyed and bored by her *discursive* remarks.

■ **disdain** V. treat with scorn or contempt. You make enemies of all you *disdain*. also N.

disgruntle V. make discontented. The passengers were *disgruntled* by the numerous delays.

Test

Word List 14   *Antonyms*

Each of the questions below consists of a word in capital letters, followed by five lettered words or phrases. Choose the lettered word or phrase that is most nearly opposite in meaning to the word in capital letters and write the letter of your choice on your answer paper.

196. DEROGATORY (A) roguish (B) immediate (C) opinionated (D) praising (E) conferred
197. DESECRATE (A) desist (B) integrate (C) confuse (D) intensify (E) consecrate
198. DESPICABLE (A) steering (B) worthy of esteem (C) inevitable (D) featureless (E) incapable
199. DESTITUTE (A) affluent (B) dazzling (C) stationary (D) characteristic (E) explanatory
200. DEVOID (A) latent (B) eschewed (C) full of (D) suspecting (E) evident
201. DEVOUT (A) quiet (B) dual (C) impious (D) straightforward (E) wrong
202. DIABOLICAL (A) mischievous (B) lavish (C) seraphic (D) azure (E) red
203. DIATRIBE (A) mass (B) range (C) eulogy (D) elegy (E) starvation
204. DIFFIDENCE (A) sharpness (B) boldness (C) malcontent (D) dialogue (E) catalog
205. DILATE (A) procrastinate (B) contract (C) conclude (D) participate (E) divert
206. DILATORY (A) narrowing (B) prompt (C) enlarging (D) portentous (E) sour
207. DIMINUTION (A) expectation (B) context (C) validity (D) appreciation (E) difficulty
208. DIPSOMANIAC (A) realist (B) thief (C) teetotaller (D) pyromaniac (E) swimmer
209. DISABUSE (A) crash (B) violate (C) renege (D) control (E) deceive
210. DISCONSOLATE (A) examining (B) thankful (C) theatrical (D) joyous (E) prominent

Word List 15   dishabille-duplicity

dishabille N. in a state of undress. Because he was certain that he would have no visitors, he lounged around the house in a state of *dishabille,* wearing only his pajamas and a pair of old bedroom slippers.

disheartened ADJ. lacking courage and hope. His failure to pass the bar exam *disheartened* him.

disheveled ADJ. untidy. Your *disheveled* appearance will hurt your chances in this interview.

■ **disinclination** N. unwillingness. Some mornings I feel a great *disinclination* to get out of bed.

disingenuous ADJ. not naive; sophisticated. Although he was young, his remarks indicated that he was *disingenuous.*

disinter V. dig up; unearth. They *disinterred* the body and held an autopsy.

disinterested ADJ. unprejudiced. The only *disinterested* person in the room was the judge.

disjointed ADJ. disconnected. His remarks were so *disjointed* that we could not follow his reasoning.

■ **dismantle** V. take apart. When the show closed, they *dismantled* the scenery before storing it.

dismember V. cut into small parts. When the Austrian Empire was *dismembered,* several new countries were established.

■ **disparage** V. belittle. Do not *disparage* anyone's contribution; these little gifts add up to large sums.

disparate ADJ. basically different; unrelated. It is difficult, if not impossible, to organize these *disparate* elements into a coherent whole.

■ **disparity** N. difference; condition of inequality. The *disparity* in their ages made no difference at all.

■ **dispassionate** ADJ. calm; impartial. In a *dispassionate* analysis of the problem, he carefully examined the causes of the conflict and proceeded to suggest suitable remedies.

■ **disperse** V. scatter. The police fired tear gar into the crowd to disperse the protesters.

dispersion N. scattering. The *dispersion* of this group throughout the world may be explained by their expulsion from their homeland.

dispirited ADJ. lacking in spirit. The coach used all the tricks at his command to buoy up the enthusiasm of his team, which had become *dispirited* at the loss of the star player.

disport V. amuse. The popularity of Florida as a winter resort is constantly increasing; each year, thousands more *disport* themselves at Miami and Palm Beach.

■ **disputatious** ADJ. argumentative; fond of argument. People avoided discussing contemporary problems with him because of his *disputatious* manner.

disquisition N. a formal systematic inquiry; an explanation of the results of a formal inquiry. In his *disquisition,* he outlined the steps he had taken in reaching his conclusions.

dissection N. analysis; cutting apart in order to examine. The *dissection* of frogs in the laboratory is particularly unpleasant to some students.

■ **dissemble** V. disguise; pretend. Even though you are trying to *dissemble* your motive in joining this group, we can see through your pretense.

disseminate V. scatter (like seeds). The invention of the radio has helped propagandists to *disseminate* their favorite doctrines very easily.

dissertation N. formal essay. In order to earn a graduate degree from many of our universities, a candidate is frequently required to prepare a *dissertation* on some scholarly subject.

dissimulate V. pretend; conceal by feigning. She tried to *dissimulate* her grief by her exuberant attitude.

dissipate V. squander. The young man quickly *dissipated* his inheritance and was soon broke.

dissolute ADJ. loose in morals. The *dissolute* life led by the ancient Romans is indeed shocking.

■ **dissonance** N. discord. Some contemporary musicians deliberately use *dissonance* to achieve certain effects.

dissuade V. advise against. He could not *dissuade* his friend from joining the conspirators.

dissuasion N. advice against. All his powers of *dissuasion* were useless; they failed to heed his warning.

distaff ADJ. female. His ancestors on the *distaff* side were equally as famous as his father's progenitors.

■ **distant** ADJ. reserved or aloof; cold in manner. His *distant* greeting made me feel unwelcome from the start. (secondary meaning)

distend V. expand; swell out. I can tell when he is under stress by the way the veins *distend* on his forehead.

distortion N. twisting out of shape. It is difficult to believe the newspaper accounts of this event because of the *distortions* and exaggerations written by the reporters.

distrait ADJ. absentminded. Because of his concentration on the problem, the professor often appeared *distrait* and unconcerned about routine.

distraught ADJ. upset; distracted by anxiety. The *distraught* parents frantically searched the ravine for their lost child.

diurnal ADJ. daily. A farmer cannot neglect his *diurnal* tasks at any time; cows, for example, must be milked regularly.

diva N. operatic singer; prima donna. Although world famous as a *diva,* she did not indulge in fits of temperament.

diverge V. vary; go in different directions from the same point. The spokes of the wheel *diverge* from the hub.

■ **divergent** ADJ. differing; deviating. The two witnesses presented the jury with remarkably *divergent* accounts of the same episode.

divers ADJ. several; differing. We could hear *divers* opinions of his ability.

■ **diverse** ADJ. differing in some characteristics; various. There are *diverse* ways of approaching this problem.

■ **diversion** N. act of turning aside; pastime. After studying for several hours, he needed a *diversion* from work. divert, V.

diversity N. variety; dissimilitude. The *diversity* of colleges in this country indicates that many levels of ability are being cared for.

divest V. strip; deprive. He was *divested* of his power to act and could no longer govern.

divination N. foreseeing the future with aid of magic. I base my opinions not on any special gift of *divination* but on the laws of probability.

divulge V. reveal. I will not tell you this news because I am sure you will *divulge* it prematurely.

docile ADJ. obedient; easily managed. As *docile* as he seems today, that old lion was once a ferocious, snarling beast.

docket N. program as for trial; book where such entries are made. The case of Smith vs. Jones was entered in the *docket* for July 15. also V.

■ **document** V. provide written evidence. She kept all the receipts from her business trip in order to *document* her expenses for the firm. also N.

doddering ADJ. shaky; infirm from old age. Although he is not as yet a *doddering* and senile old man, his ideas and opinions no longer can merit the respect we gave them years ago.

doff V. take off. A gentleman used to *doff* his hat to a lady.

doggerel N. poor verse. Although we find occasional snatches of genuine poetry in her work, most of her writing is mere *doggerel.*

■ **dogmatic** ADJ. positive; arbitrary. Do not be so *dogmatic* about that statement; it can be easily refuted.

doldrums N. blues; listlessness; slack period. Once the excitement of meeting her deadline was over, she found herself in the *doldrums.*

dolorous ADJ. sorrowful. He found the *dolorous* lamentations of the bereaved family emotionally disturbing and he left as quickly as he could.

dolt N. stupid person. I thought I was talking to a mature audience; instead, I find myself addressing a pack of *dolts* and idiots.

domicile N. home. Although his legal *domicile* was in New York City, his work kept him away from his residence for many years. also V.

domineer V. rule over tyrannically. Students prefer teachers who guide, not ones who *domineer.*

dormant ADJ. sleeping; lethargic; torpid. Sometimes *dormant* talents in our friends surprise those of us who never realized how gifted our acquaintances really are. dormancy, N.

dorsal ADJ. relating to the back of an animal. A shark may be identified by its *dorsal* fin, which projects above the surface of the ocean.

dotage N. senility. In his *dotage,* the old man bored us with long tales of events in his childhood.

doughty ADJ. courageous. Many folk tales have sprung up about this *doughty* pioneer who opened up the New World for his followers.

dour ADJ. sullen; stubborn. The man was *dour* and taciturn.

douse V. plunge into water; drench; extinguish. They *doused* each other with hoses and water balloons.

dowdy ADJ. slovenly; untidy. She tried to change her *dowdy* image by buying a new fashionable wardrobe.

dregs N. sediment; worthless residue. The *dregs* of society may be observed in this slum area of the city.

droll ADJ. queer and amusing. He was a popular guest because his *droll* anecdotes were always entertaining.

dross N. waste matter; worthless impurities. Many methods have been devised to separate the valuable metal from the *dross.*

drone N. idle person; male bee. Content to let his wife support him, the would-be writer was in reality nothing but a *drone.*

drone V. talk dully; buzz or murmur like a bee. On a gorgeous day, who wants to be stuck in a classroom listening to the teacher *drone.*

drudgery N. menial work. Cinderella's fairy godmother rescued her from a life of *drudgery.*

■ **dubious** ADJ. doubtful. He has the *dubious* distinction of being the lowest man in his class.

duenna N. attendant of young female; chaperone. Their romance could not flourish because of the presence of her *duenna.*

dulcet ADJ. sweet sounding. The *dulcet* sounds of the birds at dawn were soon drowned out by the roar of traffic passing our motel.

■ **duplicity** N. double-dealing; hypocrisy. People were shocked and dismayed when they learned of his *duplicity* in this affair, as he had always seemed honest and straightforward.

Test

Word List 15　*Synonyms and Antonyms*

Each of the following questions consists of a word in capital letters, followed by five lettered words or phrases. Choose the lettered word or phrase which is most nearly similar or the opposite of the word in capital letters and write the letter of your choice on your answer paper.

211. DISINGENUOUS (A) uncomfortable (B) eventual (C) naive (D) complex (E) enthusiastic
212. DISINTERESTED (A) prejudiced (B) horrendous (C) affected (D) arbitrary (E) bored
213. DISJOINTED (A) satisfied (B) carved (C) understood (D) connected (E) evicted
214. DISPARITY (A) resonance (B) elocution (C) relief (D) difference (E) symbolism
215. DISPASSIONATE (A) sensual (B) immoral (C) inhibited (D) impartial (E) scientific
216. DISPIRITED (A) current (B) dented (C) drooping (D) removed (E) dallying

217. DISSIPATE (A) economize (B) clean (C) accept (D) anticipate (E) withdraw
218. DISTEND (A) bloat (B) adjust (C) exist (D) materialize (E) finish
219. DISTRAIT (A) clever (B) industrial (C) absentminded (D) narrow (E) crooked
220. DIVULGE (A) look (B) refuse (C) deride (D) reveal (E) harm
221. DOFF (A) withdraw (B) take off (C) remain (D) control (E) start
222. DOGMATIC (A) benign (B) canine (C) impatient (D) petulant (E) arbitrary
223. DOTAGE (A) senility (B) silence (C) sensitivity (D) interest (F) generosity
224. DOUR (A) sullen (B) ornamental (C) grizzled (D) lacking speech (E) international
225. DROLL (A) rotund (B) amusing (C) fearsome (D) tiny (E) strange

Word List 16　durance-encroachment

durance N. restraint; imprisonment. The lecturer spoke of a *"durance* vile" to describe his years in the prison camp.

duress N. forcible restraint, especially unlawfully. The hostages were held under *duress* until the prisoners' demands were met.

dwindle V. shrink; reduce. They spent so much money that their funds *dwindled* to nothing.

dynamic ADJ. active; efficient. A *dynamic* government is necessary to meet the demands of a changing society.

dyspeptic ADJ. suffering from indigestion. All the talk about rich food made him feel *dyspeptic.* dyspepsia, N.

earthy ADJ. unrefined; coarse. His *earthy* remarks often embarrassed the women in his audience.

ebb V. recede; lessen. His fortunes began to *ebb* during the Recession. also N.

ebullient ADJ. showing excitement; overflowing with enthusiasm. His *ebullient* nature could not be repressed; he was always exuberant. ebullience, N.

■ **eccentric** ADJ. odd; whimsical; irregular. The comet passed close by the earth in its *eccentric* orbit.

eccentricity N. oddity; idiosyncrasy. Some of his friends tried to account for his rudeness to strangers as the *eccentricity* of genius.

ecclesiastic ADJ. pertaining to the church. The minister donned his *ecclesiastic* garb and walked to the pulpit. also N.

eclat N. brilliance; glory. To the delight of his audience, he completed his task with *eclat* and consummate ease.

eclecticism N. selection of elements from various sets of opinions or systems. The *eclecticism* of the group was demonstrated by their adoption of principles and practices of many forms of government.

eclipse V. darken; extinguish; surpass. The new stock market high *eclipsed* the previous record set in 1985.

ecologist N. a person concerned with the interrelationship between living organisms and their environment. The *ecologist* was concerned that the new dam would upset the natural balance of the creatures living in Glen Canyon.

ecstasy N. rapture; joy; any overpowering emotion. The announcement that the war had ended brought on an *ecstasy* of joy that resulted in many uncontrolled celebrations.

edify V. instruct; correct morally. Although his purpose was to *edify* and not to entertain his audience, many of his listeners were amused and not enlightened.

educe V. draw forth; elicit. She could not *educe* a principle that would encompass all the data.

eerie ADJ. weird. In that *eerie* setting, it was easy to believe in ghosts and other supernatural beings.

efface V. rub out. The coin had been handled so many times that its date had been *effaced*.

effectual ADJ. efficient. If we are to succeed in this endeavor, we must seek *effectual* means of securing our goals.

effeminate ADJ. having womanly traits. His voice was high-pitched and *effeminate*.

effervesce V. bubble over; show excitement. Some of us cannot stand the way she *effervesces* over trifles.

■ **effervescence** N. inner excitement; exuberance. Nothing depressed her for long; her natural *effervescence* soon reasserted itself. effervescent, ADJ.

effete ADJ. worn out; exhausted; barren. The literature of the age reflected the *effete* condition of the writers; no new ideas were forthcoming.

efficacy N. power to produce desired effect. The *efficacy* of this drug depends on the regularity of the dosage.

effigy N. dummy. The mob showed its irritation by hanging the judge in *effigy*.

efflorescent ADJ. flowering. Greenhouse gardeners are concerned with the coinciding of the plants' *efflorescent* period with certain holidays.

effluvium N. noxious smell. Air pollution has become a serious problem in our major cities; the *effluvium* and the poisons in the air are hazards to life.

effrontery N. shameless boldness. She had the *effrontery* to insult the guest.

effulgent ADJ. brilliantly radiant. The *effulgent* rays of the rising sun lit the sky.

effusion N. pouring forth. The critics objected to her literary *effusion* because it was too flowery.

effusive ADJ. pouring forth; gushing. Her *effusive* manner of greeting her friends finally began to irritate them.

egoism N. excessive interest in one's self; belief that one should be interested in one's self rather than in others. His *egoism* prevented him from seeing the needs of his colleagues.

egotism N. conceit; vanity. She thought so much of herself that we found her *egotism* unwarranted and irritating.

egregious ADJ. gross; shocking. She was an *egregious* liar and we could never believe her.

egress N. exit. Barnum's sign "To the *Egress*" fooled many people who thought they were going to see an animal and instead found themselves in the street.

ejaculation N. exclamation. He could not repress an *ejaculation* of surprise when he heard the news.

■ **elaboration** N. addition of details; intricacy. Tell what happened simply, without any *elaboration*. elaborate, V.

elation N. a rise in spirits; exaltation. She felt no *elation* at finding the purse because it was empty.

elegiacal ADJ. like an elegy; mournful. The essay on the lost crew was *elegiacal* in mood. elegy, N.

elicit V. draw out by discussion. The detectives tried to *elicit* where he had hidden his loot.

elixir N. cure-all; something invigorating. The news of her chance to go abroad acted on her like an *elixir*.

■ **eloquence** N. expressiveness; persuasive speech. The crowds were stirred by Martin Luther King's *eloquence*.

elucidate V. explain; enlighten. He was called upon to *elucidate* the disputed points in his article.

■ **elusive** ADJ. evasive; baffling; hard to grasp. His *elusive* dreams of wealth were costly to those of his friends who supported him financially. elude, V.

elusory ADJ. tending to deceive expectations; elusive. He argued that the project was an *elusory* one and would bring disappointment to all.

elysian ADJ. relating to paradise; blissful. An afternoon sail on the bay was for her an *elysian* journey.

emaciated ADJ. thin and wasted. His long period of starvation had left him *emaciated*.

emanate V. issue forth. A strong odor of sulphur *emanated* from the spring.

emancipate V. set free. At first, the attempts of the Abolitionists to *emancipate* the slaves were unpopular in New England as well as in the South.

embellish V. adorn. His handwriting was *embellished* with flourishes.

embezzlement N. stealing. The bank teller confessed his *embezzlement* of the funds.

emblazon V. deck in brilliant colors. *Emblazoned* on his shield was his family coat of arms.

embroil V. throw into confusion; involve in strife; entangle. He became *embroiled* in the heated discussion when he tried to arbitrate the dispute.

embryonic ADJ. undeveloped; rudimentary. The evil of class and race hatred must be eliminated while it is still in an *embryonic* state; otherwise, it may grow to dangerous proportions.

emend V. correct; correct by a critic. The critic *emended* the book by selecting the passages which he thought most appropriate to the text.

emendation N. correction of errors; improvement. Please initial all the *emendations* you have made in this contract.

emeritus ADJ. retired but retained in an honorary capacity. As professor *emeritus*, he retained all his honors without having to meet the obligations of daily assignments.

emetic N. substance causing vomiting. The use of an *emetic* like mustard is useful in cases of poisoning.

eminent ADJ. high; lofty. After his appointment to this *eminent* position, he seldom had time for his former friends.

emollient N. soothing or softening remedy. He applied an *emollient* to the inflamed area. Also ADJ.

emolument N. salary; compensation. In addition to the *emolument* this position offers, you must consider the social prestige it carries with it.

empirical ADJ. based on experience. He distrusted hunches and intuitive flashes; he placed his reliance entirely on *empirical* data.

empyreal ADJ. celestial; fiery. The scientific advances of the twentieth century have enabled man to invade the *empyreal* realm of the eagle.

■ **emulate** V. rival; imitate. As long as our political leaders *emulate* the virtues of the great leaders of this country, we shall flourish.

enamored ADJ. in love. Narcissus became *enamored* of his own beauty.

embed V. enclose; place in something. Tales of actual historical figures like King Alfred have become *embedded* in legends.

enclave N. territory enclosed within an alien land. The Vatican is an independent *enclave* in Italy.

encomiastic ADJ. praising; eulogistic. Some critics believe that his *encomiastic* statements about Napoleon were inspired by his desire for material advancement rather than by an honest belief in the Emperor's genius. encomium, N.

encomium N. praise; eulogy. He was sickened by the *encomiums* and panegyrics expressed by speakers who had previously been among the first to vilify the man they were now honoring.

encompass V. surround. Although we were *encompassed* by enemy forces, we were cheerful for we were well stocked and could withstand a siege until our allies joined us.

encroachment N. gradual intrusion. The *encroachment* of the factories upon the neighborhood lowered the value of the real estate.

Test

Word List 16   *Synonyms*

Each of the questions below consists of a word in capital letters, followed by five lettered words or phrases. Choose the lettered word or phrase that is most nearly similar in meaning to the word in capital letters and write the letter of your choice on your answer paper.

226. DWINDLE (A) blow (B) inhabit (C) spin (D) lessen (E) combine

227. ECSTASY (A) joy (B) speed (C) treasure (D) warmth (E) lack

228. EDIFY (A) mystify (B) suffice (C) improve (D) erect (E) entertain

229. EFFACE (A) countenance (B) encourage (C) recognize (D) blackball (E) rub out

230. EFFIGY (A) requisition (B) organ (C) charge (D) accordion (E) dummy

231. EGREGIOUS (A) pious (B) shocking (C) anxious (D) sociable (E) gloomy

232. EGRESS (A) entrance (B) bird (C) exit (D) double (E) progress

233. ELATED (A) debased (B) respectful (C) drooping (D) gay (E) charitable

234. ELUSIVE (A) deadly (B) eloping (C) evasive (D) simple (E) petrified

235. EMACIATED (A) garrulous (B) primeval (C) vigorous (D) disparate (E) thin

236. EMBELLISH (A) doff (B) don (C) balance (D) adorn (E) equalize

237. EMEND (A) cherish (B) repose (C) correct (D) assure (E) worry

238. EMENDATION (A) correction (B) interpretation (C) exhumation (D) inquiry (E) fault

239. EMINENT (A) purposeful (B) high (C) delectable (D) curious (E) urgent

240. EMANCIPATE (A) set free (B) take back (C) make worse (D) embolden (E) run away

Word List 17   encumber-eulogistic

encumber V. burden. Some people *encumber* themselves with too much luggage when they take short trips.

endearment N. fond statement. Your gifts and *endearments* cannot make me forget your earlier insolence.

endemic ADJ. prevailing among a specific group of people or in a specific area or country. This disease is *endemic* in this part of the world; more than 80 percent of the population are at one time or another affected by it.

endive N. species of leafy plant used in salads. The salad contained *endive* in addition to the ingredients she usually used.

■ **endorse** V. approve; support. Everyone waited to see which one of the rival candidates for the city council the mayor would *endorse*. (secondary meaning) endorsement, N.

endue V. provide with some quality; endow. He was *endued* with a lion's courage.

energize V. invigorate; make forceful and active. We shall have to *energize* our activities by getting new members to carry on.

enervate V. weaken. The hot days of August are *enervating*.

■ **enervation** N. lack of vigor; weakness. She was slow to recover from her illness; even a short walk to the window left her in a state of *enervation*.

■ **engender** V. cause; produce. To receive praise for real accomplishments *engenders* self-confidence in a child.

engross V. occupy fully. John was so *engrossed* in his studies that he did not hear his mother call.

■ **enhance** v. advance; improve. Your chances for promotion in this department will be *enhanced* if you take some more courses in evening school.

enigma N. puzzle. Despite all attempts to decipher the code, it remained an *enigma*.

■ **enigmatic** ADJ. obscure; puzzling. Many have sought to fathom the *enigmatic* smile of the *Mona Lisa*.

enjoin v. command; order; forbid. The owners of the company asked the court to *enjoin* the union from picketing the plant.

ennui N. boredom. The monotonous routine of hospital life induced a feeling of *ennui* which made him moody and irritable.

enormity N. hugeness (in a bad sense). He did not realize the *enormity* of his crime until he saw what suffering he had caused.

enrapture v. please intensely. The audience was *enraptured* by the freshness of the voices and the excellent orchestration.

ensconce v. settle comfortably. The parents thought that their children were *ensconced* safely in the private school and decided to leave for Europe.

ensue v. follow. The evils that *ensued* were the direct result of the miscalculations of the leaders.

enthrall v. capture; enslave. From the moment he saw her picture, he was *enthralled* by her beauty.

entice v. lure; attract; tempt. She always tried to *entice* her baby brother into mischief.

entity N. real being. As soon as the Charter was adopted, the United Nations became an *entity* and had to be considered as a factor in world diplomacy.

entomology N. study of insects. I found *entomology* the least interesting part of my course in biology; studying insects bored me.

entrance v. put under a spell; carry away with emotion. Shafts of sunlight on a wall could *entrance* her and leave her spellbound.

entreat v. plead; ask earnestly. She *entreated* her father to let her stay out till midnight.

entree N. entrance; a way in. Because of his wealth and social position, he had *entree* into the most exclusive circles.

entrepreneur N. businessman; contractor. Opponents of our present tax program argue that it discourages *entrepreneurs* from trying new fields of business activity.

enunciate v. speak distinctly. How will people understand you if you do not *enunciate?*

environ v. enclose; surround. In medieval days, Paris was *environed* by a wall. environs, N.

■ **ephemeral** ADJ. short-lived; fleeting. The mayfly is an *ephemeral* creature.

epicure N. connoisseur of food and drink. *Epicures* frequent this restaurant because it features exotic wines and dishes.

epicurean N. person who devotes himself to pleasures of the senses, especially to food. This restaurant is famous for its menu, which can cater to the most exotic whim of the *epicurean*. also ADJ.

epigram N. witty thought or saying, usually short. Poor Richard's *epigrams* made Benjamin Franklin famous.

epilogue N. short speech at conclusion of dramatic work. The audience was so disappointed in the play that many did not remain to hear the *epilogue*.

epitaph N. inscription in memory of a dead person. In his will, he dictated the *epitaph* he wanted placed on his tombstone.

epithet N. descriptive word or phrase. Homer's writings were featured by the use of such *epithets* as "rosy-fingered dawn."

epitome N. summary; concise abstract. This final book is the *epitome* of all his previous books. epitomize, v.

epoch N. period of time. The glacial *epoch* lasted for thousands of years.

equable ADJ. tranquil; steady; uniform. After the hot summers and cold winters of New England, he found the climate of the West Indies *equable* and pleasant.

equanimity N. calmness of temperament. In his later years, he could look upon the foolishness of the world with *equanimity* and humor.

equestrian N. rider on horseback. These paths in the park are reserved for *equestrians* and their steeds. also ADJ.

equilibrium N. balance. After the divorce, he needed some time to regain his *equilibrium*.

equine ADJ. resembling a horse. His long, bony face had an *equine* look to it.

equinox N. period of equal days and nights; the beginning of Spring and Autumn. The vernal *equinox* is usually marked by heavy rainstorms.

equipage N. horse-drawn carriage. The *equipage* drew up before the inn and the passengers stepped out.

equipoise N. balance; balancing force; equilibrium. The high wire acrobat used his pole as an *equipoise* to overcome the swaying caused by the wind.

equitable ADJ. fair; impartial. I am seeking an *equitable* solution to this dispute, one which will be fair and acceptable to both sides.

equity N. fairness; justice. Our courts guarantee *equity* to all.

equivocal ADJ. doubtful; ambiguous. Macbeth was misled by the *equivocal* statements of the witches.

equivocate v. lie; mislead; attempt to conceal the truth. The audience saw through his attempts to *equivocate* on the subject under discussion and ridiculed his remarks.

erode v. eat away. The limestone was *eroded* by the dripping water.

erotic ADJ. pertaining to passionate love. The *erotic* passages in this novel should be removed as they are merely pornographic.

errant ADJ. wandering. Many a charming tale has been written about the knights-*errant* who helped the weak and punished the guilty during the Age of Chivalry.

■ **erratic** ADJ. odd; unpredictable. Investors become anxious when the stock market appears *erratic*.

■ **erroneous** ADJ. mistaken; wrong. I thought my answer was correct, but it was *erroneous*.

■ **erudite** ADJ. learned; scholarly. His *erudite* writing was difficult to read because of the many allusions which were unfamiliar to most readers. erudition, N.

erudition N. high degree of knowledge and learning. Although they respected his *erudition,* the populace refused to listen to his words of caution and turned to less learned leaders.

escapade N. prank; flighty conduct. The headmaster could not regard this latest *escapade* as a boyish joke and expelled the young man.

eschew V. avoid. He tried to *eschew* all display of temper.

escutcheon N. shield-shaped surface on which coat of arms is placed. His traitorous acts placed a shameful blot on the family *escutcheon*.

■ **esoteric** ADJ. known only to the chosen few. Those students who had access to his *esoteric* discussions were impressed by the breadth of his knowledge.

espionage N. spying. In order to maintain its power, the government developed a system of *espionage* which penetrated every household.

espouse V. adopt; support. She was always ready to *espouse* a worthy cause.

esprit de corps N. comradeship; spirit. West Point cadets are proud of their *esprit de corps*.

■ **esteem** V. respect; value; judge. I esteem Ezra Pound both for his exciting poetry and for his acute comments on literature. also N.

estranged ADJ. separated. The *estranged* wife sought a divorce.

ethereal ADJ. light; heavenly; fine. Visitors were impressed by her *ethereal* beauty, her delicate charm.

ethnic ADJ. relating to races. Intolerance between *ethnic* groups is deplorable and usually is based on lack of information.

ethnology N. study of man. Sociology is one aspect of the science of *ethnology*.

etymology N. study of word parts. A knowledge of *etymology* can help you on many English tests.

eugenic ADJ. pertaining to the improvement of race. It is easier to apply *eugenic* principles to the raising of racehorses or prize cattle than to the development of human beings.

eulogistic ADJ. praising. To everyone's surprise, the speech was *eulogistic* rather than critical in tone.

Test

Word List 17   *Antonyms*

Each of the questions below consists of a word in capital letters, followed by five lettered words or phrases. Choose the lettered word or phrase that is most nearly opposite in meaning to the word in capital letters and write the letter of your choice on your answer paper.

241. ENERVATE (A) strengthen (B) sputter (C) arrange (D) scrutinize (E) agree
242. ENHANCE (A) degrade (B) doubt (C) scuff (D) gasp (E) agree
243. ENNUI (A) hate (B) excitement (C) seriousness (D) humility (E) kindness
244. ENUNCIATE (A) pray (B) request (C) deliver (D) wait (E) mumble
245. EPHEMERAL (A) sensuous (B) passing (C) popular (D) distasteful (E) eternal
246. EQUABLE (A) flat (B) decisive (C) stormy (D) rough (E) scanty

247. EQUANIMITY (A) agitation (B) stirring (C) volume (D) identity (E) luster
248. EQUILIBRIUM (A) imbalance (B) peace (C) inequity (D) directness (E) urgency
249. EQUITABLE (A) able to leave (B) able to learn (C) unfair (D) preferable (E) rough
250. EQUIVOCAL (A) mistaken (B) quaint (C) azure (D) clear (E) universal
251. ERRATIC (A) unromantic (B) free (C) popular (D) steady (E) unknown
252. ERRONEOUS (A) accurate (B) dignified (C) curious (D) abrupt (E) round
253. ERUDITE (A) professorial (B) stately (C) short (D) unknown (E) ignorant
254. ETHEREAL (A) long-lasting (B) earthy (C) ill (D) critical (E) false
255. EULOGISTIC (A) pretty (B) critical (C) brief (D) stern (E) free

Word List 18   eulogy-faculty

eulogy N. praise. All the *eulogies* of his friends could not remove the sting of the calumny heaped upon him by his enemies.

euphemism N. mild expression in place of an unpleasant one. The expression "he passed away" is a *euphemism* for "he died."

euphonious ADJ. pleasing in sound. Italian and Spanish are *euphonious* languages and therefore easily sung.

euthanasia N. mercy killing. Many people support *euthanasia* for terminally-ill patients who wish to die.

evanescent ADJ. fleeting; vanishing. For a brief moment, the entire skyline was bathed in an orange-red hue in the *evanescent* rays of the sunset.

■ **evasive** ADJ. not frank; eluding. Your *evasive* answers convinced the judge that you were withholding important evidence. evade, V.

evince V. show clearly. When he tried to answer the questions, he *evinced* his ignorance of the subject matter.

eviscerate V. disembowel; remove entrails. The medicine man *eviscerated* the animal and offered the entrails to the angry gods.

evoke V. call forth. He *evoked* much criticism by his hostile manner.

ewer N. water pitcher. The primitive conditions of the period were symbolized by the porcelain *ewer* and basin in the bedroom.

■ **exacerbate** V. worsen; embitter. This latest arrest will *exacerbate* the already existing discontent of the people and enrage them.

exaction N. exorbitant demand; extortion. The colonies rebelled against the *exactions* of the mother country.

exasperate V. vex. Johnny often *exasperates* his mother with his pranks.

exchequer N. treasury. He had been Chancellor of the *Exchequer* before his promotion to the high office he now holds.

excision N. act of cutting away. With the *excision* of the dead and dying limbs of this tree, you have not only improved its appearance but you have enhanced its chances of bearing fruit.

excoriate V. flay; abrade. These shoes are so ill-fitting that they will *excoriate* the feet and create blisters.

exculpate V. clear from blame. He was *exculpated* of the crime when the real criminal confessed.

execrable ADJ. very bad. The anecdote was in *execrable* taste and shocked the audience.

execrate V. curse; express abhorrence for. The world *execrates* the memory of Hitler and hopes that genocide will never again be the policy of any nation.

■ **execute** V. put into effect; carry out. The choreographer wanted to see how well she could *execute* a pirouette. (secondary meaning) execution, N.

exegesis N. explanation, especially of Biblical passages. I can follow your *exegesis* of this passage to a limited degree; some of your reasoning eludes me.

■ **exemplary** ADJ. serving as a model; outstanding. Her *exemplary* behavior was praised at Commencement.

exertion N. effort; expenditure of much physical work. The *exertion* spent in unscrewing the rusty bolt left her exhausted.

exhort V. urge. The evangelist will *exhort* all sinners in his audience to reform.

exhume V. dig out of the ground; remove from a grave. Because of the rumor that he had been poisoned, his body was *exhumed* in order that an autopsy might be performed.

exigency N. urgent situation. In this *exigency,* we must look for aid from our allies.

exiguous ADJ. small; minute. Grass grew there, an *exiguous* outcropping among the rocks.

exodus N. departure. The *exodus* from the hot and stuffy city was particularly noticeable on Friday evenings.

ex officio ADJ. by virtue of one's office. The Mayor was *ex officio* chairman of the committee that decided the annual tax rate. also ADV.

exonerate V. acquit; exculpate. I am sure this letter naming the actual culprit will *exonerate* you.

exorbitant ADJ. excessive. The people grumbled at his *exorbitant* prices but paid them because he had a monopoly.

exorcise V. drive out evil spirits. By incantation and prayer, the medicine man sought to *exorcise* the evil spirits which had taken possession of the young warrior.

exotic ADJ. not native; strange. Because of his *exotic* headdress, he was followed in the streets by small children who laughed at his strange appearance.

expatiate V. talk at length. At this time, please give us a brief resumé of your work; we shall permit you to *expatiate* later.

expatriate N. exile; someone who has withdrawn from his native land. Henry James was an American *expatriate* who settled in England.

■ **expedient** ADJ. suitable; practical; politic. A pragmatic politician, he was guided by what was *expedient* rather than by what was ethical. expediency, N.

■ **expedite** V. hasten. We hope you will be able to *expedite* delivery because of our tight schedule.

expeditiously ADV. rapidly and efficiently. Please adjust this matter as *expeditiously* as possible as it is delaying important work.

■ **expertise** N. specialized knowledge; expert skill. Although she was knowledgeable in a number of fields, she was hired for her particular *expertise* in computer programming.

expiate V. make amends for (a sin). He tried to *expiate* his crimes by a full confession to the authorities.

expletive N. interjection; profane oath. The sergeant's remarks were filled with *expletives* that offended the new recruits.

■ **explicit** ADJ. definite; open. Your remarks are *explicit;* no one can misinterpret them.

■ **exploit** N. deed or action, particularly a brave deed. Raoul Wallenberg was noted for his *exploits* in rescuing Jews from Hitler's forces.

■ **exploit** V. make use of, sometimes unjustly. Cesar Chavez fought attempts to *exploit* migrant farmworkers in California. exploitation, N.

expostulation N. remonstrance. Despite the teacher's scoldings and *expostulations,* the class remained unruly.

expunge V. cancel; remove. If you behave, I will *expunge* this notation from your record.

expurgate V. clean; remove offensive parts of a book. The editors felt that certain passages in the book had to be *expurgated* before it could be used in the classroom.

extant ADJ. still in existence. Although the authorities suppressed the book, many copies are *extant* and may be purchased at exorbitant prices.

extemporaneous ADJ. not planned; impromptu. Because his *extemporaneous* remarks were misinterpreted, he decided to write all his speeches in advance.

extenuate V. weaken; mitigate. It is easier for us to *extenuate* our own shortcomings than those of others.

extirpate V. root up. The Salem witch trials were a misguided attempt to *extirpate* superstition and heresy.

extol V. praise; glorify. The astronauts were *extolled* as the pioneers of the Space Age.

extort V. wring from; get money by threats, etc. The blackmailer *extorted* money from his victim.

extradition N. surrender of prisoner by one state to another. The lawyers opposed the *extradition* of their client on the grounds that for more than five years he had been a model citizen.

extraneous ADJ. not essential; external. Do not pad your paper with *extraneous* matters; stick to essential items only.

extricate V. free; disentangle. He found that he could not *extricate* himself from the trap.

extrinsic ADJ. external; not inherent; foreign. Do not be fooled by *extrinsic* causes. We must look for the intrinsic reason.

extrovert N. person interested mostly in external objects and actions. A good salesman is usually an *extrovert,* who likes to mingle with people.

extrude V. force or push out. Much pressure is required to *extrude* these plastics.

exuberant ADJ. abundant; effusive; lavish. His speeches were famous for his *exuberant* language and vivid imagery.

exude V. discharge; give forth. The maple syrup is obtained from the sap that *exudes* from the trees in early spring. exudation, N.

exult V. rejoice. We *exulted* when our team won the victory.

fabricate V. build; lie. Because of the child's tendency to *fabricate*, we had trouble believing her.

facade N. front of the building. The *facade* of the church had often been photographed by tourists because it was more interesting than the rear.

facet N. small plane surface (of a gem); a side. The stonecutter decided to improve the rough diamond by providing it with several *facets.*

facetious ADJ. humorous; jocular. Your *facetious* remarks are not appropriate at this serious moment.

facile ADJ. easy; expert. Because he was a *facile* speaker, he never refused a request to address an organization.

facilitate V. make less difficult. He tried to *facilitate* matters at home by getting a part-time job.

facsimile N. copy. Many museums sell *facsimiles* of the works of art on display.

faction N. party; clique; dissension. The quarrels and bickering of the two small *factions* within the club disturbed the majority of the members.

factious ADJ. inclined to form factions; causing dissension. Your statement is *factious* and will upset the harmony that now exists.

factitious ADJ. artificial; sham. Hollywood actresses often create *factitious* tears by using glycerine.

factotum N. handyman; person who does all kinds of work. Although we had hired him as a messenger, we soon began to use him as a general *factotum* around the office.

faculty N. mental or bodily powers; teaching staff. As he grew old, he feared he might lose his *faculties* and become useless to his employer.

Test

Word List 18 *Antonyms*

Each of the questions below consists of a word in capital letters, followed by five lettered words or phrases. Choose the lettered word or phrase that is most nearly opposite in meaning to the word in capital letters and write the letter of your choice on your answer paper.

256. EUPHONIOUS (A) strident (B) lethargic (C) literary (D) significant (E) merry
257. EVASIVE (A) frank (B) correct (C) empty (D) fertile (E) watchful
258. EXASPERATE (A) confide (B) formalize (C) placate (D) betray (E) bargain
259. EXCORIATE (A) scandalize (B) encourage (C) avoid (D) praise (E) vanquish
260. EXCULPATE (A) blame (B) prevail (C) aquire (D) ravish (E) accumulate
261. EXECRABLE (A) innumerable (B) philosophic (C) physical (D) excellent (E) meditative
262. EXECRATE (A) disobey (B) enact (C) perform (D) acclaim (E) fidget
263. EXHUME (A) decipher (B) sadden (C) integrate (D) admit (E) inter
264. EXODUS (A) neglect (B) consent (C) entry (D) gain (E) rebuke
265. EXONERATE (A) forge (B) accuse (C) record (D) doctor (E) reimburse
266. EXORBITANT (A) moderate (B) partisan (C) military (D) barbaric (E) counterfeit
267. EXTEMPORANEOUS (A) rehearsed (B) hybrid (C) humiliating (D) statesmanlike (E) picturesque
268. EXTRANEOUS (A) modern (B) decisive (C) essential (D) effective (E) expressive

269. EXTRINSIC (A) reputable (B) inherent (C) swift (D) ambitious (E) cursory

270. EXTROVERT (A) clown (B) hero (C) ectomorph (D) neurotic (E) introvert

---

Word List 19   fain-flinch

fain ADV. gladly. The knight said, "I would *fain* be your protector."

■ **fallacious** ADJ. misleading. Your reasoning must be *fallacious* because it leads to a ridiculous answer.

fallible ADJ. liable to err. I know I am *fallible,* but I feel confident that I am right this time.

fallow ADJ. plowed but not sowed; uncultivated. Farmers have learned that it is advisable to permit land to lie *fallow* every few years.

falter V. hesitate. When told to dive off the high board, she did not *falter,* but proceeded at once.

■ **fanaticism** N. excessive zeal. The leader of the group was held responsible even though he could not control the *fanaticism* of his followers. fantastic, ADJ., N.

fancied ADJ. imagined; unreal. You are resenting *fancied* insults. No one has ever said such things about you.

fancier N. breeder or dealer of animals. The dog *fancier* exhibited her prize collie at the annual Kennel Club show.

fanciful ADJ. whimsical; visionary. This is a *fanciful* scheme because it does not consider the facts.

fanfare N. call by bugles or trumpets. The exposition was opened with a *fanfare* of trumpets and the firing of cannon.

fantastic ADJ. unreal; grotesque; whimsical. Your fears are *fantastic* because no such animal as you have described exists.

farce N. broad comedy; mockery. Nothing went right; the entire interview degenerated into a *farce.* farcical, ADJ.

■ **fastidious** ADJ. difficult to please; squeamish. The waitresses disliked serving him dinner because of his very *fastidious* taste.

fatalism N. belief that events are determined by forces beyond one's control. With *fatalism,* he accepted the hardships that beset him. fatalistic, ADJ.

fathom V. comprehend; investigate. I find his motives impossible to *fathom.*

fatuous ADJ. foolish; inane. He is far too intelligent to utter such *fatuous* remarks.

fauna N. animals of a period or region. The scientist could visualize the *fauna* of the period by examining the skeletal remains and the fossils.

faux pas N. an error or slip (in manners or behavior). Your tactless remarks during dinner were a *faux pas.*

fawning ADJ. courting favor by cringing and flattering. She was constantly surrounded by a group of *fawning* admirers who hoped to win some favor.

fealty N. loyalty; faithfulness. The feudal lord demanded *fealty* of his vassals.

feasible ADJ. practical. This is an entirely *feasible* proposal. I suggest we adopt it.

febrile ADJ. feverish. In his *febrile* condition, he was subject to nightmares and hallucinations.

fecundity N. fertility; fruitfulness. The *fecundity* of his mind is illustrated by the many vivid images in his poems.

feign V. pretend. Lady Macbeth *feigned* illness in the courtyard although she was actually healthy.

feint N. trick; shift; sham blow. The boxer was fooled by his opponent's *feint* and dropped his guard. also V.

felicitous ADJ. apt; suitably expressed; well chosen. He was famous for his *felicitous* remarks and was called upon to serve as master-of-ceremonies at many a banquet.

fell ADJ. cruel; deadly. The newspapers told of the tragic spread of the *fell* disease.

felon N. person convicted of a grave crime. A convicted *felon* loses the right to vote.

ferment N. agitation; commotion. The entire country was in a state of *ferment.*

ferret V. drive or hunt out of hiding. She *ferreted* out their secret.

fervent ADJ. ardent; hot. She felt that the *fervent* praise was excessive and somewhat undeserved.

fervid ADJ. ardent. Her *fervid* enthusiasm inspired all of us to undertake the dangerous mission.

■ **fervor** N. glowing ardor. Their kiss was full of the *fervor* of first love.

fester V. generate pus. When her finger began to *fester,* the doctor lanced it and removed the splinter which had caused the pus to form.

festive ADJ. joyous; celebratory. Their wedding in the park was a *festive* occasion.

fete V. honor at a festival. The returning hero was *feted* at a community supper and dance. also N.

fetid ADJ. malodorous. The neglected wound became *fetid.*

fetish N. object supposed to possess magical powers; an object of special devotion. The native wore a *fetish* around his neck to ward off evil spirits.

fetter V. shackle. The prisoner was *fettered* to the wall.

fiasco N. total failure. Our ambitious venture ended in a *fiasco* and we were forced to flee.

fiat N. command. I cannot accept government by *fiat;* I feel that I must be consulted.

fickle ADJ. changeable; faithless. He discovered she was *fickle* and went out with many men.

fictitious ADJ. imaginary. Although this book purports to be a biography of George Washington, many of the incidents are *fictitious*.

fidelity N. loyalty. A dog's *fidelity* to its owner is one of the reasons why that animal is a favorite household pet.

fiduciary ADJ. pertaining to a position of trust. In his will, he stipulated that the bank act in a *fiduciary* capacity and manage his estate until his children became of age. also N.

figment N. invention; imaginary thing. That incident never took place; it is a *figment* of your imagination.

filch V. steal. The boys *filched* apples from the fruit stand.

filial ADJ. pertaining to a son or daughter. Many children forget their *filial* obligations and disregard the wishes of their parents.

finale N. conclusion. It is not until we reach the *finale* of this play that we can understand the author's message.

finesse N. delicate skill. The *finesse* and adroitness of the surgeon impressed the observers in the operating room.

finicky ADJ. too particular; fussy. The old lady was *finicky* about her food and ate very little.

finite ADJ. limited. It is difficult for humanity with its *finite* existence to grasp the infinite.

firebrand N. hothead; troublemaker. The police tried to keep track of all the local *firebrands* when the President came to town.

fissure N. crevice. The mountain climbers secured footholds in tiny *fissures* in the rock.

fitful ADJ. spasmodic; intermittent. After several *fitful* attempts, he decided to postpone the start of the project until he felt more energetic.

flaccid ADJ. flabby. His sedentary life had left him with *flaccid* muscles.

flagellate V. flog; whip. The Romans used to *flagellate* criminals with a whip that had three knotted strands.

flagging ADJ. weak; drooping. The encouraging cheers of the crowd lifted the team's *flagging* spirits.

■ **flagrant** ADJ. conspicuously wicked. We cannot condone such *flagrant* violations of the rules.

flail V. thresh grain by hand; strike or slap. In medieval times, warriors *flailed* their foe with a metal ball attached to a handle.

flair N. talent. She has an uncanny *flair* for discovering new artists before the public has become aware of their existence.

flamboyant ADJ. ornate. Modern architecture has discarded the *flamboyant* trimming on buildings and emphasizes simplicity of line.

flaunt V. display ostentatiously. She is not one of those actresses who *flaunt* their physical charms; she can act.

flay V. strip off skin; plunder. The criminal was condemned to be *flayed* alive.

fleck V. spot. Her cheeks, *flecked* with tears, were testimony to the hours of weeping.

■ **fledgling** ADJ. inexperienced. While it is necessary to provide these *fledgling* poets with an opportunity to present their work, it is not essential that we admire everything they write. also N.

fleece N. wool coat of a sheep. They shear sheep of their *fleece*, which they then comb into separate strands of wool.

fleece V. rob; plunder. The tricksters *fleeced* him of his inheritance.

flick N. light stroke as with a whip. The horse needed no encouragement; only one *flick* of the whip was all the jockey had to apply to get the animal to run at top speed.

flinch V. hesitate; shrink. He did not *flinch* in the face of danger but fought back bravely.

Test

Word List 19   *Synonyms and Antonyms*

Each of the following questions consists of a word in capital letters, followed by five lettered words or phrases. Choose the lettered word or phrase which is most nearly similar or the opposite of the word in capital letters and write the letter of your choice on your answer paper.

271. FANCIFUL (A) imaginative (B) knowing (C) elaborate (D) quick (E) lusty

272. FATUOUS (A) fatal (B) natal (C) terrible (D) sensible (E) tolerable

273. FEASIBLE (A) theoretical (B) impatient (C) constant (D) present (E) impractical

274. FECUNDITY (A) prophecy (B) futility (C) fruitfulness (D) need (E) dormancy

275. FEIGN (A) deserve (B) condemn (C) condone (D) attend (E) pretend

276. FELL (A) propitious (B) illiterate (C) catastrophic (D) futile (E) inherent

277. FERMENT (A) stir up (B) fill (C) ferret (D) mutilate (E) banish

278. FIASCO (A) cameo (B) mansion (C) pollution (D) success (E) gamble

279. FICKLE (A) fallacious (B) tolerant (C) loyal (D) hungry (E) stupid

280. FILCH (A) milk (B) purloin (C) itch (D) cancel (E) resent

281. FINITE (A) bounded (B) established (C) affirmative (D) massive (E) finicky

282. FLAIL (A) succeed (B) harvest (C) knife (D) strike (E) resent

283. FLAIR (A) conflagration (B) inspiration (C) bent (D) egregiousness (E) magnitude

284. FLAMBOYANT (A) old-fashioned (B) restrained (C) impulsive (D) cognizant (E) eloquent

285. FLEDGLING (A) weaving (B) bobbing (C) beginning (D) studying (E) flaying

Word List 20   flippancy-gaff

■ **flippancy** N. trifling gaiety. Your *flippancy* at this serious moment is offensive. flippant, ADJ.

floe N. mass of floating ice. The ship made slow progress as it battered its way through the ice *floes*.

flora N. plants of a region or era. Because she was a botanist, she spent most of her time studying the *flora* of the desert.

florid ADJ. flowery; ruddy. His complexion was even more *florid* than usual because of his anger.

flotilla N. small fleet. It is always an exciting and interesting moment when the fishing *flotilla* returns to port.

flotsam N. drifting wreckage. Beachcombers eke out a living by salvaging the *flotsam* and jetsam of the sea.

flourish V. grow well; prosper; decorate with ornaments. The orange trees *flourished* in the sun.

flout V. reject; mock. The headstrong youth *flouted* all authority; he refused to be curbed.

fluctuation N. wavering. Meteorologists watch the *fluctuations* of the barometer in order to predict the weather.

fluency N. smoothness of speech. He spoke French with *fluency* and ease.

fluster V. confuse. The teacher's sudden question *flustered* him and he stammered his reply.

fluted ADJ. having vertical parallel grooves (as in a pillar). All that remained of the ancient building were the *fluted* columns.

flux N. flowing; series of changes. While conditions are in such a state of *flux*, I do not wish to commit myself too deeply in this affair.

foible N. weakness; slight fault. We can overlook the *foibles* of our friends; no one is perfect.

foil N. contrast. In "Star Wars," dark, evil Darth Vader is a perfect *foil* for fair-haired, naive Luke Skywalker.

foil V. defeat; frustrate. In the end, Skywalker is able to *foil* Vader's diabolical schemes.

foist V. insert improperly; palm off. I will not permit you to *foist* such ridiculous ideas upon the membership of this group.

foment V. stir up; instigate. This report will *foment* dissension in the club.

foolhardy ADJ. rash. Don't be *foolhardy*. Get the advice of experienced people before undertaking this venture.

foppish ADJ. vain about dress and appearance. He tried to imitate the *foppish* manner of the young men of the court.

foray N. raid. The company staged a midnight *foray* against the enemy outpost.

forbearance N. patience. We must use *forbearance* in dealing with him because he is still weak from his illness.

foreboding N. premonition of evil. Caesar ridiculed his wife's *forebodings* about the Ides of March.

forensic ADJ. suitable to debate or courts of law. In her best *forensic* manner, the lawyer addressed the jury.

■ **foresight** N. ability to foresee future happenings; prudence. A wise investor, she had the foresight to buy land just before the current real estate boom.

formality N. adherence to established rules or procedures. Signing this position is a mere *formality*; it does not obligate you in any way.

formidable ADJ. menacing; threatening. We must not treat the battle lightly for we are facing a *formidable* foe.

forte N. strong point or special talent. I am not eager to play this rather serious role, for my *forte* is comedy.

fortitude N. bravery; courage. He was awarded the medal for his *fortitude* in the battle.

fortuitous ADJ. accidental; by chance. There is no connection between these two events; their timing is extremely *fortuitous*.

foster V. rear; encourage. According to the legend, Romulus and Remus were *fostered* by a she-wolf. also ADJ.

fracas N. brawl, melee. The military police stopped the *fracas* in the bar and arrested the belligerents.

fractious ADJ. unruly. The *fractious* horse unseated its rider.

frailty N. weakness. We had to pity the sick old woman because of her *frailty*.

franchise N. right granted by authority. The city issued a *franchise* to the company to operate surface transit lines on the streets for ninety-nine years. also V.

frantic ADJ. wild. At the time of the collision, many people became *frantic* with fear.

fraudulent ADJ. cheating; deceitful. The government seeks to prevent *fraudulent* and misleading advertising.

fraught ADJ. filled. Since this enterprise is *fraught* with danger, I will ask for volunteers who are willing to assume the risks.

fray N. brawl. The three musketeers were in the thick of the *fray*.

freebooter N. buccaneer. This town is a rather dangerous place to visit as it is frequented by pirates, *freebooters,* and other plunderers.

frenetic ADJ. frenzied; frantic. His *frenetic* activities convinced us that he had no organized plan of operation.

frenzied ADJ. madly excited. As soon as they smelled smoke, the *frenzied* animals milled about in their cages.

fresco N. painting on plaster (usually fresh). The cathedral is visited by many tourists who wish to admire the *frescoes* by Giotto.

freshet N. sudden flood. Motorists were warned that spring *freshets* had washed away several small bridges and that long detours would be necessary.

fret V. to be annoyed or vexed. To *fret* over your poor grades is foolish; instead, decide to work harder in the future.

friction N. clash in opinion; rubbing against. At this time when harmony is essential, we cannot afford to have any *friction* in our group.

frieze N. ornamental band on a wall. The *frieze* of the church was adorned with sculpture.

frigid ADJ. intensely cold. Alaska is in the *frigid* zone.

fritter V. waste. He could not apply himself to any task and *frittered* away his time in idle conversation.

■ **frivolity** N. lack of seriousness. We were distressed by his *frivolity* during the recent grave crisis. frivolous, ADJ.

frolicsome ADJ. prankish; gay. The *frolicsome* puppy tried to lick the face of its master.

frond N. fern leaf; palm or banana leaf. After the storm the beach was littered with the *fronds* of palm trees.

froward ADJ. disobedient; perverse; stubborn. Your *froward* behavior has alienated many of us who might have been your supporters.

frowzy ADJ. slovenly; unkempt; dirty. Her *frowzy* appearance and her cheap decorations made her appear ludicrous in this group.

fructify V. bear fruit. This peach tree should *fructify* in three years.

frugality N. thrift. In these difficult days, we must live with *frugality* or our money will be gone.

fruition N. bearing of fruit; fulfillment; realization. This building marks the *fruition* of all our aspirations and years of hard work.

frustrate V. thwart; defeat. We must *frustrate* this dictator's plan to seize control of the government.

fulcrum N. support on which a lever rests. If we use this stone as a *fulcrum* and the crowbar as a lever, we may be able to move this boulder.

fulgent ADJ. beaming; radiant. In the *fulgent* glow of the early sunrise, everything seemed bright and gleaming.

fulminate V. thunder; explode. The people against whom she *fulminated* were innocent of any wrongdoing.

fulsome ADJ. disgustingly excessive. His *fulsome* praise of the dictator annoyed his listeners.

functionary N. official. As his case was transferred from one *functionary* to another, he began to despair of ever reaching a settlement.

funereal ADJ. sad; solemn. I fail to understand why there is such a *funereal* atmosphere; we have lost a battle, not a war.

furor N. frenzy; great excitement. The story of her embezzlement of the funds created a *furor* on the Stock Exchange.

■ **furtive** ADJ. stealthy; sneaky. The boy gave a *furtive* look at his classmate's test paper.

fusion N. union; coalition. The opponents of the political party in power organized a *fusion* of disgruntled groups and became an important element in the election.

fustian ADJ. pompous; bombastic. Several in the audience were deceived by her *fustian* style; they mistook pomposity for erudition.

futile ADJ. ineffective; fruitless. Why waste your time on *futile* pursuits?

gadfly N. animal-biting fly; an irritating person. Like a *gadfly*, he irritated all the guests at the hotel; within forty-eight hours, everyone regarded him as an annoying busybody.

gaff N. hook; barbed fishing spear. When he attempted to land the sailfish, he was so nervous that he dropped the *gaff* into the sea. also V.

Test

Word List 20 *Synonyms*

Each of the questions below consists of a word in capital letters, followed by five lettered words or phrases. Choose the lettered word or phrase that is most nearly similar in meaning to the word in capital letters and write the letter of your choice on your answer paper.

286. FLORID (A) ruddy (B) rusty (C) ruined (D) patient (E) poetic
287. FOIL (A) bury (B) frustrate (C) shield (D) desire (E) gain
288. FOMENT (A) spoil (B) instigate (C) interrogate (D) spray (E) maintain
289. FOOLHARDY (A) strong (B) unwise (C) brave (D) futile (E) erudite
290. FOPPISH (A) scanty (B) radical (C) orthodox (D) dandyish (E) magnificent
291. FORAY (A) excursion (B) contest (C) ranger (D) intuition (E) fish
292. FORMIDABLE (A) dangerous (B) outlandish (C) grandiloquent (D) impenetrable (E) venerable
293. FOSTER (A) speed (B) fondle (C) become infected (D) raise (E) roll
294. FRANCHISE (A) subway (B) kiosk (C) license (D) reason (E) fashion
295. FRITTER (A) sour (B) chafe (C) dissipate (D) cancel (E) abuse
296. FRUGALITY (A) foolishness (B) extremity (C) indifference (D) enthusiasm (E) economy
297. FULGENT (A) dizzy (B) empty (C) diverse (D) shining (E) dreamy
298. FUROR (A) excitement (B) worry (C) flux (D) anteroom (E) lover
299. FURTIVE (A) underhanded (B) coy (C) brilliant (D) quick (E) abortive
300. GADFLY (A) humorist (B) nuisance (C) scholar (D) bum (E) thief

Word List 21   gainsay-gossamer

gainsay v. deny. She was too honest to *gainsay* the truth of the report.

gait N. manner of walking or running; speed. The lame man walked with an uneven *gait*.

galaxy N. the Milky Way; any collection of brilliant personalities. The deaths of such famous actors as Clark Gable, Gary Cooper and Spencer Tracy demonstrate that the *galaxy* of Hollywood superstars is rapidly disappearing.

gall N. bitterness; nerve. The knowledge of his failure filled him with *gall*.

gall v. annoy; chafe. Their taunts *galled* him.

galleon N. large sailing ship. The Spaniards pinned their hopes on the *galleon*, the large warship; the British, on the smaller and faster pinnace.

galvanize v. stimulate by shock; stir up. The entire nation was *galvanized* into strong military activity by the news of the attack on Pearl Harbor.

gambit N. opening in chess in which a piece is sacrificed. The player was afraid to accept his opponent's *gambit* because he feared a trap which as yet he could not see.

gambol v. skip; leap playfully. Watching children *gamboling* in the park is a pleasant experience. also N.

gamely ADV. Because he had fought *gamely* against a much superior boxer, the crowd gave him a standing ovation when he left the arena.

gamester N. gambler. An inveterate *gamester*, she was willing to wager on the outcome of any event, even one which involved the behavior of insects.

gamut N. entire range. In this performance, the leading lady was able to demonstrate the complete *gamut* of her acting ability.

gape v. open widely. The huge pit *gaped* before him: if he stumbled, he would fall in.

garbled ADJ. mixed up; based on false or unfair selection. The *garbled* report confused many readers who were not familiar with the facts. garble, v.

gargantuan ADJ. huge; enormous. The *gargantuan* wrestler was terrified of mice.

gargoyle N. waterspout carved in grotesque figures on building. The *gargoyles* adorning the Cathedral of Notre Dame in Paris are amusing in their grotesqueness.

garish ADJ. gaudy. She wore a *garish* rhinestone necklace.

garner v. gather; store up. She hoped to *garner* the world's literature in one library.

garnish v. decorate. Parsley was used to *garnish* the boiled potato. also N.

garrulity N. talkativeness. The man who married a dumb wife asked the doctor to make him deaf because of his wife's *garrulity* after her cure.

garrulous ADJ. loquacious; wordy. Many members avoided the company of the *garrulous* old gentleman because his constant chatter on trivial matters bored them.

gasconade N. bluster; boastfulness. Behind his front of *gasconade* and pompous talk, he tried to hide his inherent uncertainty and nervousness. also v.

gastronomy N. science of preparing and serving good food. One of the by-products of his trip to Europe was his interest in *gastronomy*; he enjoyed preparing and serving foreign dishes to his friends.

gauche ADJ. clumsy; boorish. Such remarks are *gauche* and out of place; you should apologize for making them.

gaudy ADJ. flashy; showy. Her *gaudy* taste in clothes appalled us.

gaunt ADJ. lean and angular; barren. His once round face looked surprisingly *gaunt* after he had lost weight.

gauntlet N. leather glove. Now that we have been challenged, we must take up the *gauntlet* and meet our adversary fearlessly.

gazette N. official periodical publication. He read the *gazettes* regularly for the announcement of his promotion.

genealogy N. record of descent; lineage. He was proud of his *genealogy* and constantly referred to the achievements of his ancestors.

generality N. vague statement. This report is filled with *generalities*; you must be more specific in your statements.

generic ADJ. characteristic of a class or species. You have made the mistake of thinking that his behavior is *generic*; actually, very few of his group behave the way he does.

genesis N. beginning; origin. Tracing the *genesis* of a family is the theme of "Roots."

geniality N. cheerfulness; kindliness; sympathy. This restaurant is famous and popular because of the *geniality* of the proprietor who tries to make everyone happy.

genre N. style of art illustrating scenes of common life. His painting of fisher folk at their daily tasks is an excellent illustration of *genre* art.

genteel ADJ. well-bred; elegant. We are looking for a man with a *genteel* appearance who can inspire confidence by his cultivated manner.

gentility N. those of gentle birth; refinement. Her family was proud of its *gentility* and elegance.

gentry N. people of standing; class of people just below nobility. The local *gentry* did not welcome the visits of the summer tourists and tried to ignore their presence in the community.

genuflect v. bend the knee as in worship. A proud democrat, he refused to *genuflect* to any man.

germane ADJ. pertinent; bearing upon the case at hand. The lawyer objected that the testimony being offered was not *germane* to the case at hand.

germinal ADJ. pertaining to a germ; creative. Such an idea is *germinal*; I am certain that it will influence thinkers and philosophers for many generations.

germinate v. cause to sprout; sprout. After the seeds *germinate* and develop their permanent leaves, the plants may be removed from the cold frames and transplanted to the garden.

gerrymander V. change voting district lines in order to favor a political party. The illogical pattern of the map of this congressional district is proof that the State Legislature *gerrymandered* this area in order to favor the majority party. also N.

gestate V. evolve, as in prenatal growth. While this scheme was being *gestated* by the conspirators, they maintained complete silence about their intentions.

gesticulation N. motion; gesture. Operatic performers are trained to make exaggerated *gesticulations* because of the large auditoriums in which they appear.

ghastly ADJ. horrible. The murdered man was a *ghastly* sight.

gibber V. speak foolishly. The demented man *gibbered* incoherently.

gibbet N. gallows. The bodies of the highwaymen were left dangling from the *gibbet* as a warning to other would-be transgressors.

gibe V. mock. As you *gibe* at their superstitious beliefs, do you realize that you, too, are guilty of similarly foolish thoughts?

giddy ADJ. light-hearted; dizzy. He felt his *giddy* youth was past.

gig N. two-wheeled carriage. As they drove down the street in their new *gig*, drawn by the dappled mare, they were cheered by the people who recognized them.

gingerly ADV. very carefully. To separate egg whites, first crack the egg *gingerly*.

gist N. essence. She was asked to give the *gist* of the essay in two sentences.

glaze V. cover with a thin and shiny surface. The freezing rain *glazed* the streets and made driving hazardous. also N.

glean V. gather leavings. After the crops had been harvested by the machines, the peasants were permitted to *glean* the wheat left in the fields.

glib ADJ. fluent. He is a *glib* and articulate speaker.

gloaming N. twilight. The snow began to fall in the *gloaming* and continued all through the night.

gloat V. express evil satisfaction; view malevolently. As you *gloat* over your ill-gotten wealth, do you think of the many victims you have defrauded?

glossary N. brief explanation of words used in the text. I have found the *glossary* in this book very useful; it has eliminated many trips to the dictionary.

glossy ADJ. smooth and shining. I want this photograph printed on *glossy* paper, not matte.

glower V. scowl. The angry boy *glowered* at his father.

glut V. overstock; fill to excess. The many manufacturers *glutted* the market and could not find purchasers for the many articles they had produced. also N.

glutinous ADJ. sticky; viscous. Molasses is a *glutinous* substance.

■ **glutton** N. someone who eats too much. You can be a gourmet without being a *glutton*.

gluttonous ADJ. greedy for food. The *gluttonous* boy ate all the cookies.

gnarled ADJ. twisted. The *gnarled* oak tree had been a landmark for years and was mentioned in several deeds.

gnome N. dwarf; underground spirit. In medieval mythology, *gnomes* were the special guardians and inhabitants of subterranean mines.

goad V. urge on. He was *goaded* by his friends until he yielded to their wishes. also N.

gorge V. stuff oneself. The gluttonous guest *gorged* himself with food as though he had not eaten for days.

gory ADJ. bloody. The audience shuddered as they listened to the details of the *gory* massacre.

gossamer ADJ. sheer; like cobwebs. Nylon can be woven into *gossamer* or thick fabrics. also N.

Test

Word List 21   *Synonyms*

Each of the questions below consists of a word in capital letters, followed by five lettered words or phrases. Choose the lettered word or phrase that is most nearly similar in meaning to the word in capital letters and write the letter of your choice on your answer paper.

301. GALLEON (A) liquid measure (B) ship (C) armada (D) company (E) printer's proof
302. GARISH (A) sordid (B) flashy (C) prominent (D) lusty (E) thoughtful
303. GARNER (A) prevent (B) assist (C) collect (D) compute (E) consult
304. GARNISH (A) paint (B) garner (C) adorn (D) abuse (E) banish
305. GARRULITY (A) credulity (B) senility (C) loquaciousness (D) speciousness (E) artistry
306. GARRULOUS (A) arid (B) hasty (C) sociable (D) quaint (E) talkative
307. GASCONADE (A) transparency (B) cleanliness (C) bluster (D) imposture (E) seizure
308. GAUCHE (A) rigid (B) awkward (C) swift (D) tacit (E) needy
309. GAUNT (A) victorious (B) tiny (C) stylish (D) haggard (E) nervous
310. GENUFLECT (A) falsify (B) trick (C) project (D) bend the knee (E) pronounce correctly
311. GERMANE (A) bacteriological (B) Middle European (C) prominent (D) warlike (E) relevant
312. GERMINAL (A) creative (B) excused (C) sterilized (D) primitive (F) strategic
313. GIST (A) chaff (B) summary (C) expostulation (D) expiation (E) chore

314. GLIB (A) slippery (B) fashionable (C) antiquated (D) articulate (E) anticlimactic

315. GNOME (A) fury (B) giant (C) dwarf (D) native (E) alien

Word List 22   gouge-hiatus

gouge V. tear out. In that fight, all the rules were forgotten; the adversaries bit, kicked, and tried to *gouge* each other's eyes out.

gourmand N. epicure; person who takes excessive pleasure in food and drink. The *gourmand* liked the French cuisine.

gourmet N. connoisseur of food and drink. The *gourmet* stated that this was the best onion soup she had ever tasted.

granary N. storehouse for grain. We have reason to be thankful, for our crops were good and our *granaries* are full.

grandiloquent ADJ. pompous; bombastic; using high-sounding language. The politician could never speak simply; she was always *grandiloquent*.

grandiose ADJ. imposing; impressive. His *grandiose* manner impressed those who met him for the first time.

granulate V. form into grains. Sugar that has been *granulated* dissolves more readily than lump sugar. granule, N.

graphic ADJ. pertaining to the art of delineating; vividly described. I was particularly impressed by the *graphic* presentation of the storm.

grapple V. wrestle; come to grips with. He *grappled* with the burglar and overpowered him.

gratify V. please. Her parents were *gratified* by her success.

gratis ADJ. free. The company offered to give one package *gratis* to every purchaser of one of their products. also ADJ.

gratuitous ADJ. given freely; unwarranted. I resent your *gratuitous* remarks because no one asked for them.

gratuity N. tip. Many service employees rely more on *gratuities* than on salaries for their livelihood.

■ **gravity** N. seriousness. We could tell we were in serious trouble from the *gravity* of her expression. (secondary meaning) grave, ADJ.

gregarious ADJ. sociable. She was not *gregarious* and preferred to be alone most of the time.

grimace N. a facial distortion to show feeling such as pain, disgust, etc. Even though he remained silent, his *grimace* indicated his displeasure. also V.

grisly ADJ. ghastly. She shuddered at the *grisly* sight.

grotesque ADJ. fantastic; comically hideous. On Halloween people enjoy wearing *grotesque* costumes.

grotto N. small cavern. The Blue *Grotto* in Capri can be entered only by small boats rowed by natives through a natural opening in the rocks.

grovel V. crawl or creep on ground; remain prostrate. Even though we have been defeated, we do not have to *grovel* before our conquerors.

■ **grudging** ADJ. unwilling; reluctant; stingy. We received only *grudging* support from the mayor despite his earlier promises of aid.

gruel N. liquid food made by boiling oatmeal, etc., in milk or water. Our daily allotment of *gruel* made the meal not only monotonous but also unpalatable.

grueling ADJ. exhausting. The marathon is a *grueling* race.

gruesome ADJ. grisly. People screamed when her *gruesome* appearance was flashed on the screen.

gruff ADJ. rough-mannered. Although he was blunt and *gruff* with most people, he was always gentle with children.

guffaw N. boisterous laughter. The loud *guffaws* that came from the closed room indicated that the members of the committee had not yet settled down to serious business. also V.

guile N. deceit; duplicity. She achieved her high position by *guile* and treachery.

guileless ADJ. without deceit. He is naive, simple, and *guileless;* he cannot be guilty of fraud.

guise N. appearance; costume. In the *guise* of a plumber, the detective investigated the murder case.

■ **gullible** ADJ. easily deceived. He preyed upon *gullible* people, who believed his stories of easy wealth.

gustatory ADJ. affecting the sense of taste. This food is particularly *gustatory* because of the spices it contains.

gusto N. enjoyment; enthusiasm. He accepted the assignment with such *gusto* that I feel he would have been satisfied with a smaller salary.

gusty ADJ. windy. The *gusty* weather made sailing precarious.

guttural ADJ. pertaining to the throat. *Guttural* sounds are produced in the throat or in the back of the tongue and palate.

habiliments N. garb; clothing. Although not a minister, David Belasco used to wear clerical *habiliments*.

hackles N. hairs on back and neck of a dog. The dog's *hackles* rose and he began to growl as the sound of footsteps grew louder.

hackneyed ADJ. commonplace; trite. The English teacher criticized her story because of its *hackneyed* and unoriginal plot.

haggard ADJ. wasted away; gaunt. After his long illness, he was pale and *haggard*.

haggle V. argue about prices. I prefer to shop in a store that has a one-price policy because, whenever I *haggle* with a shopkeeper, I am never certain that I paid a fair price for the articles I purchased.

halcyon ADJ. calm; peaceful. In those *halcyon* days, people were not worried about sneak attacks and bombings.

hale ADJ. healthy. After a brief illness, he was soon *hale*.

hallowed ADJ. blessed; consecrated. She was laid to rest in *hallowed* ground.

hallucination N. delusion. I think you were frightened by a *hallucination* which you created in your own mind.

■ hamper V. obstruct. The minority party agreed not to *hamper* the efforts of the leaders to secure a lasting peace.

hap N. chance; luck. In his poem *Hap*, Thomas Hardy objects to the part chance plays in our lives.

haphazard ADJ. random; by chance. His *haphazard* reading left him unacquainted with the authors of the books.

hapless ADJ. unfortunate. This *hapless* creature had never known a moment's pleasure.

harangue N. noisy speech. In her lengthy *harangue,* the principal berated the offenders. also V.

harbor V. provide a refuge for; hide. The church *harbored* illegal aliens who were political refugees.

harass V. to annoy by repeated attacks. When he could not pay his bills as quickly as he had promised, he was *harassed* by his creditors.

harbinger N. forerunner. The crocus is an early *harbinger* of spring.

harping N. tiresome dwelling on a subject. After he had reminded me several times about what he had done for me, I told him to stop *harping* on my indebtedness to him. harp, V.

harridan N. shrewish hag. Most people avoided the *harridan* because they feared her abusive and vicious language.

harrow V. break up ground after plowing; torture. I don't want to *harrow* you at this time by asking you to recall the details of your unpleasant experience.

harry V. raid. The guerrilla band *harried* the enemy nightly.

haughtiness N. pride; arrogance. I resent his *haughtiness* because he is no better than we are.

hauteur N. haughtiness. His snobbishness is obvious to all who witness his *hauteur* when he talks to those whom he considers his social inferiors.

hawser N. large rope. The ship was tied to the pier by a *hawser*.

hazardous ADJ. dangerous. Your occupation is too *hazardous* for insurance companies to consider your application.

hazy ADJ. slightly obscure. In *hazy* weather, you cannot see the top of this mountain.

■ heckler N. person who harasses others. The *heckler* kept interrupting the speaker with rude remarks. heckle, V.

hedonism N. belief that pleasure is the sole aim in life. *Hedonism* and asceticism are opposing philosophies of human behavior.

heedless ADJ. not noticing; disregarding. He drove on, *heedless* of the warnings placed at the side of the road that it was dangerous.

hegira flight, especially Mohammed's flight from Mecca to Medina. Mohammed began his *hegira* when he was 53 years old.

heinous ADJ. atrocious; hatefully bad. Hitler's *heinous* crimes will never be forgotten.

herbivorous ADJ. grain-eating. Some *herbivorous* animals have two stomachs for digesting their food.

heresy N. opinion contrary to popular belief; opinion contrary to accepted religion. He was threatened with excommunication because his remarks were considered to be pure *heresy*.

heretic N. person who maintains opinions contrary to the doctrines of the church. She was punished by the Spanish Inquisition because she was a *heretic*.

hermetically ADV. sealed by fusion so as to be airtight. After these bandages are sterilized, they are placed in *hermetically* sealed containers.

hermitage N. home of a hermit. Even in his remote *hermitage* he could not escape completely from the world.

heterogeneous ADJ. dissimilar. In *heterogeneous* groupings, we have an unassorted grouping, while in homogeneous groupings we have people or things which have common traits.

hew V. cut to pieces with ax or sword. The cavalry rushed into the melee and *hewed* the enemy with their swords.

hiatus N. gap; pause. There was a *hiatus* of twenty years in the life of Rip van Winkle.

Test

Word List 22   *Antonyms*

Each of the questions below consists of a word in capital letters, followed by five lettered words or phrases. Choose the lettered word or phrase that is most nearly opposite in meaning to the word in capital letters and write the letter of your choice on your answer paper.

316. GRANDIOSE (A) false (B) ideal (C) proud (D) simple (E) functional

317. GRATUITOUS (A) warranted (B) frank (C) ingenuous (D) frugal (E) pithy

318. GREGARIOUS (A) antisocial (B) anticipatory (C) glorious (D) horrendous (E) similar

319. GRISLY (A) suggestive (B) doubtful (C) untidy (D) pleasant (E) boarish

320. GULLIBLE (A) incredulous (B) fickle (C) tantamount (D) easy (E) stylish

321. GUSTO (A) noise (B) panic (C) atmosphere (D) gloom (E) distaste

322. GUSTY (A) calm (B) noisy (C) fragrant (D) routine (E) gloomy

323. HACKNEYED (A) carried (B) original (C) banned (D) timely (E) oratorical

324. HAGGARD (A) shrewish (B) inspired (C) plump
     (D) maidenly (E) vast
325. HALCYON (A) wasteful (B) prior (C) subsequent
     (D) puerile (E) martial
326. HAPHAZARD (A) safe (B) indifferent
     (C) deliberate (D) tense (E) conspiring
327. HAPLESS (A) cheerful (B) consistent
     (C) fortunate (D) considerate (E) shapely

328. HEGIRA (A) return (B) harem (C) oasis
     (D) panic (E) calm
329. HERETIC (A) sophist (B) believer (C) interpreter
     (D) pacifist (E) owner
330. HETEROGENEOUS (A) orthodox (B) pagan
     (C) unlikely (D) similar (E) banished

Word List 23   hibernal-imbue

hibernal ADJ. wintry. Bears prepare for their long *hibernal* sleep by overeating.

hibernate V. sleep throughout the winter. Bears are one of the many species of animals that *hibernate*.

hierarchy N. body divided into ranks. It was difficult to step out of one's place in this *hierarchy*.

hieroglyphic N. picture writing. The discovery of the Rosetta Stone enabled scholars to read the ancient Egyptian *hieroglyphics*.

■ **hilarity** N. boisterous mirth. This *hilarity* is improper on this solemn day of mourning.

hindmost ADJ. furthest behind. The coward could always be found in the *hindmost* lines whenever a battle was being waged.

■ **hindrance** N. block; obstacle. Stalled cars along the highway are a *hindrance* to traffic that tow trucks should remove without delay. hinder, V.

hireling N. one who serves for hire [usually used contemptuously]. In a matter of such importance, I do not wish to deal with *hirelings;* I must meet with the chief.

hirsute ADJ. hairy. He was a *hirsute* individual with a heavy black beard.

histrionic ADJ. theatrical. He was proud of his *histrionic* ability and wanted to play the role of Hamlet. histrionics, N.

hoary ADJ. white with age. The man was *hoary* and wrinkled when he was 70.

hoax N. trick; practical joke. Embarrassed by the *hoax,* he reddened and left the room. also V.

hogshead N. large barrel. On the trip to England, the ship carried munitions; on its return trip, *hogsheads* filled with French wines and Scotch liquors.

holocaust N. destruction by fire. Citizens of San Francisco remember that the destruction of the city was caused not by the earthquake but by the *holocaust* that followed.

holster N. pistol case. Even when he was not in uniform, he carried a *holster* and pistol under his arm.

homage N. honor; tribute. In her speech she tried to pay *homage* to a great man.

homespun ADJ. domestic; made at home. *Homespun* wit like *homespun* cloth was often coarse and plain.

homily N. sermon; serious warning. His speeches were always *homilies*, advising his listeners to repent and reform.

homogeneous ADJ. of the same kind. Educators try to put pupils of similar abilities into classes because they believe that this *homogeneous* grouping is advisable. homogeneity, N.

hone V. sharpen. To make shaving easier, he *honed* his razor with great care.

hoodwink V. deceive; delude. Having been *hoodwinked* once by the fast-talking salesman, he was extremely cautious when he went to purchase a used car.

horde N. crowd. Just before Christmas the stores are filled with *hordes* of shoppers.

hortatory ADJ. encouraging; exhortive. The crowd listened to his *hortatory* statements with ever-growing excitement; finally they rushed from the hall to carry out his suggestions.

horticultural ADJ. pertaining to cultivation of gardens. When he bought his house, he began to look for flowers and decorative shrubs, and began to read books dealing with *horticultural* matters.

hostelry N. inn. Travelers interested in economy should stay at *hostelries* and pensions rather than fashionable hotels.

hovel N. shack; small, wretched house. He wondered how poor people could stand living in such a *hovel*.

hover V. hang about; wait nearby. The police helicopter *hovered* above the accident.

hoyden N. boisterous girl. Although she is now a *hoyden*, I am sure she will outgrow her tomboyish ways and quiet down.

hubbub N. confused uproar. The marketplace was a scene of *hubbub* and excitement; in all the noise, we could not distinguish particular voices.

hubris N. arrogance; excessive self-conceit. Filled with *hubris,* Lear refused to heed his friends' warnings.

hue N. color; aspect. The aviary contained birds of every possible *hue.*

hue and cry N. outcry. When her purse was snatched, she raised such a *hue and cry* that the thief was captured.

humane ADJ. kind. His *humane* and considerate treatment of the unfortunate endeared him to all.

humdrum ADJ. dull; monotonous. After his years of adventure, he could not settle down to a *humdrum* existence.

humid ADJ. damp. She could not stand the *humid* climate and moved to a drier area.

■ **humility** N. humbleness of spirit. He spoke with a *humility* and lack of pride that impressed his listeners.

hummock N. small hill. The ascent of the *hummock* is not difficult and the view from the hilltop is ample reward for the effort.

humus N. substance formed by decaying vegetable matter. In order to improve his garden, he spread *humus* over his lawn and flower beds.

hurtle V. crash; rush. The runaway train *hurtled* towards disaster.

husbandry N. frugality; thrift; agriculture. He accumulated his small fortune by diligence and *husbandry*. husband, V.

hustings N. meetings particularly to choose candidates. Congress adjourned so that the members could attend to their political *hustings.*

hybrid N. mongrel; mixed breed. Mendel's formula explains the appearance of *hybrids* and pure species in breeding. also ADJ.

hydrophobia N. rabies; fear of water. A dog that bites a human being must be observed for symptoms of *hydrophobia.*

■ **hyperbole** N. exaggeration; overstatement. This salesman is guilty of *hyperbole* in describing his product; it is wise to discount his claims. hyperbolic, ADJ.

hyperborean ADJ. situated in extreme north; arctic; cold. The *hyperborean* blasts brought snow and ice to the countryside.

hypercritical ADJ. excessively exacting. You are *hypercritical* in your demands for perfection; we all make mistakes.

hypochondriac N. person unduly worried about his health; worrier without cause about illness. The doctor prescribed chocolate pills for his patient who was a *hypochondriac.*

■ **hypocritical** ADJ. pretending to be virtuous; deceiving. I resent his *hypocritical* posing as a friend for I know he is interested only in his own advancement. hypocrisy, N.

■ **hypothetical** ADJ. based on assumptions or hypotheses. Why do we have to consider *hypothetical* cases when we have actual case histories which we may examine? hypothesis, N.

ichthyology N. study of fish. Jacques Cousteau's programs about sea life have advanced the cause of *ichthyology.*

icon N. religious image; idol. The *icons* on the walls of the church were painted in the 13th century.

iconoclastic ADJ. attacking cherished traditions. George Bernard Shaw's *iconoclastic* plays often startled more conventional people. iconoclasm, N.

ideology N. ideas of a group of people. That *ideology* is dangerous to this country because it embraces undemocratic philosophies.

idiom N. special usage in language. I could not understand their *idiom* because literal translation made no sense.

idiosyncrasy N. peculiarity; eccentricity. One of his personal *idiosyncrasies* was his habit of rinsing all cutlery given him in a restaurant.

idiosyncratic ADJ. private; peculiar to an individual. Such behavior is *idiosyncratic;* it is as easily identifiable as a signature.

idolatry N. worship of idols; excessive admiration. Such *idolatry* of singers of country music is typical of the excessive enthusiasm of youth.

idyllic ADJ. charmingly carefree; simple. Far from the city, she led an *idyllic* existence in her rural retreat.

igneous ADJ. produced by fire; volcanic. Lava, pumice, and other *igneous* rocks are found in great abundance around Mount Vesuvius near Naples.

ignoble ADJ. of lowly origin; unworthy. This plan is inspired by *ignoble* motives and I must, therefore, oppose it.

ignominious ADJ. disgraceful. The country smarted under the *ignominious* defeat and dreamed of the day when it would be victorious. ignominy, N.

illimitable ADJ. infinite. Man, having explored the far corners of the earth, is now reaching out into *illimitable* space.

illusion N. misleading vision. It is easy to create an optical *illusion* in which lines of equal length appear different.

illusive ADJ. deceiving. This is only a mirage; let us not be fooled by its *illusive* effect.

■ **illusory** ADJ. deceptive; not real. Unfortunately, the costs of running the lemonade stand were so high that Tom's profits proved *illusory.*

imbecility N. weakness of mind. I am amazed at the *imbecility* of the readers of these trashy magazines.

imbibe V. drink in. The dry soil *imbibed* the rain quickly.

imbroglio N. a complicated situation; perplexity; entanglement. He was called in to settle the *imbroglio* but failed to bring harmony into the situation.

imbrue V. drench, stain, especially with blood. As the instigator of this heinous murder, he is as much *imbrued* in blood as the actual assassin.

imbue V. saturate, fill. His visits to the famous Gothic cathedrals *imbued* him with feelings of awe and reverence.

Test

Word List 23 *Antonyms*

Each of the questions below consists of a word in capital letters, followed by five lettered words or phrases. Choose the lettered word or phrase that is most nearly opposite in meaning to the word in capital letters and write the letter of your choice on your answer paper.

331. HIBERNAL (A) musical (B) summerlike (C) local (D) seasonal (E) discordant

332. HILARITY (A) gloom (B) heartiness (C) weakness (D) casualty (E) paucity

333. HIRSUTE (A) scaly (B) bald (C) erudite
     (D) quiet (E) long

334. HORTATORY (A) inquiring (B) denying
     (C) killing (D) frantic (E) dissuading

335. HOYDEN (A) burden (B) light (C) demure girl
     (D) game (E) traffic

336. HUBBUB (A) calm (B) fury (C) capital
     (D) axle (E) wax

337. HUMMOCK (A) unmusical (B) scorn
     (C) wakefulness (D) vale (E) vestment

338. HUSBANDRY (A) sportsmanship (B) dishonesty
     (C) wastefulness (D) friction (E) cowardice

339. HYBRID (A) productive (B) special (C) purebred
     (D) oafish (E) genius

340. HYPERBOLE (A) velocity (B) climax (C) curve
     (D) understatement (E) expansion

341. HYPERBOREAN (A) sultry (B) pacific
     (C) noteworthy (D) western (E) wooded

342. HYPERCRITICAL (A) tolerant (B) false
     (C) extreme (D) inarticulate (E) cautious

343. HYPOTHETICAL (A) rational (B) fantastic
     (C) wizened (D) opposed (E) axiomatic

344. IGNOBLE (A) produced by fire (B) worthy
     (C) given to questioning (D) huge (E) known

345. ILLUSIVE (A) not deceptive (B) not certain
     (C) not obvious (D) not coherent (E) not brilliant

Word List 24   immaculate-incessant

immaculate ADJ. pure; spotless. The West Point cadets were *immaculate* as they lined up for inspection.

imminent ADJ. impending; near at hand. The *imminent* battle will soon determine our success or failure in this conflict.

immobility N. state of being immovable. Modern armies cannot afford the luxury of *immobility*, as they are vulnerable to attack while standing still.

immolate V. offer as a sacrifice. The tribal king offered to *immolate* his daughter to quiet the angry gods.

immune ADJ. exempt. He was fortunately *immune* from the disease and could take care of the sick.

immure V. imprison; shut up in confinement. For the two weeks before the examination, the student *immured* himself in his room and concentrated upon his studies.

■ **immutable** ADJ. unchangeable. Scientists are constantly seeking to discover the *immutable* laws of nature.

impair V. worsen; diminish in value. This arrest will *impair* her reputation in the community.

impale V. pierce. He was *impaled* by the spear hurled by his adversary.

impalpable ADJ. imperceptible; intangible. The ash is so fine that it is *impalpable* to the touch but it can be seen as a fine layer covering the window ledge.

impasse N. predicament from which there is no escape. In this *impasse*, all turned to prayer as their last hope.

impassive ADJ. without feeling; not affected by pain. The American Indian has been incorrectly depicted as an *impassive* individual, undemonstrative and stoical.

impeach V. charge with crime in office; indict. The angry congressman wanted to *impeach* the President for his misdeeds.

impeccable ADJ. faultless. He was proud of his *impeccable* manners.

■ **impecunious** ADJ. without money. Now that he was wealthy, he gladly contributed to funds to assist the *impecunious* and the disabled.

impediment N. hindrance; stumbling-block. She had a speech *impediment* that prevented her speaking clearly.

impending ADJ. nearing; approaching. The entire country was saddened by the news of his *impending* death.

impenitent ADJ. not repentant. We could see by his brazen attitude that he was *impenitent*.

imperious ADJ. domineering. His *imperious* manner indicated that he had long been accustomed to assuming command.

impermeable ADJ. impervious; not permitting passage through its substance. This new material is *impermeable* to liquids.

impertinent ADJ. insolent. I regard your remarks as *impertinent* and I resent them.

imperturbability N. calmness. We are impressed by his *imperturbability* in this critical moment and are calmed by it.

imperturbable ADJ. calm; placid. He remained *imperturbable* and in full command of the situation in spite of the hysteria and panic all around him.

impervious ADJ. not penetrable; not permitting passage through. You cannot change their habits for their minds are *impervious* to reasoning.

impetuous ADJ. violent; hasty; rash. We tried to curb his *impetuous* behavior because we felt that in his haste he might offend some people.

impetus N. moving force. It is a miracle that there were any survivors since the two automobiles that collided were traveling with great *impetus*.

impiety N. irreverence; wickedness. We must regard your blasphemy as an act of *impiety*.

impinge V. infringe; touch; collide with. How could they be married without *impinging* on one another's freedom?

impious ADJ. irreverent. The congregation was offended by her *impious* remarks.

implacable ADJ. incapable of being pacified. Madame Defarge was the *implacable* enemy of the Evremonde family.

implausible ADJ. unlikely; unbelievable. Though her alibi seemed *implausible*, it in fact turned out to be true.

implement V. supply what is needed; furnish with tools. I am unwilling to *implement* this plan until I have assurances that it has the full approval of your officials. also N.

■ **implication** N. that which is hinted at or suggested. If I understand the *implications* of your remark, you do not trust our captain.

implicit ADJ. understood but not stated. It is *implicit* that you will come to our aid if we are attacked.

imply V. suggest a meaning not expressed; signify. Even though your statement does not declare that you are at war with that country, your actions *imply* that that is the actual situation.

impolitic ADJ. not wise. I think it is *impolitic* to raise this issue at the present time because the public is too angry.

imponderable ADJ. weightless. I can evaluate the data gathered in this study; the *imponderable* items are not so easily analyzed.

import N. significance. I feel that you have not grasped the full *import* of the message sent to us by the enemy.

importunate ADJ. urging; demanding. He tried to hide from his *importunate* creditors until his allowance arrived.

importune V. beg earnestly. I must *importune* you to work for peace at this time.

imposture N. assuming a false identity; masquerade. She was imprisoned for her *imposture* of a doctor.

impotent ADJ. weak; ineffective. Although he wished to break the nicotine habit, he found himself *impotent* in resisting the craving for a cigarette.

imprecate V. curse; pray that evil will befall. To *imprecate* Hitler's atrocities is not enough; we must insure against any future practice of genocide.

impregnable ADJ. invulnerable. Until the development of the airplane as a military weapon, the fort was considered *impregnable*.

imprimatur N. permission to print or publish a book. The publication of the book was delayed until the *imprimatur* of the State Education Committee was granted.

impromptu ADJ. without previous preparation. Her listeners were amazed that such a thorough presentation could be made in an *impromptu* speech.

impropriety N. state of being inappropriate. Because of the *impropriety* of his costume, he was denied entrance into the dining room.

improvident ADJ. thriftless. He was constantly being warned to mend his *improvident* ways and begin to "save for a rainy day."

improvise V. compose on the spur of the moment. She would sit at the piano and *improvise* for hours on themes from Bach and Handel.

■ **imprudent** ADJ. lacking caution; injudicious. It is *imprudent* to exercise vigorously and become overheated when you are unwell.

impugn V. doubt; challenge; gainsay. I cannot *impugn* your honesty without evidence.

impunity N. freedom from punishment. The bully mistreated everyone in the class with *impunity* for he felt that no one would dare retaliate.

imputation N. charge; reproach. You cannot ignore the *imputations* in his speech that you are the guilty party.

impute V. attribute; ascribe. If I wished to *impute* blame to the officers in charge of this program, I would come out and state it definitely and without hesitation.

■ **inadvertently** ADV. carelessly; unintentionally; by oversight. She *inadvertently* omitted two questions on the examination and mismarked her answer sheet.

inalienable ADJ. not to be taken away; nontransferable. The Declaration of Independence mentions the *inalienable* rights that all of us possess.

■ **inane** ADJ. silly; senseless. Such comments are *inane* because they do not help us solve our problem. inanity, N.

inanimate ADJ. lifeless. She was asked to identify the still and *inanimate* body.

inarticulate ADJ. speechless; producing indistinct speech. He became *inarticulate* with rage and uttered sounds without meaning.

incandescent ADJ. strikingly bright; shining with intense heat. If you leave on an *incandescent* light bulb, it quickly grows too hot to touch.

incantation N. singing or chanting of magic spells; magical formula. Uttering *incantations* to make the brew more potent, the witch doctor stirred the liquid in the caldron.

incapacitate V. disable. During the winter, many people were *incapacitated* by respiratory ailments.

incarcerate V. imprison. The warden will *incarcerate* the felon after conviction.

incarnadine V. stain crimson or blood-color. After killing Duncan, Macbeth cries that his hands are so bloodstained that they would "the multitudinous seas *incarnadine*."

incarnate ADJ. endowed with flesh; personified. Your attitude is so fiendish that you must be a devil *incarnate*.

incarnation N. act of assuming a human body and human nature. The *incarnation* of Jesus Christ is a basic tenet of Christian theology.

incendiary N. arsonist. The fire spread in such an unusual manner that the fire department chiefs were certain that it had been set by an *incendiary*. also ADJ.

incense V. enrage; infuriate. Unkindness to children *incensed* her.

incentive N. spur; motive. Students who dislike school must be given an *incentive* to learn.

inception N. start; beginning. She was involved with the project from its *inception*.

incessant ADJ. uninterrupted. The crickets kept up an *incessant* chirping which disturbed our attempts to fall asleep.

Test

Word List 24   *Synonyms and Antonyms*

Each of the following questions consists of a word in capital letters, followed by five lettered words or phrases. Choose the lettered word or phrase which is most nearly similar or the opposite of the word in capital letters and write the letter of your choice on your answer paper.

346. IMMOLATE (A) debate (B) scour (C) sacrifice (D) sanctify (E) ratify
347. IMMUTABLE (A) silent (B) changeable (C) articulate (D) loyal (E) varied
348. IMPAIR (A) separate (B) make amends (C) make worse (D) falsify (E) cancel
349. IMPALPABLE (A) obvious (B) combined (C) high (D) connecting (E) lost
350. IMPASSIVE (A) active (B) demonstrative (C) perfect (D) anxious (E) irritated
351. IMPECCABLE (A) unmentionable (B) quotable (C) blinding (D) faulty (E) hampering

352. IMPECUNIOUS (A) affluent (B) afflicted (C) affectionate (D) affable (E) afraid
353. IMPERVIOUS (A) impenetrable (B) perplexing (C) chaotic (D) cool (E) perfect
354. IMPETUOUS (A) rash (B) inane (C) just (D) flagrant (E) redolent
355. IMPOLITIC (A) campaigning (B) advisable (C) aggressive (D) legal (E) fortunate
356. IMPORTUNE (A) export (B) plead (C) exhibit (D) account (E) visit
357. IMPROMPTU (A) prompted (B) appropriate (C) rehearsed (D) foolish (E) vast
358. INALIENABLE (A) inherent (B) repugnant (C) closed to immigration (D) full (E) accountable
359. INANE (A) passive (B) wise (C) intoxicated (D) mellow (E) silent
360. INCARCERATE (A) inhibit (B) acquit (C) account (D) imprison (E) force

Word List 25   inchoate-ingenious

inchoate ADJ. recently begun; rudimentary; elementary. Before the Creation, the world was an *inchoate* mass.

incidence N. falling on a body; a casual occurrence. We must determine the angle of *incidence* of the rays of light.

incipient ADJ. beginning; in an early stage. I will go to sleep early for I want to break an *incipient* cold.

incisive ADJ. cutting; sharp. His *incisive* remarks made us see the fallacy in our plans.

incite V. arouse to action. The demagogue *incited* the mob to take action into its own hands.

inclement ADJ. stormy; unkind. I like to read a good book in *inclement* weather.

inclusive ADJ. tending to include all. This meeting will run from January 10 to February 15 *inclusive*.

incognito ADV. with identity concealed; using an assumed name. The monarch enjoyed traveling through the town *incognito* and mingling with the populace. also ADJ.

incoherence N. lack of relevance; lack of intelligibility. The bereaved father sobbed and stammered, caught up in the *incoherence* of his grief.

incommodious ADJ. not spacious. In their *incommodious* quarters, they had to improvise for closet space.

■ **incompatible** ADJ. inharmonious. The married couple argued incessantly and finally decided to separate because they were *incompatible*.

incongruity N. lack of harmony; absurdity. The *incongruity* of his wearing sneakers with formal attire amused the observers.

incongruous ADJ. not fitting; absurd. These remarks do not have any relationship to the problem at hand; they are *incongruous* and should be stricken from the record.

■ **inconsequential** ADJ. of trifling significance. Your objections are *inconsequential* and may be disregarded.

incontinent ADJ. lacking self-restraint; licentious. His *incontinent* behavior off stage shocked many people and they refused to attend the plays and movies in which he appeared.

incontrovertible ADJ. indisputable. We must yield to the *incontrovertible* evidence which you have presented and free your client.

incorporeal ADJ. immaterial; without a material body. We must devote time to the needs of our *incorporeal* mind as well as our corporeal body.

■ **incorrigible** ADJ. uncorrectable. Because he was an *incorrigible* criminal, he was sentenced to life imprisonment.

incredulity N. a tendency to disbelief. Your *incredulity* in the face of all the evidence is hard to understand.

incredulous ADJ. withholding belief; skeptical. The *incredulous* judge refused to accept the statement of the defendant.

increment N. increase. The new contract calls for a 10 percent *increment* in salary for each employee for the next two years.

incriminate V. accuse. The evidence gathered against the racketeers *incriminates* some high public officials as well.

incubate V. hatch; scheme. Inasmuch as our supply of electricity is cut off, we shall have to rely on the hens to *incubate* these eggs.

incubus N. burden; mental care; nightmare. The *incubus* of financial worry helped bring on her nervous breakdown.

inculcate V. teach. In an effort to *inculcate* religious devotion, the officials ordered that the school day begin with the singing of a hymn.

incumbent N. officeholder. The newly elected public official received valuable advice from the present *incumbent.* also ADJ.

incur V. bring upon oneself. His parents refused to pay any future debts he might *incur.*

incursion N. temporary invasion. The nightly *incursions* and hit-and-run raids of our neighbors across the border tried the patience of the country to the point where we decided to retaliate in force.

indefatigable ADJ. tireless. He was *indefatigable* in his constant efforts to raise funds for the Red Cross.

indemnify V. make secure against loss; compensate for loss. The city will *indemnify* all home owners whose property is spoiled by this project.

indenture V. bind as servant or apprentice to master. Many immigrants could come to America only after they had *indentured* themselves for several years. also N.

indicative ADJ. suggestive; implying. A lack of appetite may be *indicative* of a major mental or physical disorder.

indict V. charge. If the grand jury *indicts* the suspect, he will go to trial.

■ **indifferent** ADJ. unmoved; lacking concern. Because she felt no desire to marry, she was *indifferent* to his constant proposals.

indigenous ADJ. native. Tobacco is one of the *indigenous* plants which the early explorers found in this country.

indigent ADJ. poor. Because he was *indigent,* he was sent to the welfare office.

indignation N. anger at an injustice. He felt *indignation* at the ill-treatment of helpless animals.

indignity N. offensive or insulting treatment. Although he seemed to accept cheerfully the *indignities* heaped upon him, he was inwardly very angry.

■ **indiscriminate** ADJ. choosing at random; confused. She disapproved of her son's *indiscriminate* television viewing and decided to restrict him to educational programs.

indisputable ADJ. too certain to be disputed. In the face of these *indisputable* statements, I withdraw my complaint.

indissoluble ADJ. permanent. The *indissoluble* bonds of marriage are all too often being dissolved.

indite V. write; compose. Cyrano *indited* many letters for Christian.

■ **indolent** ADJ. lazy. The sultry weather in the tropics encourages tourists to lead an *indolent* life. indolence, N.

indomitable ADJ. unconquerable. The founders of our country had *indomitable* willpower.

indubitably ADV. beyond a doubt. Because her argument was *indubitably* valid, the judge accepted it.

induce V. persuade; bring about. They tried to *induce* labor because the baby was overdue.

inductive ADJ. pertaining to induction or proceeding from the specific to the general. The discovery of the planet Pluto is an excellent example of the results that can be obtained from *inductive* reasoning.

■ **indulgent** ADJ. humoring; yielding; lenient. An *indulgent* parent may spoil a child by creating an artificial atmosphere

inebriety N. habitual intoxication. Because of his *inebriety,* he was discharged from his position as family chauffeur.

ineffable ADJ. unutterable; cannot be expressed in speech. Such *ineffable* joy must be experienced; it cannot be described.

ineluctable ADJ. irresistible; not to be escaped. He felt that his fate was *ineluctable* and refused to make any attempt to improve his lot.

inept ADJ. unsuited; absurd; incompetent. The constant turmoil in the office proved that she was an *inept* administrator.

inert ADJ. inactive; lacking power to move. Faced with the growing corruption scandal, the bureaucracy was *inert* and did nothing.

inertia N. state of being inert or indisposed to move. Our *inertia* in this matter may prove disastrous; we must move to aid our allies immediately.

■ **inevitable** ADJ. unavoidable. Death and taxes are both *inevitable.*

inexorable ADJ. relentless; unyielding; implacable. After listening to the pleas for clemency, the judge was *inexorable* and gave the convicted man the maximum punishment allowed by law.

infallible ADJ. unerring. We must remember that none of us is *infallible;* we all make mistakes.

■ **infamous** ADJ. notoriously bad. Jesse James was an *infamous* outlaw.

infantile ADJ. childish; infantile. When will he outgrow such *infantile* behavior?

■ **infer** V. deduce; conclude. We must be particularly cautious when we *infer* that a person is guilty on the basis of circumstantial evidence.

inference N. conclusion drawn from data. I want you to check this *inference* because it may have been based on insufficient information.

infernal ADJ. pertaining to hell; devilish. They could think of no way to hinder his *infernal* scheme.

infidel N. unbeliever. The Saracens made war against the *infidels.*

infinitesimal ADJ. very small. In the twentieth century, physicists have made their greatest discoveries about the characteristics of *infinitesimal* objects like the atom and its parts.

infirmity N. weakness. Her greatest *infirmity* was lack of willpower.

■ **inflated** ADJ. exaggerated; pompous; enlarged (with air or gas). His claims about the new product were inflated; it did not work as well as he had promised.

influx N. flowing into. The *influx* of refugees into the country has taxed the relief agencies severely.

infraction N. violation. Because of his many *infractions* of school regulations, he was suspended by the dean.

infringe V. violate; encroach. I think your machine *infringes* on my patent and I intend to sue.

ingenious ADJ. clever. He came up with an *ingenious* use for styrofoam packing balls.

Test

Word List 25　*Synonyms*

Each of the questions below consists of a word in capital letters, followed by five lettered words or phrases. Choose the lettered word or phrase that is most nearly similar in meaning to the word in capital letters and write the letter of your choice on your answer paper.

361. INCLEMENT (A) unfavorable (B) abandoned (C) kindly (D) selfish (E) active
362. INCOMPATIBLE (A) capable (B) reasonable (C) faulty (D) indifferent (E) alienated
363. INCONSEQUENTIAL (A) disorderly (B) insignificant (C) subsequent (D) insufficient (E) preceding
364. INCONTINENT (A) insular (B) complaisant (C) crass (D) wanton (E) false
365. INCORRIGIBLE (A) narrow (B) straight (C) inconceivable (D) unreliable (E) unreformable
366. INCRIMINATE (A) exacerbate (B) involve (C) intimidate (D) lacerate (E) prevaricate

367. INCULCATE (A) exculpate (B) educate (C) exonerate (D) prepare (E) embarrass
368. INDIGENT (A) lazy (B) pusillanimous (C) penurious (D) affluent (E) contrary
369. INDIGNITY (A) pomposity (B) bombast (C) obeisance (D) insult (E) message
370. INDOLENCE (A) sloth (B) poverty (C) latitude (D) aptitude (E) anger
371. INDUBITABLY (A) flagrantly (B) doubtfully (C) carefully (D) carelessly (E) certainly
372. INEBRIETY (A) revelation (B) drunkenness (C) felony (D) starvation (E) gluttony
373. INEPT (A) outward (B) spiritual (C) foolish (D) clumsy (E) abundant
374. INFALLIBLE (A) final (B) unbelievable (C) perfect (D) inaccurate (E) inquisitive
375. INFIRMITY (A) disability (B) age (C) inoculation (D) hospital (E) unity

Word List 26　ingenue-invidious

ingenue N. an artless girl; an actress who plays such parts. Although she was forty, she still insisted that she be cast as an *ingenue* and refused to play more mature roles.

ingenuous ADJ. naive; young; unsophisticated. These remarks indicate that you are *ingenuous* and unaware of life's harsher realities.

ingrate N. ungrateful person. You are an *ingrate* since you have treated my gifts with scorn.

ingratiate V. become popular with. He tried to *ingratiate* himself into her parents' good graces.

inherent ADJ. firmly established by nature or habit. His *inherent* love of justice compelled him to come to their aid.

■ **inhibit** V. prohibit; restrain. The child was not *inhibited* in her responses. inhibition, N.

inimical ADJ. unfriendly; hostile. She felt that they were *inimical* and were hoping for her downfall.

inimitable ADJ. matchless; not able to be imitated. We admire Auden for his *inimitable* use of language; he is one of a kind.

iniquitous ADJ. unjust; wicked. I cannot approve of the *iniquitous* methods you used to gain your present position. iniquity, N.

■ **initiate** V. begin; originate; receive into a group. The college is about to *initiate* a program in reducing math anxiety among students.

■ **injurious** ADJ. harmful. Smoking cigarettes can be *injurious* to your health.

inkling N. hint. This came as a complete surprise to me as I did not have the slightest *inkling* of your plans.

■ **innate** ADJ. inborn. His *innate* talent for music was soon recognized by his parents.

■ **innocuous** ADJ. harmless. Let him drink it; it is *innocuous* and will have no ill effect.

innovation N. change; introduction of something new. She loved *innovations* just because they were new.

■ **innovative** ADJ. novel; introducing a change. The establishment of our SAT computer data base has enabled us to come up with some *innovative* tactics for doing well on the SAT.

innuendo N. hint; insinuation. I resent the *innuendos* in your statement more than the statement itself.

inopportune ADJ. untimely; poorly chosen. A rock concert is an *inopportune* setting for a quiet conversation.

inordinate ADJ. unrestrained; excessive. She had an *inordinate* fondness for candy.

insatiable ADJ. not easily satisfied; greedy. His thirst for knowledge was *insatiable*; he was always in the library.

inscrutable ADJ. incomprehensible; not to be discovered. I fail to understand the reasons for your outlandish behavior; your motives are *inscrutable*.

insensate ADJ. without feeling. She lay there as *insensate* as a log.

insidious ADJ. treacherous; stealthy; sly. The fifth column is *insidious* because it works secretly within our territory for our defeat.

insinuate V. hint; imply. What are you trying to *insinuate* by that remark?

■ **insipid** ADJ. tasteless; dull. I am bored by your *insipid* talk.

insolent ADJ. haughty and contemptuous. I resent your *insolent* manner.

■ **insolvent** ADJ. bankrupt; lacking money to pay. When rumors that he was *insolvent* reached his creditors, they began to press him for payment of the money due them. insolvency, N.

insomnia N. wakefulness; inability to sleep. He refused to join us in a midnight cup of coffee because he claimed it gave him *insomnia*.

insouciant ADJ. indifferent; without concern or care. Your *insouciant* attitude at such a critical moment indicates that you do not understand the gravity of the situation.

instigate V. urge; start; provoke. I am afraid that this statement will *instigate* a revolt.

insubordinate ADJ. disobedient. The *insubordinate* private was confined to the barracks.

insular ADJ. like an island; narrow-minded. In an age of such rapid means of communication, we cannot afford to be hemmed in by such *insular* ideas.

insuperable ADJ. insurmountable; invincible. In the face of *insuperable* difficulties they maintained their courage and will to resist.

■ **insurgent** ADJ. rebellious. We will not discuss reforms until the *insurgent* troops have returned to their homes. also N.

insurrection N. rebellion; uprising. Given the current state of affairs in South Africa, an *insurrection* seems unavoidable.

integrate V. make whole; combine; make into one unit. She tried to *integrate* all their activities into one program.

integrity N. wholeness; purity; uprightness. The beloved preacher was a man of great *integrity*.

integument N. outer covering or skin. The turtle takes advantage of its hard *integument* and hides within its shell when threatened.

intellect N. higher mental powers. He thought college would develop his *intellect*.

intelligentsia N. the intelligent and educated classes [often used derogatorily]. She preferred discussions about sports and politics to the literary conversations of the *intelligentsia*.

inter V. bury. They are going to *inter* the body tomorrow at Broadlawn Cemetery.

interdict V. prohibit; forbid. Civilized nations must *interdict* the use of nuclear weapons if we expect our society to live.

interim N. meantime. The company will not consider our proposal until next week; in the *interim*, let us proceed as we have in the past.

interlocutory ADJ. conversational; intermediate, not final. This *interlocutory* decree is only a temporary setback; the case has not been settled.

interloper N. intruder. The merchant thought of his competitors as *interlopers* who were stealing away his trade.

interment N. burial. *Interment* will take place in the church cemetery at 2 P.M. Wednesday.

■ **interminable** ADJ. endless. Although his speech lasted for only twenty minutes, it seemed *interminable* to his bored audience.

intermittent ADJ. periodic; on and off. Our picnic was marred by *intermittent* rains.

internecine ADJ. mutually destructive. The rising death toll on both sides indicates the *internecine* nature of this conflict.

interpolate V. insert between. She talked so much that I could not *interpolate* a single remark.

interstices N. chinks; crevices. The mountain climber sought to obtain a foothold in the *interstices* of the cliff.

intervene V. come between. She *intervened* in the argument between her two sons.

intimate V. hint. She *intimated* rather than stated her preferences.

intimidation N. fear. A ruler who maintains his power by *intimidation* is bound to develop clandestine resistance.

intractable ADJ. unruly; refractory. The horse was *intractable* and refused to enter the starting gate.

intransigence N. state of stubborn unwillingness to compromise. The *intransigence* of both parties in the dispute makes an early settlement almost impossible to obtain.

intransigent ADJ. refusing any compromise. The strike settlement has collapsed because both sides are *intransigent*.

intrepid ADJ. fearless. For his *intrepid* conduct in battle, he was promoted.

intrinsic ADJ. belonging to a thing in itself; inherent. Although the *intrinsic* value of this award is small, I shall always cherish it.

introspective ADJ. looking within oneself. We all have our *introspective* moments during which we examine our souls.

introvert N. one who is introspective; inclined to think more about oneself. In his poetry, he reveals that he is an *introvert* by his intense interest in his own problems. also V.

intrude V. trespass; enter as an uninvited person. She hesitated to *intrude* on their conversation.

intuition N. power of knowing without reasoning. She claimed to know the truth by *intuition*. intuitive, ADJ.

inundate V. overflow; flood. The tremendous waves *inundated* the town.

inured ADJ. accustomed; hardened. She became *inured* to the Alaskan cold.

invalidate V. weaken; destroy. The relatives who received little or nothing sought to *invalidate* the will by claiming that the deceased had not been in his right mind when he had signed the document.

invective N. abuse. He had expected criticism but not the *invective* which greeted his proposal.

inveigh V. denounce; utter censure or invective. He *inveighed* against the demagoguery of the previous speaker and urged that the audience reject his philosophy as dangerous.

inveigle V. lead astray; wheedle. She was *inveigled* into joining the club after an initial reluctance.

inverse ADJ. opposite. There is an *inverse* ratio between the strength of light and its distance.

invert V. turn upside down or inside out. When he *inverted* his body in a hand stand, he felt the blood rush to his head.

inveterate ADJ. deep-rooted; habitual. She is an *inveterate* smoker and cannot stop the habit.

invidious ADJ. designed to create ill will or envy. We disregarded her *invidious* remarks because we realized how jealous she was.

Test

Word List 26   *Synonyms*

Each of the questions below consists of a word in capital letters, followed by five lettered words or phrases. Choose the lettered word or phrase that is most nearly similar in meaning to the word in capital letters and write the letter of your choice on your answer paper.

376. INGENUOUS (A) clever (B) stimulating (C) naive (D) worried (E) cautious
377. INIMICAL (A) antagonistic (B) anonymous (C) fanciful (D) accurate (E) seldom
378. INNOCUOUS (A) not capable (B) not dangerous (C) not eager (D) not frank (E) not peaceful
379. INSINUATE (A) resist (B) suggest (C) report (D) rectify (E) lecture
380. INSIPID (A) witty (B) flat (C) wily (D) talkative (E) lucid
381. INTEGRATE (A) tolerate (B) unite (C) flow (D) copy (E) assume

382. INTER (A) bury (B) amuse (C) relate (D) frequent (E) abandon
383. INTERDICT (A) acclaim (B) dispute (C) prohibit (D) decide (E) fret
384. INTERMITTENT (A) heavy (B) fleet (C) occasional (D) fearless (E) responding
385. INTRACTABLE (A) culpable (B) flexible (C) unruly (D) efficient (E) base
386. INTRANSIGENCE (A) lack of training (B) stubbornness (C) novelty (D) timidity (E) cupidity
387. INTREPID (A) cold (B) hot (C) understood (D) callow (E) courageous
388. INTRINSIC (A) extrinsic (B) abnormal (C) above (D) abandoned (E) basic
389. INUNDATE (A) abuse (B) deny (C) swallow (D) treat (E) flood
390. INVEIGH (A) speak violently (B) orate (C) disturb (D) apply (E) whisper

Word List 27   invincible-laity

invincible ADJ. unconquerable. Superman is *invincible.*

inviolability N. security from being destroyed, corrupted or profaned. They respected the *inviolability* of her faith and did not try to change her manner of living.

invoke V. call upon; ask for. She *invoked* her advisor's aid in filling out her financial aid forms.

invulnerable ADJ. incapable of injury. Achilles was *invulnerable* except in his heel.

iota N. very small quantity. She hadn't an *iota* of common sense.

irascible ADJ. irritable; easily angered. Her *irascible* temper frightened me.

iridescent ADJ. exhibiting rainbowlike colors. She admired the *iridescent* hues of the oil that floated on the surface of the water.

irksome ADJ. annoying; tedious. He found working on the assembly line *irksome* because of the monotony of the operation he had to perform. irk, V.

■ **ironic** ADJ. resulting in an unexpected and contrary manner. It is *ironic* that his success came when he least wanted it.

irony N. hidden sarcasm or satire; use of words that convey a meaning opposite to the literal meaning. Gradually his listeners began to realize that the excessive praise he was lavishing was merely *irony;* he was actually denouncing his opponent.

irreconcilable ADJ. incompatible; not able to be resolved. Because the separated couple were *irreconcilable*, the marriage counselor recommended a divorce.

irrefragable ADJ. not to be disproved; indisputable. The testimonies of the witnesses provide *irrefragable* proof that my client is innocent; I demand that he be released at once.

irrelevant ADJ. not applicable; unrelated. This statement is *irrelevant* and should be disregarded by the jury.

irremediable ADJ. incurable; uncorrectable. The error she made was *irremediable;* she could see no way to repair it.

irreparable ADJ. not able to be corrected or repaired. Your apology cannot atone for the *irreparable* damage you have done to her reputation.

irrepressible ADJ. unable to be restrained or held back. Her high spirits were *irrepressible.*

■ **irresolute** ADJ. uncertain how to act; weak. She had no respect for him because he seemed weak-willed and *irresolute*.

irreverent ADJ. lacking proper respect. The worshippers resented her *irreverent* remarks about their faith.

irrevocable ADJ. unalterable. Let us not brood over past mistakes since they are *irrevocable*.

isotope N. varying form of an element. The study of the *isotopes* of uranium led to the development of the nuclear bomb.

iterate V. utter a second time; repeat. I will *iterate* the warning I have previously given to you.

itinerant ADJ. wandering; traveling. He was an *itinerant* peddler and traveled through Pennsylvania and Virginia selling his wares. also N.

itinerary N. plan of a trip. Before leaving for his first visit to France and England, he discussed his *itinerary* with people who had been there and with his travel agent.

jaded ADJ. fatigued; surfeited. He looked for exotic foods to stimulate his *jaded* appetite.

jargon N. language used by special group; gibberish. We tried to understand the *jargon* of the peddlers in the marketplace but could not find any basis for comprehension.

jaundiced ADJ. yellowed; prejudiced; envious. She gazed at the painting with *jaundiced* eyes; she knew it was better than hers.

jaunt N. trip; short journey. He took a quick *jaunt* to Atlantic City.

jaunty ADJ. stylish; perky; carefree. She wore her beret at a *jaunty* angle.

jejune ADJ. lacking interest; barren; meager. The plot of the play is *jejune* and fails to capture the interest of the audience.

jeopardy N. exposure to death or danger. She cannot be placed in double *jeopardy*.

jeremiad N. lament; complaint. His account of the event was a lengthy *jeremiad*, unrelieved by any light moments.

jettison V. throw overboard. In order to enable the ship to ride safely through the storm, the captain had to *jettison* much of his cargo.

jingoism N. extremely aggressive and militant patriotism. We must be careful to prevent a spirit of *jingoism* from spreading at this time; the danger of a disastrous war is too great.

jocose ADJ. giving to joking. The salesman was so *jocose* that many of his customers suggested that he become a "stand-up" comic.

jocular ADJ. said or done in jest. Do not take my *jocular* remarks seriously.

jocund ADJ. merry. Santa Claus is always vivacious and *jocund*.

jollity N. gaiety; cheerfulness. The festive Christmas dinner was a merry one, and old and young alike joined in the general *jollity*.

jostle V. shove; bump. In the subway he was *jostled* by the crowds.

jovial ADJ. good-natured; merry. A frown seemed out of place on his invariably *jovial* face.

jubilation N. rejoicing. There was great *jubilation* when the armistice was announced.

■ **judicious** ADJ. sound in judgment; wise. At a key moment in his life, he made a *judicious* investment that was the foundation of his later wealth.

juggernaut N. irresistible crushing force. Nothing could survive in the path of the *juggernaut*.

juncture N. crisis; joining point. At this critical *juncture*, let us think carefully before determining the course we shall follow.

junket N. a merry feast or picnic. The opposition claimed that her trip to Europe was merely a political *junket*.

junta N. group of men joined in political intrigue; cabal. As soon as he learned of its existence, the dictator ordered the execution of all of the members of the *junta*.

jurisprudence N. science of law. He was more a student of *jurisprudence* than a practitioner of the law.

juxtapose V. place side by side. Comparison will be easier if you *juxtapose* the two objects.

kaleidoscope N. tube in which patterns made by the reflection in mirrors of colored pieces of glass, etc., produce interesting symmetrical effects. People found a new source of entertainment while peering through the *kaleidoscope*; they found the ever-changing patterns fascinating.

ken N. range of knowledge. I cannot answer your question since this matter is beyond my *ken*.

kindle V. start a fire; inspire. Her teacher's praise *kindled* a spark of hope inside her.

kindred ADJ. related; belonging to the same family. Tom Sawyer and Huck Finn were two *kindred* spirits. also N.

kiosk N. summer house; open pavilion. She waited at the subway *kiosk*.

kinetic ADJ. producing motion. Designers of the electric automobile find that their greatest obstacle lies in the development of light and efficient storage batteries, the source of the *kinetic* energy needed to propel the vehicle.

kismet N. fate. *Kismet* is the Arabic word for "fate."

kith N. familiar friends. He always helped both his *kith* and kin.

kleptomaniac N. person who has a compulsive desire to steal. They discovered that the wealthy customer was a *kleptomaniac* when they caught her stealing some cheap trinkets.

knavery N. rascality. We cannot condone such *knavery* in public officials.

knead V. mix; work dough. Her hands grew strong from *kneading* bread.

knell N. tolling of a bell at a funeral; sound of the funeral bell. "The curfew tolls the *knell* of parting day." also V.

knoll N. little round hill. Robert Louis Stevenson's grave is on a *knoll* in Samoa.

labyrinth N. maze. Tom and Betty were lost in the *labyrinth* of secret caves.

lacerate V. mangle; tear. Her body was *lacerated* in the automobile crash.

lachrymose ADJ. producing tears. His voice has a *lachrymose* quality which is more appropriate at a funeral than a class reunion.

lackadaisical ADJ. affectedly languid. He was *lackadaisical* and indifferent about his part in the affair.

lackey N. footman; toady. The duke was followed by his *lackeys*.

lackluster ADJ. dull. We were disappointed by the *lackluster* performance.

■ **laconic** ADJ. brief and to the point. Many of the characters portrayed by Clint Eastwood are *laconic* types: strong men of few words.

laggard ADJ. slow; sluggish. The sailor had been taught not to be *laggard* in carrying out orders.

lagoon N. shallow body of water near a sea; lake. They enjoyed their swim in the calm *lagoon*.

laity N. laymen; persons not connected with the clergy. The *laity* does not always understand the clergy's problems.

Test

Word List 27 *Antonyms*

Each of the questions below consists of a word in capital letters, followed by five lettered words or phrases. Choose the lettered word or phrase that is most nearly opposite in meaning to the word in capital letters and write the letter of your choice on your answer paper.

391. IRKSOME (A) interesting (B) lazy (C) tireless (D) few (E) too many

392. IRRELEVANT (A) lacking piety (B) fragile (C) congruent (D) pertinent (E) varied

393. IRREPARABLE (A) legible (B) correctable (C) proverbial (D) concise (E) legal

394. IRREVERENT (A) related (B) mischievous (C) respective (D) pious (E) violent

395. JADED (A) upright (B) stimulated (C) aspiring (D) applied (E) void

396. JAUNDICED (A) whitened (B) inflamed (C) quickened (D) aged (E) unbiased

397. JEJUNE (A) youthful (B) ancient (C) strong (D) fictional (E) interesting

398. JEREMIAD (A) prophecy (B) proposition (C) praise (D) overture (E) explanation

399. JETTISON (A) salvage (B) submerge (C) descend (D) decelerate (E) repent

400. JOCULAR (A) arterial (B) bloodless (C) verbose (D) serious (E) blind

401. JUDICIOUS (A) punitive (B) unwise (C) criminal (D) licit (E) temporary

402. KITH (A) outfit (B) strangers (C) brothers (D) ceramics tool (E) quality

403. LACHRYMOSE (A) cheering (B) smooth (C) passionate (D) curt (E) tense

404. LACKADAISICAL (A) monthly (B) possessing time (C) ambitious (D) pusillanimous (E) intelligent

405. LACONIC (A) milky (B) verbose (C) wicked (D) flagrant (E) derelict

Word List 28   lambent-lout

lambent ADJ. flickering; softly radiant. They sat quietly before the *lambent* glow of the fireplace.

laminated ADJ. made of thin plates or scales. The desk was covered with a sheet of *laminated* plastic.

lampoon V. ridicule. This article *lampoons* the pretensions of some movie moguls. also N.

languid ADJ. weary; sluggish; listless. Her siege of illness left her *languid* and pallid.

■ **languish** V. lose animation; lose strength. In stories, love-lorn damsels used to *languish* and pine away.

languor N. lassitude; depression. His friends tried to overcome the *languor* into which he had fallen by taking him to parties and to the theater.

lank ADJ. long and thin. *Lank,* gaunt, Abraham Lincoln was a striking figure.

lapidary N. worker in precious stones. She employed a *lapidary* to cut the large diamond.

larceny N. theft. Because of the prisoner's record, the district attorney refused to reduce the charge from grand *larceny* to petit *larceny*.

largess N. generous gift. Lady Bountiful distributed *largess* to the poor.

lascivious ADJ. lustful. The *lascivious* books were banned by the clergy.

lassitude N. languor; weariness. The hot, tropical weather created a feeling of *lassitude* and encouraged drowsiness.

latent ADJ. dormant; hidden. Her *latent* talent was discovered by accident.

lateral ADJ. coming from the side. In order to get good plant growth, the gardener must pinch off all *lateral* shoots.

latitude N. freedom from narrow limitations. I think you have permitted your son too much *latitude* in this matter.

■ **laudable** ADJ. praiseworthy; commendable. His *laudable* deeds will be remembered by all whom he aided.

■ **laudatory** ADJ. expressing praise. The critics' *laudatory* comments helped to make her a star.

lave V. wash. The running water will *lave* away all stains.

lavish ADJ. liberal; wasteful. The actor's *lavish* gifts pleased her. also V.

lax ADJ. careless. We dislike restaurants where the service is *lax* and inattentive.

lecherous ADJ. impure in thought and act; lustful; unchaste. He is a *lecherous* and wicked old man.

lechery N. gross lewdness; lustfulness. In his youth he led a life of *lechery* and debauchery; he did not mend his ways until middle age.

lectern N. reading desk. The chaplain delivered his sermon from a hastily improvised *lectern*.

leeway N. room to move; margin. When you set a deadline, allow a little *leeway*.

■ **legacy** N. a gift made by a will. Part of my *legacy* from my parents is an album of family photographs.

legerdemain N. sleight of hand. The magician demonstrated his renowned *legerdemain*.

leniency N. mildness; permissiveness. Considering the gravity of the offense, we were surprised by the *leniency* of the sentence.

leonine N. like a lion. He was *leonine* in his rage.

lesion N. unhealthy change in structure; injury. Many *lesions* are the result of disease.

lethal ADJ. deadly. It is unwise to leave *lethal* weapons where children may find them.

■ **lethargic** ADJ. drowsy; dull. The stuffy room made her *lethargic*.

■ **levity** N. lightness. Such *levity* is improper on this serious occasion.

lewd ADJ. lustful. They found his *lewd* stories objectionable.

lexicographer N. compiler of a dictionary. The new dictionary is the work of many *lexicographers* who spent years compiling and editing the work.

lexicon N. dictionary. I cannot find this word in any *lexicon* in the library.

liaison N. officer who acts as go-between for two armies. As the *liaison*, he had to avoid offending the leaders of the two armies. also ADJ.

libation N. drink. He offered a *libation* to the thirsty prisoner.

libelous ADJ. defamatory; injurious to the good name of a person. He sued the newspaper because of its *libelous* story.

libertine N. debauched person, roué. Although she was aware of his reputation as a *libertine*, she felt she could reform him and help him break his dissolute way of life.

libidinous ADJ. lustful. They objected to his *libidinous* behavior.

libido N. emotional urges behind human activity. The psychiatrist maintained that suppression of the *libido* often resulted in maladjustment and neuroses.

libretto N. text of an opera. The composer of an opera's music is remembered more frequently than the author of its *libretto*.

licentious ADJ. wanton; lewd; dissolute. The *licentious* monarch helped bring about his country's downfall.

lieu N. instead of. They accepted his check in *lieu* of cash.

lilliputian ADJ. extremely small. The model was built on a *lilliputian* scale. also N.

limber ADJ. flexible. Hours of ballet classes kept him *limber*.

limbo N. region near heaven or hell where certain souls are kept; a prison (slang). Among the divisions of Hell are Purgatory and *Limbo*.

limn V. portray; describe vividly. He was never satisfied with his attempts to *limn* her beauty on canvas.

limpid ADJ. clear. A *limpid* stream ran through his property.

lineage N. descent; ancestry. He traced his *lineage* back to Mayflower days.

lineaments N. features of the face. She quickly sketched the *lineaments* of his face.

linguistic ADJ. pertaining to language. The modern tourist will encounter very little *linguistic* difficulty as English has become an almost universal language.

lionize V. treat as a celebrity. She enjoyed being *lionized* and adored by the public.

liquidate V. settle accounts; clear up. He was able to *liquidate* all his debts in a short period of time.

lissom ADJ. agile; lithe. As a young boy, he was *lissom* and graceful; he gave promise of developing into a fine athlete.

■ **listless** ADJ. lacking in spirit or energy. We had expected him to be full of enthusiasm and were surprised by his *listless* attitude.

litany N. supplicatory prayer. On this solemn day, the congregation responded to the prayers of the priest during the *litany* with fervor and intensity.

lithe ADJ. flexible; supple. Her figure was *lithe* and willowy.

litigation N. lawsuit. Try to settle this amicably; I do not want to start *litigation*.

litotes N. understatement for emphasis. To say,"He little realizes," when we mean that he does not realize at all, is an example of the kind of understatement we call *litotes*.

livid ADJ. lead-colored; black and blue; enraged. His face was so *livid* with rage that we were afraid that he might have an attack of apoplexy.

loath ADJ. averse; reluctant. They were both *loath* for him to go.

loathe V. detest. We *loathed* the wicked villain.

lode N. metal-bearing vein. If this *lode* which we have discovered extends for any distance, we have found a fortune.

■ **lofty** ADJ. very high. They used to tease him about his *lofty* ambitions.

loiter V. hang around; linger. The policeman told him not to *loiter* in the alley.

loll V. lounge about. They *lolled* around in their chairs watching television.

longevity N. long life. When he reached ninety, the old man was proud of his *longevity.*

lope V. gallop slowly. As the horses *loped* along, we had an opportunity to admire the ever-changing scenery

loquacious ADJ. talkative. She is very *loquacious* and can speak on the telephone for hours.

lout N. clumsy person. The delivery boy is an awkward *lout.*

Test

Word List 28   *Antonyms*

Each of the questions below consists of a word in capital letters, followed by five lettered words or phrases. Choose the lettered word or phrase that is most nearly opposite in meaning to the word in capital letters and write the letter of your choice on your answer paper.

406. LAMPOON (A) darken (B) praise (C) abandon (D) sail (E) fly

407. LANGUOR (A) vitality (B) length (C) embarrassment (D) wine (E) avarice

408. LATENT (A) trim (B) forbidding (C) execrable (D) early (E) obvious

409. LAVISH (A) hostile (B) unwashed (C) timely (D) decent (E) frugal

410. LAUDATORY (A) dirtying (B) disclaiming (C) defamatory (D) inflammatory (E) debased

411. LAX (A) salty (B) strict (C) shrill (D) boring (E) cowardly

412. LECHERY (A) trust (B) compulsion (C) zeal (D) addiction (E) purity

413. LETHARGIC (A) convalescent (B) beautiful (C) enervating (D) invigorating (E) interrogating

414. LEVITY (A) bridge (B) dam (C) praise (D) blame (E) solemnity

415. LILLIPUTIAN (A) destructive (B) proper (C) gigantic (D) elegant (E) barren

416. LIMPID (A) erect (B) turbid (C) tangential (D) timid (E) weary

417. LITHE (A) stiff (B) limpid (C) facetious (D) insipid (E) vast

418. LIVID (A) alive (B) mundane (C) positive (D) undiscolored (E) vast

419. LOATH (A) loose (B) evident (C) deliberate (D) eager (E) tiny

420. LOQUACIOUS (A) taciturn (B) sentimental (C) soporific (D) soothing (E) sedate

Word List 29   lubricity-maunder

lubricity N. slipperiness; evasiveness. He exasperated the reporters by his *lubricity;* they could not pin him down to a definite answer.

lucent ADJ. shining. The moon's *lucent* rays silvered the river.

lucid ADJ. bright; easily understood. His explanation was *lucid* and to the point.

lucrative ADJ. profitable. He turned his hobby into a *lucrative* profession.

lucre N. money. Preferring *lucre* to fame, he wrote stories of popular appeal.

ludicrous ADJ. laughable; trifling. Let us be serious; this is not a *ludicrous* issue.

lugubrious ADJ. mournful. The *lugubrious* howling of the dogs added to our sadness.

lull N. moment of calm. Not wanting to get wet, they waited under the awning for a *lull* in the rain.

luminous ADJ. shining; issuing light. The sun is a *luminous* body.

lunar ADJ. pertaining to the moon. *Lunar* craters can be plainly seen with the aid of a small telescope.

lupine ADJ. like a wolf. She was terrified of his fierce, *lupine* smile.

lurid ADJ. wild; sensational. The *lurid* stories he told shocked his listeners.

luscious ADJ. pleasing to taste or smell. The ripe peach was *luscious.*

luster N. shine; gloss. The soft *luster* of the silk in the dim light was pleasing.

lustrous ADJ. shining. Her large and *lustrous* eyes gave a touch of beauty to an otherwise drab face.

luxuriant ADJ. fertile; abundant; ornate. Farming was easy in this *luxuriant* soil.

macabre ADJ. gruesome; grisly. The city morgue is a *macabre* spot for the uninitiated.

macerate V. waste away. Cancer *macerated* his body.

Machiavellian ADJ. crafty; double-dealing. I do not think he will be a good ambassador because he is not accustomed to the *Machiavellian* maneuverings of foreign diplomats.

machinations N. schemes. I can see through your wily *machinations.*

madrigal N. pastoral song. His program of folk songs included several *madrigals* which he sang to the accompaniment of a lute.

maelstrom N. whirlpool. The canoe was tossed about in the *maelstrom.*

magnanimous ADJ. generous. The philanthropist was most *magnanimous.*

magnate N. person of prominence or influence. The steel *magnate* decided to devote more time to city politics.

magniloquent ADJ. boastful, pompous. In their stories of the trial, the reporters ridiculed the *magniloquent* speeches of the defense attorney.

magnitude N. greatness; extent. It is difficult to comprehend the *magnitude* of his crime.

maim V. mutilate; injure. The hospital could not take care of all who had been wounded or *maimed* in the railroad accident.

maladroit ADJ. clumsy; bungling. In his usual *maladroit* way, he managed to upset the cart and spill the food.

malaise N. uneasiness; distress. She felt a sudden vague *malaise* when she heard sounds at the door.

malapropism N. comic misuse of a word. Mrs. Warren's funniest *malapropism* occurs when she accuses Skitterby of being "a snare and an Andalusian."

malcontent N. person dissatisfied with existing state of affairs. He was one of the few *malcontents* in Congress; he constantly voiced his objections to the Presidential program. also ADJ.

malediction N. curse. The witch uttered *maledictions* against her captors.

malefactor N. criminal. We must try to bring these *malefactors* to justice.

malevolent ADJ. wishing evil. We must thwart his *malevolent* schemes.

■ **malicious** ADJ. dictated by hatred or spite. The *malicious* neighbor spread the gossip.

malign V. speak evil of; defame. Because of her hatred of the family, she *maligns* all who are friendly to them.

malignant ADJ. having an evil influence; virulent. This is a *malignant* disease; we may have to use drastic measures to stop its spread.

malingerer N. one who feigns illness to escape duty. The captain ordered the sergeant to punish all *malingerers* and force them to work.

mall N. public walk. The *Mall* in Central Park has always been a favorite spot for Sunday strollers.

malleable ADJ. capable of being shaped by pounding. Gold is a *malleable* metal.

malodorous ADJ. foul-smelling. The compost heap was most *malodorous* in summer.

mammal N. a vertebrate animal whose female suckles its young. Many people regard the whale as a fish and do not realize that it is a *mammal*.

mammoth ADJ. gigantic. The *mammoth* corporations of the twentieth century are a mixed blessing.

manacle V. restrain; handcuff. The police immediately *manacled* the prisoner so he could not escape. also N.

mandate N. order; charge. In his inaugural address, the President stated that he had a *mandate* from the people to seek an end to social evils such as poverty, poor housing, etc. also V.

mandatory ADJ. obligatory. These instructions are *mandatory;* any violation will be severely punished.

mangy ADJ. shabby; wretched. We finally threw out the *mangy* rug that the dog had destroyed.

maniacal ADJ. raving mad. His *maniacal* laughter frightened us.

manifest ADJ. understandable; clear. His evil intentions were *manifest* and yet we could not stop him. also V.

manifesto N. declaration; statement of policy. This statement may be regarded as the *manifesto* of the party's policy.

manifold ADJ. numerous; varied. I cannot begin to tell you how much I appreciate your *manifold* kindnesses.

manipulate V. operate with the hands. How do you *manipulate* these puppets?

manumit V. emancipate; free from bondage. Enlightened slave owners were willing to *manumit* their slaves and thus put an end to the evil of slavery in the country.

marauder N. raider; intruder. The sounding of the alarm frightened the *marauders*.

marital ADJ. pertaining to marriage. After the publication of his book on *marital* affairs, he was often consulted by married people on the verge of divorce.

maritime ADJ. bordering on the sea; nautical. The *Maritime* Provinces depend on the sea for their wealth.

■ **marred** ADJ. damaged; disfigured. She had to refinish the *marred* surface of the table. mar, V.

marrow N. soft tissue filling the bones. The frigid cold chilled the traveler to the *marrow*.

marsupial N. one of a family of mammals that nurse their offspring in a pouch. The most common *marsupial* in North America is the opossum.

martial ADJ. warlike. The sound of *martial* music is always inspiring.

martinet N. strict disciplinarian. The commanding officer was a *martinet* who observed each regulation to the letter.

masochist N. person who enjoys his own pain. The *masochist* begs, "Hit me." The sadist smiles and says, "I won't."

masticate V. chew. We must *masticate* our food carefully and slowly in order to avoid stomach disorders.

maternal ADJ. motherly. Many animals display *maternal* instincts only while their offspring are young and helpless.

matriarch N. woman who rules a family or larger social group. The *matriarch* ruled her gypsy tribe with a firm hand.

matricide N. murder of a mother by a child. A crime such as *matricide* is inconceivable.

matrix N. mold or die. The cast around the *matrix* was cracked.

maudlin ADJ. effusively sentimental. I do not like such *maudlin* pictures. I call them tearjerkers.

maul V. handle roughly. The rock star was *mauled* by his over-excited fans.

maunder V. talk incoherently; utter drivel. You do not make sense; you *maunder* and garble your words.

Test

Word List 29   *Synonyms and Antonyms*

Each of the following questions consists of a word in capital letters, followed by five lettered words or phrases. Choose the lettered word or phrase which is most nearly similar or the opposite of the word in capital letters and write the letter of your choice on your answer paper.

421. LUGUBRIOUS (A) frantic (B) cheerful (C) burdensome (D) oily (E) militant

422. LURID (A) dull (B) duplicate (C) heavy (D) painstaking (E) intelligent

423. MACABRE (A) musical (B) frightening (C) chewed (D) wicked (E) exceptional

424. MAGNILOQUENT (A) loquacious (B) bombastic (C) rudimentary (D) qualitative (E) minimizing

425. MAGNITUDE (A) realization (B) fascination (C) enormity (D) gratitude (E) interference

426. MALADROIT (A) malicious (B) starving (C) thirsty (D) tactless (E) artistic

427. MALEDICTION (A) misfortune (B) hap (C) fruition (D) correct pronunciation (E) benediction

428. MALEFACTOR (A) quail (B) lawbreaker (C) beneficiary (D) banker (E) female agent

429. MALEVOLENT (A) kindly (B) vacuous (C) ambivalent (D) volatile (E) primitive

430. MALIGN (A) intersperse (B) vary (C) emphasize (D) frighten (E) eulogize

431. MALLEABLE (A) brittle (B) blatant (C) brilliant (D) brownish (E) basking

432. MANIACAL (A) demoniac (B) saturated (C) sane (D) sanitary (E) handcuffed

433. MANIFEST (A) limited (B) obscure (C) faulty (D) varied (E) vital

434. MANUMIT (A) print (B) impress (C) enslave (D) endeavor (E) fail

435. MARTIAL (A) bellicose (B) celibate (C) divorced (D) quiescent (E) planetary

Word List 30   mausoleum-misnomer

mausoleum N. monumental tomb. His body was placed in the family *mausoleum.*

mauve ADJ. pale purple. The *mauve* tint in the lilac bush was another indication that Spring had finally arrived.

maverick N. rebel. How can you keep such a *maverick* in line?

mawkish ADJ. sickening; insipid. Your *mawkish* sighs fill me with disgust.

maxim N. proverb; a truth pithily stated. Aesop's fables illustrate moral *maxims.*

mayhem N. injury to body. The riot was marked not only by *mayhem,* with its attendant loss of life and limb, but also by arson and pillage.

meander V. to wind or turn in its course. It is difficult to sail up this stream because of the way it *meanders* through the countryside.

meddlesome ADJ. interfering. He felt his marriage was suffering because of his *meddlesome* mother-in-law.

mediate V. settle a dispute through the services of an outsider. Let us *mediate* our differences rather than engage in a costly strike.

mediocre ADJ. ordinary; commonplace. We were disappointed because he gave a rather *mediocre* performance in this role.

meditation N. reflection; thought. She reached her decision only after much *meditation.*

medley N. mixture. The band played a *medley* of Gershwin tunes.

megalomania N. mania for doing grandiose things. Developers who spend millions trying to build the world's tallest skyscraper suffer from *megalomania.*

mélange N. medley; miscellany. This anthology provides a *mélange* of the author's output in the fields of satire, criticism and political analysis.

melee N. fight. The captain tried to ascertain the cause of the *melee* that had broken out among the crew members.

mellifluous ADJ. flowing smoothly; smooth. Italian is a *mellifluous* language.

memento N. token; reminder. Take this book as a *memento* of your visit.

memorialize V. commemorate. Let us *memorialize* his great contribution by dedicating this library in his honor.

mendacious ADJ. lying; false. He was a pathological liar, and his friends learned to discount his *mendacious* stories.

mendicant N. beggar. From the moment we left the ship, we were surrounded by *mendicants* and peddlers.

menial ADJ. suitable for servants; low. I cannot understand why a person of your ability and talent should engage in such *menial* activities. also N.

mentor N. teacher. During this very trying period, she could not have had a better *mentor,* for the teacher was sympathetic and understanding.

mercantile ADJ. concerning trade. I am more interested in the opportunities available in the *mercantile* field than I am in those in the legal profession.

mercenary ADJ. interested in money or gain. I am certain that your action was prompted by *mercenary* motives. also N.

mercurial ADJ. fickle; changing. He was of a *mercurial* temperament and therefore unpredictable.

meretricious ADJ. flashy; tawdry. Her jewels were inexpensive but not *meretricious*.

meringue N. a pastry decoration made of whites of eggs. The lemon *meringue* pie is one of our specialties.

mesa N. high, flat-topped hill. The *mesa*, rising above the surrounding countryside, was the most conspicuous feature of the area.

mesmerize V. hypnotize. The incessant drone seemed to *mesmerize* him and place him in a trance.

metallurgical ADJ. pertaining to the art of removing metals from ores. During the course of his *metallurgical* research, the scientist developed a steel alloy of tremendous strength.

metamorphosis N. change of form. The *metamorphosis* of caterpillar to butterfly is typical of many such changes in animal life.

metaphor N. implied comparison. "He soared like an eagle" is an example of a simile; "He is an eagle in flight," a *metaphor*.

metaphysical ADJ. pertaining to speculative philosophy. The modern poets have gone back to the fanciful poems of the *metaphysical* poets of the seventeenth century for many of their images. metaphysics, N.

mete V. measure; distribute. He tried to be impartial in his efforts to *mete* out justice.

meteoric ADJ. swift; momentarily brilliant. We all wondered at his *meteoric* rise to fame.

■ **methodical** ADJ. systematic. An accountant must be *methodical* and maintain order among his financial records.

■ **meticulous** ADJ. excessively careful. He was *meticulous* in checking his accounts and never made mistakes.

metropolis N. large city. Every evening this terminal is filled with the thousands of commuters who are going from this *metropolis* to their homes in the suburbs.

mettle N. courage; spirit. When challenged by the other horses in the race, the thoroughbred proved its *mettle* by its determination to hold the lead.

mews N. group of stables built around a courtyard. Let us visit the *mews* to inspect the newly purchased horse.

miasma N. swamp gas; odor of decaying matter. I suspect that this area is infested with malaria as I can readily smell the *miasma*.

microcosm N. small world. In the *microcosm* of our small village, we find illustrations of all the evils that beset the universe.

mien N. demeanor; bearing. She had the gracious *mien* of a queen.

migrant ADJ. changing its habitat; wandering. These *migrant* birds return every spring. also N.

migratory ADJ. wandering. The return of the *migratory* birds to the northern sections of this country is a harbinger of spring.

milieu N. environment; means of expression. His *milieu* is watercolor although he has produced excellent oil paintings and lithographs.

militant ADJ. combative; bellicose. Although at this time he was advocating a policy of neutrality, one could usually find him adopting a more *militant* attitude. also N.

militate V. work against. Your record of lateness and absence will *militate* against your chances of promotion.

millennium N. thousand-year period; period of happiness and prosperity. I do not expect the *millennium* to come during my lifetime.

mimicry N. imitation. Her gift for *mimicry* was so great that her friends said that she should be in the theater.

minaret N. slender tower attached to a mosque. From the balcony of the *minaret* we obtained an excellent view of the town and the neighboring countryside.

minatory ADJ. threatening. All abusive and *minatory* letters received by the mayor and other public officials were examined by the police.

mincing ADJ. affectedly dainty. Yum-Yum walked across the stage with *mincing* steps.

minion N. a servile dependent. He was always accompanied by several of his *minions* because he enjoyed their subservience and flattery.

minuscule ADJ. extremely small. Why should I involve myself with a project with so *minuscule* a chance for success?

minutiae N. petty details. She would have liked to ignore the *minutiae* of daily living.

mirage N. unreal reflection; optical illusion. The lost prospector was fooled by a *mirage* in the desert.

■ **mire** V. entangle; stick in swampy ground. Their rear wheels became *mired* in mud. also N.

mirth N. merriment; laughter. Sober Malvolio found Sir Toby's *mirth* improper.

misadventure N. mischance; ill luck. The young explorer met death by *misadventure*.

misanthrope N. one who hates mankind. We thought the hermit was a *misanthrope* because he shunned our society.

misapprehension N. error; misunderstanding. To avoid *misapprehension*, I am going to ask all of you to repeat the instructions I have given.

miscegenation N. intermarriage between races. Some states passed laws against *miscegenation*.

miscellany N. mixture of writings on various subjects. This is an interesting *miscellany* of nineteenth-century prose and poetry.

mischance N. ill luck. By *mischance*, he lost his week's salary.

miscreant N. wretch; villain. His kindness to the *miscreant* amazed all of us who had expected to hear severe punishment pronounced.

misdemeanor N. minor crime. The culprit pleaded guilty to a *misdemeanor* rather than face trial for a felony.

■ **miserly** ADJ. stingy; mean. The *miserly* old man hoarded his coins not out of prudence but out of greed. miser, N.

misgivings N. doubts. Hamlet described his *misgivings* to Horatio but decided to fence with Laertes despite his foreboding of evil.

mishap N. accident. With a little care you could have avoided this *mishap*.

misnomer N. wrong name; incorrect designation. His tyrannical conduct proved to all that his nickname, King Eric the Just, was a *misnomer*.

Test

Word List 30   *Synonyms*

Each of the questions below consists of a word in capital letters, followed by five lettered words or phrases. Choose the lettered word or phrase that is most nearly similar in meaning to the word in capital letters and write the letter of your choice on your answer paper.

436. MAWKISH (A) sentimental (B) true (C) certain
     (D) devious (E) carefree
437. MEDIOCRE (A) average (B) bitter (C) medieval
     (D) industrial (E) agricultural
438. MELEE (A) heat (B) brawl (C) attempt
     (D) weapon (E) choice
439. MELLIFLUOUS (A) porous (B) honeycombed
     (C) strong (D) smooth (E) viscous
440. MENIAL (A) intellectual (B) clairvoyant
     (C) servile (D) arrogant (E) laudatory
441. MENTOR (A) guide (B) genius (C) talker
     (D) philosopher (E) stylist
442. MESMERIZE (A) remember (B) hypnotize
     (C) delay (D) bore (E) analyze

443. METICULOUS (A) steadfast (B) recent
     (C) quaint (D) painstaking (E) overt
444. MIASMA (A) dream (B) noxious fumes
     (C) scenario (D) quantity (E) total
445. MILITANT (A) combative (B) dramatic
     (C) religious (D) quaint (E) paternal
446. MINION (A) monster (B) quorum (C) majority
     (D) host (E) dependent
447. MIRAGE (A) dessert (B) illusion (C) water
     (D) mirror (E) statement
448. MISANTHROPE (A) benefactor (B) philanderer
     (C) man-hater (D) aesthete (E) epicure
449. MISCHANCE (A) gamble (B) ordinance
     (C) aperture (D) anecdote (E) adversity
450. MISDEMEANOR (A) felony (B) peccadillo
     (C) indignity (D) fiat (E) illiteracy

Word List 31   misogamy-natal

misogamy N. hatred of marriage. He remained a bachelor not because of *misogamy* but because of ill fate: his fiancee died before the wedding.

misogynist N. hater of women. She accused him of being a *misogynist* because he had been a bachelor all his life.

missile N. object to be thrown or projected. Scientists are experimenting with guided *missiles*.

missive N. letter. The ambassador received a *missive* from the Secretary of State.

mite N. very small object or creature; small coin. Gnats are annoying *mites* that sting.

■ **mitigate** V. appease. Nothing he did could *mitigate* her wrath; she was unforgiving.

mnemonic ADJ. pertaining to memory. He used *mnemonic* tricks to master new words.

mobile ADJ. movable; not fixed. The *mobile* blood bank operated by the Red Cross visited our neighborhood today. mobility, N.

mode N. prevailing style. She was not used to their lavish *mode* of living.

modicum N. limited quantity. Although his story is based on a *modicum* of truth, most of the events he describes are fictitious.

modish ADJ. fashionable. She always discarded all garments which were no longer *modish*.

modulation N. toning down; changing from one key to another. When she spoke, it was with quiet *modulation* of voice.

mogul N. powerful person. The oil *moguls* made great profits when the price of gasoline rose.

moiety N. half; part. There is a slight *moiety* of the savage in her personality which is not easily perceived by those who do not know her well.

molecule N. the smallest part of a homogeneous substance. In chemistry, we study how atoms and *molecules* react to form new substances.

mollify V. soothe. We tried to *mollify* the hysterical child by promising her many gifts.

molt V. shed or cast off hair or feathers. The male robin *molted* in the spring.

molten ADJ. melted. The city of Pompeii was destroyed by volcanic ash rather than by *molten* lava flowing from Mount Vesuvius.

momentous ADJ. very important. On this *momentous* occasion, we must be very solemn.

momentum N. quantity of motion of a moving body; impetus. The car lost *momentum* as it tried to ascend the steep hill.

monarchy N. government under a single ruler. England today remains a *monarchy*.

monastic ADJ. related to monks. Wanting to live a religious life, he took his *monastic* vows.

monetary ADJ. pertaining to money. She was in complete charge of all *monetary* matters affecting the household.

monolithic ADJ. solidly uniform; unyielding. The patriots sought to present a *monolithic* front.

monotheism N. belief in one God. Abraham was the first to proclaim his belief in *monotheism*.

monotony N. sameness leading to boredom. He took a clerical job, but soon grew to hate the *monotony* of his daily routine.

monumental ADJ. massive. Writing a dictionary is a *monumental* task.

moodiness N. fits of depression or gloom. We could not discover the cause of her recurrent *moodiness*.

moor N. marshy wasteland. These *moors* can only be used for hunting; they are too barren for agriculture.

moot ADJ. debatable. Our tariff policy is a *moot* subject.

moratorium N. legal delay of payment. If we declare a *moratorium* and delay collection of debts for six months, I am sure the farmers will be able to meet their bills.

morbid ADJ. given to unwholesome thought; gloomy. These *morbid* speculations are dangerous; we must lighten our thinking by emphasis on more pleasant matters.

mordant ADJ. biting; sarcastic; stinging. Actors feared the critic's *mordant* pen.

mores N. customs. The *mores* of Mexico are those of Spain with some modifications.

morganatic ADJ. describing a marriage between a member of a royal family and a commoner in which it is agreed that any children will not inherit title, etc. Refusing the suggestion of a *morganatic* marriage, the king abdicated from the throne when he could not marry the woman he loved.

moribund ADJ. at the point of death. The doctors called the family to the bedside of the *moribund* patient.

■ **morose** ADJ. ill-humored; sullen. When we first meet Hamlet, we find him *morose* and depressed.

mortician N. undertaker. The *mortician* prepared the corpse for burial.

mortify V. humiliate; punish the flesh. She was so *mortified* by her blunder that she ran to her room in tears.

mote N. small speck. The tiniest *mote* in the eye is very painful.

motif N. theme. This simple *motif* runs throughout the entire score.

motley ADJ. parti-colored; mixed. The captain had gathered a *motley* crew to sail the vessel.

mottled ADJ. spotted. When he blushed, his face took on a *mottled* hue.

mountebank N. charlatan; boastful pretender. The patent medicine man was a *mountebank*.

muddle V. confuse; mix up. His thoughts were *muddled* and chaotic. also N.

muggy ADJ. warm and damp. August in New York City is often *muggy*.

mugwump N. defector from a party. When he refused to support his party's nominees, he was called a *mugwump* and deprived of his seniority privileges in Congress.

mulct V. defraud a person of something. The lawyer was accused of trying to *mulct* the boy of his legacy.

multifarious ADJ. varied; greatly diversified. A career woman and mother, she was constantly busy with the *multifarious* activities of her daily life.

multiform ADJ. having many forms. Snowflakes are *multiform* but always hexagonal.

multilingual ADJ. having many languages. Because they are bordered by so many countries, the Swiss people are *multilingual*.

multiplicity N. state of being numerous. He was appalled by the *multiplicity* of details he had to complete before setting out on his mission.

mundane ADJ. worldly as opposed to spiritual. He was concerned only with *mundane* matters, especially the daily stock market quotations.

munificent ADJ. very generous. The *munificent* gift was presented to the bride by her rich uncle.

murkiness N. darkness; gloom. The *murkiness* and fog of the waterfront that evening depressed me.

murrain N. plague; cattle disease. "A *murrain* on you" was a common malediction in that period.

muse V. ponder. For a moment he *mused* about the beauty of the scene, but his thoughts soon changed as he recalled his own personal problems. also N.

musky ADJ. having the odor of musk. She left a trace of *musky* perfume behind her.

muster V. gather; assemble. Washington *mustered* his forces at Trenton.

musty ADJ. stale; spoiled by age. The attic was dark and *musty*.

mutable ADJ. changing in form; fickle. His opinions were *mutable* and easily influenced by anyone who had any powers of persuasion.

■ **muted** ADJ. silent; muffled; toned down. In the funeral parlor, the mourners' voices had a *muted* quality. mute, V.

mutilate V. maim. The torturer threatened to *mutilate* his victim.

mutinous ADJ. unruly; rebellious. The captain had to use force to quiet his *mutinous* crew.

myopic ADJ. nearsighted. In thinking only of your present needs and ignoring the future, you are being rather *myopic*.

myriad N. very large number. *Myriads* of mosquitoes from the swamps invaded our village every twilight. also ADJ.

nadir N. lowest point. Although few people realized it, the Dow-Jones averages had reached their *nadir* and would soon begin an upward surge.

naiveté N. quality of being unsophisticated. I cannot believe that such *naiveté* is unassumed in a person of her age and experience. naive, ADJ.

narcissist N. conceited person. A *narcissist* is his own best friend.

nascent ADJ. incipient; coming into being. If we could identify these revolutionary movements in their *nascent* state, we would be able to eliminate serious trouble in later years.

natal ADJ. pertaining to birth. He refused to celebrate his *natal* day because it reminded him of the few years he could look forward to.

Test

Word List 31 _Synonyms_

Each of the questions below consists of a word in capital letters, followed by five lettered words or phrases. Choose the lettered word or phrase that is most nearly similar in meaning to the word in capital letters and write the letter of your choice on your answer paper.

451. MODISH (A) sentimental (B) stylish (C) vacillating (D) contrary (E) adorned
452. MOLLIFY (A) avenge (B) attenuate (C) attribute (D) mortify (E) appease
453. MONETARY (A) boring (B) fascinating (C) fiscal (D) stationary (E) scrupulous
454. MOOT (A) visual (B) invisible (C) controversial (D) anticipatory (E) obsequious
455. MORDANT (A) dying (B) trenchant (C) fabricating (D) controlling (E) avenging
456. MORIBUND (A) dying (B) appropriate (C) leather bound (D) answering (E) undertaking
457. MOTLEY (A) active (B) disguised (C) variegated (D) somber (E) sick

458. MUGGY (A) attacking (B) fascinating (C) humid (D) characteristic (E) gelid
459. MULCT (A) swindle (B) hold (C) record (D) print (E) fertilize
460. MULTILINGUAL (A) variegated (B) polyglot (C) multilateral (D) polyandrous (E) multiplied
461. MUNDANE (A) global (B) futile (C) spatial (D) heretic (E) worldly
462. MUNIFICENT (A) grandiose (B) puny (C) philanthropic (D) poor (E) gracious
463. MUSTY (A) flat (B) necessary (C) indifferent (D) nonchalant (E) vivid
464. MYOPIC (A) visionary (B) nearsighted (C) moral (D) glassy (E) blind
465. NASCENT (A) incipient (B) ignorant (C) loyal (D) treacherous (E) unnamed

Word List 32 natation-obsidian

natation N. swimming. The Red Cross emphasizes the need for courses in *natation*.

nauseate V. cause to become sick; fill with disgust. The foul smells began to *nauseate* him.

nautical ADJ. pertaining to ships or navigation. The Maritime Museum contains many models of clipper ships, logbooks, anchors and many other items of a *nautical* nature.

nave N. main body of a church. The *nave* of the cathedral was empty at this hour.

neap ADJ. lowest. We shall have to navigate very cautiously over the reefs as we have a *neap* tide this time of the month.

nebulous ADJ. vague; hazy; cloudy. She had only a *nebulous* memory of her grandmother's face.

necrology N. obituary notice; list of the dead. The *necrology* of those buried in this cemetery is available in the office.

necromancy N. black magic; dealings with the dead. Because he was able to perform feats of *necromancy,* the natives thought he was in league with the devil.

nefarious ADJ. very wicked. He was universally feared because of his many *nefarious* deeds.

negation N. denial. I must accept his argument since you have been unable to present any *negation* of his evidence.

negligence N. carelessness. *Negligence* can prove costly near complicated machinery.

nemesis N. revenging agent. Captain Bligh vowed to be Christian's *nemesis*.

neologism N. new or newly coined word or phrase. As we invent new techniques and professions, we must also invent *neologisms* such as "microcomputer" and "astronaut" to describe them.

neophyte N. recent convert; beginner. This mountain slope contains slides that will challenge experts as well as *neophytes.*

nepotism N. favoritism (to a relative). John left his position with the company because he felt that advancement was based on *nepotism* rather than ability.

nether ADJ. lower. Tradition locates hell in the *nether* regions.

nettle V. annoy; vex. Do not let him *nettle* you with his sarcastic remarks.

nexus N. connection. I fail to see the *nexus* which binds these two widely separated events.

nib N. beak; pen point. The *nibs* of fountain pens often became clotted and corroded.

nicety N. precision; minute distinction. I cannot distinguish between such *niceties* of reasoning.

niggardly ADJ. meanly stingy; parsimonious. The *niggardly* pittance the widow receives from the government cannot keep her from poverty.

niggle V. spend too much time on minor points; carp. Let's not *niggle* over details. niggling, ADJ.

nihilism N. denial of traditional values; total skepticism. *Nihilism* holds that existence has no meaning.

nirvana N. in Buddhist teachings, the ideal state in which the individual loses himself in the attainment of an impersonal beatitude. He tried to explain the concept of *nirvana* to his skeptical students.

nocturnal ADJ. done at night. Mr. Jones obtained a watchdog to prevent the *nocturnal* raids on his chicken coops.

noisome ADJ. foul smelling; unwholesome. I never could stand the *noisome* atmosphere surrounding the slaughter houses.

nomadic ADJ. wandering. Several *nomadic* tribes of Indians would hunt in this area each year.

nomenclature N. terminology; system of names. She struggled to master scientific *nomenclature.*

nominal ADJ. in name only; trifling. He offered to drive her to the airport for only a *nominal* fee.

nonage N. immaturity. She was embarrassed by the *nonage* of her contemporaries who never seemed to grow up.

nonchalance N. indifference; lack of interest. Few people could understand how he could listen to the news of the tragedy with such *nonchalance;* the majority regarded him as callous and unsympathetic.

noncommittal ADJ. neutral; unpledged; undecided. We were annoyed by his *noncommittal* reply for we had been led to expect definite assurances of his approval.

nonentity N. nonexistence; person of no importance. Of course you are a *nonentity;* you will continue to be one until you prove your value to the community.

nonplus V. bring to a halt by confusion. In my efforts to correct this situation I felt *nonplussed* by the stupidity of my assistants.

non sequitur N. a conclusion that does not follow from the facts stated. Your term paper is full of *non sequiturs;* I cannot see how you reached the conclusions you state.

nosegay N. fragrant bouquet. These spring flowers will make an attractive *nosegay.*

nostalgia N. homesickness; longing for the past. The first settlers found so much work to do that they had little time for *nostalgia.*

nostrum N. questionable medicine. No quack selling *nostrums* is going to cheat me.

notorious ADJ. outstandingly bad; unfavorably known. Captain Kidd was a *notorious* pirate.

■ **novelty** N. something new; newness. The computer is no longer a *novelty* around the office. novel, ADJ.

novice N. beginner. Even a *novice* can do good work if he follows these simple directions.

noxious ADJ. harmful. We must trace the source of these *noxious* gases before they asphyxiate us.

nuance N. shade of difference in meaning or color. The unskilled eye of the layman has difficulty in discerning the *nuances* of color in the paintings.

nubile ADJ. marriageable. Mrs. Bennet, in *Pride and Prejudice* by Jane Austen, was worried about finding suitable husbands for her five *nubile* daughters.

nugatory ADJ. futile; worthless. This agreement is *nugatory* for no court will enforce it.

nullify V. to make invalid. Once the contract was *nullified,* it no longer had any legal force.

numismatist N. person who collects coins. The *numismatist* had a splendid collection of antique coins.

nuptial ADJ. related to marriage. Their *nuptial* ceremony was performed in Golden Gate Park.

nurture V. bring up; feed; educate. We must *nurture* the young so that they will develop into good citizens.

nutrient ADJ. providing nourishment. During the convalescent period, the patient must be provided with *nutrient* foods. also N.

oaf N. stupid, awkward person. He called the unfortunate waiter a clumsy *oaf.*

obdurate ADJ. stubborn. He was *obdurate* in his refusal to listen to our complaints.

obeisance N. bow. She made an *obeisance* as the king and queen entered the room.

obelisk N. tall column tapering and ending in a pyramid. Cleopatra's Needle is an *obelisk* in New York City's Central Park.

obese ADJ. fat. It is advisable that *obese* people try to lose weight.

obfuscate V. confuse; muddle. Do not *obfuscate* the issues by dragging in irrelevant arguments.

obituary ADJ. death notice. I first learned of her death when I read the *obituary* column in the newspaper. also N.

■ **objective** ADJ. not influenced by emotions; fair. Even though he was her son, she tried to be *objective* about his behavior.

■ **objective** N. goal; aim. A degree in medicine was her ultimate *objective.*

objurgate V. scold; rebuke severely. I am afraid she will *objurgate* us publicly for this offense.

objurgation N. severe rebuke; scolding. *Objurgations* and even threats of punishment did not deter the young hoodlums.

oblation N. the Eucharist; pious donation. The wealthy man offered *oblations* so that the Church might be able to provide for the needy.

obligatory ADJ. binding; required. It is *obligatory* that books borrowed from the library be returned within two weeks.

oblique ADJ. slanting; deviating from the perpendicular or from a straight line. The sergeant ordered the men to march *"Oblique* Right."

obliquity N. departure from right principles; perversity. His moral decadence was marked by his *obliquity* from the ways of integrity and honesty.

obliterate v. destroy completely. The tidal wave *obliterated* several island villages.

oblivion N. forgetfulness. Her works had fallen into a state of *oblivion;* no one bothered to read them.

obloquy N. slander; disgrace; infamy. I resent the *obloquy* that you are casting upon my reputation.

obnoxious ADJ. offensive. I find your behavior *obnoxious;* please mend your ways.

■ **obscure** ADJ. dark; vague; unclear. Even after I read the poem a fourth time, its meaning was still *obscure.* obscurity, N.

■ **obscure** v. darken; make unclear. At times he seemed purposely to *obscure* his meaning, preferring mystery to clarity.

obsequious ADJ. slavishly attentive; servile; sycophantic. Nothing is more disgusting to me than the *obsequious* demeanor of the people who wait upon you.

obsequy N. funeral ceremony. Hundreds paid their last respects at his *obsequies.*

obsession N. fixed idea; continued brooding. This *obsession* with the supernatural has made him unpopular with his neighbors.

obsidian N. black volcanic rock. The deposits of *obsidian* on the mountain slopes were an indication that the volcano had erupted in ancient times.

Test

Word List 32 *Antonyms*

Each of the questions below consists of a word in capital letters, followed by five lettered words or phrases. Choose the lettered word or phrase that is most nearly opposite in meaning to the word in capital letters and write the letter of your choice on your answer paper.

466. NEBULOUS (A) starry (B) clear (C) cold (D) fundamental (E) porous
467. NEFARIOUS (A) various (B) lacking (C) benign (D) pompous (E) futile
468. NEGATION (A) postulation (B) hypothecation (C) affirmation (D) violation (E) anticipation
469. NEOPHYTE (A) veteran (B) satellite (C) desperado (D) handwriting (E) violence
470. NIGGARDLY (A) protected (B) biased (C) prodigal (D) bankrupt (E) placated
471. NOCTURNAL (A) harsh (B) marauding (C) patrolling (D) daily (E) fallow
472. NOISOME (A) quiet (B) dismayed (C) fragrant (D) sleepy (E) inquisitive

473. NOTORIOUS (A) fashionable (B) renowned (C) inactive (D) intrepid (E) invincible
474. OBDURATE (A) yielding (B) fleeting (C) finite (D) fascinating (E) permanent
475. OBESE (A) skillful (B) cadaverous (C) clever (D) unpredictable (E) lucid
476. OBJURGATION (A) elegy (B) oath (C) model (D) praise (E) approval
477. OBLIGATORY (A) demanding (B) optional (C) facile (D) friendly (E) divorced
478. OBLOQUY (A) praise (B) rectangle (C) circle (D) dialogue (E) cure
479. OBSEQUIOUS (A) successful (B) democratic (C) supercilious (D) ambitious (E) lamentable
480. OBSESSION (A) whim (B) loss (C) phobia (D) delusion (E) feud

Word List 33 obsolete-pacifist

■ **obsolete** ADJ. outmoded. That word is *obsolete:* do not use it.

obstetrician N. physician specializing in delivery of babies. In modern times, the delivery of children has passed from the midwife to the more scientifically trained *obstetrician.*

■ **obstinate** ADJ. stubborn. We tried to persuade him to give up smoking, but he was *obstinate* and refused to change.

obstreperous ADJ. boisterous; noisy. The crowd became *obstreperous* and shouted their disapproval of the proposals made by the speaker.

obtrude v. push into prominence. The other members of the group object to the manner in which you *obtrude* your opinions into matters of no concern to you.

obtrusive ADJ. pushing forward. I found her a very *obtrusive* person, constantly seeking the center of the stage.

obtuse ADJ. blunt; stupid. Because he was so *obtuse,* he could not follow the teacher's reasoning and asked foolish questions.

obviate v. make unnecessary; get rid of. I hope this contribution will *obviate* any need for further collections of funds.

Occident N. the West. It will take time for the *Occident* to understand the ways and customs of the Orient.

occlude v. shut; close. A blood clot *occluded* an artery to the heart.

occult ADJ. mysterious; secret; supernatural. The *occult* rites of the organization were revealed only to members. also N.

oculist N. physician who specializes in treatment of the eyes. In many states, an *oculist* is the only one who may apply medicinal drops to the eyes for the purpose of examining them.

odious ADJ. hateful. I find the task of punishing you most *odious*.

odium N. repugnance; dislike. I cannot express the *odium* I feel at your heinous actions.

odoriferous ADJ. giving off an odor. The *odoriferous* spices stimulated her jaded appetite.

odorous ADJ. having an odor. This variety of hybrid tea rose is more *odorous* than the one you have in your garden.

odyssey N. long, eventful journey. The refugee's journey from Cambodia was a terrifying *odyssey*.

offal N. waste; garbage. In America, we discard as *offal* that which could feed families in less fortunate parts of the world.

offertory N. collection of money at religious ceremony; part of the Mass during which offerings are made. The donations collected during the *offertory* will be assigned to our mission work abroad.

officious ADJ. meddlesome; excessively trying to please. Browning informs us that the Duke resented the bough of cherries some *officious* fool brought to please the Duchess.

ogle V. glance coquettishly at; make eyes at. Sitting for hours at the sidewalk cafe, the old gentleman would *ogle* the young girls and recall his youthful romances.

olfactory ADJ. concerning the sense of smell. The *olfactory* organ is the nose.

oligarchy N. government by a few. The feudal *oligarchy* was supplanted by an autocracy.

ominous ADJ. threatening. These clouds are *ominous;* they portend a severe storm.

omnipotent ADJ. all-powerful. The monarch regarded himself as *omnipotent* and responsible to no one for his acts.

omnipresent ADJ. universally present; ubiquitous. On Christmas Eve, Santa Claus is *omnipresent*.

omniscient ADJ. all-knowing. I do not pretend to be *omniscient,* but I am positive about this fact.

omnivorous ADJ. eating both plant and animal food; devouring everything. Some animals, including man, are *omnivorous* and eat both meat and vegetables; others are either carnivorous or herbivorous.

onerous ADJ. burdensome. He asked for an assistant because his work load was too *onerous*.

onomatopoeia N. words formed in imitation of natural sounds. Words like "rustle" and "gargle" are illustrations of *onomatopoeia*.

onslaught N. vicious assault. We suffered many casualties during the unexpected *onslaught* of the enemy troops.

onus N. burden; responsibility. The emperor was spared the *onus* of signing the surrender papers; instead, he relegated the assignment to his generals.

opalescent ADJ. iridescent. The Ancient Mariner admired the *opalescent* sheen on the water.

opaque ADJ. dark; not transparent. The *opaque* window kept the sunlight out of the room.

opiate N. sleep producer; deadener of pain. By such *opiates,* she made the people forget their difficulties and accept their unpleasant circumstances.

opportune ADJ. timely; well chosen. You have come at an *opportune* moment, for I need a new secretary.

■ **opportunist** N. individual who sacrifices principles for expediency by taking advantage of circumstances. I do not know how he will vote on this question as he is an *opportunist*.

opprobrious ADJ. disgraceful. I find your conduct so *opprobrious* that I must exclude you from classes.

opprobrium N. infamy; vilification. He refused to defend himself against the slander and *opprobrium* hurled against him by the newspapers; he preferred to rely on his record.

optician N. maker and seller of eyeglasses. The patient took the prescription given him by his oculist to the *optician*.

■ **optimist** N. person who looks on the good side. The pessimist says the glass is half-empty; the *optimist* says it is half-full.

optimum ADJ. most favorable. If you wait for the *optimum* moment to act, you may never begin your project. also N.

■ **optional** ADJ. not compulsory; left to one's choice. I was impressed by the range of *optional* accessories for my microcomputer that were available. option, N.

optometrist N. one who fits glasses to remedy visual defects. Although an *optometrist* is qualified to treat many eye disorders, she may not use medicines or surgery in her examinations.

■ **opulence** N. wealth. Visitors from Europe are amazed and impressed by the *opulence* of this country.

opus N. work. Although many critics hailed his Fifth Symphony as his major work, he did not regard it as his major *opus*.

oracular ADJ. foretelling; mysterious. Oedipus could not understand the *oracular* warning he received.

oratorio N. dramatic poem set to music. The Glee Club decided to present an *oratorio* during their recital.

ordain V. command; arrange; consecrate. The king *ordained* that no foreigner should be allowed to enter the city.

ordinance N. decree. Passing a red light is a violation of a city *ordinance*.

orient V. get one's bearings; adjust. Philip spent his first day in Denver *orienting* himself to the city.

orientation N. act of finding oneself in society. Freshman *orientation* provides the incoming students with an opportunity to learn about their new environment and their place in it.

orifice N. mouthlike opening; small opening. The Howe Caverns were discovered when someone observed that a cold wind was issuing from an *orifice* in the hillside.

orison N. prayer. Hamlet greets Ophelia with the request, "Nymph, in thy *orisons,* be all my sins remembered."

ornate ADJ. excessively decorated; highly decorated. Furniture of the Baroque period can be recognized by its *ornate* carvings.

ornithologist N. scientific student of birds. Audubon's drawings of American bird life have been of interest not only to the *ornithologists* but also to the general public.

ornithology N. study of birds. Audubon's studies of American birds greatly influenced the course of *ornithology* in this country.

orotund ADJ. having a round, resonant quality; inflated speech. The politician found that his *orotund* voice was an asset when he spoke to his constituents.

orthodox ADJ. traditional; conservative in belief. Faced with a problem, he preferred to take an *orthodox* approach rather than shock anyone.

orthography N. correct spelling. Many of us find English *orthography* difficult to master because so many of our words are not written phonetically.

oscillate V. vibrate pendulumlike; waver. It is interesting to note how public opinion *oscillates* between the extremes of optimism and pessimism.

ossify V. change or harden into bone. When he called his opponent a ''bonehead,'' he implied that his adversary's brain had *ossified* and that he was not capable of clear thinking.

ostensible ADJ. apparent; professed; pretended. Although the *ostensible* purpose of this expedition is to discover new lands, we are really interested in finding new markets for our products.

ostentatious ADJ. showy; pretentious. The real hero is modest, never *ostentatious*.

ostracize V. exclude from public favor; ban. As soon as the newspapers carried the story of his connection with the criminals, his friends began to *ostracize* him. ostracism, N.

oust V. expel; drive out. The world wondered if Aquino would be able to *oust* Marcos from office.

■ **overt** ADJ. open to view. According to the United States Constitution, a person must commit an *overt* act before he may be tried for treason.

overweening ADJ. presumptuous; arrogant. His *overweening* pride in his accomplishments was not justified.

ovine ADJ. like a sheep. How *ovine* these true-believers were, following their shepherds thoughtlessly.

ovoid ADJ. egg-shaped. At Easter she had to cut out hundreds of brightly colored *ovoid* shapes.

pachyderm N. thick-skinned animal. The elephant is probably the best-known *pachyderm*.

pacifist N. one opposed to force; antimilitarist. The *pacifists* urged that we reduce our military budget and recall our troops stationed overseas.

Test

Word List 33   *Antonyms*

Each of the questions below consists of a word in capital letters, followed by five lettered words or phrases. Choose the lettered word or phrase that is most nearly opposite in meaning to the word in capital letters and write the letter of your choice on your answer paper.

481. OBSOLETE (A) heated (B) desolate (C) renovated (D) frightful (E) automatic
482. OBSTREPEROUS (A) turbid (B) quiet (C) remote (D) lucid (E) active
483. OBTUSE (A) sheer (B) transparent (C) tranquil (D) timid (E) shrewd
484. ODIOUS (A) fragrant (B) redolent (C) fetid (D) delightful (E) puny
485. ODIUM (A) noise (B) liking (C) dominant (D) hasty (E) atrium
486. OMNIPOTENT (A) weak (B) democratic (C) despotic (D) passionate (E) late
487. OMNISCIENT (A) sophisticated (B) ignorant (C) essential (D) trivial (E) isolated
488. OPIATE (A) distress (B) sleep (C) stimulant (D) laziness (E) despair
489. OPPORTUNE (A) occasional (B) fragrant (C) fragile (D) awkward (E) neglected
490. OPPORTUNIST (A) man of destiny (B) man of principle (C) changeling (D) adversary (E) colleague
491. OPPROBRIUM (A) delineation (B) aptitude (C) majesty (D) freedom (E) praise
492. OPTIMUM (A) pessimistic (B) knowledgeable (C) worst (D) minimum (E) chosen
493. OPULENCE (A) pessimism (B) patriotism (C) potency (D) passion (E) poverty
494. OROTUND (A) not reddish (B) not resonant (C) grave (D) fragile (E) not eager
495. OVERWEENING (A) humble (B) impotent (C) avid (D) acrimonious (E) exaggerated

Word List 34   paddock-peccadillo

paddock N. saddling enclosure at race track; lot for exercising horses. The *paddock* is located directly in front of the grandstand so that all may see the horses being saddled and the jockeys mounted.

paean N. song of praise or joy. *Paeans* celebrating the victory filled the air.

■ **painstaking** ADJ. showing hard work; taking great care. The new high frequency word list is the result of *painstaking* efforts on the part of our research staff.

palatable ADJ. agreeable; pleasing to the taste. Paying taxes can never be made *palatable*.

palatial ADJ. magnificent. He proudly showed us through his *palatial* home.

palaver N. discussion; misleading speech; chatter. In spite of all the *palaver* before the meeting, the delegates were able to conduct serious negotiations when they sat down at the conference table. also V.

paleontology N. study of prehistoric life. The *paleontology* instructor had a superb collection of fossils.

palette N. board on which painter mixes pigments. At the present time, art supply stores are selling a paper *palette* which may be discarded after use.

palimpsest N. parchment used for second time after original writing has been erased. Using chemical reagents, scientists have been able to restore the original writings on many *palimpsests.*

pall V. grow tiresome. The study of word lists can eventually *pall* and put one to sleep.

pallet N. small, poor bed. The weary traveler went to sleep on his straw *pallet.*

palliate V. ease pain; make less guilty or offensive. Doctors must *palliate* that which they cannot cure.

palliation N. act of making less severe or violent. If we cannot find a cure for this disease at the present time, we can, at least, endeavor to seek its *palliation.*

pallid ADJ. pale; wan. Because his occupation required that he work at night and sleep during the day, he had an exceptionally *pallid* complexion.

palpable ADJ. tangible; easily perceptible. I cannot understand how you could overlook such a *palpable* blunder.

palpitate V. throb; flutter. As he became excited, his heart began to *palpitate* more and more erratically.

paltry ADJ. insignificant; petty. This is a *paltry* sum to pay for such a masterpiece.

panacea N. cure-all; remedy for all diseases. There is no easy *panacea* that will solve our complicated international situation.

panache N. flair; flamboyance. Many performers imitate Noel Coward, but few have his *panache* and sense of style.

pandemic ADJ. widespread; affecting the majority of people. They feared the AIDS epidemic would soon reach *pandemic* proportions.

pandemonium N. wild tumult. When the ships collided in the harbor, *pandemonium* broke out among the passengers.

pander V. cater to the low desires of others. Books which *pander* to man's lowest instincts should be banned.

panegyric N. formal praise. The modest hero blushed as he listened to the *panegyrics* uttered by the speakers about his valorous act.

panoply N. full set of armor. The medieval knight in full *panoply* found his movements limited by the weight of his armor.

panorama N. comprehensive view; unobstructed view in all directions. Tourists never forget the impact of their first *panorama* of the Grand Canyon.

pantomime N. acting without dialogue. Because he worked in *pantomime,* the clown could be understood wherever he appeared. also V.

papyrus N. ancient paper made from stem of papyrus plant. The ancient Egyptians were among the first to write on *papyrus.*

parable N. short, simple story teaching a moral. Let us apply to our own conduct the lesson that this *parable* teaches.

paradox N. statement that looks false but is actually correct; a contradictory statement. Wordsworth's "The child is father to the man" is an example of *paradox.*

paragon N. model of perfection. The class disliked him because the teacher was always pointing to him as a *paragon* of virtue.

parallelism N. state of being parallel; similarity. There is a striking *parallelism* between the twins.

parameter N. limits; independent variable. We need to define the *parameters* of the problem.

paramour N. illicit lover. She sought a divorce on the grounds that her husband had a *paramour* in another town.

paranoia N. chronic form of insanity marked by delusions of grandeur or persecution. The psychiatrists analyzed his ailment as *paranoia* when he claimed that everyone hated him.

paranoiac N. mentally unsound person suffering from delusions. Although he is obviously suffering from delusions, I hesitate to call him a *paranoiac.*

parapet N. low wall at edge of roof or balcony. The best way to attack the soldiers fighting behind the *parapets* on the roof is by bombardment from the air.

paraphernalia N. equipment; odds and ends. His desk was cluttered with paper, pen, ink, dictionary and other *paraphernalia* of the writing craft.

paraphrase V. restate a passage in one's own words while retaining thought of author. In 250 words or less, *paraphrase* this article. also N.

parasite N. animal or plant living on another; toady; sycophant. The tapeworm is an example of the kind of *parasite* that may infest the human body.

parched ADJ. extremely dry; very thirsty. The *parched* desert landscape seemed hostile to life.

paregoric N. medicine that eases pain. The doctor prescribed a *paregoric* to alleviate his suffering.

pariah N. social outcast. I am not a *pariah* to be shunned and ostracized.

parity N. equality; close resemblance. I find your analogy inaccurate because I do not see the *parity* between the two illustrations.

parlance N. language; idiom. All this legal *parlance* confuses me; I need an interpreter.

parley N. conference. The peace *parley* has not produced the anticipated truce. also V.

parody N. humorous imitation; travesty. We enjoyed the clever *parodies* of popular songs which the chorus sang.

paroxysm N. fit or attack of pain, laughter, rage. When he heard of his son's misdeeds, he was seized by a *paroxysm* of rage.

parricide N. person who murders his own father; murder of a father. The jury was shocked by the details of this vicious *parricide* and found the man who had killed his father guilty of murder in the first degree.

parry V. ward off a blow. He was content to wage a defensive battle and tried to *parry* his opponent's thrusts.

parsimonious ADJ. stingy; excessively frugal. His *parsimonious* nature did not permit him to enjoy any luxuries.

■ **partial** ADJ. (1) incomplete. In this issue we have published only a *partial* list of contributors because we lack space to acknowledge everyone. (2) biased; having a liking for something. I am extremely *partial* to chocolate eclairs.

partiality N. inclination; bias. As a judge, not only must I be unbiased, but I must also avoid any evidence of *partiality* when I award the prize.

■ **partisan** ADJ. one-sided; prejudiced; committed to a party. On certain issues of conscience, she refused to take a *partisan* stand. also N.

parturition N. delivery; childbirth. The difficulties anticipated by the obstetricians at *parturition* did not materialize; it was a normal delivery.

parvenu N. upstart; newly rich person. Although extremely wealthy, he was regarded as a *parvenu* by the aristocratic members of society.

passé ADJ. old-fashioned; past the prime. Her style is *passé* and reminiscent of the Victorian era.

passive ADJ. not active; acted upon. Mahatma Gandhi urged his followers to pursue a program of *passive* resistance as he felt that it was more effective than violence and acts of terrorism.

pastiche N. imitation of another's style in musical composition or in writing. We cannot even say that her music is a *pastiche* of this composer or that; it is, rather, reminiscent of many musicians.

pastoral ADJ. rural. In these stories of *pastoral* life, we find an understanding of the daily tasks of country folk.

patent ADJ. open for the public to read; obvious. It was *patent* to everyone that the witness spoke the truth. also N.

pathetic ADJ. causing sadness, compassion, pity; touching. Everyone in the auditorium was weeping by the time he finished his *pathetic* tale about the orphaned boy.

pathological ADJ. pertaining to disease. As we study the *pathological* aspects of this disease, we must not overlook the psychological elements.

pathos N. tender sorrow; pity; quality in art or literature that produces these feelings. The quiet tone of *pathos* that ran through the novel never degenerated into the maudlin or the overly sentimental.

patina N. green crust on old bronze works; tone slowly taken by varnished painting. Judging by the *patina* on this bronze statue, we can conclude that this is the work of a medieval artist.

patois N. local or provincial dialect. His years of study of the language at the university did not enable him to understand the *patois* of the natives.

patriarch N. father and ruler of a family or tribe. In many primitive tribes, the leader and lawmaker was the *patriarch*.

patrician ADJ. noble; aristocratic. We greatly admired her well-bred, *patrician* elegance. also N.

patricide N. person who murders his father; murder of a father. The words parricide and *patricide* have exactly the same meaning.

patrimony N. inheritance from father. As predicted by his critics, he spent his *patrimony* within two years of his father's death.

■ **patronize** V. support; act superior toward. Experts in a field sometimes appear to *patronize* people who are less knowledgeable of the subject.

■ **paucity** N. scarcity. They closed the restaurant because the *paucity* of customers made it uneconomical to operate.

peccadillo N. slight offense. If we examine these escapades carefully, we will realize that they are mere *peccadilloes* rather than major crimes.

Test

Word List 34   *Synonyms and Antonyms*

Each of the following questions consists of a word in capital letters, followed by five lettered words or phrases. Choose the lettered word or phrase which is most nearly similar or the opposite of the word in capital letters and write the letter of your choice on your answer paper.

496. PAEAN (A) serf (B) pealing (C) lien (D) lament (E) folly

497. PALLET (A) bed (B) pigment board (C) bench (D) spectrum (E) quality

498. PALLIATE (A) smoke (B) quicken (C) substitute (D) alleviate (E) sadden

499. PANDEMONIUM (A) calm (B) frustration (C) efficiency (D) impishness (E) sophistication

500. PANEGYRIC (A) medication (B) panacea (C) rotation (D) vacillation (E) praise

501. PARABLE (A) equality (B) allegory (C) frenzy (D) folly (E) cuticle

502. PARADOX (A) exaggeration (B) contradiction (C) hyperbole (D) invective (E) poetic device

503. PARAMOUR (A) illicit lover (B) majority (C) importance (D) hatred (E) clandestine affair

504. PARANOIA (A) fracture (B) statement (C) quantity (D) benefaction (E) sanity

505. PARIAH (A) village (B) suburb (C) outcast (D) disease (E) benefactor

506. PARITY (A) duplicate (B) miniature (C) golf tee (D) similarity (E) event
507. PARSIMONIOUS (A) grammatical (B) syntactical (C) effective (D) extravagant (E) esoteric
508. PARTIALITY (A) completion (B) equality (C) bias (D) divorce (E) reflection
509. PASSÉ (A) scornful (B) rural (C) out-of-date (D) silly (E) barbaric
510. PASTICHE (A) imitation (B) glue (C) present (D) greeting (E) family

---

Word List 35   peculate-philander

peculate V. steal; embezzle. His crime of *peculating* public funds entrusted to his care is especially damnable.

peculation N. embezzlement; theft. Her *peculations* were not discovered until the auditors found discrepancies in the financial statements.

pecuniary ADJ. pertaining to money. I never expected a *pecuniary* reward for my work in this activity.

pedagogue N. teacher; dull and formal teacher. He could never be a stuffy *pedagogue;* his classes were always lively and filled with humor.

pedant N. scholar who overemphasizes book learning or technicalities. Her insistence that the book be memorized marked the teacher as a *pedant* rather than a scholar.

■ **pedantic** ADJ. showing off learning; bookish. What you say is *pedantic* and reveals an unfamiliarity with the realities of life.

pedestrian ADJ. ordinary; unimaginative. Unintentionally boring, he wrote page after page of *pedestrian* prose.

pediatrician N. expert in children's diseases. The family doctor advised the parents to consult a *pediatrician* about their child's ailment.

pediment N. triangular part above columns in Greek buildings. The *pediment* of the building was filled with sculptures and adorned with elaborate scrollwork.

pejorative ADJ. having a deteriorating or depreciating effect on the meaning of a word. His use of *pejorative* language indicated his contempt for his audience.

pell-mell ADV. in confusion; disorderly. The excited students dashed *pell-mell* into the stadium to celebrate the victory.

pellucid ADJ. transparent; limpid; easy to understand. After reading these stodgy philosophers, I find his *pellucid* style very enjoyable.

penance N. self-imposed punishment for sin. The Ancient Mariner said, "I have *penance* done and *penance* more will do," to atone for the sin of killing the albatross.

penchant N. strong inclination; liking. He had a strong *penchant* for sculpture and owned many statues.

pendant ADJ. hanging down from something. Her *pendant* earrings glistened in the light.

pendent ADJ. suspended; jutting; pending. The *pendent* rock hid the entrance to the cave.

penitent ADJ. repentant. When he realized the enormity of his crime, he became remorseful and *penitent.* also N.

pendulous ADJ. hanging; suspended. The *pendulous* chandeliers swayed in the breeze and gave the impression that they were about to fall from the ceiling.

pennate ADJ. having wings or feathers. The *pennate* leaves of the sumac remind us of feathers.

pensive ADJ. dreamily thoughtful; thoughtful with a hint of sadness. The *pensive* youth gazed at the painting for a long time and then sighed.

penumbra N. partial shadow (in an eclipse). During an eclipse, we can see an area of total darkness and a lighter area which is the *penumbra.*

penurious ADJ. stingy; parsimonious. He was a *penurious* man, averse to spending money even for the necessities of life.

penury N. extreme poverty. We find much *penury* and suffering in this slum area.

peon N. unskilled laborer; drudge. He was doomed to be a *peon,* to live a lowly life of drudgery and toil.

percussion ADJ. striking one object against another sharply. The drum is a *percussion* instrument. also N.

perdition N. damnation; complete ruin. He was damned to eternal *perdition.*

peregrination N. journey. His *peregrinations* in foreign lands did not bring understanding; he mingled only with fellow tourists and did not attempt to communicate with the native population.

peremptory ADJ. demanding and leaving no choice. I resent your *peremptory* attitude.

perennial N. lasting. These plants are hardy *perennials* and will bloom for many years. also ADJ.

perfidious ADJ. basely false. Your *perfidious* gossip is malicious and dangerous.

perfidy N. violation of a trust. When we learned of his *perfidy,* we were shocked and dismayed.

perforce ADV. of necessity. I must *perforce* leave, as my train is about to start.

■ **perfunctory** ADJ. superficial; listless; not thorough. He overlooked many weaknesses when he inspected the factory in his *perfunctory* manner.

perigee N. point of moon's orbit when it is nearest the earth. The rocket which was designed to take photographs of the moon was launched as the moon approached its *perigee.*

perimeter N. outer boundary. To find the *perimeter* of any quadrilateral, we add the lengths of the four sides.

peripatetic ADJ. walking about; moving. The *peripatetic* school of philosophy derives its name from the fact that Aristotle walked with his pupils while discussing philosophy with them.

■ **peripheral** ADJ. marginal; outer. We lived, not in central London, but in one of those *peripheral* suburbs that spring up on the outskirts of a great city.

periphery N. edge, especially of a round surface. He sensed that there was something just beyond the *periphery* of his vision.

peristyle N. series of columns surrounding a building or yard. The cloister was surrounded by a *peristyle* reminiscent of the Parthenon.

perjury N. false testimony while under oath. When several witnesses appeared to challenge his story, he was indicted for *perjury*.

permeable ADJ. porous; allowing passage through. Glass is *permeable* to light.

permeate V. pass through; spread. The odor of frying onions *permeated* the air.

pernicious ADJ. very destructive. He argued that these books had a *pernicious* effect on young and susceptible minds.

perpetrate V. commit an offense. Only an insane person could *perpetrate* such a horrible crime.

perpetual ADJ. everlasting. Ponce de Leon hoped to find *perpetual* youth.

peroration N. conclusion of an oration. The *peroration* was largely hortatory and brought the audience to its feet clamoring for action at its close.

perquisite N. any gain above stipulated salary. The *perquisites* attached to this job make it even more attractive than the salary indicates.

persiflage N. flippant conversation; banter. This *persiflage* is not appropriate when we have such serious problems to discuss.

personable ADJ. attractive. The man I am seeking to fill this position must be *personable* since he will be representing us before the public.

perspicacious ADJ. having insight; penetrating; astute. The brilliant lawyer was known for his *perspicacious* deductions.

perspicuity N. clearness of expression; freedom from ambiguity. One of the outstanding features of this book is the *perspicuity* of its author; her meaning is always clear.

perspicuous ADJ. plainly expressed. Her *perspicuous* comments eliminated all possibility of misinterpretation.

pert ADJ. impertinent; forward. I think your *pert* and impudent remarks call for an apology.

pertinacious ADJ. stubborn; persistent. He is bound to succeed because his *pertinacious* nature will not permit him to quit.

pertinent ADJ. suitable; to the point. The lawyer wanted to know all the *pertinent* details.

perturb V. disturb greatly. I am afraid this news will *perturb* him and cause him grief.

perturbation N. agitation. I fail to understand why such an innocent remark should create such *perturbation*.

perusal N. reading. I am certain that you have missed important details in your rapid *perusal* of this document. peruse, V.

pervade V. spread throughout. As the news of the defeat *pervaded* the country, a feeling of anger directed at the rulers who had been the cause of the disaster grew.

perverse ADJ. stubborn; intractable. Because of your *perverse* attitude, I must rate you as deficient in cooperation.

perversion N. corruption; turning from right to wrong. Inasmuch as he had no motive for his crimes, we could not understand his *perversion*.

perversity N. stubborn maintenance of a wrong cause. I cannot forgive your *perversity* in repeating such an impossible story.

■ **pessimism** N. belief that life is basically bad or evil; gloominess. The good news we have been receiving lately indicates that there is little reason for your *pessimism*.

pestilential ADJ. causing plague; baneful. People were afraid to explore the *pestilential* swamp. pestilence, N.

petrify V. turn to stone. His sudden and unexpected appearance seemed to *petrify* her.

■ **petty** ADJ. trivial; unimportant; very small. She had no major complaints to make about his work, only a few *petty* quibbles that were almost too minor to state.

petulant ADJ. touchy; peevish. The feverish patient was *petulant* and restless.

pharisaical ADJ. pertaining to the Pharisees, who paid scrupulous attention to tradition; self-righteous; hypocritical. Walter Lippman has pointed out that moralists who do not attempt to explain the moral code they advocate are often regarded as *pharisaical* and ignored.

■ **phenomena** N. observable facts; subjects of scientific investigation. We kept careful records of the *phenomena* we noted in the course of these experiments.

phial N. small bottle. Even though it is small, this *phial* of perfume is expensive.

philander V. make love lightly; flirt. Do not *philander* with my affections because love is too serious.

Test

Word List 35   *Antonyms*

Each of the questions below consists of a word in capital letters, followed by five lettered words or phrases. Choose the lettered word or phrase that is most nearly opposite in meaning to the word in capital letters and write the letter of your choice on your answer paper.

511. PEJORATIVE (A) positive (B) legal (C) determining (D) delighting (E) declaiming
512. PELLUCID (A) logistical (B) philandering (C) incomprehensible (D) vagrant (E) warranted
513. PENCHANT (A) distance (B) imminence (C) dislike (D) attitude (E) void
514. PENURIOUS (A) imprisoned (B) captivated (C) generous (D) vacant (E) abolished
515. PERFUNCTORY (A) official (B) thorough (C) insipid (D) vicarious (E) distinctive
516. PERIGEE (A) eclipse (B) planet (C) apogee (D) refugee (E) danger
517. PERIPATETIC (A) worldly (B) stationary (C) disarming (D) seeking (E) inherent
518. PERMEABLE (A) perishable (B) effective (C) plodding (D) impenetrable (E) lasting

519. PERNICIOUS (A) practical (B) comparative (C) harmless (D) tangible (E) detailed
520. PERPETUAL (A) momentary (B) standard (C) serious (D) industrial (E) interpretive
521. PERSPICUITY (A) grace (B) feature (C) review (D) difficulty (E) vagueness
522. PERT (A) polite (B) perishable (C) moral (D) deliberate (E) stubborn
523. PERTINACIOUS (A) vengeful (B) consumptive (C) superficial (D) skilled (E) advertised
524. PERTINENT (A) understood (B) living (C) discontented (D) puzzling (E) irrelevant
525. PETULANT (A) angry (B) moral (C) declining (D) underhanded (E) uncomplaining

---

Word List 36   philanthropist-precedent

philanthropist N. lover of mankind; doer of good. As he grew older, he became famous as a *philanthropist* and benefactor of the needy.

philistine N. narrow-minded person, uncultured and exclusively interested in material gain. We need more men of culture and enlightenment; we have too many *philistines* among us.

philology N. study of language. The professor of *philology* advocated the use of Esperanto as an international language.

phlegmatic ADJ. calm; not easily disturbed. The nurse was a cheerful but *phlegmatic* person.

phobia N. morbid fear. Her fear of flying was more than mere nervousness; it was a real *phobia*.

physiognomy N. face. He prided himself on his ability to analyze a person's character by studying his *physiognomy*.

physiological ADJ. pertaining to the science of the function of living organisms. To understand this disease fully, we must examine not only its *physiological* aspects but also its psychological elements.

picaresque ADJ. pertaining to rogues in literature. *Tom Jones* has been hailed as one of the best *picaresque* novels in the English language.

piebald ADJ. mottled; spotted. You should be able to identify this horse easily as it is the only *piebald* horse in the race; the others are all one color.

pied ADJ. variegated; multicolored. The *Pied* Piper of Hamelin got his name from the multicolored clothing he wore.

pillage V. plunder. The enemy *pillaged* the quiet village and left it in ruins.

pillory V. punish by placing in a wooden frame and subjecting to ridicule. Even though he was mocked and *pilloried*, he maintained that he was correct in his beliefs. also N.

pinion V. restrain. They *pinioned* his arms against his body but left his legs free so that he could move about. also N.

pinnacle N. peak. We could see the morning sunlight illuminate the *pinnacle* while the rest of the mountain lay in shadow.

■ **pious** ADJ. devout. The *pious* parents gave their children a religious upbringing. piety, N.

piquant ADJ. pleasantly tart-tasting; stimulating. The *piquant* sauce added to our enjoyment of the meal. piquancy, N.

pique N. irritation; resentment. She showed her *pique* by her refusal to appear with the other contestants at the end of the contest.

piscatorial ADJ. pertaining to fishing. He spent many happy hours at the lake in his *piscatorial* activities.

pithy ADJ. concise; meaty. I enjoy reading his essays because they are always compact and *pithy*.

pittance N. a small allowance or wage. He could not live on the *pittance* he received as a pension and had to look for an additional source of revenue.

■ **placate** V. pacify; conciliate. The teacher tried to *placate* the angry mother.

placid ADJ. peaceful; calm. After his vacation in this *placid* section, he felt soothed and rested.

plagiarism N. theft of another's ideas or writings passed off as original. The editor recognized the *plagiarism* and rebuked the culprit who had presented the manuscript as original.

■ **plagiarize** V. steal another's ideas and pass them off as one's own. The editor could tell that the writer had *plagiarized* parts of the article; he could recognize whole paragraphs from the original source.

plaintive ADJ. mournful. The dove has a *plaintive* and melancholy call.

plangent ADJ. plaintive; resounding sadly. Although we could not understand the words of the song, we got the impression from the *plangent* tones of the singers that it was a lament of some kind.

platitude N. trite remark; commonplace statement. The *platitudes* in his speech were applauded by the vast majority in his audience; only a few people perceived how trite his remarks were.

platonic ADJ. purely spiritual; theoretical; without sensual desire. Although a member of the political group, she took only a *platonic* interest in its ideals and goals.

plauditory ADJ. approving; applauding. The theatrical company reprinted the *plauditory* comments of the critics in its advertisement.

■ **plausible** ADJ. having a show of truth but open to doubt; specious. Even though your argument is *plausible,* I still would like to have more proof.

plebeian ADJ. common; pertaining to the common people. His speeches were aimed at the *plebeian* minds and emotions; they disgusted the more refined.

plebiscite N. expression of the will of a people by direct election. I think this matter is so important that it should be decided not by a handful of legislators but by a *plebiscite* of the entire nation.

plenary ADJ. complete; full. The union leader was given *plenary* power to negotiate a new contract with the employers.

plenipotentiary ADJ. fully empowered. Since he was not given *plenipotentiary* powers by his government, he could not commit his country without consulting his superiors. also N.

plenitude N. abundance; completeness. Looking in the pantry, we admired the *plenitude* of fruits and pickles we had preserved during the summer.

plethora N. excess; overabundance. She offered a *plethora* of reasons for her shortcomings.

plumb ADJ. checking perpendicularity; vertical. Before hanging wallpaper it is advisable to drop a *plumb* line from the ceiling as a guide. also N. and V.

podiatrist N. doctor who treats ailments of the feet. He consulted a *podiatrist* about his fallen arches.

podium N. pedestal; raised platform. The audience applauded as the conductor made his way to the *podium.*

poignant ADJ. keen; piercing; severe. Her *poignant* grief left her pale and weak.

polemic N. controversy; argument in support of point of view. Her essays were, for the main part, *polemics* for the party's policy.

politic ADJ. expedient; prudent; well devised. Even though he was disappointed, he did not think it *politic* to refuse this offer.

polity N. form of government of nation or state. Our *polity* should be devoted to the concept that the government should strive for the good of all citizens.

poltroon N. coward. Only a *poltroon* would so betray his comrades at such a dangerous time.

polygamist N. one who has more than one spouse at a time. He was arrested as a *polygamist* when his two wives filed complaints about him.

polyglot ADJ. speaking several languages. New York City is a *polyglot* community because of the thousands of immigrants who settle there.

■ **ponderous** ADJ. weighty; unwieldy. His humor lacked the light touch; his jokes were always *ponderous.*

porphyry N. igneous rock containing feldspar or quartz crystals. The *porphyry* used by the Egyptians in their buildings was purplish in color.

portend V. foretell; presage. The king did not know what these omens might *portend* and asked his soothsayers to interpret them.

portent N. sign; omen; forewarning. He regarded the black cloud as a *portent* of evil.

portentous ADJ. ominous; serious. I regard our present difficulties and dissatisfactions as *portentous* omens of future disaster.

portly ADJ. stately; stout. The overweight gentleman was referred to as *portly* by the polite salesclerk.

posterity N. descendants; future generations. We hope to leave a better world to *posterity.*

posthumous ADJ. after death (as of child born after father's death or book published after author's death). The critics ignored his works during his lifetime; it was only after the *posthumous* publication of his last novel that they recognized his great talent.

postprandial ADJ. after dinner. The most objectionable feature of these formal banquets is the *postprandial* speech.

postulate N. self-evident truth. We must accept these statements as *postulates* before pursuing our discussions any further. also V.

potable ADJ. suitable for drinking. The recent drought in the Middle Atlantic States has emphasized the need for extensive research in ways of making sea water *potable.* also N.

potentate N. monarch; sovereign. The *potentate* spent more time at Monte Carlo than he did at home on his throne.

potential ADJ. expressing possibility; latent. This juvenile delinquent is a *potential* murderer. also N.

potion N. dose (of liquid). Tristan and Isolde drink a love *potion* in the first act of the opera.

potpourri N. heterogeneous mixture; medley. He offered a *potpourri* of folk songs from many lands.

poultice N. soothing application applied to sore and inflamed portions of the body. He was advised to apply a flaxseed *poultice* to the inflammation.

practicable ADJ. feasible. The board of directors decided that the plan was *practicable* and agreed to undertake the project.

practical ADJ. based on experience; useful. He was a *practical* man, opposed to theory.

pragmatic ADJ. practical; concerned with practical values. This test should provide us with a *pragmatic* analysis of the value of this course.

■ **pragmatist** N. practical person. No *pragmatist* enjoys becoming involved in a game which he can never win.

prate V. speak foolishly; boast idly. Let us not *prate* about our qualities; rather, let our virtues speak for themselves.

■ **prattle** V. babble. The children *prattled* endlessly about their new toys. also N.

preamble N. introductory statement. In the *Preamble* to the Constitution, the purpose of the document is set forth.

precarious ADJ. uncertain; risky. I think this stock is a *precarious* investment and advise against its purchase.

precedent N. something preceding in time which may be used as an authority or guide for future action. This decision sets a *precedent* for future cases of a similar nature.

precedent ADJ. preceding in time, rank, etc. Our discussions, *precedent* to this event, certainly did not give you any reason to believe that we would adopt your proposal.

Test

Word List 36   *Synonyms*

Each of the questions below consists of a word in capital letters, followed by five lettered words or phrases. Choose the lettered word or phrase that is most nearly similar in meaning to the word in capital letters and write the letter of your choice on your answer paper.

526. PHLEGMATIC (A) calm (B) cryptic (C) practical
     (D) salivary (E) dishonest

527. PHYSIOGNOMY (A) posture (B) head
     (C) physique (D) face (E) size

528. PIEBALD (A) motley (B) coltish (C) hairless
     (D) thoroughbred (E) delicious

529. PILLAGE (A) hoard (B) plunder (C) versify
     (D) denigrate (E) confide

530. PINION (A) express (B) report (C) reveal
     (D) submit (E) restrain

531. PINNACLE (A) foothills (B) card game
     (C) pass (D) taunt (E) peak

532. PIOUS (A) historic (B) devout (C) multiple
     (D) fortunate (E) authoritative

533. PIQUE (A) pyramid (B) revolt (C) resentment
     (D) struggle (E) inventory

534. PLACATE (A) determine (B) transmit (C) pacify
     (D) allow (E) define

535. PLAINTIVE (A) mournful (B) senseless
     (C) persistent (D) rural (E) evasive

536. PLAGIARISM (A) theft of funds (B) theft of ideas
     (C) belief in God (D) arson (E) ethical theory

537. PLATITUDE (A) fatness (B) bravery
     (C) dimension (D) trite remark (E) strong belief

538. POLEMIC (A) blackness (B) lighting
     (C) magnetism (D) controversy (E) grimace

539. POLTROON (A) bird (B) tavern (C) soldier
     (D) coward (E) politician

540. POSTPRANDIAL (A) after dark (B) on awakening
     (C) in summer (D) after dinner (E) in winter

Word List 37   precept-propitiate

precept N. practical rule guiding conduct. "Love thy neighbor as thyself" is a worthwhile *precept*.

preciosity N. overrefinement in art or speech. Roxane, in the play *Cyrano de Bergerac*, illustrates the extent to which *preciosity* was carried in French society.

precipice N. cliff; dangerous position. Suddenly Indiana Jones found himself dangling from the edge of a *precipice*.

precipitate ADJ. headlong; rash. Do not be *precipitate* in this matter; investigate further.

precipitate V. throw headlong; hasten. We must be patient as we cannot *precipitate* these results.

precipitous ADJ. steep. This hill is difficult to climb because it is so *precipitous*.

precise ADJ. exact. If you don't give me *precise* directions and a map, I'll never find your place.

■ **preclude** V. make impossible; eliminate. This contract does not *preclude* my being employed by others at the same time that I am working for you.

precocious ADJ. advanced in development. By her rather adult manner of discussing serious topics, the child demonstrated that she was *precocious*.

precursor N. forerunner. Gray and Burns were *precursors* of the Romantic Movement in English literature.

predatory ADJ. plundering. The hawk is a *predatory* bird.

■ **predecessor** N. former occupant of a post. I hope I can live up to the fine example set by my late *predecessor* in this office.

predilection N. partiality; preference. Although the artist used various media from time to time, she had a *predilection* for watercolors.

preeminent ADJ. outstanding; superior. The king traveled to Boston because he wanted the *preeminent* surgeon in the field to perform the operation.

preempt V. appropriate beforehand. Your attempt to *preempt* this land before it is offered to the public must be resisted.

prefatory ADJ. introductory. The chairman made a few *prefatory* remarks before he called on the first speaker.

prehensile ADJ. capable of grasping or holding. Monkeys use not only their arms and legs but also their *prehensile* tails in traveling through the trees.

prelude N. introduction; forerunner. I am afraid that this border raid is the *prelude* to more serious attacks.

premeditate V. plan in advance. She had *premeditated* the murder for months, reading about common poisons and buying weed killer that contained arsenic.

premonition N. forewarning. We ignored these *premonitions* of disaster because they appeared to be based on childish fears.

premonitory ADJ. serving to warn. You should have visited a doctor as soon as you felt these *premonitory* chest pains.

preponderance N. superiority of power, quantity, etc. The rebels sought to overcome the *preponderance* of strength of the government forces by engaging in guerrilla tactics.

preponderate V. be superior in power; outweigh. I feel confident that the forces of justice will *preponderate* eventually in this dispute.

preposterous ADJ. absurd; ridiculous. The excuse he gave for his lateness was so *preposterous* that everyone laughed.

prerogative N. privilege; unquestionable right. The President cannot levy taxes; that is the *prerogative* of the legislative branch of government.

presage V. foretell. The vultures flying overhead *presaged* the discovery of the corpse in the desert.

presentiment N. premonition; foreboding. Hamlet felt a *presentiment* about his meeting with Laertes.

■ **prestige** N. impression produced by achievements or reputation. The wealthy man sought to obtain social *prestige* by contributing to popular charities.

presumption N. arrogance; effrontery. She had the *presumption* to disregard our advice.

pretentious ADJ. ostentatious; ambitious. I do not feel that your limited resources will permit you to carry out such a *pretentious* program.

preternatural ADJ. beyond that which is normal in nature. John's mother's total ability to tell when he was lying struck him as almost *preternatural.*

pretext N. excuse. He looked for a good *pretext* to get out of paying a visit to his aunt.

prevail V. induce; triumph over. He tried to *prevail* on her to type his essay for him.

prevaricate V. lie. Some people believe that to *prevaricate* in a good cause is justifiable and regard the statement as a ''white lie.''

prim ADJ. very precise and formal; exceedingly proper. Many people commented on the contrast between the *prim* attire of the young lady and the inappropriate clothing worn by her escort.

primogeniture N. seniority by birth. By virtue of *primogeniture,* the first-born child has many privileges denied his brothers and sisters.

primordial ADJ. existing at the beginning (of time); rudimentary. The Neanderthal Man is one of our *primordial* ancestors.

primp V. dress up. She *primps* for hours before a dance.

pristine ADJ. characteristic of earlier times; primitive; unspoiled. This area has been preserved in all its *pristine* wildness.

privation N. hardship; want. In his youth, he knew hunger and *privation.*

privy ADJ. secret; hidden; not public. We do not care for *privy* chamber government.

probe V. explore with tools. The surgeon *probed* the wound for foreign matter before suturing it. also N.

probity N. uprightness; incorruptibility. Everyone took his *probity* for granted; his defalcations, therefore, shocked us all.

proboscis N. long snout; nose. The elephant uses his *proboscis* to handle things and carry them from place to place.

proclivity N. inclination; natural tendency. The cross old lady has a *proclivity* to grumble.

procrastinate V. postpone; delay. It is wise not to *procrastinate;* otherwise, we find ourselves bogged down in a mass of work which should have been finished long ago.

prod V. poke; stir up; urge. If you *prod* him hard enough, he'll eventually clean his room.

■ **prodigal** ADJ. wasteful; reckless with money. The *prodigal* son squandered his inheritance. also N.

■ **prodigious** ADJ. marvelous; enormous. He marveled at her *prodigious* appetite when he saw all the food she ate.

profane V. violate; desecrate. Tourists are urged not to *profane* the sanctity of holy places by wearing improper garb. also ADJ.

profligate ADJ. dissipated; wasteful; licentious. In this *profligate* company, she lost all sense of decency. also N.

■ **profusion** N. lavish expenditure; overabundant condition. Seldom have I seen food and drink served in such *profusion* as at the wedding feast.

progenitor N. ancestor. We must not forget the teachings of our *progenitors* in our desire to appear modern.

progeny N. children; offspring. He was proud of his *progeny* but regarded George as the most promising of all his children.

prognathous ADJ. having projecting jaws. His *prognathous* face made him seem more determined than he actually was.

prognosis N. forecasted course of a disease; prediction. If the doctor's *prognosis* is correct, the patient will be in a coma for at least twenty-four hours.

prognosticate V. predict. I *prognosticate* disaster unless we change our wasteful ways.

projectile N. missile. Man has always hurled *projectiles* at his enemy whether in the form of stones or of highly explosive shells.

proletarian N. member of the working class. The aristocrats feared mob rule and gave the right to vote only to the wealthy, thus depriving the *proletarians* of a voice in government. also ADJ.

■ **prolific** ADJ. abundantly fruitful. She was a *prolific* writer and wrote as many as three books a year.

prolix ADJ. verbose; drawn out. Her *prolix* arguments irritated and bored the jury. prolixity, N.

promiscuous ADJ. mixed indiscriminately; haphazard; irregular. In the opera *La Boheme,* we get a picture of the *promiscuous* life led by the young artists of Paris.

promontory N. headland. They erected a lighthouse on the *promontory* to warn approaching ships of their nearness to the shore.

promulgate V. make known by official proclamation or publication. As soon as the Civil Service Commission *promulgates* the names of the successful candidates, we shall begin to hire members of our staff.

prone ADJ. inclined to; prostrate. She was *prone* to sudden fits of anger.

propagate V. multiply; spread. I am sure disease must *propagate* in such unsanitary and crowded areas.

propellants N. substances which propel or drive forward. The development of our missile program has forced our scientists to seek more powerful *propellants*.

propensity N. natural inclination. I dislike your *propensity* to belittle every contribution she makes to our organization.

prophylactic ADJ. used to prevent disease. Despite all *prophylactic* measures introduced by the authorities, the epidemic raged until cool weather set in. also N.

propinquity N. nearness; kinship. Their relationship could not be explained as being based on mere *propinquity:* they were more than relatives; they were true friends.

propitiate V. appease. The natives offered sacrifices to *propitiate* the gods.

Test

Word List 37   *Antonyms*

Each of the questions below consists of a word in capital letters, followed by five lettered words or phrases. Choose the lettered word or phrase that is most nearly opposite in meaning to the word in capital letters and write the letter of your choice on your answer paper.

541. PRECIPITATE (A) dull (B) anticipatory (C) cautious (D) considerate (E) welcome

542. PREFATORY (A) outstanding (B) magnificent (C) conclusive (D) intelligent (E) predatory

543. PRELUDE (A) intermezzo (B) diva (C) aria (D) aftermath (E) duplication

544. PRESUMPTION (A) assertion (B) activation (C) motivation (D) proposition (E) humility

545. PRETENTIOUS (A) ominous (B) calm (C) unassuming (D) futile (E) volatile

546. PRIM (A) informal (B) prior (C) exterior (D) private (E) cautious

547. PRISTINE (A) cultivated (B) condemned (C) irreligious (D) cautious (E) critical

548. PROBITY (A) regret (B) assumption (C) corruptibility (D) extent (E) upswing

549. PRODIGAL (A) large (B) thrifty (C) consistent (D) compatible (E) remote

550. PRODIGIOUS (A) infinitesimal (B) indignant (C) indifferent (D) indisposed (E) insufficient

551. PROFANE (A) sanctify (B) desecrate (C) define (D) manifest (E) urge

552. PROGNATHOUS (A) chewing (B) maxillary (C) receding (D) belligerent (E) impacted

553. PROLIX (A) stupid (B) indifferent (C) redundant (D) livid (E) pithy

554. PROPHYLACTIC (A) causing growth (B) causing disease (C) antagonistic (D) brushing (E) favorable

555. PROPINQUITY (A) remoteness (B) uniqueness (C) health (D) virtue (E) simplicity

Word List 38   propitious-quarry

propitious ADJ. favorable; kindly. I think it is advisable that we wait for a more *propitious* occasion to announce our plans; this is not a good time.

propound V. put forth for analysis. In your discussion, you have *propounded* several questions; let us consider each one separately.

propriety N. fitness; correct conduct. I want you to behave at this dinner with *propriety;* don't embarrass me.

propulsive ADJ. driving forward. The jet plane has a greater *propulsive* power than the engine-driven plane.

prorogue V. dismiss parliament; end officially. It was agreed that the king could not *prorogue* parliament until it had been in session for at least fifty days.

prosaic ADJ. commonplace; dull. I do not like this author because he is so unimaginative and *prosaic*.

proscenium N. part of stage in front of curtain. In the theater-in-the-round there can be no *proscenium* or *proscenium* arch.

proscribe V. ostracize; banish; outlaw. Antony, Octavius, and Lepidus *proscribed* all those who had conspired against Julius Caesar.

proselytize V. convert to a religion or belief. In these interfaith meetings, there must be no attempt to *proselytize;* we must respect all points of view.

prosody N. the art of versification. This book on *prosody* contains a rhyming dictionary as well as samples of the various verse forms.

prostrate V. stretch out full on ground. He *prostrated* himself before the idol. also ADJ.

protean ADJ. versatile; able to take on many shapes. A remarkably *protean* actor, Alec Guinness could take on any role.

protégé N. person under the protection and support of a patron. Cyrano de Bergerac refused to be a *protégé* of Cardinal Richelieu.

protocol N. diplomatic etiquette. We must run this state dinner according to *protocol* if we are to avoid offending any of our guests.

prototype N. original work used as a model by others. The crude typewriter on display in this museum is the *prototype* of the elaborate machines in use today.

protract V. prolong. Do not *protract* this phone conversation as I expect an important business call within the next few minutes.

protrude V. stick out. His fingers *protruded* from the holes in his gloves.

provenance N. origin or source of something. I am not interested in its *provenance;* I am more concerned with its usefulness than with its source.

provender N. dry food; fodder. I am not afraid of a severe winter because I have stored a large quantity of *provender* for the cattle.

provident ADJ. displaying foresight; thrifty; preparing for emergencies. In his usual *provident* manner, he had insured himself against this type of loss.

provincial ADJ. pertaining to a province; limited. We have to overcome their *provincial* attitude and get them to become more cognizant of world problems.

proviso N. stipulation. I am ready to accept your proposal with the *próviso* that you meet your obligations within the next two weeks.

■ **provoke** V. stir to anger; cause retaliation. In order to prevent a sudden outbreak of hostilities, we must not *provoke* our foe. provocation, N.

proximity N. nearness. The deer sensed the hunter's *proximity* and bounded away.

proxy N. authorized agent. Please act as my *proxy* and vote for this slate of candidates in my absence.

prude N. excessively modest person. The X-rated film was definitely not for *prudes.*

■ **prudent** ADJ. cautious; careful. A miser hoards money not because he is *prudent* but because he is greedy. prudence, N.

prune V. cut away; trim. With the help of her editor, she was able to *prune* her manuscript into publishable form.

prurient ADJ. based on lascivious thoughts. The police attempted to close the theater where the *prurient* film was being presented.

pseudonym N. pen name. Samuel Clemens' *pseudonym* was Mark Twain.

psyche N. soul; mind. It is difficult to delve into the *psyche* of a human being.

psychiatrist N. a doctor who treats mental diseases. A *psychiatrist* often needs long conferences with his patient before a diagnosis can be made.

psychopathic ADJ. pertaining to mental derangement. The *psychopathic* patient suffers more frequently from a disorder of the nervous system than from a diseased brain.

psychosis N. mental disorder. We must endeavor to find an outlet for the patient's repressed desires if we hope to combat this *psychosis.*

pterodactyl N. extinct flying reptile. The remains of *pterodactyls* indicate that these flying reptiles had a wingspan of as much as twenty feet.

puerile ADJ. childish. His *puerile* pranks sometimes offended his more mature friends.

pugilist N. boxer. The famous *pugilist* Cassius Clay changed his name to Muhammed Ali.

pugnacious ADJ. combative; disposed to fight. As a child he was *pugnacious* and fought with everyone.

puissant ADJ. powerful; strong; potent. We must keep his friendship for he will make a *puissant* ally.

pulchritude N. beauty; comeliness. I do not envy the judges who have to select this year's Miss America from this collection of female *pulchritude.*

pulmonary ADJ. pertaining to the lungs. In his researches on *pulmonary* diseases, he discovered many facts about the lungs of animals and human beings.

pulsate V. throb. We could see the blood vessels in his temple *pulsate* as he became more angry.

pummel V. beat. The severity with which he was *pummeled* was indicated by the bruises he displayed on his head and face.

punctilious ADJ. laying stress on niceties of conduct, form; precise. We must be *punctilious* in our planning of this affair, for any error may be regarded as a personal affront.

pundit N. learned Hindu; any learned man; authority on a subject. Even though he discourses on the matter like a *pundit,* he is actually rather ignorant about this topic.

pungent ADJ. stinging; caustic. The *pungent* aroma of the smoke made me cough.

punitive ADJ. punishing. He asked for *punitive* measures against the offender.

puny ADJ. insignificant; tiny; weak. Our *puny* efforts to stop the flood were futile.

purblind ADJ. dim-sighted; obtuse. In his *purblind* condition, he could not identify the people he saw.

purgatory N. place of spiritual expiation. In this *purgatory,* he could expect no help from his comrades.

purge V. clean by removing impurities; clear of charges. If you are to be *purged* of the charge of contempt of Congress, you must be willing to answer the questions previously asked. also N.

purloin V. steal. In the story, "The *Purloined* Letter," Poe points out that the best hiding place is often the most obvious place.

purport N. intention; meaning. If the *purport* of your speech was to arouse the rabble, you succeeded admirably. also V.

purveyor N. furnisher of foodstuffs; caterer. As *purveyor* of rare wines and viands, he traveled through France and Italy every year in search of new products to sell.

purview N. scope. The sociological implications of these inventions are beyond the *purview* of this book.

pusillanimous ADJ. cowardly; fainthearted. You should be ashamed of your *pusillanimous* conduct during this dispute.

putative ADJ. supposed; reputed. Although there are some doubts, the *putative* author of this work is Massinger.

putrid ADJ. foul; rotten; decayed. The gangrenous condition of the wound was indicated by the *putrid* smell when the bandages were removed. putrescence, N.

pyromaniac N. person with an insane desire to set things on fire. The detectives searched the area for the *pyromaniac* who had set these costly fires.

quack N. charlatan; impostor. Do not be misled by the exorbitant claims of this *quack;* he cannot cure you.

quadruped N. four-footed animal. Most mammals are *quadrupeds.*

quaff V. drink with relish. As we *quaffed* our ale, we listened to the gay songs of the students in the tavern.

quagmire N. bog; marsh. Our soldiers who served in Vietnam will never forget the drudgery of marching through the *quagmires* of the delta country.

quail V. cower; lose heart. He was afraid that he would *quail* in the face of danger.

quaint ADJ. odd; old-fashioned; picturesque. Her *quaint* clothes and old-fashioned language marked her as an eccentric.

■ **qualified** ADJ. limited; restricted. Unable to give the candidate full support, the mayor gave him only a *qualified* endorsement. (secondary meaning)

qualms N. misgivings. His *qualms* of conscience had become so great that he decided to abandon his plans.

quandary N. dilemma. When the two colleges to which he had applied accepted him, he was in a *quandary* as to which one he should attend.

quarantine N. isolation of person or ship to prevent spread of infection. We will have to place this house under *quarantine* until we determine the exact nature of the disease. also V.

quarry N. victim; object of a hunt. The police closed in on their *quarry.*

quarry V. dig into. They *quarried* blocks of marble out of the hillside.

Test

Word List 38   *Antonyms*

Each of the questions below consists of a word in capital letters, followed by five lettered words or phrases. Choose the lettered word or phrase that is most nearly opposite in meaning to the word in capital letters and write the letter of your choice on your answer paper.

556. PROPITIOUS (A) rich (B) induced (C) promoted (D) indicative (E) unfavorable

557. PROSAIC (A) pacified (B) reprieved (C) pensive (D) imaginative (E) rhetorical

558. PROTEAN (A) amateur (B) catholic (C) unchanging (D) rapid (E) unfavorable

559. PROTRACT (A) make circular (B) shorten (C) further (D) retrace (E) involve

560. PROVIDENT (A) unholy (B) rash (C) miserable (D) disabled (E) remote

561. PROVINCIAL (A) wealthy (B) crass (C) literary (D) aural (E) sophisticated

562. PSYCHOTIC (A) dangerous (B) clairvoyant (C) criminal (D) soulful (E) sane

563. PUERILE (A) fragrant (B) adult (C) lonely (D) feminine (E) masterly

564. PUGNACIOUS (A) pacific (B) feline (C) mature (D) angular (E) inactive

565. PUISSANT (A) pouring (B) fashionable (C) articulate (D) healthy (E) weak

566. PULCHRITUDE (A) ugliness (B) notoriety (C) bestiality (D) masculinity (E) servitude

567. PUNCTILIOUS (A) happy (B) active (C) vivid (D) careless (E) futile

568. PUNITIVE (A) large (B) humorous (C) rewarding (D) restive (E) languishing

569. PUSILLANIMOUS (A) poverty-stricken (B) chained (C) posthumous (D) courageous (E) strident

570. PUTATIVE (A) colonial (B) quarrelsome (C) undisputed (D) powerful (E) unremarkable

Word List 39   quay-recusant

quay N. dock; landing place. Because of the captain's carelessness, the ship crashed into the *quay.*

queasy ADJ. easily nauseated; squeamish. As the ship left the harbor, he became *queasy* and thought that he was going to suffer from seasickness.

quell V. put down; quiet. The police used fire hoses and tear gas to *quell* the rioters.

querulous ADJ. fretful; whining. His classmates were repelled by his *querulous* and complaining statements.

quibble V. equivocate; play on words. Do not *quibble;* I want a straightforward and definite answer. also N.

queue N. line. They stood patiently in the *queue* outside the movie theatre.

quiescent ADJ. at rest; dormant. After this geyser erupts, it will remain *quiescent* for twenty-four hours.

quietude N. tranquillity. He was impressed by the air of *quietude* and peace that pervaded the valley.

quintessence N. purest and highest embodiment. Noel Coward displayed the *quintessence* of wit.

quip N. taunt. You are unpopular because you are too free with your *quips* and sarcastic comments. also V.

quirk N. startling twist; caprice. By a *quirk* of fate, he found himself working for the man whom he had discharged years before.

quixotic ADJ. idealistic but impractical. His head is in the clouds; he is constantly presenting these *quixotic* schemes.

quizzical ADJ. bantering; comical; humorously serious. Will Rogers' *quizzical* remarks endeared him to his audiences.

quorum N. number of members necessary to conduct a meeting. The senator asked for a roll call to determine whether a *quorum* was present.

rabid ADJ. like a fanatic; furious. He was a *rabid* follower of the Dodgers and watched them play whenever he could go to the ball park.

raconteur N. story-teller. My father was a gifted *raconteur* with an unlimited supply of anecdotes.

ragamuffin N. person wearing tattered clothes. He felt sorry for the *ragamuffin* who was begging for food and gave him money to buy a meal.

rail V. scold; rant. You may *rail* at him all you want; you will never change him.

raiment N. clothing. "How can I go to the ball?" asked Cinderella. "I have no *raiment* fit to wear."

rakish ADJ. stylish; sporty. He wore his hat at a *rakish* and jaunty angle.

ramification N. branching out; subdivision. We must examine all the *ramifications* of this problem.

ramify V. divide into branches or subdivisions. When the plant begins to *ramify,* it is advisable to nip off most of the new branches.

ramp N. slope; inclined plane. The house was built with *ramps* instead of stairs in order to enable the man in the wheelchair to move easily from room to room and floor to floor.

rampant ADJ. rearing up on hind legs; unrestrained. The *rampant* weeds in the garden killed all the flowers which had been planted in the spring.

rampart N. defensive mound of earth. "From the *ramparts* we watched" as the fighting continued.

ramshackle ADJ. rickety; falling apart. The boys propped up the *ramshackle* clubhouse with a couple of boards.

rancid ADJ. having the odor of stale fat. A *rancid* odor filled the ship's galley and nauseated the crew.

rancor N. bitterness; hatred. Let us forget our *rancor* and cooperate in this new endeavor.

rankle V. irritate; fester. The memory of having been jilted *rankled* him for years.

rant V. rave; speak bombastically. As we heard him *rant* on the platform, we could not understand his strange popularity with many people.

rapacious ADJ. excessively grasping; plundering. Hawks and other *rapacious* birds may be killed at any time.

rapprochement N. reconciliation. Both sides were eager to effect a *rapprochement* but did not know how to undertake a program designed to bring about harmony.

rarefied ADJ. made less dense [of a gas]. The mountain climbers had difficulty breathing in the *rarefied* atmosphere.

raspy ADJ. grating; harsh. The sergeant's *raspy* voice grated on the recruits' ears.

ratiocination N. reasoning; act of drawing conclusions from premises. Poe's "The Gold Bug" is a splendid example of the author's use of *ratiocination*.

rationalization N. bringing into conformity with reason. All attempts at *rationalization* at this time are doomed to failure; tempers and emotions run too high for intelligent thought to prevail.

rationalize V. reason; justify an improper act. Do not try to *rationalize* your behavior by blaming your companions.

raucous ADJ. harsh and shrill. His *raucous* laughter irritated me and grated on my ears.

ravage V. plunder; despoil. The marauding army *ravaged* the countryside.

ravening ADJ. rapacious; seeking prey. We kept our fires burning all night to frighten away the *ravening* wolves.

ravenous ADJ. extremely hungry. The *ravenous* dog upset several garbage pails in its search for food.

raze V. destroy completely. The owners intend to *raze* the hotel and erect an office building on the site.

reactionary ADJ. recoiling from progress; retrograde. His program was *reactionary* since it sought to abolish many of the social reforms instituted by the previous administration. also N.

realm N. kingdom; sphere. The *realm* of possibilities for the new invention was endless.

rebate N. discount. We offer a *rebate* of ten percent to those who pay cash.

■ **rebuff** V. snub; beat back. She *rebuffed* his invitation so smoothly that he did not realize he had been snubbed.

■ **rebuttal** N. refutation; response with contrary evidence. The defense lawyer confidently listened to the prosecutor sum up his case, sure that she could answer his arguments in her *rebuttal.*

recalcitrant ADJ. obstinately stubborn. Donkeys are reputed to be the most *recalcitrant* of animals.

recant V. repudiate; withdraw previous statement. Unless you *recant* your confession, you will be punished severely.

recapitulate v. summarize. Let us *recapitulate* what has been said thus far before going ahead.

recession N. withdrawal; retreat. The *recession* of the troops from the combat area was completed in an orderly manner.

recidivism N. habitual return to crime. Prison reformers in the United States are disturbed by the high rate of *recidivism;* the number of men serving second and third terms in prison indicates the failure of the prisons to rehabilitate the inmates.

recipient N. receiver. Although he had been the *recipient* of many favors, he was not grateful to his benefactor.

reciprocal ADJ. mutual; exchangeable; interacting. The two nations signed a *reciprocal* trade agreement.

reciprocate v. repay in kind. If they attack us, we shall be compelled to *reciprocate* and bomb their territory.

recluse N. hermit. The *recluse* lived in a hut in the forest.

reconcile v. make friendly after quarrel; correct inconsistencies. Each month we *reconcile* our checkbook with the bank statement.

recondite ADJ. abstruse; profound; secret. He read many *recondite* books in order to obtain the material for his scholarly thesis.

reconnaissance N. survey of enemy by soldiers; reconnoitoring. If you encounter any enemy soldiers during your *reconnaissance,* capture them for questioning.

recourse N. resorting to help when in trouble. The boy's only *recourse* was to appeal to his father for aid.

recreant N. coward; betrayer of faith. The religious people ostracized the *recreant* who had abandoned their faith.

recrimination N. countercharges. Loud and angry *recriminations* were her answer to his accusations.

recrudescence N. reopening of a wound or sore. Keep this wound bandaged until it has completely healed to prevent its *recrudescence.*

■ **rectify** v. correct. I want to *rectify* my error before it is too late.

rectitude N. uprightness. He was renowned for his *rectitude* and integrity.

recumbent ADJ. reclining; lying down completely or in part. The command "AT EASE" does not permit you to take a *recumbent* position.

recuperate v. recover. The doctors were worried because the patient did not *recuperate* as rapidly as they had expected.

recurrent ADJ. occurring again and again. These *recurrent* attacks disturbed us and we consulted a physician.

recusant N. person who refuses to comply; applied specifically to those who refused to attend Anglican services. In that religious community, the *recusant* was shunned as a pariah.

Test

Word List 39   *Synonyms and Antonyms*

Each of the following questions consists of a word in capital letters, followed by five lettered words or phrases. Choose the lettered word or phrase which is most nearly similar or the opposite of the word in capital letters and write the letter of your choice on your answer paper.

571. QUEASY (A) toxic (B) easily upset (C) chronic (D) choleric (E) false
572. QUELL (A) boast (B) incite (C) reverse (D) wet (E) answer
573. QUIXOTIC (A) rapid (B) exotic (C) longing (D) timid (E) idealistic
574. RAGAMUFFIN (A) dandy (B) biscuit (C) exotic dance (D) light snack (E) baker
575. RAUCOUS (A) mellifluous (B) uncooked (C) realistic (D) veracious (E) anticipating
576. RAVAGE (A) rank (B) revive (C) plunder (D) pillory (E) age

577. RAZE (A) shave (B) heckle (C) finish (D) tear down (F) write
578. REACTIONARY (A) conservative (B) retrograde (C) dramatist (D) militant (E) chemical
579. REBATE (A) relinquish (B) settle (C) discount (D) cancel (E) elicit
580. RECALCITRANT (A) grievous (B) secretive (C) cowardly (D) thoughtful (E) cooperative
581. RECLUSE (A) learned scholar (B) mocker (C) social person (D) careful worker (E) daredevil
582. RECREANT (A) vacationing (B) faithful (C) indifferent (D) obliged (E) reviving
583. RECTIFY (A) remedy (B) avenge (C) create (D) assemble (E) attribute
584. RECUPERATE (A) reenact (B) engage (C) recapitulate (D) recover (E) encounter
585. RECUSANT (A) nonconformer (B) deliberator (C) abstainer (D) qualifier (E) patient

Word List 40   redolent-rescind

redolent ADJ. fragrant; odorous; suggestive of an odor. Even though it is February, the air is *redolent* of spring.

redoubtable ADJ. formidable; causing fear. The neighboring countries tried not to offend the Russians because they could be *redoubtable* foes.

redress N. remedy; compensation. Do you mean to tell me that I can get no *redress* for my injuries? also v.

■ **redundant** ADJ. superfluous; excessively wordy; repetitious. Your composition is *redundant;* you can easily reduce its length. redundancy, N.

reek V. emit (odor). The room *reeked* with stale tobacco smoke. also N.

refection N. slight refreshment. Despite our hunger, we stopped on the road for only a quick *refection*.

refectory N. dining hall. In this huge *refectory,* we can feed the entire student body at one sitting.

refraction N. bending of a ray of light. When you look at a stick inserted in water, it looks bent because of the *refraction* of the light by the water.

refractory ADJ. stubborn; unmanageable. The *refractory* horse was eliminated from the race when he refused to obey the jockey.

refulgent ADJ. radiant. We admired the *refulgent* moon and watched it for a while.

refurbish V. renovate; make bright by polishing. The flood left a deposit of mud on everything; it was necessary to *refurbish* our belongings.

refutation N. disproof of opponents' arguments. I will wait until I hear the *refutation* before deciding whom to favor.

■ **refute** V. disprove. The defense called several respectable witnesses who were able to *refute* the false testimony of the prosecution's only witness.

regal ADJ. royal. Prince Albert had a *regal* manner.

regale V. entertain. John *regaled* us with tales of his adventures in Africa.

regatta N. boat or yacht race. Many boating enthusiasts followed the *regatta* in their own yachts.

regeneration N. spiritual rebirth. Modern penologists strive for the *regeneration* of the prisoners.

regicide N. murder of a king or queen. The death of Mary Queen of Scots was an act of *regicide*.

regime N. method or system of government. When a Frenchman mentions the Old *Regime,* he refers to the government existing before the revolution.

regimen N. prescribed diet and habits. I doubt whether the results warrant our living under such a strict *regimen*.

rehabilitate V. restore to proper condition. We must *rehabilitate* those whom we send to prison.

reimburse V. repay. Let me know what you have spent and I will *reimburse* you.

reiterate V. repeat. I shall *reiterate* this message until all have understood it.

rejuvenate V. make young again. The charlatan claimed that his elixir would *rejuvenate* the aged and weary.

■ **relegate** V. banish; consign to inferior position. If we *relegate* these experienced people to positions of unimportance because of their political persuasions, we shall lose the services of valuably trained personnel.

relevancy N. pertinence; reference to the case in hand. I was impressed by the *relevancy* of your remarks; I now understand the situation perfectly. relevant, ADJ.

relinquish V. abandon. I will *relinquish* my claims to this property if you promise to retain my employees.

relish V. savor; enjoy. I *relish* a good joke as much as anyone else. also N.

remediable ADJ. reparable. Let us be grateful that the damage is *remediable*.

remedial ADJ. curative; corrective. Because he was a slow reader, he decided to take a course in *remedial* reading.

reminiscence N. recollection. Her *reminiscences* of her experiences are so fascinating that she ought to write a book.

remiss ADJ. negligent. He was accused of being *remiss* in his duty when the prisoner escaped.

remnant N. remainder. I suggest that you wait until the store places the *remnants* of these goods on sale.

remonstrate V. protest. I must *remonstrate* about the lack of police protection in this area.

■ **remorse** N. guilt; self-reproach. The murderer felt no *remorse* for his crime.

remunerative ADJ. compensating; rewarding. I find my new work so *remunerative* that I may not return to my previous employment. remuneration, N.

rend V. split; tear apart. In his grief, he tried to *rend* his garments.

render V. deliver; provide; represent. He *rendered* aid to the needy and indigent.

rendezvous N. meeting place. The two fleets met at the *rendezvous* at the appointed time. also V.

rendition N. translation; artistic interpretation of a song, etc. The audience cheered enthusiastically as she completed her *rendition* of the aria.

■ **renegade** N. deserter; apostate. Because he refused to support his fellow members in their drive, he was shunned as a *renegade*.

renege V. deny; go back on. He *reneged* on paying off his debt.

renounce V. abandon; discontinue; disown; repudiate. Joan of Arc refused to *renounce* her statements even though she knew she would be burned at the stake as a witch.

renovate V. restore to good condition; renew. They claim that they can *renovate* worn shoes so that they look like new ones.

renunciation N. giving up; renouncing. Do not sign this *renunciation* of your right to sue until you have consulted a lawyer.

reparable ADJ. capable of being repaired. Fortunately, the damages we suffered in the accident were *reparable* and our car looks brand new.

reparation N. amends; compensation. At the peace conference, the defeated country promised to pay *reparations* to the victors.

repartee N. clever reply. He was famous for his witty *repartee* and his sarcasm.

repellent ADJ. driving away; unattractive. Mosquitoes find the odor so *repellent* that they leave any spot where this liquid has been sprayed. also N.

repercussion N. rebound; reverberation; reaction. I am afraid that this event will have serious *repercussions*.

repertoire N. list of works of music, drama, etc., a performer is prepared to present. The opera company decided to include *Madame Butterfly* in its *repertoire* for the following season.

repine V. fret; complain. There is no sense *repining* over the work you have left undone.

replenish V. fill up again. The end of rationing enabled us to *replenish* our supply of canned food.

replete ADJ. filled to capacity; abundantly supplied. This book is *replete* with humorous situations.

replica N. copy. Are you going to hang this *replica* of the Declaration of Independence in the classroom or in the auditorium?

repository N. storehouse. Libraries are *repositories* of the world's best thoughts.

■ **reprehensible** ADJ. deserving blame. Your vicious conduct in this situation is *reprehensible*.

reprieve N. temporary stay. During the twenty-four-hour *reprieve*, the lawyers sought to make the stay of execution permanent. also V.

reprimand V. reprove severely. I am afraid that my parents will *reprimand* me when I show them my report card. also N.

reprisal N. retaliation. I am confident that we are ready for any *reprisals* the enemy may undertake.

■ **reproach** N. blame; censure. I want my work to be above *reproach* and without error. also V.

reprobate N. person hardened in sin, devoid of a sense of decency. I cannot understand why he has so many admirers if he is the *reprobate* you say he is.

reprobation N. severe disapproval. The students showed their *reprobation* of his act by refusing to talk with him.

reprove V. censure; rebuke. The principal *reproved* the students when they became unruly in the auditorium.

■ **repudiate** V. disown; disavow. He announced that he would *repudiate* all debts incurred by his wife.

repugnance N. loathing. She looked at the snake with *repugnance*.

■ **repulsion** N. act of driving back; distaste. The *repulsion* of the enemy forces was not accomplished bloodlessly; many of the defenders were wounded in driving the enemy back.

reputed ADJ. supposed. He is the *reputed* father of the child. also V.

requiem N. mass for the dead; dirge. They played Mozart's *Requiem* at the funeral.

requisite N. necessary requirement. Many colleges state that a student must offer three years of a language as a *requisite* for admission.

requite V. repay; revenge. The wretch *requited* his benefactors by betraying them.

■ **rescind** V. cancel. Because of public resentment, the king had to *rescind* his order.

Test

Word List 40   *Synonyms*

Each of the questions below consists of a word in capital letters, followed by five lettered words or phrases. Choose the lettered word or phrase that is most nearly similar in meaning to the word in capital letters and write the letter of your choice on your answer paper.

586. REFRACTORY (A) articulate (B) sinkable (C) vaunted (D) useless (E) unmanageable

587. REGAL (A) oppressive (B) royal (C) major (D) basic (E) entertaining

588. REITERATE (A) gainsay (B) revive (C) revenge (D) repeat (E) return

589. RELISH (A) desire (B) nibble (C) savor (D) vindicate (E) avail

590. REMISS (A) lax (B) lost (C) foolish (D) violating (E) ambitious

591. REMONSTRATE (A) display (B) restate (C) protest (D) resign (E) reiterate

592. REPARTEE (A) witty retort (B) willful departure (C) spectator (D) monologue (E) sacrifice

593. REPELLENT (A) propulsive (B) unattractive (C) porous (D) stiff (E) elastic

594. REPERCUSSION (A) reaction (B) restitution (C) resistance (D) magnificence (E) acceptance

595. REPLENISH (A) polish (B) repeat (C) reinstate (D) refill (E) refuse

596. REPLICA (A) museum piece (B) famous site (C) battle emblem (D) facsimile (E) replacement

597. REPRISAL (A) reevaluation (B) assessment (C) loss (D) retaliation (E) nonsense

598. REPROVE (A) prevail (B) rebuke (C) ascertain (D) prove false (E) scarify

599. REPUDIATE (A) besmirch (B) appropriate (C) annoy (D) reject (E) avow

600. REPUGNANCE (A) belligerence (B) tenacity (C) renewal (D) pity (E) loathing

---

Word List 41   rescission-sacrosanct

rescission N. abrogation; annulment. The *rescission* of the unpopular law was urged by all political parties.

■ **reserve** N. self-control; care in expressing oneself. She was outspoken and uninhibited; he was cautious and inclined to *reserve*. (secondary meaning)

residue N. remainder; balance. In his will, he requested that after payment of debts, the *residue* be given to his wife.

■ **resignation** N. submissiveness. He met all his troubles with an attitude of patient *resignation*. (secondary meaning) resigned, ADJ.

resilient ADJ. elastic; having the power of springing back. Steel is highly *resilient* and therefore is used in the manufacture of springs.

■ **resolution** N. determination. Nothing could shake his *resolution* to succeed despite all difficulties.

resonant ADJ. echoing; resounding; possessing resonance. His *resonant* voice was particularly pleasing.

respite N. delay in punishment; interval of relief; rest. The judge granted the condemned man a *respite* to enable his attorneys to file an appeal.

resplendent ADJ. brilliant; lustrous. The toreador wore a *resplendent* costume.

responsiveness N. state of reacting readily to appeals, orders, etc. The audience cheered and applauded, delighting the performers by its *responsiveness.*

restitution N. reparation; indemnification. He offered to make *restitution* for the window broken by his son.

restive ADJ. unmanageable; fretting under control. We must quiet the *restive* animals.

■ **restraint** N. controlling force. She dreamt of living an independent life, free of all *restraints.*

resurgent ADJ. rising again after defeat, etc. The *resurgent* nation surprised everyone by its quick recovery after total defeat.

resuscitate V. revive. The lifeguard tried to *resuscitate* the drowned child by applying artificial respiration.

retaliate V. repay in kind (usually for bad treatment). Fear that we will *retaliate* immediately deters our foe from attacking us.

retentive ADJ. holding; having a good memory. The pupil did not need to spend much time in study as he had a *retentive* mind.

■ **reticence** N. reserve; uncommunicativeness; inclination to be silent. Because of the *reticence* of the key witness, the case against the defendant collapsed.

reticulated ADJ. covered with a network; having the appearance of a mesh. She wore the *reticulated* stockings so popular with teenagers at that time.

retinue N. following; attendants. The queen's *retinue* followed her down the aisle.

retort N. quick sharp reply. Even when it was advisable for her to keep her mouth shut, she was always ready with a quick *retort.* also V.

retraction N. withdrawal. He dropped his libel suit after the newspaper published a *retraction* of its statement.

retrench V. cut down; economize. If they were to be able to send their children to college, they would have to *retrench.*

retribution N. vengeance; compensation; punishment for offenses. The evangelist maintained that an angry deity would exact *retribution* from the sinners.

retrieve V. recover; find and bring in. The dog was intelligent and quickly learned to *retrieve* the game killed by the hunter.

retroactive ADJ. of a law which dates back to a period before its enactment. Because the law was *retroactive* to the first of the year, we found she was eligible for the pension.

retrograde V. go backwards; degenerate. Instead of advancing, our civilization seems to have *retrograded* in ethics and culture. also ADJ.

retrospective ADJ. looking back on the past. It is only when we become *retrospective* that we can appreciate the tremendous advances made during this century.

revelry N. boisterous merrymaking. New Year's Eve is a night of *revelry.*

reverberate V. echo; resound. The entire valley *reverberated* with the sound of the church bells.

revere V. respect; honor. In Asian societies, people *revere* their elders.

■ **reverent** ADJ. respectful. His *reverent* attitude was appropriate in a house of worship.

reverie N. daydream; musing. He was awakened from his *reverie* by the teacher's question.

revile V. slander; vilify. He was avoided by all who feared that he would *revile* and abuse them if they displeased him.

revulsion N. sudden violent change of feeling; reaction. Many people in this country who admired dictatorships underwent a *revulsion* when they realized what Hitler and Mussolini were trying to do.

rhapsodize V. to speak or write in an exaggeratedly enthusiastic manner. She greatly enjoyed her Hawaiian vacation and *rhapsodized* about it for weeks.

rhetoric N. art of effective communication; insincere language. All writers, by necessity, must be skilled in *rhetoric.*

■ **rhetorical** ADJ. pertaining to effective communication; insincere in language. To win his audience, the speaker used every *rhetorical* trick in the book.

rheumy ADJ. pertaining to a discharge from nose and eyes. His *rheumy* eyes warned us that he was coming down with a cold.

ribald ADJ. wanton; profane. He sang a *ribald* song that offended many of the more prudish listeners.

rife ADJ. abundant; current. In the face of the many rumors of scandal, which are *rife* at the moment, it is best to remain silent.

rift N. opening; break. The plane was lost in the stormy sky until the pilot saw the city through a *rift* in the clouds.

rigor N. severity. Many settlers could not stand the *rigors* of the New England winters.

rime N. white frost. The early morning dew had frozen and everything was covered with a thin coat of *rime.*

risible ADJ. inclined to laugh; ludicrous. His remarks were so *risible* that the audience howled with laughter. risibility, N.

risqué ADJ. verging upon the improper; offcolor. Please do not tell your *risqué* anecdotes at this party.

roan ADJ. brown mixed with gray or white. You can distinguish this horse in a race because it is *roan* while all the others are bay or chestnut.

robust ADJ. vigorous; strong. The candidate for the football team had a *robust* physique.

rococo ADJ. ornate; highly decorated. The *rococo* style in furniture and architecture, marked by scrollwork and excessive decoration, flourished during the middle of the eighteenth century.

roil V. to make liquids murky by stirring up sediment. Be careful when you pour not to *roil* the wine; if you stir up the sediment you'll destroy the flavor.

roseate ADJ. rosy; optimistic. I am afraid you will have to alter your *roseate* views in the light of the distressing news that has just arrived.

roster N. list. They print the *roster* of players in the season's program.

rostrum N. platform for speech-making; pulpit. The crowd murmured angrily and indicated that they did not care to listen to the speaker who was approaching the *rostrum*.

rote N. repetition. He recited the passage by *rote* and gave no indication he understood what he was saying.

rotunda N. circular building or hall covered with a dome. His body lay in state in the *rotunda* of the Capitol.

rotundity N. roundness; sonorousness of speech. Washington Irving emphasized the *rotundity* of the governor by describing his height and circumference.

rout V. stampede; drive out. The reinforcements were able to *rout* the enemy. also N.

rubble N. fragments. Ten years after World War II, some of the *rubble* left by enemy bombings could still be seen.

rubicund ADJ. having a healthy reddish color; ruddy; florid. His *rubicund* complexion was the result of an active outdoor life.

ruddy ADJ. reddish; healthy-looking. His *ruddy* features indicated that he had spent much time in the open.

rudimentary ADJ. not developed; elementary. His dancing was limited to a few *rudimentary* steps.

rueful ADJ. regretful; sorrowful; dejected. The artist has captured the sadness of childhood in his portrait of the boy with the *rueful* countenance.

ruffian N. bully; scoundrel. The *ruffians* threw stones at the police.

ruminate V. chew the cud; ponder. We cannot afford to wait while you *ruminate* upon these plans.

rummage V. ransack; thoroughly search. When we *rummaged* through the trunks in the attic, we found many souvenirs of our childhood days. also N.

ruse N. trick; stratagem. You will not be able to fool your friends with such an obvious *ruse*.

rustic ADJ. pertaining to country people; uncouth. The backwoodsman looked out of place in his *rustic* attire.

rusticate V. banish to the country; dwell in the country. I like city life so much that I can never understand how people can *rusticate* in the suburbs.

ruthless ADJ. pitiless. The escaped convict was a dangerous and *ruthless* murderer.

saccharine ADJ. cloyingly sweet. She tried to ingratiate herself, speaking sweetly and smiling a *saccharine* smile.

sacerdotal ADJ. priestly. The priest decided to abandon his *sacerdotal* duties and enter the field of politics.

sacrilegious ADJ. desecrating; profane. His stealing of the altar cloth was a very *sacrilegious* act.

sacrosanct ADJ. most sacred; inviolable. The brash insurance salesman invaded the *sacrosanct* privacy of the office of the president of the company.

Test

Word List 41 *Antonyms*

Each of the questions below consists of a word in capital letters, followed by five lettered words or phrases. Choose the lettered word or phrase that is most nearly opposite in meaning to the word in capital letters and write the letter of your choice on your answer paper.

601. RESILIENT (A) pungent (B) foolish (C) worthy (D) insolent (E) unyielding

602. RESTIVE (A) buoyant (B) placid (C) remorseful (D) resistant (E) retiring

603. RETENTIVE (A) forgetful (B) accepting (C) repetitive (D) avoiding (E) fascinating

604. RETICENCE (A) fatigue (B) fashion (C) treachery (D) loquaciousness (E) magnanimity

605. RETROGRADE (A) progressing (B) inclining (C) evaluating (D) concentrating (E) directing

606. REVERE (A) advance (B) dishonor (C) age (D) precede (E) wake

607. RIFE (A) direct (B) scant (C) peaceful (D) grim (E) mature

608. ROBUST (A) weak (B) violent (C) vicious (D) villainous (E) hungry

609. ROTUNDITY (A) promenade (B) nave (C) grotesqueness (D) slimness (E) impropriety

610. RUBICUND (A) dangerous (B) pallid (C) remote (D) indicative (E) nonsensical

611. RUDDY (A) robust (B) witty (C) wan (D) exotic (E) creative

612. RUDIMENTARY (A) pale (B) polite (C) asinine (D) developed (E) quiescent

613. RUEFUL (A) trite (B) content (C) capable (D) capital (E) zealous

614. RUSTIC (A) urban (B) slow (C) corroded (D) mercenary (E) civilian

615. RUTHLESS (A) merciful (B) majestic (C) mighty (D) militant (E) maximum

Word List 42   sadistic-sepulcher

sadistic ADJ. inclined to cruelty. If we are to improve conditions in this prison, we must first get rid of the *sadistic* warden.

saffron ADJ. orange-colored; colored like the autumn crocus. The Halloween cake was decorated with *saffron*-colored icing.

saga N. Scandinavian myth; any legend. This is a *saga* of the sea and the men who risk their lives on it.

sagacious ADJ. keen; shrewd; having insight. He is much too *sagacious* to be fooled by a trick like that.

salient ADJ. prominent. One of the *salient* features of that newspaper is its excellent editorial page.

saline ADJ. salty. The slightly *saline* taste of this mineral water is pleasant.

sallow ADJ. yellowish; sickly in color. We were disturbed by his *sallow* complexion, which was due to jaundice.

saltatory ADJ. relating to leaping. The male members of the ballet company were renowned for their *saltatory* exploits.

salubrious ADJ. healthful. Many people with hay fever move to more *salubrious* sections of the country during the months of August and September.

salutary ADJ. tending to improve; beneficial; wholesome. The punishment had a *salutary* effect on the boy, as he became a model student.

salvage V. rescue from loss. All attempts to *salvage* the wrecked ship failed. also N.

salver N. tray. The food was brought in on silver *salvers* by the waiters.

sanctimonious ADJ. displaying ostentatious or hypocritical devoutness. You do not have to be so *sanctimonious* to prove that you are devout.

■ **sanction** V. approve; ratify. Nothing will convince me to *sanction* the engagement of my daughter to such a worthless young man.

sangfroid N. coolness in a trying situation. The captain's *sangfroid* helped to allay the fears of the passengers.

sanguinary ADJ. bloody. The battle of Iwo Jima was unexpectedly *sanguinary* with many casualties.

sanguine ADJ. cheerful; hopeful. Let us not be too *sanguine* about the outcome; something could go wrong.

sapid ADJ. savory; tasty; relishable. This chef has the knack of making most foods more *sapid* and appealing.

sapient ADJ. wise; shrewd. The students enjoyed the professor's *sapient* digressions more than his formal lectures.

■ **sarcasm** N. scornful remarks; stinging rebuke. His feelings were hurt by the *sarcasm* of his supposed friends.

sarcophagus N. stone coffin, often highly decorated. The display of the *sarcophagus* in the art museum impresses me as a morbid exhibition.

sardonic ADJ. disdainful; sarcastic; cynical. The *sardonic* humor of nightclub comedians who satirize or ridicule patrons in the audience strikes some people as amusing and others as rude.

sartorial ADJ. pertaining to tailors. He was as famous for the *sartorial* splendor of his attire as he was for his acting.

sate V. satisfy to the full; cloy. Its hunger *sated*, the lion dozed.

satellite N. small body revolving around a larger one. During the first few years of the Space Age, hundreds of *satellites* were launched by Russia and the United States.

satiate V. surfeit; satisfy fully. The guests, having eaten until they were *satiated*, now listened inattentively to the speakers.

satiety N. condition of being crammed full; glutted state; repletion. The *satiety* of the guests at the sumptuous feast became apparent when they refused the delicious dessert.

satire N. form of literature in which irony, sarcasm, and ridicule are employed to attack vice and folly.*Gulliver's Travels,* which is regarded by many as a tale for children, is actually a bitter *satire* attacking man's folly.

■ **satirical** ADJ. mocking. The humor of cartoonist Gary Trudeau often is *satirical;* through the comments of the Doonesbury characters, Trudeau ridicules political corruption and folly.

satrap N. petty ruler working for a superior despot. The monarch and his *satraps* oppressed the citizens of the country.

■ **saturate** V. soak. Their clothes were *saturated* by the rain. saturation, N.

saturnine ADJ. gloomy. Do not be misled by his *saturnine* countenance; he is not as gloomy as he looks.

satyr N. half-human, half-bestial being in the court of Dionysus, portrayed as wanton and cunning. He was like a *satyr* in his lustful conduct.

saunter V. stroll slowly. As we *sauntered* through the park, we stopped frequently to admire the spring flowers.

savant N. scholar. Our faculty includes many world-famous *savants.*

savoir faire N. tact; poise; sophistication. I envy his *savoir faire;* he always knows exactly what to do and say.

savor V. have a distinctive flavor, smell, or quality. I think your choice of a successor *savors* of favoritism.

■ **scanty** ADJ. meager; insufficient. Thinking his helping of food was *scanty,* Oliver Twist asked for more.

scapegoat N. someone who bears the blame for others. After the Challenger disaster, NASA searched for *scapegoats* on whom they could cast the blame.

scarify V. make slight incisions in; scratch. He was not severely cut; the flying glass had merely *scarified* him.

scavenger N. collector and disposer of refuse; animal that devours refuse and carrion. The Oakland *Scavenger* Company is responsible for the collection and disposal of the community's garbage.

schism N. division; split. Let us not widen the *schism* by further bickering.

scintilla N. shred; least bit. You have not produced a *scintilla* of evidence to support your argument.

scintillate V. sparkle; flash. I enjoy her dinner parties because the food is excellent and the conversation *scintillates*.

scion N. offspring. The farm boy felt out of place in the school attended by the *scions* of the wealthy and noble families.

scoff V. mock; ridicule. He *scoffed* at dentists until he had his first toothache.

scourge N. lash; whip; severe punishment. They feared the plague and regarded it as a deadly *scourge*. also V.

■ **scrupulous** ADJ. conscientious; extremely thorough. I can recommend him for a position of responsibility for I have found him a very *scrupulous* young man.

scullion N. menial kitchen worker. He acted as though he were the head chef when he was actually only a *scullion*.

scurrilous ADJ. obscene; indecent. Your *scurrilous* remarks are especially offensive because they are untrue.

scurry V. move briskly. The White Rabbit had to *scurry* to get to his appointment on time.

scuttle V. sink. The sailors decided to *scuttle* their vessel rather than surrender it to the enemy.

sebaceous ADJ. oily; fatty. The *sebaceous* glands secrete oil to the hair follicles.

secession N. withdrawal. The *secession* of the Southern states provided Lincoln with his first major problem after his inauguration.

■ **seclusion** N. isolation; solitude. One moment she loved crowds; the next, she sought *seclusion*.

secular ADJ. worldly; not pertaining to church matters; temporal. The church leaders decided not to interfere in *secular* matters.

sedate ADJ. composed; grave. The parents were worried because they felt their son was too quiet and *sedate*.

sedentary ADJ. requiring sitting. Because he had a *sedentary* occupation, he decided to visit a gymnasium weekly.

sedition N. resistance to authority; insubordination. His words, though not treasonous in themselves, were calculated to arouse thoughts of *sedition*.

sedulous ADJ. diligent. The young woman was so *sedulous* that she received a commendation for her hard work.

seethe V. be disturbed; boil. The nation was *seething* with discontent as the noblemen continued their arrogant ways.

seine N. net for catching fish. When the shad run during the spring, you may see fishermen with *seines* along the banks of our coastal rivers.

seismic ADJ. pertaining to earthquakes. The Richter scale is a measurement of *seismic* disturbances.

semblance N. outward appearance; guise. Although this book has a *semblance* of wisdom and scholarship, a careful examination will reveal many errors and omissions.

senescence N. state of growing old. He did not show any signs of *senescence* until he was well past seventy.

senility N. old age; feeble mindedness of old age. Most of the decisions are being made by the junior members of the company because of the *senility* of the president.

sensual ADJ. devoted to the pleasures of the senses; carnal; voluptuous. I cannot understand what caused him to drop his *sensual* way of life and become so ascetic.

sensuous ADJ. pertaining to the physical senses; operating through the senses. He was stimulated by the sights, sounds and smells about him; he was enjoying his *sensuous* experience.

sententious ADJ. terse; concise; aphoristic. After reading so many redundant speeches, I find his *sententious* style particularly pleasing.

septic ADJ. putrid; producing putrefaction. The hospital was in such a filthy state that we were afraid that many of the patients would suffer from *septic* poisoning.

sepulcher N. tomb. Annabel Lee was buried in the *sepulcher* by the sea.

Test

Word List 42   *Antonyms*

Each of the questions below consists of a word in capital letters, followed by five lettered words or phrases. Choose the lettered word or phrase that is most nearly opposite in meaning to the word in capital letters and write the letter of your choice on your answer paper.

616. SADISTIC (A) happy (B) quaint (C) kindhearted (D) vacant (E) fortunate

617. SAGACIOUS (A) foolish (B) bitter (C) voracious (D) veracious (E) fallacious

618. SALLOW (A) salacious (B) ruddy (C) colorless (D) permitted (E) minimum

619. SALUBRIOUS (A) salty (B) bloody (C) miasmic (D) maudlin (E) wanted

620. SALVAGE (A) remove (B) outfit (C) burn (D) lose (E) confuse

621. SANCTIMONIOUS (A) hypothetical (B) paltry (C) mercenary (D) pious (E) grateful

622. SANGUINE (A) choleric (B) sickening (C) warranted (D) irritated (E) pessimistic

623. SATIETY (A) emptiness (B) warmth (C) erectness (D) ignorance (E) straight

624. SCANTY (A) collected (B) remote (C) invisible (D) plentiful (E) straight

625. SCURRILOUS (A) savage (B) scabby (C) decent (D) volatile (E) major

626. SECULAR (A) vivid (B) clerical (D) positive (E) varying

627. SEDENTARY (A) vicarious (B) loyal
     (C) accidental (D) active (E) afraid
628. SENESCENCE (A) youth (B) romance
     (C) doldrums (D) quintessence (E) friendship
629. SENILITY (A) virility (B) loquaciousness
     (C) forgetfulness (D) youth (E) majority
630. SENTENTIOUS (A) paragraphed (B) positive
     (C) posthumous (D) pacific (E) wordy

Word List 43   sequacious-somatic

sequacious ADJ. eager to follow; ductile. The *sequacious* members of Parliament were only too willing to do the bidding of their leader.

■ **sequester** V. retire from public life; segregate; seclude. Although he had hoped for a long time to *sequester* himself in a small community, he never was able to drop his busy round of activities in the city.

seraph N. high-ranking, six-winged angel. In ''Annabel Lee'' Poe maintains that the ''winged *seraphs* of Heaven'' envied their great love.

serendipity N. gift for finding valuable things not searched for. Many scientific discoveries are a matter of *serendipity*.

serenity N. calmness; placidity. The *serenity* of the sleepy town was shattered by a tremendous explosion.

serpentine ADJ. winding; twisting. The car swerved at every curve in the *serpentine* road.

serrated ADJ. having a sawtoothed edge. The beech tree is one of many plants that have *serrated* leaves.

serried ADJ. standing shoulder to shoulder; crowded. In these days of automatic weapons, it is suicidal for troops to charge in *serried* ranks against the foe.

servile ADJ. slavish; cringing. Uriah Heep was a very *servile* individual.

severance N. division; partition; separation. The *severance* of church and state is a basic principle of our government.

■ **severity** N. harshness; plainness. The newspapers disapproved of the *severity* of the sentence.

shackle V. chain; fetter. The criminal's ankles were *shackled* to prevent his escape. also N.

sham V. pretend. He *shammed* sickness to get out of going to school. also N.

shambles N. slaughterhouse; scene of carnage. By the time the police arrived, the room was a *shambles*.

sheaf N. bundle of stalks of grain; any bundle of things tied together. The lawyer picked up a *sheaf* of papers as he rose to question the witness.

sheathe V. place into a case. As soon as he recognized the approaching men, he *sheathed* his dagger and hailed them as friends.

sherbet N. flavored dessert ice. I prefer raspberry *sherbet* to ice cream since it is less fattening.

shibboleth N. watchword; slogan. We are often misled by *shibboleths*.

shimmer V. glimmer intermittently. The moonlight *shimmered* on the water as the moon broke through the clouds for a moment. also N.

shoal N. shallow place. The ship was stranded on a *shoal* and had to be pulled off by tugs.

shoddy ADJ. sham; not genuine; inferior. You will never get the public to buy such *shoddy* material.

shrew N. scolding woman. No one wanted to marry Shakespeare's Kate because she was a *shrew*.

■ **shrewd** ADJ. clever; astute. A *shrewd* investor, he took clever advantage of the fluctuations of the stock market.

sibling N. brother or sister. We may not enjoy being *siblings,* but we cannot forget that we still belong to the same family.

sibylline ADJ. prophetic; oracular. Until their destruction by fire in 83 B.C., the *sibylline* books were often consulted by the Romans.

sidereal ADJ. relating to the stars. The study of *sidereal* bodies has been greatly advanced by the new telescope.

silt N. sediment deposited by running water. The harbor channel must be dredged annually to remove the *silt*.

simian ADJ. monkeylike. Lemurs are nocturnal mammals and have many *simian* characteristics, although they are less intelligent than monkeys.

simile N. comparison of one thing with another, using the word *like* or *as*. ''My love is like a red, red rose'' is a *simile*.

similitude N. similarity; using comparisons such as similes, etc. Although the critics deplored his use of mixed metaphors, he continued to write in *similitudes*.

simpering ADJ. smirking. I can overlook his *simpering* manner, but I cannot ignore his stupidity.

simulate V. feign. He *simulated* insanity in order to avoid punishment for his crime.

sinecure N. well-paid position with little responsibility. My job is no *sinecure;* I work long hours and have much responsibility.

sinewy ADJ. tough; strong and firm. The steak was too *sinewy* to chew.

sinister ADJ. evil. We must defeat the *sinister* forces that seek our downfall.

sinuous ADJ. winding; bending in and out; not morally honest. The snake moved in a *sinuous* manner.

sirocco N. warm, sultry wind blown from Africa to southern Europe. We can understand the popularity of the siesta in southern Spain; when the *sirocco* blows, the afternoon heat is unbearable.

■ **skeptic** N. doubter; person who suspends judgment until he has examined the evidence supporting a point of view. In this matter, I am a *skeptic;* I want proof.

skimp V. provide scantily; live very economically. They were forced to *skimp* on necessities in order to make their limited supplies last the winter.

skinflint N. miser. The old *skinflint* refused to give her a raise.

skittish ADJ. lively; frisky. She is as *skittish* as a kitten playing with a piece of string.

skulduggery N. dishonest behavior. The investigation into municipal corruption turned up new instances of *skulduggery* daily.

skulk V. move furtively and secretly. He *skulked* through the less fashionable sections of the city in order to avoid meeting any of his former friends.

slacken V. slow up; loosen. As they passed the finish line, the runners *slackened* their pace.

slake V. quench; sate. When we reached the oasis, we were able to *slake* our thirst.

slander N. defamation; utterance of false and malicious statements. Unless you can prove your allegations, your remarks constitute *slander*. also V.

slattern N. untidy or slovenly person. If you persist in wearing such sloppy clothes, people will call you a *slattern*.

sleazy ADJ. flimsy; unsubstantial. This is a *sleazy* material; it will not wear well.

sleeper N. something originally of little value or importance that in time becomes very valuable. Unnoticed by the critics at its publication, the eventual Pulitzer Prize winner was a classic *sleeper*.

sleight N. dexterity. The magician amazed the audience with his *sleight* of hand.

slither V. slip or slide. During the recent ice storm, many people *slithered* down this hill as they walked to the station.

sloth N. laziness. Such *sloth* in a young person is deplorable; go to work!

slough V. cast off. Each spring, the snake *sloughs* off its skin.

slovenly ADJ. untidy; careless in work habits. Such *slovenly* work habits will never produce good products.

sluggard N. lazy person. "You are a *sluggard,* a drone, a parasite," the angry father shouted at his lazy son.

■ **sluggish** ADJ. slow; lazy; lethargic. After two nights without sleep, she felt *sluggish* and incapable of exertion.

sluice N. artificial channel for directing or controlling the flow of water. This *sluice* gate is opened only in times of drought to provide water for irrigation.

smattering N. slight knowledge. I don't know whether it is better to be ignorant of a subject or to have a mere *smattering* of information about it.

smirk N. conceited smile. Wipe that *smirk* off your face! also V.

smolder V. burn without flame; be liable to break out at any moment. The rags *smoldered* for hours before they burst into flame.

snicker N. half-stifled laugh. The boy could not suppress a *snicker* when the teacher sat on the tack. also V.

snivel V. run at the nose; snuffle; whine. Don't you come *sniveling* to me complaining about your big brother.

sobriety N. soberness. The solemnity of the occasion filled us with *sobriety*.

sobriquet N. nickname. Despite all his protests, his classmates continued to call him by that unflattering *sobriquet*.

sodden ADJ. soaked; dull, as if from drink. He set his *sodden* overcoat near the radiator to dry.

sojourn N. temporary stay. After his *sojourn* in Florida, he began to long for the colder climate of his native New England home.

solace N. comfort in trouble. I hope you will find *solace* in the thought that all of us share your loss.

solecism N. construction that is flagrantly incorrect grammatically. I must give this paper a failing mark because it contains many *solecisms*.

solicitous ADJ. worried; concerned. The employer was very *solicitous* about the health of her employees as replacements were difficult to get.

soliloquy N. talking to oneself. The *soliloquy* is a device used by the dramatist to reveal a character's innermost thoughts and emotions.

solstice N. point at which the sun is farthest from the equator. The winter *solstice* usually occurs on December 21.

solvent ADJ. able to pay all debts. By dint of very frugal living, he was finally able to become *solvent* and avoid bankruptcy proceedings.

somatic ADJ. pertaining to the body; physical. Why do you ignore the spiritual aspects and emphasize only the corporeal and the *somatic?*

Test

Word List 43 *Synonyms and Antonyms*

Each of the following questions consists of a word in capital letters, followed by five lettered words or phrases. Choose the lettered word or phrase which is most nearly similar or the opposite of the word in capital letters and write the letter of your choice on your answer paper.

631. SERAPH (A) messenger (B) harbinger (C) demon (D) official (E) potentate

632. SERRIED (A) worried (B) embittered (C) in close order (D) fallen (E) infantile

633. SERVILE (A) moral (B) puerile (C) futile
     (D) foul (E) haughty

634. SHODDY (A) superior (B) barefoot (C) sunlit
     (D) querulous (E) garrulous

635. SIMILITUDE (A) gratitude (B) magnitude
     (C) likeness (D) aptitude (E) kindness

636. SINISTER (A) unwed (B) ministerial (C) good
     (D) returned (E) splintered

637. SKITTISH (A) tractable (B) inquiring (C) dramatic
     (D) vain (E) frisky

638. SLEAZY (A) fanciful (B) creeping (C) substantial
     (D) uneasy (E) warranted

639. SLOTH (A) penitence (B) filth (C) futility
     (D) poverty (E) industry

640. SLOUGH (A) toughen (B) trap (C) violate
     (D) cast off (E) depart

641. SLOVENLY (A) half-baked (B) loved
     (C) inappropriate (D) tidy (E) rapidly

642. SOBRIETY (A) inebriety (B) aptitude
     (C) scholasticism (D) monotony (E) aversion

643. SOBRIQUET (A) ingenue (B) livelihood
     (C) bar (D) epitaph (E) nickname

644. SOLSTICE (A) equinox (B) sunrise (C) pigsty
     (D) interstices (E) iniquity

645. SOLVENT (A) enigmatic (B) bankrupt (C) fiducial
     (D) puzzling (E) gilded

Word List 44   somber-sublime

somber ADJ. gloomy; depressing. From the doctor's grim expression, I could tell he had *somber* news.

somnambulist N. sleepwalker. The most famous *somnambulist* in literature is Lady Macbeth; her monologue in the sleepwalking scene is one of the highlights of Shakespeare's play.

somnolent ADJ. half asleep. The heavy meal and the overheated room made us all *somnolent* and indifferent to the speaker.

sonorous ADJ. resonant. His *sonorous* voice resounded through the hall.

sophist N. teacher of philosophy; quibbler; employer of fallacious reasoning. You are using all the devices of a *sophist* in trying to prove your case; your argument is specious.

sophistication N. artificiality; unnaturalness; act of employing sophistry in reasoning. *Sophistication* is an acquired characteristic, found more frequently among city dwellers than among residents of rural areas.

sophomoric ADJ. immature; shallow. Your *sophomoric* remarks are a sign of your youth and indicate that you have not given much thought to the problem.

■ **soporific** ADJ. sleep producer. I do not need a sedative when I listen to one of his *soporific* speeches. also N.

sordid ADJ. filthy; base; vile. The social worker was angered by the *sordid* housing provided for the homeless.

soupçon N. suggestion; hint; taste. A *soupçon* of garlic will improve this dish.

spangle N. small metallic piece sewn to clothing for ornamentation. The thousands of *spangles* on her dress sparkled in the glare of the stage lights.

spasmodic ADJ. fitful; periodic. The *spasmodic* coughing in the auditorium annoyed the performers.

spate N. sudden flood. I am worried about the possibility of a *spate* if the rains do not diminish soon.

spatial ADJ. relating to space. It is difficult to visualize the *spatial* extent of our universe.

spatula N. broad-bladed instrument used for spreading or mixing. The manufacturers of this frying pan recommend the use of a rubber *spatula* to avoid scratching the specially treated surface.

spawn V. lay eggs. Fish ladders had to be built in the dams to assist the salmon returning to *spawn* in their native streams. also N.

specious ADJ. seemingly reasonable but incorrect. Let us not be misled by such *specious* arguments.

spectral ADJ. ghostly. We were frightened by the *spectral* glow that filled the room.

spectrum N. colored band produced when beam of light passes through a prism. The visible portion of the *spectrum* includes red at one end and violet at the other.

sphinx-like ADJ. enigmatic; mysterious. The Mona Lisa's *sphinx-like* expression has puzzled art lovers for centuries.

splenetic ADJ. spiteful; irritable; peevish. People shunned him because of his *splenetic* temper. spleen, N.

spoliation N. pillaging; depredation. We regard this unwarranted attack on a neutral nation as an act of *spoliation* and we demand that it cease at once and that proper restitution be made.

spoonerism N. accidental transposition of sounds in successive words. When the radio announcer introduced the President as Hoobert Herver, he was guilty of a *spoonerism*.

■ **sporadic** ADJ. occurring irregularly. Although there are *sporadic* outbursts of shooting, we may report that the major rebellion has been defeated.

sportive ADJ. playful. Such a *sportive* attitude is surprising in a person as serious as you usually are.

spry ADJ. vigorously active; nimble. She was eighty years old, yet still *spry* and alert.

spume N. froth; foam. The *spume* at the base of the waterfall extended for a quarter of a mile downriver.

spurious ADJ. false; counterfeit. She tried to pay the check with a *spurious* ten-dollar bill.

spurn V. reject; scorn. The heroine *spurned* the villain's advances.

squalid ADJ. dirty; neglected; poor. It is easy to see how crime can breed in such a *squalid* neighborhood.

■ **squander** V. waste. The prodigal son *squandered* the family estate.

staccato ADJ. played in an abrupt manner; marked by abrupt sharp sound. His *staccato* speech reminded one of the sound of a machine gun.

■ **stagnant** ADJ. motionless; stale; dull. The *stagnant* water was a breeding ground for disease. stagnate, V.

staid ADJ. sober; sedate. Her conduct during the funeral ceremony was *staid* and solemn.

stalemate N. deadlock. Negotiations between the union and the employers have reached a *stalemate;* neither side is willing to budge from previously stated positions.

stalwart ADJ. strong, brawny; steadfast. His consistent support of the party has proved that he is a *stalwart* and loyal member. also N.

stamina N. strength; staying power. I doubt that she has the *stamina* to run the full distance of the marathon race.

stanch V. check flow of blood. It is imperative that we *stanch* the gushing wound before we attend to the other injuries.

■ **stanza** N. division of a poem. Do you know the last *stanza* of "The Star-Spangled Banner"?

statute N. law. We have many *statutes* in our law books which should be repealed.

statutory ADJ. created by statute or legislative action. The judicial courts review and try *statutory* crimes.

■ **steadfast** ADJ. loyal. I am sure you will remain *steadfast* in your support of the cause.

stein N. beer mug. She thought of college as a place where one drank beer from *steins* and sang songs of lost lambs.

stellar ADJ. pertaining to the stars. He was the *stellar* attraction of the entire performance.

stentorian ADJ. extremely loud. The town crier had a *stentorian* voice.

stereotyped ADJ. fixed and unvarying representation. My chief objection to the book is that the characters are *stereotyped*.

stertorous ADJ. having a snoring sound. He could not sleep because of the *stertorous* breathing of his roommates.

stilted ADJ. bombastic; inflated. His *stilted* rhetoric did not impress the college audience; they were immune to bombastic utterances.

stigma N. token of disgrace; brand. I do not attach any *stigma* to the fact that you were accused of this crime; the fact that you were acquitted clears you completely.

stigmatize V. brand; mark as wicked. I do not want to *stigmatize* this young offender for life by sending her to prison.

stint N. supply; allotted amount; assigned portion of work. He performed his daily *stint* cheerfully and willingly. also, V.

stipend N. pay for services. There is a nominal *stipend* for this position.

■ **stoic** N. person who is indifferent to pleasure or pain. The doctor called her patient a *stoic* because he had borne the pain of the examination without whimpering. also ADJ.

stoke V. to feed plentifully. They swiftly *stoked* themselves, knowing they would not have another meal until they reached camp.

stolid ADJ. dull; impassive. I am afraid that this imaginative poetry will not appeal to such a *stolid* person.

stratagem N. deceptive scheme. We saw through his clever *stratagem*.

stratum N. layer of earth's surface; layer of society. Unless we alleviate conditions in the lowest *stratum* of our society, we may expect grumbling and revolt.

striated ADJ. marked with parallel bands. The glacier left many *striated* rocks.

stricture N. critical comments; severe and adverse criticism. His *strictures* on the author's style are prejudiced and unwarranted.

strident ADJ. loud and harsh. She scolded him in a *strident* voice.

■ **stringent** ADJ. binding; rigid. I think these regulations are too *stringent*.

stultify V. cause to appear foolish or inconsistent. By changing your opinion at this time, you will *stultify* yourself.

stupor N. state of apathy; daze; lack of awareness. In his *stupor,* the addict was unaware of the events taking place around him.

stygian ADJ. gloomy; hellish; deathly. They descended into the *stygian,* half-lit sub-basement.

stymie V. present an obstacle; stump. The detective was *stymied* by the contradictory evidence in the robbery investigation. also N.

suave ADJ. smooth; bland. He is the kind of individual who is more easily impressed by a *suave* approach than by threats or bluster.

suavity N. urbanity; polish. He is particularly good in roles that require *suavity* and sophistication.

subaltern N. subordinate. The captain treated his *subalterns* as though they were children rather than commissioned officers.

subjective ADJ. occurring or taking place within the subject; unreal. Your analysis is highly *subjective;* you have permitted your emotions and your opinions to color your thinking.

subjugate V. conquer; bring under control. It is not our aim to *subjugate* our foe; we are interested only in establishing peaceful relations.

sublimate V. refine; purify. We must strive to *sublimate* these desires and emotions into worthwhile activities.

sublime ADJ. exalted; noble; uplifting. Mother Teresa has been honored for her *sublime* deeds.

Test

Word List 44   *Synonyms and Antonyms*

Each of the following questions consists of a word in capital letters, followed by five lettered words or phrases. Choose the lettered word or phrase which is most nearly similar or the opposite of the word in capital letters and write the letter of your choice on your answer paper.

646. SONOROUS (A) resonant (B) reassuring (C) repetitive (D) resinous (E) sisterly

647. SOPHOMORIC (A) unprecedented (B) mature (C) insipid (D) intellectual (E) illusionary

648. SOPORIFIC (A) dining (B) caustic (C) memorial (D) awakening (E) springing

649. SPASMODIC (A) intermittent (B) fit (C) inaccurate (D) violent (E) physical

650. SPORADIC (A) seedy (B) latent (C) vivid (D) inconsequential (E) occasional

651. SPORTIVE (A) competing (B) playful (C) indignant (D) foppish (E) fundamental

652. SPURIOUS (A) genuine (B) angry (C) mitigated (D) interrogated (E) glorious

653. SQUANDER (A) fortify (B) depart (C) roam (D) preserve (E) forfeit

654. STACCATO (A) musical (B) long (C) legato (D) sneezing (E) pounded

655. STAMINA (A) patience (B) pistils (C) weakness (D) fascination (E) patina

656. STEREOTYPED (A) original (B) antique (C) modeled (D) repetitious (E) continued

657. STILTED (A) candid (B) pompous (C) modish (D) acute (E) inarticulate

658. STRINGENT (A) binding (B) reserved (C) utilized (D) lambent (E) indigent

659. SUAVITY (A) ingeniousness (B) indifference (C) urbanity (D) constancy (E) paucity

660. SUBLIME (A) unconscious (B) respected (C) exalted (D) sneaky (E) replaced

Word List 45   subliminal-tantamount

subliminal ADJ. below the threshold. We may not be aware of the *subliminal* influences which affect our thinking.

sub rosa ADV. in strict confidence; privately. I heard of this *sub rosa* and I cannot tell you about it.

subsequent ADJ. following; later. In *subsequent* lessons, we shall take up more difficult problems.

subservient ADJ. behaving like a slave; servile; obsequious. He was proud and dignified; he refused to be *subservient* to anyone.

subsidiary ADJ. subordinate; secondary. This information may be used as *subsidiary* evidence but is not sufficient by itself to prove your argument. also N.

subsidy N. direct financial aid by government, etc. Without this *subsidy,* American ship operators would not be able to compete in world markets.

subsistence N. existence; means of support; livelihood. In these days of inflated prices, my salary provides a mere *subsistence*.

substantiate V. verify; support. I intend to *substantiate* my statement by producing witnesses.

substantive ADJ. essential; pertaining to the substance. Although the delegates were aware of the importance of the problem, they could not agree on the *substantive* issues.

subterfuge N. pretense; evasion. As soon as we realized that you had won our support by a *subterfuge,* we withdrew our endorsement of your candidacy.

■ **subtlety** N. nicety; cunning; guile; delicacy. The *subtlety* of his remarks was unnoticed by most of his audience. subtle, ADJ.

subversive ADJ. tending to overthrow or ruin. We must destroy such *subversive* publications.

succinct ADJ. brief; terse; compact. His remarks are always *succinct* and pointed.

succor N. aid; assistance; relief. We shall be ever grateful for the *succor* your country gave us when we were in need. also V.

succulent ADJ. juicy; full of richness. The citrus foods from Florida are more *succulent* to some people than those from California. also N.

succumb V. yield; give in; die. I *succumb* to temptation whenever it comes my way.

sudorific ADJ. pertaining to perspiration. Manufacturers of deodorants have made the public conscious of the need to avoid offending people with *sudorific* odors.

suffuse V. spread over. A blush *suffused* her cheeks when we teased her about her love affair.

sully V. tarnish; soil. He felt that it was beneath his dignity to *sully* his hands in such menial labor.

sultry ADJ. sweltering. He could not adjust himself to the *sultry* climate of the tropics.

summation N. act of finding the total; summary. In his *summation,* the lawyer emphasized the testimony given by the two witnesses.

sumptuary ADJ. limiting or regulating expenditures. While no *sumptuary* law has been enacted, the public will never tolerate the expenditure of so large a sum.

sumptuous ADJ. lavish; rich. I cannot recall when I have had such a *sumptuous* Thanksgiving feast.

sunder V. separate; part. Northern and southern Ireland are politically and religiously *sundered.*

sundry ADJ. various; several. My suspicions were aroused when I read *sundry* items in the newspapers about your behavior.

superannuated ADJ. retired on pension because of age. The *superannuated* man was indignant because he felt that he could still perform a good day's work.

supercilious ADJ. contemptuous; haughty. I resent your *supercilious* and arrogant attitude.

■ **superficial** ADJ. trivial; shallow. Since your report gave only a *superficial* analysis of the problem, I cannot give you more than a passing grade.

superfluity N. excess; overabundance. We have a definite lack of sincere workers and a *superfluity* of leaders.

superimpose V. place over something else. Your attempt to *superimpose* another agency in this field will merely increase the bureaucratic nature of our government.

supernal ADJ. heavenly; celestial. His tale of *supernal* beings was skeptically received.

supernumerary N. person or thing in excess of what is necessary; extra. His first appearance on the stage was as a *supernumerary* in a Shakespearean tragedy.

■ **supersede** V. cause to be set aside; replace. This regulation will *supersede* all previous rules.

supine ADJ. lying on back. The defeated pugilist lay *supine* on the canvas.

supplant V. replace; usurp. Ferdinand Marcos was *supplanted* by Corazon Aquino as president of the Philippines.

supple ADJ. flexible; pliant. The angler found a *supple* limb and used it as a fishing rod.

suppliant ADJ. entreating; beseeching. He could not resist the dog's *suppliant* whimpering, and he gave it some food. also N.

supplicate V. petition humbly; pray to grant a favor. We *supplicate* Your Majesty to grant him amnesty.

supposititious ADJ. assumed; counterfeit; hypothetical. I find no similarity between your *supposititious* illustration and the problem we are facing.

suppurate V. create pus. The surgeon refused to lance the abscess until it *suppurated*.

surcease N. cessation. He begged the doctors to grant him *surcease* from his suffering.

surfeit V. cloy; overfeed. I am *surfeited* with the sentimentality of the average motion picture film.

surly ADJ. rude; cross. Because of his *surly* attitude, many people avoided his company.

surmise V. guess. I *surmise* that he will be late for this meeting. also N.

surmount V. overcome. He had to *surmount* many obstacles in order to succeed.

■ **surpass** V. exceed. Her SAT scores *surpassed* our expectations.

■ **surreptitious** ADJ. secret. News of their *surreptitious* meeting gradually leaked out.

surrogate N. substitute. For a fatherless child, a male teacher may become a father *surrogate*.

surveillance N. watching; guarding. The FBI kept the house under constant *surveillance* in the hope of capturing all the criminals at one time.

■ **susceptible** ADJ. impressionable; easily influenced. He was a very *susceptible* young man, and so his parents worried that he might fall into bad company.

sustenance N. means of support, food, nourishment. In the tropics, the natives find *sustenance* easy to obtain, due to all the fruit trees.

suture N. stitches sewn to hold the cut edges of a wound or incision; material used in sewing. We will remove the *sutures* as soon as the wound heals. also V.

swarthy ADJ. dark; dusky. Despite the stereotypes, not all Italians are *swarthy;* many are fair and blond.

swathe V. wrap around; bandage. When I visited him in the hospital, I found him *swathed* in bandages.

swelter V. be oppressed by heat. I am going to buy an air conditioning unit for my apartment as I do not intend to *swelter* through another hot and humid summer.

■ **swindler** N. cheat. She was gullible and trusting, an easy victim for the first *swindler* who came along.

sybarite N. lover of luxury. Rich people are not always *sybarites;* some of them have little taste for a life of luxury.

sycophantic ADJ. servilely flattering. The king enjoyed the *sycophantic* attentions of his followers. sycophant, N.

syllogism N. logical formula utilizing a major premise, a minor premise and a conclusion. There must be a fallacy in this *syllogism;* I cannot accept the conclusion.

sylvan ADJ. pertaining to the woods; rustic. His paintings of nymphs in *sylvan* backgrounds were criticized as overly sentimental.

■ **symmetry** N. arrangement of parts so that balance is obtained; congruity. The addition of a second tower will give this edifice the *symmetry* which it now lacks.

synchronous ADJ. similarly timed; simultaneous with. We have many examples of scientists in different parts of the world who have made *synchronous* discoveries.

synthesis N. combining parts into a whole. Now that we have succeeded in isolating this drug, our next problem is to plan its *synthesis* in the laboratory.

synthetic ADJ. artificial; resulting from synthesis. During the twentieth century, many *synthetic* products have replaced the natural products. also N.

tacit ADJ. understood; not put into words. We have a *tacit* agreement based on only a handshake.

■ **taciturn** ADJ. habitually silent; talking little. New Englanders are reputedly *taciturn* people.

tactile ADJ. pertaining to the organs or sense of touch. His callused hands had lost their *tactile* sensitivity.

tainted ADJ. contaminated; corrupt. Health authorities are always trying to prevent the sale and use of *tainted* food.

talisman N. charm. She wore the *talisman* to ward off evil.

talon N. claw of bird. The falconer wore a leather gauntlet to avoid being clawed by the hawk's *talons*.

tantalize v. tease; torture with disappointment. Tom loved to *tantalize* his younger brother with candy; he knew the boy was forbidden to have it.

tantamount ADJ. equal. Your ignoring their pathetic condition is *tantamount* to murder.

Test

Word List 45   *Synonyms and Antonyms*

Each of the following questions consists of a word in capital letters, followed by five lettered words or phrases. Choose the lettered word or phrase which is most nearly similar or the opposite of the word in capital letters and write the letter of your choice on your answer paper.

661. SUBLIMINAL (A) radiant (B) indifferent (C) obvious (D) domestic (E) horizontal
662. SUPERANNUATED (A) senile (B) experienced (C) retired (D) attenuated (E) accepted
663. SUPERCILIOUS (A) haughty (B) highbrow (C) angry (D) inane (E) philosophic
664. SUPERFICIAL (A) abnormal (B) portentous (C) shallow (D) angry (E) tiny
665. SUPERNUMERARY (A) miser (B) extra (C) associate (D) astronomer (E) inferiority
666. SUPPLIANT (A) intolerant (B) swallowing (C) beseeching (D) finishing (E) flexible

667. SURFEIT (A) belittle (B) cloy (C) drop (D) estimate (E) claim
668. SURREPTITIOUS (A) secret (B) snakelike (C) nightly (D) abstract (E) furnished
669. SUTURE (A) stitch (B) reflection (C) knitting (D) tailor (E) past
670. SWATHED (A) wrapped around (B) waved (C) gambled (D) rapt (E) mystified
671. SYCOPHANTIC (A) quiet (B) recording (C) servilely flattering (D) frolicsome (E) eagerly awaiting
672. SYNTHETIC (A) simplified (B) doubled (C) tuneful (D) artificial (E) fiscal
673. TACIT (A) spoken (B) allowed (C) neural (D) impertinent (E) unwanted
674. TALISMAN (A) chief (B) juror (C) medicine man (D) amulet (E) gift
675. TANTALIZE (A) tease (B) wax (C) warrant (D) authorize (E) total

Word List 46   tantrum-tome

tantrum N. fit of petulance; caprice. The child learned that he could have almost anything if he went into *tantrums*.

taper N. candle. He lit the *taper* on the windowsill.

tarantula N. venomous spider. We need an antitoxin to counteract the bite of the *tarantula*.

tarn N. small mountain lake. This mountainous area is famous for its picturesque *tarns* and larger lakes.

tarry v. delay; dawdle. We can't *tarry* if we want to get to the airport on time.

tatterdemalion N. ragged fellow. Do you expect an army of *tatterdemalions* and beggars to put up a real fight?

taurine ADJ. like a bull. The bull charged into the ring, a mighty specimen of *taurine* power.

taut ADJ. tight; ready. The captain maintained that he ran a *taut* ship.

tautological ADJ. needlessly repetitious. In the sentence "It was visible to the eye," the phrase "to the eye" is *tautological*.

tautology N. unnecessary repetition; pleonasm. "Joyful happiness" is an illustration of *tautology*.

tawdry ADJ. cheap and gaudy. He won a few *tawdry* trinkets in Coney Island.

tedium N. boredom; weariness. We hope this radio will help overcome the *tedium* of your stay in the hospital.

teleology N. belief that a final purpose or design exists for the presence of individual beings or of the universe itself.

The questions propounded by *teleology* have long been debated in religious and scientific circles.

temerarious ADJ. rash. Mountain climbing at this time of year is *temerarious* and foolhardy.

temerity N. boldness; rashness. Do you have the *temerity* to argue with me?

temper v. restrain; blend; toughen. His hard times in the army only served to *temper* his strength.

temperate ADJ. restrained; self-controlled. Noted for his *temperate* appetite, he seldom gained weight.

tempo N. speed of music. I find the conductor's *tempo* too slow for such a brilliant piece of music.

temporal ADJ. not lasting forever; limited by time; secular. At one time in our history, *temporal* rulers assumed that they had been given their thrones by divine right.

temporize v. avoid committing oneself; gain time. I cannot permit you to *temporize* any longer; I must have a definite answer today.

tenacious ADJ. holding fast. I had to struggle to break his *tenacious* hold on my arm.

tenacity N. firmness; persistency; adhesiveness. It is extremely difficult to overcome the *tenacity* of a habit such as smoking.

tendentious ADJ. having an aim; designed to further a cause. The editorials in this periodical are *tendentious* rather than truth-seeking.

tenebrous ADJ. dark; gloomy. We were frightened as we entered the *tenebrous* passageways of the cave.

tenet N. doctrine; dogma. The agnostic did not accept the *tenets* of their faith.

tensile ADJ. capable of being stretched. Mountain climbers must know the *tensile* strength of their ropes.

■ **tentative** ADJ. provisional; experimental. Your *tentative* plans sound plausible; let me know when the final details are worked out.

tenuous ADJ. thin; rare; slim. The allegiance of our allies is held by rather *tenuous* ties.

tenure N. holding of an office; time during which such an office is held. He has permanent *tenure* in this position and cannot be fired.

tepid ADJ. lukewarm. During the summer, I like to take a *tepid* bath, not a hot one.

tergiversation N. evasion; fickleness. I cannot understand your *tergiversation;* I was certain that you were devoted to our cause.

termagant N. shrew; scolding, brawling woman. *The Taming of the Shrew* is one of many stories of the methods used in changing a *termagant* into a demure lady.

terminate V. to bring to an end. When his contract was *terminated* unexpectedly, he desperately needed a new job.

terminology N. terms used in a science or art. The special *terminology* developed by some authorities in the field has done more to confuse the layman than to enlighten him.

terminus N. last stop of railroad. After we reached the railroad *terminus,* we continued our journey into the wilderness on saddle horses.

terrapin N. American marsh tortoise. The flesh of the diamondback *terrapin* is considered by many epicures to be a delicacy.

terrestrial ADJ. on the earth. We have been able to explore the *terrestrial* regions much more thoroughly than the aquatic or celestial regions.

terse ADJ. concise; abrupt; pithy. I admire his *terse* style of writing; he comes directly to the point.

tertiary ADJ. third. He is so thorough that he analyzes *tertiary* causes where other writers are content with primary and secondary reasons.

tesselated ADJ. inlaid; mosaic. I recall seeing a table with a *tesselated* top of bits of stone and glass in a very interesting pattern.

testator N. maker of a will. The attorney called in his secretary and his partner to witness the signature of the *testator.*

testy ADJ. irritable; short-tempered. My advice is to avoid discussing this problem with him today as he is rather *testy* and may shout at you.

tether V. tie with a rope. Before we went to sleep, we *tethered* the horses to prevent their wandering off during the night.

thaumaturgist N. miracle worker; magician. I would have to be a *thaumaturgist* and not a mere doctor to find a remedy for this disease.

theocracy N. government of a community by religious leaders. Some Pilgrims favored the establishment of a *theocracy* in New England.

theosophy N. wisdom in divine things. *Theosophy* seeks to embrace the essential truth in all religions.

therapeutic ADJ. curative. These springs are famous for their *therapeutic* and healing qualities.

thermal ADJ. pertaining to heat. The natives discovered that the hot springs gave excellent *thermal* baths and began to develop their community as a health resort. also N.

thespian ADJ. pertaining to drama. Her success in the school play convinced her she was destined for a *thespian* career. also N.

thrall N. slave; bondage. The captured soldier was held in *thrall* by the conquering army.

threnody N. song of lamentation; dirge. When he died, many poets wrote *threnodies* about his passing.

■ **thrifty** ADJ. careful about money; economical. A *thrifty* shopper compares prices before making major purchases.

throes N. violent anguish. The *throes* of despair can be as devastating as the spasms accompanying physical pain.

throng N. crowd. *Throngs* of shoppers jammed the aisles. also V.

throttle V. strangle. The criminal tried to *throttle* the old man with his bare hands.

thwart V. baffle; frustrate. He felt that everyone was trying to *thwart* his plans and prevent his success.

thyme N. aromatic plant used for seasoning. The addition of a little *thyme* will enhance the flavor of the clam chowder.

timbre N. quality of a musical tone produced by a musical instrument. We identify the instrument producing a musical sound by its *timbre.*

timidity N. lack of self-confidence or courage. If you are to succeed as a salesman, you must first lose your *timidity* and fear of failure.

timorous ADJ. fearful; demonstrating fear. His *timorous* manner betrayed the fear he felt at the moment.

tipple V. drink (alcoholic beverages) frequently. He found that his most enjoyable evenings occurred when he *tippled* with his friends at the local pub.

tirade N. extended scolding; denunciation. Long before he had finished his *tirade,* we were sufficiently aware of the seriousness of our misconduct.

titanic ADJ. gigantic. *Titanic* waves beat against the shore during the hurricane.

tithe N. tax of one tenth. Because he was an agnostic, he refused to pay his *tithes* to the clergy. also V.

titillate V. tickle. I am here not to *titillate* my audience but to enlighten it.

titter N. nervous laugh. Her aunt's constant *titter* nearly drove her mad. also V.

titular ADJ. nominal holding of title without obligations. Although he was the *titular* head of the company, the real decisions were made by his general manager.

toady v. flatter for favors. I hope you see through those who are *toadying* you for special favors. also N.

tocsin N. alarm bell. Awakened by the sound of the *tocsin,* we rushed to our positions to await the attack.

toga N. Roman outer robe. Marc Antony pointed to the slashes in Caesar's *toga.*

tome N. large volume. He spent much time in the libraries poring over ancient *tomes.*

Test

Word List 46 *Synonyms*

Each of the questions below consists of a word in capital letters, followed by five lettered words or phrases. Choose the lettered word or phrase that is most nearly similar in meaning to the word in capital letters and write the letter of your choice on your answer paper.

676. TATTERDEMALION (A) confetti (B) crudity (C) stubborn individual (D) ragged fellow (E) artist
677. TAUTOLOGY (A) memory (B) repetition (C) tension (D) simile (E) lack of logic
678. TAWDRY (A) orderly (B) meretricious (C) reclaimed (D) filtered (E) proper
679. TEMERITY (A) timidity (B) resourcefulness (C) boldness (D) tremulousness (E) caution
680. TEMPORAL (A) priestly (B) scholarly (C) secular (D) sleepy (E) sporadic
681. TENACIOUS (A) fast running (B) intentional (C) obnoxious (D) holding fast (E) collecting

682. TENACITY (A) splendor (B) perseverance (C) tendency (D) ingratitude (E) decimation
683. TENDENTIOUS (A) biased (B) likely (C) absurd (D) festive (E) literary
684. TENTATIVE (A) prevalent (B) portable (C) mocking (D) wry (E) experimental
685. TENUOUS (A) vital (B) thin (C) careful (D) dangerous (E) necessary
686. TEPID (A) boiling (B) lukewarm (C) freezing (D) gaseous (E) cold
687. TERGIVERSATION (A) fickleness (B) conversation (C) altercation (D) swollen state (E) acquiescence
688. TESSELATED (A) striped (B) made of mosaics (C) piebald (D) uniform (E) trimmed
689. THAUMATURGIST (A) producer (B) dreamer (C) philosopher (D) thief (E) miracle worker
690. TITILLATE (A) hasten (B) fasten (C) stimulate (D) incorporate (E) enlarge

Word List 47 tonsure-ukase

tonsure N. shaving of the head, especially by person entering religious orders. His *tonsure,* even more than his monastic garb, indicated that he was a member of the religious order.

topography N. physical features of a region. Before the generals gave the order to attack, they ordered a complete study of the *topography* of the region.

torpid ADJ. dormant; dull; lethargic. The *torpid* bear had just come out of his cave after his long hibernation.

torso N. trunk of statue with head and limbs missing; human trunk. This *torso,* found in the ruins of Pompeii, is now on exhibition in the museum in Naples.

tortilla N. flat cake made of cornmeal, etc. As we traveled through Mexico, we became more and more accustomed to the use of *tortillas* instead of bread.

tortuous ADJ. winding; full of curves. Because this road is so *tortuous,* it is unwise to go faster than twenty miles an hour on it.

touchstone N. stone used to test the fineness of gold alloys; criterion. What *touchstone* can be used to measure the character of a person?

touchy ADJ. sensitive; irascible. Do not discuss this phase of the problem as he is very *touchy* about it.

toxic ADJ. poisonous. We must seek an antidote for whatever *toxic* substance he has eaten.

tract N. pamphlet; a region of indefinite size. The King granted William Penn a *tract* of land in the New World.

tractable ADJ. docile. You will find the children in this school very *tractable* and willing to learn.

traduce V. expose to slander. His opponents tried to *traduce* the candidate's reputation by spreading rumors about his past.

trajectory N. path taken by a projectile. The police tried to locate the spot from which the assassin had fired the fatal shot by tracing the *trajectory* of the bullet.

tranquillity N. calmness; peace. After the commotion and excitement of the city, I appreciate the *tranquillity* of these fields and forests.

transcend V. exceed; surpass. This accomplishment *transcends* all our previous efforts. transcendental, ADJ.

transcribe V. copy. When you *transcribe* your notes, please send a copy to Mr. Smith and keep the original for our files. transcription, N.

transgression N. violation of a law; sin. Forgive us our *transgressions;* we know not what we do.

transient ADJ. fleeting; quickly passing away; staying for a short time. This hotel caters to a *transient* trade because it is near a busy highway.

transition N. going from one state of action to another. During the period of *transition* from oil heat to gas heat, the furnace will have to be shut off.

translucent ADJ. partly transparent. We could not recognize the people in the next room because of the *translucent* curtains which separated us.

transmute V. change; convert to something different. He was unable to *transmute* his dreams into actualities.

transparent ADJ. permitting light to pass through freely; easily detected. Your scheme is so *transparent* that it will fool no one.

transpire V. exhale; become known; happen. In spite of all our efforts to keep the meeting a secret, news of our conclusions *transpired*.

trappings N. outward decorations; ornaments. He loved the *trappings* of success: the limousines, the stock options, the company jet.

traumatic ADJ. pertaining to an injury caused by violence. In his nightmares, he kept on recalling the *traumatic* experience of being wounded in battle.

travail N. painful labor. How long do you think a man can endure such *travail* and degradation without rebelling?

traverse V. go through or across. When you *traverse* this field, be careful of the bull.

travesty N. comical parody; treatment aimed at making something appear ridiculous. The ridiculous decision the jury has arrived at is a *travesty* of justice.

treacle N. syrup obtained in refining sugar. *Treacle* is more highly refined than molasses.

treatise N. article treating a subject systematically and thoroughly. He is preparing a *treatise* on the Elizabethan playwrights for his graduate degree.

trek N. travel; journey. The tribe made their *trek* further north that summer in search of game. also V.

tremor N. trembling; slight quiver. She had a nervous *tremor* in her right hand.

tremulous ADJ. trembling; wavering. She was *tremulous* more from excitement than from fear.

trenchant ADJ. cutting; keen. I am afraid of his *trenchant* wit for it is so often sarcastic.

trencherman N. good eater. He is not finicky about his food; he is a *trencherman*.

trepidation N. fear; trembling agitation. We must face the enemy without *trepidation* if we are to win this battle.

tribulation N. distress; suffering. After all the trials and *tribulations* we have gone through, we need this rest.

tribunal N. court of justice. The decision of the *tribunal* was final and the prisoner was sentenced to death.

tribute N. tax levied by a ruler; mark of respect. The colonists refused to pay *tribute* to a foreign despot.

trident N. three-pronged spear. Neptune is usually depicted as rising from the sea, carrying his *trident* on his shoulder.

trilogy N. group of three works. Romain Rolland's novel *Jean Christophe* was first published as a *trilogy*.

triolet N. eight-line stanza with rhyme scheme *a b aaa b a b*. The *triolet* is a difficult verse pattern because it utilizes only two rhymes in its eight lines.

trite ADJ. hackneyed; commonplace. The *trite* and predictable situations in many television programs alienate many viewers.

trivia N. trifles; unimportant matters. Too many magazines ignore newsworthy subjects and feature *trivia*.

troglodyte N. cave dweller. We know that the first men in this area were *troglodytes* by the artifacts we have discovered in the caves.

trope N. figure of speech. The poem abounds in *tropes* and alliterative expressions.

troth N. pledge of good faith especially in betrothal. He gave her his *troth* and vowed he would cherish her always.

truckle V. curry favor; act in an obsequious way. If you *truckle* to the lord, you will be regarded as a sycophant; if you do not, you will be considered arrogant.

truculent ADJ. aggressive; savage. They are a *truculent* race, ready to fight at any moment.

truism N. self-evident truth. Many a *truism* is well expressed in a proverb.

trumpery N. objects that are showy, valueless, deceptive. All this finery is mere *trumpery*.

truncate V. cut the top off. The top of a cone which has been *truncated* in a plane parallel to its base is a circle.

tryst N. meeting. The lovers kept their *tryst* even though they realized their danger.

tumbrel N. a farm tipcart. The *tumbrels* became the vehicles which transported the condemned people from the prisons to the guillotine.

tumid ADJ. swollen; pompous; bombastic. I especially dislike his *tumid* style; I prefer writing which is less swollen and bombastic.

tumult N. commotion; riot; noise. She could not make herself heard over the *tumult* of the mob.

tundra N. rolling, treeless plain in Siberia and arctic North America. Despite the cold, many geologists are trying to discover valuable mineral deposits in the *tundra*.

turbid ADJ. muddy; having the sediment disturbed. The water was *turbid* after the children had waded through it.

■ **turbulence** N. state of violent agitation. We were frightened by the *turbulence* of the ocean during the storm.

tureen N. deep table dish for holding soup. The waiters brought the soup to the tables in silver *tureens*.

turgid ADJ. swollen; distended. The *turgid* river threatened to overflow the levees and flood the countryside.

turmoil N. confusion; strife. Conscious he had sinned, he was in a state of spiritual *turmoil*.

turnkey N. jailer. By bribing the *turnkey*, the prisoner arranged to have better food brought to him in his cell.

turpitude N. depravity. A visitor may be denied admittance to this country if she has been guilty of moral *turpitude*.

tutelage N. guardianship; training. Under the *tutelage* of such masters of the instrument, she made rapid progress as a virtuoso.

tutelary ADJ. protective; pertaining to a guardianship. I am acting in my *tutelary* capacity when I refuse to grant you permission to leave the campus.

tycoon N. wealthy leader. John D. Rockefeller was a prominent *tycoon*.

■ **tyranny** N. oppression; cruel government. Frederick Douglass fought against the *tyranny* of slavery throughout his entire life.

tyro N. beginner; novice. For a mere *tyro*, you have produced some marvelous results.

ubiquitous ADJ. being everywhere; omnipresent. You must be *ubiquitous* for I meet you wherever I go.

ukase N. official decree, usually Russian. It was easy to flaunt the *ukases* issued from St. Petersburg; there was no one to enforce them.

Test

Word List 47   *Antonyms*

Each of the questions below consists of a word in capital letters, followed by five lettered words or phrases. Choose the lettered word or phrase that is most nearly opposite in meaning to the word in capital letters and write the letter of your choice on your answer paper.

691. TRACTABLE (A) unmanageable (B) irreligious (C) mortal (D) incapable (E) unreal

692. TRADUCE (A) exhume (B) increase (C) purchase (D) extol (E) donate

693. TRANQUILLITY (A) lack of sleep (B) lack of calm (C) emptiness (D) renewal (E) closeness

694. TRANSIENT (A) carried (B) close (C) permanent (D) removed (E) certain

695. TREMULOUS (A) steady (B) obese (C) young (D) healthy (E) unkempt

696. TRENCHERMAN (A) finicky eater (B) infantryman (C) angler (D) imbiber (E) pacifist

697. TREPIDATION (A) slowness (B) amputation (C) fearlessness (D) adroitness (E) death

698. TRITE (A) correct (B) original (C) distinguished (D) premature (E) certain

699. TRUCULENT (A) juicy (B) overflowing (C) peaceful (D) determined (E) false

700. TRUMPERY (A) silence (B) defeat (C) percussion (D) murder (E) valuables

701. TURBID (A) clear (B) improbable (C) invariable (D) honest (E) turgid

702. TURBULENCE (A) reaction (B) approach (C) impropriety (D) calm (E) hostility

703. TURGID (A) rancid (B) shrunken (C) cool (D) explosive (E) painful

704. TURPITUDE (A) amplitude (B) heat (C) wealth (D) virtue (E) quiet

705. TYRO (A) infant (B) rubber (C) personnel (D) idiot (E) expert

Word List 48   ulterior-vehement

ulterior ADJ. situated beyond; unstated. You must have an *ulterior* motive for your behavior, since there is no obvious reason for it.

ultimate ADJ. final; not susceptible to further analysis. Scientists are searching for the *ultimate* truths.

ultimatum N. last demand; warning. Since they have ignored our *ultimatum,* our only recourse is to declare war.

umbrage N. resentment; anger; sense of injury or insult. She took *umbrage* at his remarks and stormed away in a huff.

unanimity N. complete agreement. We were surprised by the *unanimity* with which our proposals were accepted by the different groups.

unassuaged ADJ. unsatisfied; not soothed. Her anger is *unassuaged* by your apology.

unassuming ADJ. modest. He is so *unassuming* that some people fail to realize how great a man he really is.

unbridled ADJ. violent. She had a sudden fit of *unbridled* rage.

uncanny ADJ. strange; mysterious. You have the *uncanny* knack of reading my innermost thoughts.

unconscionable ADJ. unscrupulous; excessive. She found the loan shark's demands *unconscionable* and impossible to meet.

uncouth ADJ. outlandish; clumsy; boorish. Most biographers portray Lincoln as an *uncouth* and ungainly young man.

unction N. the act of anointing with oil. The anointing with oil of a person near death is called extreme *unction.*

unctuous ADJ. oily; bland; insincerely suave. Uriah Heep disguised his nefarious actions by *unctuous* protestations of his '' 'umility.''

■ **undermine** V. weaken; sap. The recent corruption scandals have *undermined* many people's faith in the city government.

undulate V. move with a wavelike motion. The flag *undulated* in the breeze.

unearth V. dig up. When they *unearthed* the city, the archeologists found many relics of an ancient civilization.

unearthly ADJ. not earthly; weird. There is an *unearthly* atmosphere in her work which amazes the casual observer.

unequivocal ADJ. plain; obvious. My answer to your proposal is an *unequivocal* and absolute "No."

unerringly ADV. infallibly. My teacher *unerringly* pounced on the one typographical error in my essay.

unfaltering ADJ. steadfast. She approached the guillotine with *unfaltering* steps.

unfeigned ADJ. genuine; real. She turned so pale that I am sure her surprise was *unfeigned*.

unfledged ADJ. immature. It is hard for an *unfledged* writer to find a sympathetic publisher.

ungainly ADJ. awkward. He is an *ungainly* young man; he trips over everything.

unguent N. ointment. Apply this *unguent* to the sore muscles before retiring.

■ **uniformity** N. sameness; monotony. After a while, the *uniformity* of TV situation comedies becomes boring.

unilateral ADJ. one-sided. This legislation is *unilateral* since it binds only one party in the controversy.

unimpeachable ADJ. blameless and exemplary. Her conduct in office was *unimpeachable* and her record is spotless.

uninhibited ADJ. unrepressed. The congregation was shocked by her *uninhibited* laughter during the sermon.

unique ADJ. without an equal; single in kind. You have the *unique* distinction of being the first student whom I have had to fail in this course.

unison N. unity of pitch; complete accord. The choir sang in *unison*.

unkempt ADJ. disheveled; with uncared-for appearance. The beggar was dirty and *unkempt*.

unmitigated ADJ. harsh; severe; not lightened. I sympathize with you in your *unmitigated* sorrow.

■ **unobtrusive** ADJ. inconspicuous; not blatant. The secret service agents in charge of protecting the President tried to be as *unobtrusive* as possible.

■ **unprecedented** ADJ. novel; unparalleled. Margaret Mitchell's book *Gone with the Wind* was an *unprecedented* success.

unruly ADJ. disobedient; lawless. The only way to curb this *unruly* mob is to use tear gas.

unsavory ADJ. distasteful; morally offensive. People with *unsavory* reputations should not be allowed to work with young children.

unscathed ADJ. unharmed. They prayed he would come back from the war *unscathed*.

unseemly ADJ. unbecoming; indecent. Your levity is *unseemly* at this time of mourning.

unsullied ADJ. untarnished. I am happy that my reputation is *unsullied*.

untenable ADJ. unsupportable. I find your theory *untenable* and must reject it.

untoward ADJ. unfortunate; annoying. *Untoward* circumstances prevent me from being with you on this festive occasion.

unwitting ADJ. unintentional; not knowing. She was the *unwitting* tool of the swindlers.

unwonted ADJ. unaccustomed. He hesitated to assume the *unwonted* role of master of ceremonies at the dinner.

upbraid V. scold; reproach. I must *upbraid* him for his unruly behavior.

upshot N. outcome. The *upshot* of the rematch was that the former champion proved that he still possessed all the skills of his youth.

urbane ADJ. suave; refined; elegant. The courtier was *urbane* and sophisticated. urbanity, N.

urchin N. mischievous child (usually a boy). Get out! This store is no place for grubby *urchins!*

ursine ADJ. bearlike; pertaining to a bear. Because of its *ursine* appearance, the great panda has been identified with the bears; actually, it is closely related to the raccoon.

usurpation N. act of seizing power and rank of another. The revolution ended with the *usurpation* of the throne by the victorious rebel leader.

usury N. lending money at illegal rates of interest. The loan shark was found guilty of *usury*.

utopia N. imaginary land with perfect social and political system. Shangri-la was the name of James Hilton's Tibetan *utopia*.

uxorious ADJ. excessively devoted to one's wife. His friends laughed at him because he was so *uxorious* and submissive to his wife's desires.

■ **vacillation** N. fluctuation; wavering. His *vacillation* when confronted with a problem annoyed all of us who had to wait until he made his decision. vacillate, V.

vacuous ADJ. empty; inane. The *vacuous* remarks of the politician annoyed the audience, who had hoped to hear more than empty platitudes.

vagabond N. wanderer; tramp. In summer, college students wander the roads of Europe like carefree *vagabonds*. also ADJ.

vagary N. caprice; whim. She followed every *vagary* of fashion.

vagrant ADJ. stray; random. He tried to study, but could not collect his *vagrant* thoughts. also N.

vainglorious ADJ. boastful; excessively conceited. She was a *vainglorious* and arrogant individual.

valance N. short drapery hanging above window frame. The windows were curtainless; only the tops were covered with *valances*.

valedictory ADJ. pertaining to farewell. I found the *valedictory* address too long; leave-taking should be brief.

validate V. confirm; ratify. I will not publish my findings until I *validate* my results.

valor N. bravery. He received the Medal of Honor for his *valor* in battle.

vampire N. ghostly being that sucks the blood of the living. Children were afraid to go to sleep at night because of the many legends of *vampires*.

vanguard N. forerunners; advance forces. We are the *vanguard* of a tremendous army that is following us.

vantage N. position giving an advantage. They fired upon the enemy from behind trees, walls and any other point of *vantage* they could find.

vapid ADJ. insipid; inane. She delivered an uninspired and *vapid* address.

variegated ADJ. many-colored. He will not like this solid blue necktie as he is addicted to *variegated* clothing.

vassal N. in feudalism, one who held land of a superior lord. The lord demanded that his *vassals* contribute more to his military campaign.

vaunted ADJ. boasted; bragged; highly publicized. This much *vaunted* project proved a disappointment when it collapsed.

veer V. change in direction. After what seemed an eternity, the wind *veered* to the east and the storm abated.

vegetate V. live in a monotonous way. I do not understand how you can *vegetate* in this quiet village after the adventurous life you have led.

vehement ADJ. impetuous; with marked vigor. He spoke with *vehement* eloquence in defense of his client.

Test

Word List 48   *Antonyms*

Each of the questions below consists of a word in capital letters, followed by five lettered words or phrases. Choose the lettered word or phrase that is most nearly opposite in meaning to the word in capital letters and write the letter of your choice on your answer paper.

706. UNEARTH (A) conceal (B) gnaw (C) clean (D) fling (E) react
707. UNFEIGNED (A) pretended (B) fashionable (C) wary (D) switched (E) colonial
708. UNGAINLY (A) ignorant (B) graceful (C) detailed (D) dancing (E) pedantic
709. UNIMPEACHABLE (A) fruitful (B) rampaging (C) faulty (D) pensive (E) thorough
710. UNKEMPT (A) bombed (B) washed (C) neat (D) showy (E) tawdry
711. UNRULY (A) chatting (B) obedient (C) definite (D) lined (E) curious
712. UNSEEMLY (A) effortless (B) proper (C) conducive (D) pointed (E) informative
713. UNSULLIED (A) tarnished (B) countless (C) soggy (D) papered (E) homicidal
714. UNTENABLE (A) supportable (B) tender (C) sheepish (D) tremulous (E) adequate
715. UNWITTING (A) clever (B) intense (C) sensitive (D) freezing (E) intentional
716. VACILLATION (A) remorse (B) relief (C) respect (D) steadfastness (E) inoculation
717. VALEDICTORY (A) sad (B) collegiate (C) derivative (D) salutatory (E) promising
718. VALOR (A) admonition (B) injustice (C) cowardice (D) generosity (E) repression
719. VANGUARD (A) regiment (B) rear (C) echelon (D) protection (E) loyalty
720. VAUNTED (A) unvanquished (B) fell (C) belittled (D) exacting (E) believed

Word List 49   vellum-vogue

vellum N. parchment. Bound in *vellum* and embossed in gold, this book is a beautiful example of the binder's craft.

velocity N. speed. The train went by at considerable *velocity*.

vendetta N. blood feud. The rival mobs engaged in a bitter *vendetta*.

vendor N. seller. The fruit *vendor* sold her wares from a stall on the sidewalk.

venal ADJ. capable of being bribed. The *venal* policeman accepted the bribe offered him by the speeding motorist whom he had stopped.

veneer N. thin layer; cover. Casual acquaintances were deceived by his *veneer* of sophistication and failed to recognize his fundamental shallowness.

venerable ADJ. deserving high respect. We do not mean to be disrespectful when we refuse to follow the advice of our *venerable* leader.

■ **venerate** V. revere. In China, the people *venerate* their ancestors.

venial ADJ. forgivable; trivial. We may regard a hungry man's stealing as a *venial* crime.

venison N. the meat of a deer. The hunters dined on *venison*.

vent N. a small opening; outlet. The wine did not flow because the air *vent* in the barrel was clogged.

vent V. express; utter. He *vented* his wrath on his class.

ventral V. abdominal. We shall now examine the *ventral* plates of this serpent, not the dorsal side.

ventriloquist N. someone who can make his or her voice seem to come from another person or thing. This *ventriloquist* does an act in which she has a conversation with a wooden dummy.

venturous ADJ. daring. The five *venturous* young men decided to look for a new approach to the mountain top.

venturesome ADJ. bold. A group of *venturesome* women were the first to scale Mt. Annapurna.

venue N. location. The attorney asked for a change of *venue;* he thought his client would do better if the trial were held in a less conservative county.

veracious ADJ. truthful. I can recommend him for this position because I have always found him *veracious* and reliable.

verbalize V. to put into words. I know you don't like to talk about these things, but please try to *verbalize* your feelings.

verbatim ADV. word for word. He repeated the message *verbatim.* also ADJ.

verbiage N. pompous array of words. After we had waded through all the *verbiage*, we discovered that the writer had said very little.

■ **verbose** ADJ. wordy. This article is too *verbose;* we must edit it.

verdant ADJ. green; fresh. The *verdant* meadows in the spring are always an inspiring sight.

verge N. border; edge. Madame Curie knew she was on the *verge* of discovering the secrets of radioactive elements. also V.

verdigris N. a green coating on copper which has been exposed to the weather. Despite all attempts to protect the statue from the elements, it became coated with *verdigris.*

verisimilitude N. appearance of truth; likelihood. Critics praised her for the *verisimilitude* of her performance as Lady Macbeth. She was completely believable.

verity N. truth; reality. The four *verities* were revealed to Buddha during his long meditation.

vermicular ADJ. pertaining to a worm. The *vermicular* burrowing in the soil helps to aerate it.

vernal ADJ. pertaining to spring. We may expect *vernal* showers all during the month of April.

vernacular N. living language; natural style. Cut out those old-fashioned thee's and thou's and write in the *vernacular.* also ADJ.

versatile ADJ. having many talents; capable of working in many fields. He was a *versatile* athlete; at college he had earned varsity letters in baseball, football, and track.

vertex N. summit. Let us drop a perpendicular line from the *vertex* of the triangle to the base.

vertiginous ADJ. giddy; causing dizziness. I do not like the rides in the amusement park because they have a *vertiginous* effect on me.

vertigo N. dizziness. We test potential plane pilots for susceptibility to spells of *vertigo.*

verve N. enthusiasm; liveliness. She approached her studies with such *verve* that it was impossible for her to do poorly.

vestige N. trace; remains. We discovered *vestiges* of early Indian life in the cave.

vex N. annoy; distress. Please try not to *vex* your mother; she is doing the best she can.

■ **viable** ADJ. capable of maintaining life. The infant, though prematurely born, is *viable* and has a good chance to survive.

viand N. food. There was a variety of *viands* at the feast.

vicarious ADJ. acting as a substitute; done by a deputy. Many people get a *vicarious* thrill at the movies by imagining they are the characters on the screen.

vicissitude N. change of fortune. I am accustomed to life's *vicissitudes,* having experienced poverty and wealth, sickness and health, and failure and success.

victuals N. food. I am very happy to be able to provide you with these *victuals;* I know you are hungry.

vie V. contend; compete. When we *vie* with each other for his approval, we are merely weakening ourselves and strengthening him.

vigilance N. watchfulness. Eternal *vigilance* is the price of liberty.

vignette N. picture; short literary sketch. *The New Yorker* published her latest *vignette.*

■ **vilify** V. slander. She is a liar and is always trying to *vilify* my reputation. vilification, N.

vindicate V. clear of charges. I hope to *vindicate* my client and return him to society as a free man.

vindictive ADJ. revengeful. She was very *vindictive* and never forgave an injury.

viper N. poisonous snake. The habitat of the horned *viper,* a particularly venomous snake, is in sandy regions like the Sahara or the Sinai peninsula.

virago N. shrew. Rip Van Winkle's wife was a veritable *virago.*

virile ADJ. manly. I do not accept the premise that a man is *virile* only when he is belligerent.

virtual ADJ. in essence; for practical purposes. She is a *virtual* financial wizard when it comes to money matters.

■ **virtuoso** N. highly skilled artist. Heifetz is a violin *virtuoso.*

■ **virulent** ADJ. extremely poisonous. The virus is highly *virulent* and has made many of us ill for days.

virus N. disease communicator. The doctors are looking for a specific medicine to control this *virus.*

visage N. face; appearance. The stern *visage* of the judge indicated that she had decided to impose a severe penalty.

visceral ADJ. felt in one's inner organs. She disliked the *visceral* sensations she had whenever she rode the roller coaster.

viscid ADJ. sticky; adhesive. Glue is a *viscid* liquid.

viscous ADJ. sticky; gluey. Melted tar is a *viscous* substance.

visionary ADJ. produced by imagination; fanciful; mystical. She was given to *visionary* schemes which never materialized. also N.

vitiate V. spoil the effect of; make inoperative. Fraud will *vitiate* the contract.

vitreous ADJ. pertaining to or resembling glass. Although this plastic has many *vitreous* qualities such as transparency, it is unbreakable.

vitriolic ADJ. corrosive; sarcastic. Such *vitriolic* criticism is uncalled for.

vituperative ADJ. abusive; scolding. He became more *vituperative* as he realized that we were not going to grant him his wish.

vivacious ADJ. animated; gay. She had always been *vivacious* and sparkling.

vivisection N. act of dissecting living animals. The Society for the Prevention of Cruelty to Animals opposed *vivisec-* *tion* and deplored the practice of using animals in scientific experiments.

vixen N. female fox; ill-tempered woman. Aware that she was right once again, he lost his temper and called her a shrew and a *vixen*.

vizier N. powerful Muslim government official. The *vizier* decreed that all persons in the city were to be summoned to the ceremony.

vociferous ADJ. clamorous; noisy. The crowd grew *vociferous* in its anger and threatened to take the law into its own hands.

vogue N. popular fashion. Jeans became the *vogue* on many college campuses.

Test

Word List 49   *Synonyms and Antonyms*

Each of the following questions consists of a word in capital letters, followed by five lettered words or phrases. Choose the lettered word or phrase which is most nearly similar or the opposite of the word in capital letters and write the letter of your choice on your answer paper.

721. VENAL (A) springlike (B) honest (C) angry (D) indifferent (E) going
722. VENERATE (A) revere (B) age (C) reject (D) reverberate (E) degenerate
723. VENIAL (A) unforgivable (B) unforgettable (C) unmistaken (D) fearful (E) fragrant
724. VERACIOUS (A) worried (B) slight (C) alert (D) truthful (E) instrumental
725. VERDANT (A) poetic (B) green (C) red (D) autumnal (E) frequent
726. VERITY (A) sanctity (B) reverence (C) falsehood (D) rarity (E) household
727. VESTIGE (A) trek (B) trail (C) trace (D) trial (E) tract

728. VIABLE (A) moribund (B) salable (C) useful (D) foolish (E) inadequate
729. VIAND (A) wand (B) gown (C) food (D) orchestra (E) frock
730. VICARIOUS (A) substitutional (B) aggressive (C) sporadic (D) reverent (E) internal
731. VIGILANCE (A) bivouac (B) guide (C) watchfulness (D) mob rule (E) posse
732. VILIFY (A) erect (B) eulogize (C) better (D) magnify (E) horrify
733. VINDICTIVE (A) revengeful (B) fearful (C) divided (D) literal (E) convincing
734. VIRULENT (A) sensuous (B) malignant (C) masculine (D) conforming (E) approaching
735. VISAGE (A) doubt (B) personality (C) hermitage (D) face (E) armor

Word List 50   volatile-zephyr

■ **volatile** ADJ. evaporating rapidly; lighthearted; mercurial. Ethyl chloride is a very *volatile* liquid.

volition N. act of making a conscious choice. She selected this dress of her own *volition*.

voluble ADJ. fluent; glib. She was a *voluble* speaker, always ready to talk.

■ **voluminous** ADJ. bulky; large. Despite her family burdens, she kept up a *voluminous* correspondence with her friends.

voluptuous ADJ. gratifying the senses. The nobility during the Renaissance led *voluptuous* lives.

voracious ADJ. ravenous. The wolf is a *voracious* animal, its hunger never satisfied.

votary N. follower of a cult. She was a *votary* of every new movement in literature and art.

vouchsafe V. grant condescendingly; guarantee. I can safely *vouchsafe* you a fair return on your investment.

vulnerable ADJ. susceptible to wounds. Achilles was *vulnerable* only in his heel.

vulpine ADJ. like a fox; crafty. She disliked his sly ways, but granted him a certain *vulpine* intelligence.

vying V. contending. Why are we *vying* with each other for her favors? vie, V.

waft V. moved gently by wind or waves. Daydreaming, he gazed at the leaves which *wafted* past his window.

waggish ADJ. mischievous; humorous; tricky. He was a prankster who, unfortunately, often overlooked the damage he could cause with his *waggish* tricks.

waif N. homeless child or animal. Although he already had eight cats, he could not resist adopting yet another feline *waif.*

waive V. give up temporarily; yield. I will *waive* my rights in this matter in order to expedite our reaching a proper decision.

wallow V. roll in; indulge in; become helpless. The hippopotamus loves to *wallow* in the mud.

wan ADJ. having a pale or sickly color; pallid. Suckling asked, ''Why so pale and *wan,* fond lover?''

wane V. grow gradually smaller. From now until December 21, the winter equinox, the hours of daylight will *wane.*

wangle V. wiggle out; fake. She tried to *wangle* an invitation to the party.

wanton ADJ. unruly; unchaste; excessive. His *wanton,* drunken ways cost him many friends.

warble V. sing; babble. Every morning the birds *warbled* outside her window. also N.

warrant V. justify; authorize. Before the judge issues the injunction, you must convince her this action is *warranted.*

warranty N. guarantee; assurance by seller. The purchaser of this automobile is protected by the manufacturer's *warranty* that he will replace any defective part for five years or 50,000 miles.

warren N. tunnels in which rabbits live; crowded conditions in which people live. The tenement was a veritable *warren,* packed with people too poor to live elsewhere.

wary ADJ. very cautious. The spies grew *wary* as they approached the sentry.

wastrel N. profligate. He was denounced as a *wastrel* who had dissipated his inheritance.

wax V. increase; grow. With proper handling, his fortunes *waxed* and he became rich.

waylay V. ambush; lie in wait. They agreed to *waylay* their victim as he passed through the dark alley going home.

wean V. accustom a baby not to nurse; give up a cherished activity. He decided he would *wean* himself away from eating junk food and stick to fruits and vegetables.

weather V. endure the effects of weather or other forces. He *weathered* the changes in his personal life with difficulty, as he had no one in whom to confide.

welt N. mark from a beating or whipping. The evidence of child abuse was very clear; Jennifer's small body was covered with *welts* and bruises.

welter V. wallow. At the height of the battle, the casualties were so numerous that the victims *weltered* in their blood while waiting for medical attention.

wheedle V. cajole; coax; deceive by flattery. She knows she can *wheedle* almost anything she wants from her father.

whelp N. young wolf, dog, tiger, etc. This collie *whelp* won't do for breeding, but he'd make a fine pet.

whet V. sharpen; stimulate. The odors from the kitchen are *whetting* my appetite; I will be ravenous by the time the meal is served.

■ **whimsical** ADJ. capricious; fanciful; quaint. *Peter Pan* is a *whimsical* play.

whinny V. neigh like a horse. When he laughed through his nose, it sounded as if he *whinnied.*

whit N. smallest speck. There is not a *whit* of intelligence or understanding in your observations.

whorl N. ring of leaves around stem; ring. Identification by fingerprints is based on the difference in shape and number of the *whorls* on the fingers.

wily ADJ. cunning; artful. She is as *wily* as a fox in avoiding trouble.

wince V. shrink back; flinch. The screech of the chalk on the blackboard made her *wince.*

windfall N. fallen fruit; unexpected lucky event. This huge tax refund is quite a *windfall.*

winnow V. sift; separate good parts from bad. This test will *winnow* out the students who study from those who don't bother.

winsome ADJ. agreeable; gracious; engaging. By her *winsome* manner, she made herself liked by everyone who met her.

■ **wither** V. shrivel; decay. Cut flowers are beautiful for a day, but all too soon they *wither.*

witless ADJ. foolish; idiotic. Such *witless* and fatuous statements will create the impression that you are an ignorant individual.

witticism N. witty saying; facetious remark. What you regard as *witticisms* are often offensive to sensitive people.

wizardry N. sorcery; magic. Merlin amazed the knights with his *wizardry.*

wizened ADJ. withered; shriveled. The *wizened* old man in the home for the aged was still active and energetic.

wont N. custom; habitual procedure. As was his *wont,* he jogged two miles every morning before going to work.

worldly ADJ. engrossed in matters of this earth; not spiritual. You must leave your *worldly* goods behind you when you go to meet your Maker.

wraith N. ghost; phantom of a living person. It must be a horrible experience to see a ghost; it is even more horrible to see the *wraith* of a person we know to be alive.

wrangle V. quarrel; obtain through arguing; herd cattle. They *wrangled* over their inheritance.

wrath N. anger; fury. She turned to him, full of *wrath,* and said, ''What makes you think I'll accept lower pay for this job than you get?''

wreak V. inflict. I am afraid he will *wreak* his vengeance on the innocent as well as the guilty.

wrench V. pull; strain; twist. She *wrenched* free of her attacker and landed a powerful kick to his kneecap.

wrest V. pull away; take by violence. With only ten seconds left to play, our team *wrested* victory from their grasp.

writhe V. squirm; twist. He was *writhing* in pain, desperate for the drug his body required.

wry ADJ. twisted; with a humorous twist. We enjoy Dorothy Parker's verse for its *wry* wit.

xenophobia N. fear or hatred of foreigners. When the refugee arrived in America, he was unprepared for the *xenophobia* he found there.

yen N. longing; urge. She had a *yen* to get away and live on her own for a while.

yeoman N. man owning small estate; middle-class farmer. It was not the aristocrat but the *yeoman* who determined the nation's policies.

yoke N. join together, unite. I don't wish to be *yoked* to him in marriage, as if we were cattle pulling a plow.

yokel N. country bumpkin. At school, his classmates regarded him as a *yokel* and laughed at his rustic mannerisms.

yore N. time past. He dreamed of the elegant homes of *yore,* but gave no thought to their inelegant plumbing.

zany ADJ. crazy; comic. I can watch the Marx brothers' *zany* antics for hours.

■ **zealot** N. fanatic; person who shows excessive zeal. It is good to have a few *zealots* in our group for their enthusiasm is contagious.

zenith N. point directly overhead in the sky; summit. When the sun was at its *zenith,* the glare was not as strong as at sunrise and sunset.

zephyr N. gentle breeze; west wind. When these *zephyrs* blow, it is good to be in an open boat under a full sail.

Test

Word List 50   *Synonyms*

Each of the questions below consists of a word in capital letters, followed by five lettered words or phrases. Choose the lettered word or phrase that is most nearly similar in meaning to the word in capital letters and write the letter of your choice on your answer paper.

736. VOLUBLE (A) worthwhile (B) serious (C) terminal (D) loquacious (E) circular

737. VORACIOUS (A) ravenous (B) spacious (C) truthful (D) pacific (E) tenacious

738. VOUCHSAFE (A) borrow (B) grant (C) punish (D) desire (E) qualify

739. WAIF (A) soldier (B) urchin (C) surrender (D) breeze (E) spouse

740. WANTON (A) needy (B) passive (C) rumored (D) oriental (E) unchaste

741. WARRANTY (A) threat (B) guarantee (C) order for arrest (D) issue (E) fund

742. WASTREL (A) refuse (B) spendthrift (C) mortal (D) tolerance (E) song

743. WAYLAY (A) ambush (B) journey (C) rest (D) roadmap (E) song

744. WELKIN (A) bell (B) greeting (C) cloudy (D) pressure (E) sky

745. WHINNY (A) complain (B) hurry (C) request (D) neigh (E) gallop

746. WINDFALL (A) unexpected gain (B) widespread destruction (C) calm (D) autumn (E) wait

747. WINSOME (A) victorious (B) gracious (C) married (D) permanent (E) pained

748. WIZENED (A) magical (B) clever (C) shriveled (D) swift (E) active

749. YEOMAN (A) masses (B) middle-class farmer (C) proletarian (D) indigent person (E) man of rank

750. ZEALOT (A) beginner (B) patron (C) fanatic (D) murderer (E) leper

Answer Key

Test—Word List 1

1. E	6. E	11. A
2. A	7. B	12. E
3. C	8. E	13. A
4. D	9. A	14. D
5. B	10. A	15. C

Test—Word List 2

16. E	21. A	26. B
17. B	22. A	27. D
18. A	23. B	28. B
19. D	24. B	29. C
20. A	25. B	30. D

Test—Word List 3

31. C	36. E	41. B
32. C	37. C	42. E
33. D	38. B	43. E
34. D	39. E	44. C
35. A	40. D	45. A

Test—Word List 4

46. A	51. C	56. E
47. A	52. A	57. C
48. B	53. C	58. D
49. D	54. B	59. D
50. B	55. D	60. C

Test—Word List 5

61. E	66. A	71. D
62. D	67. C	72. C
63. B	68. C	73. C
64. C	69. B	74. B
65. C	70. C	75. D

Test—Word List 6

76. D	81. A	86. C
77. B	82. B	87. A
78. D	83. B	88. E
79. A	84. E	89. E
80. E	85. E	90. C

Test—Word List 7

91. B	96. B	101. D
92. B	97. A	102. B
93. B	98. D	103. A
94. D	99. B	104. A
95. B	100. C	105. B

Test—Word List 8

106. D	111. B	116. B
107. E	112. A	117. D
108. A	113. D	118. A
109. C	114. C	119. C
110. E	115. D	120. B

Test—Word List 9

121. D	126. E	131. A
122. E	127. A	132. D
123. E	128. D	133. C
124. C	129. B	134. B
125. C	130. E	135. A

Test—Word List 10

136. E	141. B	146. E
137. B	142. E	147. E
138. D	143. D	148. C
139. C	144. D	149. A
140. A	145. D	150. D

Test—Word List 11

151. B	156. C	161. B
152. B	157. C	162. D
153. A	158. E	163. D
154. A	159. E	164. A
155. A	160. B	165. B

Test—Word List 12

166. C	171. C	176. B
167. B	172. B	177. B
168. C	173. A	178. A
169. D	174. A	179. C
170. D	175. B	180. A

Test—Word List 13

181. A	186. A	191. C
182. E	187. B	192. B
183. D	188. C	193. E
184. D	189. B	194. A
185. A	190. C	195. A

Test—Word List 14

196. D	201. C	206. B
197. E	202. C	207. D
198. B	203. C	208. C
199. A	204. B	209. E
200. C	205. B	210. D

Test—Word List 15

211. C	216. C	221. B
212. A	217. A	222. E
213. D	218. A	223. A
214. D	219. C	224. A
215. D	220. D	225. B

Test—Word List 16

226. D	231. B	236. D
227. A	232. C	237. C
228. C	233. D	238. A
229. E	234. C	239. B
230. E	235. E	240. A

Test—Word List 17

241. A	246. C	251. D
242. A	247. A	252. A
243. B	248. A	253. E
244. E	249. C	254. B
245. E	250. D	255. B

Test—Word List 18

256. A	261. D	266. A
257. A	262. D	267. A
258. C	263. E	268. C
259. D	264. C	269. B
260. A	265. B	270. E

Test—Word List 19

271. A	276. A	281. A
272. D	277. A	282. D
273. E	278. D	283. C
274. C	279. C	284. B
275. E	280. B	285. C

Test—Word List 20

286. A	291. A	296. E
287. B	292. A	297. D
288. B	293. D	298. A
289. B	294. C	299. A
290. D	295. C	300. B

Test—Word List 21

301. B	306. E	311. E
302. B	307. C	312. A
303. C	308. B	313. B
304. C	309. D	314. D
305. C	310. D	315. C

Test—Word List 22

316. D	321. E	326. C
317. A	322. A	327. C
318. A	323. B	328. A
319. D	324. C	329. B
320. A	325. E	330. D

Test—Word List 23

331. B	336. A	341. A
332. A	337. D	342. A
333. B	338. C	343. E
334. E	339. C	344. B
335. C	340. D	345. A

Test—Word List 24

346. C	351. D	356. B
347. B	352. A	357. C
348. C	353. A	358. A
349. A	354. A	359. B
350. B	355. B	360. D

Test—Word List 25

361. A	366. B	371. E
362. E	367. B	372. B
363. B	368. C	373. D
364. D	369. D	374. C
365. E	370. A	375. A

Test—Word List 26

376. C	381. B	386. B
377. A	382. A	387. E
378. B	383. C	388. E
379. B	384. C	389. E
380. B	385. C	390. A

Test—Word List 27

391. A	396. E	401. B
392. D	397. E	402. B
393. B	398. C	403. A
394. D	399. A	404. C
395. B	400. D	405. B

Test—Word List 28

406. B	411. B	416. B
407. A	412. E	417. A
408. E	413. D	418. D
409. E	414. E	419. D
410. C	415. C	420. A

Test—Word List 29

421. B	426. D	431. A
422. A	427. E	432. C
423. B	428. B	433. B
424. B	429. A	434. C
425. C	430. E	435. A

Test—Word List 30

436. A	441. A	446. E
437. A	442. B	447. B
438. B	443. D	448. C
439. D	444. B	449. E
440. C	445. A	450. B

Test—Word List 31

451. B	456. A	461. E
452. E	457. C	462. C
453. C	458. C	463. A
454. C	459. A	464. B
455. B	460. B	465. A

Test—Word List 32

466. B	471. D	476. D
467. C	472. C	477. B
468. C	473. B	478. A
469. A	474. A	479. C
470. C	475. B	480. A

Test—Word List 33

481. C	486. A	491. E
482. B	487. B	492. C
483. E	488. C	493. E
484. D	489. D	494. B
485. B	490. B	495. A

Test—Word List 34

496. D	501. B	506. D
497. A	502. B	507. D
498. D	503. A	508. C
499. A	504. E	509. C
500. E	505. C	510. A

Test—Word List 35

511. A	516. C	521. E
512. C	517. B	522. A
513. C	518. D	523. C
514. C	519. C	524. E
515. B	520. A	525. E

Test—Word List 36

526. A	531. E	536. B
527. D	532. B	537. D
528. A	533. C	538. D
529. B	534. C	539. D
530. E	535. A	540. D

Test—Word List 37

541. C	546. A	551. A
542. C	547. A	552. C
543. D	548. C	553. E
544. E	549. B	554. B
545. C	550. A	555. A

Test—Word List 38

556. E	561. E	566. A
557. D	562. E	567. D
558. C	563. B	568. C
559. B	564. A	569. D
560. B	565. E	570. C

Test—Word List 39

571. B	576. C	581. C
572. B	577. D	582. B
573. E	578. A	583. A
574. A	579. C	584. D
575. A	580. E	585. A

Test—Word List 40

586. E	591. C	596. D
587. B	592. A	597. D
588. D	593. B	598. B
589. C	594. A	599. D
590. A	595. D	600. E

Test—Word List 41

601. E	606. B	611. C
602. B	607. B	612. D
603. A	608. A	613. B
604. D	609. D	614. A
605. A	610. B	615. A

Test—Word List 42

616. C	621. D	626. B
617. A	622. E	627. D
618. B	623. A	628. A
619. C	624. D	629. D
620. D	625. C	630. E

Test—Word List 43

631. C	636. C	641. D
632. C	637. E	642. A
633. E	638. C	643. E
634. A	639. E	644. A
635. C	640. D	645. B

Test—Word List 44

646. A	651. B	656. A
647. B	652. A	657. B
648. D	653. D	658. A
649. A	654. C	659. C
650. E	655. C	660. C

Test—Word List 45

661. C	666. C	671. C
662. C	667. B	672. D
663. A	668. A	673. A
664. C	669. A	674. D
665. B	670. A	675. A

Test—Word List 46

676. D	681. D	686. B
677. B	682. B	687. A
678. B	683. A	688. B
679. C	684. E	689. E
680. C	685. B	690. C

Test—Word List 47

691. A	696. A	701. A
692. D	697. C	702. D
693. B	698. B	703. B
694. C	699. C	704. D
695. A	700. E	705. E

Test—Word List 48

706. A	711. B	716. D
707. A	712. B	717. D
708. B	713. A	718. C
709. C	714. A	719. B
710. C	715. E	720. C

Test—Word List 49

721. B	726. C	731. C
722. A	727. C	732. B
723. A	728. A	733. A
724. D	729. C	734. B
725. B	730. A	735. D

Test—Word List 50

736. D	741. B	746. A
737. A	742. B	747. B
738. B	743. A	748. C
739. B	744. E	749. B
740. E	745. D	750. C

Basic Word Parts

In addition to reviewing the SAT High-Frequency Word List, what other quick vocabulary-building tactics can you follow when you face an SAT deadline?

One good approach is to learn how to build up (and tear apart) words. You know that words are made up of other words: the *room* in which you *store* things is the *storeroom*; the person whose job is to *keep* the *books* is the *bookkeeper*.

Just as words are made up of other words, words are also made up of word parts: prefixes, suffixes, and roots. A knowledge of these word parts and their meanings can help you determine the mean-

ings of unfamiliar words.

Most modern English words are derived from Anglo-Saxon (Old English), Latin, and Greek. Because few students nowadays study Latin and Greek (and even fewer study Anglo-Saxon!), the majority of high school juniors and seniors lack a vital tool for unlocking the meaning of unfamiliar words.

Build your vocabulary by mastering basic word parts. Learning thirty key word parts can help you unlock the meaning of over 10,000 words. Learning fifty key word parts can help you unlock the meaning of over 100,000!

Common Prefixes

Prefixes are syllables that precede the root or stem and change or refine its meaning.

Prefix	Meaning	Illustration
ab, abs	from, away from	*abduct* lead away, kidnap *abjure* renounce *abject* degraded
ad, ac, af, ag, an, ap, ar, as, at	to, forward	*adit* entrance *adjure* request earnestly *admit* allow entrance *accord* agreement, harmony *affliction* distress *aggregation* collection *annexation* add to *apparition* ghost *arraignment* indictment *assumption* arrogance, the taking for granted *attendance* presence, the persons present
ambi	both	*ambidextrous* skilled with both hands *ambiguous* of double meaning *ambivalent* having two conflicting emotions
an, a	without	*anarchy* lack of government *anemia* lack of blood *amoral* without moral sense
ante	before	*antecedent* preceding event or word *antediluvian* ancient (before the flood) *ante-nuptial* before the wedding
anti	against, opposite	*antipathy* hatred *antiseptic* against infection *antithetical* exactly opposite

Prefix	Meaning	Illustration
arch	chief, first	*archetype* original *archbishop* chief bishop *archeology* study of first or ancient times
be	over, thoroughly	*bedaub* smear over *befuddle* confuse thoroughly *beguile* deceive, charm thoroughly
bi	two	*bicameral* composed of two houses (Congress) *biennial* every two years *bicycle* two-wheeled vehicle
cata	down	*catastrophe* disaster *cataract* waterfall *catapult* hurl (throw down)
circum	around	*circumnavigate* sail around (the globe) *circumspect* cautious (looking around) *circumscribe* limit (place a circle around)
com, co, col, con, cor	with, together	*combine* merge with *commerce* trade with *communicate* correspond with *coeditor* joint editor *collateral* subordinate, connected *conference* meeting *corroborate* confirm
contra, contro	against	*contravene* conflict with *controversy* dispute
de	down, away	*debase* lower in value *decadence* deterioration *decant* pour off
demi	partly, half	*demigod* partly divine being
di	two	*dichotomy* division into two parts *dilemma* choice between two bad alternatives
dia	across	*diagonal* across a figure *diameter* distance across a circle *diagram* outline drawing
dis, dif	not, apart	*discord* lack of harmony *differ* disagree (carry apart) *disparity* condition of inequality; difference
dys	faulty, bad	*dyslexia* faulty ability to read *dyspepsia* indigestion
ex, e	out	*expel* drive out *extirpate* root out *eject* throw out

Prefix	Meaning	Illustration
extra, extro	beyond, outside	*extracurricular* beyond the curriculum *extraterritorial* beyond a nation's bounds *extrovert* person interested chiefly in external objects and actions
hyper	above; excessively	*hyperbole* exaggeration *hyperventilate* breathe at an excessive rate
hypo	beneath; lower	*hypoglycemia* low blood sugar
in, il, im, ir	not	*inefficient* not efficient *inarticulate* not clear or distinct *illegible* not readable *impeccable* not capable of sinning; flawless *irrevocable* not able to be called back
in, il, im, ir	in, on, upon	*invite* call in *illustration* something that makes clear *impression* effect upon mind or feelings *irradiate* shine upon
inter	between, among	*intervene* come between *international* between nations *interjection* a statement thrown in
intra, intro	within	*intramural* within a school *introvert* person who turns within himself
macro	large, long	*macrobiotic* tending to prolong life *macrocosm* the great world (the entire universe)
mega	great, million	*megalomania* delusions of grandeur *megaton* explosive force of a million tons of TNT
meta	involving change	*metamorphosis* change of form
micro	small	*microcosm* miniature universe *microbe* minute organism *microscopic* extremely small
mis	bad, improper	*misdemeanor* minor crime; bad conduct *mischance* unfortunate accident *misnomer* wrong name
mis	hatred	*misanthrope* person who hates mankind *misogynist* woman-hater
mono	one	*monarchy* government by one ruler *monotheism* belief in one god
multi	many	*multifarious* having many parts *multitudinous* numerous
neo	new	*neologism* newly coined word *neophyte* beginner; novice

Prefix	Meaning	Illustration
non	not	*noncommittal* undecided *nonentity* person of no importance
ob, oc, of, op	against	*obloquy* infamy; disgrace *obtrude* push into prominence *occlude* close; block out *offend* insult *opponent* someone who struggles against; foe
olig	few	*oligarchy* government by a few
pan	all, every	*panacea* cure-all *panorama* unobstructed view in all directions
para	beyond, related	*parallel* similar *paraphrase* restate; translate
per	through, completely	*permeable* allowing passage through *pervade* spread throughout
peri	around, near	*perimeter* outer boundary *periphery* edge *periphrastic* stated in a roundabout way
poly	many	*polygamist* person with several spouses *polyglot* speaking several languages
post	after	*postpone* delay *posterity* generations that follow *posthumous* after death
pre	before	*preamble* introductory statement *prefix* word part placed before a root/stem *premonition* forewarning
prim	first	*primordial* existing at the dawn of time *primogeniture* state of being the first born
pro	forward, in favor of	*propulsive* driving forward *proponent* supporter
proto	first	*prototype* first of its kind
pseudo	false	*pseudonym* pen name
re	again, back	*reiterate* repeat *reimburse* pay back
retro	backward	*retrospect* looking back *retroactive* effective as of a past date
se	away, aside	*secede* withdraw *seclude* shut away *seduce* lead astray

Prefix	Meaning	Illustration
semi	half, partly	*semiannual* every six months *semiconscious* partly conscious
sub, suc, suf, sug, sup, sus	under, less	*subway* underground road *subjugate* bring under control *succumb* yield; cease to resist *suffuse* spread through *suggest* hint *suppress* put down by force *suspend* delay
super, sur	over, above	*supernatural* above natural things *supervise* oversee *surtax* additional tax
syn, sym, syl, sys	with, together	*synchronize* time together *synthesize* combine together *sympathize* pity; identify with *syllogism* explanation of how ideas relate *system* network
tele	far	*telemetry* measurement from a distance *telegraphic* communicated over a distance
trans	across	*transport* carry across *transpose* reverse, move across
ultra	beyond, excessive	*ultramodern* excessively modern *ultracritical* exceedingly critical
un	not	*unfeigned* not pretended; real *unkempt* not combed; disheveled *unwitting* not knowing; unintentional
under	below	*undergird* strengthen underneath *underling* someone inferior
uni	one	*unison* oneness of pitch; complete accord *unicycle* one-wheeled vehicle
vice	in place of	*vicarious* acting as a substitute *viceroy* governor acting in place of a king
with	away, against	*withhold* hold back; keep *withstand* stand up against; resist

Common Roots and Stems

Roots are basic words which have been carried over into English. *Stems* are varia- tions of roots brought about by changes in declension or conjugation.

Root or Stem	Meaning	Illustration
ac, acr	sharp	*acrimonious* bitter; caustic *acerbity* bitterness of temper *acidulate* to make somewhat acid or sour
aev, ev	age, era	*primeval* of the first age *coeval* of the same age or era *medieval* or *mediaeval* of the middle ages
ag, act	do	*act* deed *agent* doer
agog	leader	*demagogue* false leader of people *pedagogue* teacher (leader of children)
agri, agrari	field	*agrarian* one who works in the field *agriculture* cultivation of fields *peregrination* wandering (through fields)
ali	another	*alias* assumed (another) name *alienate* estrange (turn away from another)
alt	high	*altitude* height *altimeter* instrument for measuring height
alter	other	*altruistic* unselfish, considering others *alter ego* a second self
am	love	*amorous* loving, especially sexually *amity* friendship *amicable* friendly
anim	mind, soul	*animadvert* cast criticism upon *unanimous* of one mind *magnanimity* greatness of mind or spirit
ann, enn	year	*annuity* yearly remittance *biennial* every two years *perennial* present all year; persisting for several years
anthrop	man	*anthropology* study of man *misanthrope* hater of mankind *philanthropy* love of mankind; charity
apt	fit	*aptitude* skill *adapt* make suitable or fit

Root or Stem	Meaning	Illustration
aqua	water	*aqueduct* passageway for conducting water *aquatic* living in water *aqua fortis* nitric acid (strong water)
arch	ruler, first	*archaeology* study of antiquities (study of first things) *monarch* sole ruler *anarchy* lack of government
aster	star	*astronomy* study of the stars *asterisk* star-like type character (∗) *disaster* catastrophe (contrary star)
aud, audit	hear	*audible* able to be heard *auditorium* place where people may be heard *audience* hearers
auto	self	*autocracy* rule by one person (self) *automobile* vehicle that moves by itself *autobiography* story of one's own life
belli	war	*bellicose* inclined to fight *belligerent* inclined to wage war *rebellious* resisting authority
ben, bon	good	*benefactor* one who does good deeds *benevolence* charity (wishing good) *bonus* something extra above regular pay
biblio	book	*bibliography* list of books *bibliophile* lover of books *Bible* The Book
bio	life	*biography* writing about a person's life *biology* study of living things *biochemist* student of the chemistry of living things
breve	short	*brevity* briefness *abbreviate* shorten *breviloquent* marked by brevity of speech
cad, cas	to fall	*decadent* deteriorating *cadence* intonation, musical movement *cascade* waterfall
cap, capt, cept, cip	to take	*capture* seize *participate* take part *precept* wise saying (originally a command)
capit, capt	head	*decapitate* remove (cut off) someone's head *captain* chief
carn	flesh	*carnivorous* flesh-eating *carnage* destruction of life *carnal* fleshly

Root or Stem	Meaning	Illustration
ced, cess	to yield, to go	*recede* go back, withdraw *antecedent* that which goes before *process* go forward
celer	swift	*celerity* swiftness *decelerate* reduce swiftness *accelerate* increase swiftness
cent	one hundred	*century* one hundred years *centennial* hundredth anniversary *centipede* many-footed, wingless animal
chron	time	*chronology* timetable of events *anachronism* a thing out of time sequence *chronicle* register events in order of time
cid, cis	to cut, to kill	*incision* a cut (surgical) *homicide* killing of a man *fratricide* killing of a brother
cit, citat	to call, to start	*incite* stir up, start up *excite* stir up *recitation* a recalling (or repeating) aloud
civi	citizen	*civilization* society of citizens, culture *civilian* member of community *civil* courteous
clam, clamat	to cry out	*clamorous* loud *declamation* speech *acclamation* shouted approval
claud, claus, clos, clud	to close	*claustrophobia* fear of close places *enclose* close in *conclude* finish
cognosc, cognit	to learn	*agnostic* lacking knowledge, skeptical *incognito* traveling under assumed name *cognition* knowledge
compl	to fill	*complete* filled out *complement* that which completes something *comply* fulfill
cord	heart	*accord* agreement (from the heart) *cordial* friendly *discord* lack of harmony
corpor	body	*incorporate* organize into a body *corporeal* pertaining to the body, fleshly *corpse* dead body
cred, credit	to believe	*incredulous* not believing, skeptical *credulity* gullibility *credence* belief

Root or Stem	Meaning	Illustration
cur	to care	*curator* person who has the care of something *sinecure* position without responsibility *secure* safe
curr, curs	to run	*excursion* journey *cursory* brief *precursor* forerunner
da, dat	to give	*data* facts, statistics *mandate* command *date* given time
deb, debit	to owe	*debt* something owed *indebtedness* debt *debenture* bond
dem	people	*democracy* rule of the people *demagogue* (false) leader of the people *epidemic* widespread (among the people)
derm	skin	*epidermis* skin *pachyderm* thick-skinned quadruped *dermatology* study of skin and its disorders
di, diurn	day	*diary* a daily record of activities, feelings, etc. *diurnal* pertaining to daytime
dic, dict	to say	*abdicate* renounce *diction* speech *verdict* statement of jury
doc, doct	to teach	*docile* obedient; easily taught *document* something that provides evidence *doctor* learned person (originally, teacher)
domin	to rule	*dominate* have power over *domain* land under rule *dominant* prevailing
duc, duct	to lead	*viaduct* arched roadway *aqueduct* artificial waterway
dynam	power, strength	*dynamic* powerful *dynamite* powerful explosive *dynamo* engine making electrical power
ego	I	*egoist* person who is self-interested *egotist* selfish person *egocentric* revolving about self
erg, urg	work	*energy* power *ergatocracy* rule of the workers *metallurgy* science and technology of metals

Root or Stem	Meaning	Illustration
err	to wander	*error* mistake *erratic* not reliable, wandering *knight-errant* wandering knight
eu	good, well, beautiful	*eupeptic* having good digestion *eulogize* praise *euphemism* substitution of pleasant way of saying something blunt
fac, fic, fec, fect	to make, to do	*factory* place where things are made *fiction* manufactured story *affect* cause to change
fall, fals	to deceive	*fallacious* misleading *infallible* not prone to error, perfect *falsify* lie
fer, lat	to bring, to bear	*transfer* bring from one place to another *translate* bring from one language to another *conifer* bearing cones, as pine trees
fid	belief, faith	*infidel* nonbeliever, heathen *confidence* assurance, belief
fin	end, limit	*confine* keep within limits *finite* having definite limits
flect, flex	bend	*flexible* able to bend *deflect* bend away, turn aside
fort	luck, chance	*fortuitous* accidental, occurring by chance *fortunate* lucky
fort	strong	*fortitude* strength, firmness of mind *fortification* strengthening *fortress* stronghold
frag, fract	break	*fragile* easily broken *infraction* breaking of a rule *fractious* unruly, tending to break rules
fug	flee	*fugitive* someone who flees *refuge* shelter, home for someone fleeing
fus	pour	*effusive* gushing, pouring out *diffuse* widespread (poured in many directions)
gam	marriage	*monogamy* marriage to one person *bigamy* marriage to two people at the same time *polygamy* having many wives or husbands at the same time
gen, gener	class, race	*genus* group of animals with similar traits *generic* characteristic of a class *gender* class organized by sex

Root or Stem	Meaning	Illustration
grad, gress	go, step	*digress* go astray (from the main point) *regress* go backwards *gradual* step by step, by degrees
graph, gram	writing	*epigram* pithy statement *telegram* instantaneous message over great distance *stenography* shorthand (writing narrowly)
greg	flock, herd	*gregarious* tending to group together as in a herd *aggregate* group, total *egregious* conspicuously bad; shocking
helio	sun	*heliotrope* flower that faces the sun *heliograph* instrument that uses the sun's rays to send signals
it, itiner	journey, road	*exit* way out *itinerary* plan of journey
jac, jact, jec	to throw	*projectile* missile; something thrown forward *trajectory* path taken by thrown object *ejaoulatory* casting or throwing out
jur, jurat	to swear	*perjure* testify falsely *jury* group of men and women sworn to seek the truth *adjuration* solemn urging
labor, laborat	to work	*laboratory* place where work is done *collaborate* work together with others *laborious* difficult
leg, lect, lig	to choose, to read	*election* choice *legible* able to be read *eligible* able to be selected
leg	law	*legislature* law-making body *legitimate* lawful *legal* lawful
liber, libr	book	*library* collection of books *libretto* the "book" of a musical play *libel* slander (originally found in a little book)
liber	free	*liberation* the fact of setting free *liberal* generous (giving freely); tolerant
log	word, study	*entomology* study of insects *etymology* study of word parts and derivations *monologue* speech by one person
loqu, locut	to talk	*soliloquy* speech by one individual *loquacious* talkative *elocution* speech

Root or Stem	Meaning	Illustration
luc	light	*elucidate* enlighten *lucid* clear *translucent* allowing some light to pass through
magn	great	*magnify* enlarge *magnanimity* generosity, greatness of soul *magnitude* greatness, extent
mal	bad	*malevolent* wishing evil *malediction* curse *malefactor* evil-doer
man	hand	*manufacture* create (make by hand) *manuscript* written by hand *emancipate* free (let go from the hand)
mar	sea	*maritime* connected with seafaring *submarine* undersea craft *mariner* seaman
mater, matr	mother	*maternal* pertaining to motherhood *matriarch* female ruler of a family, group, or state *matrilineal* descended on the mother's side
mit, miss	to send	*missile* projectile *dismiss* send away *transmit* send across
mob, mot, mov	move	*mobilize* cause to move *motility* ability to move *immovable* not able to be moved
mon, monit	to warn	*admonish* warn *premonition* foreboding *monitor* watcher (warner)
mori, mort	to die	*mortuary* funeral parlor *moribund* dying *immortal* not dying
morph	shape, form	*amorphous* formless, lacking shape *metamorphosis* change of shape *anthropomorphic* in the shape of man
mut	change	*immutable* not able to be changed *mutate* undergo a great change *mutability* changeableness, inconstancy
nat	born	*innate* from birth *prenatal* before birth *nativity* birth
nav	ship	*navigate* sail a ship *circumnavigate* sail around the world *naval* pertaining to ships

Root or Stem	Meaning	Illustration
neg	deny	*negation* denial *renege* deny, go back on one's word *renegade* turncoat, traitor
nomen	name	*nomenclature* act of naming, terminology *nominal* in name only (as opposed to actual) *cognomen* surname, distinguishing nickname
nov	new	*novice* beginner *renovate* make new again *novelty* newness
omni	all	*omniscient* all knowing *omnipotent* all powerful *omnivorous* eating everything
oper	to work	*operate* work *cooperation* working together
pac	peace	*pacify* make peaceful *pacific* peaceful *pacifist* person opposed to war
pass	feel	*dispassionate* free of emotion *impassioned* emotion-filled *impassive* showing no feeling
pater, patr	father	*patriotism* love of one's country (fatherland) *patriarch* male ruler of a family, group, or state *paternity* fatherhood
path	disease, feeling	*pathology* study of diseased tissue *apathetic* lacking feeling; indifferent *antipathy* hostile feeling
ped, pod	foot	*impediment* stumbling-block; hindrance *tripod* three-footed stand *quadruped* four-footed animal
ped	child	*pedagogue* teacher of children *pediatrician* children's doctor
pel, puls	to drive	*compulsion* a forcing to do *repel* drive back *expel* drive out, banish
pet, petit	to seek	*petition* request *appetite* craving, desire *compete* vie with others
phil	love	*philanthropist* benefactor, lover of humanity *Anglophile* lover of everything English *philanderer* one involved in brief love affairs

Root or Stem	Meaning	Illustration
pon, posit	to place	*postpone* place after *positive* definite, unquestioned (definitely placed)
port, portat	to carry	*portable* able to be carried *transport* carry across *export* carry out (of country)
poten	able, powerful	*omnipotent* all-powerful *potentate* powerful person *impotent* powerless
psych	mind	*psychology* study of the mind *psychosis* mental disorder *psychopath* mentally ill person
put, putat	to trim, to calculate	*putative* supposed (calculated) *computation* calculation *amputate* cut off
quer, ques, quir, quis	to ask	*inquiry* investigation *inquisitive* questioning *query* question
reg, rect	rule	*regicide* murder of a ruler *regent* ruler *insurrection* rebellion; overthrow of a ruler
rid, ris	to laugh	*derision* scorn *risibility* inclination to laughter *ridiculous* deserving to be laughed at
rog, rogat	to ask	*interrogate* question *prerogative* privilege
rupt	to break	*interrupt* break into *bankrupt* insolvent *rupture* a break
sacr	holy	*sacred* holy *sacrilegious* impious, violating something holy *sacrament* religious act
sci	to know	*science* knowledge *omniscient* knowing all *conscious* aware
scop	watch, see	*periscope* device for seeing around corners *microscope* device for seeing small objects
scrib, script	to write	*transcribe* make a written copy *script* written text *circumscribe* write around, limit
sect	cut	*dissect* cut apart *bisect* cut into two pieces

Root or Stem	Meaning	Illustration
sed, sess	to sit	*sedentary* inactive (sitting) *session* meeting
sent, sens	to think, to feel	*consent* agree *resent* show indignation *sensitive* showing feeling
sequi, secut, seque	to follow	*consecutive* following in order *sequence* arrangement *sequel* that which follows *non sequitur* something that does not follow logically
solv, solut	to loosen	*absolve* free from blame *dissolute* morally lax *absolute* complete (not loosened)
somn	sleep	*insomnia* inability to sleep *somnolent* sleepy *somnambulist* sleepwalker
soph	wisdom	*philosopher* lover of wisdom *sophisticated* worldly wise
spec, spect	to look at	*spectator* observer *aspect* appearance *circumspect* cautious (looking around)
spir	breathe	*respiratory* pertaining to breathing *spirited* full of life (breath)
string, strict	bind	*stringent* strict *constrict* become tight *stricture* limit, something that restrains
stru, struct	build	*constructive* helping to build *construe* analyze (how something is built)
tang, tact, ting	to touch	*tangent* touching *contact* touching with, meeting *contingent* depending upon
tempor	time	*contemporary* at same time *extemporaneous* impromptu *temporize* delay
ten, tent	to hold	*tenable* able to be held *tenure* holding of office *retentive* holding; having a good memory
term	end	*interminable* endless *terminate* end
terr	land	*terrestrial* pertaining to earth *subterranean* underground

Root or Stem	Meaning	Illustration
therm	heat	*thermostat* instrument that regulates heat *diathermy* sending heat through body tissues
tors, tort	twist	*distort* twist out of true shape or meaning *torsion* act of twisting *tortuous* twisting
tract	drag, pull	*distract* pull (one's attention) away *intractable* stubborn, unable to be dragged *attraction* pull, drawing quality
trud, trus	push, shove	*intrude* push one's way in *protrusion* something sticking out
urb	city	*urban* pertaining to a city *urbane* polished, sophisticated (pertaining to a city dweller) *suburban* outside of a city
vac	empty	*vacuous* lacking content, empty-headed *evacuate* compel to empty an area
vad, vas	go	*invade* enter in a hostile fashion *evasive* not frank; eluding
veni, vent, ven	to come	*intervene* come between *prevent* stop *convention* meeting
ver	true	*veracious* truthful *verify* check the truth *verisimilitude* appearance of truth
verb	word	*verbose* wordy *verbiage* excessive use of words *verbatim* word for word
vers, vert	turn	*vertigo* turning dizzy *revert* turn back (to an earlier state) *diversion* something causing one to turn aside
via	way	*deviation* departure from the way *viaduct* roadway (arched) *trivial* trifling (small talk at crossroads)
vid, vis	to see	*vision* sight *evidence* things seen *vista* view
vinc, vict, vanq	to conquer	*invincible* unconquerable *victory* winning *vanquish* defeat

Root or Stem	Meaning	Illustration
viv, vit	alive	*vivisection* operating on living animals *vivacious* full of life *vitality* liveliness
voc, vocat	to call	*avocation* calling, minor occupation *provocation* calling or rousing the anger of *invocation* calling in prayer
vol	wish	*malevolent* wishing someone ill *voluntary* of one's own will
volv, volut	to roll	*revolve* roll around *evolve* roll out, develop *convolution* coiled state

Common Suffixes

Suffixes are syllables which are added to a word. Occasionally, they change the meaning of the word; more frequently, they serve to change the grammatical form of the word (noun to adjective, adjective to noun, noun to verb).

Suffix	Meaning	Illustration
able, ible	capable of (adjective suffix)	*portable* able to be carried *interminable* not able to be limited *legible* able to be read
ac, ic	like, pertaining to (adjective suffix)	*cardiac* pertaining to the heart *aquatic* pertaining to the water *dramatic* pertaining to the drama
acious, icious	full of (adjective suffix)	*audacious* full of daring *perspicacious* full of mental perception *avaricious* full of greed
al	pertaining to (adjective or noun suffix)	*maniacal* insane *final* pertaining to the end *logical* pertaining to logic
ant, ent	full of (adjective or noun suffix)	*eloquent* pertaining to fluid, effective speech *suppliant* pleader (person full of requests) *verdant* green
ary	like, connected with (adjective or noun suffix)	*dictionary* book connected with words *honorary* with honor *luminary* celestial body
ate	to make (verb suffix)	*consecrate* to make holy *enervate* to make weary *mitigate* to make less severe

Suffix	Meaning	Illustration
ation	that which is (noun suffix)	*exasperation* irritation *irritation* annoyance
cy	state of being (noun suffix)	*democracy* government ruled by the people *obstinacy* stubbornness *accuracy* correctness
eer, er, or	person who (noun suffix)	*mutineer* person who rebels *lecher* person who lusts *censor* person who deletes improper remarks
escent	becoming (adjective suffix)	*evanescent* tending to vanish *pubescent* arriving at puberty
fic	making, doing (adjective suffix)	*terrific* arousing great fear *soporific* causing sleep
fy	to make (verb suffix)	*magnify* enlarge *petrify* turn to stone *beautify* make beautiful
iferous	producing, bearing (adjective suffix)	*pestiferous* carrying disease *vociferous* bearing a loud voice
il, ile	pertaining to, capable of (adjective suffix)	*puerile* pertaining to a boy or child *ductile* capable of being hammered or drawn *civil* polite
ism	doctrine, belief (noun suffix)	*monotheism* belief in one god *fanaticism* excessive zeal; extreme belief
ist	dealer, doer (noun suffix)	*fascist* one who believes in a fascist state *realist* one who is realistic *artist* one who deals with art
ity	state of being (noun suffix)	*annuity* yearly grant *credulity* state of being unduly willing to believe *sagacity* wisdom
ive	like (adjective suffix)	*expensive* costly *quantitative* concerned with quantity *effusive* gushing
ize, ise	make (verb suffix)	*victimize* make a victim of *rationalize* make rational *harmonize* make harmonious *enfranchise* make free or set free
oid	resembling, like (adjective suffix)	*ovoid* like an egg *anthropoid* resembling man *spheroid* resembling a sphere
ose	full of (adjective suffix)	*verbose* full of words *lachrymose* full of tears

Suffix	Meaning	Illustration
osis	condition (noun suffix)	*psychosis* diseased mental condition *neurosis* nervous condition *hypnosis* condition of induced sleep
ous	full of (adjective suffix)	*nauseous* full of nausea *ludicrous* foolish
tude	state of (noun suffix)	*fortitude* state of strength *beatitude* state of blessedness *certitude* state of sureness

Mathematics

Tactics, strategies, practice

10 Standard Multiple-Choice Questions

- ■ **Testing Tactics**
- ■ **Important Facts and Formulas**
- ■ **Practice Exercises**
- ■ **Answer Key**
- ■ **Answer Explanations**

The SAT assumes that you are familiar with arithmetic, elementary algebra, and plane geometry. The questions on the test are about equally divided among those three areas. You do not need to know any more advanced mathematics to do well on this part of the SAT. If you are afraid you may have forgotten some of the math that you had in ninth or tenth grade, use the review in Chapter 12 of this book. It is divided into topics, so you can concentrate on specific areas that seem unfamiliar.

There are two types of questions in the mathematics test. Quantitative comparison questions, which make up about one third of the test, are discussed specifically in the next chapter. Two thirds of the test consists of standard multiple-choice questions. The directions for these are as follows:

The following information is for your reference in solving some of the problems.

Circle of radius r. Area $= \pi r^2$; Circumference $= 2\pi r$
   The number of degrees of arc in a circle is 360.
The measure in degrees of a straight angle is 180.

Definitions of symbols:
$=$ is equal to	$\leq$ is less than or equal to
$\neq$ is unequal to	$\geq$ is greater than or equal to
$<$ is less than	$\parallel$ is parallel to
$>$ is greater than	$\perp$ is perpendicular to

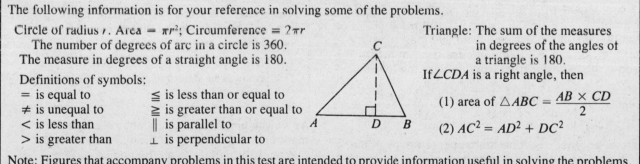

Triangle: The sum of the measures in degrees of the angles of a triangle is 180.
If $\angle CDA$ is a right angle, then

(1) area of $\triangle ABC = \dfrac{AB \times CD}{2}$

(2) $AC^2 = AD^2 + DC^2$

<u>Note</u>: Figures that accompany problems in this test are intended to provide information useful in solving the problems. They are drawn as accurately as possible EXCEPT when it is stated in a specific problem that its figure is not drawn to scale. All figures lie in a plane unless otherwise indicated. All numbers used are real numbers.

Testing Tactics

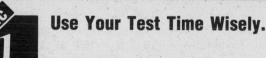

Use Your Test Time Wisely.

You are allowed 30 minutes for 25 standard multiple-choice questions. Should you give each question 30 ÷ 25 or 1.2 minutes? Absolutely not.

Although all questions carry the same point value, the first few questions in each section are easy, the next ones are more difficult, and the last ones are challenging. What does that mean to you in using the examination time wisely? It should be a signal to you that the early questions should not get the average time of 1.2 minutes each. It should also mean that, if any of the questions in the early part of the section appear difficult, perhaps you missed a point or misread the question. Also, don't be tempted to leave any of these "easy" questions unanswered, planning to return later. If you skip these questions, you will soon find yourself tackling very difficult ones without the preliminary "warm-up" the easy questions would have provided.

Let's look at some former SAT questions that appeared at the beginning of a math section. The first question appears to have a lengthy solution. Oddly enough, questions with a great deal of reading matter usually will not require much computation time. The fact that 93 percent of the students who took the test answered this question correctly indicates that it is not difficult.

A gymnast competed in a meet and received the following scores for three events: 9.5 for bars, 8.7 for balance beam, and 8.8 for floor routine. What is the average (arithmetic mean) of these three scores?

(A) 8.9   (B) 9.0   (C) 9.1   (D) 9.2   (E) 9.3

You might be tempted to quickly apply the formula for finding averages, but a shortcut (especially if you recognize the fact that this problem appears in the very early part of the test) is in order. The scores you are to average are 9.5, 8.7, and 8.8. Note that 8.7 is 0.3 away from 9.0 and 8.8 is 0.2 away from 9.0, or together they are 0.5 below 9.0. But the first quantity, 9.5, is 0.5 above 9.0, so you may conclude that the average is 9.0 and choose (B). For most people this is faster than working with the formula:

$$\text{Average} = \frac{\text{Sum}}{\text{Number of cases}} = \frac{9.5 + 8.7 + 8.8}{3} = 9.0$$

Here is another question that appeared early in the math section. Of the students who took the test, 88 percent got this one right; can you do it in a few seconds?

If $\dfrac{(20 + 50) + (30 + N)}{2} = 70$, then $N =$

(A) 30   (B) 40   (C) 50   (D) 60   (E) 70

Calculate the value of the numerator:

$$70 + 30 + N = 100 + N$$

Cross-multiply:

$$100 + N = 140 \quad \text{and} \quad N = 40$$

Choice (B) is correct. Note: The time you save on a

question like this gives you a reserve of seconds for the difficult questions near the end of the section.

The next question was number 4 on a recent SAT. Though it seems to involve much consideration, remember that questions at the beginning of a section only appear to be complicated.

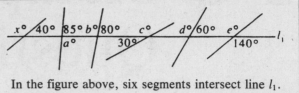

In the figure above, six segments intersect line l_1. Which of the degree measures, $a, b, c, d,$ or $e,$ is equal to x?

(A) a (B) b (C) c (D) d (E) e

First find the value of x. Note that x is the supplement of 40°. Therefore, $x = 140°$. Then, glance to the right for another angle with the 140° label. Because vertical angles have the same measure in degrees, $e = 140°$. Choice (E) is correct.

To demonstrate the fact that the questions toward the end of a section are difficult, here is one that only 18 percent of the candidates got right. Try it.

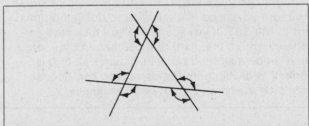

Three lines intersect as shown in the figure above. What is the sum of the degree measures of the marked angles?

(A) 360°   (B) 540°   (C) 720°   (D) 900°
(E) It cannot be determined from the information given.

As we will emphasize again later, it is advisable to mark up the geometric diagram. Assign number names, 1 through 9, to all the angles.

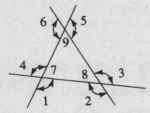

Look for relationships. What formulas come to mind? Remember 7 + 8 + 9 = 180°. What about 2 + 8, 1 + 7, and 5 + 9? Each of these pairs is supplementary. Therefore the sum is (180°)(3) or 540°. Now, to find 1 + 2 + 5, deduct the sum of 7 + 8 + 9: 1 + 2 + 5 = 540° − 180° or 360°. Now consider 3 + 4 + 5. Recall that vertical angles have the same measure in degrees. Therefore, measure of 2 = measure of 3, measure of 1 = measure of 4, and measure of 5 = measure of 6. Thus,

$$1 + 2 + 3 + 4 + 5 + 6 = 2(360°) \text{ or } 720°$$

Choice (C) is correct.

On analysis this is a difficult question because it calls into play at least three formulas.

Tactic 2: Avoid Lengthy Computations. Look for Shortcuts.

If an SAT problem reminds you of math problems that normally take 5 or 10 minutes to solve, reconsider. Perhaps you missed the point. Perhaps you misread the question. Actually, no question on the SAT should require more than 120 seconds. Does this former SAT question intimidate you?

> If $40 \cdot 20{,}000 = 8 \cdot 10^x$, then $x =$
>
> (A) 4   (B) 5   (C) 6   (D) 7   (E) 8

Look at the right side of the equation. It has a value of 8 times the x-power of 10. The left side should be transformed to 8 times some power of 10, such as 8 times 10^5. The five zeroes represent 10^5; therefore the left side = 8 times 10^5 and $x = 5$.

Here is another actual SAT question that you should use a shortcut to solve.

> If the first and last digits are interchanged in each of the following numbers, which will yield the number with the *least* value?
>
> (A) 4,321   (B) 3,241   (C) 2,431   (D) 4,231
> (E) 3,421

It isn't necessary to rewrite all the choices, interchanging the first and last digits. Here you should use your eyes, not your pencil. The first digit in all converted numbers will be 1. The second digit will be 2 for choices (B) and (D). At this point you should draw a line through (A), (C), and (E). For choice (B) the third digit will be a 4; but for the correct choice, which is (D), the third digit will be a 3. Choice C, incidentally, is designed for students who thought the question asked them to choose the number with the least value.

Tactic 3: Read the Question Carefully. Know What the Question Is Asking.

The test makers know that for most of the work problems you did in math class, the job was completed. The following actual SAT question has a little extra added on that might escape the careless reader.

> If it takes 10 people 12 hours to do a certain job, how many hours would it take 6 people, working at the same rate, to do $\frac{1}{4}$ of the same job?
>
> (A) 6   (B) 5   (C) $4\frac{1}{2}$ (D) 4   (E) $3\frac{3}{4}$

Identify this as an inverse proportion, since an increase in the number of workers will result in a decrease in the time (hours) to complete the job. If x = number of hours required by 6 people, then

$$(10 \text{ people})(12 \text{ hours}) = (6 \text{ people})(x \text{ hours})$$

Since $x = 20$, to complete $\frac{1}{4}$ of this job would require $\frac{1}{4}$ of 20 or 5 hours. Choice (B) is correct.

The following question from a former SAT has a negative sign that may escape the hasty or careless reader.

INCOME FOR THE EXCEL COMPANY January to April, 1980	
January	+ $4,700,000
February	− $4,000,000
March	+ $5,300,000
April	+ $2,000,000

Based on the table above, the average (arithmetic mean) monthly income from January to April, inclusive, for the Excel Company was

(A) $2,000,000
(B) $3,000,000
(C) $3,500,000
(D) $4,000,000
(E) $4,100,000

To obtain the average or arithmetic mean, we add and divide by 4. But why handle those big numbers? Drop the last five zeros and work in hundred thousandths. Then add: $47 + 53 + 20 = 120$, and subtract 40, obtaining 80, which when divided by 4 gives 20. Now add on the five zeros for the correct answer, $2,000,000. Choice (A) is correct.

The next SAT question has several traps for students who don't read the question carefully. Don't make the same mistake.

Sue ate $\frac{1}{3}$ of a sandwich at noon and then $\frac{1}{2}$ of the *remainder* at supper. What part of the sandwich remained uneaten?

(A) $\frac{1}{6}$ (B) $\frac{1}{5}$ (C) $\frac{1}{3}$ (D) $\frac{1}{2}$ (E) $\frac{2}{3}$

After the noon meal Sue had $\frac{2}{3}$ of the sandwich left.

Since the question asks what "remained uneaten," confine your computation to determining the part left uneaten; do not be concerned with the part eaten. At supper Sue ate $\frac{1}{2}$ of the $\frac{2}{3}$; in other words, $\frac{1}{2}$ of the $\frac{2}{3}$ was still uneaten. Since $\frac{1}{2}$ of $\frac{2}{3}$ is $\frac{1}{3}$, the correct choice is (C).

Choice (E) gives the part that was eaten, not the part that "remained uneaten." It is, therefore, not the answer to this question.

Tactic 4: Don't Panic When Faced with a Complex Problem.

Knowing what to expect in the examination room is important for success. Recognize that some questions will be difficult. When you come face to face with a problem like the one that follows, don't feel that you can't do well on the test and that you will never be accepted by any college. Wrong! Not so! This question was number 25 on a section with 25 questions. Would it comfort you to know that only 14 percent of the students who took this SAT got this question right?

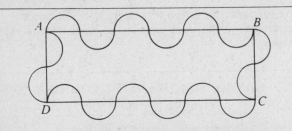

In the figure above, *ABCD* is a rectangle and the curved path is made up of 16 semicircles of equal diameter. If the total length of this curved path is 32π, then the *area* of rectangle *ABCD* is

(A) 24   (B) 32   (C) 48   (D) 64   (E) 192

Let's try the solution. We are told that the curved path is really 16 equal semicircles. Let's consider it the circumference of 8 equal circles, so that the length (circumference) of each of these circles is $\frac{32\pi}{8}$ or 4π. Using the formula for circumference, $C = \pi d$, we form the equations

$$4\pi = \pi d \quad \text{and} \quad d = 4$$

Look at *AB*. It is composed of 6 *d*'s, or 24. Look at *AD*. It is made up of 2 *d*'s, or 8.

$$\text{Area of } ABCD = 24 \times 8 \quad \text{or} \quad 192.$$

The correct choice is (E).

Tactic 5: Know Important Formulas, Concepts, Rules, and Definitions.

At the top of the first page of each math section of the SAT, you will be given some information for your reference. To save time in the examination room, however, you should have some key rules at your fingertips. For example, consider this actual SAT question.

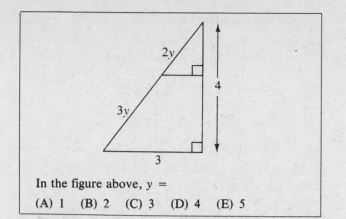

In the figure above, $y =$
(A) 1 (B) 2 (C) 3 (D) 4 (E) 5

It can be solved in seconds if you recognize that this right triangle has legs in the ratio of $3:4$ and therefore the ratio including the third side is $3:4:5$. Consequently, the side with dimension $2y + 3y$ must equal 5; $5y = 5$ and $y = 1$. Choice (A) is correct.

Tactic 6

Do Not Panic if a Question Has an Unusual Symbol.

If you encounter a question with an unusual symbol, replace the symbol with the specially designed definition that usually comes with the symbol. You should resist the temptation to skip this type of question because of its strange appearance. Some of these questions are easy. Here is one that 64 percent of the students answered correctly.

If $\lfloor x \rfloor$ is defined by the equation $\lfloor x \rfloor = \dfrac{\sqrt{x}}{2}$ for all whole numbers x, which of the following equals 5?

(A) $\lfloor 10 \rfloor$ (B) $\lfloor 20 \rfloor$ (C) $\lfloor 25 \rfloor$
(D) $\lfloor 50 \rfloor$ (E) $\lfloor 100 \rfloor$

In this case we work back from the answers given. We are looking for a quantity such that one half of its square root is equal to 5. Which ones to try? Try the easiest ones first; they are the ones whose square roots are easy to obtain. If they are to be rejected, it can be done quickly. Try choices (C) and (E). Reject (C) because $\dfrac{1}{2}(5) \neq 5$. Try (E): $\dfrac{1}{2}\sqrt{100} =$ 5. The correct answer is (E).

Here is a question that was number 30 in a section with 35 questions.

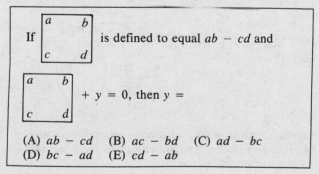

If $\begin{array}{cc} a & b \\ c & d \end{array}$ is defined to equal $ab - cd$ and $\begin{array}{cc} a & b \\ c & d \end{array} + y = 0$, then $y =$

(A) $ab - cd$ (B) $ac - bd$ (C) $ad - bc$
(D) $bc - ad$ (E) $cd - ab$

On analysis we will discover this question to be an exercise in solving a literal equation:

$$ab - cd + y = 0$$
$$y = cd - ab$$

The following two questions, shown here with their original numbers, 5 and 6, on the SAT exam, indicate that more than one question may be associated with a set of special symbols. Do not shy away from this type of problem. Actually, as you can tell from the numbers 5 and 6, you can expect these questions to be among the relatively easy ones.

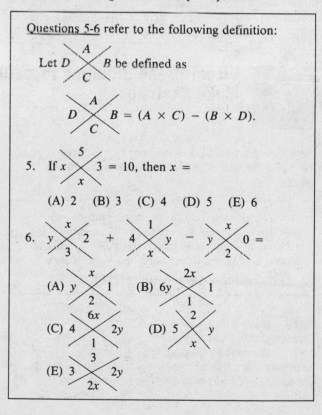

Questions 5-6 refer to the following definition:

Let $D \underset{C}{\overset{A}{\times}} B$ be defined as

$D \underset{C}{\overset{A}{\times}} B = (A \times C) - (B \times D)$.

5. If $x \underset{x}{\overset{5}{\times}} 3 = 10$, then $x =$

(A) 2   (B) 3   (C) 4   (D) 5   (E) 6

6. $y \underset{3}{\overset{x}{\times}} 2 + 4 \underset{x}{\overset{1}{\times}} y - y \underset{2}{\overset{x}{\times}} 0 =$

(A) $y \underset{2}{\overset{x}{\times}} 1$ (B) $6y \underset{1}{\overset{2x}{\times}} 1$

(C) $4 \underset{1}{\overset{6x}{\times}} 2y$ (D) $5 \underset{x}{\overset{2}{\times}} y$

(E) $3 \underset{2x}{\overset{3}{\times}} 2y$

Question 5 is an easy problem in which you solve an equation:

$$5x - 3x = 10$$
$$2x = 10$$
$$x = 5$$

Choice D is correct.

In question 6 you add similar algebraic terms and then change the result to the form of the original definition:

$$(3x - 2y) + (x - 4y) - (2x - 0)$$
$$3x + x - 2x - 2y - 4y \quad \text{or} \quad 2x - 6y$$

Only two choices are plausible: (B) and (E). Each has $2x$. Since (B) checks, don't bother with (E). Choice (B) is correct.

The next two questions, also numbered as on the actual SAT, are a bit more difficult than the last two, as the numbers 15 and 16 indicate.

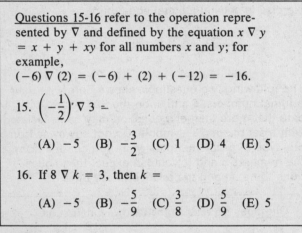

> Questions 15-16 refer to the operation represented by ∇ and defined by the equation $x \nabla y = x + y + xy$ for all numbers x and y; for example,
> $$(-6) \nabla (2) = (-6) + (2) + (-12) = -16.$$
>
> 15. $\left(-\dfrac{1}{2}\right) \nabla 3 =$
>
>   (A) -5 (B) $-\dfrac{3}{2}$ (C) 1 (D) 4 (E) 5
>
> 16. If $8 \nabla k = 3$, then $k =$
>
>   (A) -5 (B) $-\dfrac{5}{9}$ (C) $\dfrac{3}{8}$ (D) $\dfrac{5}{9}$ (E) 5

For question 15, substitute:

$$x = \left(-\frac{1}{2}\right) \quad \text{and} \quad y = 3$$
$$\left(-\frac{1}{2}\right) + 3 + \left(-\frac{1}{2}\right)(3)$$
$$\left(-\frac{1}{2}\right) + 3 + \left(-\frac{3}{2}\right)$$
$$-\frac{1}{2} + 3 - \frac{3}{2} = 3 - \frac{4}{2} \quad \text{or} \quad 3 - 2 = 1$$

Choice (C) is correct.

For question 16, solve for k, where $x = 8$ and $y = k$:

$$8 + k + 8k = 3$$
$$9k = -5$$
$$k = -\frac{5}{9}$$

Choice (B) is correct.

Visualize the Situation Presented. Make Sketches.

Here is the type of question that can be solved easily if you make a pictorial representation of the facts.

> At Central High School, the math club has 15 members and the chess club has 12 members. If a total of 13 students belong to only one of the two clubs, how many students belong to both clubs?
>
>   (A) 2   (B) 6   (C) 7   (D) 12   (E) 14

Choice (A) is incorrect. Two students belong to both clubs, but 23 belong to either the math or the chess club (i.e., to only one club).

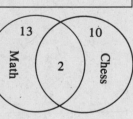

Look at (B). Six students belong to both clubs, but 15 belong to either one.

Note that (C) is correct. Go no further.

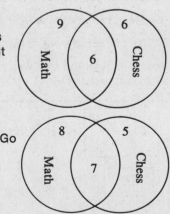

Caution: The sketches you make need not be works of art. Don't spend time showing off; your test booklet will not be inspected.

Here is another actual SAT question that asks you to visualize a situation.

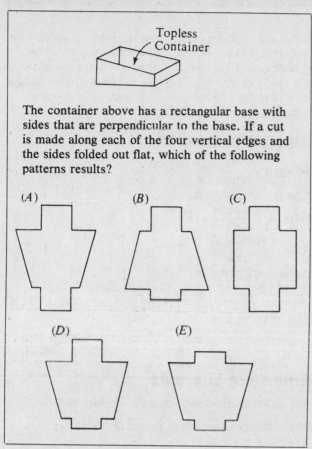

The container above has a rectangular base with sides that are perpendicular to the base. If a cut is made along each of the four vertical edges and the sides folded out flat, which of the following patterns results?

This question came early in the math section, so that you may expect it to be relatively easy despite its lengthy appearance. Choice (A) would not give the box its slant. The front and rear are the same size. This is also the reason for rejecting (E). Choice (B) has the unequal sides in the wrong positions for the direction of the slant. Choice (C) has no slant. That leaves (D) as the best representation. Choice (D) is correct.

Use the Test Booklet Wisely. Mark Up the Diagrams.

Feel free to mark up the booklet. Besides doing the scratch work in the booklet, save time by marking the diagrams given with the problems. Don't make new ones, as you did with your math textbook. Here is a former question where this practice will help.

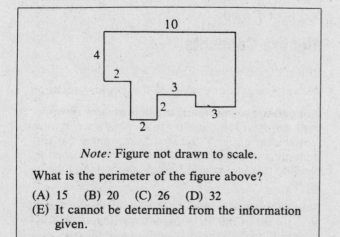

Note: Figure not drawn to scale.

What is the perimeter of the figure above?

(A) 15   (B) 20   (C) 26   (D) 32
(E) It cannot be determined from the information given.

To answer the question you must find the length of the unmarked side on the right and the unmarked side at the lower left. Drawing dotted lines, as done below, gives no clues.

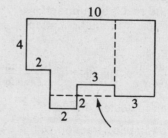

The correct choice is (E).

Important Facts and Formulas

You are most likely to do well on the mathematics section of the SAT if you know your math. All the tactics in the world cannot substitute for knowledge. In the long run, the ability to solve problems quickly and accurately is far more useful than the ability to outguess the testers.

However, not all students are gifted mathematicians, and even those who are may have forgotten some of the topics they covered a year or two ago in algebra and geometry. Almost everyone could benefit from some review. The facts and formulas that follow in this chapter provide a minimal review for those of you who are running short on time. Go over them and, as far as possible, commit them to memory.

In addition, spend as much time as you can on the review material in Chapter 12. That chapter is divided topically, so you can concentrate on topics that you have forgotten, or that you know always give you trouble.

Symbols

= equals
≠ is not equal to
> is more than
< is less than
≧ is greater than or equal to
≦ is less than or equal to

≃ is congruent to
~ is similar to
⊥ is perpendicular to
∥ is parallel to
± plus or minus

Rules for Handling Exponents

$$x^a \cdot x^b = x^{a+b}$$
$$x^a \div x^b = x^{a-b}$$
$$(x^a)^b = x^{ab}$$
$$(xy)^a = x^a y^a$$

$$\left(\frac{x}{y}\right)^a = \frac{x^a}{y^a}$$
$$x^0 = 1 \text{ if } x \neq 0$$
$$x^{-a} = \frac{1}{x^a}$$
$$x^{1/a} = \sqrt[a]{x}$$

Important Definitions

Sum is the result of addition.
Difference is the result of subtraction.
Product is the result of multiplication.
In division,

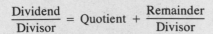

$$\frac{\text{Dividend}}{\text{Divisor}} = \text{Quotient} + \frac{\text{Remainder}}{\text{Divisor}}$$

A fraction is an indicated division.

A decimal is an implied fraction with a denominator of 10, 100, 1000, ...

A percent is a fraction with a denominator of 100.

A ratio compares two quantities by dividing one by the other.

A proportion is an equation, both sides of which are fractions.

A *positive* number is one that is greater than zero; a *negative* number is one that is less than zero. The meaning and the use of signed numbers are basic in the study of algebra. Positive numbers are preceded by a plus sign (+); negative numbers, by a minus sign (−).

Important Formulas

$$\text{Average} = \frac{\text{Sum of numbers}}{\text{Quantity of numbers}}$$

Rate × Time = Distance

$$\text{Time} = \frac{\text{Distance}}{\text{Rate}}$$

$$\text{Rate} = \frac{\text{Distance}}{\text{Time}}$$

Percentage composition

$$= \frac{\text{Quantity dissolved}}{\text{Total quantity of mixture}} \times 100$$

Part of task done

$$= \frac{\text{Time actually worked}}{\text{Time required to complete entire task}}$$

Arithmetic Concepts

Any quantity multiplied by zero is zero ($x \cdot 0 = 0$).

Any quantity except zero raised to the zero power is 1 ($x^0 = 1$ if $x \neq 0$).

If $x^2 = 4$, then $x = +2$ or -2.

Any fraction multiplied by its reciprocal equals 1:

$$\left(\frac{x}{y}\right)\left(\frac{y}{x}\right) = 1$$

Odd and Even Numbers

even + even = even
odd + odd = even
even + odd = odd
even × even = even
even × odd = even
odd × odd = odd

Algebra Concepts

Only *like* algebraic terms may be combined.

Always check your answer in the original equation.

In *algebraic expressions,* break problems down to their simplest form and try to eliminate any equivalent answer choices. In simplifying, remember to multiply and divide before adding and subtracting; simplify exponents and fractions; combine like terms.

If an expression has more than one set of parentheses, get rid of the inner parentheses first and work outward through the rest of the parentheses.

Any operation done to one side of an equation must be done to the other.

Geometry Concepts
Right Triangles
In a right triangle, (leg)^2 + (leg)^2 = (hypotenuse)^2, or $a^2 + b^2 = c^2$.

In a 30°–60°–90° triangle:

the leg opposite the 30° angle equals $\frac{1}{2}$ the hypotenuse;

the leg opposite the 60° angle equals $\frac{1}{2}$ the hypotenuse times $\sqrt{3}$;
the ratio of the shorter leg to the hypotenuse is 1:2.

In a 45°–45°–90° triangle:
the hypotenuse equals a leg times $\sqrt{2}$;

the leg equals $\frac{1}{2}$ the hypotenuse times $\sqrt{2}$.

Equilateral Triangles
In an equilateral triangle, an altitude equals $\frac{1}{2}$ the side times $\sqrt{3}$.

Areas of Polygons
Area of a rectangle = bh
Area of a square = s^2
Area of a parallelogram = bh

Area of a triangle = $\frac{1}{2} bh$

Area of a right triangle = $\frac{1}{2}$ leg × leg

Circles
Circumference of a circle = πd or $2\pi r$

Length of an arc = $\frac{n}{360} \times 2\pi r$

Area of a circle = πr^2

Coordinate Geometry
Distance between two points =
$$\sqrt{(x_1 - x_2)^2 + (y_1 - y_2)^2}$$

Coordinates of midpoint of line =

$$\frac{1}{2}(x_1 + x_2), \frac{1}{2}(y_1 + y_2)$$

Basic Quantities To Know (≈ Represents "Approximately Equals")

$\pi \approx 3.1416 \approx \frac{22}{7}$

$\sqrt{2} \approx 1.1414$

$\sqrt{3} \approx 1.732$

Important Solutions of the Pythagorean Theorem
3–4–5 triangle
5–12–13 triangle
1–1–$\sqrt{2}$ triangle (45°–45°–90°)
1–$\sqrt{3}$–2 triangle (30°–60°–90°)

Important Theorems
If two sides of a triangle are congruent, the angles opposite these sides are congruent. (Base angles of an isosceles triangle are congruent.)

The sum of the measure of the angles of a triangle is equal to a straight angle (180°).

If two angles of a triangle are congruent, the sides opposite these angles are congruent.

Two right triangles are congruent if the hypotenuse and leg of one triangle are congruent to the hypotenuse and corresponding leg of the other.

In a circle, a diameter perpendicular to a chord bisects the chord and its two arcs.

An angle inscribed in a circle is measured by one-half its intercepted arc.

An angle formed by two chords intersecting within a circle is measured by one-half the sum of the intercepted arcs.

An angle formed by two secants meeting outside a circle is measured by one-half the difference of the intercepted arcs.

An angle formed by a tangent and a secant is measured by one-half the difference of the intercepted arcs.

An angle formed by the intersection of two tangents is measured by one-half the difference of the intercepted arcs.

If two triangles have the three angles of one congruent respectively to the three angles of the other, the triangles are similar.

If, in a right triangle, the altitude is drawn upon the hypotenuse:
(a) the two triangles thus formed are similar to the given triangle and similar to each other;
(b) the length of each leg of the given triangle is the mean proportional between the hypotenuse and the projection of that leg on the hypotenuse.

If two lines are cut by a transversal and a pair of alternate interior angles are congruent, the two lines are parallel.

The opposite sides of a parallelogram are congruent and the opposite angles are congruent.

The diagonals of a parallelogram bisect each other.

If the opposite sides of a quadrilateral are congruent, the figure is a parallelogram.

If two sides of a quadrilateral are congruent and parallel, the figure is a parallelogram.

In a circle or in congruent circles, congruent chords are equally distant from the center.

Tangents drawn to a circle from an external point are equal in length.

An angle formed by a tangent and a chord drawn from the point of contact is measured by one-half its intercepted arc.

If an angle of one triangle is congruent to an angle of another triangle and the sides including these angles are proportional, the triangles are similar.

If two chords intersect within a circle, the product of the segments of one chord is equal to the product of the segments of the other.

If from a point outside a circle a tangent and a secant are drawn to the circle, the tangent is the mean proportional between the secant and its external segment.

The areas of two similar triangles are to each other as the squares of any two corresponding sides.

If two sides of a triangle are not congruent, the angles opposite these sides are not congruent and the greater angle lies opposite the greater side.

If two angles of a triangle are not congruent, the sides opposite these angles are not congruent and the greater side lies opposite the greater angle.

Practice Exercises

Mathematics Exercise A

1. What is the value of $\dfrac{x}{x-a} + \dfrac{a}{a-x}$ when x is 50 and a is 10?

   (A) 0   (B) 1   (C) 10   (D) 5   (E) 50

2. If x is doubled and y is tripled in the expression $z = \dfrac{3x}{y}$, then the value of z is

   (A) doubled   (B) tripled   (C) halved

   (D) multiplied by 6   (E) multiplied by a factor of $\dfrac{2}{3}$

3. If $x^2 + y^2 = 2$ and $x^2 - y^2 = 2$, then $x^4 - y^4 =$

   (A) 0   (B) 2   (C) 4   (D) 5   (E) 8

4. $\dfrac{8(11-2) - 5(11-2)}{3} =$

   (A) 1   (B) 11   (C) 9   (D) 3   (E) 5

5. If $27 \cdot 27 = 3 \cdot 3 \cdot x$, then $x =$

   (A) 9   (B) 27   (C) 81   (D) 243   (E) 36

6. A certain type of bacteria triples in number every 20 minutes. At the end of 5 hours there are x bacteria in the colony. In how many hours more will there be $27x$?

   (A) 1   (B) $1\dfrac{1}{3}$ (C) $1\dfrac{2}{3}$ (D) 2   (E) $\dfrac{2}{3}$

7. If $\dfrac{x}{\sqrt{2}} = \sqrt{2}$, then $x =$

   (A) 2   (B) $\sqrt{2}$ (C) $\dfrac{1}{2}$ (D) $\dfrac{1}{\sqrt{2}}$ (E) $\dfrac{\sqrt{2}}{2}$

8. If $\dfrac{1}{y} = \dfrac{1}{x-2}$, all of the following are true EXCEPT

   (A) $y - x = 2$
   (B) $y + 2 = x$
   (C) $y - x = -2$
   (D) $x - y = 2$
   (E) $x - y - 2 = 0$

9. If $x = -1$, $ax^5 + bx^3 - 4 = 0$. What is the value of this equation when $x = 1$?

   (A) 0   (B) 1   (C) 6   (D) -8 (E) -4

10. What is the area, in square inches, of a square if its diagonal is 6 inches?

    (A) 9   (B) 6   (C) 36   (D) 12   (E) 18

11. Suppose $a * b = c$ is true only if $b^c = a$. When $64 * 4 = y$, then $y =$

    (A) $\dfrac{1}{2}$ (B) 2   (C) 3   (D) 4   (E) $\dfrac{1}{4}$

12. The statement $3x - 1 \neq 2x$ is true for all values of x EXCEPT

    (A) $x \neq 1$ (B) $x = -1$ (C) $x = 1$ (D) $x > 1$
    (E) $x < 1$

13. A bag contains 28 pounds of sugar which is to be separated into packages containing 14 ounces each. How many such packages can be made?

    (A) 2   (B) 4   (C) 8   (D) 16   (E) 32

14. What is the value of $1^{3a} + 1^{2a}$?

    (A) 0   (B) 1   (C) 2   (D) 5
    (E) It cannot be determined from the information given

15. The approximate value of $\sqrt{15}$ is 3.87. Which of the following is the best approximation to $\sqrt{\dfrac{5}{3}}$?

    (A) 0.2   (B) 0.4   (C) 1.29   (D) 6.10
    (E) 3.66

16. Which of the following has the greatest value?

    (A) $\dfrac{1-\dfrac{1}{3}}{3}$ (B) $\dfrac{-3}{-\dfrac{1}{3}}$ (C) $\dfrac{-3}{\dfrac{1}{3}}$ (D) 0

    (E) $\dfrac{3-\dfrac{1}{3}}{3}$

17. When x is 1, 2, 3, or 4, the expression $x^2 + x + 17$ has the values 19, 23, 29, and 37, respectively. All of these results are prime numbers. What is the least positive integer that will not yield a prime in the formula?

    (A) 5   (B) 7   (C) 11   (D) 13   (E) 16

18. The area of $\triangle ABC =$

    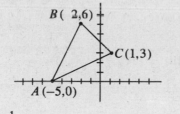

    (A) $13\dfrac{1}{2}$ (B) 12   (C) 11   (D) 9   (E) $9\dfrac{1}{2}$

19. If $y = \dfrac{3x - 6}{x}$, for what values of x will y be positive?

    (A) $x > 2$ or $x < 0$
    (B) only when x is positive
    (C) only when x is negative
    (D) $-2 < x < 2$
    (E) $-2 < x < 2$ but not 0

20. In $ABCD$, AD and BC are parallel. The length of $BC =$

    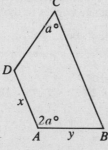

    (A) x (B) $x + y$ (C) $x + 2y$ (D) $2x + y$
    (E) $2x + 2y$

21. Suppose $a * b = c$ is true if and only if c is the remainder after a is divided by b. The value of $\dfrac{5 * 3}{10 * 6} =$

    (A) 2   (B) $\dfrac{1}{2}$ (C) 4   (D) 3   (E) 1

22. If $(0.4)(y) = 5$, then $(4.44)(y) =$

    (A) 5.055   (B) 0.555   (C) 555   (D) 55.5
    (E) 5.55

23. If $\dfrac{1}{2 - \dfrac{x}{1 - x}} = \dfrac{1}{2}$, what is the value of x?

    (A) 12   (B) -2 (C) 0   (D) 1   (E) -1

24. If $p > 1$, which of the following expressions decrease(s) as p increases?

    I. $p + \dfrac{1}{p}$

    II. $p^2 - 10p$

    III. $\dfrac{1}{p + 1}$

    (A) III only   (B) I and III only
    (C) II and III only   (D) all   (E) none

25. If y and z are consecutive integers and $z^2 = x^2 + y^2$, which of the following is true?

    (A) $z = x + y$ (B) $x^2 = 1 + 2y$
    (C) $y^2 = 2x + 1$ (D) $z = 1 + 2x$
    (E) $x = y + 2z$

Mathematics Exercise B

1. If the circumference of a circle increases from π inches to 2π inches, what change occurs in the area?

    (A) It remains the same.
    (B) It doubles.
    (C) It triples.
    (D) It quadruples.
    (E) It is halved.

2. $31(m - n) - 32(m - n) + (m - n) =$
    (A) $-n$ (B) $-m$ (C) 0   (D) 1   (E) m

3. If $3x = 2y$ and $6y = 7z$, what is the ratio of x to z?

    (A) 2:3   (B) 7:9   (C) 3:2   (D) 5:7   (E) 5:3

4. If x must be greater than 4, which of the following must have the least value?

    (A) $\dfrac{4}{x + 1}$ (B) $\dfrac{4}{x - 1}$ (C) $\dfrac{4}{x}$ (D) $\dfrac{x}{4}$

    (E) $\dfrac{x + 1}{4}$

5. $\dfrac{\dfrac{1}{5} + \dfrac{1}{10}}{\dfrac{1}{15} + \dfrac{1}{5}} =$

(A) $\dfrac{7}{15}$ (B) $\dfrac{2}{3}$ (C) $\dfrac{9}{8}$ (D) 15 (E) 5

6. Six consecutive integers are given. The sum of the first three is 27. What is the sum of the last three?

(A) 29 (B) 30 (C) 32 (D) 33 (E) 36

7. What are all values of x for which $-x = \sqrt[3]{x}$?

(A) 1 (B) 0 and -1 (C) 0 only (D) -8
(E) No values are possible.

8. If the points given in A through E are the endpoints of segments that have their other ends at the origin, which segment has a midpoint that is farthest from the origin?

(A) (3, 3) (B) (2, 5) (C) (1, 6) (D) (0, 7)
(E) (4, 3)

9. An arithmetic progression is a sequence of numbers for which each new number is found by adding a given number p to the previous number. In the arithmetic progression below, only two numbers are known.

$$-, -, \underline{5}, -, -, -, \underline{17}, -$$

What number comes after 17?

(A) 19 (B) 20 (C) 21 (D) 18 (E) 23

10. Suppose $x > y$ and $xy < 0$. Which of the following must be negative?

(A) y (B) x (C) $x - y$ (D) $x^2 - y^2$
(E) $(y - x)^2$

11. What will the result be if $\dfrac{x + 10}{2}$ is subtracted

from $\dfrac{x}{2} + 10$?

(A) 5 (B) x (C) $\dfrac{x}{2}$ (D) 0 (E) $x + 10$

12. A mathematical law states that the sum of the first n odd counting numbers is n^2. Which of the following is an example of this law?

(A) $1 + 3 = 4$
(B) $1 + 9 + 16 = 26$
(C) $1 + 2 = 3$
(D) $1 + 3 + 5 = 1 + 2(4)^2$
(E) $1 + 4 = 5$

13. What is the area of triangle ABC if, for each point (x, y) of line AB, $y = 2x - 8$.

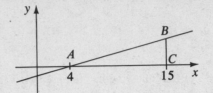

(A) 100 (B) 121 (C) 144 (D) 169 (E) 132

14. $\dfrac{y^2 + 4y - 5}{y^2 - 1} =$

(A) $\dfrac{y + 5}{y + 1}$ (B) $y + 4$ (C) $\dfrac{y + 1}{y + 5}$ (D) $\dfrac{5y}{4}$
(E) $5y$

15. $\dfrac{4^3 + 4^4}{4^3} =$

(A) 1 (B) 2 (C) 4 (D) 5 (E) 8

16. Which of the following is the simplest form of

$$\dfrac{x - \dfrac{1}{y}}{y - \dfrac{1}{x}} ?$$

(A) $\dfrac{x}{y}$ (B) $\dfrac{y}{x}$ (C) $\dfrac{x - 1}{y - 1}$ (D) $\dfrac{y - 1}{x - 1}$
(E) $\dfrac{xy - 1}{xy}$

17. If $a = b + 3$, what is the value of $(a - b)^3$?

(A) 1 (B) 8 (C) 27 (D) 64 (E) 0

18. Suppose you have 72 green marbles and 108 red marbles to sell. You decide to separate them into packages of the same size, each containing either all red or all green. What is the greatest number of marbles you can put in each package?

(A) 3 (B) 18 (C) 12 (D) 24 (E) 36

19. If the length of a rectangle is increased by 20 percent and the width is decreased by 20 percent, what percent change occurs in the area?

(A) It remains the same.
(B) It increases 5%.
(C) It decreases 4%.
(D) It increases 2%.
(E) It decreases 2%.

20. What percent of $\dfrac{1}{2}$ is $\dfrac{3}{4}$?

(A) 100% (B) 120% (C) 125% (D) 140%
(E) 150%

21. Which of the following is the square (second power) of $\sqrt{1} + \sqrt{1}$?

   (A) 1   (B) 2   (C) 4   (D) 3   (E) $1 + \sqrt{2}$

22. If $x = 1 + 3^a$ and $y = 1 + 3^{-a}$ which of the following is a formula for y in terms of x?

   (A) x (B) $x - 1$ (C) $\dfrac{1}{x-1}$ (D) $\dfrac{x}{x-1}$

   (E) $x + 1$

23. If $\dfrac{p \times p \times p}{p + p + p} = 3$, $p =$

   (A) $\dfrac{1}{3}$ (B) $\dfrac{1}{9}$ (C) 27   (D) ± 3 (E) 9

24. $S(x)$ is defined as follows:
   $S(x) = 1$ when $x > 1$,
   $S(x) = x$ when $-1 \leq x \leq 1$, and
   $S(x) = -1$ when $x < -1$.
   What is the value of $S(5) + S(4) + S(0)$?

   (A) 1   (B) 0   (C) 3   (D) 2   (E) -1

25. $5 - [7 - (9 - 11)] =$

   (A) -4 (B) 3   (C) -2 (D) 7   (E) 5

Answer Key

Mathematics Exercise A

1.	B	6.	A	11.	C	16.	B	21.	B
2.	E	7.	A	12.	C	17.	E	22.	D
3.	C	8.	A	13.	E	18.	A	23.	C
4.	C	9.	D	14.	C	19.	A	24.	A
5.	C	10.	E	15.	C	20.	B	25.	B

Mathematics Exercise B

1.	D	6.	E	11.	A	16.	A	21.	B
2.	C	7.	B	12.	A	17.	C	22.	D
3.	B	8.	D	13.	B	18.	E	23.	D
4.	A	9.	B	14.	A	19.	C	24.	D
5.	C	10.	A	15.	D	20.	E	25	A

Answer Explanations

Mathematics Exercise A

1. **B.** Instead of time-consuming substitution of values, note that $a - x = -(x - a)$. Therefore, the fractions can be combined to get $\dfrac{x-a}{x-a} = 1$ regardless of the values of x and a (as long as x does not equal a, of course).

2. **E.** The trap is to cancel the 3 in the numerator with the 3 that appears in the denominator when the denominator is tripled. If this is done, the result is $\dfrac{2x}{y}$. If cancellation is not performed, the result can be written as $\dfrac{2}{3}\left(\dfrac{3x}{y}\right)$ or $\dfrac{2}{3}z$. The obvious solution is the correct one.

3. **C.** Factor the difference between two perfect squares:
   $x^4 - y^4 = (x^2 + y^2)(x^2 - y^2) = (2)(2)$

4. **C.** The calculation is not really lengthy, but note:
   $$\dfrac{8(11-2) - 5(11-2)}{3} = \dfrac{3(11-2)}{3}$$
   $$= 11 - 2 = 9$$

5. **C.** $27 \cdot 27 = (3 \cdot 3)(9 \cdot 9)$. Thus $x = 9 \cdot 9 = 81$.

6. **A.** Since the question asks "how many hours more?" you can ignore the first 5 hours. In 20 minutes x will triple to $3x$; in 20 more minutes $3x$ will triple to $3(3x)$; and at end of 1 hour there will be $(3)(3)(3x)$ or $27x$ bacteria.

7. **A.** Cross-multiply: $\sqrt{2} \cdot \sqrt{2} = 2$, $x = 2$.

8. **A.** Since the numerators are equal, the denominators are equal. Therefore, $y = x - 2$. Choice (B) is true because, by adding 2 to each side of the equation, you get $y + 2 = x$. Choice (C) is true because, by subtracting x from both sides of the equation, you get $y - x = -2$. Choice (D) is true because, by subtracting y and adding 2, you get $x - y = 2$. Choice (E) is true because, by subtracting y, you get $x - y - 2 = 0$. Choice (A) is not true because it contradicts (C); therefore, (A) is the right answer.

9. **D.** If x is replaced by -1, $ax^5 + bx^3 - 4$ becomes $-a - b - 4$. Since you are told that $-a - b - 4 = 0$, $-4 = a + b$. If x is now replaced by 1, $ax^5 + bx^3 - 4$ becomes $a + b - 4$; hence $a + b - 4$ is $-4 - 4$ or -8.

10. E. The square has diagonals that bisect each other, are perpendicular, and separate the square into four triangles of the same area. Thus you have four right triangles with legs of length 3 and areas of $\frac{9}{2}$; and $4\left(\frac{9}{2}\right) = 18$.

11. C. By direct substitution into the formula given you get $4^y = 64$. Since $64 = 4^3$, $y = 3$.

12. C. Any value that makes $3x - 1 \neq 2x$ true makes $3x - 1 = 2x$ false. The latter is true for $x = 1$.

13. E. Changing pounds to ounces gives 28×16, but do not multiply it out. Cancel: $\dfrac{\overset{2}{\cancel{28}}(16)}{\cancel{(14)}} = 32$.

14. C. No matter what a is, $1^{3n} = 1$ and $1^{2n} = 1$.

15. C. You must change $\sqrt{\dfrac{5}{3}}$ to a form that will use the given approximation of $\sqrt{15}$:

$$\sqrt{\frac{5}{3}} = \sqrt{\frac{5 \times 3}{3 \times 3}} = \frac{\sqrt{15}}{\sqrt{9}} = \frac{\sqrt{15}}{3} = \frac{3.87}{3} = 1.29$$

16. B. (A), (B), and (E) are positive, so (C) and (D) can be eliminated since they are not positive. (E) is greater than (A) since $3 - \dfrac{1}{3}$ is greater than $1 - \dfrac{1}{3}$. (B) is 9. (E) is $\dfrac{2\frac{2}{3}}{3}$, which is $\dfrac{1}{3}$ of $2\frac{2}{3}$ and hence less than 1. A routine and lengthy approach is to simplify each of them.

17. E. Rewrite $x^2 + x + 17$ as $x(x + 1) + 17$. In order for the entire expression to have a factor, 17 must divide into either x or $x + 1$. Thus either x or $x + 1$ must equal 17. If $x = 16$ (E), $x + 1 = 17$. For any value of x less than 16, neither x nor $x + 1$ will be divisible by 17 and the number will be prime.

18. A. Draw perpendiculars to the x-axis from B and C and then add and subtract the necessary pieces.

(1) Area of triangle $ABB' = \dfrac{1}{2}(3)(6) = 9$.

(2) Area of trapezoid $BB'C'C =$
$\dfrac{1}{2}(6 + 3)3 = 13\dfrac{1}{2}$.

(3) Area of triangle $ACC' =$
$\dfrac{1}{2}(6)(3) = 9$.

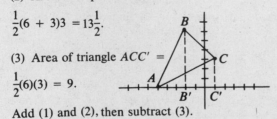

Add (1) and (2), then subtract (3).

19. A. $\dfrac{3x - 6}{x} = 3 - \dfrac{6}{x}$, which will be positive as long as $3 > \dfrac{6}{x}$. The value of $\dfrac{6}{x}$ will be less than 3 when (1)x is negative, or (2)$x > 2$.

20. B. Draw AP bisecting $\angle DAB$. $PC = x$ since $PADC$ is a parallelogram. $\angle APB$ has measure $a°$ since $\angle APB$ and $\angle C$ are corresponding angles. $PB = y$ since $\angle PAB$ and $\angle BPA$ have the same measure.

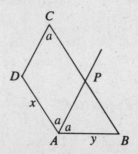

21. B. By direct division $5 * 3 = 2$ and $10 * 6 = 4$. The fraction $\dfrac{2}{4} = \dfrac{1}{2}$.

22. D.
$$0.4y = 5$$
$$0.04y = 0.5 \text{ (multiply by 0.1)}$$
$$+ \quad 4y = 50 \text{ (multiply original equation by 10)}$$
$$\overline{4.44y = 55.5}$$

23. C. Do no lengthy computation; recognize that the fractions can be equal when $\dfrac{x}{1 - x} = 0$, which means x must equal zero.

24. A. Only III. As the denominator $(p + 1)$ increases, the value of the fraction decreases.

25. B. $z = y + 1$, so $z^2 = y^2 + 2y + 1 = x^2 + y^2$. Thus $2y + 1 = x^2$.

Mathematics Exercise B

1. D. Since the circumference is doubled, the radius is doubled. The area is based on the square of the radius. Squaring the factor of 2 thus introduced makes the area change by a factor of 4.

2. C. $31(m - n) + (m - n) = 32(m - n)$. Thus the value of the expression is $32(m - n) - 32(m - n) = 0$.

3. B. Multiply both sides of $3x = 2y$ by 3 to get $9x = 6y$. Since $6y = 7z$, by substitution $9x = 7z$. Divide the latter equation by $9z$ to yield $\dfrac{x}{z} = \dfrac{7}{9}$.

4. A. Choices (D) and (E) can be excluded because greater values of x will increase the numerator and thereby the fraction. Choices (A), (B), and (C) all have the same numerator, so the fraction with the least value will be the one with the greatest denominator.

5. C. Avoid lengthy computation. Multiply the original fraction by $\dfrac{30}{30}$ to get $\dfrac{6 + 3}{2 + 6}$ or $\dfrac{9}{8}$

6. E. The sum of the last three integers must be 9 more than the sum of the first three. You can see the pattern if you let x be the first of these integers:
$$\underbrace{x, x + 1, x + 2,}_{3x + 3} \underbrace{x + 3, x + 4, x + 5}_{3x + 12}$$

7. B. Cube both sides to eliminate the radical:
$-x^3 = x$.
$-(0)^3 = 0$ and $-(-1)^3 = -1$

8. D. If the midpoint is farthest from the origin, then the endpoint will also be farthest from the origin. To save time, avoid computation; make a sketch and locate each given endpoint. Observe that D is farthest from the origin.

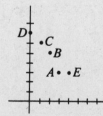

9. B. Ignore the first two terms, and get the result strictly from the definition given. The terms, starting with 5, are as follows:
$-, -, 5, 5 + p, 5 + 2p, 5 + 3p, 5 + 4p$
$5 + 4p = 17$, so p is 3 and the next term is 20.

10. A. Since xy is negative, either x or y is negative, but not both. Since $x > y$, then y must be negative.

11. A. $\dfrac{x + 10}{2} = \dfrac{x}{2} + 5$, which will leave 5 when subtracted from $\dfrac{x}{2} + 10$.

12. A. Only two choices, (A) and (D), involve sums of consecutive odd counting numbers. In (D), the sum is incorrect and it is not a square.

13. B. The length of the base can be computed: $15 - 4 = 11$. To find the height, note that the y-coordinate of B gives the height. Since $y = 2x - 8$ for each point of the line and $x = 15$ at $B, y = 22$.
Area $= \dfrac{1}{2} (11)(22) = 121$

14. A. Factor and cancel:
$$\dfrac{y^2 + 4y - 5}{y^2 - 1} = \dfrac{(y + 5)(\cancel{y - 1})}{(y + 1)(\cancel{y - 1})}$$

15. D. Divide:
$4^3 \div 4^3 = 1$ and
$4^4 \div 4^3 = 4$ or
$\dfrac{4^3 + 4^4}{4^3} = 1 + 4 = 5$

16. A. Multiply by $\dfrac{xy}{xy}$ to get
$$\dfrac{x^2y - x}{xy^2 - y} = \dfrac{x(\cancel{xy - 1})}{y(\cancel{xy - 1})} = \dfrac{x}{y}$$

17. C. If $a = b + 3$, then
$a - b = 3$ and $(a - b)^3 = 3^3 = 27$

18. E. $72 = 2 \times 2 \times 2 \times 3 \times 3$
$108 = 2 \times 2 \times 3 \times 3 \times 3$
By inspecting factors, you can see that the greatest number which will divide both is $2 \times 2 \times 3 \times 3$

19. C. $(1.20L)(0.80W) = 0.96LW$ is the new area, or a decrease of $0.04LW$ or 4%.

20. E. The fraction $\dfrac{3}{4}$ is $\dfrac{1}{2}$ plus half of $\dfrac{1}{2}$ or 100% plus 50%.

21. B. $\sqrt{1} = 1$; therefore $\sqrt{1} + \sqrt{1} = \sqrt{1 + 1} = \sqrt{2}$, which when squared gives 2.

22. D. From the given information we can conclude that

$$x - 1 = 3^a$$
$$y = 1 + 3^{-a}$$
$$y = 1 + \frac{1}{3^a} = 1 + \frac{1}{x - 1}$$
$$y = \frac{x - 1}{x - 1} + \frac{1}{x - 1} = \frac{x}{x - 1}$$

23. D. $$\frac{p^3}{3p} = 3$$
$$\frac{p^2}{3} = 3$$
$$p^2 = 9$$
$$p = \pm 3$$

24. D. From the three-part formula we may conclude that

$$S(5) = 1, \ S(4) = 1, \ S(0) = 0$$

Therefore, $1 + 1 + 0 = 2$.

25. A. Remove the innermost parentheses first:

$$5 - [7 - (9 - 11)] =$$
$$5 - [7 - (-2)] =$$
$$5 - [7 + 2] =$$
$$5 - 9 = -4$$

11 Quantitative Comparison Questions

- **■ Testing Tactics**
- **■ Principles Involving Inequalities**
- **■ Practice Exercises**
- **■ Answer Key**
- **■ Answer Explanations**

About one third of the questions in the mathematics sections of the SAT are quantitative comparison questions. You may never have seen questions quite like these before, so they require some explanation. These questions do not ask you for the solution to a problem. Instead, you will be given two quantities. Sometimes you will also be given information about the two quantities to help you compare them. Then you must decide whether one of the quantities is greater than the other, or whether they are equal. Sometimes there will not be enough information for you to be able to make a decision. The directions for these questions are as follows:

Questions 8–27 each consist of two quantities, one in Column A and one in Column B. You are to compare the two quantities and on the answer sheet blacken space

- A if the quantity in Column A is greater;
- B if the quantity in Column B is greater;
- C if the two quantities are equal;
- D If the relationship cannot be determined from the information given.

AN E RESPONSE WILL NOT BE SCORED.

	EXAMPLES		
	Column A	Column B	Answers
E1.	2×6	$2 + 6$	●ⒷⒸⒹⒺ
E2.	$180 - x$	y	ⒶⒷ●ⒹⒺ
E3.	$p - q$	$q - p$	ⒶⒷⒸ●Ⓔ

(E2 figure: $x° \diagup y°$)

Notes:

1. In certain questions, information concerning one or both of the quantities to be compared is centered above the two columns.
2. In a given question, a symbol that appears in both columns represents the same thing in Column A as it does in Column B.
3. Letters such as x, n, and k stand for real numbers.

Read those directions again, and remind yourself that there are only FOUR possible answers to these questions. Every other question on the SAT has five answer choices. These are different. You must not choose (E) for your answer. If you do, your answer will not be scored, and you might as well have saved your time and skipped the question.

Testing Tactics

The following tactics, designed to help you tackle quantitative comparison questions, use actual former SAT questions as illustrative examples.

Quantitative Comparison Questions Require Less Time.

The following question was the first in the section on quantitative comparison questions. Eighty percent of the students taking the test answered it correctly. Again we see that the early questions are warm-up questions.

Column A	Column B
$\dfrac{1}{3} - \dfrac{1}{5}$	$\dfrac{2}{15}$

You should quickly realize that you must subtract two fractions with different denominators. You choose (C) because

$$\frac{5}{15} - \frac{3}{15} = \frac{2}{15}$$

This question demonstrates that it is possible to test all phases of mathematics in the quantitative comparison format. Again, do not expect to be involved in much computation.

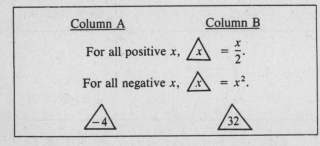

Column A	Column B
For all positive x, $\boxed{x} = \dfrac{x}{2}$.	
For all negative x, $\boxed{x} = x^2$.	
$\boxed{-4}$	$\boxed{32}$

Since the expression in Column A has a negative value, use

$$\boxed{x} = x^2 \quad \text{or} \quad (-4)^2 = 16$$

For Column B use

$$\boxed{x} = \frac{x}{2} \quad \text{or} \quad \frac{32}{2} = 16$$

The correct answer is (C).

The following former SAT question involves elementary, basic algebraic operations and should be done in 30 seconds or less.

Column A	Column B
$x(x + y) - z(x + y)$	$(x - z)(x + y)$

$$x(x + y) - z(x + y) = x^2 + xy - xz - yz$$
$$(x - z)(x + y) = x^2 - xz + xy - yz$$

Choose (C).

For the next question use your eyes, not your pencil.

Column A	Column B
List A	*List B*
6	17
13	24
19	11
8	16
14	19
The sum of 3 different numbers from list A	The sum of 3 different numbers from list B

Observe that there are many possible results of addition, depending upon whether you choose integers with large or small values. The correct answer is (D).

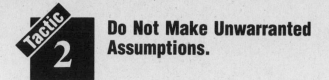

Do Not Make Unwarranted Assumptions.

In dealing with unknowns, do not assume that they are positive. And do not assume that unknowns are whole numbers. Also consider the possibility that unknowns may have zero values and fractional values less than 1. The following SAT question will trap you if you fail to see that the unknowns are positive but may have a value less than 1.

Column A	Column B
a, b, and c are positive.	
$a + b + c$	$\dfrac{1}{a + b + c}$

The correct answer is (D).

Unwarranted assumptions can also produce problems when geometric figures are involved.

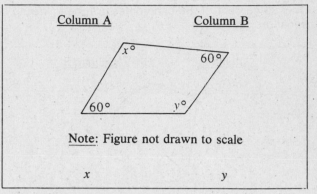

Note: Figure not drawn to scale

x	y

In the question above, you may conclude only that $x + y = 360 - 120$. Do not make the unwarranted assumption that the figure is a parallelogram, which would make $x = y$. You can conclude only that the figure is a quadrilateral, the sum of whose angles is 360°. Choose (D).

Eliminate from Consideration Any Quantity That Appears in Both Columns.

Column A	Column B
$10^6 - 2^6$	$10^6 - 3^6$

In this question note that 10^6 appears in both columns. Consider only the values of -2^6 and -3^6. The even number (2) to the sixth power will have a positive value, and the odd number (3) to the sixth power will have a larger positive value. Subtracting a larger positive number from 10^6 gives a smaller result. The correct answer is (A).

Mark Up Any Given Diagram and Expect to Do Little Computation.

Consider this question. Mark on the diagram all the information that is given.

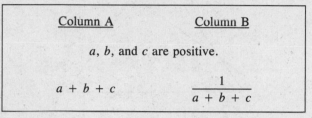

P and Q are midpoints on two sides of the rectangle and Q and R are midpoints on two sides of $\triangle PST$.

Perimeter of the shaded region	18

The diagram below (enlarged) shows how you should mark the given diagram in order to conclude that $RS = 4$ because $PR = 4$ and $RS = PR$, $TS = 6$ because it is equal to the side marked 6, $QR = 3$ because it is one-half the side marked 6. $TQ = 5$ because the right triangle TSP is a 3-4-5 triangle ($TS = 6$, $PS = 8$, and $TP = 10$). The perimeter = $4 + 6 + 3 + 5$ or 18. The correct answer is (C).

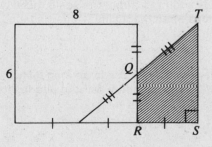

Use Important Rules, Formulas, and Relationships.

Only 36 percent of the candidates got the following question right.

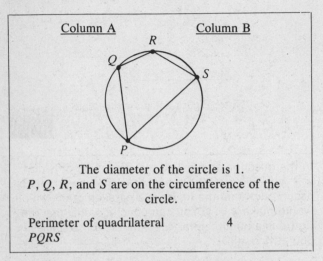

The diameter of the circle is 1.
P, Q, R, and S are on the circumference of the circle.

Column A	Column B
Perimeter of quadrilateral $PQRS$	4

Consider the important fact that the length of the diameter is the longest line segment that can be drawn within a circle. Why would the question tell you the diameter when it is obviously not one of the sides of the quadrilateral? Each side of the quadrilateral $PQRS$ is a chord with length less than 1, the diameter of the circle. Therefore, the correct answer is (B).

The next SAT question applies several formulas.

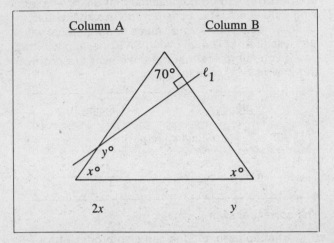

The sum of the measures in degrees of the angles of a triangle is 180. Therefore,

$$x + x + 70 = 180; \quad 2x = 180 - 70$$
$$2x = 110 \text{ (Column A)}$$

To find the value of y, consider its supplement, which is the acute angle in the right triangle and is equal to 20°. Therefore $y = 180 - 20$ or 160. Choose (B).

Principles Involving Inequalities

The preparation you do for the mathematics section as a whole will help you prepare for the quantitative comparison questions. The same areas of arithmetic, algebra, and geometry appear on both parts of the test. Do the practice exercises that appear later in this chapter to familiarize yourself with the format of these questions.

In addition, review the following principles involving inequalities:

1. You may add or subtract the same quantity from both sides of an inequality without altering its solution set.
   If $x > y$, then $x - y > 0$.

2. You may multiply or divide an inequality by the same POSITIVE quantity without altering its solution set.
   If $\frac{a}{4} > 1$, then $a > 4$.

3. If you multiply or divide an inequality by a NEGATIVE number, then you must reverse the direction of the inequality sign.
   If $-2x > 3$, then $x < \frac{-3}{2}$.

4. If unequal quantities are added to unequal quantities of the same order, the result is unequal in the same order.
   If $a > b$ and $c > d$, then $a + c > b + d$.

5. You may take the positive square root of both sides of the inequality without changing the direction of the inequality. (*Note:* You may only take square roots of a positive number.)

6. You may square both sides of an inequality if both sides are positive. The direction of the inequality remains the same. If both sides of an inequality are negative, you must switch the direction of the inequality.

7. If the first of three quantities is greater than the second, and the second is greater than the third, then the first is greater than the third. If $a > b$ and $b > c$, then $a > c$.

8. The sum of the lengths of any two sides of a triangle is greater than the length of the third side.

9. If two sides of a triangle are unequal, then the angles opposite those sides are unequal. The greater angle lies opposite the greater side.

10. The exterior angle of a triangle is greater than either remote interior angle. In the triangle shown, $c > a$ and $c > d$.

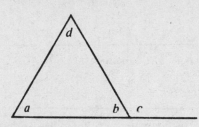

Practice Exercises

Questions 1-142 each consist of two quantities, one in Column A and one in Column B. You are to compare the two quantities and on the answer sheet blacken space

A if the quantity in Column A is greater;
B if the quantity in Column B is greater;
C if the two quantities are equal;
D If the relationship cannot be determined from the information given.

AN E RESPONSE WILL NOT BE SCORED.

	EXAMPLES		
	Column A	Column B	Answers
E1.	2×6	$2 + 6$	● Ⓑ Ⓒ Ⓓ Ⓔ
E2.	$180 - x$	y	Ⓐ Ⓑ ● Ⓓ Ⓔ
E3.	$p - q$	$q - p$	Ⓐ Ⓑ Ⓒ ● Ⓔ

(E2: $x° / y°$)

Notes:

1. In certain questions, information concerning one or both of the quantities to be compared is centered above the two columns.
2. In a given question, a symbol that appears in both columns represents the same thing in Column A as it does in Column B.
3. Letters such as x, n, and k stand for real numbers.

	Column A	Column B
1.	3^2	2^3
2.	$\dfrac{6 + \frac{3}{4}}{2 - \frac{5}{4}}$	$(3)^2$
3.	$\frac{1}{3}$ of 8	$66\frac{2}{3}\%$ of 4
4.	$\sqrt{\frac{1}{4}} + \sqrt{\frac{1}{25}}$	$\sqrt{\frac{1}{4} + \frac{1}{25}}$
5.	$x = 3$ $y = \frac{1}{6}$ $2x - 18y$	$3x - 36y$

	Column A	Column B
6.	The average of $\sqrt{0.49}$, $\frac{3}{4}$, and 0.8	75%
7.	$B = 0$ $A > 1$ $C > 1$ $2B(A + C)$	$A(B + C)$
8.	$\dfrac{n + a}{a}$	$\dfrac{n}{a} + 1$
9.	$\sqrt{\dfrac{1}{0.25}}$	4

	Column A	Column B

$$x < 0$$
$$y < 0$$

10. $x + y$ $x - y$

In triangle ABC, the measure of $\angle ACB = 60$

11. $\angle B$ $\angle A$

12. Michael has 5 green marbles and the same number of red marbles. The number of red marbles in his collection is $\frac{1}{2}$ the number of white marbles and $\frac{1}{3}$ the number of blue ones.   Philip has 35 marbles in his collection.

13. The number of posts needed by Mr. A to hold a wire fence 120 feet long if he places posts 12 feet apart in a straight line.   Mr. B uses 10 posts to support a similar wire fence.

$$0 < x < 10$$
$$0 < y < 12$$

14. x y

$$a = 1$$
$$b = -1$$

15. $\dfrac{x(a + b)}{v}$ $\dfrac{2x(a + b)}{v}$

Triangle ABC

16. $AB + BC$ AC

This concerns #17 and #18.

17. $\angle 4$ $\angle 3$

18. $\angle 4 + \angle 1$ $\angle 1 + \angle 2 + \angle 3$

	Column A	Column B

19. Mark received either an 80% or a 90% on each of four physics tests.   Sara's average for these four physics tests was 85%.

20. Ann earns $10 a day for clerical work in the dean's office.   Joan earns $50 a week for work in the dean's office during vacation periods.

21. Last week Martin received $10 in commission for selling 100 copies of a magazine.   Last week Miguel sold 100 copies of this magazine. He received his basic salary of $5 per week plus a commission of 2¢ for each of the first 25 copies sold, 3¢ for each of the next 25 copies sold, and 4¢ for each copy thereafter.

Measure of $\angle B = 30$

22. $2x$ y

In triangle ABC, $AC < AB$ and $AC > BC$
This concerns #23 and #24.

23.   angle B angle A

24.   angle B angle C

25. b $d - a$

26. $(5)(144)(6)$ $(12^2)(5^2)$

27. $7 \times 5 \times 8 \times 9$ $63 \times 4 \times 10$

28. $\dfrac{(369)(72)}{(3)(4)(5)}$ $\dfrac{(10)(8)(369)}{(2)(3)(4)}$

29. $\dfrac{0.9}{2}$ $\dfrac{3}{10}$

	Column A	Column B
30.	$\sqrt{14.4}$	1.2
31.	$\sqrt{\dfrac{1}{9} + \dfrac{1}{16}}$	$\sqrt{\dfrac{1}{16}} + \sqrt{\dfrac{1}{9}}$
32.	$\dfrac{1}{0.5}$	$\sqrt{4}$
33.	$\left(\dfrac{1}{0.07}\right)^2$	$\dfrac{1}{7}$
	$3^{n+2} = 27$	
34.	n	3
35.	$\sqrt{0.16}$	0.1π
36.	$\dfrac{1}{\sqrt{25}}$	$\dfrac{1}{(0.5)}$
	$3 - 2x < 9$	
37.	x	-3
	$a < 0$ $b < 0$	
38.	$a - b$	$a + b$
	$x > 0$ $y > 0$ $\dfrac{x}{y} > 2$	
39.	$2y$	x
40.	$\sqrt{0.25}$	$\dfrac{1}{4}$
41.	0.425	$3\sqrt{0.0196}$
42.	$\sqrt[3]{8} + 1^5$	$5\sqrt{8}$
43.	5	$\sqrt{9} + \sqrt{16}$
44.	$(0.3)^2$	$\sqrt{0.09}$
45.	a^3	a^2
46.	$n + 1$	$n - 1$
47.	$10 - \dfrac{10}{0.1}$	-90
	$x = \dfrac{1}{y + z}$	
48.	$\dfrac{5}{x}$	$5(y + z)$

	Column A	Column B
	$-10 < z < -1$	
49.	$\dfrac{1}{z^5}$	$\dfrac{1}{z^4}$
	$1 < a < 5$ $1 < b < 5$	
50.	$b - a$	$a - b$
	$0 < x < 20$ $0 < y < 24$	
51.	$\dfrac{x}{y} + 5$	$\dfrac{y}{x} + 10$
	$a : b = 1$	
52.	a	b
53.	$\sqrt{2}$	$\dfrac{2}{\sqrt{2}}$
	$x < 0$	
54.	$x^3 - 1$	1
	$a > 1$	
55.	$\dfrac{\frac{a}{2}}{\frac{2}{a}}$	$\dfrac{a^2}{2}$
56.	x^2	x^3
	$\dfrac{1}{x} = \sqrt{0.04}$	
57.	x	25
58.	$(x + y)^2$	$(x - y)^2$
59.	$\dfrac{a}{b}$	$\dfrac{a}{b} \cdot \dfrac{b}{a}$
60.	$(y + 10)$ $- (y - 2x - 30)$	$(x + 160)$ $- (120 - x)$
61.	$\dfrac{x + y}{y}$	$\dfrac{x}{y} + 1$
	$x = 2$ $y = 1$ $z = 0$	
62.	$4x + 2y - 3z^2$	10
63.	$\dfrac{x^2 - y^2}{x}$	$\dfrac{x^2 + 2xy + y^2}{x - y}$

	Column A	Column B

$$x = 2$$
$$y = 3$$

64.
$$\dfrac{xy}{\dfrac{1}{x} + \dfrac{1}{y}} \qquad\qquad 7$$

$$a > 0$$

65.
$$\dfrac{5a - 3}{6a} + \dfrac{3a + 7}{10a} \qquad \dfrac{17a + 3}{15a}$$

$$x + 13 = 4y$$
$$3x + 4y = 25$$

66. x $\qquad\qquad$ y

$$x^2 + 25 = 10x$$
$$y^2 + 36 = 12y$$

67. x $\qquad\qquad$ y

$$x = 2$$
$$y = 3$$
$$z = 4$$

68.
$$\dfrac{x^2 + y^2}{z^2} \qquad\qquad \dfrac{x + y}{z}$$

$$a - 2b = 11$$
$$5a + 4b = 27$$

69. $5a$ $\qquad\qquad$ 35

$$(x - y)^2 = 16$$
$$x^2 + y^2 = 58$$

70. xy $\qquad\qquad$ $(x - y)^2$

$$x\sqrt{0.01} = 1$$

71. x $\qquad\qquad$ 10

72.
$$\dfrac{x}{y} + \dfrac{a}{b} \qquad\qquad \dfrac{xb + ya}{by}$$

---

73. $(a + b)(a - b)$ $\qquad\qquad$ $a^2 - b^2$

$$x^2 = 4$$
$$y^2 = 9$$

74. x $\qquad\qquad$ y

---

75. 0.3% $\qquad\qquad$ $\dfrac{3}{1000}$

---

76. 0.04% of 600 $\qquad\qquad$ 4% of 600

---

77. 102 $\qquad\qquad$ 102% of 100

	Column A	Column B

78. List price of $500 with discounts of 10% and 20% | List price of $490 less 20%

The average weight of Lori, Michael, and Sara is 45 pounds.

79. The combined weight of Lori and Michael | The combined weight of Lori and Sara

---

80. Percent increase from 800 to 1,400 | Percent increase from 1,400 to 2,000

---

81. The distance covered in 3 hours at an average rate of 40 miles per hour | The distance covered traveling at 50 miles per hour for one hour and 30 miles per hour for the next 2 hours

---

82. The average rate of a motorcyclist who covers a mile in one minute and 20 seconds | The average rate of a motorist traveling for one hour and covering 45 miles

---

83. The work done by m men in h hours | The work done by n men in h hours

---

84. The record of a team that won W games and lost L games | The record of a team that won W games of the $W + L$ games played

---

Perimeter of square $ABCD = 8a$

85. Side of $ABCD$ $\qquad\qquad$ $2a$

Side of square $ABCD = 4$

86. Area of $ABCD$ $\qquad$ Perimeter of $ABCD$

---

87. Area of $\triangle ABC$ $\qquad$ Area of $\triangle DBC$

---

88. $a + b$ $\qquad\qquad$ $c + d$

---

89. a $\qquad\qquad$ b

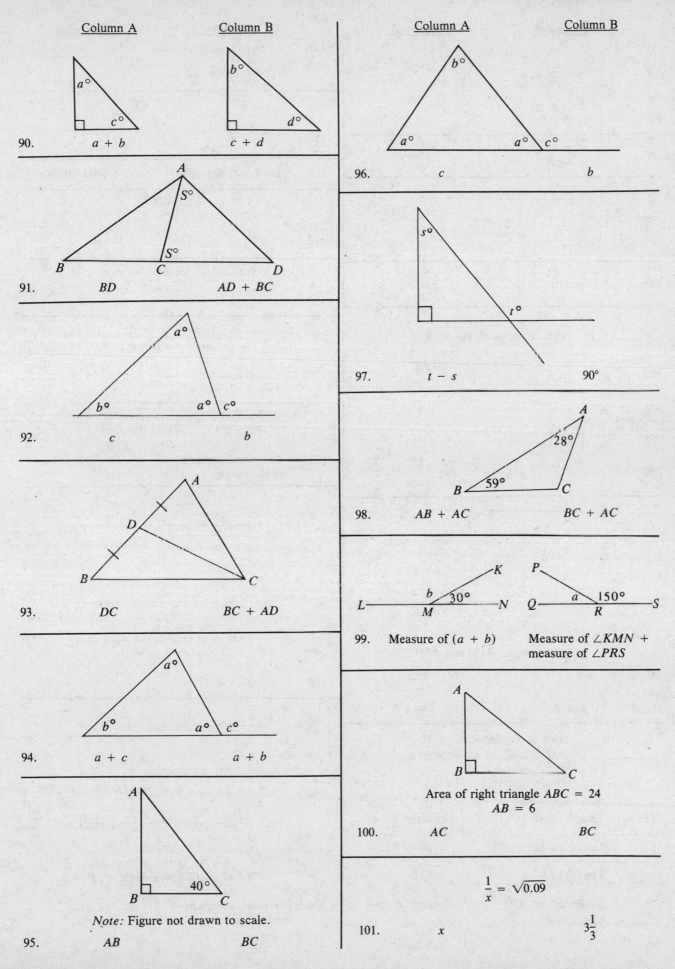

Column A | Column B
Column A | Column B

90. $a + b$ | $c + d$

91. BD | $AD + BC$

92. c | b

93. DC | $BC + AD$

94. $a + c$ | $a + b$

Note: Figure not drawn to scale.

95. AB | BC

96. c | b

97. $t - s$ | $90°$

98. $AB + AC$ | $BC + AC$

99. Measure of $(a + b)$ | Measure of $\angle KMN$ + measure of $\angle PRS$

Area of right triangle $ABC = 24$
$AB = 6$

100. AC | BC

$$\frac{1}{x} = \sqrt{0.09}$$

101. x | $3\frac{1}{3}$

	Column A	Column B

$$a + 2b = 1\frac{1}{3}$$
$$a - b = \frac{1}{3}$$

102.	$3b$	1
103.	$\dfrac{x - y}{-z}$	$\dfrac{y - x}{z}$

$$x = 0$$
$$y > 0$$

104.	$\dfrac{9x^2y^2}{27}$	$\dfrac{1}{3}$
105.	$\dfrac{4}{5}$quart	$\dfrac{1}{5}$gallon

$$a:b = c:d$$
This concerns #106–#109.

106.	$\dfrac{b}{a}$	$\dfrac{d}{c}$
107.	$a + b$	$c + d$
108.	bc	ad
109.	$\dfrac{a}{c}$	$\dfrac{b}{d}$

$$l = 110$$
This concerns #110 and #111.

110.	l	n
111.	$k + m$	$l + n$

Area of triangle $ABC = 72$
Measure of $\angle A$ = measure
of $\angle C$, which = 45°.
This concerns #112–#115.

112.	Length of AB	Length of BC
113.	Length of AB	Length of AC
114.	Length of AB	12
115.	Length of AC + length of BC	Length of AB

	Column A	Column B
116.	The average of $\sqrt{0.81}$, 60%, $1\frac{1}{2}$	3

$$7x = 196$$

117.	$\dfrac{x}{7}$	4
118.	(2)(4)(6)(8)(10)(12)(14)	(16)(14)(12)(10)(8)(6)

$$A > B$$
$$B > C$$

119.	$2A$	$B + C$

$$5 \times 5 \times 5 \times 5 = 10 \times 10 \times T$$

120.	T	10

$$\dfrac{\text{Area of circle } A}{\text{Area of circle } B} = \dfrac{1}{4}$$

121.	Four times the radius of circle A	The radius of circle B

Point O (5, 3) is the center of a circle.
Point P (5, 7) lies on the circle.

122.	The circumference of the circle	8π

ABC and DEF are straight lines.
$a = 20$, $b = 160$

123.	$a + x$	$x + y$

$AB \parallel CD$
O is the center of the circle.
EF of equilateral triangle $OEF = 5$

124.	The shortest distance from AB to CD	10

Column A	Column B

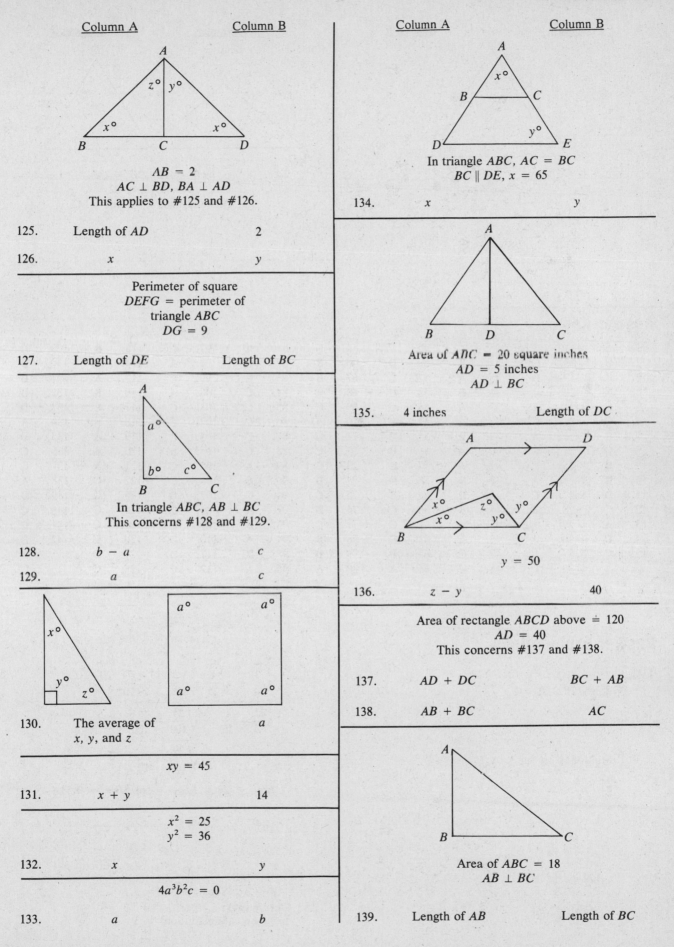

$AB = 2$
$AC \perp BD,\ BA \perp AD$
This applies to #125 and #126.

	Column A	Column B
125.	Length of AD	2
126.	x	y

Perimeter of square
$DEFG$ = perimeter of
triangle ABC
$DG = 9$

	Column A	Column B
127.	Length of DE	Length of BC

In triangle ABC, $AB \perp BC$
This concerns #128 and #129.

	Column A	Column B
128.	$b - a$	c
129.	a	c
130.	The average of x, y, and z	a

$xy = 45$

	Column A	Column B
131.	$x + y$	14

$x^2 = 25$
$y^2 = 36$

	Column A	Column B
132.	x	y

$4a^3b^2c = 0$

	Column A	Column B
133.	a	b

In triangle ABC, $AC = BC$
$BC \parallel DE$, $x = 65$

	Column A	Column B
134.	x	y

Area of ABC = 20 square inches
$AD = 5$ inches
$AD \perp BC$

	Column A	Column B
135.	4 inches	Length of DC

$y = 50$

	Column A	Column B
136.	$z - y$	40

Area of rectangle $ABCD$ above = 120
$AD = 40$
This concerns #137 and #138.

	Column A	Column B
137.	$AD + DC$	$BC + AB$
138.	$AB + BC$	AC

Area of ABC = 18
$AB \perp BC$

	Column A	Column B
139.	Length of AB	Length of BC

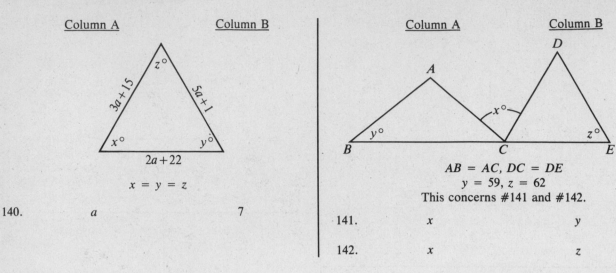

Column A   Column B

$x = y = z$

140. a 7

$AB = AC, DC = DE$
$y = 59, z = 62$
This concerns #141 and #142.

141. x y

142. x z

Answer Key

1.	A	17.	A	33.	A	49.	B	65.	C	81.	A	97.	C	113.	B	129.	D
2.	C	18.	C	34.	B	50.	D	66.	B	82.	C	98.	A	114.	C	130.	B
3.	C	19.	D	35.	A	51.	D	67.	B	83.	D	99.	C	115.	A	131.	D
4.	A	20.	D	36.	B	52.	C	68.	B	84.	C	100.	A	116.	B	132.	D
5.	C	21.	A	37.	A	53.	C	69.	C	85.	C	101.	C	117.	C	133.	D
6.	C	22.	C	38.	A	54.	B	70.	A	86.	C	102.	C	118.	B	134.	A
7.	B	23.	A	39.	B	55.	B	71.	C	87.	C	103.	C	119.	A	135.	D
8.	C	24.	B	40.	A	56.	D	72.	C	88.	C	104.	B	120.	B	136.	C
9.	B	25.	C	41.	A	57.	B	73.	C	89.	A	105.	C	121.	A	137.	C
10.	B	26.	A	42.	B	58.	D	74.	D	90.	D	106.	C	122.	C	138.	A
11.	D	27.	C	43.	B	59.	D	75.	C	91.	C	107.	D	123.	C	139.	D
12.	C	28.	B	44.	B	60.	C	76.	B	92.	A	108.	C	124.	C	140.	C
13.	A	29.	A	45.	D	61.	C	77.	C	93.	B	109.	C	125.	C	141.	C
14.	D	30.	A	46.	A	62.	C	78.	B	94.	A	110.	D	126.	C	142.	B
15.	C	31.	B	47.	C	63.	D	79.	D	95.	B	111.	D	127.	D		
16.	A	32.	C	48.	C	64.	A	80.	A	96.	A	112.	C	128.	C		

Answer Explanations

1. A. $3^2 = (3)(3) = 9$
        $2^3 = (2)(2)(2) = 8$

2. C.   Multiply Column A by $\frac{4}{4}$:
        $\frac{24 + 3}{8 - 5} = \frac{27}{3} = 9$
        $3^2 = (3)(3) = 9$

3. C. $66\frac{2}{3}\% = \frac{2}{3}$
        $\frac{1}{3}$ of 8 = $\frac{2}{3}$ of 4

4. A. $\sqrt{\frac{1}{4}} + \sqrt{\frac{1}{25}} = \frac{1}{2} + \frac{1}{5} = \frac{7}{10}$

        $\sqrt{\frac{1}{4} + \frac{1}{25}} = \sqrt{\frac{25}{100} + \frac{4}{100}}$

        $= \sqrt{\frac{29}{100}} = \frac{1}{10}\sqrt{29}$

        Since $\sqrt{29} = 5.3+$, $\frac{1}{10}$ of $5.3+ = 0.53+$

        $\frac{7}{10}$ or $0.7 > 0.53$

5. C. $2x - 18y$
        $6 - 3$ (Substitution) $= 3$
        $3x - 36y$
        $9 - 6$ (Substitution) $= 3$

6. C. *Hint:* Change all to decimals before adding.

$$\sqrt{0.49} = 0.7$$

$$\frac{3}{4} = 0.75$$

$$\frac{0.8}{2.25 \ \text{Sum}}$$

$$\frac{\text{Sum}}{3} = \text{Average} = 0.75 \text{ or } 75\%$$

Alternatively, observe that 0.75 is the median—the middle between 0.7 and 0.8—and is therefore the average.

7. B. In Column A, since $B = 0$, the value of the expression is zero. In Column B, the zero value (B) is added to a positive value (C) and is then multiplied by another positive value (A) to yield a positive value.

8. C. $\dfrac{n + a}{a} = \dfrac{n}{a} + \dfrac{a}{a}$ or $\dfrac{n}{a} + 1$

9. B. $\sqrt{\dfrac{1}{0.25}} = \dfrac{1}{0.5} = \dfrac{10}{5} = 2$

10. B. Since x and y have negative values, Column $A = -|x| - |y|$ and Column $B = -|x| + |y|$.

11. D. The only fact we may conclude is that the measure of $\angle B$ + the measure of $\angle C$ = 120°.

12. C. We must determine how many marbles Michael has. We know he has 5 green, 5 red, 10 white, and 15 blue for a total of 35.

13. A. Mr. A has $120 \div 12$ spaces between his posts. There is one post at the beginning of the fence and one more at the end of each of the 10 spaces: $1 + 10 = 11$ posts in all.

14. D. The value of x may vary from just above 0 to just below 10, and the value of y may vary from just above 0 to just below 12.

15. C. $\dfrac{x(1 - 1)}{v} = 0$

$\dfrac{2x(1 - 1)}{v} = 0$

16. A. A straight line is the shortest distance between two points.

17. A. Measure of $\angle 4$ = measure of $\angle 3$ + measure of $\angle 2$. Therefore measure of $\angle 4$ > measure of $\angle 3$.   (The measure of the exterior angle of a triangle is equal to the sum of the measures of both remote interior angles.)

18. C. Measure of $\angle 1$ + measure of $\angle 4$ = 180   (Supplementary angles)

Measure of $\angle 1$ + measure of $\angle 2$ + measure of $\angle 3$ = 180   (The sum of the measures in degrees of the angles of a triangle is 180.)

19. D. We may conclude that the sum of Sara's four tests is 340. There are many possible combinations for Mark's performance. For example, if he had three tests with 90% and one worth 80%, his average would be 87.5%.

20. D. We do not know how many days make up the work week for Joan.

21. A. Miguel's salary included (0.02)(25) or $0.50 plus (0.03)(25) or $0.75 plus (0.04)(50) = $2.00 plus $5.00, for a total of $8.25. Martin received $10.00.

22. C. In triangle ABC, $\angle C$ is inscribed in the semicircle and is therefore a right angle. ABC is a 30–60–90 triangle. Therefore, AB is the hypotenuse, and the side opposite the 30° angle $= \dfrac{1}{2}AB = \dfrac{1}{2}y$. Since $x = \dfrac{1}{2}y$, $2x = y$.

For 23, 24:

$\angle C$ is opposite the largest side of ABC.

$\angle B$ is opposite the next larger side of ABC.

$\angle A$ is opposite the shortest side of ABC.

23. A. Angle B is larger than angle A.

24. B. Angle C is larger than angle B.

25. C. $d = a + b$ (See Question 17.)

$d - a = b$ (Subtraction)

26. A. In Column B $(12)^2 = 144$. Cancel 144 from both columns and consider the other values.

Column A = (5)(6) or 30

Column B = $5^2 = 25$

27. C. Use the same principle as in #26, but proceed to cancel:

$$(7)(5)(8)(9) \qquad (63)(4)(10)$$

28. B. Cancel similar values:

$$\frac{(369)(72)}{(3)(4)(5)} \qquad \frac{(10)(8)(369)}{(2)(3)(4)}$$

$$= \frac{6}{5} \qquad\qquad = \frac{10}{3}$$

$$\frac{10}{3} > \frac{6}{5}$$

29. A. $\dfrac{0.9}{2} = \dfrac{9}{20}$

$\dfrac{3}{10} = \dfrac{6}{20}$

$\dfrac{9}{20} > \dfrac{6}{20}$

30. A. $\sqrt{14.4} = 3+$. Do not compute. Estimate to save time.
$3+ > 1.2$

31. B. $\sqrt{\dfrac{1}{9} + \dfrac{1}{16}} = \sqrt{\dfrac{16}{144} + \dfrac{9}{144}} = \sqrt{\dfrac{25}{144}} = \dfrac{5}{12}$

$\sqrt{\dfrac{1}{16}} + \sqrt{\dfrac{1}{9}} = \dfrac{1}{4} + \dfrac{1}{3} = \dfrac{7}{12}$

$\dfrac{7}{12} > \dfrac{5}{12}$

32. C. $\dfrac{1}{0.5} = \dfrac{10}{5} = 2$

$\sqrt{4} = 2$

33. A. $\dfrac{1}{0.07} = \dfrac{100}{7}$

$\dfrac{100}{7} > \dfrac{1}{7}$. Do not compute. Estimate to save time.

34. B. $3^3 = 27$
$3^{n+2} = 3^3$
$n + 2 = 3$
$n = 1$

35. A. $\sqrt{0.16} = 0.4$
$0.1\pi = (0.1)(3.14+) = 0.314+$
$0.4 > 0.314+$

36. B. $\dfrac{1}{\sqrt{25}} = \dfrac{1}{5}$

$\dfrac{1}{0.5} = \dfrac{10}{5} = 2$

37. A. $3 - 2x < 9$
$-2x < 6$ (Subtraction)
$-x < 3$ (Division by 2)
$x > -3$ (Division by -1 [the sign is reversed for division by a negative number])

38. A. Since a and b have negative values:
$a - b = -|a| + |b|$, and
$a + b = -|a| - |b|$
$+|b| > -|b|$

39. B. Since x and y have positive values:
$\dfrac{x}{y} > 2$ becomes

$x > 2y$ (Multiplication by positive y)

40. A. $\sqrt{0.25} = 0.5 = \dfrac{1}{2}$

$\dfrac{1}{2} > \dfrac{1}{4}$

41. A. Estimate the value of $\sqrt{0.0196}$ to be $0.1+$.
$\sqrt{0.0196} = 0.3+$; $0.425 > 0.3+$

42. B. $\sqrt[3]{8} = 2$ $\sqrt{8} = 2+$
$1^5 = 1$ $5(2+) = 10+$
$2 + 1 = 3$
$10+ > 3$

43. B. $\sqrt{9} = 3$; $\sqrt{16} = 4$; $3 + 4 = 7$
$7 > 5$

44. B. $(0.3)^2 = 0.09$
$\sqrt{0.09} = 0.3$
$0.3 > 0.09$

45. D. The values would vary according to whether $a = 0$, $a > 0$, or $a < 0$.

46. A. $+1 > -1$

47. C. $10 - \dfrac{10}{0.1} = 10 - \dfrac{100}{1} = -90$

$10 - 100 = -90$

48. C. $x = \dfrac{1}{y + z}$

$\dfrac{1}{x} = y + z$ (In a proportion the extremes may be interchanged.)

$\dfrac{5}{x} = 5(y + z)$ (Multiply by 5.)

49. B. Since z has a negative value, z^5 has a negative value, and z^4 has a positive value.
Therefore, $\dfrac{1}{z^4} > \dfrac{1}{z^5}$.

50. D. The values of a and b may vary, resulting in many different values for $b - a$ and for $a - b$.

51. D. See Question 50.

52. C. $a:b = 1$ may be written as
$\dfrac{a}{b} = 1$
$a = b$

53. C. $\dfrac{2}{\sqrt{2}} \cdot \dfrac{\sqrt{2}}{\sqrt{2}} = \dfrac{2\sqrt{2}}{2} = \sqrt{2}$

54. B. Since x is negative, x^3 is negative and $x^3 - 1$ also has a negative value.

55. B. $\dfrac{a}{2} \div \dfrac{2}{a} = \dfrac{a}{2} \cdot \dfrac{a}{2} = \dfrac{a^2}{4}$

   $\dfrac{a^2}{2} > \dfrac{a^2}{4}$

56. D. The value of x may vary, for example:
   $x = 0$, $x > 1$ or $x < 1$

57. B. $\dfrac{1}{x} = \sqrt{0.04}$

   $\dfrac{1}{x} = 0.2$

   $x = \dfrac{1}{0.2}$

   $x = \dfrac{10}{2} = 5$

58. D. See Question 56.

59. D. Though Column B $= \dfrac{a}{b} \cdot \dfrac{b}{a} = 1$, $\dfrac{a}{b}$ in Column A has many possible values, depending upon whether a and b are positive, negative, fractions less than 1, etc.

60. C. $(y + 10) - (y - 2x - 30)$
   $y + 10 - y + 2x + 30$
   $2x + 40$
   $(x + 160) - (120 - x)$
   $x + 160 - 120 + x$
   $2x + 40$

61. C. $\dfrac{x + y}{y} = \dfrac{x}{y} + \dfrac{y}{y} = \dfrac{x}{y} + 1$

62. C. $4x + 2y \quad - 3z^2$
   $(4)(2) + (2)(1) - 3(0)^2$
   $8 + 2 \quad - 0 = 10$

63. D. $\dfrac{x^2 - y^2}{x} \qquad \dfrac{x^2 + 2xy + y^2}{x - y}$

   $\dfrac{(x + y)(x - y)}{x} \qquad \dfrac{(x + y)^2}{x - y}$

   Do not be tempted to answer this question by factoring as shown; it can be seen by immediate examination that x and/or y may have values that are negative, positive, or zero.

64. A. $\dfrac{xy}{\dfrac{1}{x} + \dfrac{1}{y}}$

   $\dfrac{(2)(3)}{\dfrac{1}{2} + \dfrac{1}{3}} = \dfrac{6}{\dfrac{5}{6}} = (6)\left(\dfrac{6}{5}\right) = \dfrac{36}{5} = 7\dfrac{1}{5}$

   $7\dfrac{1}{5} > 7$

65. C. $\dfrac{5a - 3}{6a} + \dfrac{3a + 7}{10a}$

   $\dfrac{25a - 15}{30a} + \dfrac{9a + 21}{30a}$

   $\dfrac{34a + 6}{30a}$

   $\dfrac{17a + 3}{15a}$

66. B. Solve for x and y, and compare:
   $x + 13 = 4y \quad$ (1)
   $x - 4y = -13 \quad$ (By subtraction)
   $3x + 4y = 25 \quad$ (2)
   $4x = 12 \quad$ (By addition)
   $x = 3$
   $3 + 13 = 4y \quad$ (By substitution in (1))
   $16 = 4y$
   $4 = y$
   $y > x$

67. B. Solve for x and y and compare:
   $x^2 + 25 = 10x$
   $x^2 - 10x + 25 = 0$
   $(x - 5)(x - 5) = 0$
   $x = 5, 5$
   $y^2 + 36 = 12y$
   $y^2 - 12y + 36 = 0$
   $(y - 6)(y - 6) = 0$
   $y = 6, 6$
   $y > x$

68. B. Substitute the given values:
   $\dfrac{x^2 + y^2}{z^2} \qquad \dfrac{x + y}{z}$

   $\dfrac{4 + 9}{16} = \dfrac{13}{16} \qquad \dfrac{2 + 3}{4} = \dfrac{5}{4} = \dfrac{20}{16}$

   $\dfrac{20}{16} > \dfrac{13}{16}$

69. C. $a - 2b = 11$
   $2a - 4b = 22 \quad$ (Multiply by 2)
   $5a + 4b = 27$
   $7a = 49 \quad$ (By addition)
   $a = 7$
   $5a = 35$

70. A. $(x - y)^2 = 16$
   $x^2 - 2xy + y^2 = 16$
   $x^2 + y^2 - 2xy = 16$
   $58 - 2xy = 16 \quad$ (By substitution)
   $-2xy = -42$
   $xy = 21 \quad$ (Column A)
   $(x - y)^2 = 16 \quad$ (Column B)

71. C. $\sqrt{0.01} = 0.1$
   $(x)(0.1) = 1$
   $x = 10$

72. C. $\dfrac{x}{y} + \dfrac{a}{b}$

$\dfrac{xb}{by} + \dfrac{ay}{by} = \dfrac{xb + ay}{by}$

73. C. $(a + b)(a - b) = a^2 - b^2$

74. D. If $x^2 = 4$, $x = \pm 2$; and if $y^2 = 9$, $y = \pm 3$.

75. C. $0.3\% = \dfrac{0.3}{100} = \dfrac{3}{1000}$

76. B. 0.04% of $600 = (0.04\%)(600) = (0.0004)(600)$
4% of $600 = (0.04)(600)$
By inspection observe that $(0.0004)(600) <$ $(0.04)(600)$, and do no computation.

77. C. 100% of $100 = 100$
2% of $100 = 2$
102% of $100 = 102$

78. B. In successive discounts do not combine percents; but calculate the second discount after deducting the first discount.
$500 less 10% ($50) = $450
$450 less 20% = $450 − $90 = $360
(Column A)
$490 less 20% = $490 − $98 = $392
(Column B)

79. D. If the average weight of Lori, Sara, and Michael is 45 pounds, all we know is that their combined weights equal 135 pounds.

80. A. $\dfrac{\text{change}}{\text{original}} = \dfrac{600}{800} = \dfrac{3}{4}$ (Column A)

$\dfrac{600}{1400} = \dfrac{3}{7}$ (Column B)

No computation (or change to percent) is necessary. The change or increase is the same in both cases (600), but in Column A the original was 800 and in Column B the original was 1,400. Therefore, the percent increase must be greater for Column A.

81. A. For Column A, apply the formula
Rate × Time = Distance
$(40)(3) = 120$ miles
For Column B, apply the formula for each part of the trip:
$(50)(1) = 50$ miles
$(30)(2) = 60$ miles
Total = 110 miles

82. C. Convert 1 minute and 20 seconds to hours.
1 min. 20 sec. $= 1\dfrac{1}{3}$ min. $= \dfrac{4}{3}$ min. or
$\left(\dfrac{1}{60}\right)\left(\dfrac{4}{3}\right)$ hr. or $\dfrac{1}{45}$ hr.
Apply the formula
$\text{Rate} = \dfrac{\text{Distance (miles)}}{\text{Time (hours)}}$
$= \dfrac{1 \text{ mile}}{\dfrac{1}{45} \text{ hr.}}$ or $\dfrac{45 \text{ miles}}{1 \text{ hr.}}$ (Column A)

83. D. If $m > n$, then the work done in Column A > the work done in Column B.
If $n > m$, then the work done in Column B > the work done in Column A.
Another possibility is that m and n are equal.

84. C. In Column A, the team played a total of $W + L$ games, the same as specified in Column B.

85. C. Side of the square $= \dfrac{1}{4}$ perimeter $= \left(\dfrac{1}{4}\right)(8a)$
or $2a$.

86. C. Area $= 4^2 = 16$. Perimeter $= 4 \times 4 = 16$.

87. C. Both triangles share base BC. The altitudes of the two triangles are equal lengths between parallel segments DA and BC.

88. C. Acute angles of right triangles are complementary.

89. A. The third angle in the upper triangle $= 180°$ $- 100°$ or $80°$. Therefore, $a° = 80$ because alternate interior angles of parallel lines are equal (Column A). For Column B, $b° = 60$ because vertical angles have equal measures.

90. D. In the triangles, $a + c = 90$ and $b + d = 90$ (see Question 88). However, we cannot use this information to find $a + b$ or $c + d$.

91. C. $CD = AD$ (Since $S° = S°$)
$BD = BC + CD$ (The whole is equal to the sum of its parts.)
$BD = BC + AD$ (By substitution)

92. A. $c = b + a$ (See Question 17.)
$c > b$

93. B. $BC + BD > DC$ (see Question 16). Since $AD = BD$,
$BC + AD > DC$ (By substitution)

94. A. $a + c = 180$ (supplementary angles)
$a + b < 180$ (The sum of the measures in degrees of the angles of a triangle is 180°.)

95. B. The measure of $\angle CAB = 50°$
Side BC is opposite the larger of the two acute angles.

96. A. $c + a = 180$ (See Question 94.)
$c = 180 - a$ (By subtraction)
$b + a < 180$ (See Question 94.)
$b < 180 - a$ (By subtraction)
Therefore, $c > b$.

97. C. $t = s + 90°$ (See Question 17.)
$t - s = 90°$ (By subtraction)

98. A. The measure of $\angle C = 180° - (59° + 28°) = 93°$
AB (side opposite angle with measure of 93°) is larger than BC (side opposite angle with measure of 28°). Therefore, $AB + AC > BC + AC$.

99. C. $a = 180° - 150° = 30°$
$b = 180° - 30° = 150°$
$a + b = 180°$ (Column A)
$30° + 150° = 180°$ (Column B)

100. A. Area $= \frac{1}{2}(AB)(BC)$

$24 = \frac{1}{2}(6)(BC)$, or $BC = 8$

Observe that ABC is a 3–4–5 right triangle with sides 6–8–10. Therefore, $AC = 10$.

101. C. $\frac{1}{x} = \sqrt{0.09} = 0.3 = \frac{3}{10}$

$\frac{1}{x} = \frac{3}{10}$

$x = \frac{10}{3} = 3\frac{1}{3}$

102. C. $a - b = \frac{1}{3}$ (Given)

$-a + b = -\frac{1}{3}$ (Multiply by -1.)

$a + 2b = 1\frac{1}{3}$ (Given)

$\overline{}$

$3b = 1$ (By addition)

103. C. $\left(\dfrac{x - y}{-z}\right) \times (-1) = \dfrac{-x + y}{z}$ or $\dfrac{y - x}{z}$

104. B. Do not compute. Since $x = 0$, the value of the expression in Column A is zero.

105. C. Since 1 gallon = 4 quarts, $\frac{1}{5}$ gallon $= \frac{4}{5}$ quarts.

106. C. $a : b = c : d$ may be written as

$\dfrac{a}{b} = \dfrac{c}{d}$ or, by exchanging

means and extremes, as

$\dfrac{b}{a} = \dfrac{d}{c}$

107. D. The test for changing the terms of a proportion is that the product of the means must equal the product of the extremes. In Question 106, $bc = ad$.

108. C. See Question 107.

109. C. Note that $bc = ad$.

110. D. We can conclude only that $k + m + n = 360 - 110$.

111. D. See Question 110.

112. C. We are told that the measure of $\angle A = 45$, the measure of $\angle C = 45$, and $\angle B$ is a right angle. ABC is an isosceles right triangle, and $AB = BC$.

113. B. In a 45–45–90 triangle, the hypotenuse $=$ leg$\sqrt{2}$. $AC = AB\sqrt{2}$. Therefore, $AC > AB$. Or, more simply, the hypotenuse is always the largest side in any right triangle.

114. C. Area of $ABC = 72 = \frac{1}{2}(AB)(BC) = \frac{1}{2}(12)(12)$

$AB = 12$

115. A. In ABC, $AB = BC = 12$ and $AC = 12\sqrt{2}$
$12\sqrt{2} + 12 > 12$
Or, without computation, observe that AB is the hypotenuse and recall that a straight line is the shortest distance between two points.

116. B. Change each one to decimal form, add, and divide by 3:
$\sqrt{0.81} = 0.9$
$60\% = 0.6$
$1\frac{1}{2} = 1.5$
Total $= 3.0$
Average $= \dfrac{3.0}{3} = 1$ (Column A)
$3 > 1$

117. C. $7x = 196$
$x = 28$
$\dfrac{x}{7} = 4$

118. B. Cancel $(6)(8)(10)(12)(14)$ from both columns. The result is $(2)(4)$ in Column A and (16) in Column B.
$16 > (2)(4)$

119. A. Since $A > B$,
$$2A > 2B$$
$$B + C > 2B$$
$$2A > B + C$$

120. B. Find the value of T.
$$100T = 625$$
$$T = 6.25$$
$$10 > 6.25$$

121. A. If the area of circle B is four times the area of circle A, then the radius of B must be twice the radius of A. Four times the radius of circle A is greater than the radius of circle B.

122. C. The distance between the center of the circle $(5, 3)$ and a point on the circle $(5, 7)$ is the radius of the circle. The distance, using the formula $\sqrt{(x_1 - x_2)^2 + (y_1 - y_2)^2} = \sqrt{0 + (7 - 3)^2} = \sqrt{16} = 4$
Circumference $= 2\pi$ (radius). Since the radius $= 4$, the circumference is 8π (Column A).

123. C. If $a = 20$, $x = 160$.
If $b = 160$, $y = 20$.
$a + x = 180$ and $x + y = 180$.

124. C. The shortest distance from AB to CD is the diameter of circle O. Since triangle OEF is equilateral, radii OE and OF are equal; $EF = 5$. Therefore, the diameter $= 10$.

125. C. $AB = AD = 2$

126. C. In right triangle ABC, $x + z = 90$.
Since $\angle A$ is a right angle $y + z = 90$.
Therefore, $x = y$.

127. D. Perimeter of the square $= 9 \times 4 = 36$
Perimeter of the triangle $= 36$
Since side BC could possibly be the side of a right or an isosceles or a scalene triangle, the comparison cannot be made.

128. C. $b = 90$
$a + c = 90$
$b = a + c$
$b - a = c$

129. D. We can conclude only that $a + c = 90$.

130. B. $x + y + z = 180$; the average $= 60$
The value of a in the square $= 90$

131. D. The trap here is to conclude incorrectly that the product 45 is obtained only by $(9)(5)$.

132. D. $x = \pm 5$ and $y = \pm 6$

133. D. The terms a and b may have zero values or positive or negative nonzero values.

134. A. In triangle ABC, since $x = 65$, the measure of $\angle ABC$ + the measure of $\angle ACB = 115$ and the measure of angle $ACB = \frac{1}{2}(115)$ or $57\frac{1}{2}$.
The measure of $\angle AED =$ the measure of $\angle ACB$ since $BC \parallel DE$ and they are corresponding angles. Therefore, $y = 57\frac{1}{2}$.
Therefore, $x > y$.

135. D. Since the area of $ABC = 20$ square inches and $AD = 5$, $BC = 8$. However, we have no information about the relationship of DC to BC.

136. C. Since $y = 50$, the measure of $\angle BCD = 100$; and, since this is a parallelogram, the measure of $\angle ABC = 80$ and $x = 40$.
In the triangle, $x + y + z = 180$, or
$$40 + 50 + z = 180$$
$$z = 90$$
$z - y = 90 - 50 = 40$ (Column A)

137. C. Since the area of $ABCD = 120$, $DC = 3$ and
$AD = BC = 40$ and
$DC = AB = 3$
$AD + DC = 43 = BC + AB = 43$
Or, without computation, observe that equal sides are added to equal sides.

138. A. A straight line is the shortest distance between two points.

139. D. We may not assume that this is a special right triangle, 45–45–90 or 30–60–90.

140. C. This is an equilateral triangle.
$$5a + 1 = 3a + 15$$
$$2a = 14$$
$$a = 7$$

141. C. Since $AC = AB$,
$y =$ the measure of $\angle ACB = 59$ (Column B)
Since $DE = DC$,
$z =$ the measure of $\angle DCE = 62$
Measure of $\angle ACB + x +$ measure of $\angle DCE = 180$
$$59 + x + 62 = 180$$
$$x = 180 - 121$$
$$x = 59$$ (Column A)

142. B. See Question 141.
$x = 59$, $z = 62$

When we divide 12 by 4, the resulting quotient is 3. We say that 4 and 3 are **factors** of 12. Likewise 5 and 4 are factors of 20.

A **prime number** is a whole number greater than 1 and divisible only by itself and by 1. Examples of prime numbers are 2, 3, 5, 7. The integer 14 is not prime since it is divisible by 2 and by 7.

A collection of numbers in which each number is a successor of the number that precedes it makes up a group of **consecutive integers.** If n is an integer, then the following are consecutive integers: n, $n + 1, n + 2, n + 3, n + 4, \ldots$.

The **least common multiple** of two numbers is the smallest number that is a common multiple of both numbers. For example, the least common multiple of 2 and 3 is 6. This is useful in adding or subtracting fractions, where denominators must be the same.

Fundamental Operations

Addition

To add numbers with the same sign, add their absolute values and write the sum with their common sign.

Examples

■ $14 + 12 = 26$

■ $-8 + (-9) = -17$

To add numbers with opposite signs, find their absolute values, subtract the lesser absolute value from the greater, and then write the result with the same sign as that of the number with the greater absolute value. For example, to add -36 and $+14$, subtract 14 from 36 to get 22 and write the result as -22 since -36 has the greater absolute value.

To add three or more signed numbers you can, of course, combine them in the order given, but it is simpler to add all the positives and all the negatives, and then combine the results. Thus to add $-22 + 37 + 64 - 18 - 46 + 13 - 85$, add $37 + 64 + 13 = 114$ and $-22 - 18 - 46 - 85 = -171$. Then combine the results: $-171 + 114 = -57$.

Subtraction

Subtraction is based on the following property:

$$a - b = a + (-b)$$

This means that subtracting a number is the same as adding its opposite. The number being subtracted is called the **subtrahend;** to subtract signed numbers, simply change the sign of the subtrahend and add.

Examples

■ $27 - (-18) = 27 + 18 = 45$

■ $-37 - (-29) = -37 + 29 = -8$

■ $-26 - 14 = -26 + (-14) = -40$

Multiplication

Multiply signed numbers by multiplying their absolute values. If the numbers have the same sign, write your answer with a positive sign. If the signs are opposite, write your answer with a negative sign.

Examples

■ $(+8)(-7) = -56$

■ $(-4)(-3) = 12$

■ $(12)(10) = 120$

■ $(-7)(16) = -112$

Division

Division follows the same rule as multiplication: divide absolute values and use a positive sign for your answer if the original signs were the same, or a negative sign if they were opposite.

Examples

■ $35 \div 7 = 5$

■ $16 \div (-4) = -4$

■ $-27 \div 3 = -9$

■ $-36 \div (-9) = 4$

Divisibility requires identification of quotients that result from division. If the resulting quotient is an integer, we may say that the original dividend is divisible by the divisor. Thus 75 is divisible by 3 and by 5, but not by 2.

Helpful Tips on Divisibility

1. An integer is divisible by 2 if the last digit is evenly divisible by 2.

2. An integer is divisible by 3 if the sum of its digits is evenly divisible by 3.

3. An integer is evenly divisible by 5 if the last digit is either zero or 5.

Order of Operations

If, in a single problem, parentheses are not included to clarify the order of operations, multiplication and division are performed before addition and subtraction. Thus in the problem

$$4 \cdot 3 + 9 \div 3 - 8 \div 4$$

assume that there are parentheses at the plus and the minus sign. Therefore, $(4 \cdot 3) + (9 \div 3) - (8 \div 4)$, or $12 + 3 - 2$, yields the answer 13.

Important Laws

Law of Commutative Operations

In the operations addition and multiplication the order in which we add or multiply does not alter the correct answer. Thus $9 + 8 = 8 + 9$, and $7 \times 6 = 6 \times 7$. Subtraction is not commutative; $5 - 3 \neq 3 - 5$. Division is not commutative; $12 \div 3 \neq 3 \div 12$.

Law of Associative Operations

Similarly, in addition and multiplication we may group the figures in any manner without disturbing the correct answer. Thus $(5 + 6) + 7 = 5 + (6 + 7)$, and $(5 \cdot 6)7 = 5(6 \cdot 7)$.

Distributive Law

This law states that, if a sum is to be multiplied by a number, we may multiply each addend by the given number and add the results. The same result would be obtained if the addition was done first, followed by the multiplication. Thus $5(2 + 3 + 4) = 10 + 15 + 20 = 45$, or $5(9) = 45$.

Identity Law

The identity element for addition is zero. Thus any number plus zero, or zero plus any number, is equal to the given number. The identity element for multiplication is 1. Thus any number times 1, or 1 times any number, is equal to the given number.

Algebraic Concepts and Operations

Important Definitions

In algebra we use letters to represent numbers or sets of numbers. Such letters are called **variables.** When two variables, or a numeral and a variable, are written with no sign of operation between them, we mean that the numbers they represent are to be multiplied:

$$4abc \quad \text{means} \quad 4 \times a \times b \times c$$

When two or more numerals and variables represent numbers that are being multiplied to yield a product, these numerals and variables are called the **factors** of the product. To **factor** means to find the multipliers that yield the product. Thus 6 and 5 are factors of 30. Bear in mind, however, that 6 can also be factored into 2 times 3. To be completely factored, the number 30 must be written as $2 \times 3 \times 5$. The latter is called the **prime factorization** of 30. The numbers 2, 3, and 5 are called **primes** because they have no positive integers as factors except themselves and 1. Note, however, that 1 is not considered to be a prime even though it follows the definition.

Examples

Find the factors of 15, $6ab$, $a^2 + 2ab + b^2$, and $a^2 - b^2$.

- $15 = 5 \times 3$
- $6ab = 3 \times 2 \times a \times b$
- $a^2 + 2ab + b^2 = (a + b)(a + b)$
- $a^2 - b^2 = (a + b)(a - b)$

Factorization of algebraic expressions is discussed on page 331 under the heading "Factoring."

Any factor of a product is called the **coefficient** of the remaining factors, but the usual use of this word is to designate the numerical factor.

Examples

- The coefficient of $6ab$ is 6.
- The coefficient of $-5x^2$ is -5.
- The coefficient of x^4y^2 is 1 because $x^4y^2 = (1)(x^4y^2)$; thus the coefficient is 1.

An **exponent** indicates the number of times a numeral or variable is used as a factor.

Examples

- 2^5 means $2 \times 2 \times 2 \times 2 \times 2 = 32$.
- x^2y^4 means $x \cdot x \cdot y \cdot y \cdot y \cdot y$.

When an exponent is not a positive integer (i.e., a number belonging to the set $\{1, 2, 3, 4, \ldots\}$), it has a different use which we will review later.

A **monomial** is an expression consisting of one term; it is the product of a set of numerals and variables. Examples of monomials are $14x$ and $6ab$. If two monomials have the same variables as factors, and these variables have the same exponents, they are called **similar** or **like** terms.

A **binomial** is the sum or difference of two unlike monomials.

Examples

- $3x + 4y$

- $26x^2y - 72xy$

A **trinomial** has three terms.

Examples

- $9x^2 + 4xy - 2y^3$

- $2x^7y - 16x + 2y$

Monomials, binomials, and trinomials all belong to a family of expressions called **polynomials.** A polynomial may have any number of terms.

Fundamental Operations

Addition and Subtraction

Most algebraic additions and subtractions of like terms are carried out with the aid of a simple pattern known as the **distributive law:**

$$a(b + c) = ab + ac$$

or its corollary:

$$a(b - c) = ab - ac$$

It is used in reverse form to carry out algebraic addition and subtraction.

Examples

- $2x + 3x = (2 + 3)x = 5x$

- $8x^2y + (-3x^2y) = [8 + (-3)]x^2y = 5x^2y$

- $4x^2 - 6x^2 = (4 - 6)x^2 = -2x^2$

- $3abc^2 + abc^2 = (3 + 1)abc^2 = 4abc^2$

When adding polynomials, you will make fewer mistakes if you arrange like terms in vertical columns. For example, to add $3x^2 + 9x - 4$ and $-7x^2 - 4x + 8$, arrange your work as follows:

$$\begin{array}{r} 3x^2 + 9x - 4 \\ -7x^2 - 4x + 8 \\ \hline -4x^2 + 5x + 4 \end{array}$$

When two polynomials are to be subtracted, arrange them in vertical columns according to like terms and change the sign of every term in the subtrahend. For example, to subtract $9x^2 - 3x - 5$ from $2x^2 + 3x - 8$, change the signs of the polynomial as follows: $-9x^2 + 3x + 5$, and then add.

$$\begin{array}{r} 2x^2 + 3x - 8 \\ -9x^2 + 3x + 5 \\ \hline -7x^2 + 6x - 3 \end{array}$$

Multiplication

Before you can multiply polynomials, you must master the multiplication of variables, and thus you must understand a simple rule of exponents:

$$x^2 \cdot x^3 = x \cdot x \cdot x \cdot x \cdot x = x^5$$

The positive integer used as an exponent counts the number of times the variable (its base) is used as a factor. When multiplying factors that have the same base, add their exponents.

Examples

- $x^5 \cdot x^7 = x^{5+7} = x^{12}$

- $(x^2y)(x^3y^2) = x^{2+3} \cdot y^{1+2} = x^5y^3$

To *multiply monomials*, multiply their coefficients and add the exponents of variables with the same base.

Examples

- $(6x^2)(5x^4) = (6 \cdot 5)(x^2 \cdot x^4) = 30x^{2+4} = 30x^6$

- $(6x)(-5x^4) = (6)(-5)(x^1)(x^4) = -30x^5$

To *multiply a polynomial by a monomial*, apply the distributive law by multiplying each term of the polynomial by the monomial.

Examples

- $3x^2(5x^3 + 2x - 3y) = (3x^2)(5x^3) + (3x^2)(2x) - (3x^2)(3y) = 15x^5 + 6x^3 - 9x^2y$

- $-4x^2y(2x^2 - 3xy - 4y^2)$
  $= (-4x^2y)(2x^2) - (-4x^2y)(3xy) - (-4x^2y)(4y^2)$
  $= -8x^4y + 12x^3y^2 + 16x^2y^3$

To *multiply a polynomial by a polynomial*, multiply each term of one polynomial by each term of the other, and combine like terms.

Example

- $(3x^2 - 2x - 7)(2x - 4)$
  $= (3x^2)(2x) - (2x)(2x) - (7)(2x) + (3x^2)(-4)$
  $+ (-2x)(-4) + (-7)(-4)$
  $= 6x^3 - 4x^2 - 14x - 12x^2 + 8x + 28$
  $= 6x^3 - 16x^2 - 6x + 28$

A special case of multiplying polynomials is worth studying separately because of its use in factoring. To *multiply a binomial by a binomial*, note first how the pairs of terms are named:

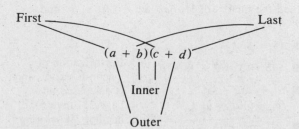

Then multiply the binomials term by term in the order F, O, I, L. Frequently the O and I terms combine to make the product a trinomial or a binomial.

Examples

■ $(x + 3)(x - 2) = x^2 - 2x + 3x - 6$
$\qquad\qquad\qquad = x^2 + x - 6$

■ $(x - 3)(x + 3) = x^2 + 3x - 3x - 9 = x^2 - 9$

Removing Parentheses

Parentheses are used as grouping symbols and as indicators of multiplication. Often it is necessary to remove the parentheses to simplify expressions that have grouped terms.

If the parentheses are preceded by a positive sign, they may be removed with no further alteration.

Example

■ $(x + y) + (3x - 2y) = x + y + 3x - 2y$
$\qquad\qquad\qquad\qquad = x + 3x + y - 2y$
$\qquad\qquad\qquad\qquad = 4x - y$

If the parentheses are preceded by a negative sign, they may be removed only if the sign of each term inside the parentheses is changed to the opposite sign.

Examples

■ $(x + y) - (3x - 2y) = x + y - 3x + 2y$
$\qquad\qquad\qquad\qquad = x - 3x + y + 2y$
$\qquad\qquad\qquad\qquad = -2x + 3y$

■ $(3x^2 + 2x) - (4x^2 - 3x + 5)$
$\quad = 3x^2 + 2x - 4x^2 + 3x - 5 = -x^2 + 5x - 5$

If the parentheses are preceded by a multiplier, carrying out the multiplication by the use of the distributive law will also remove the parentheses.

Examples

■ $(x + y) - 5(x + y) = x + y - 5x - 5y$
$\qquad\qquad\qquad\quad = -4x - 4y$

■ $4(3x^2 + 2x) - 8(x^2 + 3x - 2)$
$\quad = 12x^2 + 8x - 8x^2 - 24x + 16$
$\quad = 4x^2 - 16x + 16$

When additional grouping symbols are needed, brackets, [ ], and braces, { }, are used. If grouping symbols appear within other sets, remove one set at a time, starting with the innermost.

Example

■ $4x - \{2x - 3[(x + 2) - (3 - x)]\}$
$\quad = 4x - \{2x - 3[x + 2 - 3 + x]\}$
$\quad = 4x - \{2x - 3[2x - 1]\}$
$\quad = 4x - \{2x - 6x + 3\}$
$\quad = 4x - \{-4x + 3\}$
$\quad = 4x + 4x - 3$
$\quad = 8x - 3$

Division

To divide a monomial by a monomial, divide the coefficients algebraically and subtract the exponents of factors that have the same base.

Examples

■ $x^6 \div x^2 = x^{6-2} = x^4$

■ $-15x^6y^3 \div 3x^2y = \dfrac{-15}{3} x^{6-2}y^{3-1} = -5x^4y^2$

■ $-18x^3yz^2 \div (-6xyz) = \dfrac{-18}{-6} x^{3-1}y^{1-1}z^{2-1} = 3x^2z$
(Note that $y^0 = 1$ as long as y is any number except 0.)

To divide a polynomial by a monomial, divide each term of the dividend by the divisor.

Examples

■ $(-18x^4 - 6x^3 + 2x^2) \div 2x^2$
$\quad = \dfrac{-18x^4 - 6x^3 + 2x^2}{2x^2}$
$\quad = \dfrac{18x^4}{2x^2} + \dfrac{-6x^3}{2x^2} + \dfrac{2x^2}{2x^2}$
$\quad = -9x^2 - 3x + 1$

■ $\dfrac{6x^{3c} - 8x^{2c}}{2x^c} = \dfrac{6x^{3c}}{2x^c} - \dfrac{8x^{2c}}{2x^c}$
$\qquad\qquad = 3x^{3c-c} - 4x^{2c-c} = 3x^{2c} - 4x^c$

Factoring

To **factor** an expression means to find two or more expressions whose product is the given expression. Every expression can be written as the product of itself and 1. Any expression that cannot be factored in any other way is called **prime.**

Type 1. To factor a polynomial that has a common monomial factor, find the greatest monomial that will divide into each term of the polynomial. This is one factor. Divide the polynomial by this factor to obtain the other factor.

Example

■ Factor $4x^3y^3 - 22xy^2$.
$\quad 4x^3y^3 - 22xy^2 = 2xy^2(2x^2y - 11)$

Type 2. To factor an expression that is the difference of two perfect squares, find the square root of each term. The sum of the two square roots is one factor, and the difference of the two square roots is the other factor. This factoring rule can be easily visualized as follows:

$$a^2 - b^2 = (a + b)(a - b)$$

Example

■ Factor $x^2 - 64$.
$\quad x^2 - 64 = (x - 8)(x + 8)$

Type 3. Trinomials of the Form $ax^2 + bx + c$. When two binomials of the form $mx + n$ and $px + q$ are multiplied, the result is a trinomial with this rather complicated-looking form:

$$mpx^2 + (mq + np)x + nq$$

When the actual multiplication is carried out, of course, the result is not nearly so awesome, since the real numbers m, n, p, and q all combine to produce the simplified form

$$ax^2 + bx + c$$

For example, $(3x + 2)(5x + 7) = 3 \cdot 5 \cdot x^2 + (3 \cdot 7 + 2 \cdot 5)x + 2 \cdot 7$. The latter, however, is simply $15x^2 + 31x + 14$.

Note that the first coefficient of the trinomial is the product of the first coefficients of the factors, and the last coefficient of the trinomial is the product of the last coefficients of the factors. The middle coefficient is the sum of the products of the first and last coefficients taken in a special order: the product of the inner terms and the product of the outer terms.

To factor, you must be able to guess how this process is reversed. Your clues are the factors of the first, ax^2, and last, c, terms of the trinomial $ax^2 + bx + c$. Since several possible factorizations of ax^2 and c may exist, some of your work will involve trial and error.

Examples

■ Factor $x^2 + 8x + 12$. (Note that the factors of x^2 are just x and x, but the factors of 12 that you must try are, in pairs, 12 and 1, -12 and -1, 4 and 3, -4 and -3, 6 and 2, -6 and -2. Your job is to determine which of these will combine to give the coefficient of the middle term, 8.)
   $x^2 + 8x + 12 = (x + 6)(x + 2)$

■ Factor $x^2 - 6x + 8$.
   $x^2 - 6x + 8 = (x - 4)(x - 2)$

■ Factor $x^2 - 3x - 10$.
   $x^2 - 3x - 10 = (x - 5)(x + 2)$

Handling Roots and Radicals

If $x^2 = y$, then x is called a **square root** of y. Thus 10 is a square root of 100 since $10^2 = 100$. Also, -10 is a square root of 100 since $(-10)^2 = 100$. Every positive number has two square roots which are always the opposites of each other. Zero has only one square root, 0. Negative numbers have no square roots in the real-number system.

The **principal square root** of a number is its positive square root if the number has two roots. This principal root is indicated by the radical sign, $\sqrt{}$. Thus $\sqrt{100} = 10$ and $\sqrt{49} = 7$.

The **negative square root** is indicated by a negative sign in front of the radical. Thus $-\sqrt{100} = -10$.

A **radical** is an indicated root of a number or expression. The number under the radical sign is called the **radicand**. The **index** of the root, written as a small number in the "vee" of the radical sign, indicates the number of equal factors that must be multiplied to give the radicand. Thus

$$\sqrt[3]{8} \quad \text{means} \quad \sqrt[3]{8} \cdot \sqrt[3]{8} \cdot \sqrt[3]{8} = 8$$

Since $2 \cdot 2 \cdot 2 = 8$, it follows that $\sqrt[3]{8} = 2$.

Similarly,

$$\sqrt[5]{2} \quad \text{means} \quad \sqrt[5]{2} \cdot \sqrt[5]{2} \cdot \sqrt[5]{2} \cdot \sqrt[5]{2} \cdot \sqrt[5]{2} = 2$$

But there is no whole number or ratio of integers for which the latter equation is true, so $\sqrt[5]{2}$ is an irrational number (see below).

Where no index is written, as in $\sqrt{100}$, the number 2 is understood. Thus $\sqrt{100} = \sqrt[2]{100}$.

A **rational number** is a number that can be expressed as the ratio of two integers (where the denominator is not 0). Thus $2\frac{1}{3}$ is a rational number since $2\frac{1}{3} = \frac{7}{3}$.

An **irrational number** is a number that cannot be expressed as the ratio of two integers. Examples encountered in elementary mathematics include $\sqrt{2}$, $\sqrt[3]{5}$, and π.

Expressions involving radicals can often be simplified. Look first to see whether there are factors that can be removed from the radicand.

Examples

■ $\sqrt{8} = \sqrt{4 \cdot 2} = \sqrt{4}\sqrt{2} = 2\sqrt{2}$
■ $\sqrt{75} = \sqrt{25 \cdot 3} = 5\sqrt{3}$
■ $\sqrt[3]{54} = \sqrt[3]{27}\,\sqrt[3]{2} = 3\sqrt[3]{2}$

Like radicals are radicals that have the same index and same radicand. When all radicals in a sum or difference have been simplified, like radicals are combined.

Examples

■ $2\sqrt{5} + 5\sqrt{5} = (2 + 5)\sqrt{5} = 7\sqrt{5}$
■ $6\sqrt{3} - 3\sqrt{3} = (6 - 3)\sqrt{3} = 3\sqrt{3}$
■ $\sqrt{50} + \sqrt{2} = \sqrt{25}\sqrt{2} + \sqrt{2}$
   $= 5\sqrt{2} + \sqrt{2} = 6\sqrt{2}$
■ $3\sqrt{27} + \sqrt{108} = 3\sqrt{9}\sqrt{3} + \sqrt{36}\sqrt{3}$
   $= (3)(3)\sqrt{3} + 6\sqrt{3} = 15\sqrt{3}$
■ $4\sqrt{32} - 6\sqrt{8} = 4\sqrt{16}\sqrt{2} - 6\sqrt{4}\sqrt{2}$
   $= 4 \cdot 4\sqrt{2} - 6 \cdot 2\sqrt{2} = 4\sqrt{2}$

To simplify the radicals above, we have actually used a law that looks like this:

$$\sqrt{ab} = \sqrt{a}\sqrt{b}$$

The same law when read from right to left tells how to multiply radicals.

Examples

- $\sqrt{18}\sqrt{2} = \sqrt{18 \cdot 2} = \sqrt{36} = 6$
- $(2\sqrt{8})(3\sqrt{18}) = 2 \cdot 3\sqrt{8 \cdot 18}$
  $= 6\sqrt{144} = 6 \cdot 12 = 72$
- $\left(\frac{2}{3}\sqrt{3}\right)(9\sqrt{27}) = \left(\frac{2}{3} \cdot 9\right)(\sqrt{81}) = 54$
- $\left(\frac{1}{3}\sqrt{8}\right)(3\sqrt{2}) = \left(\frac{1}{3} \cdot 3\right)(\sqrt{16}) = 4$

To divide two radicals, first simplify each and then rationalize the denominator by multiplying the numerator and the denominator by the same factors, choosing whatever factors are necessary to make the denominator a rational number.

Examples

- $\frac{\sqrt{75}}{\sqrt{3}} = \frac{5\sqrt{3}}{\sqrt{3}} = 5$ (Remove the common factor, $\sqrt{3}$.)
- $\frac{\sqrt{6}}{\sqrt{3}} = \frac{\sqrt{6} \cdot \sqrt{3}}{\sqrt{3} \cdot \sqrt{3}} = \frac{\sqrt{18}}{3} = \frac{\sqrt{9}\sqrt{2}}{3} = \frac{3\sqrt{2}}{3} = \sqrt{2}$
- $\frac{\sqrt{5}}{\sqrt{2}} = \frac{\sqrt{5} \cdot \sqrt{2}}{\sqrt{2} \cdot \sqrt{2}} = \frac{\sqrt{10}}{2}$
- $\frac{25\sqrt{32}}{5\sqrt{2}} = \frac{25 \cdot 4\sqrt{2}}{5\sqrt{2}} = \frac{100\sqrt{2}}{5\sqrt{2}} = 20$

Solving Equations

An **equation** is a mathematical sentence which states that two expressions name the same number. Thus $4x = 20$ is an equation that is true when x is 5 and false when x is anything else.

A **root** (or **solution**) of an equation is a number that makes the equation true when used in place of the variable. The root of the equation $4x = 20$ is 5. Some equations have more than one root. The roots of the equation $x^2 - 7x + 12 = 0$ are 4 and 3.

Addition, subtraction, multiplication, or division of each side of an equation by the same quantity results in a new equation that has the same roots. (Division or multiplication by zero, of course, is excluded here as in every other place in mathematics.) These operations are used on equations whose roots are not immediately apparent in order to find new equations that are simpler.

Examples

Solve each of the following for x:

- $x - 4 = 12$
  Add 4 to each side.
  $(x - 4) + 4 = 12 + 4$
  $x = 16$

- $x + 4 = 12$
  Subtract 4 from each side.
  $x = 8$

- $4x - 5 = 3x + 2$
  $4x - 3x = 5 + 2$
  $x = 7$

- $\frac{x}{4} = 12$
  Multiply each side by 4.
  $x = 4 \cdot 12 = 48$

- $4x = 12$
  Divide each side by 4.
  $x = \frac{12}{4} = 3$

If each side of an equation is raised to the same power, the new equation will include the roots of the original, but may also have one or more additional roots that do not satisfy the original equation. As a very simple example, note that the only root of the equation $x = -3$ is -3, but that $x^2 = 9$, which is obtained by squaring each side, also has 3 as a solution.

Thus, if you find it necessary to square both sides of an equation, always check your solution set with the original equation and discard any of the added "extraneous" roots.

Examples

Solve each of the following for x:
- $3\sqrt{x + 2} - 3 = 4$
  Add 3 to each side and then divide each side by 3.
  $$\sqrt{x + 2} = \frac{7}{3}$$
  Now square each side and subtract 2.
  $$x + 2 = \frac{49}{9}$$
  $$x = \frac{31}{9}$$
  Check: $3\sqrt{\frac{31}{9} + 2} - 3 \stackrel{?}{=} 4$
  $$3\sqrt{\frac{31 + 18}{9}} - 3 \stackrel{?}{=} 4$$
  $$3\left(\frac{7}{3}\right) - 3 \stackrel{?}{=} 4$$
  $$7 - 3 \stackrel{?}{=} 4$$
  $$4 = 4$$

- $\sqrt{x} + 1 = 0$
  $\sqrt{x} = -1$; $x = 1$, but 1 does not work since $\sqrt{1} + 1 = 2$.
  Thus there is no solution.

■ A man changed a $1 bill and received 14 coins in nickels and dimes. How many nickels did he receive?

Let x = number of nickels; then $14 - x$ will be number of dimes. Also, $5x$ is value, in cents, of x nickels, and $10(14 - x)$ will be value of dimes.
$$5x + 10(14 - x) = 100$$
$$x = 8$$
8 nickels, 6 dimes

Inequalities and the Number Line

On the SAT you will be expected to know the meanings of the symbols > (is greater than), and < (is less than), as well as how to simplify mathematical sentences that use these symbols. The meanings should be intuitively clear from the descriptions above, but more formal definitions follow:

$a > b$ means that $a - b$ is a positive number.
$a < b$ means that $a - b$ is a negative number.

Examples

■ $6 > -6$ because $6 - (-6) = 12$.
■ $8 < 11$ because $8 - 11 = -3$.
■ $-4 < -1$ because $-4 - (-1) = -3$.
■ $-5 < 0$ because $-5 - 0 = -5$.

Many of the concepts of inequalities are easily understood by reference to a number line. Every point on a number line has a real number assigned to it, and every real number is assigned to some point of the line. This matching can be done as follows:

1. On a horizontal line pick any two points. Label the one on the left 0 and the one on the right 1.

2. Set compasses to the distance between these points, and mark off additional points to the right of 1;

and to the left of 0:

3. Assign the remaining rational numbers by dividing up the segments connecting the integers in proportion to the fractional values:

The irrational numbers can be assigned their approximate positions by using their approximate decimal equivalents. Thus $\sqrt{2}$ approximately equals 1.414, π approximately equals 3.14159, and so on.

When a point and a number are paired as described above, the number is called the **coordinate** of the point, and the point is called the **graph** of the number.

The inequality symbols have simple number line meanings. Thus $a > b$ means "a is to the right of b" on the number line; $a < b$ means "a is to the left of b."

To solve inequalities, you may add to, or subtract from, each side the same quantity without changing the solution set.

Examples

■ $x - 4 > 15$
Add 4 to each side.
$x > 19$

■ $x + 5 \leq 3$
Subtract 5 from each side.
$x \leq -2$

The multiplication and division laws are slightly more complicated. Each side may be multiplied or divided by a positive quantity with no change in the solution set. If, however, you multiply or divide by a negative quantity, you must reverse the direction of the inequality symbol. For example, if $3 < 4$ and you multiply each side by -1, the new inequality is $-3 > -4$.

Examples

■ Solve $3x > 12$ for x.
$x > 4$

■ Solve $-4x + 6 < 30$ for x.
$-4x < 24$
$x > -6$ (Direction is changed because each side was divided by a negative number, -4.)

■ Solve for x: $x + 3 < \frac{3}{2}x - 1$.
$$3 < \frac{1}{2}x - 1$$
$$4 < \frac{1}{2}x$$
$$8 < x, \text{ that is, } x > 8$$

■ Solve for x: $3x \geq 7x - 8$.
$-4x \geq -8$
$x \leq 2$

Two inequalities may be added if the inequality signs have the same direction by simply adding the left sides, adding the right sides, and keeping the same inequality sign. If they do not have the same direction, use the fact that $a > b$ means the same as $b < a$ to alter one of the inequalities until they do agree. Since $5 > 2$ and $8 > -1$, it follows that $5 + 8 > 2 + (-1)$.

Examples

■ If $x > 3$ and $y > 8$, then $x + y > 11$. (Add left sides and add right sides: $x + y > 11$.)

■ If $x > 16$ and $y < 15$, then $x - y > 1$ ($x > 16$, $-y > -15$, $x - y > 1$).

When it is necessary to determine which of two fractions is greater, use the following rule:

When both b and d are positive,

$$\frac{a}{b} > \frac{c}{d} \quad \text{if and only if} \quad ad > bc$$

In other words, cross-multiply each denominator with the opposite numerator, and decide which of the products is greater.

Examples

■ $\frac{7}{11} < \frac{2}{3}$ since $3 \times 7 < 2 \times 11$.

■ $-\frac{8}{17} > -\frac{5}{8}$ since $(-8)(8) > (17)(-5)$.

A rule that students have found useful on past SAT examinations is the following:

If $\frac{1}{a} < \frac{1}{b}$ and a and b are both positive or both negative, then $a > b$.

In other words, the fractions may be inverted only if the inequality symbol is reversed when both fractions have the same sign.

If a and b do not have the same sign, then the inequality symbol keeps its direction.

Examples

■ $\frac{1}{2} < \frac{3}{4}$; therefore $2 > \frac{4}{3}$.

■ If $x > 0$ and $\frac{1}{x} < \frac{1}{2}$, then $x > 2$.

■ $\frac{1}{x - 1} > \frac{1}{3}$; therefore $x - 1 < 3$.

Practice Exercises

Roots and Radicals

1. $2\sqrt{3} + 3\sqrt{3} - 4\sqrt{3}$
2. $5\sqrt{32} + 2\sqrt{50}$
3. $10\sqrt{18} - 2\sqrt{50}$
4. $4\sqrt{28} - \sqrt{63} - \sqrt{7}$
5. $\frac{1}{4}\sqrt{96} + \frac{1}{5}\sqrt{150}$
6. $2\sqrt{45} - 3\sqrt{20} + \sqrt{80}$
7. $2\sqrt{75} - 3\sqrt{50} + 2\sqrt{98}$
8. $\frac{1}{3}\sqrt{27} - \frac{1}{2}\sqrt{12}$
9. $\sqrt{7} + 3\sqrt{28} + 2\sqrt{63}$
10. $\sqrt{500} + 2\sqrt{20} - 3\sqrt{45} + \sqrt{125}$

Simplify each of the following products:

11. $(\sqrt{3})(\sqrt{12})$
12. $(\sqrt{21})(\sqrt{3})$
13. $(\sqrt{60})(\sqrt{5})$
14. $(3\sqrt{18})(\sqrt{3})$
15. $(3\sqrt{3})(\sqrt{6})$
16. $(2\sqrt{17})(3\sqrt{17})$
17. $(2\sqrt{3})(\sqrt{7})$
18. $\left(\frac{1}{5}\sqrt{9}\right)(5\sqrt{9})$
19. $\left(\frac{1}{3}\sqrt{2}\right)(\sqrt{5})$
20. $(2\sqrt{2})(8\sqrt{8})$

Simplify each of the following quotients:

21. $\sqrt{75} \div \sqrt{3}$
22. $\sqrt{24} \div \sqrt{2}$
23. $21\sqrt{75} \div 3\sqrt{3}$
24. $\frac{1}{3}\sqrt{54} \div \sqrt{3}$
25. $9\sqrt{27} \div 3\sqrt{27}$
26. $\frac{4\sqrt{20}}{\sqrt{5}}$
27. $\frac{3\sqrt{48}}{\sqrt{3}}$
28. $\frac{6\sqrt{54}}{2\sqrt{3}}$
29. $\frac{25\sqrt{21}}{5\sqrt{3}}$
30. $\frac{2\sqrt{18} + 4\sqrt{2}}{\sqrt{200}}$

Solving Equations

1. Solve for x:
$$8x - (6x - 3) = 9$$

2. Solve for a:
$$p = \frac{cn}{a}$$

3. Solve for y:
$$10y - (3y + 11) = 45$$

4. Solve for h:
$$A = \frac{h}{2}(b + b_1)$$

5. Solve for z:
$$28z - 6(3z - 5) = 40$$

6. Solve for a:
$$S = \frac{n}{2}(a + L)$$

7. Solve for n:
$$2n - (24 - n) = 30$$

8. Solve for d:
$$A = \frac{1}{4}\pi d^2$$

9. Solve for x:
$$3 + 13x = 1 - 3x$$

10. Solve for r:
$$i = Prt$$

11. Solve for y:
$$cd = y(c + d)$$

12. Solve for e:
$$S = 6e^2$$

13. Solve for x:
$$2\sqrt{x + 1} = 3$$

14. Solve for L:
$$P = 2L + 2W$$

15. Solve for π:
$$A = \pi(R + r)(R - r)$$

16. Solve for E:
$$I = \frac{E}{R}$$

17. Solve for t:
$$s = \frac{at^2}{2}$$

18. Solve for x:
$$\frac{6}{\sqrt{x + 5}} = \sqrt{x + 5}$$

19. Solve for y:
$$3\sqrt{3y + 2} - 4 = 0$$

20. Solve for s:
$$K = s^2$$

Solving Verbal Problems Algebraically

1. The highest recorded temperature in South Dakota was 109 degrees, and the lowest was -33 degrees. How many degrees difference is there between these two temperatures?

    (A) 33   (B) 71   (C) 76   (D) 109   (E) 142

2. Arnold is now $x - 10$ years old. How old will he be 10 years from now?

    (A) $x - 20$ (B) $x + 10$ (C) x (D) $10x - 10$
    (E) $x + 20$

3. How many 3-cent stamps can be purchased for c cents?

    (A) $3c$ (B) $\frac{c}{3}$ (C) $\frac{3}{c}$ (D) $300c$ (E) $\frac{3c}{100}$

4. A lending library charges c cents for the first week that a book is borrowed and f cents for each day over 1 week. What is the cost for taking out a book for d days, where d is greater than 7?

    (A) $c + fd$ (B) $c + f(d - 7)$ (C) cd
    (D) $7c + f(d - 7)$ (E) $cd + f$

5. At c cents per orange, what is the price, in dollars, for 1 dozen oranges?

    (A) $12c$ (B) $\frac{c}{12}$ (C) $\frac{12}{100c}$ (D) $\frac{c}{100}$ (E) $\frac{12c}{100}$

6. What is the total weight, in ounces, of a package containing a book that weighs p pounds, if the wrapping material weighs n ounces?

    (A) $16p + n$ (B) $16n + p$ (C) $16(n + p)$
    (D) $\frac{p}{16} + n$ (E) $n + \frac{16}{p}$

7. How many pupils are there in a class if 2 pupils remain after 4 rows of seats are filled, and 9 pupils remain after 3 rows of seats are filled?

    (A) 7   (B) 26   (C) 30   (D) 34   (E) 36

8. To send a parcel by messenger within city limits costs 60 cents for the first pound and 48 cents for each additional pound. What is the cost, in cents, of sending a parcel weighing p pounds?

    (A) $48p$ (B) $60p$ (C) $12p$ (D) $60 + 48p$
    (E) $12 + 48p$

9. Mr. Jones receives a weekly salary of $\$D$ for a 5-day work week. What is his daily salary after receiving a \$5.00 per week increase?

    (A) $D + 5$ (B) $5D$ (C) $\frac{D}{5} + 1$ (D) $\frac{D}{5} + 5$
    (E) $5D + 5$

10. A picnic attracts 240 persons. There are 20 more men than women, and 20 more adults than children. How many men are at this picnic?

    (A) 240   (B) 75   (C) 110   (D) 130   (E) 200

11. Eight years from now Eileen will be twice the age she was 6 years ago. What is her present age?

    (A) 4   (B) 8   (C) 12   (D) 20   (E) 26

12. Saul and Gladys together had \$100. After giving Gladys \$10.00, Saul finds that he has \$4.00 more than $\frac{1}{5}$ the amount Gladys now has. How much does Saul now have?

    (A) \$18.67   (B) \$20.00   (C) \$21.00   (D) \$27.50
    (E) \$35.00

13. The numerator and denominator of a fraction are in the ratio of $2:3$. If 6 is subtracted from the numerator, the result will be a fraction that has a value $\frac{2}{3}$ of the original fraction. The numerator of the original fraction is

(A) 4   (B) 6   (C) 9   (D) 18   (E) 27

14. One half of the student body at the Danby School study French, and one third of the others study Spanish. The remaining 300 do not study any foreign language. How many students are there in the Danby School?

(A) 360   (B) 550   (C) 900   (D) 1,350
(E) 1,800

15. During the month of June the Forster-Gold Fruit Company sold twice as many apricots as pears, three times as many peaches as apricots, and four times as many apples as peaches. If the company sold 300 more peaches than apricots, how many apples were sold?

(A) 75   (B) 180   (C) 300   (D) 720   (E) 1,800

16. Jill is twice as old as Shelly. In y years she will be $1\frac{1}{2}$ times as old. What is Shelly's age at present?

(A) $\frac{y}{4}$ (B) $\frac{2y}{3}$ (C) y (D) $\frac{3y}{2}$ (E) $3y$

17. The sum of six consecutive odd numbers exceeds twice the largest number by 38. Find the sum of the six numbers.

(A) 42   (B) 50   (C) 57   (D) 60   (E) 72

18. The price of a balcony seat in the Avon Theater is $\frac{1}{3}$ the price of a seat in the orchestra. When the theater is completely sold out, the total receipts from the 600 orchestra seats and the 450 balcony seats are \$4,500. What is the price of one orchestra seat?

(A) \$2.00   (B) \$2.30   (C) \$4.00   (D) \$6.00
(E) \$10.00

19. In 1950 there were twice as many radios as television sets in Manchester. By 1952, 200 more television sets had been purchased, but the number of radios still exceeded the number of television sets by 40. How many radios were there in Manchester in 1952?

(A) 160   (B) 280   (C) 320   (D) 360   (E) 480

20. Fifteen houses line Indian Creek. The average space between each house exceeds the average width of each house by 80 feet. The sidewalk, 2,920 feet in length, begins at a point 30 feet before the first house and ends at a point 30 feet beyond the last house. What is the average width, in feet, of each house?

(A) 58   (B) 59   (C) 60   (D) 61   (E) 62

Inequalities and the Number Line

In each of the following, replace the question mark with either $>$ or $<$:

1. $3 \; ? \; 6$
2. $-3 \; ? \; -6$
3. $-3 \; ? \; 6$
4. $-\frac{1}{2} \; ? \; -\frac{1}{4}$
5.   If $x > 0$, $y > 0$, and $\frac{1}{x} > \frac{1}{y}$, then $x \; ? \; y$.
6.   If $x > 0 > y$ and $\frac{1}{y} < \frac{1}{x}$, then $y \; ? \; x$.
7.   If $x > y > 0$, then $x^2 \; ? \; y^2$.
8.   If $y < x < 0$, then $x^2 \; ? \; y^2$.
9.   If $x > 1$, then $x + \frac{1}{x} \; ? \; 2$.
10.   If $x > 1 > y$, then $x^2 + y^2 \; ? \; 0$.

Solve each of the following inequalities for x, and graph the solution set on a number line:

11. $3x > 12$
12. $8x \leqq 5$
13. $4x - 12 > 0$
14. $x + 3 > 4x - 9$
15. $5 - 4x > 2x - 7$
16. $\frac{1}{x} < 5$
17. $\frac{1}{x} > 5$
18. $\frac{2}{x - 1} > \frac{1}{2}$
19. $\frac{1}{x^2} > \frac{1}{4}$
20. $\frac{1}{-\sqrt{x}} < \frac{1}{9}$

Algebraic Fractions

APPLYING FACTORING

Reduce to lowest terms:

1. $\dfrac{3x + 3}{x^2 + 2x + 1}$

2. $\dfrac{2x^2 - 2}{x + 1}$

3. $\dfrac{3y + 3z}{4y + 4z}$

4. $\dfrac{5x + 5y}{5x + 5y}$

5. $\dfrac{x^2 - 25}{3x + 15}$

6. $\dfrac{a^2 - 16}{a^2 - 8a + 16}$

7. $\dfrac{5a + 10}{a^2 + 4a + 4}$

8. $\dfrac{x^2 - 3x - 4}{x^2 + 2x + 1}$

9. $\dfrac{x^2 + 5x - 6}{x^2 - 2x + 1}$

10. $\dfrac{x^2 - 8x + 15}{x^2 + x - 12}$

11. $\dfrac{\dfrac{1}{x} + \dfrac{1}{y}}{\dfrac{1}{xy}}$

12. $\dfrac{\dfrac{1}{x}}{\dfrac{1}{x} - x}$

13. $\dfrac{1 - \dfrac{1}{m}}{\dfrac{1}{m}}$

14. $\dfrac{x - 1}{1 - x^2}$

15. $\dfrac{b - \dfrac{1}{a}}{\dfrac{1}{a}}$

16. $\dfrac{1 - a^2}{a + 1}$

17. $\dfrac{\dfrac{a}{x}}{\dfrac{b}{x^2}}$

18. $\dfrac{\dfrac{1}{a^2} + \dfrac{1}{b^2}}{\dfrac{2}{ab}}$

19. $\dfrac{1 - \dfrac{1}{a}}{1 + \dfrac{1}{a}}$

20. $\dfrac{\dfrac{x}{y} + \dfrac{y}{x}}{\dfrac{1}{xy}}$

Combine into a single fraction:

21. $\dfrac{5x}{3} + \dfrac{x}{4}$

22. $\dfrac{5x}{3} + \dfrac{2x}{4}$

23. $\dfrac{5x - 3}{6x} + \dfrac{3x + 7}{10x}$

24. $\dfrac{x + 4}{3} + \dfrac{x + 5}{4}$

25. $\dfrac{5}{2a} - \dfrac{a - b}{6a^2}$

26. $\dfrac{3}{a - 5} + \dfrac{2}{5 - a}$

27. $\dfrac{5a}{4} - \dfrac{a}{3}$

28. $\dfrac{1}{x} - \dfrac{1}{y}$

29. $\dfrac{1}{5} + \dfrac{1}{x}$

30. $\dfrac{3}{x^2} - \dfrac{2}{x}$

FUNDAMENTAL OPERATIONS

Multiply:

31. $\dfrac{3a^2b}{2} \cdot \dfrac{8}{ab^2}$

32. $\dfrac{a^2 - b^2}{12a^3} \cdot \dfrac{6a}{a - b}$

33. $\dfrac{(x + 5)^2}{25} \cdot \dfrac{5}{(x + 5)}$

34. $\left(\dfrac{a}{b} + 2\right)\left(\dfrac{a}{b} - 2\right)$

35. $\left(5 + \dfrac{5}{3a}\right)\left(\dfrac{1}{a} + 3\right)$

36. $\left(\dfrac{1}{9} - x^2\right)\left(\dfrac{9}{1 - 3x}\right)$

37. $\left(\dfrac{1}{a^2} - \dfrac{1}{b^2}\right)\left(\dfrac{2ab}{a - b}\right)$

38. $\left(x + \dfrac{x^2}{y}\right)\left(\dfrac{y^2}{y^2 - x^2}\right)$

39. $\left(\dfrac{x^2 - 1}{x - 1}\right)\left(\dfrac{x - 1}{x + 1}\right)$

40. $\left(\dfrac{x^2 + 4}{x^2 - 4}\right)\left(\dfrac{(x - 2)}{x + 2}\right)$

Divide:

41. $\left(2 + \dfrac{x}{y}\right) \div \left(2 - \dfrac{x^2}{y^2}\right)$

42. $\left(1 - \dfrac{a}{b}\right) \div \left(b - \dfrac{a^2}{b}\right)$

43. $\left(\dfrac{x^2}{y^2} - 16\right) \div \left(\dfrac{x}{y} - 4\right)$

44. $\left(5 + \dfrac{5}{3a}\right) \div \left(\dfrac{1}{9a} - a\right)$

45. $\left(\dfrac{1}{9} - x^2\right) \div \left(x - \dfrac{1}{3}\right)$

Simplify:

46. $\dfrac{\dfrac{x^2 - 4y^2}{y^2}}{\dfrac{x + 2y}{y}}$

47. $\dfrac{1 - \dfrac{3}{x}}{1 - \dfrac{9}{x^2}}$

48. $\dfrac{a + \dfrac{1}{4}}{a^2 - \dfrac{1}{16}}$

49. $\dfrac{x - \dfrac{y^2}{x}}{1 + \dfrac{y}{x}}$

50. $\dfrac{\dfrac{x}{y} - \dfrac{y}{x}}{\dfrac{y}{x} - 1}$

Answer Key

Roots and Radicals

1. $\sqrt{3}$
2. $30\sqrt{2}$
3. $20\sqrt{2}$
4. $4\sqrt{7}$
5. $2\sqrt{6}$
6. $4\sqrt{5}$

7. $10\sqrt{3} - \sqrt{2}$
8. 0
9. $13\sqrt{7}$
10. $10\sqrt{5}$
11. 6
12. $3\sqrt{7}$

13. $10\sqrt{3}$
14. $9\sqrt{6}$
15. $9\sqrt{2}$
16. 102
17. $2\sqrt{21}$
18. 9

19. $\dfrac{1}{3}\sqrt{10}$
20. 64
21. 5
22. $2\sqrt{3}$
23. 35
24. $\sqrt{2}$

25. 3
26. 8
27. 12
28. $9\sqrt{2}$
29. $5\sqrt{7}$
30. 1

Solving Equations

1. 3

2. $\dfrac{cn}{p}$

3. 8

4. $\dfrac{2A}{b + b_1}$

5. 1

6. $\dfrac{2S - nL}{n}$

7. 18

8. $\pm\sqrt{\dfrac{4A}{\pi}}$

9. $-\dfrac{1}{8}$

10. $\dfrac{i}{Pt}$

11. $\dfrac{cd}{c + d}$

12. $\pm\sqrt{\dfrac{s}{6}}$

13. $1\dfrac{1}{4}$

14. $\dfrac{P - 2W}{2}$

15. $\dfrac{A}{(R + r)(R - r)}$

16. IR

17. $\pm\sqrt{\dfrac{2s}{a}}$

18. 1

19.. $-\dfrac{2}{27}$

20. $\pm\sqrt{k}$

Solving Verbal Problems Algebraically

1. E
2. C
3. B
4. B

5. E
6. A
7. C
8. E

9. C
10. B
11. D
12. B

13. D
14. C
15. E
16. C

17. E
18. D
19. E
20. C

Inequalities and the Number Line

1. <
2. >
3. <
4. <
5. <
6. <
7. >
8. <
9. >
10. >
11. $x > 4$;
12. $x \leqq \dfrac{5}{8}$;
13. $x > 3$;

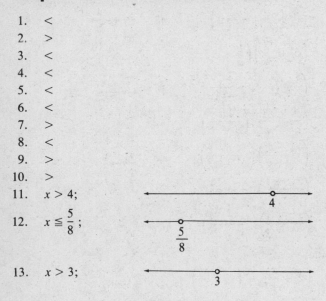

14. $x < 4$;
15. $x < 2$;
16. $x < 0$ or $x > \dfrac{1}{5}$;
17. $0 < x < \dfrac{1}{5}$;
18. $1 < x < 5$;
19. $-2 < x < 2$;
20. $-9 < \sqrt{x}$ is true

for all values of $x \geq 0$ since $\sqrt{x}$ is always positive or 0. Since $\sqrt{x}$ is in the denominator in the original inequality, $x > 0$.

Algebraic Fractions

APPLYING FACTORING

1. $\dfrac{3}{x + 1}$

2. $2x - 2$

3. $\dfrac{3}{4}$

4. 1

5. $\dfrac{x - 5}{3}$

6. $\dfrac{a + 4}{a - 4}$

7. $\dfrac{5}{a + 2}$

8. $\dfrac{x - 4}{x + 1}$

9. $\dfrac{x + 6}{x - 1}$

10. $\dfrac{x - 5}{x + 4}$

11. $x + y$

12. $\dfrac{1}{1 - x^2}$

13. $m - 1$

14. $-\dfrac{1}{x + 1}$

15. $ab - 1$

16. $1 - a$

17. $\dfrac{ax}{b}$

18. $\dfrac{b^2 + a^2}{2ab}$

19. $\dfrac{a - 1}{a + 1}$

20. $x^2 + y^2$

21. $\dfrac{23x}{12}$

22. $\dfrac{13x}{6}$

23. $\dfrac{17x + 3}{15x}$

24. $\dfrac{7x + 31}{12}$

25. $\dfrac{14a + b}{6a^2}$

26. $\dfrac{1}{a - 5}$

27. $\dfrac{11a}{12}$

28. $\dfrac{y - x}{xy}$

29. $\dfrac{x + 5}{5x}$

30. $\dfrac{3 - 2x}{x^2}$

FUNDAMENTAL OPERATIONS

31. $\dfrac{12a}{b}$

32. $\dfrac{a + b}{2a^2}$

33. $\dfrac{x + 5}{5}$

34. $\dfrac{a^2 - 4b^2}{b^2}$

35. $\dfrac{45a^2 + 30a + 5}{3a^2}$

36. $1 + 3x$

37. $-\dfrac{2b + 2a}{ab}$

38. $\dfrac{xy}{y - x}$

39. $x - 1$

40. $\dfrac{x^2 + 4}{x^2 + 4x + 4}$

41. $\dfrac{2y^2 + xy}{2y^2 - x^2}$

42. $\dfrac{1}{b + a}$

43. $\dfrac{x + 4y}{y}$

44. $\dfrac{15}{1 - 3a}$

45. $-\dfrac{3x + 1}{3}$

46. $\dfrac{x - 2y}{y}$

47. $\dfrac{x}{x + 3}$

48. $\dfrac{4}{4a - 1}$

49. $x - y$

50. $-\dfrac{x + y}{y}$

Fractions

Important Definitions

A **fraction** is an indicated division. Thus $\dfrac{1}{2}$ means 1 divided by 2. In a fraction the top number is called the **numerator** and the bottom number, the **denominator.** An **improper fraction** is one in which the numerator is greater than the denominator. Thus $\dfrac{19}{5}$ is an improper fraction.

A **mixed number** indicates the sum of a whole number and a proper fraction. Thus $3\dfrac{1}{4}$ is a mixed number representing $3 + \dfrac{1}{4}$.

In many applications it is necessary to convert mixed numbers to improper fractions. This can be done by changing the whole number to a fraction with the same denominator as the fractional part and then adding the two fractions. A shortcut that saves time is to multiply the whole number by the denominator and then add the numerator of the fractional part to get the numerator of the result. The denominator is unchanged.

Examples

■ $6\dfrac{1}{2} = \dfrac{6 \times 2 + 1}{2} = \dfrac{13}{2}$

■ $9\dfrac{5}{6} = \dfrac{6 \times 9 + 5}{6} = \dfrac{59}{6}$

To convert an improper fraction to a mixed number, divide the numerator by the denominator. Remember:

$$\dfrac{\text{Dividend}}{\text{Divisor}} = \text{Quotient} + \dfrac{\text{Remainder}}{\text{Divisor}}$$

Example

■ $\dfrac{24}{7}$ means $7\overline{)24}$.

$$\begin{array}{r} 3 \\ 7\overline{)24} \\ \underline{21} \\ 3 \end{array}$$

Therefore $\dfrac{24}{7} = 3\dfrac{3}{7}$.

Equivalent Fractions

Principle 1: $\dfrac{a}{b} = \dfrac{a}{b} \times \dfrac{c}{c} = \dfrac{ac}{bc}$ if c is not 0.

This principle says that we may multiply the numerator and denominator of a fraction by the same nonzero number without changing the value of the fraction.

Examples

■ $\dfrac{1}{4} = \dfrac{1 \times 3}{4 \times 3} = \dfrac{3}{12}$

■ $\dfrac{1}{4} = \dfrac{1 \times 7}{4 \times 7} = \dfrac{7}{28}$

By using this principle, we can write any fraction with any denominator (except zero) that we choose without changing the value of the fraction.

Examples—Changing to Equivalent Fractions with Denominators of 36

■ $\dfrac{8}{12} = \dfrac{8 \times 3}{12 \times 3} = \dfrac{24}{36}$

■ $\dfrac{1}{4} = \dfrac{1 \times 9}{4 \times 9} = \dfrac{9}{36}$

■ $\dfrac{1}{3} = \dfrac{1 \times 12}{3 \times 12} = \dfrac{12}{36}$

■ $\dfrac{4}{9} = \dfrac{4 \times 4}{9 \times 4} = \dfrac{16}{36}$

Example—Changing to an Equivalent Fraction with a Denominator of $x^2 - 4$

■ $\dfrac{3}{x - 2} = \dfrac{3(x + 2)}{(x - 2)(x + 2)} = \dfrac{3x + 6}{x^2 - 4}$

Principle 1 can also be used to simplify fractions by removing factors that appear in both the numerator and the denominator. This use can perhaps be seen more clearly if the principle is rewritten as

$$\dfrac{ac}{bc} = \dfrac{a}{b} \quad \text{if } c \text{ is not } 0$$

It is easier to apply this principle when the numerator and denominator are first factored.

Examples

■ $\dfrac{4y - 2}{2y^2 - 5y + 2} = \dfrac{2(2y - 1)}{(2y - 1)(y - 2)} = \dfrac{2}{y - 2}$

■ $\dfrac{2x - 1}{2x^2 - x} = \dfrac{2x - 1}{x(2x - 1)} = \dfrac{1}{x}$

Signs of Fractions

Principle 2: $+ \dfrac{a}{b} = + \dfrac{-a}{-b} = - \dfrac{-a}{+b} = - \dfrac{+a}{-b}$.

This principle can be simply stated as follows: If any two of the three signs of a fraction are changed, the value of the fraction will remain unchanged.

Examples—Eliminating Negative Signs

■ $\dfrac{-2}{-3} = \dfrac{2}{3}$

■ $- \dfrac{2}{-3} = \dfrac{2}{3}$

■ $\dfrac{-a - 3}{-4} = \dfrac{-(a + 3)}{-4} = \dfrac{a + 3}{4}$

■ $- \dfrac{3 - a}{-4} = \dfrac{a - 3}{-4}$

Operations Involving Fractions
Addition and Subtraction

Principle 3: $\dfrac{a}{c} + \dfrac{b}{c} = \dfrac{a + b}{c}$ and $\dfrac{a}{c} - \dfrac{b}{c} = \dfrac{a - b}{c}$.

This principle states that the sum (or difference) of two fractions which have the same denominator is a fraction with the same denominator and with a numerator that is the sum (or difference) of the original numerators. If the fractions to be combined have different denominators, use Principle 1 to change them to the same denominator. After you have found a sum or difference, be sure to reduce your answer to lowest terms.

Examples

■ $\dfrac{2}{7} + \dfrac{3}{7} + \dfrac{1}{7} = \dfrac{2 + 3 + 1}{7} = \dfrac{6}{7}$

■ $\dfrac{1}{2} + \dfrac{1}{3} + \dfrac{1}{4} = \dfrac{6}{12} + \dfrac{4}{12} + \dfrac{3}{12} = \dfrac{13}{12}$

■ $\dfrac{3}{6} - \dfrac{2}{6} = \dfrac{1}{6}$

■ $\dfrac{11}{12} - \dfrac{3}{4} = \dfrac{11}{12} - \dfrac{9}{12} = \dfrac{2}{12} = \dfrac{1}{6}$

■ $12\dfrac{3}{4} - 1\dfrac{7}{8} = \dfrac{51}{4} - \dfrac{15}{8} = \dfrac{102}{8} - \dfrac{15}{8} = \dfrac{87}{8}$

■ $\dfrac{5}{3b} + \dfrac{2}{3b} + \dfrac{1}{3b} + \dfrac{4}{3b} = \dfrac{12}{3b} = \dfrac{4}{b}$

■ $\dfrac{2a}{b} - \dfrac{c}{b} - \dfrac{a}{2b} + \dfrac{4c}{3b}$

$\quad = \dfrac{12a}{6b} - \dfrac{6c}{6b} - \dfrac{3a}{6b} + \dfrac{8c}{6b} = \dfrac{9a + 2c}{6b}$

■ $\dfrac{5}{a - 3} + \dfrac{3}{3 - a} = \dfrac{5}{a - 3} + \dfrac{-3}{a - 3} = \dfrac{2}{a - 3}$

To find the lowest common denominator (LCD) when combining fractions, proceed as follows:

1. Factor each denominator completely.

2. Form the LCD by using every factor that appears in any denominator.

3. Use each factor in the LCD as many times as it appears in the denominator in which it occurs the most times.

For example, if you wish to add $\dfrac{1}{360} + \dfrac{1}{175}$, the two denominators are 360 and 175.

$$360 = 2^3 \cdot 3^2 \cdot 5$$
$$175 = 5^2 \cdot 7$$

Thus the LCD must have 2, 3, 5, and 7 as its factors; the LCD $= 2^3 3^2 5^2 7$.

Examples

■ $\dfrac{1}{18} + \dfrac{1}{12}$

$18 = 3 \times 3 \times 2$
$12 = 2 \times 2 \times 3$
$\text{LCD} = 2 \times 2 \times 3 \times 3 = 36$

■ $\dfrac{1}{a^3bc^2} - \dfrac{3}{2b^3c}$

$\text{LCD} = 2a^3b^3c^2$

■ $\dfrac{1}{(x-1)^2(x+1)} + \dfrac{3}{x^2-1}$

$x^2 - 1 = (x+1)(x-1)$
$\text{LCD} = (x-1)^2(x+1)$

Multiplication

Principle 4: $\dfrac{a}{b} \times \dfrac{c}{d} = \dfrac{ac}{bd}$.

This principle can be stated as follows: To multiply fractions, multiply their numerators to obtain the numerator of the product and multiply their denominators to form the denominator.

Examples

■ $\dfrac{2}{7} \times \dfrac{3}{7} \times \dfrac{1}{7} = \dfrac{6}{343}$

■ $\dfrac{1}{2} \times \dfrac{1}{3} \times \dfrac{1}{4} = \dfrac{1}{24}$

■ $\dfrac{a}{b^2c} \times \dfrac{b}{ac^2} = \dfrac{ab}{ab^2c^3} = \dfrac{1}{bc^3}$

Often the product of fractions will have factors common to the numerator and the denominator, as in the last example above. As a shortcut these can be removed before the multiplication is done. If a factor appears in any numerator of the product, and in any denominator as well, it will not change the value of the product and can be removed from both.

Examples

■ $\dfrac{3}{4} \times \dfrac{20}{49} \times \dfrac{7}{25}$

$= \dfrac{3}{4} \times \dfrac{5 \cdot 4}{7 \cdot 7} \times \dfrac{7}{5 \cdot 5}$

$= \dfrac{3}{1} \times \dfrac{1}{7} \times \dfrac{1}{5} = \dfrac{3}{35}$

■ $\left(\dfrac{8x-4}{12x}\right)\left(\dfrac{2x^2+x}{4x^2-1}\right)$

$= \dfrac{4(2x-1)}{12x} \cdot \dfrac{x(2x+1)}{(2x+1)(2x-1)}$

$= \dfrac{4}{12} \times 1 = \dfrac{1}{3}$

To multiply mixed numbers, convert them to improper fractions first:

$$2\dfrac{5}{6} \times 5\dfrac{2}{3} = \dfrac{17}{6} \times \dfrac{17}{3} = \dfrac{289}{18}$$

Division

Principle 5: $\dfrac{a}{b} \div \dfrac{c}{d} = \dfrac{a}{b} \times \dfrac{d}{c}$.

This principle can be stated as follows: To divide a fraction by a fraction, invert the divisor and then multiply according to Principle 4.

Examples

■ $\dfrac{1}{2} \div \dfrac{1}{3} = \dfrac{1}{2} \times \dfrac{3}{1} = \dfrac{3}{2}$

■ $\dfrac{2}{5} \div \dfrac{8}{15} = \dfrac{2}{5} \times \dfrac{15}{8} = \dfrac{3}{4}$

To divide mixed numbers, convert to improper fractions first:

$$2\dfrac{5}{6} \div 5\dfrac{2}{3} = \dfrac{17}{6} \div \dfrac{17}{3} = \dfrac{17}{6} \times \dfrac{3}{17} = \dfrac{1}{2}$$

To divide fractions involving variables, be sure to factor after inverting and cancel any common factors before multiplying:

$$\dfrac{x+y}{x^2-xy} \div \dfrac{1}{x^2-y^2} = \dfrac{x+y}{x(x-y)} \cdot \dfrac{(x+y)(x-y)}{1}$$
$$= \dfrac{(x+y)^2}{x}$$

Simplifying Complex Fractions

A complex fraction is a fraction that has one or more fractions in its numerator and/or denominator. To simplify a complex fraction, find the LCD of all of the fractions found in the numerator and denominator. Then multiply the numerator and denominator of the complex fraction by this LCD. Your fraction will no longer be complex but may have factors common to numerator and denominator that can be removed.

Examples

■ $\dfrac{\dfrac{1}{3} + \dfrac{5}{6}}{1 - \left(\dfrac{1}{3}\right)\left(\dfrac{3}{4}\right)} \quad \text{LCD} = 12$

$= \dfrac{12\left(\dfrac{1}{3} + \dfrac{5}{6}\right)}{12\left(1 - \dfrac{1}{3} \cdot \dfrac{3}{4}\right)}$

$= \dfrac{4+10}{12-3} = \dfrac{14}{9}$

$$\dfrac{\dfrac{1}{x} + \dfrac{1}{y}}{\dfrac{1}{xy}} \qquad \text{LCD} = xy$$

$$= \dfrac{xy\left(\dfrac{1}{x} + \dfrac{1}{y}\right)}{xy\left(\dfrac{1}{xy}\right)}$$

$$= \dfrac{y + x}{1} = y + x$$

$$\dfrac{\dfrac{1}{a}}{1 - \dfrac{1}{a}} = \dfrac{\left(\dfrac{1}{a}\right)a}{\left(1 - \dfrac{1}{a}\right)a} = \dfrac{1}{a - 1}$$

$$\dfrac{\dfrac{1}{y} - \dfrac{1}{x}}{1 - \dfrac{y}{x}} = \dfrac{\left(\dfrac{1}{y} - \dfrac{1}{x}\right)xy}{\left(1 - \dfrac{y}{x}\right)xy}$$

$$= \dfrac{x - y}{xy - y^2}$$

$$= \dfrac{x - y}{y(x - y)} = \dfrac{1}{y}$$

Solving Fractional Equations

To solve an equation involving fractions, change it to an equation with no fractions. This can be done by multiplying each side by the LCD of all of the fractions that appear in the equation.

Examples

■ Solve for x:

$$\dfrac{x}{4} + \dfrac{x}{3} = \dfrac{7}{12} \qquad \text{LCD} = 12$$

$$12\left(\dfrac{x}{4} + \dfrac{x}{3}\right) = 12\left(\dfrac{7}{12}\right)$$

$$3x + 4x = 7$$

$$x = 1$$

■ Solve for x:

$$\dfrac{4x}{7 + 5x} = \dfrac{1}{3} \qquad \text{LCD} = 3(7 + 5x)$$

$$3(4x) = 1(7 + 5x)$$

$$x = 1$$

■ Solve for x:

$$\dfrac{5}{x - 2} + \dfrac{2}{2 - x} = \dfrac{3}{2} \quad \left(\text{Note that } 2 - x\right.$$

$= -(x - 2)$, so this equation is the same as

$\dfrac{5}{x - 2} - \dfrac{2}{x - 2} = \dfrac{3}{2}$). $\left.\text{LCD} = 2(x - 2)\right.$

$$2(5) - 2(2) = 3(x - 2)$$

$$x = 4$$

■ Solve for r:

$$\dfrac{1}{p} + \dfrac{1}{r} = \dfrac{1}{s} \qquad \text{LCD} = prs$$

$$rs + ps = pr$$

$$rs - pr = -ps$$

$$r(s - p) = -ps$$

$$r = \dfrac{-ps}{s - p} = \dfrac{-ps}{-(p - s)} = \dfrac{ps}{p - s}$$

■ Solve for a:

$$S = \dfrac{1}{2}n(a + 1)$$

$$2S = na + n$$

$$2S - n = na$$

$$\dfrac{2S - n}{n} = a$$

Solving Problems Involving Fractions

The word *of* frequently indicates multiplication. For example:

$$\dfrac{1}{2} \text{ of } 4 \quad \text{means} \quad \dfrac{1}{2} \cdot 4 = 2$$

and

$$\dfrac{2}{3} \text{ of } \dfrac{9}{10} \quad \text{means} \quad \dfrac{2}{3} \times \dfrac{9}{10} = \dfrac{3}{5}$$

Examples

■ Find $\dfrac{7}{8}$ of 48.

$$\dfrac{7}{8} \times 48 = 42$$

■ What is $\dfrac{1}{4}$ of $\dfrac{4}{7}$?

$$\dfrac{1}{4} \times \dfrac{4}{7} = \dfrac{1}{7}$$

■ Mr. Brown owns $\dfrac{3}{7}$ of the interest in a company and sells $\dfrac{1}{2}$ of his share to Ms. Wein. What part of the business does Ms. Wein own after this deal?

$$\dfrac{1}{2} \times \dfrac{3}{7} = \dfrac{3}{14}$$

A fraction is commonly used to indicate the ratio of some part to the whole:

$$\dfrac{\text{Part}}{\text{Whole}} = \text{Fractional part}$$

In many problems, the "part" follows the word *is* and the "whole" follows *of*.

Examples

■ What fractional part of 32 is 20?
  Part = 20, whole = 32

$$\text{Fractional part} = \dfrac{20}{32} = \dfrac{5}{8}$$

■ In a class of 26 there are 16 girls. What fractional part of the class is made up of girls?

$$\frac{16}{26} = \frac{8}{13}$$

■ What fractional part of a quarter is a nickel?

$$\frac{5}{25} = \frac{1}{5}$$

■ $6 = \frac{2}{3}x; \ x =$

$18 = 2x$

$x = 9$

■ When 300 pupils are in a lecture hall, only $\frac{2}{3}$ of the seats are occupied. How many seats are there?

Let $x =$ number of seats.

$$\frac{300}{x} = \frac{2}{3}$$

$900 = 2x$

$x = 450$

■ 5 is $\frac{1}{4}$ of what number?

$$\frac{1}{4}x = 5$$

$x = 20$

Practice Exercises

Operations Involving Fractions

Do only the odd-numbered questions. If you discover that you are very weak in your work with fractions, return to this section later, if you have the time, and work the even-numbered questions.

ADDITION

1. $\frac{1}{2} + \frac{1}{4}$

2. $\frac{1}{4} + \frac{5}{8}$

3. $\frac{1}{2} + \frac{1}{8}$

4. $\frac{2}{3} + \frac{5}{6}$

5. $\frac{1}{3} + \frac{1}{4}$

6. $\frac{1}{3} + \frac{1}{5}$

7. $\frac{1}{6} + \frac{1}{3}$

8. $\frac{1}{2} + \frac{1}{5}$

9. $\frac{2}{7} + \frac{1}{3}$

10. $\frac{1}{2} + \frac{1}{7}$

11. $\frac{1}{2} + \frac{1}{3} + \frac{1}{4}$

12. $\frac{1}{3} + \frac{3}{4} + \frac{5}{6}$

13. $\frac{1}{2} + \frac{5}{8} + \frac{1}{4}$

14. $\frac{1}{4} + \frac{1}{8} + \frac{1}{2}$

15. $\frac{1}{5} + \frac{2}{3} + \frac{1}{4}$

16. $17\frac{5}{8}$
$\underline{21\frac{3}{4}}$

17. $36\frac{5}{12}$
$\underline{24\frac{2}{3}}$

18. $8\frac{5}{6}$
$7\frac{5}{12}$
$\underline{6\frac{2}{3}}$

19. $3\frac{1}{4}$
$\underline{\frac{1}{3}}$

20. $7\frac{1}{2} + 2\frac{1}{3} + 3\frac{3}{8} + 4\frac{3}{4}$

21. $64\frac{3}{4}$
$\underline{45\frac{2}{3}}$

22. $15\frac{5}{6} + 7\frac{1}{4}$

23. $8\frac{2}{3} + 3\frac{5}{6}$

24. $9\frac{1}{2} + \frac{1}{10}$

25. $8\frac{1}{2} + \frac{1}{3}$

SUBTRACTION

26. $\frac{2}{3} - \frac{1}{6}$

27. $\frac{7}{8} - \frac{1}{2}$

28. $\frac{1}{2} - \frac{3}{8}$

29. $\frac{3}{4} - \frac{1}{2}$

30. $\frac{3}{4} - \frac{1}{6}$

31. $\frac{2}{3} - \frac{1}{9}$

32. $\frac{5}{9} - \frac{1}{3}$

33. $\frac{7}{12} - \frac{1}{3}$

34. $19\frac{2}{3}$
$\underline{-7\frac{1}{4}}$

35. $97\frac{1}{3}$
$\underline{-28\frac{5}{6}}$

36. 62
$\underline{-7\frac{5}{8}}$

37. $23\frac{1}{2}$
$\underline{-4\frac{4}{5}}$

38. $9\frac{3}{4} - \frac{1}{2}$

39. $76\frac{3}{4} - 67\frac{1}{3}$

40. $13\frac{7}{12} - 2\frac{1}{3}$

41. $44\frac{1}{2} - 3\frac{3}{4}$

42. $3\frac{1}{3} - 2\frac{1}{2}$

43. $4\frac{1}{3} - 1\frac{5}{6}$

44. $8\frac{1}{10} - 6\frac{3}{5}$

45. $9\frac{1}{2} - \frac{2}{3}$

MULTIPLICATION

46. $\frac{3}{7} \times \frac{2}{3}$

47. $\frac{5}{8} \times \frac{4}{5}$

48. $\frac{3}{8} \times \frac{4}{9}$

49. $\frac{5}{6} \times \frac{2}{5}$

50. $\frac{1}{3} \times \frac{1}{4}$

51. $\frac{2}{5} \times \frac{5}{6}$

52. $\frac{7}{8} \times 36$

53. $55 \times \frac{2}{5}$

54. $7\frac{1}{2} \times 1\frac{2}{3}$

55. $2\frac{2}{3} \times 3\frac{1}{10}$

56. $4\frac{1}{6} \times 5\frac{1}{5}$

57. $6\frac{1}{5} \times 7\frac{2}{3}$

58. $8\frac{5}{12} \times 1\frac{3}{5}$

59. $9\frac{7}{10} \times 3\frac{5}{6}$

60. $2\frac{4}{9} \times 5\frac{3}{8}$

61. $3\frac{5}{8} \times 7\frac{2}{3}$

62. $5\frac{1}{2} \times 9\frac{4}{5}$

63. $4\frac{4}{5} \times 2\frac{1}{12}$

64. $6\frac{1}{10} \times 4\frac{5}{6}$

65. $7\frac{2}{3} \times 8\frac{1}{2}$

DIVISION

66. $\dfrac{2}{3} \div \dfrac{1}{3}$

67. $\dfrac{5}{8} \div \dfrac{1}{2}$

68. $\dfrac{2}{3} \div \dfrac{5}{6}$

69. $\dfrac{1}{4} \div \dfrac{1}{3}$

70. $\dfrac{3}{4} \div \dfrac{1}{8}$

71. $\dfrac{5}{12} \div \dfrac{5}{9}$

72. $\dfrac{7}{8} \div \dfrac{3}{4}$

73. $\dfrac{5}{9} \div \dfrac{1}{6}$

74. $\dfrac{5}{6} \div \dfrac{5}{9}$

75. $\dfrac{2}{3} \div \dfrac{1}{12}$

76. $3\dfrac{1}{3} \div \dfrac{2}{3}$

77. $5\dfrac{1}{3} \div \dfrac{5}{6}$

78. $7\dfrac{1}{6} \div \dfrac{1}{3}$

79. $9\dfrac{1}{9} \div \dfrac{2}{3}$

80. $4\dfrac{3}{8} \div \dfrac{1}{4}$

81. $2\dfrac{3}{4} \div 1\dfrac{1}{8}$

82. $6\dfrac{3}{10} \div 3\dfrac{1}{5}$

83. $8\dfrac{1}{6} \div 4\dfrac{1}{4}$

84. $2\dfrac{1}{3} \div 5\dfrac{2}{5}$

85. $3\dfrac{4}{9} \div 7\dfrac{2}{3}$

86. $5\dfrac{1}{3} \div 2\dfrac{1}{5}$

87. $14\dfrac{2}{3} \div 8\dfrac{5}{6}$

88. $18\dfrac{1}{6} \div 2\dfrac{1}{3}$

89. $10\dfrac{1}{4} \div 4\dfrac{5}{8}$

90. $12\dfrac{1}{6} \div 6\dfrac{1}{8}$

91. $25\dfrac{1}{2} \div 2\dfrac{1}{5}$

92. $16\dfrac{1}{2} \div 5\dfrac{1}{2}$

93. $14\dfrac{1}{6} \div 4\dfrac{1}{5}$

94. $13\dfrac{2}{3} \div 1\dfrac{1}{2}$

95. $18\dfrac{1}{2} \div 5\dfrac{1}{3}$

96. $\left(\dfrac{1}{4} + \dfrac{5}{8}\right) \div \left(\dfrac{1}{2} + \dfrac{3}{4}\right)$

97. $\left(\dfrac{1}{4} + \dfrac{1}{8}\right) \div \left(\dfrac{3}{8} + \dfrac{1}{2}\right)$

98. $\left(\dfrac{1}{8} + \dfrac{1}{2}\right) \div \left(\dfrac{1}{2} + \dfrac{1}{3}\right)$

99. $\left(\dfrac{2}{9} + \dfrac{1}{3}\right) \div \left(\dfrac{1}{3} + \dfrac{1}{4}\right)$

100. $\left(\dfrac{3}{4} + \dfrac{1}{3}\right) \div \left(\dfrac{2}{3} + \dfrac{5}{12}\right)$

COMPLEX FRACTIONS

101. $\dfrac{\dfrac{1}{2} - \dfrac{1}{4}}{\dfrac{3}{4} - \dfrac{1}{8}}$

102. $\dfrac{\dfrac{2}{3} - \dfrac{1}{6}}{\dfrac{7}{8} - \dfrac{1}{2}}$

103. $\dfrac{\dfrac{5}{12} - \dfrac{1}{6}}{\dfrac{5}{6} - \dfrac{2}{3}}$

104. $\dfrac{\dfrac{1}{2} - \dfrac{2}{5}}{\dfrac{1}{3} - \dfrac{1}{9}}$

105. $\dfrac{\dfrac{2}{3} - \dfrac{1}{4}}{\dfrac{1}{2} - \dfrac{1}{3}}$

106. $\dfrac{\dfrac{1}{4} + \dfrac{1}{6} + \dfrac{2}{3}}{\dfrac{2}{3} - \dfrac{1}{2}}$

107. $\dfrac{2\dfrac{1}{4} + 5\dfrac{5}{6}}{\dfrac{5}{6} - \dfrac{3}{4}}$

108. $\dfrac{6\dfrac{3}{4} + 6\dfrac{1}{2}}{\dfrac{3}{4} - \dfrac{2}{3}}$

109. $\dfrac{1\dfrac{2}{3} + 4\dfrac{3}{4}}{\dfrac{7}{8} - \dfrac{1}{4}}$

110. $\dfrac{3\dfrac{1}{3} + \dfrac{1}{4}}{\dfrac{2}{3} - \dfrac{1}{4}}$

111. $\dfrac{\dfrac{7}{8} - \dfrac{1}{2}}{\dfrac{1}{4} + \dfrac{1}{6} + \dfrac{2}{3}}$

112. $\dfrac{\dfrac{2}{3} - \dfrac{1}{6}}{\dfrac{1}{2} + \dfrac{3}{4} + \dfrac{3}{8}}$

113. $\dfrac{\dfrac{11}{12} - \dfrac{1}{4}}{2\dfrac{1}{4} + 5\dfrac{5}{6}}$

114. $\dfrac{2\dfrac{1}{2} - \dfrac{1}{5}}{\dfrac{1}{2} + \dfrac{3}{5}}$

115. $\dfrac{4 - 1\dfrac{7}{8}}{\dfrac{1}{8} + \dfrac{1}{2} + \dfrac{1}{4}}$

116. $\dfrac{\dfrac{14}{15} - \dfrac{3}{5}}{\dfrac{1}{2} \div \dfrac{3}{8}}$

117. $\dfrac{4\dfrac{1}{3} \div \dfrac{2}{3}}{10\dfrac{1}{2} + 9\dfrac{3}{4}}$

118. $\dfrac{6\dfrac{2}{3} + 4\dfrac{1}{2}}{8 \times \dfrac{1}{4}}$

119. $\dfrac{48 \times \dfrac{5}{12}}{4\dfrac{7}{12} + 2\dfrac{1}{3}}$

120. $\dfrac{\dfrac{2}{5} \times 35}{\dfrac{7}{8} + \dfrac{1}{3}}$

121. $\dfrac{4\dfrac{3}{4} \times \dfrac{2}{9}}{\dfrac{1}{2} \div \dfrac{1}{4}}$

122. $\dfrac{7\frac{3}{5} - 2\frac{1}{10}}{\frac{1}{4} \times 3\frac{3}{4}}$

123. $\dfrac{9\frac{7}{8} - 3\frac{11}{12}}{\frac{7}{10} \times \frac{5}{6}}$

124. $\dfrac{4\frac{2}{5} \div 5\frac{1}{2}}{8\frac{5}{6} - 8\frac{1}{2}}$

125. $\dfrac{2\frac{2}{5} \times 2\frac{1}{3}}{\frac{2}{3} \div \frac{2}{6}}$

Fractional Equations

1. $\dfrac{x}{3} + \dfrac{x}{4} = \dfrac{7}{12}$ $x =$

   (A) $\dfrac{1}{12}$ (B) 1   (C) $3\frac{1}{2}$ (D) 7   (E) 14

2. $\dfrac{x + 2}{3} - \dfrac{x - 2}{5} = 2$ $x =$

   (A) -7 (B) 2   (C) 3   (D) 7   (E) 15

3. $\dfrac{8}{20} = \dfrac{x}{30}$ $x =$

   (A) 2   (B) $7\frac{1}{2}$ (C) 12   (D) 18   (E) 24

4. $\dfrac{2x + 3}{3} - \dfrac{x - 3}{5} = 3$ $x =$

   (A) -3 (B) $-\dfrac{11}{7}$ (C) 1   (D) 3   (E) 9

5. $\dfrac{27}{x} = \dfrac{3}{4}$ $x =$

   (A) 3   (B) 4   (C) 12   (D) 36   (E) 108

6. $\dfrac{10}{1 - 2x} = 2$ $x =$

   (A) -3 (B) -2 (C) $-\dfrac{1}{2}$ (D) 2   (E) 3

7. $\dfrac{2}{3x + 4} = \dfrac{1}{4x - 3}$ $x =$

   (A) $\dfrac{10}{11}$ (B) $\dfrac{2}{5}$ (C) 1   (D) 2   (E) 7

8. $\dfrac{rx - a}{x - 1} = s$ $x =$

   (A) $\dfrac{s - a}{s - r}$ (B) $\dfrac{a}{r}$ (C) $-\dfrac{a}{r}$ (D) $\dfrac{1 - a}{s - r}$
   (E) $\dfrac{a - 1}{s - r}$

9. $r = \dfrac{x}{1 - x}$ $x =$

   (A) 0   (B) 1   (C) r (D) $\dfrac{r}{r - 1}$ (E) $\dfrac{r}{r + 1}$

10. $\dfrac{x - 3}{2x} = \dfrac{1}{3}$ $x =$

    (A) -9 (B) $2\frac{2}{3}$ (C) 3   (D) $4\frac{1}{2}$ (E) 9

11. $\dfrac{2x}{3} + 3 = \dfrac{x}{3}$ $x =$

    (A) -9 (B) -3 (C) -1 (D) $\dfrac{3}{5}$ (E) 9

12. $\dfrac{x^2 + 4x + 2}{x^2 + 3x + 7} = 1$ $x =$

    (A) 5   (B) 9   (C) $\dfrac{2}{7}$ (D) 1   (E) $\dfrac{5}{7}$

13. $\dfrac{t}{5u} = 3, \dfrac{r}{2s} = 5, \dfrac{s}{t} = 2$ $\dfrac{u}{r} =$

    (A) $\dfrac{1}{300}$ (B) $\dfrac{3}{20}$ (C) $\dfrac{3}{5}$ (D) $\dfrac{5}{3}$ (E) 30

14. $\sqrt{\dfrac{2 + x^2}{2}} = 3$ $x =$

    (A) -4 (B) $+4$ (C) ± 4 (D) 9   (E) 16

15. If $\sqrt{\dfrac{9}{16}x^2 + \dfrac{3}{8}x + \dfrac{1}{16}} = 4$, then $x =$

    (A) 3   (B) $3\frac{1}{2}$ (C) $\dfrac{17}{3}$ (D) 16   (E) 17

16. If $\left(2 + \dfrac{1}{x}\right)\left(y\right) = \dfrac{1}{x}$, then $y =$

    (A) -2 (B) $\dfrac{1}{2}$ (C) $\dfrac{1}{2x + 1}$ (D) $\dfrac{2}{2x + 1}$
    (E) $\dfrac{2x + 1}{x^2}$

17. $\dfrac{a}{3} = 2b, b = \dfrac{c}{2}$ $c =$

    (A) $\dfrac{a}{3}$ (B) $\dfrac{12}{a}$ (C) $\dfrac{3a}{4}$ (D) $\dfrac{4a}{3}$ (E) $3a$

18. $\dfrac{3}{x} = \dfrac{a + b}{c}$ $\dfrac{x}{3} =$

    (A) $\dfrac{c}{a + b}$ (B) $\dfrac{3c}{a + b}$ (C) $3c$ (D) $3c(a + b)$
    (E) $3c + a + b$

19. $13 = \dfrac{13w}{1 - w}$ $(2w)^2 =$

    (A) $\dfrac{1}{2}$ (B) $\dfrac{1}{4}$ (C) 1   (D) 2   (E) 4

20. $\frac{1}{2}x = k = \frac{2}{3}y$ $x + y = k$ times

(A) $\frac{2}{5}$ (B) $\frac{3}{4}$ (C) $1\frac{1}{6}$ (D) $2\frac{1}{2}$ (E) $3\frac{1}{2}$

Verbal Problems Involving Fractions

1. Ten merchants agreed to purchase uniforms for a local baseball team at a total cost of M dollars. After a disagreement, two merchants dropped out of the project. By how many dollars was the cost to each merchant remaining increased?

(A) $\frac{M-20}{2}$ (B) $\frac{M}{40}$ (C) $\frac{M}{9}$ (D) $\frac{M}{2}$ (E) $2M$

2. Three-fourths of a gasoline storage tank is emptied by filling each of five trucks with the same amount of fuel. What part of the total capacity of the storage tank did each vehicle receive?

(A) $\frac{1}{5}$ (B) $\frac{1}{10}$ (C) $\frac{2}{15}$ (D) $\frac{3}{20}$ (E) $\frac{4}{15}$

3. A gasoline tank that is $\frac{1}{2}$ full has 8 gallons removed. The tank is then $\frac{1}{10}$ full. What is the capacity, in gallons, of the tank?

(A) 2.5 (B) 6.4 (C) 15.8 (D) 20 (E) 40

4. A motion was adopted by a vote of 5 to 3. What part of the total vote was against the motion?

(A) $\frac{3}{8}$ (B) $\frac{3}{5}$ (C) $\frac{5}{8}$ (D) $\frac{5}{3}$ (E) $\frac{8}{5}$

5. The indicator of an oil tank shows $\frac{1}{5}$ full. After a truck delivers 165 gallons of oil, the indicator shows $\frac{4}{5}$ full. What is the capacity, in gallons, of the tank?

(A) 55 (B) 105 (C) 140 (D) 175 (E) 275

6. Ms. Ackerman owned $\frac{5}{8}$ of an interest in a house. She sold $\frac{1}{5}$ of her interest, at cost, for $1,000. What was the total value of the house?

(A) $3,000 (B) $4,000 (C) $5,000 (D) $6,000
(E) $8,000

7. Of Ted's salary, $\frac{1}{10}$ is spent for clothing, and $\frac{1}{3}$ for food and for rent. What part of the salary is left for other expenditures and savings?

(A) $\frac{17}{30}$ (B) $\frac{3}{5}$ (C) $\frac{19}{30}$ (D) $\frac{2}{3}$ (E) $\frac{7}{10}$

8. A man leaves his estate to his wife and two sons. If the wife receives $\frac{1}{3}$ of the estate and each son receives $\frac{1}{2}$ of the remainder, find the value of the entire estate if each son receives $4,000 as his share.

(A) $6,000 (B) $12,000 (C) $16,000
(D) $18,000 (E) $24,000

9. What part of a quarter is 2 pennies, 2 nickels, and 1 dime?

(A) $\frac{1}{88}$ (B) $\frac{1}{5}$ (C) $\frac{3}{25}$ (D) $\frac{17}{25}$ (E) $\frac{22}{25}$

10. Sulfuric acid contains, by weight, 2 parts of hydrogen, 32 parts of sulfur, and 64 parts of oxygen. What part, by weight, of sulfuric acid is sulfur?

(A) $\frac{1}{4}$ (B) $\frac{16}{49}$ (C) $\frac{8}{25}$ (D) $\frac{16}{33}$ (E) $\frac{16}{30}$

11. When the gasoline gauge of an automobile shows $\frac{1}{8}$ full, 14 gallons is needed to completely fill the tank. What is the capacity, in gallons, of the gasoline tank?

(A) 15 (B) 16 (C) 18 (D) 20 (E) 98

12. A 5-foot stick is cut so that one part is $\frac{2}{3}$ of the other. How long, in inches, is the shorter segment?

(A) 3 (B) $3\frac{1}{3}$ (C) $3\frac{1}{2}$ (D) 24 (E) 36

13. A baseball team won w games and lost l games. What fractional part of its games did it win?

(A) $\frac{l}{w}$ (B) $\frac{w-l}{w}$ (C) $\frac{w}{l}$ (D) $\frac{w+l}{w}$
(E) $\frac{w}{w+l}$

14. In a graduating class with the same number of boys and of girls, $\frac{1}{8}$ of the girls and $\frac{5}{6}$ of the boys are honor students. What part of the class consists of boys who are not honor students?

(A) $\frac{1}{12}$ (B) $\frac{1}{6}$ (C) $\frac{7}{48}$ (D) $\frac{13}{48}$ (E) $\frac{35}{48}$

15. If a woman's salary is D per month and during a certain month she spends a, what fractional part of her salary does she save?

(A) $D - a$ (B) $\frac{D-a}{D}$ (C) $\frac{a}{D}$ (D) $\frac{D}{a}$
(E) $\frac{D-a}{a}$

16. A state convention attracts r representatives. Town A has a representatives, while Town B has b representatives. What part of all the representatives are from Town A?

    (A) $\dfrac{b}{r}$ (B) $\dfrac{a}{b}$ (C) $\dfrac{a}{b+r}$ (D) $\dfrac{a}{r}$ (E) $\dfrac{a}{a+r}$

17. A boy walked for $\dfrac{1}{2}$ hour and then got an automobile ride for $\dfrac{1}{3}$ hour. What part of an hour did the entire trip take?

    (A) $\dfrac{1}{6}$ (B) $\dfrac{1}{5}$ (C) $\dfrac{2}{5}$ (D) $\dfrac{5}{6}$ (E) $\dfrac{3}{2}$

18. A manufacturer of a glassware product finds that $\dfrac{1}{20}$ of the items are damaged in shipment and unsuitable for sale. How many items should be shipped so that a customer will have 190 items suitable for sale?

    (A) 152   (B) 200   (C) 228   (D) 285   (E) 380

19. Three out of five boys in Centerville graduate from high school. One third of these boys go to junior college. What fractional part of the boys in Centerville go to junior college?

    (A) $\dfrac{3}{40}$ (B) $\dfrac{1}{8}$ (C) $\dfrac{1}{5}$ (D) $\dfrac{5}{9}$ (E) $\dfrac{9}{5}$

20. If 10 parts of alcohol are mixed with 14 parts of xylol, what part of the mixture is alcohol?

    (A) $\dfrac{1}{14}$ (B) $\dfrac{1}{7}$ (C) $\dfrac{5}{12}$ (D) $\dfrac{7}{12}$ (E) $\dfrac{7}{5}$

21. If $\dfrac{2}{3}$ of the workers in a factory go on vacation in July and $\dfrac{1}{2}$ of the remainder take their vacations in August, what fraction of the workers take their vacations at other times of the year?

    (A) 0   (B) $\dfrac{1}{6}$ (C) $\dfrac{1}{3}$ (D) $\dfrac{2}{3}$ (E) $\dfrac{5}{6}$

22. Which of the following fractions is closest to $\dfrac{1}{4}$?

    (A) $\dfrac{1}{5}$ (B) $\dfrac{3}{10}$ (C) $\dfrac{3}{20}$ (D) $\dfrac{7}{20}$ (E) $\dfrac{4}{15}$

23. Susan is 4 times as old as Paul and $1\dfrac{1}{2}$ times as old as Mary. What fraction of Paul's age is Mary?

    (A) $\dfrac{3}{8}$ (B) $2\dfrac{2}{3}$ (C) $3\dfrac{3}{4}$ (D) 6   (E) $6\dfrac{1}{2}$

24. How many $\dfrac{1}{4}$-inch strips can be cut from a length of ribbon 8 feet long?

    (A) 24   (B) 32   (C) 200   (D) 320   (E) 384

25. 2 pints = 1 quart; 4 quarts = 1 gallon. What part of a gallon is 6 pints?

    (A) $\dfrac{1}{6}$ (B) $\dfrac{2}{3}$ (C) $\dfrac{3}{4}$ (D) $\dfrac{4}{3}$ (E) $\dfrac{3}{2}$

26. When the price of an article is reduced by $\dfrac{2}{7}$ of its former value, the number of articles sold is increased to $\dfrac{21}{10}$ of the original amount. The present daily receipts are what fraction of the former?

    (A) $\dfrac{3}{5}$ (B) $1\dfrac{1}{2}$ (C) $1\dfrac{2}{3}$ (D) $2\dfrac{2}{5}$ (E) $2\dfrac{1}{2}$

27. Ronald paints $\dfrac{1}{4}$ of a barn, and Meg paints $\dfrac{1}{8}$ of the remainder. What fraction of the barn is left unpainted?

    (A) $\dfrac{1}{32}$ (B) $\dfrac{11}{32}$ (C) $\dfrac{21}{32}$ (D) $\dfrac{29}{32}$ (E) $\dfrac{31}{32}$

28. Milltown has 1,600 phones, of which $\dfrac{3}{4}$ are manually operated. If $\dfrac{1}{3}$ of these are replaced by dial phones and 300 additional dial phones are installed, what fraction of the phones are now manually operated?

    (A) $\dfrac{8}{19}$ (B) $\dfrac{7}{16}$ (C) $\dfrac{11}{19}$ (D) $\dfrac{9}{16}$ (E) $\dfrac{1}{2}$

29. If $\dfrac{2}{3}$ of a yard of licorice is divided into 12 strips, what part of a foot will 2 strips be?

    (A) $\dfrac{1}{9}$ (B) $\dfrac{1}{6}$ (C) $\dfrac{1}{3}$ (D) $\dfrac{1}{2}$ (E) $\dfrac{2}{3}$

30. Each year a car depreciates a certain fraction of its value. During the first year it depreciates $\dfrac{1}{3}$ of its value, during the second year it depreciates $\dfrac{1}{4}$ of its value, and during the third year it depreciates $\dfrac{1}{5}$ of its value. What fraction of its original value is the value of a car at the end of the third year?

    (A) $\dfrac{2}{5}$ (B) $\dfrac{3}{5}$ (C) $\dfrac{13}{60}$ (D) $\dfrac{47}{60}$ (E) $\dfrac{29}{30}$

Answer Key

Operations Involving Fractions

ADDITION

1. $\frac{3}{4}$

2. $\frac{7}{8}$

3. $\frac{5}{8}$

4. $1\frac{1}{2}$

5. $\frac{7}{12}$

6. $\frac{8}{15}$

7. $\frac{1}{2}$

8. $\frac{7}{10}$

9. $\frac{13}{21}$

10. $\frac{9}{14}$

11. $1\frac{1}{12}$

12. $1\frac{11}{12}$

13. $1\frac{3}{8}$

14. $\frac{7}{8}$

15. $1\frac{7}{60}$

16. $39\frac{3}{8}$

17. $61\frac{1}{12}$

18. $22\frac{11}{12}$

19. $3\frac{7}{12}$

20. $17\frac{23}{24}$

21. $110\frac{5}{12}$

22. $23\frac{1}{12}$

23. $12\frac{1}{2}$

24. $9\frac{3}{5}$

25. $8\frac{5}{6}$

SUBTRACTION

26. $\frac{1}{2}$

27. $\frac{3}{8}$

28. $\frac{1}{8}$

29. $\frac{1}{4}$

30. $\frac{7}{12}$

31. $\frac{5}{9}$

32. $\frac{2}{9}$

33. $\frac{1}{4}$

34. $12\frac{5}{12}$

35. $68\frac{1}{2}$

36. $54\frac{3}{8}$

37. $18\frac{7}{10}$

38. $9\frac{1}{4}$

39. $9\frac{5}{12}$

40. $11\frac{1}{4}$

41. $40\frac{3}{4}$

42. $\frac{5}{6}$

43. $2\frac{1}{2}$

44. $1\frac{1}{2}$

45. $8\frac{5}{6}$

MULTIPLICATION

46. $\frac{2}{7}$

47. $\frac{1}{2}$

48. $\frac{1}{6}$

49. $\frac{1}{3}$

50. $\frac{1}{12}$

51. $\frac{1}{3}$

52. $31\frac{1}{2}$

53. 22

54. $12\frac{1}{2}$

55. $8\frac{4}{15}$

56. $21\frac{2}{3}$

57. $47\frac{8}{15}$

58. $13\frac{7}{15}$

59. $37\frac{11}{60}$

60. $13\frac{5}{36}$

61. $27\frac{19}{24}$

62. $53\frac{9}{10}$

63. 10

64. $29\frac{29}{60}$

65. $65\frac{1}{6}$

DIVISION

66. 2

67. $1\frac{1}{4}$

68. $\frac{4}{5}$

69. $\frac{3}{4}$

70. 6

71. $\frac{3}{4}$

72. $1\frac{1}{6}$

73. $3\frac{1}{3}$

74. $1\frac{1}{2}$

75. 8

76. 5

77. $6\frac{2}{5}$

78. $21\frac{1}{2}$

79. $13\frac{2}{3}$

80. $17\frac{1}{2}$

81. $2\frac{4}{9}$

82. $1\frac{31}{32}$

83. $1\frac{47}{51}$

84. $\frac{35}{81}$

85. $\frac{31}{69}$

86. $2\frac{14}{33}$

87. $1\frac{35}{53}$

88. $7\frac{11}{14}$

89. $2\frac{8}{37}$

90. $1\frac{145}{147}$

91. $11\frac{13}{22}$

92. 3

93. $3\frac{47}{126}$

94. $9\frac{1}{9}$

95. $3\frac{15}{32}$

96. $\frac{7}{10}$

97. $\frac{3}{7}$

98. $\frac{3}{4}$

99. $\frac{20}{21}$

100. 1

COMPLEX FRACTIONS

101. $\frac{2}{5}$

102. $1\frac{1}{3}$

103. $1\frac{1}{2}$

104. $\frac{9}{20}$

105. $2\frac{1}{2}$

106. $6\frac{1}{2}$

107. 97

108. 159

109. $10\frac{4}{15}$

110. $8\frac{3}{5}$

111. $\frac{9}{26}$

112. $\frac{4}{13}$

113. $\frac{8}{97}$

114. $2\frac{1}{11}$

115. $2\frac{3}{7}$

116. $\frac{1}{4}$

117. $\frac{26}{81}$

118. $5\frac{7}{12}$

119. $2\frac{74}{83}$

120. $11\frac{17}{29}$

121. $\frac{19}{36}$

122. $5\frac{13}{15}$

123. $10\frac{3}{14}$

124. $2\frac{2}{5}$

125. $2\frac{4}{5}$

Fractional Equations

1.	B	5.	D	9.	E	13.	A	17.	A
2.	D	6.	B	10.	E	14.	C	18.	A
3.	C	7.	D	11.	A	15.	B	19.	C
4.	D	8.	A	12.	A	16.	C	20.	E

Verbal Problems Involving Fractions

1.	B	7.	A	13.	E	19.	C	25.	C
2.	D	8.	B	14.	A	20.	C	26.	B
3.	D	9.	E	15.	B	21.	B	27.	C
4.	A	10.	B	16.	D	22.	E	28.	A
5.	E	11.	B	17.	D	23.	B	29.	C
6.	E	12.	D	18.	B	24.	E	30.	A

Decimals

A **decimal** is an implied fraction in which the denominator is 10, 100, 1,000, 10,000, ...

$\dfrac{3}{10}$ is written as 0.3.

$\dfrac{3}{100}$ is written as 0.03.

$\dfrac{3}{1000}$ is written as 0.003.

$33\dfrac{3}{100}$ is written as 33.03.

If a number consists of a whole number and a fraction, the whole number is written before the decimal point, and the fraction after it:

$$3\dfrac{7}{10} = 3.7$$
$$3\dfrac{72}{100} = 3.72$$
$$37\dfrac{2}{10} = 37.2$$

The value of a decimal is not changed by adding zeros after the last digit following the decimal point.

$$0.5 = 0.50 = 0.500 \quad \text{because} \quad 0.5 = \dfrac{5}{10}$$
$$0.50 = \dfrac{50}{100}; \quad 0.500 = \dfrac{500}{1000}$$

Fundamental Operations Involving Decimals

Addition

To add decimal numbers, list the numbers to be added, making certain that the decimal points are under each other, and add in the usual manner.

Examples

■ $4.25 + 12 + 6.312 + 3.2 = ?$

```
 4.25
12.
 6.312
 3.2
25.762
```

Subtraction

To subtract decimal numbers, list as described above and subtract in the usual manner.

Example

■ From 8.6 take 2.73.

```
 8.60
−2.73
 5.87
```

Multiplication

In multiplying decimal numbers, be sure that the number of decimal places in the product is equal to the combined number of decimal places in the multiplicand and the multiplier.

Example

■ Multiply 2.663 by 3.14.

```
  2.663   multiplicand (3 decimal places)
× 3.14    multiplier (2 decimal places)
 10652
  2663
 7989
836182    product
8.36182   answer after placing the decimal
            5 decimal places to the left.
```

Multiplication of decimals by 10, 100, 1000, 0.1, 0.01, 0.001, etc., can be carried out quickly by changing the position of the decimal point. To multiply by 10, move the decimal point one place to the right; to multiply by 100, move the decimal point two places to the right; etc. To multiply by 0.1, move the decimal point one place to the left; to multiply by 0.01, move the decimal point two places to the left; etc.

Examples

■ $(72.36)(10) = 723.6$

■ $(5.9824)(100) = 598.24$

■ $(0.27345)(1000) = 273.45$

■ $(0.003279)(10,000) = 32.79$

■ $(437.21)(0.1) = 43.721$

■ $(324.79)(0.01) = 3.2479$

■ $(0.0324)(0.001) = 0.0000324$

Division

In dividing decimal nuumbers, make the divisor a whole number by moving the decimal point the proper number of places to the right. Move the decimal point of the dividend the same number of places to the right. Place a decimal point in the quotient directly above the decimal point in the dividend.

Example

■ Divide 9.683 by 4.21.

$$
\begin{array}{r}
\overset{\text{quotient}}{\text{divisor)dividend}} \qquad
\begin{array}{r}
2.3 \\
4.21.\overline{)9.68.3} \\
8\ 42 \\
\hline
1\ 26\ 3 \\
1\ 26\ 3 \\
\hline
\end{array}
\end{array}
$$

When a question is worded "Find correct to two decimal places or to the nearest hundredth," it is necessary to carry the division to one more place than specified.

Example

■ Divide correct to two decimal places: $27.5 \div 8$.

$$
\begin{array}{r}
3.437 \\
8\overline{)27.500}
\end{array}
$$

If the digit just to the right of the desired decimal place is 5 or greater, add 1 to the desired decimal place number. In the example above, 3.437 becomes 3.44. If the digit just to the right of the desired decimal place is less than 5, drop it.

Example

■ Divide 0.22 by 0.7, correct to two decimal places.

$$
\begin{array}{r}
.314 = .31 \\
0.7.\overline{)0.2.200}
\end{array}
$$

Division of decimals by 10, 100, 1000, etc., can be carried out quickly by changing the position of the

decimal point. To divide by 10, move the decimal point one place to the left; to divide by 100, move the decimal point two places to the left; etc.

Examples

■ $72.36 \div 10 = 7.236$

■ $5.9824 \div 100 = 0.059824$

■ $0.27345 \div 1000 = 0.00027345$

■ $0.003279 \div 10,000 = 0.0000003279$

Converting a Fraction to a Decimal

To convert a fraction to a decimal, simply perform the indicated division. The numerator is divided by the denominator.

Examples

■ What is the decimal equivalent of $\dfrac{7}{8}$?

$$
\begin{array}{r}
0.875 \\
8\overline{)7.000}
\end{array}
$$

■ What is the decimal equivalent of $\dfrac{3}{64}$?

$$
\begin{array}{r}
0.046875 \\
64\overline{)3.000000} \\
\underline{2\ 56} \\
440 \\
\underline{384} \\
560 \\
\underline{512} \\
480 \\
\underline{448} \\
320 \\
\underline{320}
\end{array}
$$

Solving Equations Containing Decimals

To clear an equation of decimals, multiply each term on both sides of the equation by 10, 100, etc.

Example

■ Solve for x: $0.02x + 0.6 = x$.
  Multiply each term on both sides of the equation by 100:

$2x + 60 = 100x$

Subtract $2x$ from both sides of the equation:

$60 = 98x$

Divide both sides of the equation by 98:

$$x = \frac{60}{98}$$

Reduce:

$$x = \frac{30}{49}$$

Practice Exercises

1. Add 47.63 + 97.863 + 854.8 + 0.2897.
2. Add 3.876 + 48.7 + 96 + 833.97.

3. Subtract 867.4
     93.87

4. Subtract 97.637 from 121.86.

5. Multiply 873.9
       ×0.46

6. Multiply   2.7
       ×0.023

7. Multiply   48.7
       ×9.3

8. Divide, correct to two decimal places, 637.56 ÷ 8.3.

9. Divide, correct to two decimal places, 42.93 ÷ 0.76.

10. Divide, correct to two decimal places, 496 ÷ 6.9.

Solve the following for y:

11. $0.2y = 0.16$
12. $9y - 2.1 = 2.1 - 5y$
13. $2y + 3.4 = 6.8$
14. $8y + 7.3 = 9y - 5.7$
15. $23y - 39.2 = 2.8 + 2y$

Answer Key

1.	1000.5827	4.	24.223	7.	452.91	10.	71.88	13.	1.7
2.	982.546	5.	401.994	8.	76.81	11.	0.8	14.	13
3.	773.53	6.	0.0621	9.	56.49	12.	0.3	15.	2

Percents

A **percent** is a fraction with a denominator of 100. Instead of writing the denominator, we write the word *percent* or the symbol %.

Conversions

To write a percent as a fraction, drop *percent* or the % sign and write a fraction with the original number as numerator and 100 as denominator. *If a decimal is needed*, convert the fraction to a decimal by using the methods reviewed in the preceding section.

Examples

■ $1\% = \dfrac{1}{100} = 0.01$

■ $22\% = \dfrac{22}{100} = 0.22$

■ $3.7\% = \dfrac{3.7}{100} = 0.037$

■ $75\% = \dfrac{75}{100} = 0.75$

■ $\dfrac{1}{2}\% = \dfrac{\frac{1}{2}}{100} = 0.005$

■ $a\% = \dfrac{a}{100}$ (No decimal is possible without knowing more about a.)

Some percents are used often enough that it is advisable to memorize the simplified fractions to which they are equivalent:

$$33\tfrac{1}{3}\% = \tfrac{1}{3} \qquad 20\% = \tfrac{1}{5} \qquad 83\tfrac{1}{3}\% = \tfrac{5}{6}$$

$$66\tfrac{2}{3}\% = \tfrac{2}{3} \qquad 40\% = \tfrac{2}{5} \qquad 12\tfrac{1}{2}\% = \tfrac{1}{8}$$

$$25\% = \tfrac{1}{4} \qquad 60\% = \tfrac{3}{5} \qquad 37\tfrac{1}{2}\% = \tfrac{3}{8}$$

$$50\% = \tfrac{1}{2} \qquad 80\% = \tfrac{4}{5} \qquad 62\tfrac{1}{2}\% = \tfrac{5}{8}$$

$$75\% = \tfrac{3}{4} \qquad 16\tfrac{2}{3}\% = \tfrac{1}{6} \qquad 87\tfrac{1}{2}\% = \tfrac{7}{8}$$

To change a percent to a decimal, drop the % sign and move the decimal point two places to the left.

Examples

■ $5\% = 0.05$

■ $83\% = 0.83$

■ $2.3\% = 0.023$

To change a decimal to a percent, move the decimal point two places to the right and add a % sign.

Examples

■ $0.0002 = 0.02\%$

■ $0.02 = 2\%$

■ $20 = 2,000\%$

To write a fraction as a percent, first change the fraction to a decimal and then move the decimal point two places to the right and add the % sign.

Examples

■ $\dfrac{2}{5} = 0.40 = 40\%$

■ $\dfrac{3}{25} = 0.12 = 12\%$

■ $\dfrac{7}{10} = 0.7 = 70\%$

Types of Percentage Problems

Most problems in which the information is given in terms of percents, or the answer is requested as a percent, can be handled by setting up a proportion. The formula below will help.

$$\frac{\text{Part}}{\text{Whole}} = y\% = \frac{y}{100}$$

Examples

■ 2 is what percent of 5?
$$\frac{2}{5} = \frac{x}{100}$$
$$200 = 5x$$
$$40 = x; \text{ therefore } 40\%$$

■ What percent of 4 is 0.02?
$$\frac{0.02}{4} = \frac{x}{100}$$
$$4x = 2$$
$$x = \frac{1}{2}; \text{ therefore } \frac{1}{2}\%$$

■ Write $\dfrac{a}{b}$ as a percent.
$$\frac{a}{b} = \frac{x}{100}$$
$$100a = bx$$
$$x = \frac{100a}{b}; \text{ therefore } \frac{100a}{b}\%$$

■ What percent of p is q?
$$\frac{q}{p} = \frac{x}{100}$$
$$x = \frac{100q}{p}\%$$

■ t is what percent of v?
$$\frac{t}{v} = \frac{x}{100}$$
$$x = \frac{100t}{v}; \text{ therefore } \frac{100t}{v}\%$$

■ What is 20 percent of 15?
$$\frac{20}{100} = \frac{x}{15}$$
$$x = \frac{15 \times 20}{100} = 3$$

■ What is 300 percent of 7?
$$\frac{300}{100} = \frac{x}{7}$$
$$x = 21$$

■ 15 is 20 percent of what number?
$$\frac{20}{100} = \frac{15}{x}$$
$$x = 75$$

■ 7 is 5 percent of what number?
$$\frac{7}{x} = \frac{5}{100}$$
$$x = 140$$

■ 140 is $66\frac{2}{3}$ percent of what number?
$$\frac{140}{x} = \frac{66\frac{2}{3}}{100}$$
$$x = 210$$

Verbal Problems Involving Percent

To solve these problems, apply the definitions and principles that apply to percents.

Examples

■ A book sold for \$4.80 after a 20 percent discount was taken off the list price. What was the list price? If a 20% discount was taken, then \$4.80 is 80% of the list price. Let x be the list price and set up the proportion:
$$\frac{80}{100} = \frac{4.80}{x}$$
$$80x = 480$$
$$x = 6 \text{ (dollars)}$$

■ A company pays a salesman a commission of $16\frac{2}{3}$ percent and has \$20,000 left in proceeds. What was the value of the sales before the commission was deducted?

(*Hint:* The \$20,000 represents $83\frac{1}{3}\%$ of the original value.)
$$\frac{20,000}{x} = \frac{83\frac{1}{3}}{100}$$
$$x = 24,000$$

■ A radio sells for $220. If this price represents a profit of 10 percent of the cost for the seller, how much did she buy it for?
Let x = original cost. Then 10% of x, which is $0.10x$, is the profit. Thus the $220 is cost + profit, or 110% of x.

$$\frac{220}{x} = \frac{110}{100}$$
$$x = 200$$

■ If the temperature rises from 72° to 80°, what is the percent of increase?
Let $x\%$ be the percent of increase, which is a change of 8°. Therefore

$$\frac{x}{100} = \frac{8}{72}$$
$$72x = 800$$
$$x = 11\tfrac{1}{9}\%$$

Practice Exercises

Percent

1. What percent is $\frac{3}{12}$?

2. What percent of 12 is 3?

3. $12\% = \frac{3}{?}$

4. What percent of 3 is 12?

5. $40\% = \frac{?}{5}$

6. How much is 40% of 5?

7. $\frac{?}{40} = 5\%$

8. 3 is 6% of a certain number. What is the number?

9. $\frac{3}{?} = 6\%$

10. What percent of 6 is 3?

11. What percent of 3 is 6?

12. What percent of 7 is 5?

13. What percent of 5 is 7?

14. Calculate 5% of 7.

15. Calculate 7% of 5.

16. What fraction is equivalent to 325%?

17. 3% of a certain number is equal to 7. What is the number?

18. What is the fraction equivalent of 0.024%?

19. Find 600% of 0.075.

20. What percent of 0.002 is 0.0004?

21. What is 0.007% of t?

22. $0.00003 = 330\%$ of x. Find x.

23. Find 0.003% of 0.0012.

24. What percent of m is n?

25. If b is larger than d, what is the difference between 6% of b and 5% of d?

Verbal Problems Involving Percent

1. In a class of 550 students, 42 percent wish to go to college. How many students wish to attend college?
(A) 13   (B) 23   (C) 77   (D) 210   (E) 231

2. In a class of 20 boys and 28 girls, what percent of the class are girls?
(A) 41.7%   (B) 48%   (C) 58.3%   (D) 70%
(E) 71%

3. A man saved $24.00 or $37\tfrac{1}{2}$ percent of his daily salary. What was his daily salary?
(A) $40   (B) $46   (C) $64   (D) $88   (E) $90

4. Ms. Garcia deposits $700.00 in a bank that pays 3 percent interest per year. How much money will she have at the end of the year?
(A) $21.00   (B) $679.00   (C) $702.10
(D) $721.00   (E) $910.00

5. How much money would a man have to invest at the rate of 5 percent per year, to have $1,470.00 at the end of the year?
(A) $70.00   (B) $700.00   (C) $1400.00
(D) $1462.65   (E) $1540.00

6. Mr. Carson paid $4.80 for a book after receiving a discount of 20 percent of the list price. What was the list price?
(A) $3.60   (B) $3.84   (C) $5.76   (D) $6.00
(E) $8.64

7. Ms. Goodsale receives a salary of $6,000 per year plus 5 percent of all her sales over $10,000, and a special bonus of $500 if her sales exceed $20,000. What are her earnings during a year when her sales total $21,000?

(A) $6,050   (B) $6,500   (C) $6,550   (D) $7,000
(E) $7,050

8. A radio sells for $220. What was the cost, if the rate of profit was 10 percent of the cost?

(A) $198   (B) $200   (C) $210   (D) $240
(E) $242

9. The population of a city was 63,900 in 1955, an increase of $6\frac{1}{2}$ percent over a previous census. By how many persons did the population increase between these periods?

(A) 3,900   (B) 59,747   (C) 60,000   (D) 67,800
(E) 68,153

10. A department store had an end-of-winter sale of overcoats at the following prices:
    I. $80 coats reduced to $55
    II. $85 coats reduced to $60
    III. $90 coats reduced to $65
    IV. $95 coats reduced to $70
    V. $120 coats reduced to $95
    Which group of coats was offered at the greatest rate of discount from its original price?

(A) I   (B) II   (C) III   (D) IV   (E) V

11. If 54 percent of a town's population received the first two polio "shots" but 10 percent of these persons did not receive the third, what percent of the town took all three "shots"?

(A) 44%   (B) 48.6%   (C) 49.6%   (D) 59.4%
(E) 64%

12. A class of 80 is 25 percent girls. If 10 percent of the boys and 20 percent of the girls attended a picnic, what percent of the class attended?

(A) 10%   (B) 12%   (C) $12\frac{1}{2}$%   (D) 20%
(E) 30%

13. Q is what percent of 20 percent of 15?

(A) $\frac{Q}{300}$%   (B) $\frac{3}{100Q}$%   (C) $\frac{3Q}{100}$%   (D) $\frac{100}{3Q}$%
(E) $\frac{100Q}{3}$%

14. In May the average price of a bushel of corn was 25 percent above that of April. In June it was 30 percent below that of May. If the average price of corn in April was $1.60 a bushel, what was the decrease in the average price of a bushel of corn from May to June?

(A) $0.20   (B) $0.36   (C) $0.48   (D) $0.60
(E) $0.72

15. On the average an inspector rejects 0.08 percent of manufactured instruments as defective. How many instruments will he examine in order to reject 2?

(A) 25   (B) 250   (C) 2,500   (D) 25,000
(E) 250,000

16. Judy gave her sister Lucy $12.00, which is 15 percent of Judy's weekly earnings. How much does Judy have now?

(A) $10.20   (B) $68.00   (C) $69.80   (D) $80.00
(E) $92.00

17. What is the value of n after it has been decreased by $16\frac{2}{3}$ percent?

(A) $\frac{1}{6}n$ (B) $\frac{1}{3}n$ (C) $\frac{5}{6}n$ (D) $\frac{6}{7}n$ (E) $\frac{7}{6}n$

18. Eight percent of 36 is 72 percent of what number?

(A) 2.06   (B) 2.88   (C) 3.24   (D) 4   (E) 40

19. If the number of articles purchased is increased by 20 percent and the price of each is decreased by 25 percent, by what percent is the value of the purchase changed?

(A) +5%   (B) −5%   (C) +10%   (D) −10%
(E) 0%

20. X is what percent of $\frac{4}{5}$ of X?

(A) 75%   (B) 80%   (C) 120%   (D) 125%
(E) 180%

Answer Key

Percent

1.	25%	7.	2	12.	71.4%	17.	$233\frac{1}{3}$	22.	$\frac{1}{110,000}$
2.	25%	8.	50	13.	140%			23.	0.000000036
3.	25	9.	50	14.	0.35	18.	$\frac{24}{100,000}$	24.	$\frac{100n}{m}$
4.	400%	10.	50%	15.	0.35	19.	0.45		
5.	2			16.	$\frac{13}{4}$	20.	20%	25.	$\frac{6b-5d}{100}$
6.	2	11.	200%			21.	0.00007t		

Verbal Problems Involving Percent

1.	E	5.	C	9.	A	13.	E	17.	C
2.	C	6.	D	10.	A	14.	D	18.	D
3.	C	7.	E	11.	B	15.	C	19.	D
4.	D	8.	B	12.	C	16.	B	20.	D

Solving Verbal Problems

Problems Involving Averages

To find the **arithmetic mean**, or **average**, of a group of numbers, add the numbers and divide the sum by the number of numbers added. Be prepared to apply this principle to (a) whole numbers, (b) fractions, (c) decimals, (d) percentages, (e) algebraic expressions, and (f) combinations of these.

From this basic formula:

$$\frac{Sum}{Number\ of\ numbers} = Average$$

another useful formula can be developed:

$$Sum = Average \times Number\ of\ numbers$$

Helpful Tips on Averaging

1. Make certain that all units are the same. For example, to find the average height of members of an athletic team if the various heights are given in feet, in inches, or in a combination of both, you must change all figures to inches, or to feet if that is more convenient.

2. When two or more averages are to be combined into a single average, give appropriate weight to each average. If a person bought 100 shares at $50 each and later bought 200 shares of the same stock at $25 each, to calculate the **weighted average** price per share you must first find the total cost and then divide by 300.

$$\begin{array}{l} \$50 \times 100 = \$\ 5,000 \\ \$25 \times 200 = \underline{\$\ 5,000} \\ \$10,000 \end{array}$$

The 300 shares were purchased for $10,000. The average price per share is

$$\frac{\$10,000}{300} \quad or \quad \$33.33$$

To add the two purchase prices ($50 + $25 = $75) and then divide by 2 $\left(\frac{\$75}{2} = \$37.50\right)$ would

not reflect the fact that twice as many shares were bought at the lower price.

3. In problems requiring you to supply a missing value in order to obtain a specific average, first determine the required sum and then compare it with the given sum. Consider this problem: What number must be added to 5, 6, 9, and 11 to have an average of 7? You will have five numbers. The required sum is 7 × 5 or 35. The sum of 5, 6, 9, and 11 is 31. Therefore the number to be added is 4.

4. Treat algebraic expressions in a similar manner. Suppose that you have this problem: The average of two numbers is xy; if one number is x, what is the other number? The sum of the two numbers is $2xy$. If one number is x, the other number is $2xy - x$, or $x(2y - 1)$ by factoring.

Examples

■ A student in a chemistry class reports the following readings on a thermometer during an experiment: 5°, 0°, −2°, 9°. What is the average temperature?

$$\frac{5 + 0 - 2 + 9}{4} = 3$$

■ Mark has an average of 80 percent for six semesters. What grade must he earn in the next semester if he wants his average to be 82 percent? Since Mark will end up with seven grades which average 82, the total of the grades will have to be 7(82). But this total is also represented by the sum of the first six grades, 6(80), plus the last grade, which you can indicate by x. Write an equation and find x.

$$\begin{array}{l} 6(80) + x = 7(82) \\ 480 + x = 574 \\ x = 94\% \end{array}$$

The following examples demonstrate that, if the averages of two different sets of numbers are to be combined, they must be weighted in proportion to the number of members of each set.

■ A student attended Central High School for two semesters and earned an average of 90 percent. She then transferred to Union High School and averaged 85 percent for five semesters. What was her scholastic average for all seven semesters?

First find the sum of her grades for the seven terms, using the same idea as in the preceding example.

$$\frac{2(90) + 5(85)}{7} = 86.4\%$$

■ If three boys each earn an average of $5 per day and two men each earn an average of $12 per day, what are the average daily earnings of the group?

$$\frac{3(5) + 2(12)}{5} = \$7.80$$

Practice Exercises

1. What average must a student earn in her seventh semester in order to attain a scholastic average of 80 percent, if her averages for her previous semesters were as follows: Semester I, 71 percent; Semester II, 75 percent; Semesters III and IV, 80 percent; Semester V, 86 percent; and Semester VI, 88 percent?

   (A) 80%   (B) 82%   (C) 83%   (D) 84%
   (E) 85%

2. What is the average of a, b, and c?

   (A) $\frac{abc}{3}$ (B) $\frac{a + b + c}{3}$ (C) $3abc$

   (D) $\frac{abc}{a + b + c}$ (E) $\frac{a + b + c}{abc}$

3. What is the average temperature reading for a 4-day period when the daily temperature readings were 7, 0, -2, and 3?

   (A) -2 (B) 2   (C) 2.6   (D) 3   (E) -3

4. What is the average of $\frac{1}{2}, \frac{5}{6}, \frac{3}{4}, \frac{5}{12}$?

   (A) $\frac{7}{8}$ (B) $\frac{2}{5}$ (C) $\frac{5}{8}$ (D) $1\frac{3}{5}$ (E) $2\frac{1}{2}$

5. What is the average of 0.6, 6.6, 0.4, 2.4?

   (A) 1   (B) 2   (C) $2\frac{1}{2}$ (D) 10   (E) 12

6. Find the value of x if the average of 1.0, 0.8, 0.2, and x is exactly 0.6.

   (A) 0.2   (B) 0.4   (C) 0.66   (D) 1.3   (E) 2.4

7. The average of two numbers is M, and one number is N. The other number is

   (A) $2N$ (B) $2M$ (C) $2M - 2$ (D) $2M - N$
   (E) $M - N$

8. The readings in a freezer are 5°, -7°, and 8°. What must the next reading be so that the average will be 1°?

   (A) -5°   (B) -2°   (C) -1°   (D) 1°   (E) 10°

9. Mary purchases 3 pounds of mixed nuts at 89 cents per pound. Jane purchases 2 pounds of peanuts at 49 cents per pound. What is the average price, in cents, per pound for the mixture of both purchases?

   (A) 69   (B) 70   (C) 71   (D) 72   (E) 73

10. What is the average of $N - 2$, $-N$, $N + 2$, and $2N$?

    (A) $\frac{3N}{4}$ (B) N (C) $2N$ (D) $\frac{N}{4}$ (E) $4N$

11. Mr. Rich bought 50 shares of Shurshot Corporation at $60, and 2 months later purchased 25 shares of this stock at $56. At what price should he purchase 25 additional shares in order to have an average price of $58 per share?

    (A) $53   (B) $54   (C) $55   (D) $56   (E) $57

12. What is the average of one tenth, one hundredth, and one thousandth?

    (A) 0.003   (B) 0.01   (C) 0.037   (D) 0.111
    (E) 0.333

13. The average of two numbers is a. If the larger number is l, what is the smaller?

    (A) $a - l$ (B) $2a - l$ (C) $1 - \frac{1}{2}a$ (D) $l - a$

    (E) $l - 2a$

14. The variations of several barometer readings on either side of 29 inches were $+0.3$, -0.8, -0.2, 0.0, and $+0.2$ inch. What is the average, in inches, of these readings?

    (A) 28.875   (B) 28.9   (C) 29.0   (D) 29.1
    (E) 29.125

15. The average of M numbers is A, and the average of N numbers is B. What is the average of all the numbers?

    (A) $A + B$ (B) $\frac{A + B}{2}$ (C) $\frac{AM + BN}{2}$

    (D) $\frac{AM + BN}{M + N}$ (E) $\frac{AM + BN}{A + B}$

Answer Key

1.	A	4.	C	7.	D	10.	A	13.	B
2.	B	5.	C	8.	B	11.	D	14.	B
3.	B	6.	B	9.	E	12.	C	15.	D

2. To calculate the average rate for a trip involving two or more parts, regard the trip as a single trip, using the total distance and the total time. You will be applying the weighted average principle.

Example

■ A motorist travels for 3 hours at 45 miles per hour and for 2 hours at 40 miles per hour. What is her average rate for the entire trip? Determine the total distance covered by finding the distance for each part and adding the results. Then substitute total distance and total time into the formula.

$$45 \times 3 + 40 \times 2 = 135 + 80 = 215 \text{ miles}$$
$$3 + 2 = 5 \text{ hr.}$$
$$\frac{215}{5} = 43 \text{ m.p.h.}$$

3. Be on the alert for a shift in units, which occurs in several SAT problems and is well illustrated in motion problems.

Example

■ At an average rate of 30 miles per hour, how far can I go in 2 minutes?

$$\text{Rate} \times \text{Time} = \text{Distance}$$
$$\frac{\text{miles}}{\text{per hour}} \times \text{hours} = \text{miles}$$
$$2 \text{ min.} = \frac{2}{60} \text{ hr.}$$
$$\frac{30 \text{ miles}}{\text{per hour}} \times \frac{2}{60} \text{ hours} = 1 \text{ mile}$$

4. Visualize the situation presented in the problem. If two moving bodies start at the same time but from different points, at the time when they meet their rates may not be the same, but the time spent in traveling is the same for both. If one moving body leaves later and overtakes another that left earlier over the same road, then the distances covered are equal but the rates and time factors are unequal.

Example

■ Two trains start from the same station at the same time but travel in opposite directions. Their hourly rates are 35 miles per hour and 55 miles per hour, respectively. After how many hours will the trains be 540 miles apart? Let x = number of hours each train travels, since the two will travel for exactly the same time. Then $35x$ is the first train's distance, and $55x$ is the second's. Together the trains have traveled 540 miles.

$$35x + 55x = 540$$
$$90x = 540$$
$$x = 6 \text{ hr.}$$

Practice Exercises

1. How many miles can a motorist travel from 9:55 A.M. to 10:15 A.M. at a rate of 40 miles per hour?

    (A) $13\frac{1}{3}$ (B) 15   (C) 20   (D) 30   (E) 40

2. What is the average speed, in miles per hour, of a plane that covers 120 miles in 1 hour and 20 minutes?

    (A) 30   (B) 60   (C) 90   (D) 100   (E) 120

3. A man walked into the woods at the rate of 4 miles per hour and returned over the same road at the rate of 3 miles per hour. If he completed the entire trip in $3\frac{1}{2}$ hours, how far, in miles, into the woods did he walk?

    (A) 3   (B) 4   (C) 5   (D) 6   (E) 7

4. Mr. Bronson left his home at 8:00 A.M. and traveled at the average rate of 40 miles per hour until 11:30 A.M. What distance, in miles, did he cover during the period?

    (A) 100   (B) 140   (C) 160   (D) 320   (E) 340

5. A salesman travels for 2 hours at 30 miles an hour and then covers 60 miles in the next 3 hours. What is the average rate for the entire trip?

    (A) 18   (B) 24   (C) 36   (D) 45   (E) 90

6. What is the rate in miles per hour for a messenger who travels $\frac{2}{3}$ of a mile in 4 minutes?

    (A) 10   (B) 24   (C) $26\frac{2}{3}$ (D) 30   (E) 45

7. What is the distance covered by a jet plane that travels at the rate of xy miles per hour for 2 hours?

    (A) $\frac{x}{2}$ (B) $\frac{x}{y}$ (C) $2xy$ (D) $\frac{xy}{2}$ (E) $\frac{y}{2}$

8. What is the rate of a plane that covers xy miles in y hours?

    (A) x (B) $\frac{x}{y}$ (C) $2xy$ (D) $\frac{xy}{2}$ (E) y

9. At what time will a train traveling at 50 miles per hour arrive at the station, if it is 5 miles from the station at 5:00 P.M.?

    (A) 5:05   (B) 5:06   (C) 5:10   (D) 5:50
    (E) 5:55

10. A train traveling 100 miles at m miles per hour arrived at its destination 1 hour late. How many miles an hour should it have traveled to arrive on time?

    (A) $\frac{100}{m}$ (B) $\frac{100-m}{m}$ (C) $\frac{100m}{100-m}$
    (D) $\frac{100m}{100+m}$ (E) $\frac{100-m}{100m}$

11. A train covers the distance d between two cities in h hours arriving 2 hours late. What rate would permit the train to arrive on schedule?

    (A) $h-2$ (B) $\frac{d}{h}-2$ (C) $\frac{d}{h-2}$
    (D) $dh-2$ (E) $\frac{d}{h+2}$

12. A train travels from La Crosse to New Lisbon in 46 minutes. If the distance between the two cities is 59.8 miles, what is the average rate of the train in miles per hour?

    (A) 46   (B) 47   (C) 48   (D) 61   (E) 78

13. How fast is a train moving if it covers d miles in h hours?

    (A) $\frac{h}{d}$ (B) hd (C) $\frac{dh}{2}$ (D) $\frac{d}{h}$ (E) $\frac{h}{2d}$

14. A boat sails m miles upstream at the rate of r miles per hour. If the rate of the stream is s miles per hour, how long will it take the boat to return to its starting point?

    (A) $\frac{m}{r}$ (B) $\frac{m}{r+2s}$ (C) $mr-s$ (D) $\frac{m}{s}+r$
    (E) $\frac{m}{r+s}$

15. How many hours will it take a woman to travel M miles at the rate of H miles per hour?

    (A) HM (B) $\frac{H}{M}$ (C) $\frac{M}{H}$ (D) $\frac{M}{2H}$ (E) $\frac{D}{2M}$

16. A train covered d miles the first hour, e miles the second hour, and f miles the third hour. What was the average rate for the entire trip?

    (A) $\frac{def}{3}$ (B) $3def$ (C) $3(def)$ (D) $3(d+e+f)$
    (E) $\frac{1}{3}(d+e+f)$

17. A motorist traveled 60 miles at the rate of 20 miles per hour and returned over the same route at 40 miles per hour. What was the average rate for the entire trip?

    (A) $26\frac{2}{3}$ (B) 30   (C) 34   (D) $37\frac{1}{2}$ (E) 60

18. How many minutes will it take a train to cover a distance of 1 mile if its average speed is 50 miles per hour?

    (A) 0.2   (B) 0.8   (C) 1.2   (D) 2   (E) 5

19. Nancy rides her bicycle 10 miles at an average rate of 12 miles per hour and 12 miles at an average rate of 10 miles per hour. The average rate for the entire trip is approximately

    (A) 2   (B) 10   (C) 11   (D) 21   (E) 22

20. How many miles can a motorist travel from 8:55 A.M. to 9:15 A.M. if his average rate is 36 miles per hour?

    (A) 12   (B) 24   (C) 36   (D) 48   (E) 108

21. Ms. Quigley runs y yards in s seconds. What would her rate be, in yards per second, if she ran twice as far in 10 more seconds?

    (A) $\dfrac{2 + y}{100 + s}$ (B) $\dfrac{y}{2(s + 10)}$ (C) $\dfrac{2y}{10s}$

    (D) $\dfrac{2y}{s + 10}$ (E) $\dfrac{2y}{s - 10}$

22. A wheel rotates 10 times each minute and moves 20 feet during each rotation. How many feet does the wheel move in 1 hour?

    (A) 120   (B) 200   (C) 600   (D) 1,200
    (E) 12,000

23. Two automobiles travel in the same direction at 40 miles per hour and 50 miles per hour, respectively. How many hours after they are alongside of each other will they be 18 miles apart?

    (A) 0.36   (B) 0.40   (C) 0.45   (D) 1.80
    (E) 2.50

24. A mile runner is clocked at 58 seconds after the first $\frac{1}{4}$ mile (440 yards) and at 1 minute 56 seconds after he has run $\frac{1}{2}$ mile. What rate, in yards per second, must he maintain for the final two quarters if he is to run a 4-minute mile?

    (A) 7.0   (B) 7.1   (C) 7.3   (D) 7.6   (E) 7.8

25. Ms. Beedle rides her bicycle at an average rate of m kilometers per minute. Ms. Coddle walks half the distance in 3 times the length of time. What is Ms. Coddle's rate, in kilometers per minute?

    (A) $\dfrac{m}{90}$ (B) $\dfrac{m}{40}$ (C) $\dfrac{m}{10}$ (D) $\dfrac{m}{6}$ (E) $\dfrac{2m}{3}$

26. Mr. Bailey travels m miles at a miles per hour, and Mr. Barnes travels the same distance but at a slower rate of b miles per hour. What is the difference, in hours, between the time taken by Mr. Bailey and the time taken by Mr. Barnes?

    (A) $\dfrac{m}{a - b}$ (B) $\dfrac{m}{ab}$ (C) $\dfrac{2m}{a - b}$ (D) $\dfrac{m(a - b)}{ab}$

    (E) $\dfrac{m(b - a)}{ab}$

27. How much farther can a motorist traveling at 35 miles per hour for h hours travel than a motorist who travels at 40 miles per hour for $h - 2$ hours?

    (A) $70 - 5h$ (B) $80 - 5h$ (C) 45
    (D) $5h - 80$ (E) $5h + 80$

28. The "MISTRAL" connects Paris and Lyons, a distance of 320 miles. At an average rate of 78 miles per hour, how many minutes does the trip take?

    (A) 244   (B) 245   (C) 246   (D) 408   (E) 410

29. The "SUD-EXPRESS" averages a rate of 73 miles per hour in its run from Paris to Bordeaux. What is the distance, in miles, between these two cities, if the trip takes 297 minutes?

    (A) 246   (B) 361   (C) 365   (D) 369   (E) 407

30. If a wheel rotates 12 times each minute, how many degrees does it rotate in 5 seconds?

    (A) 60   (B) 150   (C) 240   (D) 360   (E) 1,800

31. By rail the trip from Boston to New York is 215 miles, while by airplane it is 188 miles. How many hours shorter is the trip by plane traveling at 225 miles per hour than by train traveling at 54 miles per hour?

    (A) 2.98   (B) 3.0   (C) 3.14   (D) 4.0   (E) 4.5

32. Mr. Walker travels a miles in b hours, and then c miles in d hours. How many hours will be needed to travel 1,000 miles if he maintains this average rate?

    (A) $\dfrac{1000}{a + c}$ (B) $\dfrac{1000}{b + d}$ (C) $\dfrac{1000}{b + c + d}$

    (D) $\dfrac{1000(b + d)}{a + c}$ (E) $\dfrac{a + c}{1000(b + d)}$

33. The elevator in an eleven-story office building travels at the rate of one floor per $\frac{1}{4}$ minute, which allows time for picking up and discharging passengers. At the main floor and at the top floor, the operator stops for 1 minute. How many complete trips will an operator make during a 7-hour period?

    (A) 20   (B) 30   (C) 60   (D) 76   (E) 120

34. How many minutes will it take a police car to respond to a call d miles away if the police car travels at m miles per hour?

    (A) $\dfrac{60m}{d}$ (B) $\dfrac{60d}{m}$ (C) $\dfrac{d}{m}$ (D) $\dfrac{dm}{60}$ (E) $\dfrac{60}{dm}$

35. Ms. Barrow travels from London to Tintern Abbey, a distance of 250 miles, in $5\frac{1}{2}$ hours. After resting for 20 minutes, she returns to London in 4 hours 40 minutes. What is her average rate, in miles per hour, for the round trip?

    (A) 43   (B) 44   (C) 45   (D) 46   (E) 48

Answer Key

1.	A	8.	A	15.	C	22.	E	29.	B
2.	C	9.	B	16.	E	23.	D	30.	D
3.	D	10.	C	17.	A	24.	B	31.	C
4.	B	11.	C	18.	C	25.	D	32.	D
5.	B	12.	E	19.	C	26.	E	33.	C
6.	A	13.	D	20.	A	27.	B	34.	B
7.	C	14.	B	21.	D	28.	C	35.	E

Ratio and Proportion Problems

Ratio

A **ratio** is an expression that compares two quantities by dividing one by the other. In a class of 10 girls and 13 boys, the ratio of girls to boys is $\frac{10}{13}$ or 10:13. The ratio of boys to girls is $\frac{13}{10}$ or 13:10.

Since a ratio may be written as a fraction, to find the maximum ratio among a given set of ratios, determine which fraction has the greatest value. In any ratio involving measured quantities the units of measure of the quantities compared must be the same.

Examples

■ A room is 120 inches long and 12 feet wide. Find the ratio of width to length. First change everything to feet; 120 inches = 10 feet.

$$\frac{12}{10} = \frac{6}{50} = \frac{3}{25}$$

■ Find the ratio of 2 ounces to 4 pounds.
Convert the 4 pounds to 64 ounces to get similar units.

$$\frac{2}{64} = \frac{1}{32}$$

■ The ratio of two numbers is 7:3, and their difference is 20. Find the numbers. Since the two numbers are not themselves 7 and 3, it follows that $\frac{7}{3}$ is a fraction that has been simplified by removing a common factor. Let n be this common factor, and represent the numbers by $7n$ and $3n$.

$$7n - 3n = 20$$
$$n = 5$$

The numbers are 35 and 15.

■ The ratio of two numbers is 16 to 33. The larger number is 264. Find the smaller. Let the common factor be n.

$$33n = 264$$
$$n = 8$$

The smaller number = $16n = 128$.

■ Two numbers are in the ratio 5 to 8. When 2 is added to each, the ratio of the resulting numbers is 2 to 3. Find the numbers.
Let $5n$ and $8n$ be the numbers. Then the resulting numbers will be $5n + 2$ and $8n + 2$, and their ratio will equal the fraction $\frac{2}{3}$.

$$\frac{5n + 2}{8n + 2} = \frac{2}{3}$$
$$n = 2$$

The numbers are 10 and 16.

Proportion

A **proportion** is an equation both sides of which are fractions. For example, $\frac{1}{2} = \frac{5}{10}$ is a proportion. A proportion consists of four terms: the first and last are the **extremes**; the second and third are the **means**. In the example just given, 1 and 10 are extremes, and 2 and 5 are means. In any proportion the product of the means equals the product of the extremes. Thus, if

$$\frac{a}{b} = \frac{c}{d}$$

then

$$ad = bc$$

Examples

■ Find the value of x if $\frac{4}{7} = \frac{16}{x}$.

$$4x = 16 \times 7$$
$$x = 28$$

■ If $7y = 3z$, then $\frac{y}{z} =$
To undo this cross-multiplication, divide both sides by $7z$.

$$\frac{7y}{7z} = \frac{3z}{7z}$$
$$\frac{y}{z} = \frac{3}{7}$$

To determine whether a problem to be solved involves a proportion, use the following test:

1. Are there two variables?

2. Does a change in one of these variables affect the other variable?

If the problem does involve a proportion, decide whether it is a direct proportion or an inverse proportion. Common sense will help you decide. This decision is important as it will determine how you should proceed.

In **direct proportion** the two variables are so related that, if both quantities are multiplied or divided by the same number, the ratio is unchanged. Some examples will help to make this clear.

1. *Conversion problems.* In converting U.S. dollars to British pounds, the more dollars you exchange, the greater will be the number of pounds you will get. In converting kilometers to miles, the greater the number of miles, the greater will be the number of kilometers. Algebraically, this may be expressed as

$$\frac{x}{y} = k, \quad \text{where the value of } k \text{ remains constant}$$

2. *Work problems where one individual is involved.* The more time spent, the greater will be the part of the task accomplished. If you have an assignment that will take 3 hours, in 1 hour you will accomplish $\frac{1}{3}$ of the task, in 2 hours $\frac{2}{3}$ of the task, and in 3 hours $\frac{3}{3}$, or the entire task.

3. *Business problems.* In partnerships, profits are distributed in direct proportion to the shares of ownership. In making purchases, consumers realize that the greater the quantity of an item bought, the greater will be the amount of money required.

4. *Recipe problems.* A recipe gives the quantities of ingredients required to produce a certain quantity of finished product. If the cook or baker wishes to produce five times the quantity indicated, he or she will multiply the quantity specified for each ingredient in the recipe by 5.

5. *Geometric problems involving similar triangles and polygons.* Corresponding sides are in proportion in similar triangles and polygons.

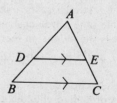

In *ABC*, if *DE* is parallel to *BC*, then $\triangle ADE$ is similar to $\triangle ABC$. If $AD = 6$, $DB = 3$, and $AE = 8$, and you must find *EC*, set up the proportion:

$$\frac{AD}{DB} = \frac{AE}{EC}$$

Then substitute:

$$\frac{6}{3} = \frac{8}{EC}$$
$$6(EC) = 24$$
$$EC = 4$$

In an **inverse proportion** an *increase* by multiplication in one variable results in a corresponding *decrease* in the other, and a *decrease* by division in one variable results in a corresponding *increase* in the other. Consider these examples.

1. When a team is working on a task, an increase in the size of the work force will produce a decrease in the time required to complete the task. On the other hand, a decrease in the size of the work force will cause an increase in the required time. Thus, if 10 workers require 6 days to complete a task, 6 persons working at the same rate will require 10 days to do the same job. Algebraically, this principle may be expressed as

$$xy = k, \quad \text{where } k \text{ has a constant level}$$

The way to identify the inverse proportion in this type of problem is to ask yourself this question: How does an increase in the work force affect the time required to complete the task?

2. If you have a fixed supply of milk for a specific number of school children for a week, and the number of children is suddenly doubled, how will that affect the number of days the supply will last? With more mouths to feed, the number of days will decrease because *k* remains the same in $xy = k$. In other words, the product of *x* and *y* remains the same, for an increase in *x* causes a decrease in *y* because the value of *k* is constant.

Examples

Will you use $\frac{x}{y} = k$ or $xy = k$?

■ If *m* books cost *d* dollars, how much will *x* books cost?

The ratio $\frac{m}{d}$ is the proportionality constant for a direct proportion between the number of books and their cost. Let *y* be the number of dollars in the cost of the *x* books, set up the proportion, and solve for *y*:

$$\frac{\text{number of books}}{\text{cost (in dollars)}} = \frac{m}{d} = \frac{x}{y}$$
$$my = dx$$
$$y = \frac{dx}{m}$$

■ If $1\frac{1}{2}$ cups of molasses can be substituted for 1 cup of sugar in a recipe, how many cups of molasses should be used in a recipe requiring $1\frac{1}{2}$ cups of sugar?

The constant of proportionality is the ratio of cups of molasses to cups of sugar. Let x be the number of cups of molasses for $1\frac{1}{2}$ cups of sugar.

$$\frac{\text{Cups of molasses}}{\text{Cups of sugar}} = \frac{1\frac{1}{2}}{1} = \frac{x}{1\frac{1}{2}}$$

$$x = \left(\frac{3}{2}\right)\left(\frac{3}{2}\right) = \frac{9}{4}$$

$$= 2\frac{1}{4} \text{ cups of molasses}$$

■ Mrs. Rosenfeld would like to have her driveway repaired. If 10 men would take 12 hours to do this job, how long would 16 men working at the same rate take?

The greater the number of people hired to do a certain job, the shorter the time required to complete the work. This is definitely an inverse proportion. Using $xy = k$, where k is the time required by 16 men, we have

$$(10)(12) = 16(x)$$
$$120 = 16x$$
$$7.5 = x$$

Practice Exercises

1. A city street has four large apartment houses and fourteen private homes. What is the ratio of apartment houses to private homes?

   (A) $\frac{2}{5}$ (B) $\frac{2}{9}$ (C) $\frac{4\frac{1}{2}}{1}$ (D) $\frac{1}{3\frac{1}{2}}$ (E) $\frac{7}{2}$

2. A mixture of nuts contains 2 pounds of cashew nuts and 2 ounces of peanuts. What is the ratio of peanuts to cashew nuts in the mixture?

   (A) 1:16 (B) 1:1 (C) 8:1 (D) 16:1 (E) 4:1

3. Candy previously sold for $1.60 per pound is now offered for 48 cents in a 6-ounce package. What is the ratio of the former price to the present price?

   (A) 3:1 (B) 5:4 (C) 10:3 (D) 3:10 (E) 4:5

4. If 3 apples cost 19 cents, how many apples can be purchased for $1.52?

   (A) 15 (B) 19 (C) 22 (D) 24 (E) 26

5. A boy makes a diagram of a plane to a scale of $\frac{1}{400}$ of actual size. If the diagram of the plane is 9.6 inches in length, what is the length, in feet, of the plane?

   (A) 96 (B) 320 (C) 384 (D) 960 (E) 3,840

6. On a map drawn to the scale $\frac{1}{2}$ inch = 200 miles, what is the distance, in miles, between two cities that are $3\frac{1}{2}$ inches apart on the map?

   (A) 300 (B) 350 (C) 700 (D) 1,200 (E) 1,400

7. How many minutes will a train traveling at the rate of 45 miles per hour take to cover a distance of $\frac{4}{5}$ mile?

   (A) 1.07 (B) 1.7 (C) 10 (D) 16 (E) 7.4

8. A motorist on the Freeway covers 0.8 mile in 1 minute. What distance, in miles, can he travel in 6 seconds?

   (A) 0.08 (B) 0.48 (C) 0.8 (D) 4.8 (E) 8

9. What is the average rate, in miles per hour, for a motorist who goes 2 miles in 3 minutes?

   (A) 20 (B) 24 (C) 32 (D) 40 (D) $66\frac{2}{3}$

10. How many miles are there in $1\frac{3}{5}$ kilometers if 1 kilometer equals $\frac{5}{8}$ mile?

    (A) $\frac{25}{64}$ (B) 1 (C) $1\frac{39}{40}$ (D) 2 (E) 24

11. If rain is falling at a rate of 2 inches per hour, how many inches will fall in 12 minutes?

    (A) $\frac{1}{360}$ (B) $\frac{2}{5}$ (C) $2\frac{1}{2}$ (D) 5 (E) 600

12. A vertical pole 6 feet high casts a shadow 4 feet long. At the same time a tree casts a shadow 64 feet long. What is the height, in feet, of the tree?

    (A) 44 (B) 72 (C) 96 (D) 192 (E) 256

13. If 2 cups of melted chocolate weigh 16 ounces, how many cups of melted chocolate can be obtained from a package of chocolate weighing 1 pound, 8 ounces?

    (A) 2.2 (B) 3 (C) 3.2 (D) 4 (E) 4.3

14. Six cups of shredded coconut weigh 1 pound. What is the weight, in ounces, of 1 cup of shredded coconut?

    (A) 0.6   (B) 0.16   (C) 1.6   (D) 2.6   (E) 4.3

15. A package of dried currants weighs 10 ounces. If 3 cups of dried currants weigh 1 pound, how many packages will a baker need for a recipe that calls for 15 cups of dried currants?

    (A) 5   (B) 8   (C) 10   (D) 50   (E) 80

16. There are 3 to 4 tablespoons of bread flour in 1 ounce. What is the maximum number of tablespoons of bread flour in 12 ounces?

    (A) 8   (B) 12   (C) 36   (D) 42   (E) 48

17. One cup of condensed, sweetened milk weighs 11 ounces. How many ounces of milk will remain unused for a recipe requiring 2 cups of milk when a housewife opens four 6-ounce cans of condensed milk?

    (A) 1   (B) 2   (C) 12   (D) 20   (E) 22

18. Two tablespoons = 1 ounce liquid; 4 tablespoons = $\frac{1}{4}$ cup. How many ounces are there in 1 cup?

    (A) 4   (B) 8   (C) 16   (D) 24   (E) 32

19. If a apples cost d dollars, how many apples can be bought for x dollars?

    (A) $\frac{ad}{x}$ (B) $\frac{d}{ax}$ (C) $\frac{dx}{a}$ (D) $\frac{a}{d}$ (E) $\frac{ax}{d}$

20. If cards are sold at the rate of 3 for 10¢, what will be the cost of 3 dozen such cards?

    (A) $0.42   (B) $1.08   (C) $1.20   (D) $1.26
    (E) $1.44

21. At the rate of 2 for 5 cents, how many envelopes can be purchased for 65 cents?

    (A) 13   (B) 26   (C) 32   (D) 34   (E) 52

22. The blueprint of a room is drawn to the scale 1 inch = 20 feet. If a room is actually 10 yards long, how long, in inches, is the line of the blueprint drawn to represent the length of the room?

    (A) $\frac{2}{3}$ (B) $1\frac{1}{2}$ (C) $1\frac{1}{3}$ (D) 2   (E) 6

23. If 4 men can clear the snow near a school in 6 hours, how many hours will it take 12 men working at the same rate to perform this task?

    (A) 2   (B) 8   (C) 12   (D) 18   (E) 24

24. If m men do a job in 10 days, how long will it take 10 men to complete this task, assuming that they work at the same rate?

    (A) $\frac{10}{m}$ (B) $\frac{100}{m}$ (C) $100m$ (D) $\frac{m}{100}$ (E) m

25. A dietician has sufficient milk to feed 13 infants for 4 weeks. How many days will this supply last if 13 more infants are added?

    (A) 2   (B) 8   (C) 14   (D) 26   (E) 56

26. In planning for a picnic, a committee purchases enough frankfurters to allow each of the 18 expected persons 3 frankfurters. If 9 additional persons come to the picnic, how many fewer frankfurters will each person be given?

    (A) 1   (B) $1\frac{1}{2}$ (C) 2   (D) $2\frac{1}{4}$ (D) $2\frac{1}{2}$

27. How many inches long is the shadow of an R-foot pole, if an r-inch ruler casts an s-inch shadow at the same time?

    (A) $\frac{12Rs}{r}$ (B) $\frac{Rs}{r}$ (C) $\frac{Rs}{12r}$ (D) $\frac{12R}{rs}$ (D) $\frac{rs}{R}$

28. If a $3\frac{2}{3}$-pound box of candy costs $3.30, what is the price per pound of the candy in the box?

    (A) 90¢   (B) $1.00   (C) $1.10   (D) $1.11
    (E) $1.21

29. A pound of commercial fertilizer occupies from 20 to 25 cubic inches, while a pound of humus occupies from 40 to 55 cubic inches. What is the maximum ratio of the amount of commercial fertilizer to humus in a 2-ton truck carrying equal amounts of each?

    (B) $\frac{1}{2}$ (B) $\frac{4}{11}$ (C) $\frac{5}{8}$ (D) $\frac{5}{11}$ (E) $\frac{9}{19}$

30. In a section of Mills City the ratio of private homes to apartment house dwellings is 5:3. If all the apartment house dwellings are brick structures and $\frac{1}{10}$ of the private homes are wooden structures, what is the maximum portion of houses that may be brick?

    (A) $\frac{3}{8}$ (B) $\frac{5}{8}$ (C) $\frac{6}{13}$ (D) $\frac{8}{13}$ (E) $\frac{15}{16}$

31. Grass seed formerly sold for 60¢ a pound is now packaged in 2-pound packages and is sold for $1.50 per package. What is the ratio of the old price to the present price of this seed?

    (A) 1:5   (B) 2:5   (C) 3:5   (D) 4:5   (E) 5:4

32. A test tube holds x cubic centimeters of water. How many test tubes are necessary to hold y cubic centimeters of water?

    (A) $\frac{y}{x}$ (B) $\frac{x}{y}$ (C) xy (D) $\frac{1}{y}$ (E) $\frac{1}{x}$

33. How many 3-cent stamps may be purchased for d dollars?

    (A) $\frac{d}{3}$ (B) $\frac{3}{d}$ (C) $\frac{d}{300}$ (D) $\frac{3}{100d}$ (E) $\frac{100d}{3}$

34. If t tables cost d dollars, what will be the cost, in dollars, of x tables?

 (A) $\dfrac{dx}{t}$ (B) $\dfrac{dt}{x}$ (C) dtx (D) $\dfrac{xt}{d}$ (E) $\dfrac{d}{t}$

35. One British gallon is equivalent to 1.20094 U.S. gallons. If an automobile travels 18 miles on a British gallon of gasoline, how many U.S. gallons would it use on a 216-mile trip?

 (A) 10   (B) 12   (C) 14.4   (D) 21.6   (E) 3,240

36. Mr. Lynch, who owns $\dfrac{3}{7}$ of a business, received $6,000 as his share of the profit for a certain year. How much will Mr. Beane receive during the same year if Mr. Beane owns $\dfrac{2}{7}$ of this business?

 (A) $1,400   (B) $1,614   (C) $2,000   (D) $2,562
 (E) $4,000

37. If 7 miles is equivalent to 11.27 kilometers, then 9.66 kilometers is equivalent to

 (A) 5 miles   (B) 6 miles   (C) 7 miles
 (D) 7.5 miles   (E) 7.9 miles

38. Mrs. Wilson left $32,000 and specified that the money be divided so that the ratio of the husband's share to the son's share was 5:3. The son received

 (A) $4,000   (B) $6,400   (C) $10,667
 (D) $12,000   (E) $20,000

39. Mary Lewis is paid $560 for a regular 35-hour week. Up to 40 hours she is paid at the regular hourly rate. For overtime more than 40 hours she receives $1\dfrac{1}{2}$ times as much as the regular hourly rate. How many hours did she work during a particular week when she earned $880?

 (A) 45   (B) 48.3   (C) 50   (D) 52   (E) 55

40. A furniture salesman averages $400 in commissions during a normal 40-hour week. During a special sale his rate of commission is increased by 25 percent. What is his average weekly commission during this period if he works 60 hours per week while the special sale is in progress?

 (A) $750   (B) $1,125   (C) $1,500   (D) $1,600
 (E) $6,000

41. At d cents per dozen what is the price, in cents, of x pencils?

 (A) $\dfrac{x}{12d}$ (B) $\dfrac{12d}{x}$ (C) $\dfrac{12x}{d}$ (D) $12dx$ (E) $\dfrac{dx}{12}$

42. Anne runs 100 yards in 9.8 seconds and then runs 440 yards in 49 seconds. What is the ratio of her average speed in the 440-yard run to her average speed in the 100-yard run?

 (A) $\dfrac{49}{43}$ (B) $\dfrac{22}{25}$ (C) $\dfrac{11}{12}$ (D) $\dfrac{12}{11}$ (E) $\dfrac{25}{22}$

43. A par
 trillion
 miles

 (A) $\dfrac{1}{63}$

44. If the
 African
 free
 would
 African
 then
 officia

 (A)

45. Appro
 denom
 $1,000
 What
 circula
 circu

 (A)
 (E)

46. Mr.
 day,
 day.
 that of
 annua

 (A) $3,600
 (E) $1

47. At 1250
 value

 (A) 6

48. In the
 quart of
 members
 member
 will
 dining

 (A) 2

49. In Euro
 per squ
 corresp
 centimete
 centimete
 inch?

 (A) 1
 (E) 3

50.   APPROXIMATE WORKING TIME
        (in minutes) REQUIRED TO PRODUCE

Commodity	U.S.S.R.	U.S.
1 Quart of Milk	42	7
1 Pound of Potatoes	7	2

How many more times efficient is the United States than the U.S.S.R. in the production of 1 quart of milk as compared to the production of 1 pound of potatoes?

(A) 1.7   (B) 2.5   (C) 3.5   (D) 6   (E) 21

Answer Key

1.	D	11.	B	21.	B	31.	D	41.	E
2.	A	12.	C	22.	B	32.	A	42.	B
3.	B	13.	B	23.	A	33.	E	43.	C
4.	D	14.	D	24.	E	34.	A	44.	B
5.	B	15.	B	25.	C	35.	C	45.	A
6.	E	16.	E	26.	A	36.	E	46.	D
7.	A	17.	B	27.	A	37.	B	47.	C
8.	A	18.	B	28.	A	38.	D	48.	A
9.	D	19.	E	29.	C	39.	C	49.	B
10.	B	20.	C	30.	E	40.	A	50.	A

Mixture and Solution Problems

The principles of fractions are used in solving problems involving mixtures or solutions. One useful formula is:

$$\frac{\text{Quantity of substance dissolved}}{\text{Total quantity of solution}} = \text{Fractional part of solution containing dissolved substance}$$

Examples

■ A 10-gallon solution of disinfectant contains 1 gallon of disinfectant. What is the percent concentration of the solution?

$$\frac{1}{10} = 10\%$$

■ How many pounds of pure salt must be added to 30 pounds of a 2 percent solution of salt and water to increase it to a 10 percent solution?

Since 2% of the 30 lb. is salt, there is 0.6 lb. of salt. Add x lb. of salt to the solution, and set up the ratio of the new amount of salt, $x + 0.6$, to the new amount of solution, $x + 30$.

$$\frac{x + 0.6}{x + 30} = \frac{1}{10}$$
$$x = 2\frac{2}{3}$$

■ How much water must be added to 3 quarts of a 10 percent solution of acid to reduce it to a 6 percent solution?

Let x be the amount of water added. Then set up the ratio of quarts of acid in the original solution to the number of quarts of new solution.

$$\frac{0.3 \text{ quart of acid in original solution}}{(3 + x) \text{ quarts of new solution}} = \frac{0.3}{3 + x} = \frac{6}{100}$$
$$x = 2$$

Practice Exercises

1. How many quarts of water must be added to 10 quarts of alcohol that is 95 percent pure in order to obtain a solution that is 50 percent pure?

(A) 0.5   (B) 5   (C) 9   (D) 10   (E) 15

2. An alloy of copper and tin is 20 percent copper. How many pounds of copper must be added to 20 pounds of the alloy in order for the resulting alloy to be 50 percent copper?

(A) 6   (B) 12   (C) 12.5   (D) 13   (E) 14

3. A certain grade of gun metal (a mixture of tin and copper) contains 16 percent tin. How much tin, in pounds, must be added to 410 pounds of this gun metal to make a mixture that is 18 percent tin?

(A) 5   (B) 6.5   (C) 7   (D) 8   (E) 10

4. Of 24 pounds of salt water, 8 percent is salt; of another mixture, 4 percent is salt. How many pounds of the second mixture should be added to the first mixture in order to get a mixture that is 5 percent salt?

(A) 18   (B) 36   (C) 54   (D) 63   (E) 72

5. How much water, in cubic centimeters, must be added to 100 cubic centimeters of 80 percent solution of boric acid to reduce it to a 50 percent solution?

(A) 30   (B) 40   (C) 50   (D) 60   (E) 84

6. How many quarts of pure alcohol must be added to 10 quarts of a mixture that is 15 percent alcohol to

make a mixture that will be 25 percent alcohol?

(A) $\frac{3}{4}$ (B) $1\frac{1}{3}$ (C) $1\frac{1}{4}$ (D) $2\frac{1}{2}$ (E) 4

7. A solution of 27 gallons of acid contains 9 gallons of pure acid. How much water, in gallons, should be added to produce a 25 percent solution of this acid?

(A) $6\frac{3}{4}$ (B) 9   (C) $15\frac{3}{4}$ (D) 18   (E) 27

8. A solution is made by mixing a quarts of pure salt with b quarts of water. What is the percent solution of the salt?

(A) $\frac{a}{a+b}\%$ (B) $\frac{100a}{a+b}\%$ (C) $\frac{100a}{b}\%$

(D) $\frac{a+b}{100}\%$ (E) $100(a+b)\%$

9. A chemist has 80 pints of a 20 percent salt solution. How many pints of pure salt must be added to produce a solution that is 30 percent pure salt?

(A) 4.6   (B) 8   (C) 11.4   (D) 16   (E) 27.4

10. How much alcohol, in pints, must be added to 80 pints of a solution of alcohol and iodine that is 20 percent iodine, in order to produce a 15 percent solution of iodine?

(A) 4.7   (B) 10.7   (C) 12   (D) 12.7   (E) 26.7

11. A pharmacist wishes to convert 100 ounces of a 3 percent tincture of iodine to a 2 percent tincture of iodine. How many ounces of alcohol should she add to her original solution?

(A) 1   (B) 50   (C) 67   (D) 100   (E) 150

12. Sixteen ounces of fresh orange juice contains 216 calories, and 16 ounces of fresh grapefruit juice contains 174 calories. If an 8-ounce mixture of these two juices contains 94 calories, what fraction of the mixture is orange juice?

(A) $\frac{1}{3}$ (B) $\frac{47}{108}$ (C) $\frac{1}{2}$ (D) $\frac{2}{3}$ (E) $\frac{47}{54}$

13. When at least 25 cigars are purchased, the price of "Corona Royals" is $9.75 for 25 and the price of "Coronas" is $4.50 for 25. What is the cost of 70 "Coronas" and 30 "Corona Royals"?

(A) $18.00   (B) $23.25   (C) $24.30   (D) $28.50
(E) $32.50

14. How many quarts of a 90 percent solution of alcohol should be mixed with a 75 percent solution of alcohol in order to make 20 quarts of 78 percent solution?

(A) 4   (B) 9   (C) 11   (D) 15   (E) 16

15. A confectioner mixes 9 parts of a grade of candy that costs p cents a pound with 4 parts of another grade of candy that costs $1\frac{1}{2}$ times as much. What is the cost, in cents, of 1 pound of this mixture?

(A) p (B) $\frac{15}{13}p$ (C) $\frac{35}{26}p$ (D) $\frac{3}{2}p$ (E) $15p$

16. A 64-pound mixture of sand and gravel is 25 percent sand. How many pounds of sand must be added to produce a mixture that is 40 percent gravel?

(A) 9.6   (B) 16   (C) 38.4   (D) 40   (E) 56

17. How many pounds of water must be added to 48 pounds of alcohol to make a solution that is 25 percent alcohol?

(A) 36   (B) 48   (C) 64   (D) 144   (E) 192

18. A 6-ounce can of frozen orange juice concentrate contains 300 calories, while an 8-ounce glass of fresh orange juice contains 100 calories. How many ounces of water should be added to a 6-ounce can of concentrate in order to produce a drink with the same caloric value per ounce as fresh orange juice? (*Note:* Water has no caloric value.)

(A) 18   (B) 24   (C) 400   (D) 3,744   (E) 3,750

19. Growell sells Grade A grass seed at 12¢ per ounce, and Grade A Plus at 35¢ per ounce. What is the cost of a 1-pound mixture containing 10 ounces of Grade A with the rest Grade A Plus?

(A) $1.65   (B) $3.30   (C) $3.40   (D) $6.80
(E) $4.70

20. A recipe for a cheese cake calls for 12 ounces of cottage cheese and 6 ounces of cream cheese. If there are 216 calories in 8 ounces of cottage cheese and 106 calories in 1 ounce of cream cheese, how many calories are there in 36 ounces of the cheese mixture?

(A) 960   (B) 972   (C) 1,920   (D) 3,816
(E) 4,788

Answer Key

1.	C	5.	D	9.	C	13.	C	17.	D
2.	B	6.	B	10.	E	14.	A	18.	A
3.	E	7.	B	11.	B	15.	B	19.	B
4.	E	8.	B	12.	A	16.	E	20.	C

Work Problems

Problems involving time spent working often require the use of fractions. For example, a student who has 4 hours of homework does $\frac{1}{4}$ of his task when he works 1 hour. A simple formula to remember is:

$$\frac{\text{Time spent working}}{\text{Time required to do job}} = \text{Fractional part of job done}$$

Examples

■ A man can paint a room in 6 hours. His son can paint the same room in 8 hours if he works alone. How long will it take the man and his son to do the job if they work together?

Let x = number of hours it will take them to finish, working together. Then in each hour they complete $\frac{1}{x}$ of the job. This $\frac{1}{x}$ represents the $\frac{1}{6}$ that the man does and the $\frac{1}{8}$ that his son completes.

$$\frac{1}{x} = \frac{1}{6} + \frac{1}{8}$$
$$\text{LCD} = 24x$$
$$24 = 4x + 3x$$
$$x = 3\frac{3}{7}$$

■ Ms. Jones can do a job in 10 days. After working 3 days, she hires a helper and the two complete the task in 5 days. How long would it have taken the helper to complete the task alone?

Each day Ms. Jones does $\frac{1}{10}$ of the job. In 3 days she does $\frac{3}{10}$ and then does another $\frac{5}{10}$ while working with the helper. If x is the number of days the helper would take to do the job alone, then he does $\frac{1}{x}$ each day and $\frac{5}{x}$ in 5 days. The sum of these fractions must equal 1, since the job was completed.

$$\frac{5}{x} + \frac{5}{10} + \frac{3}{10} = 1$$
$$\text{LCD} = 10x$$
$$50 + 5x + 3x = 10x$$
$$x = 25$$

■ One garden hose can completely fill a portable swimming pool in 80 minutes. Another garden hose can fill the same pool in half the time. How long would it take to fill the pool using both hoses?

Let x = number of minutes needed to fill the pool using both hoses. Then $\frac{1}{x}$ will be the fractional part completed in 1 minute. This represents the combined effects of the $\frac{1}{80}$ from the first hose and the $\frac{1}{40}$ from the second.

$$\frac{1}{80} + \frac{1}{40} = \frac{1}{x}$$
$$\text{LCD} = 80x$$
$$x + 2x = 80$$
$$x = 26\frac{2}{3}$$

Practice Exercises

1. Mr. Lopez can do a job in 8 days, and his son can do it in 12 days. How long would it take them to do the job if they worked together?

    (A) 4.8 (B) 5 (C) 10 (D) 15 (E) 20

2. A and B can paint a barn in 3 days. A can do it alone in 5 days. How many days would it take B to do this job alone?

    (A) 0.2 (B) 3.2 (C) 5.0 (D) 6.4 (E) 7.5

3. A machine can cut some wood in 6 minutes, and a man using a hand saw can do it in 18 minutes. After 4 minutes there is a power shortage and the wood must be cut by hand saw. How many minutes must the man work to complete the task?

    (A) 2 (B) 6 (C) 12 (D) 14 (E) 18

4. Mr. Boone can do a job in 10 days. A helper joins him after 3 days, and together they work for 4 days to complete the task. How many days would it take the helper to do the job alone?

    (A) 3 (B) $5\frac{5}{7}$ (C) 6 (D) 7 (E) $13\frac{1}{3}$

5. A pipe can fill a swimming pool in h hours. What part of the pool is filled in x hours?

    (A) hx (B) $\frac{h}{x}$ (C) $\frac{x}{h}$ (D) $h + x$ (E) $\frac{hx}{2}$

6. Three pipes are used to fill a pool with water. One pipe alone can fill the pool in 9 hours. Another can fill it in 6 hours. The third can fill it in 3 hours. How many minutes will it take to fill this pool if all three pipes are used simultaneously?

    (A) 1.63 (B) 11 (C) 54 (D) 56.4 (E) 98

7. The secretary of a club can address the envelopes for a mailing in 40 minutes. Her younger brother, who could do the entire job alone in 1 hour, assists her. How long, in minutes, would it take to address the envelopes if both work?

    (A) 0.04 (B) 0.4 (C) 8 (D) 24 (E) 50

8. Mr. Mitchell can do a job in 45 minutes, while his son would require 2 hours to do the work. How long would it take to complete this task if Mr. Mitchell was assisted by his son?

   (A) 18 min.   (B) 33 min.   (C) 35 min.
   (D) 1 hr. 21 min.   (E) 1 hr. 31 min.

9. If a woman working alone can do a job in h hours and her helper working alone can do it in k hours, how many hours would it take them to do the job if they worked together?

   (A) $\dfrac{1}{hk}$ (B) $\dfrac{h+k}{hk}$ (C) $\dfrac{h+k}{2}$ (D) $\dfrac{hk}{2}$
   (E) $\dfrac{hk}{h+k}$

10. Mr. Minelli can mow his lawn in x hours. After 2 hours it begins to rain. What part of the lawn is left unmowed?

    (A) $\dfrac{2-x}{x}$ (B) $\dfrac{x}{2}$ (C) $x-2$ (D) $\dfrac{x-2}{2}$
    (E) $\dfrac{x-2}{x}$

11. If 10 men can do a job in 20 days, how many days will it take 8 men to do the job if they work at the same rate?

    (A) 4   (B) 14   (C) 16   (D) 18   (E) 25

12. A master painter can paint a house in m days, and his two workers require w_1 and w_2 days to paint a house. If the master works as fast as the two workers together, find m in terms of w_1 and w_2.

    (A) 1   (B) $\dfrac{w_1+w_2}{w_1 w_2}$ (C) $\dfrac{w_1 w_2}{w_1+w_2}$ (D) $\dfrac{w_1}{w_2}$
    (E) $\dfrac{w_2}{w_1}$

13. A mother can do a job as fast as her two daughters working together. If one daughter does the job alone in 3 hours and the other does it alone in 6 hours, how many hours does it take the mother to do the job alone?

    (A) 1   (B) 2   (C) 3   (D) 4   (E) 5

14. Five men can paint a house in 6 days. If two of the men don't work, what will be the increase in time, in days, required to complete the job?

    (A) 4   (B) 6   (C) 8   (D) 10   (E) 12

15. In a factory, a women work b hours a day and produce c articles each day. If d women are released, how many hours a day will the remaining women have to work to produce c articles each day?

    (A) $\dfrac{ab}{d}$ (B) $\dfrac{ad}{b}$ (C) $\dfrac{a-d}{b}$ (D) $\dfrac{ab}{a-d}$
    (E) $\dfrac{b(a-d)}{d}$

16. Mr. Berg, who works twice as fast as Mr. Slocum, receives an hourly rate of pay $1\dfrac{1}{2}$ times as much as Mr. Slocum. An efficiency expert calculates that an article produced by Mr. Berg has a labor cost of 12¢. What is the labor cost, in cents, of an article produced by Mr. Slocum?

    (A) 4   (B) 8   (C) 9   (D) 16   (E) 18

17. A regular postal clerk sorts 100 letters in c seconds, while a part-time worker requires p seconds to sort 100 letters. How many seconds will it take them to sort 100 letters if they work together?

    (A) $\dfrac{p+c}{2}$ (B) $\dfrac{p+c}{pc}$ (C) $\dfrac{pc}{p+c}$
    (D) $\dfrac{100(p+c)}{pc}$ (E) $\dfrac{100pc}{p+c}$

18. Mrs. Crocker can do the dinner dishes in $\dfrac{1}{4}$ hour, while her daughter Betty takes $\dfrac{1}{2}$ hour. What part of an hour would it take to do these dishes if they worked together?

    (A) $\dfrac{1}{8}$ (B) $\dfrac{1}{6}$ (C) $\dfrac{3}{16}$ (D) $\dfrac{3}{8}$ (E) $\dfrac{4}{3}$

19. John can paint a barn in 12 days. Joseph can do the same job in 3 days, while James can paint the barn in 2 days. What part of the task would be completed in 1 day if the three boys worked together?

    (A) $\dfrac{1}{17}$ (B) $\dfrac{3}{17}$ (C) $\dfrac{11}{12}$ (D) 1   (E) $\dfrac{12}{11}$

20. If three boys can paint a fence in 2 days, what part of the job can be completed by two boys in 1 day?

    (A) $\dfrac{1}{3}$ (B) $\dfrac{2}{3}$ (C) $\dfrac{3}{4}$ (D) 1   (E) $\dfrac{4}{3}$

21. Mr. Smith works twice as fast as Mr. Legatos and three times as fast as Mr. Paruolo. If Mr. Paruolo can complete a job in 12 hours, what part of the job can Mr. Legatos do in 6 hours?

    (B) $\dfrac{1}{12}$ (B) $\dfrac{1}{3}$ (C) $\dfrac{1}{2}$ (D) $\dfrac{3}{4}$ (E) 1

22. In one half the time, Abby can produce three times as much work as Beth. Beth can do in twice the time $\dfrac{1}{3}$ as much work as Carol. If Carol does a job in 1 hour, how many hours will it take Abby to do the same job?

    (A) $\dfrac{1}{6}$ (B) $\dfrac{2}{3}$ (C) 1   (D) $\dfrac{3}{2}$ (E) 6

23. If three secretaries can type six manuscripts in 12 days, how many days will it take two secretaries to type three such manuscripts?

    (A) 4   (B) 9   (C) 12   (D) 16   (E) 36

24. Snowhite Paint Co. contracts to paint three houses. Andy can paint a house in 6 days, while Bruce would take 8 days and Carl would take 12 days. After 8 days Andy goes on vacation, and Bruce begins to work for a period of 6 days. How many days will it take Carl to complete the contract?

    (A) 7　(B) 8　(C) 11　(D) 12　(E) 13

25. Mr. Stanley mowed $\frac{3}{4}$ of his lawn in $1\frac{1}{4}$ hours. Mr. Samuels, who works twice as fast, finished mowing the lawn. How many minutes did Mr. Samuels work?

    (A) $12\frac{1}{2}$　(B) 16　(C) 25　(D) 38　(E) 50

Answer Key

1.	**A**	6.	**E**	11.	**E**	16.	**D**	21.	**D**
2.	**E**	7.	**D**	12.	**C**	17.	**C**	22.	**C**
3.	**B**	8.	**B**	13.	**B**	18.	**B**	23.	**B**
4.	**E**	9.	**E**	14.	**A**	19.	**C**	24.	**C**
5.	**C**	10.	**E**	15.	**D**	20.	**A**	25.	**A**

Basic Geometric Concepts and Coordinate Geometry

The questions appearing on the SAT that involve geometry make use of only elementary ideas concerning such simple plane figures as angles, lines, circles, and triangles and such simple solid figures as spheres and rectangular solids.

A list of geometric facts is given at the beginning of each math section of the SAT, and almost all of the geometry questions can be worked using these facts as a basis. The more experience you have with the use of these facts, however, the easier you will find the questions and the quicker you will discover the methods needed to answer them.

The skills you need to practice involve the following: area, circumference, and arc measures of circles; angle relationships in triangles; the area of a triangle; the relationship between the sides of a right triangle; the area and perimeter of a rectangle; and the volumes of rectangular and spherical solids.

To help you visualize these relationships, we have compiled a summary of facts and fundamental situations involving common geometric ideas. Be sure to master these concepts.

Important Definitions, Relationships, and Measurements

Points, Lines, and Planes

The building blocks of geometry are points, lines, and planes. A **point** indicates a position and has no length, width, or thickness. A **line** is a continuous set of points that is straight and infinitely long in two opposite directions, but has no width or thickness. A **plane** is a flat surface that extends in all directions but has no thickness.

Most geometric figures are formed by joining parts of lines—either line segments or rays. A **line segment** has two points of a line as endpoints and con-tains all points of the line that lie between the endpoints. A **ray** has one point of a line as an endpoint and contains all of the points that lie on a given side of the line.

In drawings, these figures appear like this:

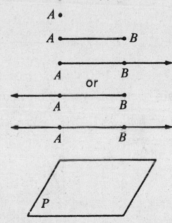

Angles and Triangles

If two different rays have the same endpoint, they form an **angle**.

The common endpoint is called the **vertex**, and the rays are called the **sides**.

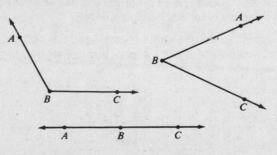

The angle directly above has rays that are opposite to each other and lie along a straight line. Such an angle is called a **straight angle**. The measure in degrees of a straight angle is 180. Degree measures of other angles are proportional to the fractional part of a straight angle that they represent.

Two angles are **adjacent** if they have the same vertex and share a common side. Adjacent angles may not overlap.

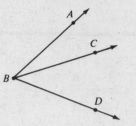

In the figure above there is one pair of adjacent angles, $\angle ABC$ and $\angle CBD$. Note that $\angle ABC$ and $\angle ABD$ are not adjacent since they overlap.

Two angles are **supplementary** if the sum of their degree measures is 180. A 60° and a 120° angle are supplementary. A 150° and a 30° angle are supplementary.

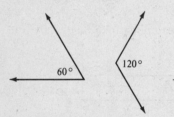

Two angles are **complementary** if the sum of their degree measures is 90. A 40° and a 50° angle are complementary. A 25° and a 65° angle are complementary.

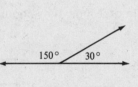

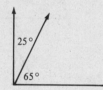

Note that two angles do not have to be adjacent to be supplementary or complementary.

An angle is a **right angle** if its measure is 90°. Note that two adjacent right angles have sides that form a line.

If two lines intersect to form right angles, the lines are **perpendicular**.

If three points of a plane do not all lie on the same line, the segments that connect these points form a **triangle**. The sum of the degree measures of the angles of a triangle is 180.

If a triangle has a right angle, it is called a **right triangle**. A triangle is **equilateral** if all sides have the same length. All of the angles of an equilateral triangle have the same degree measure, 60.

An **isosceles triangle** is one in which two sides have the same length. The angles opposite the sides of equal length have the same degree measure. These are called the **base angles**, and the side of the triangle that they share is called the **base** of the isosceles triangle.

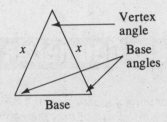

The altitude to the base of an isosceles triangle bisects the base and bisects the vertex angle.

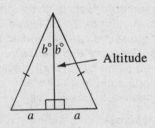

Line-Angle Relationships

Two intersecting lines form two pairs of vertical angles. Note that $\angle 1$ and $\angle 2$ are vertical angles, and $\angle a$ and $\angle b$ are vertical angles. Vertical angles have the same degree measure.

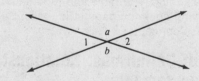

If two lines that lie in the same plane do not intersect, they are **parallel**. A line that intersects a pair of parallel lines is called a **transversal**.

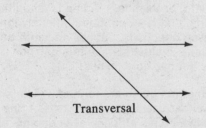

Transversal

If a pair of parallel lines is intersected by a transversal, three important angle relationships exist:

1. Alternate interior angles have the same measure:

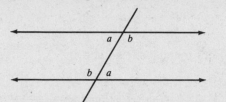

2. Corresponding angles have the same measure:

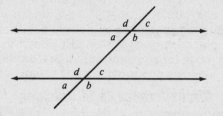

3. Interior angles on the same side of the transversal are supplementary.

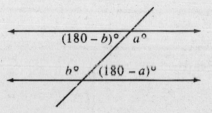

Quadrilaterals

The closed figure formed by joining four points in a plane, no three of which lie on the same line, is a **quadrilateral**.

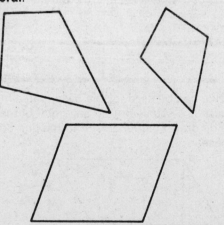

A **parallelogram** is a quadrilateral having opposite sides parallel. The opposite sides of a parallelogram are also equal in length. In the figure below, AC is parallel to and equal to BD; AB is parallel to and equal to DC.

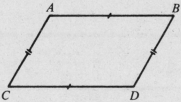

The opposite angles of a parallelogram have the same measure. Thus $\angle A$ has the same measure as $\angle D$, and $\angle B$ has the same measure as $\angle C$.

The diagonals of a parallelogram bisect each other. In the figure below, $AE = ED$ and $BE = EC$.

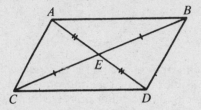

If a parallelogram has four right angles it is a **rectangle**. The diagonals of a rectangle are equal in length. Thus $AC = BD$.

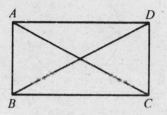

A **rhombus** is a parallelogram having all sides of the same length; $AB = BC = CD = AD$. The diagonals of a rhombus are perpendicular to each other; $AC \perp BD$.

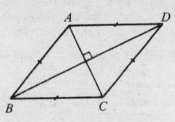

A **square** is a rectangle having all sides of the same length. Thus it has all of the properties of a parallelogram, a rectangle, and a rhombus.

A **trapezoid** is a quadrilateral having one pair of sides parallel (the *bases*) and the other pair nonparallel (the *legs*). Thus AD is parallel to BC.

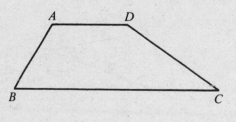

Angle-Circle Relationships

A **circle** is determined by a point and a positive number. The set of all points in a plane that are the given number of units away from the given point is a circle. The given point is its center; the given number, its radius.

A **central angle** of a circle is an angle whose vertex is the center of the circle. The measure of the arc cut off by the central angle is the same as the measure of the angle.

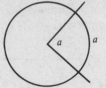

An **inscribed angle** of a circle is an angle whose vertex is a point of the circle and whose sides intersect, in the circle, two other points. The measure of an inscribed angle is half the measure of the arc it cuts off.

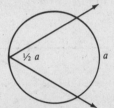

If an angle is inscribed in a semicircle, it must be a right angle.

Relationships Between the Sides of Triangles

Two triangles are **similar** if all of their pairs of corresponding angles have the same measure. Roughly speaking, triangles are similar if they have the same shape but not necessarily the same size.

Corresponding sides of similar triangles are proportional:

$$\frac{AB}{A'B'} = \frac{AC}{A'C'} = \frac{BC}{B'C'}$$

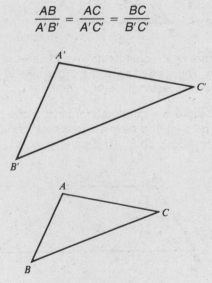

In a right triangle the square of the hypotenuse is equal to the sum of the squares of the legs. This relationship is called the **Pythagorean Theorem**.

$$(\text{leg})^2 + (\text{leg})^2 = (\text{hypotenuse})^2$$

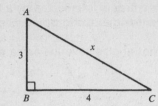

In the right triangle shown above:

$$(3)^2 + (4)^2 = x^2$$
$$9 + 16 = x^2$$
$$25 = x^2$$
$$5 = x$$

Note that the **hypotenuse** is the side opposite the right angle; it is always the longest side of the right triangle. Look for a relationship of $3:4:5$ or $5:12:13$ in right triangles and avoid lengthy computation.

Areas, Circumference, and Volumes

The area of a rectangle is the product of the length (l) and the width (w):

$$A = lw$$

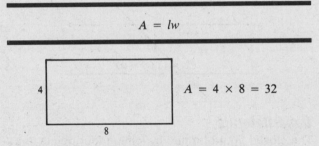

$$A = 4 \times 8 = 32$$

The area of a parallelogram is the product of the lengths of the base (b) and the altitude (h) to that base:

$$A = bh$$

Any side can be used for the base. The altitude to the base is a segment from any point of the opposite side drawn perpendicular to the line containing the base.

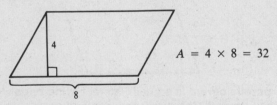

$$A = 4 \times 8 = 32$$

The area of a triangle is equal to one-half the product of the lengths of a base (b) and the altitude (h) to that base:

$$A = \frac{1}{2}bh$$

Any side may be a base. The altitude to the base is the segment from the vertex opposite the base and perpendicular to the line containing the base.

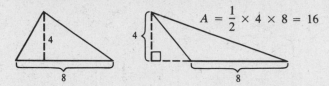

$$A = \frac{1}{2} \times 4 \times 8 = 16$$

The area of a right triangle is one-half the product of the lengths of its legs:

$$A = \frac{1}{2} (\text{leg})(\text{leg})$$

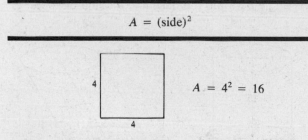

$$A = \frac{1}{2} \times 4 \times 8 = 16$$

The area of a square is the square of the length of one of its sides.

$$A = (\text{side})^2$$

$$A = 4^2 = 16$$

The area of a square is also equal to one-half the square of the length of its diagonal.

$$A = \frac{1}{2} (\text{diagonal})^2$$

$$A = \frac{1}{2} \times 8^2 = 32$$

The ratio of the areas of two similar figures is equal to the square of the ratio of the lengths of any two corresponding linear parts (sides, altitudes, medians, or angle bisectors).

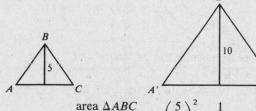

$$\frac{\text{area } \Delta ABC}{\text{area } \Delta A'B'C'} = \left(\frac{5}{10}\right)^2 = \frac{1}{4}$$

The area of a circle is equal to the product of π and the square of the radius:

$$A = \pi r^2$$

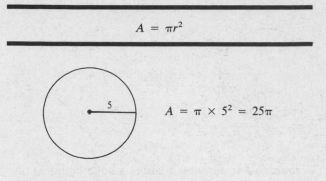

$$A = \pi \times 5^2 = 25\pi$$

The circumference of (sometimes referred to as the "distance around") a circle is the product of π and the diameter, or two times the product of π and the radius:

$$C = \pi d \quad \text{or} \quad C = 2\pi r$$

$$C = 2 \times \pi \times 5 = 10\pi$$

A **sector** of a circle is a pie-shaped region bounded by a central angle, the arc it cuts off, and two radii. Each sector of a circle represents some fractional part of the circular region. This fractional part can be found by the following formula:

$$\frac{\text{Degree measure of central angle}}{360} =$$

$$\text{Fractional part of circle}$$

Hence a 60° angle cuts off a sector that represents $\frac{1}{6}$ of the circle, and a 150° angle determines a sector that is $\frac{150}{360}$ or $\frac{5}{12}$ of the circle.

To find the area of a sector, find the area of the circle and multiply by the fractional part.

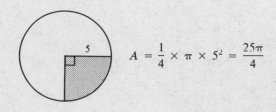

$$A = \frac{1}{4} \times \pi \times 5^2 = \frac{25\pi}{4}$$

To find the arc length of a sector, find the circumference of the circle and multiply by the fractional part.

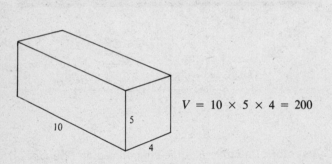

Arc length $= \dfrac{1}{4} \times 2\pi \times 5 = \dfrac{5\pi}{2}$

A **rectangular parallelepiped** is a solid figure all of whose faces are rectangles. It has six such faces. Its volume is the product of the length times the width times the height:

$$V = lwh$$

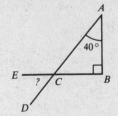

$V = 10 \times 5 \times 4 = 200$

A **cube** is a special kind of rectangular parallelepiped with length, width, and height all equal. If x is the length, width, or height, then

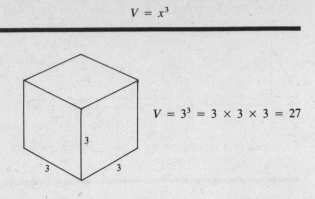

$$V = x^3$$

$V = 3^3 = 3 \times 3 \times 3 = 27$

A **cylinder** is a solid, generated by a rectangle, that revolves about one of its sides. The volume of a **cylinder** is the area of the base multiplied by the height. If the cylinder has a circular base, then

$$V = h(\pi r^2)$$

If two cylinders have the same height and the same base, they will have the same volume regardless of the angle between the base and the line of centers.

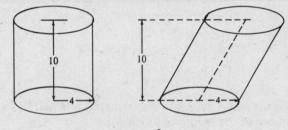

$V = 10(\pi \times 4^2) = 160\pi$

Practice Exercises

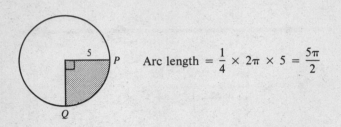

1. Angle $ECD =$
   (A) 20 (B) 25 (C) 40 (D) 50 (E) 90

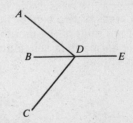

2. AD is perpendicular to CD. Angle $ADE = 140°$. Angle $EDC =$
   (A) 40° (B) 50° (C) 120° (D) 130° (E) 220°

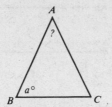

3. $AB = AC$, measure of $\angle B = a$. Measure of $\angle A =$
   (A) $a - 180$ (B) $2a - 180$ (C) $180 - 2a$
   (D) $180 - a$ (E) $\dfrac{180 - a}{2}$

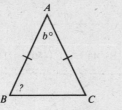

4. $AB = AC$, measure of $\angle A = b$. Measure of $\angle B =$
   (A) $b - 180$ (B) $b - 90$ (C) $180 - 2b$
   (D) $180 - b$ (E) $90 - \dfrac{b}{2}$

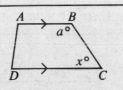

5. In $ABCD$, AB is parallel to DC. What is the value of x in terms of a?
   (A) a (B) $90 - a$ (C) $\dfrac{180 - a}{2}$ (D) $180 - a$
   (E) $360 - a$

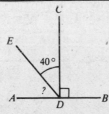

6. CD is perpendicular to AB. Angle $CDE = 40°$. Angle $EDA =$
   (A) $40°$ (B) $50°$ (C) $90°$ (D) $130°$ (E) $140°$

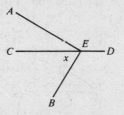

7. AE is perpendicular to BE. Angle $AEC = 25°$. Angle $x =$
   (A) $25°$ (B) $65°$ (C) $75°$ (D) $115°$ (E) $155°$

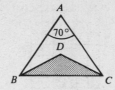

8. DB and DC are angle bisectors of isosceles triangle ABC. Angle $A = 70°$. Angle $BDC =$
   (A) $55°$ (B) $70°$ (C) $110°$ (D) $125°$ (E) $140°$

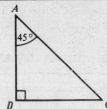

9. In triangle ABD, $AD = 13$, $AB = AD$. Altitude $AC = 12$. $BD =$
   (A) 5 (B) 10 (C) 12 (D) 13 (E) 25

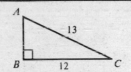

10. Area of triangle $ABC =$
    (A) 30 (B) 39 (C) 80 (D) 78 (E) 156

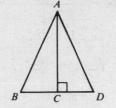

11. Area of triangle $ABC = 18$. Angle $A = 45°$. $AC =$
    (A) $3\sqrt{2}$ (B) $6\sqrt{2}$ (C) $9\sqrt{2}$ (D) $12\sqrt{2}$
    (E) $18\sqrt{2}$

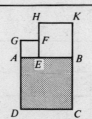

12. Area of square $GAEF = 25$. Area of square $HEBK = 100$. Area of square $ABCD =$
    (A) 125 (B) 225 (C) 600 (D) 625 (E) $5,000$

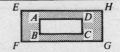

13. $AB = 10$, $BC = 30$, $EF = 20$, $EH = 60$. Area of the shaded portion =
    (A) 300 (B) 600 (C) 900 (D) $1,200$ (E) $1,800$

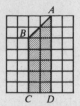

14. Area of *ABCD* =

    (A) 6   (D) 10   (C) 12   (D) 14   (E) 16

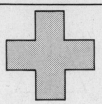

15. The area of the cross formed by cutting four equal
    squares from a larger square = 20. The perimeter
    of the cross =

    (A) 24   (B) $12\sqrt{5}$ (C) $16\sqrt{5}$ (D) 48   (E) 64

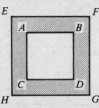

16. Each side of square *ACDB* = 8. The width of the
    border between square *EHGF* and *ACDB* = 2. The
    area of the shaded portion =

    (A) 36   (B) 40   (C) 48   (D) 80   (E) 100

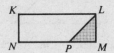

17. $MP = \frac{1}{3}$ of *MN*, the base of rectangle *KNML*.
    Area of triangle *LMP* = 8. Area of *KNML* =

    (A) 24   (B) 32   (C) 48   (D) 72   (E) 96

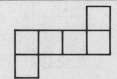

18. The area of each square = 16. The perimeter of
    the figure =

    (A) 24   (B) 40   (C) 44   (D) 48   (E) 56

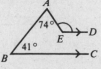

19. *ED* is parallel to *BC*. Angle *A* = 74°. Angle *B* =
    41°. Angle *AED* =

    (A) 41°   (B) 65°   (C) 74°   (D) 106°   (E) 115°

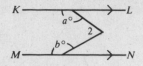

20. *KL* is parallel to *MN*. What is the value, in
    degrees, of ∠2?

    (A) $180 - a + b$ (B) $180 + a + b$
    (C) $360 - a + b$ (D) $360 - a - b$ (E) $b - a$

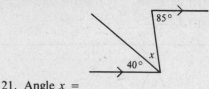

21. Angle *x* =

    (A) 40°   (B) 45°   (C) 50°   (D) 85°   (E) 125°

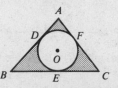

22. Angle *a* =

    (A) 30°   (B) 60°   (C) 70°   (D) 150°   (E) 160°

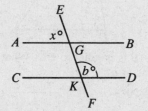

23. What is the value of *x* in terms of *b*?

    (A) *b*   (B) $b - 180$ (C) $90 - b$ (D) $180 - b$
    (E) $\dfrac{360 - b}{2}$

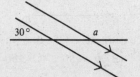

24. Circle *O* is inscribed in triangle *ABC*. *BD* = 4, *AF*
    = 3, *EC* = 5. The perimeter of triangle *ABC* =

    (A) 12   (B) 15   (C) 17   (D) 24
    (E) none of these

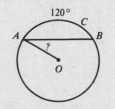

25. Arc *ACB* = 120°. Angle *BAO* =

    (A) 12°   (B) 30°   (C) 45°   (D) 60°   (E) 120°

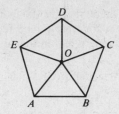

26. $AB = BC = CD = DE = EA$, and $AO = OB = OC = OD = OE$. The measure of $\angle BOA =$

(A) 15   (B) 30   (C) 45   (D) 60   (E) 72

27. If the radius of a circle is increased by 50 percent, the area of the circle is increased by

(A) 25%   (B) 50%   (C) 100%   (D) 125%
(E) 250%

28. If the radius of a circle is increased by 50 percent, the circumference is increased by

(A) 25%   (B) 50%   (C) 100%   (D) 125%
(E) 250%

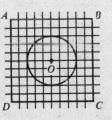

29. Area of circle $O = 9\pi$ square inches. The area, in square inches, of $ABCD =$

(A) 64   (B) 72   (C) 81   (D) 100   (E) 216

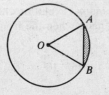

30. In circle O, $OA = 6$. Angle $AOB = 60°$. The area of the shaded portion =

(A) 2π (B) $4\pi - \sqrt{3}$ (C) $6\pi - 9\sqrt{3}$
(D) $36\pi - 9\sqrt{3}$ (E) $36\pi - 36$

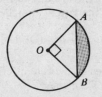

31. In circle O, $OA = 6$. AO is perpendicular to OB. The area of the shaded portion =

(A) 2π (B) $\pi - 2$ (C) $6\pi - 9\sqrt{3}$
(D) $9\pi - 18$ (E) $36\pi - 9\sqrt{3}$

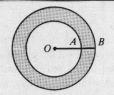

32. If $r = 2$, the area of $ABCD =$

(A) 36   (B) 12π (C) 36π (D) 144
(E) $144 - 36\pi$

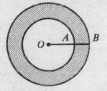

33. Radius $OA = 6$. $AB = 2$. The area of the shaded portion =

(A) 4π (B) 18π (C) 28π (D) 32π (E) 36π

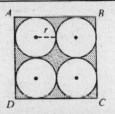

34. Radius $r = 2$. The area of the shaded portion =

(A) 16   (B) $16 - 2\pi$ (C) 48π (D) $64 - 4\pi$
(E) $64 - 16\pi$

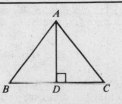

35. In circle O, $OB = 6$ and $AB = 2$. The ratio of the shaded portion to the small circle =

(A) 1:9   (B) 1:3   (C) 4:5   (D) 5:4   (E) 3:4

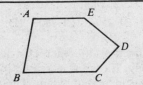

36. If AE is parallel to BC, then $\angle E + \angle D + \angle C =$

(A) 60°   (B) 100°   (C) 180°   (D) 360°
(E) none of these

37. $AB = AC = 5$. $BC = 6$. Altitude $AD =$

(A) 4   (B) 5   (C) $5\sqrt{2}$ (D) $5\sqrt{3}$ (E) 6

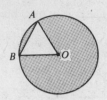

38. AB = radius OA; area of triangle AOB = $4\sqrt{3}$. Area of circle O =

(A) 4π (B) 8π (C) 16π (D) $24\sqrt{3}$

(E) $24\pi\sqrt{3}$

39. A rectangular fish tank is 3 feet long by 2 feet wide and contains water to a height of 1 foot. If all the water is poured into a second tank that is 4 feet long and 1 foot wide, how high, in feet, will the water level be in the second tank?

(A) 0.5   (B) 0.66   (C) 1.5   (D) 5.0   (E) 6.0

40. A room is 12 feet × 27 feet. What is the cost of carpeting the room at $11.00 per square yard?

(A) $29.70
(B) $396.00
(C) $45.64
(D) $225.00
(E) $1,188.00

41. The length of a rectangle is $4l$, and the width is $3w$. What is its perimeter?

(A) $4l + 3w$ (B) $7lw$ (C) $12lw$ (D) $14lw$

(E) $8l + 6w$

42. A wheel that has an area of πs^2 rolls a distance of m feet. How many revolutions does it make?

(A) $\dfrac{\pi s^2}{m}$ (B) $\dfrac{m}{\pi s^2}$ (C) $\dfrac{m}{2\pi s}$ (D) $\dfrac{2\pi s}{m}$

(E) $2\pi sm$

43. The width of a rectangle is $\dfrac{4}{5}$ of its length. If its perimeter is 72, what is its area?

(A) 160   (B) 250   (C) 280   (D) 320   (E) 500

44. The length and width of a rectangle are l and w, respectively. If each is increased by a units, the perimeter is increased by how many units?

(A) a (B) $2a$ (C) $4a$ (D) a^2 (E) $4a^2$

45. A square has the same area as a triangle whose base is 12 inches and whose altitude is 24 inches. What is the length, in inches, of the side of the square?

(A) 6   (B) 12   (C) 36   (D) 144   (E) 288

46. A circular flower bed whose diameter is 4 feet is increased so that the diameter is 12 feet. How many times larger is the new flower bed?

(A) $\sqrt{8}$ (B) 3   (C) 8   (D) 9   (E) 64

47. A rectangular lot 50 feet by 100 feet is surrounded on all sides by a concrete walk 5 feet wide. Find the number of square feet in the surface of the walk.

(A) 1,600   (B) 5,250   (C) 5,500   (D) 6,100
(E) 6,600

48. A picture 12 inches by 20 inches is surrounded by a 2-inch mat. Find the area, in square inches, of the mat.

(A) 68   (B) 96   (C) 112   (D) 144   (E) 352

49. A seesaw is balanced at its center at a point 3 feet above the ground. What is the highest, in feet, one end can rise above the ground?

(A) 3   (B) $3\sqrt{2}$ (C) 5   (D) 6   (E) 9

50. The scale of a map is $\dfrac{3}{4}$ inch = 12 miles. What is the area, in square miles, of a plot represented on this map by a square whose side is 1 inch?

(A) 4   (B) 9   (C) 16   (D) 81   (E) 256

51. A wheel has a radius of $3\dfrac{1}{2}$ feet. How many revolutions will the wheel make in traveling 242 feet? $\left(\text{Use } \pi = \dfrac{22}{7}.\right)$

(A) 3.3   (B) 5.5   (C) 11   (D) 22   (E) 80

52. The ratio of the surface areas of two cubes is 1:4. What is the ratio of their volumes?

(A) 1:2   (B) 1:4   (C) $\dfrac{1}{2}$:4   (D) 1:8   (E) 1:16

53. The diameter of the front wheel of a tricycle is 8 inches and of each of the two back wheels 3 inches. How many revolutions has each of the back wheels made when the front wheel has turned 1,440°?

(A) $2\dfrac{2}{3}$ (B) 4   (C) $10\dfrac{2}{3}$ (D) 24   (E) 96

54. An angle is 30° more than one-half its complement. Find the angle.

(A) 20°   (B) 30°   (C) 50°   (D) 60°   (E) 75°

55. Two sides of a triangle are 12 and 8 inches, respectively. If the altitude to the former is 4 inches, the altitude to the latter, in inches, is

(A) $\dfrac{8}{3}$ (B) 3   (C) 6   (D) 12   (E) 24

56. What is the area of a circle inscribed in a square having a side of 6 inches?

(A) 6π (B) 9π (C) 16π (D) 18π (E) 36π

57. What is the area of a square inscribed in a circle whose area is 25π?

(A) 25   (B) 50   (C) 75   (D) 100   (E) 125

58. The circumference of the base of a cylinder is 16π inches. The height of the cylinder is equal to the diameter of the base. How many gallons does the cylinder hold? (231 cu. in. = 1 gal.)

    (A) 1.10   (B) 3.5   (C) 4   (D) 13.9   (E) 16

59. What is the perimeter of a right triangle whose legs are 36 and 48?

    (A) 60   (B) 84   (C) 120   (D) 132   (E) 144

60. The angles of a quadrilateral are in the ratio of $1:2:3:4$. Find the largest angle.

    (A) 72°   (B) 90°   (C) 120°   (D) 144°   (E) 180°

Answer Key

1. D	11. B	21. B	31. D	41. E	51. C
2. D	12. B	22. D	32. D	42. C	52. D
3. C	13. C	23. D	33. C	43. D	53. C
4. E	14. C	24. D	34. E	44. C	54. C
5. D	15. A	25. B	35. D	45. B	55. C
6. B	16. D	26. E	36. D	46. D	56. B
7. B	17. C	27. D	37. A	47. A	57. B
8. D	18. E	28. B	38. C	48. D	58. D
9. B	19. E	29. D	39. C	49. D	59. E
10. A	20. D	30. C	40. B	50. E	60. D

Coordinate Geometry

Many of the techniques of algebra can be applied to geometry when the points of a plane are assigned pairs of real numbers that indicate the positions of these points. This can be done by first drawing a pair of perpendicular number lines, **axes**, in the plane that intersect at the origin of each line.

One axis is drawn horizontal, the **x-axis**, and one vertical, the **y-axis**. The positive ray of the x-axis points to the right, and the positive ray of the y-axis points upward.

To label a given point in the plane, draw perpendicular lines from the point to each of the axes and find the number-line coordinates on these axes. To avoid confusion, always record the x-coordinate first and the y-coordinate second, separating them with a comma and enclosing the pair of numbers in parentheses to indicate that the order of the numbers has special meaning.

Example

■ In the diagram observe the coordinates of each point, A–J.

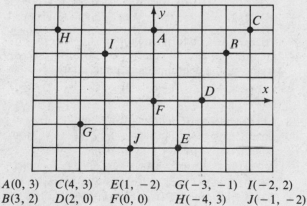

A(0, 3)   C(4, 3)   E(1, −2)   G(−3, −1)   I(−2, 2)
B(3, 2)   D(2, 0)   F(0, 0)   H(−4, 3)   J(−1, −2)

To find the distance between any two points use the *distance formula*. According to this formula, if point P_1 has coordinates (x_1, y_1) and point P_2 is (x_2, y_2), the distance between the points is

$$\sqrt{(x_1 - x_2)^2 + (y_1 - y_2)^2}$$

In the example above, the length of AC is $\sqrt{16 + 0} = \sqrt{16}$ and $\sqrt{16} = 4$. In that example the length of $FE = \sqrt{5}$.

To find the coordinates of the midpoint of a segment whose endpoints are given, use the *midpoint formula*. According to this formula, if point $P_1 = (x_1, y_1)$ and $P_2 = (x_2, y_2)$, the coordinates of the midpoint of the segment whose endpoints are P_1 and P_2 are

$$\left(\frac{x_1 + x_2}{2}, \frac{y_1 + y_2}{2}\right)$$

Examples

■ If $(3, -1)$ and $(-4, 2)$ are the coordinates of the endpoints of a segment, find the coordinates of the midpoint.

$$\left(\frac{3 + (-4)}{2}, \frac{-1 + 2}{2}\right) = \left(-\frac{1}{2}, \frac{1}{2}\right)$$

The midpoint is

$$\left(-\frac{1}{2}, \frac{1}{2}\right)$$

■ If $(3, -1)$ is one endpoint of a segment and $(5, 0)$ is its midpoint, find the coordinates of the other endpoint.

Let (x, y) be the other endpoint.

$$\frac{x + 3}{2} = 5 \qquad \frac{y - 1}{2} = 0$$
$$x = 7 \qquad\quad y = 1$$

The other endpoint is $(7, 1)$.

Practice Exercises

1. A line segment AB is drawn from point $(2, 3)$ and point $(4, 7)$. What are the coordinates of the midpoint?

    (A) $(5, 3)$ (B) $(3, 5)$ (C) $(6, 10)$ (D) $(2, 4)$
    (E) $(4, 2)$

2. What is the distance from point $A(3, 4)$ to point $B(-3, -4)$?

    (A) 0 (B) 5 (C) 10 (D) 13 (E) 14

3. Point $P(4, 2)$ is the midpoint of line OPC, where O is at origin $(0, 0)$. The coordinates of C are

    (A) $(2, 1)$ (B) $(4, 8)$ (C) $(4, 4)$ (D) $(8, 2)$
    (E) $(8, 4)$

4. Point $P(0, -4)$ is the midpoint of line AB, where the coordinates of point A are $(-2, -5)$. The coordinates of point B are

    (A) $(-4, -10)$ (B) $(2, -5)$ (C) $(2, 5)$
    (D) $(2, -3)$ (E) $(2, 3)$

5. The vertices of triangle ABC are $(-1, 2)$, $(-1, 1)$, and $(-3, 2)$. Triangle ABC is

    (A) obtuse (B) isosceles (C) right
    (D) equilateral (E) either isosceles or equilateral

6. The vertices of triangle DEF are $(1, 2)$, $(-1, 1)$, and $(-3, 2)$. Triangle DEF is

    (A) equilateral (B) acute
    (C) either equilateral or obtuse (D) isosceles
    (E) neither isosceles nor right

7. Triangle ABC has the following vertices: $A(1, 1)$, $B(9, 4)$, and $C(1, 7)$. Which of the following statements is true?

    (A) $AB = BC$ (B) $AB = AC$ (C) $AB > BC$
    (D) $AB < BC$ (E) $AC = BC$

8. The vertices of triangle ABC are as follows: $A(2, 3)$, $B(8, 3)$, and $C(6, 7)$. Median BM is drawn. The coordinates of point M are

    (A) $(5, 4)$ (B) $(4, 5)$ (C) $(6, 4.5)$ (D) $(4, 6)$
    (E) $(4, 6.5)$

9. The vertices of square $ABCD$ are as follows: $(4, 0)$, $(4, 4)$, $(8, 4)$, and $(8, 0)$. The area of $ABCD$ equals

    (A) 2 (B) 4 (C) 8 (D) 12 (E) 16

10. The vertices of triangle ABC are $(2, 2)$, $(2, 6)$, and $(6, 2)$. The area of triangle ABC is

    (A) 8 (B) 10 (C) 12 (D) 14 (E) 16

11. What is the area of a square whose points (corners) are $(0, 4)$, $(4, 0)$, $(0, -4)$, and $(-4, 0)$?

    (A) 4 (B) 8 (C) 16 (D) 32 (E) 64

12. The area of a circle whose center is at $(0, 0)$ is 9π. The circle passes through all of the following points EXCEPT

    (A) $(-3, 0)$ (B) $(3, 0)$ (C) $(0, 3)$ (D) $(0, -3)$
    (E) $(3, 3)$

13. Quadrilateral $ABCD$ has the following points as its vertices: $(2, 2)$, $(6, 2)$, $(-2, -2)$, and $(6, -2)$. The area of $ABCD$ is

    (A) 4 (B) 8 (C) 24 (D) 32 (E) 64

14. AB is a diameter of a circle whose center is O. The coordinates of point A are $(-2, 0)$. The coordinates of point B are $(2, 0)$. The circle passes through a point whose coordinates are

    (A) $(-2, -2)$, (B) $(-2, 2)$ (C) $(0, 4)$
    (D) $(0, -2)$ (E) $(2, 2)$

15. A circle whose center is at origin O passes through point $P(4, 3)$. The length of the radius of this circle is

    (A) 3 (B) 3.5 (C) 4 (D) 4.5 (E) 5

16. The coordinates of a point equally distant from $A(4, -2)$ and $B(4, 6)$ and on the y-axis are

    (A) $(0, 2)$ (B) $(0, 4)$ (C) $(0, 8)$ (D) $(2, 0)$
    (E) $(2, 2)$

17. Triangle ABC is formed by joining point $A(6, 5)$, point $B(-3, 2)$, and point $C(9, -4)$. If median AM is drawn, the coordinates of point M are

    (A) $(-1, 3)$ (B) $(-6, -2)$ (C) $(-6, 2)$
    (D) $(3, 1)$ (E) $(3, -1)$

18. Line segment AB is drawn from point $(-3, 4)$ to point $(-3, -4)$. Line segment CD is drawn from point $(3, 3)$ to point $(3, -5)$. Which of the following is always true?

    (A) $AB > CD$ (B) $AB < CD$ (C) $AB \parallel CD$
    (D) AB intersects CD (E) $AB \perp CD$

19. If all points 3 units from (0, 0) are joined, the result will be a

(A) square with perimeter of 12 units
(B) triangle with area of $9\sqrt{3}$
(C) circle with diameter of 3 units
(D) circle with radius of 3 units
(E) rectangle with area of 9 units

20. The locus of points equidistant from a given line is a pair of lines that are

(A) perpendicular   (B) equal   (C) bisected
(D) broken   (E) parallel

21. The following points are joined: $(-2, -2)$, $(-1, -1)$, $(1, 1)$, $(2, 2)$. All of the following correctly describe the result EXCEPT

(A) The line formed is parallel to the x-axis.
(B) A straight line is formed.
(C) The line formed bisects the right angle formed by the coordinates of the axes.
(D) Any point on the line formed is equidistant from the x-axis and the y-axis.
(E) The line formed passes through the origin.

22. The perpendicular bisector of AB, where AB is formed by joining point (3, 6) and point (3, 0), is a line

(A) parallel to the y-axis, passing through (0, 0)
(B) parallel to the x-axis, passing through (3, 3)
(C) passing through (3, 3) and (0, 0)
(D) intersecting AB at (3, 0)
(E) intersecting AB at (3, 6)

23. Point $(-2, 6)$ is the center of a circle that is tangent to the x-axis. The coordinates of the point of tangency are

(A) $(-2, 0)$ (B) (0, 4)   (C) $(-2, -6)$
(D) $(0, -2)$ (E) (6, 0)

24. What is the area of a triangle with vertices at (5, 3), (11, 3), and (8, 8)?

(A) 7   (B) 15   (C) 24   (D) 30   (E) 64

25. KL is drawn from point (1, 6) to point $(1, -6)$. Of the following line segments, which would be parallel to KL?

(A) from point (1, 6) to point (6, 1)
(B) from point $(-1, -6)$ to point $(-6, -1)$
(C) from point $(-1, -1)$ to point $(-6, -6)$
(D) from point $(-6, -6)$ to point $(-6, 6)$
(E) from point (1, 1) to point (6, 6)

Answer Key

1.	B	6.	D	11.	D	16.	A	21.	A
2.	C	7.	A	12.	E	17.	E	22.	B
3.	E	8.	B	13.	C	18.	C	23.	A
4.	D	9.	E	14.	D	19.	D	24.	B
5.	C	10.	A	15.	E	20.	E	25.	D

Interpreting Data

A **graph** is a pictorial representation of data that gives an overall view of facts, omitting minor details. General conclusions can be drawn after examining the data.

The ability to interpret a pictorial representation of facts and figures is important for success in college-level work. This justifies the inclusion of this type of question on the Scholastic Aptitude Test. In addition, this type of question lends itself to testing the ability to apply basic principles of arithmetic, algebra, and geometry.

Helpful Tips on Coping with Graph Questions

1. Examine the entire graph. Get the general meaning of the picture.

2. Avoid lengthy computation. Most of these questions can be answered by estimating or applying the given choices to the facts presented.

3. Use only the information given; do not add information from your own background knowledge.

4. Be careful to use the correct units in answering the question. Do not confuse decimals with percentages.

5. Make sure your conclusion is reasonable.

Types of Graphs

Line graphs are used to show how a quantity changes. Very often the quantity is measured as time changes. If the line goes up, the quantity is increasing; if the line is horizontal, the quantity is not changing. To measure the height of a point on the graph, it is not necessary to use a ruler. Use your pencil or a piece of paper as a straightedge. Graph V in the Practice Exercises is a good illustration. Some graphs deal with two factors (Graph II), in which case comparisons are made.

Bar graphs can be either vertical or horizontal (Graph I). Quantities are compared by the height or length of the bar.

Circle graphs (Graphs III and IV) are used to show how various sectors share in the whole.

Practice Exercises

COST OF SEED PER FIFTY POUNDS

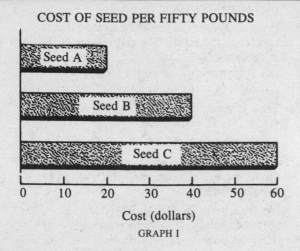

Cost (dollars)

GRAPH I

QUESTIONS 1–4 REFER TO GRAPH I.

1. What is the cost of $12\frac{1}{2}$ pounds of Seed B?

   (A) $10.   (B) $20.   (C) $40.   (D) $60.   (E) $75.

2. How many pounds of Seed C will I get for $30?

   (A) $12\frac{1}{2}$ (B) 25   (C) 50   (D) 100   (E) 900

3. The price of 1 pound of Seed C is what percent of the price of 1 pound of Seed B?

   (A) 20%   (B) $33\frac{1}{3}$%   (C) $66\frac{2}{3}$%   (D) 120%

   (E) 150%

4. What is the ratio of the price of 20 pounds of Seed B to the price of 20 pounds of Seed A?

   (A) 1:1   (B) 1:2   (C) 2:1   (D) 2:3   (E) 4:1

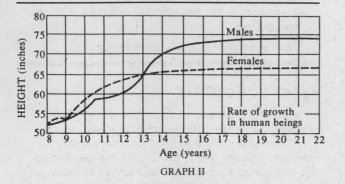

GRAPH II

QUESTIONS 5–9 REFER TO GRAPH II.

5. How many years old is a male when he reaches the height of an 11-year-old female?

   (A) 10   (B) 11   (C) 12   (D) 12.2   (E) 12.5

6. How many years old is a male when he is $\frac{1}{2}$ foot taller than the female of the same age?

   (A) 10.5   (B) 13   (C) 15   (D) 17   (E) 20

7. How many years old is a female when she is 4 feet 7 inches tall?

   (A) 9.2   (B) 9.5   (C) 9.6   (D) 13.3   (E) 21

8. According to this graph, how many years elapse between the occasions when males and females of the same age are also of the same height?

   (A) 4   (B) 8   (C) 9   (D) 13   (E) 22

9. How old is a male when he is 20 percent taller than a female is at the age of 10.5 years?

   (A) 10   (B) 10.5   (C) 14   (D) 14.5   (E) 15.2

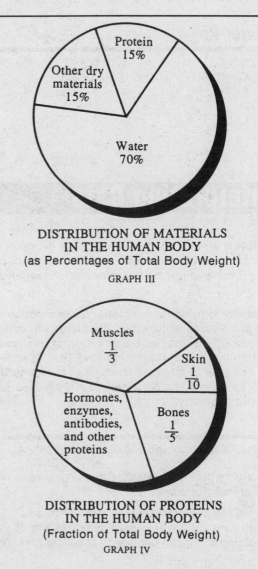

DISTRIBUTION OF MATERIALS IN THE HUMAN BODY
(as Percentages of Total Body Weight)

GRAPH III

DISTRIBUTION OF PROTEINS IN THE HUMAN BODY
(Fraction of Total Body Weight)

GRAPH IV

QUESTIONS 10–17 REFER TO GRAPHS III AND IV.

10. In terms of total body weight, the distribution of materials other than water and protein is equal to

    (A) $\frac{1}{15}$ (B) $\frac{85}{100}$ (C) $\frac{1}{20}$ (D) $\frac{3}{20}$ (E) $\frac{1}{5}$

11. A person weighing 170 pounds would, according to these graphs, be composed of water weighing

    (A) 17 lb. (B) 70 lb. (C) 100 lb. (D) 119 lb. (E) 153 lb.

12. How many degrees of the circle should be used to represent the distribution of protein?

    (A) 15 (B) 45 (C) 54 (D) 60 (E) 90

13. What percent of the entire body weight is made up of skin?

    (A) 0.15 (B) 1.0 (C) 1.5 (D) 10 (E) 15

14. If the weight of the bones of an individual is represented by x pounds, the weight, in pounds, of the skin of this individual is represented by

    (A) $\frac{1}{x+5}$ (B) $\frac{1}{x-5}$ (C) $2x$ (D) $\frac{x}{2}$ (E) $\frac{x}{5}$

15. What part of the proteins in the body is made up of muscles and skin?

    (A) $\frac{15}{1300}$ (B) $\frac{1}{130}$ (C) $\frac{1}{13}$ (D) $\frac{13}{30}$ (E) $\frac{1}{30}$

16. The ratio of the distribution of protein in muscle to the distribution of protein in skin is

    (A) 3:1 (B) 1:3 (C) 3:10 (D) $3\frac{1}{3}$:1 (E) 30:1

17. The human body, according to the data furnished by the graphs, is composed mainly of

    (A) proteins (B) hormones, enzymes, antibodies, and other proteins (C) muscles (D) bones (E) water

QUESTIONS 18–20 REFER TO GRAPH V.

18. When the temperature is 10 degrees on the Celsius scale, the number of degrees on the Fahrenheit scale is

    (A) 10 (B) 32 (C) 42 (D) 50 (E) 68

19. All of the following statements are true EXCEPT

    (A) If the Fahrenheit temperature that is equivalent to a Celsius reading of 60° is decreased by 10%, the resulting Celsius temperature is approximately 55°.
    (B) 90° on the Celsius scale corresponds to approximately 194° on the Fahrenheit scale.
    (C) 90° on the Fahrenheit scale corresponds to approximately 32° on the Celsius scale.
    (D) 0° on the Fahrenheit scale corresponds to approximately 0° on the Celsius scale.
    (E) Fahrenheit degrees equal approximately $\frac{9}{5}$ Celsius degrees plus 32°.

20. What will be the increase in the reading of the Fahrenheit scale when the Celsius reading is increased by 20 degrees?

    (A) 20° (B) 32° (C) 36° (D) 58° (E) 273°

SOLUBILITY-TEMPERATURE RELATIONSHIPS FOR VARIOUS SALTS

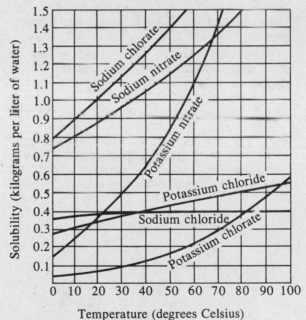

GRAPH VI

QUESTIONS 21–26 REFER TO GRAPH VI.

21. Which of the following salts has the greatest solubility?

    (A) Potassium chlorate at 81°C.
    (B) Potassium chloride at 45°C.
    (C) Potassium nitrate at 29°C.
    (D) Sodium chloride at 21°C.
    (E) Sodium chloride at 85°C.

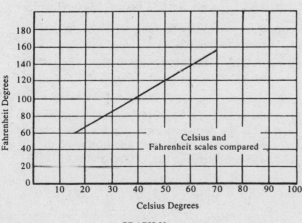

GRAPH V

22. Approximately how many kilograms of potassium nitrate can be dissolved in 10 liters of water at 23°C.?

    (A) 0.04   (B) 0.4   (C) 0.35   (D) 3.0   (E) 4.0

23. By what percent is the solubility of potassium chlorate in water increased as the water is heated from 29°C. to 62°C.?

    (A) 15   (B) 25   (C) 35   (D) 150   (E) 250

24. If 1 mole of potassium chloride weighs 0.07456 kilogram, approximately how many moles of potassium chloride can be dissolved in 100 liters of water at 36°C.?

    (A) 0.002   (B) 0.2   (C) 5   (D) 50   (E) 500

25. For which of the following pairs of salts is there NOT a temperature between 10°C. and 90°C. at which the salts have the same solubility?
    (A) Potassium chloride and sodium chloride
    (B) Potassium nitrate and sodium nitrate
    (C) Potassium chlorate and potassium nitrate
    (D) Potassium chlorate and sodium chloride
    (E) Potassium chloride and potassium nitrate

26. Which of the following salts has the greatest change in solubility, in kilograms per liter of water, between 15°C. and 25°C.?

    (A) Potassium chlorate   (B) Potassium nitrate
    (C) Sodium chloride   (D) Sodium chloride
    (E) Sodium nitrate

ANALYSIS OF ORDINARY LIFE INSURANCE PURCHASES IN THE UNITED STATES, 1955
(From 1956 Fact Book, permission of Institute of Life Insurance)

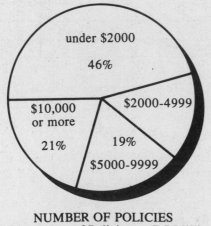

NUMBER OF POLICIES
Total Number of Policies — 7.5 Million

GRAPH VII

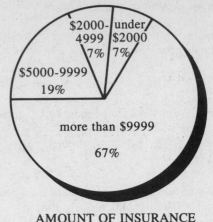

AMOUNT OF INSURANCE
Total Value of All Policies — $30.8 Billions

GRAPH VIII

QUESTIONS 27–31 REFER TO GRAPHS VII AND VIII.

27. How many MORE ordinary life insurance policies were purchased for amounts of $2,000 or more, than for amounts under $2,000, in the United States in 1955? (Answer in millions.)

    (A) 0.3   (B) 0.6   (C) 4.0   (D) 2,864   (E) 2,649

28. Approximately what part of the money invested in life insurance purchased in the United States in 1955 was for amounts less than $10,000?

    (A) $\frac{1}{7}$ (B) $\frac{1}{5}$ (C) $\frac{1}{3}$ (D) $\frac{2}{3}$ (E) $\frac{4}{5}$

29. What was the average amount, in dollars, of all the ordinary life insurance policies purchased in the United States in 1955?

    (A) 2,310   (B) 2,435   (C) 3,428   (D) 4,107
    (E) 16,240

30. Of the insurance policies for amounts of more than $10,000, $\frac{8}{21}$ were for less than $25,000. How many policies of $25,000 or more were purchased? (Answer in millions.)

    (A) 0.225   (B) 0.386   (C) 0.493   (D) 0.793
    (E) 0.975

31. If the radius of each of the circles in the graph is 1, what is the perimeter enclosing the area representing the amount of ordinary life insurance over $9,999 purchased in the United States in 1955?

    (A) 2   (B) $\frac{2}{3}\pi$ (C) $\frac{2}{3}\pi + 2$ (D) $\frac{4}{3}\pi$

    (E) $\frac{4}{3}\pi + 2$

MEDIAN AGE AT FIRST MARRIAGE

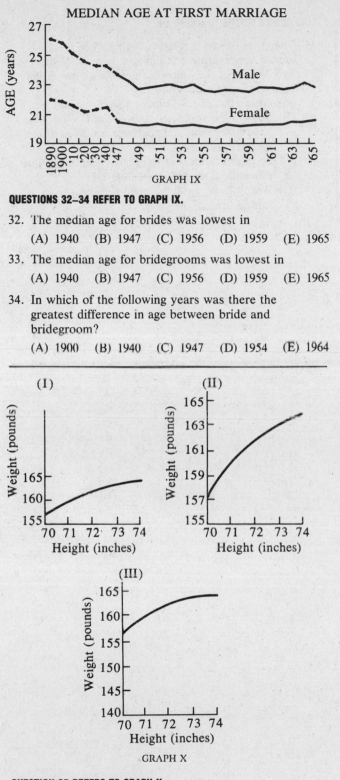

GRAPH IX

QUESTIONS 32–34 REFER TO GRAPH IX.

32. The median age for brides was lowest in

    (A) 1940   (B) 1947   (C) 1956   (D) 1959   (E) 1965

33. The median age for bridegrooms was lowest in

    (A) 1940   (B) 1947   (C) 1956   (D) 1959   (E) 1965

34. In which of the following years was there the greatest difference in age between bride and bridegroom?

    (A) 1900   (B) 1940   (C) 1947   (D) 1954   (E) 1964

GRAPH X

QUESTION 35 REFERS TO GRAPH X.

Following are the average heights, in inches, and weights, in pounds, of a given population:

Height	Weight
74	165
73	163
72	162
71	160
70	157

35. Which of the graphs—I, II, or III— represents these data correctly?

    (A) I   (B) II   (C) III   (D) All are correct.
    (E) None is correct.

YEARLY INCOME OF XYZ COMPANY

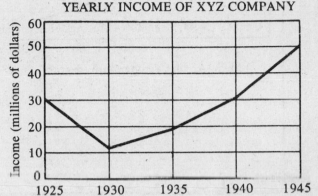

GRAPH XI

QUESTIONS 36–37 REFER TO GRAPH XI.

36. We are justified in concluding that
    (A) higher prices were charged by XYZ Company in 1945.
    (B) the income of XYZ Company increased more rapidly in the 1935–1940 period than in the preceding 5 years.
    (C) the number of sales of XYZ Company has been increasing since 1930.
    (D) there was a depression in 1930.

37. Approximately what was the average annual income of the company from 1930 to 1940?

    (A) $15,000,000   (B) $20,000,000
    (C) $25,000,000   (D) $30,000,000

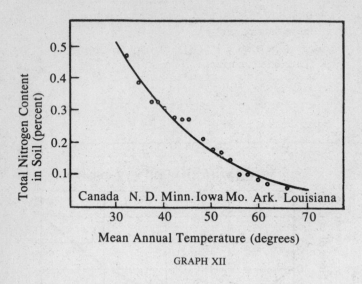

GRAPH XII

QUESTION 38 REFERS TO GRAPH XII.

38. The graph shows a relationship between mean annual temperature and nitrogen content of the soil. Which of the following statements can BEST be inferred from the graph?
    (A) Heat "bakes out" nitrogen from the soil.
    (B) Soils in the southern parts of the United States have lower nitrogen content than do northern midwestern soils.
    (C) Southern farmers have greater need to fertilize thin soils than do Canadian farmers.
    (D) Warmth may be substituted for nitrogen in raising farm crops.

Answer Key

1.	A	9.	E	17.	E	25.	C	33.	D
2.	B	10.	D	18.	D	26.	B	34.	A
3.	E	11.	D	19.	D	27.	B	35.	A
4.	C	12.	C	20.	C	28.	C	36.	B
5.	E	13.	C	21.	C	29.	D	37.	B
6.	C	14.	D	22.	E	30.	E	38.	B
7.	A	15.	D	23.	D	31.	E		
8.	A	16.	D	24.	E	32.	C		

13 The Test of Standard Written English (TSWE)

- ■ **Testing Tactics**
- ■ **12 Common Grammar and Usage Errors**
- ■ **Practice Exercises**
- ■ **Answer Key**
- ■ **Answer Explanations**

The Test of Standard Written English (TSWE) is not counted in your SAT score. It is scored separately, and, according to the College Board, is intended only to help colleges place students in the appropriate freshman English class. Therefore, you should probably not spend too much of your study time preparing for this section. At the same time, you don't want to approach it too casually. You don't want the college of your choice to think that your terrific verbal SAT score was a mistake.

The questions test your ability to recognize clear, correct standard written English, the kind of writing your college professors will expect on the papers you write for them. You'll be expected to know

basic grammar, such as subject-verb agreement, pronoun-antecedent agreement, correct verb tense; correct sentence structure, such as how to recognize a dangling participle or when two parts of a sentence are not clearly connected; and correct diction.

There are two different kinds of questions on the TSWE: usage questions and sentence correction ones. Most of them, 35 of the 50, to be exact, are usage questions, in which you have to find the error in the underlined sections of a sentence. You do not have to correct the sentence or explain what is wrong. Here are the directions.

Directions: The following sentences contain problems in grammar, usage, diction (choice of words), and idiom.

      Some sentences are correct.
      No sentence contains more than one error.

You will find that the error, if there is one, is underlined and lettered. Assume that elements of the sentence that are not underlined are correct and cannot be changed. In choosing answers, follow the requirements of standard written English.

If there is an error, select the one underlined part that must be changed to make the sentence correct and blacken the corresponding space on your answer sheet.

If there is no error, blacken answer space Ⓔ.

EXAMPLE:

The region has a climate <u>so severe that</u> plants
                 A

<u>growing</u> there rarely <u>had been</u> more than twelve
   B   C

inches <u>high</u>. <u>No error</u>
     D   E

SAMPLE ANSWER
Ⓐ Ⓑ ● Ⓓ Ⓔ

In the sentence correction questions, you will have five different versions of the same sentence, and you must choose the best one. Here are the directions.

Directions: In each of the following sentences, some part or all of the sentence is underlined. Below each sentence you will find five ways of phrasing the underlined part. Select the answer that produces the most effective sentence, one that is clear and exact, without awkwardness or ambiguity, and blacken the corresponding space on your answer sheet. In choosing answers, follow the requirements of standard written English. Choose the answer that best expresses the meaning of the original sentence.

Answer (A) is always the same as the underlined part. Choose answer (A) if you think the original sentence needs no revision.

EXAMPLE:

Laura Ingalls Wilder published her first book
and she was sixty-five years old then.

(A) and she was sixty-five years old then
(B) when she was sixty-five years old
(C) at age sixty-five years old
(D) upon reaching sixty-five years
(E) at the time when she was sixty-five

SAMPLE ANSWER

Ⓐ ● Ⓒ Ⓓ Ⓔ

Testing Tactics

Remember That the Error, If There Is One, Must Be in the Underlined Part of the Sentence.

You don't have to worry about improvements that could be made to the rest of the sentence. The only errors you need to consider are those in the underlined parts. For example, if you have a sentence in which the subject is plural and the verb is singular, you could call either one the error. But if only the verb is underlined, the error for that sentence is the verb. For example:

Mr. Brown is one of the commuters who takes
        A   B
the 7:30 train from Brooktown every morning.
               C   D
No error
  E

Since *who* refers to *commuters,* it is plural, and needs a plural verb, so the error is B. If you were writing this sentence yourself, you could correct it any number of other ways. You could say, "Mr. Brown is a commuter who takes . . ." or "Mr. Brown, a commuter, takes . . ." or "Mr. Brown, who is one of the commuters, takes . . ." However, the actual question doesn't offer you any of these possibilities. You have to choose from the underlined choices. Don't waste your time considering other ways to fix the sentence.

Use Your Ear for the Language.

Remember, you don't have to name the error, or be able to explain why it is wrong. All you have to do is recognize that something is wrong. If a word sounds wrong to you, it probably is, even if you don't know why.

See if your ear helps you with this question.

In my history class I learned why the American
      A   B
colonies opposed the British, how they organized
               C
the militia, and the work of the Continental
                      D
Congress. No error
         E

The last part of this sentence probably sounds funny to you—awkward, strange, wooden. You may not know exactly what it is, but something sounds wrong here. If you followed your instincts and chose D as the error, you would be right. The error is a lack of parallel structure. The sentence is listing three things you learned, and they should all be in the same form. Since the first two are clauses, the third should be too: "In my history class I learned why the American colonies opposed the British, how they organized the militia, and how the Continental Congress worked."

Look First for the Most Common Errors.

Most of the sentences will have errors. If you are having trouble finding mistakes, check for some of the more common errors: subject-verb agreement, pronoun-antecedent problems, misuse of adjectives and adverbs, dangling modifiers. But only look for errors in the underlined parts of the sentence. This should not take very long. For example:

Marilyn and I ran fast as we could, but we
       A   B
missed our train which made us late for work.
            C   D

No error
  E

Imagine that you have this sentence, and you can't see what is wrong with it. Start at the beginning and check each answer choice. *I* is part of the subject, so it is the right case. *Fast* can be an adverb, so it is being used correctly. *Which* is a pronoun, and needs a noun for its antecedent. The only available one is *train*, but that doesn't make sense. (The train didn't make us late—*missing* the train made us late.) So there is your error.

Once you have checked each answer choice, if you still can't find an error, choose E, "No error." A certain number of questions have no errors.

If You Spot an Error in the Underlined Section, Eliminate Any Answer That Repeats It.

(This tactic only applies to sentence correction questions.)

If something in the underlined section strikes you as an obvious error, you can immediately ignore any answer choices that repeat it. Remember, you still don't have to be able to explain what is wrong. You just need to find a correct equivalent. If the error you found is absent from more than one of the choices, look over those choices again to see if they add any new errors.

Try an example to see how this tactic works.

Being as I had studied for the test with a tutor, I was confident.

(A) Being as I had studied for the test
(B) Being as I studied for the test
(C) Since I studied for the test
(D) Since I had studied for the test
(E) Because I studied for the test

Since you immediately recognize that *being as* is not acceptable as a conjunction in standard written English, you can eliminate choices A and B right away. But you also know that both *since* and *because* are perfectly acceptable substitutes, so you have to look more closely at the remaining choices. The only other changes they make are in the tense of the verb. Since the studying occurred before the taking of the test, the past perfect tense, *had studied,* is correct, so the answer is Choice D. Even if you hadn't known that, you could have figured it out. Since *because* and *since* are both acceptable, and since choices C and E both use the same verb, *studied,* those two choices must be wrong. Otherwise, they would both be right, and the SAT doesn't have questions with two right answers.

Find the Changes in the Answers.

(This tactic only applies to sentence correction questions.)

If you don't see the error in the underlined section, look at the answer choices to see what is changed. The changes will tell you what kind of problem is being tested in this question. For example:

> The panel narrowed the field of applicants to the three <u>whom it thought were</u> best qualified for the position because of training and experience.
>
> (A) whom it thought were
> (B) of whom it thought were
> (C) who it thought was
> (D) whom it thought was
> (E) who it thought were

You can see right away that you have to choose between *who* and *whom* and between *was* and *were*. You can immediately eliminate Choice B—any choice that turns the sentence into gibberish is the wrong answer. To decide the pronoun question, check on the way it is used in the sentence. In this sentence, it is the subject of the verb *was* or *were* and therefore it must be *who*. This leaves you with choices C and E. Now you want to know if you need a plural or a singular verb. Since *who* refers to *three*, it is plural, and needs the plural verb *were*. The correct answer is E.

Make Sure That All Parts of the Sentence Are Logically Connected.

(This tactic only applies to sentence correction questions.)

Not all parts of a sentence are created equal. Some parts should be subordinated to the rest, connected with subordinating conjunctions or relative pronouns, not just added on with *and*. Overuse of *and* frequently makes sentences sound babyish.

Take, for example, this question.

> The leader always had loyal supporters <u>and they loved him</u>.
>
> (A) and they loved him
> (B) and they loving him
> (C) what loved him
> (D) who loved him
> (E) which loved him

The original version of this sentence doesn't have any grammatical errors, but it is a poor sentence because it doesn't connect its two clauses logically. The second clause is merely adding information about the supporters, so it should be turned into an adjective clause, introduced by a relative pronoun. Choices D and E both seem to fit, but you know that *which* should never be used to refer to people, so Choice D is obviously the correct answer.

Similarly, those parts of a sentence that are logically equal should always be presented in similar form

(parallel construction). Can you spot the error in parallel structure in the next question?

> In this chapter we'll analyze both types of questions, <u>suggest useful techniques for tackling them, providing some sample items for you to try</u>.
>
> (A) suggest useful techniques for tackling them, providing some sample items for you to try
> (B) suggest useful techniques for tackling them, providing some sample items which you can try
> (C) suggest useful techniques for tackling them, and provide some sample items for you to try
> (D) and suggest useful techniques for tackling them by providing some sample items for you to try
> (E) having suggested useful techniques for tackling them and provided some sample items for you to try

To answer questions like this correctly, you must pay attention to what the sentence means. You must first decide whether or not *analyzing, suggesting,* and *providing* are logically equal in importance here. Since they are—they are all activities that "we" will do—they should be given equal emphasis. Choice C is the one that correctly provides the parallel structure.

12 Common Grammar and Usage Errors

Some errors are more common than others on the TSWE. Here are a dozen that appear frequently on the examination. Watch out for them when you do the practice exercises and when you take the SAT.

1. The Run-on Sentence

Mary's party was very exciting, it lasted until two a.m.

It is raining today, I need a raincoat.

You may also have heard this error called a comma splice. It can be corrected by making two sentences instead of one:

Mary's party was very exciting. It lasted until two a.m.

or by using a semicolon in place of the comma:

Mary's party was very exciting; it lasted until two a.m.

or by proper compounding:

Mary's party was very exciting and lasted until two a.m.

You can also correct this error with proper subordination. The second example above could be corrected:

Since it is raining today, I need a raincoat.

It is raining today, so I need a raincoat.

2. The Sentence Fragment

Since John was talking during the entire class, making it impossible for anyone to concentrate.

This is the opposite of the first error. Instead of too much in one sentence, here you have too little. Do not be misled by the length of the fragment. It must have a main clause before it can be a complete sentence. All you have in this example is the cause. You still need a result. For example, the sentence could be corrected:

Since John was talking during the entire class, making it impossible for anyone to concentrate, the teacher made him stay after school.

3. Error in the Case of a Noun or Pronoun

Between you and I, this test is not really very difficult.

Case problems usually involve personal pronouns, which are in the nominative case (*I, he, she, we, they, who*) when they are used as subjects or predicate nominatives, and in the objective case (*me, him, her, us, them, whom*) when they are used as direct objects, indirect objects, and objects of prepositions. In this example, if you realize that *between* is a preposition, you know that *I* should be changed to the objective *me* because it is the object of a preposition.

4. Error in Subject-Verb Agreement

Harvard College, along with several other Ivy League schools, are sending students to the conference.

Phrases starting with *along with* or *as well as* or *in addition to* that are placed in between the subject and the verb do not affect the verb. The subject of this sentence is *Harvard College*, so the verb should be *is sending*.

There is three bears living in that house.

Sentences that begin with *there* have the subject after the verb. The subject of this sentence is *bears*, so the verb should be *are*.

5. Error in Pronoun-Antecedent Agreement

Every one of the girls on the team is trying to do their best.

Every pronoun must have a specific noun or noun substitute for an antecedent, and it must agree with that antecedent in number (singular or plural). In this example, *their* refers to *one* and must be singular:

Every one of the girls on the team is trying to do her best.

6. Error in the Tense or Form of a Verb

After the sun set behind the mountain, a cool breeze sprang up and brought relief from the heat.

Make sure the verbs in a sentence appear in the proper sequence of tenses, so that it is clear what happened when. Since according to the sentence, the breeze did not appear until after the sun had finished setting, the setting belongs in the past perfect tense:

After the sun had set behind the mountain, a cool breeze sprang up and brought relief from the heat.

7. Failure to Use the Subjunctive Mood When Needed

If I was your parent, I would ground you for a month.

The subjunctive mood is not very common in English, but it is used to indicate a condition contrary to fact. Since I am not your parent, the subjunctive is needed in this example:

If I were your parent, I would ground you for a month.

8. Error in Comparison

I can go to California or Florida. I wonder which is best.

When you are comparing only two things, you should use the comparative form of the adjective, not the superlative:

I wonder which is better.

Comparisons must also be complete and logical.

The rooms on the second floor are larger than the first floor.

It would be a strange building that had rooms larger than an entire floor. Logically, this sentence should be corrected to:

The rooms on the second floor are larger than those on the first floor.

9. Misuse of Adjectives and Adverbs

She did good on the test.
They felt badly about leaving their friends.

These are the two most common ways that adjectives and adverbs are misused. In the first example, when you are talking about how someone did, you want the adverb *well*, not the adjective *good*:

She did well on the test.

In the second example, after a linking verb like *feel*, you want a predicate adjective to describe the subject:

They felt bad about leaving their friends.

10. Dangling Modifiers

Reaching for the book, the ladder slipped out from under him.

A participial phrase at the beginning of the sentence should describe the subject of the sentence. Since it doesn't make sense to think of a ladder reaching for a book, this participle is left dangling with nothing to modify. The sentence needs some rewriting:

When he reached for the book, the ladder slipped out from under him.

11. Lack of Parallel Structure

In his book on winter sports, the author discusses ice-skating, skiing, hockey, and how to fish in an ice-covered lake.

Logically, equal and similar ideas belong in similar form. This shows that they are equal. In this sentence, the author discusses four sports, and all four should be presented the same way:

In his book on winter sports, the author discusses ice skating, skiing, hockey, and fishing in an ice-covered lake.

12. Error in Diction or Idiom

The affects of the storm could be seen everywhere.

Your ear for the language will help you handle these errors, especially if you are accustomed to reading standard English. These questions test you on words that are frequently misused, on levels of usage (informal versus formal), and on standard English idioms. In this example, the verb *affect,* meaning "to influence," has been confused with the noun *effect,* meaning "result."

The effects of the storm could be seen everywhere.

Practice Exercises

The exercise that follows will give you practice in answering the two types of questions you'll find on the TSWE: usage questions and sentence correction questions. When you've completed the exercise, check your answers against the answer key. Then, read the answer explanations for any questions you either answered incorrectly or omitted.

TSWE Exercise

Directions: The following sentences contain problems in grammar, usage, diction (choice of words), and idiom.

Some sentences are correct.
No sentence contains more than one error.

You will find that the error, if there is one, is underlined and lettered. Assume that elements of the sentence that are not underlined are correct and cannot be changed. In choosing answers, follow the requirements of standard written English.

If there is an error, select the one underlined part that must be changed to make the sentence correct and blacken the corresponding space on your answer sheet.

If there is no error, blacken answer space Ⓔ.

EXAMPLE:
The region has a climate so severe that plants
                                A
growing there rarely had been more than twelve
         B   C
inches high. No error
        D   E

SAMPLE ANSWER
Ⓐ Ⓑ ⬤ Ⓓ Ⓔ

1. We were already to leave for the amusement park
            A   B
   when John's car broke down; we were forced to
                    C   D
   postpone our outing. No error
                        E

2. By order of the Student Council, the wearing of
   A   B
   slacks by we girls in school has been permitted.
            C   D
   No error
   E

3. Each one of the dogs in the show require a special
   A   B   C
   kind of diet. No error
   D   E

4. The major difficulty confronting the authorities was
                        A   B
   the reluctance of the people to talk; they had been
                                C
   warned not to say nothing to the police. No error
        D   E

5. If I were you, I would never permit him
        A   B
   to take part in such an exhausting and painful
   C   D
   activity. No error
            E

6. Stanford White, who is one of America's
                   A
   most notable architects, have designed many
   B   C
   famous buildings, among them the original
                     D
   Madison Square Garden. No error
                          E

7. The notion of allowing the institution of slavery
              A   B
   to continue to exist in a democratic society had no
   C
   appeal to either the violent followers of John

   Brown nor the peaceful disciples of Sojourner
         D
   Truth. No error
          E

8. Some students <u>prefer</u> watching filmstrips to
                 A
<u>textbooks</u> because they feel <u>uncomfortable with</u>
   B   C
the presentation <u>of</u> information in a non-oral form.
                 D
<u>No error</u>
E

9. <u>There</u> was so much conversation <u>in back of</u> me
   A   B
<u>that</u> I <u>couldn't</u> hear the actors on the stage.
   C   D
<u>No error</u>
E

10. This book is <u>too</u> elementary; <u>it can help</u> neither
                 A   B
you <u>nor</u> <u>I</u> . <u>No error</u>
    C   D   E

11. In a way <u>we</u> may say <u>that</u> we <u>have reached</u> the
             A   B   C
<u>end of</u> the Industrial Revolution. <u>No error</u>
D   E

12. <u>Although</u> the books are <u>altogether</u> on the shelf,
    A   B
<u>they</u> are not arranged in <u>any kind of</u> order.
C   D
<u>No error</u>
E

13. The <u>reason for</u> my <u>prolonged absence</u> from class
        A   B
<u>was</u> <u>because</u> I was ill for three weeks. <u>No error</u>
C   D   E

14. <u>According to</u> researchers, the weapons and work
    A
implements <u>used by</u> Cro-Magnon hunters appear
           B
<u>being</u> <u>actually quite</u> "modern." <u>No error</u>
C   D   E

15. Since we were caught <u>completely unawares</u>, the
                         A
<u>affect</u> of Ms. Rivera's remarks <u>was startling</u>; some
B   C
were shocked, <u>but</u> others were angry. <u>No error</u>
              D   E

16. The committee <u>had intended</u> both <u>you and I</u> to
                  A   B
speak at the assembly; <u>however</u>, <u>only</u> one of us
                       C   D
will be able to talk. <u>No error</u>
E

17. The existence of rundown "welfare hotels"

<u>in which</u> homeless families <u>reside</u> at enormous
A   B
<u>cost to</u> the taxpayer provides a shameful
C
<u>commentary of</u> America's commitment to house
D
the poor. <u>No error</u>
E

18. We have heard that the <u>principal</u> has decided
                          A
<u>whom</u> the prize winners <u>will be</u> <u>and</u> will announce
B   C   D
the names in the assembly today. <u>No error</u>
E

19. <u>As soon as</u> the sun <u>had rose</u> <u>over</u> the mountains,
    A   B   C
the valley became <u>unbearably hot</u> and stifling.
                  D
<u>No error</u>
E

20. <u>They</u> are both <u>excellent books</u>, but this one <u>is</u>
    A   B   C
<u>best</u>. <u>No error</u>
D   E

21. Although the news <u>had come</u> as a surprise <u>to all</u> in
                      A   B
the room, everyone tried to do <u>their</u> work
                               C
<u>as though</u> nothing had happened. <u>No error</u>
D   E

22. <u>Even</u> well-known fashion designers have difficulty
    A
staying on top <u>from one season to another</u>
               B
<u>because of</u> <u>changeable moods</u> and needs in the
C   D
marketplace. <u>No error</u>
E

23. Arms control has been <u>under discussion</u> for
                              A
    decades with the Soviet Union, <u>but</u> solutions
                                      B
    <u>are still</u> <u>alluding</u> the major powers. <u>No error</u>
      C   D   E

24. Perhaps sports enthusiasts are realizing <u>that</u>
                                             A
    jogging is <u>not easy on</u> joints and tendons, for the
                B
    <u>latest</u> fad <u>is being walking</u>. <u>No error</u>
      C   D   E

25. Technological advances <u>can cause</u> factual data to
                             A
    become obsolete within a <u>short time</u>; <u>yet</u>, students
                                B   C
    should concentrate on <u>reasoning skills</u>, not facts.
                            D
    <u>No error</u>
      E

26. <u>If</u> anyone cares <u>to join</u> me in this campaign, <u>either</u>
     A   B   C
    now or in the near future, <u>they</u> will be welcomed
                                D
    gratefully. <u>No error</u>
                  E

27. The poems <u>with which</u> he occasionally
                A
    <u>deigned to regale</u> the fashionable world were
      B
    <u>invariably bad</u>—stereotyped, bombastic, and
      C
    <u>even ludicrous</u>. <u>No error</u>
      D   E

28. <u>Ever since</u> the <u>quality of</u> teacher education came
      A   B
    under public scrutiny, suggestions for <u>upgrading</u>
                                              C
    the profession <u>are abounding</u>. <u>No error</u>
                     D   E

29. <u>Because</u> the door was locked and bolted, the
      A
    police <u>were</u> forced <u>to break</u> into the apartment
             B   C
    <u>through</u> the bedroom window. <u>No error</u>
      D   E

30. I <u>will</u> <u>always</u> remember <u>you</u> <u>standing by</u> me and
       A   B   C   D
    offering me encouragement. <u>No error</u>
                                 E

31. With special training, capuchin monkeys

    <u>can enable</u> quadriplegics <u>as well as</u> other
      A   B
    handicapped individuals <u>to become</u>
                              C
    <u>increasingly independent</u>. <u>No error</u>
      D   E

32. <u>Contrary to</u> what had previously been reported,
      A
    the conditions <u>governing</u> the truce between Libya
                     B
    and Chad <u>arranged by</u> the United Nations <u>has</u> not
               C   D
    yet been revealed. <u>No error</u>
                         E

33. Avid readers generally either admire <u>or</u> dislike
                                           A
    Ernest Hemingway's journalistic <u>style of</u> writing;
                                      B
    <u>few have</u> no opinion of him. <u>No error</u>
      C   E

34. In 1986, the nuclear disaster at Chernobyl

    <u>has aroused</u> intense speculation <u>about</u> the longterm
      A   B
    <u>effects of</u> radiation that continued for
      C
    <u>the better part of</u> a year. <u>No error</u>
      D   E

35. Howard Hughes, <u>who</u> <u>became</u> the subject of
                     A   B
    bizarre rumors <u>as a result of</u> his extreme
                     C
    reclusiveness, was well-known as an aviator,
    industrialist, and <u>in producing motion pictures</u>.
                         D
    <u>No error</u>
      E

Directions: In each of the following sentences, some part or all of the sentence is underlined. Below each sentence you will find five ways of phrasing the underlined part. Select the answer that produces the most effective sentence, one that is clear and exact, without awkwardness or ambiguity, and blacken the corresponding space on your answer sheet. In choosing answers, follow the requirements of standard written English. Choose the answer that best expresses the meaning of the original sentence.

Answer (A) is always the same as the underlined part. Choose answer (A) if you think the original sentence needs no revision.

EXAMPLE: SAMPLE ANSWER
Laura Ingalls Wilder published her first book
and she was sixty-five years old then.

(A) and she was sixty-five years old then
(B) when she was sixty-five years old
(C) at age sixty-five years old
(D) upon reaching sixty-five years
(E) at the time when she was sixty-five

36. The child is neither encouraged to be critical or to examine all the evidence before forming an opinion.

(A) neither encouraged to be critical or to examine
(B) neither encouraged to be critical nor to examine
(C) either encouraged to be critical or to examine
(D) encouraged either to be critical nor to examine
(E) not encouraged either to be critical or to examine

37. The process by which the community influence the actions of its members is known as social control.

(A) influence the actions of its members
(B) influences the actions of its members
(C) had influenced the actions of its members
(D) influences the actions of their members
(E) will influence the actions of its members

38. Play being recognized as an important factor in improving mental and physical health and thereby reducing human misery and poverty.

(A) Play being recognized as
(B) By recognizing play as
(C) Their recognizing play as
(D) Recognition of it being
(E) Play is recognized as

39. To be sure, there would be scarcely any time left over for other things if school children would have been expected to have considered all sides of every matter on which they hold opinions.

(A) would have been expected to have considered
(B) should have been expected to have considered
(C) were expected to consider
(D) will be expected to have been considered
(E) were expected to be considered

40. Using it wisely, leisure promotes health, efficiency and happiness.

(A) Using it wisely
(B) If it is used wisely
(C) Having used it wisely
(D) Because of its wise use
(E) Because of usefulness

41. In giving expression to the play instincts of the human race, new vigor and effectiveness are afforded by recreation to the body and to the mind.

(A) new vigor and effectiveness are afforded by recreation to the body and to the mind
(B) recreation affords new vigor and effectiveness to the body and to the mind
(C) there are afforded new vigor and effectiveness to the body and to the mind
(D) by recreation the body and mind are afforded new vigor and effectiveness
(E) the body and the mind afford new vigor and effectiveness to themselves by recreation

42. Depending on skillful suggestion, argument is seldom used in advertising.

(A) Depending on skillful suggestion, argument is seldom used in advertising.
(B) Argument is seldom used by advertisers, who depend instead on skillful suggestion.
(C) Skillful suggestion is depended on by advertisers instead of argument.
(D) Suggestion, which is more skillful, is used in place of argument by advertisers.
(E) Instead of suggestion, depending on argument is used by skillful advertisers.

43. When this war is over, no nation will <u>either be isolated in war or peace</u>.

    (A) either be isolated in war or peace
    (B) be either isolated in war or peace
    (C) be isolated in neither war nor peace
    (D) be isolated either in war or in peace
    (E) be isolated neither in war or peace

44. Thanks to the prevailing westerly winds, dust <u>blowing east from the drought-stricken plains</u> travels halfway across the continent to fall on the cities of the East Coast.

    (A) blowing east from the drought-stricken plains
    (B) that, blowing east from the drought-stricken plains,
    (C) from the drought-stricken plains blowing east
    (D) that is from the drought-stricken plains and blows east
    (E) blowing east that is from the plains that are drought-stricken

45. Americans are learning that their concept of a research worker <u>toiling alone in a laboratory and who discovers miraculous cures</u> has been highly idealized and glamorized.

    (A) toiling alone in a laboratory and who discovers miraculous cures
    (B) toiling in a laboratory and discovers miraculous cures
    (C) toiling alone in a laboratory to discover miraculous cures
    (D) who toil alone in the laboratory and discover miraculous cures
    (E) who has toiled alone hoping to discover miraculous cures

46. However many mistakes have been made in our past, the tradition of America, <u>not only the champion of freedom but also fair play</u>, still lives among millions who can see light and hope scarcely anywhere else.

    (A) not only the champion of freedom but also fair play
    (B) the champion of not only freedom but also of fair play
    (C) the champion not only of freedom but also of fair play
    (D) not only the champion but also freedom and fair play
    (E) not the champion of freedom only, but also fair play

47. <u>Examining the principal movements sweeping through the world, it can be seen</u> that they are being accelerated by the war.

    (A) Examining the principal movements sweeping through the world, it can be seen
    (B) Having examined the principal movements sweeping through the world, it can be seen
    (C) Examining the principal movements sweeping through the world can be seen
    (D) Examining the principal movements sweeping through the world, we can see
    (E) It can be seen examining the principal movements sweeping through the world

48. <u>The FCC is broadening its view on what constitutes indecent programming</u>, radio stations are taking a closer look at their broadcasters' materials.

    (A) The FCC is broadening its view on what constitutes indecent programming
    (B) The FCC, broadening its view on what constitutes indecent programming, has caused
    (C) The FCC is broadening its view on what constitutes indecent programming, as a result
    (D) Since the FCC is broadening its view on what constitutes indecent programming
    (E) The FCC, having broadened its view on what constitutes indecent programming

49. As district attorney, Elizabeth Holtzman not only has the responsibility of supervising a staff of dedicated young lawyers <u>but she has the task of maintaining good relations with the police also</u>.

    (A) but she has the task of maintaining good relations with the police also
    (B) but she also has the task of maintaining good relations with the police
    (C) but also has the task of maintaining good relations with the police
    (D) but she has the task to maintain good relations with the police also
    (E) but also she has the task to maintain good relations with the police

50. Many politicians are now trying to take uncontroversial positions on <u>issues; the purpose being to allow them to appeal</u> to as wide a segment of the voting population as possible.

    (A) issues; the purpose being to allow them to appeal
    (B) issues in order to appeal
    (C) issues, the purpose is to allow them to appeal
    (D) issues and the purpose is to allow them to appeal
    (E) issues; that was allowing them to appeal

Answer Key

1.	A	11.	E	21.	C	31.	E	41.	B
2.	C	12.	B	22.	E	32.	D	42.	B
3.	B	13.	D	23.	D	33.	D	43.	D
4.	D	14.	C	24.	D	34.	A	44.	A
5.	E	15.	B	25.	C	35.	D	45.	C
6.	C	16.	C	26.	D	36.	E	46.	C
7.	D	17.	D	27.	E	37.	B	47.	D
8.	B	18.	B	28.	D	38.	E	48.	D
9.	B	19.	B	29.	E	39.	C	49.	C
10.	D	20.	D	30.	C	40.	B	50.	B

Answer Explanations

1. A. Should be *all ready*. *All ready* means the group is ready; *already* means prior to a given time, previously.

2. C. Should be *us*. The expression *us girls* is the object of the preposition *by*.

3. B. Should be *requires*. Verb should agree with the subject (*each one*).

4. D. Should be *to say anything*. *Not to say nothing* is a double negative.

5. E. Sentence is correct.

6. C. Error in agreement. Since the subject is Stanford White (singular), change *have designed* to *has designed*.

7. D. Error in use of correlatives. Change *nor* to *or*. The correct form of the correlative pairs *either* with *or*.

8. B. Error in parallel structure. Change *textbooks* to *reading textbooks*. To have parallel structure, the linked sentence elements must share the same grammatical form.

9. B. Error in diction. Change *in back of* to *behind*.

10. D. Should be *me*. Pronoun is the object of the verb *can help*.

11. E. Sentence is correct.

12. B. Should be *all together*. *All together* means in a group; *altogether* means entirely.

13. D. Improper use of *because*. Change to *that* (*The reason . . . was that. . . .*).

14. C. Incorrect verbal. Change the participle *being* to the infinitive *to be*.

15. B. Error in diction. Change *affect* (a verb meaning to influence or pretend) to *effect* (a noun meaning result).

16. C. Should be *me*. Subjects of infinitives are in the objective case.

17. D. Error in diction. Change *commentary of* to *commentary on*.

18. B. Should be *who*. The pronoun is the predicate complement of *will be* and is in the nominative case.

19. B. Should be *had risen*. The past participle of the verb *to rise* is *risen*.

20. D. Should be *better*. Do not use the superlative when comparing two things.

21. C. Should be *his or her* instead of *their*. The antecedent of the pronoun is *everyone* (singular).

22. E. Sentence is correct.

23. D. Error in diction. Change *alluding* (meaning to refer indirectly) to *eluding* (meaning to evade).

24. D. Confusion of verb and gerund (verbal noun). Change *is being walking* to *is walking*.

25. C. Error in sentence connector. Change *yet* to *therefore* or another similar connector to clarify the connection between the clauses.

26. D. Should be *he or she*. The antecedent of the pronoun is *anyone* (singular).

27. E. Sentence is correct.

28. D. Error in tense. Change *are abounding* to *have abounded*. The present perfect tense talks about an action that occurs at one time, but is seen in relation to another time.

29. E. Sentence is correct.

30. C. Should be *your*. The pronoun modifying a gerund (verbal noun) should be in the possessive case.

31. E. Sentence is correct.

32. D. Error in agreement. Since the subject is *conditions* (plural), change *has* to *have*.

33. D. Error in pronoun. Since the sentence speaks about Hemingway's style rather than about Hemingway, the phrase should read *of it*, not *of him*.

34. A. Error in tense. Change *has aroused* to *aroused*. The present perfect tense (*has aroused*) is used for indefinite time. In this sentence, the time is defined as *the better part of a year*.

35. D. Lack of parallel structure. Change *in producing motion pictures* to *motion picture producer*.

36. E. This question involves two aspects of correct English. *Neither* should be followed by *nor*; *either* by *or*. Choices A and D are, therefore, incorrect. The words *neither . . . nor* and *either . . . or* should be placed before the two items being discussed—*to be critical* and *to examine*. Choice E meets both requirements.

37. B. This question tests agreement. Agreement between subject and verb and pronoun and antecedent are both involved. *Community* (singular) needs a singular verb, *influences*. Also, the pronoun which refers to *community* should be singular (*its*).

38. E. This is an incomplete sentence or fragment. The sentence needs a verb to establish a principal clause. Choice E provides the verb (*is recognized*) and presents the only complete sentence in the group.

39. C. *Would have been expected* is incorrect as a verb in a clause introduced by the conjunction *if*. *Had been expected* or *were expected* is preferable. *To have considered* does not follow correct sequence of tense and should be changed to *to consider*.

40. B. One way of correcting a dangling participle is to change the participial phrase to a clause. Choices B and D substitute clauses for the phrase. However, Choice D changes the meaning of the sentence. Choice B is correct.

41. B. As it stands, the sentence contains a dangling modifier. This is corrected by making *recreation* the subject of the sentence, in the process switching from the passive to the active voice. Choice E also provides a subject for the sentence; however, the meaning of the sentence is changed in Choice E.

42. B. As presented, the sentence contains a dangling participle, *depending*. Choice B corrects this error. The other choices change the emphasis presented by the author.

43. D. *Either . . . or* should precede the two choices offered (*in war* and *in peace*).

44. A. Sentence is correct.

45. C. In the underlined phrase, you will find two modifiers of *worker*—*toiling* and *who discovers*. The first is a participial phrase and the second a clause. This results in an error in parallel structure. Choice B also has an error in parallel structure. Choice C corrects this by eliminating one of the modifiers of *worker*. Choice D corrects the error in parallel structure but introduces an error in agreement between subject and verb—*who* (singular) and and *toil* (plural). Choice E changes, the tense and also the meaning of the original sentence.

46. C. Parallel structure requires that *not only* and *but also* immediately precede the words they limit.

47. D. Choices A, B, and E are incorrect because of the dangling participle. Choice C is incoherent. Choice D correctly eliminates the dangling participle by introducing the subject *we*.

48. D. The punctuation in Choices A and C creates a run-on sentence. Choices B and E are both ungrammatical. Choice D corrects the run-on sentence by changing the beginning clause into an adverb clause that starts with the subordinating conjunction *since*.

49. C. Since the words *not only* immediately precede the verb in the first half of the sentence, the words *but also* should immediately precede the verb in the second half. This error in parallel structure is corrected in Choice C.

50. B. The punctuation in Choices A, C, D, and E creates an incomplete sentence or fragment. Choice B corrects the run-on phrase by linking the elements with *in order to*.

PART FOUR

Test Yourself

14 Six Model Scholastic Aptitude Tests

- **6 Model Tests**
- **Answer Keys**
- **Self-Evaluations**
- **Answer Explanations**

You are now about to take a major step in preparing yourself to handle an actual SAT. Before you are 6 Model Tests patterned after current published SATs. Up to now, you've concentrated on specific areas and on general testing techniques. You've mastered tactics and worked on drills. Now you have a chance to test yourself—thoroughly, repeatedly—before you walk in that test center door.

These 6 Model Tests resemble the actual SAT in format, in difficulty, and in content. When you take them, take them as if they *were* the actual SAT.

Build Your Stamina

Don't start and stop and take time out for a soda or for an important phone call. To do well on the SAT, you have to focus on the test, the test, and nothing but the test for hours at a time. Most high school students have never had to sit through a three-hour examination before they take their first SAT. To survive a three-hour exam takes *stamina,* and, as marathon runners know, the only way to build stamina is to put in the necessary time.

Refine Your Skills

You know how to maximize your score by tackling easy questions first and by eliminating wrong answers whenever you can. Put these skills into practice. If you find yourself spending too much time on any one question, skip it and move on. Remember to check frequently to make sure you are answering the questions in the right spots. This is a great chance for you to get these skills down pat.

Spot Your Weak Points

Do you need a bit more drill in a particular area? After you take each test, consult the self-evaluation section and the answer explanations for that test to pinpoint any areas that need work. Don't just evaluate your scores. Build your skills. Read the answer explanations for each question you answered incorrectly, each question you omitted, and each question you answered correctly but found hard. The answer explanation section is tailor-made to help you. You'll find reminders of tactics, definitions of terms, explanations of why the correct answer works. You'll even find an occasional shortcut or two and an explanation of why that incorrect answer didn't work.

Use the answer explanation section to help you spot specific types of questions that you want to review. Suppose, for example, you've omitted answering several reading questions on a test. Going through the answer explanations, you find they all belong to the Inference type. You know right then that you can boost your score by mastering that specific skill.

Take a Deep Breath— and Smile!

It's hard to stay calm when those around you are tense, and you're bound to run into some pretty tense people when you take the SAT. (Not everyone works through this book, unfortunately.) So you may experience a slight case of "exam nerves" on the big day. Don't worry about it.

1. Being keyed up for an examination isn't always bad: you may outdo yourself because you are so worked up.

2. Total panic is unlikely to set in: you know too much.

You know you can handle a three-hour test.

You know you can handle the sorts of questions you'll find on the SAT.

You know you can omit several questions and *still* score high. Answer only 50–60% of the questions correctly and you'll still get an average or better than average score (and dozens of solid, well-known colleges are out there right now, looking for serious students with just that kind of score). Answer more than that correctly and you should wind up with a superior score.

Make Your Practice Pay—Approximate the Test

1. Complete an entire Model Test at one sitting.

2. Use a clock or timer.

3. Allow *precisely* 30 minutes for each section. (If you have time left over, review your answers or recheck the way you've marked your answer sheet.)

4. After each section, give yourself a five-minute break.

5. Allow no talking in the test room.

6. Work rapidly without wasting time.

Answer Sheet–Test 1

Start with number 1 for each new section. If a section has fewer than 50 questions, leave the extra spaces blank.

Section 1

1. Ⓐ Ⓑ Ⓒ Ⓓ Ⓔ   11. Ⓐ Ⓑ Ⓒ Ⓓ Ⓔ   21. Ⓐ Ⓑ Ⓒ Ⓓ Ⓔ   31. Ⓐ Ⓑ Ⓒ Ⓓ Ⓔ   41. Ⓐ Ⓑ Ⓒ Ⓓ Ⓔ
2. Ⓐ Ⓑ Ⓒ Ⓓ Ⓔ   12. Ⓐ Ⓑ Ⓒ Ⓓ Ⓔ   22. Ⓐ Ⓑ Ⓒ Ⓓ Ⓔ   32. Ⓐ Ⓑ Ⓒ Ⓓ Ⓔ   42. Ⓐ Ⓑ Ⓒ Ⓓ Ⓔ
3. Ⓐ Ⓑ Ⓒ Ⓓ Ⓔ   13. Ⓐ Ⓑ Ⓒ Ⓓ Ⓔ   23. Ⓐ Ⓑ Ⓒ Ⓓ Ⓔ   33. Ⓐ Ⓑ Ⓒ Ⓓ Ⓔ   43. Ⓐ Ⓑ Ⓒ Ⓓ Ⓔ
4. Ⓐ Ⓑ Ⓒ Ⓓ Ⓔ   14. Ⓐ Ⓑ Ⓒ Ⓓ Ⓔ   24. Ⓐ Ⓑ Ⓒ Ⓓ Ⓔ   34. Ⓐ Ⓑ Ⓒ Ⓓ Ⓔ   44. Ⓐ Ⓑ Ⓒ Ⓓ Ⓔ
5. Ⓐ Ⓑ Ⓒ Ⓓ Ⓔ   15. Ⓐ Ⓑ Ⓒ Ⓓ Ⓔ   25. Ⓐ Ⓑ Ⓒ Ⓓ Ⓔ   35. Ⓐ Ⓑ Ⓒ Ⓓ Ⓔ   45. Ⓐ Ⓑ Ⓒ Ⓓ Ⓔ
6. Ⓐ Ⓑ Ⓒ Ⓓ Ⓔ   16. Ⓐ Ⓑ Ⓒ Ⓓ Ⓔ   26. Ⓐ Ⓑ Ⓒ Ⓓ Ⓔ   36. Ⓐ Ⓑ Ⓒ Ⓓ Ⓔ   46. Ⓐ Ⓑ Ⓒ Ⓓ Ⓔ
7. Ⓐ Ⓑ Ⓒ Ⓓ Ⓔ   17. Ⓐ Ⓑ Ⓒ Ⓓ Ⓔ   27. Ⓐ Ⓑ Ⓒ Ⓓ Ⓔ   37. Ⓐ Ⓑ Ⓒ Ⓓ Ⓔ   47. Ⓐ Ⓑ Ⓒ Ⓓ Ⓔ
8. Ⓐ Ⓑ Ⓒ Ⓓ Ⓔ   18. Ⓐ Ⓑ Ⓒ Ⓓ Ⓔ   28. Ⓐ Ⓑ Ⓒ Ⓓ Ⓔ   38. Ⓐ Ⓑ Ⓒ Ⓓ Ⓔ   48. Ⓐ Ⓑ Ⓒ Ⓓ Ⓔ
9. Ⓐ Ⓑ Ⓒ Ⓓ Ⓔ   19. Ⓐ Ⓑ Ⓒ Ⓓ Ⓔ   29. Ⓐ Ⓑ Ⓒ Ⓓ Ⓔ   39. Ⓐ Ⓑ Ⓒ Ⓓ Ⓔ   49. Ⓐ Ⓑ Ⓒ Ⓓ Ⓔ
10. Ⓐ Ⓑ Ⓒ Ⓓ Ⓔ   20. Ⓐ Ⓑ Ⓒ Ⓓ Ⓔ   30. Ⓐ Ⓑ Ⓒ Ⓓ Ⓔ   40. Ⓐ Ⓑ Ⓒ Ⓓ Ⓔ   50. Ⓐ Ⓑ Ⓒ Ⓓ Ⓔ

Section 2

1. Ⓐ Ⓑ Ⓒ Ⓓ Ⓔ   11. Ⓐ Ⓑ Ⓒ Ⓓ Ⓔ   21. Ⓐ Ⓑ Ⓒ Ⓓ Ⓔ   31. Ⓐ Ⓑ Ⓒ Ⓓ Ⓔ   41. Ⓐ Ⓑ Ⓒ Ⓓ Ⓔ
2. Ⓐ Ⓑ Ⓒ Ⓓ Ⓔ   12. Ⓐ Ⓑ Ⓒ Ⓓ Ⓔ   22. Ⓐ Ⓑ Ⓒ Ⓓ Ⓔ   32. Ⓐ Ⓑ Ⓒ Ⓓ Ⓔ   42. Ⓐ Ⓑ Ⓒ Ⓓ Ⓔ
3. Ⓐ Ⓑ Ⓒ Ⓓ Ⓔ   13. Ⓐ Ⓑ Ⓒ Ⓓ Ⓔ   23. Ⓐ Ⓑ Ⓒ Ⓓ Ⓔ   33. Ⓐ Ⓑ Ⓒ Ⓓ Ⓔ   43. Ⓐ Ⓑ Ⓒ Ⓓ Ⓔ
4. Ⓐ Ⓑ Ⓒ Ⓓ Ⓔ   14. Ⓐ Ⓑ Ⓒ Ⓓ Ⓔ   24. Ⓐ Ⓑ Ⓒ Ⓓ Ⓔ   34. Ⓐ Ⓑ Ⓒ Ⓓ Ⓔ   44. Ⓐ Ⓑ Ⓒ Ⓓ Ⓔ
5. Ⓐ Ⓑ Ⓒ Ⓓ Ⓔ   15. Ⓐ Ⓑ Ⓒ Ⓓ Ⓔ   25. Ⓐ Ⓑ Ⓒ Ⓓ Ⓔ   35. Ⓐ Ⓑ Ⓒ Ⓓ Ⓔ   45. Ⓐ Ⓑ Ⓒ Ⓓ Ⓔ
6. Ⓐ Ⓑ Ⓒ Ⓓ Ⓔ   16. Ⓐ Ⓑ Ⓒ Ⓓ Ⓔ   26. Ⓐ Ⓑ Ⓒ Ⓓ Ⓔ   36. Ⓐ Ⓑ Ⓒ Ⓓ Ⓔ   46. Ⓐ Ⓑ Ⓒ Ⓓ Ⓔ
7. Ⓐ Ⓑ Ⓒ Ⓓ Ⓔ   17. Ⓐ Ⓑ Ⓒ Ⓓ Ⓔ   27. Ⓐ Ⓑ Ⓒ Ⓓ Ⓔ   37. Ⓐ Ⓑ Ⓒ Ⓓ Ⓔ   47. Ⓐ Ⓑ Ⓒ Ⓓ Ⓔ
8. Ⓐ Ⓑ Ⓒ Ⓓ Ⓔ   18. Ⓐ Ⓑ Ⓒ Ⓓ Ⓔ   28. Ⓐ Ⓑ Ⓒ Ⓓ Ⓔ   38. Ⓐ Ⓑ Ⓒ Ⓓ Ⓔ   48. Ⓐ Ⓑ Ⓒ Ⓓ Ⓔ
9. Ⓐ Ⓑ Ⓒ Ⓓ Ⓔ   19. Ⓐ Ⓑ Ⓒ Ⓓ Ⓔ   29. Ⓐ Ⓑ Ⓒ Ⓓ Ⓔ   39. Ⓐ Ⓑ Ⓒ Ⓓ Ⓔ   49. Ⓐ Ⓑ Ⓒ Ⓓ Ⓔ
10. Ⓐ Ⓑ Ⓒ Ⓓ Ⓔ   20. Ⓐ Ⓑ Ⓒ Ⓓ Ⓕ   30. Ⓐ Ⓑ Ⓒ Ⓓ Ⓔ   40. Ⓐ Ⓑ Ⓒ Ⓓ Ⓔ   50. Ⓐ Ⓑ Ⓒ Ⓓ Ⓔ

Section 3

1. Ⓐ Ⓑ Ⓒ Ⓓ Ⓔ   11. Ⓐ Ⓑ Ⓒ Ⓓ Ⓔ   21. Ⓐ Ⓑ Ⓒ Ⓓ Ⓔ   31. Ⓐ Ⓑ Ⓒ Ⓓ Ⓔ   41. Ⓐ Ⓑ Ⓒ Ⓓ Ⓔ
2. Ⓐ Ⓑ Ⓒ Ⓓ Ⓔ   12. Ⓐ Ⓑ Ⓒ Ⓓ Ⓔ   22. Ⓐ Ⓑ Ⓒ Ⓓ Ⓔ   32. Ⓐ Ⓑ Ⓒ Ⓓ Ⓔ   42. Ⓐ Ⓑ Ⓒ Ⓓ Ⓔ
3. Ⓐ Ⓑ Ⓒ Ⓓ Ⓔ   13. Ⓐ Ⓑ Ⓒ Ⓓ Ⓔ   23. Ⓐ Ⓑ Ⓒ Ⓓ Ⓔ   33. Ⓐ Ⓑ Ⓒ Ⓓ Ⓔ   43. Ⓐ Ⓑ Ⓒ Ⓓ Ⓔ
4. Ⓐ Ⓑ Ⓒ Ⓓ Ⓔ   14. Ⓐ Ⓑ Ⓒ Ⓓ Ⓔ   24. Ⓐ Ⓑ Ⓒ Ⓓ Ⓔ   34. Ⓐ Ⓑ Ⓒ Ⓓ Ⓔ   44. Ⓐ Ⓑ Ⓒ Ⓓ Ⓔ
5. Ⓐ Ⓑ Ⓒ Ⓓ Ⓔ   15. Ⓐ Ⓑ Ⓒ Ⓓ Ⓔ   25. Ⓐ Ⓑ Ⓒ Ⓓ Ⓔ   35. Ⓐ Ⓑ Ⓒ Ⓓ Ⓔ   45. Ⓐ Ⓑ Ⓒ Ⓓ Ⓔ
6. Ⓐ Ⓑ Ⓒ Ⓓ Ⓔ   16. Ⓐ Ⓑ Ⓒ Ⓓ Ⓔ   26. Ⓐ Ⓑ Ⓒ Ⓓ Ⓔ   36. Ⓐ Ⓑ Ⓒ Ⓓ Ⓔ   46. Ⓐ Ⓑ Ⓒ Ⓓ Ⓔ
7. Ⓐ Ⓑ Ⓒ Ⓓ Ⓔ   17. Ⓐ Ⓑ Ⓒ Ⓓ Ⓔ   27. Ⓐ Ⓑ Ⓒ Ⓓ Ⓕ   37. Ⓐ Ⓑ Ⓒ Ⓓ Ⓔ   47. Ⓐ Ⓑ Ⓒ Ⓓ Ⓔ
8. Ⓐ Ⓑ Ⓒ Ⓓ Ⓔ   18. Ⓐ Ⓑ Ⓒ Ⓓ Ⓔ   28. Ⓐ Ⓑ Ⓒ Ⓓ Ⓔ   38. Ⓐ Ⓑ Ⓒ Ⓓ Ⓔ   48. Ⓐ Ⓑ Ⓒ Ⓓ Ⓔ
9. Ⓐ Ⓑ Ⓒ Ⓓ Ⓔ   19. Ⓐ Ⓑ Ⓒ Ⓓ Ⓔ   29. Ⓐ Ⓑ Ⓒ Ⓓ Ⓔ   39. Ⓐ Ⓑ Ⓒ Ⓓ Ⓔ   49. Ⓐ Ⓑ Ⓒ Ⓓ Ⓔ
10. Ⓐ Ⓑ Ⓒ Ⓓ Ⓔ   20. Ⓐ Ⓑ Ⓒ Ⓓ Ⓔ   30. Ⓐ Ⓑ Ⓒ Ⓓ Ⓔ   40. Ⓐ Ⓑ Ⓒ Ⓓ Ⓔ   50. Ⓐ Ⓑ Ⓒ Ⓓ Ⓔ

Start with number 1 for each new section. If a section has fewer than 50 questions, leave the extra spaces blank.

Section 4

1. Ⓐ Ⓑ Ⓒ Ⓓ Ⓔ	11. Ⓐ Ⓑ Ⓒ Ⓓ Ⓔ	21. Ⓐ Ⓑ Ⓒ Ⓓ Ⓔ	31. Ⓐ Ⓑ Ⓒ Ⓓ Ⓔ	41. Ⓐ Ⓑ Ⓒ Ⓓ Ⓔ
2. Ⓐ Ⓑ Ⓒ Ⓓ Ⓔ	12. Ⓐ Ⓑ Ⓒ Ⓓ Ⓔ	22. Ⓐ Ⓑ Ⓒ Ⓓ Ⓔ	32. Ⓐ Ⓑ Ⓒ Ⓓ Ⓔ	42. Ⓐ Ⓑ Ⓒ Ⓓ Ⓔ
3. Ⓐ Ⓑ Ⓒ Ⓓ Ⓔ	13. Ⓐ Ⓑ Ⓒ Ⓓ Ⓔ	23. Ⓐ Ⓑ Ⓒ Ⓓ Ⓔ	33. Ⓐ Ⓑ Ⓒ Ⓓ Ⓔ	43. Ⓐ Ⓑ Ⓒ Ⓓ Ⓔ
4. Ⓐ Ⓑ Ⓒ Ⓓ Ⓔ	14. Ⓐ Ⓑ Ⓒ Ⓓ Ⓔ	24. Ⓐ Ⓑ Ⓒ Ⓓ Ⓔ	34. Ⓐ Ⓑ Ⓒ Ⓓ Ⓔ	44. Ⓐ Ⓑ Ⓒ Ⓓ Ⓔ
5. Ⓐ Ⓑ Ⓒ Ⓓ Ⓔ	15. Ⓐ Ⓑ Ⓒ Ⓓ Ⓔ	25. Ⓐ Ⓑ Ⓒ Ⓓ Ⓔ	35. Ⓐ Ⓑ Ⓒ Ⓓ Ⓔ	45. Ⓐ Ⓑ Ⓒ Ⓓ Ⓔ
6. Ⓐ Ⓑ Ⓒ Ⓓ Ⓔ	16. Ⓐ Ⓑ Ⓒ Ⓓ Ⓔ	26. Ⓐ Ⓑ Ⓒ Ⓓ Ⓔ	36. Ⓐ Ⓑ Ⓒ Ⓓ Ⓔ	46. Ⓐ Ⓑ Ⓒ Ⓓ Ⓔ
7. Ⓐ Ⓑ Ⓒ Ⓓ Ⓔ	17. Ⓐ Ⓑ Ⓒ Ⓓ Ⓔ	27. Ⓐ Ⓑ Ⓒ Ⓓ Ⓔ	37. Ⓐ Ⓑ Ⓒ Ⓓ Ⓔ	47. Ⓐ Ⓑ Ⓒ Ⓓ Ⓔ
8. Ⓐ Ⓑ Ⓒ Ⓓ Ⓔ	18. Ⓐ Ⓑ Ⓒ Ⓓ Ⓔ	28. Ⓐ Ⓑ Ⓒ Ⓓ Ⓔ	38. Ⓐ Ⓑ Ⓒ Ⓓ Ⓔ	48. Ⓐ Ⓑ Ⓒ Ⓓ Ⓔ
9. Ⓐ Ⓑ Ⓒ Ⓓ Ⓔ	19. Ⓐ Ⓑ Ⓒ Ⓓ Ⓔ	29. Ⓐ Ⓑ Ⓒ Ⓓ Ⓔ	39. Ⓐ Ⓑ Ⓒ Ⓓ Ⓔ	49. Ⓐ Ⓑ Ⓒ Ⓓ Ⓔ
10. Ⓐ Ⓑ Ⓒ Ⓓ Ⓔ	20. Ⓐ Ⓑ Ⓒ Ⓓ Ⓔ	30. Ⓐ Ⓑ Ⓒ Ⓓ Ⓔ	40. Ⓐ Ⓑ Ⓒ Ⓓ Ⓔ	50. Ⓐ Ⓑ Ⓒ Ⓓ Ⓔ

Section 5

1. Ⓐ Ⓑ Ⓒ Ⓓ Ⓔ	11. Ⓐ Ⓑ Ⓒ Ⓓ Ⓔ	21. Ⓐ Ⓑ Ⓒ Ⓓ Ⓔ	31. Ⓐ Ⓑ Ⓒ Ⓓ Ⓔ	41. Ⓐ Ⓑ Ⓒ Ⓓ Ⓔ
2. Ⓐ Ⓑ Ⓒ Ⓓ Ⓔ	12. Ⓐ Ⓑ Ⓒ Ⓓ Ⓔ	22. Ⓐ Ⓑ Ⓒ Ⓓ Ⓔ	32. Ⓐ Ⓑ Ⓒ Ⓓ Ⓔ	42. Ⓐ Ⓑ Ⓒ Ⓓ Ⓔ
3. Ⓐ Ⓑ Ⓒ Ⓓ Ⓔ	13. Ⓐ Ⓑ Ⓒ Ⓓ Ⓔ	23. Ⓐ Ⓑ Ⓒ Ⓓ Ⓔ	33. Ⓐ Ⓑ Ⓒ Ⓓ Ⓔ	43. Ⓐ Ⓑ Ⓒ Ⓓ Ⓔ
4. Ⓐ Ⓑ Ⓒ Ⓓ Ⓔ	14. Ⓐ Ⓑ Ⓒ Ⓓ Ⓔ	24. Ⓐ Ⓑ Ⓒ Ⓓ Ⓔ	34. Ⓐ Ⓑ Ⓒ Ⓓ Ⓔ	44. Ⓐ Ⓑ Ⓒ Ⓓ Ⓔ
5. Ⓐ Ⓑ Ⓒ Ⓓ Ⓔ	15. Ⓐ Ⓑ Ⓒ Ⓓ Ⓔ	25. Ⓐ Ⓑ Ⓒ Ⓓ Ⓔ	35. Ⓐ Ⓑ Ⓒ Ⓓ Ⓔ	45. Ⓐ Ⓑ Ⓒ Ⓓ Ⓔ
6. Ⓐ Ⓑ Ⓒ Ⓓ Ⓔ	16. Ⓐ Ⓑ Ⓒ Ⓓ Ⓔ	26. Ⓐ Ⓑ Ⓒ Ⓓ Ⓔ	36. Ⓐ Ⓑ Ⓒ Ⓓ Ⓔ	46. Ⓐ Ⓑ Ⓒ Ⓓ Ⓔ
7. Ⓐ Ⓑ Ⓒ Ⓓ Ⓔ	17. Ⓐ Ⓑ Ⓒ Ⓓ Ⓔ	27. Ⓐ Ⓑ Ⓒ Ⓓ Ⓔ	37. Ⓐ Ⓑ Ⓒ Ⓓ Ⓔ	47. Ⓐ Ⓑ Ⓒ Ⓓ Ⓔ
8. Ⓐ Ⓑ Ⓒ Ⓓ Ⓔ	18. Ⓐ Ⓑ Ⓒ Ⓓ Ⓔ	28. Ⓐ Ⓑ Ⓒ Ⓓ Ⓔ	38. Ⓐ Ⓑ Ⓒ Ⓓ Ⓔ	48. Ⓐ Ⓑ Ⓒ Ⓓ Ⓔ
9. Ⓐ Ⓑ Ⓒ Ⓓ Ⓔ	19. Ⓐ Ⓑ Ⓒ Ⓓ Ⓔ	29. Ⓐ Ⓑ Ⓒ Ⓓ Ⓔ	39. Ⓐ Ⓑ Ⓒ Ⓓ Ⓔ	49. Ⓐ Ⓑ Ⓒ Ⓓ Ⓔ
10. Ⓐ Ⓑ Ⓒ Ⓓ Ⓔ	20. Ⓐ Ⓑ Ⓒ Ⓓ Ⓔ	30. Ⓐ Ⓑ Ⓒ Ⓓ Ⓔ	40. Ⓐ Ⓑ Ⓒ Ⓓ Ⓔ	50. Ⓐ Ⓑ Ⓒ Ⓓ Ⓔ

Section 6

1. Ⓐ Ⓑ Ⓒ Ⓓ Ⓔ	11. Ⓐ Ⓑ Ⓒ Ⓓ Ⓔ	21. Ⓐ Ⓑ Ⓒ Ⓓ Ⓔ	31. Ⓐ Ⓑ Ⓒ Ⓓ Ⓔ	41. Ⓐ Ⓑ Ⓒ Ⓓ Ⓔ
2. Ⓐ Ⓑ Ⓒ Ⓓ Ⓔ	12. Ⓐ Ⓑ Ⓒ Ⓓ Ⓔ	22. Ⓐ Ⓑ Ⓒ Ⓓ Ⓔ	32. Ⓐ Ⓑ Ⓒ Ⓓ Ⓔ	42. Ⓐ Ⓑ Ⓒ Ⓓ Ⓔ
3. Ⓐ Ⓑ Ⓒ Ⓓ Ⓔ	13. Ⓐ Ⓑ Ⓒ Ⓓ Ⓔ	23. Ⓐ Ⓑ Ⓒ Ⓓ Ⓔ	33. Ⓐ Ⓑ Ⓒ Ⓓ Ⓔ	43. Ⓐ Ⓑ Ⓒ Ⓓ Ⓔ
4. Ⓐ Ⓑ Ⓒ Ⓓ Ⓔ	14. Ⓐ Ⓑ Ⓒ Ⓓ Ⓔ	24. Ⓐ Ⓑ Ⓒ Ⓓ Ⓔ	34. Ⓐ Ⓑ Ⓒ Ⓓ Ⓔ	44. Ⓐ Ⓑ Ⓒ Ⓓ Ⓔ
5. Ⓐ Ⓑ Ⓒ Ⓓ Ⓔ	15. Ⓐ Ⓑ Ⓒ Ⓓ Ⓔ	25. Ⓐ Ⓑ Ⓒ Ⓓ Ⓔ	35. Ⓐ Ⓑ Ⓒ Ⓓ Ⓔ	45. Ⓐ Ⓑ Ⓒ Ⓓ Ⓔ
6. Ⓐ Ⓑ Ⓒ Ⓓ Ⓔ	16. Ⓐ Ⓑ Ⓒ Ⓓ Ⓔ	26. Ⓐ Ⓑ Ⓒ Ⓓ Ⓔ	36. Ⓐ Ⓑ Ⓒ Ⓓ Ⓔ	46. Ⓐ Ⓑ Ⓒ Ⓓ Ⓔ
7. Ⓐ Ⓑ Ⓒ Ⓓ Ⓔ	17. Ⓐ Ⓑ Ⓒ Ⓓ Ⓔ	27. Ⓐ Ⓑ Ⓒ Ⓓ Ⓔ	37. Ⓐ Ⓑ Ⓒ Ⓓ Ⓔ	47. Ⓐ Ⓑ Ⓒ Ⓓ Ⓔ
8. Ⓐ Ⓑ Ⓒ Ⓓ Ⓔ	18. Ⓐ Ⓑ Ⓒ Ⓓ Ⓔ	28. Ⓐ Ⓑ Ⓒ Ⓓ Ⓔ	38. Ⓐ Ⓑ Ⓒ Ⓓ Ⓔ	48. Ⓐ Ⓑ Ⓒ Ⓓ Ⓔ
9. Ⓐ Ⓑ Ⓒ Ⓓ Ⓔ	19. Ⓐ Ⓑ Ⓒ Ⓓ Ⓔ	29. Ⓐ Ⓑ Ⓒ Ⓓ Ⓔ	39. Ⓐ Ⓑ Ⓒ Ⓓ Ⓔ	49. Ⓐ Ⓑ Ⓒ Ⓓ Ⓔ
10. Ⓐ Ⓑ Ⓒ Ⓓ Ⓔ	20. Ⓐ Ⓑ Ⓒ Ⓓ Ⓔ	30. Ⓐ Ⓑ Ⓒ Ⓓ Ⓔ	40. Ⓐ Ⓑ Ⓒ Ⓓ Ⓔ	50. Ⓐ Ⓑ Ⓒ Ⓓ Ⓔ

Remove answer sheet by cutting on dotted line

SECTION 1 Time—30 minutes
45 Questions

For each question in this section, choose the best answer and blacken the corresponding space on the answer sheet.

Each question below consists of a word in capital letters, followed by five lettered words or phrases. Choose the word or phrase that is most nearly opposite in meaning to the word in capital letters. Since some of the questions require you to distinguish fine shades of meaning, consider all the choices before deciding which is best.

Example:

GOOD: (A) sour   (B) bad   (C) red
(D) hot   (E) ugly   Ⓐ ● Ⓒ Ⓓ Ⓔ

1. FERTILE: (A) useful   (B) hospitalized
(C) gloomy   (D) barren   (E) isolated

2. PREDICAMENT: (A) untroubled state
(B) friendly nature   (C) sudden wealth
(D) afterthought   (E) postscript

3. IMBECILITY: (A) crime   (B) intelligence
(C) assurance   (D) belligerence   (E) culpability

4. GRATIFY: (A) waste   (B) stupefy
(C) displease   (D) argue   (E) acknowledge

5. MANGLE: (A) travel alone   (B) plan jointly
(C) speak gently   (D) make whole
(E) handle ineffectively

6. ERRATIC: (A) dominant   (B) predictable
(C) peaceful   (D) perishable   (E) holy

7. OBLITERATE: (A) dazzle   (B) establish
(C) prefer   (D) conclude   (E) contact

8. STOLID: (A) burglarized   (B) unstable
(C) petulant   (D) giddy   (E) insufficient

9. AVERSE: (A) eager   (B) poetic   (C) frantic
(D) finished   (E) greedy

10. ORNATE: (A) wanton   (B) severe   (C) bizarre
(D) fruitful   (E) superfluous

11. CONSUMMATE: (A) convict   (B) undertake
(C) starve   (D) reveal   (E) fashion

12. SCHISM: (A) union   (B) undertaking
(C) failure   (D) plot   (E) doctrine

13. NEOPHYTE: (A) dancer   (B) expert
(C) menace   (D) singer   (E) fencer

14. SYCOPHANT: (A) lunatic   (B) coward
(C) preacher   (D) faith healer
(E) dignified leader

15. EXPATIATE: (A) alienate   (B) approve
(C) demonstrate   (D) summarize   (E) return

Each sentence below has one or two blanks, each blank indicating that something has been omitted. Beneath the sentence are five lettered words or sets of words. Choose the word or set of words that best fits the meaning of the sentence as a whole.

Example:

Although its publicity has been ----, the film itself is intelligent, well-acted, handsomely produced, and altogether ----.

(A) tasteless..respectable (B) extensive..moderate
(C) sophisticated..amateur (D) risqué..crude
(E) perfect..spectacular

● Ⓑ Ⓒ Ⓓ Ⓔ

16. The present expansion of the military strength of our old enemy to the north must fill us with ----.

(A) guilt   (B) amazement   (C) admiration
(D) apprehension   (E) repugnance

17. We could not warm to the candidate, whose speech contained nothing but empty promises, ----, and clichés.

(A) candor   (B) platitudes   (C) anger
(D) ingenuity   (E) threats

18. By dint of much practice, Dr. Elizabeth Wheeler became ---- and was able to manipulate her surgical tools with either hand.

(A) practical   (B) tricky   (C) ambiguous
(D) ambidextrous   (E) ambivalent

19. Like many other reformers, Alice Paul, author of the Equal Rights Amendment introduced in Congress in 1923, received little honor in her lifetime but has gained considerable fame ----.

(A) posthumously   (B) anonymously
(C) privately   (D) prematurely   (E) previously

20. The hypocrite ---- feelings which he does not possess but which he feels he should display.

(A) conceals   (B) decries   (C) betrays
(D) simulates   (E) condones

GO ON TO THE NEXT PAGE ➡

1 1 1 1 1 1 1 1 1 1 1 1

Each passage below is followed by questions based on its content. Answer all questions following a passage on the basis of what is stated or implied in that passage.

Charlotte Stanhope was at this time about thirty-five-years old; and, whatever may have been her faults, she had none of those which
Line belong to old young ladies. She neither dressed
(5) young, nor talked young, nor indeed looked young. She appeared to be perfectly content with her time of life, and in no way affected the graces of youth. She was a fine young woman; and had she been a man, would have been a fine young
(10) man. All that was done in the house, and was not done by servants, was done by her. She gave the orders, paid the bills, hired and dismissed the domestics, made the tea, carved the meat, and managed everything in the Stanhope household.
(15) She, and she alone, could ever induce her father to look into the state of his wordly concerns. She, and she alone, could in any degree control the absurdities of her sister. She, and she alone, prevented the whole family from falling into utter
(20) disrepute and beggary. It was by her advice that they now found themselves very unpleasantly situated in Barchester.

So far, the character of Charlotte Stanhope is not unprepossessing. But it remains to be said,
(25) that the influence which she had in her family, though it had been used to a certain extent for their wordly well-being, had not been used to their real benefit, as it might have been. She had aided her father in his indifference to his
(30) professional duties, counselling him that his livings were as much his individual property as the estates of his elder brother were the property of that worthy peer. She had for years past stifled every little rising wish for a return to
(35) England which the reverend doctor had from time to time expressed. She had encouraged her mother in her idleness in order that she herself might be mistress and manager of the Stanhope household. She had encouraged and fostered the
(40) follies of her sister, though she was always willing, and often able, to protect her from their probable result. She had done her best, and had thoroughly succeeded in spoiling her brother, and turning him loose upon the world an idle man
(45) without a profession, and without a shilling that he could call his own.

Miss Stanhope was a clever woman, able to talk on most subjects, and quite indifferent as to what the subject was. She prided herself on her
(50) freedom from English prejudice, and she might have added, from feminine delicacy. On religion she was a pure freethinker, and with much want of true affection, delighted to throw out her own views before the troubled mind of her father. To

(55) have shaken what remained of his Church of England faith would have gratified her much; but the idea of his abandoning his preferment in the church had never once presented itself to her
(60) mind. How could he indeed, when he had no income from any other source?

21. The passage as a whole is best characterized as

(A) a description of the members of a family
(B) a portrait of a young woman's moral and intellectual character
(C) an illustration of the evils of egotism
(D) an analysis of family dynamics in aristocratic society
(E) a contrast between a virtuous daughter and her disreputable family

22. The tone of the passage is best described as

(A) self-righteous and moralistic
(B) satirical and candid
(C) sympathetic and sentimental
(D) bitter and disillusioned
(E) indifferent and unfeeling

23. On the basis of the passage, which of the following statements about Dr. Stanhope can most logically be made?

(A) He is even more indolent than his wife.
(B) He resents having surrendered his authority to his daughter.
(C) He feels remorse for his professional misconduct.
(D) He has little left of his initial religious beliefs.
(E) He has disinherited his son without a shilling.

24. It can be inferred from the passage that Charlotte's mother (lines 36–39) is which of the following?

 I. An affectionate wife and mother
 II. A model of the domestic arts
 III. A woman of unassertive character

(A) I only   (B) II only   (C) III only   (D) I and III only   (E) II and III only

25. The passage suggests that Charlotte possesses all of the following characteristics EXCEPT

(A) an inappropriate flirtatiousness
(B) a lack of reverence
(C) a materialistic nature
(D) a managing disposition
(E) a touch of coarseness

GO ON TO THE NEXT PAGE

1   1   1   1   1   1   1   1   1   1   1

In most North American tribes, specialization by the artist's sex and role in the group determined the kind of object to be decorated and the
Line style to be employed in creating the decoration.
(5) Men almost exclusively produced compositions depicting life forms as well as supernatural beings. Men were the representational artists. Women, on the other hand, traditionally made abstract, geometric compositions. This specializa-
(10) tion persists in a general way even today.

Among Plains Indians the abstract designs that were the prerogative of the women have survived in greater number than those with figures which were painted by men. This geometric art was
(15) probably older than the figurative, coming out of such antecedents of Woodland culture as were later evolved into weaving, quillwork, and bead-work. The patterns were classical in form—circles and arcs, triangles, rectangles, and hyperbo-
(20) las. Colors were primarily red, yellow, blue, and green, applied evenly and flat, and usually outlined. The women's geometric art appears on many objects, but principally on hide robes and abundant boxes, bags, and other utilitarian recep-
(25) tacles.

The most influential Plains art form was the narrative composition, which was created to tell a story, often heroic or highly personal, celebrating a deed of courage. These representational
(30) works were generally drafted by a group of men—often the individuals who had performed the deeds being recorded—who drew on untailored hide robes and tepee liners made of skins. The paintings usually filled the entire field; often
(35) they were conceived at different times as separate pictorial vignettes documenting specific actions. In relationship to each other, these vignettes suggest a narrative. Composition was focused on the center of the skin, where the
(40) action was depicted and the figures were larger and more numerous. Often the composition is centrifugal, without top or bottom, suggesting that the hide was painted to be shown on the ground surrounded by viewers.
(45) The earliest known hide paintings (ca. 1700) were highly individualistic and were revealed to the artist through his vision quests and dreams. Among Plains tribes the initiation into adulthood of the male was linked to his discovery of a per-
(50) sonal omen or "medicine" through visions, dreams, and hallucinations. The result of these very important quests were images which were protective against both natural and supernatural enemies. The images were not only mystical but
(55) might also relate to specific life or dream events which supported the importance and identity of a male. The emblems thus obtained (they could even be bought by those impoverished of visions)

were painted in a flat, highly stylized manner in
(60) which perspective and volume were suggested by the overlapping of planes. This narrative and religious style developed from a private iconography to something new in the early 1800s when encounters with Anglos brought both new materi-
(65) als and subject matter. The confrontation also gave rise to a previously unconscious expression of Indian group solidarity. Cloth came into use as a substitute for animal hides; and the focus of Plains art on the group rather than the individual
(70) became emphatic.

26. Which of the following titles best summarizes the content of the passage?

(A) The Ongoing Influence of Plains Indian Art
(B) Male and Female in Tribal Life
(C) Indian Art as Narrative and Dream
(D) Design Specialization In Plains Art
(E) The History of Indian Representational Art

27. The author cites specific examples of the work of Plains artists primarily to

(A) show the differences between male and female decorative styles
(B) emphasize the functional role of art in Indian life
(C) describe the techniques employed in the creation of particular works
(D) illustrate the changes made by Anglo influence on Plains art
(E) explore the spiritual significance of representational design

28. With which of the following statements regarding male Plains artists prior to 1800 would the author most likely agree?

I. They tended to work corporately on projects.
II. They believed art had power to ward off danger.
III. They derived their designs from classical forms.

(A) I only   (B) III only   (C) I and II only
(D) II and III only   (E) I, II, and III

29. According to the passage, dream visions were important to the Plains artist because they

(A) enabled him to foresee influences on his style
(B) suggested the techniques and methods of his art
(C) determined his individual aesthetic philosophy
(D) expressed his sense of tribal solidarity
(E) revealed the true form of his spiritual guardian

GO ON TO THE NEXT PAGE

1 1 1 1 1 1 1 1 1 1 1 1 1

30. In its narrative aspect, Plains art resembles LEAST

(A) a cartoon strip made up of several panels
(B) a portrait bust of a chieftain in full headdress
(C) an epic recounting the adventures of a legendary hero
(D) a chapter from the autobiography of a prominent leader
(E) a mural portraying scenes from the life of George Washington

---

Select the word or set of words that best completes each of the following sentences.

---

31. While a great deal of change and modernization has taken place in India since 1947, the basic economic arrangements, values, and family roles have been generally ---- .

(A) overturned (B) stable (C) modified
(D) complicated (E) appropriate

32. Deloria has his detractors among Indians and whites, but his critics have had amazingly ---- success at shaking his self-confidence or ---- his reputation.

(A) great..repairing
(B) widespread..bolstering
(C) little..denting
(D) small..enhancing
(E) poor..restoring

33. The linguistic ---- of refugee children is reflected in their readiness to adopt the language of their new homeland.

(A) conservatism (B) inadequacy
(C) adaptability (D) philosophy (E) structure

34. The socially-conditioned desire to be approved and liked may lead a woman speaker to project ---- image that distracts from the content of her speech and is often ---- as childish behavior.

(A) an irritating..hailed
(B) a frantic..viewed
(C) a vivacious..applauded
(D) an amorous..questioned
(E) an endearing..interpreted

35. She kept her late parents' furniture, not for any ---- value it had, but for purely ---- reasons.

(A) potential..monetary
(B) ornamental..aesthetic
(C) financial..pecuniary
(D) intrinsic..sentimental
(E) personal..accidental

Each question below consists of a related pair of words or phrases, followed by five lettered pairs of words or phrases. Select the lettered pair that best expresses a relationship similar to that expressed in the original pair.

Example:

YAWN : BOREDOM :: (A) dream : sleep
(B) anger : madness (C) smile : amusement
(D) face : expression (E) impatience : rebellion

Ⓐ Ⓑ ● Ⓓ Ⓔ

---

36. WORDS : WRITER :: (A) honor : thief
(B) mortar : bricklayer (C) child : teacher
(D) batter : baker (E) laws : policeman

37. MUSEUM : EXHIBIT :: (A) sculptor : statue
(B) prison : cell (C) hall : corridor
(D) painting : frame (E) theater : performance

38. SNOW : DRIFT :: (A) mountain : boulder
(B) sand : dune (C) pane : glass
(D) desert : oasis (E) mud : rain

39. BASEMENT : ATTIC :: (A) baseball : football
(B) root : crown (C) garage : house
(D) heel : toe (E) chimney : roof

40. ARIA : DIVA :: (A) pool : swimmer
(B) soliloquy : actor (C) opera : operetta
(D) solo : chorus (E) circumference : arena

41. GRAIN : SILO :: (A) tree : acorn (B) seed : plant
(C) water : bucket (D) druggist : doctor
(E) furlong : mile

42. CHEER : DREARY :: (A) stress : efficient
(B) courage : timorous (C) disdain : pertinent
(D) pity : humorous (E) rejection : despondent

43. SHRUG : INDIFFERENCE :: (A) grin : deference
(B) wave : fatigue (C) nod : assent
(D) blink : scorn (E) scowl : desire

44. ANGER : CHOLERIC :: (A) wrath : ironic
(B) love : bucolic (C) island : volcanic
(D) greed : avaricious (E) pride : malicious

45. INTEREST : USURY :: (A) frugality : parsimony
(B) pleasure : use (C) thought : enjoyment
(D) anger : wrath (E) situation : position

IF YOU FINISH BEFORE TIME IS CALLED, YOU MAY CHECK YOUR WORK ON THIS SECTION ONLY. DO NOT WORK ON ANY OTHER SECTION IN THE TEST.

S T O P

2   2 2 2 2 2 2 2 2 2   2

In this section solve each problem, using any available space on the page for scratchwork. Then decide which is the best of the choices given and blacken the corresponding space on the answer sheet.

The following information is for your reference in solving some of the problems.

Circle of radius r: Area = πr^2; Circumference = $2\pi r$
    The number of degrees of arc in a circle is 360.
The measure in degrees of a straight angle is 180.

Definitions of symbols:
= is equal to $\leq$ is less than or equal to
$\neq$ is unequal to $\geq$ is greater than or equal to
< is less than $\parallel$ is parallel to
> is greater than $\perp$ is perpendicular to

Triangle: The sum of the measures in degrees of the angles of a triangle is 180.
If $\angle CDA$ is a right angle, then

(1) area of $\triangle ABC = \dfrac{AB \times CD}{2}$

(2) $AC^2 = AD^2 + DC^2$

Note: Figures that accompany problems in this test are intended to provide information useful in solving the problems. They are drawn as accurately as possible EXCEPT when it is stated in a specific problem that its figure is not drawn to scale. All figures lie in a plane unless otherwise indicated. All numbers used are real numbers.

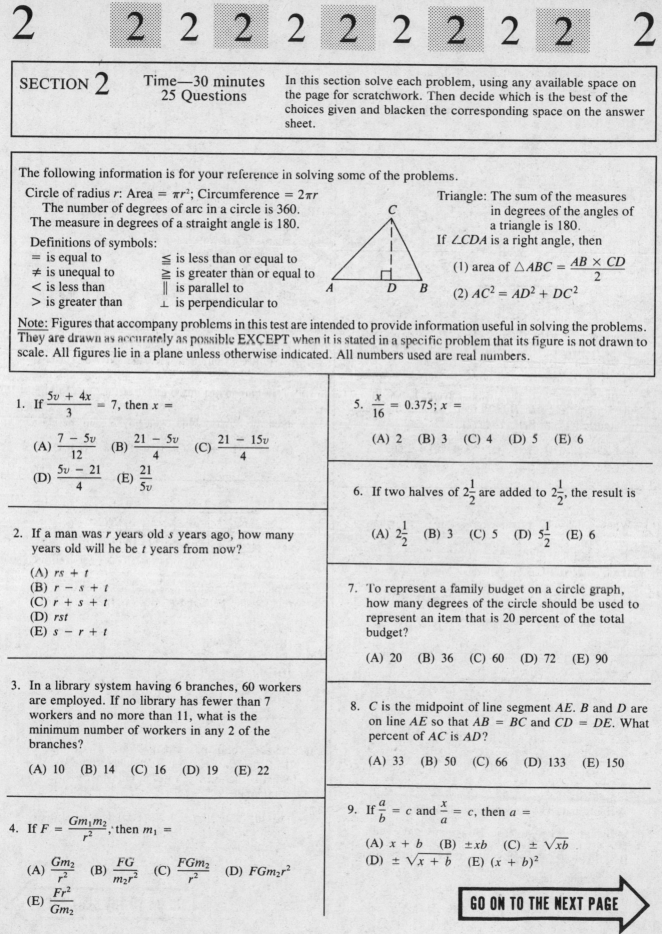

1. If $\dfrac{5v + 4x}{3} = 7$, then $x =$

    (A) $\dfrac{7 - 5v}{12}$ (B) $\dfrac{21 - 5v}{4}$ (C) $\dfrac{21 - 15v}{4}$

    (D) $\dfrac{5v - 21}{4}$ (E) $\dfrac{21}{5v}$

2. If a man was r years old s years ago, how many years old will he be t years from now?

    (A) $rs + t$
    (B) $r - s + t$
    (C) $r + s + t$
    (D) rst
    (E) $s - r + t$

3. In a library system having 6 branches, 60 workers are employed. If no library has fewer than 7 workers and no more than 11, what is the minimum number of workers in any 2 of the branches?

    (A) 10   (B) 14   (C) 16   (D) 19   (E) 22

4. If $F = \dfrac{Gm_1 m_2}{r^2}$, then $m_1 =$

    (A) $\dfrac{Gm_2}{r^2}$ (B) $\dfrac{FG}{m_2 r^2}$ (C) $\dfrac{FGm_2}{r^2}$ (D) $FGm_2 r^2$

    (E) $\dfrac{Fr^2}{Gm_2}$

5. $\dfrac{x}{16} = 0.375$; $x =$

    (A) 2   (B) 3   (C) 4   (D) 5   (E) 6

6. If two halves of $2\frac{1}{2}$ are added to $2\frac{1}{2}$, the result is

    (A) $2\frac{1}{2}$ (B) 3   (C) 5   (D) $5\frac{1}{2}$ (E) 6

7. To represent a family budget on a circle graph, how many degrees of the circle should be used to represent an item that is 20 percent of the total budget?

    (A) 20   (B) 36   (C) 60   (D) 72   (E) 90

8. C is the midpoint of line segment AE. B and D are on line AE so that $AB = BC$ and $CD = DE$. What percent of AC is AD?

    (A) 33   (B) 50   (C) 66   (D) 133   (E) 150

9. If $\dfrac{a}{b} = c$ and $\dfrac{x}{a} = c$, then $a =$

    (A) $x + b$ (B) $\pm xb$ (C) $\pm \sqrt{xb}$
    (D) $\pm \sqrt{x + b}$ (E) $(x + b)^2$

GO ON TO THE NEXT PAGE

10. If 0.6 is the average of 0.2, 0.8, 1.0, and x, what is the numerical value of x?

(A) 0.2   (B) 0.4   (C) 0.67   (D) 1.3   (E) 2.4

11. If $\frac{2x}{5} = 9$, then $\frac{2x}{9} =$

(A) $\frac{4}{5}$ (B) $2\frac{1}{2}$ (C) 5   (D) $16\frac{1}{5}$ (E) $22\frac{1}{2}$

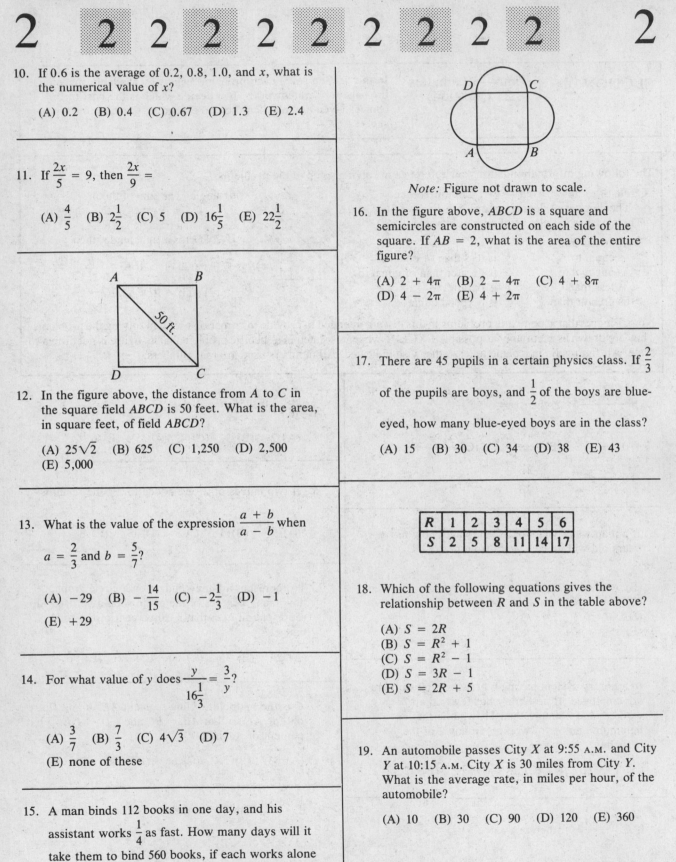

12. In the figure above, the distance from A to C in the square field $ABCD$ is 50 feet. What is the area, in square feet, of field $ABCD$?

(A) $25\sqrt{2}$ (B) 625   (C) 1,250   (D) 2,500
(E) 5,000

13. What is the value of the expression $\frac{a + b}{a - b}$ when $a = \frac{2}{3}$ and $b = \frac{5}{7}$?

(A) -29 (B) $-\frac{14}{15}$ (C) $-2\frac{1}{3}$ (D) -1

(E) $+29$

14. For what value of y does $\frac{y}{16\frac{1}{3}} = \frac{3}{y}$?

(A) $\frac{3}{7}$ (B) $\frac{7}{3}$ (C) $4\sqrt{3}$ (D) 7

(E) none of these

15. A man binds 112 books in one day, and his assistant works $\frac{1}{4}$ as fast. How many days will it take them to bind 560 books, if each works alone on alternate days?

(A) $\frac{1}{8}$ (B) $\frac{1}{2}$ (C) 2   (D) 4   (E) 8

Note: Figure not drawn to scale.

16. In the figure above, $ABCD$ is a square and semicircles are constructed on each side of the square. If $AB = 2$, what is the area of the entire figure?

(A) $2 + 4\pi$ (B) $2 - 4\pi$ (C) $4 + 8\pi$
(D) $4 - 2\pi$ (E) $4 + 2\pi$

17. There are 45 pupils in a certain physics class. If $\frac{2}{3}$ of the pupils are boys, and $\frac{1}{2}$ of the boys are blue-eyed, how many blue-eyed boys are in the class?

(A) 15   (B) 30   (C) 34   (D) 38   (E) 43

R	1	2	3	4	5	6
S	2	5	8	11	14	17

18. Which of the following equations gives the relationship between R and S in the table above?

(A) $S = 2R$
(B) $S = R^2 + 1$
(C) $S = R^2 - 1$
(D) $S = 3R - 1$
(E) $S = 2R + 5$

19. An automobile passes City X at 9:55 A.M. and City Y at 10:15 A.M. City X is 30 miles from City Y. What is the average rate, in miles per hour, of the automobile?

(A) 10   (B) 30   (C) 90   (D) 120   (E) 360

GO ON TO THE NEXT PAGE

2   2   2   2   2   2   2   2   2   2

20. How many 3-pound weights are needed to balance twelve 4-pound weights?

   (A) 4   (B) 9   (C) 13   (D) 16   (E) 48

21. To which of the following is $\dfrac{a}{b} - \dfrac{a}{c}$ equal?

   (A) $\dfrac{a}{b-c}$ (B) $\dfrac{1}{b-c}$ (C) $\dfrac{1}{bc}$ (D) $\dfrac{ab-ac}{bc}$
   (E) $\dfrac{ac-ab}{bc}$

22. If $r = \dfrac{s}{3}$ and $4r = 5t$, what is s in terms of t?

   (A) $\dfrac{4t}{15}$ (B) $\dfrac{15t}{4}$ (C) $4t$ (D) $5t$ (E) $60t$

23. If $\dfrac{n}{7} + \dfrac{n}{5} = \dfrac{12}{35}$, what is the numerical value of n?

   (A) 1   (B) $\sqrt{12}$ (C) 6   (D) 17.5   (E) 35

24. A can of food feeds 3 kittens or 2 adult cats. If I have 8 cans of food, and I feed 12 kittens, how many adult cats can I feed with the remainder?

   (A) 2   (B) 4   (C) 8   (D) 12   (E) 18

25. 234, 256, 273, 281, 218x.
   If it is assumed that x is greater than 1, which one of the following CANNOT be the average of the five numbers listed above?

   (A) 218   (B) 255   (C) 271   (D) 281
   (E) 2.839

IF YOU FINISH BEFORE TIME IS CALLED, YOU MAY CHECK YOUR WORK ON THIS SECTION ONLY. DO NOT WORK ON ANY OTHER SECTION IN THE TEST.   **S T O P**

SECTION 3   Time—30 minutes
50 Questions

The questions in this section measure skills that are important to writing well. In particular, they test your ability to recognize and use language that is clear, effective, and correct according to the requirements of standard written English, the kind of English found in most college textbooks.

Directions: The following sentences contain problems in grammar, usage, diction (choice of words), and idiom.

Some sentences are correct.
No sentence contains more than one error.

You will find that the error, if there is one, is underlined and lettered. Assume that elements of the sentence that are not underlined are correct and cannot be changed. In choosing answers, follow the requirements of standard written English.

If there is an error, select the one underlined part that must be changed to make the sentence correct and blacken the corresponding space on your answer sheet.

If there is no error, blacken answer space ⓔ.

EXAMPLE:

The region has a climate so severe that plants
                         A

growing there rarely had been more than twelve
        B   C

inches high. No error
       D   E

SAMPLE ANSWER
Ⓐ Ⓑ ● Ⓓ Ⓔ

1. Being that my car is getting its annual tune-up, I
   A   B

   will not be able to pick you up tomorrow morning.
   C   D

   No error
   E

2. The teacher with her capable aides
                A

   have complete control of the situation; I
   B

   look forward to a very uneventful trip. No error
   C   D   E

3. We can't hardly believe that the situation is
      A

   so serious as to justify such precautions as you
   B   C

   have taken. No error
   D   E

4. No one but he knew which questions were going to
          A B   C   D

   be asked on this test. No error
                    E

5. You are being quite cynical when you say
                A

   that the reason why we have such a large turnout
   B   C

   is because we are serving refreshments. No error
   D   E

6. Although I am playing golf for more than three
   A   B   C

   years, I cannot manage to break 90. No error
                    D   E

7. I have found that a mild salt solution is more
     A

   affective than the commercial preparations
   B   C

   available in drug stores in the treatment of this
                          D

   ailment. No error
           E

GO ON TO THE NEXT PAGE

3   3 3 3 3 3 3 3 3 3 3   **3**

8. If I have to make a choice <u>between</u> John, Henry,
   A   B
   and <u>her</u>, I think I'll select Henry because of his
         C
   self-control <u>during</u> moments of stress. <u>No error</u>
                D   E

9. This new information is <u>so important that</u> we must
                              A
   inform the authorities; <u>bring</u> this to the office
                            B
   <u>at once</u> and give <u>it</u> to Mr. Brown. <u>No error</u>
    C   D   E

10. <u>In order to</u> raise public consciousness concerning
     A
    environmental problems, <u>everyone</u> should
                             B
    distribute leaflets, write to <u>his or her</u> Congressman,
                                   C
    <u>as well as signing</u> the necessary petitions.
     D
    <u>No errors</u>
     E

11. Scientists recently discovered the wreckage of the

    Titanic, <u>which</u> sank after <u>it</u> struck an iceberg,
              A   B
    <u>furthermore</u> it was not possible for them to <u>raise</u> it.
     C   D
    <u>No error</u>
     E

12. Scientists <u>show</u> that change, <u>whether</u> good or bad,
               A   B
    leads to stress, <u>and</u> that the <u>accumulation from</u>
                      C   D
    stress-related changes can cause major illness.

    <u>No error</u>
     E

13. These awards, I <u>can assure</u> you, <u>will be given</u> not
                    A   B
    <u>only</u> to the best player, but also to the <u>best</u> team in
     C   D
    today's tournament. <u>No error</u>
                         E

14. We have spent <u>all together</u> <u>too much</u> money on
                   A   B
    this project; we have <u>exceeded</u> our budget and
                          C
    <u>can expect</u> no additional funds until the beginning
     D
    of the new year. <u>No error</u>
                      E

15. <u>After</u> John broke his ankle, the teacher <u>had wanted</u>
     A   B
    <u>us all</u>—Frank, Helen, you, and <u>me</u>—to visit him in
     C   D
    the hospital. <u>No error</u>
                   E

16. Between thirty <u>and</u> forty students <u>seem willing</u> to
                   A   B
    volunteer; <u>the rest</u> are not <u>planning to</u> participate
                C   D
    in the program. <u>No error</u>
                     E

17. <u>Farther</u> along the road, another contestant
     A
    <u>was trying</u> to repair the tire on his <u>new shiny</u>
     B   C
    bicycle <u>so that</u> he could win the race. <u>No error</u>
             D   E

18. The horse <u>that</u> won the trophies <u>differed with</u> the
              A   B
    <u>other</u> horses in <u>overall appearance</u> as well as
     C   D
    ability. <u>No error</u>
              E

19. The business executive, <u>planning</u> to attend the
                            A
    conference in New Orleans, <u>could not decide</u>
                                B
    whether to travel on or <u>remaining at</u> the hotel was
                             C
    the <u>better</u> choice. <u>No error</u>
         D   E

20. He is not the <u>kind of a person</u> who accepts such
                   A
    treatment <u>passively</u>; <u>he</u> is certain <u>to seek</u> revenge.
                B   C   D
    <u>No error</u>
     E

21. John, <u>together with</u> other members of the
                A
    Association, <u>has risen</u> over two thousand dollars
                  B
    toward the <u>establishment of</u> an <u>annual</u> scholarship
                C   D
    for disadvantaged students. <u>No error</u>
                                 E

GO ON TO THE NEXT PAGE

22. In order for he and I to be able to attend, we
        A   B   C

    will need to receive tickets within the week.
    D

    No error
    E

23. I feel badly about the present conflict because I do
        A   B

    not know how to resolve it without hurting either
                                        C

    you or him. No error
        D   E

24. A new production of the opera *Aida* has just been
                                            A

    announced; it will be sang on an outdoor stage
              B   C

    with live animals. No error
    D   E

25. Unless two or more members object to him joining
        A   B

    the club, we shall have to accept his application
                               C

    for membership. No error
    D   E

Directions: In each of the following sentences, some part or all of the sentence is underlined. Below each sentence you will find five ways of phrasing the underlined part. Select the answer that produces the most effective sentence, one that is clear and exact, without awkwardness or ambiguity, and blacken the corresponding space on your answer sheet. In choosing answers, follow the requirements of standard written English. Choose the answer that best expresses the meaning of the original sentence.

Answer (A) is always the same as the underlined part. Choose answer (A) if you think the original sentence needs no revision.

EXAMPLE:
Laura Ingalls Wilder published her first book
and she was sixty-five years old then.

(A) and she was sixty-five years old then
(B) when she was sixty-five years old
(C) at age sixty-five years old
(D) upon reaching sixty-five years
(E) at the time when she was sixty-five

SAMPLE ANSWER

Ⓐ ● Ⓒ Ⓓ Ⓔ

---

26. Although serfs were lucky to drink their ale from cracked wooden bowls, nobles customarily drunk their wine from elaborately chased drinking horns.

    (A) drunk their wine from
    (B) have drinked their wine from
    (C) drank their wine from
    (D) had drunken their wine from
    (E) drinking their wine from

27. Before the search party reached the scene of the accident, the rain began to fall, making rescue efforts more difficult.

    (A) the rain began to fall
    (B) the rain had began to fall
    (C) it began to rain
    (D) the rain had begun to fall
    (E) it started to rain

28. For many students, keeping a journal during college seems satisfying their need for self-expression.

    (A) keeping a journal during college seems satisfying their need
    (B) keeping a journal during college seems to satisfy their need
    (C) keeping a journal during college seeming satisfying their need
    (D) to keep a journal during college seems satisfying their need
    (E) the keeping of a journal during college seems to satisfy their need

GO ON TO THE NEXT PAGE →

3   3 3 3 3 3 3 3 3 3 3 3

29. Peter Martin began to develop his own choreographic style, but he was able to free himself from the influence of Balanchine.

(A) style, but he was able to
(B) style; but he was able to
(C) style only when he was able to
(D) style only when he is able to
(E) style: only when he was able to

30. Irregardless of the outcome of this dispute, our two nations will remain staunch allies.

(A) Irregardless of the outcome
(B) Regardless of how the outcome
(C) With regard to the outcome
(D) Regardless of the outcome
(E) Disregarding the outcome

31. With the onset of winter the snows began to fall, we were soon forced to remain indoors most of the time.

(A) the snows began to fall, we were soon forced to remain indoors
(B) the snows began to fall; we were soon forced to remain indoors
(C) the snows began to fall: we were soon forced to remain indoors
(D) the snows began to fall, having forced us to remain indoors
(E) the snows had begun to fall; we were soon forced to remain indoors

32. "Araby," along with several other stories from Joyce's *Dubliners,* are going to be read at Town Hall by noted Irish actress Siobhan McKenna.

(A) are going to be read
(B) were going to be read
(C) are gone to be read
(D) is going to be read
(E) is gone to be read

33. In 1980 the Democrats lost not only the executive branch, but also their majority in the United States Senate.

(A) lost not only the executive branch, but also their majority
(B) lost not only the executive branch, but also its majority
(C) not only lost the executive branch, but their majority also
(D) lost the executive branch, but also their majority
(E) lost not only the executive branch, but their majority also

34. Before considering an applicant for this job, he must have a degree in electrical engineering as well as three years experience in the field.

(A) Before considering an applicant for this job, he must have
(B) Before considering an applicant for this job, he should have
(C) We will not consider an applicant for this job without
(D) To consider an applicant for this job, he must have
(E) We will not consider an applicant for this job if he does not have

35. To invest intelligently for the future, mutual funds provide an excellent opportunity for the average investor.

(A) To invest intelligently for the future, mutual funds
(B) As an intelligent investment for the future, mutual funds
(C) Investing intelligently for the future, mutual funds
(D) To invest with intelligence, mutual funds
(E) Having invested intelligently, you must determine that mutual funds

36. She was told to give the award to whomever she thought had contributed most to the welfare of the student body.

(A) to whomever she thought
(B) to whoever she thought
(C) to the senior whom she thought
(D) to whomsoever
(E) to him whom she thought

37. Since he is lying the book on the table where it does not belong.

(A) Since he is lying the book on the table where it does not belong.
(B) He is lying the book on the table where it does not belong.
(C) Because he is laying the book on the table where it does not belong.
(D) Since he is laying the book on the table where it does not belong.
(E) He is laying the book on the table where it does not belong.

38. Mary is as fast as, if not faster than, anyone in her class and should be on the team.

(A) as fast as, if not faster than, anyone
(B) as fast, if not faster than, anyone else
(C) as fast, if not more fast than, anyone
(D) as fast as, if not faster than, anyone else
(E) as swift as, if not faster than, anyone

GO ON TO THE NEXT PAGE

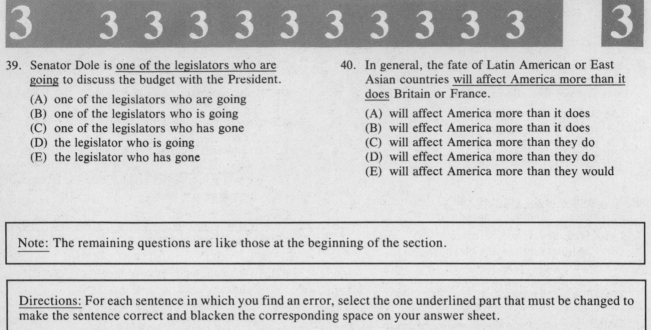

39. Senator Dole is <u>one of the legislators who are going</u> to discuss the budget with the President.

   (A) one of the legislators who are going
   (B) one of the legislators who is going
   (C) one of the legislators who has gone
   (D) the legislator who is going
   (E) the legislator who has gone

40. In general, the fate of Latin American or East Asian countries <u>will affect America more than it does</u> Britain or France.

   (A) will affect America more than it does
   (B) will effect America more than it does
   (C) will affect America more than they do
   (D) will effect America more than they do
   (E) will affect America more than they would

Note: The remaining questions are like those at the beginning of the section.

Directions: For each sentence in which you find an error, select the one underlined part that must be changed to make the sentence correct and blacken the corresponding space on your answer sheet.

If there is no error, blacken answer space Ⓔ.

EXAMPLE:

The region has a climate <u>so severe that</u> plants
                              A

<u>growing there</u> rarely <u>had been</u> more than twelve
      B   C

inches <u>high</u>. <u>No error</u>
        D   E

SAMPLE ANSWER

Ⓐ Ⓑ ● Ⓓ Ⓔ

---

41. The lieutenant <u>reminded</u> his men that the only
                          A
    information <u>to be given</u> to the captors was <u>each</u>
                     B   C
    individual's name, rank, and

    <u>what his serial number was</u>. <u>No error</u>
                  D   E

42. <u>When</u> the teacher ordered the student <u>to go to</u> the
        A   B
    dean's office <u>as a result of</u> the class disruption, she
                         C
    surprised us because she usually <u>will handle</u> her
                                            D
    own discipline problems. <u>No error</u>
                                    E

43. He was the author <u>whom</u> I <u>believed</u> was
                          A   B
    <u>most likely</u> to receive the <u>coveted</u> award. <u>No error</u>
         C   D   E

44. Please give this scholarship <u>to whoever</u> in the
                                       A
    graduating class <u>has done</u> the most <u>to promote</u>
                           B   C
    <u>goodwill</u> in the community. <u>No error</u>
         D   E

45. Both lawyers <u>interpreted</u> the statute <u>differently</u>,
                      A   B
    <u>and</u> they needed a judge to settle <u>its</u> dispute.
     C   D
    <u>No error</u>
        E

46. All of the team members, except <u>him</u>, <u>has</u>
                                         A   B
    anticipated <u>interest from</u> the national leagues, and
                      C
    now practice twice <u>as long</u>. <u>No error</u>
                            D   E

47. Everybody <u>but</u> him has paid <u>their</u> dues; we
                   A   B
    <u>must seek</u> ways to make him understand the
         C
    <u>need for</u> prompt payment. <u>No error</u>
         D   E

GO ON TO THE NEXT PAGE ➡

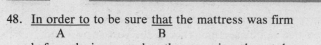

48. In order to to be sure <u>that</u> the mattress was firm
　　 <u>A</u>　　　　　　　　<u>B</u>

　　 before placing an order, the man gingerly <u>sat down</u>
　　　　　　　　　　　　　　　　　　　　　　 <u>C</u>

　　 and <u>laid back</u>. <u>No error</u>
　　　　　 <u>D</u>　　 <u>E</u>

49. <u>Since</u> she found the climate of Arizona
　　 <u>A</u>

　　 <u>very healthy</u>, she decided <u>to move</u> to Phoenix
　　　 <u>B</u>　　　　　　　　　 <u>C</u>

　　 <u>as soon as</u> possible. <u>No error</u>
　　　 <u>D</u>　　　　　　 <u>E</u>

50. The data <u>which</u> he presented <u>was</u> not <u>pertinent</u> to
　　　　　　 <u>A</u>　　　　　　 <u>B</u>　　　 <u>C</u>

　　 the matter <u>under discussion</u>. <u>No error</u>
　　　　　　　 <u>D</u>　　　　　 <u>E</u>

IF YOU FINISH BEFORE TIME IS CALLED, YOU MAY CHECK YOUR WORK ON
THIS SECTION ONLY. DO NOT WORK ON ANY OTHER SECTION IN THE TEST.　　**S T O P**

SECTION 4   Time—30 minutes   For each question in this section, choose the best answer and
40 Questions   blacken the corresponding space on the answer sheet.

Each question below consists of a word in capital letters, followed by five lettered words or phrases. Choose the word or phrase that is most nearly opposite in meaning to the word in capital letters. Since some of the questions require you to distinguish fine shades of meaning, consider all the choices before deciding which is best.

Example:

GOOD: (A) sour   (B) bad   (C) red
(D) hot   (E) ugly

Each sentence below has one or two blanks, each blank indicating that something has been omitted. Beneath the sentence are five lettered words or sets of words. Choose the word or set of words that best fits the meaning of the sentence as a whole.

Example:

Although its publicity has been ----, the film itself is intelligent, well-acted, handsomely produced, and altogether ----.

(A) tasteless..respectable   (B) extensive..moderate
(C) sophisticated..amateur   (D) risqué..crude
(E) perfect..spectacular

1. PARDON: (A) separate   (B) anger   (C) pursue
(D) blame   (E) commit

2. FAMISHED: (A) satisfied   (B) exiled
(C) sheltered   (D) unknown   (E) thirsty

3. YIELDING: (A) silent   (B) unable to hope
(C) disinclined to bend   (D) exposed to danger
(E) compromised

4. MENIAL: (A) feminine   (B) physical
(C) indifferent   (D) dignified   (E) irrelevant

5. GARGANTUAN: (A) fearful of death
(B) tiny in size   (C) sparsely settled
(D) unlikely to succeed   (E) eager to please

6. SCRUPULOUS: (A) unclearly stated
(B) careless of detail   (C) resistant to change
(D) wholly convinced   (E) clean of person

7. MOLLIFY: (A) annoy   (B) possess   (C) alter
(D) intimidate   (E) liquefy

8. BELLICOSITY: (A) ugliness   (B) outrage
(C) stupidity   (D) unusualness   (E) pacifism

9. GARRULITY: (A) flamboyance   (B) profanity
(C) reticence   (D) incongruity   (E) insipidness

10. QUIXOTIC: (A) sluggish   (B) practical
(C) vapid   (D) fashionable   (E) irritable

11. The doctor felt that the ---- was using up valuable time that he needed for really sick patients.

(A) kleptomaniac   (B) hypochondriac
(C) dipsomaniac   (D) invalid   (E) psychiatrist

12. It is the task of the International Wildlife Preservation Commission to prevent endangered species from becoming ---- in order that future generations may ---- the great diversity of animal life.

(A) tamed..recollect   (B) evolved..value
(C) extinct..enjoy   (D) specialized..anticipate
(E) widespread..appreciate

13. It is remarkable that a man so in the public eye, so highly praised and imitated, can retain his ---- .

(A) magniloquence   (B) dogmas   (C) bravado
(D) idiosyncrasies   (E) humility

14. As a sportscaster, Cosell is apparently never ---- ; he makes ---- comments about every boxing match he covers.

(A) excited..hysterical   (B) relevant..pertinent
(C) satisfied..disparaging   (D) amazed..awe-struck
(E) impressed..laudatory

15. It is difficult to translate a foreign text literally because we cannot capture the ---- of the original passage exactly.

(A) novelty   (B) explanations   (C) connotations
(D) affluence   (E) alienation

GO ON TO THE NEXT PAGE

4 4 4 4 4 4 4 4 4 4 4 4

Each question below consists of a related pair of words or phrases, followed by five lettered pairs of words or phrases. Select the lettered pair that best expresses a relationship similar to that expressed in the original pair.

Example:

YAWN : BOREDOM ::   (A) dream : sleep
(B) anger : madness   (C) smile : amusement
(D) face : expression   (E) impatience : rebellion

Ⓐ Ⓑ ● Ⓓ Ⓔ

16. HEART : PUMP ::   (A) lungs : collapse
(B) appendix : burst   (C) stomach : digest
(D) intestine : twist   (E) teeth : ache

17. STANZA : POEM ::   (A) flag : anthem
(B) story : building   (C) mural : painting
(D) program : recital   (E) rhyme : prose

18. MONGREL : COLLIE ::   (A) goose : gosling
(B) gem : ruby   (C) alloy : iron   (D) pony : bridle
(E) bleat : sheep

19. MASON : TROWEL ::   (A) potter : clay
(B) doctor : degree   (C) carpenter : adze
(D) preacher : sermon   (E) sculptor : museum

20. MASTER : SERVANT ::   (A) judge : jury
(B) monarch : subject   (C) serf : peasant
(D) capital : labor   (E) landlord : tenant

21. AMULET : EVIL ::   (A) fort : attack
(B) fire : hose   (C) murder : crime
(D) police : law   (E) bracelet : greed

22. AMASS : WEALTH ::   (A) lavish : bribes
(B) garner : grain   (C) disperse : enemy
(D) refund : deposit   (E) weigh : value

23. INIQUITOUS : MALEFACTOR ::
(A) conspicuous : leader
(B) egregious : philanthropist
(C) reprehensible : altruist
(D) modest : benefactor
(E) mischievous : prankster

24. CONNOISSEUR : PAINTING ::   (A) egotist : self
(B) gourmet : viands   (C) miser : gold
(D) jury : criminal   (E) artist : critic

25. CARTOGRAPHER : GAZETTEER ::
(A) conductor : newspaper
(B) novice : expert
(C) author : composer
(D) lexicographer : dictionary
(E) cartoonist : pencil

GO ON TO THE NEXT PAGE

4 4 4 4 4 4 4 4 4 4 4 4

Each passage below is followed by questions based on its content. Answer all questions following a passage on the basis of what is <u>stated</u> or <u>implied</u> in that passage.

One potential hideaway that until now has been completely ignored is De Witt Isle, off the coast of Tasmania (a large island southeast of *Line* Australia). Its assets are 4,000 acres of jagged
(5) rocks, tangled undergrowth and trees twisted and bent by battering winds. Settlers have avoided it like the plague, but bandicoots (ratlike marsupials native to Australia), wallabies, eagles, and penguins think De Witt is just fine.
(10) So does Jane Cooper, 18, a pert Melbourne high school graduate, who emigrated there with three goats, several chickens and a number of cats brought along to stand guard against the bandicoots. Why De Witt? "I was frightened at
(15) the way life is lived today in our cities," says Jane. "I wanted to be alone, to have some time to think and find out about myself."

She has been left alone to write poems and start work on a book, play the flute and dive for
(20) crayfish and abalone to supplement her diet of cereal, canned goods and homegrown vegetables.

Her solitary life isn't easy. "Dear God," she wrote in her diary on her first day ashore, "how I love this island . . . but I don't know if I'm
(25) strong enough to stay. I found myself walking along the rocks crying." Then her mood began to change: "I'm going to conquer this island. I won't let it beat me . . . I had been feeling so sorry for myself that I was unaware of the beauty
(30) that surrounded me." Recently she sent a letter home via the local fishermen. She wrote: "I feel very old and very young. I'm more determined than ever to stay here." She had made a friend—a penguin named Mickey Mouse—and she is
(35) beginning to feel that "this is my world and my life . . . it is so beautiful here I can't imagine Melbourne any longer." To millions of city-bound Australians, Jane has become something of a heroine.

26. Which statement can best be made on the basis of the passage?

(A) Jane never doubted her ability to survive.
(B) The Isle's weather proved quite an obstacle.
(C) The local fishermen trust Jane.
(D) Jane is basically rather unemotional.
(E) Jane's days on the Isle are very full ones.

27. It may be inferred from the end of the passage that Jane

(A) is still rather lonesome
(B) has apparently won the battle
(C) will probably go home
(D) is deceiving herself
(E) greatly needs encouragement

28. In the first paragraph, which word is used in an ironic sense?

(A) hideaway   (B) coast   (C) assets
(D) winds   (E) bandicoots

There is an enormous difference in the ways in which various public officials respond to public pressures, and in the means and methods they employ to deal with them. The best possess understanding of the forces that must be taken into account, determination not to be swerved from the path of public interest, a willingness to make enemies along with a gift for avoiding them, and faith that public support will be forthcoming for the correct course. The poorest are over-hesitant, evasive, preoccupied with their relationships with their colleagues, superiors, the press or the political support on which they lean. They will make no move unless the gallery is packed. They confront all embarrassments with a stale general formula.

29. The title that best expresses the ideas of this passage is:

(A) Political Pressure Groups
(B) Mistakes for Public Officials to Make
(C) Characteristics of Public Officials
(D) Gaining Political Support
(E) Avoiding Political Enemies

30. According to the passage, the best public officials

(A) insist on unanimous support for their ideas
(B) uniformly follow well-established general procedures
(C) respond to pressure groups
(D) have confidence in the public
(E) are cautious in dealing with their constituents

GO ON TO THE NEXT PAGE

31. The author mentions all of the following faults of poor public officials EXCEPT

   (A) corruption
   (B) lack of candor
   (C) indecision
   (D) uninventiveness
   (E) lack of independence

   Throughout extensive areas of the tropics the tall and stately primeval forest has given way to eroded land, scrub, and the jumble of secondary growth. Just as the virgin forests of Europe and North America were laid low by man's improvidence, so those of the tropics are now vanishing—only their destruction may be encompassed in decades instead of centuries. A few authorities hold that, except for government reserves, the earth's great rain forests may vanish within a generation. The economic loss will be incalculable, for the primary rain forests are rich sources of timber (mahogany, teak) and such by-products as resins, gums, cellulose, camphor and rattans. No one, indeed, can compute their resources, for of the thousands of species that compose the forest cover, there are only a few whose physical and chemical properties have been studied with a view to commercial use.

   Most important of all, the primeval rain forest is a reservoir of specimens, a dynamic center of evolution whence the rest of the world's plant life has been continually enriched with new forms. These extensive reserves must be defended from the acquisitive hand of man, whose ruthless ax would expose them to the ravages of sun and rain.

32. According to the passage, the primary reason for conservation of the great rain forests is that they

   (A) are areas of botanical evolution
   (B) are not ready for man's ruthless ax
   (C) are the chief source of income of governments
   (D) provide major sources of material for chemical industries
   (E) need further development before they can be used commercially

33. As used in the passage, the word "primeval" (paragraph 2, line 1) means

   (A) first in importance
   (B) commercial
   (C) gorgeous
   (D) untouched
   (E) forbidden to man

34. The ideas of the author would probably be most strongly supported by

   (A) lumber company representatives
   (B) conservationists and botanists
   (C) chemical manufacturers
   (D) government representatives
   (E) the "man on the street"

35. According to the passage, the result of chopping down the tropical rain forest has been

   (A) an increase in government reserves
   (B) a surge in plant evolution
   (C) damage to the soil
   (D) a decrease of commercial exploitation
   (E) a renewal of European and North American forests

GO ON TO THE NEXT PAGE

For me, scientific knowledge is divided into mathematical sciences, natural sciences or sciences dealing with the natural world (physical and biological sciences), and sciences dealing with mankind (psychology, sociology, all the sciences of cultural achievements, every kind of historical knowledge). Apart from these sciences is philosophy, about which we will talk shortly. In the first place, all this is pure or theoretical knowledge, sought only for the purpose of understanding, in order to fulfill the need to understand that is intrinsic and consubstantial to man. What distinguishes man from animal is that he knows and needs to know. If man did not know that the world existed, and that the world was of a certain kind, that he was in the world and that he himself was of a certain kind, he wouldn't be man. The technical aspects of applications of knowledge are equally necessary for man and are of the greatest importance, because they also contribute to defining him as man and permit him to pursue a life increasingly more truly human.

But even while enjoying the results of technical progress, he must defend the primacy and autonomy of pure knowledge. Knowledge sought directly for its practical applications will have immediate and foreseeable success, but not the kind of important result whose revolutionary scope is in large part unforeseen, except by the imagination of the Utopians. Let me recall a well-known example. If the Greek mathematicians had not applied themselves to the investigation of conic sections, zealously and without the least suspicion that it might someday be useful, it would not have been possible centuries later to navigate far from shore. The first men to study the nature of electricity could not imagine that their experiments, carried on because of mere intellectual curiosity, would eventually lead to modern electrical technology, without which we can scarcely conceive of contemporary life. Pure knowledge is valuable for its own sake, because the human spirit cannot resign itself to ignorance. But, in addition, it is the foundation for practical results that would not have been reached if this knowledge had not been sought disinterestedly.

36. The author includes among the sciences all of the following EXCEPT

(A) chemistry (B) astronomy (C) economics
(D) anthropology (E) literature

37. The author indicates that most important advances made by mankind come from

(A) technical applications
(B) apparently useless information
(C) the natural sciences
(D) the study of philosophy
(E) the biological sciences

38. The author points out that the Greeks who studied conic sections

(A) invented modern mathematical applications
(B) were interested in navigation
(C) were unaware of the value of their studies
(D) worked with electricity
(E) were forced to resign themselves to failure

39. The title below that best expresses the ideas of this passage is

(A) Technical Progress
(B) A Little Learning Is a Dangerous Thing
(C) Man's Distinguishing Characteristics
(D) Learning for Its Own Sake
(E) The Difference Between Science and Philosophy

40. It can be inferred from the passage that to the author man's need to know is chiefly important in that it

(A) allows the human race to progress technically
(B) encompasses both the physical and social sciences
(C) demonstrates human vulnerability
(D) defines his essential humanity
(E) has increased as our knowledge of the world has grown

IF YOU FINISH BEFORE TIME IS CALLED, YOU MAY CHECK YOUR WORK ON THIS SECTION ONLY. DO NOT WORK ON ANY OTHER SECTION IN THE TEST. S T O P

5

SECTION 5   Time—30 minutes
35 Questions

In this section solve each problem, using any available space on the page for scratchwork. Then decide which is the best of the choices given and blacken the corresponding space on the answer sheet.

The following information is for your reference in solving some of the problems.

Circle of radius r: Area $= \pi r^2$; Circumference $= 2\pi r$
  The number of degrees of arc in a circle is 360.
The measure in degrees of a straight angle is 180.

Definitions of symbols:
$=$ is equal to $\leq$ is less than or equal to
$\neq$ is unequal to $\geq$ is greater than or equal to
$<$ is less than $\parallel$ is parallel to
$>$ is greater than $\perp$ is perpendicular to

Triangle: The sum of the measures in degrees of the angles of a triangle is 180.
If $\angle CDA$ is a right angle, then

(1) area of $\triangle ABC = \dfrac{AB \times CD}{2}$

(2) $AC^2 = AD^2 + DC^2$

Note: Figures that accompany problems in this test are intended to provide information useful in solving the problems. They are drawn as accurately as possible EXCEPT when it is stated in a specific problem that its figure is not drawn to scale. All figures lie in a plane unless otherwise indicated. All numbers used are real numbers.

1. $\dfrac{1}{r} = 3$ and $s = 3$; then $r =$

(A) s (B) $3 - s$ (C) $\dfrac{1}{s}$ (D) $-s$ (E) $9s$

2. If 2 parts of sand are mixed with 3 parts of gravel, what part of the total mixture is sand?

(A) $\dfrac{1}{3}$ (B) $\dfrac{2}{5}$ (C) $\dfrac{3}{5}$ (D) $\dfrac{2}{3}$ (E) $\dfrac{3}{2}$

3. If $2.3y = 46$, then $y =$

(A) 2 (B) 20 (C) 105.5 (D) 200 (E) 1058

4. $\dfrac{8}{10} - \dfrac{12}{15} =$

(A) -1 (B) 0 (C) 1 (D) $\dfrac{4}{15}$ (E) $\dfrac{8}{5}$

5. Which of the following is the equivalent of $\dfrac{1}{N + \dfrac{1}{N}}$?

(A) 1 (B) $\dfrac{1}{2N}$ (C) $\dfrac{2}{N}$ (D) $\dfrac{N}{N + 1}$

(E) $\dfrac{N}{N^2 + 1}$

6. Which of the following fractions has the smallest value?

(A) $\dfrac{5}{4}$ (B) $\dfrac{6}{5}$ (C) $\dfrac{13}{10}$ (D) $\dfrac{29}{25}$ (E) $\dfrac{59}{50}$

7. When 30 percent of the maximum supply of a certain article is on the market, what is the price, in cents, of the article according to the graph above?

(A) 47 (B) 49 (C) 52 (D) 56 (E) 66

GO ON TO THE NEXT PAGE

5

Questions 8–27 each consist of two quantities, one in Column A and one in Column B. You are to compare the two quantities and on the answer sheet blacken space

A   if the quantity in Column A is greater;
B   if the quantity in Column B is greater;
C   if the two quantities are equal;
D   If the relationship cannot be determined from the information given.

AN E RESPONSE WILL NOT BE SCORED.

	EXAMPLES		
	Column A	Column B	Answers
E1.	2×6	$2 + 6$	⬤ⒷⒸⒹⒺ
E2.	$180 - x$	y	ⒶⒷ⬤ⒹⒺ
E3.	$p - q$	$q - p$	ⒶⒷⒸ⬤Ⓔ

(E2: figure with angles $x°$ and $y°$)

Notes:

1.   In certain questions, information concerning one or both of the quantities to be compared is centered above the two columns.
2.   In a given question, a symbol that appears in both columns represents the same thing in Column A as it does in Column B.
3.   Letters such as x, n, and k stand for real numbers.

	Column A	Column B
	$\dfrac{1}{x} < 0$	
8.	x	1
	$x = y^2 - 1 = 3$	
9.	x	y
	$x^2 = 25$	
10.	x	5
11.	$\dfrac{1}{x} \div \dfrac{1}{\frac{1}{x}}$	$\dfrac{1}{x} \cdot \dfrac{1}{x}$
	$0 < x < 31$ x is divisible by 3 and 9.	
12.	x	27
13.	$\dfrac{1}{3}$ of (4 yards 2 feet)	1 yard 4 feet

	Column A	Column B
	$x^n = 1$	
14.	x	1
	$x > 1$	
15.	$\sqrt{\dfrac{2x}{y}} \times \sqrt{\dfrac{xy}{2}}$	x
	$x = \dfrac{1}{2}$	
16.	$\dfrac{\frac{3}{4}}{1 + x}$	x

GO ON TO THE NEXT PAGE

5

SUMMARY DIRECTIONS FOR COMPARISON QUESTIONS

Answer: A   if the quantity in Column A is greater;
B   if the quantity in Column B is greater;
C   if the two quantities are equal;
D   if the relationship cannot be determined from the information given.

AN E RESPONSE WILL NOT BE SCORED.

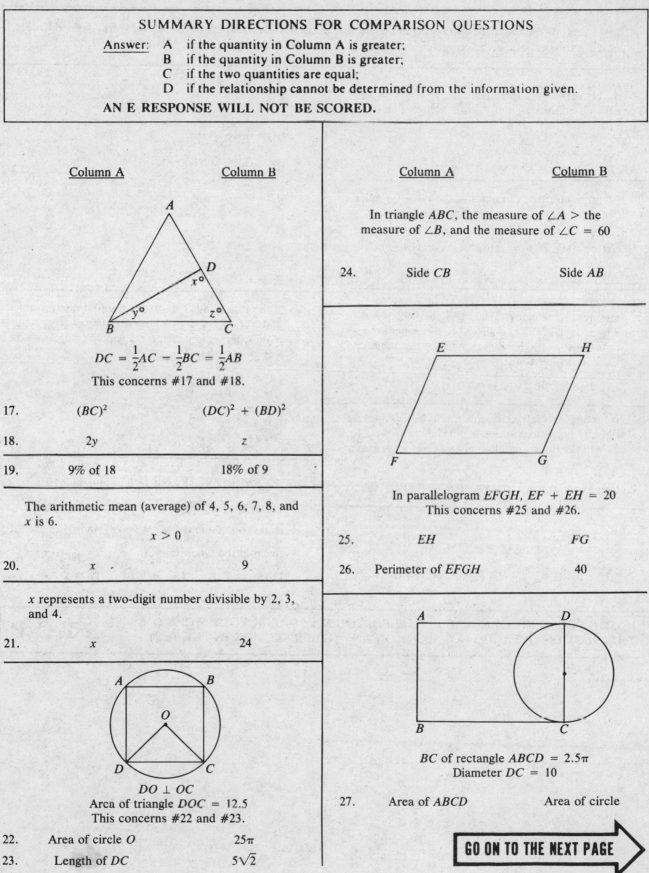

Column A   Column B

$$DC = \frac{1}{2}AC = \frac{1}{2}BC = \frac{1}{2}AB$$
This concerns #17 and #18.

17. $(BC)^2$ $(DC)^2 + (BD)^2$

18. $2y$ z

19.   9% of 18   18% of 9

The arithmetic mean (average) of 4, 5, 6, 7, 8, and x is 6.

$$x > 0$$

20. x 9

x represents a two-digit number divisible by 2, 3, and 4.

21. x 24

$DO \perp OC$
Area of triangle $DOC = 12.5$
This concerns #22 and #23.

22.   Area of circle O 25π
23.   Length of DC $5\sqrt{2}$

Column A   Column B

In triangle ABC, the measure of $\angle A >$ the measure of $\angle B$, and the measure of $\angle C = 60$

24.   Side CB Side AB

In parallelogram $EFGH$, $EF + EH = 20$
This concerns #25 and #26.

25. EH FG
26.   Perimeter of $EFGH$ 40

BC of rectangle $ABCD = 2.5\pi$
Diameter $DC = 10$

27.   Area of $ABCD$ Area of circle

GO ON TO THE NEXT PAGE

5

Solve each of the remaining problems in this section using any available space for scratchwork. Then decide which is the best of the choices given and blacken the corresponding space on the answer sheet.

28. If $\boxdot$ is defined by the equation $x \boxdot y = x + xy + y$ for all numbers x and y, what is the value of z if $8 \boxdot z = 3$?

   (A) -5 (B) $-\dfrac{5}{9}$ (C) $\dfrac{3}{8}$ (D) $\dfrac{5}{9}$ (E) 5

29. An airplane travels m miles at the rate of h miles per hour. How many hours does the trip take?

   (A) $\dfrac{h}{m}$ (B) $h + m$ (C) $\dfrac{m}{h}$ (D) $-m + h$
   (E) $m - h$

30. A nurse gives her patient one tablet every 45 minutes. How many tablets will she need for a 9-hour tour of duty, if she gives the patient the first tablet at the beginning, and the last tablet at the end, of her tour?

   (A) 8   (B) 10   (C) 11   (D) 12   (E) 13

31. If an airplane starts at point R and travels 14 miles directly north to S, then 48 miles directly west to T, what is the straightline distance, in miles, from T to R?

   (A) 25   (B) 34   (C) 50   (D) 62   (E) 2,500

32. If $2x - 3 = 2$, then $x - \dfrac{1}{2} =$

   (A) 2   (B) $2\dfrac{1}{2}$ (C) 3   (D) $4\dfrac{1}{2}$ (E) $5\dfrac{1}{2}$

33. $\dfrac{2}{s}\cdot\dfrac{t}{t} - \dfrac{3}{t - s} =$

   (A) $\dfrac{1}{s^2 + 2st + t^2}$

   (B) $\dfrac{-1}{s - t}$

   (C) $\dfrac{-1}{t - s}$

   (D) $\dfrac{5}{s - t}$

   (E) $\dfrac{5}{t - s}$

34. If the taxi fare is c cents for the first quarter-mile and s cents for each additional quarter-mile, what is the charge, in cents, for a trip of x miles, where x is greater than 1?

   (A) $c + s(4x - 1)$
   (B) $c + s(x - 1)$
   (C) $c + sx$
   (D) sx
   (E) $(c - 1)s + x$

35. The water in a fish tank $1\dfrac{1}{4}$ feet by 8 inches is 7 inches high. If the water is poured into a tank 13 inches by 20 inches, what height, in inches, will it reach in the larger tank?

   (A) 0.27   (B) 0.31   (C) 1.7   (D) 3.2   (E) 4.6

IF YOU FINISH BEFORE TIME IS CALLED, YOU MAY CHECK YOUR WORK ON THIS SECTION ONLY. DO NOT WORK ON ANY OTHER SECTION IN THE TEST.   **S T O P**

6   6   6   6   6   6   6   6   6   6   6

SECTION 6   Time—30 minutes   For each question in this section, choose the best answer and
45 Questions   blacken the corresponding space on the answer sheet.

Each question below consists of a word in capital letters, followed by five lettered words or phrases. Choose the word or phrase that is most nearly opposite in meaning to the word in capital letters. Since some of the questions require you to distinguish fine shades of meaning, consider all the choices before deciding which is best.

Example:

GOOD: (A) sour   (B) bad   (C) red
(D) hot   (E) ugly   Ⓐ ● Ⓒ Ⓓ Ⓔ

1. INEVITABLE: (A) infrequent   (B) visible
    (C) vital   (D) enviable   (E) avoidable

2. GRAPHIC: (A) leaden   (B) literary
    (C) elementary   (D) lacking vividness
    (E) enlarged in size

3. HILARITY: (A) depth   (B) fog   (C) anger
    (D) gloom   (E) abundance

4. INARTICULATE: (A) distinct   (B) remote
    (C) sudden   (D) favorable   (E) zestful

5. FESTER: (A) soothe   (B) heal   (C) stain
    (D) erase   (E) decelerate

6. APATHY: (A) friendliness   (B) timeliness
    (C) concern   (D) anger   (E) insolence

7. AFFLUENCE: (A) lack of effect
    (B) loss of stability   (C) poverty
    (D) appeasement   (E) vigilance

8. RESTRAINT: (A) excess   (B) renewal
    (C) woe   (D) wakefulness   (E) division

9. INSIPIDNESS: (A) sparkling liveliness
    (B) consuming thirst   (C) blooming health
    (D) correct behavior   (E) instant dislike

10. CASTIGATE: (A) enthrone   (B) classify
    (C) close   (D) praise   (E) rehabilitate

11. EPHEMERAL: (A) relevant   (B) waspish
    (C) intelligent   (D) active   (E) permanent

12. DASTARD: (A) neighbor   (B) intelligent person
    (C) brave person   (D) ancestor   (E) lover

13. FELICITOUS: (A) inappropriate   (B) expert
    (C) congratulatory   (D) histrionic   (E) frantic

14. RECONDITE: (A) ambushed
    (B) simple to understand   (C) difficult to control
    (D) outlandish   (E) auxiliary

15. SENTENTIOUS: (A) roundabout   (B) rewarding
    (C) adverbial   (D) cautionary   (E) detrimental

Each sentence below has one or two blanks, each blank indicating that something has been omitted. Beneath the sentence are five lettered words or sets of words. Choose the word or set of words that best fits the meaning of the sentence as a whole.

Example:

Although its publicity has been ----, the film itself is intelligent, well-acted, handsomely produced, and altogether ----.

(A) tasteless..respectable   (B) extensive..moderate
(C) sophisticated..amateur   (D) risqué..crude
(E) perfect..spectacular   ● Ⓑ Ⓒ Ⓓ Ⓔ

16. I regret that we shall be unable to ---- all who have requested rooms for the weekend of graduation.

(A) correlate   (B) accommodate   (C) elucidate
(D) saturate   (E) intimidate

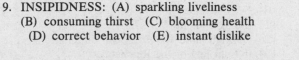
GO ON TO THE NEXT PAGE

6 6 6 6 6 6 6 6 6 6 6

17. Like foolish people who continue to live near an active volcano, many of us are ---- about the ---- of atomic warfare and its attendant destruction.

   (A) worried..possibility
   (B) unconcerned..threat
   (C) excited..power
   (D) cheered..possession
   (E) irritated..news

18. For all the ---- involved in the study of seals, we Arctic researchers have occasional moments of pure ---- over some new idea or discovery.

   (A) tribulations..despair
   (B) hardships..exhilaration
   (C) confusions..bewilderment
   (D) inconvenience..panic
   (E) thrills..delight

19. Despite the growing ---- of Hispanic actors in the American theater, many Hispanic experts feel that the Spanish-speaking population is ---- on the stage.

   (A) decrease..inappropriate
   (B) emergence..visible
   (C) prominence..underrepresented
   (D) skill..alienated
   (E) number..misdirected

20. The ---- tables of the insurance companies indicate that the life expectancy of Americans is ---- .

   (A) statistical..stimulating
   (B) accounting..exaggerated
   (C) authorial..waning
   (D) arithmetic..normal
   (E) actuarial..waxing

Each passage below is followed by questions based on its content. Answer all questions following a passage on the basis of what is <u>stated</u> or <u>implied</u> in that passage.

The establishment of the Third Reich influenced events in American history by starting a chain of events which culminated in war between
Line Germany and the United States. The complete
(5) destruction of democracy, the persecution of Jews, the war on religion, the cruelty and barbarism of the Nazis, and especially, the plans of Germany and her allies, Italy and Japan, for world conquest caused great indignation in this
(10) country and brought on fear of another world war. While speaking out against Hitler's atrocities, the American people generally favored isolationist policies and neutrality. The Neutrality Acts of 1935 and 1936 prohibited trade with any
(15) belligerents or loans to them. In 1937 the President was empowered to declare an arms embargo in wars between nations at his discretion.
   American opinion began to change somewhat after President Roosevelt's "quarantine the
(20) aggressor" speech at Chicago (1937) in which he severely criticized Hitler's policies. Germany's seizure of Austria and the Munich Pact for the partition of Czechoslovakia (1938) also aroused the American people. The conquest of Czecho-
(25) slovakia in March, 1939, was another rude awakening to the menace of the Third Reich. In August, 1939, came the shock of the Nazi-Soviet Pact and in September the attack on Poland and the outbreak of the European war. The United
(30) States attempted to maintain neutrality in spite of sympathy for the democracies arrayed against the Third Reich. The Neutrality Act of 1939 repealed the arms embargo and permitted "cash and carry" exports of arms to belligerent nations. A
(35) strong national defense program was begun. A draft act was passed (1940) to strengthen the military services. A Lend-Lease Act (1941) authorized the President to sell, exchange, or lend materials to any country deemed necessary by
(40) him for the defense of the United States. Help was given to Britain by exchanging certain overage destroyers for the right to establish American bases in British territory in the Western Hemisphere. In August, 1941, President Roosevelt and
(45) Prime Minister Churchill met and issued the Atlantic Charter which proclaimed the kind of a world which should be established after the war. In December, 1941, Japan launched the attack on the United States at Pearl Harbor. Immediately
(50) thereafter, Germany declared war on the United States.

21. One item occurring before 1937 that the author does NOT mention in his list of actions that alienated the American public was

   (A) the hounding and oppression of religious groups
   (B) Nazi savagery and atrocities
   (C) the agreements with Italy
   (D) German plans for European domination
   (E) the burning of the Reichstag

GO ON TO THE NEXT PAGE ➔

6   6   6   6   6   6   6   6   6   6   6

22. The author is primarily concerned with

    (A) evaluating various legislative efforts to strengthen national defense
    (B) summarizing the events that led up to America's involvement in the war
    (C) criticizing the atrocities perpetrated by the Third Reich
    (D) explaining a basic distinction between American and German policy
    (E) describing the social and psychological effects of war

23. During the years 1933–36, American foreign policy may best be described as being one of

    (A) overt belligerence
    (B) deliberate uninvolvement
    (C) moral indignation
    (D) veiled contempt
    (E) reluctant admiration

24. According to the passage, all of the following events occurred in 1939 EXCEPT

    (A) the invasion of Poland
    (B) the invasion of Czechoslovakia
    (C) the passing of the Neutrality Act
    (D) the passing of the Lend-Lease Act
    (E) the outbreak of the war in Europe

25. According to the passage, the Lend-Lease Act was designed primarily to

    (A) strengthen our national defense
    (B) provide battleships to the Allies
    (C) encourage belligerent nations
    (D) promote the Atlantic Charter
    (E) avenge Pearl Harbor

The history of mammals dates back at least to Triassic time. Development was retarded, however, until the sudden acceleration of evolutional
Line change that occurred in the oldest Paleocene.
(5) This led in Eocene time to increase in average size, larger mental capacity, and special adaptations for different modes of life. In the Oligocene Epoch, there was further improvement, with some appearance of some new lines and extinc-
(10) tion of others. Miocene and Pliocene time was marked by culmination of several groups and continued approach toward modern characters. The peak of the career of mammals in variety and average large size was attained in the Mio-
(15) cene.

The adaptation of mammals to almost all possible modes of life parallels that of the reptiles in Mesozoic time, and except for greater intelli-

gence, the mammals do not seem to have done
(20) much better than corresponding reptilian forms. The bat is doubtless a better flying animal than the pterosaur, but the dolphin and whale are hardly more fishlike than the ichthyosaur. Many swift-running mammals of the plains, like the
(25) horse and the antelope, must excel any of the dinosaurs. The tyrannosaur was a more ponderous and powerful carnivore than any flesh-eating mammal, but the lion or tiger is probably a more efficient and dangerous beast of prey because of
(30) a superior brain. The significant point to observe is that different branches of the mammals gradually fitted themselves for all sorts of life, grazing on the plains and able to run swiftly (horse, deer, bison), living in rivers and swamps (hippopota-
(35) mus, beaver), dwelling in trees (sloth, monkey), digging underground (mole, rodent), feeding on flesh in the forest (tiger) and plain (wolf), swimming in the sea (dolphin, whale, seal) and flying in the air (bat). Man is able by mechanical means
(40) to conquer the physical world and adapt himself to almost any set of conditions.

This adaptation produces gradual changes of form and structure. It is biologically characteristic of the youthful, plastic stage of a group. Early
(45) in its career, an animal assemblage seems to possess capacity for change, which, as the unit becomes old and fixed, disappears. The generalized types of organisms retain longest the ability to make new adjustments when required, and it is
(50) from them that new, fecund stocks take origin— certainly not from any specialized end products. So, in the mammals, we witness the birth, plastic spread in many directions, increasing specialization, and in some branches, the extinction, which
(55) we have learned from observation of the geological record of life is a characteristic of the evolution of life.

26. The statements made by the writer are based on evidence

    (A) developed by Charles Darwin
    (B) found by comparing animals and present day reptiles
    (C) found by going to different time periods
    (D) that cannot be definitely established
    (E) gained by studying fossil remains

GO ON TO THE NEXT PAGE

6 6 6 6 6 6 6 6 6 6 6 6 6

27. From this passage, we may conclude that the pterosaur

(A) resembled the bat
(B) was a mammal that lived in the Mesozoic
(C) was a flying reptile
(D) lived in the sea
(E) evolved during the Miocene period

28. According to the passage, the greatest number of forms of mammalian life is found in the

(A) Triassic period
(B) Eocene period
(C) Oligocene period
(D) Pliocene period
(E) Miocene period

29. That the mammals which succeeded the reptiles in geologic time were superior is illustrated by the statement that

(A) the tiger has a brain that surpasses that of the tyrranosaur
(B) the deer runs more swiftly than the lion
(C) the whale is more fishlike than the ichthyosaur
(D) the tiger is more powerful than the carnivorous reptiles
(E) the dinosaurs were slow moving animals

30. *Saur* in such words as pterosaur, dinosaur, and tyrranosaur probably means

(A) large
(B) reptilian
(C) living in Mesozoic time
(D) inefficient
(E) flying

Select the word or set of words that best completes each of the following sentences.

31. By developing skill in the use of sign language, he was able to overcome his ---- difficulties during his recent trip to Japan.

(A) peripatetic   (B) linguistic   (C) plausible
(D) monetary   (E) territorial

32. Even though they knew their competitors' plans were ---- than their own, they refused to ---- their pace.

(A) better..slow
(B) less advanced..relax
(C) more developed..delay
(D) weaker..increase
(E) more suitable..disregard

33. The credit manager said the company would report to private credit bureaus and collection agencies the names of more than two thousand ---- borrowers, whom he described as "deadbeats."

(A) potential   (B) delinquent   (C) acceptable
(D) insubstantial   (E) esteemed

34. Thomas Hardy's novels are said to suffer from the "long arm of coincidence" because too many events seem to have ---- rather than ---- connection.

(A) a surprising..a factual
(B) an exhilarating..a central
(C) an accidental..a causal
(D) an underlying..an actual
(E) a realistic..a casual

35. Your ---- in the face of all the evidence we have presented is proof of our assertion that you are ----.

(A) gullibility..well-informed
(B) disbelief..openminded
(C) acquiescence..acquisitive
(D) skepticism..indifferent
(E) incredulity..opinionated

Each question below consists of a related pair of words or phrases, followed by five lettered pairs of words or phrases. Select the lettered pair that best expresses a relationship similar to that expressed in the original pair.

Example:

YAWN : BOREDOM :: (A) dream : sleep
(B) anger : madness   (C) smile : amusement
(D) face : expression   (E) impatience : rebellion

Ⓐ Ⓑ ● Ⓓ Ⓔ

36. NOVELIST:PLOT :: (A) architect:blueprint
(B) dramatist:acts   (C) sculptor:chisel
(D) magician:legerdemain   (E) composer:notes

37. WINCE:PAIN :: (A) pardon:tolerance
(B) blush:embarrassment   (C) cry:anger
(D) sing:gaiety   (E) march:patriotism

GO ON TO THE NEXT PAGE

6   6 6 6 6 6 6 6 6 6 6

38. ABHOR:DISLIKE :: (A) chastise:punish
(B) vanquish:defeat   (C) qualify:limit
(D) demolish:damage   (E) cultivate:garden

39. DREGS:WINE :: (A) wheat:bread
(B) nectar:ambrosia   (C) fruit:grapes
(D) gold:ore   (E) slag:iron

40. HECKLER:JEER :: (A) snob:flatter
(B) grumbler:complain   (C) mentor:repent
(D) laughingstock:mock   (E) miser:weep

41. SLINK:STEALTH :: (A) whine:querulousness
(B) snarl:mockery   (C) disguise:alias
(D) praise:friendship   (E) invest:capital

42. AMUSING:UPROARIOUS ::
(A) puzzling:dumbfounding
(B) quiet:noisy
(C) intractable:stubborn
(D) petty:narrow-minded
(E) exhausted:weary

43. STANCH:BLEEDING :: (A) dam:flood
(B) divert:traffic   (C) squander:money
(D) induce:nausea   (E) color:facts

44. CARAPACE:TURTLE :: (A) speed:hare
(B) chameleon:lizard   (C) amphibian:frog
(D) shell:snail   (E) kennel:dog

45. SEDULOUS:DILIGENT :: (A) ambitious:vain
(B) haughty:obsequious   (C) lush:barren
(D) ingenuous:naive   (E) devious:diverse

IF YOU FINISH BEFORE TIME IS CALLED, YOU MAY CHECK YOUR WORK ON
THIS SECTION ONLY. DO NOT WORK ON ANY OTHER SECTION IN THE TEST.   **S T O P**

Answer Key

Note: The answers to the math sections are keyed to the corresponding review areas in Chapter 12. The numbers in parentheses after each answer refer to topics as listed below. (Note that to review for number 16, Quantitative Comparison, study Chapter 11.)

1. Fundamental Operations
2. Algebraic Operations
3. Using Algebra
4. Roots and Radicals
5. Inequalities
6. Fractions
7. Decimals
8. Percent
9. Averages
10. Motion
11. Ratio and Proportion
12. Mixtures and Solutions
13. Work
14. Coordinate Geometry
15. Geometry
16. Quantitative Comparison
17. Data Interpretation

Section 1   Verbal

1.	D	10.	B	19.	A	28.	C	37.	E
2.	A	11.	B	20.	D	29.	E	38.	B
3.	B	12.	A	21.	B	30.	B	39.	B
4.	C	13.	B	22.	B	31.	B	40.	B
5.	D	14.	E	23.	D	32.	C	41.	C
6.	B	15.	D	24.	C	33.	C	42.	B
7.	B	16.	D	25.	A	34.	E	43.	C
8.	D	17.	B	26.	D	35.	D	44.	D
9.	A	18.	D	27.	A	36.	D	45.	A

Section 2   Math

1.	B (2)	6.	C (1)	11.	C (2, 6)	16.	E (15)	21.	E (2, 6)
2.	C (3)	7.	D (15)	12.	C (15)	17.	A (6)	22.	B (2)
3.	C (1)	8.	E (15)	13.	A (2)	18.	D (2)	23.	A (2, 6)
4.	E (2)	9.	C (2)	14.	D (2)	19.	C (10)	24.	C (11)
5.	E (2)	10.	B (7, 9)	15.	E (1, 13)	20.	D (1)	25.	A (9)

Section 3   Test of Standard Written English

1.	A	11.	C	21.	B	31.	B	41.	D
2.	B	12.	D	22.	B	32.	D	42.	D
3.	A	13.	E	23.	A	33.	A	43.	A
4.	B	14.	A	24.	C	34.	E	44.	E
5.	D	15.	B	25.	B	35.	B	45.	D
6.	B	16.	E	26.	C	36.	B	46.	B
7.	B	17.	E	27.	A	37.	E	47.	B
8.	B	18.	B	28.	B	38.	D	48.	D
9.	B	19.	C	29.	C	39.	A	49.	E
10.	D	20.	A	30.	D	40.	A	50.	B

Section 4   Verbal

1.	D	9.	C	17.	B	25.	D	33.	D
2.	A	10.	B	18.	C	26.	E	34.	B
3.	C	11.	B	19.	C	27.	B	35.	C
4.	D	12.	C	20.	B	28.	C	36.	E
5.	B	13.	E	21.	A	29.	C	37.	B
6.	B	14.	C	22.	B	30.	D	38.	C
7.	A	15.	C	23.	E	31.	A	39.	D
8.	E	16.	C	24.	B	32.	A	40.	D

Section 5   Math

1.	C (2)	8.	B (5, 16)	15.	C (4, 16)	22.	C (15, 16)	29.	C (10)
2.	B (6, 12)	9.	A (2, 16)	16.	C (2, 6, 16)	23.	C (15, 16)	30.	E (1)
3.	B (2)	10.	D (2, 16)	17.	C (15, 16)	24.	A (15, 16)	31.	C (15)
4.	B (6)	11.	C (2, 6, 16)	18.	C (15, 16)	25.	C (15, 16)	32.	A (2)
5.	E (2, 6)	12.	D (5, 16)	19.	C (8, 16)	26.	C (15, 16)	33.	D (2, 6)
6.	D (6)	13.	B (1, 16)	20.	B (9, 16)	27.	C (15, 16)	34.	A (3)
7.	B (8, 17)	14.	D (4, 16)	21.	D (1, 16)	28.	B (2)	35.	D (15)

Section 6   Verbal

1.	E	10.	D	19.	C	28.	E	37.	B
2.	D	11.	E	20.	E	29.	A	38.	D
3.	D	12.	C	21.	E	30.	B	39.	E
4.	A	13.	A	22.	B	31.	B	40.	B
5.	B	14.	B	23.	B	32.	B	41.	A
6.	C	15.	A	24.	D	33.	B	42.	A
7.	C	16.	B	25.	A	34.	C	43.	A
8.	A	17.	B	26.	E	35.	E	44.	D
9.	A	18.	B	27.	C	36.	A	45.	D

Self-Evaluation

The model SAT test you have just completed has the same format as the actual SAT. As you take more of the model tests in this chapter, you will lose any SAT "stage fright" you might have.

Use the steps that follow to evaluate your performance on Model SAT Test 1. (Note: You'll find the charts referred to in steps 1–5 on the next four pages.)

■ **STEP 1**   Use the Answer Key to check your answers for each section.

■ **STEP 2**   For each section, count the number of correct and incorrect answers (remember that you don't count omitted answers), and enter the numbers on the appropriate lines of the chart "Calculate Your Raw Score." Then do the indicated calculations to get your Raw Verbal Score, your Raw TSWE Score, and your Raw Math Score.

■ **STEP 3**   Consult the chart "Evaluate Your Performance" to see how well you did.

■ **STEP 4**   To pinpoint the specific areas in which you need to improve, circle the numbers of the questions that you either left blank or got wrong on the "Identify Your Weaknesses" charts. This will tell you where to concentrate your efforts to get the most out of your study time. The chart for the math sections gives you page references for review and practice by skill areas. The charts for the verbal and TSWE sections refer you to the appropriate chapters to study for each question type.

■ **STEP 5**   Do the review and practice indicated on the charts wherever you had a concentration of circles.

Important: Remember that, in addition to evaluating your scores, you should read all of the answer explanations for questions you answered incorrectly, questions you omitted, and questions you answered correctly but found difficult. Reviewing the answer explanations will help you understand concepts and strategies, and may point out shortcuts.

Calculate Your Raw Score

Verbal

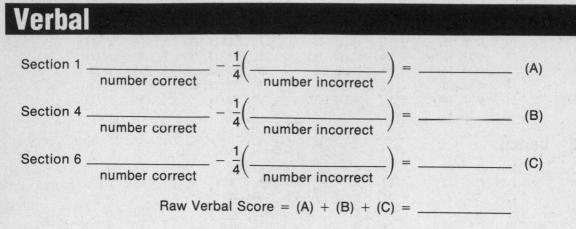

Section 1 _____ − $\frac{1}{4}$(_____) = _____ (A)
number correct   number incorrect

Section 4 _____ − $\frac{1}{4}$(_____) = _____ (B)
number correct   number incorrect

Section 6 _____ − $\frac{1}{4}$(_____) = _____ (C)
number correct   number incorrect

Raw Verbal Score = (A) + (B) + (C) = _____

TSWE

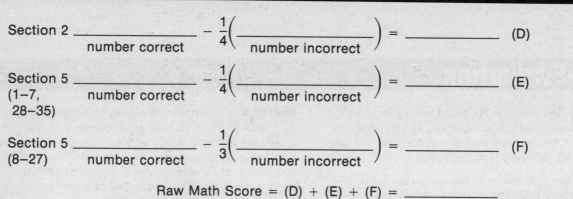

Section 3 _____ − $\frac{1}{4}$(_____) = Raw TSWE Score = _____
number correct   number incorrect

Math

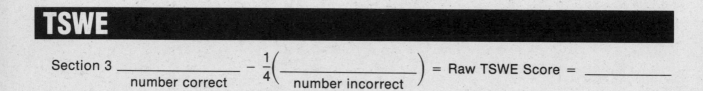

Section 2 _____ − $\frac{1}{4}$(_____) = _____ (D)
number correct   number incorrect

Section 5
(1–7, _____ − $\frac{1}{4}$(_____) = _____ (E)
28–35) number correct   number incorrect

Section 5
(8–27) _____ − $\frac{1}{3}$(_____) = _____ (F)
number correct   number incorrect

Raw Math Score = (D) + (E) + (F) = _____

Evaluate Your Performance
Verbal, TSWE, Math

	Verbal	TSWE	Math
Excellent	111–130	45–60	52–60
Very Good	91–110	41–45	45–51
Good	81–90	36–40	36–44
Above Average	61–80	31–35	30–35
Average	45–60	26–30	20–29
Below Average	below 45	below 26	below 20

Identify Your Weaknesses

Verbal

Question Type	Question Numbers			Chapter to Study
	Section 1	Section 4	Section 6	
Antonym	1, 2, 3, 4, 5, 6, 7, 8, 9, 10, 11, 12, 13, 14, 15	1, 2, 3, 4, 5, 6, 7, 8, 9, 10	1, 2, 3, 4, 5, 6, 7, 8, 9, 10, 11, 12, 13, 14, 15	Chapter 5
Analogy	36, 37, 38, 39, 40, 41, 42, 43, 44, 45	16, 17, 18, 19, 20, 21, 22, 23, 24, 25	36, 37, 38, 39, 40, 41, 42, 43, 44, 45	Chapter 6
Sentence Completion	16, 17, 18, 19, 20, 31, 32, 33, 34, 35	11, 12, 13, 14, 15	16, 17, 18, 19, 20, 31, 32, 33, 34, 35	Chapter 7
Reading Comprehension	21, 22, 23, 24, 25, 26, 27, 28, 29, 30	26, 27, 28, 29, 30, 31, 32, 33, 34, 35, 36, 37, 38, 39, 40	21, 22, 23, 24, 25, 26, 27, 28, 29, 30	Chapter 8

TSWE

Question Type	Question Numbers	Chapter to Study
Usage	1, 2, 3, 4, 5, 6, 7, 8, 9, 10, 11, 12, 13, 14, 15, 16, 17, 18, 19, 20, 21, 22, 23, 24, 25, 41, 42, 43, 44, 45, 46, 47, 48, 49, 50	Chapter 13
Sentence Correction	26, 27, 28, 29, 30, 31, 32, 33, 34, 35, 36, 37, 38, 39, 40	Chapter 13

Identify Your Weaknesses

Math

Skill Area	Question Numbers		Pages to Study
	Section 2	Section 5	
Fundamental Operations	3, 6, 15, 20	13, 21, 30	328–29
Algebraic Operations	1, 4, 5, 9, 11, 13, 14, 18, 21, 22, 23	1, 3, 9, 10, 11, 14, 15, 16, 28, 32, 33	329–34
Using Algebra	2	34	334–35
Fractions	11, 17, 21, 23	2, 4, 5, 6, 8, 11, 16, 33	341–45
Decimals and Percents	10	7, 19	351–55
Verbal Problems	10, 19, 25	20, 29	357–58
Ratio and Proportion	24		362–64
Geometry	7, 8, 12, 16	17, 18, 22, 23, 24, 25, 26, 27, 31, 35	371–76
Inequalities		8, 12	335–36
Quantitative Comparison		8, 9, 10, 11, 12, 13, 14, 15, 16, 17, 18, 19, 20, 21, 22, 23, 24, 25, 26, 27	309–13
Data Interpretation		7	383–88
Roots and Radicals		14, 15	332–33

Answer Explanations
Section 1   Verbal

1. D. *Fertile* means fruitful or productive, able to produce children or crops. Its opposite is *barren*, unproductive, unable to produce children or crops.
Context Clue: Think of "fertile fields."

2. A. A *predicament* is a difficult, perplexing situation, one with no easy way out. Its opposite is *untroubled state*.

3. B. *Imbecility* is mental weakness. Its opposite is *intelligence*.
Context Clue: Think of "weak-minded imbecility."

4. C. To *gratify* is to give pleasure to; to satisfy or please. Its opposite is to *displease*.
Context Clue: "She wished to gratify her parents by getting good grades."

5. D. To *mangle* is to cut or mutilate; to destroy. Its opposite is to *make whole*.
Context Clue: Think of "a mangled wreck."

6. B. *Erratic* means eccentric or odd, something you are unable to foretell or predict. Its opposite is *predictable*.
Context Clue: Think of "an erratic pitcher"; you can never predict when he will throw a wild pitch.

7. B. To *obliterate* something is to wipe it out or remove it. Its opposite is to build something up or *establish* it.
Context Clue: Think of "obliterating a grade of F."

8. D. *Stolid* means unemotional, not easily aroused or excited. Its opposite is *giddy*, which means exuberant and light-hearted.

9. A. *Averse* means unwilling, disinclined, tending to avoid something one dislikes. Its opposite is *eager*.
Context Clue: Think of someone "averse to tests."

10. B. *Ornate* means highly adorned or decorated. Its opposite is *severe*, which means austere or plain.
Context Clue: Think of "ornate Victorian mansions."

11. B. To *consummate* means to complete or achieve. If you consummate a merger, you bring it to completion. Its opposite is to begin or *undertake*.

12. A. A *schism* is a division or split, a breach in unity. Its opposite is *union*.
Context Clue: Think of "a schism dividing the Church."

13. B. A *neophyte* is a beginner, someone new at doing something. Its opposite is *expert*.
Word Parts Clue: *Neo* means new.

14. E. A *sycophant* is a flattering follower, someone who fawns on a superior, a "yes-man." Its opposite is *dignified leader*.

15. D. To *expatiate* is to expand upon or elaborate in detail. Its opposite is to *summarize* or state concisely, giving only the main points.

16. D. *Apprehension* means fear for the future. It is logical to feel fear or anxiety for the future when a neighboring enemy country begins to expand its armed forces.
Remember, before you look at the answer choices, read the sentence and think of a word that makes sense.
Likely Words: anxiety, fear.

(Argument Pattern)

17. B. The word *platitudes* (trite, commonplace remarks) complements *empty promises* and *clichés* (overworked phrases). The three linked phrases support the same thought.
Remember to watch for signal words that link one part of the sentence to another. The presence of *and* linking items in a series indicates that the missing word may be a synonym or near-synonym for the other linked words.

(Support Signal)

18. D. Someone able to manipulate things with both hands is *ambidextrous*, capable of using both hands with equal ease.
The presence of *and* indicates that the missing word supports or explains the other linked words.

(Definition Pattern)

19. A. *Posthumously* means after one's death. Someone who failed to gain fame during her lifetime could only receive it *after* death.
Word Parts Clue: *Post* means after.

20. D. A *hypocrite* (someone who pretends to be virtuous) would fake feelings he thinks he should show. *Simulates* means pretends or feigns.
Choice A is incorrect. It would not be logical for a hypocrite to *conceal* or hide something he thinks he should display.

Choice B is incorrect. It would not be logical for a hypocrite to *decry* or criticize a feeling he thinks he should show.

Choice C is incorrect. If a hypocrite does not possess certain feelings, he cannot *betray* them or reveal them unintentionally.

Choice E is incorrect. It would not be logical for a hypocrite to merely *condone* or excuse a feeling he thinks he should show.

21. B. The passage as a whole is a portrait of Charlotte Stanhope's moral and intellectual temperament or character. The opening sentence of each paragraph describes some aspect of her behavior or character which the paragraph then goes on to develop. Remember, when asked to find the main idea, be sure to check the opening and summary sentences of each paragraph.

Choice A is incorrect. While the various members of the family are described, they are described only in relationship to Charlotte.

Choice C is incorrect. Although Charlotte may well be selfish or egotistical, she does do some good for others. The passage does not illustrate the evils of egotism.

Choice D is incorrect. The passage analyzes Charlotte; it discusses the members of her family only in relationship to her.

Choice E is incorrect. While Charlotte has her virtues, the passage stresses her faults. While her family may not be described as admirable, nothing suggests they are disreputable (not well-esteemed or well-regarded).

(Main Idea)

22. B. The author presents Charlotte *candidly* and openly: her faults are not concealed. The author also presents her *satirically*: her weaknesses and those of her family are mocked or made fun of. If you find the characters in a passage foolish or pompous, the author may well be writing satirically.

Choice A is incorrect. While the author is concerned with Charlotte's moral character, he is not *moralistic* or *self-righteous*; he is describing her character, not preaching a sermon against her.

Choice C is incorrect. The author is unsympathetic to Charlotte's faults and he is not *sentimental* or emotionally excessive about her.

Choice D is incorrect. *Bitterness* is too strong a term to describe the author's tone. He has no reason to be bitter.

Choice E is incorrect. While the author's tone is not highly emotional, it is better to describe it as satiric than as *unfeeling*.

(Attitude/Tone)

23. D. Lines 54–56 mention the troubled mind of Dr. Stanhope, and state that Charlotte would have enjoyed shaking "*what remained* of his Church of England faith." The phrase "what remained" implies that little is left of Dr. Stanhope's original religious faith.

Choice A is incorrect. There is no comparison made between the two elder Stanhopes. Both are *indolent* (lazy).

Choice B is incorrect. Since only Charlotte could persuade her father to look after his affairs (lines 15–16), he apparently was willing to let her manage matters for him and willingly surrendered his authority.

Choice C is incorrect. There is no evidence in the passage that Dr. Stanhope feels regret or remorse.

Choice E is incorrect. While Charlotte's brother is described as moneyless (line 45), there is no evidence in the passage that Dr. Stanhope has disinherited him.

(Inference)

24. C. There is no evidence in the passage that Charlotte's mother is an affectionate wife and mother; similarly, there is no evidence that she is excellent in the "domestic arts" (making tea; managing the household—the very tasks assumed by Charlotte).

Statements I and II are incorrect. Only Statement III is correct. The sole mention of Charlotte's mother (lines 36–37) states that she was encouraged in her idleness by Charlotte. She lacks the willpower to resist Charlotte's encouragements. Thus, she shows herself to be a woman of unassertive, pliable character.

(Specific Details)

25. A. The first paragraph emphasizes that Charlotte "in no way affected the graces of youth." Her manner is that of an assured mistress of a household, not of a flirt.

Choice B is incorrect. Charlotte was a freethinker (one who denies established belief) and thus lacked reverence or respect for religion.

Choice C is incorrect. Charlotte is concerned with her family's worldly well-being and makes her father attend to his material concerns. Thus, she has a materialistic nature.

Choice D is incorrect. Charlotte manages everything and everyone.

Choice E is incorrect. Charlotte's coarseness (vulgarity; crudeness) is implied in the reference to her "freedom . . . from feminine delicacy" (lines 50–51).

(Inference)

26. D. The opening sentence introduces the subject of "specialization by the artist's sex and role

in the group" and its impact on style. These artists specialize or limit themselves to certain set designs. The subsequent paragraphs discuss the men's and women's traditional designs. The title that best summarizes this content is *Design Specialization in Plains Art*. Choice A is incorrect. The passage does not discuss the continuing or ongoing effect of Plains art.

Choice B is too broad to be correct. The passage deals specifically with male and female *artistic roles* in the tribe, not with male and female roles in general.

Choice C is too narrow to be correct. While the passage discusses male Indian art in terms of narrative and dream, it also discusses several other topics.

Choice E is too narrow to be correct. The passage deals with Indian abstract or geometrical art as well as Indian representational art.

Remember, when asked to choose a title, watch out for choices that are too specific or too broad.

(Main Idea/Title)

27. A. Throughout the passage the author is supporting his thesis that male and female Indian artists specialized in different sorts of designs. Thus, when he describes specific examples of their work, he is doing so to point out these differences in decorative styles.

Choice B is incorrect. The passage mentions that women's art, for example, appears on functional objects (lines 22–25); however, it stresses these objects' designs, not their usefulness.

Choice C is incorrect. The passage mentions artistic materials and patterns in some detail; it barely touches on technique (*how* the artist worked).

Choices D and E are incorrect. By the time the author mentions Anglo influence (lines 60–64) and the spiritual significance of emblems (lines 47–60), he no longer is discussing specific works of art.

(Inference)

28. C. You can arrive at the correct answer by the process of elimination.

The author would agree with Statement I. He states in lines 29–31 that Indian men worked in groups (*corporately*) on projects. Therefore, you can eliminate Choices B and D.

The author also would agree with Statement II. He states in lines 53–54 that the dream images or emblems were "protective against . . . enemies" and thus could *ward off danger*. Therefore, you can eliminate Choice A.

The author would *not* agree with Statement

III. In lines 18–20 he assigns the use of classical or abstract forms not to the men, but to the women. Therefore, you can eliminate Choice E.

Only Choice C remains. It is the correct answer.

(Specific Details)

29. E. Lines 45–54 talk of the discovery of personal omens or emblems through dream quests and tell of their protective nature. These emblems can thus be described as *spiritual guardians*.

Choices A and C are incorrect. They are not mentioned in the passage.

Choice B is incorrect. The dream vision suggested the artist's subject matter (his omen or emblem), not his methods or technique.

Choice D is also incorrect. Group solidarity is mentioned in the passage, but *not* in connection with dreams.

(Specific Details)

30. B. Choice B, the portrait bust, lacks a narrative aspect: it tells no heroic story. Therefore, it does *not* resemble Plains art in its narrative aspect. Choice B is correct.

Choice A, the cartoon strip, has a narrative aspect: it tells a story in panels or "pictorial vignettes."

Choice C, the epic, has a narrative aspect: it tells a heroic story.

Choice D, the autobiography, tells a personal story.

Choice E, the mural showing scenes from the life of George Washington, an American hero, clearly resembles Plains art.

(Inference)

31. B. Despite the changes produced by modernization, certain aspects of Indian life have remained *stable* (firmly established; resistant to change).

Watch for signal words that link one part of the sentence to another. *While* in the opening clause signals a contrast. This indicates that the missing word must be an antonym or near-antonym for *change*.

(Contrast Signal)

32. C. The fact that Deloria has detractors or critics leads one to expect his confidence might be shaken. However, the opposite has occurred. The critics have had *little* success at shaking his self-confidence or *denting* or damaging his reputation.

Note the use of *but* signalling the contrast.

(Contrast Signal)

33. C. A readiness to adopt or adjust to new things is *adaptability*.
Remember, before you look at the answer choices, read the sentence and think of a word that makes sense.
Likely Words: "versatility," "ability."

(Definition Pattern)

34. E. The desire to be liked may lead one to project an *endearing* image, one that arouses tender or affectionate feelings. Such behavior might well be *interpreted* or viewed as childish in a public speaker.

(Examples)

35. D. *Intrinsic* value is inherent value, value that essentially belongs to an object, not merely *sentimental* value. She did not keep the furniture because it was worth money or was beautiful (inherent, "real" value). She kept it for emotional reasons (sentimental value). The words *not for . . . but for* signal a contrast, telling you that the missing words must be antonyms or near-antonyms. You can immediately eliminate Choices B and C as synonym or near-synonym pairs.

(Contrast Signal)

36. D. A *writer* creates a book out of *words*. A *baker* creates a cake out of *batter*.

(Worker and Material)

37. E. A *museum* is the place where an *exhibit* or show is held. A *theater* is the place where a *performance* is held.

(Function)

38. B. A ridge of *snow* is a *drift*. A ridge of *sand* is a *dune*.

(Definition)

39. B. The *basement* is the lowest portion of a house; the *attic* is the highest portion. The *root* is the lowest portion of a tree; the *crown* is the highest portion.

(Spatial Sequence)

40. B. An *aria* (operatic song) is performed by a *diva* (great female singer). A *soliloquy* (monologue directly addressed to the audience) is performed by an *actor*.

(Worker and Action)

41. C. *Grain* is kept in a *silo*; *water* is kept in a *bucket*.

(Function)

42. B. *Dreary* (gloomy, cheerless, depressing) means lacking *cheer* (comfort). *Timorous* (fearful, timid) means lacking *courage*.
Remember, consider secondary meanings of the capitalized words as well as their primary meanings.

(Antonym Variant)

43. C. A *shrug* indicates *indifference* or lack of concern; a *nod* indicates *assent* or agreement.

(Action and Its Significance)

44. D. A person characterized by *anger* is defined as *choleric*; a person characterized by *greed* is defined as *avaricious*.
Beware Eye-Catchers: Choice A is incorrect. Don't be fooled because *anger* is a synonym for *wrath*.

(Synonym Variant)

45. A. *Usury* is an excessive or extreme form of *interest*; *parsimony* (stinginess) is an extreme form of *frugality* (economy or thrift).

(Degree of Intensity)

Section 2 Math

1. B. Cross-multiply: $5v + 4x = 21$
Subtract $5v$: $\qquad 4x = 21 - 5v$
Divide by 4: $\qquad x = \dfrac{21 - 5v}{4}$

2. C. If the man was r years old s years ago, he is now $r + s$ years; t years hence he will be $r + s + t$.

3. C. To keep the number of workers in 2 branches to a minimum, the other 4 branches would have to have the maximum, 11 each. This accounts for 44 of the 60 workers, leaving 16 for the remaining 2 branches.

4. E. $$\frac{F}{1} = \frac{Gm_1m_2}{r^2}$$
Cross-multiply: $\quad Fr^2 = Gm_1m_2$
Divide by Gm_2: $\quad \dfrac{Fr^2}{Gm_2} = m_1$

5. E. Cross-multiply: $\quad x = 16 \times 0.375$
Since $\qquad 0.375 = \dfrac{3}{8}$,
$$x = 6$$

6. C. Two halves of $2\frac{1}{2} = 2\frac{1}{2}$
$$2\frac{1}{2} + 2\frac{1}{2} = 5$$

7. D.   There are 360° in a circle; 20% (or $\frac{1}{5}$) of
$360° = 72°$.

8. E. AD is larger than AC. It is
$\frac{3}{2}$ or $1\frac{1}{2}$ or 150% as large. $\overline{\underset{A\quad B\quad C\quad D\quad E}{}}$

9. C. $\frac{a}{b}$ and $\frac{x}{a}$ are each equal to c and therefore
equal to each other.

$$\frac{a}{b} = \frac{x}{a}$$

Cross-multiply: $a^2 = bx$
Extract the square root
of both sides: $a = \pm\sqrt{bx}$

10. B.   Since 0.6 is the average:
$$\frac{0.2 + 0.8 + 1.0 + x}{4} = 0.6$$

Cross-multiply: $2.4 = 2 + x$
$x = 0.4$

11. C.   In a proportion, the two means (or extremes)
may be interchanged.
Since $\frac{2x}{5} = \frac{9}{1}$, interchanging the means, 9 and
5, we get $\frac{2x}{9} = \frac{5}{1}$ or 5.

12. C.   In right triangle ADC
$x^2 + x^2 = 50^2$
$2x^2 = 2500$
$x^2 = 1250$
Area of square = s^2, where
s = side of square
Area of square = x^2 or
1250

13. A.   Substitute values:
$$\frac{a + b}{a - b} = \frac{\frac{2}{3} + \frac{5}{7}}{\frac{2}{3} - \frac{5}{7}}$$

Multiply numerator and denominator by 21:
$$\frac{14 + 15}{14 - 15} = \frac{29}{-1} = -29$$

14. D. $\dfrac{y}{16\frac{1}{3}} = \dfrac{3}{y}$

$\dfrac{y}{\frac{49}{3}} = \dfrac{3}{y}$

$y^2 = 49$
$y = 7$

15. E.   A man binds 112 books in 1 day, and his
assistant works one quarter as fast and binds
28 books in 1 day. Since they work on
alternate days, they produce 112 + 28 or 140
books each pair of days, so it takes $\frac{560}{140}$ or 4
pairs of days, or 8 days, to produce 560
books.

16. E.   Each side = 2
Area of square = 4
The four semicircles equal 2 circles with
diameter = 2, radius = 1.
Area of one circle = $\pi(1)^2$ or π
Area of two circles = 2π
Therefore area of the entire figure = $4 + 2\pi$

17. A.   Since there are 45 pupils in the class, and $\frac{2}{3}$
are boys, there are 30 boys in the class. If $\frac{1}{2}$ of
the boys are blue-eyed, 15 boys are blue-eyed.

18. D.   The best way to do this is to start with answer
choice (A) and substitute the values of the
table in each of the of the possible answers.
Choice (A) is not correct because, when $R =$
2, S does not = 5. Choice (B) is not correct
because, when $R = 3$, S does not = 8.
Choice (C) is not correct because, when $R =$
1, S does not = 2. Choice (D), $S = 3R - 1$,
is satisfied by all values in the table: (3×1)
$- (1) = 2$, $(3 \times 2) - 1 = 5$, $(3 \times 3) - 1 =$
8, $(4 \times 3) - 1 = 11$, $(5 \times 3) - 1 = 14$, and
$(6 \times 3) - 1 = 17$. Choice (E) is not correct
because, when $R = 1$, S does not = 2.

19. C.   The auto travels 30 miles from X to Y in 20
min. At this rate the car averages 90 miles in
60 min. or 1 hr.

20. D.   Twelve 4-lb. weights weigh 48 lb. It takes 16
3-lb. weights to weigh 48 lb.

21. E. $\dfrac{a}{b} - \dfrac{a}{c}$

Use bc as a common denominator: $\dfrac{ac - ab}{bc}$.

22. B. $4r = 5t$ $4r = 5t$
Divide by 4: $r = \dfrac{5t}{4}$

$r = \dfrac{s}{3}$

To get s in terms of t, r must be eliminated:
$\dfrac{s}{3} = \dfrac{5t}{4}$ (since each fraction equals r)
Cross-multiply: $4s = 15t$
Divide by 4: $s = \dfrac{15t}{4}$

23. A. $\dfrac{n}{7} + \dfrac{n}{5} = \dfrac{12}{35}$

Multiply each side by 35: $5n + 7n = 12$
$$12n = 12$$
$$n = 1$$

24. C. Twelve kittens consume 4 cans. The remaining 4 cans can feed 8 cats.

25. A. Since x is greater than 1, 218x is greater than 218. Since none of the numbers is less than 218, it is impossible for the average of the numbers to be 218. The average of a group of numbers cannot be less than the smallest of the numbers or greater than the largest of the numbers. If x is large, the average of the numbers may be 2,839.

Section 3   Test of Standard Written English

1. A. Error in diction. Change *Being that* to *Since*.

2. B. Error in agreement between subject and verb. Change *have control* to *has control*.

3. A. Double negative. Change *can't* to *can*.

4. B. Error in case. *But*, as used in this sentence, is a preposition meaning *except*. Change *he* to *him*.

5. D. Change *reason . . . is because* to *reason . . . is that*.

6. B. Error in tense. Change *am playing* to *have been playing*.

7. B. Error in diction. Change *affective* to *effective*.

8. B. Error in diction. *Among* should be used when three or more items are being considered.

9. B. Error in diction. Change *bring* to *take*.

10. D. Lack of parallel structure. Change *as well as signing* to *and sign* in order to match the other items in the list.

11. C. Incorrect sentence connector. Change *furthermore* to the coordinating conjunction *but* to clarify the relationship between the clauses.

12. D. Error in diction. Change *accumulation from* to *accumulation of*.

13. E. Sentence is correct.

14. A. Error in diction. *Altogether* is correct.

15. B. Error in tense. Change *had wanted* to *wanted*.

16. E. Sentence is correct.

17. E. Sentence is correct.

18. B. Error in diction. Change *differ with* (which relates to difference of opinion) to *differ from* (which relates to difference in appearance).

19. C. Lack of parallel structure. Change *remaining at* to the infinitive *to remain at* in order to match *to travel on*.

20. A. Avoid the expression *kind of a person*. Omit the article (*a*).

21. B. Error in diction. The verb *to rise* means to ascend; the verb *to raise* means to cause to rise. Therefore, change *has risen* to *raised*.

22. B. Error in case. Change *he and I* to *him and me*.

23. A. The verb *feels* should be followed by an adjective (*bad*).

24. C. Error in tense. Change *will be sang* to *will be sung*.

25. B. Error in case. Change *him* to *his*.

26. C. Choice C uses *drank*, the correct form of the irregular verb *drink*.

27. A. Sentence is correct as written.

28. B. *Seems satisfying their need* is unidiomatic. *Seems to satisfy their need* is correct (Choice B).

29. C. Choice C corrects the error in conjunction use.

30. D. *Irregardless* is a nonstandard use of *regardless*.

31. B. The run-on sentence is corrected in Choice B.

32. D. The phrase *along with several other stories* is not part of the subject of the sentence. The subject is ''*Araby*'' (singular); the verb should be *is going to be read* (singular).

33. A. Choice B introduces an error in agreement. Choices C, D, and E misuse the *not only . . . but also* construction.

34.. E.   The dangling modifier is corrected in Choice E.

35. B.   The dangling construction is corrected in Choices B and E. However, only Choice B retains the meaning of the original sentence.

36. B.   The error in case is corrected in Choice B. *Whoever* is the subject of the verb *had contributed*.

37. E.   In this question we find two errors. Both the sentence fragment and the misuse of the intransitive verb *lie* are corrected in Choice E.

38. D.   The faulty comparison is corrected in Choice D.

39. A.   The original sentence is correct. The subject of *are going* is *legislators* (plural). Therefore, Choices B and C are incorrect. Choices D and E change the meaning of the original sentence.

40. A.   The original sentence is correct. The singular pronoun *it* refers to the subject of the main clause, *fate* (singular).

41. D.   Lack of parallel structure. Change the clause *what his serial number was* to a noun (*serial number*) to match the other items in the list.

42. D.   Error in tense. Change *will handle* to *handled*.

43. A.   Error in case. Change *whom* to *who*.

44. E.   Sentence is correct.

45. D.   Error in agreement. Since the antecedent of *its* is *lawyers*, change *its* to *their*.

46. B.   Error in tense. Delete the word *has* to make the verb *anticipated*.

47. B.   Error in agreement. *Everybody* is a singular pronoun. Change *their* to *his or her*.

48. D.   Error in diction. The verb *to lay* (past tense is *laid*) means to put or to place; the verb *to lie* (past tense is *lay*) means to recline. Therefore, change *laid back* to *lay back*.

49. E.   Sentence is correct.

50. B.   Error in agreement. *Data* is a plural noun. Change *was* to *were*.

Section 4   Verbal

1. D.   *Pardon* means excuse or condone. The opposite of pardon is *blame*.

2. A.   *Famished* means starving or extremely hungry. The opposite of famished is *satisfied* or *stuffed*.
Context Clue: "I'm famished. When do we eat?"

3. C.   A person or thing that is *yielding* is flexible or easily bent. Its opposite is unyielding or *disinclined to bend*.

4. D.   *Menial* means lowly or servile; degrading. Its opposite is haughty or *dignified*.
Context Clue: Think of "menial labor."

5. B.   *Gargantuan* means extremely large, gigantic. Its opposite is *tiny in size*.
Context Clue: Think of "a gargantuan helping of food."

6. B.   *Scrupulous* means careful in attending to details; precise and exact. Its opposite is *careless of detail*.
Context Clue: Think of "scrupulous care." Remember to consider secondary meanings of the capitalized word as well as its primary meaning. *Scrupulous* is also used as a synonym for *honest* and *conscientious*, as in "scrupulous conduct," for example. Its opposite in this sense would be *dishonest* or *unprincipled*. It is not used with this meaning here.

7. A.   *Mollify* means to soothe; to appease or placate. Its opposite is *annoy*.
Context Clue: Think of trying to "mollify his anger."

8. E.   *Bellicosity* means aggressive hostility or warlike spirit. Its opposite is *pacifism* (opposition to violence).
Context Clue: Think of "frightened by his bellicosity."
Word Parts Clue: *Belli-* means war.
When you are unsure of a word's exact meaning, consider whether it has a positive or negative sense. If you have only seen it used in negative contexts, its antonym must be a word that appears in positive contexts. By eliminating the negative words *ugliness*, *outrage*, and *stupidity*, you narrow down your answer choices to two words.

9. C.   *Garrulity* means talkativeness. Its opposite is *reticence* (reserve; inclination not to talk).
Context Clue: Think of "long-winded garrulity."

10. B. *Quixotic* means impractical or visionary; idealistic, like Don Quixote. Its opposite is realistic or *practical*.
Context Clue: Think of "a quixotic gesture." Don Quixote tried to attack windmills because he thought they were wicked giants.

11. B. A *hypochondriac* suffers from unwarranted fear of illness. Such a person would be likely to take up a good deal of a doctor's time complaining about imaginary diseases.
Beware Eye-Catchers: Choice D is incorrect. An invalid is a disabled or sickly person. Such a person would have a legitimate claim on a doctor's time.

(Definition)

12. C. Preservationists would not wish a species to die out or become *extinct*, but would instead want it to survive for the *enjoyment* of generations to come.

(Definition)

13. E. It is difficult for a celebrity to keep his *humility* or sense of his own *unimportance* while the world is telling him how important he is.
Remember, before you look at the choices, read the sentence and think of a word that makes sense.
Likely Words: modesty, humbleness, humility.

14. C. Someone *never satisfied* would be likely to make *disparaging* (belittling or carping) comments.
Remember to watch for signal words that link one part of the sentence to another. The use of "never" in the opening clause sets up a contrast. The missing words must be antonyms or near-antonyms. You can immediately eliminate Choices A, B, and D as synonym or near-synonym pairs.

(Contrast Signal)

15. C. *Connotations* (the implications or overtones a word carries in addition to its primary meaning) are most difficult to translate.
Remember, before you look at the choices, read the sentence and think of a word that makes sense.
Likely Words: subtleties, nuances, meaning.

(Cause & Effect Signal)

16. C. The function of the *heart* is to *pump*; the function of the *stomach* is to *digest*.

(Function)

17. B. A *stanza* is a subdivision of a *poem*; a *story* is a subdivision of a *building*.

(Part to Whole)

18. C. A *mongrel* is of mixed breed while a *collie* is of pure breed. An *alloy* is a mixture of metals. *Iron* is a single metal.
Choice A is incorrect. A gosling is a young goose.
Choice B is incorrect. A ruby is a kind of gem.
Choice D is incorrect. A bridle is a piece of restraining harness for a horse or pony.
Choice E is incorrect. A bleat is the cry of a sheep.

(Part to Whole)

19. C. A *trowel* is a tool used by a *mason*; an *adze* is a tool used by a *carpenter*.
Remember, if more than one answer appears to fit the relationship in your sentence, look for a narrower approach. "A mason uses a trowel" is too broad a framework; it could fit both Choices A and C. While a *potter* uses *clay* in his work, it is his material, not his tool.

(Worker and Tool)

20. B. A *servant* serves his *master*; a *subject* serves his *monarch*.
Beware Eye-Catchers: Choice E is incorrect. Although a *landlord* and a *tenant* have a "working relationship," the tenant does not serve the landlord.

(Function)

21. A. An *amulet* is a charm designed to repel *evil*; a *fort* is a stronghold designed to repel *attack*.

(Function)

22. B. One seeks to *amass* (gather) *wealth* to preserve it; one seeks to *garner* (collect) *grain* to store it.

(Function)

23. E. A *malefactor* (evildoer) is by definition *iniquitous* (wicked); a *prankster* (person who plays tricks on others) is by definition *mischievous*.

(Defining Characteristic)

24. B. A *connoisseur* is an expert in the field of art or *paintings*. A *gourmet* is an expert in the field of food or *viands*.
Remember, if more than one answer appears to fit the relationship in your sentence, look for a narrower approach. "A connoiseur

enjoys paintings'' is too broad a framework; it could fit Choices B and C. A miser enjoys gold, but he is not necessarily a discerning judge of its artistic or aesthetic qualities.

(Function)

25. D.   A *cartographer* (map drawer) is a maker of *gazetteers* (geographical dictionaries). A *lexicographer* is a writer of *dictionaries*.

(Worker and Creation)

26. E.   The third paragraph in particular gives a picture of a busy program; that, plus Jane's response to the beauty of the island, supports the statement that her days are full ones.
Choice A is incorrect. In lines 24–25 she doubts whether she is strong enough to stay.
Choice B is incorrect. Line 5 mentions trees twisted by battering winds, but nowhere in the passage does it suggest that Jane had difficulties with the weather.
Choice C is incorrect. Line 31 mentions the local fishermen, but the passage nowhere indicates that Jane has gained their trust.
Choice D is incorrect. "Frightened," "walking along the rocks crying," and "feeling so sorry for myself" indicate that Jane is emotional rather than unemotional.

(Inference)

27. B.   Jane states in the last paragraph that she cannot imagine life in Melbourne any longer and that she is more determined than ever to stay. Her love for the island has won over her loneliness. She has apparently *won the battle*.
Choice A is incorrect. Jane does not speak of loneliness; she speaks of feeling at home.
Choices C, D, and E are incorrect. Nothing in the passage's conclusion suggests any of these possibilities.

(Inference)

28. C.   Irony may be defined as a figure of speech in which words express a meaning that is the opposite of the supposedly intended meaning. Thus, to call jagged rocks, twisted trees, and tangled undergrowth "assets" or items of value is an ironical description.
Choice A is incorrect. The island is literally Jane's hideaway. The word is used without irony.
Choices B and D are incorrect. "Wind" and "coast" are similarly used without irony.
Choice E is incorrect. As lines 7–8 state, "bandicoot," though an odd word, is the correct term for a species of Australian rat. It is used without irony.

(Technique)

29. C.   The introductory or topic sentence indicates that the passage will be about the ways public officials respond to pressure. The passage then divides public officials into two groups, good and bad, and discusses their characteristics.
Choice A is incorrect. Political pressure groups are not specifically mentioned in the passage.
Choice B is incorrect. The passage discusses types of public officials, not mistakes that public officials make.
Choices D and E are incorrect. Both are too specific to be suitable titles.
Remember, when asked to choose a title, watch out for choices that are too specific or too broad.

(Main Idea/Title)

30. D.   The author states that the best public officials have "faith that public support will be forthcoming." Thus, they have *confidence* in the public.
Choice A is incorrect. Poor public officials need a packed gallery and a show of unanimous support.
Choice B is incorrect. Nothing in the passage suggests it.
Choice C is incorrect. The best public officials are not "swerved from the path of public interest," even by pressure groups.
Choice E is incorrect. Poor public officials are "overhesitant" and worry about how they are viewed by their constituents.

(Specific Details)

31. A.   Choice A is NOT mentioned in the passage. Therefore, Choice A is the correct choice. All the other characteristics are mentioned in the passage.
Choice B is incorrect. The passage states that poor public officials are *evasive* (avoiding arguments or controversy by verbal dodges and tricks). They lack candor.
Choice C is incorrect. According to the passage, they are *overhesitant* or indecisive.
Choice D is incorrect. The passage states that they use *stale formulas*; they lack inventiveness.
Choice E is incorrect. According to the passage, they worry about their colleagues, their audience; they lack independence.

(Specific Details)

32. A.   The opening sentence of the second paragraph supports Choice A. The existence of the rain forest as a source of new, evolving life forms is "most important of all."

(Specific Details)

33. D.   The rain forest is still "primeval" because it has been untouched since earliest times. It is a reservoir whose contents must not be touched or exposed to axes and the destructive effects of rain and sun.

Remember, when asked to give the meaning of an unfamiliar word, look for nearby context clues.

(Word from Context)

34. B.   The author's contention that these forests should be preserved would probably be most strongly supported by conservationists and botanists. Lumber company representatives, chemical manufacturers, and government representatives all would have logical reasons for exploiting these resources. The views of the "man on the street" would likely be mixed.

(Inference)

35. C.   In the opening sentence, the author indicates that the primeval forests have given way to "eroded land," land that has been damaged by wind and rain.

Remember, when asked about specific details in the passage, spot key words in the question and scan the passage to find them (or their synonyms).

(Specific Details)

36. E.   In the opening sentence, the author includes both the physical sciences (chemistry, astronomy) and the social sciences (economics, anthropology) under the sciences. He nowhere mentions literature.

(Specific Details)

37. B.   The illustrations given by the author in the second paragraph indicate how "useless" study of conic sections and electricity has been of unexpected and tremendous value to humanity.

Choice A is incorrect. The concluding sentence points out that many practical results have come about through the disinterested pursuit of knowledge that seemed to have no technical application or use.

Choices C, D, and E are incorrect. The author favors no one discipline or field of learning.

(Specific Details)

38. C.   In the second paragraph we are told that the Greeks studied conic sections "without the least suspicion that it might someday be useful." In other words, they were *unaware* of the value of their studies.

Choice A is incorrect. The Greeks were

dealing not with applied mathematics, but with pure mathematics.

Choice B is incorrect. The application of the theory of conic sections to navigational problems took place "centuries later" than the time of the Greek mathematicians.

Choice D is incorrect. The reference to electricity comes after the reference to the Greek mathematicians.

Choice E is incorrect. The reference to resigning oneself applies not to the Greeks but to the "human spirit."

(Specific Details)

39. D.   The author is stressing the value of pure research or "learning for its own sake."

Choice A is incorrect. The passage stresses the primacy of pure knowledge; it is first in importance.

Choice B is incorrect. The passage values learning.

Choices C and E are incorrect. Both are far too broad.

Remember, when asked to choose a title, watch out for choices that are too specific or too broad.

(Main Idea/Title)

40. D.   The third sentence states that the need to understand "is intrinsic and consubstantial to man." In other words, it is an essential part of humanity's substance or nature, the part that distinguishes the human from the animal. The author stresses this point strongly. This implies that to the author man's need to know is chiefly important in that it *defines his essential humanity.*

Choice A is incorrect. The author enjoys the results of technical progress, but defends the primacy of pure knowledge. This suggests that he would disagree with the idea that the need to know is important chiefly because it enables technical progress.

Choices B, C, and E are incorrect. There is nothing in the passage to suggest them.

(Inference)

Section 5   Math

1. C.   Since $\frac{1}{r} = 3$ and $s = 3$, $s = \frac{1}{r}$. (Things equal to the same thing are equal to each other.)

$$s = \frac{1}{r}$$

Cross-multiply: $rs = 1$

Divide by s: $r = \frac{1}{s}$

2. B.   If 2 parts of sand are mixed with 3 parts of gravel, there are 5 parts of mixture. Since there are 2 parts of sand, $\frac{2}{5}$ of the mixture is sand.

3. B.
$$2.3y = 46$$
Multiply by 10: $23y = 460$
Divide by 23: $y = 20$

4. B.   Reduce the fractions: $\frac{8}{10} = \frac{4}{5}$ and $\frac{12}{15} = \frac{4}{5}$
$$\frac{4}{5} - \frac{4}{5} = 0$$

5. E. $\dfrac{1}{N + \dfrac{1}{N}}$
Multiply numerator and denominator by N:
$$\frac{N}{N^2 + 1}$$

6. D.   100 is the common denominator.
$$\frac{5}{4} = \frac{125}{100} \qquad \frac{6}{5} = \frac{120}{100} \qquad \frac{13}{10} = \frac{130}{100}$$
$$\frac{29}{25} = \frac{116}{100} \qquad \frac{59}{50} = \frac{118}{100}$$
The smallest fraction is $\frac{116}{100}$ or $\frac{29}{25}$.

7. B.   By looking at the graph half-way between 20 and 40 on the horizontal-axis, we can see that the market price is slightly less than 50, or 49.

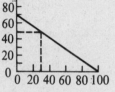

8. B.   The value of the fraction is negative; therefore the denominator must be negative since the numerator has a positive value. Therefore the value of x is less than 1.

9. A. $y^2 - 1 = 3$
$y^2 = 4$
$y = \pm 2$
Since $x = 3$, x is larger than y.

10. D.   Since $x^2 = 25$, $x = \pm 5$. If $x = +5$, the correct choice would be (C).
However, if $x = -5$, then the correct choice would be (B).

11. C.   In Column A, $\dfrac{1}{x} \div \dfrac{1}{x}$ or $\dfrac{1}{x} \div \dfrac{x}{1}$
or $\dfrac{1}{x} \cdot \dfrac{1}{x}$ or $\dfrac{1}{x^2}$
In Column B, $\dfrac{1}{x} \cdot \dfrac{1}{x} = \dfrac{1}{x^2}$

12. D.   The value of x could be 9, 18, or 27.

13. B.   4 yd. = 12 ft.
4 yd. 2 ft. = 14 ft.
$\frac{1}{3}$ of (4 yd. 2 ft.) = $\frac{14}{3} = 4\frac{2}{3}$ ft.
1 yd. 4 ft. = 7 ft.

14. D.   If n has a value of zero, then x could have any positive value except zero.
If n has a value of 1, then x could be equal to 1.
If n has an even integral value, then x could be ± 1.

15. C. $\sqrt{\dfrac{2x}{y}} \cdot \sqrt{\dfrac{xy}{2}} = \sqrt{\dfrac{2x^2 y}{2y}} = \sqrt{x^2} = x$

16. C. $\dfrac{\dfrac{3}{4}}{1 + \dfrac{1}{2}}$
Multiply numerator and denominator by 4:
$$\frac{3}{4 + 2} = \frac{3}{6} = \frac{1}{2}$$

17. C.   If $\frac{1}{2}AC = \frac{1}{2}BC = \frac{1}{2}AB$, then $AC = AB = BC$.
The triangle is equilateral, and $z = 60$. Since BD divides AC so that $AD = DC$, it is also perpendicular, forming right triangle BDC, and $x = 90$. This question is an application of the Pythagorean Theorem.

18. C. $y = 30$ and $z = 60$.

19. C. $(0.09)(18) = (0.18)(9)$

20. B.   Since the average of six values is 6, the sum must be 36. Without x, the sum = 30; therefore $x = 6$.

21. D.   There are several possible values of x: 12, 24, 48, ...

22. C.   Radii OD and OC are equal legs of right triangle DOC.
Area of $DOC = \frac{1}{2}$ (leg) (leg) = 12.5 or (leg)^2
= 25. Therefore leg = 5. Since the leg (or radius) = 5, the area of the circle = 25π.

23. C. DC is the hypotenuse of isosceles right triangle DOC. By the Pythagorean Theorem $(DC)^2 = (5)^2 + (5)^2$ or $(DC)^2 = 50$ or $DC = \sqrt{50}$ or $5\sqrt{2}$.
Alternatively, recognize that the hypotenuse of the isosceles right triangle equals a leg times $\sqrt{2}$. Therefore the hypotenuse is $5\sqrt{2}$.

24. **A.** Since the measure of $\angle C = 60$, m $\angle A$ + m $\angle B$ = 120, and therefore m $\angle A$ is more than $\frac{1}{2}$ of 120, since A is larger than B (given). CB lies opposite the angle with a measure of more than $60°$ and is therefore larger than side AB, which lies opposite the angle with a measure of $60°$.

25. **C.** Since this is a parallelogram, $EH = FG$.

26. **C.** $EF + EH = \frac{1}{2}$ the perimeter.

27. **C.** Area of $ABCD = (BC)(DC)$ or $(2.5\pi)(10)$ or 25π.
    Area of circle $= \pi r^2$.
    Since diameter $= 10$, radius $= 5$ and area $= \pi r^2$ or 25π.

28. **B.** $8 + 8z + z = 3$
    $$9z = -5$$
    $$z = -\frac{5}{9}$$

29. **C.** Recall the formula: $\dfrac{\text{Distance}}{\text{Rate}} = \text{Time}$

    Substitute: $\dfrac{m}{h} = \text{time}$

30. **E.** There are 9×60 or 540 min. in 9 hr. The nurse needs a tablet when she begins and one every 45 min. for 540 min. Hence $\frac{540}{45}$ or 12 tablets are needed for the 12 45-min. periods in the 9 hr. tour. Adding the tablet she gives at the beginning, she needs 13 tablets.

31. **C.** Applying the Pythagorean Theorem to this right triangle:
    $(TR)^2 = (ST)^2 + (SR)^2$
    The Straight-line distance
    $RT = \sqrt{14^2 + 48^2}$ or 50.
    Or note that choices (A) and (B) can be ruled out since they are less than the distance from S to T alone. Choice (E) is obviously too large. Choice (D) is incorrect because it equals the sum of the distances from R to S and from S to T. This leaves choice (C).

32. **A.**
    $$2x - 3 = 2$$
    Add 3: $\quad 2x = 5$
    Divide by 2: $\quad x = \dfrac{5}{2}$
    Find $x - \frac{1}{2}$ by substitution: $\dfrac{5}{2} - \dfrac{1}{2} = 2$

33. **D.** If the two fractions have similar denominators, the problem is simplified.
    $$\frac{3}{t-s} \text{ or } \frac{3}{-s+t} = \frac{-3}{s-t}$$
    because the numerator and denominator are multiplied by -1. The problem now is
    $$\frac{2}{s-t} - \frac{-3}{s-t} \text{ or } \frac{5}{s-t}.$$

34. **A.** There are $4x$ quarter-miles in a trip of x miles, and c cents is the charge for the first $\frac{1}{4}$ mile. The remaining quarter miles $(4x - 1)$ are s cents each or $s(4x - 1)$ cents. The total cost for the trip is $c + s(4x - 1)$ cents.

35. **D.** The dimensions of the first tank are 7 in., 8 in., and $1\frac{1}{4}$ ft. (15 in.). The volume is $7 \times 8 \times 15$ cu. in. or 840 cu. in.
    The volume (840 cu. in.) occupied in the second tank $= 13$ in. $\times 20$ in. $\times H$ in. or $260H$ cu. in.
    Since $260H = 840$, $H = \dfrac{42}{13}$ or 3.2.

Section 6   Verbal

1. **E.** The opposite of *inevitable* (inescapable) is *avoidable*.
   Context Clue: Think of "inevitable conclusion."

2. **D.** *Graphic* means vivid or striking. Its opposite is *lacking vividness*.
   Context Clue: Think of a "graphic description."

3. **D.** *Hilarity* means merriment or cheerfulness. Its opposite is *gloom*.
   Context Clue: Think of "the hilarity of circus clowns."

4. **A.** An *inarticulate* expression is unintelligible. An articulate one is *distinct*.
   Context Clue: Think of "inarticulate mumbling."

5. **B.** To *fester* means to rot or grow putrid. Its opposite is to *heal*.
   Context Clue: Think of "a festering wound."

6. **C.** *Apathy* means indifference or lack of concern. Its opposite is *concern*.
   Context Clue: Think of "the apathy of non-voters."
   Word Parts Clue: *A-* or *An-* means not; *path-* means feel. *Apathy* means the state of not feeling, of not being concerned.

7. C. *Affluence* means riches or wealth. Its opposite is *poverty*.
Context Clue: Think of "living in affluence."

8. A. *Restraint* means moderation. Its opposite is *excess*.
Remember to consider secondary meanings of the capitalized word as well as its primary meaning. You may think of *restraint* as a controlling force, something like handcuffs, but that is not the sense in which it is used here.

9. A. *Insipidness* means dullness or lack of flavor. Its opposite is animation or *sparkling liveliness*.
Context Clue: Think of being bored by "the insipidness of a dull party."
Beware Eye-Catchers: Choice B is incorrect. *Insipidness* has nothing to do with being thirsty and wanting to sip.

10. D. To *castigate* is to punish or criticize severely. Its opposite is to *praise*.
Context Clue: Think of "castigating sinners."

11. E. *Ephemeral* means short-lived, transitory. Its opposite is *permanent*.
Context Clue: Think of "ephemeral as a Mayfly."

12. C. A *dastard* is a coward. Its opposite is a *brave person*.
Context Clue: Think of "a cowardly dastard."

13. A. *Felicitous* means apt and well-chosen. Its opposite is *inappropriate*.
Context Clue: Think of "a felicitous remark."

14. B. *Recondite* means difficult to understand. Its opposite is *simple to understand*.
Context Clue: Think of "a recondite treatise."

15. A. A *sententious* statement is pithy and to the point. Its opposite is *roundabout*.
Beware Eye-Catchers: Choice C is incorrect. Sentences and adverbs are both grammatical terms. However, sententious and adverbial are unrelated.

16. B. To be unable to provide rooms for people is to be unable to *accommodate* them.

17. B. Many writers have compared people who seem *unconcerned* about the *threat* of atomic warfare to people who live in areas of danger and lack the sense to move away.
Remember, in double-blank sentences, go through the answer choices, testing the *first* words in each choice and eliminating those that don't fit.
Choice A does not fit. *Foolish* people would be *unworried* rather than worried about living near an active volcano.
Choice C also seems unlikely. Even extremely foolish people would not be *cheered* about atomic warfare.

(Examples)

18. B. In spite of the difficulties or *hardships* involved in their research, the researchers have some moments of *exhilaration* or cheer.
Remember to watch for signal words that link one part of the sentence to another. The use of "for all the" in the opening clause sets up a contrast. The missing words must be antonyms or near-antonyms. You can immediately eliminate Choices A, C, and E as synonym or near-synonym pairs.

(Contrast Signal)

19. C. Although some Hispanic actors are *prominent* (widely and popularly known), the group as a whole is *underrepresented* (not represented adequately).
Remember to watch for signal words that link one part of the sentence to another. The use of "despite" in the opening phrase sets up a contrast. The missing words must be antonyms or near-antonyms. Only Choice C is such a pair.

(Contrast Signal)

20. E. *Actuarial* (pertaining to statistics of mortality rates) tables indicate that the life expectancy of Americans is on the rise or *waxing*.
Remember, in double-blank sentences, go through the answer choices, testing the *first* words in each choice and eliminating those that don't fit. You can immediately eliminate *authorial*, Choice C, *accounting*, Choice B, and *arithmetic*, Choice D. None of these terms are particularly relevant to insurance and life expectancy.

(Definition)

21. E. Choice E is mentioned nowhere in the passage. Therefore, Choice E is correct.
Choice A is incorrect. Lines 5–6 mention the persecution of religious groups.
Choice B is incorrect. Lines 6–7 mention the "cruelty and barbarism" of the Nazis.
Choice C is incorrect. Lines 7–9 mention the pact between Germany and Italy.
Choice D is incorrect. Lines 7–9 mention Germany's plans for "world conquest."
Remember, when asked about specific details

in the passage, spot key words in the question and scan the passage to find them (or their synonyms).
Key Words: oppression, savagery, Italy, domination, Reichstag.

(Specific Details)

22. B.   The detailed listing of dates and battles and legislative acts provides a summary of this chain of events. The opening sentences of both paragraphs and the concluding sentence of the passage all support Choice B.
Choice A is incorrect. The passage mentions efforts to strengthen national defense only in passing.
Choice C is incorrect. While the opening paragraph lists German atrocities, the bulk of the passage is not devoted to criticizing these crimes.
Choice D is incorrect. The passage does not contrast two policies; it summarizes a chain of events.
Choice E is incorrect. The author is concerned with the specific factors leading up to a particular war, not with the effects of war in general.

(Main Idea)

23. B.   Choice B, *deliberate uninvolvement*, best expresses America's general policy of neutrality.
Choice A is incorrect. America was neutral, not openly warlike.
Choice C is incorrect. While Americans were indignant over German atrocities, American policy was one of neutrality or uninvolvement.
Choices D and E can be ruled out immediately. Neither attitude makes sense in the context.
Remember, when asked about specific details in the passage, spot key words in the question and scan the passage to find them (or their synonyms).
Key Words: belligerence, uninvolvement, indignation.

(Specific Details)

24. D.   Choice D is stated in the second paragraph as having occurred in 1941, *not* in 1939. Therefore, Choice D is correct. All of the other choices are specifically mentioned as having taken place in 1939.
For a question involving specific details about a date and about the names of historical events, scan the passage looking for capitalized names and for the date. Capitalized words and numbers are easy to locate.
Key Words: Poland, Czechoslovakia, Neutrality, Lend-Lease, 1939, war.

(Specific Details)

25. A.   The justification for the Lend-Lease Act was that it improved our national defense.

(Specific Details)

26. E.   The last sentence of the passage mentions observing "the geological record of life," or, in other words, *studying fossil remains*.
Choice A is incorrect. The passage contains no mention of Darwin.
Choice B is incorrect. The reptiles under discussion are not present day specimens.
Choice C is incorrect. The idea is physically impossible.
Choice D is incorrect. The dating in lines 1–15 is very detailed and definite. The author does not seem to be in doubt.

(Specific Details)

27. C.   In the second paragraph, the author shows how the adaptation of mammals parallels that of ancient reptiles. As an illustration, he compares the flying abilities of the bat (a mammal) to those of the pterosaur (a reptile).
Choice A is incorrect. The pterosaur no more resembles a bat in appearance than a horse resembles a dinosaur.
Choice B is incorrect. The pterosaur was not a mammal but a reptile.
Choice D is incorrect. The ichthyosaur (referred to as somewhat fishlike) is an aquatic form of reptile; the pterosaur is an avian or birdlike form.
Choice E is incorrect. Lines 13–15 state that the mammals, not the reptiles, evolved in the Miocene.

(Inference)

28. E.   The passage attributes the peak or high point of mammalian existence in terms of variety and size to the Miocene (lines 13–15).

(Specific Details)

29. A.   Lines 28–30 mention the lion or tiger as "a more efficient and dangerous beast of prey *because of a superior brain*."
Choice B is incorrect. Deers and lions are both mammals.
Choice C is incorrect. The passage denies that the whale is particularly more fishlike than the ichthyosaur. Also, it never holds up "fishlike-ness" as a measure of superiority.
Choice D is incorrect. The passage states the direct opposite.
Choice E is plausible, but incorrect. The passage measures superiority in terms of intelligence, not of speed.

(Inference)

30. B.   Since these three animals were reptiles, we may assume that *saur* means reptile or reptilian.
Remember, when asked to make inferences, base your answers on what the passage implies, not what it states directly.

(Inference)

31. B.   Sign language is useful when words are unavailable or when a person has linguistic difficulties, as in dealing with a foreign language.
Remember, before you look at the choices, read the sentence and think of a word that makes sense.
Likely Words: translation, language, vocabulary.

(Examples)

32. B.   Although we might expect people to *relax* their pace on learning that their competitors' plans were *less advanced*, these people refuse. *Even though* sets up an unexpected contrast. Choice A is incorrect. It would be logical in a competitive world to try to work faster rather than *slower* to overcome any advantages a competitor's product might have. This answer lacks *even though*'s sense of an *unexpected* contrast.
Choice C is incorrect for similar reasons. Choices D and E make no sense.

(Contrast Signal)

33. B.   "Deadbeats" are borrowers who default on their loans, persons who do not repay what they borrow. These people are *delinquent* or neglectful of an obligation. Note how the phrase set off by the comma defines the missing word.

(Definition)

34. C.   A *causal* connection involves cause and effect. Causal is the opposite of *accidental* or due to chance.
Remember to watch for signal words that link one part of the sentence to another. The use of "rather than" sets up a contrast. The missing words must be antonyms or near-antonyms.

(Contrast Signal)

35. E.   Disbelief or *incredulity* in the face of strong evidence indicates a closed or *opinionated* mind, not an openminded one.

(Argument Pattern)

36. A.   Just as a *novelist* creates a *plot* as a guide for a novel in progress, an *architect* creates a *blueprint* as a guide for a building in progress.
Remember, if more than one answer appears to fit the relationship in your sentence, look for a narrower approach. "A novelist uses a plot" is too broad a framework; it could fit Choices B, C, D, and E.

(Worker and Creation)

37. B.   Those who *wince* indicate *pain*; those who *blush* indicate *embarrassment*.

(Action and Its Significance)

38. D.   *Abhor* (hate) is more extreme than *dislike*; *demolish* is more extreme than *damage*.

(Degree of Intensity)

39. E.   Just as the *dregs* (sediment) must be separated from *wine*, *slag* must be separated from *iron*.

(Defining Characteristic)

40. B.   A *heckler* is someone who *jeers* or mocks; a *grumbler*, someone who *complains*.
Beware Eye-Catchers: Choice D is incorrect. A heckler does the jeering; a laughingstock, however, is the one who gets mocked.

(Definition)

41. A.   To *slink* is to show *stealth*, to move sneakily; to *whine* is to show *querulousness*, to speak petulantly.

(Defining Characteristic)

42. A.   Something *uproarious* is extremely *amusing*; something *dumbfounding* is extremely *puzzling*.
Note that Choices C, D, and E are all pairs of synonyms. Eliminate them: the correct answer must belong to a different analogy type.

(Degree of Intensity)

43. A.   One must *stanch bleeding* to stop the flow of blood; one must *dam* a *flood* to prevent an overflow of water.

(Function)

44. D.   A *carapace* (hard case) protects a *turtle*; a *shell* protects a *snail*.

(Function)

45. D.   *Sedulous* (industrious) and *diligent* are synonyms; likewise *ingenuous* (innocent; unsophisticated) and *naive* are synonyms.

(Synonyms)

Answer Sheet–Test 2

Start with number 1 for each new section. If a section has fewer than 50 questions, leave the extra spaces blank.

Section 1

1. Ⓐ Ⓑ Ⓒ Ⓓ Ⓔ	11. Ⓐ Ⓑ Ⓒ Ⓓ Ⓔ	21. Ⓐ Ⓑ Ⓒ Ⓓ Ⓔ	31. Ⓐ Ⓑ Ⓒ Ⓓ Ⓔ	41. Ⓐ Ⓑ Ⓒ Ⓓ Ⓔ
2. Ⓐ Ⓑ Ⓒ Ⓓ Ⓔ	12. Ⓐ Ⓑ Ⓒ Ⓓ Ⓔ	22. Ⓐ Ⓑ Ⓒ Ⓓ Ⓔ	32. Ⓐ Ⓑ Ⓒ Ⓓ Ⓔ	42. Ⓐ Ⓑ Ⓒ Ⓓ Ⓔ
3. Ⓐ Ⓑ Ⓒ Ⓓ Ⓔ	13. Ⓐ Ⓑ Ⓒ Ⓓ Ⓔ	23. Ⓐ Ⓑ Ⓒ Ⓓ Ⓔ	33. Ⓐ Ⓑ Ⓒ Ⓓ Ⓔ	43. Ⓐ Ⓑ Ⓒ Ⓓ Ⓔ
4. Ⓐ Ⓑ Ⓒ Ⓓ Ⓔ	14. Ⓐ Ⓑ Ⓒ Ⓓ Ⓔ	24. Ⓐ Ⓑ Ⓒ Ⓓ Ⓔ	34. Ⓐ Ⓑ Ⓒ Ⓓ Ⓔ	44. Ⓐ Ⓑ Ⓒ Ⓓ Ⓔ
5. Ⓐ Ⓑ Ⓒ Ⓓ Ⓔ	15. Ⓐ Ⓑ Ⓒ Ⓓ Ⓔ	25. Ⓐ Ⓑ Ⓒ Ⓓ Ⓔ	35. Ⓐ Ⓑ Ⓒ Ⓓ Ⓔ	45. Ⓐ Ⓑ Ⓒ Ⓓ Ⓔ
6. Ⓐ Ⓑ Ⓒ Ⓓ Ⓔ	16. Ⓐ Ⓑ Ⓒ Ⓓ Ⓔ	26. Ⓐ Ⓑ Ⓒ Ⓓ Ⓔ	36. Ⓐ Ⓑ Ⓒ Ⓓ Ⓔ	46. Ⓐ Ⓑ Ⓒ Ⓓ Ⓔ
7. Ⓐ Ⓑ Ⓒ Ⓓ Ⓔ	17. Ⓐ Ⓑ Ⓒ Ⓓ Ⓔ	27. Ⓐ Ⓑ Ⓒ Ⓓ Ⓔ	37. Ⓐ Ⓑ Ⓒ Ⓓ Ⓔ	47. Ⓐ Ⓑ Ⓒ Ⓓ Ⓔ
8. Ⓐ Ⓑ Ⓒ Ⓓ Ⓔ	18. Ⓐ Ⓑ Ⓒ Ⓓ Ⓔ	28. Ⓐ Ⓑ Ⓒ Ⓓ Ⓔ	38. Ⓐ Ⓑ Ⓒ Ⓓ Ⓔ	48. Ⓐ Ⓑ Ⓒ Ⓓ Ⓔ
9. Ⓐ Ⓑ Ⓒ Ⓓ Ⓔ	19. Ⓐ Ⓑ Ⓒ Ⓓ Ⓔ	29. Ⓐ Ⓑ Ⓒ Ⓓ Ⓔ	39. Ⓐ Ⓑ Ⓒ Ⓓ Ⓔ	49. Ⓐ Ⓑ Ⓒ Ⓓ Ⓔ
10. Ⓐ Ⓑ Ⓒ Ⓓ Ⓔ	20. Ⓐ Ⓑ Ⓒ Ⓓ Ⓔ	30. Ⓐ Ⓑ Ⓒ Ⓓ Ⓔ	40. Ⓐ Ⓑ Ⓒ Ⓓ Ⓔ	50. Ⓐ Ⓑ Ⓒ Ⓓ Ⓔ

Section 2

1. Ⓐ Ⓑ Ⓒ Ⓓ Ⓔ	11. Ⓐ Ⓑ Ⓒ Ⓓ Ⓔ	21. Ⓐ Ⓑ Ⓒ Ⓓ Ⓔ	31. Ⓐ Ⓑ Ⓒ Ⓓ Ⓔ	41. Ⓐ Ⓑ Ⓒ Ⓓ Ⓔ
2. Ⓐ Ⓑ Ⓒ Ⓓ Ⓔ	12. Ⓐ Ⓑ Ⓒ Ⓓ Ⓔ	22. Ⓐ Ⓑ Ⓒ Ⓓ Ⓔ	32. Ⓐ Ⓑ Ⓒ Ⓓ Ⓔ	42. Ⓐ Ⓑ Ⓒ Ⓓ Ⓔ
3. Ⓐ Ⓑ Ⓒ Ⓓ Ⓔ	13. Ⓐ Ⓑ Ⓒ Ⓓ Ⓔ	23. Ⓐ Ⓑ Ⓒ Ⓓ Ⓔ	33. Ⓐ Ⓑ Ⓒ Ⓓ Ⓔ	43. Ⓐ Ⓑ Ⓒ Ⓓ Ⓔ
4. Ⓐ Ⓑ Ⓒ Ⓓ Ⓔ	14. Ⓐ Ⓑ Ⓒ Ⓓ Ⓔ	24. Ⓐ Ⓑ Ⓒ Ⓓ Ⓔ	34. Ⓐ Ⓑ Ⓒ Ⓓ Ⓔ	44. Ⓐ Ⓑ Ⓒ Ⓓ Ⓔ
5. Ⓐ Ⓑ Ⓒ Ⓓ Ⓔ	15. Ⓐ Ⓑ Ⓒ Ⓓ Ⓔ	25. Ⓐ Ⓑ Ⓒ Ⓓ Ⓔ	35. Ⓐ Ⓑ Ⓒ Ⓓ Ⓔ	45. Ⓐ Ⓑ Ⓒ Ⓓ Ⓔ
6. Ⓐ Ⓑ Ⓒ Ⓓ Ⓔ	16. Ⓐ Ⓑ Ⓒ Ⓓ Ⓔ	26. Ⓐ Ⓑ Ⓒ Ⓓ Ⓔ	36. Ⓐ Ⓑ Ⓒ Ⓓ Ⓔ	46. Ⓐ Ⓑ Ⓒ Ⓓ Ⓔ
7. Ⓐ Ⓑ Ⓒ Ⓓ Ⓔ	17. Ⓐ Ⓑ Ⓒ Ⓓ Ⓔ	27. Ⓐ Ⓑ Ⓒ Ⓓ Ⓔ	37. Ⓐ Ⓑ Ⓒ Ⓓ Ⓔ	47. Ⓐ Ⓑ Ⓒ Ⓓ Ⓔ
8. Ⓐ Ⓑ Ⓒ Ⓓ Ⓔ	18. Ⓐ Ⓑ Ⓒ Ⓓ Ⓔ	28. Ⓐ Ⓑ Ⓒ Ⓓ Ⓔ	38. Ⓐ Ⓑ Ⓒ Ⓓ Ⓔ	48. Ⓐ Ⓑ Ⓒ Ⓓ Ⓔ
9. Ⓐ Ⓑ Ⓒ Ⓓ Ⓔ	19. Ⓐ Ⓑ Ⓒ Ⓓ Ⓔ	29. Ⓐ Ⓑ Ⓒ Ⓓ Ⓔ	39. Ⓐ Ⓑ Ⓒ Ⓓ Ⓔ	49. Ⓐ Ⓑ Ⓒ Ⓓ Ⓔ
10. Ⓐ Ⓑ Ⓒ Ⓓ Ⓔ	20. Ⓐ Ⓑ Ⓒ Ⓓ Ⓔ	30. Ⓐ Ⓑ Ⓒ Ⓓ Ⓔ	40. Ⓐ Ⓑ Ⓒ Ⓓ Ⓔ	50. Ⓐ Ⓑ Ⓒ Ⓓ Ⓔ

Section 3

1. Ⓐ Ⓑ Ⓒ Ⓓ Ⓔ	11. Ⓐ Ⓑ Ⓒ Ⓓ Ⓔ	21. Ⓐ Ⓑ Ⓒ Ⓓ Ⓔ	31. Ⓐ Ⓑ Ⓒ Ⓓ Ⓔ	41. Ⓐ Ⓑ Ⓒ Ⓓ Ⓔ
2. Ⓐ Ⓑ Ⓒ Ⓓ Ⓔ	12. Ⓐ Ⓑ Ⓒ Ⓓ Ⓔ	22. Ⓐ Ⓑ Ⓒ Ⓓ Ⓔ	32. Ⓐ Ⓑ Ⓒ Ⓓ Ⓔ	42. Ⓐ Ⓑ Ⓒ Ⓓ Ⓔ
3. Ⓐ Ⓑ Ⓒ Ⓓ Ⓔ	13. Ⓐ Ⓑ Ⓒ Ⓓ Ⓔ	23. Ⓐ Ⓑ Ⓒ Ⓓ Ⓔ	33. Ⓐ Ⓑ Ⓒ Ⓓ Ⓔ	43. Ⓐ Ⓑ Ⓒ Ⓓ Ⓔ
4. Ⓐ Ⓑ Ⓒ Ⓓ Ⓔ	14. Ⓐ Ⓑ Ⓒ Ⓓ Ⓔ	24. Ⓐ Ⓑ Ⓒ Ⓓ Ⓔ	34. Ⓐ Ⓑ Ⓒ Ⓓ Ⓔ	44. Ⓐ Ⓑ Ⓒ Ⓓ Ⓔ
5. Ⓐ Ⓑ Ⓒ Ⓓ Ⓔ	15. Ⓐ Ⓑ Ⓒ Ⓓ Ⓔ	25. Ⓐ Ⓑ Ⓒ Ⓓ Ⓔ	35. Ⓐ Ⓑ Ⓒ Ⓓ Ⓔ	45. Ⓐ Ⓑ Ⓒ Ⓓ Ⓔ
6. Ⓐ Ⓑ Ⓒ Ⓓ Ⓔ	16. Ⓐ Ⓑ Ⓒ Ⓓ Ⓔ	26. Ⓐ Ⓑ Ⓒ Ⓓ Ⓔ	36. Ⓐ Ⓑ Ⓒ Ⓓ Ⓔ	46. Ⓐ Ⓑ Ⓒ Ⓓ Ⓔ
7. Ⓐ Ⓑ Ⓒ Ⓓ Ⓔ	17. Ⓐ Ⓑ Ⓒ Ⓓ Ⓔ	27. Ⓐ Ⓑ Ⓒ Ⓓ Ⓔ	37. Ⓐ Ⓑ Ⓒ Ⓓ Ⓔ	47. Ⓐ Ⓑ Ⓒ Ⓓ Ⓔ
8. Ⓐ Ⓑ Ⓒ Ⓓ Ⓔ	18. Ⓐ Ⓑ Ⓒ Ⓓ Ⓔ	28. Ⓐ Ⓑ Ⓒ Ⓓ Ⓔ	38. Ⓐ Ⓑ Ⓒ Ⓓ Ⓔ	48. Ⓐ Ⓑ Ⓒ Ⓓ Ⓔ
9. Ⓐ Ⓑ Ⓒ Ⓓ Ⓔ	19. Ⓐ Ⓑ Ⓒ Ⓓ Ⓔ	29. Ⓐ Ⓑ Ⓒ Ⓓ Ⓔ	39. Ⓐ Ⓑ Ⓒ Ⓓ Ⓔ	49. Ⓐ Ⓑ Ⓒ Ⓓ Ⓔ
10. Ⓐ Ⓑ Ⓒ Ⓓ Ⓔ	20. Ⓐ Ⓑ Ⓒ Ⓓ Ⓔ	30. Ⓐ Ⓑ Ⓒ Ⓓ Ⓔ	40. Ⓐ Ⓑ Ⓒ Ⓓ Ⓔ	50. Ⓐ Ⓑ Ⓒ Ⓓ Ⓔ

Remove answer sheet by cutting on dotted line

Start with number 1 for each new section. If a section has fewer than 50 questions, leave the extra spaces blank.

Section 4

1. Ⓐ Ⓑ Ⓒ Ⓓ Ⓔ	11. Ⓐ Ⓑ Ⓒ Ⓓ Ⓔ	21. Ⓐ Ⓑ Ⓒ Ⓓ Ⓔ	31. Ⓐ Ⓑ Ⓒ Ⓓ Ⓔ	41. Ⓐ Ⓑ Ⓒ Ⓓ Ⓔ
2. Ⓐ Ⓑ Ⓒ Ⓓ Ⓔ	12. Ⓐ Ⓑ Ⓒ Ⓓ Ⓔ	22. Ⓐ Ⓑ Ⓒ Ⓓ Ⓔ	32. Ⓐ Ⓑ Ⓒ Ⓓ Ⓔ	42. Ⓐ Ⓑ Ⓒ Ⓓ Ⓔ
3. Ⓐ Ⓑ Ⓒ Ⓓ Ⓔ	13. Ⓐ Ⓑ Ⓒ Ⓓ Ⓔ	23. Ⓐ Ⓑ Ⓒ Ⓓ Ⓔ	33. Ⓐ Ⓑ Ⓒ Ⓓ Ⓔ	43. Ⓐ Ⓑ Ⓒ Ⓓ Ⓔ
4. Ⓐ Ⓑ Ⓒ Ⓓ Ⓔ	14. Ⓐ Ⓑ Ⓒ Ⓓ Ⓔ	24. Ⓐ Ⓑ Ⓒ Ⓓ Ⓔ	34. Ⓐ Ⓑ Ⓒ Ⓓ Ⓔ	44. Ⓐ Ⓑ Ⓒ Ⓓ Ⓔ
5. Ⓐ Ⓑ Ⓒ Ⓓ Ⓔ	15. Ⓐ Ⓑ Ⓒ Ⓓ Ⓔ	25. Ⓐ Ⓑ Ⓒ Ⓓ Ⓔ	35. Ⓐ Ⓑ Ⓒ Ⓓ Ⓔ	45. Ⓐ Ⓑ Ⓒ Ⓓ Ⓔ
6. Ⓐ Ⓑ Ⓒ Ⓓ Ⓔ	16. Ⓐ Ⓑ Ⓒ Ⓓ Ⓔ	26. Ⓐ Ⓑ Ⓒ Ⓓ Ⓔ	36. Ⓐ Ⓑ Ⓒ Ⓓ Ⓔ	46. Ⓐ Ⓑ Ⓒ Ⓓ Ⓔ
7. Ⓐ Ⓑ Ⓒ Ⓓ Ⓔ	17. Ⓐ Ⓑ Ⓒ Ⓓ Ⓔ	27. Ⓐ Ⓑ Ⓒ Ⓓ Ⓔ	37. Ⓐ Ⓑ Ⓒ Ⓓ Ⓔ	47. Ⓐ Ⓑ Ⓒ Ⓓ Ⓔ
8. Ⓐ Ⓑ Ⓒ Ⓓ Ⓔ	18. Ⓐ Ⓑ Ⓒ Ⓓ Ⓔ	28. Ⓐ Ⓑ Ⓒ Ⓓ Ⓔ	38. Ⓐ Ⓑ Ⓒ Ⓓ Ⓔ	48. Ⓐ Ⓑ Ⓒ Ⓓ Ⓔ
9. Ⓐ Ⓑ Ⓒ Ⓓ Ⓔ	19. Ⓐ Ⓑ Ⓒ Ⓓ Ⓔ	29. Ⓐ Ⓑ Ⓒ Ⓓ Ⓔ	39. Ⓐ Ⓑ Ⓒ Ⓓ Ⓔ	49. Ⓐ Ⓑ Ⓒ Ⓓ Ⓔ
10. Ⓐ Ⓑ Ⓒ Ⓓ Ⓔ	20. Ⓐ Ⓑ Ⓒ Ⓓ Ⓔ	30. Ⓐ Ⓑ Ⓒ Ⓓ Ⓔ	40. Ⓐ Ⓑ Ⓒ Ⓓ Ⓔ	50. Ⓐ Ⓑ Ⓒ Ⓓ Ⓔ

Section 5

1. Ⓐ Ⓑ Ⓒ Ⓓ Ⓔ	11. Ⓐ Ⓑ Ⓒ Ⓓ Ⓔ	21. Ⓐ Ⓑ Ⓒ Ⓓ Ⓔ	31. Ⓐ Ⓑ Ⓒ Ⓓ Ⓔ	41. Ⓐ Ⓑ Ⓒ Ⓓ Ⓔ
2. Ⓐ Ⓑ Ⓒ Ⓓ Ⓔ	12. Ⓐ Ⓑ Ⓒ Ⓓ Ⓔ	22. Ⓐ Ⓑ Ⓒ Ⓓ Ⓔ	32. Ⓐ Ⓑ Ⓒ Ⓓ Ⓔ	42. Ⓐ Ⓑ Ⓒ Ⓓ Ⓔ
3. Ⓐ Ⓑ Ⓒ Ⓓ Ⓔ	13. Ⓐ Ⓑ Ⓒ Ⓓ Ⓔ	23. Ⓐ Ⓑ Ⓒ Ⓓ Ⓔ	33. Ⓐ Ⓑ Ⓒ Ⓓ Ⓔ	43. Ⓐ Ⓑ Ⓒ Ⓓ Ⓔ
4. Ⓐ Ⓑ Ⓒ Ⓓ Ⓔ	14. Ⓐ Ⓑ Ⓒ Ⓓ Ⓔ	24. Ⓐ Ⓑ Ⓒ Ⓓ Ⓔ	34. Ⓐ Ⓑ Ⓒ Ⓓ Ⓔ	44. Ⓐ Ⓑ Ⓒ Ⓓ Ⓔ
5. Ⓐ Ⓑ Ⓒ Ⓓ Ⓔ	15. Ⓐ Ⓑ Ⓒ Ⓓ Ⓔ	25. Ⓐ Ⓑ Ⓒ Ⓓ Ⓔ	35. Ⓐ Ⓑ Ⓒ Ⓓ Ⓔ	45. Ⓐ Ⓑ Ⓒ Ⓓ Ⓔ
6. Ⓐ Ⓑ Ⓒ Ⓓ Ⓔ	16. Ⓐ Ⓑ Ⓒ Ⓓ Ⓔ	26. Ⓐ Ⓑ Ⓒ Ⓓ Ⓔ	36. Ⓐ Ⓑ Ⓒ Ⓓ Ⓔ	46. Ⓐ Ⓑ Ⓒ Ⓓ Ⓔ
7. Ⓐ Ⓑ Ⓒ Ⓓ Ⓔ	17. Ⓐ Ⓑ Ⓒ Ⓓ Ⓔ	27. Ⓐ Ⓑ Ⓒ Ⓓ Ⓔ	37. Ⓐ Ⓑ Ⓒ Ⓓ Ⓔ	47. Ⓐ Ⓑ Ⓒ Ⓓ Ⓔ
8. Ⓐ Ⓑ Ⓒ Ⓓ Ⓔ	18. Ⓐ Ⓑ Ⓒ Ⓓ Ⓔ	28. Ⓐ Ⓑ Ⓒ Ⓓ Ⓔ	38. Ⓐ Ⓑ Ⓒ Ⓓ Ⓔ	48. Ⓐ Ⓑ Ⓒ Ⓓ Ⓔ
9. Ⓐ Ⓑ Ⓒ Ⓓ Ⓔ	19. Ⓐ Ⓑ Ⓒ Ⓓ Ⓔ	29. Ⓐ Ⓑ Ⓒ Ⓓ Ⓔ	39. Ⓐ Ⓑ Ⓒ Ⓓ Ⓔ	49. Ⓐ Ⓑ Ⓒ Ⓓ Ⓔ
10. Ⓐ Ⓑ Ⓒ Ⓓ Ⓔ	20. Ⓐ Ⓑ Ⓒ Ⓓ Ⓔ	30. Ⓐ Ⓑ Ⓒ Ⓓ Ⓔ	40. Ⓐ Ⓑ Ⓒ Ⓓ Ⓔ	50. Ⓐ Ⓑ Ⓒ Ⓓ Ⓔ

Section 6

1. Ⓐ Ⓑ Ⓒ Ⓓ Ⓔ	11. Ⓐ Ⓑ Ⓒ Ⓓ Ⓔ	21. Ⓐ Ⓑ Ⓒ Ⓓ Ⓔ	31. Ⓐ Ⓑ Ⓒ Ⓓ Ⓔ	41. Ⓐ Ⓑ Ⓒ Ⓓ Ⓔ
2. Ⓐ Ⓑ Ⓒ Ⓓ Ⓔ	12. Ⓐ Ⓑ Ⓒ Ⓓ Ⓔ	22. Ⓐ Ⓑ Ⓒ Ⓓ Ⓔ	32. Ⓐ Ⓑ Ⓒ Ⓓ Ⓔ	42. Ⓐ Ⓑ Ⓒ Ⓓ Ⓔ
3. Ⓐ Ⓑ Ⓒ Ⓓ Ⓔ	13. Ⓐ Ⓑ Ⓒ Ⓓ Ⓔ	23. Ⓐ Ⓑ Ⓒ Ⓓ Ⓔ	33. Ⓐ Ⓑ Ⓒ Ⓓ Ⓔ	43. Ⓐ Ⓑ Ⓒ Ⓓ Ⓔ
4. Ⓐ Ⓑ Ⓒ Ⓓ Ⓔ	14. Ⓐ Ⓑ Ⓒ Ⓓ Ⓔ	24. Ⓐ Ⓑ Ⓒ Ⓓ Ⓔ	34. Ⓐ Ⓑ Ⓒ Ⓓ Ⓔ	44. Ⓐ Ⓑ Ⓒ Ⓓ Ⓔ
5. Ⓐ Ⓑ Ⓒ Ⓓ Ⓔ	15. Ⓐ Ⓑ Ⓒ Ⓓ Ⓔ	25. Ⓐ Ⓑ Ⓒ Ⓓ Ⓔ	35. Ⓐ Ⓑ Ⓒ Ⓓ Ⓔ	45. Ⓐ Ⓑ Ⓒ Ⓓ Ⓔ
6. Ⓐ Ⓑ Ⓒ Ⓓ Ⓔ	16. Ⓐ Ⓑ Ⓒ Ⓓ Ⓔ	26. Ⓐ Ⓑ Ⓒ Ⓓ Ⓔ	36. Ⓐ Ⓑ Ⓒ Ⓓ Ⓔ	46. Ⓐ Ⓑ Ⓒ Ⓓ Ⓔ
7. Ⓐ Ⓑ Ⓒ Ⓓ Ⓔ	17. Ⓐ Ⓑ Ⓒ Ⓓ Ⓔ	27. Ⓐ Ⓑ Ⓒ Ⓓ Ⓔ	37. Ⓐ Ⓑ Ⓒ Ⓓ Ⓔ	47. Ⓐ Ⓑ Ⓒ Ⓓ Ⓔ
8. Ⓐ Ⓑ Ⓒ Ⓓ Ⓔ	18. Ⓐ Ⓑ Ⓒ Ⓓ Ⓔ	28. Ⓐ Ⓑ Ⓒ Ⓓ Ⓔ	38. Ⓐ Ⓑ Ⓒ Ⓓ Ⓔ	48. Ⓐ Ⓑ Ⓒ Ⓓ Ⓔ
9. Ⓐ Ⓑ Ⓒ Ⓓ Ⓔ	19. Ⓐ Ⓑ Ⓒ Ⓓ Ⓔ	29. Ⓐ Ⓑ Ⓒ Ⓓ Ⓔ	39. Ⓐ Ⓑ Ⓒ Ⓓ Ⓔ	49. Ⓐ Ⓑ Ⓒ Ⓓ Ⓔ
10. Ⓐ Ⓑ Ⓒ Ⓓ Ⓔ	20. Ⓐ Ⓑ Ⓒ Ⓓ Ⓔ	30. Ⓐ Ⓑ Ⓒ Ⓓ Ⓔ	40. Ⓐ Ⓑ Ⓒ Ⓓ Ⓔ	50. Ⓐ Ⓑ Ⓒ Ⓓ Ⓔ

Remove answer sheet by cutting on dotted line

MODEL SAT TEST 2

SECTION 1	Time—30 minutes 40 Questions	For each question in this section, choose the best answer and blacken the corresponding space on the answer sheet.

Each question below consists of a word in capital letters, followed by five lettered words or phrases. Choose the word or phrase that is most nearly opposite in meaning to the word in capital letters. Since some of the questions require you to distinguish fine shades of meaning, consider all the choices before deciding which is best.

Example:

GOOD: (A) sour　(B) bad　(C) red
(D) hot　(E) ugly

Ⓐ ● Ⓒ Ⓓ Ⓔ

Each sentence below has one or two blanks, each blank indicating that something has been omitted. Beneath the sentence are five lettered words or sets of words. Choose the word or set of words that best fits the meaning of the sentence as a whole.

Example:

Although its publicity has been ----, the film itself is intelligent, well-acted, handsomely produced, and altogether ----.

(A) tasteless..respectable　(B) extensive..moderate
(C) sophisticated..amateur　(D) risqué..crude
(E) perfect..spectacular

● Ⓑ Ⓒ Ⓓ Ⓔ

1. HESITATE: (A) dishearten　(B) reprove
(C) decide　(D) signify　(E) stumble

2. STAMINA:
(A) lack of stability
(B) lack of endurance
(C) lack of restraint
(D) sudden disturbance
(E) extreme unwillingness

3. BUSTLE: (A) repair　(B) cooperate fully
(C) move slowly　(D) speak clearly　(E) reject

4. IMPASSIVE: (A) strange　(B) meager
(C) stationary　(D) agitated　(E) noble

5. PRODIGIOUS: (A) intellectual　(B) adult
(C) microscopic　(D) intense　(E) religious

6. SPECIOUS: (A) typical　(B) narrow
(C) golden　(D) genuine　(E) earthly

7. VERBOSITY: (A) contradiction　(B) timidity
(C) terseness　(D) insignificance　(E) anger

8. INSTIGATE: (A) choose randomly
(B) approve vigorously　(C) waive
(D) inhibit　(E) presume

9. LICENSE: (A) restraint　(B) pertinence
(C) bane　(D) jurisdiction　(E) gluttony

10. SEDULOUS: (A) imitative　(B) seditious
(C) heavy　(D) indolent　(E) contrary

11. John Gielgud crowns a distinguished career of playing Shakespearean roles by giving a performance that is ----.

(A) mediocre　(B) outmoded　(C) superficial
(D) unsurpassable　(E) insipid

12. Those interested in learning more about how genetics applies to trees will have to ---- the excellent technical journals where most of the pertinent material is ----.

(A) subscribe to..ignored
(B) suffer through..located
(C) rely on..unrepresented
(D) resort to..found
(E) complain about..published

13. It is said that the custom of shaking hands originated when primitive men held out empty hands to indicate that they had no ---- weapons and were thus ---- disposed.

(A) lethal..clearly
(B) concealed..amicably
(C) hidden..harmfully
(D) murderous..ill
(E) secret..finally

GO ON TO THE NEXT PAGE

1 1 1 1 1 1 1 1 1 1 1

14. Satire, fiercer and more demanding than comedy in its moral intentions, measures human conduct not against ---- but against ---- .

    (A) a norm..an ideal
    (B) a standard..a model
    (C) an objective..a goal
    (D) a philosophy..a viewpoint
    (E) a rule..a yardstick

15. Rent control restrictions on small apartment owners may unfortunately ---- rather than alleviate housing problems.

    (A) resolve   (B) diminish   (C) castigate
    (D) minimize   (E) exacerbate

Each question below consists of a related pair of words or phrases, followed by five lettered pairs of words or phrases. Select the lettered pair that best expresses a relationship similar to that expressed in the original pair.

Example:

YAWN : BOREDOM :: (A) dream : sleep
(B) anger : madness   (C) smile : amusement
   (D) face : expression   (E) impatience : rebellion

Ⓐ Ⓑ ● Ⓓ Ⓔ

---

16. PEA : POD :: (A) orange : section
    (B) bean : crock   (C) pumpkin : stem
       (D) nut : shell   (E) potato : stew

17. CANDLE : TALLOW :: (A) banana : peel
    (B) temple : altar   (C) statue : bronze
       (D) fireplace : hearth   (E) furniture : polish

18. THERMOMETER : HEAT ::
    (A) filament : light
    (B) chronometer : color
    (C) odometer : waves
    (D) Geiger counter : radiation
    (E) barometer : electricity

19. AIRPLANE : HANGAR :: (A) ship : channel
    (B) jet : runway   (C) helicopter : pad
    (D) motorcycle : sidecar   (E) automobile : garage

20. SIP : GULP :: (A) giggle : guffaw   (B) eat : dine
    (C) marry : divorce   (D) fret : worry
     (E) hunt : fish

21. SPINE : CACTUS :: (A) backbone : man
    (B) quill : porcupine   (C) root : oak   (D) pit : olive
     (E) binding : book

22. SCOLD : REBUKE :: (A) dislike : loathe
    (B) implore : request   (C) hesitate : waver
     (D) delete : insert   (E) suffer : retain

23. MARSUPIAL : OPOSSUM :: (A) rodent : squirrel
    (B) fish : whale   (C) kangaroo : hare
       (D) unicorn : lion   (E) carnivore : herbivore

24. CREST : TROUGH :: (A) apex : summit
    (B) crown : zenith   (C) shoulder : knee
     (D) peak : valley   (E) bread : loaf

25. TITANIC : LILLIPUTIAN ::
    (A) gigantic : monstrous
    (B) disastrous : ingenious
    (C) oceanic : aquatic
    (D) obese : emaciated
    (E) powerful : wicked

GO ON TO THE NEXT PAGE

1   1   1   1   1   1   1   1   1   1   1   1   1

Each passage below is followed by questions based on its content. Answer all questions following a passage on the basis of what is stated or implied in that passage.

The artist of the Renaissance was an all-round man. From his studio one could order a painting for the church altar, a carved wedding chest, a silver ewer, or a crucifix. The master of the workshop might be sculpturing a Venus for the Duke's garden while his apprentices were roughing-out a reredos for the new chapel. Many of the well-known painters of that golden period were goldsmiths, armorers, workers in glass, enamel or iron. They were so out of necessity: what the Renaissance patron demanded, the Renaissance artist stood ready to supply. The engineer was artist and the artist was engineer. The great Leonardo, famous today as the painter of *The Last Supper* and *Mona Lisa,* was perhaps equally well known in the sixteenth century for his engineering projects and his scientific experiments. Our own Thomas A. Edison pronounced him the greatest inventive genius of his time. Even present day scholars who have been able to trace the prominent influence of Leonardo's predecessors on his scientific theories and designs still credit Da Vinci with a breadth of interest and a range of skills unique in any age.

26. Which of the following is the best title for the passage?

(A) The Great Leonardo
(B) Edison and Sixteenth Century Scientists
(C) The Golden Period of Art
(D) Masters and Apprentices
(E) The Versatile Renaissance Artist

27. In order to support his thesis about the Renaissance artist, the author uses which of the following?

   I. Exaggeration of fact
   II. Listing of examples
   III. Reference to an authority

(A) I only   (B) II only   (C) III only
(D) I and II only   (E) II and III only

28. The author's attitude toward the diversity of interest shown by Renaissance artists is one of

(A) skepticism   (B) admiration   (C) irony
(D) resentment   (E) determination

Next to his towering masterpiece, *Moby Dick, Billy Budd* is Melville's greatest work. It has the tone of a last testament, and the manuscript was
Line neatly tied up by his wife, Elizabeth, and kept in
(5) a trunk for some thirty years. It was not until 1924 that it was first published. Slowly it has become recognized as the remarkable work it is.

Billy Budd has been dramatized for Broadway, done on T.V., made into an opera, and reached a
(10) highly satisfying form in Ustinov's movie.

Scholars disagree, somewhat violently, about what Melville was trying to say. Nonetheless, he did succeed in making it evident that he was recounting a duel between Good and Evil.
(15) Several times he remarked that Billy Budd is as innocent and ignorant as Adam before the fall. His enemy Mate Claggart is like Satan, Adam's tempter, in Milton's *Paradise Lost.*

When Billy Budd destroys Claggart and is
(20) sentenced to be hanged according to the letter of the law, controversy exists as to whether the Captain is simply a mortal man preserving order or a Jehovah-like figure, dispensing cruel justice.

Melville, it is claimed, cleverly took pains to
(25) hide his heretical feelings. *Billy Budd* is written as if told by a pious, God-loving man.

Ironically, Melville's iconoclasm has largely misfired, for the story today is accepted as either one of simple suspense or a reverent parable of
(30) God, Satan, and Adam. Meanwhile the scholars are still arguing, and *Billy Budd* remains like a porcupine, thorny, with interesting ambiguities.

29. Regarding *Billy Budd,* critics seem to differ about the book's

(A) plot   (B) theme   (C) mood   (D) setting
(E) introduction

30. The passage states that the character of Billy Budd was

(A) Satanic   (B) ambiguous   (C) naive
(D) brutal   (E) vain

31. The passage indicates that the Captain

(A) disobeyed the law
(B) treated his crew very badly
(C) disliked Billy intensely
(D) was incapable of action
(E) was responsible for discipline

32. The author's purpose in writing this passage seems to be to

(A) point out the diverse critical perceptions of *Billy Budd*
(B) argue that *Billy Budd* is stylistically polished
(C) defend Melville against his contemporary critics
(D) denounce Melville's iconoclasm as irreligious
(E) describe Melville's growth as a literary artist

GO ON TO THE NEXT PAGE ⇨

1 1 1 1 1 1 1 1 1 1 1

Our ignorance of the complex subject of social insurance was and remains colossal. For years American business leaders delighted in maligning
Line the British social insurance schemes. Our
(5) industrialists condemned them without ever finding out what they were about. Even our universities displayed no interest. Contrary to the interest in this subject taken by organized labor abroad, our own labor movements bitterly
(10) opposed the entire program of social insurance up to a few years ago. Since the success of any reform depends largely upon a correct public understanding of the principles involved, the adoption of social insurance measures presented
(15) peculiar difficulties for the United States under our Federal type of government of limited powers, our constitutional and judicial handicaps, our long conditioning to individualism, the traditional hostility to social reform by both
(20) capital and labor, the general inertia, and our complete lack of trained administrative personnel without which even the best law can be ineffective. Has not bitter experience taught us that far more important than the passage of a
(25) law, which is at best only a declaration of intention, is a ready public opinion prepared to enforce it?

33. According to this writer, what attitude have we shown in this country toward social insurance?

(A) We have been extremely doubtful that it will work, but have been willing to give it a chance.
(B) We have opposed it on the grounds of a careful study of its defects.
(C) We have shown an unintelligent and rather blind antagonism toward it.
(D) We have been afraid that it would not work under our type of government.
(E) We have resented it because of the extensive propaganda in favor of it.

34. To what does the phrase "our long conditioning to individualism" (line 18) refer?

(A) Our habit of expecting to depend on ourselves
(B) Our increasing dependence on the Federal Government
(C) Our long distrust of "big business"
(D) Our policies of high protective tariff
(E) Our unwillingness to accept reforms

35. Which of these ideas is expressed in this passage?

(A) The surest way to cure a social evil is to get people to pass a law against it.
(B) Legislation alone cannot effect social reforms.
(C) The American people are seriously uninformed about all social problems.
(D) Our type of government makes social reform impossible.
(E) Capital and labor retard social progress.

(This passage was written prior to 1950.)

We now know that what constitutes practically all of matter is empty space: relatively enormous voids in which revolve with lightning veloc-
Line ity infinitesimal particles so utterly small that
(5) they have never been seen or photographed. The existence of these particles has been demonstrated by mathematical physicists and their operations determined by ingenious laboratory experiments. It was not until 1911 that experiments by
(10) Sir Ernest Rutherford revealed the architecture of the mysterious atom. Moseley, Bohr, Fermi, Millikan, Compton, Urey, and others have also worked on the problem.
Matter is composed of molecules whose
(15) average diameter is about 1/125 millionth of an inch. Molecules are composed of atoms so small that about 5 million could be placed in a row on the period at the end of this sentence. Long thought to be the ultimate, indivisible constituent
(20) of matter, the atom has been found to consist roughly of a proton, the positive electrical element in the atomic nucleus, surrounded by electrons, the negative electric elements swirling about the proton.

36. The main purpose of this passage is to

(A) honor the pioneering work of Sir Ernest Rutherford and his followers
(B) refute the existence of submicroscopic particles
(C) illustrate how scientists measure molecular diameter
(D) summarize the then current findings on the composition of matter
(E) analyze evidence against one theory of atomic structure

GO ON TO THE NEXT PAGE

1   1   1   1   1   1   1   1   1   1   1

37. The style of the passage can best be described as

    (A) expository   (B) persuasive
     (C) contemplative   (D) oratorical
      (E) deprecatory

38. According to the passage, all of the following were true of the center of the atom EXCEPT that it

    (A) had not yet been seen by the naked eye
    (B) contained both positive and negative elements
    (C) was very little larger than a molecule
    (D) followed experimentally determinable
        processes
    (E) was smaller than 1/125 millionth of an inch

39. By referring to the period at the end of the sentence (lines 17–18), the author intends to point up the atom's

    (A) density   (B) mystery   (C) velocity
     (D) consistency   (E) minuteness

40. Which of the following relationships most closely parallels the relationship between the proton and the electrons described in the passage?

    (A) A hawk to its prey
    (B) A blueprint to a framework
    (C) A planet to its satellites
    (D) A magnet to iron filings
    (E) A compound to its elements

IF YOU FINISH BEFORE TIME IS CALLED, YOU MAY CHECK YOUR WORK ON THIS SECTION ONLY. DO NOT WORK ON ANY OTHER SECTION IN THE TEST.

S T O P

$2 \quad 2 \quad 2 \quad 2 \quad 2 \quad 2 \quad 2 \quad 2 \quad 2 \quad 2 \quad 2$

SECTION 2   Time—30 minutes   In this section, solve each problem, using any available space on
25 Questions   the page for scratchwork. Then decide which is the best of the
choices given and blacken the corresponding space on the answer
sheet.

The following information is for your reference in solving some of the problems.

Circle of radius r: Area $= \pi r^2$; Circumference $= 2\pi r$
  The number of degrees of arc in a circle is 360.
The measure in degrees of a straight angle is 180.

Definitions of symbols:
$=$ is equal to $\leqq$ is less than or equal to
$\neq$ is unequal to $\geqq$ is greater than or equal to
$<$ is less than $\parallel$ is parallel to
$>$ is greater than $\perp$ is perpendicular to

Triangle: The sum of the measures
  in degrees of the angles of
  a triangle is 180.
If $\angle CDA$ is a right angle, then

(1) area of $\triangle ABC = \dfrac{AB \times CD}{2}$

(2) $AC^2 = AD^2 + DC^2$

Note: Figures that accompany problems in this test are intended to provide information useful in solving the problems.
They are drawn as accurately as possible EXCEPT when it is stated in a specific problem that its figure is not drawn to
scale. All figures lie in a plane unless otherwise indicated. All numbers used are real numbers.

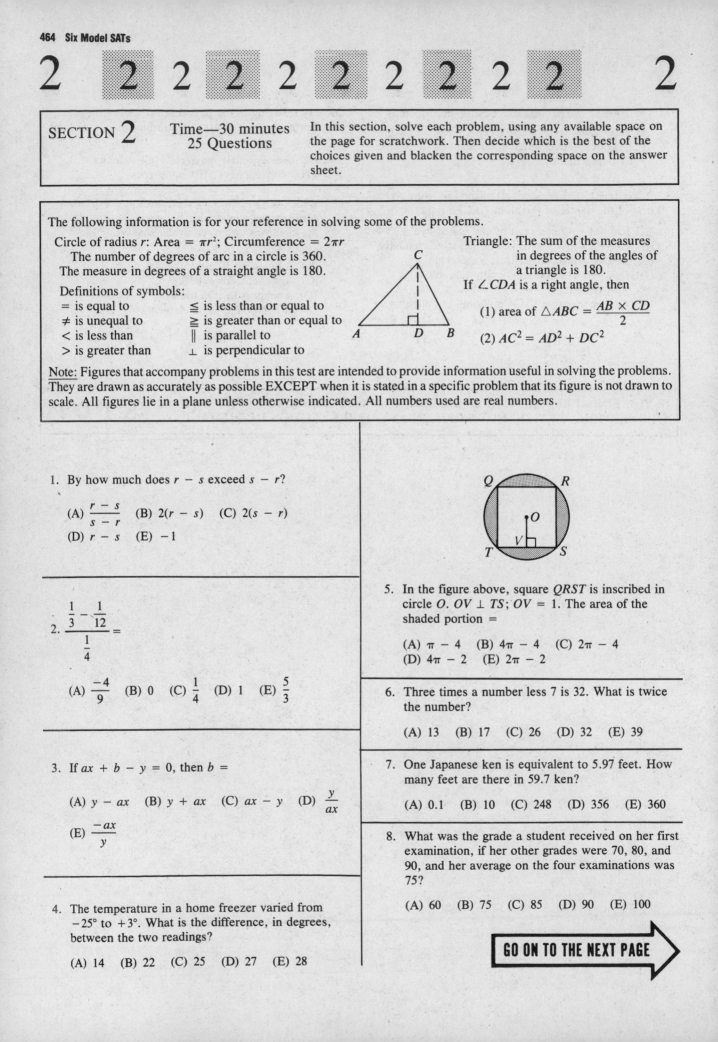

1. By how much does $r - s$ exceed $s - r$?

(A) $\dfrac{r - s}{s - r}$ (B) $2(r - s)$ (C) $2(s - r)$
(D) $r - s$ (E) -1

2. $\dfrac{\frac{1}{3} - \frac{1}{12}}{\frac{1}{4}} =$

(A) $\dfrac{-4}{9}$ (B) 0 (C) $\dfrac{1}{4}$ (D) 1 (E) $\dfrac{5}{3}$

3. If $ax + b - y = 0$, then $b =$

(A) $y - ax$ (B) $y + ax$ (C) $ax - y$ (D) $\dfrac{y}{ax}$

(E) $\dfrac{-ax}{y}$

4. The temperature in a home freezer varied from
$-25°$ to $+3°$. What is the difference, in degrees,
between the two readings?

(A) 14   (B) 22   (C) 25   (D) 27   (E) 28

5. In the figure above, square $QRST$ is inscribed in
circle O. $OV \perp TS$; $OV = 1$. The area of the
shaded portion $=$

(A) $\pi - 4$ (B) $4\pi - 4$ (C) $2\pi - 4$
(D) $4\pi - 2$ (E) $2\pi - 2$

6. Three times a number less 7 is 32. What is twice
the number?

(A) 13   (B) 17   (C) 26   (D) 32   (E) 39

7. One Japanese ken is equivalent to 5.97 feet. How
many feet are there in 59.7 ken?

(A) 0.1   (B) 10   (C) 248   (D) 356   (E) 360

8. What was the grade a student received on her first
examination, if her other grades were 70, 80, and
90, and her average on the four examinations was
75?

(A) 60   (B) 75   (C) 85   (D) 90   (E) 100

GO ON TO THE NEXT PAGE

2   2 2 2 2 2 2 2 2 2   2

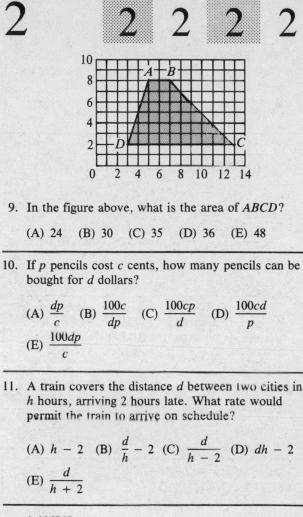

9. In the figure above, what is the area of *ABCD*?

(A) 24 (B) 30 (C) 35 (D) 36 (E) 48

10. If *p* pencils cost *c* cents, how many pencils can be bought for *d* dollars?

(A) $\dfrac{dp}{c}$ (B) $\dfrac{100c}{dp}$ (C) $\dfrac{100cp}{d}$ (D) $\dfrac{100cd}{p}$

(E) $\dfrac{100dp}{c}$

11. A train covers the distance *d* between two cities in *h* hours, arriving 2 hours late. What rate would permit the train to arrive on schedule?

(A) $h - 2$ (B) $\dfrac{d}{h} - 2$ (C) $\dfrac{d}{h - 2}$ (D) $dh - 2$

(E) $\dfrac{d}{h + 2}$

12. $\dfrac{1.116963}{0.369}$ is exactly equal to

(A) 3.023 (B) 3.024 (C) 3.025 (D) 3.026
(E) 3.027

13. Mr. Stanley will be *x* years old 5 years hence. How old was he 5 years ago?

(A) $x - 5$ (B) $x + 10$ (C) $x - 10$
(D) $5x - 5$ (E) $7x$

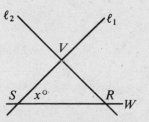

14. In the figure above, ℓ_1 is perpendicular to ℓ_2 at *V*. If the measure of angle *VSR* is *x* degrees, which of the following expresses the measure, in degrees, of angle *VRW*?

(A) $90 - x$ (B) $90 + x$ (C) $x - 90$
(D) $180 - x$ (E) 135

15. To send a parcel to Zone 7 the cost is 30¢ for the first pound and 15.5¢ for each additional pound. What is the cost, in cents, of sending a package weighing 48 ounces to Zone 7? (16 ounces = 1 pound.)

(A) 46 (B) 59 (C) 61 (D) 64 (E) 90

16. For $Z \neq 0$, let *Z* be defined by

$$Z = \frac{Z}{Z + \dfrac{1}{Z}}.$$

What is the value of $\dfrac{1}{2}Z$?

(A) $\dfrac{1}{5}$ (B) $\dfrac{1}{2}$ (C) 2 (D) $2\dfrac{1}{2}$ (E) 5

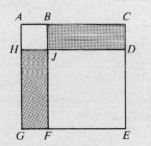

17. In the figure above, *ABJH*, *JDEF*, and *ACEG* are squares. If $\dfrac{BC}{AB} = 3$, then what is the value of $\dfrac{\text{area } BCDJ}{\text{area } HJFG}$?

(A) $\dfrac{1}{9}$ (B) $\dfrac{1}{3}$ (C) 1 (D) 3 (E) 9

18. If $r = 18$ and $\dfrac{r}{s} = \dfrac{6}{y}$, then $\dfrac{y}{s} =$

(A) $\dfrac{1}{3}$ (B) $3\dfrac{1}{6}$ (C) $3\dfrac{1}{3}$ (D) 6 (E) 18

19. A corporation has 8 departments, each with 10–16 bureaus. In each bureau there are at least 40 but no more than 60 workers. If 10 percent of the workers in each bureau are typists, what is the minimum number of typists in a department?

(A) 40 (B) 65 (C) 96 (D) 320 (E) 768

GO ON TO THE NEXT PAGE

2　2　2　2　2　2　2　2　2　2　2

20. Two thirds of the faculty of a high school are women. Twelve of the men of the faculty are unmarried, while $\frac{3}{5}$ of the male teachers are married. The total number of faculty members in this school is

　(A) 30　(B) 50　(C) 60　(D) 72　(E) 90

21. The state of Oklahoma had eight congressmen in 1940 and six in 1950. What was the percent change in representation?

　(A) -75　(B) $-33\frac{1}{3}$　(C) -25　(D) $+25$
　(E) $+75$

22. If 10 percent of $r = 20$ percent of s,
　　20 percent of $s = 30$ percent of t, and
　　100 percent of $r = x$ percent of t,
　　then $x =$

　(A) 20　(B) $33\frac{1}{3}$　(C) 40　(D) $166\frac{2}{3}$　(E) 300

23. What is the maximum number of glass tumblers (each with a circumference of 4π inches) that can be placed on a table 48 inches × 32 inches?

　(A) 36　(B) 48　(C) 92　(D) 96　(E) 192

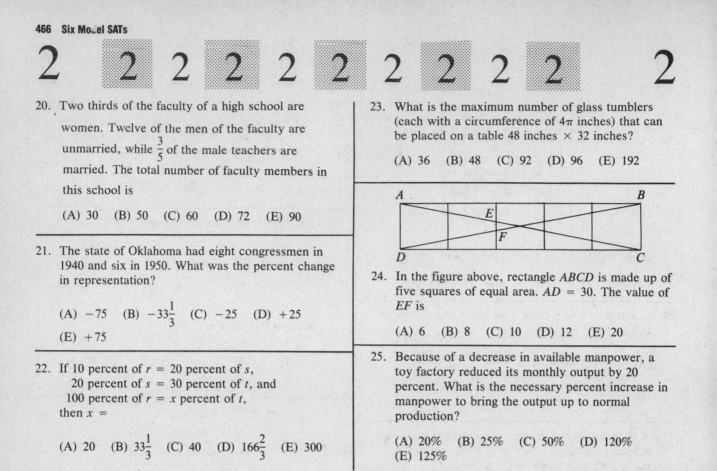

24. In the figure above, rectangle $ABCD$ is made up of five squares of equal area. $AD = 30$. The value of EF is

　(A) 6　(B) 8　(C) 10　(D) 12　(E) 20

25. Because of a decrease in available manpower, a toy factory reduced its monthly output by 20 percent. What is the necessary percent increase in manpower to bring the output up to normal production?

　(A) 20%　(B) 25%　(C) 50%　(D) 120%
　(E) 125%

IF YOU FINISH BEFORE TIME IS CALLED, YOU MAY CHECK YOUR WORK ON THIS SECTION ONLY. DO NOT WORK ON ANY OTHER SECTION IN THE TEST.　**S T O P**

3 3 3 3 3 3 3 3 3 3 3

SECTION 3   Time—30 minutes
50 Questions

The questions in this section measure skills that are important to writing well. In particular, they test your ability to recognize and use language that is clear, effective, and correct according to the requirements of standard written English, the kind of English found in most college textbooks.

Directions: The following sentences contain problems in grammar, usage, diction (choice of words), and idiom.

Some sentences are correct.
No sentence contains more than one error.

You will find that the error, if there is one, is underlined and lettered. Assume that elements of the sentence that are not underlined are correct and cannot be changed. In choosing answers, follow the requirements of standard written English.

If there is an error, select the one underlined part that must be changed to make the sentence correct and blacken the corresponding space on your answer sheet.

If there is no error, blacken answer space Ⓔ.

EXAMPLE:
The region has a climate so severe that plants
                                A
growing there rarely had been more than twelve
     B   C
inches high. No error
       D   E

SAMPLE ANSWER
Ⓐ Ⓑ ● Ⓓ Ⓔ

1. Please help me decide which of the two activities
              A   B
to choose—going to the theater with John or
                                        C
to attend tonight's dinner-dance at the hotel.
   D
No error
   E

2. When I have to decide which of two applicants for
              A   B
a job to hire, I find myself giving the position to
                        C
the one who uses the best English. No error
                        D   E

3. Because I was seated on the dais just in back of
   A   B   C
the speaker, I could see the audience's reaction to
                                              D
his vituperative remarks. No error
                              E

4. A complete system of checks and balances
   have been incorporated in our Constitution
        A   B
from inception to protect the principle of equality.
   C   D
No error
   E

5. Dr. Martin Luther King, who led a bus boycott
                            A   B
to eliminate bus segregation, will be
forever remembered for his speech, "I Have a
        C   D
Dream." No error
         E

6. As a result of the bad weather, she is the only one
   A   B
of my friends who plan to attend the graduation
                  C   D
exercises. No error
              E

7. When the fire started to burn, we added kindling
   A   B
and newspaper so that it would get stronger and
                  C
throw off more heat. No error
   D   E

8. During the recent gasoline shortage, the amount of
   A   B
accidents on our highways decreased markedly.
                            C   D
No error
   E

GO ON TO THE NEXT PAGE

3 3 3 3 3 3 3 3 3 3 3 3

9. <u>Having secured</u> the ball on a fumble, <u>we</u> <u>took</u>
    A   B C
    <u>advantage of</u> our opponent's error and scored a
    D
    field goal. <u>No error</u>
                 E

10. <u>Although</u> Mr. Jimenez <u>is</u> in this country <u>for only</u>
     A   B   C
    two years, he talks <u>like</u> a native. <u>No error</u>
                       D   E

11. These cars <u>are</u> not ready for delivery as <u>they</u> come
            A   B
    <u>off of</u> the assembly line; they must be tested
    C
    before <u>being sold</u>. <u>No error</u>
            D   E

12. <u>Because</u> Charles received a <u>number of</u> free tickets
    A   B
    for the World Series, he asked whether I <u>will go</u> to
                                        C
    the game with <u>him</u>. <u>No error</u>
                D   E

13. Your argument is no <u>different from</u> <u>the last speaker</u>
                          A   B
    who also <u>opposes</u> this <u>timely</u> legislation. <u>No error</u>
            C   D   E

14. Every woman in the ward <u>fervently</u> hopes that
                            A
    <u>their</u> child <u>will be</u> a normal and <u>healthy baby</u>.
    B   C   D
    <u>No error</u>
      E

15. After <u>consideration of</u> all census polls, <u>we</u> realized
          A   B
    that the population of California <u>is larger</u>
                               C
    <u>then that of any other state</u> in the United States.
                 D
    <u>No error</u>
      E

16. <u>Due to</u> the <u>excessively high</u> interest rate on
    A   B
    installment buying, <u>it</u> is <u>advisable</u> to purchase
                     C   D
    things on a cash basis. <u>No error</u>
                     E

17. <u>Because of</u> unfavorable weather, <u>few</u> funds, and a
    A   B
    burned-out sorority house, the party <u>had to be</u>
                                  C
    postponed <u>indefinitely</u>. <u>No error</u>
              D   E

18. <u>Bear in mind</u> that <u>since</u> words are tools, <u>only</u>
    A   B   C
    experienced writers <u>are permitted in taking</u>
                             D
    liberties in writing style. <u>No error</u>
                        E

19. The man <u>who</u> <u>is laying</u> in the aisle <u>needs</u> medical
             A   B   C
    attention <u>immediately</u>. <u>No error</u>
                D   E

20. The technique discussed in this article <u>enables</u> a
                                         A
    student to learn <u>more quickly</u> and
                      B
    <u>to have remembered</u> for a <u>longer</u> period of time.
             C   D
    <u>No error</u>
      E

21. <u>Even if</u> you go shopping <u>quite late</u>, will you please
    A   B
    <u>bring</u> <u>this</u> note to the store's manager? <u>No error</u>
    C   D   E

22. <u>Despite the fact that</u> <u>some states</u> have resisted, the
          A   B
    Congress <u>have passed</u> legislation <u>permitting</u>
             C   D
    highway speed limits to 65 miles per hour on rural
    Interstates. <u>No error</u>
              E

23. Mohandas Gandhi, <u>to who</u> the title "Father of
                  A
    Passive Resistance" <u>may be given</u>, <u>bravely led</u> the
                    B   C
    nationalist movement in India <u>against</u> British rule.
                          D
    <u>No error</u>
      E

24. I am not <u>certain</u> <u>if</u> I <u>should discuss</u> my promotion
           A   B   C
    with <u>him</u> or not. <u>No error</u>
        D   E

25. <u>When descending</u> from 37,000 feet <u>to make</u> <u>our</u>
    A   B   C
    landing, the pressure <u>affected</u> our ears. <u>No error</u>
                       D   E

GO ON TO THE NEXT PAGE

3 3 3 3 3 3 3 3 3 3 3

Directions: In each of the following sentences, some part or all of the sentence is underlined. Below each sentence you will find five ways of phrasing the underlined part. Select the answer that produces the most effective sentence, one that is clear and exact, without awkwardness or ambiguity, and blacken the corresponding space on your answer sheet. In choosing answers, follow the requirements of standard written English. Choose the answer that best expresses the meaning of the original sentence.

Answer (A) is always the same as the underlined part. Choose answer (A) if you think the original sentence needs no revision.

EXAMPLE: SAMPLE ANSWER
Laura Ingalls Wilder published her first book   Ⓐ ● Ⓒ Ⓓ Ⓔ
and she was sixty-five years old then.

(A) and she was sixty-five years old then
(B) when she was sixty-five years old
(C) at age sixty-five years old
(D) upon reaching sixty-five years
(E) at the time when she was sixty-five

26. We are more concerned that the best possible candidate be hired than that bureaucratic affirmative action rules be followed to the letter.

(A) than that bureaucratic affirmative action rules be followed
(B) and not about following bureaucratic affirmative action rules
(C) than that one should follow bureaucratic affirmative action rules
(D) than your following bureaucratic affirmative action rules
(E) and not in any bureaucratic affirmative action rules being followed

27. By the government failing to keep its pledges will earn the distrust of all other nations in the alliance.

(A) By the government failing to keep its pledges
(B) Because the government failed to keep its pledges
(C) Since the government has failed to keep its pledges
(D) Failing to keep its government pledges
(E) If the government fails to keep its pledges, it

28. Although I calculate that he will be here any minute, I cannot wait much longer for him to arrive.

(A) Although I calculate that he will be here
(B) Although I reckon that he will be here
(C) Because I calculate that he will be here
(D) Although I am confident that he will be here
(E) Because I am confident that he will be here

29. Bernard Malamud was a forty-year-old college professor in Oregon and his short story "The Magic Barrel" was published in *The Partisan Review*.

(A) Oregon and his short story "The Magic Barrel"
(B) Oregon, his short story "The Magic Barrel"
(C) Oregon; his short story "The Magic Barrel"
(D) Oregon when his short story "The Magic Barrel"
(E) Oregon, furthermore, his short story "The Magic Barrel"

30. Being as how a dangerous cloud of radiation was released at the Chernobyl nuclear plant, that accident can be considered the most serious in the history of nuclear energy.

(A) Being as how a dangerous cloud of radiation was released
(B) Because a dangerous cloud of radiation was released
(C) Due to the release of a dangerous cloud of radiation
(D) In addition to a dangerous cloud of radiation being released
(E) Releasing a dangerous cloud of radiation

31. In keeping with the hallowed Russian tradition of putting on a show to impress the visitors, the capital being painted and festooned with banners and portraits of Marx and Lenin.

(A) the capital being painted and festooned
(B) the capital been painted and festooned
(C) the capital painted and being festooned
(D) the capital's painting and festooning
(E) the capital has been painted and festooned

GO ON TO THE NEXT PAGE

32. Employers have begun to provide health club facilities for their employees because exercise builds stamina, decreases tension, and absenteeism is reduced.

   (A) decreases tension, and absenteeism is reduced
   (B) tension is decreased, and absenteeism reduced
   (C) decreases tension, and reducing absenteeism
   (D) decreases tension, and reduces absenteeism
   (E) decreasing tension, and absenteeism is reduced

33. She not only was competent but also friendly in nature.

   (A) She not only was competent but also friendly
   (B) She not was only competent but friendly also
   (C) She not only was competent but friendly also
   (D) She was not only competent but also friendly
   (E) She was not only competent but friendly also

34. The dean informed us that the applicant had not and never will be accepted by the college because of his high school record.

   (A) applicant had not and never will be accepted by the college because of his high school record
   (B) applicant had not and never would be accepted by the college because of his high school record
   (C) applicant had not been and never will be accepted by the college because of his high school record
   (D) applicant had not and never could be accepted by the college because of his high school record
   (E) applicant had not been and never would be accepted by the college because of his high school record

35. Numerous American industries have lost sales to foreign imports, in addition to which, to regain profits, some companies have merged with foreign plants.

   (A) imports, in addition to which, to regain profits
   (B) imports; to regain profits
   (C) imports; as a result, to regain profits
   (D) imports, to regain profits
   (E) imports, yet to regain profits

36. New York City hosted a four-day extravaganza for the Statue of Liberty during the July 4, 1986 weekend; the purpose being to celebrate Miss Liberty's one hundredth birthday.

   (A) weekend; the purpose being to celebrate
   (B) weekend because of celebrating
   (C) weekend, the purpose being to celebrate
   (D) weekend to celebrate
   (E) weekend, for the purpose of celebrating

37. If he were to win the medal, I for one would be disturbed.

   (A) If he were to win the medal
   (B) If he was to win the medal
   (C) If he wins the medal
   (D) If he is the winner of the medal
   (E) In the event that he wins the medal

38. The scouts were told to take an overnight hike, pitch camp, prepare dinner, and that they should be in bed by 9 P.M.

   (A) to take an overnight hike, pitch camp, prepare dinner, and that they should be in bed by 9 P.M.
   (B) to take an overnight hike, pitch camp, prepare dinner, and that they should go to bed by 9 P.M.
   (C) to take an overnight hike, pitch camp, prepare dinner, and be in bed by 9 P.M.
   (D) to take an overnight hike, pitching camp, preparing dinner, and going to bed by 9 P.M.
   (E) to engage in an overnight hike, pitch camp, prepare dinner, and that they should be in bed by 9 P.M.

39. We want the teacher to be the one who has the best rapport with the students.

   (A) We want the teacher to be the one
   (B) We want the teacher to be he
   (C) We want him to be the teacher
   (D) We desire that the teacher be him
   (E) We anticipate that the teacher will be him

40. Most students like to read these kind of books during their spare time.

   (A) these kind of books
   (B) these kind of book
   (C) this kind of book
   (D) this kinds of books
   (E) those kind of books

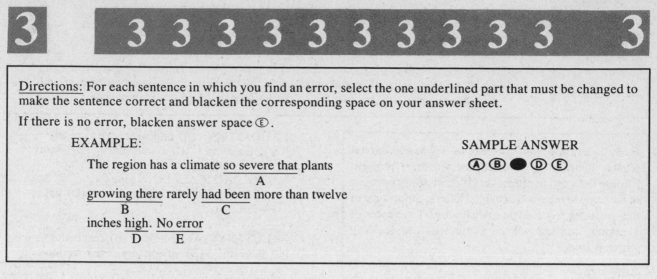

41. <u>Although</u> I am willing to <u>go along with</u> your idea, I
        A   B
cannot <u>enthuse</u> over <u>its chances</u> of success.
              C   D
<u>No error</u>
    E

42. If you plan <u>to become</u> an English major, <u>you</u>
                      A   B
should learn grammar, read <u>lots of</u> books, as well
                                      C
as <u>practicing</u> your writing skills. <u>No error</u>
      D   E

43. Mark Twain <u>may have published</u> the novel *Tom*
                        A
Sawyer one hundred years ago, <u>on the other hand,</u>
                                            B
<u>his</u> characters Tom and Becky still appeal to
  C
readers <u>of all ages.</u> <u>No error</u>
              D   E

44. By breaking the world's record, the boys <u>whom</u> I
                                                    A
<u>predicted would win</u> the contest have <u>incredibly</u>
          B   C
<u>lived up to</u> my expectations. <u>No error</u>
      D   E

45. <u>Despite</u> the bright sunlight, you <u>can scarcely</u> see
        A   B
the birds <u>because of</u> <u>their</u> protective coloration.
                C   D
<u>No error</u>
    E

46. <u>If</u> you read the material <u>quickly</u> and then review it,
  A   B
<u>one finds</u> that the main idea is <u>easily retained.</u>
      C   D
<u>No error</u>
    E

47. Valentina Tereshkova became the first woman in

space in June, 1963, <u>but this was</u> <u>only</u> two years
                              A   B
<u>after</u> Yuri Gagarin <u>became</u> the first man in space in
  C   D
April, 1961. <u>No error</u>
                    E

48. <u>Even though</u> the meal <u>is</u> under control, everything
        A   B
<u>depends upon</u> <u>them</u> arriving on time. <u>No error</u>
        C   D   E

49. Some of the solutions that businesses

<u>have proposed</u> <u>in order to</u> accommodate
        A   B
<u>working mothers</u> include flexible work hours,
        C
nursery centers, and <u>allowing</u> work rotation.
                          D
<u>No error</u>
    E

50. <u>It</u> seems rather <u>ironic</u> that while <u>many of</u>
  A   B   C
astronomy's major events are visible in the

southern hemisphere, the largest telescopes

<u>have been located</u> in the northern hemisphere.
        D
<u>No error</u>
    E

4   4 4 4 4

SECTION **4**   Time—30 minutes   For each question in this section, choose the best answer and
              45 Questions   blacken the corresponding space on the answer sheet.

Each question below consists of a word in capital letters, followed by five lettered words or phrases. Choose the word or phrase that is most nearly <u>opposite</u> in meaning to the word in capital letters. Since some of the questions require you to distinguish fine shades of meaning, consider all the choices before deciding which is best.

Example:

  GOOD: (A) sour   (B) bad   (C) red
  (D) hot   (E) ugly   Ⓐ ● Ⓒ Ⓓ Ⓔ

1. WRINKLE: (A) keep pure   (B) make smooth
   (C) alert   (D) obstruct   (E) assure

2. CALLOUS: (A) concerned   (B) blameless
   (C) irritated   (D) noxious   (E) careless

3. BLUR: (A) give approval   (B) grow in size
   (C) become simpler   (D) make clear
   (E) move slowly

4. DEMURE: (A) objective   (B) complete
   (C) bold   (D) illiterate   (E) intolerant

5. URBANITY: (A) openness   (B) rural area
   (C) naive manner   (D) caution   (E) restlessness

6. DISSUADE: (A) urge strongly   (B) extract
   (C) diminish in strength   (D) divide equally
   (E) antagonize

7. DEFERENCE: (A) support   (B) vanity
   (C) postponement   (D) value   (E) disrespect

8. ORTHODOX: (A) matchless   (B) convex
   (C) massive   (D) plain   (E) heretical

9. FERVOR: (A) candor   (B) futility
   (C) freedom   (D) responsibility
   (E) indifference

10. SUCCOR: (A) hindrance   (B) regret
    (C) rancor   (D) levity   (E) growth

11. PHLEGMATIC: (A) dogmatic   (B) lenient
    (C) repetitious   (D) excitable   (E) adept

12. LAUDATORY: (A) imposing   (B) unjust
    (C) defamatory   (D) clandestine   (E) scanty

13. LACKADAISICAL: (A) copious
    (B) enthusiastic   (C) harmonious   (D) livid
    (E) fortunate

14. SALUTARY: (A) harmful   (B) respectful
    (C) flavorful   (D) valedictory   (E) anxious

15. BANE: (A) ignorance   (B) sensitivity
    (C) source of bliss   (D) lack of permission
    (E) proclivity

Each sentence below has one or two blanks, each blank indicating that something has been omitted. Beneath the sentence are five lettered words or sets of words. Choose the word or set of words that <u>best</u> fits the meaning of the sentence as a whole.

Example:

Although its publicity has been ----, the film itself is intelligent, well-acted, handsomely produced, and altogether ----.

(A) tasteless..respectable (B) extensive..moderate
 (C) sophisticated..amateur (D) risqué..crude
  (E) perfect..spectacular

              ● Ⓑ Ⓒ Ⓓ Ⓔ

16. One argument against the welfare system is that it ---- the recipient's independence.

   (A) supports   (B) saps   (C) hastens
   (D) renews   (E) corrects

17. Despite the numerous films he had to his credit and his reputation for technical ---- , the moviemaker lacked originality; all his films were sadly ---- of the work of others.

   (A) skill..independent
   (B) ability..unconscious
   (C) expertise..derivative
   (D) competence..contradictory
   (E) blunders..enamored

GO ON TO THE NEXT PAGE ▷

4   4 4 4 4 4 4 4 4 4 4   4

18. He urged that we take particular care of the ----
chemicals to prevent their evaporation.

    (A) insoluble   (B) superficial   (C) extraneous
    (D) volatile   (E) insipid

19. Despite all its ---- , a term of enlistment in the
Peace Corps can be both stirring and satisfying to
a college graduate still undecided on a career.

    (A) rewards   (B) renown   (C) adventures
    (D) romance   (E) frustrations

20. The judge ruled that the evidence was inadmissible
on the grounds that it was not ---- to the issue at
hand.

    (A) germane   (B) consistent   (C) inchoate
    (D) luminous   (E) manifest

Each passage below is followed by questions based on its content. Answer all questions following a passage on the
basis of what is <u>stated</u> or <u>implied</u> in that passage.

The matron had given her leave to go out as
soon as the women's tea was over and Maria
looked forward to her evening out. The kitchen
Line was spick and span: the cook said you could see
(5) yourself in the big copper boilers. The fire was
nice and bright and on one of the side-tables
were four very big barmbracks. These barmbracks seemed uncut; but if you went closer you
would see that they had been cut into long thick
(10) even slices and were ready to be handed round at
tea. Maria had cut them herself.

     Maria was a very, very small person indeed
but she had a very long nose and a very long
chin. She talked a little through her nose, always
(15) soothingly: "*Yes, my dear*," and "*No, my
dear*." She was always sent for when the women
quarrelled over their tubs and always succeeded
in making peace. One day the matron had said to
her:

(20)   "Maria, you are a veritable peace-maker!"
     And the sub-matron and two of the Board
ladies had heard the compliment. And Ginger
Mooney was always saying what she wouldn't do
to the dummy who had charge of the irons if it
(25) wasn't for Maria. Everyone was so fond of
Maria.

     When the cook told her everything was ready,
she went into the women's room and began to
pull the big bell. In a few minutes the women
(30) began to come in by twos and threes, wiping
their steaming hands in their petticoats and
pulling down the sleeves of their blouses over
their red steaming arms. They settled down
before their huge mugs which the cook and the
(35) dummy filled up with hot tea, already mixed with
milk and sugar in huge tin cans. Maria super-
intended the distribution of the barmbrack and
saw that every woman got her four slices. There
was a great deal of laughing and joking during the

(40) meal. Lizzie Fleming said Maria was sure to get
the ring and, though Fleming had said that for so
many Hallow Eves, Maria had to laugh and say
she didn't want any ring or man either; and when
she laughed her grey-green eyes sparkled with
(45) disappointed shyness and the tip of her nose
nearly met the tip of her chin. Then Ginger Mooney lifted her mug of tea and proposed Maria's
health while all the other women clattered with
their mugs on the table, and said she was sorry
(50) she hadn't a sup of porter to drink it in. And
Maria laughed again till the tip of her nose nearly
met the tip of her chin and till her minute body
nearly shook itself asunder because she knew
that Mooney meant well though, of course, she
(55) had the notions of a common woman.

21. The author's primary purpose in the second
paragraph is to

    (A) introduce a central character
    (B) describe working conditions in a public
        institution
    (C) compare two women of different social classes
    (D) illustrate the value of peace-makers in society
    (E) create suspense about Maria's fate

22. The language of the passage most resembles the
language of

    (A) a mystery novel
    (B) an epic
    (C) a fairy tale
    (D) institutional board reports
    (E) a sermon

GO ON TO THE NEXT PAGE

23. It can be inferred from the passage that Maria
would most likely view the matron as which of the
following?

   (A) A political figurehead
   (B) An inept administrator
   (C) A demanding taskmaster
   (D) An intimate friend
   (E) A benevolent superior

24. We may infer from the care with which Maria has
cut the barmbracks that

   (A) she fears the matron
   (B) she is in a hurry to leave
   (C) she expects the Board members for tea
   (D) it is a dangerous task
   (E) she takes pride in her work

25. It can be inferred from the passage that all the
following are characteristic of Maria EXCEPT

   (A) a deferential nature
   (B) eagerness for compliments
   (C) respect for authority
   (D) dreams of matrimony
   (E) reluctance to compromise

There can be no doubt that the emergence of
the Negro writer in the post-war period stemmed,
in part, from the fact that he was inclined to
Line exploit the opportunity to write about himself. It
(5) was more than that, however. The movement
that has variously been called the "Harlem
Renaissance," the "Black Renaissance," and the
"New Negro Movement" was essentially a part
of the growing interest of American literary
(10) circles in the immediate and pressing social and
economic problems. This growing interest
coincided with two developments in Negro life
that fostered the growth of the New Negro
Movement. These two factors, the keener
(15) realization of injustice and the improvement of
the capacity for expression, produced a crop of
Negro writers who constituted the "Harlem
Renaissance."
   The literature of the Harlem Renaissance was,
(20) for the most part, the work of a race-conscious
group. Through poetry, prose, and song, the
writers cried out against social and economic
wrongs. They protested against segregation and
lynching. They demanded higher wages, shorter
(25) hours, and better conditions of work. They stood
for full social equality and first-class citizenship.
The new vision of social and economic freedom
which they had did not force them to embrace
the several foreign ideologies that sought to sink
(30) their roots in some American groups during the
period.

The writers of the Harlem Renaissance, bitter
and cynical as some of them were, gave little
attention to the propaganda of the socialists and
(35) communists. The editor of the *Messenger*
ventured the opinion that the New Negro was the
"product of the same world-wide forces that
have brought into being the great liberal and
radical movements that are now seizing the reins
(40) of power in all the civilized countries of the
world." Such forces may have produced the New
Negro, but the more articulate of the group did
not resort to advocating the type of political
action that would have subverted American
(45) constitutional government. Indeed, the writers of
the Harlem Renaissance were not so much
revolting against the system as they were
protesting its inefficient operation. In this
approach they proved as characteristically
(50) American as any writers of the period. Like his
contemporaries, the Negro writer was merely
becoming more aware of America's pressing
problems; and like the others, he was willing to
use his art, not only to contribute to the great
(55) body of American culture but also to improve the
culture of which he was a part.
   It seems possible, moreover, for the historian
to assign to the Negro writer a role that he did
not assume. There were doubtless many who
(60) were not immediately concerned with the
injustices heaped on the Negro. Some contrived
their poems, novels, and songs merely for the
sake of art, while others took up their pens to
escape the sordid aspects of their existence. If
(65) there is an element of race in their writings, it is
because the writings flow out of their individual
and group experiences. This is not to say that
such writings were not effective as protest
literature, but rather that not all the authors were
(70) conscious crusaders for a better world. As a
matter of fact, it was this detachment, this
objectivity, that made it possible for many of the
writers of the Harlem Renaissance to achieve a
nobility of expression and a poignancy of feeling
(75) in their writings that placed them among the
masters of recent American literature.

GO ON TO THE NEXT PAGE

4   4   4   4   4   4   4   4   4

26. The author is primarily concerned with

(A) arguing that the literature of the Harlem
Renaissance arose from the willingness of
Black writers to portray their own lives
(B) depicting the part played by socially-conscious
Black writers in a world-wide ideological and
literary crusade
(C) providing examples of the injustices protested
by the writers of the Harlem Renaissance
(D) describing the social and political background
that led to the blossoming of the Harlem
Renaissance
(E) analyzing stages in the development of the
New Negro Movement into the Harlem
Renaissance

27. In reference to the achievements of the Harlem
Renaissance, the passage conveys primarily a
sense of

(A) protest
(B) betrayal
(C) nostalgia
(D) urgency
(E) admiration

28. Which of the following is implied by the statement
that the writers of the Harlem Renaissance "were
not so much revolting against the system as they
were protesting its inefficient operation" (lines 46–
48)?

(A) Black writers played only a minor part in
protesting the injustices of the period.
(B) Left to itself, the system was sure to operate
efficiently.
(C) Black writers in general were not opposed to
the system as such.
(D) In order for the system to operate efficiently,
Blacks must seize the reins of power in
America.
(E) Black writers were too caught up in aesthetic
philosophy to identify the true nature of the
conflict.

29. With which of the following statements regarding
the writers of the Harlem Renaissance would the
author most likely agree?

(A) They needed to increase their commitment to
international solidarity.
(B) Their awareness of oppression caused them to
reject American society.
(C) They transformed their increasing social and
political consciousness into art.
(D) Their art suffered from their over-involvement
in political crusades.
(E) Their detachment from their subject matter
lessened the impact of their works.

30. The information in the passage suggests that the
author is most likely

(A) a historian who is concerned with presenting
socially conscious Black writers as loyal
Americans
(B) a literary critic who questions the conclusions
of the historians
(C) an educator involved in fostering creative
writing projects for minority youths
(D) a Black writer of fiction interested in
discovering new facts about his literary roots
(E) a researcher with questions about the validity
of his sources

Select the word or set of words that best completes each
of the following sentences.

31. He is much too ---- in his writings: he writes a
page when a sentence should suffice.

(A) devious   (B) lucid   (C) verbose
(D) efficient   (E) pleasant

32. Because our supply of fossil fuel has been sadly
---- , we must find ---- sources of energy.

(A) stored..hoarded
(B) compensated..significant
(C) exhausted..inefficient
(D) increased..available
(E) depleted..alternate

33. Because he was ---- in the performance of his
duties, his employers could not ---- his work.

(A) derelict..quarrel over
(B) dilatory..grumble at
(C) undisciplined..object to
(D) assiduous..complain about
(E) mandatory..count on

34. The ---- pack of wolves ---- the herd of cattle in
their relentless search for a stray calf.

(A) voracious..stalked
(B) mendacious..pursued
(C) meandering..harassed
(D) pacific..followed
(E) nocturnal..guided

GO ON TO THE NEXT PAGE

35. The heretofore peaceful natives, seeking ---- the treachery of their supposed allies, became, ---- enough according to their perspective, embittered and vindictive.

    (A) acquiescence in..understandably
    (B) magnanimity towards..logically
    (C) evidence of..impartially
    (D) retribution for..justifiably
    (E) exoneration of..ironically

Each question below consists of a related pair of words or phrases, followed by five lettered pairs of words or phrases. Select the lettered pair that <u>best</u> expresses a relationship similar to that expressed in the original pair.

Example:

    YAWN : BOREDOM :: (A) dream : sleep
    (B) anger : madness   (C) smile : amusement
    (D) face : expression   (E) impatience : rebellion

                           Ⓐ Ⓑ ● Ⓓ Ⓔ

---

36. ROOSTER : HEN :: (A) pigeon : dove
    (B) dog : cat   (C) gander : gosling
    (D) swan : drake   (E) gander : goose

37. QUART : PINT :: (A) liter : meter
    (B) pound : ton   (C) fathom : mile   (D) inch : yard
    (E) minute : second

38. VIOLA : INSTRUMENT :: (A) color : sound
    (B) spectrum : shade   (C) trumpet : drum
    (D) chisel : tool   (E) fiddle : bass

39. TRUNK : BOUGH :: (A) hook : eye
    (B) leaf : branch   (C) detour : highway
    (D) torso : arm   (E) keg : flask

40. COBBLER : SHOES ::
    (A) mechanic : automobile
    (B) carpenter : saw
    (C) painter : easel
    (D) spy : plans
    (E) interrogator : questions

41. FELICITY : SORROW ::
    (A) celerity : speed
    (B) agility : clumsiness
    (C) concept : scheme
    (D) congratulations : benediction
    (E) ignorance : bliss

42. TIME : SCYTHE ::
    (A) liberty : sickle
    (B) justice : scales
    (C) honesty : badge
    (D) ignorance : chains
    (E) freedom : mountaintop

43. PROPITIATE : APPEASE ::
    (A) disturb : agitate
    (B) inaugurate : terminate
    (C) profess : vindicate
    (D) mollify : incite
    (E) renovate : raze

44. ASSURANCE : FEAR :: (A) opiate : pain
    (B) insurance : premium   (C) cigarette : cough
    (D) confidence : man   (E) narcotic : drug

45. OSTRACISM : CENSURE ::
    (A) love : marriage
    (B) success : promotion
    (C) applause : approval
    (D) editing : composition
    (E) loyalty : tribute

IF YOU FINISH BEFORE TIME IS CALLED, YOU MAY CHECK YOUR WORK ON THIS SECTION ONLY. DO NOT WORK ON ANY OTHER SECTION IN THE TEST.   **S T O P**

5

In this section solve each problem, using any available space on the page for scratchwork. Then decide which is the best of the choices given and blacken the corresponding space on the answer sheet.

The following information is for your reference in solving some of the problems.

Circle of radius r: Area $= \pi r^2$; Circumference $= 2\pi r$
   The number of degrees of arc in a circle is 360.
The measure in degrees of a straight angle is 180.

Definitions of symbols:
= is equal to $\leqq$ is less than or equal to
$\neq$ is unequal to $\geqq$ is greater than or equal to
< is less than $\parallel$ is parallel to
> is greater than $\perp$ is perpendicular to

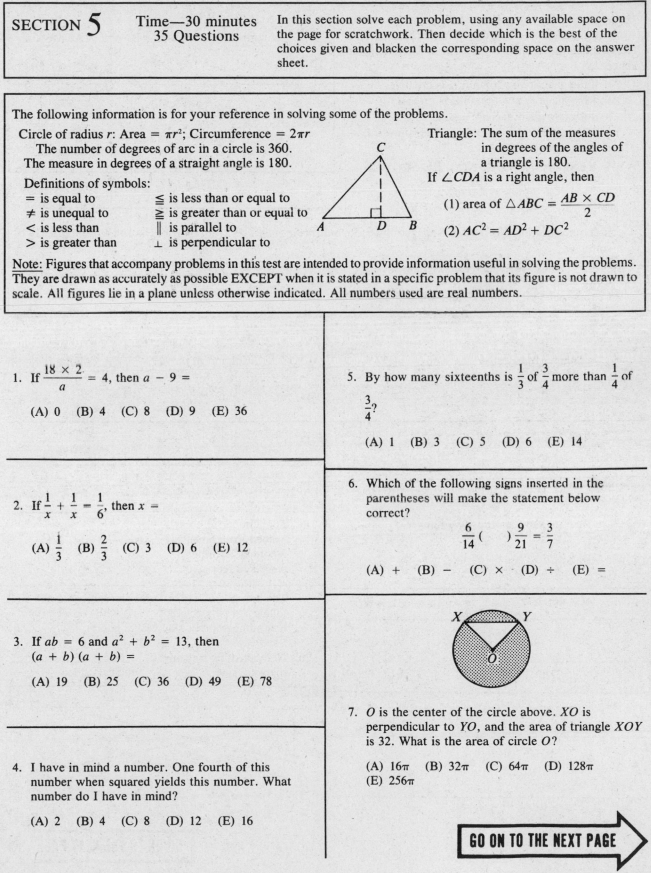

Triangle: The sum of the measures in degrees of the angles of a triangle is 180.
If $\angle CDA$ is a right angle, then

(1) area of $\triangle ABC = \dfrac{AB \times CD}{2}$

(2) $AC^2 = AD^2 + DC^2$

Note: Figures that accompany problems in this test are intended to provide information useful in solving the problems. They are drawn as accurately as possible EXCEPT when it is stated in a specific problem that its figure is not drawn to scale. All figures lie in a plane unless otherwise indicated. All numbers used are real numbers.

1. If $\dfrac{18 \times 2}{a} = 4$, then $a - 9 =$

   (A) 0   (B) 4   (C) 8   (D) 9   (E) 36

2. If $\dfrac{1}{x} + \dfrac{1}{x} = \dfrac{1}{6}$, then $x =$

   (A) $\dfrac{1}{3}$ (B) $\dfrac{2}{3}$ (C) 3   (D) 6   (E) 12

3. If $ab = 6$ and $a^2 + b^2 = 13$, then $(a + b)(a + b) =$

   (A) 19   (B) 25   (C) 36   (D) 49   (E) 78

4. I have in mind a number. One fourth of this number when squared yields this number. What number do I have in mind?

   (A) 2   (B) 4   (C) 8   (D) 12   (E) 16

5. By how many sixteenths is $\dfrac{1}{3}$ of $\dfrac{3}{4}$ more than $\dfrac{1}{4}$ of $\dfrac{3}{4}$?

   (A) 1   (B) 3   (C) 5   (D) 6   (E) 14

6. Which of the following signs inserted in the parentheses will make the statement below correct?

   $$\dfrac{6}{14} (\quad) \dfrac{9}{21} = \dfrac{3}{7}$$

   (A) +   (B) −   (C) ×   (D) ÷   (E) =

7. O is the center of the circle above. XO is perpendicular to YO, and the area of triangle XOY is 32. What is the area of circle O?

   (A) 16π (B) 32π (C) 64π (D) 128π
   (E) 256π

GO ON TO THE NEXT PAGE

5

Questions 8–27 each consist of two quantities, one in Column A and one in Column B. You are to compare the two quantities and on the answer sheet blacken space

A if the quantity in Column A is greater;
B if the quantity in Column B is greater;
C if the two quantities are equal;
D If the relationship cannot be determined from the information given.

AN E RESPONSE WILL NOT BE SCORED.

EXAMPLES		
Column A	Column B	Answers
E1. 2×6	$2 + 6$	●ⒷⒸⒹⒺ
E2. $180 - x$	y	ⒶⒷ●ⒹⒺ
E3. $p - q$	$q - p$	ⒶⒷⒸ●Ⓔ

For E2: $x°\ \ y°$ (angle diagram)

Notes:

1. In certain questions, information concerning one or both of the quantities to be compared is centered above the two columns.
2. In a given question, a symbol that appears in both columns represents the same thing in Column A as it does in Column B.
3. Letters such as x, n, and k stand for real numbers.

	Column A	Column B
8.	$\dfrac{n+7}{3} + \dfrac{n-3}{4}$	$\dfrac{7n+19}{7}$

$5 \times 5 \times 5 \times R = 3 \times 3 \times 3 \times 3$

	Column A	Column B
9.	5	R

$a > c$
$b < d$
a, b, c, and d are positive integers.

	Column A	Column B
10.	$\dfrac{a}{b}$	$\dfrac{c}{d}$
11.	$9 \times 682 \times 7$	$10 \times 682 \times 6$

$-10 < r < -1$

	Column A	Column B
12.	$\dfrac{1}{r^7}$	$\dfrac{1}{r^6}$
13.	$\dfrac{c^2 d^2 e^2}{c^3 d^3 e^3}$	$\dfrac{cde}{3}$

$n^2 > 0$

	Column A	Column B
14.	n	0

$x \neq 0$
$x^2 = xy$

	Column A	Column B
15.	x	y

	Column A	Column B
16.	$\dfrac{1}{2} + \dfrac{1}{3}$	$\dfrac{2}{5}$
17.	0.4%	$\dfrac{4}{1000}$
18.	0.0005	$\dfrac{1}{2}\%$
19.	The number of posts needed for a fence 144 feet long, with posts placed 12 feet apart	12 posts

The houses on Jordan Drive are numbered as follows: west side (1801–1837) with consecutive odd numbers; east side has 18 hours.

	Column A	Column B
20.	Number of houses on the west side	Number of houses on the east side

(diagram: intersecting lines forming angles $a°$, $b°$, $x°$, $c°$, $d°$)

	Column A	Column B
21.	$a + b + c + d$	$2x$

GO ON TO THE NEXT PAGE ⟶

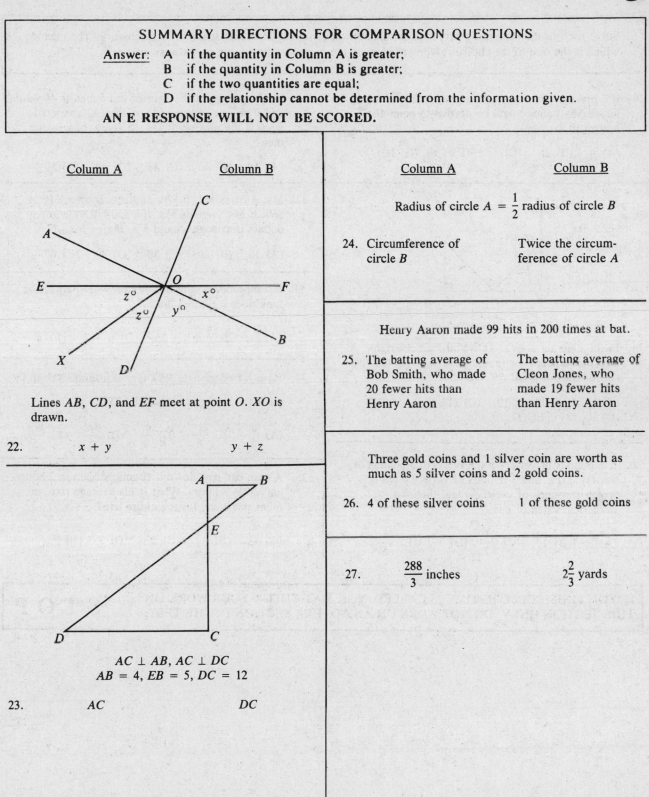

Column A   Column B

Lines *AB*, *CD*, and *EF* meet at point *O*. *XO* is drawn.

22. $x + y$ $y + z$

$AC \perp AB$, $AC \perp DC$
$AB = 4$, $EB = 5$, $DC = 12$

23.   *AC*   *DC*

Column A   Column B

Radius of circle $A = \frac{1}{2}$ radius of circle B

24. Circumference of   Twice the circum-
    circle B ference of circle A

Henry Aaron made 99 hits in 200 times at bat.

25. The batting average of   The batting average of
    Bob Smith, who made   Cleon Jones, who
    20 fewer hits than   made 19 fewer hits
    Henry Aaron   than Henry Aaron

Three gold coins and 1 silver coin are worth as much as 5 silver coins and 2 gold coins.

26. 4 of these silver coins   1 of these gold coins

27. $\dfrac{288}{3}$ inches $2\dfrac{2}{3}$ yards

5

Solve each of the remaining problems in this section using any available space for scratchwork. Then decide which is the best of the choices given and blacken the corresponding space on the answer sheet.

28. If $2p$ painters can paint $2h$ houses in $2w$ weeks, how many painters will be needed to paint $4h$ houses in $4w$ weeks?

    (A) p (B) $2p$ (C) $4p$ (D) $8p$ (E) $16p$

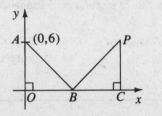

29. In the diagram above, AOB and PCB are right isosceles triangles with equal areas. What are the coordinates of point P?

    (A) (6, 0)   (B) (6, 12)   (C) (12, 0)
    (D) (0, 12)   (E) (12, 6)

30. If 7 pounds of variety p tea is worth 5 pounds of variety q tea, and 3 pounds of variety p tea is worth x pounds of variety q tea, then the numerical value of x is

    (A) $\frac{5}{7}$ (B) $1\frac{2}{3}$ (C) $2\frac{1}{7}$ (D) $3\frac{5}{7}$ (E) $4\frac{1}{5}$

31. If the average of the ages of three men is 44 years, and if no one of them is less than 42 years old, what is the maximum age, in years, of any one man?

    (A) 44   (B) 46   (C) 48   (D) 49   (E) 50

32. Ms. A owes Ms. B \$70, and Ms. B owes Ms. A \$60. If Ms. A gives Ms. B a \$50 bill, how many dollars in change should Ms. B give Ms. A?

    (A) 10   (B) 20   (C) 30   (D) 40   (E) 60

33. If a pipe fills a tank in h hours, what part of the tank does it fill in 2 hours?

    (A) $\frac{2}{h}$ (B) $\frac{h}{2}$ (C) $2h$ (D) $h + 2$ (E) $h - 2$

34. Base RT of triangle RST is $\frac{4}{5}$ of altitude SV. If SV equals c, the area of triangle $RST =$

    (A) $\frac{2c}{5}$ (B) $\frac{2c^2}{5}$ (C) $\frac{c^2}{2}$ (D) $\frac{4c^2}{5}$ (E) $\frac{8c^2}{5}$

35. A man can row down a 10-mile stream in 2 hours and up in 5 hours. What is his average rate, in miles per hour, for the entire trip?

    (A) $1\frac{3}{7}$ (B) $3\frac{1}{2}$ (C) $2\frac{6}{7}$ (D) 3 (E) 7

IF YOU FINISH BEFORE TIME IS CALLED, YOU MAY CHECK YOUR WORK ON THIS SECTION ONLY. DO NOT WORK ON ANY OTHER SECTION IN THE TEST.   **S T O P**

6   6   6   6   6   6   6   6   6   6   6

The following information is for your reference in solving some of the problems.

Circle of radius r: Area $= \pi r^2$; Circumference $= 2\pi r$
  The number of degrees of arc in a circle is 360.
The measure in degrees of a straight angle is 180.

Definitions of symbols:

$=$ is equal to	$\leq$ is less than or equal to
$\neq$ is unequal to	$\geq$ is greater than or equal to
$<$ is less than	$\parallel$ is parallel to
$>$ is greater than	$\perp$ is perpendicular to

Triangle: The sum of the measures in degrees of the angles of a triangle is 180.
If $\angle CDA$ is a right angle, then

(1) area of $\triangle ABC = \dfrac{AB \times CD}{2}$

(2) $AC^2 = AD^2 + DC^2$

Note: Figures that accompany problems in this test are intended to provide information useful in solving the problems. They are drawn as accurately as possible EXCEPT when it is stated in a specific problem that its figure is not drawn to scale. All figures lie in a plane unless otherwise indicated. All numbers used are real numbers.

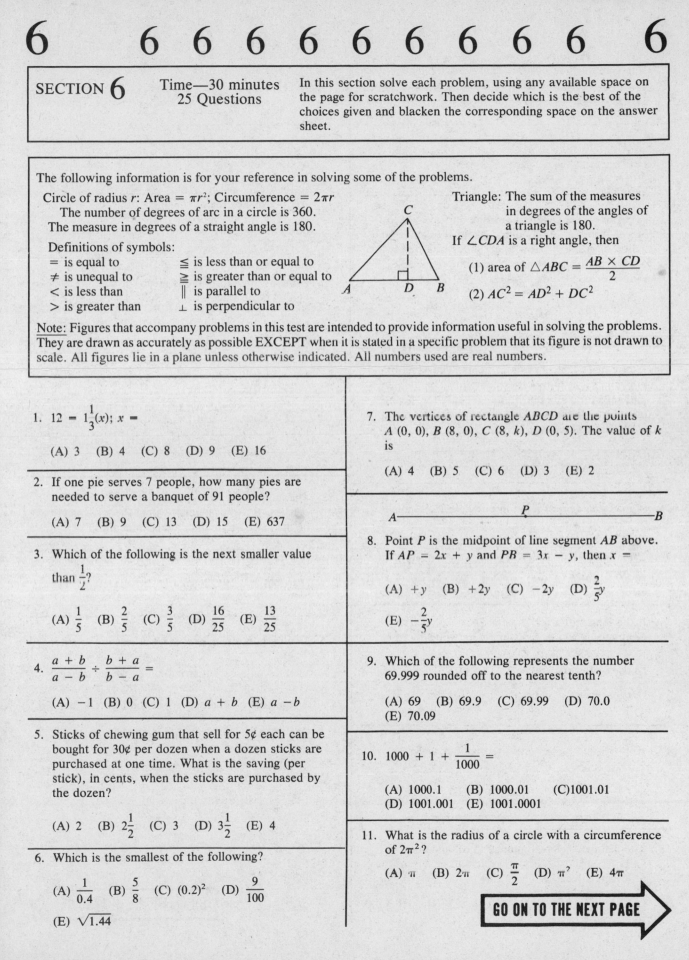

1. $12 = 1\frac{1}{3}(x)$; $x =$

    (A) 3   (B) 4   (C) 8   (D) 9   (E) 16

2. If one pie serves 7 people, how many pies are needed to serve a banquet of 91 people?

    (A) 7   (B) 9   (C) 13   (D) 15   (E) 637

3. Which of the following is the next smaller value than $\frac{1}{2}$?

    (A) $\frac{1}{5}$ (B) $\frac{2}{5}$ (C) $\frac{3}{5}$ (D) $\frac{16}{25}$ (E) $\frac{13}{25}$

4. $\dfrac{a+b}{a-b} \div \dfrac{b+a}{b-a} =$

    (A) -1 (B) 0 (C) 1 (D) $a+b$ (E) $a-b$

5. Sticks of chewing gum that sell for 5¢ each can be bought for 30¢ per dozen when a dozen sticks are purchased at one time. What is the saving (per stick), in cents, when the sticks are purchased by the dozen?

    (A) 2   (B) $2\frac{1}{2}$ (C) 3   (D) $3\frac{1}{2}$ (E) 4

6. Which is the smallest of the following?

    (A) $\dfrac{1}{0.4}$ (B) $\dfrac{5}{8}$ (C) $(0.2)^2$ (D) $\dfrac{9}{100}$

    (E) $\sqrt{1.44}$

7. The vertices of rectangle $ABCD$ are the points $A(0, 0)$, $B(8, 0)$, $C(8, k)$, $D(0, 5)$. The value of k is

    (A) 4   (B) 5   (C) 6   (D) 3   (E) 2

8. Point P is the midpoint of line segment AB above. If $AP = 2x + y$ and $PB = 3x - y$, then $x =$

    (A) $+y$ (B) $+2y$ (C) $-2y$ (D) $\frac{2}{5}y$

    (E) $-\frac{2}{5}y$

9. Which of the following represents the number 69.999 rounded off to the nearest tenth?

    (A) 69   (B) 69.9   (C) 69.99   (D) 70.0
    (E) 70.09

10. $1000 + 1 + \dfrac{1}{1000} =$

    (A) 1000.1   (B) 1000.01   (C) 1001.01
    (D) 1001.001   (E) 1001.0001

11. What is the radius of a circle with a circumference of $2\pi^2$?

    (A) π (B) 2π (C) $\dfrac{\pi}{2}$ (D) π^2 (E) 4π

GO ON TO THE NEXT PAGE

6 6 6 6 6 6 6 6 6 6 6

12. The sum of three positive consecutive integers is a. In terms of a the smallest of these integers may be expressed as

(A) $\dfrac{a}{3} - 6$ (B) $a - 6$ (C) $\dfrac{a-3}{3}$ (D) $\dfrac{a}{3}$

(E) $\dfrac{a+6}{3}$

13. A car uses one gallon of gasoline in traveling 15 miles. Another automobile can travel m miles on a gallon of gasoline. How many miles can the second car travel on the amount of gasoline required by the first car in going 60 miles?

(A) $\dfrac{m}{4}$ (B) m (C) $4m$ (D) $\dfrac{m}{9}$ (E) $9m$

14. A box of 12 tablets costs 21 cents. The same brand is packaged also in bottles containing 100 tablets and sells for $1.50 per bottle. What is the saving, in cents, per dozen tablets when the larger amount is purchased?

(A) 3   (B) 4   (C) 30   (D) 36   (E) 40

15. A man can do $\dfrac{1}{8}$ of a job in one day. How much of it can he do in x days?

(A) $\dfrac{x}{8}$ (B) $\dfrac{8}{x}$ (C) $x + 8$ (D) $8 - x$ (E) $8x$

16. If the length of a rectangle is $3u + 2v$, and its perimeter is $10u + 6v$, what is its width?

(A) $v + 2u$ (B) $2v + 4u$ (C) $2v + \dfrac{7}{2}u$

(D) $4v + 7u$ (E) $6v + 10u$

17. $W = i^2r$ and $r = \dfrac{E}{i}$; E, in terms of W and r, =

(A) $\dfrac{1}{Wr}$ (B) Wr (C) $\sqrt{Wr}$ (D) $\dfrac{W}{r}$ (E) w^2r^2

18. The distance between point $P(3, 0)$ and point Q is 5. The coordinates of point Q could be any of the following EXCEPT

(A) $(3, -5)$ (B) $(3, 5)$ (C) $(8, 0)$ (D) $(-8, 0)$
(E) $(-2, 0)$

19. In the figure above, radius $OA = 6.5$ and chord $AC = 5$. The area of triangle ABC =

(A) 16   (B) 18   (C) 24   (D) 30   (E) 36

20. If the average (arithmetic mean) of a, a, a, a, 36, and 44 is 20, then a =

(A) 10   (B) 20   (C) 25   (D) 30   (E) 40

21. $ab - 2cd = p$, $ab - 2cd = q$, and $6cd - 3ab = r$; $\dfrac{p}{r} =$

(A) -3 (B) $-\dfrac{1}{3}$ (C) $\dfrac{1}{3}$ (D) 1   (E) 3

22. The length of a rectangle is increased by 50 percent. By what percent would the width have to be decreased to maintain the same area?

(A) $33\dfrac{1}{3}\%$ (B) 50%   (C) $66\dfrac{2}{3}\%$ (D) 150%

(E) 200%

23. In a certain office, $\dfrac{1}{3}$ of the workers are women, $\dfrac{1}{2}$ of the women are married, and $\dfrac{1}{3}$ of the married women have children. If $\dfrac{3}{4}$ of the men are married and $\dfrac{2}{3}$ of the married men have children, what part of the workers are without children?

(A) $\dfrac{5}{18}$ (B) $\dfrac{4}{9}$ (C) $\dfrac{17}{36}$ (D) $\dfrac{11}{18}$ (E) $\dfrac{2}{3}$

GO ON TO THE NEXT PAGE

6   6   6   6   6   6   6   6   6   6   6

24. A woman travels in her yacht downstream at d knots and returns the same distance upstream at u knots. What is her average rate, in knots, for the round trip? (1 knot = 1 nautical mile per hour.)

(A) $\dfrac{du}{2}$ (B) $\dfrac{d + u}{2}$ (C) $\dfrac{du}{d + 2}$ (D) $\dfrac{2du}{d + u}$

(E) $\dfrac{d + u}{2du}$

25. At 10 A.M. water begins to pour into a cylindrical can 14 inches high and 4 inches in diameter at the rate of 8 cubic inches every 10 minutes. At what time will it begin to overflow? (Use $\pi = \dfrac{22}{7}$.)

(A) 1:20 P.M.   (B) 1:40 P.M.   (C) 3:40 P.M.
(D) 6:20 P.M.   (E) 6:40 P.M.

IF YOU FINISH BEFORE TIME IS CALLED, YOU MAY CHECK YOUR WORK ON THIS SECTION ONLY. DO NOT WORK ON ANY OTHER SECTION IN THE TEST.   S T O P

Answer Key

Note: The answers to the math sections are keyed to the corresponding review areas in Chapter 12. The numbers in parentheses after each answer refer to topics as listed below. (Note that to review for number 16, Quantitative Comparison, study Chapter 11.)

1. Fundamental Operations
2. Algebraic Operations
3. Using Algebra
4. Roots and Radicals
5. Inequalities
6. Fractions
7. Decimals
8. Percent
9. Averages
10. Motion
11. Ratio and Proportion
12. Mixtures and Solutions
13. Work
14. Coordinate Geometry
15. Geometry
16. Quantitative Comparison
17. Data Interpretation

Section 1 Verbal

1.	C	9.	A	17.	C	25.	D	33.	C
2.	B	10.	D	18.	D	26.	E	34.	A
3.	C	11.	D	19.	E	27.	E	35.	B
4.	D	12.	D	20.	A	28.	B	36.	D
5.	C	13.	B	21.	B	29.	B	37.	A
6.	D	14.	A	22.	C	30.	C	38.	C
7.	C	15.	E	23.	A	31.	E	39.	E
8.	D	16.	D	24.	D	32.	A	40.	C

Section 2 Math

1.	B (2)	6.	C (3)	11.	C (10)	16.	A (2)	21.	C (8)
2.	D (6)	7.	D (11)	12.	E (1, 6)	17.	C (15)	22.	E (2, 8)
3.	A (2)	8.	A (9)	13.	C (3)	18.	A (2)	23.	D (15)
4.	E (3)	9.	D (14, 15)	14.	B (15)	19.	A (8, 17)	24.	A (15)
5.	C (15)	10.	E (11)	15.	C (3)	20.	E (6)	25.	B (8)

Section 3 Test of Standard Written English

1.	D	11.	C	21.	C	31.	E	41.	C
2.	D	12.	C	22.	C	32.	D	42.	D
3.	C	13.	B	23.	A	33.	D	43.	B
4.	A	14.	B	24.	B	34.	E	44.	A
5.	E	15.	D	25.	A	35.	B	45.	E
6.	D	16.	A	26.	A	36.	D	46.	C
7.	E	17.	E	27.	E	37.	A	47.	A
8.	B	18.	D	28.	D	38.	C	48.	D
9.	E	19.	B	29.	D	39.	A	49.	D
10.	B	20.	C	30.	B	40.	C	50.	D

Section 4 Verbal

1.	B	10.	A	19.	E	28.	C	37.	E
2.	A	11.	D	20.	A	29.	C	38.	D
3.	D	12.	C	21.	A	30.	A	39.	D
4.	C	13.	B	22.	C	31.	C	40.	A
5.	C	14.	A	23.	E	32.	E	41.	B
6.	A	15.	C	24.	E	33.	D	42.	B
7.	E	16.	B	25.	E	34.	A	43.	A
8.	E	17.	C	26.	D	35.	D	44.	A
9.	E	18.	D	27.	E	36.	E	45.	C

Sections 5   Math

1. A (2)	8. D (2, 16)	15. C (2, 16)	22. D (15, 16)	29. E (14, 15)
2. E (2, 6)	9. A (1, 16)	16. A (1, 6, 16)	23. C (15, 16)	30. C (12)
3. B (2)	10. A (5, 16)	17. C (6, 8, 16)	24. C (15, 16)	31. C (9)
4. E (3)	11. A (1, 16)	18. B (7, 8, 16)	25. D (6, 16)	32. D (1)
5. A (6)	12. B (5, 16)	19. A (1, 16)	26. C (3, 16)	33. A (13)
6. E (6)	13. D (4, 16)	20. A (1, 16)	27. C (1, 16)	34. B (15)
7. C (15)	14. D (4, 5, 16)	21. C (15, 16)	28. B (11, 13)	35. C (10)

Section 6   Math

1. D (1, 6)	6. C (1, 6, 7)	11. A (15)	16. A (15)	21. B (2)
2. C (11)	7. B (14)	12. C (3)	17. C (2)	22. A (8, 15)
3. B (6)	8. B (2)	13. C (11)	18. D (14)	23. D (6)
4. A (2, 6)	9. D (1)	14. A (1)	19. D (15)	24. D (10)
5. B (1)	10. D (6, 7)	15. A (3)	20. A (9)	25. B (15)

Self-Evaluation

The model SAT test you have just completed has the same format as the actual SAT. As you take more of the model tests in this chapter, you will lose any SAT "stage fright" you might have.

Use the steps that follow to evaluate your performance on Model SAT Test 2. (Note: You'll find the charts referred to in steps 1–5 on the next four pages.)

■ **STEP 1**   Use the Answer Key to check your answers for each section.

■ **STEP 2**   For each section, count the number of correct and incorrect answers (remember that you don't count omitted answers), and enter the numbers on the appropriate lines of the chart "Calculate Your Raw Score." Then do the indicated calculations to get your Raw Verbal Score, your Raw TSWE Score, and your Raw Math Score.

■ **STEP 3**   Consult the chart "Evaluate Your Performance" to see how well you did.

■ **STEP 4**   To pinpoint the specific areas in which you need to improve, circle the numbers of the questions that you either left blank or got wrong on the "Identify Your Weaknesses" charts. This will tell you where to concentrate your efforts to get the most out of your study time. The chart for the math sections gives you page references for review and practice by skill areas. The charts for the verbal and TSWE sections refer you to the appropriate chapters to study for each question type.

■ **STEP 5**   Do the review and practice indicated on the charts wherever you had a concentration of circles.

Important: Remember that in addition to evaluating your scores, you should read all of the answer explanations for questions you answered incorrectly, questions you omitted, and questions you answered correctly but found difficult. Reviewing the answer explanations will help you understand concepts and strategies, and may point out short-cuts.

Calculate Your Raw Score

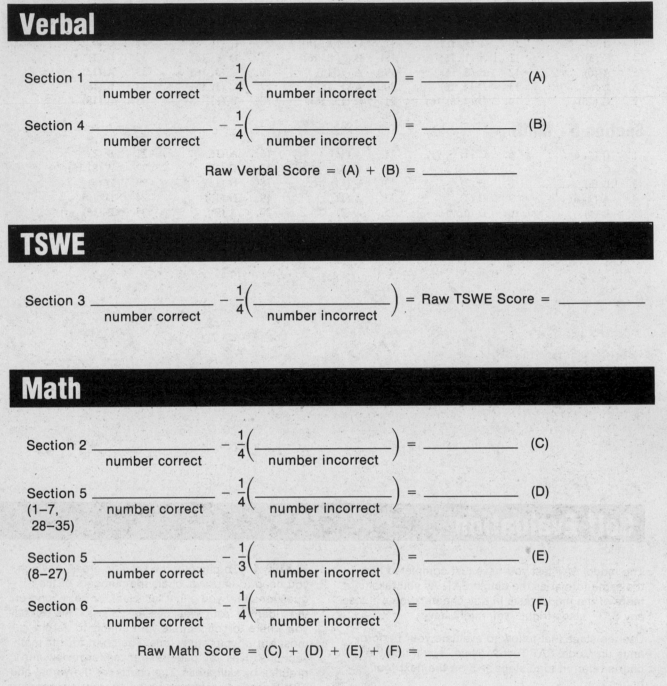

Verbal

Section 1 _____ $-\frac{1}{4}\left(\phantom{\rule{8em}{0ex}}\right)$ = _____ (A)
  number correct   number incorrect

Section 4 _____ $-\frac{1}{4}\left(\phantom{\rule{8em}{0ex}}\right)$ = _____ (B)
  number correct   number incorrect

Raw Verbal Score = (A) + (B) = _____

TSWE

Section 3 _____ $-\frac{1}{4}\left(\phantom{\rule{8em}{0ex}}\right)$ = Raw TSWE Score = _____
  number correct   number incorrect

Math

Section 2 _____ $-\frac{1}{4}\left(\phantom{\rule{8em}{0ex}}\right)$ = _____ (C)
  number correct   number incorrect

Section 5 _____ $-\frac{1}{4}\left(\phantom{\rule{8em}{0ex}}\right)$ = _____ (D)
(1–7,   number correct   number incorrect
 28–35)

Section 5 _____ $-\frac{1}{3}\left(\phantom{\rule{8em}{0ex}}\right)$ = _____ (E)
(8–27)   number correct   number incorrect

Section 6 _____ $-\frac{1}{4}\left(\phantom{\rule{8em}{0ex}}\right)$ = _____ (F)
  number correct   number incorrect

Raw Math Score = (C) + (D) + (E) + (F) = _____

Evaluate Your Performance

Verbal, TSWE, Math

	Verbal	TSWE	Math
Excellent	75–85	46–50	75–85
Very Good	65–74	41–45	61–74
Good	50–64	36–40	55–60
Above Average	40–49	31–35	45–54
Average	33–39	26–30	35–44
Below Average	below 33	below 26	below 35

Identify Your Weaknesses

Verbal

Question Type	Question Numbers		Chapter to Study
	Section 1	Section 4	
Antonym	1, 2, 3, 4, 5, 6, 7, 8, 9, 10	1, 2, 3, 4, 5, 6, 7, 8, 9, 10, 11, 12, 13, 14, 15	Chapter 5
Analogy	16, 17, 18, 19, 20, 21, 22, 23, 24, 25	36, 37, 38, 39, 40, 41, 42, 43, 44, 45	Chapter 6
Sentence Completion	11, 12, 13, 14, 15	16, 17, 18, 19, 20, 31, 32, 33, 34, 35	Chapter 7
Reading Comprehension	26, 27, 28, 29, 30, 31, 32, 33, 34, 35, 36, 37, 38, 39, 40	21, 22, 23, 24, 25, 26, 27, 28, 29, 30	Chapter 8

TSWE

Question Type	Question Numbers	Chapter to Study
Usage	1, 2, 3, 4, 5, 6, 7, 8, 9, 10, 11, 12, 13, 14, 15, 16, 17, 18, 19, 20, 21, 22, 23, 24, 25, 41, 42, 43, 44, 45, 46, 47, 48, 49, 50	Chapter 13
Sentence Correction	26, 27, 28, 29, 30, 31, 32, 33, 34, 35, 36, 37, 38, 39, 40	Chapter 13

Identify Your Weaknesses

Math

	Question Numbers			Pages to Study
Skill Area	**Section 2**	**Section 5**	**Section 6**	
Fundamental Operations	12	9, 11, 16, 19, 20, 27, 32	1, 5, 6, 9, 14, 22	328–29
Algebraic Operations	1, 2, 3, 18	1, 2, 3, 8, 15	4, 8, 17, 21	329–34
Using Algebra	4, 6, 13, 15, 16, 22, 26	4, 26	12, 15	334–35
Fractions	12, 20	5, 6, 16, 17, 18, 25	1, 3, 4, 10, 23	341–45
Decimals and Percents	19, 21, 22, 25	17, 18	10, 22	351–55
Verbal Problems	8, 11	28, 30, 31, 32, 33, 35	13, 15, 20, 24	357–58
Ratio and Proportion	7, 10	28	2, 13	362–64
Geometry	5, 9, 14, 17, 23, 24	7, 21, 22, 23, 24, 34	8, 11, 16, 18, 19, 22, 25	371–76
Coordinate Geometry		29	7, 18	381–82
Inequalities		10, 12, 14		335–36
Quantitative Comparison		8, 9, 10, 11, 12, 13, 14, 15, 16, 17, 18, 19, 20, 21, 22, 23, 24, 25, 26, 27		309–13
Roots and Radicals		13, 14		332–33

Answer Explanations
Section 1   Verbal

1. **C.** To *hesitate* means to waver, to hold back momentarily because of doubt or indecision. Its opposite is to *decide*.
Context Clue: "If you have a question, don't hesitate to ask!"

2. **B.** *Stamina* means physical strength, the power to endure fatigue and physical hardship. Its opposite is *lack of endurance*.
Context Clue: Think of "building up stamina."

3. **C.** To *bustle* is to move with great energy, to hustle. Its opposite is to *move slowly*.
Context Clue: Think of "the hustle and bustle of the big city."

4. **D.** *Impassive* means devoid of emotion, lacking feeling. Its opposite is *agitated*, excited or disturbed.
Context Clue: Think of "cold and impassive."
Word Parts Clue: *Im-* means not, *pass-* means feel. Someone impassive seems not to feel.

5. **C.** *Prodigious* means enormous, extraordinary in size. Its opposite is *microscopic* or tiny.
Context Clue: Think of someone you know who has "a prodigious appetite."

6. **D.** *Specious* means having a false look of truth or genuineness. Its opposite is *genuine* (true).
Context Clue: "Specious arguments don't hold up."
Beware Eye-Catchers: Choice B is incorrect. The capitalized word is specious, not spacious (the antonym of narrow).

7. **C.** *Verbosity* means wordiness; long-windedness. Its opposite is *terseness* or brevity; shortness of speech.
Context Clue: Think of "speeches marred by verbosity."

8. **D.** To *instigate* is to urge on or incite; to provoke. Its opposite is to *inhibit*, to repress or discourage from free activity.
Context Clue: Think of "instigating a riot."

9. **A.** *License* means excessive or undue freedom. Its opposite is *restraint* or control.
Context Clue: Think of "liberty degenerating into license."

10. **D.** *Sedulous* means persevering or diligent; hard-working. Its opposite is *indolent* or lazy.
Context Clue: "A sedulous student gets good grades."

11. **D.** One crowns a career with a triumph, in this case an *unsurpassable* performance. Remember, before you look at the choices, read the sentence and think of a word that makes sense. Words like magnificent, superlative, and matchless come to mind. Note that you are looking for a word with positive associations. Therefore, you can eliminate any word with negative ones. Choices A, B, C, and E all have negative associations. Only Choice D can be correct.

(Examples)

12. **D.** Students of genetics will have to turn or *resort to* respected journals where relevant information is *found*.
Choice A is incorrect. Excellent journals would be unlikely to ignore relevant material.
Choice B is incorrect. An interested student of genetics would enjoy reading an excellent journal in the field. Such a student would not be likely to suffer through it.
Choice C is incorrect. Pertinent material logically would be represented in an excellent technical journal.
Choice E is incorrect. We would be unlikely to complain about excellent technical journals.

(Argument Pattern)

13. **B.** By showing that they have no hidden or *concealed* weapons, they were showing themselves to be friendly or *amicably* disposed.
Because the first word of any one of these answer choices could work, you have to try out each entire answer pair before eliminating any of the choices.

(Cause and Effect Signal)

14. **A.** Since satire is more demanding than comedy, it must measure human conduct against a higher standard than comedy does. Thus, satire measures conduct against *an ideal* (a standard of perfection); comedy measures conduct against *a norm* (an average standard). Remember to watch for signal words that link one part of the sentence to another. The use of "not against . . . but against" sets up a contrast. The missing words must be antonyms or near-antonyms. You can immediately eliminate Choices C, D, and E as synonym or near-synonym pairs.

(Contrast Signal)

15. **E.** Rather than alleviating or easing problems, rent control may worsen or *exacerbate* them. The signal words "rather than" indicate that the missing word must be an antonym or near-antonym for alleviate.

You can immediately eliminate *resolve*, *diminish* and *minimize*, which make no sense in the context.

(Contrast Signal)

16. D.   Just as the *pea* grows within the *pod*, the *nut* grows within the *shell*.

(Part to Whole)

17. C.   A *candle* may be made of *tallow*; a *statue*, of *bronze*.

(Part to Whole)

18. D.   A *thermometer* measures temperature or *heat*; a *Geiger counter* measures *radiation*.
Choice A is incorrect. A filament (the conductor inside a light bulb) gives off light; it doesn't measure light.
Choice B is incorrect. A chronometer measures time, not color.
Choice C is incorrect. An odometer measures distance, not waves.
Choice E is incorrect. A barometer measures atmospheric pressure, not electricity.

(Function)

19. E.   A *hangar* is a place for servicing and storing *airplanes*; a *garage* is a place for servicing and storing *automobiles*.
If your original sentence was "An airplane is found in a hangar," Choices A, B, C, and E would all have made good analogies. If more than one answer appears to fit your original sentence, you need to state the relationship more precisely.

(Definition)

20. A.   To *gulp* is more extreme than to *sip*; to *guffaw* (laugh loudly and boisterously) is more extreme than to *giggle*.

(Degree of Intensity)

21. B.   A *spine* is a sharp-pointed outgrowth on a *cactus*; a *quill* is a sharp-pointed bristle on a *porcupine*.

(Part to Whole)

22. C.   *Scold* and *rebuke* are synonyms, as are *hesitate* and *waver*.
You need to know the exact meanings of words in order to spot the difference between synonyms and degree of intensity analogies.
Choice A is incorrect. Dislike and loathe (hate) are not synonyms. The relationship is one of Degree of Intensity.
Choice B is incorrect. Implore (beg; beseech; ask urgently) and request (ask) are not synonyms. Again, the relationship is one of Degree of Intensity.

(Synonyms)

23. A.   One example of a *marsupial* (mammal that carries its young in a pouch) is an *opossum*; one example of a *rodent* is a *squirrel*.
Answering some analogy questions requires specialized technical vocabulary typically used in high school science, literature, and social science classes.

(Class to Member)

24. D.   The *crest* is a wave's high point; the *trough*, its low point. Similarly a *peak* is a high point of land; a *valley*, a low point.

(Spatial Sequence)

25. D.   *Titanic* (enormous) and *lilliputian* (tiny or puny) are antonyms. *Obese* (corpulent, excessively fat) and *emaciated* (extremely lean, wasted away) are antonyms also.

(Antonyms)

26. E.   The opening sentence describes the Renaissance artist as an "all-round man." The passage then develops the idea of the Renaissance artist's versatility or adaptability. Remember, when asked to find the main idea, be sure to check the opening and summary sentences of each paragraph.

(Main Idea/Title)

27. E.   You can arrive at the correct answer by the process of elimination.
Statement I is untrue. The author does not exaggerate facts to make his point about the Renaissance artist. Therefore, you can eliminate Choices A and D.
Statement II is true. The author does list examples to back up his point. Therefore, you can eliminate Choice C.
Statement III is true. The author cites Edison as an authority on Leonardo. Therefore, you can eliminate Choice B. Only Choice E is left. It is the correct answer.

(Technique)

28. B.   The author admires the diversity of interest shown by the Renaissance artists. He describes them and their various interests in wholly positive terms. Note the words "famous," "well-known," "genius," "great." Remember, when asked to determine the author's attitude or mood, always look for words that convey emotion or paint pictures.

(Attitude/Tone)

29. B.   The last paragraph indicates that at least two interpretations of the book are currently in favor.
The second paragraph states that critics disagree about what Melville "was trying to

say.'' In other words, they disagree about his message or *theme*.
Choice A is incorrect. Critics do not disagree about Melville's plot or story line. They agree that Budd destroys Mate Claggart, and that the Captain sentences Budd to be hanged. However, they disagree about what this plot *means*.
Choices C, D, and E are incorrect. They are not mentioned in the passage.

(Specific Details)

30. C.   In lines 15–16 the author mentions Melville's comparison of Billy Budd to ''Adam before the fall,'' man without sin. Budd is innocent and ignorant. In other words, he is *naive*.
Choice A is incorrect. Claggart, not Budd, is like Satan (line 17).
Choice B is incorrect. The book *Billy Budd* is ambiguous (open to various interpretations). However, the character Billy Budd is described explicitly as naive.
Choices D and E are incorrect. There is nothing in the passage to indicate that Budd is either brutal (savage, crude) or vain (conceited, proud).
Remember, when asked about specific details in the passage, spot key words in the question and scan the passage to find them (or their synonyms).

(Specific Details)

31. E.   The phrase ''preserving order'' (line 22) indicates that the Captain had charge of maintaining discipline.
Choice A is incorrect. Lines 19–21 state specifically that Budd has been sentenced to be hanged ''according to the letter of the law.'' Therefore, the Captain has obeyed the law, not disobeyed it.
Choices B, C, and D are not mentioned in the passage.
Remember, when asked about specific details in the passage, spot key words in the question and scan the passage to find them (or their synonyms).
Key Words: Captain, law, discipline.

(Specific Details)

32. A.   Choice A is correct. The bulk of the passage deals with critical perceptions of Melville's novelette. Note the phrases ''scholars dis—agree'' (line 11), ''controversy exists'' (line 21), and ''scholars are still arguing'' (lines 30–31).
Choice B is incorrect. The author is not arguing about *Billy Budd*'s merits; he is summarizing other people's arguments about its meaning.

Choices C and D are incorrect. The author is not taking sides in the scholarly argument; he is merely reporting it. Thus, he is neither defending nor denouncing Melville.
Choice E is incorrect. The author is discussing only one work by Melville. Therefore, he is not describing Melville's artistic growth.

(Main Idea)

33. C.   The passage describes the extreme lack of interest in and knowledge of social insurance in this country. It also describes the aversion to such programs, using negative terms such as ''maligning'' or slandering (line 3), ''bitterly opposed'' (lines 9–10), and ''traditional hostility'' (line 19).
Remember, when asked about specific details in the passage, spot key words in the question and scan the passage to find them (or their synonyms).
Key Words: ''give a chance,'' ''careful study,'' ''antagonism,'' ''propaganda,'' ''afraid.''

(Specific Details)

34. A.   Individualism is a theory that stresses the independence of the individual. It stresses individual thought, action, and interests. To condition someone is to prepare him or her to respond in a given way. Thus, ''our long conditioning to individualism'' is our psychological and social preparation, our habit, that leads us to expect to depend on ourselves.

(Word from Context)

35. B.   The concluding sentence of the passage indicates that the passage of a law (*legislation*) is less important than public opinion in bringing about social reform.
Choice A is incorrect. It is contradicted by the concluding sentence.
Choice C is incorrect. The passage states that Americans are underinformed about the problem of social insurance. It does not say that they are underinformed about *all* social problems. Be suspicious of statements that leave no room for exceptions. Correct SAT reading comprehension answers seldom are phrased in terms of *always* or *never*, *universally*, *every*, *none*, or *all*.
Choice D is incorrect. Our type of government sets difficulties in the way of social reform (lines 14–17). It does not make it *impossible*. Again, suspect answers phrased in absolutes.
Choice E is incorrect. Labor abroad supports social insurance (lines 7–9). Labor at home no longer opposes it (lines 9–11). Therefore, the statement is untrue.

(Specific Details)

36. D. Choice D is correct. In the opening and closing sentences of the passage, the author sums up what "we now know" and informs the reader what "has been found" about the composition of matter (what constitutes matter).

Remember, when asked to find the main idea, be sure to check the opening and summary sentences of each paragraph.

(Main Idea)

37. A. An *expository* style is one that attempts to inform or explain.

Choice B is incorrect. The author is not attempting to persuade or sway his audience. The author is merely attempting to convey agreed-on facts.

Choice C is incorrect. The author is not reflecting or meditating on this subject. He is explaining it.

Choice D is incorrect. The author is neither making a speech nor striving for eloquence.

Choice E is incorrect. The author mentions the physicists' "ingenious laboratory experiments." He is positive rather than negative (belittling, deprecatory) about their work.

(Technique)

38. C. The passage states that molecules are made of atoms; logically, therefore, an atom is smaller, not larger, than the molecule to which it belongs.

Choice A is incorrect. Line 5 states atoms "have never been seen or photographed."

Choice B is incorrect. Lines 19–24 mention its positive and negative electric elements.

Choice D is incorrect. Lines 6–9 note the ingenious laboratory experiments that determine its operations or processes.

Choice E is incorrect. Lines 14–15 mention the average diameter of a molecule is 1/125 millionth of an inch. Atoms are smaller yet.

Remember, when asked about specific details in the passage, spot key words in the question and scan the passage to find them (or their synonyms).

(Specific Details)

39. E. The comparison emphasizes the smallness or *minuteness* of atoms.

Remember, when asked to make inferences, base your answers on what the passage implies, not what it states directly.

(Inference)

40. C. The satellites *circle* the planet. The electrons *swirl around* the proton. The relationships are comparable.

Choice A is incorrect. A hawk *swoops down* upon its prey. The proton does not swoop down upon the electrons.

Choice B is incorrect. A blueprint is an outline or plan. A framework is a skeletal structure. The relationships are not comparable.

Choice D is incorrect. Iron filings are *drawn or attracted* to a magnet. Electrons *swirl around* a proton.

Choice E is incorrect. A compound *is made up* of elements. A proton is not made up of electrons.

(Inference)

Section 2   Math

1. B.
$$(r - s) - (s - r)$$
$$r - s - s + r$$
Combine similar terms: $2r - 2s$
Factor: $2(r - s)$

2. D. $\dfrac{\frac{1}{3} - \frac{1}{12}}{\frac{1}{4}}$

Multiply numerator and denominator by 12:

$$\frac{4 - 1}{3} = \frac{3}{3} = 1$$

3. A. $ax + b - y = 0$
$$b = y - ax$$

4. E. From $-25°$ to $0° = 25°$
From $0°$ to $+3° = 3°$
Total $= 28°$

5. C. Draw $OA \perp QR$.
AV = side of square = 2
Area of square = 4
Draw radius OS.

$VS = \dfrac{1}{2}ST$ (side of square)

$ = 1$ (radius drawn $\perp$ to chord bisects chord)

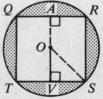

Since the hypotenuse of an isosceles right triangle = leg $\sqrt{2}$, $OS = \sqrt{2}$. Or, using the Pythagorean Theorem, in right triangle OVS,
$(OV)^2 + (VS)^2 = (OS)^2$
or $1 + 1 = (OS)^2$
$2 = (OS)^2$
$\sqrt{2} = OS$ (radius of circle)

Area of circle = $\pi(\sqrt{2})^2$ or 2π
Area of circle − area of square = area of shaded portion
$2\pi - 4$ = area of shaded portion

6. C.   Let x = the number.
$3x - 7 = 32$ (given)
$3x = 39$
$x = 13$
Twice the number, or $2x$, = 26

7. D. $\dfrac{\text{ken}}{\text{feet}} = \dfrac{1}{5.97} = \dfrac{59.7}{x}$

$x = (5.97)(59.7)$ (in a proportion, the
$x = 356.409$ or 356 ft.   product of the means equals the product of the extremes)

Alternatively, you may estimate that $(60)(6) = 360$, and choose the answer that is slightly less than 360.

8. A.   Average = 75.
Sum of all grades = (75)(4) = 300
Sum of three grades   = 240   (given)
Grade on first examination = 60

9. D.   Draw altitudes AE, BF.
Area of figure = areas of triangle AED + triangle BFC + rectangle $AEFB$

Area of triangle AED =
$\dfrac{bh}{2}$ or $\dfrac{(2 \text{ units})(6 \text{ units})}{2}$ or 6 square units
Area of triangle BFC =
$\dfrac{bh}{2}$ or $\dfrac{(6 \text{ units})(6 \text{ units})}{2}$ or 18 square units
Area of rectangle $AEFB$ =
bh or $(2 \text{ units})(6 \text{ units})$ or 12 square units
Sum = 36 square units

Or apply formula for area of trapezoid:

Area = $\dfrac{1}{2}h(b + b_1)$

Area = $\dfrac{1}{2}(6)(10 + 2)$

Area = 36 square units

10. E.   Let x = number of pencils that can be bought for d dollars (or $100d$ cents).

$\dfrac{\text{number of pencils}}{\text{cost per pencil (in cents)}} = \dfrac{P}{c} = \dfrac{x}{100d}$

$cx = 100dp$ (in a proportion, the product of the means equals the product of the extremes)

$x = \dfrac{100dp}{c}$ (division by c)

11. C. $\dfrac{\text{Distance}}{\text{Time}}$ = Rate
$h - 2$ = time that would result in arrival on schedule
$\dfrac{d}{h - 2}$ = rate that would result in arrival on schedule

12. E.   Since the question indicates that the quotient is *exactly* one of the answers, the correct answer must obviously have, as its last digit, 7, which when multiplied by 9 (the last digit of the denominator) will yield 3 (last digit of the numerator).

13. C.   Mr. Stanley is now $x - 5$ years old. Five years ago, Mr. Stanley was $(x - 5) - 5$ years old. $(x - 5) - 5 = x - 10$

14. B.

Angle SVR is a right angle.
$\angle SVR = 90°$
$\angle VSR = x°$
$\angle VRW = \angle SVR + \angle VSR$
(the exterior angle of a triangle equals the sum of both remote interior angles)
$\angle VRW = 90° + x°$
Or:
Angles $SVR + VSR + VRS = 180°$
(the sum of the angles of a triangle = 180°)
$\angle VRS = 180° - (90° + x)$ or $90° - x°$
$\angle VRS + \angle VRW = 180°$
$\angle VRW = 180° - (90° - x°)$
$\angle VRW = 180° - 90° + x°$
$\angle VRW = 90° + x°$

15. C.   48 oz. = 3 lb.
Cost of first pound = 30¢
Cost of 2 lb. = 31¢
Total cost = 61¢

16. A.   By substitution:

$\dfrac{\frac{1}{2}}{\frac{1}{2} + \frac{1}{\frac{1}{2}}} = \dfrac{\frac{1}{2}}{\frac{1}{2} + 2} = \dfrac{\frac{1}{2}}{2\frac{1}{2}}$

$= \dfrac{\frac{1}{2}}{\frac{5}{2}} = \dfrac{1}{2} \cdot \dfrac{2}{5} = \dfrac{1}{5}$

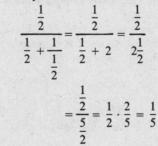

17. C. Let $x = AB$.

Then $BC = 3x \left(\dfrac{BC}{AB} = 3 \right)$

$AC = 4x$ (side of square)
Area of $BCDJ = 3x^2$
Area of $HJFG = 3x^2$

$\dfrac{\text{area of } BCDJ}{\text{area of } HJFG} = \dfrac{3x^2}{3x^2} = \dfrac{1}{1}$

18. A. $r = 18$

$\dfrac{r}{s} = \dfrac{6}{y}$

$\dfrac{18}{s} = \dfrac{6}{y}$ (by substitution)

$\dfrac{y}{s} = \dfrac{6}{18}$ (in a proportion, the extremes may be interchanged)

$\dfrac{y}{s} = \dfrac{1}{3}$

19. A. A department has at least 10 bureaus. A bureau has at least 40 workers. Therefore one department has at least 400 workers. 10% of 400 = 40 typists.

20. E. If $\dfrac{2}{3}$ of the faculty are women, $\dfrac{1}{3}$ are men.

If $\dfrac{3}{5}$ of the male teachers are married, $\dfrac{2}{5}$ are unmarried.

Then $\dfrac{2}{5}$ of $\dfrac{1}{3}$ or $\dfrac{2}{15}$ of the faculty are unmarried men.

Let x = total number of faculty members.

$\dfrac{2}{15}x$ = number of unmarried male teachers

$\dfrac{2x}{15} = 12$

$2x = 180$

$x = 90$

21. C. $\dfrac{\text{Change}}{\text{Original}} \times 100$ = Percent change

$\dfrac{-2}{8}$ or $\left(-\dfrac{1}{4} \right) \times 100$ = percent change

-25% = change

22. E. $0.1r = 0.2s$
$0.2s = 0.3t$
$0.1r = 0.3t$ (things equal to the same thing are equal to each other)
$r = 3t$ (multiply by 10)
$100\% \, r = 300\% \, t$ (convert to percent)

23. D. (Diameter)(π) = Circumference
(Diameter)(π) = 4π in.

Diameter = $\dfrac{4\pi}{\pi}$ or 4 in.   (division)

Since the length is 48 in., a maximum of 12 tumblers can be placed across the length. Since the width is 32 inches, a maximum of 8 tumblers can be placed across the width of the table. Total number of tumblers will be 12 × 8 or 96.

24. A. Triangle AGD is similar to triangle GEF. (They have a common angle, and EF is parallel to AD.)

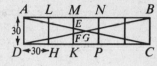

Altitude of triangle AGD =

$DH + HK + \dfrac{1}{2}KP$ or 75

Altitude of triangle $GEF = \dfrac{1}{2}KP$ or 15

$\dfrac{\text{altitude of } AGD}{\text{altitude of } GEF} = \dfrac{75}{15} = \dfrac{5}{1}$

$\dfrac{30}{EF} = \dfrac{5}{1}$

$5(EF) = 30$

$EF = 6$

25. B. Let $x\%$ or $\dfrac{x}{100}$ = increase of manpower required to return to normal (100%) production. Then 80% (present production) + $x\%$ of present output = 100% (normal output)

$\dfrac{80}{100} + \left(\dfrac{x}{100} \cdot \dfrac{80}{100} \right) = 100\%$

$\dfrac{4}{5} + \dfrac{4x}{500} = 1$

$400 + 4x = 500$

$4x = 100$

$x = 25\%$

Section 3   Test of Standard Written English

1. D. Violation of parallel structure. Change *to attend* to *attending*.

2. D. Faulty comparison. When comparing two persons or things, use the comparative form (*better*) instead of the superlative (*best*).

3. C. Faulty diction. Use *behind* instead of *in back of*.

4. A. Error in agreement. A system *has been incorporated* is correct.

5. E. Sentence is correct.

6. D. Error in agreement. The antecedent of *who* is *one*. Change *plan* to *plans*.

7. E. Sentence is correct.

8. B. Faulty diction. Change *amount of* to *number of*.

9. E. Sentence is correct.

10. B. Wrong tense. Change *is* to *has been*.

11. C. Faulty diction. Delete *of*.

12. C. Error in tense. Change *will go* to *would go*.

13. B. Faulty comparison. Do not compare a person with a thing. Correct form: *Your argument is no different from that of the last speaker.* . . .

14. B. Lack of agreement. Woman (singular) requires a singular pronoun. Change *their* to *her*.

15. D. Faulty diction. The conjunction *than* helps to make a comparison, not *then*.

16. A. Error in diction. Do not use *due to* when you mean *because of*.

17. E. Sentence is correct.

18. D. Faulty verbal. Change *in taking* to the infinitive *to take*.

19. B. Wrong word. Use *lying* instead of *laying*.

20. C. Lack of parallel structure. Change *to have remembered* to *to remember*.

21. C. Faulty diction. Use *take* instead of *bring*.

22. C. Error in agreement. The antecedent, *Congress*, is singular. Change *have passed* to *has passed*.

23. A. Error in case. Change *who* to *whom*. It is the object of the preposition *to*.

24. B. Faulty diction. Use *if* to indicate a condition. Substitute *whether*.

25. A. Dangling participle. Change to a subordinate clause—*When we descended.* . . .

26. A. The sentence's use of parallel structure is effective and correct.

27. E. This choice corrects the sentence fragment.

28. D. Do not use *calculate* when you mean *think*.

29. D. The addition of *when* makes the sentence more effective by tightening up the relationship between the clauses.

30. B. Choice B expresses the author's meaning directly and concisely. All other choices are either indirect or ungrammatical.

31. E. This choice corrects the sentence fragment.

32. D. Changing *absenteeism is reduced* to *reduces absenteeism* maintains parallel structure.

33. D. This choice eliminates the error in parallel structure.

34. E. Omission of important word and error in verb tense are corrected in choice E.

35. B. Choices A, D, and E are run-on sentences. Choice C is verbose.

36. D. Choice A contains a sentence fragment. Choices B, C, and E are verbose.

37. A. Sentence is correct.

38. C. This sentence does not violate parallel structure.

39. A. Sentence is correct.

40. C. Error in agreement. *Kind* is singular and requires a singular modifier (*this*).

41. C. Faulty diction. Change *enthuse* to *be enthusiastic*.

42. D. Lack of parallel structure. Change *practicing* to *practice*.

43. B. Error in sentence connector. Change *on the other hand* to *but* in order to express the relationship between the clauses.

44. A. Error in case. Change *whom* to *who*. *Who* is the subject of *would win*.

45. E. Sentence is correct.

46. C. Unnecessary switch in pronouns. Change *one finds* to *you find*.

47. A. Wordiness and inappropriate coordinate

conjunction. Eliminate *but this was* to tighten the sentence.

48. D. Error in case. Change the objective form *them* to the possessive form *their*, to reflect *their* arrival.

49. D. Lack of parallel structure. Eliminate *allowing*.

50. D. Error in tense. Change *have been located* to *are located*.

Section 4   Verbal

1. B. To *wrinkle* is to crease or rumple. Its opposite is to *make smooth*.
Context Clue: "Don't wrinkle your shirt!"

2. A. *Callous* means insensitive and uncaring; hardened. Its opposite is *concerned*.
Context Clue: Think of "callous about suffering."

3. D. To *blur* is to make dim or obscure. Its opposite is to *make clear*.
Context Clue: Think of "fog blurring the windshield."

4. C. *Demure* means markedly quiet and modest. Its opposite is *bold*.
Context Clue: Think of "demure and reserved."

5. C. *Urbanity* means sophistication, a worldly manner. Its opposite is a *naive* (unsophisticated) *manner*.
Context Clue: Think of "civilized urbanity."
Beware Eye-Catchers: Choice B is incorrect. The opposite of a rural area is an urban area, not urbanity.

6. A. To *dissuade* is to discourage, to persuade *not* to do something. Its opposite is to *urge strongly*.
Context Clue: "She dissuaded him from running away."

7. E. *Deference* means respectful regard. Its opposite is *disrespect*.
Context Clue: Think of "in deference to his wishes."

8. E. *Orthodox* means holding correct views. Its opposite is *heretical* (holding opinions and views contrary to popular belief).
Word Parts Clue: *Ortho-* means correct; *dox-* means belief.

9. E. *Fervor* means intensity of feeling or enthusiasm. Its opposite is apathy or *indifference*, lack of feeling.
Context Clue: Think of "cheering with fervor."

10. A. *Succor* means aid or assistance. Its opposite is *hindrance* or obstacle.
Context Clue: Think of "begging for succor."

11. D. *Phlegmatic* means not easily excited, sluggish. Its opposite is *excitable*.
Context Clue: Think of someone "too phlegmatic to budge."

12. C. *Laudatory* means admiring or expressing praise. Its opposite is *defamatory*, slanderous.
Context Clue: "Thank you for your laudatory remarks."

13. B. *Lackadaisical* means lacking enthusiasm or vigor; listless. Its opposite is energetic or *enthusiastic*.
Context Clue: "He was too lackadaisical to succeed."

14. A. *Salutary* means wholesome, beneficial, healthful. Its opposite is *harmful*.
Word Parts Clue: *Salu-* or *salut-* means health.

15. C. *Bane* means a curse or fatal element, something that brings about destruction or death. Its opposite is *source of bliss*, something that brings about happiness and joy.
Context Clue: "Tests were the bane of my existence."

16. B. To *sap* or weaken the recipient's self-sufficiency would be contrary to the recipient's true welfare.
The phrase "argument *against*" is your clue to look for a "negative" verb. Therefore, you can eliminate any answer choices with positive verbs.
Choices A, C, and D all have positive associations. If the welfare system supported, hastened, or renewed independence in people, that would be an argument for the system, not against it. Choice E makes no sense in the sentence. That leaves you with Choice B.

(Examples)

17. C. *Derivative* means unoriginal. Unoriginal work derives from or comes from the work of others. The moviemaker is unoriginal despite his reputation for skill or *expertise*.
The word "sadly" is your clue to look for a negative word to fill in the second blank. Therefore, you can eliminate any word with positive associations.

(Definition)

18. D. *Volatile* substances tend to evaporate.

(Definition)

19. E. *Frustrations* or limitations are by definition
not satisfying.
Remember to watch for signal words that link
one part of the sentence to another. The use
of "Despite" in the opening clause sets up a
contrast. The missing word must be an
antonym for "stirring and satisfying."
Note, too, that you are looking for a word
with negative associations. Therefore, you can
eliminate any word with positive ones.
Choices A, B, C, and D all have positive
associations. Only Choice E can be correct.

(Contrast Signal)

20. A. *Germane*, meaning pertinent or relevant, is the
only appropriate choice. A judge might
logically rule not to admit material because it
was irrelevant.
On the grounds that is equivalent to *because*.

(Cause and Effect Signal)

21. A. In this paragraph, the author pays particular
attention to Maria's appearance, her behavior,
her effect on others. If she had been
introduced previously in the text, there would
be no need to present these details about her
in the second paragraph.

(Main Idea)

22. C. The descriptions of the bright and shiny
kitchen where you "could see yourself in the
big copper boilers" and of tiny, witch-like
Maria with her long nose and long chin belong
to the realm of fairy tales.

(Technique)

23. E. The passage mentions the matron twice: once,
in the opening line, where she gives Maria
permission to leave work early; once, in lines
18–20, where she pays Maria a compliment.
Given this information, we can logically infer
that Maria views the matron positively, finding
her a benevolent or kindly supervisor.
Choices A, B, and C are incorrect. Nothing in
the passage suggests Maria has a negative
view of the matron.
Choice D is incorrect. Given Maria's menial
position, it is unlikely she and the matron
would be close or intimate friends.

(Inference)

24. E. To slice loaves so neatly and invisibly takes a
great deal of care. The author specifically
states Maria has cut the loaves and
emphasizes the importance of her having done

so by placing this sentence at the end of the
paragraph (a key position). As the subsequent
paragraphs point up, Maria is hungry for
compliments. Just as she takes pride in her
peace-making, she takes pride in her ability to
slice barmbracks evenly.

(Inference)

25. E. Maria helps others to compromise or become
reconciled; she herself is not necessarily
unwilling to compromise.
Choice A is implied in the passage as
characteristic of Maria. She speaks soothingly
and respectfully. Therefore, Choice A is
incorrect.
Choice B is implied in the passage as
characteristic of Maria. Maria's response to
Ginger Mooney's toast shows her enjoyment
of being noticed in this way. Therefore,
Choice B is incorrect.
Choice C is implied in the passage as
characteristic of Maria. Maria's obedience to
the cook and to the matron shows her respect
for authority. Therefore, Choice C is
incorrect.
Choice D is implied in the passage as
characteristic of Maria. Maria's disappointed
shyness and her forced laughter about a
wedding ring and husband show that she has
wistful dreams of marriage. Therefore, Choice
D is incorrect.

(Inference)

26. D. The concluding sentence of the opening
paragraph mentions factors that produced the
crop of Black writers who made up the
Harlem Renaissance. The subsequent
paragraph continues the discussion of these
social and political factors.
Choice A is incorrect. Although the opening
sentence indicates that the willingness of
Black writers to portray their own lives was a
contributing factor to the Harlem Renaissance,
the next sentence makes it clear that this
willingness was only *part* of what was going
on.
Choice B is incorrect. The author is concerned
with these writers as part of an American
literary movement, not a worldwide crusade.
Choice C is incorrect. The author cites
examples of specific injustices in passing.
Choice E is incorrect. It is unsupported by the
passage.

(Main Idea)

27. E. The author's use of such terms as "nobility of
expression" and "masters of recent American
literature" makes it clear his attitude is one of
admiration.
Remember, when asked to determine the

author's attitude or tone, look for words which convey emotion or which paint pictures.

(Attitude/Tone)

28. **C.** The fact that the writers were more involved with fighting problems in the system than with attacking the system itself suggests that fundamentally they *were not opposed to* the democratic system of government.
Choice A is incorrect. The fact that they did not revolt against the system does not necessarily imply that they played a minor part in fighting abuses of the system.
Choices B, D, and E are incorrect. None are suggested by the statement.
Remember, when asked to make inferences, base your answers on what the passage implies, not what it states directly.

(Inference)

29. **C.** In lines 8–11, the author mentions the growing interest in social and economic problems among the writers of the Harlem Renaissance. They used poetry, prose, and song to cry out against social and economic wrongs. Thus, they transformed their growing social and political interest into art.
Choice A is incorrect. The author distrusts the "foreign ideologies" (line 29) with their commitment to international solidarity.
Choice B is incorrect. The author states they wished to improve American culture.
Choices D and E are incorrect. Neither is implied by the author.

(Inference)

30. **A.** Both the author's reference to historical interpretations of the Negro writer's role (lines 57–59) and the author's evident concern to distinguish Negro writers from those who "embraced" socialist and communist propaganda (lines 32–35) suggest he is a historian interested in presenting these writers as loyal Americans.
Choice B is incorrect. The author touches on literature only in relation to historical events.
Choices C, D, and E are incorrect. There is nothing to support any of these interpretations in the passage.

(Inference)

31. **C.** *Verbose* means overly wordy. The second clause of the sentence provides an example that brings the abstract term *verbose* to life.

(Examples)

32. **E.** The *depletion* or exhaustion of our energy sources would lead us to seek *alternative* sources.

Remember, in double-blank sentences, go through the answer choices, testing the *first* words in each choice and eliminating those that don't fit.
Note that you are looking for a word with negative associations. Therefore, you can eliminate any word with positive ones. Choices A, B, and D all have positive associations. Only Choice C or Choice E can be correct. Turning to the second words of these two choices, you can eliminate Choice C: it would make no sense to seek *inefficient* energy sources.

(Cause and Effect Signal)

33. **D.** *Assiduous* work, work performed industriously or diligently, should not lead employers to *complain*.
Note that the use of *because* in the opening clause signals that a cause and effect relationship is at work here.

(Cause and Effect Signal)

34. **A.** *Voracious* (craving or eating large quantities of food) animals *stalk* or pursue their prey.
Remember, in double-blank sentences, go through the answer choices, testing the *first* words in each choice and eliminating those that don't fit. Relentless wolves would not be described as *mendacious* (lying), *meandering* (rambling), or *pacific* (peaceful). You can immediately eliminate Choices B, C, and D.

35. **D.** Given treachery on the part of their allies, it is likely the natives would seek vengeance or *retribution*. It is also likely that they would feel *justified* in doing so.
Test the first words in each answer choice. Betrayed natives who have become bitter would be unlikely to seek *acquiescence* (agreement) or *magnanimity* (generosity of spirit; nobility of mind) or *exoneration* (vindication). You can immediately rule out Choices A, B, and E.

36. **E.** The *rooster* is the male of the species; the *hen*, the female. Likewise, the *gander* is the male of its species; the *goose*, the female.

(Gender)

37. **E.** In measuring liquids, *pint* immediately precedes *quart*; in measuring time, *second* immediately precedes *minute*.

(Sequence)

38. **D.** A *viola* is a kind of *instrument*; a *chisel* is a kind of *tool*.

(Member and Class)

39. D. Just as a *bough* branches off from a tree's *trunk*, an *arm* branches off from a person's *torso*.

(Part to Whole)

40. A. A *cobbler* repairs *shoes*, and a *mechanic* repairs *automobiles*.
Remember, if more than one answer appears to fit the relationship in your sentence, look for a narrower approach. "A cobbler works with shoes" is too broad a framework; it could fit Choices B, C, D, and E. You need to find a more specific relationship between the original pair.

(Function)

41. B. *Felicity* (happiness; bliss) and *sorrow* are antonyms; *agility* (nimbleness) and *clumsiness* are antonyms.

(Antonyms)

42. B. The symbol of *time* is a bearded gentleman carrying a *scythe*; the symbol of *justice* is a blindfolded lady carrying a *scale*.

(Symbol and the Abstraction It Represents)

43. A. *Propitiate* (conciliate; soothe) and *appease* are synonyms; likewise, *disturb* and *agitate* are synonyms. Use the process of elimination to improve your guessing odds. The word pairs in Choices B, D, and E are all antonyms. Since they all belong to the same analogy type, none of the three can be the correct answer. Eliminate all three.

(Synonyms)

44. A. *Assurance* will allay (calm or quiet) *fear*; an *opiate* will allay *pain*.

(Function)

45. C. *Ostracism* (banishment from society) signifies *censure* (expression of disapproval). *Applause* signifies *approval*.

(Action and Its Significance)

Section 5

1. A. $$\frac{36}{a} = 4$$
$$4a = 36$$
$$a = 9$$
$$a - 9 = 0$$

2. E. $$\frac{1}{x} + \frac{1}{x} = \frac{1}{6}$$
Multiply by $6x$: $6 + 6 = x$
$$12 = x$$

3. B. $(a + b)(a + b) = a^2 + 2ab + b^2$
Substitute: $a^2 + b^2 = 13$
and $2ab = 12$
Therefore sum = 25

4. E. Let x be the number.
$$\left(\frac{x}{4}\right)^2 = \frac{x^2}{16} = x$$
$$x^2 = 16x$$
$$x = 16$$

5. A. $\frac{1}{3}$ of $\frac{3}{4} = \frac{3}{12}$ or $\frac{1}{4}$ or $\frac{4}{16}$.
$\frac{1}{4}$ of $\frac{3}{4} = \frac{3}{16}$.
$\frac{4}{16}$ is $\frac{1}{16}$ more than $\frac{3}{16}$.

6. E. Reduce the fractions:
$\frac{6}{14} = \frac{3}{7}$ $\frac{9}{21} = \frac{3}{7}$; $\frac{3}{7} (\ ) \frac{3}{7} = \frac{3}{7}$
The answer is obviously $=$.

7. C. Area of triangle $XOY =$
$\frac{1}{2} bh$ or $\frac{1}{2}(XO)(YO)$
Since $YO = XO = r$
$$32 = \frac{1}{2}r^2$$
$$r^2 = 64$$
Area of circle $= \pi r^2 = 64\pi$
(Note that we do not find the value of r, only to square it again.)

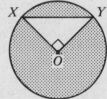

8. D. $\dfrac{n + 7}{3} + \dfrac{n - 3}{4}$
$\dfrac{4n + 28 + 3n - 9}{12}$
$\dfrac{7n + 19}{12}$
The numerators are the same, but the fraction in Column B has a smaller denominator. If $7n + 19$ has a positive value, Column B would be the larger; however, if $7n + 19$ has a negative value, Column A would be the larger.

9. A. It is not really necessary to calculate R. Observe that Column B has four factors of 3. If Column A had four factors of 5, it would be larger than Column B, instead of equal to it. Therefore $R < 5$

10. A. Since $a > c$ and $b < d$, the fraction in Column A has a larger numerator and a smaller denominator than the fraction in Column B.

11. **A.** Since both columns have 682 in common, consider only 9×7 in Column A and 10×6 in Column B.
$63 > 60$

12. **B.** The value of r is between -1 and -10. For any of these values r^7 will be negative. For example, if $r = -2$, then
$$\frac{1}{r^7} = \frac{1}{-128} \text{ or } -\frac{1}{128}$$
For any of these values for r, r^6 will have a positive value. For example, if $r = -2$, then
$$\frac{1}{r^6} = \frac{1}{64}.$$
$$\frac{1}{64} > -\frac{1}{128}$$

13. **D.** $\dfrac{c^2 d^2 e^2}{c^3 d^3 e^3}$ or $\dfrac{1}{cde}$ may be larger than, smaller than, or equal to $\dfrac{cde}{3}$, depending upon the values of c, d, and e.

14. **D.** Since $n^2 > 0$, n may have a negative value, and then $n < 0$. Also, since $n^2 > 0$, n may have a positive value, in which case $n > 0$.

15. **C.** $x^2 = xy$
Divide by x:
$x = y$.

16. **A.** $\dfrac{1}{2} + \dfrac{1}{3} = \dfrac{5}{6} = \dfrac{25}{30}$ $\dfrac{2}{5} = \dfrac{12}{30}$

17. **C.** $0.4\% = \dfrac{0.4}{100} = \dfrac{4}{1000}$

18. **B.** $\dfrac{1}{2}\% = 0.5\% = 0.005$
$0.005 > 0.0005$

19. **A.** The length of the fence (144 ft.) $\div$ the distance between the posts (12 ft.) equals 12 spaces between posts. However, the first space has 1 post at the beginning, and there is a post at the end of each of the 12 spaces. Thus there are 13 posts.

20. **A.** There are 19 houses on the west side. From #1 to #37 inclusive, there are 19 odd numbers.

21. **C.** The measure of an exterior angle of a triangle equals the sum of the measures of both remote interior angles. Therefore $x = a + b$ and $x = c + d$. By addition, $2x = a + b + c + d$.

22. **D.** Since y is common to both columns, consider x and z. No information is given about their relationship.

23. **C.** Since vertical angles 1 and 2 are equal, right triangle ABE is similar to right triangle DEC, and $\dfrac{AB}{DC} = \dfrac{AE}{EC}$.
In ABE, hypotenuse $BE = 5$, and $AB = 4$; then leg $AE = 3$.
In DEC, if $AB = 4$, and $DC = 12$, and since $AE = 3$, then $EC = 9$, because $\dfrac{4}{12} = \dfrac{3}{EC}$,
$4EC = 36$, $EC = 9$.
$AC = AE + EC = 3 + 9 = 12$.

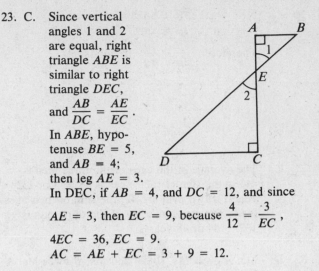

24. **C.** Circumference $= 2\pi r$. If radius of $A = \dfrac{1}{2}$ radius of B, then circumference of $A = \dfrac{1}{2}$ circumference of B. This may be stated as follows: twice the circumference of A equals the circumference of B.

25. **D.** For Bob and Cleon the numbers of times at bat are not given. The batting average depends upon the number of hits as compared with the total times at bat.

26. **C.** Let g = the value of each gold coin, and let s = the value of each silver coin. Then
$3g + 1s = 5s + 2g$ (given)
$1g = 4s$

27. **C.** 2 yd. = 72 in.
$\dfrac{2}{3}$ yd. = 24 in.
$2\dfrac{2}{3}$ yd. = 96 in. $\dfrac{288}{3}$ in. = 96 in.

28. **B.** If the amount of work to be done is doubled, and the time for the work is doubled, the job may be done by the same number of workers. Thus, if $2p$ painters paint $2h$ houses in $2w$ weeks, $2p$ painters can paint $4h$ houses (work doubled) in $4w$ weeks (time doubled).

29. **E.** Since the triangles are isosceles, $AO = OB$ and $BC = PC$. Since the areas are equal, $PC = AO$ and $OB = BC$.

30. C.
$$7p = 5q$$
$$3p = xq$$
Therefore: $\dfrac{7p}{3p} = \dfrac{5q}{xq}$ (by division)
$$\frac{7}{3} = \frac{5}{x}$$
$$7x = 15$$
$$x = 2\frac{1}{7}$$

31. C.   The average of the ages of the three men is 44, so the sum of their ages is 44×3 or 132 years. If two men are 42, the sum of their ages is 84. The maximum age of the third man is $132 - 84$ or 48 years.

32. D.   Ms. *A* owes Ms. *B* \$70 and Ms. *B* owes Ms. *A* \$60, so Ms. *A* owes Ms. *B* \$10. If Ms. *A* gives Ms. *B* \$50 (\$40 more than she owes Ms. *B*), Ms. *B* must give Ms. *A* \$40 in change.

33. A.   Substitute a number for the letter. Let $h = 7$. If the tank fills in $7(h = 7)$ hr., $\dfrac{2}{7}$ of it fills in 2 hr. Substituting h for 7, you find that $\dfrac{2}{h}$ of the tank fills in 2 hr.

34. B.   Area of triangle
$$= \frac{1}{2} \text{ Base} \times \text{Altitude}$$
$$= \frac{1}{2}\left(\frac{4}{5}c\right)(c)$$
$$= \frac{2c^2}{5}$$

35. C.   Average rate $= \dfrac{\text{(Total) distance}}{\text{(Total) time}}$. The total distance up and down the stream $= 20$ miles, and the time $= 5$ plus 2 or 7 hr. The average rate $= \dfrac{20}{7}$ or $2\dfrac{6}{7}$ m.p.h.

Section 6

1. D. $12 = 1\frac{1}{3}(x)$
$$12 = \frac{4}{3}x$$
$$36 = 4x$$
$$9 = x$$

2. C. $\dfrac{\text{quantity of pie}}{\text{number of people served}} = \dfrac{1}{7} = \dfrac{x}{91}$
$$7x = 91$$
$$x = 13$$

3. B. $\dfrac{1}{5} = 0.20$; $\dfrac{2}{5} = 0.40$; $\dfrac{3}{5} = 0.60$; $\dfrac{16}{25} = 0.64$;
$\dfrac{13}{25} = 0.52$; $\dfrac{2}{5}$ is next smaller than $\dfrac{1}{2}$ or 0.50.

4. A. $\dfrac{a + b}{a - b} \div \dfrac{b + a}{b - a}$
$$\frac{a + b}{a - b} \cdot \frac{b - a}{b + a}$$
$$\frac{1}{a - b} \cdot \frac{-a + b}{1}$$
$$\frac{1}{a - b} \cdot -\frac{a - b}{1}$$
$$\frac{1}{a - b} \cdot -\frac{a - b}{1} \text{ or } -1$$

5. B. $30¢ \div 12 = 2\frac{1}{2}¢$ each when purchased by the dozen. $5¢ - 2\frac{1}{2} = 2\frac{1}{2}¢$ saving per stick.

6. C. $\dfrac{1}{0.4} = \dfrac{10}{4} = 2\dfrac{1}{2}$ or 250%
$$\frac{5}{8} = 62\frac{1}{2}\%$$
$$(0.2)^2 = 0.04 = 4\%$$
$$\frac{9}{100} = 9\%$$
$\sqrt{1.44} = 1.2 = 120\%$
4% or $(0.2)^2$ is smallest.

7. B. k is the y-coordinate of point C. Point C is the same distance above the x-axis, as is point D. The y-coordinate of point D is 5. Therefore the y-coordinate of point C is 5. Thus $k = 5$.

8. B. $3x - y = 2x + y$
$x - y = y$ (subtract $2x$)
$x = 2y$ (add y)

9. D.   Since the hundredths unit (9) is more than 5, the tenths unit is raised from 9 to 10 so that the digits 69 become 70, and the number 69.999 becomes 70.0 to the nearest tenth.

10. **D.** Since $1000 + 1 = 1001$ and the fraction $\frac{1}{1000}$ written as a decimal is 0.001, the correct answer is 1001.001.

11. **A.** $2(\pi)(\text{radius}) = \text{circumference}$
$2(\pi)(\text{radius}) = 2\pi^2$ (given)
$\quad\quad\text{radius} = \pi$ (divide by 2π)

12. **C.** Let $x = $ smallest integer.
Then $x + 1 = $ next consecutive
$\quad\quad\quad\quad\quad$ positive integer,
and $x + 2 = $ next consecutive
$\quad\quad\quad\quad\quad$ positive integer.
$3x + 3 = $ sum of the three integers
$3x + 3 = a$ (given)
$\quad 3x = a - 3 \quad$ and $\quad x = \dfrac{a - 3}{3}$.

13. **C.** First car uses 1 gallon for 15 miles.
Therefore, it uses 4 gallons for 60 miles.
Since the second car can travel m miles on 1 gallon, it can travel $4m$ miles on 4 gallons.

14. **A.** When purchased in box of 12, cost per tablet
$= \dfrac{21\cent}{12}$ or $1\frac{3}{4}\cent$.
When purchased in bottle of 100, cost per tablet $= \dfrac{\$1.50}{100}$ or $1\frac{1}{2}\cent$
Saving per tablet by purchasing in bottle $=$
$1\frac{3}{4}\cent - 1\frac{1}{2}\cent$ or $\frac{1}{4}\cent$
Therefore saving per dozen $= 12\left(\frac{1}{4}\cent\right)$ or $3\cent$.

15. **A.** If a man does $\frac{1}{8}$ of his work in 1 day, in x days he will do x times as much or $\dfrac{x}{8}$.

16. **A.** Perimeter of rectangle
$= 2(\text{Length}) + 2(\text{Width})$
Let $x = $ width.
Perimeter of rectangle $= 2(3u + 2v) + 2x$
Perimeter of rectangle $= 6u + 4v + 2x$
$10u + 6v = 6u + 4v + 2x$
$\quad 4u + 2v = 2x$
$\quad\quad\quad x = 2u + v$

17. **C.** Eliminate i, to find E in terms of W and r.
$r = \dfrac{E}{i}$
$ir = E$
$i = \dfrac{E}{r}$
$W = i^2 r$
$W = \dfrac{E}{r} \cdot \dfrac{E}{r} \cdot r$ (by substitution)
$W = \dfrac{E^2}{r}$
$Wr = E^2$
$E = \sqrt{Wr}$

18. **D.** If two points have one coordinate the same, the distance between them is the difference between the two other coordinates.
(A) $0 - (-5) = 5$ (B) $5 - 0 = 5$
(C) $8 - 3 = 5$ (D) $3 - (-8) \neq 5$
(E) $3 - (-2) = 5$

19. **D.** Radius $AO = 6.5$
Diameter $AB = 13$
Angle C is a right angle (an angle inscribed in a semicircle is a right angle).
Triangle ABC is a right triangle.
$\quad (13)^2 = (5)^2 + (CB)^2$
$\quad 169 = 25 + (CB)^2$
$(CB)^2 = 144$
$\quad CB = 12$
Or recognize that ABC is a 5-12-13 right triangle and therefore $CB = 12$.
Area of triangle $ABC = \dfrac{1}{2}(AC)(CB)$
Area of triangle $ABC = \dfrac{1}{2}(5)(12)$ or 30

20. **A.** $\quad (20)(6) = 120$ (sum)
$36 + 44 = 80$
$120 - 80 = 40$
$\quad\quad 4u = 40$
$\quad\quad\ a = 10$

21. **B.** $\quad p = ab - 2cd$
$\quad 3p = 3ab - 6cd$
$-3p = -3ab + 6cd$
$\quad r = -3ab + 6cd$
$-3p = r$ (things equal to the same thing are equal to each other)
$\dfrac{-3p}{r} = 1$ (division by r)
$\dfrac{p}{r} = -\dfrac{1}{3}$ (division by -3)
$ab - 2cd = q$ is irrelevant.

22. **A.** Area of original rectangle $= lw$
Length of new rectangle
$= l + \dfrac{1}{2}l$
Let $x = $ decrease in width.
Width of new rectangle
$= w - x$
Area of new rectangle
$= \left(l + \dfrac{1}{2}l\right)(w - x) = lw$
$\left(\dfrac{3}{2}l\right)(w - x) = lw$
$\dfrac{3lw}{2} - \dfrac{3lx}{2} = lw$
$3lw - 3lx = 2lw$
$\quad\quad -3lx = 2lw - 3lw$
$\quad\quad -3lx = \quad\ -lw$
$\quad\quad -3x = \quad\ -\dfrac{lw}{l}$
$\quad\quad\ 3x = w$
$\quad\quad\quad\ x = \dfrac{1}{3}w \quad$ or $\quad 33\frac{1}{3}\% w$

23. D. $\frac{1}{2}$ of $\frac{1}{3}$, or $\frac{1}{6}$, of the workers are married women.

$\frac{1}{3}$ of $\frac{1}{6}$, or $\frac{1}{18}$, of the workers are married women who have children.

Since $\frac{1}{3}$ of the workers are women, $\frac{2}{3}$ of the workers are men.

$\frac{3}{4}$ of $\frac{2}{3}$, or $\frac{1}{2}$, of the workers are married men.

$\frac{2}{3}$ of $\frac{1}{2}$, or $\frac{1}{3}$, of the workers are married men who have children.

$\frac{1}{18} + \frac{1}{3}$, or $\frac{7}{18}$, of the workers have children.

Therefore $\frac{11}{18}$ of the workers do not have children.

24. D.   Let x = distance (one way) traveled by yacht.

$$\frac{\text{Distance}}{\text{Rate}} = \text{Time}$$

$$\frac{x}{d} = \text{time downstream}$$

$$\frac{x}{u} = \text{time upstream}$$

$$\frac{x}{d} + \frac{x}{u} \;\; \text{or} \;\; \frac{ux + dx}{du} = \text{total time}$$

$2x$ = total distance

$$\frac{\text{Total distance}}{\text{Total time}} = \text{Average rate for round trip}$$

$$\frac{2x}{\frac{ux + dx}{du}} = \text{average rate for round trip}$$

$$= 2x \div \frac{ux + dx}{du}$$

$$= 2x \cdot \frac{du}{ux + dx}$$

$$= 2x \cdot \frac{du}{x(u + d)}$$

$$= \frac{2du}{u + d}$$

25. B.   Volume of water in can
$$= (\text{Area of base})(\text{height})$$
Volume of water in can
$$= (\pi)(\text{Radius})^2(\text{Height})$$
Volume of water in can
$$= \left(\frac{22}{7}\right)(4)(14) \text{ or } 176 \text{ cu. in.}$$

To find the time for 176 cu. in. we have a direct proportion.

Let x = number of minutes required for 176 cu. in.

$$\frac{\text{cubic inches}}{\text{minutes}} = \frac{8}{10} = \frac{176}{x}$$

$$8x = 1760$$

$$x = 220 \text{ min.}$$

Since 220 min. = 3 hr. and 40 min., the water which began to flow at 10 A.M. will begin to overflow at 1:40 P.M.

Answer Sheet–Test 3

Start with number 1 for each new section. If a section has fewer than 50 questions, leave the extra spaces blank.

Section 1

1. Ⓐ Ⓑ Ⓒ Ⓓ Ⓔ
2. Ⓐ Ⓑ Ⓒ Ⓓ Ⓔ
3. Ⓐ Ⓑ Ⓒ Ⓓ Ⓔ
4. Ⓐ Ⓑ Ⓒ Ⓓ Ⓔ
5. Ⓐ Ⓑ Ⓒ Ⓓ Ⓔ
6. Ⓐ Ⓑ Ⓒ Ⓓ Ⓔ
7. Ⓐ Ⓑ Ⓒ Ⓓ Ⓔ
8. Ⓐ Ⓑ Ⓒ Ⓓ Ⓔ
9. Ⓐ Ⓑ Ⓒ Ⓓ Ⓔ
10. Ⓐ Ⓑ Ⓒ Ⓓ Ⓔ

11. Ⓐ Ⓑ Ⓒ Ⓓ Ⓔ
12. Ⓐ Ⓑ Ⓒ Ⓓ Ⓔ
13. Ⓐ Ⓑ Ⓒ Ⓓ Ⓔ
14. Ⓐ Ⓑ Ⓒ Ⓓ Ⓔ
15. Ⓐ Ⓑ Ⓒ Ⓓ Ⓔ
16. Ⓐ Ⓑ Ⓒ Ⓓ Ⓔ
17. Ⓐ Ⓑ Ⓒ Ⓓ Ⓔ
18. Ⓐ Ⓑ Ⓒ Ⓓ Ⓔ
19. Ⓐ Ⓑ Ⓒ Ⓓ Ⓔ
20. Ⓐ Ⓑ Ⓒ Ⓓ Ⓔ

21. Ⓐ Ⓑ Ⓒ Ⓓ Ⓔ
22. Ⓐ Ⓑ Ⓒ Ⓓ Ⓔ
23. Ⓐ Ⓑ Ⓒ Ⓓ Ⓔ
24. Ⓐ Ⓑ Ⓒ Ⓓ Ⓔ
25. Ⓐ Ⓑ Ⓒ Ⓓ Ⓔ
26. Ⓐ Ⓑ Ⓒ Ⓓ Ⓔ
27. Ⓐ Ⓑ Ⓒ Ⓓ Ⓔ
28. Ⓐ Ⓑ Ⓒ Ⓓ Ⓔ
29. Ⓐ Ⓑ Ⓒ Ⓓ Ⓔ
30. Ⓐ Ⓑ Ⓒ Ⓓ Ⓔ

31. Ⓐ Ⓑ Ⓒ Ⓓ Ⓔ
32. Ⓐ Ⓑ Ⓒ Ⓓ Ⓔ
33. Ⓐ Ⓑ Ⓒ Ⓓ Ⓔ
34. Ⓐ Ⓑ Ⓒ Ⓓ Ⓔ
35. Ⓐ Ⓑ Ⓒ Ⓓ Ⓔ
36. Ⓐ Ⓑ Ⓒ Ⓓ Ⓔ
37. Ⓐ Ⓑ Ⓒ Ⓓ Ⓔ
38. Ⓐ Ⓑ Ⓒ Ⓓ Ⓔ
39. Ⓐ Ⓑ Ⓒ Ⓓ Ⓔ
40. Ⓐ Ⓑ Ⓒ Ⓓ Ⓔ

41. Ⓐ Ⓑ Ⓒ Ⓓ Ⓔ
42. Ⓐ Ⓑ Ⓒ Ⓓ Ⓔ
43. Ⓐ Ⓑ Ⓒ Ⓓ Ⓔ
44. Ⓐ Ⓑ Ⓒ Ⓓ Ⓔ
45. Ⓐ Ⓑ Ⓒ Ⓓ Ⓔ
46. Ⓐ Ⓑ Ⓒ Ⓓ Ⓔ
47. Ⓐ Ⓑ Ⓒ Ⓓ Ⓔ
48. Ⓐ Ⓑ Ⓒ Ⓓ Ⓔ
49. Ⓐ Ⓑ Ⓒ Ⓓ Ⓔ
50. Ⓐ Ⓑ Ⓒ Ⓓ Ⓔ

Section 2

1. Ⓐ Ⓑ Ⓒ Ⓓ Ⓔ
2. Ⓐ Ⓑ Ⓒ Ⓓ Ⓔ
3. Ⓐ Ⓑ Ⓒ Ⓓ Ⓔ
4. Ⓐ Ⓑ Ⓒ Ⓓ Ⓔ
5. Ⓐ Ⓑ Ⓒ Ⓓ Ⓔ
6. Ⓐ Ⓑ Ⓒ Ⓓ Ⓔ
7. Ⓐ Ⓑ Ⓒ Ⓓ Ⓔ
8. Ⓐ Ⓑ Ⓒ Ⓓ Ⓔ
9. Ⓐ Ⓑ Ⓒ Ⓓ Ⓔ
10. Ⓐ Ⓑ Ⓒ Ⓓ Ⓔ

11. Ⓐ Ⓑ Ⓒ Ⓓ Ⓔ
12. Ⓐ Ⓑ Ⓒ Ⓓ Ⓔ
13. Ⓐ Ⓑ Ⓒ Ⓓ Ⓔ
14. Ⓐ Ⓑ Ⓒ Ⓓ Ⓔ
15. Ⓐ Ⓑ Ⓒ Ⓓ Ⓔ
16. Ⓐ Ⓑ Ⓒ Ⓓ Ⓔ
17. Ⓐ Ⓑ Ⓒ Ⓓ Ⓔ
18. Ⓐ Ⓑ Ⓒ Ⓓ Ⓔ
19. Ⓐ Ⓑ Ⓒ Ⓓ Ⓔ
20. Ⓐ Ⓑ Ⓒ Ⓓ Ⓔ

21. Ⓐ Ⓑ Ⓒ Ⓓ Ⓔ
22. Ⓐ Ⓑ Ⓒ Ⓓ Ⓕ
23. Ⓐ Ⓑ Ⓒ Ⓓ Ⓔ
24. Ⓐ Ⓑ Ⓒ Ⓓ Ⓕ
25. Ⓐ Ⓑ Ⓒ Ⓓ Ⓔ
26. Ⓐ Ⓑ Ⓒ Ⓓ Ⓔ
27. Ⓐ Ⓑ Ⓒ Ⓓ Ⓔ
28. Ⓐ Ⓑ Ⓒ Ⓓ Ⓔ
29. Ⓐ Ⓑ Ⓒ Ⓓ Ⓔ
30. Ⓐ Ⓑ Ⓒ Ⓓ Ⓔ

31. Ⓐ Ⓑ Ⓒ Ⓓ Ⓔ
32. Ⓐ Ⓑ Ⓒ Ⓓ Ⓔ
33. Ⓐ Ⓑ Ⓒ Ⓓ Ⓔ
34. Ⓐ Ⓑ Ⓒ Ⓓ Ⓔ
35. Ⓐ Ⓑ Ⓒ Ⓓ Ⓔ
36. Ⓐ Ⓑ Ⓒ Ⓓ Ⓔ
37. Ⓐ Ⓑ Ⓒ Ⓓ Ⓔ
38. Ⓐ Ⓑ Ⓒ Ⓓ Ⓔ
39. Ⓐ Ⓑ Ⓒ Ⓓ Ⓔ
40. Ⓐ Ⓑ Ⓒ Ⓓ Ⓔ

41. Ⓐ Ⓑ Ⓒ Ⓓ Ⓔ
42. Ⓐ Ⓑ Ⓒ Ⓓ Ⓔ
43. Ⓐ Ⓑ Ⓒ Ⓓ Ⓔ
44. Ⓐ Ⓑ Ⓒ Ⓓ Ⓔ
45. Ⓐ Ⓑ Ⓒ Ⓓ Ⓔ
46. Ⓐ Ⓑ Ⓒ Ⓓ Ⓔ
47. Ⓐ Ⓑ Ⓒ Ⓓ Ⓔ
48. Ⓐ Ⓑ Ⓒ Ⓓ Ⓔ
49. Ⓐ Ⓑ Ⓒ Ⓓ Ⓔ
50. Ⓐ Ⓑ Ⓒ Ⓓ Ⓔ

Section 3

1. Ⓐ Ⓑ Ⓒ Ⓓ Ⓔ
2. Ⓐ Ⓑ Ⓒ Ⓓ Ⓔ
3. Ⓐ Ⓑ Ⓒ Ⓓ Ⓔ
4. Ⓐ Ⓑ Ⓒ Ⓓ Ⓔ
5. Ⓐ Ⓑ Ⓒ Ⓓ Ⓔ
6. Ⓐ Ⓑ Ⓒ Ⓓ Ⓔ
7. Ⓐ Ⓑ Ⓒ Ⓓ Ⓔ
8. Ⓐ Ⓑ Ⓒ Ⓓ Ⓔ
9. Ⓐ Ⓑ Ⓒ Ⓓ Ⓔ
10. Ⓐ Ⓑ Ⓒ Ⓓ Ⓔ

11. Ⓐ Ⓑ Ⓒ Ⓓ Ⓔ
12. Ⓐ Ⓑ Ⓒ Ⓓ Ⓔ
13. Ⓐ Ⓑ Ⓒ Ⓓ Ⓔ
14. Ⓐ Ⓑ Ⓒ Ⓓ Ⓔ
15. Ⓐ Ⓑ Ⓒ Ⓓ Ⓔ
16. Ⓐ Ⓑ Ⓒ Ⓓ Ⓔ
17. Ⓐ Ⓑ Ⓒ Ⓓ Ⓔ
18. Ⓐ Ⓑ Ⓒ Ⓓ Ⓔ
19. Ⓐ Ⓑ Ⓒ Ⓓ Ⓔ
20. Ⓐ Ⓑ Ⓒ Ⓓ Ⓔ

21. Ⓐ Ⓑ Ⓒ Ⓓ Ⓔ
22. Ⓐ Ⓑ Ⓒ Ⓓ Ⓔ
23. Ⓐ Ⓑ Ⓒ Ⓓ Ⓔ
24. Ⓐ Ⓑ Ⓒ Ⓓ Ⓔ
25. Ⓐ Ⓑ Ⓒ Ⓓ Ⓔ
26. Ⓐ Ⓑ Ⓒ Ⓓ Ⓔ
27. Ⓐ Ⓑ Ⓒ Ⓓ Ⓔ
28. Ⓐ Ⓑ Ⓒ Ⓓ Ⓔ
29. Ⓐ Ⓑ Ⓒ Ⓓ Ⓔ
30. Ⓐ Ⓑ Ⓒ Ⓓ Ⓔ

31. Ⓐ Ⓑ Ⓒ Ⓓ Ⓔ
32. Ⓐ Ⓑ Ⓒ Ⓓ Ⓔ
33. Ⓐ Ⓑ Ⓒ Ⓓ Ⓔ
34. Ⓐ Ⓑ Ⓒ Ⓓ Ⓔ
35. Ⓐ Ⓑ Ⓒ Ⓓ Ⓔ
36. Ⓐ Ⓑ Ⓒ Ⓓ Ⓔ
37. Ⓐ Ⓑ Ⓒ Ⓓ Ⓔ
38. Ⓐ Ⓑ Ⓒ Ⓓ Ⓔ
39. Ⓐ Ⓑ Ⓒ Ⓓ Ⓔ
40. Ⓐ Ⓑ Ⓒ Ⓓ Ⓔ

41. Ⓐ Ⓑ Ⓒ Ⓓ Ⓔ
42. Ⓐ Ⓑ Ⓒ Ⓓ Ⓔ
43. Ⓐ Ⓑ Ⓒ Ⓓ Ⓔ
44. Ⓐ Ⓑ Ⓒ Ⓓ Ⓔ
45. Ⓐ Ⓑ Ⓒ Ⓓ Ⓔ
46. Ⓐ Ⓑ Ⓒ Ⓓ Ⓔ
47. Ⓐ Ⓑ Ⓒ Ⓓ Ⓔ
48. Ⓐ Ⓑ Ⓒ Ⓓ Ⓔ
49. Ⓐ Ⓑ Ⓒ Ⓓ Ⓔ
50. Ⓐ Ⓑ Ⓒ Ⓓ Ⓔ

Start with number 1 for each new section. If a section has fewer than 50 questions, leave the extra spaces blank.

Section 4

1. Ⓐ Ⓑ Ⓒ Ⓓ Ⓔ	11. Ⓐ Ⓑ Ⓒ Ⓓ Ⓔ	21. Ⓐ Ⓑ Ⓒ Ⓓ Ⓔ	31. Ⓐ Ⓑ Ⓒ Ⓓ Ⓔ	41. Ⓐ Ⓑ Ⓒ Ⓓ Ⓔ
2. Ⓐ Ⓑ Ⓒ Ⓓ Ⓔ	12. Ⓐ Ⓑ Ⓒ Ⓓ Ⓔ	22. Ⓐ Ⓑ Ⓒ Ⓓ Ⓔ	32. Ⓐ Ⓑ Ⓒ Ⓓ Ⓔ	42. Ⓐ Ⓑ Ⓒ Ⓓ Ⓔ
3. Ⓐ Ⓑ Ⓒ Ⓓ Ⓔ	13. Ⓐ Ⓑ Ⓒ Ⓓ Ⓔ	23. Ⓐ Ⓑ Ⓒ Ⓓ Ⓔ	33. Ⓐ Ⓑ Ⓒ Ⓓ Ⓔ	43. Ⓐ Ⓑ Ⓒ Ⓓ Ⓔ
4. Ⓐ Ⓑ Ⓒ Ⓓ Ⓔ	14. Ⓐ Ⓑ Ⓒ Ⓓ Ⓔ	24. Ⓐ Ⓑ Ⓒ Ⓓ Ⓔ	34. Ⓐ Ⓑ Ⓒ Ⓓ Ⓔ	44. Ⓐ Ⓑ Ⓒ Ⓓ Ⓔ
5. Ⓐ Ⓑ Ⓒ Ⓓ Ⓔ	15. Ⓐ Ⓑ Ⓒ Ⓓ Ⓔ	25. Ⓐ Ⓑ Ⓒ Ⓓ Ⓔ	35. Ⓐ Ⓑ Ⓒ Ⓓ Ⓔ	45. Ⓐ Ⓑ Ⓒ Ⓓ Ⓔ
6. Ⓐ Ⓑ Ⓒ Ⓓ Ⓔ	16. Ⓐ Ⓑ Ⓒ Ⓓ Ⓔ	26. Ⓐ Ⓑ Ⓒ Ⓓ Ⓔ	36. Ⓐ Ⓑ Ⓒ Ⓓ Ⓔ	46. Ⓐ Ⓑ Ⓒ Ⓓ Ⓔ
7. Ⓐ Ⓑ Ⓒ Ⓓ Ⓔ	17. Ⓐ Ⓑ Ⓒ Ⓓ Ⓔ	27. Ⓐ Ⓑ Ⓒ Ⓓ Ⓔ	37. Ⓐ Ⓑ Ⓒ Ⓓ Ⓔ	47. Ⓐ Ⓑ Ⓒ Ⓓ Ⓔ
8. Ⓐ Ⓑ Ⓒ Ⓓ Ⓔ	18. Ⓐ Ⓑ Ⓒ Ⓓ Ⓔ	28. Ⓐ Ⓑ Ⓒ Ⓓ Ⓔ	38. Ⓐ Ⓑ Ⓒ Ⓓ Ⓔ	48. Ⓐ Ⓑ Ⓒ Ⓓ Ⓔ
9. Ⓐ Ⓑ Ⓒ Ⓓ Ⓔ	19. Ⓐ Ⓑ Ⓒ Ⓓ Ⓔ	29. Ⓐ Ⓑ Ⓒ Ⓓ Ⓔ	39. Ⓐ Ⓑ Ⓒ Ⓓ Ⓔ	49. Ⓐ Ⓑ Ⓒ Ⓓ Ⓔ
10. Ⓐ Ⓑ Ⓒ Ⓓ Ⓔ	20. Ⓐ Ⓑ Ⓒ Ⓓ Ⓔ	30. Ⓐ Ⓑ Ⓒ Ⓓ Ⓔ	40. Ⓐ Ⓑ Ⓒ Ⓓ Ⓔ	50. Ⓐ Ⓑ Ⓒ Ⓓ Ⓔ

Section 5

1. Ⓐ Ⓑ Ⓒ Ⓓ Ⓔ	11. Ⓐ Ⓑ Ⓒ Ⓓ Ⓔ	21. Ⓐ Ⓑ Ⓒ Ⓓ Ⓔ	31. Ⓐ Ⓑ Ⓒ Ⓓ Ⓔ	41. Ⓐ Ⓑ Ⓒ Ⓓ Ⓔ
2. Ⓐ Ⓑ Ⓒ Ⓓ Ⓔ	12. Ⓐ Ⓑ Ⓒ Ⓓ Ⓔ	22. Ⓐ Ⓑ Ⓒ Ⓓ Ⓔ	32. Ⓐ Ⓑ Ⓒ Ⓓ Ⓔ	42. Ⓐ Ⓑ Ⓒ Ⓓ Ⓔ
3. Ⓐ Ⓑ Ⓒ Ⓓ Ⓔ	13. Ⓐ Ⓑ Ⓒ Ⓓ Ⓔ	23. Ⓐ Ⓑ Ⓒ Ⓓ Ⓔ	33. Ⓐ Ⓑ Ⓒ Ⓓ Ⓔ	43. Ⓐ Ⓑ Ⓒ Ⓓ Ⓔ
4. Ⓐ Ⓑ Ⓒ Ⓓ Ⓔ	14. Ⓐ Ⓑ Ⓒ Ⓓ Ⓔ	24. Ⓐ Ⓑ Ⓒ Ⓓ Ⓔ	34. Ⓐ Ⓑ Ⓒ Ⓓ Ⓔ	44. Ⓐ Ⓑ Ⓒ Ⓓ Ⓔ
5. Ⓐ Ⓑ Ⓒ Ⓓ Ⓔ	15. Ⓐ Ⓑ Ⓒ Ⓓ Ⓔ	25. Ⓐ Ⓑ Ⓒ Ⓓ Ⓔ	35. Ⓐ Ⓑ Ⓒ Ⓓ Ⓔ	45. Ⓐ Ⓑ Ⓒ Ⓓ Ⓔ
6. Ⓐ Ⓑ Ⓒ Ⓓ Ⓔ	16. Ⓐ Ⓑ Ⓒ Ⓓ Ⓔ	26. Ⓐ Ⓑ Ⓒ Ⓓ Ⓔ	36. Ⓐ Ⓑ Ⓒ Ⓓ Ⓔ	46. Ⓐ Ⓑ Ⓒ Ⓓ Ⓔ
7. Ⓐ Ⓑ Ⓒ Ⓓ Ⓔ	17. Ⓐ Ⓑ Ⓒ Ⓓ Ⓔ	27. Ⓐ Ⓑ Ⓒ Ⓓ Ⓔ	37. Ⓐ Ⓑ Ⓒ Ⓓ Ⓔ	47. Ⓐ Ⓑ Ⓒ Ⓓ Ⓔ
8. Ⓐ Ⓑ Ⓒ Ⓓ Ⓔ	18. Ⓐ Ⓑ Ⓒ Ⓓ Ⓔ	28. Ⓐ Ⓑ Ⓒ Ⓓ Ⓔ	38. Ⓐ Ⓑ Ⓒ Ⓓ Ⓔ	48. Ⓐ Ⓑ Ⓒ Ⓓ Ⓔ
9. Ⓐ Ⓑ Ⓒ Ⓓ Ⓔ	19. Ⓐ Ⓑ Ⓒ Ⓓ Ⓔ	29. Ⓐ Ⓑ Ⓒ Ⓓ Ⓔ	39. Ⓐ Ⓑ Ⓒ Ⓓ Ⓔ	49. Ⓐ Ⓑ Ⓒ Ⓓ Ⓔ
10. Ⓐ Ⓑ Ⓒ Ⓓ Ⓔ	20. Ⓐ Ⓑ Ⓒ Ⓓ Ⓔ	30. Ⓐ Ⓑ Ⓒ Ⓓ Ⓔ	40. Ⓐ Ⓑ Ⓒ Ⓓ Ⓔ	50. Ⓐ Ⓑ Ⓒ Ⓓ Ⓔ

Section 6

1. Ⓐ Ⓑ Ⓒ Ⓓ Ⓔ	11. Ⓐ Ⓑ Ⓒ Ⓓ Ⓔ	21. Ⓐ Ⓑ Ⓒ Ⓓ Ⓔ	31. Ⓐ Ⓑ Ⓒ Ⓓ Ⓔ	41. Ⓐ Ⓑ Ⓒ Ⓓ Ⓔ
2. Ⓐ Ⓑ Ⓒ Ⓓ Ⓔ	12. Ⓐ Ⓑ Ⓒ Ⓓ Ⓔ	22. Ⓐ Ⓑ Ⓒ Ⓓ Ⓔ	32. Ⓐ Ⓑ Ⓒ Ⓓ Ⓔ	42. Ⓐ Ⓑ Ⓒ Ⓓ Ⓔ
3. Ⓐ Ⓑ Ⓒ Ⓓ Ⓔ	13. Ⓐ Ⓑ Ⓒ Ⓓ Ⓔ	23. Ⓐ Ⓑ Ⓒ Ⓓ Ⓔ	33. Ⓐ Ⓑ Ⓒ Ⓓ Ⓔ	43. Ⓐ Ⓑ Ⓒ Ⓓ Ⓔ
4. Ⓐ Ⓑ Ⓒ Ⓓ Ⓔ	14. Ⓐ Ⓑ Ⓒ Ⓓ Ⓔ	24. Ⓐ Ⓑ Ⓒ Ⓓ Ⓔ	34. Ⓐ Ⓑ Ⓒ Ⓓ Ⓔ	44. Ⓐ Ⓑ Ⓒ Ⓓ Ⓔ
5. Ⓐ Ⓑ Ⓒ Ⓓ Ⓔ	15. Ⓐ Ⓑ Ⓒ Ⓓ Ⓔ	25. Ⓐ Ⓑ Ⓒ Ⓓ Ⓔ	35. Ⓐ Ⓑ Ⓒ Ⓓ Ⓔ	45. Ⓐ Ⓑ Ⓒ Ⓓ Ⓔ
6. Ⓐ Ⓑ Ⓒ Ⓓ Ⓔ	16. Ⓐ Ⓑ Ⓒ Ⓓ Ⓔ	26. Ⓐ Ⓑ Ⓒ Ⓓ Ⓔ	36. Ⓐ Ⓑ Ⓒ Ⓓ Ⓔ	46. Ⓐ Ⓑ Ⓒ Ⓓ Ⓔ
7. Ⓐ Ⓑ Ⓒ Ⓓ Ⓔ	17. Ⓐ Ⓑ Ⓒ Ⓓ Ⓔ	27. Ⓐ Ⓑ Ⓒ Ⓓ Ⓔ	37. Ⓐ Ⓑ Ⓒ Ⓓ Ⓔ	47. Ⓐ Ⓑ Ⓒ Ⓓ Ⓔ
8. Ⓐ Ⓑ Ⓒ Ⓓ Ⓔ	18. Ⓐ Ⓑ Ⓒ Ⓓ Ⓔ	28. Ⓐ Ⓑ Ⓒ Ⓓ Ⓔ	38. Ⓐ Ⓑ Ⓒ Ⓓ Ⓔ	48. Ⓐ Ⓑ Ⓒ Ⓓ Ⓔ
9. Ⓐ Ⓑ Ⓒ Ⓓ Ⓔ	19. Ⓐ Ⓑ Ⓒ Ⓓ Ⓔ	29. Ⓐ Ⓑ Ⓒ Ⓓ Ⓔ	39. Ⓐ Ⓑ Ⓒ Ⓓ Ⓔ	49. Ⓐ Ⓑ Ⓒ Ⓓ Ⓔ
10. Ⓐ Ⓑ Ⓒ Ⓓ Ⓔ	20. Ⓐ Ⓑ Ⓒ Ⓓ Ⓔ	30. Ⓐ Ⓑ Ⓒ Ⓓ Ⓔ	40. Ⓐ Ⓑ Ⓒ Ⓓ Ⓔ	50. Ⓐ Ⓑ Ⓒ Ⓓ Ⓔ

Remove answer sheet by cutting on dotted line

The following information is for your reference in solving some of the problems.

Circle of radius r: Area $= \pi r^2$; Circumference $= 2\pi r$
   The number of degrees of arc in a circle is 360.
The measure in degrees of a straight angle is 180.

Definitions of symbols:
$=$ is equal to $\leqq$ is less than or equal to
$\neq$ is unequal to $\geqq$ is greater than or equal to
$<$ is less than $\parallel$ is parallel to
$>$ is greater than $\perp$ is perpendicular to

Triangle: The sum of the measures in degrees of the angles of a triangle is 180.
If $\angle CDA$ is a right angle, then

(1) area of $\triangle ABC = \dfrac{AB \times CD}{2}$

(2) $AC^2 = AD^2 + DC^2$

Note: Figures that accompany problems in this test are intended to provide information useful in solving the problems. They are drawn as accurately as possible EXCEPT when it is stated in a specific problem that its figure is not drawn to scale. All figures lie in a plane unless otherwise indicated. All numbers used are real numbers.

---

1. If $9x - 5 = 3y$, then $\dfrac{9x - 5}{3} =$

   (A) $\dfrac{y}{3}$ (B) $\dfrac{3}{y}$ (C) y (D) $3y$ (E) $y + 3$

2. 9 percent of what number is 27?

   (A) 24 (B) 30 (C) 243 (D) 300 (E) 330

3. If $\dfrac{x}{64} = 0.875$, then $x =$

   (A) 48 (B) 54 (C) 56 (D) 58 (E) 62

4. What is the thickness, in inches, of a pipe that has an outer diameter of 2.5 inches and an inner diameter of 2.1 inches?

   (A) 0.2 (B) 0.4 (C) 0.8 (D) 3.2 (E) 4.6

5. Which of the following is divisible by 2 and 7?

   (A) 361 (B) 362 (C) 363 (D) 364 (E) 365

6. The pupils in a classroom can be seated in r rows, with s seats in each row, leaving two seats vacant. Express in terms of r and s the number of pupils in the classroom.

   (A) $2 - rs$ (B) $2r - s$ (C) $2s - r$
   (D) $rs + 2$ (E) $rs - 2$

7. If the total cost of a oranges is D dollars, what is the cost, in cents, of x oranges?

   (A) $\dfrac{100Dx}{a}$ (B) $\dfrac{100D}{ax}$ (C) $\dfrac{100D}{x}$ (D) $\dfrac{Dx}{100a}$

   (E) $\dfrac{Da}{100x}$

8. A fence 320 feet long has wooden posts each 40 feet apart. How many posts are there?

   (A) 7 (B) 8 (C) 9 (D) 10 (E) 11

9. If $x = -2$ and $\dfrac{1}{y} = -4$, what is the value of y in terms of x?

   (A) $x - 6$ (B) $2x$ (C) $\dfrac{x}{2}$ (D) $\dfrac{1}{2x}$ (E) $x + 6$

10. How many eighths are there in $37\dfrac{1}{2}$ percent?

   (A) 3 (B) 4 (C) 4.8 (D) 5 (E) 7

11. A bag of chicken feed will feed 18 chickens for 54 days. For how many days will it feed 12 chickens?

   (A) 36 (B) 37 (C) 53 (D) 72 (E) 81

GO ON TO THE NEXT PAGE

1 1 1 1 1 1 1 1 1 1 1

12. A picture in an art museum is 6 feet wide and 8 feet long. If its frame has a width of 6 inches, what is the ratio of the area of the frame to the area of the picture?

(A) $\frac{5}{16}$ (B) $\frac{5}{4}$ (C) $\frac{4}{5}$ (D) $\frac{5}{12}$ (E) $\frac{3\frac{1}{5}}{1}$

13. To indicate on a circle graph that $\frac{2}{5}$ of a graduating class is going to college, how many degrees should there be in the central angle of the portion drawn to represent this group?

(A) 36   (B) 40   (C) 72   (D) 80   (E) 144

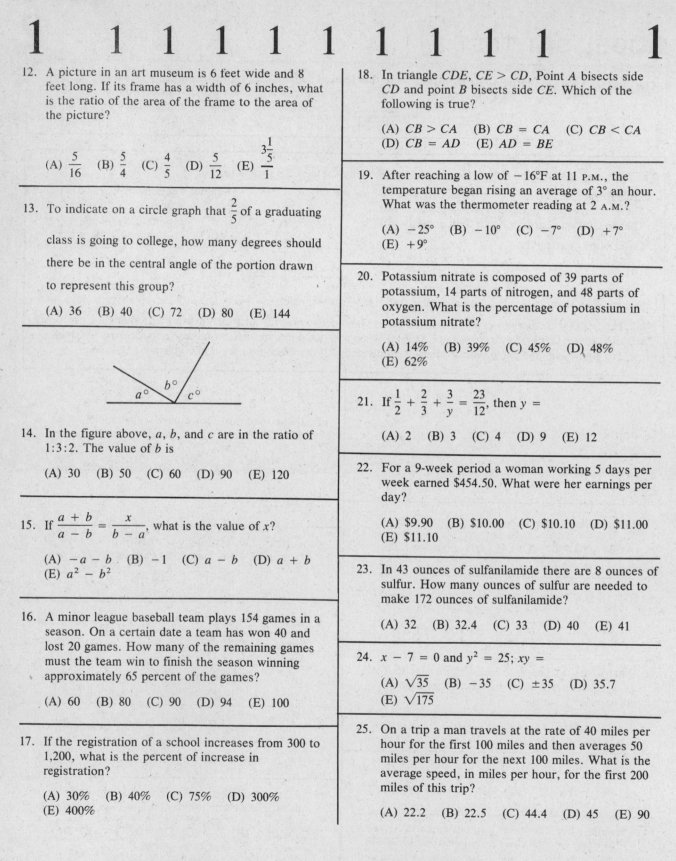

14. In the figure above, a, b, and c are in the ratio of $1:3:2$. The value of b is

(A) 30   (B) 50   (C) 60   (D) 90   (E) 120

15. If $\frac{a + b}{a - b} = \frac{x}{b - a}$, what is the value of x?

(A) $-a - b$ (B) -1 (C) $a - b$ (D) $a + b$
(E) $a^2 - b^2$

16. A minor league baseball team plays 154 games in a season. On a certain date a team has won 40 and lost 20 games. How many of the remaining games must the team win to finish the season winning approximately 65 percent of the games?

(A) 60   (B) 80   (C) 90   (D) 94   (E) 100

17. If the registration of a school increases from 300 to 1,200, what is the percent of increase in registration?

(A) 30%   (B) 40%   (C) 75%   (D) 300%
(E) 400%

18. In triangle CDE, $CE > CD$, Point A bisects side CD and point B bisects side CE. Which of the following is true?

(A) $CB > CA$ (B) $CB = CA$ (C) $CB < CA$
(D) $CB = AD$ (E) $AD = BE$

19. After reaching a low of $-16°F$ at 11 P.M., the temperature began rising an average of $3°$ an hour. What was the thermometer reading at 2 A.M.?

(A) $-25°$ (B) $-10°$ (C) $-7°$ (D) $+7°$
(E) $+9°$

20. Potassium nitrate is composed of 39 parts of potassium, 14 parts of nitrogen, and 48 parts of oxygen. What is the percentage of potassium in potassium nitrate?

(A) 14%   (B) 39%   (C) 45%   (D) 48%
(E) 62%

21. If $\frac{1}{2} + \frac{2}{3} + \frac{3}{y} = \frac{23}{12}$, then $y =$

(A) 2   (B) 3   (C) 4   (D) 9   (E) 12

22. For a 9-week period a woman working 5 days per week earned $454.50. What were her earnings per day?

(A) $9.90   (B) $10.00   (C) $10.10   (D) $11.00
(E) $11.10

23. In 43 ounces of sulfanilamide there are 8 ounces of sulfur. How many ounces of sulfur are needed to make 172 ounces of sulfanilamide?

(A) 32   (B) 32.4   (C) 33   (D) 40   (E) 41

24. $x - 7 = 0$ and $y^2 = 25$; $xy =$

(A) $\sqrt{35}$ (B) -35 (C) ± 35 (D) 35.7
(E) $\sqrt{175}$

25. On a trip a man travels at the rate of 40 miles per hour for the first 100 miles and then averages 50 miles per hour for the next 100 miles. What is the average speed, in miles per hour, for the first 200 miles of this trip?

(A) 22.2   (B) 22.5   (C) 44.4   (D) 45   (E) 90

IF YOU FINISH BEFORE TIME IS CALLED, YOU MAY CHECK YOUR WORK ON THIS SECTION ONLY. DO NOT WORK ON ANY OTHER SECTION IN THE TEST.   **STOP**

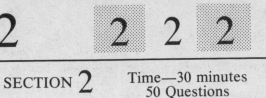

SECTION 2   Time—30 minutes   The questions in this section measure skills that are important to
              50 Questions   writing well. In particular, they test your ability to recognize and
                                     use language that is clear, effective, and correct according to the
                                     requirements of standard written English, the kind of English
                                     found in most college textbooks.

Directions: The following sentences contain problems in grammar, usage, diction (choice of words), and idiom.

Some sentences are correct.
No sentence contains more than one error.

You will find that the error, if there is one, is underlined and lettered. Assume that elements of the sentence that are not underlined are correct and cannot be changed. In choosing answers, follow the requirements of standard written English.

If there is an error, select the one underlined part that must be changed to make the sentence correct and blacken the corresponding space on your answer sheet.

If there is no error, blacken answer space Ⓔ.

EXAMPLE:

The region has a climate so severe that plants
                          A
growing there rarely had been more than twelve
      B   C
inches high. No error
       D   E

SAMPLE ANSWER
Ⓐ Ⓑ ● Ⓓ Ⓔ

1. After his heart attack, he was ordered to lay in bed
   A   B   C
   and rest for two weeks. No error
            D   E

2. While my aunt and I were traveling through our
         A   B   C
   National Parks, my aunt was frightened by a bear.
                                D

   No error
   E

3. Only recently, the newly organized football
   A   B
   association added two new teams to their league.
               C   D

   No error
   E

4. In view of the controversy with the school board,
   A
   neither the teachers nor the principal are being
                        B   C
   considered for promotion at this time. No error
                           D   E

5. The prospective purchaser of the house left the
       A
   premises because he was asked to pay a
                          B
   considerable higher price than he was able to
   C   D
   afford. No error
          E

6. While we have rummaged through the attic, we
              A   B
   found not only an album of our trip to Europe, but
         C
   also a multitude of old news clippings. No error
              D   E

7. Of all the members of the United States team,
      A   B
   Greg Lemond became the first to win the
                  C   D
   prestigious Tour de France bike race. No error
                                          E

GO ON TO THE NEXT PAGE

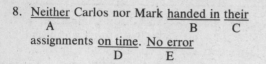

2 2 2 2 2 2 2 2 2 2   2

8. Neither Carlos nor Mark handed in their
    <u>A</u>   <u>B</u>   <u>C</u>
    assignments on time. No error
                 <u>D</u>   <u>E</u>

9. Before we adopt this legislation, we ought to
              <u>A</u>   <u>B</u>
    consider the affect the new law will have on our
                 <u>C</u>   <u>D</u>
    retired and disabled citizens. No error
                                   <u>E</u>

10. The legendary Henry Aaron has established an
                              <u>A</u>
    enviable record, and it probably will not
    <u>B</u>   <u>C</u>
    be broken during the next fifty years. No error
    <u>D</u>   <u>E</u>

11. Mathematics is not his favorite subject; he finds
                <u>A</u>   <u>B</u>
    them too confusing. No error
    <u>C</u> <u>D</u>   <u>E</u>

12. Toni Cade Bambara, who is a black American
                        <u>A</u>
    writer, has been active in civil rights and women's
            <u>B</u>
    issues, nor is she attuned to Afro-American
            <u>C</u>   <u>D</u>
    relationships. No error
                   <u>E</u>

13. The boom of video cassette records can be
                                        <u>A</u>
    attributed to numerous things, including being price
    <u>B</u>   <u>C</u>   <u>D</u>
    reduction, time shift approval, and the growth of

    rental stores. No error
                  <u>E</u>

14. With the passage of the Tax Reform Act of 1986,
              <u>A</u>
    the most comprehensive changes in the federal tax
        <u>B</u>
    system since World War II is taking place.
           <u>C</u>   <u>D</u>
    No error
    <u>E</u>

15. After a six-month study semester abroad, she was
    <u>A</u>   <u>B</u>
    happy to get home to comfortable familiar
    <u>C</u>   <u>D</u>
    surroundings and appetizing food. No error
                                      <u>E</u>

16. Much more experimental data are required before
    <u>A</u>   <u>B</u>   <u>C</u>
    we can accept this theory. No error
                <u>D</u>   <u>E</u>

17. Because he has been warned only about the danger
                 <u>A</u>   <u>B</u>
    of walking on the railroad trestle, he dared
       <u>C</u>
    several of his friends to walk on the tracks. No error
    <u>D</u>   <u>E</u>

18. Where is it possible to find if it was Lowell or
                                 <u>A</u> <u>B</u>   <u>C</u>
    Longfellow who wrote "Hiawatha"? No error
              <u>D</u>   <u>E</u>

19. Choosing between you and she is very difficult;
    <u>A</u>   <u>B</u> <u>C</u>
    both of you are fully qualified. No error
                    <u>D</u>   <u>E</u>

20. After the incident was over, neither the passengers
    <u>A</u>   <u>B</u>
    nor the bus driver were able to identify the youngsters
                       <u>C</u>
    who had created the disturbance. No error
        <u>D</u>   <u>E</u>

21. The suspenseful play "The Mystery of Edwin
        <u>A</u>
    Drood" permits its audience to determine the
                 <u>B</u>
    ending; unfortunately, the play has a new unique
           <u>C</u>   <u>D</u>
    ending for each performance. No error
                                 <u>E</u>

22. The Philippine government changed hands when
                            <u>A</u>   <u>B</u>
    Marcos failed satisfying his countrymen that he
                 <u>C</u>
    had won the presidential election, and Corazon

    Aquino took over. No error
          <u>D</u>   <u>E</u>

23. Was it they who were involved in the recent
    <u>A</u> <u>B</u> <u>C</u>
    unruly demonstration? No error
    <u>D</u>   <u>E</u>

24. We must regard any statement about this
       <u>A</u>
    controversy, whatever the source, as gossip until
                 <u>B</u>   <u>C</u>
    they are confirmed. No error
    <u>D</u>   <u>E</u>

25. She is the only one of the applicants who are
                <u>A</u>   <u>B</u> <u>C</u>
    fully qualified for the position. No error
    <u>D</u>   <u>E</u>

GO ON TO THE NEXT PAGE ➤

2   2 2 2 2 2 2 2 2 2   2

Directions: In each of the following sentences, some part or all of the sentence is underlined. Below each sentence you will find five ways of phrasing the underlined part. Select the answer that produces the most effective sentence, one that is clear and exact, without awkwardness or ambiguity, and blacken the corresponding space on your answer sheet. In choosing answers, follow the requirements of standard written English. Choose the answer that best expresses the meaning of the original sentence.

Answer (A) is always the same as the underlined part. Choose answer (A) if you think the original sentence needs no revision.

EXAMPLE:
Laura Ingalls Wilder published her first book and she was sixty-five years old then.

(A) and she was sixty-five years old then
(B) when she was sixty-five years old
(C) at age sixty-five years old
(D) upon reaching sixty-five years
(E) at the time when she was sixty-five

SAMPLE ANSWER
Ⓐ ● Ⓒ Ⓓ Ⓔ

26. Fifty-three thousand shouting enthusiasts filled the stadium, they had come to watch the first game of the season and to cheer the home team.

(A) enthusiasts filled the stadium, they had come
(B) enthusiasts filled the stadium to come
(C) enthusiasts, filling the stadium, had come
(D) enthusiasts filled the stadium; and had come
(E) enthusiasts filling the stadium, who had come

27. During the judging of the animals at the show, the judges could not decide whether Brown's collie or Jones's terrier was the best dog.

(A) whether Brown's collie or Jones's terrier was the best
(B) if Brown's collie or Jones's terrier was the better
(C) whether Brown's collie or Jones's terrier was the better
(D) if Brown's collie or Jones's terrier was the best
(E) whether Brown's collie or Jones's terrier had been the best

28. Finally reviewing the extensive evidence against the defendant, he was found guilty.

(A) Finally reviewing the extensive evidence against the defendant,
(B) Reviewing the extensive evidence against the defendant,
(C) The jury finally reviewed the evidence concerning the defendant,
(D) When the jury finally reviewed the extensive evidence against the defendant,
(E) The jury finally reviewed the evidence against the defendant,

29. Paul Gauguin was married and had family responsibilities and he ran away to the South Seas to paint.

(A) Paul Gauguin was married and had family responsibilities and he
(B) Although being married and having family responsibilities, Paul Gauguin
(C) Although Paul Gauguin was married and had family responsibilities, he
(D) Being married, and therefore having family responsibilities, Paul Gauguin
(E) Despite the fact that Paul Gauguin was married and had family responsibilities, he

30. A key difference between mice and voles is tail length, a mouse's tail is twice as long as the tail of a vole.

(A) length, a mouse's tail is
(B) length; a mouse's tail is
(C) length, the tail of a mouse is
(D) length; a mouse's tail, it is
(E) length, mice's tails are

GO ON TO THE NEXT PAGE

2 2 2 2 2 2 2 2 2 2 2

31. As a retired executive, he is now busier than ever; he makes his living by speaking before business and philanthropic groups, writing books and articles, and he is a director of three major corporations.

(A) by speaking before business and philanthropic groups, writing books and articles, and he is a director of

(B) by speaking before business and philanthropic groups, and he writes books and articles as well as being a director of

(C) by speaking before business and philanthropic groups, and he writes books and articles, and directs

(D) by speaking before business and philanthropic groups, writing books and articles, and directing

(E) by speaking before business and philanthropic groups, in addition to writing books and articles, and he is a director of

32. The President has established a special commission for the space program; the purpose being to investigate the causes of the Challenger disaster.

(A) program; the purpose being to

(B) program; whose purpose is to

(C) program, the purpose is to

(D) program to

(E) program; in order to

33. When Harriet Tubman decided to help runaway slaves escape to the North, she knew that her mission would bring her into danger in both South and North.

(A) When Harriet Tubman decided to help runaway slaves escape

(B) When Harriet Tubman decides to help runaway slaves escape

(C) When Harriet Tubman decided about helping runaway slaves escape

(D) After the decision by Harriet Tubman to help runaway slaves escape

(E) After Harriet Tubman's making of the decision to help runaway slaves escape

34. The growing impoverishment of women and children in American society distresses Senator Moynihan, and he is also infuriated.

(A) distresses Senator Moynihan, and he is also infuriated

(B) distresses Senator Moynihan, infuriating him

(C) distresses and infuriates Senator Moynihan

(D) is distressing to Senator Moynihan, making him furious

(E) is a cause of distress to Senator Moynihan, and of fury

35. Being a successful reporter demands powers of observation, fluency, and persistence.

(A) Being a successful reporter demands

(B) Being a successful reporter who demands

(C) To be a successful reporter who demands

(D) Being a successful reporter demanding

(E) To be a successful reporter demanding

36. I don't object to John's bill payment if he doesn't expect any favors from me in return.

(A) John's bill payment if he doesn't

(B) whether John pays the bill but he mustn't not

(C) having John pay the bill whether he doesn't

(D) John's payment of the bill but he shouldn't

(E) John's paying the bill as long as he doesn't

37. Had I been at the scene of the accident, I could have administered first aid to the victims.

(A) Had I been at the scene of the accident

(B) If I were at the scene of the accident

(C) If I was at the scene of the accident

(D) I should have been at the scene of the accident

(E) I should have been at the scene of the accident, and

38. The Northern Lights, or Aurora Borealis, is so named because it is a light display that takes place in the northern skies.

(A) because it is a light display that takes place

(B) as a light display taking place

(C) because of taking place

(D) due to the fact that it is a light display

(E) contrary to the fact of taking place

39. It is not for you to assume responsibility; it is, rather, me who is the guilty person in this matter.

(A) me who is

(B) me who am

(C) I who is

(D) I who are

(E) I who am

40. At least, you are original; I have never heard that kind of an excuse until now.

(A) that kind of an excuse

(B) that sort of an excuse

(C) that kinds of excuse

(D) them kinds of excuses

(E) that kind of excuse

GO ON TO THE NEXT PAGE

2 2 2 2 2 2 2 2 2 2 2 2

Note: The remaining questions are like those at the beginning of the section.

Directions: For each sentence in which you find an error, select the one underlined part that must be changed to make the sentence correct and blacken the corresponding space on your answer sheet.

If there is no error, blacken answer space Ⓔ.

EXAMPLE:

The region has a climate so severe that plants
                        A
growing there rarely had been more than twelve
    B   C
inches high. No error
       D   E

SAMPLE ANSWER

Ⓐ Ⓑ ● Ⓓ Ⓔ

41. I have been thinking lately about the monsters   or
        A
    fantasies or whatever—that frightened myself as a
            B   C   D
    child. No error
            E

42. We admired his many attempts bravely to enter the
        A   B   C   D
    burning building. No error
                      E

43. He worked in the lumber camps during the
                                    A
    summer not because of the money but because he
              B   C
    wanted to strengthen his muscles by doing hard
                                            D
    physical labor. No error
                    E

44. That book is liable to become a best seller because
        A   B
    it is well-written, full of suspense, and very
                        C   D
    entertaining. No error
                  E

45. According to a random poll taken by National
        A   B
    Wildlife, the top three threats to the environment
    is water pollution, air pollution, and hazardous
    C   D
    wastes. No error
            E

46. His three children, Ruth, Frank, and Ellis, are
    very talented youngsters, but the latter shows the
                              A   B   C
    most promise. No error
    D   E

47. Passing antidrug legislation, calling for more
    A
    education, and to aid Bolivia in raids on cocaine
                  B
    dealers are all ways that the United States is
              C
    fighting back against "crack" use. No error
                  D   E

48. Cajun cooking, which uses special prepared spices,
                              A
    has always been well-known in Louisiana, but it is
                                             B
    only now becoming known in other parts of the
    C   D
    country. No error
             E

49. It seems strange to realize that when Harvey
    A   B   C
    Firestone organized the Firestone Tire and Rubber
    Company in 1900, rubber tires had been a novelty.
                                   D
    No error
    E

50. The same laser technology that is being used on
                                       A
    compact disks is also under application to
                  B   C
    computers to achieve additional memory. No error
              D   E

IF YOU FINISH BEFORE TIME IS CALLED, YOU MAY CHECK YOUR WORK ON
THIS SECTION ONLY. DO NOT WORK ON ANY OTHER SECTION IN THE TEST.

STOP

3 3 3 3 3 3 3 3 3 3 3

SECTION 3   Time—30 minutes   For each question in this section, choose the best answer and
              45 Questions   blacken the corresponding space on the answer sheet.

Each question below consists of a word in capital letters, followed by five lettered words or phrases. Choose the word or phrase that is most nearly opposite in meaning to the word in capital letters. Since some of the questions require you to distinguish fine shades of meaning, consider all the choices before deciding which is best.

Example:

  GOOD: (A) sour   (B) bad   (C) red
  (D) hot   (E) ugly   Ⓐ ● Ⓒ Ⓓ Ⓔ

1. HEARTEN: (A) keep cool   (B) speak softly
   (C) slow down   (D) deceive   (E) discourage

2. SPACIOUS: (A) erroneous   (B) airless
   (C) cramped   (D) earthy   (E) aquatic

3. SIMULATED: (A) depressed   (B) genuine
   (C) prosaic   (D) reckoned   (E) inharmonious

4. FIENDISH: (A) unique   (B) disdainful
   (C) valid   (D) angelic   (E) permanent

5. DWINDLE: (A) loiter   (B) leave behind
   (C) think back   (D) follow   (E) increase

6. REVERE: (A) awake   (B) protrude   (C) divert
   (D) dishonor   (E) pretend

7. UNMARRED: (A) beneficial   (B) uncomfortable
   (C) hostile   (D) spoiled   (E) irritated

8. DESIST: (A) continue   (B) dismay   (C) elevate
   (D) fall apart   (E) speak well of

9. DISPARAGE: (A) equal   (B) praise
   (C) tolerate   (D) cultivate   (E) endow

10. DISSIDENCE: (A) noise   (B) glamor
    (C) treason   (D) agreement   (E) negligence

11. ANOMALOUS: (A) essential   (B) regular
    (C) outstanding   (D) protected   (E) prolific

12. QUELL: (A) withhold   (B) extol   (C) heed
    (D) incur   (E) incite

13. PUERILE: (A) adult   (B) candid
    (C) imperfect   (D) questionable   (E) attractive

14. DISCERNMENT: (A) loss of credibility
    (B) propensity   (C) morbidity   (D) impudence
    (E) lack of insight

15. LASSITUDE: (A) discovery   (B) sobriety
    (C) width   (D) strife   (E) liveliness

Each sentence below has one or two blanks, each blank indicating that something has been omitted. Beneath the sentence are five lettered words or sets of words. Choose the word or set of words that best fits the meaning of the sentence as a whole.

Example:

Although its publicity has been ----, the film itself is intelligent, well-acted, handsomely produced, and altogether ----.

(A) tasteless..respectable   (B) extensive..moderate
  (C) sophisticated..amateur   (D) risqué..crude
  (E) perfect..spectacular

                                  ● Ⓑ Ⓒ Ⓓ Ⓔ

16. Archaeologists are involved in ---- Mayan temples in Central America, uncovering the old ruins in order to learn more about the civilization they represent.

(A) demolishing   (B) incapacitating
  (C) excavating   (D) worshiping   (E) adapting

17. Afraid that the ---- nature of the plays being presented would corrupt the morals of their audiences, the Puritans closed the theatres in 1642.

(A) mediocre   (B) fantastic   (C) profound
  (D) lewd   (E) witty

18. The governor's imposition of martial law on the once-peaceful community was the last straw, so far as the lawmakers were concerned: the legislature refused to function until martial law was ----.

(A) reaffirmed   (B) reiterated   (C) inaugurated
  (D) rescinded   (E) prolonged

GO ON TO THE NEXT PAGE ⇒

3 3 3 3 3 3 3 3 3 3 3

19. The sergeant suspected that the private was ---- in order to avoid going on the ---- campaign scheduled for that morning.

(A) malingering..arduous
(B) proselytizing..interminable
(C) invalidating..threatened
(D) exemplary..leisurely
(E) disgruntled..strenuous

20. The columnist was almost ---- when he mentioned his friends, but he was unpleasant and even ---- when he discussed people who irritated him.

(A) recalcitrant..laconic
(B) reverential..acrimonious
(C) sensitive..remorseful
(D) insipid..militant
(E) benevolent..stoical

Each passage below is followed by questions based on its content. Answer all questions following a passage on the basis of what is <u>stated</u> or <u>implied</u> in that passage.

I remember to start with that day in Sacramento—a California now nearly thirty years past—when I first entered a classroom, able to understand some fifty stray English words.

The third of four children, I had been preceded to a neighborhood Roman Catholic school by an older brother and sister. Each afternoon they returned, as they left in the morning, always together, speaking in Spanish as they climbed the five steps of the porch. And their mysterious books, wrapped in shopping-bag paper, remained on the table next to the door, closed firmly behind them.

An accident of geography sent me to a school where all my classmates were white, many the children of doctors and lawyers and business executives. All my classmates certainly must have been uneasy on that first day of school—as most children are uneasy—to find themselves apart from their families in the first institution of their lives. But I was astonished.

The nun said, in a friendly but oddly impersonal voice, "Boys and girls, this is Richard Rodriguez." (I heard her sound out: *Rich-heard Road-ree-guess*.) It was the first time I had heard anyone name me in English. "Richard," the nun repeated more slowly, writing my name down in her black leather book. Quickly I turned to see my mother's face dissolve in a watery blur behind the pebbled glass door.

In the early years of my boyhood, my parents coped very well in America. My father had steady work. My mother managed at home. They were nobody's victims. Optimism and ambition led them to a house (our home) many blocks from the Mexican south side of town. We lived among *gringos* and only a block from the biggest, whitest houses. It never occurred to my parents that they couldn't live wherever they chose. Nor was the Sacramento of the fifties bent on teaching them a contrary lesson. My mother and father were more annoyed than intimidated by those two or three neighbors who tried initially to make us unwelcome. ("Keep your brats away from my sidewalk!") But despite all they achieved, perhaps because they had so much to

achieve, any deep feeling of ease, the confidence of "belonging" in public, was withheld from them both. They regarded the people at work, the faces in crowds, as very distant from us. They were the others, *los gringos*. That term was interchangeable in their speech with another, even more telling, *los americanos*.

21. The family members in the passage are discussed primarily in terms of

(A) the different personalities of each
(B) the common heritage they shared
(C) the ambitions they possessed
(D) their interaction with the English-speaking world
(E) their struggle against racial discrimination

22. For which of the following reasons was the author's experience different from that of his fellow pupils on his first day of school?

(A) He felt deserted because his mother had left him.
(B) He was startled by being addressed in English.
(C) His older brother and sister had told him lies about the school.
(D) He had never before seen a nun.
(E) He had never previously encountered white children.

23. The author's attitude toward his parents can best be described as

(A) admiring   (B) contemptuous   (C) indifferent
(D) envious   (E) diffident

GO ON TO THE NEXT PAGE

3   3 3 3 3 3 3 3 3 3 3   3

24. Which of the following statements regarding Mexican-Americans in Sacramento would be most true to the author's experiences?

(A) They were unable to find employment.
(B) They felt estranged from the community as a whole.
(C) They found a ready welcome in white neighborhoods.
(D) They took an active part in public affairs.
(E) They were unaware of academic institutions.

25. The word "telling" as used in the last sentence means

(A) outspoken   (B) interchangeable
  (C) unutterable   (D) embarrassing
    (E) revealing

Of the 197 million square miles making up the surface of the globe, 71 percent is covered by interconnecting bodies of marine water; the Pacific Ocean alone covers half the Earth and averages near 14,000 feet in depth. The *continents*—Eurasia, Africa, North America, South America, Australia, and Antarctica—are the portions of the *continental masses* rising above sea level. The submerged borders of the continental masses are the *continental shelves,* beyond which lie the deep-sea basins.

The oceans attain their greatest depths not in their central parts, but in certain elongated furrows, or long narrow troughs, called *deeps.* These profound troughs have a peripheral arrangement, notably around the borders of the Pacific and Indian oceans. The position of the deeps near the continental masses suggests that the deeps, like the highest mountains, are of recent origin, since otherwise they would have been filled with waste from the lands. This suggestion is strengthened by the fact that the deeps are frequently the sites of world-shaking earthquakes. For example, the "tidal wave" that in April, 1946, caused widespread destruction along Pacific coasts resulted from a strong earthquake on the floor of the Aleutian Deep.

The topography of the ocean floors is none too well known, since in great areas the available soundings are hundreds or even thousands of miles apart. However, the floor of the Atlantic is becoming fairly well known as a result of special surveys since 1920. A broad, well-defined ridge—the mid-Atlantic ridge—runs north and south between Africa and the two Americas, and numerous other major irregularities diversify the Atlantic floor. Closely spaced soundings show that many parts of the oceanic floors are as rugged as mountainous regions of the continents. Use of the recently perfected method of echo sounding is rapidly enlarging our knowledge of submarine topography. During World War II great strides were made in mapping submarine surfaces, particularly in many parts of the vast Pacific basin.

The continents stand on the average 2870 feet—slightly more than half a mile—above sea level. North America averages 2300 feet; Europe averages only 1150 feet; and Asia, the highest of the larger continental subdivisions, averages 3200 feet. The highest point on the globe, Mount Everest in the Himalayas, is 29,000 feet above the sea; and as the greatest known depth in the sea is over 35,000 feet, the maximum *relief* (that is, the difference in altitude between the lowest and highest points) exceeds 64,000 feet, or exceeds 12 miles. The continental masses and the deep-sea basins are relief features of the first order; the deeps, ridges, and volcanic cones that diversify the sea floor, as well as the plains, plateaus, and mountains of the continents, are relief features of the second order. The lands are unendingly subject to a complex of activities summarized in the term *erosion*, which first sculptures them in great detail and then tends to reduce them ultimately to sea level. The modeling of the landscape by weather, running water, and other agents is apparent to the keenly observant eye and causes thinking people to speculate on what must be the final result of the ceaseless wearing down of the lands. Long before there was a science of geology, Shakespeare wrote "the revolution of the times makes mountains level."

26. It can be inferred from the passage that the largest ocean is the

(A) Atlantic   (B) Pacific   (C) Indian
    (D) Aleutian Deep   (E) Arctic

27. According to the passage, the peripheral furrows or *deeps* are found

(A) only in the Pacific and Indian oceans
(B) near earthquakes
(C) near the shore
(D) in the center of the ocean
(E) to be 14,000 feet in depth in the Pacific

28. The passage indicates that the continental masses

(A) comprise 29 percent of the earth's surface
(B) consist of six continents
(C) rise above sea level
(D) are partially underwater
(E) are relief features of the second order

29. The "revolution of the times" as used in the final sentence means

(A) the passage of years
(B) the current rebellion
(C) the science of geology
(D) the action of the ocean floor
(E) the overthrow of natural forces

GO ON TO THE NEXT PAGE ⟩

3   3 3 3 3 3 3 3 3 3 3   3

30. From this passage, it can be inferred that earthquakes

    (A) occur only in the peripheral furrows
    (B) occur more frequently in newly formed land or sea formations
    (C) are a prime cause of soil erosion
    (D) will ultimately "make mountains level"
    (E) are caused by the weight of the water

Select the word or set of words that best completes each of the following sentences.

---

31. The incidence of smoking among women, formerly ---- , has grown to such a degree that lung cancer, once a minor problem, has become the chief ---- of cancer-related deaths among women.

    (A) negligible..cause
    (B) minor..antidote
    (C) pre-eminent..cure
    (D) relevant..modifier
    (E) pervasive..opponent

32. An experienced politician who knew better than to launch a campaign in troubled political waters, she intended to wait for a more ---- occasion before she announced her plans.

    (A) propitious   (B) provocative   (C) unseemly
    (D) questionable   (E) theoretical

33. You have valid arguments on your side, and your case is ----; nevertheless, your ---- attitude will alienate any potential supporters.

    (A) ingenious..fascinating
    (B) just..altruistic
    (C) pretentious..logical
    (D) persuasive..truculent
    (E) dramatic..tortuous

34. Wemmick, the soul of kindness in private, is obliged in ---- to be uncompassionate and even ---- on behalf of his employer, the harsh lawyer Jaggers.

    (A) conclusion..careless
    (B) principle..contradictory
    (C) theory..esoteric
    (D) court..judicious
    (E) public..ruthless

35. To the relief of the archaeologists, although two of the three human burial pits had been ---- , possibly by animals rummaging through them, one was ---- .

    (A) destroyed..despoiled
    (B) disturbed..intact
    (C) verified..extant
    (D) impeded..fragmentary
    (E) elevated..desecrated

Each question below consists of a related pair of words or phrases, followed by five lettered pairs of words or phrases. Select the lettered pair that best expresses a relationship similar to that expressed in the original pair.

Example:

    YAWN : BOREDOM ::   (A) dream : sleep
    (B) anger : madness   (C) smile : amusement
    (D) face : expression   (E) impatience : rebellion

    Ⓐ Ⓑ ● Ⓓ Ⓔ

---

36. BARBER:SHEARS ::
    (A) baker:batter
    (B) dentist:drill
    (C) patient:prescription
    (D) architect:blueprint
    (E) butcher:sausages

37. PUCK:HOCKEY ::   (A) net:tennis
    (B) goal:soccer   (C) ball:golf   (D) rod:fishing
    (E) helmet:football

38. POODLE:DOG ::   (A) witch:cat
    (B) porpoise:fish   (C) fodder:cow
    (D) whale:mammal   (E) stable:horse

39. HILLOCK:MOUNTAIN ::   (A) hassock:stool
    (B) pond:lake   (C) spice:herb   (D) gravel:sand
    (E) tree:lumber

40. FROWN:DISPLEASURE ::   (A) blush:pallor
    (B) smile:commiseration   (C) sneer:contempt
    (D) snore:relief   (E) smirk:regret

41. PRIDE:LION ::   (A) bevy:quail   (B) lair:bear
    (C) fish:minnow   (D) flag:banner
    (E) anger:symbol

42. MENTOR:COUNSEL ::   (A) poet:criticism
    (B) plea:mercy   (C) bodyguard:protection
    (D) sermon:conscience   (E) judge:lawyer

43. CHAUVINISM:COUNTRY ::
    (A) frugality:money
    (B) patriotism:authority
    (C) gluttony:food
    (D) jingoism:loyalty
    (E) criticism:book

GO ON TO THE NEXT PAGE

44. FRUGAL : PARSIMONIOUS ::
   (A) joyful : ecstatic
   (B) cautious : wise
   (C) honorable : loyal
   (D) poor : miserly
   (E) eager : anxious

45. CONVENTION : MORES ::
   (A) caprice : whimsicality
   (B) corruption : acquiescence
   (C) popularity : infamy
   (D) culpability : penance
   (E) innovation : prodigy

IF YOU FINISH BEFORE TIME IS CALLED, YOU MAY CHECK YOUR WORK ON THIS SECTION ONLY. DO NOT WORK ON ANY OTHER SECTION IN THE TEST.

S T O P

4 4 4 4 4 4 4 4 4 4 4 4 4

SECTION 4   Time—30 minutes   For each question in this section, choose the best answer and
40 Questions   blacken the corresponding space on the answer sheet.

Each question below consists of a word in capital letters, followed by five lettered words or phrases. Choose the word or phrase that is most nearly <u>opposite</u> in meaning to the word in capital letters. Since some of the questions require you to distinguish fine shades of meaning, consider all the choices before deciding which is best.

Example:

GOOD: (A) sour   (B) bad   (C) red
(D) hot   (E) ugly   Ⓐ ● Ⓒ Ⓓ Ⓔ

1. INTERVENE: (A) remain uninvolved
(B) replace temporarily   (C) oppose directly
(D) judge innocent   (E) admit publicly

2. ASTRONOMICAL: (A) shallow   (B) minute
(C) internal   (D) irrational   (E) ordinary

3. TRIVIA: (A) important matters
(B) abstract matters   (C) local concerns
(D) specialized concerns   (E) value judgments

4. LENIENCY: (A) wealth   (B) severity
(C) status   (D) brevity   (E) defense

5. EXTRICATE: (A) ensnare   (B) simplify
(C) leave whole   (D) stand aside   (E) indicate

6. TERSE: (A) irate   (B) quiet   (C) verbose
(D) shouted   (E) retroactive

7. FURTIVE: (A) meager   (B) reluctant
(C) apathetic   (D) aboveboard   (E) affable

8. AMELIORATE: (A) proceed   (B) intensify
(C) persuade   (D) worsen   (E) convene

9. FALLOW: (A) ruddy   (B) mature
(C) cultivated   (D) decorated   (E) visible

10. ASCETIC: (A) wanton   (B) spurious
(C) diverse   (D) indecisive   (E) prosaic

Each sentence below has one or two blanks, each blank indicating that something has been omitted. Beneath the sentence are five lettered words or sets of words. Choose the word or set of words that best fits the meaning of the sentence as a whole.

Example:

Although its publicity has been ----, the film itself is intelligent, well-acted, handsomely produced, and altogether ----.

(A) tasteless..respectable   (B) extensive..moderate
(C) sophisticated..amateur   (D) risqué..crude
(E) perfect..spectacular   ● Ⓑ Ⓒ Ⓓ Ⓔ

11. Quick-breeding and immune to most pesticides, cockroaches are so ---- that even a professional exterminator may fail to ---- them.

(A) vulnerable..eradicate
(B) widespread..discern
(C) fragile..destroy
(D) hardy..eliminate
(E) numerous..detect

12. Underlying historical events which influenced two great American peoples, citizens of Canada and of the United States, to work out their problems through the years with harmony and ---- benefit constitute a story both colorful and fascinating.

(A) mutual   (B) marginal   (C) conflicting
(D) insufficient   (E) lamentable

13. To many thoughtful people, the tremendous coverage of sporting events by television stations presents a ---- : the instrument which has made us a sports-conscious nation is also the instrument which may destroy amateur and professional athletics in this country.

(A) nuance   (B) hyperbole   (C) handicap
(D) paradox   (E) digression

GO ON TO THE NEXT PAGE ⇒

14. The actor's stories of backstage feuds and rivalry might be thought ---- were there not so many corroborating anecdotes from other theatrical personalities.

(A) pantomime   (B) ambiguity   (C) approbation
(D) hyperbole   (E) vainglory

15. The ---- ambassador was but ---- linguist; yet he insisted on speaking to foreign dignitaries in their own tongues without resorting to a translator's aid.

(A) eminent..an indifferent
(B) visiting..a notable
(C) revered..a talented
(D) distinguished..a celebrated
(E) ranking..a sensitive

Each question below consists of a related pair of words or phrases, followed by five lettered pairs of words or phrases. Select the lettered pair that best expresses a relationship similar to that expressed in the original pair.
Example:

YAWN : BOREDOM ::   (A) dream : sleep
(B) anger : madness   (C) smile : amusement
(D) face : expression   (E) impatience : rebellion

Ⓐ Ⓑ ● Ⓓ Ⓔ

16. AUTOMOBILE:GASOLINE ::
(A) train:caboose
(B) cow:milk
(C) airplane:propeller
(D) man:food
(E) disease:germs

17. COMPOSER:SYMPHONY::
(A) playwright:rehearsal
(B) actor:comedy
(C) conductor:orchestra
(D) director:movie
(E) poet:sonnet

18. WEARISOME:REFRESHING ::
(A) wrathful:irate
(B) tedious:dull
(C) original:scintillating
(D) lengthy:brief
(E) truthful:courageous

19. FOLLOW:STALK ::   (A) regret:rejoice
(B) look:spy   (C) execute:condemn
(D) lurk:hide   (E) beckon:gesture

20. DAMPEN:DRENCH ::   (A) glide:drift
(B) gambol:play   (C) simmer:boil
(D) stagnate:flow   (E) ignite:quench

21. BACTERIUM:COLONY ::
(A) microbe:disease
(B) fish:shoal
(C) stockade:settlement
(D) virus:immunization
(E) sovereign:kingdom

22. ALLAY:PAIN ::
(A) mollify:fright
(B) cancel:order
(C) arbitrate:dispute
(D) mitigate:punishment
(E) testify:court

23. EXERTION:FATIGUE ::
(A) school:graduation
(B) exercise:muscles
(C) sedation:tranquillity
(D) effort:results
(E) morality:lechery

24. ENMITY:FOE ::   (A) civility:pacifist
(B) avarice:miser   (C) vanity:celebrity
(D) piety:atheist   (E) humility:friend

25. SHUN:PARIAH ::
(A) hunt:predator
(B) transmute:alchemist
(C) beg:mendicant
(D) flatter:sycophant
(E) ridicule:butt

GO ON TO THE NEXT PAGE

4   4 4 4 4 4 4 4 4 4 4 4   4

Each passage below is followed by questions based on its content. Answer all questions following a passage on the basis of what is stated or implied in that passage.

(This passage was written prior to 1960.)

Of all the strange experiences that may await the astronaut, none will be quite so strange, the experts agree, as weightlessness. This phenomenon will occur as soon as the spaceship reaches a speed at which the rocket's centrifugal force cancels the pull of the earth's gravity, and when it does, the space man, whether settling into orbit or making for Venus or Mars, will know for certain that he has arrived in outer space. He will weigh nothing. The air in his cabin will weigh nothing. The warm carbon dioxide he breathes out, being no lighter than the air in the cabin, will not rise, so he will have to exhale forcibly. Momentum, the force whirling the ship on its course, will rule its interior as well, and with possibly weird results. All objects that are not in some way fastened down—a map, a flashlight, a pencil—will float freely, subjecting the space man to a haphazard crossfire. If he were to drink water from an ordinary tumbler, the water might dash into his nostrils, float there, and drown him. Ordinary tumblers will not be used, however; plastic squeeze bottles will. ("The proper-size orifice is being worked out," I was told by Major Henry G. Wise, of the Human Forces Division, Air Force Directorate of Research and Development.) Far more startling than the movements of objects, though, will be the space man's own movements. Normally in making a movement of any kind, a man has to overcome the body's inertia plus its weight; a weightless man has only the inertia to overcome, and the chances are that it will take a long time for his muscles to grow accustomed to the fact. "What would be a normal step on earth would . . . send the 'stepper' sailing across the cabin or somersaulting wildly in the air," the Air University Command and Staff School study declares. "A mere sneeze could propel the victim violently against the cabin wall and result in possible injury."

26. The best title for this passage is:
   (A) Miracles in the Air
   (B) New Scientific Frontiers
   (C) Overcoming Inertia
   (D) Momentum and Astrogation
   (E) Lack of Gravity in Space

27. We may infer from the passage that in space
   (A) involuntary reflex movements may have unexpected dangers
   (B) weightlessness will cancel the pull of centrifugal force
   (C) a man may drown in the course of sneezing
   (D) men weigh less than the air in the cabin
   (E) men must expend greater force to overcome inertia

28. According to the passage, weightlessness occurs when
   (A) carbon dioxide rises and displaces ordinary air
   (B) the rocket's centripetal force cancels the pull of the earth's gravity
   (C) the missile's trajectory escapes the range of the earth's gravity
   (D) the rocket's speed offsets the force of gravity
   (E) inertia equals the speed of the missile

29. The author indicates that one task of the Human Factors Division of the Air Force is to
   (A) analyze warm carbon dioxide
   (B) define the momentum of floating bodies
   (C) apply centrifugal force
   (D) reduce colds in the stratosphere
   (E) contrive appropriate devices for drinking

30. The passage is most probably an excerpt from which of the following?
   (A) A proposal for an Air Force research project
   (B) A scholarly article for a technical audience
   (C) A chapter from an advanced physics textbook
   (D) A column from a popular science magazine
   (E) The memoirs of a pioneer astronaut

Rumor is the most primitive way of spreading stories—by passing them on from mouth to mouth. But civilized countries in normal times have better sources of news than rumor. They have radio, television, and newspapers. In times of stress and confusion, however, rumor emerges and becomes rife. At such times the different kinds of news are in competition: the press, television, and radio versus the grapevine.

Especially do rumors spread when war requires censorship on many important matters. The customary news sources no longer give out enough information. Since the people cannot learn through legitimate channels all that they are anxious to learn, they pick up "news" wherever they can and when this happens, rumor thrives.

Rumors are often repeated even by those who do not believe the tales. There is a fascination about them. The reason is that the cleverly designed rumor gives expression to something deep in the hearts of the victims—the fears, suspicions, forbidden hopes, or daydreams which they hesitate to voice directly. Pessimistic rumors about defeat and disasters show that the people who repeat them are worried and anxious. Optimistic rumors about record production or peace soon coming point to complacency or confidence—and often to overconfidence.

GO ON TO THE NEXT PAGE

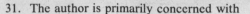

31. The author is primarily concerned with

(A) the nature of rumor
(B) the fascination of rumors
(C) rumor as primitive man's newspaper
(D) the breeding places of rumors
(E) creating a case against rumor

32. The author suggests that rumors usually

(A) alarm their hearers
(B) are hardy in their growth
(C) are disheartening
(D) can be suppressed by censorship
(E) reflect a lack of confidence in government

33. According to the passage, people who repeat a rumor as truth want to do so because they

(A) are impressed with the antiquity of this method of spreading news
(B) are naturally gullible and willing to be duped
(C) have a deeply ingrained pessimistic strain
(D) find that the rumor reflects their own unexpressed beliefs
(E) fear the truth and seek to cushion themselves against it

34. The author states that during wartime the regular sources of news present only

(A) optimistic reports
(B) pessimistic reports
(C) limited information
(D) government propaganda
(E) distorted and biased viewpoints

35. Which of the following best describes the author's personal attitude toward rumor?

(A) Excited enthusiasm
(B) Morbid curiosity
(C) Acute indignation
(D) Philosophical interest
(E) Ready credulity

The *range in frequencies* of musical sounds is approximately 20–20,000 cycles per second (Hz). Some people can hear higher frequencies than others. Longitudinal waves whose frequencies are higher than those within the audible range are called *ultrasonic* frequencies. Ultrasonic frequencies are used in sonar for such purposes as submarine detection and depth finding. Ultrasonic frequencies are also being tried for sterilizing food since these frequencies kill some bacteria. Sound waves of all frequencies in the audible range travel at the same speed in the same medium. In the audible range, the higher the frequency of the sound the higher is the *pitch*. The term *supersonic* refers to speed greater than sound. An airplane traveling at supersonic speed is moving at a speed greater than the speed of sound in air at that

temperature. *Mach 1* means a speed equal to that of sound; *Mach 2* means a speed equal to twice that of sound, etc.

Musical sounds have three basic *characteristics*: pitch, loudness, and quality or timbre. As was indicated above, *pitch* is determined largely by the frequency of the wave reaching the ear. The higher the frequency the higher is the pitch. *Loudness* depends on the amplitude of the wave reaching the ear. For a given frequency, the greater the amplitude of the wave the louder the sound. To discuss quality of sound we need to clarify the concept of overtones. Sounds are produced by vibrating objects; if these objects are given a gentle push, they usually vibrate at one definite frequency producing a pure tone. This is the way a tuning fork is usually used. When objects vibrate freely after a force is momentarily applied, they are said to produce their *natural frequency*. Some objects, like strings and air columns, can vibrate naturally at more than one frequency at a time. The lowest frequency which an object can produce when vibrating freely is known as the object's *fundamental frequency*; other frequencies that the object can produce are known as its *overtones*. The *quality* of a sound depends on the number and relative amplitude of the overtones present in the wave reaching the ear.

36. The primary purpose of the passage is to

(A) show the impossibility of hearing sounds above 20,000 Hz
(B) define the nature and quality of musical sounds
(C) analyze what gives a work of art its musical quality
(D) explain the applications of ultrasonic frequencies
(E) explore the influence of wave length on musical appreciation

37. The style and content of this passage indicate that it is most likely an excerpt from

(A) a proposal by an innovative composer of atonal music
(B) an informal article written for a popular magazine
(C) a scholarly monograph on aesthetics
(D) a college textbook on music theory
(E) a critique of music education in the schools

38. According to the author, the timbre of a musical sound is dependent on

(A) fundamentals (B) amplitude (C) frequency
  (D) overtones   (E) speed

GO ON TO THE NEXT PAGE

4

39. According to the passage, ultrasonic frequencies are

(A) inaudible
(B) excessively fast
(C) characterized by a great amplitude
(D) death rays
(E) less than 20,000 Hz

40. Which of the following individuals would be most likely to use terms like Mach 5 or Mach 9?

(A) a helicopter pilot
(B) a musician
(C) an astronaut
(D) a submarine navigator
(E) a biologist

IF YOU FINISH BEFORE TIME IS CALLED, YOU MAY CHECK YOUR WORK ON THIS SECTION ONLY. DO NOT WORK ON ANY OTHER SECTION IN THE TEST.

S T O P

5

SECTION 5   Time—30 minutes   In this section solve each problem, using any available space on
35 Questions   the page for scratchwork. Then decide which is the best of the
choices given and blacken the corresponding space on the answer
sheet.

The following information is for your reference in solving some of the problems.

Circle of radius r: Area $= \pi r^2$; Circumference $= 2\pi r$
  The number of degrees of arc in a circle is 360.
The measure in degrees of a straight angle is 180.

Definitions of symbols:
$=$ is equal to $\leqq$ is less than or equal to
$\neq$ is unequal to $\geqq$ is greater than or equal to
$<$ is less than $\parallel$ is parallel to
$>$ is greater than $\perp$ is perpendicular to

Triangle: The sum of the measures
in degrees of the angles of
a triangle is 180.
If $\angle CDA$ is a right angle, then

(1) area of $\triangle ABC = \dfrac{AB \times CD}{2}$

(2) $AC^2 = AD^2 + DC^2$

Note: Figures that accompany problems in this test are intended to provide information useful in solving the problems. They are drawn as accurately as possible EXCEPT when it is stated in a specific problem that its figure is not drawn to scale. All figures lie in a plane unless otherwise indicated. All numbers used are real numbers.

1. $\dfrac{3.6x^4 y}{0.9xy^4} =$

(A) $\dfrac{0.4x^3}{y^4}$ (B) $\dfrac{0.04x}{y^3}$ (C) $\dfrac{4x^3}{y^3}$ (D) $\dfrac{4y^3}{x^3}$

(E) $\dfrac{4x^4}{y^3}$

2. A student attending a school for 3 semesters has a scholastic average of 85 percent. She transfers to another school and after 4 semesters earns an average of 90 percent in this school. What is her average for her work in both schools?

(A) 82%   (B) 87%   (C) 87.5%   (D) 87.9%
(E) 88%

3. Three boys have marbles in the ratio of 19:5:3. If the boy with the least number has 9 marbles, how many marbles does the boy with the greatest number have?

(A) 27   (B) 33   (C) 57   (D) 81   (E) 171

4. The distance between Portland, Oregon, and Santa Fe, New Mexico, is 1,800 miles. How long, in hours, would a train with an average speed of 60 miles per hour take to make the trip?

(A) 30   (B) 39   (C) 48   (D) 300   (E) 480

5. If the cost of 500 articles is d dollars, how many of these articles can be bought for x dollars?

(A) $\dfrac{500d}{x}$ (B) $\dfrac{500}{dx}$ (C) $\dfrac{dx}{500}$ (D) $\dfrac{500x}{d}$ (E) $\dfrac{d}{500x}$

6. Point B is on line segment AC, and point E is on line segment DF. If $AB > DE$ and $BC = EF$, then

(A) $AC < DF$ (B) $AC = DF$ (C) $AC > DF$
(D) $DF > AC$ (E) $EF > DF$

7. A candy dealer makes up a mixture of 3 parts of candy costing him 60¢ per pound with 2 parts candy costing him 70¢ per pound, and 2 parts candy costing him 50¢ per pound. At what price, in cents, per pound should he sell this mixture to make a profit of 25 percent?

(A) 50   (B) 60   (C) 65   (D) 70   (E) 75

GO ON TO THE NEXT PAGE

5

Questions 8–27 each consist of two quantities, one in Column A and one in Column B. You are to compare the two quantities and on the answer sheet blacken space

A   if the quantity in Column A is greater;
B   if the quantity in Column B is greater;
C   if the two quantities are equal;
D   If the relationship cannot be determined from the information given.

AN E RESPONSE WILL NOT BE SCORED.

	EXAMPLES		
	Column A	Column B	Answers
E1.	2×6	$2 + 6$	●ⒷⒸⒹⒺ
E2.	$180 - x$	y	ⒶⒷ●ⒹⒺ
E3.	$p - q$	$q - p$	ⒶⒷⒸ●Ⓔ

For E2: $x°$ $y°$

Notes:
1. In certain questions, information concerning one or both of the quantities to be compared is centered above the two columns.
2. In a given question, a symbol that appears in both columns represents the same thing in Column A as it does in Column B.
3. Letters such as x, n, and k stand for real numbers.

	Column A	Column B
8.	$3\frac{1}{2}\%$	$\dfrac{35}{1000}$
9.	$\sqrt{0.04}$	$(0.2)^2$
10.	$\left(\dfrac{1}{2}\right)\left(\dfrac{7}{8}\right)$	$87\frac{1}{2}\%$
11.	$\left(\dfrac{1}{2}\right)^2$	23%
12.	0.3	$\dfrac{0.7}{2}$
13.	$\dfrac{X}{Y}$	$\dfrac{X}{Y} \cdot \dfrac{Y}{X}$

$-1 < a < 1$
$-1 < b < 0$

14.	a	b

	Column A	Column B
15.	$\dfrac{2x - \dfrac{y-5}{6}}{\dfrac{y-5}{3} - 4x}$	-0.5

Circleville is 23 kilometers from Center City, and Centerville is 46 kilometers from Center City.

16.	Distance from Circle-ville to Centerville	23 kilometers

$z°$ $y°$

$x°$ $x°$

This concerns #17 and #18.

17.	z	45
18.	45	x

GO ON TO THE NEXT PAGE ⇒

5

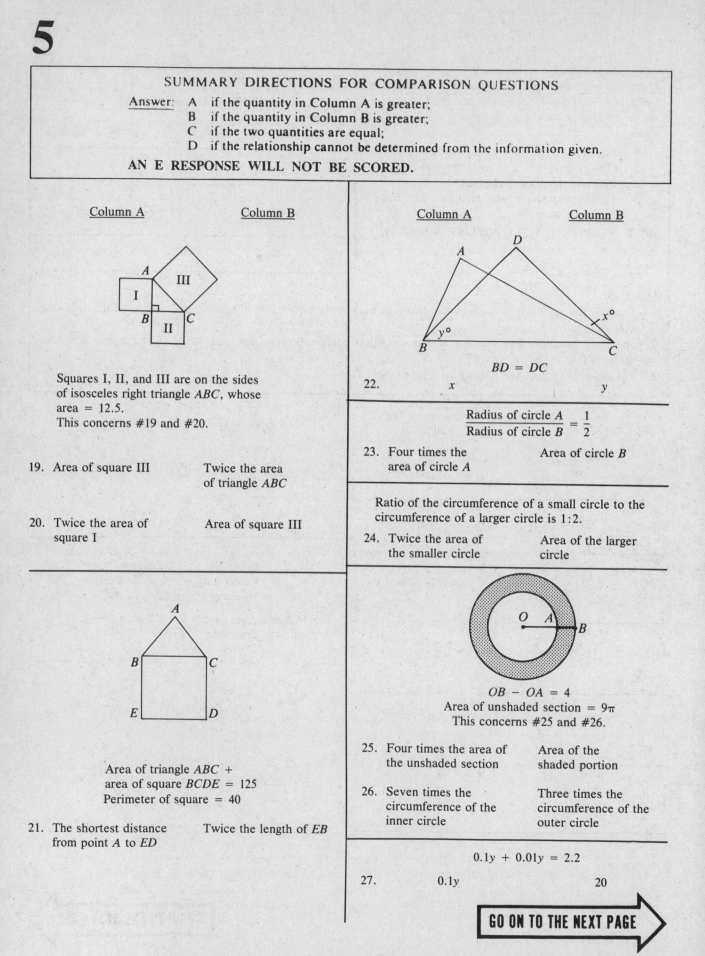

Column A   Column B

Squares I, II, and III are on the sides
of isosceles right triangle ABC, whose
area = 12.5.
This concerns #19 and #20.

19. Area of square III   Twice the area
                                 of triangle ABC

20. Twice the area of   Area of square III
     square I

Area of triangle ABC +
area of square $BCDE$ = 125
Perimeter of square = 40

21. The shortest distance   Twice the length of EB
     from point A to ED

Column A   Column B

$$BD = DC$$

22. x y

$$\frac{\text{Radius of circle } A}{\text{Radius of circle } B} = \frac{1}{2}$$

23. Four times the   Area of circle B
     area of circle A

Ratio of the circumference of a small circle to the
circumference of a larger circle is 1:2.

24. Twice the area of   Area of the larger
     the smaller circle   circle

$$OB - OA = 4$$
Area of unshaded section = 9π
This concerns #25 and #26.

25. Four times the area of   Area of the
     the unshaded section   shaded portion

26. Seven times the   Three times the
     circumference of the   circumference of the
     inner circle   outer circle

$$0.1y + 0.01y = 2.2$$

27. $0.1y$ 20

GO ON TO THE NEXT PAGE

5

Solve each of the remaining problems in this section using any available space for scratchwork. Then decide which is the best of the choices given and blacken the corresponding space on the answer sheet.

28. If 8 men can do a job in 12 days, what is the percentage increase in the number of days required to do the job when 2 men are released?

   (A) 25%   (B) $33\frac{1}{3}$%   (C) 50%   (D) 67%

   (E) 75%

29. One side of a rectangle is x inches. If the perimeter is p inches, what is the length, in inches, of the other side? Answer in terms of p and x.

   (A) $p - x$ (B) $p - 2x$ (C) $\dfrac{p - x}{2}$

   (D) $\dfrac{p - 2x}{2}$ (E) $2p - 2x$

30. $\dfrac{ca^2 - cb^2}{-a - b}$ is equivalent to cb plus

   (A) ac (B) $-ca$ (C) 1   (D) -1 (E) c

31. The coordinates of A and B are $(2a, 2b)$ and $(4a, 6b)$, respectively. The coordinates of the midpoint of AB in terms of a and b are

   (A) $(3a, 4b)$ (B) $(3b, 4a)$ (C) $(6a, 8b)$
   (D) $(6b, 8a)$ (E) $(3a, 6b)$

32. If $x^2 + y^2 = 8$ and $xy = 7$, then $(x + y)^2 =$

   (A) 14   (B) 16   (C) 22   (D) 30   (E) 49

33. A student does $\dfrac{1}{3}$ of her homework and then goes to dinner. After dinner she completes $\dfrac{3}{4}$ of the remainder of her assignments and then decides to go to a basketball game. What part of her homework will be left uncompleted if she spends no additional time on her assignments?

   (A) $\dfrac{1}{6}$ (B) $\dfrac{5}{12}$ (C) $\dfrac{1}{2}$ (D) $\dfrac{7}{12}$ (E) $\dfrac{2}{3}$

34. A train traveling at 30 miles per hour is stopped $1\frac{1}{2}$ miles from its destination at 1:00 P.M. At what time would the train have arrived at its destination if it were not for the delay?

   (A) 1:02   (B) 1:03   (C) 1:04   (D) 1:45
   (E) 2:20

35. If 9 men take 15 days to complete a task, how many days would be required to complete this task if 3 additional men were employed?

   (A) $4\dfrac{3}{4}$ (B) 10   (C) $11\dfrac{1}{4}$ (D) 12   (E) 16

IF YOU FINISH BEFORE TIME IS CALLED, YOU MAY CHECK YOUR WORK ON THIS SECTION ONLY. DO NOT WORK ON ANY OTHER SECTION IN THE TEST.   **S T O P**

6 6 6 6 6 6 6 6 6 6 6

SECTION 6   Time—30 minutes   For each question in this section, choose the best answer and
40 Questions   blacken the corresponding space on the answer sheet.

Each question below consists of a word in capital letters, followed by five lettered words or phrases. Choose the word or phrase that is most nearly opposite in meaning to the word in capital letters. Since some of the questions require you to distinguish fine shades of meaning, consider all the choices before deciding which is best.

Example:

GOOD: (A) sour   (B) bad   (C) red
(D) hot   (E) ugly
Ⓐ ● Ⓒ Ⓓ Ⓔ

---

1. CONFUSE: (A) accept willingly (B) tell apart
(C) abandon (D) remember
(E) refuse to speak

2. SCARCITY: (A) abundance   (B) mediocrity
(C) apathy   (D) lateness   (E) courage

3. HARMONIOUS: (A) incompetent   (B) basic
(C) quarrelsome   (D) remote
(E) unceremonious

4. SQUALID: (A) unconventional   (B) objective
(C) serene   (D) clean   (E) shrunken

5. INCENSE: (A) deflate   (B) calm   (C) perfume
(D) frighten   (E) disable

6. AMASS: (A) protract   (B) distribute
(C) startle   (D) embellish   (E) delude

7. MENDACIOUS: (A) beggarly   (B) regal
(C) veracious   (D) autonomous   (E) violent

8. INNUENDO:
(A) novel thought
(B) direct accusation
(C) primary cause
(D) unwarranted attack
(E) ordinary occurrence

9. FALLACIOUS: (A) intelligent   (B) mournful
(C) destitute   (D) valid   (E) extraneous

10. DIN: (A) magnitude   (B) silence   (C) fragrance
(D) formality   (E) diffidence

Each sentence below has one or two blanks, each blank indicating that something has been omitted. Beneath the sentence are five lettered words or sets of words. Choose the word or set of words that best fits the meaning of the sentence as a whole.

Example:

Although its publicity has been ----, the film itself is intelligent, well-acted, handsomely produced, and altogether ----.

(A) tasteless..respectable (B) extensive..moderate
(C) sophisticated..amateur (D) risqué..crude
(E) perfect..spectacular
● Ⓑ Ⓒ Ⓓ Ⓔ

---

11. The civil rights movement did not emerge from obscurity into national prominence overnight; on the contrary, it captured the public's imagination only ----.

(A) fruitlessly   (B) unimpeachably
(C) momentarily   (D) expeditiously
(E) gradually

12. The seventeenth-century writer Mary Astell was a rare phenomenon, a single woman who maintained and even ---- a respectable reputation while earning a living by her pen.

(A) eclipsed   (B) impaired   (C) decimated
(D) avoided   (E) enhanced

13. He bore the pain ---- and did not wince or whimper when the incision was made.

(A) histrionically   (B) stoically
(C) sardonically   (D) poorly   (E) marginally

14. Police officers who advocate strict enforcement of the law claim that the ---- shown by judges to first offenders ---- many young people to embark on a career of crime.

(A) tolerance..implores
(B) indifference..causes
(C) clemency..encourages
(D) understanding..forces
(E) harshness..stimulates

GO ON TO THE NEXT PAGE

6   6 6 6 6   6   6   6   6   6   6

15. This latest biography of Malcolm X is a nuanced and sensitive picture of a very complex man, ---- analysis of his personality.

   (A) an ineffectual   (B) a telling
   (C) a ponderous   (D) a simplistic
    (E) an overblown

Each question below consists of a related pair of words or phrases, followed by five lettered pairs of words or phrases. Select the lettered pair that best expresses a relationship similar to that expressed in the original pair.

Example:

  YAWN : BOREDOM :: (A) dream : sleep
  (B) anger : madness (C) smile : amusement
   (D) face : expression (E) impatience : rebellion

           Ⓐ Ⓑ ● Ⓓ Ⓔ

---

16. DOLLAR:DIME :: (A) week:day
   (B) hour:minute   (C) meter:centimeter
    (D) degree:minute   (E) decade:year

17. SPARK:BLAZE :: (A) nick:gash
   (B) ember:coal   (C) flag:badge
    (D) wind:banner   (E) flood:shower

18. BIZARRE:EXOTIC ::
   (A) dawdling:hasty
   (B) foreign:native
   (C) modish:outlandish
   (D) dumbfounded:astonished
   (E) nervous:pensive

19. ALLOY:METALS :: (A) tin:lead
   (B) hybrid:mongrels   (C) medley:ore
    (D) cake:ingredients   (E) gold:rings

20. FRIVOLOUS:SERIOUSNESS ::
   (A) acute:perception
   (B) meticulous:organization
   (C) outspoken:reticence
   (D) lavish:money
   (E) industrious:perseverance

21. OLFACTORY:NOSE :: (A) peripheral:eyes
   (B) gustatory:tongue   (C) ambulatory:patient
    (D) tactile:ears   (E) perfunctory:skin

22. BRONZE:PATINA :: (A) wood:veneer
   (B) plaque:honor   (C) mold:yeast
    (D) iron:rust   (E) lead:tin

23. CARDIOLOGY:HEART ::
   (A) pathology:maps
   (B) apology:sorrow
   (C) tautology:education
   (D) pharmacology:drugs
   (E) orthography:religion

24. TURNCOAT:TREACHEROUS ::
   (A) seamstress:generous
   (B) firebrand:mysterious
   (C) mountebank:serious
   (D) spoilsport:notorious
   (E) killjoy:lugubrious

25. MELLIFLUOUS:CACOPHONY ::
   (A) vinegary:acidity
   (B) fragrant:noisomeness
   (C) sweet:euphony
   (D) somber:discord
   (E) ironic:sarcasm

GO ON TO THE NEXT PAGE

6 6 6 6 6 6 6 6 6 6 6 6

Each passage below is followed by questions based on its content. Answer all questions following a passage on the basis of what is <u>stated</u> or <u>implied</u> in that passage.

The money-changers have two irregular modes of making a profit by their traffic: if they state the fair price of silver to the customer, they cheat him in the weight; if their scales and their method of weighing are accurate, they diminish the price of silver accordingly. But when they have to do with Tartars, they employ neither of these methods of fraud: on the contrary, they weigh the silver scrupulously, and sometimes allow a little overweight, and they pay them above the market price. In fact, they appear to be quite losers by the transaction, and so they would be, if the weight and the price of the silver alone were considered. Their advantage is derived, in these cases, from their manner of calculating the amount. When they come to reduce the silver into sapeks, they do indeed reduce it, making the most flagrant miscalculations, which the Tartars, who can count nothing beyond their beard, are quite incapable of detecting, and which they, accordingly, adopt implicitly, and even with satisfaction, always considering they have sold their bullion well, since they know that the full weight has been allowed, and that the full market price has been given.

26. The primary purpose of this passage appears to be to
(A) defend the economic practices of the money-changers
(B) compare the character of the Tartars with that of the money-changers
(C) denounce the gullibility of the Tartars in financial transactions
(D) explain the relationship between price and weight
(E) describe techniques the money-changers use to take advantage of their customers

27. Which of the following statements about Tartars is supported by the passage?
(A) Tartars hide valuables in their beards.
(B) Tartars are careful about weight and market price.
(C) Tartars sell sapeks for silver.
(D) Tartars cheat their customers by employing fraudulent methods of weighing their goods.
(E) Tartars seek an unfair price for their sapeks.

28. We can infer from this passage that the money-changers
(A) are aware that Tartars are poor mathematicians
(B) have fixed prices for their transactions
(C) convert bullion into pure silver
(D) lose by their transactions with the Tartars
(E) make less profit from the Tartars than from their other customers

Free unrhymed verse has been practiced for some thousands of years and reaches back to the incantation which linked verse with the ritual dance. It produced a communal emotion: the aim of the cadenced phrases was to create a state of mind. The general coloring of free rhythms in the poetry of today is very different. The predominant pattern of poetry today is that of speech rhythm, composed in the sequence of the musical phrase, not in the sequence of the metronome, the regular beat. In the twenties, conventional rhyme fell into almost complete disuse. This liberation from rhyme became as well a liberation of rhyme. Freed of its exacting task of supporting lame verse, it could be applied with greater effect where wanted for some special effect. Such break in the tradition of rhymed verse had the healthy effect of giving it a fresh start, released from the hampering convention of too familiar cadences. This refreshing and subtilizing of the use of rhyme can be seen everywhere in the poetry of today.

29. The title that best expresses the ideas of this passage is
(A) Primitive Poetry
(B) The Origin of Poetry
(C) Rhyme and Rhythm in Modern Verse
(D) Classification of Poetry
(E) Purpose in Poetry

30. According to the author contemporary or free unrhymed verse shares all the following attributes EXCEPT
(A) phrasing analogous to the patterns of speech
(B) rejection of the traditions of rhymed verse
(C) unconventional use of rhyme
(D) metronomic regularity of beat
(E) rhythmic patterns akin to musical phrases

31. The author's attitude toward the use of free unrhymed verse is one of
(A) approval   (B) skepticism   (C) indifference
   (D) anxiety   (E) tolerance

GO ON TO THE NEXT PAGE

6 6 6 6 6 6 6 6 6 6 6 6

The same high mental faculties which first led man to believe in unseen spiritual agencies, then in fetishism, polytheism, and ultimately in monotheism, would infallibly lead him, as long as his reasoning powers remained poorly developed, to various strange superstitions and customs. Many of these are terrible to think of—such as the sacrifice of human beings to a blood-loving god; the trial of innocent persons by the ordeal of poison or fire; witchcraft; devil-worship; necromancy—yet it is well occasionally to reflect on these superstitions, these conjurations of diabolic occult powers, for they show us what an infinite debt of gratitude we owe for the improvement of our reason to science, and to the accumulated knowledge science has granted us.

32. According to this author, we are under an obligation to science for our

(A) original intellectual capacity
(B) belief in fetishism
(C) development of laws to protect the innocent
(D) liberation from irrational primitive beliefs
(E) powers of conjuration

33. This passage most likely is part of a treatise on

(A) witchcraft
(B) theology
(C) scientific method
(D) anthropology
(E) organic evolution

34. The author would most likely agree with which of the following statements?

(A) Monotheism motivated primitive people to the sacrifice of human beings.
(B) Monotheism evolved with the development of the intellect.
(C) Polytheism preceded the belief in unseen spiritual forces.
(D) Polytheism was the antithesis of superstition.
(E) Fetishism is derived from monotheism.

35. It can be inferred that the author considers the kind of underdeveloped reasoning described in the passage to be a cause of

(A) vacillation   (B) apathy   (C) spontaneity
(D) barbarity   (E) skepticism

When we next saw Miss Emily, she had grown fat and her hair was turning gray. During the next few years it grew grayer and grayer until it attained an even pepper-and-salt iron-gray, when it ceased turning. Up to the day of her death at seventy-four it was still that vigorous iron-gray, like the hair of an active man.

From that time on her front door remained closed, save for a period of six or seven years, when she was about forty, during which she gave lessons in china-painting. She fitted up a studio in one of the downstairs rooms, where the daughters and granddaughters of Colonel Sartoris' contemporaries were sent to her with the same regularity and in the same spirit that they were sent to church on Sundays with a twenty-five-cent piece for the collection plate. Meanwhile her taxes had been remitted.

Then the newer generation became the backbone and the spirit of the town, and the painting pupils grew up and fell away and did not send their children to her with boxes of color and tedious brushes and pictures cut from the ladies' magazines. The front door closed on the last one and remained closed for good. When the town got free postal delivery, Miss Emily alone refused to let them fasten the metal numbers above her door and attach a mailbox to it. She would not listen to them.

36. The major subject of the passage is

(A) Miss Emily's attempt to earn a living
(B) the mystery of Miss Emily's sudden aging
(C) the indifference of the townfolk
(D) the nature of Miss Emily's personal feelings
(E) Miss Emily's changing relationship with the town

37. It can be inferred from the passage that Colonel Sartoris' contemporaries sent their daughters to Miss Emily because

(A) they admired Miss Emily's skill at painting china
(B) they wished a tactful way of providing her with money
(C) their daughters lacked ladylike accomplishments
(D) they knew she was offering lessons for a limited time
(E) she provided her pupils with religious instruction

GO ON TO THE NEXT PAGE

6 6 6 6 6 6 6 6 6 6 6

There are exceptions to the rule of male insects being smaller than female, and some of these exceptions are intelligible. Size and strength would be an advantage to the males which fight for the possession of the females, and in these cases, as with the stag-beetle (Lucanus), the males are larger than the females. There are, however, other beetles which are not known to fight together, of which the males exceed the females in size, and the meaning of this fact is not known, but in some of these cases, as with the huge Dynastes and Megasoma, we can at least see that there would be no necessity for the males to be smaller than the females, in order to be matured before them, for these beetles are not short-lived, and there would be ample time for the pairing of the sexes.

38. According to the author, the traits of the male Lucanus include which of the following?

    I. Belligerence
   II. Active intelligence
  III. Superior bulk

(A) I only
(B) III only
(C) I and III only
(D) II and III only
(E) I, II, and III

39. It can be inferred from the name "stag-beetles" that the members of this species most likely

(A) are warm-blooded mammals
(B) are herbivorous by nature
(C) have appendages that resemble horns
(D) are as short-lived as their namesakes
(E) take one mate for their lifetimes

40. The paragraph preceding this one probably

(A) discusses a generalization about the size of insects
(B) develops the concept that male insects do not live long after maturity
(C) describes the distinguishing marks of female insects
(D) discusses the role of intelligence in male insects
(E) compares male and female sexual roles

IF YOU FINISH BEFORE TIME IS CALLED, YOU MAY CHECK YOUR WORK ON THIS SECTION ONLY. DO NOT WORK ON ANY OTHER SECTION IN THE TEST. **STOP**

Answer Key

Note: The answers to the math sections are keyed to the corresponding review areas in Chapter 12. The numbers in parentheses after each answer refer to topics as listed below. (Note that to review for number 16, Quantitative Comparison, study Chapter 11.)

1. Fundamental Operations
2. Algebraic Operations
3. Using Algebra
4. Roots and Radicals
5. Inequalities
6. Fractions
7. Decimals
8. Percent
9. Averages
10. Motion
11. Ratio and Proportion
12. Mixtures and Solutions
13. Work
14. Coordinate Geometry
15. Geometry
16. Quantitative Comparison
17. Data Interpretation

Section 1   Math

1. C (2)	6. E (3)	11 E (11)	16. A (8)	21. C (2, 6)
2. D (8)	7. A (11)	12. A (11, 15)	17. D (12)	22. C (1)
3 C (6, 7)	8. C (1)	13. E (15)	18. A (5, 15)	23. A (3, 12)
4. A (1, 15)	9. D (2)	14. D (11, 15)	19. C (1)	24. C (2)
5. D (1)	10. A (6, 8)	15. A (2)	20. B (8)	25 C (10)

Section 2   Test of Standard Written English

1. C	11. C	21. C	31. D	41. D
2. E	12. C	22. C	32. D	42. C
3. D	13. D	23. E	33. A	43. B
4. C	14. D	24. D	34. C	44. B
5. C	15. D	25. C	35. A	45. C
6. A	16. E	26. C	36. E	46. B
7. E	17. A	27. C	37. A	47. B
8. C	18. A	28. D	38. A	48. A
9. C	19. B	29. C	39. E	49. D
10. C	20. C	30. B	40. E	50. C

Section 3   Verbal

1. E	10. D	19. A	28. D	37. C
2. C	11. B	20. B	29. A	38. D
3. B	12. E	21. D	30. B	39. B
4. D	13. A	22. B	31. A	40. C
5. E	14. E	23. A	32. A	41. A
6. D	15. E	24. B	33. D	42. C
7. D	16. C	25. E	34. E	43. C
8. A	17. D	26. B	35. B	44. A
9. B	18. D	27. C	36. B	45. A

Section 4   Verbal

1. A	9. C	17. E	25. E	33. D
2. B	10. A	18. D	26. E	34. C
3. A	11. D	19. B	27. A	35. D
4. B	12. A	20. C	28. D	36. B
5. A	13. D	21. B	29. E	37. D
6. C	14. D	22. D	30. D	38. D
7. D	15. A	23. C	31. A	39. A
8. D	16. D	24. B	32. B	40. C

Section 5 Math

1.	C (4, 7)	8.	C (6, 8, 16)	15.	C (2, 6, 16)	22.	B (15, 16)	29.	D (15)
2.	D (9)	9.	A (4, 16)	16.	D (15, 16)	23.	C (15, 16)	30.	B (2)
3.	C (11)	10.	B (6, 8, 16)	17.	C (15, 16)	24.	B (15, 16)	31.	A (14)
4.	A (10)	11.	A (4, 8, 16)	18.	C (15, 16)	25.	B (15, 16)	32.	C (2)
5.	D (11)	12.	B (6, 7, 16)	19.	A (15, 16)	26.	C (15, 16)	33.	A (6)
6.	C (5, 15)	13.	D (6, 16)	20.	C (15, 16)	27.	B (2, 7, 16)	34.	B (10)
7.	E (12)	14.	D (5, 16)	21.	B (15, 16)	28.	B (8, 13)	35.	C (11, 13)

Section 6 Verbal

1.	B	9.	D	17.	A	25.	B	33.	C
2.	A	10.	B	18.	D	26.	E	34.	B
3.	C	11.	E	19.	D	27.	B	35.	D
4.	D	12.	E	20.	C	28.	A	36.	E
5.	B	13.	B	21.	B	29.	C	37.	B
6.	B	14.	C	22.	D	30.	D	38.	C
7.	C	15.	B	23.	D	31.	A	39.	C
8.	B	16.	E	24.	E	32.	D	40.	A

Self-Evaluation

The model SAT test you have just completed has the same format as the actual SAT. As you take more of the model tests in this chapter, you will lose any SAT "stage fright" you might have.

Use the steps that follow to evaluate your performance on Model SAT Test 3. (Note: You'll find the charts referred to in steps 1–5 on the next four pages.)

■ **STEP 1** Use the Answer Key to check your answers for each section.

■ **STEP 2** For each section, count the number of correct and incorrect answers (remember that you don't count omitted answers), and enter the numbers on the appropriate lines of the chart "Calculate Your Raw Score." Then do the indicated calculations to get your Raw Verbal Score, your Raw TSWE Score, and your Raw Math Score.

■ **STEP 3** Consult the chart "Evaluate Your Performance" to see how well you did.

■ **STEP 4** To pinpoint the specific areas in which you need to improve, circle the numbers of the questions that you either left blank or got wrong on the "Identify Your Weaknesses" charts. This will tell you where to concentrate your efforts to get the most out of your study time. The chart for the math sections gives you page references for review and practice by skill areas. The charts for the verbal and TSWE sections refer you to the appropriate chapters to study for each question type.

■ **STEP 5** Do the review and practice indicated on the charts wherever you had a concentration of circles.

Important: Remember that, in addition to evaluating your scores, you should read all of the answer explanations for questions you answered incorrectly, questions you omitted, and questions you answered correctly but found difficult. Reviewing the answer explanations will help you understand concepts and strategies, and may point out shortcuts.

Calculate Your Raw Score

Verbal

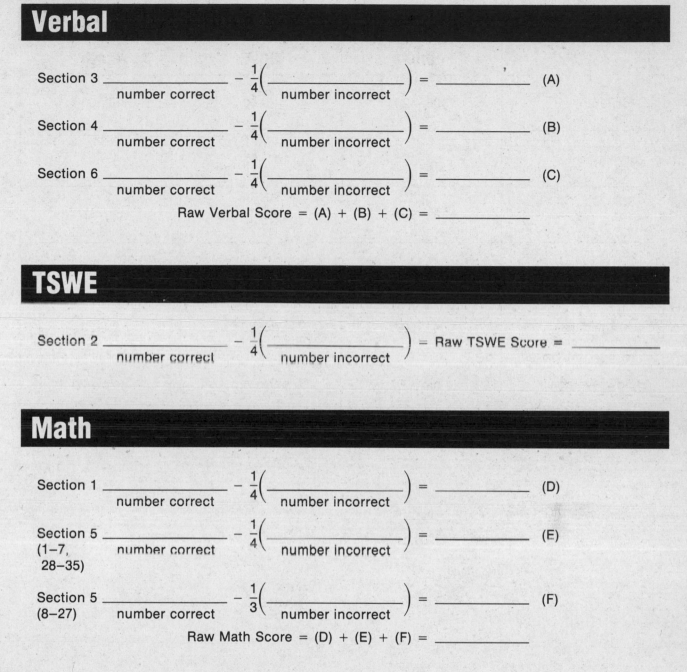

Section 3 _____ − $\frac{1}{4}$(_____) = _____ (A)
number correct   number incorrect

Section 4 _____ − $\frac{1}{4}$(_____) = _____ (B)
number correct   number incorrect

Section 6 _____ − $\frac{1}{4}$(_____) = _____ (C)
number correct   number incorrect

Raw Verbal Score = (A) + (B) + (C) = _____

TSWE

Section 2 _____ − $\frac{1}{4}$(_____) = Raw TSWE Score = _____
number correct   number incorrect

Math

Section 1 _____ − $\frac{1}{4}$(_____) = _____ (D)
number correct   number incorrect

Section 5 _____ − $\frac{1}{4}$(_____) = _____ (E)
(1–7,   number correct   number incorrect
28–35)

Section 5 _____ − $\frac{1}{3}$(_____) = _____ (F)
(8–27)   number correct   number incorrect

Raw Math Score = (D) + (E) + (F) = _____

Evaluate Your Performance

Verbal, TSWE, Math

	Verbal	TSWE	Math
Excellent	106–125	46–50	52–60
Very Good	91–105	41–45	45–51
Good	81–90	36–40	36–44
Above Average	61–80	31–35	30–35
Average	41–60	26–30	20–29
Below Average	below 40	below 26	below 20

Identify Your Weaknesses

Verbal

Question Type	Question Numbers			Chapter to Study
	Section 3	Section 4	Section 6	
Antonym	1, 2, 3, 4, 5, 6, 7, 8, 9, 10, 11, 12, 13, 14, 15	1, 2, 3, 4, 5, 6, 7, 8, 9, 10	1, 2, 3, 4, 5, 6, 7, 8, 9, 10	Chapter 5
Analogy	36, 37, 38, 39, 40, 41, 42, 43, 44, 45	16, 17, 18, 19, 20, 21, 22, 23, 24, 25	16, 17, 18, 19, 20, 21, 22, 23, 24, 25	Chapter 6
Sentence Completion	16, 17, 18, 19, 20, 31, 32, 33, 34, 35	11, 12, 13, 14, 15	11, 12, 13, 14, 15	Chapter 7
Reading Comprehension	21, 22, 23, 24, 25, 26, 27, 28, 29, 30	26, 27, 28, 29, 30, 31, 32, 33, 34, 35, 36, 37, 38, 39, 40	26, 27, 28, 29, 30, 31, 32, 33, 34, 35, 36, 37, 38, 39, 40	Chapter 8

TSWE

Question Type	Question Numbers	Chapter to Study
Usage	1, 2, 3, 4, 5, 6, 7, 8, 9, 10, 11, 12, 13, 14, 15, 16, 17, 18, 19, 20, 21, 22, 23, 24, 25, 41, 42, 43, 44, 45, 46, 47, 48, 49, 50	Chapter 13
Sentence Correction	26, 27, 28, 29, 30, 31, 32, 33, 34, 35, 36, 37, 38, 39, 40	Chapter 13

Identify Your Weaknesses

Math

	Question Numbers		
Skill Area	**Section 1**	**Section 5**	**Pages to Study**
Fundamental Operations	4, 5, 8, 19, 22		328–29
Algebraic Operations	1, 9, 15, 21, 24	15, 27, 30, 32	329–34
Using Algebra	6, 23		334–35
Fractions	3, 10, 21	8, 10, 12, 13, 15, 33	341–45
Decimals and Percents	2, 3, 10, 16, 17, 20	1, 8, 10, 11, 12, 27, 28	351–55
Verbal Problems	5, 14, 15, 17, 23, 25	2, 3, 4, 5, 7, 28, 34, 35	357–58
Ratio and Proportion	7, 11, 12, 14	3, 5, 35	362–64
Geometry	4, 12, 13, 14, 18	6, 16, 17, 18, 19, 20, 21, 22, 23, 24, 25, 26, 29, 31	371–76
Inequalities	18	6, 14	335–36
Quantitative Companion		8, 9, 10, 11, 12, 13, 14, 15, 16, 17, 18, 19, 20, 21, 22, 23, 24, 25, 26, 27	309–13
Roots and Radicals		1, 9, 11	332–33

Answer Explanations

Section 1   Math

1. C. $9x - 5 = 3y$
$$\frac{9x - 5}{3} = \frac{3y}{3}$$
$$\frac{9x - 5}{3} = y$$

2. D.   Let x = the number.
$$0.09x = 27$$
$$9x = 2700$$
$$x = 300$$

3. C. $0.875 = 87\frac{1}{2}\% = \frac{7}{8}$
$$\frac{x}{64} = \frac{7}{8}$$
$$8x = 7(64)$$
$$x - 7(8) - 56$$

It is not necessary to multiply 64 by 7.

4. A.   Shaded area represents thickness of pipe. Difference of radii equals thickness of pipe.

Radius of outer dimension = 1.25 in.
Radius of inner dimension = 1.05 in.
Difference = 0.2 in.

5. D.   Because one of the numbers is 2, consider only the even numbers. Since $362 \div 7 = 51+$, the correct answer is 364.

6. E.   If all seats were occupied, there would be rs pupils. Since 2 seats remain vacant, there are $rs - 2$ students in the classroom.

7. A. D dollars = $100D$ cents
Let y = cost (in cents) of x oranges.
$$\frac{\text{number of oranges}}{\text{cost (in cents)}} = \frac{a}{100D} = \frac{x}{y}$$
$$ay = 100Dx$$
$$y = \frac{100Dx}{a}$$

8. C. $\dfrac{\text{Length of fence}}{\text{Distance between posts}} = \text{Number of spaces}$
$$\frac{320 \text{ ft.}}{40 \text{ ft.}} = 8 \text{ spaces}$$
There is 1 post at the beginning of the first space, and there is 1 post at the end of each of the 8 spaces. Thus there are $1 + 8$ or 9 posts.

9. D. $\dfrac{1}{y} = -4$
$$\frac{1}{2y} = -2 \quad \text{(divide by 2)}$$
$$x = -2 \quad \text{(given)}$$
$$x = \frac{1}{2y} \quad \text{(things equal to the same thing are equal to each other)}$$
$$2xy = 1 \quad \text{(multiply by } 2y\text{)}$$
$$y = \frac{1}{2x} \quad \text{(divide by } 2x\text{)}$$

10. A.   If you have memorized fraction–percent equivalents, you recognize that there are three eighths in $37\frac{1}{2}\%$.

Alternatively, let x = number of eighths in $37\frac{1}{2}\%$.
$$\frac{x}{8} = 37\frac{1}{2}\%$$
$$\frac{x}{8} = \frac{37.5}{100}$$
$$100x - 300$$
$$x - 3$$

11. E.   This is an inverse proportion.
Let x = number of days that a bag of feed can take care of 12 chickens.
$$\frac{18 \text{ chickens}}{12 \text{ chickens}} = \frac{x}{54 \text{ days}}$$
$$\frac{3}{2} = \frac{x}{54}$$
$$2x = 3(54)$$
$$2x = 162$$
$$x = 81 \text{ days}$$

12. A.   Area of outside rectangle minus area of inside rectangle equals area of frame.
Area of inside rectangle (picture) = (6 ft.) (8 ft.) or 48 sq. ft. Area of outside rectangle = (7 ft.) (9 ft.) or 63 sq. ft.
Area of frame = 15 sq. ft.

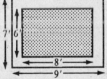

$$\frac{\text{area of frame}}{\text{area of picture}} = \frac{15 \text{ sq. ft.}}{48 \text{ sq. ft.}} = \frac{15}{48} = \frac{5}{16}$$

13. E. $\frac{2}{5}$ of 360° or $\frac{2}{5} \times 360°$ or 144°

14. D. $a + b + c = 180°$
Let x = base of ratios.
$$x + 3x + 2x = 180°$$
$$6x = 180°$$
$$x = 30°$$
Angles a, b, and c = 30, 90, and 60, respectively
Angle b = 90

15. A. $\dfrac{a + b}{a - b} = \dfrac{x}{b - a}$

$\dfrac{a + b}{a - b} = \dfrac{x}{-a + b}$

$\dfrac{a + b}{a - b} = \dfrac{-x}{a - b}$ (multiply numerator and denominator by $-$)

$a + b = -x$ (multiply both sides of the equation by $a - b$)

$x = -a - b$ (multiply by -1)

16. A. Let x = number of remaining games that must be won.

$\dfrac{\text{Total games won}}{\text{Total games played}} = \text{Percent games won}$

$\dfrac{40 + x}{154} = \dfrac{65}{100}$

$4000 + 100x = 10010$

$100x = 6010$

$x = 60 \text{ games}$

17. D. $\dfrac{\text{increase}}{\text{original}} = \dfrac{900}{300} = 3 = \dfrac{300}{100} = 300\%$

18. A. CB is one half of CE, and CA is one half of CD. Since $CE > CD$, one half of CE (or CB) > one half of CD (or CA). Doubles, triples, halves, thirds, etc., of unequal quantities are unequal in the same order.

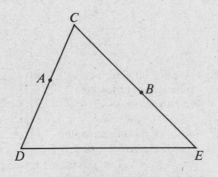

19. C. Time elapsed from 11 P.M. to 2 A.M. = 3 hr.
Rise in temperature = $(3°) (3) = 9°F$.
$-16°F. + 9°F. = -7°F.$

20. B. $\dfrac{\text{Parts of potassium}}{\text{Parts of potassium + nitrogen + oxygen}}$
= Part of potassium in potassium nitrate
$= \dfrac{39}{39 + 14 + 48}$ or $\dfrac{39}{101}$ or 0.386 or 39%

21. C. $\dfrac{1}{2} + \dfrac{2}{3} + \dfrac{3}{y} = \dfrac{23}{12}$ (multiply by $12y$)

$6y + 8y + 36 = 23y$

$6y + 8y - 23y = -36$

$-9y = -36$

$y = 4$

22. C. During the 9-week period the woman worked 45 days. Since her total earnings were $454.50, her earnings per day were

$\dfrac{\$454.50}{45}$ or $\$10.10$

23. A. Let x = number of ounces of sulfur necessary to make 172 oz. of sulfanilamide.

$\dfrac{\text{quantity of sulfur (ounces)}}{\text{quantity of sulfanilamide (ounces)}} = \dfrac{8}{43} = \dfrac{x}{172}$

$43x = (172)(8)$

$43x = 1376$

$x = 32$

24. C. $x - 7 = 0$ $y^2 = 25$
       $x = 7$ $y = \pm 5$
                 $xy = (7)(\pm 5)$
                 $xy = \pm 35$

25. C. $\dfrac{\text{Distance}}{\text{Rate}} = \text{Time}$

$\dfrac{100}{40} = 2\dfrac{1}{2}$ hr. (time for first part of trip)

$\dfrac{100}{50} = 2$ hr. (time for second part of trip)

Total time $= 4\dfrac{1}{2}$ hr.

Total distance = 200 miles

$\dfrac{\text{Distance}}{\text{Time}} = \text{Rate}$

$\dfrac{200}{4\frac{1}{2}} = 44.4$ m.p.h.

Section 2   Test of Standard Written English

1. C. Wrong word. Use *lie* instead of *lay*.

2. E. Sentence is correct.

3. D. Error in agreement between pronoun and antecedent. Since antecedent is *association*, change *their* to *its*.

4. C. Error in agreement. In a neither–nor construction the verb agrees with the noun or pronoun which comes immediately before the verb. *Principal is being considered* is correct.

5. C. Misuse of adjective for adverb. Change *considerable* to *considerably*.

6. A. Error in tense. Change *have rummaged* to *were rummaging*.

7. E.   Sentence is correct.

8. C.   Error in agreement. Change *their* to *his*.

9. C.   Error in diction. Use *effect* instead of *affect*.

10. C.   Error in subordination. Delete the comma and substitute *that* for *and it*. The second clause describes Aaron's record.

11. C.   Error in agreement. Change *them* to *it*.

12. C.   Incorrect coordinate conjunction. Change conjunction and word order for *nor is she* to *and she is* to clarify the relationship between the clauses.

13. D.   Error in diction. The word *being* is unnecessary. Change *including being* to *including*.

14. D.   Error in agreement. *Changes* requires a plural verb. Change *is* to *are*.

15. D.   Misuse of adjective for adverb. Change *comfortable* to *comfortably*.

16. E.   Sentence is correct.

17. A.   Error in tense. Change *has been warned* to *had been warned*.

18. A.   Faulty diction. Use *if* to indicate a condition. Substitute *whether*.

19. B.   Error in case. Change *she* to *her*.

20. C.   Error in agreement. In a neither–nor construction the verb agrees with the noun or pronoun which comes immediately before the verb. *Driver was able to identify* is correct.

21. C.   Incorrect sentence connector. Change the conjunctive adverb *unfortunately* to *therefore* to clarify the relationship between the clauses.

22. C.   Faulty verbal. Change *satisfying* to the infinitive *to satisfy*.

23. E.   Sentence is correct.

24. D.   Error in agreement. Change *they are* to *it is*.

25. C.   Error in agreement. The antecedent of *who* is *one*. Therefore, *who is* is correct.

26. C.   Choices A, D, and E are run-on sentences. Choice B is constructed awkwardly.

27. C.   When comparing two things, you should use the comparative degree (*better*) rather than the superlative degree (*best*).

28. D.   Choices A and B have dangling modifiers. Choices C and E create run-on sentences.

29. C.   The subordinating conjunction *Although* best connects the sentence's two clauses.

30. B.   Choices A, C, and E are run-on sentences; Choice D is unidiomatic.

31. D.   Parallel structure is maintained in Choice D. The parallelism is violated in the other choices.

32. D.   Choices A, B, and E contain sentence fragments; Choice C creates a comma splice.

33. A.   The past tense and the subordinating conjunction *When* are correctly used in Choice A.

34. C.   Choice C expresses the author's meaning directly and concisely. All other choices are either indirect or ungrammatical.

35. A.   Choices B, C, D, and E are sentence fragments.

36. E.   Choice E expresses the author's meaning directly and concisely. All other choices are either indirect or ungrammatical.

37. A.   The sentence uses the subjunctive mood correctly.

38. A.   Sentence is correct.

39. E.   The errors in case and agreement are corrected in Choice E. *I* should be used instead of *me* because it is the predicate nominative of the verb *is*. *Who*, having as its antecedent the pronoun *I*, is a first person singular pronoun. The first person singular verb *am* should be used.

40. E.   The article (*a*, *an*) should not follow *kind of*.

41. D.   The reflexive pronoun *myself* cannot be used as the object of the verb *frightened*. Change *myself* to *me*.

42. C.   Misuse of adverb for adjective. Change *his many attempts bravely to enter* to *his many brave attempts to enter*.

43. B.   Lack of parallel structure. Change *not because of the money* to *not because he needed the money* (a clause) to parallel the clause that follows *but*.

44. B.   Error in diction. Change *liable* to *likely*.

45. C.   Error in agreement. Change *is* to *are*.

46. B.   Error in diction. *Latter* should not be used to refer to more than two items. Change *latter* to *last*.

47. B.   Lack of parallel structure. Change *to aid* to *aiding*.

48. A.   Misuse of adjective for adverb. Change *special prepared* to *specially prepared*.

49. D.   Error in tense. Change *had been* to *were*.

50. C.   Lack of parallel structure. Change *under application* to *being applied*.

Section 3   Verbal

1. E.   To *hearten* means to encourage or cheer. Its opposite is to *discourage*.
Context Clue: Think of "heartened by victory."

2. C.   *Spacious* means amply large, vast. Its opposite is restricted or *cramped*.
Remember to read all the choices before you finally decide which is best. *Airless* or stuffy may seem a good antonym for *spacious*. *Cramped*, however, is a better one.
Context Clue: Think of "a spacious room."

3. B.   *Simulated* means pretended or counterfeit; its opposite is *genuine* or real.
Context Clue: Think of "simulated pearls."

4. D.   *Fiendish* means devilish or wicked. Its opposite is *angelic*.

5. E.   To *dwindle* is to diminish or decrease. Its opposite is to *increase*.
Context Clue: Think of "a dwindling amount of cash."

6. D.   To *revere* is to honor and admire profoundly. Its opposite is to *dishonor*.

7. D.   *Unmarred* means without blemish; not spoiled or scarred. Its opposite is *spoiled*.

8. A.   To *desist* is to stop or cease to do something. Its opposite is to *continue*.
Context Clue: Think of "cease and desist."

9. B.   To *disparage* something is to speak slightingly of it; to belittle it. Its opposite is to *praise*.
Context Clue: Think of "disparaging the opposition."

10. D.   *Dissidence* is disagreement or dissent. Its opposite is *agreement*.
Context Clue: Think of "political dissidence."

11. B.   *Anomalous* means abnormal; peculiar; deviating from the norm. Its opposite is *regular*.
Context Clue: Think of getting "an anomalous result" in the lab.

12. E.   To *quell* is to put down or suppress; put an end to. Its opposite is to *incite* or prompt to action.
Context Clue: Think of police "quelling a riot."

13. A.   *Puerile* means childlike. Its opposite is *adult* (mature).
Context Clue: Think of "puerile behavior."

14. E.   *Discernment* is acuteness of judgment; insight. Its opposite is *lack of insight*.
Context Clue: Think of "fine discernment."

15. E.   *Lassitude* means languor, weariness of body or mind, lack of energy. Its opposite is *liveliness*.

16. C.   To uncover buried ruins is to *excavate* them. Notice the use of the comma to set off the phrase that defines the missing word.

(Definition)

17. D.   Puritans (members of a religious group following a pure standard of morality) would be offended by *lewd* (lecherous, obscene) material and would fear it might corrupt theatre-goers.

(Argument Pattern)

18. D.   *Rescind* means to cancel or withdraw. The lawmakers were so angered by the governor's enactment of martial law that they refused to work till it was cancelled.

19. A.   *Malingering* means pretending illness to avoid duty. Faced with an *arduous* or hard campaign, one might well wish to avoid work.

20. B. The columnist almost said *reverential* (worshipful) things about those he liked, but he savagely attacked those he disliked. "Even" here serves as an intensifier. *Acrimonious* (stinging or bitter in nature) continues the idea of unpleasantness.

(Contrast Signal)

21. D. Richard's introduction to school, his parents' reaction to their unfriendly neighbors, his brother and sister's silence about their classroom experiences—all these instances illustrate the family members' interaction with the English-speaking world.

(Specific Details)

22. B. The author's statement that it "was the first time I had heard anyone name me in English" supports Choice B. In addition to finding himself apart from his family, the usual experience of new pupils, he finds himself stripped of his name, his identity. Being addressed in such a strange and impersonal manner rattles him.
Choice A is incorrect. All the students were uneasy to find themselves separated from their families.
Choices C and D are incorrect. Nothing in the passage supports them.
Choice E is incorrect. The narrator lived in a gringo neighborhood; he must have seen white children.

(Inference)

23. A. The author's assertions in the last paragraph that his parents coped very well and that they were nobody's victims, indicate that his basic attitude toward them is admiring.

(Attitude/Tone)

24. B. Statement B is true to the author's experience: they felt estranged from the gringos' world.
Choice A is incorrect. Richard's father found steady work.
Choice C is incorrect. Although Sacramento as a whole was not determined to keep Mexicans out of white neighborhoods, some neighbors tried to frighten away Richard's family.
Choice D is incorrect. Lacking confidence in public, Richard's parents remained detached from community affairs.
Choice E is incorrect. Richard's parents sent their children to Roman Catholic schools; they were involved with academic institutions.

(Specific Details)

25. E. For Richard's parents to call white people *los americanos*, "the Americans," implies that on some level they do not consider themselves

Americans. This is a *telling* or *revealing* comment that points up the degree of alienation Richard's parents felt.

(Word from Context)

26. B. We are told that 71% of the earth is covered by water and that the Pacific Ocean covers half the earth. The Pacific is obviously the largest ocean.

(Inference)

27. C. The peripheral furrows or *deeps* are discussed in the second paragraph. We are told that these deeps are near the continental masses, and therefore, near the shore.

(Specific Details)

28. D. The last sentence of the first paragraph discusses the submerged or *underwater* portions of the continental masses.
Key Words: masses, per cent, sea level, submerged, relief.

(Specific Details)

29. A. Terms such as "unendingly," "ultimately," and "ceaseless" indicate that the mountains are made level over an enormous *passage of years*.

(Word from Context)

30. B. The passage states that the *deeps*, the site of frequent earthquakes, are of recent origin. This implies that newly formed land and sea formations have a greater frequency of earthquake occurrence than older formations. Remember, when asked to make inferences, base your answers on what the passage implies, not what it states directly.

(Inference)

31. A. What was once a minor problem is now a major cause of death; what was formerly *negligible* (insignificant; minor and thus of no consequence) has become the chief *cause* of cancer-related deaths. Note how the two phrases set off by commas ("formerly. . ."; "once. . .") balance one another and are similar in meaning.
Remember, in double-blank sentences, go through the answer choices, testing the *first* words in each choice and eliminating those that don't fit.

32. A. *Propitious* means favorable. It would be sensible to wait for a favorable moment to reveal plans.
Remember, before you look at the choices,

read the sentence and think of a word that makes sense.
Likely Words: appropriate, fitting, favorable.

(Examples)

33. D. A *truculent* (aggressive) attitude will harm even a *persuasive* case.
Note that the verb *alienate* signals you that the second missing word has negative associations. Therefore, you can eliminate any answer choice with positive ones.
Choices A, B, and C all have positive associations. Only Choices D or E can be correct.

(Contrast Signal)

34. E. Wemmick's private kindness is contrasted with his *public* harshness or *ruthlessness*.
Note here the use of "even" as an intensifier: to be *ruthless* or relentless is more blameworthy than merely to be *uncompassionate* or hard-hearted.

35. B. Archaeologists prefer to deal with *intact* sites, sites that have not yet been *disturbed*.
The use of "although" in the opening clause sets up a contrast. The missing words must be antonyms or near-antonyms.

(Contrast Signal)

36. B. The *barber* uses his *shears* (scissors) to trim hair; the *dentist* uses his *drill* to bore holes in teeth.

(Worker and Tool)

37. C. A *puck* (a black rubber disk) is struck by a stick in playing *hockey*. A *ball* is struck by a club in playing *golf*.
Remember, if more than one answer appears to fit the relationship in your sentence, look for a narrower approach. "A puck is used in playing hockey" is too broad in this case.

(Function)

38. D. A *poodle* is one kind of *dog*; a *whale* is one kind of *mammal*.

(Class and Member)

39. B. A *hillock* is defined as a little hill, a natural elevation of land smaller than a *mountain*. A *pond* is a body of water smaller than a *lake*.

40. C. A *frown* (wrinkling of the brow) shows *displeasure*; a *sneer* (curling of the lip) shows *contempt* (scorn).

(Action and Its Significance)

41. A. A *pride* is a company or group of *lions*. Similarly, a *bevy* is a flock of birds, especially *quails*.
Note the use of a secondary meaning of the familiar-looking noun *pride*.
Use the process of elimination to find the correct answer. If you know that a pride is a group of lions, you can eliminate Choices B, C, D, and E: a lair is a bear's den, not a group of bears. By process of elimination, a *bevy* must be a group of quails.

(Part to Whole)

42. C. A *mentor* (wise and trusted counselor) provides one with *counsel* (advice). A *bodyguard* provides one with *protection*.

(Definition)

43. C. *Chauvinism* is excessive patriotism or extreme love of *country*. *Gluttony* is extreme desire for *food*.

(Definition)

44. A. A *parsimonious* (stingy) person is extremely *frugal* (economical); an *ecstatic* (rapturously delighted) person is extremely *joyful*.

(Degree of Intensity)

45. A. *Convention* (accepted social usage or customs) is a synonym for *mores* (customs). *Caprice* (tendency to change one's mind fancifully) is a synonym for *whimsicality*.

(Synonyms)

Section 4   Verbal

1. A. To *intervene* is to come between, as in an action; to intercede. Its opposite is to *remain uninvolved*.
Remember to break down unfamiliar words into recognizable parts.
Word Parts Clue: *Inter-* means between; *vene* means come. *Intervene* means to come between.

2. B. *Astronomical* means extremely large. Its opposite is *minute* (extremely small).
Remember to consider secondary meanings of the capitalized word as well as its primary meaning. The primary meaning of *astronomical* is "related to astronomy; pertaining to the study of the stars."
Context Clue: Think of "astronomical costs."

3. A. *Trivia* are unimportant matters, trifles. The opposite of trivia is *important matters*.
Context Clue: Think of questions about trivia in the game *Trivial Pursuit*.

4. B. *Leniency* means mercy, forbearance. Its opposite is harshness or *severity*.
Context Clue: Think of "the leniency of the court."

5. A. To *extricate* is to disentangle or free. Its opposite is to *ensnare*.
Context Clue: Think of "extricating yourself from a briar patch."

6. C. *Terse* means brief, succinct, concise. Its opposite is *verbose* (overly wordy).
Word Parts Clue: *Verb-* means word. *Verbose* means wordy.
Context Clue: Think of "terse comments."

7. D. *Furtive* means sly, stealthy, like a thief. Its opposite is *aboveboard* or open.
Context Clue: Think of "a furtive peek."

8. D. To *ameliorate* is to improve or make better. Its opposite is to *worsen*.
Context Clue: Think of "ameliorating working conditions."

9. C. *Fallow* means unsown, as in land left unseeded. Its opposite is *cultivated* or agriculturally improved.
Remember to consider less familiar meanings of the answer choices as well as their more familiar meanings. *Cultivated* means educated and refined; it also means tilled or agriculturally improved.
Context Clue: Think of "cultivated fields."

10. A. *Ascetic* means severely abstinent; austere or self-denying. It is the opposite of *wanton* (immoral or unrestrained).
Context Clue: Think of "an ascetic holy man."

11. D. Immune to most pesticides, cockroaches are thus tough or *hardy* and hard to *eliminate*.
Remember, in double-blank sentences, go through the answer choices, testing the *first* words in each choice and eliminating those that don't fit. You can immediately eliminate Choices A and C.

12. A. The sentence discusses a benefit *shared by both* countries or *mutual*.
Remember to watch for signal words that link one part of the sentence to another. The presence of *and* linking the positive terms "harmony" and "benefit" indicates that you are looking for a word without negative associations. Therefore, you can eliminate any word with negative ones. Choices B, C, D, and E all have negative associations.

13. D. The fact that television by its coverage may both create interest in a sport and kill interest in that sport is a contradiction or *paradox*.
(Examples)

14. D. Note the use of "might." Without the support of other stories, the actor's stories might not be believed. If people need such supporting testimony, their first response to the stories must be one of disbelief. They must think them exaggerations or *hyperbole*. "Were there not" is a short way of saying "If there were not."

15. A. This is a case in which you can't eliminate any of the answer choices from checking the first words of each answer pair: all are terms that could describe an ambassador. In this case, the *eminent* ambassador was only an *indifferent* (mediocre) linguist; nevertheless, he insisted on trying to speak foreign languages without help.
Remember to watch for signal words that link one part of the sentence to another. The use of "yet" in the second clause sets up a contrast.
Note that "but" here means "only." That's your clue to expect a belittling or negative word.
(Contrast Signal)

16. D. *Gasoline* provides the energy for an *automobile*; *food*, the energy for *man*.
(Function)

17. E. A *symphony* is written by a *composer*; a *sonnet* is written by a *poet*.
(Worker and the Article Created)

18. D. *Wearisome* (fatiguing; tiresome) and *refreshing* are opposites; *lengthy* and *brief* are opposites.
(Antonyms)

19. B. To *stalk* someone is to *follow* or draw near him stealthily or secretly. Similarly, to *spy* on someone is to *look* at or observe him stealthily.
(Manner)

20. C. To *dampen* something is less intense than to *drench* it; to *simmer* something is less intense than to *boil* it.
(Degree of Intensity)

21. B. A *bacterium* is a member of a *colony* (group of bacteria growing together). A *fish* is a member of a *shoal* or school.
(Member and Group)

22. D. To *allay pain* is to lessen it; to *mitigate* a *punishment* is to reduce its severity.

(Function)

23. C. *Exertion* (vigorous effort) causes *fatigue*; *sedation* (administration of a tranquilizing drug) causes *tranquility* or calm.

(Cause and Effect)

24. B. A *foe* or enemy feels *enmity* or hate. A *miser* or skinflint feels *avarice* or greed.

(Defining Characteristic)

25. E. By definition, one *shuns* (avoids) a *pariah* (outcast). Likewise, one *ridicules* a *butt* (laughingstock).
Remember to watch out for errors stemming from reversals. *Pariah* is the object of the verb *shun*; he is the person being shunned. In contrast, *predator* is the subject of the verb *hunt*; he is the person who hunts, *not* the person being hunted. The grammatical relationship is reversed.

(Defining Characteristic)

26. E. The passage discusses aspects of weightlessness or lack of gravity in space. Remember, when asked to choose a title, watch out for choices that are too specific or too broad. Choices C and D are too specific; Choices A and B, too broad.

(Main Idea/Title)

27. A. The last sentence supports Choice A. Sneezes are "involuntary reflex movements" that in space may have unexpectedly dangerous effects.

(Inference)

28. D. The second sentence states that at a certain speed the rocket's centrifugal force will cancel the pull of earth's gravity.
Note that Choice B is incorrect because it uses the term "centripetal" instead of "centrifugal."

(Specific Details)

29. E. The sentence in parentheses indicates that the Human Factors Division is working on the structure of a device for drinking.
Remember, when asked about specific details in the passage, spot key words in the question and scan the passage to find them (or their synonyms).
Key Words: Human Factors Division.

(Specific Details)

30. D. The use of simple, concrete examples (pens, flashlights, sneezes) and of vivid pictures (drowning in a glass of water; somersaulting in the air) indicates the passage is taken from a magazine for the general public rather than for an audience accustomed to reading about advanced technology. So does the colloquial, personal writing style.

(Inference)

31. A. While Choices B, C, D, and E are mentioned at different points in the passage, Choice A is best because the nature of rumor is treated *throughout* the three paragraphs.

(Main Idea)

32. B. Rumor has persisted since primitive times even when better sources of information have been at hand. Therefore, we may say that rumor is *hardy* or vigorous in growth. Remember, when asked to make inferences, base your answers on what the passage implies, not what it states directly.

(Inference)

33. D. According to the passage, rumor expresses "something deep in the heart" of the believer. In other words, it *reflects* his own unexpressed beliefs.
Remember, when asked about specific details in the passage, spot key words in the question and scan the passage to find them (or their synonyms).
Key Words: truth, belief.

(Specific Details)

34. C. The second sentence of the second paragraph indicates that in wartime people do not receive "enough information." Their information therefore is *limited*.

(Specific Details)

35. D. The author is studying rumor, analyzing its nature and its popularity. Taking no strong stand for or against it, he maintains a philosophical or scholarly interest in it as a subject for study.
Choice A is incorrect. The author is sufficiently interested in rumor to describe its workings at some length. However, he is not wildly enthusiastic about it.
Choice B is incorrect. The author is curious about rumor, but not morbidly or unhealthily so.
Choice C is incorrect. It is unsupported by the passage.
Choice E is incorrect. The author is not gullible about rumors; he studies them, but does not necessarily believe them.

(Attitude/Tone)

36. **B.** The passage aims to define certain technical terms in music. The introductory sentences of both paragraphs refer to the range in frequencies and basic characteristics of musical sounds. Italics are used to highlight the particular terms being defined.

Remember, when asked to find the main idea, be sure to check the opening and summary sentences of each paragraph.

(Main Idea)

37. **D.** A stress on defining new terminology is characteristic of college textbooks. The emphasis on the musical nature of the sounds under consideration makes it likely that this particular textbook covers music theory and not the physics of the ear, for example.

(Inference)

38. **D.** In the first sentence of the second paragraph, we are told that quality and timbre are synonyms. In the concluding sentence of the second paragraph, we learn that quality depends on overtones. Thus, timbre depends on overtones.

(Specific Details)

39. **A.** Ultrasonic frequencies are defined in the passage as being "higher than those within the audible range." Thus, ultrasonic frequencies are *inaudible*.

Choices B, C, and E are incorrect. They are not supported by the passage.

Choice D is incorrect. Although these frequencies kill some bacteria, it is not indicated that they are "death rays."

(Specific Details)

40. **C.** Astronauts, traveling at speeds of thousands of miles per hour, would be traveling many times faster than the speed of sound. Thus, they would be most likely to use terms like Mach 5 or Mach 9.

Choices A and D are incorrect. Helicopter pilots and submarine navigators travel at speeds below the speed of sound.

Choices B and E are also incorrect. Musicians and biologists customarily work with audible sound.

(Inference)

Section 5

1. **C.** $\dfrac{3.6x^4y}{0.9xy^4} = \dfrac{4x^4y}{xy^4} = \dfrac{4x^3}{y^3}$

2. **D.** This is an example of weighted average.

$85\% \times 3 = 255$
$90\% \times 4 = \underline{360}$
$\text{Sum} = \overline{615}$
Number of cases $= 7$
$\dfrac{615}{7} = 87.85\%$ or 87.9%

3. **C.** According to the information furnished, the ratio of the number of marbles of the boy with the greatest number to those of the boy with the least number is $19:3$. Since the boy with the least number actually has 9 marbles (3×3), the boy with the greatest number has 19×3 or 57 marbles.

$\dfrac{\text{boy}}{\text{marbles}} = \dfrac{3}{9} = \dfrac{19}{x}$
$3x = 171$
$x = 57$

4. **A.** $\dfrac{\text{Distance}}{\text{Rate}} = \text{Time}$

$\dfrac{1800 \text{ miles}}{60 \text{ m.p.h.}} = 30 \text{ hr.}$

5. **D.** Let $y = $ number of articles that can be bought for x dollars.

$\dfrac{\text{number of articles}}{\text{cost (in dollars)}} = \dfrac{500}{d} = \dfrac{y}{x}$
$dy = 500x$
$y = \dfrac{500x}{d}$

6. **C.** If equal quantities are added to unequal quantities, the sums are unequal in the same order.

$A \text{———————}\overset{B}{|}\text{———} C$
$D \text{————————}\overset{E}{|}\text{——} F$

7. **E.** Assume that a *part* represents a pound.

3 lb. at 60¢ per pound cost $1.80
2 lb. at 70¢ per pound cost 1.40
2 lb. at 50¢ per pound cost $\underline{1.00}$
Total cost of mixture $= \overline{\$4.20}$
Number of pounds in mixture $= 7$
Cost per pound $= 60$¢
Profit per pound (25%) $= 15$¢
Selling price $= 75$¢

8. **C.** $3\dfrac{1}{2}\% = 3.5\% = \dfrac{3.5}{100} = \dfrac{35}{1000}$

9. **A.** $\sqrt{0.04} = 0.2$
$\phantom{\sqrt{0.04} }(0.2)^2 = 0.04$
$\phantom{\sqrt{0.04} }0.2 > 0.04$

10. B.   Since $\frac{7}{8} = 87\frac{1}{2}\%$, half of $\frac{7}{8}$ is less than $87\frac{1}{2}\%$.

11. A. $\left(\frac{1}{2}\right)^2 = \left(\frac{1}{4}\right) = 25\%$

12. B. $\frac{0.7}{2} = 0.35$

$0.35 > 0.3$

13. D. $\frac{X}{Y} \cdot \frac{Y}{X} = 1$

$\frac{X}{Y}$ may be equal to, smaller than, or larger

than 1.

14. D.   The value of a could be zero, or some positive
fraction less than 1, or some negative fraction
more than -1.
The value of b could be some negative
fraction more than -1.

15. C. $\dfrac{2x - \dfrac{y-5}{6}}{\dfrac{y-5}{3} - 4x}$

Multiply numerator and denominator by 6:
$\dfrac{6(2x) - (y-5)}{2(y-5) - 24x} = \dfrac{12x - y + 5}{2y - 10 - 24x}$

$\dfrac{12x - y + 5}{24x + 2y - 10} = -\dfrac{1}{2}$ or -0.5

16. D.   Center City is
located at point O.
Circleville could be
located at any point
on the circumference
of the circle with a
radius of 23 km.
Centerville could be
located at any point
on the circumference
with a radius of 46 km.
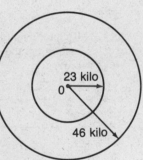
The distance from Circleville and Centerville
could be the straight-line distance from any
point on the circumference of one of these
circles to any point on the circumference of
the other circle. Obviously there are
innumerable possibilities, some equal to 23 km
and some greater than 23 km.

17. C.   In the right triangle ABC,
$x = 45$.
In right triangle BDA,
$z = 45$.

18. C.   In right triangle ABC, since the acute angles
are equal to $\frac{1}{2}$ of 90°, $x = 45$.

19. A.   Area of triangle $ABC = \frac{1}{2}(\text{leg} \times \text{leg}) = 12.5$,
or $(\text{leg})^2 = 25$. Therefore leg = 5
Area of square I or II = 5^2 or 25
Since $AB = BC = 5$, hypotenuse $AC = 5\sqrt{2}$
Area of square III = $(5\sqrt{2})^2$ or 50
Twice the area of $ABC = 25$ (given)

20. C.   See #19.

21. B.   Each side of square
$BCDE = 10$
Area of $ABC =$
$125 - 100$ or 25
Area of $ABC =$
$\frac{1}{2}(BC)(AF) = 25$
$\frac{1}{2}(10)(AF) = 25$
$AF = 5$
$FG = BE = CD = 10$
$AFG = 15$ and $2(EB) = 20$
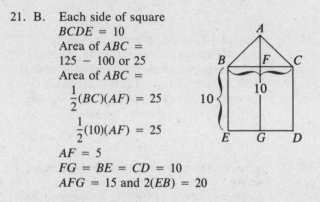

22. B.   If $BD = DC$,
then $y = x + z$
and $y > x$.
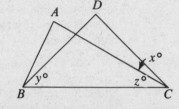

23. C.   Area of circle = πr^2
If the radius of circle B is twice the radius of
circle A, then the area of circle B is 4 times
the area of circle A. In other words, 4 times
the area of circle A = the area of circle B.

24. B.   Circumference = $2\pi r$
If the circumference of one circle is twice that
of another circle, then the radius of the larger
circle is twice that of the smaller circle. The
area of the larger circle, however, will be 4
times the area of the smaller circle.

25. B.   Since the area of the unshaded section = 9π,
the radius $OA = 3$. Since $OB - OA = 4$, OB
$= 7$.
The area of the shaded plus the unshaded
portion = 49π.
The shaded portion = $49\pi - 9\pi$ or 40π.
Four times the unshaded section = 36π.

26. C.   The circumference of the inner circle = 6π.
$(7)(6\pi) = 42\pi$.
The circumference of the outer circle = 14π.
$(3)(14\pi) = 42\pi$.

27. B. $0.1y + 0.01y = 2.2$
$10y + 1y = 220$
$11y = 220$
$y = 20$
$0.1y = 2$

28. B. $\dfrac{8 \text{ men}}{6 \text{ men}} = \dfrac{x \text{ days}}{12 \text{ days}}$ (an inverse proportion)

$6x = 96$

$x = 16$ days   (time required when 2 men are released)

Increase in time = 4 days

$\dfrac{4 \text{ days (increase)}}{12 \text{ days (original)}} = \dfrac{1}{3} = 33\dfrac{1}{3}\%$

29. D.   Perimeter = 2(Length + Width)
Let y = width.
$p = 2(x + y)$
$p = 2x + 2y$
$2y = p - 2x$
$y = \dfrac{p - 2x}{2}$

30. B. $\dfrac{ca^2 - cb^2}{-a - b}$

$-\dfrac{ca^2 - cb^2}{a + b}$ (multiply numerator and denominator by -1)

$-\dfrac{c(a^2 - b^2)}{a + b}$ (factor)

$-\dfrac{c(a + b)(a - b)}{a + b}$ (factor and divide by $a + b$)

$-c(a - b)$

$-ac + bc$ or $bc - ac$ (remove parentheses)

31. A.   Use the formulas:

x mid. $= \dfrac{x_1 + x_2}{2}$ and y mid. $= \dfrac{y_1 + y_2}{2}$.

In this case, $x_1 = 2a$, $x_2 = 4a$, $y_1 = 2b$, $y_2 = 6b$.

x mid. $= \dfrac{2a + 4a}{2} = \dfrac{6a}{2} = 3a$

y mid. $= \dfrac{2b + 6b}{2} = \dfrac{8b}{2} = 4b$

32. C. $(x + y)^2 = x^2 + 2xy + y^2$
$x^2 + y^2 = 8$ (given)
$xy = 7$ (given)
$2xy = 14$ (multiply)
$x^2 + 2xy + y^2 = 8 + 14$ or 22

33. A.   Before dinner $\dfrac{2}{3}$ of the student's homework is not done. After dinner she does $\dfrac{3}{4}$ of $\dfrac{2}{3}$, or $\dfrac{1}{2}$.

Since $\dfrac{1}{3}$ was done before dinner and $\dfrac{1}{2}$ was done after dinner, $\dfrac{1}{3} + \dfrac{1}{2}$, or $\dfrac{5}{6}$, of her homework was done. Therefore $\dfrac{1}{6}$ of her homework was uncompleted.

34. B.   The train had a distance of $1\dfrac{1}{2}$ miles to cover.

$\dfrac{\text{Distance}}{\text{Rate}} = \text{Time}$

$\dfrac{1.5 \text{ miles}}{30 \text{ m.p.h.}} = \dfrac{1}{20}$ hr. or 3 min.

Since the train was stopped at 1:00 P.M., it would have arrived at 1:03 P.M.

35. C.   This is an inverse proportion.
Let x = days required with $9 + 3$ men.

$\dfrac{9 \text{ men}}{12 \text{ men}} = \dfrac{x}{15 \text{ days}}$

$12x = 135$

$x = 11\dfrac{1}{4}$ days

Section 6   Verbal

1. B.   To *confuse* is to fail to distinguish between; to make unclear. Its opposite is to *tell apart*.

2. A.   *Scarcity* means smallness of supply; insufficiency. Its opposite is *abundance* or plentifulness.

3. C.   *Harmonious* means marked by agreement. Its opposite is *quarrelsome*.
Context Clue: Think of "a harmonious household."

4. D.   *Squalid* means filthy and neglected. Its opposite is *clean*.
Context Clue: Think of "a squalid slum."

5. B.   To *incense* means to make angry or enrage. Its opposite is to *calm*.
Remember to consider secondary meanings of the capitalized word as well as its primary meaning. *Incense* here is a verb, not a noun meaning fragrance. The fact that the answer choices are clearly verbs tells you the capitalized word is also a verb.
Context Clue: He was incensed over the damage to his car.

6. B.   To *amass* is to gather or collect. Its opposite is to *distribute*.
Context Clue: "She amassed a fortune."

7. C.   *Mendacious* means lying or dishonest. Its opposite is *veracious* (truthful).

8. B.   An *innuendo* is a sly hint or suggestion, especially a disparaging or derogatory one. Its opposite is a *direct accusation*.
Context Clue: Think of "innuendos about cheating."

9. D. *Fallacious* means logically unsound or misleading. Its opposite is *valid* or sound. Context Clue: Think of "a fallacious argument."

10. B. *Din* means a loud noise; an uproar. Its opposite is *silence*. Context Clue: She could barely hear him above the din.

11. E. The first clause states that the movement did not become famous instantly or "overnight." Instead, it gained fame step by step, or *gradually*. Remember to watch for signal words that link one part of the sentence to another. The use of "on the contrary" here sets up a contrast. The missing word must be an antonym for overnight.

(Contrast Signal)

12. E. The intensifier "even" indicates that Astell did more than merely maintain a good reputation; she improved or *enhanced* it.

(Intensifier Signal)

13. B. *Stoically* describes how a person bears pain with great courage. The presence of *and* linking the two clauses indicates that the missing word continues the thought expressed in the phrase "did not wince or whimper."

(Support Signal)

14. C. Law enforcement officers in favor of strict or rigid enforcement of the law would be against *clemency* (leniency) to offenders, especially if this leniency *encouraged* them to commit further crimes.

(Argument Pattern)

15. B. The biography is described positively as "nuanced" (subtle) and "sensitive." To complete the thought, we need another positive term. A *telling* analysis is effective; it reveals much that would otherwise go unnoticed. Note that you are looking for a word with positive associations. Therefore, you can eliminate any word with negative ones. Choices A, C, D, and E all have negative associations. Only Choice B can be correct.

16. E. A *dime* is one-tenth of a *dollar* and a *year* is one-tenth of a *decade*. The relationship is one of Part to Whole. Here it is mathematical in nature.

(Part to Whole)

17. A. A *spark* (fiery particle) is less intense than a *blaze* (bright fire); a *nick* (chip or minor cut) is less deep than a *gash* (long, deep wound).

(Degree of Intensity)

18. D. *Bizarre* and *exotic* are synonyms; both mean strange. Similarly, *dumbfounded* and *astonished* are synonyms.

(Synonyms)

19. D. An *alloy* is a mixture of *metals*. A *cake* is a mixture of *ingredients*.

(Part to Whole)

20. C. Someone *frivolous* (light or trifling) lacks *seriousness*; someone *outspoken* lacks *reticence* (reserve; tendency to silence). Choice D is incorrect. Someone lavish (extravagant) spends money freely; he does not necessarily lack it.

(Antonym Variant)

21. B. *Olfactory* refers to the sense of smell; the organ involved in this is the *nose*. *Gustatory* refers to the sense of taste; the organ involved is the *tongue*.

(Defining Characteristic)

22. D. Ancient *bronze* works are coated with a greenish rust called *patina*. Exposed *iron* also becomes coated with rust.

(Defining Characteristic)

23. D. *Cardiology* is the study of the *heart*; *pharmacology* is the science of *drugs*. Word Parts Clue: *Card-* (as in cardiac) means heart; *-logy* means science or study.

(Definition)

24. E. A *turncoat* (renegade; someone who switches to the opposite party) is by definition *treacherous*; a *killjoy* (someone who spoils the pleasure of others) is by definition *lugubrious* or gloomy.

(Definition)

25. B. *Cacophony* (harsh dissonance) could not be defined as *mellifluous* (sweet-sounding). *Noisomeness* (offensiveness of smell) could not be defined as *fragrant*. The relationship resembles that in Antonyms.

(Antonym Variant)

26. E. The first sentence clearly states that money changers have "irregular modes" of making a profit, and the rest of the paragraph offers a

description of the different techniques they use.
Choice A is incorrect. The author is not arguing in favor of the cheating, but merely describing it.
Choice B is incorrect. The author describes practices, not character.
Choices C and D are incorrect. Neither is supported by the passage.

(Main Idea)

27. B. The last sentence mentions the Tartars' satisfaction at having been allowed full weight and having received full market price. This supports the statement that they are careful about weight and market price.
Choice A is incorrect. Nothing in the passage suggests it.
Choice C is incorrect. The reverse is true.
Choice D is incorrect. The Tartars are the ones who are cheated, not the ones who cheat.
Choice E is incorrect. Nothing in the passage suggests it.

(Specific Details)

28. A. The last sentence mentions the money-changers' "flagrant miscalculations." They would not dare to miscalculate so openly if they thought the Tartars had the mathematical skills to detect them. Remember, when asked to make inferences, base your answers on what the passage implies, not what it states directly.

(Inference)

29. C. After the first two sentences, which introduce the subject of free unrhymed verse, the entire passage is devoted to a discussion of the place and purpose of rhythm and rhyme in modern poetry.
Choices A, B, D, and E are incorrect. All are too broad to be good titles for a passage on contemporary free unrhymed verse.
Remember, when asked to choose a title, watch out for choices that are too specific or too broad.

(Main Idea/Title)

30. D. Metronomic regularity of beat is not an attribute of free verse. The fourth sentence states that free verse is composed "not in the sequence of the metronome, the regular beat."
Therefore, Choice D is correct.
Choice A is an attribute of free verse. The rhythm of free verse is speech rhythm. Therefore Choice A is incorrect.
Choice B is an attribute of free verse. Free verse abandoned traditional rhyme. Therefore,

Choice B is incorrect.
Choice C is an attribute of free verse. Free verse uses rhyme for some special effect. Choice C is incorrect.
Choice E is an attribute of free verse. The pattern of free verse is "composed in the sequence of the musical phrase." Choice E is incorrect.

31. A. The use of free unrhymed verse has had a "refreshing" and "healthy" effect on modern poetry which the author views with *approval*. Remember, when asked to determine the author's attitude or tone, look for words which convey emotion or which paint pictures.

(Attitude/Tone)

32. D. The paragraph's conclusion reminds us of the terrible deeds mankind did because of superstition and impresses on us the "debt of gratitude" we owe science for freeing us from such *irrational primitive beliefs*.
Remember, when asked about specific details in the passage, spot key words in the question and scan the passage to find them (or their synonyms).
Key Words: obligation, science.

(Specific Details)

33. C. Since the passage ends with a note of gratitude to science and to scientific knowledge, we may most logically assume that the author will continue to discuss science and scientific methods.
Choices A and B are incorrect. The author considers both witchcraft and theology to be superstitions and would be unlikely to spend the effort to write a treatise or systematic explanation of a subject which he rejects.
Choice D is incorrect. The author rejects primitive customs; he only reflects on them occasionally.
Choice E is incorrect. Nothing in the passage suggests it.

(Inference)

34. B. The opening sentence lists a sequence of beliefs in order of development. Monotheism is the last of the beliefs in this sequence. It thus evolved as man's intellect or high mental faculties evolved.

(Inference)

35. D. Lines 4–10 state that poorly developed reasoning powers led man to superstitions and to terrible, bloodthirsty customs. Thus, this sort of underdeveloped reasoning led to savagery or *barbarity*.

(Inference)

36. E.   The passage records Miss Emily's interactions
with the town (few as they were) for a period
of over thirty-five years.
Choice A is too specific. Miss Emily's attempt
to earn a living is only one incident in the
thirty-year span. Choices B, C, and D are
undeveloped in the passage.

(Main Idea)

37. B.   The fact that Miss Emily's pupils are sent to
her "in the same spirit that they were sent to
church on Sundays with a twenty-five-cent
piece for the collection plate" implies that
their visits to her serve a similar charitable
purpose. This is reinforced by the statement
that she had been excused from paying taxes.

(Inference)

38. C.   Choice C is correct. You can arrive at it by
the process of elimination.
Statement I is true. The male Lucanus fights
for the female; he exhibits *belligerence* or
quarrelsomeness. Therefore, you can eliminate
Choices B and D.
Statement II is untrue. The intelligence of the
male Lucanus is unmentioned. Therefore, you
can eliminate Choice E.

Statement III is true. The male Lucanus is
larger than the female. Therefore, you can
eliminate Choice A. Only Choice C is left. It
is the correct answer.

(Specific Details)

39. C.   Just as tiger-lilies take their name from their
tiger-like stripes, so too stag-beetles take their
name from their stag-like appearance. A stag's
most obvious physical attribute is its horns; a
stag-beetle has appendages that resemble
horns.

(Inference)

40. A.   The clue lies in the first sentence. It is fair to
assume that, if the author is discussing
exceptions to a rule, that rule has been
discussed in a preceding paragraph. This
would be a rule or generalization about the
size of insects.
Remember, when asked to make inferences,
base your answers on what the passage
implies, not what it states directly.

(Inference)

Answer Sheet–Test 4

Start with number 1 for each new section. If a section has fewer than 50 questions, leave the extra spaces blank.

Remove answer sheet by cutting on dotted line

Section 1

1. Ⓐ Ⓑ Ⓒ Ⓓ Ⓔ	11. Ⓐ Ⓑ Ⓒ Ⓓ Ⓔ	21. Ⓐ Ⓑ Ⓒ Ⓓ Ⓔ	31. Ⓐ Ⓑ Ⓒ Ⓓ Ⓔ	41. Ⓐ Ⓑ Ⓒ Ⓓ Ⓔ
2. Ⓐ Ⓑ Ⓒ Ⓓ Ⓔ	12. Ⓐ Ⓑ Ⓒ Ⓓ Ⓔ	22. Ⓐ Ⓑ Ⓒ Ⓓ Ⓔ	32. Ⓐ Ⓑ Ⓒ Ⓓ Ⓔ	42. Ⓐ Ⓑ Ⓒ Ⓓ Ⓔ
3. Ⓐ Ⓑ Ⓒ Ⓓ Ⓔ	13. Ⓐ Ⓑ Ⓒ Ⓓ Ⓔ	23. Ⓐ Ⓑ Ⓒ Ⓓ Ⓔ	33. Ⓐ Ⓑ Ⓒ Ⓓ Ⓔ	43. Ⓐ Ⓑ Ⓒ Ⓓ Ⓔ
4. Ⓐ Ⓑ Ⓒ Ⓓ Ⓔ	14. Ⓐ Ⓑ Ⓒ Ⓓ Ⓔ	24. Ⓐ Ⓑ Ⓒ Ⓓ Ⓔ	34. Ⓐ Ⓑ Ⓒ Ⓓ Ⓔ	44. Ⓐ Ⓑ Ⓒ Ⓓ Ⓔ
5. Ⓐ Ⓑ Ⓒ Ⓓ Ⓔ	15. Ⓐ Ⓑ Ⓒ Ⓓ Ⓔ	25. Ⓐ Ⓑ Ⓒ Ⓓ Ⓔ	35. Ⓐ Ⓑ Ⓒ Ⓓ Ⓔ	45. Ⓐ Ⓑ Ⓒ Ⓓ Ⓔ
6. Ⓐ Ⓑ Ⓒ Ⓓ Ⓔ	16. Ⓐ Ⓑ Ⓒ Ⓓ Ⓔ	26. Ⓐ Ⓑ Ⓒ Ⓓ Ⓔ	36. Ⓐ Ⓑ Ⓒ Ⓓ Ⓔ	46. Ⓐ Ⓑ Ⓒ Ⓓ Ⓔ
7. Ⓐ Ⓑ Ⓒ Ⓓ Ⓔ	17. Ⓐ Ⓑ Ⓒ Ⓓ Ⓔ	27. Ⓐ Ⓑ Ⓒ Ⓓ Ⓔ	37. Ⓐ Ⓑ Ⓒ Ⓓ Ⓔ	47. Ⓐ Ⓑ Ⓒ Ⓓ Ⓔ
8. Ⓐ Ⓑ Ⓒ Ⓓ Ⓔ	18. Ⓐ Ⓑ Ⓒ Ⓓ Ⓔ	28. Ⓐ Ⓑ Ⓒ Ⓓ Ⓔ	38. Ⓐ Ⓑ Ⓒ Ⓓ Ⓔ	48. Ⓐ Ⓑ Ⓒ Ⓓ Ⓔ
9. Ⓐ Ⓑ Ⓒ Ⓓ Ⓔ	19. Ⓐ Ⓑ Ⓒ Ⓓ Ⓔ	29. Ⓐ Ⓑ Ⓒ Ⓓ Ⓔ	39. Ⓐ Ⓑ Ⓒ Ⓓ Ⓔ	49. Ⓐ Ⓑ Ⓒ Ⓓ Ⓔ
10. Ⓐ Ⓑ Ⓒ Ⓓ Ⓔ	20. Ⓐ Ⓑ Ⓒ Ⓓ Ⓔ	30. Ⓐ Ⓑ Ⓒ Ⓓ Ⓔ	40. Ⓐ Ⓑ Ⓒ Ⓓ Ⓔ	50. Ⓐ Ⓑ Ⓒ Ⓓ Ⓔ

Section 2

1. Ⓐ Ⓑ Ⓒ Ⓓ Ⓔ	11. Ⓐ Ⓑ Ⓒ Ⓓ Ⓔ	21. Ⓐ Ⓑ Ⓒ Ⓓ Ⓔ	31. Ⓐ Ⓑ Ⓒ Ⓓ Ⓔ	41. Ⓐ Ⓑ Ⓒ Ⓓ Ⓔ
2. Ⓐ Ⓑ Ⓒ Ⓓ Ⓔ	12. Ⓐ Ⓑ Ⓒ Ⓓ Ⓔ	22. Ⓐ Ⓑ Ⓒ Ⓓ Ⓔ	32. Ⓐ Ⓑ Ⓒ Ⓓ Ⓔ	42. Ⓐ Ⓑ Ⓒ Ⓓ Ⓔ
3. Ⓐ Ⓑ Ⓒ Ⓓ Ⓔ	13. Ⓐ Ⓑ Ⓒ Ⓓ Ⓔ	23. Ⓐ Ⓑ Ⓒ Ⓓ Ⓔ	33. Ⓐ Ⓑ Ⓒ Ⓓ Ⓔ	43. Ⓐ Ⓑ Ⓒ Ⓓ Ⓔ
4. Ⓐ Ⓑ Ⓒ Ⓓ Ⓔ	14. Ⓐ Ⓑ Ⓒ Ⓓ Ⓔ	24. Ⓐ Ⓑ Ⓒ Ⓓ Ⓔ	34. Ⓐ Ⓑ Ⓒ Ⓓ Ⓔ	44. Ⓐ Ⓑ Ⓒ Ⓓ Ⓔ
5. Ⓐ Ⓑ Ⓒ Ⓓ Ⓔ	15. Ⓐ Ⓑ Ⓒ Ⓓ Ⓔ	25. Ⓐ Ⓑ Ⓒ Ⓓ Ⓔ	35. Ⓐ Ⓑ Ⓒ Ⓓ Ⓔ	45. Ⓐ Ⓑ Ⓒ Ⓓ Ⓔ
6. Ⓐ Ⓑ Ⓒ Ⓓ Ⓔ	16. Ⓐ Ⓑ Ⓒ Ⓓ Ⓔ	26. Ⓐ Ⓑ Ⓒ Ⓓ Ⓔ	36. Ⓐ Ⓑ Ⓒ Ⓓ Ⓔ	46. Ⓐ Ⓑ Ⓒ Ⓓ Ⓔ
7. Ⓐ Ⓑ Ⓒ Ⓓ Ⓔ	17. Ⓐ Ⓑ Ⓒ Ⓓ Ⓔ	27. Ⓐ Ⓑ Ⓒ Ⓓ Ⓔ	37. Ⓐ Ⓑ Ⓒ Ⓓ Ⓔ	47. Ⓐ Ⓑ Ⓒ Ⓓ Ⓔ
8. Ⓐ Ⓑ Ⓒ Ⓓ Ⓔ	18. Ⓐ Ⓑ Ⓒ Ⓓ Ⓔ	28. Ⓐ Ⓑ Ⓒ Ⓓ Ⓔ	38. Ⓐ Ⓑ Ⓒ Ⓓ Ⓔ	48. Ⓐ Ⓑ Ⓒ Ⓓ Ⓔ
9. Ⓐ Ⓑ Ⓒ Ⓓ Ⓔ	19. Ⓐ Ⓑ Ⓒ Ⓓ Ⓔ	29. Ⓐ Ⓑ Ⓒ Ⓓ Ⓔ	39. Ⓐ Ⓑ Ⓒ Ⓓ Ⓔ	49. Ⓐ Ⓑ Ⓒ Ⓓ Ⓔ
10. Ⓐ Ⓑ Ⓒ Ⓓ Ⓔ	20. Ⓐ Ⓑ Ⓒ Ⓓ Ⓔ	30. Ⓐ Ⓑ Ⓒ Ⓓ Ⓔ	40. Ⓐ Ⓑ Ⓒ Ⓓ Ⓔ	50. Ⓐ Ⓑ Ⓒ Ⓓ Ⓔ

Section 3

1. Ⓐ Ⓑ Ⓒ Ⓓ Ⓔ	11. Ⓐ Ⓑ Ⓒ Ⓓ Ⓔ	21. Ⓐ Ⓑ Ⓒ Ⓓ Ⓔ	31. Ⓐ Ⓑ Ⓒ Ⓓ Ⓔ	41. Ⓐ Ⓑ Ⓒ Ⓓ Ⓔ
2. Ⓐ Ⓑ Ⓒ Ⓓ Ⓔ	12. Ⓐ Ⓑ Ⓒ Ⓓ Ⓔ	22. Ⓐ Ⓑ Ⓒ Ⓓ Ⓔ	32. Ⓐ Ⓑ Ⓒ Ⓓ Ⓔ	42. Ⓐ Ⓑ Ⓒ Ⓓ Ⓔ
3. Ⓐ Ⓑ Ⓒ Ⓓ Ⓔ	13. Ⓐ Ⓑ Ⓒ Ⓓ Ⓔ	23. Ⓐ Ⓑ Ⓒ Ⓓ Ⓔ	33. Ⓐ Ⓑ Ⓒ Ⓓ Ⓔ	43. Ⓐ Ⓑ Ⓒ Ⓓ Ⓔ
4. Ⓐ Ⓑ Ⓒ Ⓓ Ⓔ	14. Ⓐ Ⓑ Ⓒ Ⓓ Ⓔ	24. Ⓐ Ⓑ Ⓒ Ⓓ Ⓔ	34. Ⓐ Ⓑ Ⓒ Ⓓ Ⓔ	44. Ⓐ Ⓑ Ⓒ Ⓓ Ⓔ
5. Ⓐ Ⓑ Ⓒ Ⓓ Ⓔ	15. Ⓐ Ⓑ Ⓒ Ⓓ Ⓔ	25. Ⓐ Ⓑ Ⓒ Ⓓ Ⓔ	35. Ⓐ Ⓑ Ⓒ Ⓓ Ⓔ	45. Ⓐ Ⓑ Ⓒ Ⓓ Ⓔ
6. Ⓐ Ⓑ Ⓒ Ⓓ Ⓔ	16. Ⓐ Ⓑ Ⓒ Ⓓ Ⓔ	26. Ⓐ Ⓑ Ⓒ Ⓓ Ⓔ	36. Ⓐ Ⓑ Ⓒ Ⓓ Ⓔ	46. Ⓐ Ⓑ Ⓒ Ⓓ Ⓔ
7. Ⓐ Ⓑ Ⓒ Ⓓ Ⓔ	17. Ⓐ Ⓑ Ⓒ Ⓓ Ⓔ	27. Ⓐ Ⓑ Ⓒ Ⓓ Ⓔ	37. Ⓐ Ⓑ Ⓒ Ⓓ Ⓔ	47. Ⓐ Ⓑ Ⓒ Ⓓ Ⓔ
8. Ⓐ Ⓑ Ⓒ Ⓓ Ⓔ	18. Ⓐ Ⓑ Ⓒ Ⓓ Ⓔ	28. Ⓐ Ⓑ Ⓒ Ⓓ Ⓔ	38. Ⓐ Ⓑ Ⓒ Ⓓ Ⓔ	48. Ⓐ Ⓑ Ⓒ Ⓓ Ⓔ
9. Ⓐ Ⓑ Ⓒ Ⓓ Ⓔ	19. Ⓐ Ⓑ Ⓒ Ⓓ Ⓔ	29. Ⓐ Ⓑ Ⓒ Ⓓ Ⓔ	39. Ⓐ Ⓑ Ⓒ Ⓓ Ⓔ	49. Ⓐ Ⓑ Ⓒ Ⓓ Ⓔ
10. Ⓐ Ⓑ Ⓒ Ⓓ Ⓔ	20. Ⓐ Ⓑ Ⓒ Ⓓ Ⓔ	30. Ⓐ Ⓑ Ⓒ Ⓓ Ⓔ	40. Ⓐ Ⓑ Ⓒ Ⓓ Ⓔ	50. Ⓐ Ⓑ Ⓒ Ⓓ Ⓔ

Start with number 1 for each new section. If a section has fewer than 50 questions, leave the extra spaces blank.

Section 4

1. Ⓐ Ⓑ Ⓒ Ⓓ Ⓔ	11. Ⓐ Ⓑ Ⓒ Ⓓ Ⓔ	21. Ⓐ Ⓑ Ⓒ Ⓓ Ⓔ	31. Ⓐ Ⓑ Ⓒ Ⓓ Ⓔ	41. Ⓐ Ⓑ Ⓒ Ⓓ Ⓔ
2. Ⓐ Ⓑ Ⓒ Ⓓ Ⓔ	12. Ⓐ Ⓑ Ⓒ Ⓓ Ⓔ	22. Ⓐ Ⓑ Ⓒ Ⓓ Ⓔ	32. Ⓐ Ⓑ Ⓒ Ⓓ Ⓔ	42. Ⓐ Ⓑ Ⓒ Ⓓ Ⓔ
3. Ⓐ Ⓑ Ⓒ Ⓓ Ⓔ	13. Ⓐ Ⓑ Ⓒ Ⓓ Ⓔ	23. Ⓐ Ⓑ Ⓒ Ⓓ Ⓔ	33. Ⓐ Ⓑ Ⓒ Ⓓ Ⓔ	43. Ⓐ Ⓑ Ⓒ Ⓓ Ⓔ
4. Ⓐ Ⓑ Ⓒ Ⓓ Ⓔ	14. Ⓐ Ⓑ Ⓒ Ⓓ Ⓔ	24. Ⓐ Ⓑ Ⓒ Ⓓ Ⓔ	34. Ⓐ Ⓑ Ⓒ Ⓓ Ⓔ	44. Ⓐ Ⓑ Ⓒ Ⓓ Ⓔ
5. Ⓐ Ⓑ Ⓒ Ⓓ Ⓔ	15. Ⓐ Ⓑ Ⓒ Ⓓ Ⓔ	25. Ⓐ Ⓑ Ⓒ Ⓓ Ⓔ	35. Ⓐ Ⓑ Ⓒ Ⓓ Ⓔ	45. Ⓐ Ⓑ Ⓒ Ⓓ Ⓔ
6. Ⓐ Ⓑ Ⓒ Ⓓ Ⓔ	16. Ⓐ Ⓑ Ⓒ Ⓓ Ⓔ	26. Ⓐ Ⓑ Ⓒ Ⓓ Ⓔ	36. Ⓐ Ⓑ Ⓒ Ⓓ Ⓔ	46. Ⓐ Ⓑ Ⓒ Ⓓ Ⓔ
7. Ⓐ Ⓑ Ⓒ Ⓓ Ⓔ	17. Ⓐ Ⓑ Ⓒ Ⓓ Ⓔ	27. Ⓐ Ⓑ Ⓒ Ⓓ Ⓔ	37. Ⓐ Ⓑ Ⓒ Ⓓ Ⓔ	47. Ⓐ Ⓑ Ⓒ Ⓓ Ⓔ
8. Ⓐ Ⓑ Ⓒ Ⓓ Ⓔ	18. Ⓐ Ⓑ Ⓒ Ⓓ Ⓔ	28. Ⓐ Ⓑ Ⓒ Ⓓ Ⓔ	38. Ⓐ Ⓑ Ⓒ Ⓓ Ⓔ	48. Ⓐ Ⓑ Ⓒ Ⓓ Ⓔ
9. Ⓐ Ⓑ Ⓒ Ⓓ Ⓔ	19. Ⓐ Ⓑ Ⓒ Ⓓ Ⓔ	29. Ⓐ Ⓑ Ⓒ Ⓓ Ⓔ	39. Ⓐ Ⓑ Ⓒ Ⓓ Ⓔ	49. Ⓐ Ⓑ Ⓒ Ⓓ Ⓔ
10. Ⓐ Ⓑ Ⓒ Ⓓ Ⓔ	20. Ⓐ Ⓑ Ⓒ Ⓓ Ⓔ	30. Ⓐ Ⓑ Ⓒ Ⓓ Ⓔ	40. Ⓐ Ⓑ Ⓒ Ⓓ Ⓔ	50. Ⓐ Ⓑ Ⓒ Ⓓ Ⓔ

Section 5

1. Ⓐ Ⓑ Ⓒ Ⓓ Ⓔ	11. Ⓐ Ⓑ Ⓒ Ⓓ Ⓔ	21. Ⓐ Ⓑ Ⓒ Ⓓ Ⓔ	31. Ⓐ Ⓑ Ⓒ Ⓓ Ⓔ	41. Ⓐ Ⓑ Ⓒ Ⓓ Ⓔ
2. Ⓐ Ⓑ Ⓒ Ⓓ Ⓔ	12. Ⓐ Ⓑ Ⓒ Ⓓ Ⓔ	22. Ⓐ Ⓑ Ⓒ Ⓓ Ⓔ	32. Ⓐ Ⓑ Ⓒ Ⓓ Ⓔ	42. Ⓐ Ⓑ Ⓒ Ⓓ Ⓔ
3. Ⓐ Ⓑ Ⓒ Ⓓ Ⓔ	13. Ⓐ Ⓑ Ⓒ Ⓓ Ⓔ	23. Ⓐ Ⓑ Ⓒ Ⓓ Ⓔ	33. Ⓐ Ⓑ Ⓒ Ⓓ Ⓔ	43. Ⓐ Ⓑ Ⓒ Ⓓ Ⓔ
4. Ⓐ Ⓑ Ⓒ Ⓓ Ⓔ	14. Ⓐ Ⓑ Ⓒ Ⓓ Ⓔ	24. Ⓐ Ⓑ Ⓒ Ⓓ Ⓔ	34. Ⓐ Ⓑ Ⓒ Ⓓ Ⓔ	44. Ⓐ Ⓑ Ⓒ Ⓓ Ⓔ
5. Ⓐ Ⓑ Ⓒ Ⓓ Ⓔ	15. Ⓐ Ⓑ Ⓒ Ⓓ Ⓔ	25. Ⓐ Ⓑ Ⓒ Ⓓ Ⓔ	35. Ⓐ Ⓑ Ⓒ Ⓓ Ⓔ	45. Ⓐ Ⓑ Ⓒ Ⓓ Ⓔ
6. Ⓐ Ⓑ Ⓒ Ⓓ Ⓔ	16. Ⓐ Ⓑ Ⓒ Ⓓ Ⓔ	26. Ⓐ Ⓑ Ⓒ Ⓓ Ⓔ	36. Ⓐ Ⓑ Ⓒ Ⓓ Ⓔ	46. Ⓐ Ⓑ Ⓒ Ⓓ Ⓔ
7. Ⓐ Ⓑ Ⓒ Ⓓ Ⓔ	17. Ⓐ Ⓑ Ⓒ Ⓓ Ⓔ	27. Ⓐ Ⓑ Ⓒ Ⓓ Ⓔ	37. Ⓐ Ⓑ Ⓒ Ⓓ Ⓔ	47. Ⓐ Ⓑ Ⓒ Ⓓ Ⓔ
8. Ⓐ Ⓑ Ⓒ Ⓓ Ⓔ	18. Ⓐ Ⓑ Ⓒ Ⓓ Ⓔ	28. Ⓐ Ⓑ Ⓒ Ⓓ Ⓔ	38. Ⓐ Ⓑ Ⓒ Ⓓ Ⓔ	48. Ⓐ Ⓑ Ⓒ Ⓓ Ⓔ
9. Ⓐ Ⓑ Ⓒ Ⓓ Ⓔ	19. Ⓐ Ⓑ Ⓒ Ⓓ Ⓔ	29. Ⓐ Ⓑ Ⓒ Ⓓ Ⓔ	39. Ⓐ Ⓑ Ⓒ Ⓓ Ⓔ	49. Ⓐ Ⓑ Ⓒ Ⓓ Ⓔ
10. Ⓐ Ⓑ Ⓒ Ⓓ Ⓔ	20. Ⓐ Ⓑ Ⓒ Ⓓ Ⓔ	30. Ⓐ Ⓑ Ⓒ Ⓓ Ⓔ	40. Ⓐ Ⓑ Ⓒ Ⓓ Ⓔ	50. Ⓐ Ⓑ Ⓒ Ⓓ Ⓔ

Section 6

1. Ⓐ Ⓑ Ⓒ Ⓓ Ⓔ	11. Ⓐ Ⓑ Ⓒ Ⓓ Ⓔ	21. Ⓐ Ⓑ Ⓒ Ⓓ Ⓔ	31. Ⓐ Ⓑ Ⓒ Ⓓ Ⓔ	41. Ⓐ Ⓑ Ⓒ Ⓓ Ⓔ
2. Ⓐ Ⓑ Ⓒ Ⓓ Ⓔ	12. Ⓐ Ⓑ Ⓒ Ⓓ Ⓔ	22. Ⓐ Ⓑ Ⓒ Ⓓ Ⓔ	32. Ⓐ Ⓑ Ⓒ Ⓓ Ⓔ	42. Ⓐ Ⓑ Ⓒ Ⓓ Ⓔ
3. Ⓐ Ⓑ Ⓒ Ⓓ Ⓔ	13. Ⓐ Ⓑ Ⓒ Ⓓ Ⓔ	23. Ⓐ Ⓑ Ⓒ Ⓓ Ⓔ	33. Ⓐ Ⓑ Ⓒ Ⓓ Ⓔ	43. Ⓐ Ⓑ Ⓒ Ⓓ Ⓔ
4. Ⓐ Ⓑ Ⓒ Ⓓ Ⓔ	14. Ⓐ Ⓑ Ⓒ Ⓓ Ⓔ	24. Ⓐ Ⓑ Ⓒ Ⓓ Ⓔ	34. Ⓐ Ⓑ Ⓒ Ⓓ Ⓔ	44. Ⓐ Ⓑ Ⓒ Ⓓ Ⓔ
5. Ⓐ Ⓑ Ⓒ Ⓓ Ⓔ	15. Ⓐ Ⓑ Ⓒ Ⓓ Ⓔ	25. Ⓐ Ⓑ Ⓒ Ⓓ Ⓔ	35. Ⓐ Ⓑ Ⓒ Ⓓ Ⓔ	45. Ⓐ Ⓑ Ⓒ Ⓓ Ⓔ
6. Ⓐ Ⓑ Ⓒ Ⓓ Ⓔ	16. Ⓐ Ⓑ Ⓒ Ⓓ Ⓔ	26. Ⓐ Ⓑ Ⓒ Ⓓ Ⓔ	36. Ⓐ Ⓑ Ⓒ Ⓓ Ⓔ	46. Ⓐ Ⓑ Ⓒ Ⓓ Ⓔ
7. Ⓐ Ⓑ Ⓒ Ⓓ Ⓔ	17. Ⓐ Ⓑ Ⓒ Ⓓ Ⓔ	27. Ⓐ Ⓑ Ⓒ Ⓓ Ⓔ	37. Ⓐ Ⓑ Ⓒ Ⓓ Ⓔ	47. Ⓐ Ⓑ Ⓒ Ⓓ Ⓔ
8. Ⓐ Ⓑ Ⓒ Ⓓ Ⓔ	18. Ⓐ Ⓑ Ⓒ Ⓓ Ⓔ	28. Ⓐ Ⓑ Ⓒ Ⓓ Ⓔ	38. Ⓐ Ⓑ Ⓒ Ⓓ Ⓔ	48. Ⓐ Ⓑ Ⓒ Ⓓ Ⓔ
9. Ⓐ Ⓑ Ⓒ Ⓓ Ⓔ	19. Ⓐ Ⓑ Ⓒ Ⓓ Ⓔ	29. Ⓐ Ⓑ Ⓒ Ⓓ Ⓔ	39. Ⓐ Ⓑ Ⓒ Ⓓ Ⓔ	49. Ⓐ Ⓑ Ⓒ Ⓓ Ⓔ
10. Ⓐ Ⓑ Ⓒ Ⓓ Ⓔ	20. Ⓐ Ⓑ Ⓒ Ⓓ Ⓔ	30. Ⓐ Ⓑ Ⓒ Ⓓ Ⓔ	40. Ⓐ Ⓑ Ⓒ Ⓓ Ⓔ	50. Ⓐ Ⓑ Ⓒ Ⓓ Ⓔ

Remove answer sheet by cutting on dotted line

SECTION 1	Time—30 minutes 35 Questions	In this section, solve each problem, using any available space on the page for scratchwork. Then decide which is the best of the choices given and blacken the corresponding space on the answer sheet.

The following information is for your reference in solving some of the problems.

Circle of radius r: Area $= \pi r^2$; Circumference $= 2\pi r$
  The number of degrees of arc in a circle is 360.
The measure in degrees of a straight angle is 180.

Definitions of symbols:
$=$ is equal to $\qquad$ $\leqq$ is less than or equal to
$\neq$ is unequal to $\qquad$ $\geqq$ is greater than or equal to
$<$ is less than $\qquad$ $\parallel$ is parallel to
$>$ is greater than $\qquad$ $\perp$ is perpendicular to

Triangle: The sum of the measures
in degrees of the angles of
a triangle is 180.
If $\angle CDA$ is a right angle, then

$\quad$ (1) area of $\triangle ABC = \dfrac{AB \times CD}{2}$

$\quad$ (2) $AC^2 = AD^2 + DC^2$

Note: Figures that accompany problems in this test are intended to provide information useful in solving the problems. They are drawn as accurately as possible EXCEPT when it is stated in a specific problem that its figure is not drawn to scale. All figures lie in a plane unless otherwise indicated. All numbers used are real numbers.

---

1. If $r = \dfrac{rs}{1 - s}$, then $s^2 + 2s + 1 =$

  (A) 2   (B) $2\frac{1}{4}$ (C) $2\frac{1}{2}$ (D) 22   (E) 24

2. A merchant paid $30.00 for an article. She wishes to place a price tag on it that will enable her to offer a 10 percent discount on the price marked on the tag and still make a profit of 20 percent on the cost. What price should she mark on the tag?

  (A) $33.00   (B) $36.00   (C) $39.60   (D) $40.00
  (E) $42.40

3. Ten minutes after a plane leaves the airport, it is reported to be 40 miles away. What is the average speed, in miles per hours, of the plane?

  (A) 66   (B) 240   (C) 400   (D) 600   (E) 660

4. Martin used $\dfrac{1}{3}$ of his inheritance to pay off the

  mortgage on his house and $\dfrac{3}{5}$ of what was left to

  purchase a new automobile. How much was left

  from his total $30,000 inheritance after these two

  expenditures?

  (A) $2,000   (B) $4,000   (C) $6,000   (D) $8,000
  (E) $12,000

5. What part of a quarter is two pennies, two nickels, and one dime?

  (A) $\dfrac{3}{25}$ (B) $\dfrac{22}{25}$ (C) $\dfrac{1}{22}$ (D) $\dfrac{1}{5}$ (E) $\dfrac{3}{5}$

6. A man binds s sets of books in d days. If there are b books in a set, how many books does the man bind in one day?

  (A) $\dfrac{d}{bs}$ (B) $\dfrac{s}{bd}$ (C) $\dfrac{bd}{s}$ (D) $\dfrac{bs}{d}$ (E) $\dfrac{ds}{b}$

7. An Erlenmeyer flask can hold 0.6 liter. How many flasks are needed to hold 3.6 liters?

  (A) 3   (B) 4.2   (C) 6   (D) 12   (E) 21.6

GO ON TO THE NEXT PAGE ➡

1 1 1 1 1 1 1 1 1 1 1

Questions 8–27 each consist of two quantities, one in Column A and one in Column B. You are to compare the two quantities and on the answer sheet blacken space

A   if the quantity in Column A is greater;
B   if the quantity in Column B is greater;
C   if the two quantities are equal;
D   If the relationship cannot be determined from the information given.

AN E RESPONSE WILL NOT BE SCORED.

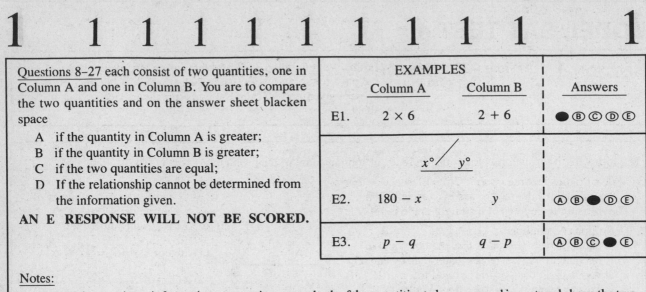

	EXAMPLES		
	Column A	Column B	Answers
E1.	2×6	$2 + 6$	● Ⓑ Ⓒ Ⓓ Ⓔ
E2.	$180 - x$	y	Ⓐ Ⓑ ● Ⓓ Ⓔ
E3.	$p - q$	$q - p$	Ⓐ Ⓑ Ⓒ ● Ⓔ

Notes:

1. In certain questions, information concerning one or both of the quantities to be compared is centered above the two columns.
2. In a given question, a symbol that appears in both columns represents the same thing in Column A as it does in Column B.
3. Letters such as x, n, and k stand for real numbers.

	Column A	Column B
8.	$\dfrac{1}{7}$	0.0142
9.	$\sqrt{\dfrac{1}{0.25}}$	2
10.	5% of 500	2.5
11.	Time elapsed from 2:55 P.M. to 3:15 P.M. on the same afternoon	$\dfrac{1}{3}$ hour

	Column A	Column B
12.	$\dfrac{(15)(16)}{x} = (5)(4)(3)$ x	4
13.	Area of square $ABCD = 25$ $AB + BC + CD$	20
14.	Area of isosceles right triangle $ABC = 18$ Length of leg AB	Length of hypotenuse AC

GO ON TO THE NEXT PAGE

1 1 1 1 1 1 1 1 1 1 1 1

SUMMARY DIRECTIONS FOR COMPARISON QUESTIONS

Answer: A   if the quantity in Column A is greater;
           B   if the quantity in Column B is greater;
           C   if the two quantities are equal;
           D   if the relationship cannot be determined from the information given.

AN E RESPONSE WILL NOT BE SCORED.

Column A   Column B

ABCD is a square.
Diagonal $BD = 6\sqrt{2}$
This concerns #15 and #16.

15.   Perimeter of ABCD   24

16.   Area of ABD   18

In triangle ABC, AB = BC, and the measure of angle B = the measure of angle C

17.   The measure of angle | The measure of
B + the measure of | angle B + the
angle C | measure of angle A

$$36 - 7x = 8$$

18.   7   x

$$z > 0$$

19. $\dfrac{z+6}{8}$ $\dfrac{z+3}{4}$

Column A   Column B

In triangle ABC, AB = 5, BC = 8

20.   Area of ABC   20

ABC is an equilateral triangle.
AB = 5x, BC = 2y

21.   Value of AC $\dfrac{2}{5}y$

$$\dfrac{3a}{4} = 9$$

22.   6a   36

$$z = 0$$

23. $x(y + z)$ xy

$$x^2 + y^2 = 12$$
$$xy = 9$$

24. $(x + y)^2$ 12

25.   Square with area | Square with perimeter
of 25 square units | of 20 units

$$x^2 - 7x + 12 = 0$$

26.   x   5

27.   Area of rectangle | Area of rectangle
ABCD with perimeter | EFGH with perimeter
36 units | 36 units

GO ON TO THE NEXT PAGE →

1 1 1 1 1 1 1 1 1 1 1

Solve each of the remaining problems in this section using any available space for scratchwork. Then decide which is the best of the choices given and blacken the corresponding space on the answer sheet.

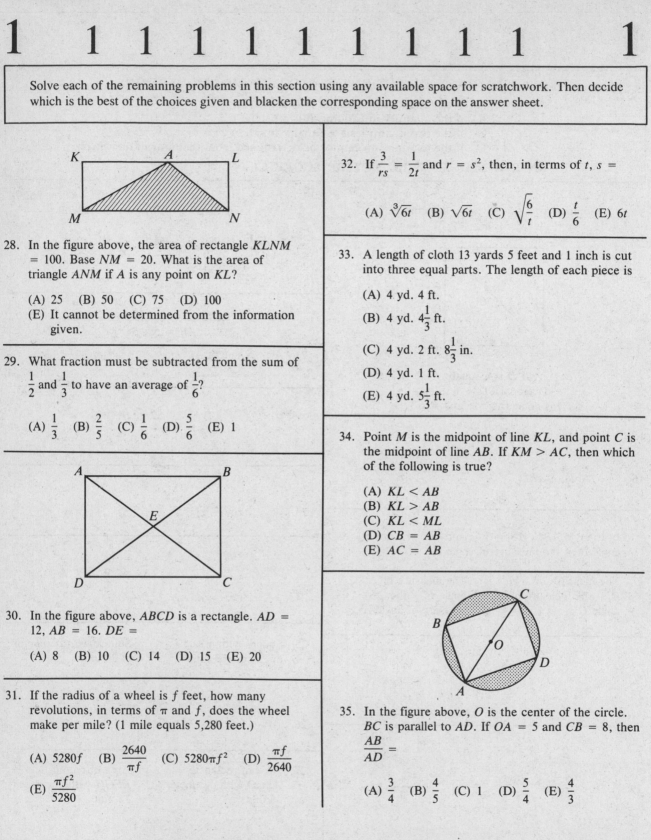

28. In the figure above, the area of rectangle $KLNM$ = 100. Base NM = 20. What is the area of triangle ANM if A is any point on KL?

    (A) 25   (B) 50   (C) 75   (D) 100
    (E) It cannot be determined from the information given.

29. What fraction must be subtracted from the sum of $\frac{1}{2}$ and $\frac{1}{3}$ to have an average of $\frac{1}{6}$?

    (A) $\frac{1}{3}$ (B) $\frac{2}{5}$ (C) $\frac{1}{6}$ (D) $\frac{5}{6}$ (E) 1

30. In the figure above, $ABCD$ is a rectangle. $AD =$ 12, $AB = 16$. $DE =$

    (A) 8   (B) 10   (C) 14   (D) 15   (E) 20

31. If the radius of a wheel is f feet, how many revolutions, in terms of π and f, does the wheel make per mile? (1 mile equals 5,280 feet.)

    (A) $5280f$ (B) $\frac{2640}{\pi f}$ (C) $5280\pi f^2$ (D) $\frac{\pi f}{2640}$

    (E) $\frac{\pi f^2}{5280}$

32. If $\frac{3}{rs} = \frac{1}{2t}$ and $r = s^2$, then, in terms of t, $s =$

    (A) $\sqrt[3]{6t}$ (B) $\sqrt{6t}$ (C) $\sqrt{\frac{6}{t}}$ (D) $\frac{t}{6}$ (E) $6t$

33. A length of cloth 13 yards 5 feet and 1 inch is cut into three equal parts. The length of each piece is

    (A) 4 yd. 4 ft.

    (B) 4 yd. $4\frac{1}{3}$ ft.

    (C) 4 yd. 2 ft. $8\frac{1}{3}$ in.

    (D) 4 yd. 1 ft.

    (E) 4 yd. $5\frac{1}{3}$ ft.

34. Point M is the midpoint of line KL, and point C is the midpoint of line AB. If $KM > AC$, then which of the following is true?

    (A) $KL < AB$
    (B) $KL > AB$
    (C) $KL < ML$
    (D) $CB = AB$
    (E) $AC = AB$

35. In the figure above, O is the center of the circle. BC is parallel to AD. If $OA = 5$ and $CB = 8$, then $\frac{AB}{AD} =$

    (A) $\frac{3}{4}$ (B) $\frac{4}{5}$ (C) 1   (D) $\frac{5}{4}$ (E) $\frac{4}{3}$

IF YOU FINISH BEFORE TIME IS CALLED, YOU MAY CHECK YOUR WORK ON THIS SECTION ONLY. DO NOT WORK ON ANY OTHER SECTION IN THE TEST.   **S T O P**

2 2 2 2 2 2 2 2 2 2 2

SECTION 2   Time—30 minutes   For each question in this section, choose the best answer and
40 Questions   blacken the corresponding space on the answer sheet.

Each question below consists of a word in capital letters, followed by five lettered words or phrases. Choose the word or phrase that is most nearly opposite in meaning to the word in capital letters. Since some of the questions require you to distinguish fine shades of meaning, consider all the choices before deciding which is best.

Example:

GOOD: (A) sour (B) bad (C) red
(D) hot (E) ugly Ⓐ ● Ⓒ Ⓓ Ⓔ

1. CONTAMINATE: (A) make official
   (B) make pure (C) make peaceful
   (D) give back (E) devour

2. PERTURBED: (A) unready (B) whipped
   (C) colorless (D) soothed (E) intruded

3. INGRATITUDE: (A) self-respect (B) closeness
   (C) affluence (D) brevity (E) thankfulness

4. ENLIGHTEN: (A) obscure (B) shorten
   (C) weigh down (D) take away (E) extricate

5. SCANTY: (A) clean (B) outer (C) profuse
   (D) serious (E) remodeled

6. GAUCHE: (A) righteous (B) measured
   (C) merry (D) tactful (E) indignant

7. BENEDICTION: (A) curse (B) psalm
   (C) verse (D) failure (E) proclamation

8. VACILLATE: (A) stand firm (B) keep private
   (C) irritate (D) identify (E) infect

9. PUGNACIOUS: (A) devious (B) candid
   (C) arbitrary (D) conciliatory (E) minuscule

10. HEINOUS: (A) loquacious (B) multifarious
    (C) limited (D) noble (E) arterial

Each sentence below has one or two blanks, each blank indicating that something has been omitted. Beneath the sentence are five lettered words or sets of words. Choose the word or set of words that best fits the meaning of the sentence as a whole.

Example:

Although its publicity has been ----, the film itself is intelligent, well-acted, handsomely produced, and altogether ----.

(A) tasteless..respectable (B) extensive..moderate
(C) sophisticated..amateur (D) risqué..crude
(E) perfect..spectacular

● Ⓑ Ⓒ Ⓓ Ⓔ

11. Although in his seventies at the time of the interview, Picasso proved alert and insightful, his faculties ---- despite the inevitable toll of the years.

(A) atrophied (B) diminished (C) intact
(D) useless (E) impaired

12. At such a serious moment in our history, your ---- is inappropriate and in bad taste.

(A) courtesy (B) levity (C) pertinence
(D) solemnity (E) maturation

13. People who take megadoses of vitamins and minerals should take care, though beneficial in small quantities, in large amounts these substances may have ---- effects.

(A) admirable (B) redundant (C) intangible
(D) toxic (E) minor

14. A prison term could not deter him from his ---- ways for with him stealing was a disease.

(A) benevolent (B) judicious (C) impossible
(D) humane (E) larcenous

15. Finally initiated into the tribe after having willingly undergone many trials, the explorer hoped to be no longer ---- the ---- rites of the primitive people.

(A) impressed by..inauthentic
(B) excluded from..esoteric
(C) distressed by..arbitrary
(D) acquainted with..supernatural
(E) welcome at..barbaric

GO ON TO THE NEXT PAGE

2   2   2   2   2   2   2   2   2   2   2

Each question below consists of a related pair of words or phrases, followed by five lettered pairs of words or phrases. Select the lettered pair that best expresses a relationship similar to that expressed in the original pair.

Example:

YAWN : BOREDOM :: (A) dream : sleep
(B) anger : madness   (C) smile : amusement
(D) face : expression   (E) impatience : rebellion

Ⓐ Ⓑ ● Ⓓ Ⓔ

16. DOG : MAMMAL :: (A) wolf : pack
(B) tree : forest   (C) insect : antenna
(D) snake : reptile   (E) kennel : house

17. TELLER : BANK :: (A) guest : motel
(B) architect : blueprint   (C) actor : rehearsal
(D) patient : hospital   (E) teacher : school

18. GOGGLES : EYES :: (A) dentures : teeth
(B) earrings : ears   (C) helmet : head
(D) leather : hide   (E) pebbles : feet

19. SILO : CORN :: (A) vault : valuables
(B) wheat : husk   (C) shoes : bunion
(D) mineral : vegetable   (E) oil : grain

20. LINIMENT : ACHE :: (A) cotton : bandage
(B) antiseptic : symptom   (C) salve : sore
(D) injection : syringe   (E) vaccine : remedy

21. FUNDAMENTAL : INCIDENTAL ::
(A) religious : conservative
(B) comprehensive : complete
(C) serene : romantic
(D) vain : humble
(E) clever : shrewd

22. VISIONARY : PRACTICAL ::
(A) dilletante : amateurish
(B) braggart : modest
(C) rebel : revolutionary
(D) connoisseur : cultivated
(E) retainer : loyal

23. TUMBLER : BEVERAGE ::
(A) quiver : arrows
(B) juggler : orange
(C) quibbler : revenge
(D) magician : prestidigitation
(E) gambler : lottery

24. EPHEMERAL : MAYFLY ::
(A) torrid : zone
(B) graceful : gazelle
(C) herbivorous : tiger
(D) expensive : elephant
(E) experimental : animal

25. INSUBORDINATION : PUNISHMENT ::
(A) abstinence : crime
(B) tolerance : segregation
(C) autonomy : government
(D) disobedience : reward
(E) diligence : promotion

GO ON TO THE NEXT PAGE

2   2 2 2 2 2 2 2 2 2 2   2

Each passage below is followed by questions based on its content. Answer all questions following a passage on the basis of what is <u>stated</u> or <u>implied</u> in that passage.

When I arrived at a few minutes before seven, I found the platoon assembled and ready to go. It was cold, and in the ranks the men were shivering and dancing up and down to keep warm. I was only the second-in-command of the platoon at that time, under instruction from a senior lieutenant, who was the platoon commander. Punctually at seven I said to Broadhurst, "March off, Sergeant. To the aerodrome, at the double."

Broadhurst asked doubtfully whether we hadn't better wait for the platoon commander, who had not turned up. Unversed in the ways of the army, I said, "No, march off. The men are cold." We doubled off.

Three or four minutes later the platoon commander, who had about fourteen years of service, appeared. He was in a towering rage. He rushed straight up to Broadhurst and asked him furiously what he meant by marching off without permission.

Broadhurst said, "I'm sorry, sir."

My feet wouldn't move. My mouth wouldn't open. I made a gigantic effort and said, "Sir—" But the lieutenant had given Broadhurst a final blast and taken command. I looked at Broadhurst, but he was busy. After parade I apologized to him, but I never explained to the lieutenant. Broadhurst told me the incident wasn't worth worrying about.

Does this seem a small crime to remember all one's life? I don't think so. It was the worst thing that I ever did in the army, because in it I showed cowardice and disloyalty. The only excuses I could find for myself were that it happened quickly and that I was very young. It had a result, though. I had been frightened of the lieutenant, frightened of being reprimanded, frightened of failure even in the smallest endeavor. I discovered now that being ashamed of yourself is worse than any fear. Duty, orders, loyalty, obedience—all things boiled down to one simple idea: whatever the consequences, a man must act so that he can live with himself.

26. It can be inferred from the passage that the narrator never explained the truth to the platoon commander because

(A) army custom forbade his doing so
(B) he felt that the incident was unimportant
(C) he hoped that Broadhurst would do it for him
(D) he feared the reaction of the platoon commander
(E) the episode happened too quickly

27. Which statement can most safely be made about the platoon commander?

(A) He refused to give the narrator any instructions.
(B) He gave command of the troops to Broadhurst.
(C) He lacked experience as a soldier.
(D) He expected his subordinates to execute orders on their own.
(E) He observed army customs to the letter.

28. From the passage the reader can most logically infer that Broadhurst was

(A) familiar with army routine
(B) proud of the platoon
(C) friendly with the platoon commander
(D) higher in rank than the platoon commander
(E) inconsiderate of the narrator

29. In looking back on the episode which he describes in the first five paragraphs, the narrator concludes that the episode

(A) proved that he had been improperly trained in army discipline
(B) caused him to "lose face" with the troops
(C) helped him to gain self-understanding
(D) showed his greater power over the troops
(E) encouraged him to obey orders without question

30. It is most probable that *before* this episode took place

(A) plans had been made for the troops to march
(B) the narrator had not been told the time of departure
(C) plans had been made for Broadhurst to stay behind
(D) the narrator had given several incorrect orders
(E) the platoon commander had relied greatly upon the narrator

GO ON TO THE NEXT PAGE

If you watch a lamp which is turned very rapidly on and off, and you keep your eyes open, "persistence of vision" will bridge the gaps of darkness between the flashes of light, and the lamp will seem to be continuously lit. This "optical afterglow" explains the magic produced by the stroboscope, an instrument which seems to freeze the swiftest motions while they are still going on, and to stop time itself dead in its tracks. The "magic" is all in the eye of the beholder.

In its simplest model the stroboscope takes the form of a rotating disk. Evenly spaced holes around its edge provide "peepholes" through which you can catch glimpses of a rotating object such as a spinning truck tire or a shaft. As the disk of the stroboscope rotates, its speed is synchronized with the speed of the spinning tire. In that way, as both the disk and the tire spin on, the solid area between the peepholes repeatedly cuts off your line of sight. You see a series of static images: the truck tire freezes in mid-spin. It's all done in the blink of an eye.

31. According to the author, the "magic" of the stroboscope is due to

    (A) continuous lighting
    (B) intense cold
    (C) slow motion
    (D) behavior of the human eye
    (E) a lapse of time

32. The author attributes the occurrence of "persistence of vision" to

    (A) changes in time
    (B) winking
    (C) rapid flashes
    (D) gaps of darkness
    (E) afterimpressions

33. The passage is most probably an excerpt from which of the following:

    (A) A proposal for a scientific research project
    (B) The diary of a celebrated magician
    (C) A medical textbook that deals with eye disease
    (D) A manual on stroboscope assembly
    (E) An informal article written for a general audience

34. The primary purpose of the passage is to

    (A) describe the technological advances that went into producing the stroboscope
    (B) account for the optical conditions that bring about the stroboscope's effects
    (C) analyze the advantages of visual accuracy
    (D) speculate about the relationship between movement and time
    (E) define the scientific basis of magic

For centuries we have enjoyed certain blessings: a stable law, before which the poor man and the rich man were equal; freedom within that law to believe what we pleased; a system of government which gave the ultimate power to the ordinary man. We have lived by toleration, rational compromise and freely expressed opinion, and we have lived very well. But we have come to take these things for granted, like the air we breathe. They have lost all glamor for us since they have become too familiar. Indeed it is a mark of the intellectual to be rather critical and contemptuous of them. Young men have acquired a cheap reputation by sneering at the liberal spirit in politics, and questioning the value of free discussion, toleration, and compromise.

35. The title that best expresses the ideas of this paragraph is:

    (A) The Value of Free Discussion
    (B) Respect for Law and Order
    (C) The Weakness of the Democratic Way of Life
    (D) Characteristics of Democracy
    (E) Unappreciated Advantages of Democratic Life

36. The writer's attitude toward young intellectuals is

    (A) indifferent   (B) respectful   (C) critical
    (D) generous   (E) angry

The stability that had marked the Iroquois Confederacy's generally pro-British position was shattered with the overthrow of James II in 1688,
Line the colonial uprisings that followed in
(5) Massachusetts, New York, and Maryland, and the commencement of King William's War against Louis XIV of France. The increasing French threat to English hegemony in the interior of North America was signalized by French-led
(10) or French-inspired attacks on the Iroquois and on outlying colonial settlements in New York and New England. The high point of the Iroquois response was the spectacular raid of August 5, 1689, in which the Iroquois virtually wiped out
(15) the French village of Lachine, just outside Montreal. A counterraid by the French on the English village of Schenectady in March, 1690, instilled an appropriate measure of fear among the English and their Iroquois allies.
(20)   The Iroquois position at the end of the war, which was formalized by treaties made during the summer of 1701 with the British and the French, and which was maintained throughout most of the eighteenth century, was one of "aggressive
(25) neutrality" between the two competing European powers. Under the new system the Iroquois initiated a peace policy toward the "far Indians," tightened their control over the nearby tribes, and induced both English and French to support
(30) their neutrality toward the European powers by appropriate gifts and concessions.
    By holding the balance of power in the sparsely settled borderlands between English and French settlements, and by their willingness to
(35) use their power against one or the other nation if not appropriately treated, the Iroquois played the game of European power politics with effectiveness. The system broke down, however, after the French became convinced that the Iroquois were
(40) compromising the system in favor of the English and launched a full-scale attempt to establish French physical and juridical presence in the Ohio Valley, the heart of the borderlands long claimed by the Iroquois. As a consequence of the
(45) ensuing Great War for Empire, in which Iroquois neutrality was dissolved and European influence moved closer, the play-off system lost its efficacy and a system of direct bargaining supplanted it.

37. The author's primary purpose in this passage is to
(A) denounce the imperialistic policies of the French
(B) disprove the charges of barbarism made against the Iroquois
(C) expose the French government's exploitation of the Iroquois balance of power
(D) describe and assess the effect of European military power on Iroquois policy
(E) show the inability of the Iroquois to engage in European-style diplomacy

38. It can be inferred from the passage that the author's attitude toward the Iroquois leadership can best be described as one of
(A) suspicion of their motives
(B) respect for their competence
(C) indifference to their fate
(D) dislike of their savagery
(E) pride in their heritage

39. With which of the following statements would the author be LEAST likely to agree?
(A) The Iroquois were able to respond effectively to French acts of aggression.
(B) James II's removal from the throne caused dissension to break out among the colonies.
(C) The French begrudged the British their alleged high standing among the Iroquois.
(D) Iroquois negotiations involved playing one side against the other.
(E) The Iroquois ceased to hold the balance of power early in the eighteenth century.

40. The author attributes such success as the Iroquois policy of aggressive neutrality had to
(A) their readiness to fight either side
(B) ties of loyalty to the British
(C) French physical presence in the borderlands
(D) the confusion of the European forces
(E) European reliance on formal treaties

IF YOU FINISH BEFORE TIME IS CALLED, YOU MAY CHECK YOUR WORK ON THIS SECTION ONLY. DO NOT WORK ON ANY OTHER SECTION IN THE TEST.   **STOP**

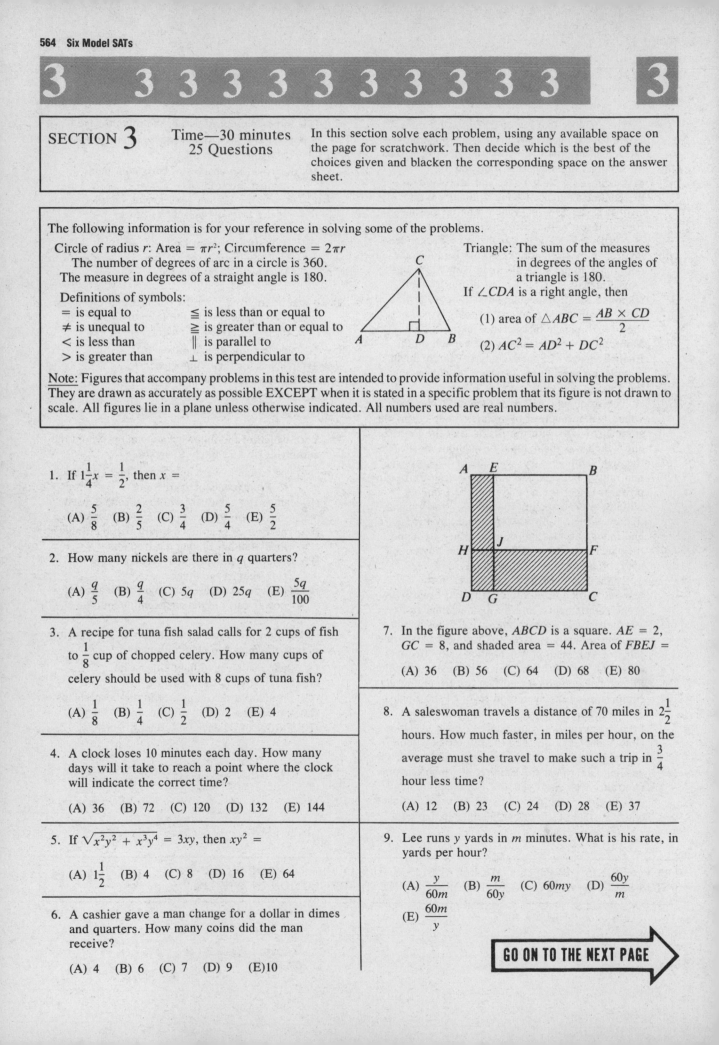

3 3 3 3 3 3 3 3 3 3 3 3

SECTION 3   Time—30 minutes   In this section solve each problem, using any available space on
             25 Questions   the page for scratchwork. Then decide which is the best of the
                                choices given and blacken the corresponding space on the answer
                                sheet.

The following information is for your reference in solving some of the problems.

Circle of radius r: Area $= \pi r^2$; Circumference $= 2\pi r$
   The number of degrees of arc in a circle is 360.
The measure in degrees of a straight angle is 180.

Definitions of symbols:
$=$ is equal to $\leqq$ is less than or equal to
$\neq$ is unequal to $\geqq$ is greater than or equal to
$<$ is less than $\parallel$ is parallel to
$>$ is greater than $\perp$ is perpendicular to

Triangle: The sum of the measures
   in degrees of the angles of
   a triangle is 180.
If $\angle CDA$ is a right angle, then

(1) area of $\triangle ABC = \dfrac{AB \times CD}{2}$

(2) $AC^2 = AD^2 + DC^2$

Note: Figures that accompany problems in this test are intended to provide information useful in solving the problems.
They are drawn as accurately as possible EXCEPT when it is stated in a specific problem that its figure is not drawn to
scale. All figures lie in a plane unless otherwise indicated. All numbers used are real numbers.

1. If $1\frac{1}{4}x = \frac{1}{2}$, then $x =$

   (A) $\frac{5}{8}$ (B) $\frac{2}{5}$ (C) $\frac{3}{4}$ (D) $\frac{5}{4}$ (E) $\frac{5}{2}$

2. How many nickels are there in q quarters?

   (A) $\frac{q}{5}$ (B) $\frac{q}{4}$ (C) $5q$ (D) $25q$ (E) $\frac{5q}{100}$

3. A recipe for tuna fish salad calls for 2 cups of fish
   to $\frac{1}{8}$ cup of chopped celery. How many cups of
   celery should be used with 8 cups of tuna fish?

   (A) $\frac{1}{8}$ (B) $\frac{1}{4}$ (C) $\frac{1}{2}$ (D) 2 (E) 4

4. A clock loses 10 minutes each day. How many
   days will it take to reach a point where the clock
   will indicate the correct time?

   (A) 36 (B) 72 (C) 120 (D) 132 (E) 144

5. If $\sqrt{x^2y^2 + x^3y^4} = 3xy$, then $xy^2 =$

   (A) $1\frac{1}{2}$ (B) 4 (C) 8 (D) 16 (E) 64

6. A cashier gave a man change for a dollar in dimes
   and quarters. How many coins did the man
   receive?

   (A) 4 (B) 6 (C) 7 (D) 9 (E) 10

7. In the figure above, $ABCD$ is a square. $AE = 2$,
   $GC = 8$, and shaded area $= 44$. Area of $FBEJ =$

   (A) 36 (B) 56 (C) 64 (D) 68 (E) 80

8. A saleswoman travels a distance of 70 miles in $2\frac{1}{2}$
   hours. How much faster, in miles per hour, on the
   average must she travel to make such a trip in $\frac{3}{4}$
   hour less time?

   (A) 12 (B) 23 (C) 24 (D) 28 (E) 37

9. Lee runs y yards in m minutes. What is his rate, in
   yards per hour?

   (A) $\frac{y}{60m}$ (B) $\frac{m}{60y}$ (C) $60my$ (D) $\frac{60y}{m}$

   (E) $\frac{60m}{y}$

GO ON TO THE NEXT PAGE

3   3 3 3 3 3 3 3 3 3 3   3

10. If $x = -2$, $y = 3$, and $a = -1$, what is the value of $\dfrac{3y^2 - x^2}{\frac{1}{2}a^3}$?

(A) 0   (B) 1   (C) 8   (D) -8 (E) -46

11. $abc = dbc + e$; $bc =$

(A) $\dfrac{e}{a - d}$ (B) $bc + e$ (C) $\dfrac{abc + e}{a}$ (D) ae

(E) $\dfrac{ae}{d}$

12. A man works d days and earns w dollars more than p dollars. What are his average earnings, in dollars, per day?

(A) $\dfrac{p}{w + d}$ (B) $\dfrac{d + p}{w}$ (C) $\dfrac{d + w}{p}$ (D) $\dfrac{p + d}{w}$

(E) $\dfrac{p + w}{d}$

13. The distance between Montreal and Washington, D.C., is 600 miles. A train leaving Washington at 7:00 A.M. arrives at 3 P.M. What is the average speed, in miles per hour, of the train?

(A) 24   (B) 37.5   (C) 48   (D) 75   (E) 150

14. Bath towels formerly sold for 80¢ each are now offered at $9.00 per dozen. What is the ratio of the old price to the new price?

(A) 5:1   (B) 16:15   (C) 15:16   (D) 8:45 (E) 45:8

15. In the figure above, the area of $ABCD =$

(A) 5   (B) 8   (C) 10   (D) 16   (E) 20

16. A pond 100 feet in diameter is surrounded by a circular grass walk that is 2 feet wide. In terms of π, how many square feet of grass are there on the walk?

(A) 98π (B) 100π (C) 102π (D) 202π (E) 204π

17. Sally's marks are 70, 90, 65, 85, and 75. What must her mark be on the next test to raise her average to 80 percent?

(A) 73   (B) 81   (C) 90   (D) 92.5   (E) 95

18. $\dfrac{1}{2} + \dfrac{3}{4} \div \left(\dfrac{5}{6} \times \dfrac{7}{8}\right) - \dfrac{9}{10} =$

(A) $\dfrac{22}{35}$ (B) $\dfrac{57}{70}$ (C) $\dfrac{35}{22}$ (D) $\dfrac{12}{7}$ (E) 22

19. What is the maximum total weight in ounces, of ten eggs, if four of them weigh 15 to 25 ounces each, and the others weigh from 20 to 25 ounces each?

(A) 180   (B) 210   (C) 220   (D) 225   (E) 250

20. Which of the following is an equation of the locus of points in the coordinate plane that are at a distance of 5 units from the origin?

(A) $x = 5$
(B) $y = 5$
(C) $x^2 + y^2 = 5$
(D) $x^2 + y^2 = 25$
(E) $x^2 + y^2 = 0$

21. If the degree measures of the angles of an isosceles triangle are $x + 24$, $4x - 12$, and $\dfrac{3x}{2} + 12$, how many degrees are there in the vertex angle of the triangle?

(A) 24   (B) 30   (C) 48   (D) 84   (E) 108

22. If $x\sqrt{0.09} = 3$, then $x =$

(A) $\dfrac{1}{10}$ (B) $\dfrac{3}{10}$ (C) $\dfrac{1}{3}$ (D) 1   (E) 10

23. Which of the following statements is (are) true of the length of segments on line ℓ above?

   I. $AB + BC = AD - CD$
  II. $AD - BC = AB + CD$
  III. $AB + CD = AD$

(A) I only
(B) II only
(C) I and III only
(D) I and II only
(E) I, II, and III

GO ON TO THE NEXT PAGE ▷

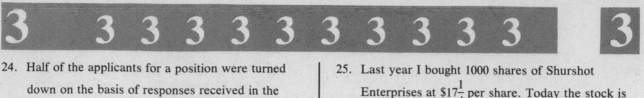

24. Half of the applicants for a position were turned down on the basis of responses received in the mail. Three others were eliminated after personal interviews, leaving $\frac{2}{5}$ of the total number of applicants for the position. How many applicants were there for the position?

(A) 10 (B) 20 (C) 30 (D) 40 (E) 50

25. Last year I bought 1000 shares of Shurshot Enterprises at $17\frac{1}{4}$ per share. Today the stock is quoted at $17\frac{3}{8}$. Without considering brokerage fees and taxes, how many shares should I sell today in order to make a profit of $100?

(A) 40 (B) 80 (C) 400 (D) 800 (E) 1,000

IF YOU FINISH BEFORE TIME IS CALLED, YOU MAY CHECK YOUR WORK ON THIS SECTION ONLY. DO NOT WORK ON ANY OTHER SECTION IN THE TEST.   S T O P

4   4   4   4

SECTION 4   Time—30 minutes
45 Questions   For each question in this section, choose the best answer and
blacken the corresponding space on the answer sheet.

Each question below consists of a word in capital
letters, followed by five lettered words or phrases.
Choose the word or phrase that is most nearly opposite
in meaning to the word in capital letters. Since some of
the questions require you to distinguish fine shades of
meaning, consider all the choices before deciding
which is best.

Example:

GOOD: (A) sour   (B) bad   (C) red
(D) hot   (E) ugly

Ⓐ ● Ⓒ Ⓓ Ⓔ

1. VIVACIOUS: (A) unattractive   (B) hungry
   (C) spiritless   (D) inquisitive   (E) unsteady

2. PRONE: (A) available   (B) disproved
   (C) haggard   (D) amateur   (E) disinclined

3. COLLABORATE: (A) work alone   (B) depart
   (C) fashion   (D) discard   (E) quiet down

4. SEGREGATE: (A) educate   (B) unite
   (C) falsify   (D) tolerate   (E) restore

5. TAUT: (A) unschooled   (B) practiced
   (C) eventual   (D) loose   (E) momentous

6. CIRCUMSPECT: (A) disregarded   (B) rash
   (C) angular   (D) indolent   (E) effective

7. ALOOF: (A) scholarly   (B) deadly
   (C) gregarious   (D) graceful   (E) immense

8. PROXIMITY: (A) substitution   (B) caution
   (C) essence   (D) relief   (E) distance

9. PARAGON: (A) bad example
   (B) house of worship   (C) cause of dispute
   (D) hexagon   (E) adversity

10. CAJOLE: (A) distinguish   (B) bully   (C) fulfill
    (D) repay promptly   (E) speak calmly

11. CALLOW: (A) experienced   (B) reddish
    (C) frenzied   (D) articulate   (E) magnificent

12. DIVERGENCE: (A) urgency   (B) enhancement
    (C) altercation   (D) confluence   (E) opulence

13. NADIR: (A) perimeter   (B) conjunction
    (C) periphery   (D) apex   (E) sphere

14. INVIDIOUS: (A) visible
    (B) creating good will   (C) unable to divide
    (D) suggestive   (E) subtle

15. ENCOMIUM: (A) recompense   (B) penalty
    (C) loss   (D) opprobrium   (E) adumbration

Each sentence below has one or two blanks, each blank
indicating that something has been omitted. Beneath
the sentence are five lettered words or sets of words.
Choose the word or set of words that best fits the meaning of the sentence as a whole.

Example:

Although its publicity has been ----, the film itself is
intelligent, well acted, handsomely produced, and
altogether ----.

(A) tasteless..respectable   (B) extensive..moderate
(C) sophisticated..amateur   (D) risqué..crude
(E) perfect..spectacular

● Ⓑ Ⓒ Ⓓ Ⓔ

16. The critics were distressed that an essayist of such
    glowing ---- could descend to writing such dull,
    uninteresting prose.

    (A) obscurity   (B) ill-repute   (C) shallowness
    (D) promise   (E) amiability

17. The testimony of eyewitnesses is notoriously ---- ;
    emotion and excitement all too often cause our
    minds to distort what we see.

    (A) judicious   (B) interdependent   (C) credible
    (D) unreliable   (E) gratifying

18. News of the shocking attack on Pearl Harbor ----
    the nation into action.

    (A) predicted   (B) allured   (C) assuaged
    (D) solicited   (E) galvanized

GO ON TO THE NEXT PAGE

19. When the colonel learned that headquarters had been unable to send him the needed reinforcements, he ---- the order for the scheduled attack.

   (A) countermanded   (B) relinquished
     (C) remarked   (D) vitiated   (E) confounded

20. At the church the visitors ---- with the ---- parents of the children drowned in the lake.

   (A) mingled..indifferent
   (B) chatted..sociable
   (C) commiserated..bereaved
   (D) rejoiced..maudlin
   (E) lamented..mirthful

Each passage below is followed by questions based on its content. Answer all questions following a passage on the basis of what is <u>stated</u> or <u>implied</u> in that passage.

The curtain rises; the Cardinal and Daniel de Bosola enter from the right. In appearance, the Cardinal is something between an El Greco
Line cardinal and a Van Dyke noble lord. He has the
(5) tall, spare form—the elongated hands and features—of the former; the trim pointed beard, the imperial repose, the commanding authority of the latter. But the El Greco features are not really those of asceticism or inner mystic spiritu-
(10) ality. They are the index to a cold, refined but ruthless cruelty in a highly civilized controlled form. Neither is the imperial repose an aloof mood of proud detachment. It is a refined expression of satanic pride of place and talent.
(15) To a degree, the Cardinal's coldness is artificially cultivated. He has defined himself against his younger brother Duke Ferdinand and is the opposite to the overwrought emotionality of the latter. But the Cardinal's aloof mood is not
(20) one of bland detachment. It is the deliberate detachment of a methodical man who collects his thoughts and emotions into the most compact and formidable shape—that when he strikes, he may strike with the more efficient and devastating
(25) force. His easy movements are those of the slowly circling eagle just before the swift descent with the exposed talons. Above all else, he is a man who never for a moment doubts his destined authority as a governor. He derisively and
(30) sharply rebukes his brother the Duke as easily and readily as he mocks his mistress Julia. If he has betrayed his hireling Bosola, he uses his brother as the tool to win back his "familiar." His court dress is a long brilliant scarlet
(35) cardinal's gown with white cuffs and a white collar turned back over the red, both collar and cuffs being elaborately scalloped and embroidered. He wears a small cape, reaching only to the elbows. His cassock is buttoned to the
(40) ground, giving a heightened effect to his already tall presence. Richelieu would have adored his neatly trimmed beard. A richly jeweled and orna-
mented cross lies on his breast, suspended from his neck by a gold chain.
(45) Bosola, for his part, is the Renaissance "familiar" dressed conventionally in somber black with a white collar. He wears a chain about his neck, a suspended ornament, and a sword. Although a "bravo," he must not be thought of
(50) as a leather-jacketed, heavy-booted tough, squat and swarthy. Still less is he a sneering, leering, melodramatic villain of the Victorian gaslight tradition. Like his black-and-white clothes, he is a colorful contradiction, a scholar-assassin, a
(55) humanist-hangman; introverted and introspective, yet ruthless in action; moody and reluctant, yet violent. He is a man of scholarly taste and subtle intellectual discrimination doing the work of a hired ruffian. In general effect, his impersonator
(60) must achieve suppleness and subtlety of nature, a highly complex, compressed, yet well restrained intensity of temperament. Like Duke Ferdinand, he is inwardly tormented, but not by undiluted passion. His dominant emotion is an intellectual-
(65) ized one: that of disgust at a world filled with knavery and folly, but in which he must play a part and that a lowly, despicable one. He is the kind of rarity that Browning loved to depict in his Renaissance monologues.

21. The primary purpose of the passage appears to be to

   (A) provide historical background on the Renaissance church
   (B) describe ecclesiastical costuming and pageantry
   (C) analyze the appearance and moral nature of two dramatic figures
   (D) compare and contrast the subjects of two historical paintings
   (E) denounce the corruption of the nobility in Renaissance Italy

GO ON TO THE NEXT PAGE ▷

4   4 4 4 4 4 4 4 4 4 4   4

22. It can be inferred from the passage that the Cardinal and Bosola

(A) are feuding brothers
(B) are noble lords
(C) together govern the church
(D) are characters in a play
(E) resemble one another in looks

23. In lines 25–27 the author most likely compares the movements of the Cardinal to those of a circling eagle in order to emphasize his

(A) flightiness
(B) love of freedom
(C) eminence
(D) sense of spirituality
(E) mercilessness

24. As used in line 49, the word *bravo* most nearly means

(A) a shout of approbation
(B) a medallion
(C) a clergyman
(D) a humanist
(E) a paid killer

25. The author of this passage assumes that the reader is

(A) familiar with the paintings of El Greco and Van Dyke
(B) disgusted with a world filled with cruelty and folly
(C) ignorant of the history of the Roman Catholic Church
(D) uninterested in psychological distinctions
(E) unacquainted with the writing of Browning

Peyton Farquhar was a well-to-do planter, of an old and highly respected Alabama family. Being a slave-owner, and, like other slave-owners, a politician, he was naturally an original secessionist and ardently devoted to the Southern cause. Circumstances had prevented him from taking service with the gallant army which had fought the disastrous campaigns ending with the fall of Corinth, and he chafed under the inglorious restraint, longing for the release of his energies, the larger life of the soldier, the opportunity for distinction. That opportunity, he felt, would come, as it comes to all in war time. Meanwhile, he did what he could. No service was too humble for him to perform in aid of the South, no adventure too perilous for him to undertake if consistent with the character of a civilian who was at heart a soldier, and who in good faith and without too much qualification assented to at least a part of the frankly villainous dictum that all is fair in love and war.

One evening while Farquhar and his wife were sitting near the entrance to his grounds, a grey-clad soldier rode up to the gate and asked for a drink of water. Mrs. Farquhar was only too happy to serve him with her own white hands. While she was gone to fetch the water, her husband approached the dusty horseman and inquired eagerly for news from the front.

"The Yanks are repairing the railroads," said the man, "and are getting ready for another advance. They have reached the Owl Creek bridge, put it in order, and built a stockade on the other bank, The commandant has issued an order, which is posted everywhere, declaring that any civilian caught interfering with the railroad, its bridges, tunnels, or trains, will be summarily hanged. I saw the order."

"How far is it to the Owl Creek bridge?" Farquhar asked.

"About thirty miles."

"Is there no force on this side of the creek?"

"Only a picket post half a mile out, on the railroad, and a single sentinel at this end of the bridge."

"Suppose a man—a civilian and a student of hanging—should elude the picket post and perhaps get the better of the sentinel," said Farquhar, smiling, "what could he accomplish?"

The soldier reflected. "I was there a month ago," he replied. "I observed that the flood of last winter had lodged a great quantity of driftwood against the wooden pier at the end of the bridge. It is now dry and would burn like tow."

The lady had now brought the water, which the soldier drank. He thanked her ceremoniously, bowed to her husband, and rode away. An hour later, after nightfall, he repassed the plantation, going northward in the direction from which he had come. He was a Yankee scout.

26. Peyton Farquhar would most likely consider which of the following a good example of how a citizen should behave in wartime?

(A) He should use even underhanded methods to support his cause.
(B) He should enlist in the army without delay.
(C) He should turn to politics as a means of enforcing his will.
(D) He should avoid involving himself in disastrous campaigns.
(E) He should concentrate on his duties as a planter.

GO ON TO THE NEXT PAGE

27. It can be inferred from the second paragraph that Mrs. Farquhar is

   (A) sympathetic to the Confederate cause
   (B) uninterested in news of the war
   (C) too proud to perform menial tasks
   (D) reluctant to ask her slaves to fetch water
   (E) inhospitable by nature

28. As used in the next-to-last paragraph, tow is

   (A) an act of hauling something
   (B) a tugboat
   (C) a railroad bridge
   (D) a highly combustible substance
   (E) a picket post

29. This passage was most likely taken from

   (A) a history textbook
   (B) Peyton Farquhar's autobiography
   (C) a story set in Civil War times
   (D) a commentary on the effects of Federal orders on civilians
   (E) a treatise on military strategy

30. We may infer from the passage that

   (A) the soldier had deserted from the Southern army
   (B) the soldier has lost his sense of direction
   (C) the scout has been tempting Farquhar into an unwise action
   (D) Farquhar knew the soldier was a Yankee scout
   (E) the soldier returned to the plantation unwillingly

Select the word or set of words that **best** completes each of the following sentences.

---

31. After three years in Paris, he was filled with ---- and longed for the familiar scenes of New York City.

   (A) glee (B) chagrin (C) nostalgia
    (D) lethargy (E) anxiety

32. We had not realized how much people ---- the library's old borrowing policy until we received complaints once it had been ---- .

   (A) enjoyed..continued
   (B) disliked..administered
   (C) respected..imitated
   (D) ignored..lauded
   (E) appreciated..superseded

33. Not only the ---- are fooled by propaganda; we can all be ---- if we are not wary.

   (A) ignorant..distressed
   (B) gullible..misled
   (C) people..puzzled
   (D) masses..scorned
   (E) uncultured..cultivated

34. No real life hero of ancient or modern days can surpass James Bond with his nonchalant ---- of death and the ---- with which he bears torture.

   (A) contempt..distress
   (B) disregard..fortitude
   (C) veneration..guile
   (D) concept..terror
   (E) impatience..fickleness

35. Unlike the highly ---- Romantic poets of the previous century, Arnold and his fellow Victorian poets were ---- and interested in moralizing.

   (A) rhapsodic..lyrical
   (B) frenetic..distraught
   (C) emotional..didactic
   (D) sensitive..strange
   (E) dramatic..warped

Each question below consists of a related pair of words or phrases, followed by five lettered pairs of words or phrases. Select the lettered pair that **best** expresses a relationship similar to that expressed in the original pair.

Example:

   YAWN : BOREDOM :: (A) dream : sleep
   (B) anger : madness   (C) smile : amusement
    (D) face : expression   (E) impatience : rebellion

   Ⓐ Ⓑ ● Ⓓ Ⓔ

---

36. JOURNALIST:TYPEWRITER ::
   (A) surgeon:bones
   (B) carpenter:lumber
   (C) poet:beauty
   (D) floorwalker:flower
   (E) electrician:pliers

37. MUTTON:SHEEP :: (A) bleat:lamb
   (B) sow:pig   (C) hide:buffalo   (D) beef:steer
    (E) calf:cow

GO ON TO THE NEXT PAGE

4 4 4 4 4 4 4 4 4 4 4 4

38. ENTRY:DIARY :: (A) sonnet:ballad
(B) paragraph:prose   (C) missive:epistle
(D) episode:serial   (E) book:dustjacket

39. MURAL:WALL :: (A) statue:courtyard
(B) painting:portrait   (C) quarry:stone
(D) etching:paper   (E) water color:tempera

40. LIBRETTO:AUTHOR :: (A) aria:tenor
(B) score:composer   (C) drama:reviewer
(D) chisel:sculptor   (E) portfolio:architect

41. TETHER:HORSE :: (A) safari:tiger
(B) specimen:animal   (C) brand:calf
(D) feed:dog   (E) manacle:prisoner

42. PORTENTOUS:OMINOUS ::
(A) heavy:threatening
(B) magnificent:treacherous
(C) applicable:pertinent
(D) good:evil
(E) showy:serious

43. PECKISH:STARVING :: (A) proper:seemly
(B) rural:urban   (C) plain:hideous
(D) drunken:sober   (E) sterile:contaminated

44. POET:ECLOGUE ::
(A) philosopher:nature
(B) dramatist:scenery
(C) sculptor:marble
(D) seamstress:gown
(E) astronomer:planet

45. VIRTUOSO:EXPERIENCED ::
(A) rogue:knavish
(B) democrat:dictatorial
(C) saint:dissolute
(D) leader:deferential
(E) evildoer:repentant

IF YOU FINISH BEFORE TIME IS CALLED, YOU MAY CHECK YOUR WORK ON
THIS SECTION ONLY. DO NOT WORK ON ANY OTHER SECTION IN THE TEST.   **S T O P**

5

The following information is for your reference in solving some of the problems.

Circle of radius r: Area = πr^2; Circumference = $2\pi r$
  The number of degrees of arc in a circle is 360.
The measure in degrees of a straight angle is 180.

Definitions of symbols:

= is equal to	≤ is less than or equal to
≠ is unequal to	≥ is greater than or equal to
< is less than	‖ is parallel to
> is greater than	⊥ is perpendicular to

Triangle: The sum of the measures in degrees of the angles of a triangle is 180.

If

(1) area of $\triangle ABC = \dfrac{AB \times CD}{2}$

(2) $AC^2 = AD^2 + DC^2$

<u>Note:</u> Figures that accompany problems in this test are intended to provide information useful in solving the problems. They are drawn as accurately as possible EXCEPT when it is stated in a specific problem that its figure is not drawn to scale. All figures lie in a plane unless otherwise indicated. All numbers used are real numbers.

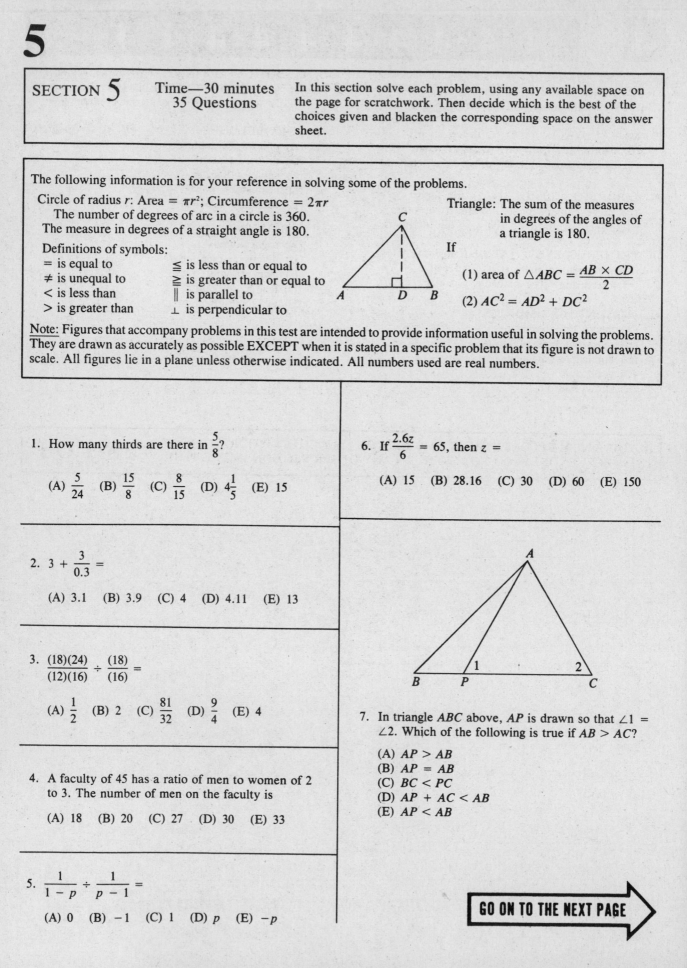

1. How many thirds are there in $\frac{5}{8}$?

  (A) $\frac{5}{24}$ (B) $\frac{15}{8}$ (C) $\frac{8}{15}$ (D) $4\frac{1}{5}$ (E) 15

2. $3 + \dfrac{3}{0.3} =$

  (A) 3.1 (B) 3.9 (C) 4 (D) 4.11 (E) 13

3. $\dfrac{(18)(24)}{(12)(16)} \div \dfrac{(18)}{(16)} =$

  (A) $\frac{1}{2}$ (B) 2 (C) $\frac{81}{32}$ (D) $\frac{9}{4}$ (E) 4

4. A faculty of 45 has a ratio of men to women of 2 to 3. The number of men on the faculty is

  (A) 18 (B) 20 (C) 27 (D) 30 (E) 33

5. $\dfrac{1}{1-p} \div \dfrac{1}{p-1} =$

  (A) 0 (B) −1 (C) 1 (D) p (E) $-p$

6. If $\dfrac{2.6z}{6} = 65$, then $z =$

  (A) 15 (B) 28.16 (C) 30 (D) 60 (E) 150

7. In triangle ABC above, AP is drawn so that $\angle 1 = \angle 2$. Which of the following is true if $AB > AC$?

  (A) $AP > AB$
  (B) $AP = AB$
  (C) $BC < PC$
  (D) $AP + AC < AB$
  (E) $AP < AB$

GO ON TO THE NEXT PAGE

5

Questions 8–27 each consist of two quantities, one in Column A and one in Column B. You are to compare the two quantities and on the answer sheet blacken space

  A if the quantity in Column A is greater;
  B if the quantity in Column B is greater;
  C if the two quantities are equal;
  D If the relationship cannot be determined from the information given.

AN E RESPONSE WILL NOT BE SCORED.

EXAMPLES		
Column A	Column B	Answers
E1. 2×6	$2 + 6$	●ⒷⒸⒹⒺ
E2. $180 - x$	y	ⒶⒷ●ⒹⒺ
E3. $p - q$	$q - p$	ⒶⒷⒸ●Ⓔ

E2 figure: $x° \diagup y°$

Notes:

1. In certain questions, information concerning one or both of the quantities to be compared is centered above the two columns.
2. In a given question, a symbol that appears in both columns represents the same thing in Column A as it does in Column B.
3. Letters such as x, n, and k stand for real numbers.

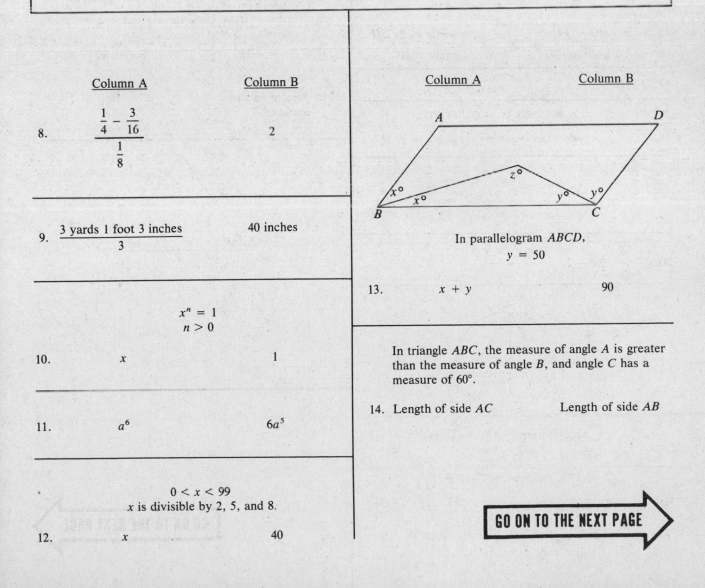

	Column A	Column B
8.	$\dfrac{\dfrac{1}{4} - \dfrac{3}{16}}{\dfrac{1}{8}}$	2
9.	$\dfrac{3 \text{ yards 1 foot 3 inches}}{3}$	40 inches

$$x^n = 1$$
$$n > 0$$

	Column A	Column B
10.	x	1
11.	a^6	$6a^5$

$$0 < x < 99$$
x is divisible by 2, 5, and 8.

	Column A	Column B
12.	x	40

In parallelogram $ABCD$,
$$y = 50$$

	Column A	Column B
13.	$x + y$	90

In triangle ABC, the measure of angle A is greater than the measure of angle B, and angle C has a measure of 60°.

	Column A	Column B
14.	Length of side AC	Length of side AB

GO ON TO THE NEXT PAGE

5

SUMMARY DIRECTIONS FOR COMPARISON QUESTIONS

Answer: A if the quantity in Column A is greater;
B if the quantity in Column B is greater;
C if the two quantities are equal;
D if the relationship cannot be determined from the information given.

AN E RESPONSE WILL NOT BE SCORED.

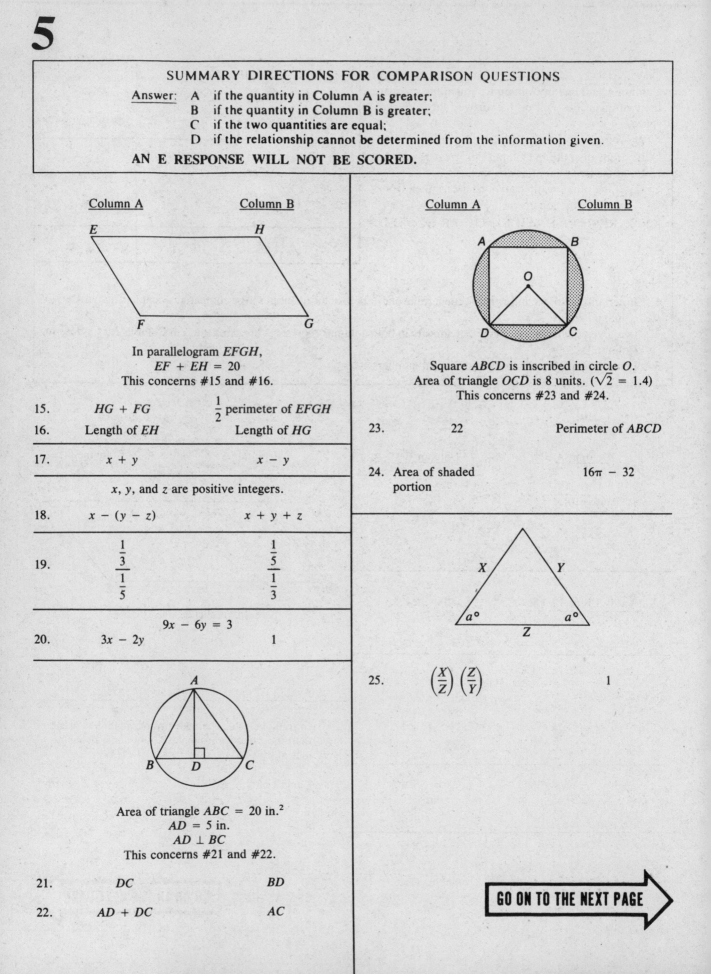

Column A   Column B

In parallelogram *EFGH*,
$EF + EH = 20$
This concerns #15 and #16.

15. $HG + FG$ $\frac{1}{2}$ perimeter of *EFGH*

16.   Length of *EH*   Length of *HG*

17. $x + y$ $x - y$

x, *y*, and *z* are positive integers.

18. $x - (y - z)$ $x + y + z$

19. $\dfrac{\frac{1}{3}}{\frac{1}{5}}$ $\dfrac{\frac{1}{5}}{\frac{1}{3}}$

$9x - 6y = 3$

20. $3x - 2y$ 1

Area of triangle $ABC = 20$ in.^{2}
$AD = 5$ in.
$AD \perp BC$
This concerns #21 and #22.

21. DC BD

22. $AD + DC$ AC

Column A   Column B

Square *ABCD* is inscribed in circle *O*.
Area of triangle *OCD* is 8 units. ($\sqrt{2} = 1.4$)
This concerns #23 and #24.

23.   22   Perimeter of *ABCD*

24.   Area of shaded portion $16\pi - 32$

25. $\left(\dfrac{X}{Z}\right)\left(\dfrac{Z}{Y}\right)$ 1

GO ON TO THE NEXT PAGE

5

Column A   Column B

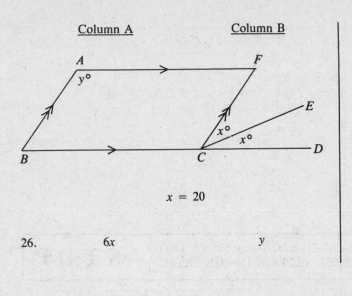

$x = 20$

26. $6x$ y

Column A   Column B

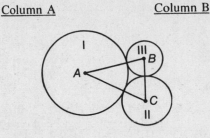

A, B, and C are centers of circles I, II, and III, respectively.
Area of circle I $= 25\pi$, area of circle II $= 16\pi$, area of circle III $= 9\pi$

27. Perimeter of triangle   12
     ABC

Solve each of the remaining problems in this section using any available space for scratchwork. Then decide which is the best of the choices given and blacken the corresponding space on the answer sheet.

28. A man buys 2,750 eggs for $100 and loses 350 of these eggs because of breakage. If he sells the remaining eggs at 70¢ per dozen, what percent of his original investment is his profit?

(A) 14%   (B) 20%   (C) 40%   (D) 45%
(E) 50%

29. A broad jumper makes an average standing jump of 8 feet. In how many jumps will he cover y yards?

(A) $\dfrac{y}{8}$ (B) $\dfrac{3y}{8}$ (C) $8y$ (D) $\dfrac{8y}{3}$ (E) $24y$

30. Of Ms. Kelly's salary, $\dfrac{1}{10}$ is spent for clothing, $\dfrac{1}{3}$ for food, and $\dfrac{1}{5}$ for rent. What percent of her salary is left for other expenditures and savings?

(A) $36\dfrac{2}{3}\%$ (B) $37\dfrac{2}{3}\%$ (C) $42\dfrac{1}{3}\%$ (D) $46\dfrac{2}{3}\%$

(E) $63\dfrac{1}{3}\%$

31. If a pipe fills a cistern in h hours, how much of the cistern does it fill in one hour?

(A) $\dfrac{1}{h}$ (B) $\dfrac{x}{h}$ (C) hx (D) $\dfrac{h}{x}$ (E) h

32. What is the average height of three boys if one boy is x inches, and the other boys are each y inches tall?

(A) $x + 2y$ (B) $\dfrac{x + y}{3}$ (C) $\dfrac{x + 2y}{3}$

(D) $\dfrac{x + 3y}{3}$ (E) $\dfrac{2y - x}{3}$

33. In the figure above, BC equals one half of AB. The area of right triangle ABC equals 64 square feet. What is the length of hypotenuse AC to the nearest foot?

(A) 12   (B) 14   (C) 18   (D) 24   (E) 32

GO ON TO THE NEXT PAGE

5

34. If 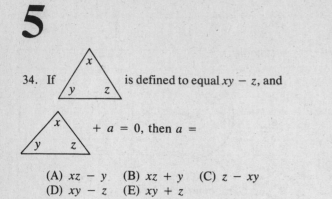 is defined to equal $xy - z$, and

$+ a = 0$, then $a =$

(A) $xz - y$ (B) $xz + y$ (C) $z - xy$
(D) $xy - z$ (E) $xy + z$

35. If $x = a + \dfrac{1}{2} = \dfrac{a + 3}{2}$, then $x =$

(A) $\dfrac{1}{2}$ (B) 1   (C) 2   (D) $2\dfrac{1}{2}$ (E) 5

IF YOU FINISH BEFORE TIME IS CALLED, YOU MAY CHECK YOUR WORK ON
THIS SECTION ONLY. DO NOT WORK ON ANY OTHER SECTION IN THE TEST.   **S T O P**

6 • 6 6 6 6 6 6 6 6 6 6 6

SECTION 6   Time—30 minutes
50 Questions

The questions in this section measure skills that are important to writing well. In particular, they test your ability to recognize and use language that is clear, effective, and correct according to the requirements of standard written English, the kind of English found in most college textbooks.

Directions: The following sentences contain problems in grammar, usage, diction (choice of words), and idiom.

    Some sentences are correct.
    No sentence contains more than one error.

You will find that the error, if there is one, is underlined and lettered. Assume that elements of the sentence that are not underlined are correct and cannot be changed. In choosing answers, follow the requirements of standard written English.

If there is an error, select the one underlined part that must be changed to make the sentence correct and blacken the corresponding space on your answer sheet.

If there is no error, blacken answer space Ⓔ.

EXAMPLE:

The region has a climate so severe that plants
                          A

growing there rarely had been more than twelve
         B   C

inches high. No error
        D   E

SAMPLE ANSWER
Ⓐ Ⓑ ● Ⓓ Ⓔ

1. I only bought what was necessary; I was not
     A   B   C
   extravagant. No error
      D   E

2. Bailing vigorously, we managed to remain afloat
   A   B   C
   until we were rescued by the Coast Guard.
              D
   No error
      E

3. We had ought to finish our trip before dark because
        A   B
   it gets very cold after the sun goes down. No error
   C   D   E

4. It is not you who are at fault; rather, it is I who is
              A   B   C   D
   to blame. No error
            E

5. Because of its efficacy in treating many ailments
      A
   and because it has brought about miraculous cures,
                 B
   penicillin has become an important addition to the
                C   D
   druggist's stock. No error
                    E

6. After the rain had fallen steadily for five days, then
                  A   B   C
   the football field was a massive sea of mud.
                          D
   No error
      E

7. I cannot force myself to like that kind of a person
                  A   B   C
   because his smugness repels me. No error
                        D   E

8. I believe that story about the fight because he
             A   B
   himself had told us the story was true. No error
   C   D   E

9. The ship had almost completely sank by the time
                A   B   C
   the rescuers arrived on the scene. No error
                D   E

GO ON TO THE NEXT PAGE

6 6 6 6 6 6 6 6 6 6 6 6

10. Since you do not participate in any of the class
    A _____ B
    activities, I must conclude that you are
    _____C
    disinterested. No error
    D _____ E

11. Marc Chagall, who recently died, painted many
    _____ A _____ B
    beautiful executed fantasies both in the United
    _____ C _____ D
    States and France. No error
    _____ E

12. Although many people complain about his attitude,
    _____ A
    it seems perfectly all right to myself. No error
    B __ C _____ D _____ E

13. The America's Cup, which was first won by the
    _____ A
    United States yacht *America*, grew out of the
    _____ B
    London Exposition of 1951 and now becoming a
    _____ C
    world yachting championship. No error
    D _____ E

14. On the contrary, you will find that Ms. Keene is
    _____ A ____ B
    better qualified than him for the executive
    C _____ D
    position. No error
    _____ E

15. Sometimes speed reading aids in comprehension,
    _____ A
    but remember that turning the pages rapidly does
    B _____ C _____ D
    not guarantee rapid comprehension. No error
    _____ E

16. The Salem witchcraft trials in 1692 inspired Arthur
    Miller to write *The Crucible*, to serve for a parable
    _____ A _____ B
    for America during the era of McCarthyism.
    _____ C ____ D
    No error
    E

17. The fishing fleet left the harbor when the fishermen
    _____ A ____ B _____ C
    heard that a school of bluefish were near the
    _____ D
    wreck. No error
    _____ E

18. After five years of booming markets and
    _____ A
    unparalleled expansion, Wall Street's major
    securities firms planning to slow their growth that
    _____ B _____ C
    has transformed them into sprawling global
    _____ D
    behemoths. No error
    _____ E

19. Neither the reporters nor the editor were
    _____ A _____ B
    satisfied with the salary offer made by the
    _____ C _____ D
    publisher. No error
    _____ E

20. Thurgood Marshall became the first of a number of
    _____ A _____ B
    black Supreme Court Justices when he was
    _____ C
    appointed of this position by President Lyndon
    _____ D
    Johnson. No error
    _____ E

21. When she spoke with the police, she reported her
    _____ A
    loss, stating that a large quantity of clothing and
    _____ B
    of valuable books were missing. No error
    _____ C _____ D _____ E

22. "Babbittry," a term used to describe a typically
    _____ A _____ B
    conservative businessman, was derived from
    _____ C ____ D
    Sinclair Lewis' novel *Babbitt*. No error
    _____ E

23. The article was rejected because of its length,
    _____ A
    verbosity, and because it presented only one point
    B _____ C _____ D
    of view. No error
    _____ E

24. Because of the triage practice used in hospitals,
    _____ A
    some of them waiting in the emergency room
    _____ B
    had been there for more than an hour. No error
    _____ C _____ D _____ E

25. Neither of the defendants were prepared for
    _____ A
    several of the arguments brought into the open and
    _____ B _____ C
    deftly handled by the prosecution. No error
    _____ D _____ E

GO ON TO THE NEXT PAGE

6. 6 6 6 6 6 6 6 6 6 6 6

<u>Directions:</u> In each of the following sentences, some part or all of the sentence is underlined. Below each sentence you will find five ways of phrasing the underlined part. Select the answer that produces the most effective sentence, one that is clear and exact, without awkwardness or ambiguity, and blacken the corresponding space on your answer sheet. In choosing answers, follow the requirements of standard written English. Choose the answer that best expresses the meaning of the original sentence.

Answer (A) is always the same as the underlined part. Choose answer (A) if you think the original sentence needs no revision.

EXAMPLE:

Laura Ingalls Wilder published her first book <u>and she was sixty-five years old then.</u>

(A) and she was sixty-five years old then
(B) when she was sixty-five years old
(C) at age sixty-five years old
(D) upon reaching sixty-five years
(E) at the time when she was sixty-five

SAMPLE ANSWER

Ⓐ ● Ⓒ Ⓓ Ⓔ

26. With the exception of <u>Frank and i, everyone in the class finished</u> the assignment before the bell rang.

(A) Frank and I, everyone in the class finished
(B) Frank and me, everyone in the class finished
(C) Frank and me, everyone in the class had finished
(D) Frank and I, everyone in the class had finished
(E) Frank and me everyone in the class finished

27. Many middle class individuals find that they cannot obtain good medical attention, <u>despite they need it badly</u>.

(A) despite they need it badly
(B) despite their bad need of it
(C) in spite of they need it badly
(D) however much their need of it were
(E) therefore, they need it badly

28. The form of terrorism that makes diplomats its target reached Sweden in <u>1975, the West German embassy in Stockholm was seized</u> by Germans linked to the Baader-Meinhof gang.

(A) 1975, the West German embassy in Stockholm was seized
(B) 1975, and the West German embassy in Stockholm was seized
(C) 1975, despite the West German embassy in Stockholm was seized
(D) 1975, when the West German embassy in Stockholm was seized
(E) 1975, the West German embassy in Stockholm's being seized

29. Arlington National Cemetery, <u>the site of the Tomb of the Unknown Soldier, is located on</u> the former Custis estate in Virginia.

(A) the site of the Tomb of the Unknown Soldier, is located on
(B) being the cite of the Tomb of the Unknown Soldier, has been located at
(C) where is located the Tomb of the Unknown Soldier, is at
(D) being the site of the Tomb of the Unknown Soldier, is at
(E) which includes the site of the Tomb of the Unknown Soldier, is located by

30. In the normal course of events, <u>Juan will graduate high school, he will enter</u> college in two years.

(A) Juan will graduate high school, he will enter
(B) Juan will graduate high school and enter
(C) Juan will be graduated from high school and enter
(D) Juan will have graduated from high school and enter
(E) Juan will graduate high school; he will enter

GO ON TO THE NEXT PAGE

6 6 6 6 6 6 6 6 6 6 6

31. It would have been wrong, even had it been possible, to force a parliamentary democracy down the throats of the Iranians.

(A) wrong, even had it been possible,
(B) wrong; even had it been possible,
(C) wrong, it had been even possible,
(D) wrong, even if possible it had been,
(E) wrong: even if it had been possible,

32. The number of California condors, decimated by increasing human intrusions into traditional condor breeding grounds, are currently given as fewer than thirty.

(A) are currently given as fewer than thirty
(B) currently are given as fewer than thirty
(C) is currently given as fewer than thirty
(D) were given currently as fewer than thirty
(E) are currently going to be given as fewer than thirty

33. Many economists maintain that the current low interest rates not only promote investment in the stock market but also made it more profitable.

(A) but also made it more profitable
(B) but also makes it more profitable
(C) but also made it more able to profit
(D) but made it also more profitable
(E) but also make it more profitable

34. Ever since the bombing of Cambodia, there has been much opposition from they who maintain that it was an unauthorized war.

(A) from they who maintain that it was an unauthorized war
(B) from they who maintain that it had been an unauthorized war
(C) from those who maintain that it was unauthorized
(D) from they maintaining that it was unauthorized
(E) from they maintaining that it had been unauthorized

35. During the winter of 1973, Americans discovered the need to conserve energy and attempts were made to meet the crisis.

(A) discovered the need to conserve energy and attempts were made to meet the crisis
(B) discovered the need to conserve energy and that the crisis had to be met
(C) discovered the need to conserve energy and made attempts to meet the crisis
(D) needed to conserve energy and to meet the crisis
(E) needed to conserve energy and attempts were made to meet the crisis

36. When one eats in this restaurant, you often find that the prices are high and that the food is poorly prepared.

(A) When one eats in this restaurant, you often find
(B) When you eat in this restaurant, one often finds
(C) When you eat in this restaurant, you often find
(D) If you eat in this restaurant, you often find
(E) When one ate in this restaurant, he often found

37. The giving of foreign aid is a tool of national policy, the hoped-for return is often indirect and long term.

(A) policy, the hoped-for return is often indirect and long term
(B) policy, however the hoped-for return is often indirect and long term
(C) policy, though the hoped-for return is often indirect and long term
(D) policy; albeit the hoped-for return is often indirect and long term
(E) policy; despite the hoped-for return is often indirect and long term

38. Strict economic sanctions that have been imposed against the Union of South Africa ban investments in that country and numerous metals may not be imported.

(A) ban investments in that country and numerous metals may not be imported
(B) ban investments there and the importation of numerous metals
(C) ban investing there and numerous metals may not be imported
(D) ban investments in that country, also, numerous metals may not be imported
(E) ban investing there and numerous metals have not been imported

39. Feeding natural wildlife during fall migration, not advocated being that it entices them to stay and possibly starve during the winter.

(A) not advocated being that it entices them to stay and possibly starve
(B) is not advocated since it entices them to stay and possibly starve
(C) is not advocated, being that it entices them to stay, perhaps starving
(D) has not been advisable because of eating patterns
(E) is not advocated; they can starve

GO ON TO THE NEXT PAGE ▷

6   6 6 6 6 6 6 6 6 6 6 6

40. John was <u>imminently qualified for the position</u>
<u>because he had studied computer programming and</u>
<u>how to operate an IBM machine.</u>

(A) imminently qualified for the position because
he had studied computer programming and
how to operate an IBM machine

(B) imminently qualified for the position since
studying computer programming and the
operation of an IBM machine

(C) eminently qualified for the position because he
had studied computer programming and how
to operate an IBM machine

(D) eminently qualified for the position because he
had studied computer programming and the
operation of an IBM machine

(E) eminently qualified because he had studied
computer programming and how to operate
an IBM machine

<u>Note:</u> The remaining questions are like those at the beginning of the section.

<u>Directions:</u> For each sentence in which you find an error, select the one underlined part that must be changed to
make the sentence correct and blacken the corresponding space on your answer sheet.

If there is no error, blacken answer space Ⓔ.

EXAMPLE:

The region has a climate <u>so severe that</u> plants
                  A

<u>growing</u> there rarely <u>had been</u> more than twelve
  B   C

inches <u>high</u>. <u>No error</u>
     D   E

SAMPLE ANSWER

Ⓐ Ⓑ ● Ⓓ Ⓔ

---

41. <u>In accordance with</u> the family's wishes, the doctor
    A

did not <u>place</u> the patient on life support systems,
        B

<u>still</u> <u>merely</u> made him comfortable. <u>No error</u>
 C   D   E

42. <u>In spite of</u> the Watergate scandal, former President
   A

Richard M. Nixon will <u>always be wanting</u>
                B

<u>to be remembered</u> for his <u>finesse in</u> foreign affairs.
    C   D

<u>No error</u>
 E

43. The <u>increase of</u> <u>working mothers</u> in the labor
     A   B

force, from 28% in 1976 to 52% in 1984, signals a
                                C

need for <u>additional</u> social and economic services in
        D

the future. <u>No error</u>
          E

44. In 1887, a <u>severe blizzard</u> in the Great Plains <u>killed</u>
        A   B

<u>millions of</u> cattle, ending the frontier cattle
  C

industry and <u>limiting</u> the need for the cowboy.
          D

<u>No error</u>
 E

45. <u>Following</u> opposition to some of her rulings, Prime
  A

Minister Indira Gandhi <u>was assassinated in</u>
                B   C

October 31, 1984; she was <u>succeeded by</u> her son,
                     D

Rajiv. <u>No error</u>
     E

GO ON TO THE NEXT PAGE

6   6   6   6   6   6   6   6   6   6   6

46. I am not <u>too eager</u> to go to this play <u>being that</u> it
          A   B   C
did not get <u>good</u> reviews. <u>No error</u>
            D   E

47. The New York Mets <u>won</u> the 1986 World Series
                        A
<u>by defeating</u> the Boston Red Sox <u>during</u> the
    B   C
seventh game in a <u>valiant final</u> effort. <u>No error</u>
                    D   E

48. The <u>small compact</u> sedan that Carlos <u>rented</u> gives
          A   B
a different <u>kind of ride</u> <u>than</u> does the heavier car
             C   D
he drives in the city. <u>No error</u>
                        E

49. <u>Because</u> Maria likes <u>spontaneous feedback</u>, she
      A   B
finds <u>talking</u> to her friends on the telephone a
       C
pleasure and <u>to write</u> letters an inconvenience.
              D
<u>No error</u>
E

50. <u>In the rush</u> to get to the <u>quarterly meeting</u>, one of
      A   B
the board members <u>forgot</u> <u>their</u> presentation.
                    C   D
<u>No error</u>
E

IF YOU FINISH BEFORE TIME IS CALLED, YOU MAY CHECK YOUR WORK ON
THIS SECTION ONLY. DO NOT WORK ON ANY OTHER SECTION IN THE TEST.   S T O P

Answer Key

Note: The answers to the math sections are keyed to the corresponding review areas in Chapter 12. The numbers in parentheses after each answer refer to topics as listed below. (Note that to review for number 16, Quantitative Comparison, study Chapter 11.)

1. Fundamental Operations
2. Algebraic Operations
3. Using Algebra
4. Roots and Radicals
5. Inequalities
6. Fractions
7. Decimals
8. Percent
9. Averages
10. Motion
11. Ratio and Proportion
12. Mixtures and Solutions
13. Work
14. Coordinate Geometry
15. Geometry
16. Quantitative Comparison
17. Data Interpretation

Section 1   Math

1.	B (2)	8.	A (1, 16)	15.	C (15, 16)	22.	A (2, 16)	29.	A (9)
2.	D (8)	9.	C (4, 16)	16.	C (15, 16)	23.	C (2, 16)	30.	B (15)
3.	B (10)	10.	A (8, 16)	17.	C (15, 16)	24.	A (2, 16)	31.	B (15)
4.	D (6)	11.	C (1, 6, 16)	18.	A (2, 16)	25.	C (15, 16)	32.	A (2, 4)
5.	B (6)	12.	C (2, 16)	19.	B (2, 16)	26.	B (2, 16)	33.	C (1)
6.	D (11, 13)	13.	B (15, 16)	20.	D (15, 16)	27.	D (15, 16)	34.	B (5, 15)
7.	C (11)	14.	B (15, 16)	21.	A (2, 16)	28.	B (15)	35.	A (15)

Section 2   Verbal

1.	B	9.	D	17.	E	25.	E	33.	E
2.	D	10.	D	18.	C	26.	D	34.	B
3.	E	11.	C	19.	A	27.	E	35.	E
4.	A	12.	B	20.	C	28.	A	36.	C
5.	C	13.	D	21.	D	29.	C	37.	D
6.	D	14.	E	22.	B	30.	A	38.	B
7.	A	15.	B	23.	A	31.	D	39.	E
8.	A	16.	D	24.	B	32.	E	40.	A

Section 3   Math

1.	B (6)	6.	C (1)	11.	A (2)	16.	E (15)	21.	D (15)
2.	C (1, 11)	7.	B (15)	12.	E (3)	17.	E (9)	22.	E (2, 4)
3.	C (11)	8.	A (10)	13.	D (10)	18.	A (1, 6)	23.	D (15)
4.	B (3, 11)	9.	D (10, 11)	14.	B (11)	19.	E (1)	24.	C (6)
5.	C (2, 4)	10.	E (2, 4)	15.	C (14)	20.	D (14)	25.	D (6)

Section 4   Verbal

1.	C	10.	B	19.	A	28.	D	37.	D
2.	E	11.	A	20.	C	29.	C	38.	D
3.	A	12.	D	21.	C	30.	C	39.	D
4.	B	13.	D	22.	D	31.	C	40.	B
5.	D	14.	B	23.	E	32.	E	41.	E
6.	B	15.	D	24.	E	33.	B	42.	C
7.	C	16.	D	25.	A	34.	B	43.	C
8.	E	17.	D	26.	A	35.	C	44.	D
9.	A	18.	E	27.	A	36.	E	45.	A

Section 5   Math

1.	B (6)	8.	B (6, 16)	15.	C (15, 16)
2.	E (6, 7)	9.	A (1, 16)	16.	D (15, 16)
3.	B (1, 6)	10.	D (4, 16)	17.	D (2, 16)
4.	A (11)	11.	D (4, 16)	18.	B (2, 16)
5.	B (2)	12.	D (5, 16)	19.	A (6, 16)
6.	E (1, 8)	13.	C (15, 16)	20.	C (2, 16)
7.	E (5, 15)	14.	B (15, 16)	21.	D (15, 16)

22.	A (15, 16)	29.	B (11)
23.	B (15, 16)	30.	A (6, 8)
24.	C (15, 16)	31.	A (11, 13)
25.	C (15, 16)	32.	C (9)
26.	B (15, 16)	33.	C (15)
27.	A (15, 16)	34.	C (2)
28.	C (1, 8)	35.	D (2)

Section 6   Test of Standard Written English

1.	A	11.	C	21.	D	31.	A	41.	C
2.	E	12.	D	22.	E	32.	C	42.	B
3.	A	13.	C	23.	C	33.	E	43.	A
4.	D	14.	D	24.	B	34.	C	44.	E
5.	B	15.	E	25.	A	35.	C	45.	C
6.	C	16.	B	26.	C	36.	C	46.	B
7.	C	17.	D	27.	B	37.	C	47.	E
8.	E	18.	B	28.	D	38.	B	48.	E
9.	B	19.	B	29.	A	39.	B	49.	D
10.	D	20.	D	30.	C	40.	D	50.	D

Self-Evaluation

The model SAT test you have just completed has the same format as the actual SAT. As you take more of the model tests in this chapter, you will lose any SAT "stage fright" you might have.

Use the steps that follow to evaluate your performance on Model SAT Test 4. (Note: You'll find the charts referred to in steps 1–5 on the next four pages.)

■ **STEP 1**   Use the Answer Key to check your answers for each section.

■ **STEP 2**   For each section, count the number of correct and incorrect answers (remember that you don't count omitted answers), and enter the numbers on the appropriate lines of the chart "Calculate Your Raw Score." Then do the indicated calculations to get your Raw Verbal Score, your Raw TSWE Score, and your Raw Math Score.

■ **STEP 3**   Consult the chart "Evaluate Your Performance" to see how well you did.

■ **STEP 4**   To pinpoint the specific areas in which you need to improve, circle the numbers of the questions that you either left blank or got wrong on the "Identify Your Weaknesses" charts. This will tell you where to concentrate your efforts to get the most out of your study time. The chart for the math sections gives you page references for review and practice by skill areas. The charts for the verbal and TSWE sections refer you to the appropriate chapters to study for each question type.

■ **STEP 5**   Do the review and practice indicated on the charts wherever you had a concentration of circles.

Important: Remember that, in addition to evaluating your scores, you should read all of the answer explanations for questions you answered incorrectly, questions you omitted, and questions you answered correctly but found difficult. Reviewing the answer explanations will help you understand concepts and strategies, and may point out shortcuts.

Calculate Your Raw Score

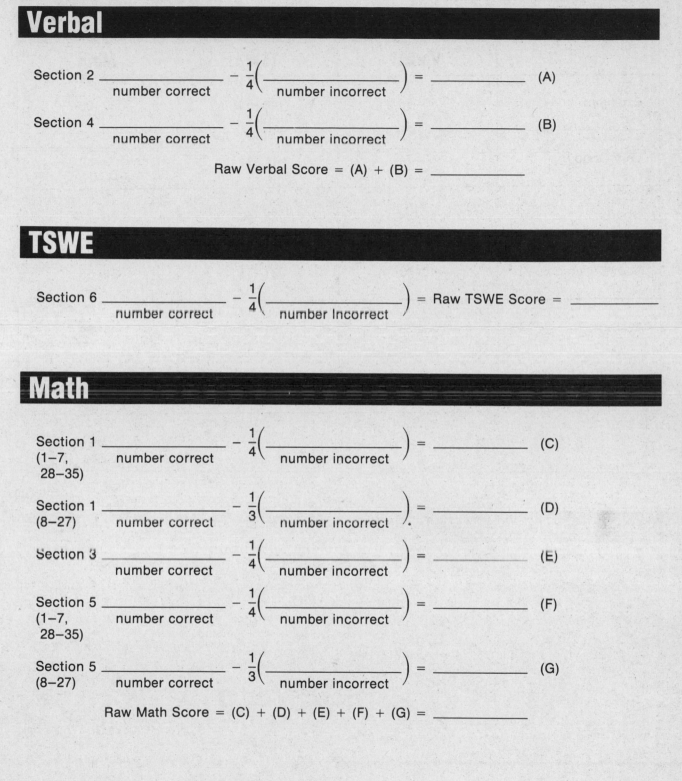

Verbal

Section 2 _____ − $\frac{1}{4}$(_____) = _____ (A)
                number correct   number incorrect

Section 4 _____ − $\frac{1}{4}$(_____) = _____ (B)
                number correct   number incorrect

Raw Verbal Score = (A) + (B) = _____

TSWE

Section 6 _____ − $\frac{1}{4}$(_____) = Raw TSWE Score = _____
                number correct   number Incorrect

Math

Section 1   _____ − $\frac{1}{4}$(_____) = _____ (C)
(1–7,   number correct   number incorrect
28–35)

Section 1   _____ − $\frac{1}{3}$(_____) = _____ (D)
(8–27)   number correct   number incorrect

Section 3   _____ − $\frac{1}{4}$(_____) = _____ (E)
                  number correct   number incorrect

Section 5   _____ − $\frac{1}{4}$(_____) = _____ (F)
(1–7,   number correct   number incorrect
28–35)

Section 5   _____ − $\frac{1}{3}$(_____) = _____ (G)
(8–27)   number correct   number incorrect

Raw Math Score = (C) + (D) + (E) + (F) + (G) = _____

Evaluate Your Performance

Verbal, TSWE, Math

	Verbal	TSWE	Math
Excellent	75–85	46–50	83–95
Very Good	65–74	44–45	72–82
Good	50–64	36–40	60–71
Above Average	40–49	31–35	55–59
Average	33–39	26–30	45–54
Below Average	below 33	below 26	below 45

Identify Your Weaknesses

Verbal

| Question Type | Question Numbers | | Chapter to Study |
	Section 2	Section 4	
Antonym	1, 2, 3, 4, 5, 6, 7, 8, 9, 10	1, 2, 3, 4, 5, 6, 7, 8, 9, 10, 11, 12, 13, 14, 15	Chapter 5
Analogy	16, 17, 18, 19, 20, 21, 22, 23, 24, 25	36, 37, 38, 39, 40, 41, 42, 43, 44, 45	Chapter 6
Sentence Completion	11, 12, 13, 14, 15	16, 17, 18, 19, 20, 31, 32, 33, 34, 35	Chapter 7
Reading Comprehension	26, 27, 28, 29, 30, 31, 32, 33, 34, 35, 36, 37, 38, 39, 40	21, 22, 23, 24, 25, 26, 27, 28, 29, 30	Chapter 8

TSWE

Question Type	Question Numbers	Chapter to Study
Usage	1, 2, 3, 4, 5, 6, 7, 8, 9, 10, 11, 12, 13, 14, 15, 16, 17, 18, 19, 20, 21, 22, 23, 24, 25, 41, 42, 43, 44, 45, 46, 47, 48, 49, 50	Chapter 13
Sentence Correction	26, 27, 28, 29, 30, 31, 32, 33, 34, 35, 36, 37, 38, 39, 40	Chapter 13

Identify Your Weaknesses

Math

Skill Area	Question Numbers			Pages to Study
	Section 1	**Section 3**	**Section 5**	
Fundamental Operations	8, 11, 33	2, 6, 18, 19, 23	3, 6, 9, 28	328–29
Algebraic Operations	1, 12, 18, 19, 21, 22, 23, 24, 26, 32	5, 10, 11, 22	5, 17, 18, 20, 34, 35	329–34
Using Algebra		4, 12		334–35
Fractions	4, 5, 11	1, 18, 24, 25	1, 2, 3, 8, 19, 30	341–45
Decimals and Percents	2, 10		2, 6, 28, 30	351–55
Verbal Problems	3, 6, 29	8, 9, 13, 17, 22	32	357–58
Ratio and Proportion	6, 7	2, 3, 4, 9, 14	4, 29, 31	362–64
Geometry	13, 14, 15, 16, 17, 20, 25, 27, 28, 30, 31, 34, 35	7, 15, 16, 21, 23	7, 13, 14, 15, 16, 21, 22, 23, 24, 25, 26, 27, 33	371–76
Coordinate Geometry		15, 20		381–82
Inequalities	34		7, 12	335–36
Quantitative Comparison	8, 9, 10, 11, 12, 13, 14, 15, 16, 17, 18, 19, 20, 21, 22, 23, 24, 25, 26, 27		8, 9, 10, 11, 12, 13, 14, 15, 16, 17, 18, 19, 20, 21, 22, 23, 24, 25, 26, 27	309–13
Roots and Radicals	9, 32	5, 10, 22	10, 11	332–33

Answer Explanations

Section 1 Math

1. B.
$$r = \frac{rs}{1-s}$$
Multiply by $1-s$: $rs = r(1-s)$
Divide by r: $s = 1-s$
Add s: $2s = 1$
Divide by 2: $s = \frac{1}{2}$

Substitute $s = \frac{1}{2}$:
$$s^2 + 2s + 1 = ?$$
$$\left(\frac{1}{2}\right)^2 + (2)\left(\frac{1}{2}\right) + 1 = ?$$
$$\frac{1}{4} + 1 + 1 = 2\frac{1}{4}$$

2. D. Profit = 20% of $30 (cost) or $6
Selling price = $36
Tag price − Discount = Selling price
Let x = tag price (in dollars).
$x - 10\% \, x = \$36$
$x - 0.1x = \$36$
$10x - 1x = 360$ (multiply by 10)
$9x = 360$
$x = \$40$

3. B. Time = 10 min. or $\frac{1}{6}$ hr.
Distance = 40 miles
$$\text{Average rate} = \frac{\text{Distance}}{\text{Time}}$$
$$\text{Average rate} = \frac{40 \text{ miles}}{\frac{1}{6} \text{ hr.}} \text{ or 240 m.p.h.}$$

4. D. After spending $\frac{1}{3}$ of his inheritance, Martin used $\frac{3}{5}$ of the remaining $\frac{2}{3}$ for the automobile.

Another way of putting this is to say that $\frac{2}{5}$ of the $\frac{2}{3}$ (or $\frac{4}{15}$) was left after satisfying the mortgage and buying the car.

$\frac{4}{15}$ of the original $30,000 = $8,000.

5. B. $\dfrac{2 \text{ pennies} + 2 \text{ nickels} + 1 \text{ dime}}{1 \text{ quarter}} = \dfrac{22\cent}{25\cent} = \dfrac{22}{25}$

6. D. Let x = number of sets of books the man binds in 1 day.
$$\frac{s \text{ sets}}{d \text{ days}} = \frac{x \text{ sets}}{1 \text{ day}}$$
$$dx = s$$
$$x = \frac{s}{d}$$
Since there are b books in one set, there are $(b)\left(\dfrac{s}{d}\right)$ or $\dfrac{bs}{d}$ books in $\dfrac{s}{d}$ sets.

7. C. Divide $\dfrac{3.6}{0.6} = \dfrac{36}{6} = 6$, or set up a direct proportion.
Let x = number of flasks necessary to hold 3.6 liters.
$$\frac{\text{number of flasks}}{\text{number of liters}} = \frac{1}{0.6} = \frac{x}{3.6}$$
$0.6x = 3.6$ (product of means equals product of extremes)
$6x = 36$ (multiply by 10)
$x = 6$

8. A. Multiply both by 7.
Column A = 1 and Column B = 0.0994.
$1 > 0.0994$

9. C. $\sqrt{\dfrac{1}{0.25}} = \sqrt{\dfrac{100}{25}} = \sqrt{4} = 2$

10. A. 5% of 500 = 25

11. C. Between 2:55 and 3:15, 20 min. (or $\frac{1}{3}$ hr.) elapses.

12. C. Since 15 is common to both columns, consider only $\dfrac{16}{x} = 4$. Since $4x = 16$, $x = 4$.

13. B. Since the area = 25, each side = 5.
The sum of three sides of the square = 15

14. B. $\dfrac{x^2}{2} = 18$
$x^2 = 36$
$x = 6$

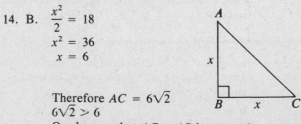

Therefore $AC = 6\sqrt{2}$
$6\sqrt{2} > 6$
Or observe that $AC > AB$ because the hypotenuse is always the longest side in any right triangle.

15. C.   In square, $ABCD$, AB = AD. Therefore, right triangle ABD is isosceles. Since BD = $6\sqrt{2}$, then AB = AD = 6. Perimeter = $6 \times 4 = 24$.

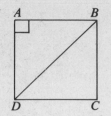

16. C.   Area = $\frac{1}{2}(6)(6) = 18$

17. C. $AB = BC$ (given)
Since the measure of $\angle B$ equals the measure of $\angle C$, $AB = AC$. Therefore triangle ABC is equilateral, and $m\angle A = m\angle B = m\angle C$ and $m\angle B + m\angle C = m\angle B + m\angle A$.

18. A. $36 - 8 = 7x$
$\quad\quad 28 = 7x$
$\quad\quad\quad 4 = x$
$7 > 4$

19. B.   Multiply both columns by 8. Column A = $z + 6$, and Column B = $2z + 6$.
$2z > z$, since z is positive.
Therefore $2z + 6 > z + 6$.

20. D.   We may not assume that ABC is a right triangle. If it were a right triangle, and if we assumed that side AC is the hypotenuse, then the area of ABC would be $\frac{1}{2}(5)(8)$ or 20.

21. A. $AC = BC = 2y > \frac{2}{5}y$

22. A. $3a = 36$ (cross-multiply)
$6a = 72$
$6a > 36$

23. C.   Remove parentheses: $x(y + z) = xy + xz$.
Since $z = 0$, $xy + xz = xy$.

24. A. $(x + y)^2 = x^2 + 2xy + y^2$. Since $xy = 9$, $2xy = 18$; and since $x^2 + y^2 = 12$, $(x + y)^2 = 30$ (Column A).

25. C.   Area of square = $(Side)^2$. If area = 25 units, side = 5 units. Since perimeter of square = side $\times$ 4, square with perimeter of 20 units has side = 5 units.

26. B.   Solve by factoring: $x^2 - 7x + 12 = 0$
$\quad\quad (x - 4)(x - 3) = 0$
$\quad\quad\quad\quad\quad x = 4, 3$

27. D.   With a perimeter of 36 units, the sides may have values of 4 and 14, 15 and 3, or 16 and 2. Note how the value of the area would differ; 4 $\times$ 14 is not equal to 15 $\times$ 3 or 16 $\times$ 2.

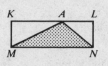

28. B.   Observe that the rectangle and the triangle share the same base, MN, and that the altitude of the rectangle is equal to the altitude of the triangle. Since the area of the triangle = $\frac{1}{2}bh$, and the area of the rectangle = bh, the area of the triangle = $\frac{1}{2}(100)$, or 50.

29. A.   Average $\times$ Number of cases = Sum
$$\left(\frac{1}{6}\right)(3) = \frac{1}{2}$$
Sum of $\frac{1}{2} + \frac{1}{3} = \frac{5}{6}$
Let x = fraction to be subtracted from $\frac{5}{6}$ to yield $\frac{1}{2}$.
$$\frac{5}{6} - x = \frac{1}{2}$$
$5 - 6x = 3$ (multiply by 6)
$\quad -6x = -2$
$\quad\quad 6x = 2$
$\quad\quad\quad x = \frac{1}{3}$

The alert student will see that subtracting $\frac{1}{3}$ from $\left(\frac{1}{2} + \frac{1}{3}\right)$ yields $\frac{1}{2}$.

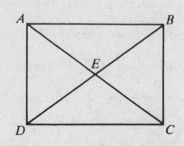

30. B.   In right triangle BAD, BD is the hypotenuse.
$(AB)^2 + (AD)^2 = (BD)^2$
(Pythagorean theorem)

$(16)^2 + (12)^2 = (BD)^2$
$256 + 144 = (BD)^2$
$400 = (BD)^2$
$20 = BD$

Alternatively, ABD is a 3-4-5 right triangle with $AD = 4(3)$ and $AB = 4(4)$, so $BD = 4(5)$ or 20. $DE = \frac{1}{2}BD$ or 10 (diagonals of a rectangle bisect each other)

31. B. $\dfrac{\text{Distance covered by moving wheel}}{\text{Circumference}}$
= Number of revolutions made
Since radius equals f feet,
circumference = 2π (radius) or $2\pi f$.
$\dfrac{5280 \text{ ft.}}{2\pi f \text{ ft.}}$ or $\dfrac{2640}{\pi f}$ ft.

32. A.   Eliminate r to find s in terms of t:

$\dfrac{3}{rs} = \dfrac{1}{2t}$

$rs = 6t$ (product of means equals product of extremes)

$r = \dfrac{6t}{s}$ (divide by s)

$r = s^2$ (given)

$s^2 = \dfrac{6t}{s}$ (things equal to the same thing are equal to each other)

$s^3 = 6t$ (product of means equals product of extremes)

$s = \sqrt[3]{6t}$ (extract cube root of both sides of the equation)

33. C.   Divide the number of yards, of feet, and of inches, in turn, by 3, the number of equal parts.
(1) $3\overline{)13}$ yd. = 4 yd. + 1 yd. remaining
1 yd. = 3 ft.; 5 ft. + 3 ft. = 8 ft.
(2) $3\overline{)8}$ ft. = 2 ft. + 2 ft. remaining.
2 ft. = 24 in.; 1 in. + 24 in. = 25 in.
(3) $3\overline{)25}$ in. = $8\frac{1}{3}$ in.

$3\overline{)13}$ yd. 5 ft. 1 in. = 4 yd. 2 ft. $8\frac{1}{3}$ in.

34. B. $KM = \frac{1}{2}KL$ and $AC = \frac{1}{2}AB$. Since $KM > AC$, $KL > AB$ since doubles, triples, etc., of unequal quantities are unequal in the same order.

K———————————M—————————L

A————————C—————B

35. A.   Triangle ABC is a 3-4-5 right triangle with $BC = 2(4)$ and $AC = 2(5)$, so $AB = 2(3)$ or 6. Or note that $\angle B$ is a right angle (an angle inscribed in a semicircle is a right angle).
Diameter $AC = 10$
$(AC)^2 = (BC)^2 + (AB)^2$
$(10)^2 = (8)^2 + (AB)^2$
$100 = 64 + (AB)^2$
$36 = (AB)^2$
$AB = 6$
$CB = DA$
$CB = 8$
$DA = 8$
$\dfrac{AB}{AD} = \dfrac{6}{8}$ or $\dfrac{3}{4}$

Section 2   Verbal

1. B.   To *contaminate* is to taint or pollute. Its opposite is *make pure*.
Context Clue: Think of "contaminated water."

2. D.   *Perturbed* means agitated or disturbed. Its opposite is *soothed*.
Context Clue: Think of "perturbed by bad news."

3. E.   *Ingratitude* means ungratefulness or unthankfulness. Its opposite is *thankfulness*.
Context Clue: Think of "shameful ingratitude."

4. A.   To *enlighten* is to inform; to make clear to someone. Its opposite is *obscure* (becloud; confuse).
Context Clue: Think of being "enlightened as well as entertained" by a show on TV.

5. C.   The opposite of *scanty* (meager) is *profuse* (abundant).
Context Clue: Think of "a scanty supply of food."

6. D.   The opposite of *gauche* (clumsy, lacking in social graces) is *tactful* (socially skillful).
Context Clue: Think of "a gauche remark."

7. A.   The opposite of *benediction* (blessing) is *curse*.
Remember to try to break down unfamiliar words into recognizable parts.
Word Parts Clue: *Bene-* means good; *dict-* means say. A *benediction* is a good saying or blessing.

8. A.   To *vacillate* means to waver or be indecisive. Its opposite is to *stand firm*.
Context Clue: Think of "vacillating between two choices."

9. D.   *Pugnacious* means combative or belligerent. Its opposite is *conciliatory* or reconciling. Context Clue: Think of "a pugnacious fighter."

10. D.   *Heinous* means hateful, odious, atrocious. Its opposite is *noble* or excellent, admirable. Context Clue: Think of "a heinous crime."

11. C.   If one is alert and insightful, one's faculties (mental powers) are *intact* (sound or whole). Note how the phrase set off by the comma restates and clarifies the idea that Picasso has continued to be perceptive and alert.

(Definition)

12. B.   *Levity* (frivolity) is inappropriate during serious moments. The phrase set off by the comma serves to explain why the behavior is inappropriate to the occasion. Word Parts Clue: *Lev-* means light. *Levity* means lightness of mind or character.

13. D.   Something beneficial or helpful in small amounts may be *toxic* (poisonous) in large amounts. Remember to watch for signal words that link one part of the sentence to another. The use of "though" in the second clause sets up a contrast. The missing word must be an antonym or near-antonym for beneficial.

(Argument Pattern)

14. E.   If his stealing is a disease, the criminal will be unable to give up his *larcenous* (thieving) ways. Remember to watch for signal words that link one part of the sentence to another. The use of "for" in the second clause is a cause signal.

(Cause and Effect Signal)

15. B.   To initiate someone is to introduce that person into the secret knowledge of a group. Until his initiation, the explorer would have been *excluded from* the *esoteric* or private and confidential rites of the tribe. Remember, in double-blank sentences, go through the answer choices, testing the *first* words in each choice and eliminating those that don't fit. You can immediately eliminate Choices D and E.

16. D.   A *dog* is a *mammal*; a *snake*, a *reptile*.

(Member and Class)

17. E.   A *teller's* working place is a *bank*; a *teacher's*, a *school*.

(Worker and Workplace)

18. C.   *Goggles* protect the *eyes*. A *helmet* protects the *head*. The sentence "Goggles are worn on the eyes" is too broad. Answer Choice B could appear to fit that framework.

(Function)

19. A.   *Corn* is stored in a *silo*; *valuables* are stored in a *vault*.

(Function)

20. C.   One puts *liniment* on an *ache* to promote healing, just as one puts *salve* on a *sore*.

(Function)

21. D.   *Fundamental* (essential) and *incidental* (casual or chance) are antonyms; so are *vain* and *humble*.

(Antonyms)

22. B.   A *visionary* (dreamer) is not *practical*; a *braggart* (boaster) is not *modest*.

(Antonym Variant)

23. A.   A *tumbler* is a container for *beverages*; a *quiver* is a container for *arrows*. Consider secondary meanings of the capitalized words as well as their primary meanings. Here a *tumbler* is a stemless drinking glass, not an acrobat.

(Definition)

24. B.   A *mayfly* is known to be *ephemeral* (short-lived); a *gazelle* is known to be *graceful*.

(Defining Characteristic)

25. E.   *Insubordination* (disobedience) may lead to *punishment*; *diligence* (industry) may lead to *promotion*.

(Cause and Effect)

26. D.   In the last paragraph of the passage we are told that the speaker "had been frightened of the lieutenant, frightened of being reprimanded." Choices A and C are not supported by the passage. Choice B is incorrect. It is Broadhurst, not the narrator, who dismisses the incident as not worth worrying about. Choice E is incorrect. The fact that things happened so fast explains why the narrator didn't speak to the platoon commander immediately. It does not explain why he didn't discuss the matter with him afterwards.

(Inference)

27. E. The outburst of the platoon commander at Broadhurst indicates that he expected his subordinates not to act "without permission." In doing so, he observed army customs to the letter.
Choices A, B, C, and D are not supported by the passage.

(Inference)

28. A. Broadhurst's questioning of the narrator's order to march indicates that he was familiar with army routine.
Choices B and C are not implied by the passage.
Choice D is contradicted by the passage. Broadhurst is lower in rank than the platoon commander: he cannot act without the commander's permission.
Choice E is contradicted by the passage. Both by questioning a foolish order and by dismissing the incident as unimportant, Broadhurst is considerate of the narrator.
Remember, when asked to make inferences, base your answers on what the passage implies, not what it states directly.

(Inference)

29. C. The last two sentences of the passage suggest that he has discovered a new sense of himself, a new self-understanding.

(Inference)

30. A. The opening sentence states that the men were "assembled and ready to go." We can logically assume that some time earlier plans had been made for them to do so. None of the other choices are suggested by the passage.

(Inference)

31. D. The last sentence of the opening paragraph supports this choice.
Choice A is incorrect. The passage mentions flashes of light, not continuous lighting.
Choice B is incorrect. "Freeze" here means to stop suddenly, not to chill.
Choices C and E are incorrect. They are unsupported by the passage.
Remember, when asked about specific details in the passage, spot key words in the question and scan the passage to find them (or their synonyms).
Key Words: "magic," eye.

(Specific Details)

32. E. The phrase "optical afterglow" supports the idea that *afterimpressions* are the basis for persistence of vision.

(Specific Details)

33. E. The use of simple, everyday comparisons to help the reader understand the phenomenon suggests that the passage comes from an informal, popular article.

(Inference)

34. B. The passage presents an explanation of what lies behind stroboscopic effects. Note the use of "explains" in the second sentence.
Choice A is incorrect. The passage does not discuss any technological advances. To the degree that it discusses technology at all, it describes the stroboscope's most primitive form.
Choices C, D, and E are incorrect. They are unsupported by the passage.

(Main Idea)

35. E. The passage points out the values of democratic life and indicates how these values are mocked and derided. Choice E emphasizes the fact that we fail to appreciate our advantages.
Choices A and B are incorrect. Free discussion and government by law are two of the specific advantages of democracy the passage mentions. They are too narrow in scope to cover the passage as a whole.
Choice C is incorrect. The passage talks of the advantages of the democratic way of life, not the weaknesses.
Choice D is incorrect. It is far too broad.
Remember, when asked to choose a title, watch out for choices that are too specific or too broad.

(Main Idea/Title)

36. C. Since the author uses words like "cheap" and "sneering," we may assume that he is *critical*.
Remember, when asked to determine the author's attitude or tone, look for words that convey emotion or paint pictures.

(Attitude/Tone)

37. D. The opening sentence describes the shattering of the Iroquois leadership's pro-British policy. The remainder of the passage describes how Iroquois policy changed to reflect changes in European military goals.
Choice A is incorrect. The passage is expository, not accusatory.
Choice B is incorrect. Nothing in the passage suggests such charges were made against the Iroquois.
Choice C is incorrect. It is unsupported by the passage.
Choice E is incorrect. The passage demonstrates the Iroquois were able to play European power politics.

Remember, when asked to find the main idea, be sure to check the opening and summary sentences of each paragraph.

(Main Idea)

38. B. In lines 36–38, the author states that the Iroquois "played the game of European power politics with effectiveness." Thus, he shows *respect for their competence*.
None of the other choices is supported by the passage.
Remember, when asked to determine the author's attitude or tone, look for words that convey value judgments.

(Inference)

39. E. Lines 20–33 indicate that in the early 1700's and through most of the eighteenth century the Iroquois *did* hold the balance of power. Therefore, Choice E is the correct answer.
Choice A is incorrect. The raid on Lachine was an effective response to French aggression, as was the Iroquois-enforced policy of aggressive neutrality.
Choice B is incorrect. James II's overthrow was followed by colonial uprisings.
Choice C is incorrect. In response to the Iroquois leaders' supposed favoring of the British (lines 39–46), the French went to war.
Choice D is incorrect. This sums up the policy of aggressive neutrality.

(Inference)

40. A. Lines 34–35 indicate that the Iroquois played the game of power politics with effectiveness "by their willingness to use their power against one or the other nation." In other words, they were ready to fight either side.
Choice B is incorrect. Ties of loyalty may actually have hampered the Iroquois; the French fear that the Iroquois were compromising the system in favor of the British led to the eventual breakdown of the policy of neutrality.
Choice C is incorrect. French presence in the borderlands would have been a challenge to Iroquois power.
Choices D and E are incorrect. They are unsupported by the passage.

(Specific Details)

Section 3

1. B. $1\frac{1}{4}x = \frac{1}{2}$

$\frac{5}{4}x = \frac{1}{2}$

$5x = 2$ (multiply by 4)

$x = \frac{2}{5}$ (divide by 5)

2. C. Since there are 5 nickels in 1 quarter, there are $5q$ nickels in q quarters.

3. C. Let x = amount of celery needed for 8 cups of tuna fish.

$$\frac{\text{cups of tuna fish}}{\text{cups of chopped celery}} = \frac{2}{\frac{1}{8}} = \frac{8}{x}$$

$$2x = 1$$

$$x = \frac{1}{2}$$

4. B. When the clock loses 12 hr., or 720 min., it will reach a point where it will indicate the correct time.
Let x = number of days needed for the clock to lose 12 hr. or 720 min.

$$\frac{\text{minutes lost}}{\text{time (in days)}} = \frac{10}{1} = \frac{720}{x}$$

$$10x = 720$$

$$x = 72$$

5. C. $\sqrt{x^2y^2 + x^3y^4} = 3xy$

$\sqrt{x^2y^2(1 + xy^2)} = 3xy$ (factor)

$xy\sqrt{1 + xy^2} = 3xy$ (remove x^2y^2 from under the radical sign)

$\sqrt{1 + xy^2} = \dfrac{3xy}{xy}$ (divide by xy)

$\sqrt{1 + xy^2} = 3$

$(\sqrt{1 + xy^2})^2 = (3)^2$

$1 + xy^2 = 9$

$xy^2 = 8$ (subtract 1)

6. C. If the cashier had given the man 4 quarters, he would not have had to give him any dimes. If the cashier had given the man 3 quarters, he would have had to give him a nickel in addition to 2 dimes. If the cashier had given the man 1 quarter, he would have had to give him 7 dimes and 1 nickel. This is contrary to the given statement that the change consisted of dimes and quarters. If the cashier gave the man 2 quarters, he would then also give him 5 dimes. Therefore the change consisted of 2 + 5 or 7 coins.

7. B. Since $GC = 8$, $EB = 8$.
$AB = AE + EB$
$AB = 2 + 8$ or 10
Area of square = (Side)²
Area of square $ABCD$ = $(10)^2$ or 100
Area of $FBEJ$ = area of square $ABCD$ − area of shaded portion
Area of shaded portion = 44
Area of $FBEJ$ = 100 − 44 or 56

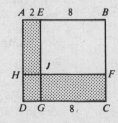

8. A. $\dfrac{\text{Distance}}{\text{Time}} = \text{Rate}$

$\dfrac{70 \text{ miles}}{2\frac{1}{2} \text{ hr.}} = 28 \text{ m.p.h.}$

Desired time $= 2\frac{1}{2}$ hr. $- \frac{3}{4}$ hr. or $1\frac{3}{4}$ hr.

Desired rate $= \dfrac{\text{Distance}}{\text{Time}}$

or $\dfrac{70 \text{ miles}}{1\frac{3}{4} \text{ hr.}}$ or 40 m.p.h.

Since the saleswoman's rate was 28 m.p.h., she should travel 12 m.p.h. faster to achieve a rate of 40 m.p.h.

9. D. $\dfrac{\text{yards}}{\text{minutes}} = \dfrac{y}{m} = \dfrac{x}{60}$

$mx = 60y$

$x = \dfrac{60y}{m}$ (divide by m)

10. E. $\dfrac{3y^2 - x^2}{\frac{1}{2}a^3}$

Substitute:

$\dfrac{3(3)(3) - (-2)(-2)}{\frac{1}{2}(-1)(-1)(-1)}$

$\dfrac{27 - 4}{-\frac{1}{2}}$

$\dfrac{23}{-\frac{1}{2}}$

$(23)\left(-\dfrac{2}{1}\right) = -46$

11. A.

$abc = dbc + e$

$abc - dbc = e$ (subtract dbc)

$bc(a - d) = e$ (factor)

$\dfrac{bc(a - d)}{(a - d)} = \dfrac{e}{a - d}$ (divide by $a - d$)

$bc = \dfrac{e}{a - d}$

12. E. The man earns $p + w$ dollars.
Since he works d days, his average earnings per day are $\dfrac{p + w}{d}$.

13. D. The time spent is 8 hr.

$\dfrac{\text{Distance}}{\text{Time}} = \text{Average rate}$

$\dfrac{600 \text{ miles}}{8 \text{ hr.}} = 75 \text{ m.p.h.}$

14. B. The former price is 80¢ each. The new price is $9.00 per dozen, or 75¢ each.

$\dfrac{\text{old price}}{\text{new price}} = \dfrac{80\cent}{75\cent} = \dfrac{16}{15}$ or $16:15$

15. C. Draw AC.
Area of triangle $ABC =$
$\frac{1}{2}$ base AC (4 units) $\times$ altitude BE (2 units) or $\frac{1}{2}(4)(2)$
or 4 units
Area of triangle $DAC =$
$\frac{1}{2}$ base AC (4 units) $\times$ altitude DF (3 units or
$\frac{1}{2}(4)(3)$ or 6 units

Area of $ABCD =$ area of triangle $ABC +$ area of triangle DAC
Area of $ABCD = 4 + 6$ or 10 units

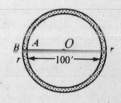

16. E. Radius $OA = 50$ ft.
Area of circle $= \pi r^2$
Area of circle with radius
$OA = \pi(50)^2$ or 2500π
sq. ft.
Radius $OB = 52$ ft.
Area of circle with radius
$OB = \pi(52)^2$ or 2704π
square ft.
Difference between areas of the two circles equals area of circular grass walk.
$2704\pi - 2500\pi = 204\pi$ sq. ft.

17. E. Average $\times$ Number of test marks
$\qquad\qquad\qquad = $ Sum of all test marks
$80 \times 6 = 480$
Sum of tests already taken $= 385$
Mark necessary on next test $= 480 - 385$ or 95%

18. A. $\dfrac{1}{2} + \dfrac{3}{4} \div \left(\dfrac{5}{6} \times \dfrac{7}{8}\right) - \dfrac{9}{10}$

$\dfrac{1}{2} + \dfrac{3}{4} \div \left(\dfrac{35}{48}\right) - \dfrac{9}{10}$

$\dfrac{1}{2} + \dfrac{3}{4} \times \dfrac{48}{35} - \dfrac{9}{10}$

$\dfrac{1}{2} + \dfrac{3}{\cancel{4}} \times \dfrac{\overset{12}{\cancel{48}}}{35} - \dfrac{9}{10}$

$\dfrac{1}{2} + \dfrac{36}{35} - \dfrac{9}{10}$ (70 is L.C.D.)

$\dfrac{35 + 72 - 63}{70}$ or $\dfrac{44}{70} = \dfrac{22}{35}$

19. E. Maximum weight of 4 eggs $= (25 \text{ oz.})(4)$ or 100 oz.
Maximum weight of remaining 6 eggs $= (25 \text{ oz.})(6)$ or 150 oz.
Combined maximum weight $= 250$ oz.

20. **D.** The locus of points that are at a fixed distance from a given point is a circle whose radius is the fixed distance and whose center is the fixed point.

An equation of a circle with center at the origin is of the form $x^2 + y^2 = r^2$, where r is the radius of the circle.

In this case, $r = 5$.

Therefore, an equation of the circle with center at origin is
$$x^2 + y^2 = (5)^2$$
or
$$x^2 + y^2 = 25$$

21. **D.** The sum of the angles of a triangle $= 180°$.

$$(x + 24) + (4x - 12) + \left(\frac{3x}{2} + 12\right) = 180°$$

$$x + 24 + 4x - 12 + \frac{3x}{2} + 12 = 180°$$

$$2x + 48 + 8x - 24 + 3x + 24 = 360°$$
$$\text{(multiply by 2)}$$
$$13x + 48 = 360$$
$$13x = 312$$
$$x = 24$$

One angle $= (x + 24)$ or $48°$
Another angle $= (4x - 12)$ or $84°$
Another angle $= \left(\frac{3x}{2} + 12\right)$ or $48°$

The $84°$ angle must be the vertex angle since the base angles of an isosceles triangle are equal.

22. **E.** $\sqrt{0.09} = 0.3$
$$x\sqrt{0.09} = 3$$
$$(x)(0.3) = 3$$
$$0.3x = 3$$
$$3x = 30$$
$$x = 10$$

23. **D.** I. $AD - CD = AC$, and $AB + BC = AC$
II. $AD - BC = AB + CD$
III. is not true because $AB + CD = AD - BC$.

24. **C.** Let $x =$ number of applicants.
$$\frac{x}{2} - 3 = \frac{2x}{5}$$
$$5x - 30 = 4x$$
$$x = 30$$

25. **D.** $17\frac{3}{8} - 17\frac{1}{4} = \frac{1}{8}$ (profit per share)

Let $x =$ number of shares to be sold.
$$(x)\left(\frac{1}{8}\right) = \text{total profit for shares sold}$$
$$\frac{x}{8} = 100$$
$$x = 800$$

Section 4 Verbal

1. **C.** *Vivacious* means lively or spirited. Its opposite is *spiritless* or unanimated.
Context Clue: Think of "a vivacious cheerleader."
Word Parts Clue: *Viv-* means life. Someone vivacious is full of life.

2. **E.** *Prone* means having a tendency or an inclination toward something. Its opposite is *disinclined*.
Context Clue: Think of "accident prone."

3. **A.** *Collaborate* means to work together with another person. Its opposite is *work alone*.
Word Parts Clue: *Co-* or *col-* means together.
Context Clue: "Sam Brownstein and Mitch Weiner collaborated on this book."

4. **B.** *Segregate* means to set apart or separate; to isolate. Its opposite is *unite* or unify.
Word Parts Clue: *Se-* means apart; *greg-* means a herd or group. To segregate someone is to set him apart from the group.
Beware Eye-Catchers: Choice D is incorrect. *Tolerate* means to endure, permit or bear. *Tolerate* and *segregate* often appear in the same context, but they are not antonyms.

5. **D.** *Taut* means drawn tight; stretched. Its opposite is *loose* or lax.
Context Clue: Think of "a taut wire."

6. **B.** *Circumspect* means cautious or careful. Its opposite is *rash* or careless.
Remember, consider secondary meanings of words as well as their primary meanings. Everyone knows the noun *rash*: a chickenpox rash, for example. Here, *rash* is an adjective that means careless.
Word Parts Clue: *Circum-* means around; *spect-* means look. Someone *circumspect* looks around carefully; he is cautious.

7. **C.** *Aloof* means remote, physically or spiritually distant. Its opposite is *gregarious* or sociable; fond of company.
Word Parts Clue: Remember, *greg* means a herd or group. Someone *gregarious* enjoys being part of a group.

8. **E.** *Proximity* means closeness, nearness. Its opposite is *distance*.
Context Clue: Think of "close proximity."
Word Parts Clue: *Prox-* means next or near.

9. **A.** A *paragon* is a model of excellence, a good example for others to copy. Its opposite is a *bad example*.

Beware Eye-Catchers: Word endings are deceptive. A *paragon* is someone or something almost perfect. A *hexagon* is a six-sided geometrical figure.

10. B.   To *cajole* is to wheedle or coax; to persuade by flattery. Its opposite is to *bully* or force to act by means of threats.

11. A.   *Callow* means inexperienced or immature. Its opposite is *experienced*.
Context Clue: Think of "a callow youth."

12. D.   *Divergence* means a drawing apart; a branching off. Its opposite is *confluence*, a coming together or flowing together, as of rivers or crowds.
Context Clue: Think of "the divergence of two paths."

13. D.   The *nadir* is the lowest point, or bottom. Its opposite is the zenith or *apex*.
Context Clue: Think of "the nadir of his hopes."

14. B.   *Invidious* means causing dislike or resentment; promoting ill will. Its opposite is *creating good will*.
Context Clue: Think of "invidious comparisons," "invidious slanders."

15. D.   An *encomium* is a formal expression of high praise. Its opposite is *opprobrium* or reproach.
Context Clue: Think of "an encomium for the returning hero."

16. D.   The critics would regret any lapse on the part of a *promising* writer.
The adjective *glowing* is your clue that you are looking for a word with positive associations. Therefore, you can eliminate any word with negative ones. Choices A, B, and C have negative associations. Only Choices D or E can be correct.

17. D.   If we see things in a distorted or altered fashion, our testimony is *unreliable*.
Note how the second clause serves to clarify or define the meaning of the missing word. Remember, before you look at the choices, read the sentence and think of a word that makes sense.
Likely Words: undependable, misleading.

(Definition)

18. E.   To *galvanize* is to rouse by shock: you react as if someone's touched you with a live wire. If news is shocking, you feel *galvanized*. The term "galvanized into action" is a set phrase or cliché.

19. A.   Without reinforcement the attack would be difficult; therefore, the colonel would probably *countermand* or cancel the order.
Note the use of the "when . . . then" structure. "When this happened, then that happened." Here "when . . . then" signals cause and effect.

(Cause and Effect Signal)

20. C.   To *commiserate* (express feelings of sympathy) with *bereaved* parents, parents saddened by death, would be appropriate. Remember, in double-blank sentences, go through the answer choices, testing the *first* words in each choice and eliminating those that don't fit. You can immediately eliminate Choice B, *chatted*, and Choice D, *rejoiced*.

21. C.   The author provides the reader both with physical details of dress and bearing and with comments about the motivations and emotions of Bosola and the Cardinal.
Choice A is incorrect. The passage scarcely mentions the church.
Choice B is incorrect. The description of ecclesiastical costumes is only one item in the description of the Cardinal.
Choice D is incorrect. The persons described are characters in a play, not figures in paintings.
Choice E is incorrect. The author's purpose is description, not accusation.

(Main Idea)

22. D.   From the opening lines, in which the curtain rises and the two men "enter from the right" (as a stage direction would say), and from the later references to gaslit Victorian melodrama, we can infer that Bosola and the Cardinal are characters in a play.
Choice A is incorrect. The Cardinal's brother is Duke Ferdinand.
Choices B and C are incorrect. Lines 58–67 describe Bosola as doing the work of a "hired ruffian" and playing a "lowly, despicable" role. He is a servant, not a noble lord or a lord of the church.
Choice E is unsupported by the passage.

(Inference)

23. E.   The eagle is poised to strike "with exposed talons." It, like the Cardinal, collects itself to strike with greater force. The imagery accentuates the Cardinal's *mercilessness*.
Choice A is incorrect. The Cardinal is not *flighty* (light-headed and irresponsible); he is cold and calculating.
Choice B is incorrect. He loves power, not freedom.
Choice C is incorrect. An eagle poised to strike with bared claws suggests violence, not

eminence (fame and high position).
Choice D is incorrect. Nothing in the passage
suggests he is spiritual.
Beware Eye-Catchers: "Eminence" is a title
of honor applied to cardinals in the Roman
Catholic church. Choice D may attract you for
this reason.

(Inference)

24. E.   Although Bosola is not a leather-jacketed
hoodlum, he *is* a hired assassin (despite his
scholarly taste).

(Word from Context)

25. A.   The casual references to the elongated hands
and features in El Greco's work and to the
trim beards and commanding stances in the
work of Van Dyke imply that the author
assumes the reader has seen examples of both
painters' art.
Remember, when asked to make inferences,
base your answers on what the passage
implies, not what it states directly.

(Inference)

26. A.   Farquhar's ready agreement with the saying
that all is fair in love and war implies his
willingness to use underhanded or unfair
methods to support the Southern cause.

(Inference)

27. A.   Mrs. Farquhar's readiness to fetch water for
the gray-clad Confederate soldier suggests
some degree of sympathy on her part for the
Confederate cause.
Choices B and D are incorrect. There is
nothing in the passage to suggest either of
them.
Choices C and E are incorrect. Mrs.
Farquhar's action in hospitably performing the
menial task of fetching water "with her own
white hands" contradicts them.

(Inference)

28. D.   The phrase "burn like tow" and the reference
to dry driftwood suggest that tow will catch
fire readily.
Remember, when asked to give the meaning of
an unfamiliar word, look for nearby context
clues.

(Word from Context)

29. C.   The use of dialogue suggests a work of fiction;
so do the descriptive adjectives and the
narrative style.

(Inference)

30. C.   The scout is a Yankee soldier disguised as a
member of the enemy. By coming to the
Farquhars' in Confederate disguise, he is able
to learn they are sympathetic to the enemy.
By telling Farquhar of the work on the bridge,
stressing both the lack of guards and the
abundance of fuel, he is tempting Farquhar
into an attack on the bridge (and into an
ambush). The scout's job is to locate potential
enemies and draw them out from cover.

(Inference)

31. C.   A longing for familiar scenes is *nostalgia* or
homesickness.
Remember, before you look at the choices,
read the sentence and think of a word that
makes sense.
Likely Words: homesickness, nostalgia,
yearning.

(Definition)

32. E.   Borrowers would complain that an old,
appreciated borrowing policy had been set
aside or *superseded*.
Remember, in double-blank sentences, go
through the answer choices, testing the *first*
words in each choice and eliminating those
that don't fit. The fact that the new policy has
received complaints indicates that the old
policy was viewed positively. You can
immediately eliminate Choice B, *disliked*, and
Choice D, *ignored*. Both are negative terms.

33. B.   We can expect *gullible* (easily deceived)
people to be most easily fooled or *misled* by
propaganda.
The use of "not only" sets up a contrast. Not
only fools, but also clever people (in their
moments off guard) can fall for propaganda.

(Contrast Signal)

34. B.   Heroic virtues include *disregard* or ignoring of
death and *fortitude* or courage in the face of
torture. Through it all, Bond remains
nonchalant or cool.

(Examples)

35. C.   The Romantic poets can be described as
emotional; Arnold and the later "moralizing"
Victorian era poets can be described as
didactic (interested in teaching).
Remember to watch for signal words that link
one part of the sentence to another. The use
of "unlike" in the opening clause sets up a
contrast. The missing words must be
antonyms or near-antonyms. You can
immediately eliminate Choices A and B as
synonym or near-synonym pairs.

(Contrast Signal)

36. E. A *typewriter* is a tool used by a *journalist*; a pair of *pliers* is a tool used by an electrician.

(Worker and Tool)

37. D. The meat of a *sheep* is called *mutton*; the meat of a *steer* is called *beef*.

(Definition)

38. D. An *entry* is one day's record that is part of a *diary*; an *episode* is one separate performance that is part of a *serial*.

(Part to Whole)

39. D. A *mural* (wall painting) is painted on a *wall*; an *etching* is imprinted on *paper*.

(Defining Characteristic)

40. B. A *libretto* (the words of an opera or musical play) is written by an *author*; the *score* (musical arrangement), by a *composer*.

(Worker and Article Created)

41. E. To restrict the movements of a *horse*, a *tether* is used. To restrict those of a *prisoner*, *manacles* are used.

(Function)

42. C. *Portentous* (threatening) and *ominous* are synonyms. *Applicable* (relevant) and *pertinent* are synonyms also.

(Synonyms)

43. C. *Peckish* (slightly hungry) is less extreme a condition than *starving*. *Plain* (homely, unattractive) is less extreme a condition than *hideous* (extremely ugly).

(Degree of Intensity)

44. D. A *poet* writes or creates an *eclogue* (short pastoral poem); a *seamstress* sews or creates a *gown*.

(Worker and Article Created)

45. A. A *virtuoso* (expert performer) is by definition *experienced*; a *rogue* (scoundrel) is by definition *knavish*.

(Synonym Variant)

Section 5

1. B. Let x = number of thirds in $\frac{5}{8}$.

$$\frac{x}{3} = \frac{5}{8}$$
$$8x = 15$$
$$x = \frac{15}{8}$$

2. E. $3 + \dfrac{3}{0.3}$

$3 + \dfrac{30}{3}$

$3 + 10 = 13$

3. B. $\dfrac{(18)(24)}{(12)(16)} \div \dfrac{18}{16}$

$\dfrac{(18)(24)}{(12)(16)} \cdot \dfrac{16}{18}$

$\dfrac{\overset{2}{\cancel{(18)}}(24)}{\cancel{(12)}\cancel{(16)}} \cdot \dfrac{\cancel{16}}{\cancel{18}} = 2$

4. A. $2x + 3x = 45$
$x = 9$
$2x = 18$ (number of men)

5. B. $\dfrac{1}{1-p} \div \dfrac{1}{p-1}$

$\dfrac{1}{1-p} \cdot \dfrac{p-1}{1}$

$\dfrac{1}{-p+1} \cdot \dfrac{p-1}{1}$

$\dfrac{-1}{p-1} \cdot (p-1)$ (multiply numerator and denominator by -1)

$\dfrac{-1}{\cancel{p-1}} \cdot \cancel{(p-1)} = -1$

6. E. $\dfrac{2.6z}{6} = 65$

$2.6z = (65)(6)$ (multiply by 6)
$2.6x = 390$
$26z = 3900$ (multiply by 10)
$z = 150$ (divide by 26)

7. E. $AP = AC$ since $\angle 1 = \angle 2$. If $AB > AC$, then also $AB > AP$ (or $AP < AB$). A quantity may be substituted for its equal any place it occurs.

8. B. Multiply both numerator and denominator of the complex fraction by 16:

$$\frac{16\left(\frac{1}{4} - \frac{3}{16}\right)}{16\left(\frac{1}{8}\right)} = \frac{4-3}{2} = \frac{1}{2}$$

9. A. $\dfrac{3 \text{ yd. } 1 \text{ ft. } 3 \text{ in.}}{3} = 1$ yd. 5 in. or 41 in.

10. D. If n = an even whole number, then $x = \pm 1$.
    If n = an odd whole number, then $x = +1$.

11. D. $a^6 = (a)(a)(a)(a)(a)(a)$
    $6a^5 = (6)(a)(a)(a)(a)(a)$
    The quantity in Column A would be equal to the quantity in Column B only if the value of a were equal to 6.

12. D. The value of x could be 40 or 80.

13. C. If $y = 50$, then the measure of $\angle DCB = 100$, the measure of $\angle ABC = 80$, and $x = 40$. Therefore $x + y = 90$.

14. B. The information given tells us that the measure of $\angle A$ is greater than the measure of $\angle B$. Since $A + B = 120$, the measure (in degrees) of $\angle A$ is greater than 60, and $\angle B$ has a measure of less than 60. Side AC lies opposite the smallest angle of the triangle.

15. C. The sum of the lengths of two adjacent sides of a parallelogram equals one-half the perimeter.

16. D. We cannot correctly answer the question because we may not assume that this figure is equilateral.

17. D. Zero, positive, and negative values may be assigned to x and/or y.

18. B. In Column A, $x - (y - z) = x - y + z$. Since y is positive, $y > -y$.

19. A. In Column A:
    $\dfrac{1}{3} \div \dfrac{1}{5} = \left(\dfrac{1}{3}\right)(5) = \dfrac{5}{3} = 1\dfrac{2}{3}$
    In Column B:
    $\dfrac{1}{5} \div \dfrac{1}{3} = \left(\dfrac{1}{5}\right)(3) = \dfrac{3}{5}$

20. C. $9x - 6y = 3$ (given)
    $3x - 2y = 1$ (division by 3)

21. D. We may not assume that BC passes through the center of the circle. We may not assume that $AB = AC$. We may only find the value of BC from the data furnished.

22. A. The sum of the lengths of 2 sides of a triangle is greater than the length of the third side. A straight line is the shortest distance between 2 points.

23. B. Since $ABCD$ is a square, $\angle DOC$ is a right angle and OD and OC are radii, DOC is an isosceles right triangle.
    Area of $DOC = \dfrac{1}{2}(OD)(OC)$ or 8. Therefore $OD = OC = 4$. $(DC)^2 = (4)^2 + (4)^2$, and $DC = \sqrt{32}$ or $4\sqrt{2}$.
    Perimeter of $ABCD = (4)(4\sqrt{2})$ or $16\sqrt{2}$ or $(16)(1.4)$ or 22.4.

24. C. Area of shaded portion = area of circle (16π) minus area of the square $[(4\sqrt{2})^2$ or 32]. Area of shaded portion = $16\pi - 32$.

25. C. $\left(\dfrac{X}{Z}\right)\left(\dfrac{Z}{Y}\right) = \dfrac{X}{Y}$
    X and Y are opposite equal angles, and therefore $X = Y$ and $\dfrac{X}{Y} = 1$.

26. B. Since $x = 20$, the measure of $\angle FCD = 40$.
    Measure of $\angle FCB = 140$ (supplement)
    Measure of $\angle FAB$ = Measure of $\angle FCB$ (opposite angles of a parallelogram)
    Therefore $y = 140$ and $y > 6x$.

27. A. Radius of I = 5
    Radius of II = 4
    Radius of III = 3
    $AB = 5 + 3 = 8$
    $BC = 3 + 4 = 7$
    $AC = 5 + 4 = 9$
    Perimeter of $ABC = 24$

28. C. Since the man loses 350 eggs, he sells $2750 - 350$ or 2400 eggs.
    2400 eggs = 200 dozen.
    If he sells these at 70¢ per dozen, he receives $140.
    Selling price − Cost = Profit
    $\$140 - \$100 = \$40$
    $\dfrac{\text{Profit}}{\text{Original investment}} \times 100 = \begin{array}{l}\text{Percent profit}\\ \text{on original}\\ \text{investment}\end{array}$
    $\dfrac{\$40}{\$100} \times 100 = 40$

29. B. Average distance covered by one jump
    × Number of jumps = Total distance
    $\dfrac{\text{Total distance covered}}{\text{Average distance covered by one jump}}$
    = Number of jumps
    $\dfrac{3y \text{ ft.}}{8 \text{ ft.}}$ = number of jumps
    (convert to similar units)
    $\dfrac{3y}{8}$ = number of jumps

30. A. $\dfrac{1}{10} + \dfrac{1}{3} + \dfrac{1}{5}$ = part of salary spent

$\dfrac{1}{10} + \dfrac{1}{3} + \dfrac{1}{5}$ (LCD = 30)

$\dfrac{3 + 10 + 6}{30}$ or $\dfrac{19}{30}$ is part of salary spent.

Therefore $\dfrac{11}{30}$ is left for other expenditures and savings.

$\dfrac{11}{30} = 0.36\dfrac{2}{3}$ or $36\dfrac{2}{3}\%$

31. A. The basic principle involved is similar to that of a work problem. Apply the formula

$\dfrac{\text{Time actually worked}}{\text{Time required to complete the task}}$ = Part of task done

$\dfrac{1 \text{ hr.}}{h \text{ hr.}} = \dfrac{1}{h}$

32. C. Sum of height of 3 boys = $x + y + y$ or $x + 2y$ in

Average = $\dfrac{\text{Sum}}{\text{Number of cases}}$ or $\dfrac{x + 2y}{3}$

33. C. Let $x = BC$; then $AB = 2x$.
Area of triangle ABC

$= \dfrac{1}{2}(b)(h)$ or

$\left(\dfrac{1}{2}\right)(x)(2x)$ or x^2

Area is given equal to 64 sq. ft.
$x^2 = 64$
$x = 8$
$BC = 8; AB = 16$

$(8)^2 + (16)^2 = (AC)^2$ (Pythagorean Theorem)

$64 + 256 = (AC)^2$
$(AC)^2 = 320$
$AC = \sqrt{320}$ or approximately 18 ft.

34. C. $xy - z + a = 0$
$a = z - xy$

35. D. Solve for a first:

$a + \dfrac{1}{2} = \dfrac{a + 3}{2}$

$2a + 1 = a + 3$
$a = 2$

Substitute $a = 2$:

$x = 2 + \dfrac{1}{2}$ or $2\dfrac{1}{2}$

Section 6   Test of Standard Written English

1. A. Misplaced modifier. *I bought only* is preferable.

2. E. Sentence is correct.

3. A. Error in diction. Change *had ought* to *ought*.

4. D. Lack of agreement. The antecedent of *who* is *I. Who*, therefore, should be followed by *am*.

5. B. Lack of parallel structure. Change clause to a phrase in order to parallel the preceding phrase. Change *it has brought about* to *of its*.

6. C. Error in sentence connector. Both *after* and *then* are sentence connectors, but only one should be used to avoid redundancy. Delete *then*.

7. C. Error in diction. Delete the article *a*.

8. E. Sentence is correct.

9. B. Error in tense. The past perfect tense of *sink* is *had sunk*.

10. D. Error in diction. Use *uninterested* instead of *disinterested*.

11. C. Misuse of adjective instead of adverb. Change *beautiful* to *beautifully*.

12. D. Misuse of pronoun. *Myself* (reflexive pronoun) must be preceded in the same sentence by either the pronoun *I* or *me*. It should not be used in place of *me* (personal pronoun).

13. C. Error in tense. Change *now becoming* to *became*.

14. D. Error in case. Since *than* is a conjunction, a verb is understood after its use. Change *him (is)* to *he (is)*.

15. E. Sentence is correct.

16. B. Error in diction. Change *to serve for* to *to serve as*.

17. D. Lack of agreement. *School* is singular and should be followed by *was* (singular).

18. B. Incomplete sentence. By changing *planning* to *plan*, we correct the error.

19. B. Lack of agreement. In a neither-nor construction the verb agrees with the noun or pronoun which comes immediately before the verb. The verb should agree with *editor* (singular). Change *were* to *was*.

20. D. Error in diction. Change *appointed of* to *appointed to*.

21. D. Lack of agreement. The subject is *quantity* (singular) and requires a singular verb *was missing*.

22. E. Sentence is correct.

23. C. Lack of parallel structure. Change *because it presented* to *presentation of*.

24. B. Misuse of pronoun. Change *them* (personal pronoun) to *those* (indefinite demonstrative pronoun).

25. A. Error in agreement. The indefinite pronoun *neither* requires a singular verb. Change *were prepared* to *was prepared*.

26. C. This corrects the two errors in this sentence— the error in case (*me* for *I*) and the error in tense (*had finished* for *finished*).

27. B. *Despite* should be used as a preposition.

28. D. The addition of the conjunction *when* corrects the run-on sentence and shows the relationship between the two clauses.

29. A. Sentence is correct.

30. C. This corrects the two errors in the sentence— the idiom error *graduate high school* and the run-on sentence.

31. A. The inverted word order used with the subjunctive (*had it been*) is correct.

32. C. As the subject of a sentence *The number* generally is considered a singular and therefore requires a singular verb (*is given*).

33. E. Changing *made* to *make* corrects the sequence of tenses.

34. C. *From* is a preposition and requires a pronoun in the objective case—*from those* (*people*).

35. C. This corrects the lack of parallel structure.

36. C. Unnecessary shift of pronoun. Do not shift from *you* to *one*.

37. C. The addition of the conjunction *though* corrects the run-on sentence.

38. B. This corrects the lack of parallel structure.

39. B. Choice B expresses the author's meaning directly and concisely. All other choices are either indirect or ungrammatical.

40. D. Choice D corrects the error in diction and the error in parallel structure.

41. C. Error in sentence connector. Change *still* to *but* in order to clarify the connection between the clauses.

42. B. Error in tense. Change *always be wanting* to *always want*.

43. A. Error in diction. The information provided pertains to percent, not to actual numbers. Therefore, change *increase of* to *increasing rate of*.

44. E. Sentence is correct.

45. C. Error in diction. Change *in* to *on*.

46. B. Error in sentence connector. Change *being that* to *since*.

47. E. Sentence is correct.

48. E. Sentence is correct.

49. D. Lack of parallel structure. Change *to write* to *writing*.

50. D. Error in agreement. The antecedent of *their* is *one*. Therefore, change *their* to either *his* or *her*.

Answer Sheet–Test 5

Start with number 1 for each new section. If a section has fewer than 50 questions, leave the extra spaces blank.

Remove answer sheet by cutting on dotted line

Section 1

1. Ⓐ Ⓑ Ⓒ Ⓓ Ⓔ	11. Ⓐ Ⓑ Ⓒ Ⓓ Ⓔ	21. Ⓐ Ⓑ Ⓒ Ⓓ Ⓔ	31. Ⓐ Ⓑ Ⓒ Ⓓ Ⓔ	41. Ⓐ Ⓑ Ⓒ Ⓓ Ⓔ
2. Ⓐ Ⓑ Ⓒ Ⓓ Ⓔ	12. Ⓐ Ⓑ Ⓒ Ⓓ Ⓔ	22. Ⓐ Ⓑ Ⓒ Ⓓ Ⓔ	32. Ⓐ Ⓑ Ⓒ Ⓓ Ⓔ	42. Ⓐ Ⓑ Ⓒ Ⓓ Ⓔ
3. Ⓐ Ⓑ Ⓒ Ⓓ Ⓔ	13. Ⓐ Ⓑ Ⓒ Ⓓ Ⓔ	23. Ⓐ Ⓑ Ⓒ Ⓓ Ⓔ	33. Ⓐ Ⓑ Ⓒ Ⓓ Ⓔ	43. Ⓐ Ⓑ Ⓒ Ⓓ Ⓔ
4. Ⓐ Ⓑ Ⓒ Ⓓ Ⓔ	14. Ⓐ Ⓑ Ⓒ Ⓓ Ⓔ	24. Ⓐ Ⓑ Ⓒ Ⓓ Ⓔ	34. Ⓐ Ⓑ Ⓒ Ⓓ Ⓔ	44. Ⓐ Ⓑ Ⓒ Ⓓ Ⓔ
5. Ⓐ Ⓑ Ⓒ Ⓓ Ⓔ	15. Ⓐ Ⓑ Ⓒ Ⓓ Ⓔ	25. Ⓐ Ⓑ Ⓒ Ⓓ Ⓔ	35. Ⓐ Ⓑ Ⓒ Ⓓ Ⓔ	45. Ⓐ Ⓑ Ⓒ Ⓓ Ⓔ
6. Ⓐ Ⓑ Ⓒ Ⓓ Ⓔ	16. Ⓐ Ⓑ Ⓒ Ⓓ Ⓔ	26. Ⓐ Ⓑ Ⓒ Ⓓ Ⓔ	36. Ⓐ Ⓑ Ⓒ Ⓓ Ⓔ	46. Ⓐ Ⓑ Ⓒ Ⓓ Ⓔ
7. Ⓐ Ⓑ Ⓒ Ⓓ Ⓔ	17. Ⓐ Ⓑ Ⓒ Ⓓ Ⓔ	27. Ⓐ Ⓑ Ⓒ Ⓓ Ⓔ	37. Ⓐ Ⓑ Ⓒ Ⓓ Ⓔ	47. Ⓐ Ⓑ Ⓒ Ⓓ Ⓔ
8. Ⓐ Ⓑ Ⓒ Ⓓ Ⓔ	18. Ⓐ Ⓑ Ⓒ Ⓓ Ⓔ	28. Ⓐ Ⓑ Ⓒ Ⓓ Ⓔ	38. Ⓐ Ⓑ Ⓒ Ⓓ Ⓔ	48. Ⓐ Ⓑ Ⓒ Ⓓ Ⓔ
9. Ⓐ Ⓑ Ⓒ Ⓓ Ⓔ	19. Ⓐ Ⓑ Ⓒ Ⓓ Ⓔ	29. Ⓐ Ⓑ Ⓒ Ⓓ Ⓔ	39. Ⓐ Ⓑ Ⓒ Ⓓ Ⓔ	49. Ⓐ Ⓑ Ⓒ Ⓓ Ⓔ
10. Ⓐ Ⓑ Ⓒ Ⓓ Ⓔ	20. Ⓐ Ⓑ Ⓒ Ⓓ Ⓔ	30. Ⓐ Ⓑ Ⓒ Ⓓ Ⓔ	40. Ⓐ Ⓑ Ⓒ Ⓓ Ⓔ	50. Ⓐ Ⓑ Ⓒ Ⓓ Ⓔ

Section 2

1. Ⓐ Ⓑ Ⓒ Ⓓ Ⓔ	11. Ⓐ Ⓑ Ⓒ Ⓓ Ⓔ	21. Ⓐ Ⓑ Ⓒ Ⓓ Ⓔ	31. Ⓐ Ⓑ Ⓒ Ⓓ Ⓔ	41. Ⓐ Ⓑ Ⓒ Ⓓ Ⓔ
2. Ⓐ Ⓑ Ⓒ Ⓓ Ⓔ	12. Ⓐ Ⓑ Ⓒ Ⓓ Ⓔ	22. Ⓐ Ⓑ Ⓒ Ⓓ Ⓔ	32. Ⓐ Ⓑ Ⓒ Ⓓ Ⓔ	42. Ⓐ Ⓑ Ⓒ Ⓓ Ⓔ
3. Ⓐ Ⓑ Ⓒ Ⓓ Ⓔ	13. Ⓐ Ⓑ Ⓒ Ⓓ Ⓔ	23. Ⓐ Ⓑ Ⓒ Ⓓ Ⓔ	33. Ⓐ Ⓑ Ⓒ Ⓓ Ⓔ	43. Ⓐ Ⓑ Ⓒ Ⓓ Ⓔ
4. Ⓐ Ⓑ Ⓒ Ⓓ Ⓔ	14. Ⓐ Ⓑ Ⓒ Ⓓ Ⓔ	24. Ⓐ Ⓑ Ⓒ Ⓓ Ⓔ	34. Ⓐ Ⓑ Ⓒ Ⓓ Ⓔ	44. Ⓐ Ⓑ Ⓒ Ⓓ Ⓔ
5. Ⓐ Ⓑ Ⓒ Ⓓ Ⓔ	15. Ⓐ Ⓑ Ⓒ Ⓓ Ⓔ	25. Ⓐ Ⓑ Ⓒ Ⓓ Ⓔ	35. Ⓐ Ⓑ Ⓒ Ⓓ Ⓔ	45. Ⓐ Ⓑ Ⓒ Ⓓ Ⓔ
6. Ⓐ Ⓑ Ⓒ Ⓓ Ⓔ	16. Ⓐ Ⓑ Ⓒ Ⓓ Ⓔ	26. Ⓐ Ⓑ Ⓒ Ⓓ Ⓔ	36. Ⓐ Ⓑ Ⓒ Ⓓ Ⓔ	46. Ⓐ Ⓑ Ⓒ Ⓓ Ⓔ
7. Ⓐ Ⓑ Ⓒ Ⓓ Ⓔ	17. Ⓐ Ⓑ Ⓒ Ⓓ Ⓔ	27. Ⓐ Ⓑ Ⓒ Ⓓ Ⓕ	37. Ⓐ Ⓑ Ⓒ Ⓓ Ⓔ	47. Ⓐ Ⓑ Ⓒ Ⓓ Ⓔ
8. Ⓐ Ⓑ Ⓒ Ⓓ Ⓔ	18. Ⓐ Ⓑ Ⓒ Ⓓ Ⓔ	28. Ⓐ Ⓑ Ⓒ Ⓓ Ⓔ	38. Ⓐ Ⓑ Ⓒ Ⓓ Ⓔ	48. Ⓐ Ⓑ Ⓒ Ⓓ Ⓔ
9. Ⓐ Ⓑ Ⓒ Ⓓ Ⓔ	19. Ⓐ Ⓑ Ⓒ Ⓓ Ⓔ	29. Ⓐ Ⓑ Ⓒ Ⓓ Ⓔ	39. Ⓐ Ⓑ Ⓒ Ⓓ Ⓔ	49. Ⓐ Ⓑ Ⓒ Ⓓ Ⓔ
10. Ⓐ Ⓑ Ⓒ Ⓓ Ⓔ	20. Ⓐ Ⓑ Ⓒ Ⓓ Ⓔ	30. Ⓐ Ⓑ Ⓒ Ⓓ Ⓔ	40. Ⓐ Ⓑ Ⓒ Ⓓ Ⓔ	50. Ⓐ Ⓑ Ⓒ Ⓓ Ⓔ

Section 3

1. Ⓐ Ⓑ Ⓒ Ⓓ Ⓔ	11. Ⓐ Ⓑ Ⓒ Ⓓ Ⓔ	21. Ⓐ Ⓑ Ⓒ Ⓓ Ⓔ	31. Ⓐ Ⓑ Ⓒ Ⓓ Ⓔ	41. Ⓐ Ⓑ Ⓒ Ⓓ Ⓔ
2. Ⓐ Ⓑ Ⓒ Ⓓ Ⓔ	12. Ⓐ Ⓑ Ⓒ Ⓓ Ⓔ	22. Ⓐ Ⓑ Ⓒ Ⓓ Ⓔ	32. Ⓐ Ⓑ Ⓒ Ⓓ Ⓔ	42. Ⓐ Ⓑ Ⓒ Ⓓ Ⓔ
3. Ⓐ Ⓑ Ⓒ Ⓓ Ⓔ	13. Ⓐ Ⓑ Ⓒ Ⓓ Ⓔ	23. Ⓐ Ⓑ Ⓒ Ⓓ Ⓔ	33. Ⓐ Ⓑ Ⓒ Ⓓ Ⓔ	43. Ⓐ Ⓑ Ⓒ Ⓓ Ⓔ
4. Ⓐ Ⓑ Ⓒ Ⓓ Ⓔ	14. Ⓐ Ⓑ Ⓒ Ⓓ Ⓔ	24. Ⓐ Ⓑ Ⓒ Ⓓ Ⓔ	34. Ⓐ Ⓑ Ⓒ Ⓓ Ⓔ	44. Ⓐ Ⓑ Ⓒ Ⓓ Ⓔ
5. Ⓐ Ⓑ Ⓒ Ⓓ Ⓔ	15. Ⓐ Ⓑ Ⓒ Ⓓ Ⓔ	25. Ⓐ Ⓑ Ⓒ Ⓓ Ⓔ	35. Ⓐ Ⓑ Ⓒ Ⓓ Ⓔ	45. Ⓐ Ⓑ Ⓒ Ⓓ Ⓔ
6. Ⓐ Ⓑ Ⓒ Ⓓ Ⓔ	16. Ⓐ Ⓑ Ⓒ Ⓓ Ⓔ	26. Ⓐ Ⓑ Ⓒ Ⓓ Ⓔ	36. Ⓐ Ⓑ Ⓒ Ⓓ Ⓔ	46. Ⓐ Ⓑ Ⓒ Ⓓ Ⓔ
7. Ⓐ Ⓑ Ⓒ Ⓓ Ⓔ	17. Ⓐ Ⓑ Ⓒ Ⓓ Ⓔ	27. Ⓐ Ⓑ Ⓒ Ⓓ Ⓔ	37. Ⓐ Ⓑ Ⓒ Ⓓ Ⓔ	47. Ⓐ Ⓑ Ⓒ Ⓓ Ⓔ
8. Ⓐ Ⓑ Ⓒ Ⓓ Ⓔ	18. Ⓐ Ⓑ Ⓒ Ⓓ Ⓔ	28. Ⓐ Ⓑ Ⓒ Ⓓ Ⓔ	38. Ⓐ Ⓑ Ⓒ Ⓓ Ⓔ	48. Ⓐ Ⓑ Ⓒ Ⓓ Ⓔ
9. Ⓐ Ⓑ Ⓒ Ⓓ Ⓔ	19. Ⓐ Ⓑ Ⓒ Ⓓ Ⓔ	29. Ⓐ Ⓑ Ⓒ Ⓓ Ⓔ	39. Ⓐ Ⓑ Ⓒ Ⓓ Ⓔ	49. Ⓐ Ⓑ Ⓒ Ⓓ Ⓔ
10. Ⓐ Ⓑ Ⓒ Ⓓ Ⓔ	20. Ⓐ Ⓑ Ⓒ Ⓓ Ⓔ	30. Ⓐ Ⓑ Ⓒ Ⓓ Ⓔ	40. Ⓐ Ⓑ Ⓒ Ⓓ Ⓔ	50. Ⓐ Ⓑ Ⓒ Ⓓ Ⓔ

Start with number 1 for each new section. If a section has fewer than 50 questions, leave the extra spaces blank.

Section 4

1. Ⓐ Ⓑ Ⓒ Ⓓ Ⓔ	11. Ⓐ Ⓑ Ⓒ Ⓓ Ⓔ	21. Ⓐ Ⓑ Ⓒ Ⓓ Ⓔ	31. Ⓐ Ⓑ Ⓒ Ⓓ Ⓔ	41. Ⓐ Ⓑ Ⓒ Ⓓ Ⓔ
2. Ⓐ Ⓑ Ⓒ Ⓓ Ⓔ	12. Ⓐ Ⓑ Ⓒ Ⓓ Ⓔ	22. Ⓐ Ⓑ Ⓒ Ⓓ Ⓔ	32. Ⓐ Ⓑ Ⓒ Ⓓ Ⓔ	42. Ⓐ Ⓑ Ⓒ Ⓓ Ⓔ
3. Ⓐ Ⓑ Ⓒ Ⓓ Ⓔ	13. Ⓐ Ⓑ Ⓒ Ⓓ Ⓔ	23. Ⓐ Ⓑ Ⓒ Ⓓ Ⓔ	33. Ⓐ Ⓑ Ⓒ Ⓓ Ⓔ	43. Ⓐ Ⓑ Ⓒ Ⓓ Ⓔ
4. Ⓐ Ⓑ Ⓒ Ⓓ Ⓔ	14. Ⓐ Ⓑ Ⓒ Ⓓ Ⓔ	24. Ⓐ Ⓑ Ⓒ Ⓓ Ⓔ	34. Ⓐ Ⓑ Ⓒ Ⓓ Ⓔ	44. Ⓐ Ⓑ Ⓒ Ⓓ Ⓔ
5. Ⓐ Ⓑ Ⓒ Ⓓ Ⓔ	15. Ⓐ Ⓑ Ⓒ Ⓓ Ⓔ	25. Ⓐ Ⓑ Ⓒ Ⓓ Ⓔ	35. Ⓐ Ⓑ Ⓒ Ⓓ Ⓔ	45. Ⓐ Ⓑ Ⓒ Ⓓ Ⓔ
6. Ⓐ Ⓑ Ⓒ Ⓓ Ⓔ	16. Ⓐ Ⓑ Ⓒ Ⓓ Ⓔ	26. Ⓐ Ⓑ Ⓒ Ⓓ Ⓔ	36. Ⓐ Ⓑ Ⓒ Ⓓ Ⓔ	46. Ⓐ Ⓑ Ⓒ Ⓓ Ⓔ
7. Ⓐ Ⓑ Ⓒ Ⓓ Ⓔ	17. Ⓐ Ⓑ Ⓒ Ⓓ Ⓔ	27. Ⓐ Ⓑ Ⓒ Ⓓ Ⓔ	37. Ⓐ Ⓑ Ⓒ Ⓓ Ⓔ	47. Ⓐ Ⓑ Ⓒ Ⓓ Ⓔ
8. Ⓐ Ⓑ Ⓒ Ⓓ Ⓔ	18. Ⓐ Ⓑ Ⓒ Ⓓ Ⓔ	28. Ⓐ Ⓑ Ⓒ Ⓓ Ⓔ	38. Ⓐ Ⓑ Ⓒ Ⓓ Ⓔ	48. Ⓐ Ⓑ Ⓒ Ⓓ Ⓔ
9. Ⓐ Ⓑ Ⓒ Ⓓ Ⓔ	19. Ⓐ Ⓑ Ⓒ Ⓓ Ⓔ	29. Ⓐ Ⓑ Ⓒ Ⓓ Ⓔ	39. Ⓐ Ⓑ Ⓒ Ⓓ Ⓔ	49. Ⓐ Ⓑ Ⓒ Ⓓ Ⓔ
10. Ⓐ Ⓑ Ⓒ Ⓓ Ⓔ	20. Ⓐ Ⓑ Ⓒ Ⓓ Ⓔ	30. Ⓐ Ⓑ Ⓒ Ⓓ Ⓔ	40. Ⓐ Ⓑ Ⓒ Ⓓ Ⓔ	50. Ⓐ Ⓑ Ⓒ Ⓓ Ⓔ

Section 5

1. Ⓐ Ⓑ Ⓒ Ⓓ Ⓔ	11. Ⓐ Ⓑ Ⓒ Ⓓ Ⓔ	21. Ⓐ Ⓑ Ⓒ Ⓓ Ⓔ	31. Ⓐ Ⓑ Ⓒ Ⓓ Ⓔ	41. Ⓐ Ⓑ Ⓒ Ⓓ Ⓔ
2. Ⓐ Ⓑ Ⓒ Ⓓ Ⓔ	12. Ⓐ Ⓑ Ⓒ Ⓓ Ⓔ	22. Ⓐ Ⓑ Ⓒ Ⓓ Ⓔ	32. Ⓐ Ⓑ Ⓒ Ⓓ Ⓔ	42. Ⓐ Ⓑ Ⓒ Ⓓ Ⓔ
3. Ⓐ Ⓑ Ⓒ Ⓓ Ⓔ	13. Ⓐ Ⓑ Ⓒ Ⓓ Ⓔ	23. Ⓐ Ⓑ Ⓒ Ⓓ Ⓔ	33. Ⓐ Ⓑ Ⓒ Ⓓ Ⓔ	43. Ⓐ Ⓑ Ⓒ Ⓓ Ⓔ
4. Ⓐ Ⓑ Ⓒ Ⓓ Ⓔ	14. Ⓐ Ⓑ Ⓒ Ⓓ Ⓔ	24. Ⓐ Ⓑ Ⓒ Ⓓ Ⓔ	34. Ⓐ Ⓑ Ⓒ Ⓓ Ⓔ	44. Ⓐ Ⓑ Ⓒ Ⓓ Ⓔ
5. Ⓐ Ⓑ Ⓒ Ⓓ Ⓔ	15. Ⓐ Ⓑ Ⓒ Ⓓ Ⓔ	25. Ⓐ Ⓑ Ⓒ Ⓓ Ⓔ	35. Ⓐ Ⓑ Ⓒ Ⓓ Ⓔ	45. Ⓐ Ⓑ Ⓒ Ⓓ Ⓔ
6. Ⓐ Ⓑ Ⓒ Ⓓ Ⓔ	16. Ⓐ Ⓑ Ⓒ Ⓓ Ⓔ	26. Ⓐ Ⓑ Ⓒ Ⓓ Ⓔ	36. Ⓐ Ⓑ Ⓒ Ⓓ Ⓔ	46. Ⓐ Ⓑ Ⓒ Ⓓ Ⓔ
7. Ⓐ Ⓑ Ⓒ Ⓓ Ⓔ	17. Ⓐ Ⓑ Ⓒ Ⓓ Ⓔ	27. Ⓐ Ⓑ Ⓒ Ⓓ Ⓔ	37. Ⓐ Ⓑ Ⓒ Ⓓ Ⓔ	47. Ⓐ Ⓑ Ⓒ Ⓓ Ⓔ
8. Ⓐ Ⓑ Ⓒ Ⓓ Ⓔ	18. Ⓐ Ⓑ Ⓒ Ⓓ Ⓔ	28. Ⓐ Ⓑ Ⓒ Ⓓ Ⓔ	38. Ⓐ Ⓑ Ⓒ Ⓓ Ⓔ	48. Ⓐ Ⓑ Ⓒ Ⓓ Ⓔ
9. Ⓐ Ⓑ Ⓒ Ⓓ Ⓔ	19. Ⓐ Ⓑ Ⓒ Ⓓ Ⓔ	29. Ⓐ Ⓑ Ⓒ Ⓓ Ⓔ	39. Ⓐ Ⓑ Ⓒ Ⓓ Ⓔ	49. Ⓐ Ⓑ Ⓒ Ⓓ Ⓔ
10. Ⓐ Ⓑ Ⓒ Ⓓ Ⓔ	20. Ⓐ Ⓑ Ⓒ Ⓓ Ⓔ	30. Ⓐ Ⓑ Ⓒ Ⓓ Ⓔ	40. Ⓐ Ⓑ Ⓒ Ⓓ Ⓔ	50. Ⓐ Ⓑ Ⓒ Ⓓ Ⓔ

Section 6

1. Ⓐ Ⓑ Ⓒ Ⓓ Ⓔ	11. Ⓐ Ⓑ Ⓒ Ⓓ Ⓔ	21. Ⓐ Ⓑ Ⓒ Ⓓ Ⓔ	31. Ⓐ Ⓑ Ⓒ Ⓓ Ⓔ	41. Ⓐ Ⓑ Ⓒ Ⓓ Ⓔ
2. Ⓐ Ⓑ Ⓒ Ⓓ Ⓔ	12. Ⓐ Ⓑ Ⓒ Ⓓ Ⓔ	22. Ⓐ Ⓑ Ⓒ Ⓓ Ⓔ	32. Ⓐ Ⓑ Ⓒ Ⓓ Ⓔ	42. Ⓐ Ⓑ Ⓒ Ⓓ Ⓔ
3. Ⓐ Ⓑ Ⓒ Ⓓ Ⓔ	13. Ⓐ Ⓑ Ⓒ Ⓓ Ⓔ	23. Ⓐ Ⓑ Ⓒ Ⓓ Ⓔ	33. Ⓐ Ⓑ Ⓒ Ⓓ Ⓔ	43. Ⓐ Ⓑ Ⓒ Ⓓ Ⓔ
4. Ⓐ Ⓑ Ⓒ Ⓓ Ⓔ	14. Ⓐ Ⓑ Ⓒ Ⓓ Ⓔ	24. Ⓐ Ⓑ Ⓒ Ⓓ Ⓔ	34. Ⓐ Ⓑ Ⓒ Ⓓ Ⓔ	44. Ⓐ Ⓑ Ⓒ Ⓓ Ⓔ
5. Ⓐ Ⓑ Ⓒ Ⓓ Ⓔ	15. Ⓐ Ⓑ Ⓒ Ⓓ Ⓔ	25. Ⓐ Ⓑ Ⓒ Ⓓ Ⓔ	35. Ⓐ Ⓑ Ⓒ Ⓓ Ⓔ	45. Ⓐ Ⓑ Ⓒ Ⓓ Ⓔ
6. Ⓐ Ⓑ Ⓒ Ⓓ Ⓔ	16. Ⓐ Ⓑ Ⓒ Ⓓ Ⓔ	26. Ⓐ Ⓑ Ⓒ Ⓓ Ⓔ	36. Ⓐ Ⓑ Ⓒ Ⓓ Ⓔ	46. Ⓐ Ⓑ Ⓒ Ⓓ Ⓔ
7. Ⓐ Ⓑ Ⓒ Ⓓ Ⓔ	17. Ⓐ Ⓑ Ⓒ Ⓓ Ⓔ	27. Ⓐ Ⓑ Ⓒ Ⓓ Ⓔ	37. Ⓐ Ⓑ Ⓒ Ⓓ Ⓔ	47. Ⓐ Ⓑ Ⓒ Ⓓ Ⓔ
8. Ⓐ Ⓑ Ⓒ Ⓓ Ⓔ	18. Ⓐ Ⓑ Ⓒ Ⓓ Ⓔ	28. Ⓐ Ⓑ Ⓒ Ⓓ Ⓔ	38. Ⓐ Ⓑ Ⓒ Ⓓ Ⓔ	48. Ⓐ Ⓑ Ⓒ Ⓓ Ⓔ
9. Ⓐ Ⓑ Ⓒ Ⓓ Ⓔ	19. Ⓐ Ⓑ Ⓒ Ⓓ Ⓔ	29. Ⓐ Ⓑ Ⓒ Ⓓ Ⓔ	39. Ⓐ Ⓑ Ⓒ Ⓓ Ⓔ	49. Ⓐ Ⓑ Ⓒ Ⓓ Ⓔ
10. Ⓐ Ⓑ Ⓒ Ⓓ Ⓔ	20. Ⓐ Ⓑ Ⓒ Ⓓ Ⓔ	30. Ⓐ Ⓑ Ⓒ Ⓓ Ⓔ	40. Ⓐ Ⓑ Ⓒ Ⓓ Ⓔ	50. Ⓐ Ⓑ Ⓒ Ⓓ Ⓔ

Remove answer sheet by cutting on dotted line

MODEL SAT TEST 5   1 1 1 1 1 1   1

SECTION 1   Time—30 minutes   For each question in this section, choose the best answer and
40 Questions   blacken the corresponding space on the answer sheet.

Each question below consists of a word in capital letters, followed by five lettered words or phrases. Choose the word or phrase that is most nearly opposite in meaning to the word in capital letters. Since some of the questions require you to distinguish fine shades of meaning, consider all the choices before deciding which is best.

Example:

GOOD: (A) sour   (B) bad   (C) red
(D) hot   (E) ugly   Ⓐ ● Ⓒ Ⓓ Ⓔ

1. RELEASE: (A) evade   (B) grasp
(C) distinguish   (D) exclude   (E) reassert

2. NOVICE: (A) failure   (B) prophet   (C) native
(D) expert   (E) benefactor

3. IMMACULATE: (A) thin   (B) extravagant
(C) indifferent   (D) anxious   (E) stained

4. DAWDLE: (A) alter   (B) lift   (C) loosen
(D) hasten   (E) locate

5. PROFUSION: (A) division   (B) scarcity
(C) sanction   (D) confusion   (E) acceptance

6. SQUEAMISH: (A) not easily disturbed
(B) trivial in effect   (C) disorganized
(D) persuasive   (E) feverish

7. CULPABLE: (A) unable   (B) innocent
(C) contradictory   (D) prolific   (E) scarred

8. ENGENDER: (A) balance
(B) handle ineffectively   (C) alter suddenly
(D) suppress   (E) discriminate

9. EMBELLISH: (A) pacify
(B) conceal deliberately   (C) alter radically
(D) disfigure   (E) exhort

10. OBDURATE: (A) inconclusive   (B) yielding
(C) squalid   (D) inevitable   (E) perceptive

Each sentence below has one or two blanks, each blank indicating that something has been omitted. Beneath the sentence are five lettered words or sets of words. Choose the word or set of words that best fits the meaning of the sentence as a whole.

Example:

Although its publicity has been ----, the film itself is intelligent, well-acted, handsomely produced, and altogether ----.

(A) tasteless..respectable (B) extensive..moderate
(C) sophisticated..amateur (D) risqué..crude
(E) perfect..spectacular   ● Ⓑ Ⓒ Ⓓ Ⓔ

11. He felt that the uninspiring routine of office work was too ---- for someone of his talent and creativity.

(A) diverse   (B) insatiable   (C) exacting
(D) enthralling   (E) prosaic

12. The museum arranged the fossils in ---- order, placing the older fossils dating from the Late Ice Age on the first floor and the more recent fossils on the second floor.

(A) alphabetical (B) chronological (C) random
(D) arbitrary   (E) retrospective

13. ---- merciful by nature, the judge was single-minded and ---- in his strict adherence to the letter of the law.

(A) While..unjust
(B) Although..implacable
(C) However..dilatory
(D) Truly..vindictive
(E) Though..lenient

GO ON TO THE NEXT PAGE

1 1 1 1 1 1 1 1 1 1 1

14. Surrounded by a retinue of sycophants who invariably ---- her singing, Callas wearied of the constant adulation and longed for honest criticism.

(A) orchestrated   (B) thwarted   (C) assailed
(D) extolled   (E) reciprocated

15. There is nothing ---- or provisional about Moore's early critical pronouncements; she deals ---- with what were then radical new developments in poetry.

(A) tentative..confidently
(B) positive..expertly
(C) dogmatic..arbitrarily
(D) shallow..superficially
(E) imprecise..inconclusively

Each question below consists of a related pair of words or phrases, followed by five lettered pairs of words or phrases. Select the lettered pair that best expresses a relationship similar to that expressed in the original pair.

Example:

YAWN : BOREDOM ::   (A) dream : sleep
(B) anger : madness   (C) smile : amusement
   (D) face : expression   (E) impatience : rebellion

Ⓐ Ⓑ ● Ⓓ Ⓔ

---

16. STAGE : ACTOR ::   (A) quarry : sculptor
(B) library : lecturer   (C) baton : conductor
   (D) safe : banker   (E) rink : skater

17. SPRINT : FEET ::   (A) cook : recipe
(B) yodel : eyes   (C) deal : cards
   (D) massage : hands   (E) strum : guitar

18. BEAM : DELIGHT ::   (A) frown : indifference
(B) glower : anger   (C) yawn : assurance
   (D) grin : compassion   (E) snarl : grief

19. CREST : WAVE ::   (A) basin : water
(B) crown : tree   (C) sand : dune
   (D) mountain : range   (E) dregs : wine

20. UNATTRACTIVE : HIDEOUS ::
(A) complex : confused
(B) dormant : sleeping
(C) marred : spoiled
(D) thrifty : parsimonious
(E) profane : sacred

21. ENTREPRENEUR : PROFITS ::
(A) philanthropist : charity
(B) organizer : union
(C) charlatan : converts
(D) hermit : companionship
(E) scholar : knowledge

22. CONGENIAL : ANIMOSITY ::
(A) friendly : opposition
(B) hostile : arrogance
(C) courteous : bias
(D) amicable : affability
(E) modest : vanity

23. MAXIM : PROVERBIAL ::
(A) generalization : specific
(B) question : interrogative
(C) dialogue : poetic
(D) hypothesis : ingenious
(E) symbol : obscure

24. ASCETIC : INTEMPERANCE ::
(A) hypocrite : brevity
(B) fanatic : zeal
(C) bigot : idolatry
(D) altruist : fidelity
(E) miser : extravagance

25. DIATRIBE : INVECTIVE ::
(A) elegy : mirth
(B) encomium : praise
(C) statute : limitation
(D) circumlocution : clarity
(E) parody : performance

GO ON TO THE NEXT PAGE

1   1 1 1 1 1 1 1 1 1 1   1

Each passage below is followed by questions based on its content. Answer all questions following a passage on the basis of what is stated or implied in that passage.

Once upon a time I taught school in the hills of Tennessee, where the broad dark vale of the Mississippi begins to roll and crumple to greet the Alleghanies. I was a Fisk student then, and all Fisk men thought that Tennessee was theirs alone, and in vacation time they sallied forth in lusty bands to meet the county school-commissioners. Young and happy, I too went, and I shall not soon forget that summer, seventeen years ago.

First, there was a Teacher's Institute at the county-seat; and there distinguished guests of the superintendent taught the teachers fractions and spelling and other mysteries—white teachers in the morning, Negroes at night. A picnic now and then, and a supper, and the rough world was softened by laughter and song. I remember how—But I wander.

There came a day when all the teachers left the Institute and began the hunt for schools. I learn from hearsay (for my mother was mortally afraid of firearms) that the hunting of ducks and bears and men is wonderfully interesting, but I am sure that the man who has never hunted a country school has something to learn of the pleasures of the chase. I see now the white, hot roads lazily rise and fall and wind before me under the burning July sun; I feel the deep weariness of heart and limb as ten, eight, six miles stretch relentlessly ahead; I feel my heart sink heavily as I hear again and again, "Got a teacher? Yes." So I walked on and on—horses were too expensive—until I had wandered beyond railways, beyond stage lines, to a land of "varmints" and rattlesnakes, where the coming of a stranger was an event, and men lived and died in the shadow of one blue hill.

26. The passage as a whole is best characterized as

    (A) an example of the harsh realities of searching for employment
    (B) a description of the achievements of a graduate of a prestigious school
    (C) an analysis of teacher education in a rural setting
    (D) an account of one man's recollections of a memorable time in his life
    (E) an illustration of the innocence and gullibility of youth

27. To the author, his journey through the Tennessee countryside seemed to be all of the following EXCEPT

    (A) gratifying   (B) interminable   (C) tiring
    (D) carefree   (E) discouraging

28. The author's attitude toward his school-hunting days is primarily one of

    (A) exasperation   (B) nostalgia   (C) bitterness
    (D) self-reproach   (E) amusement

Vanity was the beginning and end of Sir Walter Elliot's character: vanity of person and of situation. He had been remarkably handsome in his youth, and at fifty-four was still a very fine man. Few women could think more of their personal appearance than he did, nor could the valet of any new-made lord be more delighted with the place he held in society. He considered the blessing of beauty as inferior only to the blessing of a baronetcy; and the Sir Walter Elliot, who united these gifts, was the constant object of his warmest respect and devotion.

His good looks and his rank had one fair claim on his attachment, since to them he must have owed a wife of very superior character to anything deserved by his own. Lady Elliot had been an excellent woman, sensible and amiable, whose judgment and conduct, if they might be pardoned the youthful infatuation which made her Lady Elliot, had never required indulgence afterwards. She had humored, or softened, or concealed his failings, and promoted his real respectability for seventeen years; and though not the very happiest being in the world herself, had found enough in her duties, her friends, and her children, to attach her to life, and make it no matter of indifference to her when she was called on to quit them. Three girls, the two eldest sixteen and fourteen, was an awful legacy for a mother to bequeath, an awful charge rather, to confide to the authority and guidance of a conceited, silly father. She had, however, one very intimate friend, a sensible, deserving woman, who had been brought, by strong attachment to herself, to settle close by her, in the village of Kellynch; and on her kindness and advice Lady Elliot mainly relied for the best help and maintenance of the good principles and instruction which she had been anxiously giving her daughters.

This friend and Sir Walter did *not* marry, whatever might have been anticipated on that head by their acquaintance. Thirteen years had passed away since Lady Elliot's death, and they were still near neighbors and intimate friends, and one remained a widower, the other a widow.

GO ON TO THE NEXT PAGE

1 1 1 1 1 1 1 1 1 1 1

29. According to the passage, Sir Walter Elliot's vanity centered on his

    I. physical attractiveness
    II. possession of a title
    III. superiority of character

    (A) I only   (B) II only   (C) I and II   (D) I and III   (E) I, II, and III

30. The narrator speaks well of Lady Elliot for all of the following EXCEPT

    (A) her concealment of Sir Walter's shortcomings
    (B) her choice of an intimate friend
    (C) her guidance of her three daughters
    (D) her judgment in falling in love with Sir Walter
    (E) her performance of her wifely duties

31. It can be inferred that over the years Lady Elliot was less than happy because of

    (A) her lack of personal beauty
    (B) her separation from her most intimate friend
    (C) the disparity between her character and that of her husband
    (D) the inferiority of her place in society
    (E) her inability to teach good principles to her wayward daughters

32. The passage indicates that Lady Elliot viewed her approaching death with

    (A) pious submissiveness
    (B) maternal distress
    (C) detached indifference
    (D) angry defiance
    (E) humorous indulgence

33. The phrase "make it no matter of indifference to her when she was called upon to quit them" is an example of

    (A) ironic understatement
    (B) effusive sentiment
    (C) metaphorical expression
    (D) personification
    (E) parable

If Shakespeare needs any excuse for the exuberance of his language (the high key in which he pitched most of his dramatic dialogue), *Line* it should be remembered that he was doing on *(5)* the plastic stage of his own day what on the pictorial stage of our own day is not so much required. Shakespeare's dramatic figures stood out on a platform-stage, without background, with the audience on three sides of it. And the *(10)* whole of his atmosphere and environment had to

come from the gestures and language of the actors. When they spoke, they provided their own scenery, which we now provide for them. They had to do a good deal more (when they *(15)* spoke) than actors have to do today in order to give the setting. They carried the scenery on their backs, as it were, and spoke it in words.

34. The title that best expresses the ideas of this passage is:

    (A) The Scenery of the Elizabethan Stage
    (B) The Importance of Actors in the Shakespearean Drama
    (C) The Influence of the Elizabethan Stage on Shakespeare's Style
    (D) Dramatic Dialogue for the Pictorial Stage
    (E) Suitable Gestures for the Elizabethan Stage

35. According to the passage, in comparison with actors of Shakespeare's time, actors of today

    (A) convey the settings in their words
    (B) pitch their voices in a lower key
    (C) depend more on elaborate settings
    (D) have to do more to make the setting clear
    (E) use many more gestures

36. The nature of the stage for which Shakespeare wrote made it necessary for him to

    (A) employ only highly dramatic situations
    (B) depend on scenery owned by the actors themselves
    (C) have the actors shift the scenery
    (D) create atmosphere through the dialogue
    (E) restrict backgrounds to familiar types of scenes

37. The primary purpose of this passage is to

    (A) explain the flamboyance of Shakespeare's style
    (B) apologize for Shakespeare's grave excesses
    (C) describe the flexibility of the modern stage
    (D) make a distinction between Shakespeare and contemporary dramatists
    (E) describe the decline of the Elizabethan stage

GO ON TO THE NEXT PAGE

1   1 1 1 1 1 1 1 1 1   1

The opposite of adaptive divergence is an interesting and fairly common expression of evolution. Whereas related groups of organisms take on widely different characters in becoming adapted to unlike environments in the case of adaptive divergence, we find that unrelated groups of organisms exhibit adaptive convergence when they adopt similar modes of life or become suited for special sorts of environments. For example, invertebrate marine animals living firmly attached to the sea bottom or to some foreign object tend to develop a subcylindrical or conical form. This is illustrated by coral individuals, by many sponges, and even by the diminutive tubes of bryozoans. Adaptive convergence in taking this coral-like form is shown by some brachiopods and pelecypods that grew in fixed position. More readily appreciated is the streamlined fitness of most fishes for moving swiftly through water; they have no neck, the contour of the body is smoothly curved so as to give minimum resistance, and the chief propelling organ is a powerful tail fin. The fact that some fossil reptiles (ichthyosaurs) and modern mammals (whales, dolphins) are wholly fishlike in form is an expression of adaptive convergence, for these air breathing reptiles and mammals, which are highly efficient swimmers, are not closely related to fishes. Unrelated or distantly related organisms that develop similarity of form are sometimes designated as homeomorphs (having same form).

Line
(5)

(10)

(15)

(20)

(25)

(30)

38. The author mentions dolphins and ichthyosaurs (lines 24–25) as examples of

(A) modern mammalian life forms that are aquatic
(B) species of slightly greater mobility than brachiopods
(C) air-breathing reptiles closely related to fish
(D) organisms that have evolved into a fishlike form
(E) invertebrate and vertebrate marine animals

39. According to the author, adaptive convergence and adaptive divergence are

(A) manifestations of evolutionary patterns
(B) hypotheses unsupported by biological phenomena
(C) ways in which plants and animals adjust to a common environment
(D) demonstrated by brachiopods and pelecypods
(E) compensatory adjustments made in response to an unlike environment

40. It can be inferred that in the paragraph immediately preceding this passage the author mentioned

(A) marine intelligence
(B) adaptive divergence
(C) air-breathing reptiles
(D) environmental impacts
(E) organisms with similar forms

IF YOU FINISH BEFORE TIME IS CALLED, YOU MAY CHECK YOUR WORK ON THIS SECTION ONLY. DO NOT WORK ON ANY OTHER SECTION IN THE TEST.   **S T O P**

SECTION **2**   Time—30 minutes   In this section solve each problem, using any available space on
                 25 Questions   the page for scratchwork. Then decide which is the best of the
                                    choices given and blacken the corresponding space on the answer
                                    sheet.

The following information is for your reference in solving some of the problems.

Circle of radius r: Area $= \pi r^2$; Circumference $= 2\pi r$
   The number of degrees of arc in a circle is 360.
The measure in degrees of a straight angle is 180.

Definitions of symbols:
$=$ is equal to	$\leqq$ is less than or equal to
$\neq$ is unequal to	$\geqq$ is greater than or equal to
$<$ is less than	$\parallel$ is parallel to
$>$ is greater than	$\perp$ is perpendicular to

Triangle: The sum of the measures
in degrees of the angles of
a triangle is 180.
If $\angle CDA$ is a right angle, then

(1) area of $\triangle ABC = \dfrac{AB \times CD}{2}$

(2) $AC^2 = AD^2 + DC^2$

Note: Figures that accompany problems in this test are intended to provide information useful in solving the problems.
They are drawn as accurately as possible EXCEPT when it is stated in a specific problem that its figure is not drawn to
scale. All figures lie in a plane unless otherwise indicated. All numbers used are real numbers.

---

1. If 0.3 percent of $x = 2{,}163$, then $x =$

   (A) 721 (B) 7,210 (C) 72,100 (D) 721,000
   (E) 7,210,000

2. How many cents are there in $(x + 2)$ dimes?

   (A) 10 (B) 12 (C) 20 (D) $x + 20$
   (E) $10x + 20$

3. A family travels 30 miles during the first hour of a
   motor trip, and covers 40 miles during the second
   hour. What is the average speed, in miles per
   hour, for the first 2 hours of the trip?

   (A) 30 (B) 35 (C) 40 (D) 60 (E) 70

4. What part of a yard is 6 inches?

   (A) $\dfrac{1}{12}$ (B) $\dfrac{1}{4}$ (C) $\dfrac{1}{3}$ (D) $\dfrac{1}{6}$ (E) $\dfrac{1}{2}$

5. In the figure above, if the measure of $\angle 1 = 145$
   and the measure of $\angle 2 = 125$, then the measure of
   $\angle 3 =$

   (A) 35 (B) 50 (C) 65 (D) 90 (E) 135

6. The perimeter of a square is p inches. What is the
   area of this square in terms of p?

   (A) $\dfrac{p^2}{16}$ (B) $\dfrac{p^2}{4}$ (C) $\dfrac{p^2}{2}$ (D) p^2 (E) $2p^2$

7. $7x - 5y = 13$ and $2x - 7y = 26$; $9x - 12y =$

   (A) 13 (B) 26 (C) 39 (D) 40 (E) 52

8. A motorist leaves at 9:00 A.M. and stops for repairs
   at 9:20 A.M. If the distance covered was 18 miles,
   what was the average velocity, in miles per hour,
   for this part of the trip?

   (A) 5.4 (B) 6 (C) 54 (D) 36 (E) 60

9. Beth has 85 cents in nickels and dimes—12 coins
   in all. How many coins are nickels?

   (A) 5 (B) 6 (C) 7 (D) 8 (E) 9

10. A man 5 feet 8 inches tall casts a shadow of 8 feet.
    What is the height, in feet, of a pole that casts a
    shadow of 96 feet at the same time?

    (A) $4\dfrac{1}{4}$ (B) 13 (C) 39 (D) 68 (E) 132

GO ON TO THE NEXT PAGE

2   2 2 2 2 2 2 2 2 2   2

11. 1 angstrom unit = 0.0001 micron. How many angstrom units are there in 0.01 micron?

(A) 0.001 (B) 0.01 (C) 1 (D) 100
(E) 1,000

12. A fertilizer contains 32 percent nitrate, and 10 percent of the nitrate is pure nitrogen. What percent of the fertilizer is pure nitrogen?

(A) 0.32% (B) 3.2% (C) 22% (D) 32%
(E) 42%

13. Which of the following fractions is closest in value to $\frac{2}{3}$?

(A) $\frac{11}{19}$ (B) $\frac{13}{19}$ (C) $\frac{14}{19}$ (D) $\frac{15}{19}$ (E) $\frac{16}{19}$

14. One cup of cornstarch weighs $\frac{1}{4}$ pound. Four cups of flour weigh one pound. What is the weight, in pounds, of one cup of a mixture of equal parts of flour and cornstarch?

(A) $\frac{1}{4}$ (B) $\frac{1}{2}$ (C) 1 (D) 2 (E) 4

15. A baseball team has won 15 games and lost 9. If these games represent $16\frac{2}{3}$ percent of the games to be played, how many more games must the team win to average 0.750 for the season?

(A) 28 (B) 75 (C) 80 (D) 87 (E) 93

16. In triangle CDE above, $AD = BE$ and $CD < CE$. Which of the following is true?

(A) $CA > CB$ (B) $CA < CB$ (C) $CB > CE$
(D) $CD < CA$ (E) $AB \parallel DE$

17. If p pounds of apples cost D dollars, how many pounds can I get for c cents?

(A) $\frac{pc}{100}$ (B) $100pc$ (C) $100Dpc$ (D) $\frac{100D}{pc}$

(E) $\frac{pc}{100D}$

18. Eight telephone poles are each 15 feet apart. What is the distance, in feet, from the first to the last pole?

(A) 30 (B) 60 (C) 85 (D) 105 (E) 120

19. $2a = \frac{b}{2}\sqrt{2} = \frac{c}{2.5}\sqrt{2}$. In which of the following are a, b, and c arranged in descending order of value?

(A) a, b, c (B) b, c, a (C) a, c, b
(D) c, b, a (E) c, a, b

20. The area of one circle is 144π. The area of another circle is 196π. The ratio of the diameter of the smaller circle to the diameter of the larger circle is

(A) $\frac{2}{3}$ (B) $\frac{3}{7}$ (C) $\frac{4}{7}$ (D) $\frac{3}{14}$ (E) $\frac{6}{7}$

21. A checker is placed on a rectangular table 3 inches from one side of the table and 4 inches from the adjacent side. How far, in inches, is the checker from the nearest corner of the table?

(A) $\sqrt{3}$ (B) $3\frac{1}{2}$ (C) $\sqrt{5}$ (D) $\sqrt{7}$ (E) 5

22. If x is increased by 25 percent, then by what percent is x^2 increased?

(A) $6\frac{1}{4}\%$ (B) 25% (C) 50% (D) $56\frac{1}{4}\%$

(E) $156\frac{1}{4}\%$

23. Which of the following is the equation of the locus of points whose ordinates are equal to -3?

(A) $x = 3$ (B) $x = -3$ (C) $y = 3$
(D) $y = -3$ (E) $y = \pm 3$

GO ON TO THE NEXT PAGE

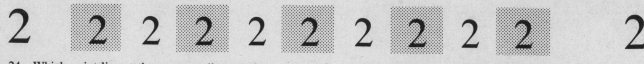

24. Which point lies at the greatest distance from the origin?

(A) $(0, -9)$ (B) $(-2, 9)$ (C) $(-7, -6)$
(D) $(8, 5)$ (E) $(0, 0)$

25. If a man walks W miles in H hours, and then R miles in the same length of time, what is his average rate for the entire trip?

(A) $\dfrac{R + W}{H}$ (B) $\dfrac{2(R + W)}{H}$ (C) $\dfrac{R + W}{2H}$
(D) $\dfrac{H}{R - W}$ (E) $\dfrac{RW - H}{2}$

IF YOU FINISH BEFORE TIME IS CALLED, YOU MAY CHECK YOUR WORK ON THIS SECTION ONLY. DO NOT WORK ON ANY OTHER SECTION IN THE TEST.   **S T O P**

3   3 3 3 3 3 3 3 3 3 3   3

SECTION 3   Time—30 minutes   For each question in this section, choose the best answer and
45 Questions   blacken the corresponding space on the answer sheet.

Each question below consists of a word in capital letters, followed by five lettered words or phrases. Choose the word or phrase that is most nearly opposite in meaning to the word in capital letters. Since some of the questions require you to distinguish fine shades of meaning, consider all the choices before deciding which is best.

Example:

GOOD: (A) sour   (B) bad   (C) red
(D) hot   (E) ugly   Ⓐ ● Ⓒ Ⓓ Ⓔ

1. CURIOUS: (A) impulsive   (B) reliable
(C) silent   (D) ordinary   (E) permanent

2. COMMENCE: (A) graduate   (B) terminate
(C) send away   (D) hold back   (E) exaggerate

3. COMPLY: (A) disobey   (B) hint   (C) supply
(D) endure   (E) disorganize

4. SERENITY: (A) ignorance   (B) formality
(C) commotion   (D) simplicity
(E) incompetence

5. IMPAIR: (A) duplicate   (B) despair
(C) improve   (D) continue   (E) expose

6. LAVISH: (A) sparing   (B) unwashed
(C) vexed   (D) nervous   (E) hostile

7. CANDID: (A) frantic   (B) incapable
(C) urgent   (D) reserved   (E) indecisive

8. PROVOKE: (A) shout   (B) regret   (C) mollify
(D) deny   (E) intensify

9. PROFOUND: (A) lost   (B) greatly admired
(C) unwilling to move   (D) lacking in depth
(E) supercilious

10. TACITURNITY: (A) wordiness (B) tactlessness
(C) irony   (D) escalation   (E) futility

11. ALIENATE: (A) renovate   (B) conciliate
(C) deviate   (D) rectify   (E) eliminate

12. CRYPTIC: (A) ghastly   (B) lawful
(C) perceptive   (D) identical
(E) unconcealed

13. LOATH: (A) despicable   (B) adoring
(C) fragrant   (D) choleric   (E) avid

14. AMENABLE: (A) inactive   (B) discursive
(C) irreparable   (D) contentious
(E) embarrassed

15. RAUCOUS: (A) impartial   (B) bloody
(C) gentle   (D) vacuous   (E) innocuous

Each sentence below has one or two blanks, each blank indicating that something has been omitted. Beneath the sentence are five lettered words or sets of words. Choose the word or set of words that best fits the meaning of the sentence as a whole.

Example:

Although its publicity has been ----, the film itself is intelligent, well-acted, handsomely produced, and altogether ----.

(A) tasteless..respectable (B) extensive..moderate
(C) sophisticated..amateur (D) risqué..crude
(E) perfect..spectacular
● Ⓑ Ⓒ Ⓓ Ⓔ

16. She pointed out that his resume was ---- because it merely recorded his previous positions and failed to highlight the specific skills he had mastered in each job.

(A) disinterested   (B) inadequate
(C) conclusive   (D) obligatory   (E) detailed

17. Because it was already known that retroviruses could cause cancer in animals, it seemed only ---- to search for similar cancer-causing viruses in human beings.

(A) culpable   (B) charitable   (C) hypothetical
(D) logical   (E) negligent

GO ON TO THE NEXT PAGE

18. Her ---- is always a source of irritation: she never uses a single word when she can use a long clause or sentence.

    (A) frivolity (B) verbosity (C) ambivalence
    (D) cogency (E) rhetoric

19. His gloomy assessment that the damage was irreparable convinced the rest of us that he was ----.

    (A) a hypocrite (B) an innovator
    (C) a malefactor (D) an anarchist
    (E) a pessimist

20. It is ---- to try to destroy pests completely with chemical poisons, for as each new chemical pesticide is introduced, the insects gradually become ---- to it.

    (A) useless..drawn
    (B) pointless..vulnerable
    (C) futile..resistant
    (D) wicked..indifferent
    (E) worthwhile..immune

Each passage below is followed by questions based on its content. Answer all questions following a passage on the basis of what is <u>stated</u> or <u>implied</u> in that passage.

Mr. Speaker, ours is an open society. It is a pluralistic society. Its strength lies in its institutions. Those institutions remain viable only as
Line long as the majority of our citizens retain a
(5) meaningful belief in them. As long as Americans feel that their institutions are responsive to the wishes of the people, we shall endure and prevail.

Everyone will admit freely that today there is
(10) a crisis in our institutions and the faith people have in them. No institution is more basic than the Congress—in this case the House of Representatives, in which we have the privilege to serve.

(15) Over the past year or so, the Nation has been awakened to the fact that the House—this House—our institution—has been less than responsive to the requirements of modern times. The Nation has read one article after the other
(20) that finds this institution wanting. One of the most pertinent and irrefutable accusations has to do with the fact that the House operates with too great an emphasis on secrecy, with too great an imbalance of power and too little attention paid
(25) to the wishes of the majority of its Members. In effect, this House of the people has been operating all too often in an undemocratic manner. manner.

We cannot pretend to stand for pluralistic
(30) democracy for the Nation if we daily deny the democratic process in our procedures and deliberations. This is what is going on each day, nonetheless. It is folly to deny the need for reform. We only add fuel to the fires already
(35) being set by reactionaries of every stripe who have a vested interest in the failure of democracy. They anticipate reaction, claiming our lack

of response as reason enough for seeking the overthrow of the society we are all a part of.
(40) Reform on our part in response to a proven need will cut short the fuse of rebellion, cut short those who seek the defeat of democracy.

Such reform can only be accomplished through existing institutions; it can only be
(45) accomplished through reform of them, beginning with the rules and procedures of the House of Representatives. We must let the people and their news media see what is transpiring here in their name, rather than shut them out in the
(50) name of fear and breach of security. This is their House, and they have a right to know what is happening here.

Mr. Speaker, we should have little to hide from the people. The national security argument
(55) has been worked to death. Recently, an article in the Wall Street Journal by Dr. Edward Teller, no raving liberal, attacks secrecy for its own sake. We defeat our own purposes by being overly secretive.

(60) By closing the House of the people to those very same people, we only alienate growing segments of society, stifle the democratic process and undermine the foundations of the institution and the Nation we all love so deeply. If we do
(65) not take the initiative in instituting reform, we merely reaffirm the worst that has been stated about the lack of progressivism in the Congress. We add strength to the arguments of the radical revolutionaries among us. We contribute to the
(70) erosion of this House and its role.

GO ON TO THE NEXT PAGE

3 3 3 3 3 3 3 3 3 3 3

21. Which of the following does the author appear to value LEAST?

(A) Legislative reforms
(B) Press coverage of Congressional sessions
(C) His responsiveness to his constituents
(D) The rhetoric of left wing extremists
(E) The opinion of Dr. Edward Teller

22. The author's primary purpose in this passage is to

(A) encourage Congress to limit the powers of the media
(B) call for an end to undemocratic practices in Congress
(C) answer the radicals who want to overthrow the government
(D) define the powers of Congressional committees
(E) analyze the needs for security of governmental agencies

23. This passage is most likely an excerpt from

(A) an informal essay in a popular magazine
(B) a play about conflict in the Federal government
(C) a speech entered in the Congressional Record
(D) a college history textbook
(E) the personal memoirs of a political leader

24. The author's attitude toward closed Congressional hearings is one of

(A) cautious skepticism
(B) grudging tolerance
(C) outright rejection
(D) wholehearted acceptance
(E) fundamental indifference

25. The tone of the passage as a whole is best described as

(A) satirical   (B) cautionary   (C) alienated
(D) objective   (E) elegiac

When the child was about ten years old, he invited his sister, Mrs. Penniman, to come and stay with him. His sister Lavinia had married a
Line poor clergyman, of a sickly constitution and a
(5) flowery style of eloquence, and then, at the age of thirty-three, had been left a widow—without children, without fortune—with nothing but the memory of Mr. Penniman's flowers of speech, a certain vague aroma of which hovered about her
(10) own conversation. Nevertheless, he had offered her a home under his own roof, which Lavinia accepted with the alacrity of a woman who had spent the ten years of her married life in the town of Poughkeepsie. The Doctor had not proposed
(15) to Mrs. Penniman to come and live with him

indefinitely; he had suggested that she should make an asyluum of his house while she looked about for unfurnished lodgings. It is uncertain whether Mrs. Penniman ever instituted a search
(20) for unfurnished lodgings, but it is beyond dispute that she never found them. She settled herself with her brother and never went away, and, when Catherine was twenty years old, her Aunt Lavinia was still one of the most striking features
(25) of her immediate entourage. Mrs. Penniman's own account of the matter was that she had remained to take charge of her niece's education. She had given this account, at least, to every one but the Doctor, who never asked for explanations
(30) which he could entertain himself any day with inventing. Mrs. Penniman, moreover, though she had a good deal of a certain sort of artificial assurance, shrunk, for indefinable reasons, from presenting herself to her brother as a fountain of
(35) instruction. She had not a high sense of humor, but she had enough to prevent her from making this mistake; and her brother, on his side, had enough to excuse her, in her situation, for laying him under contribution during a considerable part
(40) of a lifetime. He thus, at the end of six months, accepted his sister's permanent presence as an accomplished fact, and as Catherine grew older, perceived that there were in effect good reasons why she should have a companion of her own
(45) imperfect sex. He was extremely polite to Lavinia, scrupulously, formally polite; and she had never seen him in anger but once in her life, when he lost his temper in a theological discussion with her late husband. With her he
(50) never discussed theology, nor, indeed, discussed anything; he contented himself with making known, very distinctly in the form of a lucid ultimatum, his wishes with regard to Catherine.

Once, when the girl was about twelve years
(55) old, he had said to her—
"Try to make a clever woman of her, Lavinia; I should like her to be a clever woman."

Mrs. Penniman, at this, looked thoughtful a moment. "My dear Austin," she then inquired,
(60) "do you think it is better to be clever than to be good?"

"Of course I wish Catherine to be good," the Doctor said next day; "but she won't be any the less virtuous for not being a fool. I am not afraid
(65) of her being wicked; she will never have the salt of malice in her character. She is 'as good as good bread,' as the French say; but six years hence I don't want to have to compare her to good bread-and-butter."

GO ON TO THE NEXT PAGE

3 3 3 3 3 3 3 3 3 3 3 3

(70) "Are you afraid she will be insipid? My dear brother, it is I who supply the butter; so you needn't fear!" said Mrs. Penniman, who had taken in hand the child's "accomplishments," overlooking her at the piano, where Catherine
(75) displayed a certain talent, and going with her to the dancing-class, where it must be confessed that she made but a modest figure.

26. In the passage the doctor is portrayed most specifically as

   (A) humane and benevolent
   (B) casual and easy-going
   (C) sadly ineffectual
   (D) civil but imperious
   (E) habitually irate

27. From the description of how Mrs. Penniman came to live in her brother's home (lines 1–25), we may infer all of the following EXCEPT that

   (A) she readily became dependent on her brother
   (B) she was married at the age of twenty-three
   (C) she was physically delicate and in ill health
   (D) she had not found living in Poughkeepsie particularly gratifying
   (E) she occasionally echoed an ornate manner of speech

28. It can be inferred that the Doctor views children primarily as

   (A) a source of joy and comfort in old age
   (B) innocent sufferers for the sins of their fathers
   (C) clay to be molded into an acceptable image
   (D) the chief objective of the married state
   (E) their parents' sole chance for immortality

29. The remarks about Catherine in the last paragraph reveal her

   (A) limited skill as a dancer
   (B) virtuosity as a pianist
   (C) shyness with her dancing partners
   (D) indifference to cleverness
   (E) reluctance to practice

30. Which of the following best conveys the meaning of the statement "she will never have the salt of malice in her character" (lines 65–66)?

   (A) She will never be wounded by the animosity and ill-will of others.
   (B) She will always lack the liveliness that a touch of mischievousness in her could provide.
   (C) She will never suffer from remorse over her own vindictiveness of spirit.
   (D) She has rejected the evil-minded ways of the world, dedicating herself to a religious calling.
   (E) She will always resent her father for his malicious and domineering ways.

Select the word or set of words that best completes each of the following sentences.

31. This book is the most inane and ---- work I have read all year; I begrudge every dime I spent on it.

   (A) profitable (B) trivial (C) factual
   (D) relevant (E) diverting

32. There will always be tension between the wishes (and often needs) of a democracy's espionage and security services for secrecy, and the principle that a democracy's servants should be ---- to the public for what they do.

   (A) unanswerable (B) accountable
   (C) essential (D) immaterial (E) vulnerable

33. Given the similarity of backgrounds of the townspeople and their impatience with legal technicalities, we were optimistic that the town meeting would quickly arrive at ---- .

   (A) an impasse (B) an evasion
   (C) a consensus (D) a disparity (E) an amendment

34. He sold ---- which he claimed was good for ---- stomach distress, headaches, fever, muscular disorders, and seasickness.

   (A) a remedy..expediting
   (B) a potion..exacerbating
   (C) a panacea..alleviating
   (D) an infirmity..relieving
   (E) a concoction..dissolving

35. As the staggering dimensions of the problem became known, ---- awareness of how much more needed to be learned ---- sympathetic political leaders to increase appropriations for research to unlock the secrets of Alzheimer's Disease.

   (A) diminished..reminded
   (B) heightened..stimulated
   (C) waning..encouraged
   (D) growing..disinclined
   (E) maturing..polarized

GO ON TO THE NEXT PAGE ➡

3   3 3 3 3 3 3 3 3 3 3   3

Each question below consists of a related pair of words or phrases, followed by five lettered pairs of words or phrases. Select the lettered pair that best expresses a relationship similar to that expressed in the original pair.

Example:

YAWN : BOREDOM :: (A) dream : sleep
(B) anger : madness   (C) smile : amusement
(D) face : expression   (E) impatience : rebellion

Ⓐ Ⓑ ● Ⓓ Ⓔ

36. CHIEF : TRIBE :: (A) mascot : troop
(B) voter : senate   (C) partner : marriage
(D) captain : team   (E) musician : band

37. ATLAS : MAPS :: (A) album : photographs
(B) road : signs   (C) automobile : wheels
(D) star : planets   (E) circus : acrobats

38. JACKKNIFE : DIVER :: (A) sword : fencer
(B) fairway : golfer   (C) strike : umpire
(D) cartwheel : gymnast   (E) easel : painter

39. VIRUS : COLD :: (A) serum : measles
(B) infection : gangrene   (C) lungs : pneumonia
(D) bonus : salary   (E) equator : heat

40. INVENTORY : MERCHANDISE ::
(A) repertory : theater
(B) roster : members
(C) gadget : profits
(D) bankruptcy : debts
(E) dormitory : college

41. INTEREST : FASCINATION ::
(A) dislike : abhorrence
(B) delusion : gullibility
(C) exertion : fatigue
(D) science : witchcraft
(E) bonfire : torch

42. RENEGADE : FAITH :: (A) glutton : appetite
(B) zealot : suspicion   (C) visionary : dream
(D) maverick : herd   (E) hermit : cave

43. INDIGENT : WEALTHY ::
(A) irate : sober
(B) taciturn : silent
(C) meticulous : painstaking
(D) frivolous : serious
(E) scholarly : witty

44. WAN : COLOR ::
(A) altruistic : unselfishness
(B) corpulent : weight
(C) insipid : flavor
(D) pallid : texture
(E) enigmatic : puzzle

45. LABYRINTHINE : MAZE ::
(A) circuitous : logic
(B) perfidious : treachery
(C) insolvent : funds
(D) orderly : chaos
(E) fastidious : taste

IF YOU FINISH BEFORE TIME IS CALLED, YOU MAY CHECK YOUR WORK ON THIS SECTION ONLY. DO NOT WORK ON ANY OTHER SECTION IN THE TEST.   **S T O P**

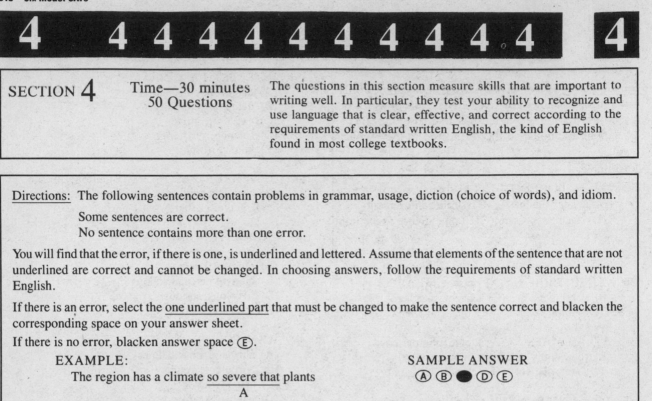

4 4 4 4 4 4 4 4 4 4 4 4 4

SECTION 4   Time—30 minutes   The questions in this section measure skills that are important to
                50 Questions   writing well. In particular, they test your ability to recognize and
                                 use language that is clear, effective, and correct according to the
                                 requirements of standard written English, the kind of English
                                 found in most college textbooks.

Directions: The following sentences contain problems in grammar, usage, diction (choice of words), and idiom.

       Some sentences are correct.
       No sentence contains more than one error.

You will find that the error, if there is one, is underlined and lettered. Assume that elements of the sentence that are not underlined are correct and cannot be changed. In choosing answers, follow the requirements of standard written English.

If there is an error, select the one underlined part that must be changed to make the sentence correct and blacken the corresponding space on your answer sheet.

If there is no error, blacken answer space Ⓔ.

       EXAMPLE: SAMPLE ANSWER
       The region has a climate so severe that plants   Ⓐ Ⓑ ● Ⓓ Ⓔ
                                   A
       growing there rarely had been more than twelve
            B   C
       inches high. No error
            D   E

1. Notice the immediate affect this drug has on the
              A   B   C
   behavior of the rats in the cage. No error
        D   E

2. I believe the commissioner and she to be honest:
                    A
   nevertheless, corruption by public officials and
       B
   their staffs appears to be a continual political
                  C   D
   problem. No error
            E

3. In spite of official denials, news sources recently
      A
   reported that the bombs that hit Tripoli in 1986
            B
   were really intended to kill Muammar al-Qaddafi.
        C   D
   No error
      E

4. Are you going to lie there all day and refuse to see
      A   B   C   D
   your friends? No error
                 E

5. Neither the teacher nor her pupils were enthused
   A   B   C
   about going on the field trip. No error
       D   E

6. While Egyptian President Anwar El-Sadat was
   A
   reviewing a military parade in 1981, a band of
                                         B
   commandos had shot him and others
             C
   in the vicinity. No error
       D   E

7. Please do not be aggravated by his bad manners
                    A   B
   since he is merely trying to attract attention.
   C   D
   No error
   E

GO ON TO THE NEXT PAGE

4   4 4 4 4 4 4 4 4 4 4   4

8. Neither the opera singers <u>or</u> the general public
                              A
   <u>had seen</u> <u>as much glitter</u> in years as they did
        B   C
   during *Turandot,* the <u>finale of</u> the opera season.
                               D
   <u>No error</u>
        E

9. His story about the <u>strange beings</u> in a space ship
                              A
   was <u>so</u> <u>incredulous</u> <u>that</u> no one believed him.
        B   C   D
   <u>No error</u>
        E

10. The hot air ballon had burst as they <u>were preparing</u>
                                               A
    <u>for launch</u>, and the platform <u>had broke</u> <u>as a result</u>.
         B   C   D
    <u>No error</u>
         E

11. I fail <u>to understand</u> <u>why</u> you are seeking my
                A   B
    <u>council</u> after the way you <u>ignored</u> my advice last
         C   D
    week. <u>No error</u>
               E

12. Ann Landers, <u>whose</u> name is a household word
                     A
    <u>to millions of</u> readers, <u>are</u> <u>well-known</u> for family
         B   C   D
    advice. <u>No error</u>
                 E

13. Between <u>you and I</u>, the highway department must
                 A
    review bridge construction <u>across the country</u>
                                     B
    <u>in order to</u> avoid major catastrophes <u>resulting from</u>
         C   D
    metal fatigue. <u>No error</u>
                        E

14. Child custody in surrogate mother cases is just

    <u>one of the many</u> controversial issues <u>which</u> <u>are</u>
         A   B   C
    currently being <u>decided upon</u> in the courts.
                         D
    <u>No error</u>
         E

15. John usually eats a quick lunch, <u>ignoring</u> the
                                          A
    question of <u>whether</u> <u>what</u> he eats is <u>healthy or</u> not.
                     B   C   D
    <u>No error</u>
         E

16. <u>If</u> you continue to drive <u>so recklessly</u>, you
     A   B
    <u>are likely</u> to have a serious accident in the <u>very</u>
         C   D
    near future. <u>No error</u>
                      E

17. The general <u>along with</u> the members of his
                     A
    general staff <u>seem</u> to favor <u>immediate retaliation</u> at
         B   C   D
    this time. <u>No error</u>
                    E

18. We resented <u>him</u> <u>criticizing</u> our efforts because he
                     A   B
    <u>had ignored</u> our requests for assistance
         C
    <u>up to that time</u>. <u>No error</u>
         D   E

19. Casey Jones, <u>who</u> was killed in the <u>line of</u> duty,
                     A   B
    <u>became</u> a hero to fellow railroad workers and
         C
    <u>was to be immortalized</u> by a ballad. <u>No error</u>
         D   E

20. <u>Whether</u> self-government is <u>to be retained</u> by the
     A   B
    county, voters <u>must go</u> to the polls to defeat the
                        C
    <u>new, deceptive</u> proposition. <u>No error</u>
         D   E

21. In the controversy <u>against</u> TV evangelism, no one
                            A
    seems <u>to have noticed</u> that the <u>most</u> influential
              B   C
    preacher in America is not Jerry Falwell or John

    Cardinal O'Connor <u>but</u> Bill Cosby. <u>No error</u>
                           D   E

GO ON TO THE NEXT PAGE ▷

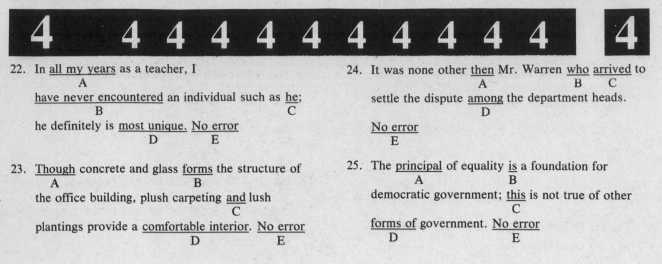

22. In all my years as a teacher, I
        A
    have never encountered an individual such as he;
            B   C
    he definitely is most unique. No error
                    D   E

23. Though concrete and glass forms the structure of
        A   B
    the office building, plush carpeting and lush
                                          C
    plantings provide a comfortable interior. No error
                        D   E

24. It was none other then Mr. Warren who arrived to
                        A   B   C
    settle the dispute among the department heads.
                        D
    No error
    E

25. The principal of equality is a foundation for
            A   B
    democratic government; this is not true of other
                          C
    forms of government. No error
    D   E

Directions: In each of the following sentences, some part or all of the sentence is underlined. Below each sentence you will find five ways of phrasing the underlined part. Select the answer that produces the most effective sentence, one that is clear and exact, without awkwardness or ambiguity, and blacken the corresponding space on your answer sheet. In choosing answers, follow the requirements of standard written English. Choose the answer that best expresses the meaning of the original sentence.

Answer (A) is always the same as the underlined part. Choose answer (A) if you think the original sentence needs no revision.

EXAMPLE:

Laura Ingalls Wilder published her first book
and she was sixty-five years old then.

(A) and she was sixty-five years old then
(B) when she was sixty-five years old
(C) at age sixty-five years old
(D) upon reaching sixty-five years
(E) at the time when she was sixty-five

SAMPLE ANSWER

Ⓐ ● Ⓒ Ⓓ Ⓔ

26. The police officer refused to permit us to enter the
    apartment, saying that he had orders to stop him
    going into the building.

    (A) stop him going
    (B) prevent him going
    (C) stop his going
    (D) stop us going
    (E) stop our going

27. After conducting the orchestra for six concerts,
    Beethoven's *Ninth Symphony* was scheduled.

    (A) After conducting
    (B) After he conducted
    (C) Because he had conducted
    (D) Although he conducted
    (E) After he had conducted

28. Jackie Robinson became the first black player in
    major league baseball, he paved the way for black
    athletes to be accepted on the field.

    (A) Jackie Robinson became the first black player
        in major league baseball, he
    (B) Jackie Robinson, in becoming the first black
        player in major league baseball, he
    (C) Jackie Robinson became the first black player
        in major league baseball; he
    (D) Jackie Robinson, the first black player in
        major league baseball; he
    (E) Jackie Robinson had become the first black
        player in major league baseball; and he

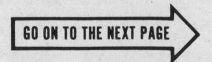

GO ON TO THE NEXT PAGE

4 4 4 4 4 4 4 4 4 4 4 4

29. Sitting in the Coliseum, <u>the music couldn't hardly be heard because of</u> the cheering and yelling of the spectators.

   (A) the music couldn't hardly be heard because of
   (B) the music couldn't hardly be heard due to
   (C) the music could hardly be heard due to
   (D) we could hardly hear the music due to
   (E) we could hardly hear the music because of

30. <u>If I would have known about</u> the traffic jam at the bridge, I would have taken an alternate route.

   (A) If I would have known about
   (B) If I could of known about
   (C) If I would of known about
   (D) If I was aware of
   (E) Had I known about

31. Across the nation, <u>curricular changes sweeping the universities as schools</u> reassess the knowledge that educated people should know.

   (A) curricular changes sweeping the universities as schools
   (B) curricular changes are sweeping the universities as schools
   (C) changes are sweeping the curricular since schools
   (D) curricular changes sweeping the universities causing schools to
   (E) curricular changes sweep the universities, but schools

32. If you have enjoyed <u>these kind of programs,</u> write to your local public television station and ask for more.

   (A) these kind of programs
   (B) those kind of programs
   (C) these kinds of programs
   (D) these kind of a program
   (E) this kind of a program

33. In her critique of the newly opened restaurant, the reviewer discussed the elaborate menu, the impressive wine <u>list, and how the waiters functioned</u>.

   (A) list, and how the waiters functioned
   (B) list and how the waiters functioned
   (C) list, and the excellent service
   (D) list and even the excellent service
   (E) list, and how the waiters usually function

34. Contemporary poets are not abandoning rhyme, <u>but some avoiding it</u>.

   (A) but some avoiding it
   (B) but it is avoided by some of them
   (C) but it is being avoided
   (D) but some are avoiding it
   (E) but it has been being avoided by some

35. <u>Your complaint is no different from the last customer</u> who expected a refund.

   (A) Your complaint is no different from the last customer
   (B) Your complaint is no different from that of the last customer
   (C) Your complaint is similar to the last customer
   (D) Your complaint is no different then that of the last customer
   (E) Your complaint is the same as the last customer

36. According to the review board, <u>many laboratory tests were ordered by the staff of the hospital that</u> had no medical justification.

   (A) many laboratory tests were ordered by the staff of the hospital that
   (B) many laboratory tests were ordered by the staff of the hospital who
   (C) the staff of the hospital ordered many laboratory tests that
   (D) the staff of the hosppital, who ordered many laboratory tests that
   (E) the ordering of many laboratory tests by the staff of the hospital which

37. <u>Confident about the outcome, President Reagan along with his staff are traveling</u> to the conference.

   (A) Confident about the outcome, President Reagan along with his staff are traveling
   (B) Confident about the outcome, President Reagan's party are traveling
   (C) Confident about the outcome, President Reagan along with his staff is traveling
   (D) With confidence about the outcome, President Reagan along with his staff are traveling
   (E) President Reagan along with his staff is traveling confidently about the outcome

38. <u>Helen Keller was blind and deaf from infancy and she</u> learned to communicate using both sign language and speech.

   (A) Helen Keller was blind and deaf from infancy and she
   (B) Although blind and deaf from infancy, Helen Keller
   (C) Although being blind and deaf from the time she was an infant, Helen Keller
   (D) Being blind and deaf from infancy, Helen Keller
   (E) Helen Keller, being blind and deaf from infancy, she

GO ON TO THE NEXT PAGE

4 4 4 4 4 4 4 4 4 4 4 4

39. Standing alone beside her husband's grave, <u>grief overwhelmed the widow and she wept inconsolably</u>.

    (A) grief overwhelmed the widow and she wept inconsolably

    (B) grief overwhelmed the widow, who wept inconsolably

    (C) grief overwhelmed the widow that wept inconsolably

    (D) the widow was overwhelmed by grief and wept inconsolably

    (E) the widow was overwhelmed by grief, she wept inconsolably

40. The difference between Liebniz and Schopenhauer is that <u>the former is optimistic; the latter, pessimistic</u>.

    (A) the former is optimistic; the latter, pessimistic

    (B) the former is optimistic, the latter, pessimistic

    (C) while the former is optimistic; the latter, pessimistic

    (D) the former one is optimistic; the latter one is a pessimist

    (E) the former is optimistic; the latter being pessimistic

---

<u>Note</u>: The remaining questions are like those at the beginning of the section.

<u>Directions</u>: For each sentence in which you find an error, select the one underlined part that must be changed to make the sentence correct and blacken the corresponding space on your answer sheet.

If there is no error, blacken answer space Ⓔ.

    EXAMPLE:

        The region has a climate <u>so severe that</u> plants
                            A

        <u>growing there</u> rarely <u>had been</u> more than twelve
           B   C

        inches <u>high</u>. <u>No error</u>
            D   E

SAMPLE ANSWER

Ⓐ Ⓑ ● Ⓓ Ⓔ

---

41. Joe DiMaggio, <u>whose</u> style was one of
             A
<u>quiet excellence</u>. was consistently the New York
    B
Yankee's <u>outstanding player</u> <u>during</u> his thirteen
              C   D
years on the team. <u>No error</u>
                E

42. If Ms. Rivera <u>was</u> <u>truly</u> happy, she would not
            A   B
<u>constantly</u> complain <u>that</u> she has no purpose in
    C   D
life. <u>No error</u>
      E

43. I <u>was</u> <u>kept awake</u> by the baby's <u>continuous crying</u>
  A   B   C
<u>during</u> the night. <u>No error</u>
  D   E

44. The office memoranda <u>was</u> circulated, but <u>nobody</u>
              A   B
responded; <u>hence</u>, <u>few supplies</u> were ordered.
          C   D
<u>No error</u>
  E

45. Juan and <u>myself</u> were <u>among</u> a <u>number of</u> players
         A   B   C
<u>to be awarded</u> badges for excellence in team
    D
sports. <u>No error</u>
       E

46. <u>Both</u> of the teams must <u>try and come</u> <u>in order to</u>
  A   B   C
<u>infuse</u> the school with team spirit. <u>No error</u>
  D   E

GO ON TO THE NEXT PAGE

4   4 4 4 4 4 4 4 4 4 4   4

47. <u>Unless</u> one visits a historic site <u>like</u> Williamsburg,
      A   B
the lives <u>of them</u> who founded this country cannot
              C
<u>fully be understood.</u> <u>No error</u>
        D   E

48. Fernando expected <u>to have gone</u> to college in the
                              A
fall, <u>but</u> his score on the scholarship exam was not
        B
high enough <u>to merit</u> the financial help <u>he needed</u>.
                    C   D
<u>No error</u>
    E

49. <u>Although</u> you may wish to take various vitamins
      A
<u>to ensure</u> proper nutrition, <u>one</u> should <u>really</u>
        B   C   D
consult a doctor beforehand. <u>No error</u>
                                  E

50. <u>Having read</u> for <u>more than</u> four hours without a
      A   B
rest, the book <u>fell</u> <u>from</u> his hands. <u>No error</u>
                  C   D   E

IF YOU FINISH BEFORE TIME IS CALLED, YOU MAY CHECK YOUR WORK ON
THIS SECTION ONLY. DO NOT WORK ON ANY OTHER SECTION IN THE TEST.   **S T O P**

5

1. What number divided by 50 gives 3.6 percent?

   (A) 1.8   (B) 3.6   (C) 7.2   (D) 18   (E) 36

2. An article sells for $65.00. This price gives the retailer a profit of 30 percent on her costs. What will be the new retail price if she cuts her profit to 10 percent of costs?

   (A) $42   (B) $45.50   (C) $50   (D) $50.05
   (E) $55

3. A picture is 36 inches long and 16 inches wide. If its frame is one inch wide, what is the area, in square inches, of the frame?

   (A) 100   (B) 108   (C) 476   (D) 576   (E) 684

4. A graduating class of 356 votes to choose a president. With five candidates seeking office, what is the least number of votes a successful candidate could receive and yet have more votes than any other candidate?

   (A) 71   (B) 72   (C) 89   (D) 178   (E) 179

5. In the figure above, the measure of $\angle A =$

   (A) 15   (B) 45   (C) 60   (D) 80   (E) 120

6. A home owner uses $\frac{1}{2}$ of his available oil to heat his home during one week of extremely cold weather. If the tank was $\frac{3}{4}$ full at the beginning of the week, what part of the full capacity did he use this week?

   (A) $\frac{3}{16}$ (B) $\frac{1}{4}$ (C) $\frac{3}{8}$ (D) $\frac{5}{8}$ (E) $\frac{2}{3}$

7. Mr. Rosenfeld works 5 days a week and binds 35 sets of books each week. If there are 7 books in a set, how many books does he bind each day?

   (A) 1   (B) 7   (C) 25   (D) 35   (E) 49

GO ON TO THE NEXT PAGE

5

Questions 8–27 each consist of two quantities, one in Column A and one in Column B. You are to compare the two quantities and on the answer sheet blacken space

A   if the quantity in Column A is greater;
B   if the quantity in Column B is greater;
C   if the two quantities are equal;
D   If the relationship cannot be determined from the information given.

AN E RESPONSE WILL NOT BE SCORED.

EXAMPLES		
Column A	Column B	Answers
E1. 2×6	$2 + 6$	●ⒷⒸⒹⒺ
E2. $180 - x$	y	ⒶⒷ●ⒹⒺ
E3. $p - q$	$q - p$	ⒶⒷⒸ●Ⓔ

Notes:

1.   In certain questions, information concerning one or both of the quantities to be compared is centered above the two columns.
2.   In a given question, a symbol that appears in both columns represents the same thing in Column A as it does in Column B.
3.   Letters such as x, n, and k stand for real numbers.

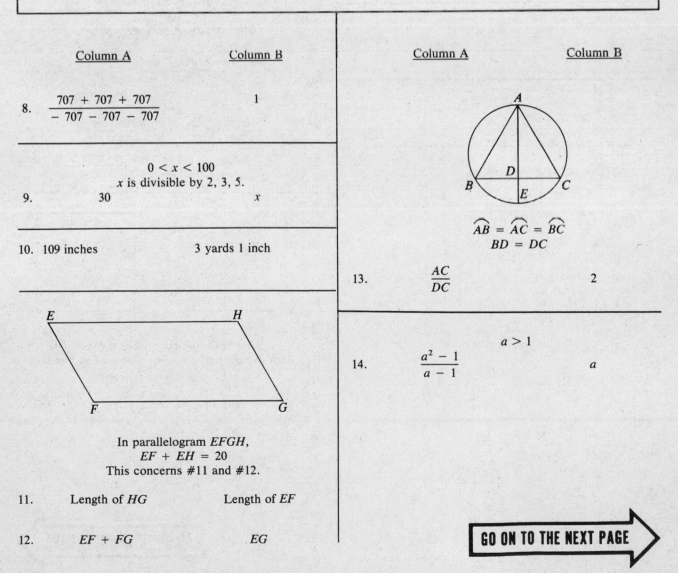

Column A   Column B

8. $\dfrac{707 + 707 + 707}{-707 - 707 - 707}$ 1

$0 < x < 100$
x is divisible by 2, 3, 5.

9.   30 x

10.   109 inches   3 yards 1 inch

In parallelogram $EFGH$,
$EF + EH = 20$
This concerns #11 and #12.

11.   Length of HG Length of EF

12. $EF + FG$ EG

Column A   Column B

$\overset{\frown}{AB} = \overset{\frown}{AC} = \overset{\frown}{BC}$
$BD = DC$

13. $\dfrac{AC}{DC}$ 2

$a > 1$

14. $\dfrac{a^2 - 1}{a - 1}$ a

GO ON TO THE NEXT PAGE

5

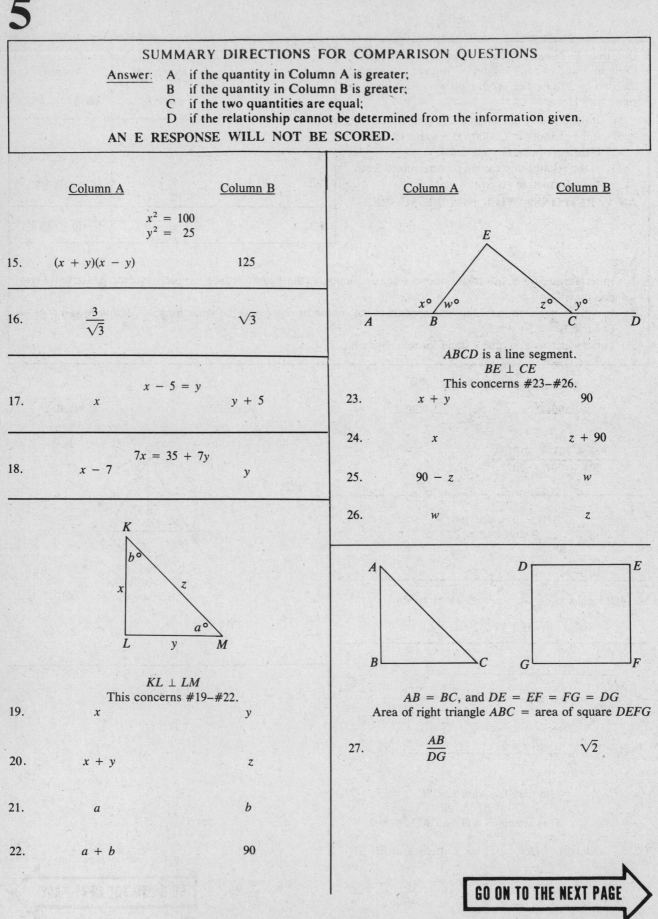

	Column A	Column B
	$x^2 = 100$ $y^2 = 25$	
15.	$(x + y)(x - y)$	125
16.	$\dfrac{3}{\sqrt{3}}$	$\sqrt{3}$
	$x - 5 = y$	
17.	x	$y + 5$
	$7x = 35 + 7y$	
18.	$x - 7$	y

$KL \perp LM$
This concerns #19–#22.

	Column A	Column B
19.	x	y
20.	$x + y$	z
21.	a	b
22.	$a + b$	90

$ABCD$ is a line segment.
$BE \perp CE$
This concerns #23–#26.

	Column A	Column B
23.	$x + y$	90
24.	x	$z + 90$
25.	$90 - z$	w
26.	w	z

$AB = BC$, and $DE = EF = FG = DG$
Area of right triangle ABC = area of square $DEFG$

	Column A	Column B
27.	$\dfrac{AB}{DG}$	$\sqrt{2}$

GO ON TO THE NEXT PAGE

5

Solve each of the remaining problems in this section using any available space for scratchwork. Then decide which is the best of the choices given and blacken the corresponding space on the answer sheet.

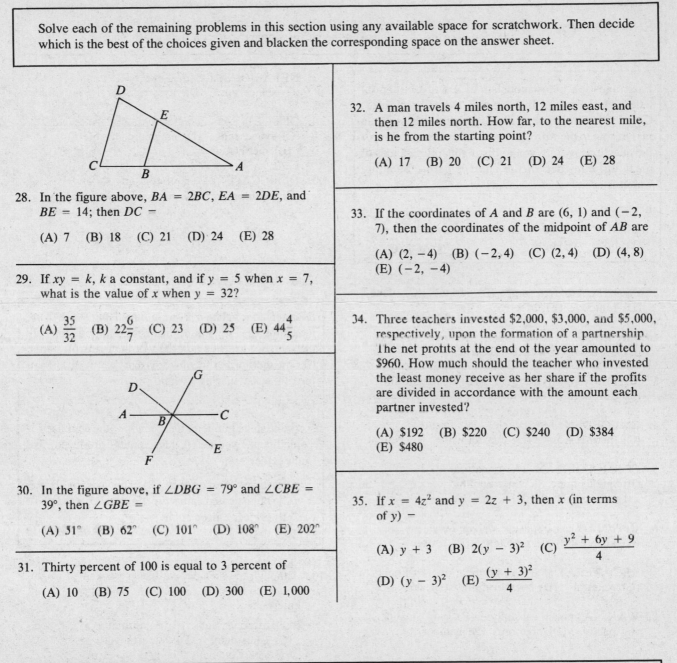

28. In the figure above, $BA = 2BC$, $EA = 2DE$, and $BE = 14$; then $DC =$

    (A) 7   (B) 18   (C) 21   (D) 24   (E) 28

29. If $xy = k$, k a constant, and if $y = 5$ when $x = 7$, what is the value of x when $y = 32$?

    (A) $\dfrac{35}{32}$ (B) $22\dfrac{6}{7}$ (C) 23   (D) 25   (E) $44\dfrac{4}{5}$

30. In the figure above, if $\angle DBG = 79°$ and $\angle CBE = 39°$, then $\angle GBE =$

    (A) 51°   (B) 62°   (C) 101°   (D) 108°   (E) 202°

31. Thirty percent of 100 is equal to 3 percent of

    (A) 10   (B) 75   (C) 100   (D) 300   (E) 1,000

32. A man travels 4 miles north, 12 miles east, and then 12 miles north. How far, to the nearest mile, is he from the starting point?

    (A) 17   (B) 20   (C) 21   (D) 24   (E) 28

33. If the coordinates of A and B are (6, 1) and $(-2, 7)$, then the coordinates of the midpoint of AB are

    (A) $(2, -4)$ (B) $(-2, 4)$ (C) $(2, 4)$ (D) $(4, 8)$
    (E) $(-2, -4)$

34. Three teachers invested $2,000, $3,000, and $5,000, respectively, upon the formation of a partnership. The net profits at the end of the year amounted to $960. How much should the teacher who invested the least money receive as her share if the profits are divided in accordance with the amount each partner invested?

    (A) $192   (B) $220   (C) $240   (D) $384
    (E) $480

35. If $x = 4z^2$ and $y = 2z + 3$, then x (in terms of y) =

    (A) $y + 3$ (B) $2(y - 3)^2$ (C) $\dfrac{y^2 + 6y + 9}{4}$

    (D) $(y - 3)^2$ (E) $\dfrac{(y + 3)^2}{4}$

IF YOU FINISH BEFORE TIME IS CALLED, YOU MAY CHECK YOUR WORK ON THIS SECTION ONLY. DO NOT WORK ON ANY OTHER SECTION IN THE TEST.   **S T O P**

6 6 6 6 6 6 6 6 6 6 6

SECTION **6**   Time—30 minutes   For each question in this section, choose the best answer and
45 Questions   blacken the corresponding space on the answer sheet.

Each question below consists of a word in capital
letters, followed by five lettered words or phrases.
Choose the word or phrase that is most nearly <u>opposite</u>
in meaning to the word in capital letters. Since some of
the questions require you to distinguish fine shades of
meaning, consider all the choices before deciding
which is best.

Example:

GOOD: (A) sour   (B) bad   (C) red
(D) hot   (E) ugly   Ⓐ ● Ⓒ Ⓓ Ⓔ

1. PUNCTUAL: (A) tardy (B) serious (C) blunt
   (D) remote (E) effective

2. ENCLOSE: (A) give away   (B) take out
   (C) prevent (D) exert (E) begin

3. MATERNAL: (A) eternal (B) uncomfortable
   (C) unrelated (D) unmotherly (E) disobedient

4. EMBOLDEN: (A) dawdle (B) frighten
   (C) distract from (D) quarrel with (E) retreat

5. COSMOPOLITAN: (A) unnatural
   (B) intellectual (C) metropolitan
    (D) provincial (E) inexpensive

6. UPHOLD: (A) oppose (B) tie down
   (C) keep calm (D) hasten (E) restore

7. ADULTERATION: (A) purification (B) fidelity
   (C) renewal (D) complication (E) gloss

8. WAX: (A) polish carefully (B) grow smaller
   (C) pacify (D) urge on (E) hamper

9. RANT: (A) watch closely (B) speak calmly
   (C) design carefully (D) support strongly
    (E) think swiftly

10. PARE: (A) augment (B) jeopardize
    (C) distract (D) chasten (E) devour

11. PALATABLE: (A) partial (B) habitable
    (C) scarce (D) distasteful (E) harmless

12. CUPIDITY: (A) lechery (B) altruism
    (C) malice (D) despondency (E) simplicity

13. NEFARIOUS: (A) negative (B) unique
    (C) slanderous (D) mysterious (E) honorable

14. DULCET: (A) cacophonous (B) iridescent
    (C) evanescent (D) incomprehensible
     (E) ineffectual

15. DESICCATE: (A) saturate (B) satiate
    (C) castigate (D) destroy (E) immunize ·

Each sentence below has one or two blanks, each blank
indicating that something has been omitted. Beneath
the sentence are five lettered words or sets of words.
Choose the word or set of words that <u>best</u> fits the meaning of the sentence as a whole.

Example:

Although its publicity has been ----, the film itself is
intelligent, well-acted, handsomely produced, and
altogether ----.

(A) tasteless..respectable (B) extensive..moderate
 (C) sophisticated..amateur (D) risqué..crude
  (E) perfect..spectacular
                                    ● Ⓑ Ⓒ Ⓓ Ⓔ

16. Although the members of Congress wanted to go
    home, no hope for an early ---- could be
    entertained.

    (A) postponement (B) compromise
     (C) adjustment (D) adjournment
      (E) bereavement

17. I can think of nothing more ---- than arriving at the
    theater and discovering that I had left the tickets at
    home.

    (A) vicious (B) erroneous (C) vexatious
     (D) banal (E) capricious

GO ON TO THE NEXT PAGE

6   6 6 6 6 6 6 6 6 6   6

18. Fearful of public exposure, he tried to ---- the issue by bringing up ---- factors.

(A) clarify..ambiguous
(B) becloud..irrelevant
(C) hasten..additional
(D) aggravate..incriminating
(E) resolve..enigmatic

19. Her critics maintained that you could tell she was an actress by her ---- manner of speech.

(A) affectionate   (B) romantic   (C) affected
(D) digressive   (E) cultivated

20. The author makes no attempt to gloss over the disagreeable sides of Strindberg's personality, such as his hysterical jealousies and suspicions, which did much to ---- his marriages and ---- many of his friends.

(A) destroy..alienate
(B) distort..appease
(C) enliven..misconstrue
(D) further..mollify
(E) wreck..diversify

Each passage below is followed by questions based on its content. Answer all questions following a passage on the basis of what is stated or <u>implied</u> in that passage.

One crying evil of his time that Dickens says very little about is child labor. There are plenty of pictures of suffering children in his books, but
Line usually they are suffering in schools rather than
(5) in factories. The one detailed account of child labor that he gives is the description in *David Copperfield* of little David washing bottles in Murdstone & Grinby's warehouse. This, of course, is autobiography. Dickens himself, at the
(10) age of ten, had worked in Warren's blacking factory in the Strand, very much as he describes it here. It was a terribly bitter memory to him, partly because he felt the whole incident to be discreditable to his parents, and he even
(15) concealed it from his wife till long after they were married. Looking back on this period, he says in *David Copperfield*:

It is a matter of some surprise to me, even now, that I can have been so easily thrown
(20) away at such an age. A child of excellent abilities and with strong powers of observation, quick, eager, delicate, and soon hurt bodily and mentally, it seems wonderful to me that nobody should have made any sign in my
(25) behalf. But none was made; and I became, at ten years old, a little laboring hind in the service of Murdstone & Grinby.

And again, having described the rough boys among whom he worked:

(30) No words can express the secret agony of my soul as I sunk into this companionship . . . and felt my hopes of growing up to be a learned and distinguished man crushed in my bosom.

(35) Obviously it is not David Copperfield who is speaking, it is Dickens himself. He uses almost the same words in the autobiography that he began and abandoned a few months earlier. Of course Dickens is right in saying that a gifted
(40) child ought not to work ten hours a day pasting labels on bottles, but what he does not say is that *no* child ought to be condemned to such a fate, and there is no reason for inferring that he thinks it. David escapes from the warehouse, but Mick
(45) Walker and Mealy Potatoes and the others are still there, and there is no sign that this troubles Dickens particularly. As usual, he displays no consciousness that the *structure* of society can be changed. He despises politics, does not believe
(50) that any good can come out of Parliament—he had been a Parliamentary shorthand writer, which was no doubt a disillusioning experience—and he is slightly hostile to the most hopeful movement of his day, trade unionism. In *Hard Times* trade
(55) unionism is represented as something not much better than a racket, something that happens because employers are not sufficiently paternal. Stephen Blackpool's refusal to join the union is rather a virtue in Dickens' eyes. Also, as Mr.
(60) Jackson has pointed out, the apprentices' association in *Barnaby Rudge*, to which Sam Tappertit belongs, is probably a hit at the illegal or barely legal unions of Dickens' own day, with their secret assemblies, passwords and so forth.
(65) Obviously he wants the workers to be decently treated, but there is no sign that he wants them to take their destiny into their own hands, least of all by open violence.

GO ON TO THE NEXT PAGE

6   6   6   6   6   6   6   6   6   6   6

21. The primary purpose of the passage is to
    (A) evoke sympathy for Dickens' childhood
        sufferings
    (B) defend the growth of trade unionism in
        Victorian England
    (C) explain differences between Dickens' early
        and later novels
    (D) describe working conditions during Dickens'
        lifetime
    (E) discuss gaps and weaknesses in Dickens'
        social criticism

22. The author mentions the fate of Mealy Potatoes
    (lines 44–47) as an example of
    (A) the evils of trade unionism
    (B) Dickens' excellence in portraying children
    (C) the abuse suffered by gifted children
    (D) Dickens' apparent acceptance of child labor
    (E) Dickens' sympathy for the oppressed

23. According to the passage, Dickens' attitude toward
    his childhood experience in the blacking factory
    was primarily one of
    (A) resentment   (B) nostalgia   (C) annoyance
     (D) skepticism   (E) enthusiasm

24. It can be inferred from lines 49–57 that Dickens
    believed factory labor problems could best be
    handled by
    (A) nonviolent protest marches
    (B) benevolent factory owners
    (C) worker collectives
    (D) decent labor unions
    (E) parliamentary intervention

25. The author's comments on Dickens' Parliamentary
    career chiefly suggest which of the following
    sayings?
    (A) Politics makes strange bedfellows.
    (B) Familiarity breeds contempt.
    (C) All's well that ends well.
    (D) When in Rome, do as the Romans do.
    (E) Nothing succeeds like success.

    The distinction often made between learning
and instinct is exemplified by two theoretical
approaches to the study of behavior: ethology
Line and behaviorist psychology. Ethology is usually
(5) thought of as the study of instinct. In the
ethological world view most animal behavior is
governed by four basic factors: sign stimuli
(instinctively recognized cues), motor programs
(innate responses to cues), drive (controlling
(10) motivational impulses) and imprinting (a
restricted and seemingly aberrant form of
learning).

    Three of these factors are found in the egg-
rolling response of geese, a behavior studied by
(15) Konrad Z. Lorenz and Nikolaas Tinbergen, who
together with Karl Frisch were the founders of
ethology. Geese incubate their eggs in mound-
shaped nests built on the ground, and it
sometimes happens that the incubating goose
(20) inadvertently knocks an egg out of the nest. Such
an event leads to a remarkable behavior. After
settling down again on its nest, the goose
eventually notices the errant egg. The animal
then extends its neck to fix its eyes on the egg,
(25) rises and rolls the egg back into the nest gently
with its bill. At first glance this might seem to be
a thoughtful solution to a problem. As it happens,
however, the behavior is highly stereotyped and
innate. Any convex object, regardless of color
(30) and almost regardless of size, triggers the
response; beer bottles are particularly effective.

    In this example the convex features that trig-
ger the behavior are the ethologists' sign stimuli.
The egg-rolling response itself is the motor pro-
(35) gram. The entire behavior is controlled by a drive
that appears about two weeks before the geese
lay eggs and persists until about two weeks after
the eggs hatch. Geese also exhibit imprinting:
during a sensitive period soon after hatching,
(40) goslings will follow almost any receding object
that emits an innately recognized "kum-kum"
call and thereafter treat the object as a parent.

    Classical behaviorist psychologists see the
world quite differently from ethologists. Behav-
(45) iorists are primarily interested in the study of
learning under strictly controlled conditions and
have traditionally treated instinct as irrelevant to
learning. Behaviorists believe nearly all the
responses of higher animals can be divided into
(50) two kinds of learning called classical conditioning
and operant conditioning.

    Classical conditioning was discovered in dogs
by the Russian physiologist Ivan P. Pavlov. In
his classic experiment he showed that if a bell is
(55) rung consistently just before food is offered to a
dog, eventually the dog will learn to salivate at
the sound of the bell. The important factors in
classical conditioning are the unconditioned stimulus (the innately recognized cue, equivalent to
(60) the ethological sign stimulus, which in this case is
food), the unconditioned response (the innately
triggered behavioral act, equivalent to the ethological motor program, which in this case is sali-
vation) and the conditioned stimulus (the stimulus
(65) the animal is conditioned to respond to, which in
this case is the bell). Early behaviorists believed
any stimulus an animal was capable of sensing
could be linked, as a conditioned stimulus, to any
unconditioned response.

GO ON TO THE NEXT PAGE ➡

6   6 6 6 6 6 6 6 6 6   6

(70) In operant conditioning, the other major category of learning recognized by most behaviorists, animals learn a behavior pattern as the result of trial-and-error experimentation they undertake in order to obtain a reward or avoid a punishment.
(75) In the classic example a rat is trained to press a lever to obtain food. The experimenter shapes the behavior by rewarding the rat at first for even partial performance of the desired response. For example, at the outset the rat might be rewarded
(80) simply for facing the end of the cage in which the lever sits. Later the experimenter requires increasingly precise behavior, until the response is perfected. Early behaviorists thought any behavior an animal was capable of performing
(85) could be taught, by means of operant conditioning, as a response to any cue or situation.

26. The passage is chiefly concerned with

(A) comparing the effectiveness of ethology with that of other behavioral theories
(B) presenting a new theory to replace ethology and behaviorist psychology
(C) discussing how two differing theories explain behavioral processes
(D) disputing the hypotheses of Pavlov and other classical behaviorists
(E) explaining the processes that control innate behavior

27. The author cites Lorenz, Tinbergen, and Frisch for their

(A) studies of the egg-rolling response in geese
(B) pioneering work studying instinctual behavior
(C) rejection of imprinting as a form of learning
(D) use of stringently controlled laboratory settings
(E) invalidation of the behaviorist approach

28. It can be inferred from lines 26–27 that the goose's behavior in replacing the egg is remarkable because it

(A) appears purposeful and intelligent
(B) is triggered by the egg
(C) refutes current ethological theories
(D) is a response to sign stimuli
(E) lasts for only four weeks

29. According to the passage, behaviorist learning theories take into account which of the following characteristics of animals?

   I. Their unconditioned response to certain fundamental stimuli, such as food.
   II. Their ability to learn through being imprinted at an early age.
   III. Their tendency to shun negative stimuli.

(A) I only   (B) II only   (C) III only   (D) I and II only   (E) I and III only

30. In exploring these two approaches to the study of behavior, the author does all of the following EXCEPT

(A) define a term
(B) point out functional parallels
(C) refer to an experimental study
(D) illustrate through an example
(E) settle an argument

Select the word or set of words that best completes each of the following sentences.

---

31. The townspeople immediately suspected ---- worker of the theft of the Mayor's car.

(A) an itinerant   (B) an indolent
(C) an indefatigable   (D) a productive
(E) a conscientious

32. The usual solution proposed for the chronic ---- of affordable housing in America is to build new houses, often with Federal subsidies to ---- the cost to the buyer.

(A) scarcity..conceal
(B) deterioration..repair
(C) excess..eliminate
(D) undersupply..augment
(E) shortage..reduce

33. Black women authors such as Zora Neale Hurston, originally ---- by both white and black literary establishments to obscurity as minor novelists, are being rediscovered by black feminist critics today.

(A) inclined   (B) relegated   (C) subjected
(D) diminished   (E) characterized

GO ON TO THE NEXT PAGE

6 6 6 6 6 6 6 6 6 6 6

34. Even when a judge does not say anything ---- , his or her tone of voice can signal a point of view to jurors and thus ---- the jury in a criminal trial.

(A) coherent..circumvent
(B) questionable..perjure
(C) prejudicial..influence
(D) material..convene
(E) constructive..corrupt

35. So intense was his ambition to attain the pinnacle of worldly success that not even the opulence and lavishness of his material possessions seemed ---- the ---- of that ambition.

(A) necessary for..fulfillment
(B) adequate to..fervor
(C) appropriate to..ebullience
(D) relevant to..languor
(E) consonant with..insignificance

Each question below consists of a related pair of words or phrases, followed by five lettered pairs of words or phrases. Select the lettered pair that best expresses a relationship similar to that expressed in the original pair.

Example:

YAWN : BOREDOM :: (A) dream : sleep
(B) anger : madness (C) smile : amusement
(D) face : expression (E) impatience : rebellion

Ⓐ Ⓑ ● Ⓓ Ⓔ

36. CAUTION:ACCIDENT :: (A) carelessness:pain
(B) worry:disaster (C) sanitation:health
(D) policeman:criminal (E) radar:collision

37. BUILDING:STORY :: (A) narration:tale
(B) ladder:rung (C) brick:wall
(D) mountain:peak (E) construction:design

38. SCALPEL:SURGEON :: (A) stethoscope:nurse
(B) cleaver:butcher (C) palette:painter
(D) shoe:cobbler (E) handcuffs:detective

39. RUDDER:STEER :: (A) anchor:drift
(B) rocket:launch (C) paddle:row
(D) chain:clank (E) river:flow

40. INSIPID:PIQUANCY :: (A) timid:boldness
(B) provocative:taste (C) apathetic:indifference
(D) lenient:clemency (E) rapid:celerity

41. VIRTUE:INTEGRITY :: (A) vice:sloth
(B) verity:truth (C) purity:honesty
(D) vanity:ambition (E) death:immortality

42. TIMOROUS:FEAR :: (A) apprehensive:ignore
(B) loquacious:listen (C) pugnacious:resign
(D) compassionate:pity (E) pessimistic:hope

43. EPIGRAM:CONCISE :: (A) riddle:inane
(B) fable:ancient (C) anecdote:humorous
(D) epic:lengthy (E) epitaph:moral

44. ENTOMOLOGY:INSECTS ::
(A) phraseology:behavior
(B) toxicology:poisons
(C) icthyology:dinosaurs
(D) orthography:religion
(E) archaeology:circles

45. PROTEAN:IMMUTABLE ::
(A) specious:plausible
(B) pacific:bellicose
(C) deleterious:harmful
(D) vital:inevitable
(E) incessant:contiguous

IF YOU FINISH BEFORE TIME IS CALLED, YOU MAY CHECK YOUR WORK ON THIS SECTION ONLY. DO NOT WORK ON ANY OTHER SECTION IN THE TEST. **S T O P**

Answer Key

Note: The answers to the math sections are keyed to the corresponding review areas in Chapter 12. The numbers in parentheses after each answer refer to topics as listed below. (Note that to review for number 16, Quantitative Comparison, study Chapter 11.)

1. Fundamental Operations
2. Algebraic Operations
3. Using Algebra
4. Roots and Radicals
5. Inequalities
6. Fractions
7. Decimals
8. Percent
9. Averages
10. Motion
11. Ratio and Proportion
12. Mixtures and Solutions
13. Work
14. Coordinate Geometry
15. Geometry
16. Quantitative Comparison
17. Data Interpretation

Section 1   Verbal

1.	B	9.	D	17.	D	25.	B	33.	A
2.	D	10.	B	18.	B	26.	D	34.	C
3.	E	11.	E	19.	B	27.	D	35.	C
4.	D	12.	B	20.	D	28.	B	36.	D
5.	D	13.	D	21.	E	29.	C	37.	A
6.	A	14.	D	22.	E	30.	D	38.	D
7.	B	15.	A	23.	B	31.	C	39.	A
8.	D	16.	E	24.	E	32.	B	40.	B

Section 2   Math

1.	D (8)	6.	A (15)	11.	D (11)	16.	B (15)	21.	E (5, 15)
2.	E (3)	7.	C (2)	12.	B (8)	17.	E (11)	22.	D (4, 8)
3.	B (10)	8.	C (10)	13.	B (6)	18.	D (1)	23.	D (14)
4.	D (6)	9.	C (3)	14.	A (1, 6)	19.	D (2, 4)	24.	D (14)
5.	D (15)	10.	D (11)	15.	E (8)	20.	E (11, 15)	25.	C (10)

Section 3   Verbal

1.	D	10.	A	19.	E	28.	C	37.	A
2.	B	11.	B	20.	C	29.	A	38.	D
3.	A	12.	E	21.	D	30.	B	39.	B
4.	C	13.	E	22.	B	31.	B	40.	B
5.	C	14.	D	23.	C	32.	B	41.	A
6.	A	15.	C	24.	C	33.	C	42.	D
7.	D	16.	B	25.	B	34.	C	43.	D
8.	C	17.	D	26.	D	35.	B	44.	C
9.	D	18.	B	27.	C	36.	D	45.	B

Section 4   Test of Standard Written English

1.	B	11.	C	21.	A	31.	B	41.	E
2.	A	12.	C	22.	D	32.	C	42.	A
3.	E	13.	A	23.	B	33.	C	43.	C
4.	E	14.	D	24.	A	34.	D	44.	A
5.	C	15.	E	25.	A	35.	B	45.	A
6.	C	16.	E	26.	E	36.	C	46.	B
7.	A	17.	C	27.	E	37.	C	47.	C
8.	A	18.	A	28.	C	38.	B	48.	A
9.	C	19.	D	29.	E	39.	D	49.	C
10.	C	20.	A	30.	E	40.	A	50.	A

Section 5   Math

1.	A (8)	8.	B (6, 16)	15.	B (4, 16)	22.	C (15, 16)	29.	A (11)
2.	E (8)	9.	D (1, 16)	16.	C (4, 16)	23.	A (15, 16)	30.	C (15)
3.	B (15)	10.	C (1, 16)	17.	C (2, 16)	24.	C (15, 16)	31.	E (8)
4.	B (1)	11.	C (15, 16)	18.	B (2, 16)	25.	C (15, 16)	32.	B (15)
5.	C (15)	12.	A (15, 16)	19.	D (15, 16)	26.	D (15, 16)	33.	C (14)
6.	C (6)	13.	C (15, 16)	20.	A (15, 16)	27.	C (15, 16)	34.	A (11)
7.	E (1)	14.	A (2, 16)	21.	D (15, 16)	28.	C (15)	35.	D (2)

Section 6   Verbal

1.	A	10.	A	19.	C	28.	A	37.	B
2.	B	11.	D	20.	A	29.	E	38.	B
3.	D	12.	B	21.	E	30.	E	39.	C
4.	B	13.	E	22.	D	31.	A	40.	A
5.	D	14.	A	23.	A	32.	E	41.	A
6.	A	15.	A	24.	B	33.	B	42.	D
7.	A	16.	D	25.	B	34.	C	43.	D
8.	B	17.	C	26.	C	35.	B	44.	B
9.	B	18.	B	27.	B	36.	E	45.	B

Self-Evaluation

The model SAT test you have just completed has the same format as the actual SAT. As you take more of the model tests in this chapter, you will lose any SAT "stage fright" you might have.

Use the steps that follow to evaluate your performance on Model SAT Test 5 (Note: You'll find the charts referred to in steps 1–5 on the next four pages.)

■ **STEP 1**   Use the Answer Key to check your answers for each section.

■ **STEP 2**   For each section, count the number of correct and incorrect answers (remember that you don't count omitted answers), and enter the numbers on the appropriate lines of the chart "Calculate Your Raw Score." Then do the indicated calculations to get your Raw Verbal Score, your Raw TSWE Score, and your Raw Math Score.

■ **STEP 3**   Consult the chart "Evaluate Your Performance" to see how well you did.

■ **STEP 4**   To pinpoint the specific areas in which you need to improve, circle the numbers of the questions that you either left blank or got wrong on the "Identify Your Weaknesses" charts. This will tell you where to concentrate your efforts to get the most out of your study time. The chart for the math sections gives you page references for review and practice by skill areas. The charts for the verbal and TSWE sections refer you to the appropriate chapters to study for each question type.

■ **STEP 5**   Do the review and practice indicated on the charts wherever you had a concentration of circles.

Important: Remember that, in addition to evaluating your scores, you should read all of the answer explanations for questions you answered incorrectly, questions you omitted, and questions you answered correctly but found difficult. Reviewing the answer explanations will help you understand concepts and strategies, and may point out shortcuts.

Calculate Your Raw Score

Verbal

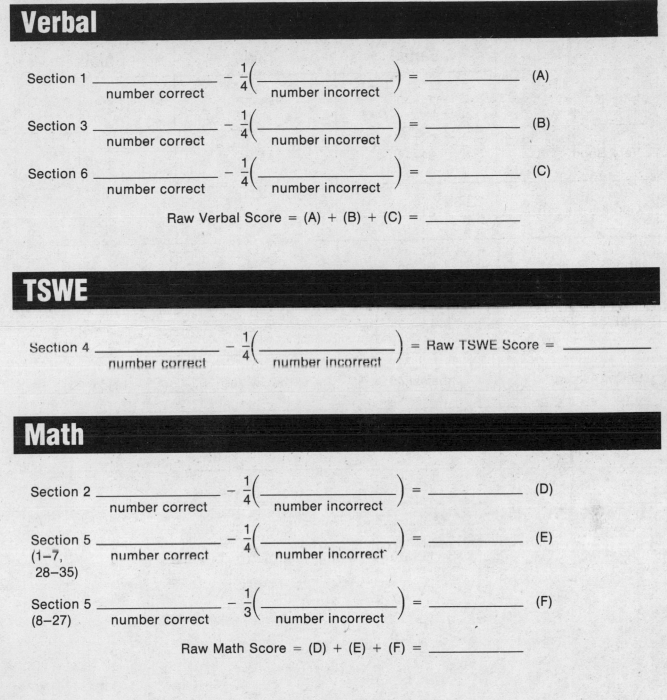

Section 1 _____ $-\frac{1}{4}\Big($ _____ $\Big)=$ _____ (A)
 number correct   number incorrect

Section 3 _____ $-\frac{1}{4}\Big($ _____ $\Big)=$ _____ (B)
 number correct   number incorrect

Section 6 _____ $-\frac{1}{4}\Big($ _____ $\Big)=$ _____ (C)
 number correct   number incorrect

Raw Verbal Score = (A) + (B) + (C) = _____

TSWE

Section 4 _____ $-\frac{1}{4}\Big($ _____ $\Big)=$ Raw TSWE Score = _____
 number correct   number incorrect

Math

Section 2 _____ $-\frac{1}{4}\Big($ _____ $\Big)=$ _____ (D)
 number correct   number incorrect

Section 5 _____ $-\frac{1}{4}\Big($ _____ $\Big)=$ _____ (E)
(1–7,   number correct   number incorrect
28–35)

Section 5 _____ $-\frac{1}{3}\Big($ _____ $\Big)=$ _____ (F)
(8–27)   number correct   number incorrect

Raw Math Score = (D) + (E) + (F) = _____

Evaluate Your Performance

Verbal, TSWE, Math

	Verbal	TSWE	Math
Excellent	111–130	46–50	52–60
Very Good	91–110	41–45	45–51
Good	81–90	36–40	36–44
Above Average	61–80	31–35	30–35
Average	45–60	26–30	20–29
Below Average	below 45	below 26	below 20

Identify Your Weaknesses

Verbal

Question Type	Question Numbers			Chapter to Study
	Section 1	**Section 3**	**Section 6**	
Antonym	1, 2, 3, 4, 5, 6, 7, 8, 9, 10	1, 2, 3, 4, 5, 6, 7, 8, 9, 10, 11, 12, 13, 14, 15	1, 2, 3, 4, 5, 6, 7, 8, 9, 10, 11, 12, 13, 14, 15	Chapter 5
Analogy	16, 17, 18, 19, 20, 21, 22, 23, 24, 25	36, 37, 38, 39, 40, 41, 42, 43, 44, 45	36, 37, 38, 39, 40, 41, 42, 43, 44, 45	Chapter 6
Sentence Completion	11, 12, 13, 14, 15	16, 17, 18, 19, 20, 31, 32, 33, 34, 35	16, 17, 18, 19, 20, 31, 32, 33, 34, 35	Chapter 7
Reading Comprehension	26, 27, 28, 29, 30, 31, 32, 33, 34, 35, 36, 37, 38, 39, 40	21, 22, 23, 24, 25, 26, 27, 28, 29, 30	21, 22, 23, 24, 25, 26, 27, 28, 29, 30, 31	Chapter 8

TSWE

Question Type	Question Numbers	Chapter to Study
Usage	1, 2, 3, 4, 5, 6, 7, 8, 9, 10, 11, 12, 13, 14, 15, 16, 17, 18, 19, 20, 21, 22, 23, 24, 25, 41, 42, 43, 44, 45, 46, 47, 48, 49, 50	Chapter 13
Sentence Correction	26, 27, 28, 29, 30, 31, 32, 33, 34, 35, 36, 37, 38, 39, 40	Chapter 13

Identify Your Weaknesses

Math

Skill Area	Question Numbers		Pages to Study
	Section 2	Section 5	
Fundamental Operations	14, 18	4, 7, 9, 10	328–29
Algebraic Operations	7, 19	14, 17, 18, 35	329–34
Using Algebra	2, 9		334–35
Fractions	4, 13, 14	6, 8	341–45
Decimals and Percents	1, 12, 15, 22	1, 2, 31	351–55
Verbal Problems	3, 8, 9, 25		357–58
Ratio and Proportion	10, 11, 17, 20	29, 34	362–64
Geometry	5, 6, 16, 20, 21	3, 5, 11, 12, 13, 19, 20, 21, 22, 23, 24, 25, 26, 27, 28, 30, 32	371–76
Coordinate Geometry	23, 24	33	381–82
Inequalities	16		335–36
Quantitative Comparison		8, 9, 10, 11, 12, 13, 14, 15, 16, 17, 18, 19, 20, 21, 22, 23, 24, 25, 26, 27	309–13
Roots and Radicals	19, 22	15, 16	332–33

Answer Explanations

Section 1 Verbal

1. B. To *release* means to let go or set free. Its opposite is to seize or *grasp*.
   Context Clue: Think of "release the prisoner."

2. D. A *novice* is an inexperienced beginner. The opposite of a novice is an *expert*.
   Context Clue: Think of "a pretty good score for a novice."
   Word Parts Clue: *Nov-* means new. A *novice* is someone new in a field.

3. E. *Immaculate* means spotlessly clean, flawless. Its opposite is *stained*.
   Context Clue: "She always hands in *immaculate* work."

4. D. To *dawdle* is to loiter or to waste time. Its opposite is to *hasten* or hurry up.
   Context Clue: "Don't *dawdle*," says the mother to the slow-walking child.

5. B. *Profusion* means abundance or plentifulness. Its opposite is *scarcity*, lack or insufficiency of supply.
   Context Clue: Think of "a profusion of blessings." (Hint: If you can't think of any phrases using the word *profusion*, try thinking of one using the adjective form *profuse*. "*Profuse* bleeding" may come to mind.)
   Beware Eye-Catchers: Choice D is incorrect. *Pro* and *con* may be opposites (as in "votes *pro*" versus "votes *con*") but *profusion* and *confusion* are not opposites.

6. A. *Squeamish* means easily disturbed or disgusted; easily nauseated. Its opposite is *not easily disturbed*.
   Context Clue: Think of "squeamish about blood."

7. B. *Culpable* means deserving blame. Its opposite is *innocent*.
   Context Clue: Think of "culpable negligence."

8. D. To *engender* is to bring forth or cause to exist. Its opposite is to *suppress* or put an end to; to abolish.
   Context Clue: "Hatred engenders violence."

9. D. To *embellish* something is to adorn it, to enhance it by adding improvements to it. Its opposite would be to *disfigure* or spoil something.
   Word Parts Clue: *Em-* or *en-* means cause to be; *bell* here means beautiful. To embellish something is to cause it to be beautiful.
   Note: *Bellus* (beauty) can all too easily be confused with *bellum* (war).

10. B. *Obdurate* means hard; stubborn; unyielding. Its opposite is submissive or *yielding*.
    Context Clue: Think of "obdurate in his determination."

11. E. The subject considers himself talented and creative and thinks office work is uninspiring, dull, in a word *prosaic*.
    Note that the missing word must be a synonym or near-synonym for "uninspiring." Connected by the linking verb *was*, both words describe or define the office routine.

    (Definition)

12. B. A *chronological* order is one arranged in order of time. The missing word is an adjective describing the order in which the museum arranged the fossils. The second part of the sentence defines that order: from older to more recent in time.
    Word Parts Clue: *Chron-* means time.

    (Definition)

13. B. *Although* the judge had a merciful nature, nevertheless he was strict and unbending (*implacable*) in sticking to the law.
    Note that *while, although, however,* and *though* all are contrast signals. Look at the second word in each of these four choices to see if it is an antonym or near-antonym for "merciful by nature." You can immediately eliminate Choices C and E.
    Choice A is incorrect. *Unjust* means lacking in fairness, not lacking in mercy.
    Choice D is incorrect. Someone *truly* merciful by nature would not be *vindictive* or vengeful.

    (Contrast Signal)

14. D. Callas longed for honest criticism. She had grown tired of *adulation* (praise) because she had been surrounded by a group of people who constantly *extolled* (praised) her singing. (A retinue of sycophants is a group of flatterers in attendance on an important personage.)
    Remember, before you look at the choices, read the sentence and think of a word that makes sense.
    Likely Words: praised, admired.

    (Examples)

15. A. Moore's criticism was *not* unsure (*tentative*) or "provisional." It was sure or confident: she writes *confidently*.
    Remember to watch for signal words that link one part of the sentence to another. The presence of *or* linking items in a series indicates that the missing word may be a synonym or near-synonym for "provisional," the other linked word.

This sentence contrasts two ideas *without* using a signal word. The contrast is implicit in the juxtaposition of the two clauses.

(Contrast Pattern)

16. E. An *actor* performs on a *stage*. A *skater* performs at a *rink*.

(Worker and Workplace)

17. D. One function of *feet* is to *sprint*. One function of *hands* is to *massage*.

(Function)

18. B. To *beam* (smile radiantly) is to show *delight*. To *glower* (scowl sullenly) is to show *anger*.

(Action and Significance)

19. B. The *crest* is the top of a *wave*. The *crown* is the top of the *tree*.

(Part to Whole)

20. D. A *hideous* person is one who is extremely *unattractive*. A *parsimonious* person is one who is extremely frugal or *thrifty*.

(Degree of Intensity)

21. E. An *entrepreneur* (the organizer of a business venture) seeks *profits*. A *scholar* seeks *knowledge*.
Note: A *charlatan* doesn't seek true *converts*; a charlatan seeks gullible fools to swindle.

(Person and Objective [Thing Sought])

22. E. Someone *congenial* (agreeable, friendly) is without *animosity* (ill will, hatred). Someone *modest* (humble) is without *vanity* (conceit, pride).

(Antonym Variant)

23. B. A *maxim* is defined as an expression that is *proverbial* in nature. A *question* is defined as an expression that is *interrogative* in nature.

(Definition)

24. E. An *ascetic* (person who leads a life of self-denial) shuns *intemperance* (lack of moderation; indulgence in passions). A *miser* (person who lives wretchedly in order to save money) shuns *extravagance* (wasteful spending).

(Person and Thing Avoided)

25. B. A *diatribe* is a bitter and abusive speech. It consists of *invective* (abuse). An *encomium* is a laudatory speech. It consists of *praise*.

(Definition)

26. D. Both in dwelling on the author's happiness in setting out on his hunt for a school and in picturing the physical details of his journey, the passage recounts the author's *recollections of a memorable time in his life*.
Choice A is incorrect. In addition to portraying the harsh realities of his search, the author also describes the exhilaration and joy.
Choice B is incorrect. The passage focuses on the author's reminiscences of the early stages of his career, not on his eventual achievements.
Choice C is incorrect. The passage is narrative and descriptive, not analytic or explanatory.
Choice E is incorrect. The author, while young and happy, is not portrayed as innocent or gullible (easy to fool).

(Main Idea)

27. D. The author does *not* portray his journey as *carefree* (free from care or worry): he feels both weariness and anxiety.
Choice A is incorrect. The author talks of "the pleasures of the chase" and of sallying forth lustily to hunt a school. The hunt, while tiring, has its rewards: it is gratifying (pleasing).
Choice B is incorrect. The road stretches "relentlessly" (mercilessly) ahead; the journey seems interminable (endless).
Choice C is incorrect. The author feels "weariness . . . of limb" (fatigue); the journey seems tiring.
Choice E is incorrect. The author's heart "sink(s) heavily"; the journey is discouraging or disheartening.
Remember, when asked about specific details in the passage, spot key words in the question and scan the passage to find them (or their synonyms).

(Specific Details)

28. B. Particularly in the first two paragraphs, the author sentimentally yearns for his happy youth ("Young and happy, . . . I shall not soon forget"; "the rough world was softened by laughter and song"). His attitude is one of *nostalgia*.
Remember, when asked to determine the author's attitude or tone, look for words that convey emotion or paint pictures.

(Attitude/Tone)

29. C. Choice C is correct. You can arrive at it by the process of elimination.
Statement I is true. Sir Walter's vanity was "vanity of person." He was vain about his personal appearance, his *physical attractiveness*. Therefore, you can eliminate Choice B.

Statement II is true. Sir Walter's vanity was also vanity "of situation." He was vain about his position in society, his titled rank. Therefore, you can eliminate Choices A and D.
Statement III is untrue. Sir Walter's wife, not Sir Walter, was superior in character. Therefore, you can eliminate Choice E.
Only Choice C is left. It is the correct answer.

(Specific Details)

30. D. The narrator does *not* commend Lady Elliot for falling in love with Sir Walter, calling it a "youthful infatuation," the only misjudgment in an otherwise blameless life.
Choice A is incorrect. The narrator speaks well of Lady Elliot for concealing Sir Walter's shortcomings: she has "promoted his real respectability."
Choice B is incorrect. The narrator commends Lady Elliot for her choice of a friend: she has chosen "a sensible, deserving woman," one who even moves into the neighborhood to be near her.
Choice C is incorrect. The narrator speaks well of the way Lady Elliot guides her daughters: she has given them "good principles and instruction."
Choice E is incorrect. The narrator clearly commends Lady Elliot in her performance of her duties as a wife.

(Specific Details)

31. C. The narrator's statement that Lady Elliot was "not the very happiest being in the world herself" is preceded by a list of all Lady Elliot had to do to cover up for her "conceited, silly" husband. Thus we can infer that the cause of her unhappiness was the difference or *disparity* between her character and that of her husband.
Choice A is incorrect. Nothing in the passage suggests Lady Elliot lacks beauty. Indeed, we suspect that Sir Walter, so conscious of his own beauty, would not have chosen an unattractive wife.
Choice B is incorrect. Lady Elliot's best friend had moved to be near her; they were not separated.
Choice D is incorrect. Lady Elliot's social position was, at least in Sir Walter's eyes, superior, not inferior.
Choice E is incorrect. Nothing in the passage suggests that Lady Elliot's daughters were wayward.

(Inference)

32. B. The narrator tells little directly of Lady Elliot's feelings about dying. However, such phrases as "Three girls . . . was an awful

legacy to bequeath" and "anxiously giving her daughters (instruction)" show us something of her mind. Her concern centers not on herself but on those she must leave behind: her daughters. Her feeling is one of *maternal* (motherly) *distress*.
Choice A is incorrect. Nothing in the passage suggests resignation or pious submissiveness on her part.
Choice C is incorrect. She was *not* indifferent to dying: the narrator states directly that quitting her family (in other words, dying) was "no matter of indifference to her."
Choices D and E are also incorrect. Both are unsupported by the passage.

(Specific Details)

33. A. Lady Elliot in "quitting her family" is not simply taking a trip: she is dying. We expect a person facing death to react strongly, emotionally. Instead, the narrator states that Lady Elliot was merely attached enough to life to make dying no matter of indifference to her. That is clearly an *understatement*. It is an example of *irony*, the literary technique that points up the contradictions in life, in this case the contradiction between the understated expression and the deeply-felt reality.

(Technique)

34. C. The passage discusses the limitations of the Elizabethan stage and the ways in which Shakespeare's style was influenced by these limitations.
Choice A is incorrect. The passage focuses on Shakespeare's language as it was affected by the stage of his day.
Choice B is incorrect. While mentioned in the passage, this is not the central theme of the passage.
Choice D is incorrect. The passage is concerned with the plastic stage of Shakespeare's time, not the present day pictorial stage.
Choice E is incorrect. It is too specific to be a suitable title for the passage.
Remember, when asked to choose a title, watch out for choices that are too specific or too broad.

(Main Idea/Title)

35. C. Today, actors do not have to provide the background and setting with their words and gestures. They can rely on elaborate scenery and lighting effects to create the setting and atmosphere.
Choice A is incorrect. Lines 9–17 indicate that Elizabethan actors, not modern actors, had to convey settings through language and gesture.

Choice B is incorrect. It misinterprets the use of "pitch" and "key" in lines 2–3.
Choice D is incorrect. Elizabethan actors had to do more to make the setting clear.
Choice E is incorrect. It is unsupported by the passage.

36. D.   Lines 9–10 state that "the whole of his atmosphere" came from the actors' language or *dialogue*.
Choice A is incorrect. It is unsupported by the passage.
Choice B is incorrect. The actors did not *physically* provide the scenery; they *figuratively* provided it. There was no actual physical scenery on stage.
Choice C is incorrect. The actors had no actual physical scenery to shift.
Choice E is incorrect. There is nothing in the passage to suggest it.

(Specific Details)

37. A.   The author sets up a hypothetical situation ("*If* Shakespeare needs any excuse for the exuberance of language . . .") and goes on to explain why Shakespeare's dialogue is more colorful and flamboyant than its modern counterpart.
Choice B is incorrect. The author clearly admires Shakespeare and does not condemn his "exuberance" as grave (serious) excesses.
Choice C is incorrect. The author only touches on the modern stage in passing.
Choice D is incorrect. The author's purpose is to explain something about Shakespeare's language, not to draw a general contrast between him and modern playwrights.
Choice E is incorrect. It is unmentioned in the passage.

(Main Idea)

38. D.   Ichthyosaurs and dolphins are described as "wholly fishlike in form" (lines 25–26).
Choice A is incorrect. Ichthyosaurs are fossil reptiles, not modern mammals (line 24).
Choice B is incorrect. Brachiopods (line 17) are coral-like forms that grow in *fixed* or stationary positions; dolphins have far more than *slightly greater mobility* than such creatures.
Choice C is incorrect. Dolphins are air-breathing mammals (line 25), not air-breathing reptiles.
Choice E is incorrect. Both Ichthyosaurs and dolphins have backbones; neither of them are stationary *invertebrates*.
Remember, when asked about specific details in the passage, spot key words in the question and scan the passage to find them (or their synonyms).

(Specific Details)

39. A.   The opening sentence states that the "*opposite* of adaptive divergence is an . . . expression of evolution." In other words, *adaptive convergence* (the opposite of adaptive divergence) is a manifestation of an evolutionary pattern. The second sentence describes adaptive divergence as the process by which related organisms adapt to unlike environments. It also is a manifestation of evolution, the process by which a species develops its distinguishing characteristics.
Choice B is incorrect. The passage shows how biological phenomena (fossils, coral individuals) illustrate or support the theory of adaptive convergence.
Choice C is incorrect. Only adaptive convergence deals with plants and animals adjusting to a *common* environment; adaptive divergence deals with their adjusting to *unlike* environments.
Choice D is incorrect. Brachiopods and pelecypods are mentioned only in connection with adaptive convergence.
Choice E is incorrect. Only adaptive divergence deals with compensatory adjustments to *unlike* environments; adaptive convergence deals with adjustments to a *common* environment.
Remember, when asked about specific details in the passage, spot key words in the question and scan the passage to find them (or their synonyms).

(Specific Details)

40. B.   Note how the passage begins. "The opposite of adaptive divergence is interesting. Whereas . . . in the case of adaptive divergence (X happens), . . . organisms exhibit adaptive convergence when (Y happens)." The topic of the passage is adaptive *convergence*. From the fact that adaptive convergence is introduced in terms of adaptive divergence, and that little explanation of adaptive divergence is given, you can infer that the author has previously informed the reader about adaptive divergence.
When you are asked to infer or reason about the contents of the paragraph preceding the passage you're reading, pay particular attention to the opening lines of your text.

(Inference)

Section 2

1. D. $0.3\%x = 2163$

$$\frac{0.3}{100}x = 2163$$

$$\frac{3}{1000}x = 2163$$

$$3x = 2{,}163{,}000$$

$$x = 721{,}000$$

2. E. Since there are 10 cents in one dime, in $(x + 2)$ dimes there are $10(x + 2)$ or $10x + 20$ cents.

3. B. Distance covered $= 30$ miles $+ 40$ miles or 70 miles.
Time spent traveling $= 2$ hr.
$$\frac{\text{Distance}}{\text{Time}} = \text{Average speed}$$
$$\frac{70}{2} = 35 \text{ m.p.h.}$$

4. D. $\dfrac{6 \text{ in.}}{1 \text{ yd.}}$ or $\dfrac{6 \text{ in.}}{3 \text{ ft.}}$ or $\dfrac{6 \text{ in.}}{36 \text{ in.}}$ or $\dfrac{6}{36}$ or $\dfrac{1}{6}$

5. D. $\angle 1 + \angle 4 = 180°$
$145° + \angle 4 = 180°$
$\angle 4 = 35°$
$\angle 2 + \angle 5 = 180°$
$125° + \angle 5 = 180°$
$\angle 5 = 55°$
$\angle 4 + \angle 5 +$
$\angle 3 = 180°$
(the sum of the angle measures of a triangle equals 180°)
$35° + 55° + \angle 3 = 180°$
$\angle 3 = 90°$

6. A. Since the sides of a square are equal, each side equals $\dfrac{1}{4}$ of the perimeter. Since the perimeter equals p inches, each side equals $\dfrac{p}{4}$.
Area of square $= (\text{Side})^2$
Area of square $= \left(\dfrac{p}{4}\right)^2$ or $\dfrac{p^2}{16}$

7. C. $7x - 5y = 13$
$\underline{2x - 7y = 26}$
$9x - 12y = 39$ (if equals are added to equals, the results are equal)

8. C. Time spent $= 20$ min. or $\dfrac{1}{3}$ hr.
Distance covered $= 18$ miles
$$\frac{\text{Distance}}{\text{Time}} = \text{Average velocity}$$
$\dfrac{18}{\frac{1}{3}}$ or $18 \div \dfrac{1}{3}$ or $18 \cdot \dfrac{3}{1} = 54$ m.p.h.

9. C. Let $n =$ number of nickels.
Since there are 12 coins in all, $12 - n =$ number of dimes.
Value of all nickels $= 5n$ cents
Value of all dimes $= 10(12 - n)$ or $120 - 10n$ cents

Value of all coins $= 5n + 120 - 10n$ cents
$5n + 120 - 10n = 85$
$-5n = -35$
$5n = 35$
$n = 7$

10. D. Let $x =$ height of pole (in feet).
$$\frac{\text{height of object (in feet)}}{\text{length of shadow (in feet)}} = \frac{5\frac{2}{3}}{8} = \frac{x}{96}$$
(5 ft. 8 in. $= 5\dfrac{2}{3}$ ft.)
$8x = \left(5\dfrac{2}{3}\right)(96)$ (product of the means equals product of the extremes)
$8x = 544$
$x = 68$ ft.

11. D. Let $x =$ number of angstrom units.
$$\frac{\text{angstrom units}}{\text{micron}} = \frac{1}{0.0001} = \frac{x}{0.01}$$
$0.0001x = 0.01$
$x = 100$ (multiply by 10,000)
Alternatively, from 0.0001 micron to 0.01 micron involves a move of the decimal point 2 places to the right (that is, multiplication by 100). A corresponding operation changes 1 angstrom unit to 100 angstrom units.

12. B. 10% of 32%, or $\dfrac{1}{10}$ of 32%, $= 3.2\%$.

13. B. Let $x =$ number of nineteenths equal to exactly $\dfrac{2}{3}$.
$$\frac{x}{19} = \frac{2}{3}$$
$3x = 38$
$x = 12\dfrac{2}{3}$
Therefore $\dfrac{12\frac{2}{3}}{19} = \dfrac{2}{3}$
$\dfrac{13}{19}$ is the fraction with closest value to $\dfrac{2}{3}$.

14. A. Since the cup contains equal parts of flour and cornstarch, the mixture contains $\dfrac{1}{2}$ cup of flour and $\dfrac{1}{2}$ cup of cornstarch. Since 1 cup of cornstarch weighs $\dfrac{1}{4}$ lb., $\dfrac{1}{2}$ cup of cornstarch weighs $\dfrac{1}{8}$ lb. Since 4 cups of flour weigh 1 lb., 1 cup weighs $\dfrac{1}{4}$ lb. and $\dfrac{1}{2}$ cup weighs $\dfrac{1}{8}$ lb.
The weight of flour and cornstarch in 1 cup $= \dfrac{1}{8} + \dfrac{1}{8}$ or $\dfrac{1}{4}$ lb.

15. E. The team has played 24 games. If 24 games represents $16\frac{2}{3}\%$ or $\frac{1}{6}$ of the games, then 100% (total games played) = (24) (6) or 144 games. To finish the season with a record of 0.750, the team must win a total of (0.750) (144) or 108 games. Since the team has already won 15 games, it must win 93 additional games.

16. B. Since $CD < CE$ and $AD = BE$, $CA < CB$ because, if equal quantities are subtracted from unequal quantities, the remainders are unequal in the same order.

17. E. $\$D = 100D¢$
    Let x = number of pounds that can be bought for $c¢$.
    $$\frac{\text{pounds of apples}}{\text{cost (in cents)}} = \frac{p}{100D} = \frac{x}{c}$$
    $$100Dx = pc$$
    $$x = \frac{pc}{100D}$$

18. D. Distance between first pole and second pole = 15 ft.
    Distance between first pole and third pole = 30 ft., etc.
    Distance between first pole and eighth pole = 105 ft.
    In other words, there are 7 spaces of 15 ft. each between the first and the eighth pole.
    $7 \times 15 = 105$

19. D. To eliminate square roots, square each term:
    $$4a^2 = \frac{2b^2}{4} = \frac{2c^2}{6.25}$$
    Or
    $$4a^2 = \frac{b^2}{2} = \frac{c^2}{3.125}$$
    Since the terms are equal, the letter with the smallest coefficient will be the greatest.
    Therefore c is the greatest and a is the least.
    In descending order the letters are c, b, a.

20. E. Area of one circle = $\pi(\text{radius})^2$
    $$144\pi = \pi r^2$$
    $$144 = r^2 \quad (\text{divide by } \pi)$$
    $$r = 12$$
    Diameter = 24
    Area of other circle = 196π
    $$196\pi = \pi r^2$$
    $$196 = r^2 \quad (\text{divide by } \pi)$$
    $$r = 14$$
    Diameter = 28
    $$\frac{\text{diameter of smaller circle}}{\text{diameter of larger circle}} = \frac{24}{28} \text{ or } \frac{6}{7} \text{ or } 6:7$$

21. E. Let A be the location of checker; then AD is the distance from nearest corner.
    $DC = AB = 3$ in.
    In right triangle ADC, leg $AC = 4$ in. and leg $DC = 3$ in.
    $$(AD)^2 = (AC)^2 + (DC)^2$$
    $$(AD)^2 = (4)^2 + (3)^2$$
    $$(AD)^2 = 16 + 9$$
    $$(AD)^2 = 25$$
    $$AD = 5$$
    Instead of applying the Pythagorean Theorem, you might observe the 3-4-5 relationship. If $DC = 3$ and $AC = 4$, then $AD = 5$.

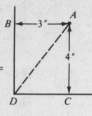

22. D. $(x + 25\%x)^2 = \left(x + \frac{1}{4}x\right)^2$
    $$= \left(1\frac{1}{4}x\right)^2 = \left(\frac{5}{4}x\right)^2$$
    $$= \frac{25}{16}x^2 = 1.56\frac{1}{4}x^2$$
    $(1x)^2 = 100\%x^2$
    Difference between $(x + 25\%x)^2$ and $(x)^2$ is $(156\frac{1}{4}\%x^2 - 100\%x^2)$ or $56\frac{1}{4}\%x^2$ or an increase of $56\frac{1}{4}\%$.

23. D. Ordinate refers to the y-value of a point.
    Ordinates are equal to -3; this means
    $$\begin{array}{ccc} \downarrow & \downarrow & \downarrow \\ y & = & -3 \end{array}$$
    The equation is $y = -3$.

24. D. Point $(0, 0)$ lies on the origin.
    Distance $OA = 9$.
    Distance $OB = \sqrt{(-2 - 0)^2 + (9 - 0)^2}$
    $= \sqrt{4 + 81} = \sqrt{85}$.
    Distance $OC = \sqrt{(-7 - .0)^2 + (-6 - 0)^2}$
    $= \sqrt{49 + 36} = \sqrt{85}$.
    Distance $OD = \sqrt{(8 - 0)^2 + (5 - 0)^2}$
    $= \sqrt{64 + 25} = \sqrt{89}$.

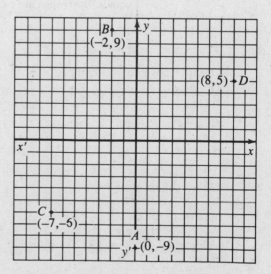

To compare these distances, note that distance $OA = 9 = \sqrt{81}$.
Thus distance OD is the greatest of the four distances.

25. C.   Distance covered $= R$ miles $+ W$ miles
$$\frac{\text{Distance}}{\text{Time}} = \text{Average rate}$$
$$\frac{R + W}{2H}$$

Section 3   Verbal

1. D.   *Curious* means odd, extraordinary, unpredictable. Its opposite is *ordinary*.
Remember to consider secondary meanings of the capitalized word as well as its primary meaning. *Curious* has other meanings in addition to "inquisitive."
Context Clue: "Curiouser and curiouser," said Alice in Wonderland.

2. B.   To *commence* means to start or begin. Its opposite is to *terminate* or end.
Context Clue: The captain ordered, "Commence firing!"

3. A.   To *comply* is to assent or agree; to go along. Its opposite is to *disobey*.
Context Clue: "He *complied* with her request."

4. C.   *Serenity* means calm; tranquillity. Its opposite is disturbance or *commotion*.
Context Clue: Think of "serenity of mind."

5. C.   To *impair* something is to damage it. Its opposite is to *improve* or strengthen; to repair.
Context Clue: "Drinking impairs your judgment."

6. A.   *Lavish* means extravagant, possibly even excessive. Its opposite is *sparing* (restrained, economical).
Context Clue: Think of "lavish hospitality."

7. D.   *Candid* means frank, holding nothing back. Its opposite is *reserved*, always holding something back, restrained.
Context Clue: Think of "a candid opinion."

8. C.   To *provoke* is to incite or arouse; to stir up. Its opposite is to *mollify*, to pacify or soothe.
Context Clue: "I hit him because he provoked me."
Word Parts Clue: *Pro-* means forth. *Voke* or *voc-* means call. To *provoke* someone is to call forth an emotional or physical reaction.

9. D.   *Profound* means deep. Its opposite is shallow or *lacking in depth*.
Context Clue: Think of "a profound sigh," "profound relief."

10. A.   *Taciturnity* means reticence, reluctance to join in conversation. Its opposite is *wordiness*.
Word Parts Clue: *Tacit* means unspoken or silent.

11. B.   To *alienate* someone is to estrange him, to make him a stranger to you. Its opposite is to *conciliate*, to mollify or pacify, to bring people together.
Context Clue: Think of "to alienate someone's affections."

12. E.   *Cryptic* means obscure, enigmatic, hidden. Its opposite is open or *unconcealed*.
Beware Eye-Catchers: Choice A is incorrect. Don't be fooled by mental associations with *Tales from the Crypt* and similar horror movies; *cryptic* has nothing to do with *ghastly*.

13. E.   *Loath* is an adjective meaning reluctant or unwilling. Its opposite is *avid* or eager.
Context Clue: "The lovers were *loath* to part."
Beware Eye-Catchers: Choice A is incorrect. Don't confuse *loath* and *loathe* (hate; feel disgust for).

14. D.   *Amenable* means readily brought to give in or submit. Its opposite is *contentious*, which means belligerent or quarrelsome.
Context Clue: "He was *amenable* to her suggestion."

15. C.   *Raucous* is harsh, shrill, grating. Its opposite is *gentle*, soft.
Context Clue: Think of "the raucous cries of the crows."

16. B.   The words "merely" and "failed to highlight" indicate that the woman is dissatisfied with the job-seeker's resume. It lacks some qualities she thinks it needs. It is *inadequate*, not up to standards, deficient.
Note that you are looking for a word with negative associations. Therefore, you can eliminate any word with positive ones. Choices C and E both have positive associations. Only Choices A, B, or D can be correct.

(Examples)

17. D.   Most medical research is aimed at helping human beings. Therefore, having discovered something about the cause of a disease

affecting animals, it would be perfectly reasonable or *logical* for researchers to wish to apply their findings to the treatment of humans.
Remember, watch for signal words that link one part of the sentence to another. The use of "because" in the opening clause is a cause signal. Ask yourself what would be a logical next step to finding out that a kind of virus caused cancer in animals.

(Cause and Effect Signal)

18. B.   The subject's *verbosity*, her tendency to use too many words, is what's irritating. The second clause defines the first.

(Definition)

19. E.   Someone who looks at damage and says it can never be repaired is *not* hopeful or optimistic. He's all too ready to believe things are in the worst possible state; in short, he is a *pessimist*.

(Examples)

20. C.   It would be pointless or *futile* to try to poison pests chemically if the creatures eventually became *resistant* to or able to withstand the effect of each new poison you introduced. Remember, watch for signal words that link one part of the sentence to another. The conjunction "for" connecting the two halves of the sentence signals you to expect a *cause and effect* relationship between them.

(Cause and Effect Signal)

21. D.   The author does *not* value the rhetoric of left wing extremists. He does not want to "add strength to the arguments of the radical revolutionaries among us" (lines 68–69).
Choice A is incorrect. The author values *legislative reform*; he argues in its favor throughout the passage.
Choice B is incorrect. The author values *press coverage of Congressional sessions*: he advocates "letting the people and their news media see what is transpiring here" in lines 47–48.
Choice C is incorrect. The author values his *responsiveness to his constituents,* his ability to respond to the wishes of the people. He maintains in lines 2–8 that it is this responsiveness on the part of our institutions that makes our way of life prevail.
Choice E is incorrect. The author apparently values *the opinion of Dr. Edward Teller*: he quotes Teller in order to back up his argument against Congressional secretiveness.

(Specific Details)

22. B.   Throughout the passage the author repeatedly calls for reform. He points out the failings of the House. In particular, he asserts that "this House of the people has been operating . . . in an undemocratic manner" (lines 26–27). Such *undemocratic practices* must come to an end.
Choice A is incorrect. The author wishes to grant the media access to Congress (lines 47–52); he does not seek to limit their powers.
Choice C is incorrect. While he mentions the radical revolutionaries in our midst, he does so only in passing (lines 68–69): his primary purpose is not to answer their arguments, but to make an argument of his own.
Choice D is incorrect. The author never mentions stregthening the powers of Congressional committees.
Choice E is incorrect. Although the author mentions in passing the needs for security of governmental agencies, he dismisses these needs as less important than the public's need (and right) to know what's going on.

(Main Idea)

23. C.   The opening lines alone should give you the answer to this question. "Mr. Speaker, ours is an open society." What you have here is a speech addressed to the Speaker of the House of Representatives by a Member of that House. Such speeches are commonly recorded or entered in the Congressional Record. They are not commonly given in full in college history textbooks, nor are they the sort of speeches commonly found in plays (they're too undramatic, for one thing).

(Inference)

24. C.   In lines 60–64 the author directly rejects closed Congressional hearings. Closed hearings undermine the very foundations of Congress and of democracy itself. He demands reform. His attitude is one of outright, complete rejection.
Choice A is incorrect. The author is not merely being skeptical (suspicious, unwilling to believe) when he discusses closed hearings.
Choice B is incorrect. The author attacks closed hearings. He does not accept or tolerate them grudgingly (reluctantly).
Choice D is incorrect. The author certainly does not accept closed hearings enthusiastically or wholeheartedly.
Choice E is incorrect. The author is not basically indifferent to closed hearings; he would not have spent so much time arguing against them if he were.

(Attitude/Tone)

25. B.   The passage is *cautionary* in tone. The author is warning his audience, giving them lots of advice.

Choice A is incorrect. *Satirical* means ironic, mocking, critical in a witty or humorous manner. The author is far too involved in the issue to make witty, mocking remarks.

Choice C is incorrect. The author is concerned. He has not been made indifferent or *alienated*.

Choice D is incorrect. *Objective* means fair, unprejudiced, undistorted by emotion. The author's prejudices against "radical revolutionaries" and his use of emotionally loaded phrases like "stifle the democratic process" and "Nation we all love so deeply" make his lack of objectivity clear.

Choice E is incorrect. The author is not *elegiac*, sorrowfully lamenting a death. He is issuing a warning.

(Attitude/Tone)

26. D. The Doctor is *civil*: "polite . . . , scrupulously, formally polite" (lines 45–46); he is also domineering or *imperious*, never discussing anything, but issuing ultimatums instead (lines 51–53).

Choice A is incorrect. While the Doctor provides his widowed sister with a home, he does not do so in a particularly kindly or benevolent manner.

Choice B is incorrect. The Doctor is formal, not casual.

Choice C is incorrect. The Doctor is not powerless or ineffectual. He is the center of authority in his home.

Choice E is incorrect. The Doctor is not habitually angry or irate; his sister has seen him in a temper only once in her life (lines 46–49).

(Specific Details)

27. C. The author portrays Mrs. Penniman's late husband as sickly. Nothing in the passage, however, allows us to infer that *she* is sickly.

Choice A is incorrect. The passage cites Mrs. Penniman's "alacrity" or willingness to accept her brother's offer. Thus, she readily becomes dependent on him.

Choice B is incorrect. The passage states that Mrs. Penniman was widowed at the age of thirty-three and that she had been married for ten years, which means that she was married at twenty-three.

Choice D is incorrect. The passage describes Mrs. Penniman's willingness to move as "the alacrity of a woman who had spent the ten years of her married life in Poughkeepsie." This suggests she did not think much of Poughkeepsie.

Choice E is incorrect. The memory of Mr. Penniman's "flowers of speech" hovered about Mrs. Penniman's conversation (lines 7–

10). This suggests she at times echoed her late husband's ornate conversational style.

(Inference)

28. C. The Doctor asks his sister to try to make a clever woman of his daughter (lines 56–57). This implies that he views children as *clay to be molded*.

Choices A, B, D, and E are all unsupported by the passage.

(Inference)

29. A. In stating that Catherine "made but a modest figure" on the dance floor, the passage suggests her moderate or *limited skill as a dancer*. "But" here means only. Her skill was *only* modest or limited.

Choice B is incorrect. *Virtuosity* means expertise, extreme skill or talent. Catherine had only "a certain talent" at the piano, not the talent of an expert.

Choice C is incorrect. *Modest* here means moderate or limited. It does not necessarily imply shyness on her part.

Choice D is incorrect. Nothing in the passage suggests Catherine is indifferent to cleverness.

Choice E is incorrect. It is unsupported by the passage.

(Inference)

30. B. "Salt" here means an element that gives liveliness, piquancy, or zest. The Doctor knows that Catherine is good. She will never have the spirit of malice or mischievousness in her to make her lively and interesting. Thus, he hopes that cleverness will prevent her turning out insipid or dull.

(Word from Context)

31. B. One feels displeasure at (begrudges) having spent money on a *trivial* (unimportant, insignificant) book.

Remember to watch for signal words that link one part of the sentence to another. The presence of *and* linking two items in a series indicates that the missing word may be a synonym or near-synonym for the other linked word. In this case, *trivial* is a near-synonym for the negative term *inane* (lacking sense; silly).

Note that you are looking for a word with negative associations. Therefore, you can eliminate any word with positive ones. Choices A, C, D, and E all have positive associations. Only Choice B can be correct.

(Examples)

32. B. A democracy's servants should be *accountable* (answerable) to the public for what they do.

Note that the wording "tension between X . . . and Y" indicates that the two linked phrases contrast in some respect.

(Contrast Pattern)

33. C. Because the townspeople were similar in background and were impatient with legal nonsense, we were hopeful (optimistic) the town meeting would quickly come to an agreement or *consensus*.
Remember, watch for signal words that link one part of the sentence to another. The use of "Given" in the opening phrase is a cause signal.
Word Parts Clue: *Con-* means together. *Sens* or *sent* means think or feel. People who think together can easily come to a *consensus*, a general accord.

(Cause and Effect Signal)

34. C. He sold a cure-all or *panacea* which he claimed was good for *alleviating* or relieving all sorts of illnesses.
Remember, in double-blank sentences, go through the answer choices, testing the *first* words in each choice and eliminating those that don't fit. You can immediately eliminate Choice D.

(Definition)

35. B. Knowledge of the extent of the problem has increased. Therefore, awareness of how much more there is to learn also has increased or been *heightened*. This heightened awareness has *stimulated* or encouraged sympathetic leaders to increase the funds.
Remember, in double-blank sentences, go through the answer choices, testing the *first* words in each choice and eliminating those that don't fit. You can immediately eliminate Choices A, C, and E.

(Argument Pattern)

36. D. The *chief* is the leader of the *tribe*. The *captain* is the leader of the *team*.

(Function)

37. A. An *atlas* is a book of *maps*. An *album* is a book of *photographs*.

(Part to Whole)

38. D. A *diver* performs a *jackknife* (a special kind of dive). A *gymnast* performs a *cartwheel* (a special kind of acrobatic feat).

(Function)

39. B. A *virus* causes a *cold*. An *infection* causes *gangrene*.

Beware Eye-Catchers: Choice A is incorrect. A *serum* provides protection against *measles*. It does not cause measles.

(Cause and Effect)

40. B. An *inventory* lists *merchandise* or assets. A *roster* lists *members* (the *roster* of the New York Mets lists team members, for example).

(Defining Characteristic)

41. A. *Interest* is a less intense feeling than *fascination*. *Dislike* is a less intense feeling than *abhorrence* (loathing, detestation).

(Degree of Intensity)

42. D. A *renegade* denies or turns away from his *faith*. A *maverick* (an unbranded calf who doesn't follow its mother; a member of a group who refuses to conform) turns away from the *herd*.

(Person and Thing Avoided)

43. D. *Indigent* (poor, needy) is the opposite of rich or *wealthy*. *Frivolous* (light-minded, superficial) is the opposite of *serious*.

(Antonyms)

44. C. Something *wan* (pale) is lacking in *color*. Something *insipid* (tasteless, uninteresting) is lacking in *flavor*.

(Antonym Variant)

45. B. A *maze* (an intricate pattern of interconnecting and branching passages) is by definition *labyrinthine* or mazelike. *Treachery* (treason or betrayal of trust) is by definition *perfidious* (deceitful; treacherous).

(Definition)

Section 4   Test of Standard Written English

1. B. Error in diction. *Affect* is a verb and should not be used in place of *effect*.

2. A. Error in case. The subject of an infinitive (*to be*) should be in the objective case. Therefore, change *commissioner and she* to *commissioner and her*.

3. E. Sentence is correct.

4. E. Sentence is correct.

5. C. Error in diction. There is no such verb as *enthuse*. Change *enthused* to *enthusiastic*.

6. C.   Error in tense. Change *had shot* to *shot*.

7. A.   Error in diction. Use *irritated* instead of *aggravated*.

8. A.   Incorrect correlative conjunction. Change *neither . . . or* to *neither . . . nor*.

9. C.   Error in diction. Change *incredulous* to *incredible*.

10. C.   Error in tense. Change *had broke* to *had broken*.

11. C.   Error in diction. Change *council* to *counsel*.

12. C.   Error in agreement. The subject, *Ann Landers*, is singular; the verb should be singular—*is*.

13. A.   Error in case. The preposition *between* requires the objective case. Therefore, change *you and I* to *you and me*.

14. D.   Error in diction. Issues are *decided* or *settled*. The actual choice made is what is *decided upon*. Delete *upon*.

15. E.   Sentence is correct.

16. E.   Sentence is correct.

17. C.   Error in agreement. The subject, *general*, is singular; the verb should be singular—*seems*.

18. A.   Error in case. The possessive pronoun precedes a gerund. Change *him* to *his*.

19. D.   Error in tense. Change *was to be immortalized* to *was immortalized*.

20. A.   Faulty diction. Change *whether* to *if* in order to indicate a condition.

21. A.   Error in diction. Change *against* to *over*.

22. D.   Incorrect use of superlative form of adjective. *Unique* does not need *more* or *most*. Delete *most*.

23. B.   Error in agreement. The verb should agree with the compound subject *concrete and glass* rather than the predicate noun *structure*. Therefore, change *forms* to *form*.

24. A.   Error in comparison. After the comparative *other*, use the subordinating conjunction *than*.

25. A.   Error in diction. Change *principal* (meaning "chief") to *principle* (meaning "fundamental truth").

26. E.   The noun or pronoun preceding a gerund (*going*) should be in the possessive case.

27. E.   The dangling modifier is best corrected in Choice E. Choices B and D introduce an error in tense. Choice C changes the meaning of the sentence.

28. C.   Choices A and B are run-on sentences. Choices D and E are ungrammatical.

29. E.   The dangling modifier and the double negative are corrected in Choice E.

30. E.   The correct use of the subjunctive mood to indicate a condition contrary to fact is found in Choice E.

31. B.   Choice B expresses the author's meaning directly and concisely. All other choices are indirect, ungrammatical, or fail to retain the meaning of the original statement.

32. C.   *Kind* should be modified by *this* or *that*; *kinds*, by *these* or *those*.

33. C.   Parallel structure is retained in Choice C.

34. D.   This corrects the sentence fragment smoothly.

35. B.   The faulty comparison is corrected in Choice B.

36. C.   Choice C corrects the misplaced modifier and eliminates the unnecessary use of the passive voice.

37. C.   The phrase *along with his staff* is not part of the subject of the sentence. The subject is *President Reagan* (singular); the verb should be *is traveling* (singular).

38. B.   The use of the subordinating conjunction *Although* and the deletion of unnecessary words strengthen this sentence.

39. D.   Choices A, B, and C have dangling modifiers; Choice E creates a run-on sentence.

40. A.   The use of the semicolon to separate the pair of clauses is correct.

41. E.   Sentence is correct.

42. A. Error in mood. Since the past tense of the subjunctive mood expresses a condition contrary to fact, change *was* to *were*.

43. C. Error in diction. Change *continuous* to *continual*.

44. A. Error in agreement. *Memoranda* is a plural noun. Change *was* to *were*.

45. A. Misuse of pronoun. *Myself* (reflexive pronoun) should not be used in place of *I* (personal pronoun).

46. B. Incorrect idiom. Use *to* before an infinitive verb of purpose. Change *try and come* to *try to come*.

47. C. Misuse of pronoun. Change *them* (personal pronoun) to *those* (indefinite demonstrative pronoun).

48. A. Error in tense. Use the infinitive after verbs of intention, even if they are in the past tense. Change *to have gone* to *to go*.

49. C. Unnecessary switch in pronouns. Change *one* to *you*.

50. A. Dangling participle. Change to *After he had read for more*.

Section 5

1. A. $\dfrac{x}{50} = 3.6\%$

$\dfrac{x}{50} = \dfrac{3.6}{100}$

$100x = 180$

$x = 1.8$

2. E. Let x = cost of article.

Cost + Profit = Selling price

$x + (30\%)(x) = \$65$

$x + 0.3x = 65$

$10x + 3x = 650$ (multiply by 10)

$13x = 650$

$x = \$50$ (cost)

Cost + Profit = Selling price

$\$50 + (10\%)(\$50)$ = selling price

$\$50 + \$5 = \$55$

3. B. Area of frame equals area of outside rectangle minus area of picture.
Area of outside rectangle = (38)(18) or 684 sq. in.
Area of picture
= (36)(16) or 576 sq. in.
Area of frame = 684 − 576 or 108 sq. in.

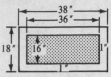

4. B. Let x = least number of votes received by the successful candidate.
$x - 1$ = maximum number of votes a defeated candidate can receive
$4(x - 1)$ or $4x - 4$ = maximum number of votes all defeated candidates can receive
$x + 4x - 4 = 356$ (total number of votes cast)

$5x = 360$

$x = 72$

Alternatively, consider that the successful candidate must get more than $\dfrac{1}{5}$ of all the votes cast. One fifth of 356 is $71\dfrac{1}{5}$. Therefore the successful candidate must receive 72 votes.

5. C. Since the sum of the measures of the angles of a triangle = 180°,

$9x + 8x + 7x = 180$

$24x = 180$

$x = 7.5°$

$\angle A$ or $8x = 8(7.5)$ or 60°

6. C. The home owner used $\dfrac{1}{2}$ of his $\dfrac{3}{4}$ of available oil.

$\dfrac{1}{2} \times \dfrac{3}{4} = \dfrac{3}{8}$

7. E. Since Mr. Rosenfeld binds 35 sets in 5 days, he binds 7 sets each day. Since there are 7 books in each set, he binds 49 books each day.

8. B. Don't take the time to do any computation. The numerator and the denominator have the same absolute value but differ in sign. Therefore the quotient is −1.

9. D. x may be 30 or 60 or 90.

10. C. 3 yd. 1 in. = 109 in.

11. C. Opposite sides of a parallelogram are congruent.

12. A. A straight line is the shortest distance between two points.

13. C.   Because the arcs are equal, ABC is an equilateral triangle. AE bisects BC (given); therefore DC is $\frac{1}{2}$ of any side of ABC.

14. A. $\dfrac{a^2 - 1}{a - 1} = \dfrac{(a + 1)(a - 1)}{(a - 1)} = a + 1$

   $a + 1 > a$

15. B. $(x + y)(x - y) = x^2 - y^2 = 100 - 25 = 75$
   $125 > 75$

16. C.   In Column A:
   $\dfrac{3}{\sqrt{3}} \cdot \dfrac{\sqrt{3}}{\sqrt{3}} = \dfrac{3\sqrt{3}}{3} = \sqrt{3}$

17. C. $x - 5 = y$
   $x = y + 5$

18. B. $7x = 35 + 7y$
   $7x - 35 = 7y$
   $x - 5 = y$
   $(x - 5) > (x - 7)$

19. D.   We may not assume any relationship between the lengths of the legs of the triangle.

20. A.   The sum of the lengths of two sides of a triangle is greater than the third side.

21. D. $a + b = 90$, but we have no information regarding the relationship of the legs of the triangle.

22. C.   The acute angles of a right triangle are complementary.

23. A. $\angle BEC$ is a right angle. Therefore
   $w + z = 90$
   Since $w + x + z + y = 360$ and $w + z = 90$,
   $x + y = 270$.

24. C.   The measure of exterior $\angle(x) = z +$ measure of $\angle BEC$.

25. C.   Since $w + z = 90$,
   $90 - z = w$ (by subtraction).

26. D. $w + z = 90$, but we have no data concerning the relative sizes of w and z.

27. C.   Let $s =$ side of square. Then
   Area of square $= s^2$
   $s^2 =$ area of triangle ABC (given)
   Therefore $AB = BC = s\sqrt{2}$
   for $s^2 = \dfrac{(s\sqrt{2})(s\sqrt{2})}{2}$
   Therefore $\dfrac{AB}{DG} = \dfrac{s\sqrt{2}}{s}$ or $\sqrt{2}$

28. C.   Let $x = CB$.
   Then $BA = 2x$ and
   $CA = 3x$
   Let $y = DE$.
   Then $EA = 2y$ and
   $DA = 3y$

   Triangle ABE is similar to triangle ADC since they have the common angle A and the including sides are in proportion as:
   $\dfrac{AE}{AD} = \dfrac{AB}{AC} = \dfrac{2}{3}$
   Also, $\dfrac{BE}{DC} = \dfrac{2}{3}$ or $\dfrac{2}{3} = \dfrac{14}{DC}$ or $\dfrac{2}{3} = \dfrac{14}{21}$
   $DC = 21$

29. A. $xy = k$
   $(7)(5) = k$ (substitution)
   $35 = k$
   $(x)(32) = k$
   $(x)(32) = 35$
   $32x = 35$
   $x - \dfrac{35}{32}$ (division by 32)

30. C. $\angle DBE = 180°$
   (a straight angle)
   $\angle GBC =$
   $180° - (79° + 39°)$
   $\angle GBC =$
   $180° - 118°$
   $\angle GBC = 62°$
   $\angle GBE =$
   $\angle GBC + \angle CBE$
   $\angle GBE = 62° + 39°$ or $101°$

31. E. $(30\%)(100) = (0.30)(100) = 30$
   $(3\%)(x) = 30$
   $0.03x = 30$
   $3x = 3000$
   $x = 1000$

32. B.   Draw AF parallel to BC.
   Extend DC to F, forming rectangle $CFAB$.

   $FA = CB = 12$
   $CF = BA = 4$
   In right triangle DFA,
   $DF = 16$, $FA = 12$
   DA (the hypotenuse) $= 20$
   Or DFA is a 3-4-5 right triangle with $FA = 4(3)$ or 12 and $DF = 4(4)$ or 16. Therefore $DA = 4(5)$ or 20.

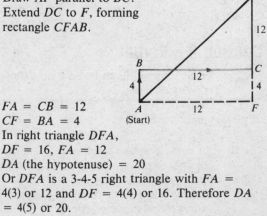

33. C. Let M be the midpoint of AB.

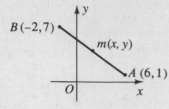

x-midpoint $= \dfrac{x_1 + x_2}{2}$

y-midpoint $= \dfrac{y_1 + y_2}{2}$

$x_{mid} = \dfrac{-2 + 6}{2} = \dfrac{4}{2} = 2$

$y_{mid} = \dfrac{7 + 1}{2} = \dfrac{8}{2} = 4$

The coordinates of the midpoint of AB are (2, 4).

34. A. The total amount of money invested is $10,000. The teacher who invested the least amount of money invested $\dfrac{\$2000}{\$10,000}$ or $\dfrac{1}{5}$ of the investment. Since she is entitled to $\dfrac{1}{5}$ of the profit, her profit will be $\dfrac{1}{5}$ of $960 or $192.

35. D. To eliminate z, solve for z in one equation and substitute in the other given equation.

$y = 2z + 3$

$y - 3 = 2z$

$\dfrac{y - 3}{2} = z$

Substitute: $x = 4\left(\dfrac{y - 3}{2}\right)^2$

$x = \cancel{4}\left(\dfrac{y - 3}{\cancel{2}}\right)\left(\dfrac{y - 3}{\cancel{2}}\right)$

$x = (y - 3)^2$

Section 6   Verbal

1. A. To be *punctual* is to be on time. Its opposite is *tardy* or late.
Context Clue: "Be punctual for your appointment."

2. B. To *enclose* means to close in or surround; to confine; to place in a parcel or envelope. Its opposite is to *take out*.
Context Clue: "Please enclose a self-addressed stamped envelope."

3. D. *Maternal* means motherly. Its opposite is *unmotherly*.
Context Clue: "That woman lacks all natural maternal feelings!"

4. B. To *embolden* someone is to make that person brave. Its antonym is to *frighten*.
Look for words you know hidden within larger words. In *embolden* you can spot *bold*, brave.

5. D. *Cosmopolitan* means sophisticated, polished, worldly. Its opposite is limited in viewpoint or *provincial*.
Remember, break down unfamiliar words into recognizable parts.
Word Parts Clue: *Cosm-* means world. *Cosmopolitan* means worldly.

6. A. To *uphold* is to support or defend. Its opposite is to *oppose*.
Beware Eye-Catchers: Choice B is incorrect. Don't let the presence of *up-* in uphold attract your attention to *down* in tie down.
Context Clue: Think of "uphold the law."

7. A. *Adulteration* means debasement or corruption; the addition of inferior ingredients to a product. Its opposite is *purification* or cleansing.
Context Clue: Think of "criminal adulteration of food."

8. B. *Wax* means to grow larger. Its opposite is to *grow smaller* or wane.
Remember to consider secondary meanings of the capitalized word as well as its primary meaning. *Wax* here does not refer to polishing.
Context Clue: "The child waxed tall."

9. B. To *rant* is to speak wildly or violently, to rave. Its opposite is to *speak calmly*.
Context Clue: Think of "rant and rave."

10. A. To *pare* is to trim off excess, to reduce or diminish. Its opposite is to increase or *augment*.
Context Clue: Think of having to "pare expenses" or "pare potatoes."

11. D. *Palatable* comes from the word *palate*, the part of your mouth that is concerned with taste. *Palatable* means agreeable to the palate. Its opposite is *distasteful*, disagreeable to the taste.
Context Clue: "The food was surprisingly palatable."

12. B. *Cupidity* means avarice or greed. Its opposite is *altruism*, unselfishness, devotion to the interests of others.

Beware Eye-Catchers: Choice A is incorrect. Cupidity is related to greed, not to lechery or lust.
Word Parts Clue: *Altr-* means other. Altruism is concern for others.

13. E. *Nefarious* means heinously, enormously wicked. Its opposite is *honorable*, noble.
Context Clue: Think of "a nefarious plot."

14. A. *Dulcet* means melodious, sweet to the ear. Its opposite is *cacophonous* or harsh-sounding.
Context Clue: Think of the musical instrument known as the *dulcimer*.
Word Parts Clue: *Caco-* means bad. *Phon-* means sound. Something cacophonous sounds bad.

15. A. *Desiccate* means dry up, deprive of moisture. Its opposite is *saturate*, to soak thoroughly.
Context Clue: Think of "desiccated like a mummy."

16. D. Before the members of Congress can go home, there must be an *adjournment* (formal closing of the session and disbanding).

(Definition)

17. C. To get to the theater without one's tickets would clearly be annoying or *vexatious*.
Note how the meaning of *vexatious* is made vivid by the concrete example of an annoying experience.

(Examples)

18. B. Someone fearful of public exposure doesn't want to clear things up or settle them; he wants to confuse or *becloud* the issue. One way to do so is to bring up *irrelevant* or unrelated matters.
Note that "Fearful of public exposure" here is used as a short way of saying "*Because* he was fearful of public exposure."
Remember, in double-blank sentences, go through the answer choices, testing the *first* words in each choice and eliminating those that don't fit. You can immediately eliminate Choice C.

(Argument Pattern)

19. C. An *affected* (artificially assumed; unnatural) manner of speech would be a likely quality to criticize in an actress.
The key phrase here is "Her critics maintained . . ." A person's critics generally make negative remarks; therefore, you can assume that the missing word is a negative term. Choices A, B, and E all are positive terms and therefore you can eliminate them.

20. A. Strindberg's disagreeableness *destroyed* his marriages and *alienated* or made strangers out of his friends.
Remember, in double-blank sentences, go through the answer choices, testing the *first* words in each choice and eliminating those that don't fit.
Note that you are looking for words that describe the consequences or effects of disagreeable behavior. These would be words with negative associations. Therefore, you can eliminate any words with positive ones.
Choices C and D have positive associations. Only Choices A, B, or E can be correct.

(Argument Pattern)

21. E. The opening sentence of the passage states that Dickens says very little about the evils of child labor. The author is pointing out the lack of strong political and social consciousness as a *weakness* in Dickens' social criticism.
Choice A is incorrect. The author is concerned with the sufferings of *all* child laborers, not merely with those of the young Dickens.
Choice B is incorrect. The passage is discussing Dickens' reactions to trade unionism; trade unionism itself is not the subject.
Choice C is incorrect. The passage mentions the novels only insofar as they serve to illustrate Dickens' views on social and political issues.
Choice D is incorrect. The author scarcely describes working conditions at all.

(Main Idea)

22. D. The author says that "there is no sign" that Dickens is troubled by Mealy Potatoes' fate. Dickens thus apparently accepts the institution of child labor for "rough boys." Only quick, gifted children are to be spared.
Choice A is incorrect. Trade unionism has nothing to do with Mealy Potatoes' fate.
Choice B is incorrect. The author is not complimenting Dickens.
Choice C is incorrect. Nothing in the passage suggests Mealy Potatoes was a gifted child.
Choice E is incorrect. Dickens apparently lacks sympathy for Mealy Potatoes; the author says there is nothing to suggest Dickens was troubled by the boy's fate.

(Specific Details)

23. A. Choice A is correct. Dickens was bitter and filled with *resentment* that he had suffered in this way.
Choice B is incorrect. Dickens felt no wistful yearning or *nostalgia* for these particular scenes from his childhood.

Choice C is incorrect. Dickens' feelings were stronger than mere irritation or *annoyance*.
Choice D is incorrect. Dickens' attitude had nothing to do with *skepticism* or disbelief.
Choice E is incorrect. Dickens was certainly not *enthusiastic* about his sufferings.

(Attitude/Tone)

24. B. If trade unionism and similar labor movements arise because employers are not fatherly enough, greater paternalism and *benevolence* (kindliness) on the owners' parts should cure such labor problems.
Choice A is incorrect. Lines 65–68 state "there is no sign" Dickens wanted the workers to take their destiny into their own hands. This implies that he would not have favored protest marches, even nonviolent ones.
Choices C and D are incorrect. Dickens apparently opposed apprentices' associations and similar labor organizations.
Choice E is incorrect. The passage states that Dickens disbelieved "that any good can come out of Parliament."

(Inference)

25. B. The author states that Dickens' time as a Parliamentary shorthand writer "was no doubt a disillusioning experience." This disillusionment led to his despising politics. In other words, his *familiarity* with Parliament *bred contempt*.

(Inference)

26. C. The opening sentence states that ethology and behaviorist psychology (*two differing theories*) illustrate the distinction between learning and instinct (*behavioral processes*). The discussion of these two theories that follows explains the behavioral processes.
Choice A is incorrect. The passage does not suggest that one behavioral theory is more effective than another.
Choice B is incorrect. The passage sums up current theories; it does not propose a new one in their place.
Choice D is incorrect. The passage presents Pavlov's arguments in the course of explaining behaviorist psychology; it does not dispute them.
Choice E is incorrect. The passage is concerned with learned behavior as well as instinctive or innate behavior.

(Main Idea)

27. B. In lines 15–17, the author states that Lorenz and Tinbergen were, with Frisch, the founders of ethology (the study of instinct).

Choice A is incorrect. Only Lorenz and Tinbergen are cited for their work with the egg-rolling response in geese; nothing in the passage suggests that Frisch worked with egg-rolling.
Choice C is incorrect. It is unsupported by the passage.
Choice D is incorrect. Behaviorists, not ethologists, are cited as favoring strictly controlled conditions (line 44–47).
Choice E is incorrect. Nothing in the passage suggests the ethologists have invalidated the behaviorists' approach.

(Specific Details)

28. A. What is remarkable about the goose's response is that "at first glance (it) might seem to be a thoughtful solution to a problem." This suggests that the appearance of *purpose and intelligence* is what makes the act remarkable or noteworthy.
Choice B is incorrect. This is an aspect of the goose's response; it is not what makes the goose's response noteworthy. It is not remarkable for an egg-rolling response to be triggered by an egg.
Choice C is incorrect. The egg-rolling response supports ethological theories; it does not refute or disprove them.
Choice D is incorrect. This is an aspect of the goose's response, not what makes the goose's response noteworthy.
Choice E is incorrect. It is both inaccurate factually (the response lasts longer than four weeks) and not an aspect of the goose's response that would be noteworthy.
Remember, when asked to make inferences, base your answers on what the passage implies, not what it states directly.

(Inference)

29. E. Choice E is correct. You can arrive at it by the process of elimination.
Statement I is true. Behaviorists such as Pavlov worked with the unconditioned responses of animals. Therefore, you can eliminate Choices B and C.
Statement II is untrue. Imprinting is a term current among ethologists, not behaviorists (line 10–12). Therefore, you can eliminate Choice D.
Statement III is true. Behaviorists assume animals act in order to obtain rewards or avoid punishments (*shun negative stimuli*). Therefore, you can eliminate Choice A.
Only Choice E is left. It is the correct answer.

(Specific Details)

30. E. The author does *not* settle any arguments; he merely presents differing theories without

attempting to resolve their differences.
Choice A is incorrect. The author defines terms throughout the entire passage.
Choice B is incorrect. The author points out equivalents (*functional parallels*) between the two systems.
Choice C is incorrect. The author refers to experimental studies involving both classical and operant conditioning.
Choice D is incorrect. The author uses the example of beer bottles to illustrate what sort of convex objects evoke the egg-rolling response from geese (lines 29–31).

(Technique)

31. **A.** Townspeople would be most likely to suspect an *itinerant* or migrant worker, a person without roots in the town, of committing a theft.
Note that you are looking for a word with negative associations. Therefore, you can eliminate any word with positive ones. Choices C, D, and E all have positive associations. Only Choice A or Choice B can be correct.

32. **E.** Building new houses would be a solution for a *shortage* or scarcity of houses. Such a program might logically involve Federal subsidies (financial grants) to cut or *reduce* the buyer's cost.
Remember, in double-blank sentences, go through the answer choices, testing the *first* words in each choice and eliminating those that don't fit. You can immediately eliminate Choices B and C.

33. **B.** To be *relegated* to obscurity (banished, put out of sight) is to be counted a person of no importance at all. For these black writers to be *rediscovered* today, they must first have gone through a period of obscurity.
Note that the "originally X . . . today Y" structure sets up a contrast between the missing word and *rediscovered*. "Relegated to obscurity" is a set phrase or cliché for being banished to oblivion or *forgotten*.

(Contrast Pattern)

34. **C.** Judges are supposed to instruct the jury about the laws relevant to the case; they are not supposed to *influence* the jury in their decision about the facts of the case. However, a person's tone of voice can convey a great deal of information about his or her feelings. The judge does not have to say anything overtly *prejudicial* (damaging; leading to premature judgment); the judge's opinions can still get across.
Note that the "Even when X does not . . . Y

does" structure sets up a contrast between the two clauses.

(Contrast Pattern)

35. **B.** His ambition was so great that nothing he had satisfied him; nothing seemed great enough to match his ambition's intensity or strength. In other words, nothing seemed *adequate to* his ambition's intensity or *fervor*.
Note that the "So . . . that" structure signals cause and effect. *Because* his ambition for worldly success was so great, no amount of worldly goods was enough for him.

(Argument Pattern)

36. **E.** *Caution* can prevent an *accident*. *Radar* can prevent a *collision* (crash).

(Function)

37. **B.** A *story* (horizontal floor) is part of a *building*. A *rung* (horizontal bar) is part of a *ladder*. Remember, consider secondary meanings of the capitalized words as well as their primary meanings.

(Part to Whole)

38. **B.** A *scalpel* is used by a *surgeon* for cutting. A *cleaver* is used by a *butcher* for cutting. Remember, if more than one answer appears to fit the relationship in your sentence, look for a narrower approach. "A surgeon uses a scalpel" is too broad a framework. It would fit Choices A, C, E, and possibly even D.

(Worker and Tool)

39. **C.** A *rudder* is used to *steer* (direct) a boat. A *paddle* is used to *row* a boat.

(Function)

40. **A.** Something *insipid* (tasteless, uninteresting) lacks *piquancy* (tartness, sharpness to the palate). Someone *timid* (fearful, shy) lacks *boldness*.

(Antonym Variant)

41. **A.** One of the *virtues* (forms of moral excellence) is *integrity* (honesty). One of the *vices* (forms of wickedness) is *sloth* (indolence; extreme laziness).

(Class and Member)

42. **D.** Someone *timorous* (fearful) *fears*. Someone *compassionate* (sympathetic; full of pity) *pities*.

(Synonym Variant)

43. D. An *epigram* (short, witty saying) is by definition *concise* (brief). An *epic* (long narrative poem) is by definition *lengthy*.

Choice A is incorrect. A *riddle* is by definition mysterious or puzzling. It is not necessarily silly or *inane*.

Choice B is incorrect. A *fable* (story illustrating a moral truth) is by definition illustrative or moral. It is not necessarily *ancient*. Modern writers use the fable form.

Choice C is incorrect. A *humorous anecdote* is just one possible type of short human interest narrative.

Choice E is incorrect. An *epitaph* (inscription on a tomb) is not by definition *moral*.

(Defining Characteristic)

44. B. Whenever a word ends in *-ology*, it's most likely the name of a field of study. *Entomology* is the study of *insects*. *Toxicology* is the study of *poisons*.

(Definition)

45. B. *Protean* (capable of change; exceedingly variable) is the opposite of *immutable*, unable to change, unchanging. *Pacific* (peaceful) is the opposite of *bellicose* (warlike; quarrelsome).

Word Parts Clue: *Im-* means not. *Mut-* means change. *Immutable* means not able to change.

Word History: The sea god Proteus could change into different shapes. *Protean* means capable of change.

If you have two answer choices that belong to the same analogy type, both cannot be the correct answer. If two answer choices both belong to the Antonym, Synonyms, or Degree of Intensity types, *neither* can be the correct answer. Choice A (*specious* and *plausible*) and Choice C (*deleterious* and *harmful*) are both synonym pairs. Neither can be correct.

(Antonyms)

Answer Sheet–Test 6

Start with number 1 for each new section. If a section has fewer than 50 questions, leave the extra spaces blank.

Section 1

1. Ⓐ Ⓑ Ⓒ Ⓓ Ⓔ	11. Ⓐ Ⓑ Ⓒ Ⓓ Ⓔ	21. Ⓐ Ⓑ Ⓒ Ⓓ Ⓔ	31. Ⓐ Ⓑ Ⓒ Ⓓ Ⓔ	41. Ⓐ Ⓑ Ⓒ Ⓓ Ⓔ
2. Ⓐ Ⓑ Ⓒ Ⓓ Ⓔ	12. Ⓐ Ⓑ Ⓒ Ⓓ Ⓔ	22. Ⓐ Ⓑ Ⓒ Ⓓ Ⓔ	32. Ⓐ Ⓑ Ⓒ Ⓓ Ⓔ	42. Ⓐ Ⓑ Ⓒ Ⓓ Ⓔ
3. Ⓐ Ⓑ Ⓒ Ⓓ Ⓔ	13. Ⓐ Ⓑ Ⓒ Ⓓ Ⓔ	23. Ⓐ Ⓑ Ⓒ Ⓓ Ⓔ	33. Ⓐ Ⓑ Ⓒ Ⓓ Ⓔ	43. Ⓐ Ⓑ Ⓒ Ⓓ Ⓔ
4. Ⓐ Ⓑ Ⓒ Ⓓ Ⓔ	14. Ⓐ Ⓑ Ⓒ Ⓓ Ⓔ	24. Ⓐ Ⓑ Ⓒ Ⓓ Ⓔ	34. Ⓐ Ⓑ Ⓒ Ⓓ Ⓔ	44. Ⓐ Ⓑ Ⓒ Ⓓ Ⓔ
5. Ⓐ Ⓑ Ⓒ Ⓓ Ⓔ	15. Ⓐ Ⓑ Ⓒ Ⓓ Ⓔ	25. Ⓐ Ⓑ Ⓒ Ⓓ Ⓔ	35. Ⓐ Ⓑ Ⓒ Ⓓ Ⓔ	45. Ⓐ Ⓑ Ⓒ Ⓓ Ⓔ
6. Ⓐ Ⓑ Ⓒ Ⓓ Ⓔ	16. Ⓐ Ⓑ Ⓒ Ⓓ Ⓔ	26. Ⓐ Ⓑ Ⓒ Ⓓ Ⓔ	36. Ⓐ Ⓑ Ⓒ Ⓓ Ⓔ	46. Ⓐ Ⓑ Ⓒ Ⓓ Ⓔ
7. Ⓐ Ⓑ Ⓒ Ⓓ Ⓔ	17. Ⓐ Ⓑ Ⓒ Ⓓ Ⓔ	27. Ⓐ Ⓑ Ⓒ Ⓓ Ⓔ	37. Ⓐ Ⓑ Ⓒ Ⓓ Ⓔ	47. Ⓐ Ⓑ Ⓒ Ⓓ Ⓔ
8. Ⓐ Ⓑ Ⓒ Ⓓ Ⓔ	18. Ⓐ Ⓑ Ⓒ Ⓓ Ⓔ	28. Ⓐ Ⓑ Ⓒ Ⓓ Ⓔ	38. Ⓐ Ⓑ Ⓒ Ⓓ Ⓔ	48. Ⓐ Ⓑ Ⓒ Ⓓ Ⓔ
9. Ⓐ Ⓑ Ⓒ Ⓓ Ⓔ	19. Ⓐ Ⓑ Ⓒ Ⓓ Ⓔ	29. Ⓐ Ⓑ Ⓒ Ⓓ Ⓔ	39. Ⓐ Ⓑ Ⓒ Ⓓ Ⓔ	49. Ⓐ Ⓑ Ⓒ Ⓓ Ⓔ
10. Ⓐ Ⓑ Ⓒ Ⓓ Ⓔ	20. Ⓐ Ⓑ Ⓒ Ⓓ Ⓔ	30. Ⓐ Ⓑ Ⓒ Ⓓ Ⓔ	40. Ⓐ Ⓑ Ⓒ Ⓓ Ⓔ	50. Ⓐ Ⓑ Ⓒ Ⓓ Ⓔ

Section 2

1. Ⓐ Ⓑ Ⓒ Ⓓ Ⓔ	11. Ⓐ Ⓑ Ⓒ Ⓓ Ⓔ	21. Ⓐ Ⓑ Ⓒ Ⓓ Ⓔ	31. Ⓐ Ⓑ Ⓒ Ⓓ Ⓔ	41. Ⓐ Ⓑ Ⓒ Ⓓ Ⓔ
2. Ⓐ Ⓑ Ⓒ Ⓓ Ⓔ	12. Ⓐ Ⓑ Ⓒ Ⓓ Ⓔ	22. Ⓐ Ⓑ Ⓒ Ⓓ Ⓔ	32. Ⓐ Ⓑ Ⓒ Ⓓ Ⓔ	42. Ⓐ Ⓑ Ⓒ Ⓓ Ⓔ
3. Ⓐ Ⓑ Ⓒ Ⓓ Ⓔ	13. Ⓐ Ⓑ Ⓒ Ⓓ Ⓔ	23. Ⓐ Ⓑ Ⓒ Ⓓ Ⓔ	33. Ⓐ Ⓑ Ⓒ Ⓓ Ⓔ	43. Ⓐ Ⓑ Ⓒ Ⓓ Ⓔ
4. Ⓐ Ⓑ Ⓒ Ⓓ Ⓔ	14. Ⓐ Ⓑ Ⓒ Ⓓ Ⓔ	24. Ⓐ Ⓑ Ⓒ Ⓓ Ⓔ	34. Ⓐ Ⓑ Ⓒ Ⓓ Ⓔ	44. Ⓐ Ⓑ Ⓒ Ⓓ Ⓔ
5. Ⓐ Ⓑ Ⓒ Ⓓ Ⓔ	15. Ⓐ Ⓑ Ⓒ Ⓓ Ⓔ	25. Ⓐ Ⓑ Ⓒ Ⓓ Ⓔ	35. Ⓐ Ⓑ Ⓒ Ⓓ Ⓔ	45. Ⓐ Ⓑ Ⓒ Ⓓ Ⓔ
6. Ⓐ Ⓑ Ⓒ Ⓓ Ⓔ	16. Ⓐ Ⓑ Ⓒ Ⓓ Ⓔ	26. Ⓐ Ⓑ Ⓒ Ⓓ Ⓔ	36. Ⓐ Ⓑ Ⓒ Ⓓ Ⓔ	46. Ⓐ Ⓑ Ⓒ Ⓓ Ⓔ
7. Ⓐ Ⓑ Ⓒ Ⓓ Ⓔ	17. Ⓐ Ⓑ Ⓒ Ⓓ Ⓔ	27. Ⓐ Ⓑ Ⓒ Ⓓ Ⓔ	37. Ⓐ Ⓑ Ⓒ Ⓓ Ⓔ	47. Ⓐ Ⓑ Ⓒ Ⓓ Ⓔ
8. Ⓐ Ⓑ Ⓒ Ⓓ Ⓔ	18. Ⓐ Ⓑ Ⓒ Ⓓ Ⓔ	28. Ⓐ Ⓑ Ⓒ Ⓓ Ⓔ	38. Ⓐ Ⓑ Ⓒ Ⓓ Ⓔ	48. Ⓐ Ⓑ Ⓒ Ⓓ Ⓔ
9. Ⓐ Ⓑ Ⓒ Ⓓ Ⓔ	19. Ⓐ Ⓑ Ⓒ Ⓓ Ⓔ	29. Ⓐ Ⓑ Ⓒ Ⓓ Ⓔ	39. Ⓐ Ⓑ Ⓒ Ⓓ Ⓔ	49. Ⓐ Ⓑ Ⓒ Ⓓ Ⓔ
10. Ⓐ Ⓑ Ⓒ Ⓓ Ⓔ	20. Ⓐ Ⓑ Ⓒ Ⓓ Ⓔ	30. Ⓐ Ⓑ Ⓒ Ⓓ Ⓔ	40. Ⓐ Ⓑ Ⓒ Ⓓ Ⓔ	50. Ⓐ Ⓑ Ⓒ Ⓓ Ⓔ

Section 3

1. Ⓐ Ⓑ Ⓒ Ⓓ Ⓔ	11. Ⓐ Ⓑ Ⓒ Ⓓ Ⓔ	21. Ⓐ Ⓑ Ⓒ Ⓓ Ⓔ	31. Ⓐ Ⓑ Ⓒ Ⓓ Ⓔ	41. Ⓐ Ⓑ Ⓒ Ⓓ Ⓔ
2. Ⓐ Ⓑ Ⓒ Ⓓ Ⓔ	12. Ⓐ Ⓑ Ⓒ Ⓓ Ⓔ	22. Ⓐ Ⓑ Ⓒ Ⓓ Ⓔ	32. Ⓐ Ⓑ Ⓒ Ⓓ Ⓔ	42. Ⓐ Ⓑ Ⓒ Ⓓ Ⓔ
3. Ⓐ Ⓑ Ⓒ Ⓓ Ⓔ	13. Ⓐ Ⓑ Ⓒ Ⓓ Ⓔ	23. Ⓐ Ⓑ Ⓒ Ⓓ Ⓔ	33. Ⓐ Ⓑ Ⓒ Ⓓ Ⓔ	43. Ⓐ Ⓑ Ⓒ Ⓓ Ⓔ
4. Ⓐ Ⓑ Ⓒ Ⓓ Ⓔ	14. Ⓐ Ⓑ Ⓒ Ⓓ Ⓔ	24. Ⓐ Ⓑ Ⓒ Ⓓ Ⓔ	34. Ⓐ Ⓑ Ⓒ Ⓓ Ⓔ	44. Ⓐ Ⓑ Ⓒ Ⓓ Ⓔ
5. Ⓐ Ⓑ Ⓒ Ⓓ Ⓔ	15. Ⓐ Ⓑ Ⓒ Ⓓ Ⓔ	25. Ⓐ Ⓑ Ⓒ Ⓓ Ⓔ	35. Ⓐ Ⓑ Ⓒ Ⓓ Ⓔ	45. Ⓐ Ⓑ Ⓒ Ⓓ Ⓔ
6. Ⓐ Ⓑ Ⓒ Ⓓ Ⓔ	16. Ⓐ Ⓑ Ⓒ Ⓓ Ⓔ	26. Ⓐ Ⓑ Ⓒ Ⓓ Ⓔ	36. Ⓐ Ⓑ Ⓒ Ⓓ Ⓔ	46. Ⓐ Ⓑ Ⓒ Ⓓ Ⓔ
7. Ⓐ Ⓑ Ⓒ Ⓓ Ⓔ	17. Ⓐ Ⓑ Ⓒ Ⓓ Ⓔ	27. Ⓐ Ⓑ Ⓒ Ⓓ Ⓔ	37. Ⓐ Ⓑ Ⓒ Ⓓ Ⓔ	47. Ⓐ Ⓑ Ⓒ Ⓓ Ⓔ
8. Ⓐ Ⓑ Ⓒ Ⓓ Ⓔ	18. Ⓐ Ⓑ Ⓒ Ⓓ Ⓔ	28. Ⓐ Ⓑ Ⓒ Ⓓ Ⓔ	38. Ⓐ Ⓑ Ⓒ Ⓓ Ⓔ	48. Ⓐ Ⓑ Ⓒ Ⓓ Ⓔ
9. Ⓐ Ⓑ Ⓒ Ⓓ Ⓔ	19. Ⓐ Ⓑ Ⓒ Ⓓ Ⓔ	29. Ⓐ Ⓑ Ⓒ Ⓓ Ⓔ	39. Ⓐ Ⓑ Ⓒ Ⓓ Ⓔ	49. Ⓐ Ⓑ Ⓒ Ⓓ Ⓔ
10. Ⓐ Ⓑ Ⓒ Ⓓ Ⓔ	20. Ⓐ Ⓑ Ⓒ Ⓓ Ⓔ	30. Ⓐ Ⓑ Ⓒ Ⓓ Ⓔ	40. Ⓐ Ⓑ Ⓒ Ⓓ Ⓔ	50. Ⓐ Ⓑ Ⓒ Ⓓ Ⓔ

Start with number 1 for each new section. If a section has fewer than 50 questions, leave the extra spaces blank.

Section 4

1. Ⓐ Ⓑ Ⓒ Ⓓ Ⓔ	11. Ⓐ Ⓑ Ⓒ Ⓓ Ⓔ	21. Ⓐ Ⓑ Ⓒ Ⓓ Ⓔ	31. Ⓐ Ⓑ Ⓒ Ⓓ Ⓔ	41. Ⓐ Ⓑ Ⓒ Ⓓ Ⓔ
2. Ⓐ Ⓑ Ⓒ Ⓓ Ⓔ	12. Ⓐ Ⓑ Ⓒ Ⓓ Ⓔ	22. Ⓐ Ⓑ Ⓒ Ⓓ Ⓔ	32. Ⓐ Ⓑ Ⓒ Ⓓ Ⓔ	42. Ⓐ Ⓑ Ⓒ Ⓓ Ⓔ
3. Ⓐ Ⓑ Ⓒ Ⓓ Ⓔ	13. Ⓐ Ⓑ Ⓒ Ⓓ Ⓔ	23. Ⓐ Ⓑ Ⓒ Ⓓ Ⓔ	33. Ⓐ Ⓑ Ⓒ Ⓓ Ⓔ	43. Ⓐ Ⓑ Ⓒ Ⓓ Ⓔ
4. Ⓐ Ⓑ Ⓒ Ⓓ Ⓔ	14. Ⓐ Ⓑ Ⓒ Ⓓ Ⓔ	24. Ⓐ Ⓑ Ⓒ Ⓓ Ⓔ	34. Ⓐ Ⓑ Ⓒ Ⓓ Ⓔ	44. Ⓐ Ⓑ Ⓒ Ⓓ Ⓔ
5. Ⓐ Ⓑ Ⓒ Ⓓ Ⓔ	15. Ⓐ Ⓑ Ⓒ Ⓓ Ⓔ	25. Ⓐ Ⓑ Ⓒ Ⓓ Ⓔ	35. Ⓐ Ⓑ Ⓒ Ⓓ Ⓔ	45. Ⓐ Ⓑ Ⓒ Ⓓ Ⓔ
6. Ⓐ Ⓑ Ⓒ Ⓓ Ⓔ	16. Ⓐ Ⓑ Ⓒ Ⓓ Ⓔ	26. Ⓐ Ⓑ Ⓒ Ⓓ Ⓔ	36. Ⓐ Ⓑ Ⓒ Ⓓ Ⓔ	46. Ⓐ Ⓑ Ⓒ Ⓓ Ⓔ
7. Ⓐ Ⓑ Ⓒ Ⓓ Ⓔ	17. Ⓐ Ⓑ Ⓒ Ⓓ Ⓔ	27. Ⓐ Ⓑ Ⓒ Ⓓ Ⓔ	37. Ⓐ Ⓑ Ⓒ Ⓓ Ⓔ	47. Ⓐ Ⓑ Ⓒ Ⓓ Ⓔ
8. Ⓐ Ⓑ Ⓒ Ⓓ Ⓔ	18. Ⓐ Ⓑ Ⓒ Ⓓ Ⓔ	28. Ⓐ Ⓑ Ⓒ Ⓓ Ⓔ	38. Ⓐ Ⓑ Ⓒ Ⓓ Ⓔ	48. Ⓐ Ⓑ Ⓒ Ⓓ Ⓔ
9. Ⓐ Ⓑ Ⓒ Ⓓ Ⓔ	19. Ⓐ Ⓑ Ⓒ Ⓓ Ⓔ	29. Ⓐ Ⓑ Ⓒ Ⓓ Ⓔ	39. Ⓐ Ⓑ Ⓒ Ⓓ Ⓔ	49. Ⓐ Ⓑ Ⓒ Ⓓ Ⓔ
10. Ⓐ Ⓑ Ⓒ Ⓓ Ⓔ	20. Ⓐ Ⓑ Ⓒ Ⓓ Ⓔ	30. Ⓐ Ⓑ Ⓒ Ⓓ Ⓔ	40. Ⓐ Ⓑ Ⓒ Ⓓ Ⓔ	50. Ⓐ Ⓑ Ⓒ Ⓓ Ⓔ

Section 5

1. Ⓐ Ⓑ Ⓒ Ⓓ Ⓔ	11. Ⓐ Ⓑ Ⓒ Ⓓ Ⓔ	21. Ⓐ Ⓑ Ⓒ Ⓓ Ⓔ	31. Ⓐ Ⓑ Ⓒ Ⓓ Ⓔ	41. Ⓐ Ⓑ Ⓒ Ⓓ Ⓔ
2. Ⓐ Ⓑ Ⓒ Ⓓ Ⓔ	12. Ⓐ Ⓑ Ⓒ Ⓓ Ⓔ	22. Ⓐ Ⓑ Ⓒ Ⓓ Ⓔ	32. Ⓐ Ⓑ Ⓒ Ⓓ Ⓔ	42. Ⓐ Ⓑ Ⓒ Ⓓ Ⓔ
3. Ⓐ Ⓑ Ⓒ Ⓓ Ⓔ	13. Ⓐ Ⓑ Ⓒ Ⓓ Ⓔ	23. Ⓐ Ⓑ Ⓒ Ⓓ Ⓔ	33. Ⓐ Ⓑ Ⓒ Ⓓ Ⓔ	43. Ⓐ Ⓑ Ⓒ Ⓓ Ⓔ
4. Ⓐ Ⓑ Ⓒ Ⓓ Ⓔ	14. Ⓐ Ⓑ Ⓒ Ⓓ Ⓔ	24. Ⓐ Ⓑ Ⓒ Ⓓ Ⓔ	34. Ⓐ Ⓑ Ⓒ Ⓓ Ⓔ	44. Ⓐ Ⓑ Ⓒ Ⓓ Ⓔ
5. Ⓐ Ⓑ Ⓒ Ⓓ Ⓔ	15. Ⓐ Ⓑ Ⓒ Ⓓ Ⓔ	25. Ⓐ Ⓑ Ⓒ Ⓓ Ⓔ	35. Ⓐ Ⓑ Ⓒ Ⓓ Ⓔ	45. Ⓐ Ⓑ Ⓒ Ⓓ Ⓔ
6. Ⓐ Ⓑ Ⓒ Ⓓ Ⓔ	16. Ⓐ Ⓑ Ⓒ Ⓓ Ⓔ	26. Ⓐ Ⓑ Ⓒ Ⓓ Ⓔ	36. Ⓐ Ⓑ Ⓒ Ⓓ Ⓔ	46. Ⓐ Ⓑ Ⓒ Ⓓ Ⓔ
7. Ⓐ Ⓑ Ⓒ Ⓓ Ⓔ	17. Ⓐ Ⓑ Ⓒ Ⓓ Ⓔ	27. Ⓐ Ⓑ Ⓒ Ⓓ Ⓔ	37. Ⓐ Ⓑ Ⓒ Ⓓ Ⓔ	47. Ⓐ Ⓑ Ⓒ Ⓓ Ⓔ
8. Ⓐ Ⓑ Ⓒ Ⓓ Ⓔ	18. Ⓐ Ⓑ Ⓒ Ⓓ Ⓔ	28. Ⓐ Ⓑ Ⓒ Ⓓ Ⓔ	38. Ⓐ Ⓑ Ⓒ Ⓓ Ⓔ	48. Ⓐ Ⓑ Ⓒ Ⓓ Ⓔ
9. Ⓐ Ⓑ Ⓒ Ⓓ Ⓔ	19. Ⓐ Ⓑ Ⓒ Ⓓ Ⓔ	29. Ⓐ Ⓑ Ⓒ Ⓓ Ⓔ	39. Ⓐ Ⓑ Ⓒ Ⓓ Ⓔ	49. Ⓐ Ⓑ Ⓒ Ⓓ Ⓔ
10. Ⓐ Ⓑ Ⓒ Ⓓ Ⓔ	20. Ⓐ Ⓑ Ⓒ Ⓓ Ⓔ	30. Ⓐ Ⓑ Ⓒ Ⓓ Ⓔ	40. Ⓐ Ⓑ Ⓒ Ⓓ Ⓔ	50. Ⓐ Ⓑ Ⓒ Ⓓ Ⓔ

Section 6

1. Ⓐ Ⓑ Ⓒ Ⓓ Ⓔ	11. Ⓐ Ⓑ Ⓒ Ⓓ Ⓔ	21. Ⓐ Ⓑ Ⓒ Ⓓ Ⓔ	31. Ⓐ Ⓑ Ⓒ Ⓓ Ⓔ	41. Ⓐ Ⓑ Ⓒ Ⓓ Ⓔ
2. Ⓐ Ⓑ Ⓒ Ⓓ Ⓔ	12. Ⓐ Ⓑ Ⓒ Ⓓ Ⓔ	22. Ⓐ Ⓑ Ⓒ Ⓓ Ⓔ	32. Ⓐ Ⓑ Ⓒ Ⓓ Ⓔ	42. Ⓐ Ⓑ Ⓒ Ⓓ Ⓔ
3. Ⓐ Ⓑ Ⓒ Ⓓ Ⓔ	13. Ⓐ Ⓑ Ⓒ Ⓓ Ⓔ	23. Ⓐ Ⓑ Ⓒ Ⓓ Ⓔ	33. Ⓐ Ⓑ Ⓒ Ⓓ Ⓔ	43. Ⓐ Ⓑ Ⓒ Ⓓ Ⓔ
4. Ⓐ Ⓑ Ⓒ Ⓓ Ⓔ	14. Ⓐ Ⓑ Ⓒ Ⓓ Ⓔ	24. Ⓐ Ⓑ Ⓒ Ⓓ Ⓔ	34. Ⓐ Ⓑ Ⓒ Ⓓ Ⓔ	44. Ⓐ Ⓑ Ⓒ Ⓓ Ⓔ
5. Ⓐ Ⓑ Ⓒ Ⓓ Ⓔ	15. Ⓐ Ⓑ Ⓒ Ⓓ Ⓔ	25. Ⓐ Ⓑ Ⓒ Ⓓ Ⓔ	35. Ⓐ Ⓑ Ⓒ Ⓓ Ⓔ	45. Ⓐ Ⓑ Ⓒ Ⓓ Ⓔ
6. Ⓐ Ⓑ Ⓒ Ⓓ Ⓔ	16. Ⓐ Ⓑ Ⓒ Ⓓ Ⓔ	26. Ⓐ Ⓑ Ⓒ Ⓓ Ⓔ	36. Ⓐ Ⓑ Ⓒ Ⓓ Ⓔ	46. Ⓐ Ⓑ Ⓒ Ⓓ Ⓔ
7. Ⓐ Ⓑ Ⓒ Ⓓ Ⓔ	17. Ⓐ Ⓑ Ⓒ Ⓓ Ⓔ	27. Ⓐ Ⓑ Ⓒ Ⓓ Ⓔ	37. Ⓐ Ⓑ Ⓒ Ⓓ Ⓔ	47. Ⓐ Ⓑ Ⓒ Ⓓ Ⓔ
8. Ⓐ Ⓑ Ⓒ Ⓓ Ⓔ	18. Ⓐ Ⓑ Ⓒ Ⓓ Ⓔ	28. Ⓐ Ⓑ Ⓒ Ⓓ Ⓔ	38. Ⓐ Ⓑ Ⓒ Ⓓ Ⓔ	48. Ⓐ Ⓑ Ⓒ Ⓓ Ⓔ
9. Ⓐ Ⓑ Ⓒ Ⓓ Ⓔ	19. Ⓐ Ⓑ Ⓒ Ⓓ Ⓔ	29. Ⓐ Ⓑ Ⓒ Ⓓ Ⓔ	39. Ⓐ Ⓑ Ⓒ Ⓓ Ⓔ	49. Ⓐ Ⓑ Ⓒ Ⓓ Ⓔ
10. Ⓐ Ⓑ Ⓒ Ⓓ Ⓔ	20. Ⓐ Ⓑ Ⓒ Ⓓ Ⓔ	30. Ⓐ Ⓑ Ⓒ Ⓓ Ⓔ	40. Ⓐ Ⓑ Ⓒ Ⓓ Ⓔ	50. Ⓐ Ⓑ Ⓒ Ⓓ Ⓔ

Remove answer sheet by cutting on dotted line

MODEL SAT TEST 6 1 1 1 1 1 1 1

| SECTION 1 | Time—30 minutes 25 Questions | In this section solve each problem, using any available space on the page for scratchwork. Then decide which is the best of the choices given and blacken the corresponding space on the answer sheet. |

The following information is for your reference in solving some of the problems.

Circle of radius r: Area = πr^2; Circumference = $2\pi r$
The number of degrees of arc in a circle is 360.
The measure in degrees of a straight angle is 180.

Definitions of symbols:

= is equal to	$\leqq$ is less than or equal to
$\neq$ is unequal to	$\geqq$ is greater than or equal to
< is less than	$\parallel$ is parallel to
> is greater than	$\perp$ is perpendicular to

Triangle: The sum of the measures in degrees of the angles of a triangle is 180.
If $\angle CDA$ is a right angle, then

(1) area of $\triangle ABC = \dfrac{AB \times CD}{2}$

(2) $AC^2 = AD^2 + DC^2$

Note: Figures that accompany problems in this test are intended to provide information useful in solving the problems. They are drawn as accurately as possible EXCEPT when it is stated in a specific problem that its figure is not drawn to scale. All figures lie in a plane unless otherwise indicated. All numbers used are real numbers.

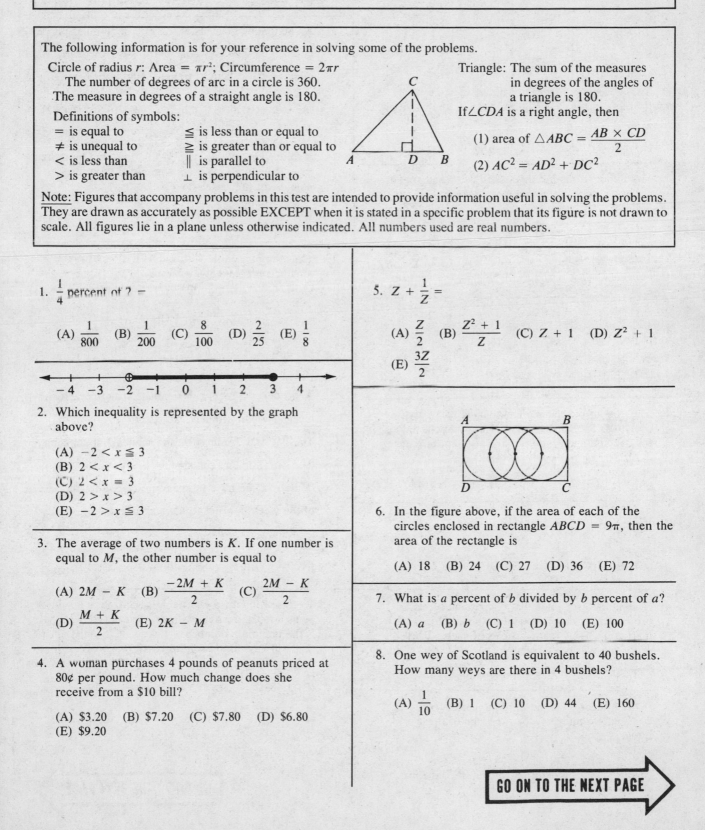

1. $\frac{1}{4}$ percent of 2 =

(A) $\dfrac{1}{800}$ (B) $\dfrac{1}{200}$ (C) $\dfrac{8}{100}$ (D) $\dfrac{2}{25}$ (E) $\dfrac{1}{8}$

2. Which inequality is represented by the graph above?

(A) $-2 < x \leqq 3$
(B) $2 < x < 3$
(C) $2 < x = 3$
(D) $2 > x > 3$
(E) $-2 > x \leqq 3$

3. The average of two numbers is K. If one number is equal to M, the other number is equal to

(A) $2M - K$ (B) $\dfrac{-2M + K}{2}$ (C) $\dfrac{2M - K}{2}$

(D) $\dfrac{M + K}{2}$ (E) $2K - M$

4. A woman purchases 4 pounds of peanuts priced at 80¢ per pound. How much change does she receive from a $10 bill?

(A) $3.20   (B) $7.20   (C) $7.80   (D) $6.80
(E) $9.20

5. $Z + \dfrac{1}{Z} =$

(A) $\dfrac{Z}{2}$ (B) $\dfrac{Z^2 + 1}{Z}$ (C) $Z + 1$ (D) $Z^2 + 1$

(E) $\dfrac{3Z}{2}$

6. In the figure above, if the area of each of the circles enclosed in rectangle $ABCD = 9\pi$, then the area of the rectangle is

(A) 18   (B) 24   (C) 27   (D) 36   (E) 72

7. What is a percent of b divided by b percent of a?

(A) a (B) b (C) 1   (D) 10   (E) 100

8. One wey of Scotland is equivalent to 40 bushels. How many weys are there in 4 bushels?

(A) $\dfrac{1}{10}$ (B) 1   (C) 10   (D) 44   (E) 160

GO ON TO THE NEXT PAGE ⟹

1 1 1 1 1 1 1 1 1 1 1

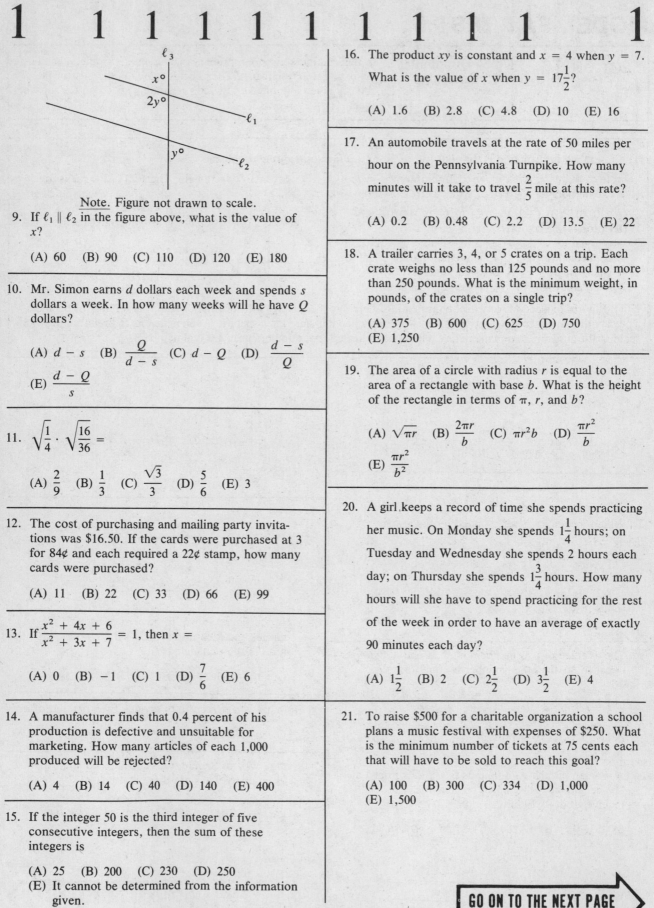

Note. Figure not drawn to scale.

9. If $\ell_1 \parallel \ell_2$ in the figure above, what is the value of x?

(A) 60 (B) 90 (C) 110 (D) 120 (E) 180

10. Mr. Simon earns d dollars each week and spends s dollars a week. In how many weeks will he have Q dollars?

(A) $d - s$ (B) $\dfrac{Q}{d - s}$ (C) $d - Q$ (D) $\dfrac{d - s}{Q}$

(E) $\dfrac{d - Q}{s}$

11. $\sqrt{\dfrac{1}{4}} \cdot \sqrt{\dfrac{16}{36}} =$

(A) $\dfrac{2}{9}$ (B) $\dfrac{1}{3}$ (C) $\dfrac{\sqrt{3}}{3}$ (D) $\dfrac{5}{6}$ (E) 3

12. The cost of purchasing and mailing party invitations was $16.50. If the cards were purchased at 3 for 84¢ and each required a 22¢ stamp, how many cards were purchased?

(A) 11 (B) 22 (C) 33 (D) 66 (E) 99

13. If $\dfrac{x^2 + 4x + 6}{x^2 + 3x + 7} = 1$, then $x =$

(A) 0 (B) -1 (C) 1 (D) $\dfrac{7}{6}$ (E) 6

14. A manufacturer finds that 0.4 percent of his production is defective and unsuitable for marketing. How many articles of each 1,000 produced will be rejected?

(A) 4 (B) 14 (C) 40 (D) 140 (E) 400

15. If the integer 50 is the third integer of five consecutive integers, then the sum of these integers is

(A) 25 (B) 200 (C) 230 (D) 250
(E) It cannot be determined from the information given.

16. The product xy is constant and $x = 4$ when $y = 7$. What is the value of x when $y = 17\dfrac{1}{2}$?

(A) 1.6 (B) 2.8 (C) 4.8 (D) 10 (E) 16

17. An automobile travels at the rate of 50 miles per hour on the Pennsylvania Turnpike. How many minutes will it take to travel $\dfrac{2}{5}$ mile at this rate?

(A) 0.2 (B) 0.48 (C) 2.2 (D) 13.5 (E) 22

18. A trailer carries 3, 4, or 5 crates on a trip. Each crate weighs no less than 125 pounds and no more than 250 pounds. What is the minimum weight, in pounds, of the crates on a single trip?

(A) 375 (B) 600 (C) 625 (D) 750
(E) 1,250

19. The area of a circle with radius r is equal to the area of a rectangle with base b. What is the height of the rectangle in terms of π, r, and b?

(A) $\sqrt{\pi r}$ (B) $\dfrac{2\pi r}{b}$ (C) $\pi r^2 b$ (D) $\dfrac{\pi r^2}{b}$

(E) $\dfrac{\pi r^2}{b^2}$

20. A girl keeps a record of time she spends practicing her music. On Monday she spends $1\dfrac{1}{4}$ hours; on Tuesday and Wednesday she spends 2 hours each day; on Thursday she spends $1\dfrac{3}{4}$ hours. How many hours will she have to spend practicing for the rest of the week in order to have an average of exactly 90 minutes each day?

(A) $1\dfrac{1}{2}$ (B) 2 (C) $2\dfrac{1}{2}$ (D) $3\dfrac{1}{2}$ (E) 4

21. To raise $500 for a charitable organization a school plans a music festival with expenses of $250. What is the minimum number of tickets at 75 cents each that will have to be sold to reach this goal?

(A) 100 (B) 300 (C) 334 (D) 1,000
(E) 1,500

GO ON TO THE NEXT PAGE

1   1   1   1   1   1   1   1   1   1   1

22. If the side of a square is increased by 150 percent, by what percent is the area increased?

(A) 125%   (B) 225%   (C) 300%   (D) 525%
(E) 625%

23. A circle whose center is the point $(-2, 6)$ is tangent to the x-axis. The coordinates of the point of tangency arc

(A) $(0, 6)$ (B) $(-2, 0)$ (C) $(0, -2)$ (D) $(6, 0)$
(E) $(-2, -2)$

24. For $K \neq 0$, let $\boxed{K}$ be defined by $\boxed{K} = K^2 + \dfrac{1}{K^2}$. Then $\boxed{2} =$

(A) 1   (B) 2   (C) 4   (D) $4\dfrac{1}{4}$ (E) $4\dfrac{1}{2}$

25. To obtain an average of exactly $\dfrac{3}{10}$, what fraction must be added to $\dfrac{3}{5}, \dfrac{1}{4}, \dfrac{1}{10}, \dfrac{1}{2}$?

(A) $\dfrac{1}{20}$ (B) $\dfrac{2}{3}$ (C) $\dfrac{6}{5}$ (D) $\dfrac{29}{20}$ (E) $\dfrac{3}{2}$

IF YOU FINISH BEFORE TIME IS CALLED, YOU MAY CHECK YOUR WORK ON THIS SECTION ONLY. DO NOT WORK ON ANY OTHER SECTION IN THE TEST.   **S T O P**

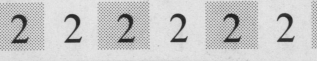

SECTION 2   Time—30 minutes   The questions in this section measure skills that are important to
50 Questions   writing well. In particular, they test your ability to recognize and
use language that is clear, effective, and correct according to the
requirements of standard written English, the kind of English
found in most college textbooks.

<u>Directions:</u> The following sentences contain problems in grammar, usage, diction (choice of words), and idiom.

     Some sentences are correct.
     No sentence contains more than one error.

You will find that the error, if there is one, is underlined and lettered. Assume that elements of the sentence that are not underlined are correct and cannot be changed. In choosing answers, follow the requirements of standard written English.

If there is an error, select the <u>one underlined part</u> that must be changed to make the sentence correct and blacken the corresponding space on your answer sheet.

If there is no error, blacken answer space Ⓔ.

EXAMPLE:
     The region has a climate <u>so severe that</u> plants
                       A

     <u>growing there</u> rarely <u>had been</u> more than twelve
         B   C

     inches <u>high.</u> <u>No error</u>
          D   E

SAMPLE ANSWER
Ⓐ Ⓑ ● Ⓓ Ⓔ

---

1. <u>As</u> <u>some of</u> the conglomerates gain more power,
   A   B
the legal codes <u>regarding</u> bankruptcy and
            C
monopoly <u>will need</u> further consideration. <u>No error</u>
       D   E

2. In 1777, the Second Continental Congress

<u>has adopted</u> a resolution <u>to designate</u> the design for
   A   B
the American flag, <u>but</u> no flags were issued <u>until</u>
             C   D
1783. <u>No error</u>
      E

3. The Joneses moved to Arizona <u>because</u> <u>they</u>
                       A   B
thought the climate in that state <u>was</u> very
                       C
<u>healthful.</u> <u>No error</u>
   D   E

4. He <u>dashed into</u> the burning building, <u>irregardless</u> of
      A   B
the risk <u>involved</u>, to warn the <u>sleeping occupants</u>.
         C   D
<u>No error</u>
   E

5. <u>According to</u> Ms. Lynch's portfolio, <u>there</u> is little
     A   B
doubt that she and her staff <u>is</u> <u>eminently qualified</u>
                     C   D
for the assignment. <u>No error</u>
                E

6. Neither the Republican members of the committee

<u>who</u> supported the proposed legislation <u>or</u> the
   A   B
Democratic members who opposed it controlled a

<u>clear majority</u>; the votes of the independents <u>were</u>
   C   D
crucial. <u>No error</u>
        E

7. <u>No one</u> can predict <u>what</u> the <u>affect</u> of the Iran–
   A   B   C
Contra disclosures <u>will be</u> on American politics in
               D
the near future. <u>No error</u>
             E

GO ON TO THE NEXT PAGE

2   2 2 2 2 2 2 2 2 2   2

8. <u>In order to</u> give adequate attention to all students,
      A

   many teachers <u>prefer</u> team teaching, <u>which</u> divides
              B   C

   students according to <u>his and her</u> abilities.
                     D

   <u>No error</u>
     E

9. I was <u>irritated by</u> <u>you</u> coming into the room <u>as</u> you
          A   B   C

   did—<u>shouting</u> and screaming. <u>No error</u>
        D   E

10. He <u>has lain</u> down his book and is sleeping; <u>reading</u>
       A   B

    in a <u>dimly lit</u> room can be <u>very</u> tiring. <u>No error</u>
        C   D   E

11. He worked <u>very hard</u> in order <u>to provide</u> for <u>their</u>
           A   B   C

    family's comfort <u>and</u> his children's educations.
                 D

    <u>No error</u>
      E

12. That <u>kind of a</u> compromise is repugnant to me
         A

    <u>because</u> <u>it</u> violates the basic <u>principles</u> of our
      B   C   D

    party. <u>No error</u>
         E

13. Just <u>like</u> prehistoric man, some <u>groups of</u>
       A   B

    southwestern Indians <u>have dwelled</u> in caves along
                     C

    steep, rocky ledges. <u>No error</u>
       D   E

14. I <u>find</u> that sculpture <u>more unusual</u> <u>than</u> any of the
      A   B   C

    other sculptures exhibited <u>during</u> this special
                      D

    exhibit. <u>No error</u>
          E

15. <u>One</u> of the basic economic reactions is <u>that</u> as
     A   B

    bond prices fall, stock prices <u>rise</u>, and
                     C

    <u>an increase in interest rates</u>. <u>No error</u>
          D   E

16. <u>Some of</u> the major networks <u>have created</u>
      A   B

    <u>special prepared</u> news stories about life on city
        C

    streets <u>to publicize</u> the plight of the homeless.
            D

    <u>No error</u>
      E

17. <u>Some women</u> have made a <u>clear-cut choice</u>
       A   B

    between a career and motherhood; others have

    been creating a <u>balance</u> between the two. <u>No error</u>
      C   D   E

18. The renter of the car <u>initialed</u> the clause in the
                  A

    contract <u>to show</u> that he was <u>aware</u> that he
           B   C

    <u>was liable</u> for the first fifty dollars of any damages
      D

    to the automobile. <u>No error</u>
             E

19. The population explosion, <u>rather</u> unexpected
                     A

    <u>according to</u> educators, <u>have caught</u> them at a
       B   C

    disadvantage with <u>a dearth of</u> classrooms.
                 D

    <u>No error</u>
      E

20. For such a long trip, someone should <u>have chosen</u>
                           A

    a different bus line, <u>for</u> this bus has <u>fewer comforts</u>
              B   C

    then any of the others. <u>No error</u>
     D   E

GO ON TO THE NEXT PAGE

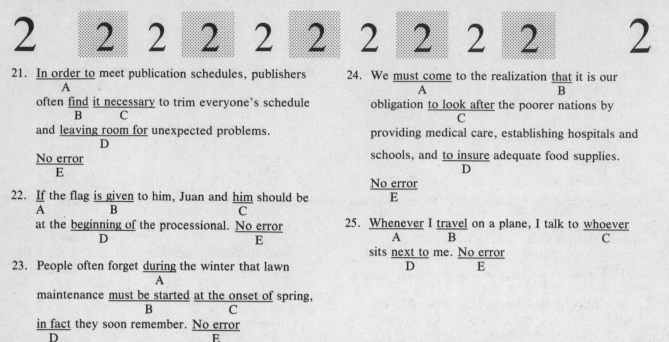

21. In order to meet publication schedules, publishers
      A
    often find it necessary to trim everyone's schedule
         B   C
    and leaving room for unexpected problems.
                D
    No error
      E

22. If the flag is given to him, Juan and him should be
      A   B   C
    at the beginning of the processional. No error
             D   E

23. People often forget during the winter that lawn
                          A
    maintenance must be started at the onset of spring,
                    B   C
    in fact they soon remember. No error
      D   E

24. We must come to the realization that it is our
        A   B
    obligation to look after the poorer nations by
                C
    providing medical care, establishing hospitals and
    schools, and to insure adequate food supplies.
                        D
    No error
      E

25. Whenever I travel on a plane, I talk to whoever
      A   B   C
    sits next to me. No error
          D   E

Directions: In each of the following sentences, some part or all of the sentence is underlined. Below each sentence you will find five ways of phrasing the underlined part. Select the answer that produces the most effective sentence, one that is clear and exact, without awkwardness or ambiguity, and blacken the corresponding space on your answer sheet. In choosing answers, follow the requirements of standard written English. Choose the answer that best expresses the meaning of the original sentence.

Answer (A) is always the same as the underlined part. Choose answer (A) if you think the original sentence needs no revision.

EXAMPLE:

Laura Ingalls Wilder published her first book and she was sixty-five years old then.

(A) and she was sixty-five years old then
(B) when she was sixty-five years old
(C) at age sixty-five years old
(D) upon reaching sixty-five years
(E) at the time when she was sixty-five

SAMPLE ANSWER

(A) ● (C) (D) (E)

---

26. If I would have realized the danger involved in this assignment, I would not have asked you to undertake it.

    (A) If I would have realized
    (B) If I should have realized
    (C) If I had realized
    (D) When I realized
    (E) Because I did not realize

27. The imminent historian stood in bed, recuperating from a viral infection, while his paper was being read at the convention.

    (A) imminent historian stood
    (B) imminent historian remained
    (C) eminent historian stayed
    (D) eminent historian stood
    (E) eminent historian had remained

28. At the zoo, the brightly-plumaged birds that fluttered overhead like tropical flowers in a breeze.

    (A) birds that fluttered
    (B) birds fluttering
    (C) birds which fluttered
    (D) birds fluttered
    (E) birds aflutter

GO ON TO THE NEXT PAGE

2   2 2 2 2 2 2 2 2 2   2

29. In India, Mahatma Gandhi was more than a
    <u>political leader he was</u> the enlightened one
    embodying the soul of the nation.

    (A) political leader he was
    (B) political leader; he was
    (C) political leader, he was
    (D) political leader which was
    (E) political leader, although he was

30. When the National Association for the
    Advancement of Colored People examined
    discrimination in the music business recently, <u>its
    report concentrating on offstage employment
    opportunities</u>.

    (A) its report concentrating on offstage
        employment opportunities
    (B) its report having concentrated on offstage
        employment opportunities
    (C) its report concentrated on offstage
        employment opportunities
    (D) its report concentrating in offstage
        employment opportunities
    (E) its report concentrated in offstage employment
        opportunities

31. <u>Some doctors volunteer to serve the poor in
    addition to their regular practices, they find</u> healing
    the poor provides different insights than healing
    the rich.

    (A) Some doctors volunteer to serve the poor in
        addition to their regular practices, they find
    (B) Besides their regular practices, some doctors
        serve the poor to find
    (C) In addition to running their regular practices,
        some doctors volunteer to serve the poor;
        they find that
    (D) Some doctors, in volunteering to serve the
        poor, find
    (E) Running their regular practices and serving the
        poor helps some doctors realize that

32. <u>Because of a teacher shortage in the math and
    science disciplines, educators are encouraging</u>
    retired scientists and engineers to pursue a second
    career in teaching.

    (A) Because of a teacher shortage in the math and
        science disciplines, educators are
        encouraging
    (B) Educators, faced with a teacher shortage in
        technical disciplines have encouraged
    (C) In addition to a teacher shortage in the math
        and science areas, educators encourage
    (D) Teacher shortages in the math and science
        disciplines have forced educators to hire
    (E) Because there is a teacher shortage in the
        math and science disciplines, educators
        encourage

33. <u>Neither the principal or the teachers had been
    satisfied with the addition of a crossing guard, and</u>
    wanted a traffic light installed at the street
    crossing.

    (A) Neither the principal or the teachers had been
        satisfied with the addition of a crossing
        guard, and
    (B) Neither the principal nor the teachers were
        satisfied with the addition of a crossing
        guard; they
    (C) Because neither the principal or the teachers
        had been satisfied with the addition of a
        crossing guard, they
    (D) As a result of the addition of a crossing guard,
        the principal and teachers
    (E) Neither the principal nor the teachers feels the
        crossing guard is sufficient; and they

34. Most of the students like to read <u>these kind of
    detective stories</u> for their supplementary reading.

    (A) these kind of detective stories
    (B) these kind of detective story
    (C) this kind of detective story
    (D) this kinds of detective story
    (E) those kind of detective story

35. Because of his throat ailment, the tenor <u>has not
    and apparently never will sing</u> again.

    (A) had not and apparently never will sing
    (B) has not sung and apparently never will
    (C) has not and apparently never would sing
    (D) has not sung and apparently never will sing
    (E) had not and apparently never will sing

36. Having the best record for attendance, <u>the school
    awarded him a medal</u> at graduation.

    (A) the school awarded him a medal
    (B) the school awarded a medal to him
    (C) he was awarded a medal by the school
    (D) a medal was awarded to him by the school
    (E) a school medal was awarded to him

37. Several regulations were <u>proposed by the president
    of the university that</u> had a sexist bias, according
    to women students.

    (A) Several regulations were proposed by the
        president of the university that
    (B) Several regulations were proposed by the
        president of the university who
    (C) The proposal of several regulations by the
        president of the university which
    (D) The president of the university, who proposed
        several regulations that
    (E) The president of the university proposed
        several regulations that

GO ON TO THE NEXT PAGE

2 2 2 2 2 2 2 2 2 2 2

38. The difference between the candidates is that <u>one is radical; the other, conservative.</u>

  (A) one is radical; the other, conservative
  (B) one is radical; the other being conservative
  (C) while one is radical; the other, conservative
  (D) one is radical, the other, conservative
  (E) one is radical, although the other is more conservative

39. <u>Police academies, on seeing as how new recruits lack basic driving skills, are teaching</u> recruits the basics on test fields and neighborhood streets.

  (A) Police academies, on seeing as how new recruits lack basic driving skills, are teaching
  (B) Since new police recruits lack basic driving skills, police academies are teaching
  (C) Police academies, because new recruits are lacking of basic driving skills, teach
  (D) As a result of new recruits lacking basic driving skills, police academies are teaching
  (E) Even though new recruits lack basic driving skills, police academies are teaching

40. <u>Because he spoke out against Hitler's policies was why Dietrich Bonhoeffer, a Lutheran pastor in Nazi Germany, was arrested and eventually hanged by the Gestapo.</u>

  (A) Because he spoke out against Hitler's policies was why Dietrich Bonhoeffer, a Lutheran pastor in Nazi Germany, was arrested and eventually hanged by the Gestapo.
  (B) Dietrich Bonhoeffer, a Lutheran pastor in Nazi Germany, was arrested and eventually hanged by the Gestapo because he spoke out against Hitler's policies.
  (C) Because he spoke out against Hitler's policies, Dietrich Bonhoeffer, a Lutheran pastor in Nazi Germany, was arrested and eventually hung by the Gestapo.
  (D) Dietrich Bonhoeffer, a Lutheran pastor in Nazi Germany, being arrested and eventually hung because he spoke out against Hitler's policies.
  (E) A Lutheran pastor in Nazi Germany, Dietrich Bonhoeffer spoke out against Hitler's policies so that he was arrested and eventually hung.

Note: The remaining questions are like those at the beginning of the section.

Directions: For each sentence in which you find an error, select the one underlined part that must be changed to make the sentence correct and blacken the corresponding space on your answer sheet.

If there is no error, blacken answer space Ⓔ.

  EXAMPLE:

   The region has a climate <u>so severe that</u> plants
                          A
   <u>growing</u> there rarely <u>had been</u> more than twelve
      B   C
   inches <u>high</u>. <u>No error</u>
        D   E

SAMPLE ANSWER

Ⓐ Ⓑ ● Ⓓ Ⓔ

---

41. The legislator stated that he <u>had opposed</u> the
                       A
   proposed tax because <u>it</u> was <u>not only</u> regressive
              B   C
   but also <u>because of its being</u> unnecessary. <u>No error</u>
           D   E

42. <u>Snowing</u> <u>heavily</u> for six hours, road conditions
     A   B
   were <u>very hazardous</u> and traffic <u>was snarled</u> on
         C   D
   most roads. <u>No error</u>
          E

43. <u>Be assured</u> that I am <u>not unmindful</u> <u>of the fact</u> that
     A   B   C
   we owe a vote of thanks <u>to whomever</u> made this
                    D
   news public. <u>No error</u>
           E

GO ON TO THE NEXT PAGE →

2   2 2 2 2 2 2 2 2 2 2   2

44. While in San Francisco, we should try and see as
    A   B
    many of the famous places as possible. No error
    C   D   E

45. On the contrary, martial arts not only increase a
    A   B
    person's fighting ability, but aid also
                               C
    the development of perfect form and
    D
    concentration. No error
                   E

46. A growing number of medical patients long for the
              A
    old-fashioned general practitioner; one feels that
                                         B   C
    medical specialization leads to

    impersonal treatment. No error
    D   E

47. I advise you to try to become his friend because he
      A   B
    may be very helpful and because of his position on
                                    C
    the committee that will decide this case. No error
                         D   E

48. Until recently, sun worshippers thought that a
    A   B
    deep tan was healthful; now it is evident that
                  C   D
    suntans can cause skin damage. No error
                                   E

49. Many people smoke; some of them who smoke
                                A
    heavily don't realize they are addicted until they
    B   C
    try to let go and quit. No error
           D   E

50. Some sports fans prefer watching the news

    to newspapers because they get the highlights,
    A   B   C
    without having to search for the information.
                   D

    No error
    E

IF YOU FINISH BEFORE TIME IS CALLED, YOU MAY CHECK YOUR WORK ON
THIS SECTION ONLY. DO NOT WORK ON ANY OTHER SECTION IN THE TEST.   S T O P

3 3 3 3 3 3 3 3 3 3 3 3

SECTION 3   Time—30 minutes   For each question in this section, choose the best answer and
              45 Questions   blacken the corresponding space on the answer sheet.

Each question below consists of a word in capital letters, followed by five lettered words or phrases. Choose the word or phrase that is most nearly opposite in meaning to the word in capital letters. Since some of the questions require you to distinguish fine shades of meaning, consider all the choices before deciding which is best.

Example:

GOOD: (A) sour   (B) bad   (C) red
(D) hot   (E) ugly   Ⓐ ● Ⓒ Ⓓ Ⓔ

1. NEGLIGENT: (A) painstaking   (B) irrelevant
   (C) rewarding   (D) authentic   (E) emphatic

2. RETRACT: (A) expose   (B) disagree
   (C) pursue   (D) extend   (E) stifle

3. CONSISTENT: (A) ill-mannered
   (B) thickheaded   (C) self-contradictory
   (D) broad-minded   (E) far-sighted

4. ESTRANGEMENT: (A) insignificance
   (B) reconciliation   (C) sincerity   (D) normality
   (E) meekness

5. STERILIZE: (A) deplete   (B) facilitate
   (C) vaccinate   (D) contaminate   (E) abstain

6. ENMESH: (A) disentangle   (B) enlarge
   (C) adorn   (D) throw away   (E) hold together

7. CORROBORATE: (A) protect   (B) deny
   (C) repent   (D) isolate   (E) urge

8. REPREHENSIBLE: (A) frightened   (B) alert
   (C) obscure   (D) commendable   (E) incredible

9. REPROVE: (A) supply with evidence
   (B) lack experience   (C) determine innocence
   (D) falsify   (E) praise

10. UNOBTRUSIVE: (A) glaring   (B) fragmentary
    (C) endurable   (D) deflated   (E) scornful

11. FLAUNT: (A) conceal   (B) dispose
    (C) accelerate   (D) enhance   (E) rebuff

12. EQUANIMITY: (A) loss of freedom
    (B) lack of agreement   (C) lack of composure
    (D) self-sufficiency   (E) hasty action

13. INGENUOUS: (A) sophisticated   (B) identical
    (C) changeable   (D) secretive   (E) unoriginal

14. SANGUINE: (A) furtive   (B) pacific
    (C) restrictive   (D) heedless   (E) pessimistic

15. HEDONISM: (A) pragmatism   (B) formality
    (C) hard-heartedness   (D) self-denial
    (E) cowardice

Each sentence below has one or two blanks, each blank indicating that something has been omitted. Beneath the sentence are five lettered words or sets of words. Choose the word or set of words that best fits the meaning of the sentence as a whole.

Example:

Although its publicity has been ----, the film itself is intelligent, well-acted, handsomely produced, and altogether ----.

(A) tasteless..respectable (B) extensive..moderate
(C) sophisticated..amateur (D) risqué..crude
(E) perfect..spectacular

● Ⓑ Ⓒ Ⓓ Ⓔ

16. His critical reviews were enjoyed by many of his audience, but the subjects of his analysis dreaded his comments; he was vitriolic, devastating, irritating and never ---- .

(A) analytic   (B) personal   (C) constructive
(D) uncharitable   (E) controversial

17. Despite the team members' resentment of the new coach's training rules, they ---- them as long as he did not ---- them too strictly.

(A) embraced..follow
(B) condemned..formulate
(C) questioned..interpret
(D) challenged..implement
(E) tolerated..apply

GO ON TO THE NEXT PAGE →

18. Given the ---- state of the published evidence, we do not argue here that exposure to low-level microwave energy is either hazardous or safe.

   (A) inconclusive   (B) satisfactory
   (C) definitive   (D) immaculate   (E) exemplary

19. The negotiation sessions were at times surprisingly ----, frequently degenerating into a welter of accusations and counter-accusations.

   (A) perspicacious   (B) phlegmatic   (C) sedate
   (D) acrimonious   (E) propitious

20. Because of its inclination to ---- , most Indian art is ---- Japanese art, where symbols have been minimized and meaning has been conveyed by the merest suggestion.

   (A) exaggerate..related to
   (B) imitate..superior to
   (C) understate..reminiscent of
   (D) overdraw..similar to
   (E) sentimentalize..supportive of

Each passage below is followed by questions based on its content. Answer all questions following a passage on the basis of what is stated or implied in that passage.

Sir Thomas was indeed the life of the party, who at his suggestion now seated themselves round the fire. He had the best right to be the talker; and the delight of his sensations in being again in his own house, in the center of his family, after such a separation, made him communicative and chatty in a very unusual degree; and he was ready to answer every question of his two sons almost before it was put. All the little particulars of his proceedings and events, his arrivals and departures, were most promptly delivered, as he sat by Lady Bertram and looked with heartfelt satisfaction at the faces around him—interrupting himself more than once, however, to remark on his good fortune in finding them all at home—coming unexpectedly as he did—all collected together exactly as he could have wished, but dared not depend on.

By not one of the circle was he listened to with such unbroken unalloyed enjoyment as by his wife, whose feelings were so warmed by his sudden arrival, as to place her nearer agitation than she had been for the last twenty years. She had been *almost* fluttered for a few minutes, and still remained so sensibly animated as to put away her work, move Pug from her side, and give all her attention and all the rest of her sofa to her husband. She had no anxieties for anybody to cloud *her* pleasure; her own time had been irreproachably spent during his absence; she had done a great deal of carpet work and made many yards of fringe; and she would have answered as freely for the good conduct and useful pursuits of all the young people as for her own. It was so agreeable to her to see him again, and hear him talk, to have her ear amused and her whole comprehension filled by his narratives, that she began particularly to feel how dreadfully she must have missed him, and how impossible it would have been for her to bear a lengthened absence.

Mrs. Norris was by no means to be compared in happiness to her sister. Not that *she* was incommoded by many fears of Sir Thomas's disapprobation when the present state of his house should be known, for her judgment had been so blinded, that she could hardly be said to show any sign of alarm; but she was vexed by the *manner* of his return. It had left her nothing to do. Instead of being sent for out of the room, and seeing him first, and having to spread the happy news through the house, Sir Thomas, with a very reasonable dependence perhaps on the nerves of his wife and children, had sought no confidant but the butler, and had been following him almost instantaneously into the drawing-room. Mrs. Norris felt herself defrauded of an office on which she had always depended, whether his arrival or his death were to be the thing unfolded; and was now trying to be in a bustle without having any thing to bustle about. Would Sir Thomas have consented to eat, she might have gone to the housekeeper with troublesome directions; but Sir Thomas resolutely declined all dinner; he would take nothing, nothing till tea came—he would rather wait for tea. Still Mrs. Norris was at intervals urging something different; and in the most interesting moment of his passage to England, when the alarm of a French privateer was at the height, she burst through his recital with the proposal of soup. "Sure, my dear Sir Thomas, a basin of soup would be a much better thing for you than tea. Do have a basin of soup."

Sir Thomas could not be provoked. "Still the same anxiety for everybody's comfort, my dear Mrs. Norris," was his answer. "But indeed I would rather have nothing but tea."

GO ON TO THE NEXT PAGE

21. Which of the following titles best describes the passage?

   (A) An Unexpected Return
   (B) The Conversation of the Upper Class
   (C) Mrs. Norris's Grievance
   (D) A Romantic Reunion
   (E) An Account of a Voyage Abroad

22. We can infer from the opening paragraph that Sir Thomas is customarily

   (A) unwelcome at home
   (B) tardy in business affairs
   (C) dissatisfied with life
   (D) more restrained in speech
   (E) lacking in family feeling

23. The passage suggests that Sir Thomas's sudden arrival

   (A) was motivated by concern for his wife
   (B) came as no surprise to Lady Bertram
   (C) was timed by him to coincide with a family reunion
   (D) was expected by the servants
   (E) was received with mixed emotions

24. Sir Thomas's attitude toward Mrs. Norris can best be described as one of

   (A) sharp irritation
   (B) patient forbearance
   (C) solemn disapproval
   (D) unreasoned alarm
   (E) unmixed delight

25. The office of which Mrs. Norris feels herself defrauded is most likely that of

   (A) butler
   (B) housekeeper
   (C) wife
   (D) traveler
   (E) message-bearer

My new mistress proved to be all she
appeared when I first met her at the door—a
woman of the kindest heart and feelings. She had
never had a slave under her control previously to

(5) myself, and prior to her marriage she had been
dependent upon her own industry for a living.
She was by trade a weaver; and by constant
application to her business, she had been in a
good degree preserved from the blighting and

(10) dehumanizing effects of slavery. I was utterly
astonished at her goodness. I scarcely knew how
to behave towards her. My early instruction was
all out of place. The crouching servility, usually
so acceptable a quality in a slave, did not answer

(15) when manifested toward her. Her favor was not
gained by it; she seemed to be disturbed by it.
She did not deem it impudent or unmannerly for
a slave to look her in the face. The meanest slave
was put fully at ease in her presence, and none

(20) left without feeling better for having seen her.
But alas! this kind heart had but a short time to
remain such. The fatal poison of irresponsible
power was already in her hands, and soon
commenced its infernal work.

(25) Very soon after I went to live with Mr. and
Mrs. Auld, she very kindly commenced to teach
me the A, B, C. After I had learned this, she
assisted me in learning to spell words of three or
four letters. Just at this point of my progress, Mr.

(30) Auld found out what was going on, and at once
forbade Mrs. Auld to instruct me further, telling
her, that it was unlawful, as well as unsafe, to
teach a slave to read. Further, he said, "If you
give a slave an inch, he will take an ell. A slave

(35) should know nothing but to obey his master—to
do as he is told to do. Learning would *spoil* the
best slave in the world. Now," said he, "if you
teach that boy (speaking of myself) how to read,
there would be no keeping him. It would forever

(40) unfit him to be a slave. He would at once
become unmanageable, and of no value to his
master. As to him, it could do him no good, but a
great deal of harm. It would make him
discontented and unhappy." These words sank

(45) deep into my heart, stirred up sentiments within
that lay slumbering, and called into existence an
entirely new train of thought. I now understood
what had been to me a most perplexing
difficulty—to wit, the white man's power to

(50) enslave the black man. From that moment I
understood the pathway from slavery to freedom.
Though conscious of the difficulty of learning
without a teacher, I set out with high hope, and a
fixed purpose, at whatever cost of trouble, to

(55) learn how to read. The very decided manner with
which my master spoke, and strove to impress
his wife with the evil consequences of giving me
instruction, served to convince me that he was
deeply sensible of the truths he was uttering. It

(60) gave me the best assurance that I might rely with
the utmost confidence on the results which, he
said, would flow from teaching me to read. What
he most dreaded, that I most desired. What he
most loved, that I most hated. That which to him

(65) was a great evil, to be carefully shunned, was to
me a great good, to be diligently sought; and the
argument which he so warmly urged, against my
learning to read, only served to inspire me with a
desire and determination to learn. In learning to

(70) read, I owe almost as much to the bitter
opposition of my master, as to the kindly aid of
my mistress. I acknowledge the benefit of both.

GO ON TO THE NEXT PAGE →

3 3 3 3 3 3 3 3 3 3 3

26. The author's main purpose in this passage is to

 (A) describe a disagreement between a woman and her husband
 (B) analyze the reasons for prohibiting the education of slaves
 (C) describe a slave's discovery of literacy as a means to freedom
 (D) dramatize a slave's change in attitude toward his mistress
 (E) portray the downfall of a kindhearted woman

27. It can be inferred from the passage that all of the following were characteristic of Mrs. Auld at the time the author first met her EXCEPT

 (A) diligence in labor
 (B) dislike of fawning
 (C) gentleness of spirit
 (D) disdain for convention
 (E) benevolent nature

28. For which of the following reasons does Mr. Auld forbid his wife to educate her slave?

 I. Providing slaves with an education violates the law.
 II. He believes slaves lack the capacity for education.
 III. He fears education would leave the slave less submissive.

 (A) I only   (B) III only   (C) I and II only
 (D) I and III only   (E) I, II, and III

29. The tone of the author in acknowledging his debt to his master (lines 69–72) can best be described as

 (A) sentimental and nostalgic
 (B) cutting and ironic
 (C) petulant and self-righteous
 (D) resigned but wistful
 (E) angry and impatient

30. Which of the following definitions of "education" is closest to the author's view of education as presented in the passage?

 (A) Education makes people easy to govern, but impossible to enslave.
 (B) Education is the best provision for old age.
 (C) Education has for its object the formation of character.
 (D) Education has produced a vast population able to read but unable to distinguish what is worth reading.
 (E) Education begins and ends with the knowledge of human nature.

Select the word or set of words that best completes each of the following sentences.

31. Irony can, after a fashion, become a mode of escape: to laugh at the terrors of life is in some sense to ---- them.

 (A) exaggerate   (B) revitalize   (C) corroborate
 (D) evade   (E) license

32. Tacitus' descriptions of Germanic tribal customs were ---- by the ---- state of communications in his day, but they match the accounts of other contemporary writers.

 (A) defined..inconsequential
 (B) limited..primitive
 (C) enriched..antiquated
 (D) contradicted..thriving
 (E) muddled..suspended

33. No matter how ---- the revelations of the coming years may be, they will be hard put to match those of the past decade, which have ---- transformed our view of the emergence of Mayan civilization.

 (A) minor..dramatically
 (B) profound..negligibly
 (C) striking..radically
 (D) bizarre..nominally
 (E) questionable..possibly

34. Black religion was in part a protest movement—a protest against a system and a society that was ---- designed to ---- the dignity of a segment of God's creation.

 (A) unintentionally..reflect
 (B) explicitly..foster
 (C) inevitably..assess
 (D) deliberately..demean
 (E) provocatively..enhance

35. Every major civilization of which we have knowledge has generally been ----, rather than hindered by the existence of ---- in the usual chain of military and political emergencies, during which peaceful periods advances in science, art, and philosophy were allowed to develop.

 (A) halted..fluctuations
 (B) helped..digressions
 (C) undisturbed..patterns
 (D) assisted..portents
 (E) aided..hiatuses

GO ON TO THE NEXT PAGE

36. SCRAPBOOK : CLIPPINGS ::
    (A) newspaper : headlines
    (B) record : label
    (C) album : stamps
    (D) almanac : dates
    (E) bulletin : tacks

37. AVALANCHE : SNOW :: (A) igloo : ice
    (B) deluge : water   (C) sleet : hail   (D) dew : rain
     (E) current : air

38. ISLAND : ARCHIPELAGO :: (A) team : player
    (B) sphere : hemisphere   (C) star : galaxy
     (D) multitude : horde   (E) continent : peninsula

39. DISBAND : ORGANIZATION ::
    (A) merge : corporation
    (B) demobilize : army
    (C) discharge : employer
    (D) expand : capacity
    (E) respect : order

40. SHIP : FOUNDER :: (A) government : reform
    (B) union : strike   (C) business : organize
     (D) building : collapse   (E) crew : muster

41. SQUIRM : DISCOMFORT ::
    (A) chortle : distress
    (B) fume : anger
    (C) snarl : confusion
    (D) waddle : embarrassment
    (E) shrug : determination

42. SUPPORT : ADVOCATE :: (A) shun : outcast
    (B) reward : victor   (C) applaud : performer
     (D) denounce : accuser   (E) donate : financier

43. STEADFAST : LOYALTY ::
    (A) ambivalent : honesty
    (B) courageous : valor
    (C) ponderous : thought
    (D) infamous : repute
    (E) deadpan : emotion

44. RUTHLESS : SYMPATHY ::
    (A) pathetic : pity
    (B) belligerent : detachment
    (C) lethargic : fatigue
    (D) heedless : intelligence
    (E) outspoken : reticence

45. CLIQUE : EXCLUSIVE ::
    (A) congregation : benevolent
    (B) entourage : attentive
    (C) coterie : modest
    (D) troupe : renowned
    (E) flock : unruly

IF YOU FINISH BEFORE TIME IS CALLED, YOU MAY CHECK YOUR WORK ON THIS SECTION ONLY. DO NOT WORK ON ANY OTHER SECTION IN THE TEST.   **S T O P**

4   4 4 4 4 4 4 4 4 4 4 4   4

SECTION **4**   Time—30 minutes   For each question in this section, choose the best answer and
40 Questions   blacken the corresponding space on the answer sheet.

Each question below consists of a word in capital letters, followed by five lettered words or phrases. Choose the word or phrase that is most nearly opposite in meaning to the word in capital letters. Since some of the questions require you to distinguish fine shades of meaning, consider all the choices before deciding which is best.

Example:

GOOD: (A) sour   (B) bad   (C) red
(D) hot   (E) ugly   Ⓐ ● Ⓒ Ⓓ Ⓔ

1. FLEXIBLE: (A) massive   (B) unbending
   (C) elderly   (D) probable   (E) remarkable

2. AMPLIFY: (A) oppose   (B) irritate   (C) satisfy
   (D) diminish   (E) deceive

3. RECKLESS: (A) powerful   (B) unkind
   (C) cautious   (D) anonymous   (E) plentiful

4. AGITATOR: (A) lunatic   (B) peacemaker
   (C) wise investor   (D) gifted amateur
   (E) accurate reporter

5. ARBITRARY: (A) beneficial   (B) popular
   (C) reasonable   (D) minute   (E) competitive

6. GULLIBLE: (A) able to succeed
   (B) willing to spend   (C) ready to listen
   (D) hard to fool   (E) aiming to please

7. PROFANE: (A) act impolite
   (B) ward off danger   (C) sanctify
   (D) congregate   (E) smother

8. INDIGENOUS: (A) foreign   (B) unpatriotic
   (C) exhausted   (D) impudent   (E) shallow

9. PUSILLANIMITY: (A) righteousness
   (B) immensity   (C) courage   (D) insularity
   (E) prevalence

10. EVANESCENCE: (A) lack of thought
    (B) need for assistance   (C) innocuousness
    (D) permanence   (E) negligence

Each sentence below has one or two blanks, each blank indicating that something has been omitted. Beneath the sentence are five lettered words or sets of words. Choose the word or set of words that best fits the meaning of the sentence as a whole.

Example:

Although its publicity has been ----, the film itself is intelligent, well-acted, handsomely produced, and altogether ----.

(A) tasteless..respectable   (B) extensive..moderate
(C) sophisticated..amateur   (D) risqué..crude
(E) perfect..spectacular

● Ⓑ Ⓒ Ⓓ Ⓔ

11. Either the Polynesian banquets at Waikiki are ----, or the one I visited was a poor example.

(A) delicious   (B) impeccable   (C) overrated
(D) untasted   (E) unpopular

12. Lee, who refrained from excesses in his personal life, differed markedly from Grant, who ---- notorious drinking bouts with his cronies.

(A) deprecated   (B) minimized   (C) indulged in
(D) shunned   (E) compensated for

13. The college librarian initiated a new schedule of fines for overdue books with the ----, if not the outright encouragement, of the faculty library committee.

(A) skepticism   (B) acquiescence   (C) scorn
(D) applause   (E) disapprobation

14. He was habitually so docile and ---- that his friends could not understand his sudden outburst against his employers.

(A) complacent   (B) incorrigible   (C) truculent
(D) erratic   (E) hasty

15. In the absence of native predators to stop their spread, imported deer ---- to such an inordinate degree that they overgrazed the countryside and ---- the native vegetation.

(A) thrived..threatened
(B) propagated..cultivated
(C) suffered..abandoned
(D) flourished..scrutinized
(E) dwindled..eliminated

GO ON TO THE NEXT PAGE ⇒

Each question below consists of a related pair of words or phrases, followed by five lettered pairs of words or phrases. Select the lettered pair that best expresses a relationship similar to that expressed in the original pair.

Example:

YAWN : BOREDOM :: (A) dream : sleep (B) anger : madness   (C) smile : amusement   (D) face : expression   (E) impatience : rebellion

Ⓐ Ⓑ ● Ⓓ Ⓔ

16. BRAKE : AUTOMOBILE ::   (A) pad : helicopter (B) ship : fleet   (C) reins : horse   (D) helmet : motorcycle   (E) boot : saddle

17. AREA : SQUARE ::   (A) diagonal : rectangle (B) volume : cube   (C) angle : triangle   (D) radius : circle   (E) base : cylinder

18. TALLY : VOTES ::   (A) census : population (B) taxation : revenue   (C) government : laws   (D) team : athletes   (E) election : candidates

19. TERMITE : WOOD ::   (A) moth : wool (B) silkworm : silk   (C) oyster : shell   (D) anthracite : coal   (E) terrace : stone

20. CEASE-FIRE : HOSTILITIES ::
(A) alimony : divorce
(B) battery : missiles
(C) lull : storm
(D) bonfire : kindling
(E) apology : insult

21. COLLEAGUES : PROFESSION ::
(A) kinsfolk : family
(B) spectators : game
(C) exiles : country
(D) rivals : team
(E) passengers : subway

22. INTEREST : USURY ::   (A) concern : disregard (B) thrift : prodigality   (C) debit : credit   (D) frugality : parsimony   (E) pleasure : utility

23. CACOPHONY : EAR ::   (A) calligraphy : eye (B) piquancy : taste   (C) stench : nose   (D) tracheotomy : throat   (E) retina : eye

24. EULOGY : PRAISE ::   (A) elegy : death (B) slander : disparagement   (C) paean : anger   (D) reproof : confirmation   (E) satire : vanity

25. EMBROIL : STRIFE ::   (A) chafe : restriction (B) embarrass : pride   (C) emulate : model   (D) annul : marriage   (E) imperil : danger

Each passage below is followed by questions based on its content. Answer all questions following a passage on the basis of what is stated or implied in that passage.

It is no secret that I am not one of those naturalists who suffer from cities, or affect to do so, nor do I find a city unnatural or uninteresting, or a rubbish heap of follies. It has always seemed to me there is something more than mechanically admirable about a train that arrives on time, a fire department that comes when you call it, a light that leaps into the room at a touch, and a clinic that will fight for the health of a penniless man and mass for him the agencies of mercy, the X-ray, the precious radium, the anesthetics and the surgical skill. For, beyond any pay these services receive, stands out the pride in perfect performance. And above all, I admire the noble impersonality of civilization that does not inquire where the recipient stands on religion or politics or race. I call this beauty, and I call it spirit— not some mystical soulfulness that nobody can define, but the spirit of man, that has been a million years a-growing.

26. The title that best expresses the ideas of this paragraph is

(A) The Spirit of the City
(B) Advantages of a City Home
(C) Disagreement among Naturalists
(D) Estimable Characteristics of Cities
(E) Tolerance in the City

27. The tone of the author can best be described as

(A) impersonal   (B) humble   (C) tolerant (D) assertive   (E) mystical

GO ON TO THE NEXT PAGE

4 **4** **4** **4** **4** **4** **4** **4** **4** **4** **4** **4**

28. The author's primary purpose in this passage is to

    (A) defend cities against their detractors
    (B) expose the deficiency of free urban services
    (C) question the affectations of other naturalists
    (D) explore the influence of mysticism on city life
    (E) compare the advantages of urban and rural life

29. The aspect of city life most commendable to this author is its

    (A) punctuality
    (B) free benefits
    (C) impartial service
    (D) mechanical improvement
    (E) health clinics

30. The author implies that efficient operation of public utilities is

    (A) needlessly expensive
    (B) of no special interest
    (C) admired by most naturalists
    (D) mechanically commendable
    (E) spiritual in quality

Scattered around the globe are more than 100 small regions of isolated volcanic activity known to geologists as hot spots. Unlike most of the world's volcanoes, they are not always found at the boundaries of the great drifting plates that make up the earth's surface; on the contrary, many of them lie deep in the interior of a plate. Most of the hot spots move only slowly, and in some cases the movement of the plates past them has left trails of extinct volcanoes. The hot spots and their volcanic trails are milestones that mark the passage of the plates.

That the plates are moving is now beyond dispute. Africa and South America, for example, are receding from each other as new material is injected into the sea floor between them. The complementary coastlines and certain geological features that seem to span the ocean are reminders of where the two continents were once joined. The relative motion of the plates carrying these continents has been constructed in detail, but the motion of one plate with respect to another cannot readily be translated into motion with respect to the earth's interior. It is not possible to determine whether both continents are moving (in opposite directions) or whether one continent is stationary and the other is drifting away from it. Hot spots, anchored in the deeper layers of the earth, provide the measuring instruments needed to resolve the question. From an analysis of the hot-spot population it appears that the African plate is stationary and that it has not moved during the past 30 million years.

The significance of hot spots is not confined to their role as a frame of reference. It now appears that they also have an important influence on the geophysical processes that propel the plates across the globe. When a continental plate comes to rest over a hot spot, the material welling up from deeper layers creates a broad dome. As the dome grows it develops deep fissures; in at least a few cases the continent may rupture entirely along some of these fissures, so that the hot spot initiates the formation of a new ocean. Thus just as earlier theories have explained the mobility of the continents, so hot spots may explain their mutability.

31. According to the passage, which of the following statements indicate that Africa and South America once adjoined one another?

    I. They share certain common topographic traits.
    II. Their shorelines are physical counterparts.
    III. The African plate has been stable for 30 million years.

    (A) I only   (B) II only   (C) I and II only
    (D) II and III only   (E) I, II, and III

32. According to the passage, the hot spot theory eventually may prove useful in interpreting

    (A) the boundaries of the plates
    (B) the depth of the ocean floor
    (C) the relative motion of the plates
    (D) current instruments of measurement
    (E) major changes in continental shape

GO ON TO THE NEXT PAGE

4 4 4 4 4 4 4 4 4 4 4 4

Certitude is not the test of certainty. We have been cocksure of many things that were not so. If I may quote myself again, property, friendship, *Line* and truth have a common root in time. One
(5) cannot be wrenched from the rocky crevices into which one has grown for many years without feeling that one is attacked in one's life. What we most love and revere generally is determined by early associations. I love granite rocks and
(10) barberry bushes, no doubt because with them were my earliest joys that reach back through the past eternity of my life. But while one's experience thus makes certain preferences dogmatic for oneself, recognition of how they
(15) came to be so leaves one able to see that others, poor souls, may be equally dogmatic about something else. And this again means skepticism. Not that one's belief or love does not remain. Not that we would not fight and die for it if
(20) important—we all, whether we know it or not, are fighting to make the kind of world that we should like—but that we have learned to recognize that others will fight and die to make a different world, with equal sincerity of belief.
(25) Deep-seated preferences cannot be argued about—you cannot argue a man into liking a glass of beer—and therefore, when differences are sufficiently far-reaching, we try to kill the other man rather than let him have his way. But
(30) that is perfectly consistent with admitting that, so far as appears, his grounds are just as good as ours.

33. With which of the following statements would the author be most likely to agree?

   I. The degree of assurance we feel about an issue is directly proportional to the truth of that issue.
   II. Early associations determine later preferences to a considerable degree.
   III. Knowing why we have certain preferences destroys our faith in their worth.

   (A) I only   (B) II only   (C) III only
   (D) I and II   (E) II and III

34. The author uses the phrase "wrenched from the rocky crevices into which one has grown" (lines 5–6) to describe disturbing

   (A) trenches in wartime   (D) belief in an afterlife
   (B) grave sites   (E) barberry leaves
   (C) fixed preferences

35. The reference to the glass of beer (line 27) is introduced primarily to

   (A) make an abstract assertion concrete
   (B) introduce a note of impatience
   (C) illustrate the power of alcohol
   (D) demonstrate the author's preferences
   (E) weaken the argument for skepticism

Of the poetry of the United States different opinions have been entertained, and prejudice on the one side, and partiality on the other, have *Line* equally prevented a just and rational estimate of
(5) its merits. Abroad, our literature has fallen under unmerited contumely from those who were but slenderly acquainted with the subject on which they professed to decide; and at home, it must be confessed that the swaggering and pompous
(10) pretensions of many have done not a little to provoke and excuse the ridicule of foreigners. Either of these extremes exerts an injurious influence on the cause of letters in our country. To encourage exertion and embolden merit to
(15) come forward, it is necessary that they should be acknowledged and rewarded—few will have the confidence to solicit what has been withheld from claims as strong as theirs, or the courage to tread a path which presents no prospect but the
(20) melancholy wrecks who have gone before them. National gratitude—national pride—every high and generous feeling that attaches us to the land of our birth, or that exalts our character as individuals, ask of us that we should foster the
(25) infant literature of our country, and that genius and industry, employing their efforts to hasten its perfection, should receive from our hands, that celebrity which reflects as much honor on the nation which confers it as on those to whom it is
(30) extended. On the other hand, it is not necessary for these purposes, it is even detrimental to bestow on mediocrity the praise due to excellence, and still more so is the attempt to persuade ourselves and others into an admiration
(35) of the faults of favorite writers. We make but a contemptible figure in the eyes of the world, and set ourselves up as objects of pity to our posterity, when we affect to rank the poets of our own country with those mighty masters of song
(40) who have flourished in Greece, Italy and Britain.

36. The author's main purpose in writing this passage is to

   (A) assert the greatness of our poetry
   (B) answer foreign critics who sneer at American literature
   (C) deplore the lack of good writing in this country
   (D) discuss the need for encouraging our writers appropriately
   (E) deplore the extravagant claims made on behalf of American authors

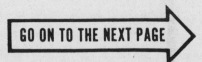
GO ON TO THE NEXT PAGE

4 4 4 4 4 4 4 4 4 4 4 4

37. By the phrase "the melancholy wrecks who have gone before them" (line 20), the author of the passage most probably means

(A) shipwrecked vessels on transatlantic crossings
(B) damaged national pride
(C) underappreciated authors of previous generations
(D) Greek, Italian, and British masters of song
(E) writers of elegies, odes, and laments

38. The author would most likely agree with all of the following statements EXCEPT

(A) American literature is less mature than its European counterpart.
(B) Foreign critics possess a wide knowledge of American verse.
(C) It is both pretentious and self-defeating to overrate minor poets.
(D) Americans need to create a literary climate that nourishes artists.
(E) Many gifted poets languish in undeserved obscurity.

39. The author's attitude toward the state of American poetry is primarily one of

(A) fascinated curiosity
(B) bitter disillusionment
(C) pretended indifference
(D) passionate chauvinism
(E) measured enthusiasm

40. As used in line 6, "contumely" most likely means

(A) praise   (B) evaluation   (C) rudeness
    (D) domination   (E) publication

IF YOU FINISH BEFORE TIME IS CALLED, YOU MAY CHECK YOUR WORK ON THIS SECTION ONLY. DO NOT WORK ON ANY OTHER SECTION IN THE TEST.   **S T O P**

5

The following information is for your reference in solving some of the problems.

Circle of radius r: Area $= \pi r^2$; Circumference $= 2\pi r$
   The number of degrees of arc in a circle is 360.
The measure in degrees of a straight angle is 180.

Definitions of symbols:
$=$ is equal to $\leq$ is less than or equal to
$\neq$ is unequal to $\geq$ is greater than or equal to
$<$ is less than $\parallel$ is parallel to
$>$ is greater than $\perp$ is perpendicular to

Triangle: The sum of the measures in degrees of the angles of a triangle is 180.
If $\angle CDA$ is a right angle, then

(1) area of $\triangle ABC = \dfrac{AB \times CD}{2}$

(2) $AC^2 = AD^2 + DC^2$

Note: Figures that accompany problems in this test are intended to provide information useful in solving the problems. They are drawn as accurately as possible EXCEPT when it is stated in a specific problem that its figure is not drawn to scale. All figures lie in a plane unless otherwise indicated. All numbers used are real numbers.

1. Which of the following numbers is divisible by 2, 3, and 5?

   (A) 600   (B) 606   (C) 665   (D) 666   (E) 669

2. What grade did a student receive on his first examination, if the grades on his other examinations were 50 percent, 70 percent, and 90 percent, and his average on the four examinations was 75 percent?

   (A) 60%   (B) 65%   (C) 75%   (D) 80%
   (E) 90%

3. The length of a fence around a perfectly rectangular plot is 160 feet. Which of the following could be the length of one of its sides?

   I. 20 feet
   II. 40 feet
   III. 60 feet

   (A) I only   (B) II only   (C) III only   (D) I and III   (E) II and III

4. If $4y - x - 10 = 0$ and $3x = 2y$, then $xy =$

   (A) $\dfrac{2}{3}$ (B) 1   (C) $1\dfrac{1}{3}$ (D) 5   (E) 6

5. If $a = \dfrac{b}{2}$, then $b + 2 =$

   (A) $\dfrac{a}{2}$ (B) a (C) $2a + 2$ (D) $2a$ (E) $a - 2$

6. A man works a times as fast as any one of his helpers. If the man does a job in h hours, how many hours are required for w helpers to do the job?

   (A) $\dfrac{ah}{w}$ (B) $\dfrac{aw}{h}$ (C) $\dfrac{w}{ah}$ (D) awh (E) $\dfrac{a}{wh}$

7. A monkey climbs 30 feet at the beginning of each hour and falls back 20 feet during each hourly period. If he begins his ascent at 8:00 A.M., at what time will he first make contact with a point 120 feet distant from the ground?

   (A) 4 P.M.   (B) 5 P.M.   (C) 6 P.M.   (D) 7 P.M.
   (E) 8 P.M.

GO ON TO THE NEXT PAGE

5

Questions 8–27 each consist of two quantities, one in Column A and one in Column B. You are to compare the two quantities and on the answer sheet blacken space

A   if the quantity in Column A is greater;
B   if the quantity in Column B is greater;
C   if the two quantities are equal;
D   If the relationship cannot be determined from the information given.

AN E RESPONSE WILL NOT BE SCORED.

	EXAMPLES			
	Column A	Column B		Answers
E1.	2×6	$2 + 6$		●ⒷⒸⒹⒺ
E2.	$180 - x$	y		ⒶⒷ●ⒹⒺ
E3.	$p - q$	$q - p$		ⒶⒷⒸ●Ⓔ

For E2, angle diagram: $x°$ / $y°$

Notes:
1. In certain questions, information concerning one or both of the quantities to be compared is centered above the two columns.
2. In a given question, a symbol that appears in both columns represents the same thing in Column A as it does in Column B.
3. Letters such as x, n, and k stand for real numbers.

	Column A	Column B
8.	105% of 25	26

$$\frac{48}{x} = 4$$

	Column A	Column B
9.	$16\frac{2}{3}\%$ of 72	x
10.	$\frac{1}{2}$	$\sqrt{\frac{1}{4}}$
11.	$\sqrt{\frac{1}{25}}$	20%
12.	$\sqrt{14.4}$	4

	Column A	Column B
13.	The time required to cover $\frac{1}{2}$ mile traveling at 20 miles per hour	The time required to cover $\frac{1}{3}$ mile traveling at 30 miles per hour
14.	The number of revolutions made by the wheel of a bicycle (diameter of $\frac{7}{\pi}$ feet) covering a distance of 70 feet	The number of revolutions made by the wheel of a motorcycle (diameter of $\frac{10}{\pi}$ feet) covering a distance of 100 feet

GO ON TO THE NEXT PAGE

5

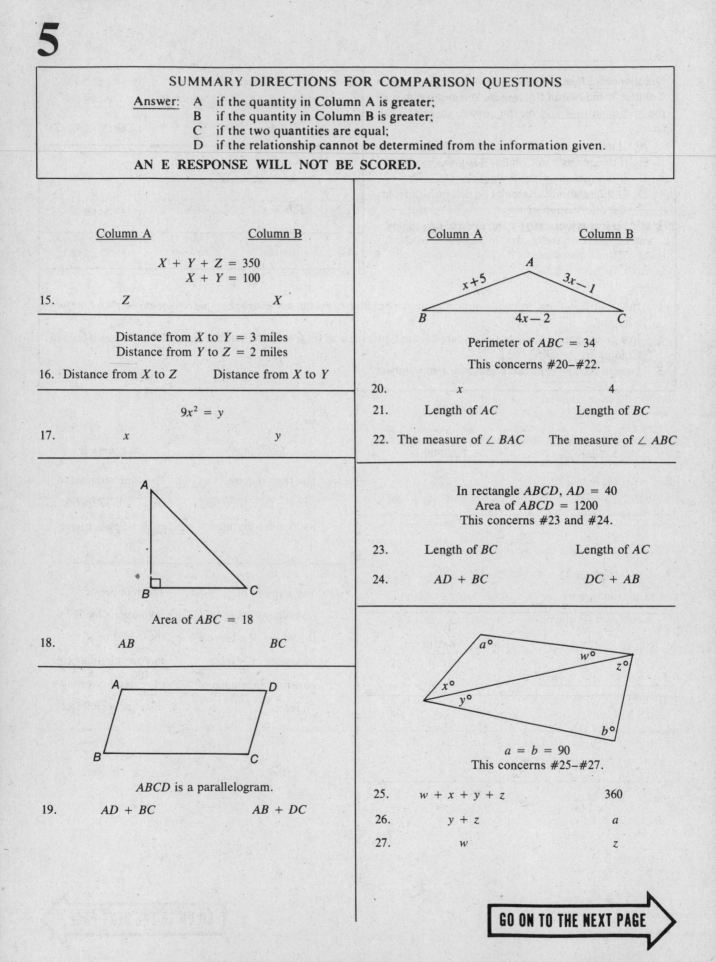

Column A   Column B

$$X + Y + Z = 350$$
$$X + Y = 100$$

15. Z X

Distance from X to Y = 3 miles
Distance from Y to Z = 2 miles

16. Distance from X to Z Distance from X to Y

$$9x^2 = y$$

17. x y

Area of ABC = 18

18. AB BC

$ABCD$ is a parallelogram.

19. $AD + BC$ $AB + DC$

Column A   Column B

Perimeter of ABC = 34

This concerns #20–#22.

20. x 4

21.   Length of AC Length of BC

22. The measure of $\angle BAC$ The measure of $\angle ABC$

In rectangle $ABCD$, AD = 40
Area of $ABCD$ = 1200
This concerns #23 and #24.

23.   Length of BC Length of AC

24. $AD + BC$ $DC + AB$

$a = b = 90$
This concerns #25–#27.

25. $w + x + y + z$ 360

26. $y + z$ a

27. w z

GO ON TO THE NEXT PAGE

5

Solve each of the remaining problems in this section using any available space for scratchwork. Then decide which is the best of the choices given and blacken the corresponding space on the answer sheet.

28. How many 5-gallon cans of milk will be needed to fill 120 pint bottles?

   (A) 3   (B) 6   (C) 9   (D) 12   (E) 24

29. Mr. Fixit can lubricate 6 cars, and change the oil and the filter on these cars, in an 8-hour workday. At that rate how long will it take him to provide these services for 5 automobiles?

   (A) less than 6 hr.
   (B) 6 hr. 23 min.
   (C) 6 hr. 40 min.
   (D) 7 hr. 15 min.
   (E) more than 7 hr.

30. Mr. Walker covered a distance of 55 miles in 4 hours by driving his car at 40 miles per hour part of the way and walking the remainder of the way at 5 miles per hour. What part of the total distance did he go by car?

   (A) $\frac{3}{11}$ (B) $\frac{8}{11}$ (C) $\frac{1}{8}$ (D) $\frac{3}{8}$ (E) $\frac{1}{3}$

31. At a masquerade party the judges eliminate $\frac{1}{4}$ of the eligible contestants after each half hour. If 256 contestants were present at the party, how many would still be eligible for a prize after 2 hours?

   (A) 0   (B) 16   (C) 32   (D) 64   (E) 81

32. Ms. Jenkins owned $\frac{5}{8}$ of an interest in a house. She sold $\frac{1}{5}$ of her interest, at cost, for $1,000. What is the total value of the house?

   (A) $3,000   (B) $5,000   (C) $6,000   (D) $8,000
   (E) $9,000

33. A salesman sold a book at 105 percent of the marked price instead of discounting the marked price by 5 percent. If he sold the book for $4.20, what was the price for which he should have sold the book?

   (A) $3.40   (B) $3.80   (C) $4.20   (D) $4.40
   (E) $4.60

34. After several tryouts 20 percent of a football squad was discharged. The coach then had 32 players. How many players were on the squad at first?

   (A) 24   (B) 26   (C) 39   (D) 40   (E) 80

35. If the sum of a set of different odd integers is exactly zero, which of the following will ALWAYS be true?
   I. The product of integers in the set is zero.
   II. The average of the set is zero.
   III. The number of integers in the set is an even number.

   (A) I only   (B) II only   (C) I and III
   (D) II and III   (E) I, II, and III

IF YOU FINISH BEFORE TIME IS CALLED, YOU MAY CHECK YOUR WORK ON THIS SECTION ONLY. DO NOT WORK ON ANY OTHER SECTION IN THE TEST.   **S T O P**

6 6 6 6 6 6 6 6 6 6 6

SECTION 6   Time—30 minutes   In this section solve each problem, using any available space on
              25 Questions   the page for scratchwork. Then decide which is the best of the
                                  choices given and blacken the corresponding space on the answer
                                  sheet.

The following information is for your reference in solving some of the problems.

Circle of radius r: Area $= \pi r^2$; Circumference $= 2\pi r$
  The number of degrees of arc in a circle is 360.
The measure in degrees of a straight angle is 180.

Definitions of symbols:
= is equal to $\leq$ is less than or equal to
$\neq$ is unequal to $\geq$ is greater than or equal to
< is less than $\parallel$ is parallel to
> is greater than $\perp$ is perpendicular to

Triangle: The sum of the measures
  in degrees of the angles of
  a triangle is 180.
If $\angle CDA$ is a right angle, then

(1) area of $\triangle ABC = \dfrac{AB \times CD}{2}$

(2) $AC^2 = AD^2 + DC^2$

Note: Figures that accompany problems in this test are intended to provide information useful in solving the problems.
They are drawn as accurately as possible EXCEPT when it is stated in a specific problem that its figure is not drawn to
scale. All figures lie in a plane unless otherwise indicated. All numbers used are real numbers.

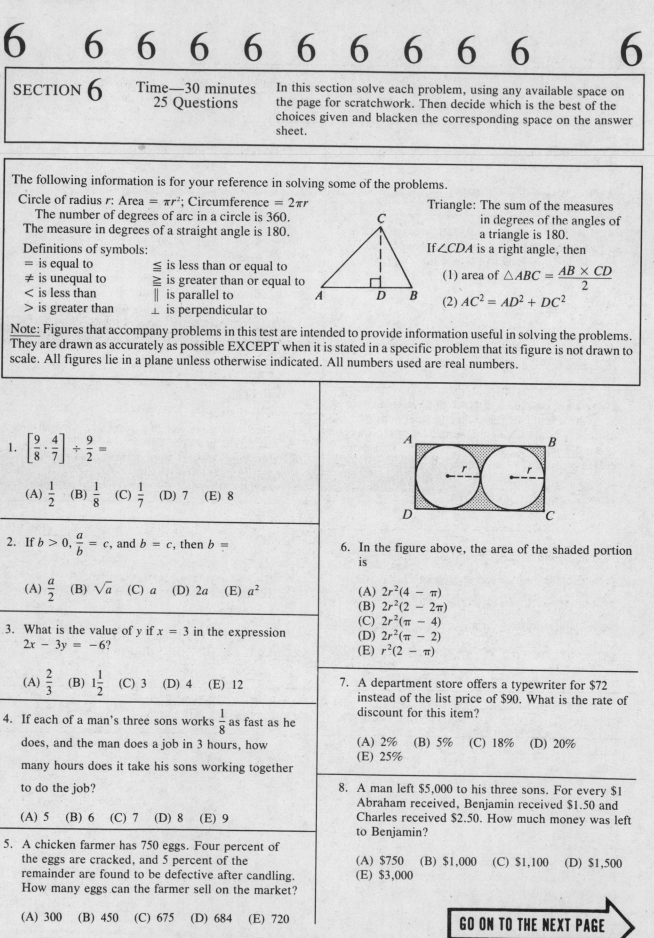

1. $\left[\dfrac{9}{8} \cdot \dfrac{4}{7}\right] \div \dfrac{9}{2} =$

(A) $\dfrac{1}{2}$ (B) $\dfrac{1}{8}$ (C) $\dfrac{1}{7}$ (D) 7   (E) 8

2. If $b > 0$, $\dfrac{a}{b} = c$, and $b = c$, then $b =$

(A) $\dfrac{a}{2}$ (B) $\sqrt{a}$ (C) a (D) $2a$ (E) a^2

3. What is the value of y if $x = 3$ in the expression
$2x - 3y = -6$?

(A) $\dfrac{2}{3}$ (B) $1\dfrac{1}{2}$ (C) 3   (D) 4   (E) 12

4. If each of a man's three sons works $\dfrac{1}{8}$ as fast as he
does, and the man does a job in 3 hours, how
many hours does it take his sons working together
to do the job?

(A) 5   (B) 6   (C) 7   (D) 8   (E) 9

5. A chicken farmer has 750 eggs. Four percent of
the eggs are cracked, and 5 percent of the
remainder are found to be defective after candling.
How many eggs can the farmer sell on the market?

(A) 300   (B) 450   (C) 675   (D) 684   (E) 720

6. In the figure above, the area of the shaded portion
is

(A) $2r^2(4 - \pi)$
(B) $2r^2(2 - 2\pi)$
(C) $2r^2(\pi - 4)$
(D) $2r^2(\pi - 2)$
(E) $r^2(2 - \pi)$

7. A department store offers a typewriter for $72
instead of the list price of $90. What is the rate of
discount for this item?

(A) 2%   (B) 5%   (C) 18%   (D) 20%
(E) 25%

8. A man left $5,000 to his three sons. For every $1
Abraham received, Benjamin received $1.50 and
Charles received $2.50. How much money was left
to Benjamin?

(A) $750   (B) $1,000   (C) $1,100   (D) $1,500
(E) $3,000

GO ON TO THE NEXT PAGE

6   6 6 6 6 6 6 6 6 6   6

9. The El Capitan of the Santa Fe travels a distance of 152.5 miles from La Junta to Garden City in 2 hours. What is the average speed, in miles per hour?

(A) 15.25   (B) 31.5   (C) 30.5   (D) 71
(E) 76.3

10. A salesman traveled for 5 hours at an average rate of 40 miles per hour. He then developed motor trouble and returned to his original starting point in 10 hours. What was his average rate, in miles per hour, on the return trip?

(A) 10   (B) 15   (C) 20   (D) 26.6   (E) 40

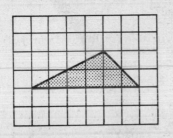

11. How many square units are there in the shaded triangle above?

(A) 4   (B) 6   (C) 8   (D) 9   (E) 12

12. John and James painted a barn for $100. If John worked 8 days and James worked 12 days, how much should James receive for his work?

(A) $32   (B) $40   (C) $60   (D) $75   (E) $80

13. If a carload contains from 12 to 18 boxed refrigerators, what is the least number of refrigerators contained in 4 carloads?

(A) 24   (B) 36   (C) 48   (D) 60   (E) 72

14. Of the values 45.9, 49.5, 59.4, and x (where x is more than 45), which of the following CANNOT possibly be the average?

(A) 45   (B) 55   (C) 56   (D) 550   (E) 555

15. Of 25 tulip bulbs that are planted each year, from 20 to 22 produce flowers. What is the maximum percentage of flowers produced in any one year?

(A) 12   (B) 20   (C) 22   (D) 80   (E) 88

16. How long is the shadow of a 35-foot tree, if a 98-foot tree casts a 42-foot shadow at the same time?

(A) 8   (B) 9   (C) 12   (D) 13   (E) 15

17. How many points are 2 inches from a given line and 3 inches from a point on that line?

(A) 1 point   (B) 2 points   (C) 3 points
(D) 4 points   (E) 5 points

18. Which of the following is greater than $\frac{1}{4}$?

(A) 0.04   (B) $\left(\frac{1}{4}\right)^2$ (C) $\frac{1}{0.04}$ (D) $(0.04)^2$
(E) $\frac{0.04}{4}$

19. Three high schools supplied student workers for a summer project. High School A supplied 7 students for 3 days; High School B, 4 students for 5 days; and High School C, 5 students for 9 days. The total wages earned by all students were $774. If each student received the same daily wage, how much did the group of students working from High School B receive for the work?

(A) $56.80   (B) $180   (C) $193.50   (D) $227.65
(E) $90

20. Ms. Baker finds that she gets 7 miles on a gallon of gasoline. After having the carburetor overhauled, she uses only $\frac{5}{7}$ as much gasoline. How much further, in miles, can she now ride on one gallon of gasoline?

(A) $1\frac{2}{5}$ (B) 2   (C) $2\frac{4}{5}$ (D) 5   (E) $9\frac{4}{5}$

21. $2.4 \sqrt{\dfrac{x^4 y^2}{16} + \dfrac{y^2 x^4}{9}} =$

(A) xy (B) xy^2 (C) $x^2 y$ (D) $x\sqrt{y}$ (E) $y\sqrt{x}$

GO ON TO THE NEXT PAGE

6 6 6 6 6 6 6 6 6 6 6

22. In the figure above, $AE \perp ED$, $CD \perp ED$, $DC \perp CB$; $ED = 13$, $CD = 3$, $CB = 2$, $AE = 11$. Then $AB =$

(A) 8　(B) 13　(C) 14　(D) 15　(E) 17

23. If books bought at prices ranging from $2.00 to $3.50 are sold at prices ranging from $3.00 to $4.25, what is the greatest possible profit that may be made in selling 8 books?

(A) $2.50　(B) $4.00　(C) $6.00　(D) $9.00
(E) $18.00

24. Which two of the following are equal?

I. $1 + \dfrac{x}{y}$

II. y

III. $\dfrac{y^2 + 2xy}{xy}$

IV. $\dfrac{y}{x}$

V. $\dfrac{2x + y}{x}$

(A) I and III　(B) I and IV　(C) I and V
(D) III and V　(E) II and V

25. A salesperson reports an increase in sales by 20 percent. What is the ratio of the current sales to the original?

(A) 1:5　(B) 4:5　(C) 6:5　(D) 5:4　(E) 5:1

IF YOU FINISH BEFORE TIME IS CALLED, YOU MAY CHECK YOUR WORK ON THIS SECTION ONLY. DO NOT WORK ON ANY OTHER SECTION IN THE TEST.　**S T O P**

Answer Key

Note: The answers to the math sections are keyed to the corresponding review areas in Chapter 12. The numbers in parentheses after each answer refer to topics as listed below. (Note that to review for number 16, Quantitative Comparison, study Chapter 11.)

1. Fundamental Operations
2. Algebraic Operations
3. Using Algebra
4. Roots and Radicals
5. Inequalities
6. Fractions
7. Decimals
8. Percent
9. Averages
10. Motion
11. Ratio and Proportion
12. Mixtures and Solutions
13. Work
14. Coordinate Geometry
15. Geometry
16. Quantitative Comparison
17. Data Interpretation

Section 1   Math

1.	B (8)	6.	E (15)	11.	B (4)	16.	A (11)	21.	D (1)
2.	A (5)	7.	C (8)	12.	C (1)	17.	B (10, 11)	22.	D (8, 15)
3.	E (9)	8.	A (11)	13.	C (2)	18.	A (1)	23.	B (14)
4.	D (1)	9.	A (15)	14.	A (8)	19.	D (15)	24.	D (2)
5.	B (2)	10.	B (2)	15.	D (1, 9)	20.	D (9)	25.	A (9)

Section 2   Test of Standard Written English

1.	E	11.	C	21.	D	31.	C	41.	D
2.	A	12.	A	22.	C	32.	A	42.	A
3.	E	13.	E	23.	D	33.	B	43.	D
4.	B	14.	E	24.	D	34.	C	44.	B
5.	C	15.	D	25.	E	35.	D	45.	C
6.	B	16.	C	26.	C	36.	C	46.	B
7.	C	17.	C	27.	C	37.	E	47.	C
8.	D	18.	E	28.	D	38.	A	48.	E
9.	B	19.	C	29.	B	39.	B	49.	A
10.	A	20.	D	30.	C	40.	B	50.	A

Section 3   Verbal

1.	A	10.	A	19.	D	28.	D	37.	B
2.	D	11.	A	20.	C	29.	B	38.	C
3.	C	12.	C	21.	A	30.	A	39.	B
4.	B	13.	A	22.	D	31.	D	40.	D
5.	D	14.	E	23.	E	32.	B	41.	B
6.	A	15.	D	24.	B	33.	C	42.	D
7.	B	16.	C	25.	E	34.	D	43.	B
8.	D	17.	E	26.	C	35.	E	44.	E
9.	E	18.	A	27.	D	36.	C	45.	B

Section 4   Verbal

1.	B	9.	C	17.	B	25.	E	33.	B
2.	D	10.	D	18.	A	26.	D	34.	C
3.	C	11.	C	19.	A	27.	D	35.	A
4.	B	12.	C	20.	C	28.	A	36.	D
5.	C	13.	B	21.	A	29.	C	37.	C
6.	D	14.	A	22.	D	30.	E	38.	B
7.	C	15.	A	23.	C	31.	C	39.	E
8.	A	16.	C	24.	B	32.	E	40.	C

Section 5   Math

1.	A (1)	8.	A (8, 16)	15.	D (2, 16)	22.	A (15, 16)	29.	C (11)
2.	E (9)	9.	C (2, 8, 16)	16.	D (15, 16)	23.	B (15, 16)	30.	B (10)
3.	D (15)	10.	C (4, 16)	17.	D (2, 16)	24.	A (15, 16)	31.	E (6)
4.	E (2)	11.	C (4, 8, 16)	18.	D (15, 16)	25.	B (15, 16)	32.	D (6)
5.	C (2)	12.	B (4, 16)	19.	D (15, 16)	26.	C (15, 16)	33.	B (8)
6.	A (13)	13.	A (10, 16)	20.	C (15, 16)	27.	D (15, 16)	34.	D (8)
7.	B (1)	14.	C (2, 16)	21.	B (15, 16)	28.	A (1)	35.	D (1)

Section 6   Math

1.	C (1)	6.	A (15)	11.	B (14)	16.	E (11)	21.	C (4)
2.	B (2)	7.	D (8)	12.	C (1, 6)	17.	D (15)	22.	E (15)
3.	D (2)	8.	D (6, 11)	13.	C (1)	18.	C (6, 8)	23.	E (8)
4.	D (13)	9.	E (10)	14.	A (9)	19.	B (1)	24.	D (6)
5.	D (3, 8)	10.	C (10)	15.	E (8)	20.	C (11)	25.	C (8, 11)

Self-Evaluation

If you have been doing the model tests in order, you have just completed the last model test. By now you should be totally familiar with the types of questions you will find on the SAT and with the format of the exam.

Do the self-evaluation procedures for this test just as you did for the five model tests you've already taken. Here are the step-by-step procedures that you should follow.

■ **STEP 1**   Use the Answer Key to check your answers for each section.

■ **STEP 2**   For each section, count the number of correct and incorrect answers (remember that you don't count omitted answers), and enter the numbers on the appropriate lines of the chart "Calculate Your Raw Score." Then do the indicated calculations to get your Raw Verbal Score, your Raw TSWE Score, and your Raw Math Score.

■ **STEP 3**   Consult the chart "Evaluate Your Performance" to see how well you did.

■ **STEP 4**   To pinpoint the specific areas in which you need to improve, circle the numbers of the questions that you either left blank or got wrong on the "Identify Your Weaknesses" charts. This will tell you where to concentrate your efforts to get the most out of your study time. The chart for the math sections gives you page references for review and practice by skill areas. The charts for the verbal and TSWE sections refer you to the appropriate chapters to study for each question type.

■ **STEP 5**   Do the review and practice indicated on the charts wherever you had a concentration of circles.

Important: Remember that, in addition to evaluating your scores, you should read all of the answer explanations for questions you answered incorrectly, questions you omitted, and questions you answered correctly but found difficult. Reviewing the answer explanations will help you understand concepts and strategies, and may point out short-cuts.

Calculate Your Raw Score

Verbal

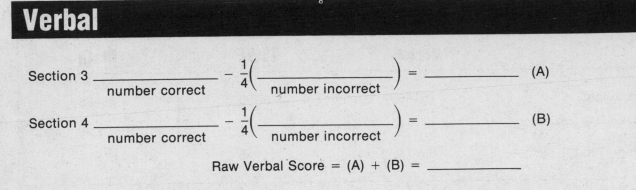

Section 3 $\underline{\hspace{3cm}}$ $- \frac{1}{4}\left(\underline{\hspace{3cm}} \right) =$ $\underline{\hspace{2cm}}$ (A)
number correct   number incorrect

Section 4 $\underline{\hspace{3cm}}$ $- \frac{1}{4}\left(\underline{\hspace{3cm}} \right) =$ $\underline{\hspace{2cm}}$ (B)
number correct   number incorrect

Raw Verbal Score = (A) + (B) = $\underline{\hspace{3cm}}$

TSWE

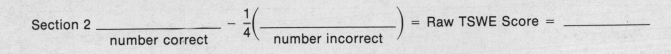

Section 2 $\underline{\hspace{3cm}}$ $- \frac{1}{4}\left(\underline{\hspace{3cm}} \right) =$ Raw TSWE Score = $\underline{\hspace{2cm}}$
number correct   number incorrect

Math

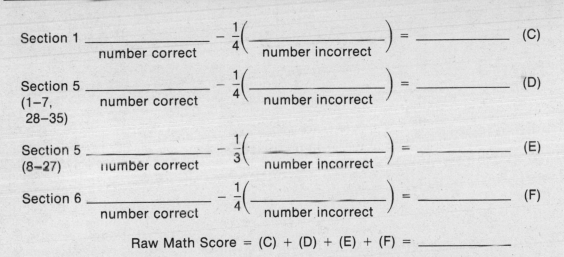

Section 1 $\underline{\hspace{3cm}}$ $- \frac{1}{4}\left(\underline{\hspace{3cm}} \right) =$ $\underline{\hspace{2cm}}$ (C)
number correct   number incorrect

Section 5 $\underline{\hspace{3cm}}$ $- \frac{1}{4}\left(\underline{\hspace{3cm}} \right) =$ $\underline{\hspace{2cm}}$ (D)
(1–7,   number correct   number incorrect
28–35)

Section 5 $\underline{\hspace{3cm}}$ $- \frac{1}{3}\left(\underline{\hspace{3cm}} \right) =$ $\underline{\hspace{2cm}}$ (E)
(8–27)   number correct   number incorrect

Section 6 $\underline{\hspace{3cm}}$ $- \frac{1}{4}\left(\underline{\hspace{3cm}} \right) =$ $\underline{\hspace{2cm}}$ (F)
number correct   number incorrect

Raw Math Score = (C) + (D) + (E) + (F) = $\underline{\hspace{3cm}}$

Evaluate Your Performance

Verbal, TSWE, Math

	Verbal	TSWE	Math
Excellent	75–85	46–50	75–85
Very Good	65–74	41–45	61–74
Good	50–64	36–40	55–60
Above Average	40–49	31–35	45–54
Average	33–39	26–30	35–44
Below Average	below 33	below 26	below 35

Identify Your Weaknesses

Verbal

Question Type	Question Numbers		Chapter to Study
	Section 3	Section 4	
Antonym	1, 2, 3, 4, 5, 6, 7, 8, 9, 10, 11, 12, 13, 14, 15	1, 2, 3, 4, 5, 6, 7, 8, 9, 10	Chapter 5
Analogy	36, 37, 38, 39, 40, 41, 42, 43, 44, 45	16, 17, 18, 19, 20, 21, 22, 23, 24, 25	Chapter 6
Sentence Completion	16, 17, 18, 19, 20, 31, 32, 33, 34, 35	11, 12, 13, 14, 15	Chapter 7
Reading Comprehension	21, 22, 23, 24, 25, 26, 27, 28, 29, 30	26, 27, 28, 29, 30, 31, 32, 33, 34, 35, 36, 37, 38, 39, 40	Chapter 8

TSWE

Question Type	Question Numbers	Chapter to Study
Usage	1, 2, 3, 4, 5, 6, 7, 8, 9, 10, 11, 12, 13, 14, 15, 16, 17, 18, 19, 20, 21, 22, 23, 24, 25, 41, 42, 43, 44, 45, 46, 47, 48, 49, 50	Chapter 13
Sentence Correction	26, 27, 28, 29, 30, 31, 32, 33, 34, 35, 36, 37, 38, 39, 40	Chapter 13

Identify Your Weaknesses

Math

Skill Area	Question Numbers			Pages to Study
	Section 1	Section 5	Section 6	
Fundamental Operations	4, 12, 15, 18, 21	1, 3, 7, 28, 35	1, 12, 13, 19	328–29
Algebraic Operations	5, 10, 13, 24	4, 5, 9, 14, 15, 17	2	329–34
Fractions		31, 32	8, 12, 18, 24	341–45
Decimals and Percents	1, 7, 14, 22	8, 9, 11, 33, 34	5, 7, 15, 18, 23, 25	351–55
Verbal Problems	3, 12, 17, 20	2, 6, 13, 30, 32	4, 9, 10, 20	357–58
Ratio and Proportion	8, 16, 17	29	8, 16, 20, 25	362–64
Geometry	6, 9, 19, 22	3, 16, 18, 19, 20, 21, 22, 23, 24, 25, 26, 27	6, 16, 17, 22	371–76
Coordinate Geometry	23		11	381–82
Inequalities	2			335–36
Quantitative Comparison		8, 9, 10, 11, 12, 13, 14, 15, 16, 17, 18, 19, 20, 21, 22, 23, 24, 25, 26, 27		309–13
Roots and Radicals	11	11, 12	21	332–33

Answer Explanations

Section 1   Math

1. **B.** $\frac{1}{4}\% = \frac{\frac{1}{4}}{100}$ or $\frac{1}{4} \div 100$ or $\frac{1}{4} \cdot \frac{1}{100} = \frac{1}{400}$

   $\frac{1}{400}$ of 2 or $\frac{1}{400} \cdot \frac{2}{1} = \frac{1}{200}$

2. **A.** The thickened line between -2 and 3 represents all the numbers whose points (coordinates) are on the line. The open circle at -2 indicates that -2 is not part of the set, while the solid circle at 3 indicates that 3 is a member of the set. Thus the inequality shown is all numbers more than -2 and less than or equal to 3.

3. **E.** Since the average is K, the sum of the two numbers is $2K$.
   Since one number is M, the other number is $2K - M$.

4. **D.** At 80¢ per pound, the cost of 4 lb. is $3.20. The change is $10.00 - $3.20 or $6.80.

5. **B.** $Z + \frac{1}{Z} = \frac{Z^2}{Z} + \frac{1}{Z} = \frac{Z^2 + 1}{Z}$

6. **E.** If the area $= 9\pi$, then each radius $= 3$,
   $$AD = 2r = 6$$
   $$AB = 4r = 12$$
   Area of $ABCD = 6 \times 12 = 72$

   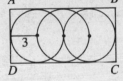

7. **C.** $a\% = \frac{a}{100}$ $b\% = \frac{b}{100}$

   $\left(\frac{a}{100} \cdot b\right) \div \left(\frac{b}{100} \cdot a\right)$

   $\frac{ab}{100} \div \frac{ab}{100}$

   Any quantity divided by itself equals 1.

8. **A.** This is a direct proportion.
   Let $x =$ number of weys in 4 bushels.
   $$\frac{\text{weys}}{\text{bushels}} = \frac{1}{40} = \frac{x}{4}$$
   $$40x = 4$$
   $$x = \frac{4}{40} \text{ or } \frac{1}{10}$$

   Or, since 4 bushels is $\frac{1}{10}$ of 40 bushels, it is equivalent to $\frac{1}{10}$ wey.

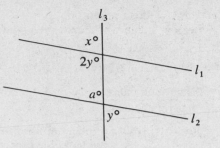

9. **A.** $a = y$ because vertical angles are congruent
   $2y + a$ or $2y + y = 3y$
   $$3y = 180$$
   $$y = 60$$
   $$2y = 120$$
   $x = 180 - 120$ or 60

10. **B.** In 1 week Mr. Simon saves $(d - s)$ dollars.
    To save Q dollars will require $\frac{Q}{d - s}$ weeks.

11. **B.** $\sqrt{\frac{1}{4}} \cdot \sqrt{\frac{16}{36}}$

    $\frac{1}{2} \cdot \frac{4}{6}$

    $\frac{1}{2} \cdot \frac{\overset{2}{\cancel{4}}}{6} = \frac{1}{3}$

12. **C.** Each card costs 84¢ $\div$ 3 or 28¢.
    Each mailing costs   22¢.
    Cost of purchasing and
    mailing one card = $\overline{50¢.}$
    Total cost, $16.50, $\div$ $0.50 = 33 cards

13. **C.** $x^2 + 4x + 6 = x^2 + 3x + 7$
    $4x + 6 = 3x + 7$ (subtract x^2)
    $x + 6 = 7$ (subtract $3x$)
    $x = 1$ (subtract 6)

14. **A.** 0.4% of 1,000 articles will be rejected.
    $0.4\% = \frac{0.4}{100} = \frac{4}{1000}$

    $\frac{4}{1000} \cdot \frac{1000}{1} = 4$

15. **D.** The third (middle) integer is the arithmetic mean. Apply the formula:
    Sum = Average × Number of numbers
    Sum = $50 \times 5 = 250$

16. **A.** $xy = k$
    $(4)(7) = k$
    $28 = k$
    $xy = k$
    $(x)(17.5) = 28$
    $x = \frac{28}{17.5}$ or 1.6

17. B. This is a direct proportion.
Let x = number of minutes required to travel $\frac{2}{5}$ mile.

$$\frac{\text{distance (in miles)}}{\text{time (in minutes)}} = \frac{50}{60} = \frac{\frac{2}{5}}{x}$$

$50x = \left(\frac{2}{5}\right)(60)$ (product of means equals product of extremes)

$50x = 24$

$x = \frac{24}{50}$ or 0.48

18. A. Minimum number of crates on a trip = 3
Minimum weight of a crate = 125 lb.
Minimum weight of crates on a trip = 375 lb.

19. D. Area of circle = $\pi(\text{radius})^2$
Area of circle = πr^2
Area of rectangle = πr^2 (given)
Area of rectangle = (Base) (Altitude)
Area of rectangle = (b) (altitude)
$\pi r^2 = (b)$ (altitude)
$\frac{\pi r^2}{b}$ = altitude (division by b)

20. D. To have an average of 90 min. (or $1\frac{1}{2}$ hr.) per day, the total time spent practicing for the week must equal $(7)\left(1\frac{1}{2}\right)$ or $10\frac{1}{2}$ hr. From Monday to Thursday the girl has practiced $1\frac{1}{4} + 2 + 2 + 1\frac{3}{4}$ or 7 hr. She must therefore spend $3\frac{1}{2}$ additional hours practicing for the rest of the week.

21. D. To raise $500 in addition to the expenses of $250 the school must receive $750 for tickets. At 75¢ per ticket, $\frac{\$750}{\$0.75}$ or 1,000 tickets must be sold.

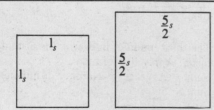

22. D. Let s = side of original square.
$s + 150\%s$ or $s + 1\frac{1}{2}s$ or $2\frac{1}{2}s$ or $\frac{5}{2}s$ = side of new square
Area of square = $(\text{Side})^2$
Area of original square = $(s)^2$ or s^2

Area of new square = $\left(\frac{5s}{2}\right)^2$ or $\frac{25s^2}{4}$ or $6\frac{1}{4}s^2$

Area of new square = $6\frac{1}{4}s^2$ (or $625\%s^2$)

Area of original square = $1s^2$ (or $100\%s^2$)

Increase = 525% of s^2

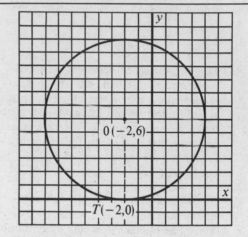

23. B. Observe that the point of tangency is at $(-2, 0)$.
Radius OT is $\perp$ to the x-axis since a radius is $\perp$ to a tangent at the point of contact. Thus OT is parallel to the y-axis, and point T, like point O, is 2 units to the left of the y-axis. Thus $x = -2$.
Since the point T lies on the x-axis, $y = 0$. The coordinates of the point of tangency, point T, are $(-2, 0)$.

y x $T(-2, 0)$ $O(-2, 6)$

24. D. Substitute: $(2) = (2)^2 + \frac{1}{2^2} = 4 + \frac{1}{4} = 4\frac{1}{4}$

25. A. To attain an average of $\frac{3}{10}$, the sum of the five fractions must be $5\left(\frac{3}{10}\right)$ or $\frac{15}{10}$.

$\frac{3}{5} + \frac{1}{4} + \frac{1}{10} + \frac{1}{2}$

$\frac{12}{20} + \frac{5}{20} + \frac{2}{20} + \frac{10}{20} = \frac{29}{20}$

The sum of the four fractions = $\frac{29}{20}$

The fraction to be added must be $\frac{15}{10} - \frac{29}{20}$

or $\frac{30}{20} - \frac{29}{20} = \frac{1}{20}$.

Section 2   Test of Standard Written English

1. E. Sentence is correct.

2. A. Error in tense. Change *has adopted* to *adopted*.

3. E.   Sentence is correct.

4. B.   Error in diction. Change *irregardless* to *regardless*.

5. C.   Error in agreement. The subject *she and her staff* is plural; the verb should be plural—*are*.

6. B.   Error in diction. Change *or* to *nor*.

7. C.   Error in diction. Change *affect* to *effect*.

8. D.   Error in agreement. Change *his and her* to *their*.

9. B.   Error in case. Change *you* to *your*.

10. A.   Error in diction. The verb *to lie* (past participle is *lain*) means to recline; the verb *to lay* (past participle is *laid*) means to put or place. Therefore, change *has lain* to *has laid*.

11. C.   Error in agreement. Change *their* to *his*.

12. A.   Error in diction. Omit *a*.

13. E.   Sentence is correct.

14. E.   Sentence is correct.

15. D.   Lack of parallel structure. Change *an increase in interest rates* to *interest rates increase*.

16. C.   Misuse of adjective for adverb. Change *special prepared* to *specially prepared*.

17. C.   Error in tense. Change *been creating* to *created*.

18. E.   Sentence is correct.

19. C.   Error in agreement. The subject *explosion* is singular. Therefore, change *have caught* to *has caught*.

20. D.   Faulty diction. The conjunction *than* helps to make a comparison, not *then*.

21. D.   Lack of parallel structure. Change *leaving room for* to *to leave room for*.

22. C.   Error in case. Change *him* to *he*.

23. D.   Error in sentence connector. Change *in fact* to *but* in order to clarify the relationship between the clauses.

24. D.   Error in parallel structure. Change *to insure* to *insuring*.

25. E.   Sentence is correct.

26. C.   The past perfect tense is required in an "if" clause.

27. C.   The two errors in diction (*imminent* for *eminent* and *stood* for *stayed*) are corrected in Choice C.

28. D.   This corrects the sentence fragment.

29. B.   Choice B corrects the run-on sentence.

30. C.   Choice C corrects the sentence fragment.

31. C.   Choice C corrects the run-on sentence and expresses the author's meaning directly and concisely. All other choices are indirect, ungrammatical, or do not retain the meaning of the original sentence.

32. A.   Sentence is correct as given.

33. B.   Choice B corrects the conjunction *neither . . . nor* (not *neither . . . or*) as well as the run-on sentence, and retains the meaning of the original sentence.

34. C.   Use *this kind of story* or *these kinds of stories*.

35. D.   The omission of the correct verb form is corrected in Choice D.

36. C.   The dangling participle construction is corrected in C.

37. E.   Choice E corrects the misplaced modifier and eliminates the unnecessary use of the passive voice.

38. A.   The use of the semicolon to separate the pair of clauses is correct.

39. B.   Choice B expresses the author's meaning directly and concisely. All other choices are indirect, ungrammatical, or do not retain the meaning of the original sentence.

40. B.   Choice B eliminates the excessive wordiness of the original sentence without introducing any errors in diction.

41. D.   Lack of parallel structure. Delete *because of its being*.

42. A.   Dangling participle. Change *Snowing* to *Because it had snowed*.

43. D. Error in case. Change *to whomever* to *to whoever*. It is the subject of the verb *made*.

44. B. Misuse of conjunction. Use *to* before an infinitive verb of purpose. Change *try and see* to *try to see*.

45. C. Error in conjunction. Since the correlative conjunction is *not only . . . but also*, change *but aid also* to *but also aid*.

46. B. Unnecessary switch in pronouns. It is the *patients* (plural noun) who feel there is a problem. Change *one feels* to *they feel*.

47. C. Lack of parallel structure. Change *of his* to *he has a*.

48. E. Sentence is correct.

49. A. Misuse of pronoun. Change *them* (personal pronoun) to *those* (demonstrative pronoun).

50. A. Lack of parallel structure. Change *to newspapers* to *to reading newspapers*.

Section 3   Verbal

1. A. *Negligent* means neglectful or careless; inattentive. Its opposite is *painstaking*, showing steady, earnest care.

2. D. To *retract* means to draw or pull back. Its opposite is to stick out or project; to *extend*. Remember to try to break down unfamiliar words into recognizable parts.
Word Parts Clue: *Re-* means back; *tract-* means to drag or pull. *Retract* means to pull back.

3. C. *Consistent* means harmonious, showing no disagreement or contradiction. Its opposite is *self-contradictory* or inconsistent.
Context Clue: Think of "telling a consistent story."

4. B. *Estrangement* means alienation; the destruction of friendship or affection. Its opposite is *reconciliation*, restoration to friendship.
Context Clue: Think of "his estrangement from his family."

5. D. To *sterilize* is to destroy living germs or microorganisms, in a sense, to cleanse. Its opposite is to *contaminate*, to corrupt or infect.
Context Clue: Think of "sterilized needles."

6. A. To *enmesh* is to catch or entangle in (as if caught in a net). Its opposite is to *disentangle* (to extricate or free).
Context Clue: Think of "enmeshed in a web of lies."

7. B. To *corroborate* is to confirm, to support with evidence. Its opposite is to *deny*.
Context Clue: "She corroborated his account."

8. D. *Reprehensible* means blameworthy, deserving censure. Its opposite is *commendable* or praiseworthy.
Context Clue: Think of "a reprehensible traitor."

9. E. To *reprove* is to rebuke or scold. Its opposite is to *praise*.
Context Clue: Think of "reproving naughty children."

10. A. *Unobtrusive* means not blatantly obvious or noticeable. Its opposite is *glaring* or painfully obvious.
Remember to consider secondary meanings of words as well as their primary meanings. *Glaring* has other meanings in addition to scowling to show anger.
Context Clue: Think of "a quiet, unobtrusive manner."

11. A. To *flaunt* is to display something ostentatiously, to show it off. Its opposite is to *conceal* or hide.
Context Clue: "If you've got it, flaunt it!"

12. C. *Equanimity* means emotional balance; evenness of disposition. Its opposite is *lack of composure*, lack of poise.
Word Parts Clue: *Equ-* means even or equal; *anim-* means mind. *Equanimity* is evenness of mind.

13. A. *Ingenuous* means naive, innocent, unsophisticated. Its opposite is *sophisticated* or worldly.
Context Clue: Think of "an ingenuous sweet young thing."

14. E. *Sanguine* means anticipating the best; optimistic; confident. Its opposite is *pessimistic* or expecting the worst.
Context Clue: Think of "sanguine expectations."

15. D. *Hedonism* is the doctrine that pleasure or happiness is the only good thing in life; it advocates self-indulgence. Its opposite is *self-denial* or restraint.
Context Clue: Think of "selfish hedonism."

16. C. The reviewer was vitriolic (as biting as acid), devastating (destructive), and irritating (annoying). He was not *constructive* or helpful.
Never signals a contrast. The missing word must be an antonym or near-antonym for the three adjectives in the series.
Note that you are looking for a word with positive associations. Therefore, you can eliminate any word with negative ones.
Choices D and E have negative associations. Only Choices A, B, or C can be correct.
Choice C is preferable.

(Contrast Signal)

17. E. The team members *tolerated* or put up with the coach's rules as long as the coach was not too strict in *applying* them.
Despite signals a contrast. You expect people who resent rules to fight them or disobey them. Instead, the team members put up with them.
Remember, in double-blank sentences, go through the answer choices, testing the *first* words in each choice and eliminating those that don't fit. You can immediately eliminate Choices B, C, and D.

(Contrast Signal)

18. A. If we still cannot make up our minds whether low-level microwave radiation is dangerous or safe, our evidence must be too weak for us to be able to decide; it must be *inconclusive*.
Remember, before you look at the choices, read the sentence and think of a word that makes sense.
Likely Words: incomplete, uncorroborated, unverified.

(Argument Pattern)

19. D. The negotiations have degenerated or deteriorated; they have become *acrimonious* or bitter.
The phrase following the blank gives an example of what the sessions are like. They are degenerating into a welter or turmoil of accusations.
Note that you are looking for a word with negative associations. Therefore, you can eliminate any word with positive ones.
Choices A, C, and E all have positive associations. Only Choice B or Choice D can be correct. *Phlegmatic* (slow and stolid; undemonstrative) is an inappropriate word to describe a wild turmoil of accusations. By process of elimination, the correct answer must be *acrimonious*, Choice D.

(Examples)

20. C. Indian art recalls (*is reminiscent of*) Japanese art because, like Japanese art, it minimizes; it *understates*.
The clause following "Japanese art" gives *examples* of what Japanese art is like: it suggests; it does not state directly or overstate. Look at the first word of each answer pair. If the first word means states directly or overstates, then the second word must mean "is unlike," because it is unlike Japanese art to overstate. If the first word means suggests or understates, then the second word must mean "is like," because it is like Japanese art to understate.

(Examples)

21. A. The phrases "coming unexpectedly as he did" and "his sudden arrival" support the idea that Sir Thomas has returned unexpectedly. Note that these key phrases are found in the closing sentence of the first paragraph and in the opening sentence of the second paragraph. Sir Thomas' unexpected return is central to the passage.
Choice B is incorrect. Although the persons talking belong to the upper classes, as a title "The Conversation of the Upper Class" is too vague.
Choice C is incorrect. Mrs. Norris's complaint or grievance (the subject of the third paragraph) is too narrow in scope to be an appropriate title for the passage as a whole.
Choice D is incorrect. Although Lady Bertram is quite pleased to have her husband home again, their reunion is placid rather than emotional or romantic.
Choice E is incorrect. Although Sir Thomas gives an account of his voyage in the first paragraph, the passage places its emphasis on the reactions of his family to his surprising return.
Remember, when asked to choose a title, watch out for choices that are too specific or too broad.

(Main Idea/Title)

22. D. By stating that his joy at his return "made him communicative and chatty in a very unusual degree," the opening paragraph implies that Sir Thomas is usually *more restrained in speech*.
Choice A is incorrect. Nothing in the passage suggests he is usually unwelcome in his own home.
Choices B and C are incorrect. Neither is supported by the opening paragraph.
Choice E is incorrect. Sir Thomas' delight at finding his family together "exactly as he could have wished" indicates he does not lack family feeling.

Remember, when asked to make inferences, base your answers on what the passage implies, not what it states directly.

(Inference)

23. **E.** The opening sentence of the second paragraph states that none of the members of his family listened to him with such "unbroken unalloyed enjoyment" as his wife did. Her enjoyment was complete and unmixed with other emotions. Later the passage states emphatically that Sir Thomas' wife "had no anxieties for anybody to cloud *her* pleasure." The author italicizes the word *her* to suggest that others in the group have anxieties and face Sir Thomas' arrival *with mixed emotions*.
Choice A is incorrect. It is unsupported by the passage.
Choice B is incorrect. Lady Bertram's fluttered or discomposed state on his arrival indicates her surprise.
Choice C is incorrect. The last sentence of the first paragraph indicates that Sir Thomas did not expect to find his whole family at home. Therefore, he had not timed his arrival to coincide with a reunion.
Choice D is incorrect. Sir Thomas has had to seek out the butler and confide the news of his arrival to him. Therefore, the servants had not expected his arrival.

(Inference)

24. **B.** Refusing to be provoked by Mrs. Norris's interruptions, Sir Thomas demonstrates *patient forbearance* or restraint.
Choice A is incorrect. Sir Thomas "could not be provoked." Therefore, he showed no irritation.
Choice C is incorrect. Sir Thomas remarks courteously on Mrs. Norris's anxiety for everybody's comfort. This implies that he in general approves rather than disapproves of her concern.
Choice D is incorrect. It is unsupported by the passage.
Choice E is incorrect. Given Mrs. Norris's interruptions of his story, it is unlikely Sir Thomas would view her with *unmixed delight*.

(Inference)

25. **E.** Mrs. Norris has looked forward to spreading the news of Sir Thomas's return (or of his death!). The office she has lost is that of herald or message-bearer.
Choice A is incorrect. Mrs. Norris wishes to give orders to the butler, not to be the butler.
Choice B is incorrect for much the same reason.
Choice C is incorrect. Mrs. Norris is the sister of Sir Thomas's wife; the passage does not

indicate that she has any desire to be his wife.
Choice D is incorrect. Mrs. Norris wishes to give news of the traveler, not to be the traveler.

(Inference)

26. **C.** The author's purpose in this passage is to show how he discovered that learning to read was vital for him if he wanted to be free. The bulk of the passage deals with learning to read—the author's introduction to it, his master's arguments against it, his own increased determination to succeed in it.
Choice A is incorrect. It is the cause of their disagreement that is central, not the existence of their disagreement.
Choice B is incorrect. The author lists, but does not analyze, the master's reasons for forbidding his wife to teach her slave.
Choice D is incorrect. It is unsupported by the passage.
Choice E is a possible answer, but not as good as Choice C. Only the last two sentences of the first paragraph stress Mrs. Auld's moral downfall.

(Main Idea)

27. **D.** The passage does not suggest that a *disdain* or scorn for convention is typical of Mrs. Auld.
Choice A is incorrect. Mrs. Auld was noted for "constant application to her business" (lines 7–8). This implies that *diligence in labor* was one of her characteristics.
Choice B is incorrect. Mrs. Auld seemed "disturbed" by "crouching servility" (lines 13–16). This implies that a *dislike of fawning* was one of her characteristics.
Choice C is incorrect. Mrs. Auld was kindhearted (lines 1–3) and able to put people at ease (lines 18–19). This implies that *gentleness of spirit* was one of her characteristics.
Choice E is incorrect. Mrs. Auld voluntarily began to teach the narrator. She wished him well. This implies that a *benevolent nature* was one of her characteristics.

(Inference)

28. **D.** Choice D is correct. You can arrive at it by the process of elimination.
Statement I is true. In line 32 Mr. Auld tells his wife that instructing slaves is unlawful: it *violates the law*. Therefore, you can eliminate Choice B.
Statement II is untrue. Since Mr. Auld is so concerned that education would spoil his slaves, he must believe that slaves *can* be taught. Therefore, you can eliminate Choices C and E.
Statement III is true. Mr. Auld states that a

slave who was able to read would become "unmanageable" (line 41). Therefore, you can eliminate Choice A.

Only Choice D is left. It is the correct answer.

(Specific Details)

29. B. The author's tone is strongly ironic. He knows full well that, in opposing his education, his master did not intend to *benefit* him. Thus, by acknowledging his "debt" to his master, the author is underlining his master's defeat.

Choice A is incorrect. The author is not filled with loving sentiment and warmth when he thinks of his harsh master.

Choice C is incorrect. The author neither whines nor congratulates himself on his own moral superiority.

Choice D is incorrect. The author is not resigned or submissive; he certainly is not wistful or longing for the days gone by.

Choice E is incorrect. Although the author still feels anger at the institution of slavery, when he thinks of his master's defeat he feels triumphant as well.

(Attitude/Tone)

30. A. The author wholly believes his master's statement that learning would make him unmanageable. In other words, education would make him *impossible to enslave*.

Choice B is incorrect. The author is concerned with education for freedom, not for old age.

Choices C, D, and E are incorrect. They are unsupported by the passage.

(Inference)

31. D. If irony has become a way of escape, then its job is to help people escape or *evade* life's terrors.

Note that the second clause defines what is meant by irony as a *mode of escape*. It clarifies the phrase's meaning.

(Definition)

32. B. Tacitus' descriptions were *limited* or hindered by the crude (*primitive*) state of communications.

But signals a contrast. The fact that Tacitus' descriptions match those of other writers of his time implies that they are reasonable descriptions for that period. They are adequate *in spite of* the limitations they suffered from.

(Contrast Signal)

33. C. If future archaeological discoveries will be "hard put to match" the revelations of the past ten years, the past decade's discoveries must have been truly remarkable ones, ones that *radically* or fundamentally changed the field. Even *striking* or dramatic discoveries could not compare with such revelations.

34. D. One would protest a system *deliberately* or intentionally designed to *demean* (degrade or debase) human dignity.

Choices A, B, and E are incorrect. One would be unlikely to protest a system that reflected, fostered (nourished), or enhanced (improved) human dignity.

Choice C is also incorrect. *Assess* (evaluate) is inappropriate in the context.

(Definition)

35. E. Civilization is helped or *aided* by *hiatuses* (interruptions or gaps) in the chain of wars. These interruptions are the peaceful periods during which the arts of civilization flourish. *Rather than* signals a contrast. The first missing word must be an antonym or near-antonym for "hindered."

(Contrast Signal)

36. C. A *scrapbook* is a blank book for keeping a collection of *clippings*. An *album* is a blank book for keeping a collection of *stamps*.

(Part to Whole)

37. B. An *avalanche* is a sudden great or overwhelming rush of *snow*. A *deluge* is a sudden great or overwhelming rush of *water*.

(Defining Characteristic)

38. C. An *archipelago* is a cluster of *islands*. A *galaxy* is a cluster of *stars*.

(Part to Whole)

39. B. To *disband* an *organization* is to dismiss it from service or break it up. To *demobilize* an *army* is to dismiss it from service or break it up.

Remember to watch out for errors stemming from reversals. Choice C is incorrect. The employer is the person who discharges or dismisses someone from service. He is not the one who is discharged.

(Defining Characteristic)

40. D. A *ship* that *founders* gives way and sinks. A *building* that *collapses* gives way and falls down.

(Function)

41. B. To *squirm* or wriggle is to show *discomfort* (mental or physical uneasiness). To *fume* or seethe is to show *anger*.

(Action and Its Significance)

42. D. An *advocate* (defender) by definition argues for or *supports* a cause or person. An *accuser* by definition publicly blames or *denounces* a cause or person.

    Remember to watch out for errors stemming from reversals. Advocates support. In contrast, outcasts *are shunned*. Victors *are rewarded*. Performers *are applauded*. Ask yourself who is performing the action.

    (Defining Characteristic)

43. B. Someone *steadfast* (faithful, loyal) shows *loyalty*. Someone *courageous* (brave) shows *valor* (bravery, courage).

    (Synonym Variant)

44. E. Someone *ruthless* (merciless, pitiless) lacks *sympathy*. Someone *outspoken* (candid, frank, unreserved in speech) lacks *reticence* (reserve, restraint in speaking).

    (Antonym Variant)

45. B. A *clique* (narrow, exclusive group of persons) is by definition *exclusive* (inclined to shut others out). An *entourage* (group of attendants) is by definition *attentive* (characterized by paying attention).

    (Defining Characteristic)

Section 4   Verbal

1. B. *Flexible* means pliable, able to be twisted or bent without breaking. Its opposite is *unbending*.
   Word Parts Clue: *Flex-* means bend; *-ible* means able. *Flexible* means able to be bent.
   Context Clue: Think of "flexible rules."

2. D. To *amplify* is to enlarge or expand. Its opposite is to lessen or *diminish*.
   Word Parts Clue: *Ample* means abundant, plentiful; more than adequate in size or scope. To amplify something is to further increase its size or scope.

3. C. *Reckless* means careless, thoughtless, foolhardy. Its opposite is *cautious* or careful.
   Context Clue: Think of "reckless driving."

4. B. An *agitator* stirs things up. A *peacemaker* calms things down.
   Context Clue: Think of "troublesome agitators."

5. C. *Arbitrary* means capricious, unreasonable, unsupported. Its opposite is *reasonable*.
   Context Clue: Think of "making arbitrary demands."

6. D. *Gullibility* is the quality of being easily cheated or fooled. Its opposite is *hardness to fool*.
   Word Parts Clue: A *gull* is a dupe or fool.

7. C. To *profane* something is to treat it with irreverence, to desecrate or debase it. Its opposite is to *sanctify* it or make it holy.
   Context Clue: Think of "profaning a holy place."

8. A. *Indigenous* means native. Its opposite is *foreign* or alien.
   Context Clue: Think of "plants indigenous to Florida," "indigenous inhabitants."

9. C. *Pusillanimity* means cowardliness, faint-heartedness, timidity. Its opposite is *courage*.

10. D. *Evanescence* is the quality of being transient, fleeting, impermanent. Its opposite is *permanence* or durability.
    Context Clue: Think of "the evanescence of a rainbow."
    Word Parts Clue: *Van-* is related to vanish. *Evanescence* is the process of vanishing.

11. C. The sentence implies that Polynesian banquets are usually reputed to be good. The speaker was disappointed by the banquet. Two possibilities exist: either this banquet was a poor one, or the banquets in general are *overrated* (too highly valued).
    Note how the "either . . . or" structure sets up a contrast between the two clauses.

    (Contrast Signal)

12. C. Since Lee avoided or refrained from excesses, Grant, his opposite, must have *indulged in* or satisfied his taste for excesses.
    The key words in this sentence are "differed markedly." They set up the contrast between the two men.
    Note that you are looking for a word that suggests Grant enjoyed drinking. Therefore, you can eliminate any word that suggests he disliked or disapproved of it. Choices A, B, and D all suggest dislike or disapproval. Only Choice C or Choice D can be correct.

    (Contrast Pattern)

13. B. The librarian has the committee's *acquiescence* or agreement; they assent but do not go so far as to encourage or spur on the librarian. Their support is of a lesser degree.
    Note how the "with the . . . if not the" structure signals that the two nouns must differ in meaning to some degree.
    Remember, before you look at the choices, read the sentence and think of a word that makes sense.

Likely Words: agreement, permission, consent, approval.

14. A. His friends could not understand his outburst because he was usually submissive (*docile*) and satisfied (*complacent*).
Remember to watch for signal words that link one part of the sentence to another. The presence of *and* linking items in a series indicates that the missing word may be a synonym or near-synonym for the other linked words. In this case, *docile* and *complacent* are near-synonyms.

(Support Signal)

15. A. With no enemies to stop their spread, the deer must have done well or *thrived*. They did so extremely well that they "overgrazed" or ate too much grass. This *threatened* (was bad for) the vegetation.
Note how the "so . . . that" structure signals cause and effect.
Remember, in double-blank sentences, go through the answer choices, testing the *first* words in each choice and eliminating those that don't fit. You can immediately eliminate Choices C and E.

(Cause and Effect Signal)

16. C. A *brake* slows or stops an *automobile*. *Reins* slow or stop a *horse*.

(Function)

17. B. *Area* measures the size of a *square*. *Volume* measures the size of a *cube*.

(Defining Characteristic)

18. A. A *tally* is a recorded account of *votes*. A *census* is a recorded account of *population*.
Beware Eye-Catchers: Choice E is incorrect. An election is a choice among candidates; it is not a recorded account of candidates.

(Definition)

19. A. A *termite* feeds on (and eats away) *wood*. In its larval stage, a *moth* feeds on (and eats away) *wool*.
Beware Eye-Catchers: Choice B is incorrect. A silkworm makes silk; it does not feed on it.

(Function)

20. C. A *cease-fire* is a temporary pause in *hostilities* (acts of warfare). A *lull* is a temporary pause in a *storm*.

(Defining Characteristic)

21. A. *Colleagues* (professional associates) share a common *profession*. *Kinsfolk* (relatives) share a common *family*.

(Defining Characteristic)

22. D. *Usury* (exorbitant interest) is an excessive or extreme form of *interest*. *Parsimony* (miserliness; excessive thrift) is an excessive or extreme form of *frugality* (economy; thrift).
Use the process of elimination to improve your guessing odds. The word pairs in Choices A, B, and C are all antonyms. Since they all belong to the same analogy type, none of the three can be the correct answer. Eliminate all three.

(Degree of Intensity)

23. C. *Cacophony* (harsh discordant sound) is distasteful to the *ear*. A *stench* (foul smell) is distasteful to the *nose*.
Remember, if more than one answer appears to fit the relationship in your sentence, look for a narrower approach. "Cacophony is perceived by the ear" is too general a framework. It would fit both Choice A and Choice C.

(Defining Characteristic)

24. B. A *eulogy* is an expression of *praise*. A *slander* (statement damaging someone's reputation) is an expression of *disparagement* (depreciation, scorn).
Beware Eye-Catchers: Choice A is incorrect. An elegy is an expression of sorrow over a death. It is not an expression of death.

(Definition)

25. E. To *embroil* someone is to involve him in conflict or *strife*. To *imperil* someone is to involve him in peril or *danger*.

(Defining Characteristic)

26. D. Throughout the passage, characteristics of a city which the author finds admirable or *estimable* are mentioned.
Choice A is incorrect. "The Spirit of the City" is far too general a title to be appropriate.
Choice B is incorrect. It is too specific, restricting itself to the advantages of a city home, ignoring those of the city in general.
Choice C is incorrect. The disagreements of naturalists are only touched on in passing.
Choice E is incorrect. It too is only touched on in passing.

(Main Idea/Title)

27. D. The author makes strong positive statements about cities ("I call this beauty . . . I call it spirit"); he is *assertive*.

Choice A is incorrect. The author admires the impersonality of civilization; he himself is not emotionally uninvolved or impersonal.
Choice B is incorrect. The author is not self-effacing or humble as he states his beliefs.
Choice C is incorrect. The author admires tolerance—lack of concern about "religion or politics or race." However, his tone is not tolerant.
Choice E is incorrect. The author is scornful of "mystical soulfulness." He himself is not mystical.
Remember, when asked to determine the author's attitude or tone, look for words that convey emotion or paint pictures.

(Attitude/Tone)

28. A.   This passage is a defense of cities. By differentiating himself from naturalists who criticize cities, the author establishes himself as one who defends cities.
Choice B is incorrect. The author discusses the good points about free urban services, not their bad points or deficiencies.
Choice C is incorrect. The author discusses other naturalists' faults only in passing. Questioning them is not his main purpose.
Choice D is incorrect. It is supported by the passage.
Choice E is incorrect. He never touches on rural life.

(Main Idea)

29. C.   The use of the phrase "and above all" in the next to last sentence emphasizes the author's appreciation of the impersonal or *impartial service*.
Choices A, B, and E are incorrect. While the author admires these different attributes, they are not the aspects of city life he finds *most* commendable.
Choice D is incorrect. It is unsupported by the passage.

(Specific Details)

30. E.   In the last sentence, the author associates the impersonal provision of city services—public utilities—with the spirit of man. Thus, to operate these public utilities efficiently is to perform a service that is *spiritual* as well as practical.
Choice A is incorrect. The author is not complaining about the cost of services.
Choice B is incorrect. The author is interested in this efficient operation.
Choice C is incorrect. The author implies the opposite.
Choice D is incorrect. The author calls this efficient operation *more than* mechanically admirable; it is *spiritually* admirable.

(Inference)

31. C.   Choice C is correct. You can arrive at it by the process of elimination.
Statement I is correct. There are "certain geographical features that seem to span the ocean." These indicate the continents were once joined. Therefore, you can eliminate Choices B and D.
Statement II is correct. The "complementary coastlines" are *physical counterparts*. This indicates the continents were once joined. Therefore, you can eliminate Choice A.
Statement III is not correct. Though it is true that the African plate has been stable for ages, this fact is not stated as proof that Africa and South America once were joined. Therefore, you can eliminate Choice E.
Only Choice C is left. It is the correct answer.

(Specific Details)

32. E.   The concluding sentence of the passage states that hot spots someday "may explain (the continents') mutability," their tendency to change in shape, even break apart and form a new ocean.
Choice A is incorrect. Hot spots are seldom located near the boundaries of plates. Thus, they would be unlikely to provide useful information about plate boundaries.
Choice B is incorrect. It is unsupported by the passage.
Choice C is incorrect. Hot spots have proved useful in studying the *respective* motion of the plates, not their relative motion.
Choice D is incorrect. According to the passage, hot spots have served as measuring instruments in determining the respective motion of the plates. They have not been used to interpret instruments of measurement.

(Specific Details)

33. B.   Choice B is correct. You can arrive at it by the process of elimination.
The author would disagree with Statement I. According to lines 1–2, "We have been cocksure of many things that were not so." The confidence or degree of assurance we feel about an issue is *not necessarily* related to the issue's truth. Therefore, you can eliminate Choices A and D.
The author would agree with Statement II. Lines 7–9 state that "what we most love and revere generally is determined by early associations." Therefore, you can eliminate Choice C.
The author would disagree with Statement III. Even though we realize that everyone's grounds for belief "are just as good as ours," our belief or faith still remains (lines 18–20). Knowing why we have preferences does not

destroy our faith in their worth. Therefore, you can eliminate Choice E.
Only Choice B is left. It is the correct answer.

(Inference)

34. **C.** Throughout the passage the author is discussing our long-term fixed preferences. To give us a sense of what it is like to disturb such deep-seated feelings, he creates an image of tearing up a tough mountain plant whose roots go deep into the rock.

(Technique)

35. **A.** In lines 25–27, the author states firmly that "deep-seated preferences cannot be argued about." Then, to support his opinion, the author gives a common everyday example: "you cannot argue a man into liking a glass of beer." The author substitutes a concrete physical act (*liking a glass of beer*) for an abstract phrase (*deep-seated preference*).

(Technique)

36. **D.** The author's primary purpose is to convince people of the need to influence the cause of letters in our country positively. Throughout the passage he argues that we should foster the literature of our country, praising the good and criticizing the bad.
Choice A is incorrect. The author stresses that our infant literature cannot stand comparison with the literary masterpieces of Britain, Italy, and Greece (lines 37–42).
Choice B is incorrect. It is insufficiently broad. While the author rebukes the foreign critics, he also rebukes American boasters who overpraise American verse (lines 9–12).
Choice C is incorrect. The author asserts that we should reward American literary "genius and industry" (lines 27–32) and condemns those who scorn our literature.
Choice E is incorrect. It is insufficiently broad. While the author rebukes those who overrate American authors, he also rebukes the prejudiced foreign critics who underrate them.

(Main Idea)

37. **C.** The author states that few writers are confident enough to believe their work can win them fame when they see other writers' work, work just as good as theirs, ignored. Few writers are brave enough to stick to a career that has destroyed generations of American writers before them. These ignored writers of previous generations are the *melancholy wrecks* American writers see—the only "prospect before them."
Remember, when asked to give the meaning of

an unfamiliar word, look for nearby context clues.

(Word from Context)

38. **B.** The author does not suggest that foreign critics possess a wide knowledge of American verse: they are "but slenderly acquainted" with it.
Choice A is incorrect. The author refers to the "infant literature of our country" and compares it unfavorably with the works of Europe's "mighty masters of song." This implies that he would agree *American literature is less mature* than European.
Choice C is incorrect. The author states that it is "detrimental to bestow on mediocrity the praise due to excellence (lines 33–35)." Doing so makes us "a contemptible figure" to others. This implies that the author would agree it is *pretentious* (self-important; pompous and conceited) and *self-defeating* to do so.
Choice D is incorrect. The author's main point is that Americans need to create an environment that nourishes writers.
Choice E is incorrect. Lines 16–22 indicate both that not every worthy artist is bold enough to come forward with his work and that many who do come forward receive no reward. The writer might well agree that many gifted poets languish in obscurity.

(Inference)

39. **E.** While the author is enthusiastic about the prospects for poetry in America, he is not excessive in his enthusiasm. Instead, he measures out both praise and blame judiciously. His attitude is one of *measured enthusiasm*.
Choice A is incorrect. He is interested, not *fascinated*; objective, not full of wonder.
Choice B is incorrect. The author is hopeful that the climate for literature in America will improve. He is not *bitter and disillusioned*.
Choice C is incorrect. The author makes no pretence of being unconcerned. He clearly cares about American poetry.
Choice D is incorrect. *Chauvinism* means blind patriotism, excessive devotion to American poetry not because it is good but simply because it is American. That is not the author's attitude.
Remember, when asked to determine the author's attitude or tone, look for words that convey emotion or paint pictures.

(Attitude/Tone)

40. **C.** The opening sentence sets up a contrast between the prejudice against American literature shown by foreigners and the over enthusiasm shown by Americans. The

second sentence continues this contrast. *Contumely* (rude language, insults) in the second sentence balances *prejudice* in the first: it is a negative word.

(Word from Context)

Section 5 · Math

1. A. Since the number must be divisible by 5, consider only 600 and 665. Since it must be even (divisible by 2), choose (A): 600.

2. E. If average of four examinations was 75%, sum of all examination marks was (75%)(4) or 300%.
Sum of three examinations is 50 + 70 + 90 or 210%.
Therefore the first examination grade was 90%.

3. D. II is incorrect because, if it is assumed that 40 ft. is the length of one side, the opposite side will also equal 40. Then $\frac{1}{2}$ of 80 or 40 will be the lengths of the other sides, making the plot a square. If the sides are assumed to be 20 and 60, then the perimeter is 20 + 20 + 60 + 60 or 160 ft.

4. E. $4y - x - 10 = 0$
$$4y = x + 10$$
$$2y = 3x \quad \text{(given)}$$
$$4y = 6x \quad \text{(multiply by 2)}$$
$$6x = x + 10 \quad \text{(things equal to the same thing are equal to each other)}$$
$$5x = 10 \quad \text{(subtract } x\text{)}$$
$$x = 2 \quad \text{(divide by 5)}$$
$$3x = 2y \quad \text{(given)}$$
$$6 = 2y \quad \text{(substitute value of } x\text{)}$$
$$y = 3 \quad \text{(divide by 2)}$$
$$xy = 6 \quad \text{(substitute values of } x \text{ and } y\text{)}$$

5. C. Solve for b: $a = \frac{b}{2}$
$$b = 2a$$
$$b + 2 = 2a + 2$$

6. A. If the man can do the job in h hours, each of the helpers will take ah hours to do the job. Let x = number of hours required by w helpers to do the job. This is an inverse proportion.
$$\frac{1 \text{ helper}}{w \text{ helpers}} = \frac{x \text{ hr.}}{ah \text{ hr.}}$$
$$wx = ah \quad \text{(product of means equals product of extremes)}$$
$$x = \frac{ah}{w} \quad \text{(divide by } w\text{)}$$

Or, if a helper takes ah hr. to do the job, then w helpers will take $\frac{ah}{w}$ hr.

7. B. At the very beginning of each hour the monkey ascends 30 ft. and during the hour falls back 20 ft. Thus the monkey gains (30 − 20) or 10 ft. by the end of each hour. In 9 hr. (from 8 A.M. to 5 P.M.) he will have gained 90 ft.
At 5 P.M., which is the *beginning* of the tenth hour, he ascends 30 ft. to reach a point 120 ft. above the ground.

8. A. 100% of 25 = 25;
  5% of 25 = 1.25
105% of 25 = 26.25

9. C. $4x = 48; x = 12$
$16\frac{2}{3}\% = \frac{1}{6}; \frac{1}{6}$ of 72 = 12

10. C. $\sqrt{\frac{1}{4}} = \frac{1}{2}$

11. C. $\sqrt{\frac{1}{25}} = \frac{1}{5} = 20\%$

12. B. $\sqrt{14.4} = 3.79$ or $3+$; $3.79 < 4$

13. A. Time $= \dfrac{\text{Distance}}{\text{Rate}}$
Time $= \dfrac{\frac{1}{2}\text{mile}}{20 \text{ m.p.h.}} = \dfrac{1}{40}$ hr.
Time $= \dfrac{\frac{1}{3}\text{mile}}{30 \text{ m.p.h.}} = \dfrac{1}{90}$ hr.

14. C. $\dfrac{\text{Distance}}{\text{Circumference}} = $ Number of revolutions
Circumference $= \pi D$
Circumference $= (\pi) \cdot \dfrac{7}{(\pi)} = 7$
Circumference $= (\pi) \cdot \dfrac{10}{(\pi)} = 10$

$\dfrac{70 \text{ ft.}}{7 \text{ ft.}} = 10$ revolutions (Column A)
$\dfrac{100 \text{ ft.}}{10 \text{ ft.}} = 10$ revolutions (Column B)

15. D. If $X + Y = 100$, then $100 + Z = 350$ and $Z = 250$.
However, since Y could be either positive or negative, X could be either greater than or less than 250.

16. D. If Y is at the center of both circles, then Z could be anywhere on the circumference of the circle with radius $= 2$, and X could be at any point on the circumference with radius $= 3$. There are many possibilities for the location of X in respect to the location of Z.

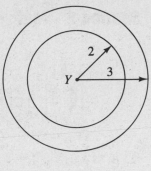

17. D. If x is > 1, x^2 will be greater than 1, and y will be greater than x since $y = 9x^2$.
    However, if x is a small positive number, say $x = 0.01$, x^2 will equal 0.0001 and y will be 0.0009 and therefore less than x.

18. D. From the information given, we can deduce only that $\frac{1}{2}$ the product of these two values equals 18.

19. D. We may conclude only that $AD = BC$ and $AB = DC$.

20. C. $x + 5 + 3x - 1 + 4x - 2 = 34$ (given)
    $$8x + 2 = 34$$
    $$8x = 32$$
    $$x = 4$$

21. B. Since $x = 4$ (see #20),
    $$AC = 3x - 1 \text{ or } 11$$
    $$BC = 4x - 2 \text{ or } 14$$

22. A. Since $AC = 11$ and $BC = 14$ (see #21), measure of $\angle BAC >$ measure of $\angle ABC$.

23. B. Observe that AC is the hypotenuse of right triangle ABC, of which BC is a leg. The hypotenuse is the longest side of a right triangle.
    Or, Since $AD = 40$, BC also $= 40$. Since the area of $ABCD = 1200$, $AB = 30$. ABC is a right triangle. Since the legs are 40 and 30, the hypotenuse (AC) must be 50, and $AC > BC$.

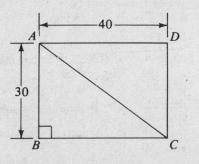

24. A. $AD + BC = 80$ (see #23)
    $DC + AB = 60$

25. B. Since $a = 90$, $x + w = 90$
    Since $b = 90$, $y + z = 90$
    $w + x + y + z = 180$

26. C. $y + z = 90$ (see #25)

27. D. No data given to determine the relative sizes.

28. A. 5 gallons $= 20$ quarts $= 40$ pints
    $$\frac{120 \text{ pint bottles}}{40 \text{ pints in each can}} = 3 \text{ cans}$$

29. C. Let $x =$ time (in hours) required to service 5 cars.
    $$\frac{\text{number of cars}}{\text{time (in hours)}} = \frac{6}{8} = \frac{5}{x}$$
    $$6x = 40$$
    $$x = 6\frac{2}{3} \text{ hr. or 6 hr. 40 min.}$$

30. B. Let $x =$ distance covered by driving car.
    $55 - x =$ distance covered by walking
    Rate riding $= 40$ m.p.h.
    Rate walking $= 5$ m.p.h.
    $$\frac{\text{Distance}}{\text{Rate}} = \text{Time}$$
    Time driving car $= \dfrac{x}{40}$
    Time walking $= \dfrac{55 - x}{5}$
    Total time $= 4$ hr.   (given)
    $$\frac{x}{40} + \frac{55 - x}{5} = 4$$
    $x + 8(55 - x) = 160$ (multiply by 40)
    $$x + 440 - 8x = 160$$
    $$-7x = -280$$
    $$7x = 280$$
    $$x = 40 \quad \text{(distance covered by driving car)}$$
    $$\frac{\text{distance covered by driving car}}{\text{total distance}} = \frac{40}{55} = \frac{8}{11}$$

31. E. At the end of the first half hour, $\frac{1}{4}$ of 256 or 64 contestants are eliminated and 192 remain eligible. At the end of the first hour, $\frac{1}{4}$ of 192 or 48 contestants are eliminated and 144 remain eligible. After $1\frac{1}{2}$ hr., $\frac{1}{4}$ of 144 or 36 contestants are eliminated and 108 remain eligible. After 2 hour., $\frac{1}{4}$ of 108 or 27 contestants are eliminated and 81 contestants remain eligible.

Another method is to consider that, at the end of the first half hour, $\frac{3}{4}$ of the contestants remain eligible. At the end of the first hour, $\frac{3}{4}$ of these, or $\frac{3}{4} \times \frac{3}{4} = \frac{9}{16}$ of the original contestants, remain eligible. After $1\frac{1}{2}$ hr., $\frac{3}{4} \times \frac{9}{16} = \frac{27}{64}$ remain eligible. After 2 hr., $\frac{3}{4} \times \frac{27}{64} = \frac{81}{256}$ of the 256 original contestants are still eligible.

$$\frac{81}{\cancel{256}} \times \frac{\cancel{256}}{1} = 81$$

32. D. Ms. Jenkins sold $\frac{1}{5}$ of $\frac{5}{8}$, or $\frac{1}{8}$, of the house. Since this represents \$1,000, $\frac{8}{8}$ (the whole house) has a value of \$8,000.

33. B. Let x = Marked price.
$$\frac{105x}{100} = \$4.20 \qquad \text{(product of means equals}$$
$$105x = 420 \qquad\qquad \text{product of extremes)}$$

$$x = \$4.00 \qquad \text{(division by 105)}$$

\$4.00 less 5% discount = \$3.80

34. D. Let x = number of players who were on the squad at first.
$$x - 20\% \text{ of } x = 32$$
$$x - 0.2x = 32$$
$$10x - 2x = 320 \quad \text{(multiply by 10)}$$
$$8x = 320$$
$$x = 40$$

35. D. I. Since no integer is zero (all are odd), the product of these integers cannot be zero.
II. Since the sum is zero, the average must be zero.
III. The sum of all the negative integers must be the negative of the sum of all the positive integers in order for the total sum to be zero. If there is an even number of positive (odd) integers, their sum will be even and there will also have to be an even number of negative (odd) integers to balance this sum. If there is an odd number of positive (odd) integers, their sum will be odd and there will also have to be an odd number of negative (odd) integers to balance this sum. In either case the total number of positive and negative integers will be even.

Section 6 Math

1. C. $\left[\dfrac{9}{8} \cdot \dfrac{4}{7}\right] \div \dfrac{9}{2}$
$$\left[\frac{\cancel{9}}{\cancel{8}} \cdot \frac{\cancel{4}}{7}\right] \cdot \left[\frac{\cancel{2}}{\cancel{9}}\right] = \frac{1}{7}$$

2. B. $\dfrac{a}{b} = c$
$b = c$
$b = \dfrac{a}{b}$ (things equal to the same thing are equal to each other)
$b^2 = a$ (multiply by b)
$b = \sqrt{a}$ (extract square root)

3. D. $2x - 3y = -6$
$6 - 3y = -6$
$-3y = -12$
$y = 4$

4. D. Each son takes 8 times as much time as the father (or 24 hr. each). With the 3 sons working, $\frac{1}{3}$ the time, or $\frac{1}{3}$ or 24 hr. = 8 hr., would be required.

5. D. 4% of 750 or (0.04)(750) or 30 eggs cracked.
750 − 30 = 720 eggs remain.
5% of 720 or (0.05)(720) or 36 eggs were found defective after candling.
720 − 36 or 684 eggs can be sold.

6. A. Area of shaded portion equals area of rectangle $ABCD$ minus area of the two circles.
Length of rectangle = four radii (4r).
Width of rectangle = two radii (2r).

Area of rectangle = (Base)(Altitude)
Area of rectangle = (4r) (2r) or $8r^2$
Area of one circle = πr^2
Area of two circles = $2\pi r^2$
Area of shaded portion = $8r^2 - 2\pi r^2$
Or $2r^2(4 - \pi)$ (factoring)

7. D. List price − Discount = Selling price
\$90 − discount = \$72
Discount = \$18
$\dfrac{\text{Discount}}{\text{List price}} \times 100$ = Rate of discount
$$\frac{18}{90} \times 100 = 20$$

8. D. For every $5 left by the father, Benjamin received $1.50.

Benjamin received $\frac{\$1.50}{\$5.00}$ or $\frac{3}{10}$ of the money left.

$\frac{3}{10}$ of $5,000 (amount left by father) = $1,500

9. E. Distance = 152.5 miles
Time = 2 hr.

$\frac{\text{Distance}}{\text{Time}}$ = Average speed

$\frac{152.5}{2}$ = 76.25 or 76.3 m.p.h.

10. C. Distance = (Rate) (Time)
Distance = (40 m.p.h.) (5 hr.)
Distance (one way) = 200 miles

Average rate for return trip = $\frac{\text{Distance}}{\text{Time}}$

Average rate for return trip = $\frac{200 \text{ miles}}{10 \text{ hr.}}$

or 20 m.p.h.

11. B. Area of triangle = $\frac{1}{2}$ (Base)(Altitude)

Area of triangle = $\frac{1}{2}$ (6 units)(2 units)

Area of triangle = 6 square units

12. C. Total number of days required to paint the barn was 20 days.

James worked $\frac{12}{20}$ or $\frac{3}{5}$ of the total days.

He should receive $\frac{3}{5}$ of $100 or $60.

13. C. The least number of refrigerators in a carload is 12.
The least number in 4 carloads is (4) (12) or 48.

14. A. Since x equals more than 45, each of the four values is more than 45 and the average of the numbers cannot possibly be 45.

15. E. The maximum number of bulbs that produce flowers = 22

$\frac{22}{25} \times 100$ = percent that produce flowers

$\frac{22}{\cancel{25}} \times \frac{\cancel{100}^{4}}{1} = 88$

16. E. Let x = length of shadow of 35-ft. tree.

$\frac{\text{length of object (in feet)}}{\text{length of shadow (in feet)}} = \frac{35}{x} = \frac{98}{42}$

$\frac{35}{x} = \frac{14}{6}$

$\frac{35}{x} = \frac{7}{3}$

$7x = 105$

$x = 15$

17. D. The locus of points 2 in. from line AB consists of two parallel lines, P_1P_2 and P_3P_4. The locus of points 3 in. from point C is a circle with C as center and 3 in. as radius. Points P_1, P_2, P_3, P_4 are both 2 in. from AB and 3 in. from C.

18. C. $0.04 = 4\%$

$\left(\frac{1}{4}\right)^2 = \frac{1}{16} = 6\frac{1}{4}\%$

$\frac{1}{0.04} = \frac{100}{4} = 25 = 2500\%$

$(0.04)^2 = 0.0016 = 0.16\%$

$\frac{0.04}{4} = \frac{4}{400} = \frac{1}{100} = 1\%$

19. B. The number of work-days involved is:
School A: $7 \times 3 = 21$
School B: $4 \times 5 = 20$
School C: $5 \times 9 = 45$

86 total

$\$774 \div 86 = \$9$ per student per day
$20 \times \$9 = \$180$

20. C. After the carburetor was overhauled, the efficiency is $\frac{5}{7}$ gallon for 7 miles. Find the new miles per gallon and subtract from the former efficiency (miles per gallon). Set up a ratio.

Let x = miles per gallon with overhauled carburetor.

$\frac{\text{gallons of gasoline}}{\text{miles}} = \frac{\frac{5}{7}}{7} = \frac{1}{x}$

$\frac{5}{7}x = 7$

$5x = 49$

$x = 9\frac{4}{5}$

The question asks, "How much *further* can she ride?" Therefore: $9\frac{4}{5} - 7 = 2\frac{4}{5}$

21. C. $2.4 \sqrt{\dfrac{x^4 y^2}{16} + \dfrac{y^2 x^4}{9}}$

$2.4 \sqrt{\dfrac{9x^4 y^2 + 16 y^2 x^4}{144}}$ (144 is LCD)

$2.4 \sqrt{\dfrac{25 x^4 y^2}{144}}$ (combine fractions)

$2.4 \left(\dfrac{5 x^2 y}{12}\right)$ (extract square root)

$\dfrac{12 x^2 y}{12}$ (multiply)

$x^2 y$ (cancel)

22. E.   Draw CF parallel to DE, forming rectangle $FEDC$.

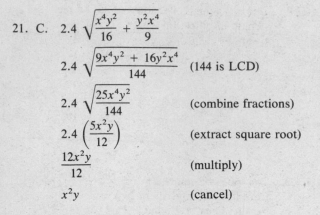

$FC = ED = 13$
$FB = FC + CB$
$FB = 13 + 2$ or 15
$FE = CD = 3$
$AF = AE - FE$
$AF = 11 - 3$ or 8

Recognize that AFB is an 8-15-17 right triangle and thus $AB = 17$.
Or apply the Pythagorean Theorem:

$(AB)^2 = (AF)^2 + (FB)^2$ (Pythagorean theorem)

$(AB)^2 = (8)^2 + (15)^2$
$(AB)^2 = 64 + 225$
$(AB)^2 = 289$
  $AB = 17$ (extract square root)

23. E.   To ascertain the greatest profit, we must assume the maximum selling price and minimum cost for 8 books.

Minimum cost of 8 books at $2.00 per book = $16.00

Maximum selling price of 8 books at $4.25 per book = $34.00

Greatest possible profit = $18.00

24. D.   I. $1 + \dfrac{x}{y} = \dfrac{y + x}{y}$

II. y

III. $\dfrac{y^2 + 2xy}{xy} = \dfrac{y(y + 2x)}{xy} = \dfrac{y + 2x}{x}$

IV. $\dfrac{y}{x}$

V. $\dfrac{2x + y}{x}$ or $\dfrac{y + 2x}{x}$

III and V are equal.

25. C.   If 100% represents the salesperson's original sales, then 120% represents the current sales.

$\dfrac{\text{current sales}}{\text{original sales}} = \dfrac{120\%}{100\%} = \dfrac{120}{100} = \dfrac{6}{5}$ or $6:5$

PART FIVE

Organize Your Admissions Game Plan

15 Getting into College

- **Choosing a College**
- **From Application to Acceptance**
- **Meeting the Cost**

Choosing a College

Not long ago colleges had to turn away some well-qualified applicants because of the great number of college-bound high school seniors and the limited space for the entering freshman class. But what is the case today? Since 1977 there has been a steady decline in the number of high school graduates. From almost 3.2 million in 1977, it is estimated that the number will be reduced to 2.3 million by 1992, a decline of almost one quarter. Many colleges are therefore facing difficulties. To avoid closing, some colleges have merged. A number of women's institutions have become coeducational. Schools may not have lowered their standards, but many schools with very high standards are now seeking students in ways they haven't before. In other words, it is now a buyer's market: qualified applicants can usually count on acceptance by one or more of their first-choice colleges.

Gathering Information

College Directories

There are a number of guides available. *Profiles of American Colleges* (Barron's Educational Series, Inc., Hauppauge, N.Y. 11788) is a comprehensive directory. It has complete, succinct descriptions of 1,500 four-year colleges including such items as admission standards, costs, student life, and courses of study. Colleges are indexed alphabetically and by admissions competitive rating. Two charts present at-a-glance data about the colleges regarding costs, enrollments, and standardized entrance examination scores; and career pursuits related to major fields of study. Other valuable information regarding applying to college, financial aid, selecting a major, and information for international students is also included. Another Barron's book, *Index of College Majors*, offers a systematic approach to college selection by means of an index of major programs of study available at these 1,500 colleges. For instance, if you are interested in attending a four-year college that offers a major in Urban Studies, you will find it easy to identify these colleges in your area or other geographical areas.

The College Catalog

Consult college catalogs in your school or public library and write for those in which you seem to have a genuine interest. Observe the number of courses offered. Look for the strength of the faculty in the subject areas that are of most interest to you. Remember that a fantastic physics department is of no use to you if you never plan to enter a science laboratory. A magnificent music department will not help you if you are tone deaf. Examine descriptions of the library, science laboratories, and other facilities in areas of interest to you. Information in a catalog may save you a time-consuming, expensive visit to a campus that is not a college for you.

Exploring the Campus

Planning Your Visit to a College Campus

If the college you are visiting is near your home, you should walk on the college grounds often and talk to currently enrolled students about the college. You should become familiar with the buildings, visit the library, and ask permission to enter laboratories, classrooms, and dormitories. If practical, you should inquire whether you may receive a guided tour.

In most cases, however, the college of interest to you may be far from home. This involves expense and special preparation. From a practical point of view, these visits should be confined to those colleges in which you have a sincere interest. Be alert to advertisements on your school bulletin boards and in local papers of group tours to several campuses during a school holiday period. These relatively inexpensive trips are generally organized by bus companies or travel agents.

There are at least two schemes for making visits to colleges:

1. The visit planned through the admissions office, complete with a formal interview and a guided campus tour.

2. The visit informally arranged with a student you know who already attends the school. In this case, a casual weekend visit should be planned during which time you can ask questions and examine all the interesting places and facilities on campus.

Ideally, if time and money permit, you should plan both types of visits to the two or three schools you are most seriously considering.

If you are taking the trip on your own, you should make certain arrangements ahead of time. If you are planning a formal visit, you should write to the admissions office telling them of your contemplated trip. Perhaps you should give them an alternate date to suit the convenience of the busy office. In many cases a member of the staff will chat with you, perhaps take notes of impressions made by you, and you may leave with a feeling of encouragement to file an application.

To save time and money, try to include colleges in the same geographic area on the same trip. It is foolish to attempt to visit more than two colleges in one day; in fact, it is advisable to devote at least a full day to exploring each of those universities you are seriously considering. If an overnight stay is involved, be sure to make reservations considerably in advance. Some colleges are in a position to recommend accommodations in their areas. If the opportunity exists, ask to spend the night in a typical dormitory with the students themselves.

If possible, your parents should accompany you. Most colleges are interested in seeing parents, though they may want some time alone with the prospective student. The wise parent and prospective student will withhold judgment of a college until they get back home and an objective judgment can be made about the entire trip.

Relax throughout the visit. Don't make it a hasty, pressure-filled shopping trip. Regard it as an inspection, an educational experience, where you are learning first hand about institutions you have heard about. You'll find that the trip will tell you more about the college you really want and what colleges expect of you.

Just before you make the trip, re-read the catalog.

Make notes on specific things you would like to see, such as a particular arts center or a language laboratory. Make notes on specific questions you have. When you speak to a college official, do not hesitate to discuss finances, scholarships, and work opportunities as well as your high school record. After all, if you decide to apply to this college, its officials are going to learn of your financial situation eventually. Tactfully, you may ask for some estimate of your chances for admission. Most probably you will not get any firm commitment, but a word of encouragement may be sufficient at this time.

What You Should Look for on the Campus Tour

Devote a good deal of time to an examination of the college library. Get an idea of the size of its collections, its study facilities, and other special features such as listening rooms. Make time in your visit to attend several classes, possibly choosing those that are of special interest to you. Be sure to visit a typical dormitory room, dining hall, student lounge, the college's athletic and recreational facilities, and, if you so desire, fraternity or sorority houses. If a student guide accompanies you on your tour, feel free to ask about any aspect of college life. The guide will welcome some clue about your interests—sports, dramatics, debate, and so forth—and may include a visit to the headquarters for such activities if time permits. But it's up to you to see what interests you—the responsibility is not the guide's.

Whether you are touring the campus alone or with your parents, make it your business to talk to students. Tell them who you are. Very often they will tell you that they were in your position a few years ago. Observe their patterns of speech, their dress, and ask yourself if you belong there. Feel free to ask them about gripes; more than likely, they'll unburden their likes and dislikes without being asked.

Obtain a copy of the college newspaper. What problems seem to face the students? Does the newspaper seem to reflect the atmosphere of the campus? What is the general tone, morale, and quality of the paper?

After the visit, make some notes on your reactions to the college; they'll be useful later on when you're trying to evaluate various institutions, and they may suggest some additional points for discussion with your guidance counselors and parents.

How the College Board Can Help You Select a College

The Admissions Testing Program (ATP) of the College Board can help you select a college that will satisfy your educational goals through its Student Search Service, which is free. The Student Search Service helps colleges find students with characteristics they are seeking. To take advantage of this service, you simply indicate on your registration form for the SAT that you want to participate.

From Application to Acceptance

Applying for Admission

The first step in the application procedure is to obtain applications from the colleges you're planning to apply to. You do this by writing (a postcard is quite acceptable) or calling the admissions office of each school and asking them to mail you an application.

When you receive the application forms, you will be asked to deliver certain parts to your high school authorities so that they may fill out the data in connection with the evaluation of your school record. Your parents may be asked to fill out one section with information regarding your personal health. Another part of the application will delve into your family background, your past history, and your interests and hobbies, as well as your plans for the future. You will be asked to fill out certain parts in your own handwriting. Don't worry about your handwriting. It is too late to change it now, but do be careful about neatness.

Filling Out the Application

Neatness counts. Read the entire application before you start to write, and then put it away in a safe place. Writing for a second application may not count in your favor. When you are ready to answer the questions, jot down the facts you must collect. Collect all your data on scrap paper and have some reliable person such as a teacher or guidance counselor review the answers and make suggestions for the necessary mechanical corrections. Some colleges require that all parts of the application be completed in the handwriting of the applicant. In such cases, write out the corrected answers very carefully. If permitted, type or print the answers on the application form.

If a photograph is requested, choose one that is simple and does you justice. Do not use a snapshot with extraneous background. It is not wise to use a photograph that shows you in unusual dress or attire.

Many applications require you to write an essay. This is an interesting, decisive, and revealing part of the application. A superb, original, thoughtful, literate, and mature life story can tip the scales in your favor, if all the phases of the application are satisfactory. A poor essay, on the other hand, might provide sufficient reason for rejection. This does not mean that you should hire a "ghost writer." Members of an admissions board are quick to detect "masterpieces" written by well-meaning parents or friends of the family. The next chapter, "Writing Your Application Essay," will show you how to write your own masterpiece.

Evaluation of Your School Record

This is by far the most significant part of the application. Officers of admissions committees were not at all surprised at a recent study that showed that about half of the first year dropouts left school for academic reasons, which included poor grades in college and poor high school preparation.

Some colleges communicate with your high school as soon as your application is filed. Others ask you to deliver a special form to your principal, headmaster, or guidance counselor. The college will want to know if you have met or will meet the entrance requirements. They will therefore request a transcript of your high school record.

In examining this record, the committee looks for grades and the subjects completed. They look for subjects that gave the applicant difficulty and take into account such extenuating circumstances as temporary illness, or lack of interest in certain (but not all) subjects. They attempt to determine whether the student elected challenging courses, and are on the lookout for students who took easy courses in order to raise their averages.

Your standing in the class is quite significant. This is a direct way of comparing you with the other students in your graduating class. If you have high grades, but a low rank in your class, it is sometimes a sign that the marking system in your school suffers from inflation. If you attend a specialized school for selected or gifted pupils, then class standing needs special consideration, for you are being compared with special students. Finally, if you attend a very small school, your achievement involves small numbers and therefore carries less significance.

Extracurricular Activities

Activities outside the classroom, both in school and in the community, are important. They afford the opportunity to develop personal talents, to pursue special interests, and to stimulate qualities of initiative and leadership. However, admissions officers are not impressed with a long list of rather insignificant activities, most of which merely involved occasional passive attendance at meetings. These make an attractive listing in a high school yearbook but do not impress the scrutinizing eye of a college admissions officer, who is more concerned with any elected and appointed offices you might have held, and those activities you might have engaged in which suggest definite signs of leadership in your character, and who is also very interested in your ability to play an unusual musical instrument, paint a canvas, or write a line of poetry.

Certainly no good college will entirely put aside its other standards for admission for a good extracurricular record. However, all other things being equal, in choosing one of two applicants, the admissions office will generally choose the student who participated in out-of-class activities.

Letters of Reference

Many colleges will ask you to submit the names and addresses of people who will furnish information regarding your character. Of course, common courtesy requires that you first ask the individual for permission to use his or her name. In choosing these individuals, it is well to bear in mind that they will be requested to give answers to such questions as:

1. Are you related to the applicant?
2. How long have you known the applicant?
3. In what capacity have you been in contact with the applicant?
4. Give any evidences of good moral character, leadership, maturity, and consideration for others that you have had the opportunity to observe in the applicant.

Some colleges send you forms to be given to people who can furnish information about your character. It is courteous to supply each of these people with a stamped envelope addressed to the office of admissions. The people you might ask for recommendations include:

1. teacher of a subject in which you excel
2. instructor, teacher, or coach of a creative activity in which you excel (e.g., art, music, drama)
3. advisor of a club or service activity in which you participated
4. coach of a team on which you served
5. scout leader
6. sponsor of a youth group
7. religious leader
8. professional or business person active in your community
9. camp counselor or director
10. employer of your part-time or summer position
11. public official

Keep in mind that college personnel are not likely to be swayed by letters containing empty platitudes and sweeping praise. They read scores of these letters every day. Certainly they want to know your accomplishments and strong points, those things which make you different from the other applicants; but at the same time they are anxious to learn about a flesh and blood person, *not* the subject of some glorious ode. The typically general, impersonal recommendation of some well-known personality will have less impact on admissions officers than a warm, sensitive letter from a less well-known individual who intimately knows you and is therefore in a better position to appraise your particular qualities.

Avoid suggesting as references individuals who will not answer the college questionnaire promptly. Likewise, do not use individuals who might not show good judgment, neatness, or taste in corresponding with the admissions office of the college.

The Personal Interview

There is no uniformity among the schools as to the time for holding the interview. It may occur after all other factors determining admission have been inspected and tentatively approved, or it may occur before the secondary school records and test scores have been received. In addition, while some schools require an interview, others consider the interview only a way to give you more information about the school.

If an interview is required, you should write early in the school year for an appointment. If the interview is optional but you can arrange for one, you should also make an appointment. (Where distance makes a visit impractical, a local alumnus may be assigned to talk with you.) Plan your trip to the college so that you arrive punctually. Your appearance and dress should be in good taste. Remember you are not going to a formal dance, nor to a sporting event. Make certain that your shoes are shined, your hair is combed, and your fingernails are clean. Dress conservatively. Be careful about odors of perfumes, tobacco, or foods. This is the day when you should start breaking the habit of chewing gum.

As far as the interview itself is concerned, the best advice is to *be yourself*. Since this is not an interview for a role as actor or actress, you should relax and answer all questions with frankness and honesty. If you do not possess a particular characteristic for which they are looking, you may not be happy at this school. The interviewer may give you some valuable counsel and send you off to the school where you really belong.

If you haven't ever experienced such an interview you will be wondering about the topics of conversation and the general tone of this event. It will be informal, and it is safe to say that it will be conducted on a most pleasant level. You will perhaps discuss people and things you like or dislike. Again, be honest. Perhaps the official interviewing you likes jazz music himself. Even if he doesn't, he won't hold it against you if you do. Don't hide your distastes or weaknesses. Some of our poor high school mathematics students have gone on to become college professors in other fields.

You may be asked about your career plans. If you are not certain about your future, state that as a fact. It is not a sign of weakness. Most students enter college with only vague ideas about what they want to do after graduation. If you have applied to other colleges, don't hesitate to mention them if that question comes up.

Towards the close of the interview you may be given an opportunity to ask questions about the college. Don't feel that you have to ask a question and then hastily compose a question which may show your unfamiliarity with data furnished in the catalog. It may be wiser to say that you have no questions to ask about the school.

Your College Board Scores

Colleges use standardized scores to enable them to compare students from different schools. A high school record alone cannot be a yardstick of academic promise. Grading standards differ among high schools. Class standing in a small high school is not as significant as it is in a large city school. The standing in a specialized school is of little significance except for those at the very top. Entrance examinations afford equal opportunity to each college-bound student.

Do not, however, feel that you are a failure because you fell short of an 800 on your SAT. Bear in mind that the average SAT scores on a national basis are somewhere between 400 and 500 reported on a scale of 200 to 800. Even highly competitive schools admit students with a wide range of scores.

A college that reported a median score of 610 in the verbal part of the SAT for its freshman class indicated that 25% of freshmen scored between 550 and 559, 14% received 500 to 549, and 6% had scores between 400 and 450. For the mathematics part of the SAT the same school reported a median score of 700, but 20% of the admitted students received scores between 500 and 599.

Another school, reporting an average of 669 in the verbal part of the SAT for the 500 accepted applicants, indicated that 33 of them scored between 550 and 599, and 10 scored below 550. It is interesting to note that this school failed to accept 15 applicants with SAT verbal scores of 700 to 749 and one applicant with a score above 750.

Thus we see that College Board scores are important, but additional criteria are used. It is well to repeat that SAT scores are used to *supplement* such factors as high school grades, class rank, and personal qualities. Another factor that admissions officers are reporting is that they are giving special consideration to applicants with low SAT scores from deprived areas or to applicants for whom English is not the native language. Of course, these college-bound students must present evidence of academic promise.

To Sum It Up

You will gain admission to college on the basis of your school record, your personality, your extracurricular activities, the impressions you made on others, and your performance on college entrance examinations. Your acceptance is an indication that the college has faith in your ability to succeed in that school.

Meeting the Cost

Types of Financial Aid

The main types of financial aid are grants and scholarships, loans, and student employment. Grants are awarded on the basis of need and do not have to be repaid. These may come from government agencies, college funds, or special programs. Scholarships are similar to grants, and usually are awarded on the basis of academic achievement and/or financial need. College employment offices often furnish on- or off-campus jobs to help supplement other forms of aid. Finally, low-interest loans that do not have to be repaid until after graduation can help pay for college.

Chief Sources of Financial Aid

There are four main sources of financial aid: the federal government, state governments, private sources, and the colleges themselves.

Federal Government

The federal government has five main student aid programs: the Pell Grant Program, the Supplemental Educational Opportunity Grant (SEOG), the College Work-Study Program (CWS), Carl Perkins Loans (formerly, National Direct Student Loans), and Guaranteed Student Loans (GSL).

The Pell Grant Program, the largest of the federal student aid grant programs, and SEOG are the two main federal grant programs. They are both based on need, and they do not have to be repaid. College Work-Study is a student employment program that provides on- and off-campus jobs for students who demonstrate need. Carl Perkins Loans and GSL are both low-interest loan programs, also based on demonstrated need. Monies borrowed through these loan programs do not have to be repaid until after graduation.

In addition to the federal student aid programs already mentioned, the Veterans Administration provides two types of funds—G.I. Bill benefits and War Orphan benefits—to veterans of all wars and to the children of deceased or entirely disabled veterans whose disability or death was service-related. Contact a local office of the Veterans Administration for details on eligibility.

State Governments

Most states have some type of scholarship or grant program for residents. These are usually based on achievement in high school and scores on college entrance examinations, but need is often also a determining factor. Often the scholarship or grant applies only if the student attends a college in that state. Some states also have loan programs and student employment programs.

Private Sources

Many individual scholarships are available from labor unions, benevolent societies, patriotic organizations, and business. Look in your high school guidance office and in your local library for information on private scholarships such as these as well as local scholarships available in your community. Awards made available by local fraternal societies, women's clubs, civic and business organizations, ethnic and religious groups, alumni, and PTAs are numerous but usually modest in dollars and cents value. Your parents' employer or labor union may turn out to be another source of aid.

The largest independently funded scholarship program in the United States is administered by the National Merit Scholarship Corporation and is funded by company foundations and colleges and universities. Scholarship recipients are selected on the basis of their score on the Preliminary Scholastic Aptitude Test/National Merit Scholarship Qualifying Test (PSAT/NMSQT), other academic factors, and their character. For further information, write to the National Merit Scholarship Corporation, One American Plaza, Evanston, Illinois 60201, and ask for the PSAT/NMSQT Student Bulletin.

Colleges

Nearly every college offers a number of scholarships and grants that range from partial payment of tuition to complete payment of all expenses. These grants are awarded in recognition of academic achievement and/or financial need. Special scholarships may be given to attract outstanding athletes or students with special talents in such areas as music, drama, or journalism.

In addition to their own scholarship and grant funds, colleges often act as agents of distribution for federal and state programs.

Since each college has different scholarships, grants, loans, and student-employment opportunities to offer, and since there is an often enormous difference in the amount of money available for student aid from one college to another, it is important that you get your information about student aid directly from the financial aid office of each college you are thinking of applying to.

How to Apply for Financial Aid

Most need-based financial aid programs, whether they are government programs, private programs, or individual college programs, require applicants to file either the Financial Aid Form (FAF) of the College Scholarship Service or the Family Financial Statement (FFS) of the American College Testing Program to apply for the various types of aid available. Both financial aid forms ask the applicant to itemize all family information and financial data pertinent to the candidate's application for aid.

It is important to find out which form or forms the colleges you are applying to require. Some schools will want their own aid application filed in addition to either the FAF or the FFS. And some government and private programs request additional forms as well; they use the FAF or FFS as an initial qualifying form but then require a separate application for their program.

Both FAF and FFS forms are available from your high school guidance counselor or local college financial aid offices.

We've left the two most important facts about applying for financial aid for last: (1) you must apply for financial aid; you are not automatically considered for aid when you apply to a college; and (2) apply as early as possible so that you have the best possible chance at a share of the available funds before they are used up on applicants who applied for aid earlier. There is no getting away from the fact that you'll have to do some research, and that you and your parents will have to spend some time filling out some rather detailed forms. But there is no way to get around this paperwork when you're applying for any kind of financial aid. So be patient and be thorough; hopefully, your efforts will pay off.

16 Writing Your Application Essay

- **What the Colleges Look For**
- **The Questions That Colleges Ask**
- **Pitfalls to Avoid**
- **Composing Your Essay**
- **Presenting Your Essay**
- **In Addition to Your Essay**

On the day you seal and mail your college application, your job—at least for the present—is done. But the work of the admissions committee at the college of your choice has just begun. At selective colleges—those that receive three or more applications for each place in the freshman class—college officials screen applications with agonizing care.

Each section of your application, from SAT scores to extra-curricular activities, contributes another piece to your portrait. But a thoughtful, well-written essay endows your portrait with life. It is like a window into your mind and personality. Unlike an A in chemistry or a B+ in English, it reveals your uniqueness, your attitudes on life, your creativity, your aims, and your drive. And perhaps most important, it demonstrates your writing ability. The gift of saying what you want to say in clear, correct, and interesting language sometimes offsets shortcomings in almost any other part of your application.

What the Colleges Look For

Colleges seek a generous mix of bright, confident, and positive students who will contribute actively to campus life for the next four years. Basically, your essay tells the colleges whether you're the sort of person they are looking for. It puts the finishing touches on your application. A three-sport high school athlete, for example, could use the essay to prove that his mind is as fit as his body. A serious scholar could prove that he has a sense of humor. Whatever your attributes, admissions people want you to think of your essay as an opportunity to present yourself honestly, openly, and intelligently.

Your transcript and list of activities have already told them what you have done. From your essay they hope to learn why.

Although you probably won't be admitted to a college solely on the strength of your essay, a well-written and sincere piece of writing can tip the balance in your favor. Conversely, a poor and sloppy essay can shut the door in your face. Nevertheless, some college officials claim, fewer than half of all application essays show evidence of real, honest effort. Still, at every college that requires an essay, your work will be read thoughtfully and seriously. At most colleges a team of two or more people will read every essay. At one prestigious school, up to five admissions people sometimes read an essay before the applicant is accepted. It's that important, according to that school's officials.

Colleges Want to Know What Makes You Tick

Because colleges want to get to know you, the cardinal rule of writing an application essay is to be yourself. Don't make the fatal mistake of trying to guess what a college wants. Admissions people don't want anything in particular except for you to portray yourself accurately and honestly. They don't ask trick questions on an application.

Pick a subject you care about—something significant and familiar to you. Nothing will flop faster than an impersonal essay full of sweeping generalizations about issues in the news or philosophical questions that have puzzled scholars for ages. If you're interested in current events, that's fine, but admissions people can read about apartheid and nuclear disarmament in *Newsweek*. If you're going to write about a current issue, make sure you have

715

done more than read the newspaper: go to a rally, march in a parade, circulate a petition, give a speech in your history class. In short, show personal commitment and involvement in whatever you write about.

Try to make your essay the one that only you could write. After all, it should set you apart in some way from every other applicant. That doesn't mean it must be worthy of a Pulitzer Prize, only that it ought to be uniquely personal. It ought to sound like you.

The Questions That Colleges Ask

Colleges have invented numerous ways to test your essay-writing skills. Sometimes you're assigned just one 250 to 300 word essay, sometimes more. Some applications give you choices, others don't. While some give you no directions on what to write—as though to test your ingenuity—others state specific guidelines, in part to see whether you can follow directions.

Although application questions differ in detail from one college to the next, they all ask you to write about the same general subject: YOU! Your task is always the same—to project personal qualities not apparent in other places on your application.

The mass of application questions fall into five broad categories, each with opportunities for you to project yourself onto the paper, but each with perils to watch out for:

1. Why go to college, and why here?
2. Who are you?
3. Would you tell us a story about yourself?
4. What is important to you?
5. What would you like to tell us about yourself?

Responses to these questions frequently overlap. If, for instance, you were to write an essay that describes an important personal value—say, your love of the outdoors—you might frame it in the form of a story about a rafting trip down the Colorado River. At the same time you would be defining who you are—in this case, perhaps an adventurous out-doorsman or a recently-converted city-slicker.

Why Go to College? Why Here?

From questions about your plans for the future, colleges hope to discern your route for the next four years. What will the college experience mean to you? Will you study or will you party? Have you thought about why you're going to college at all? Expecting a look at your educational map, colleges often make inquiries such as these:

Why do you want to go to college?

Why do you want to go to this college in particular?

What are your career objectives and how will college help you achieve them?

How will this college help you fulfill your goals and aspirations?

What will your presence add to this college?

No one answer to such questions is preferable to another. If you aim to be a physicist for IBM, that's fine. But no college seeks to fill its classrooms with only one type of student. In the main, colleges try to keep their enrollments balanced. It's not a weakness, therefore, to admit that you don't know how you want to spend the rest of your life. College is for exploring. In fact, liberal-arts students frequently come to campuses with receptive and open minds. More than likely, they'll rummage through many of the offerings on which a college has built its reputation.

As you explain your intentions to a college, consider these essay-writing hints:

DO

■ Answer the question.

■ Scrutinize the college's offerings before writing a word. If you expect to major in, say, ecology, be sure the college has an environmental studies program.

■ Think hard about what *you* hope to get out of college, avoiding clichés such as "I want an education," and "I want to get a good, well-paying job," and "I want to be a success in my chosen field."

■ Try to figure out why this college appeals to you. Did the college reps make it sound exciting? Did you visit the campus and feel good vibrations? Is there a particular program that has attracted your interest?

■ Focus on educational or personal reasons for going to college, not on social, economic, or family reasons.

DON'T

■ Don't flatter the college. Yale, Stanford, and all the other top colleges already know that they're good.

■ Don't stress that you love the college's location, size, or appearance. By applying there, you have implied that those characteristics are acceptable to you.

■ Don't tell a college that it's your "safe" school.

■ Don't write that you're going to college because you don't know what else to do.

Finally, don't take any of these precautions as the last word in application essay-writing. Use them at your discretion. But don't ignore them unless you have a sound reason for doing so. Jim D, for example, came right out and told Bowdoin he wanted to go there precisely because of its location. "Like Thoreau," Jim wrote, "I feel most alive near wild streams and forests."

Answers That Worked

Marian T's after school work in a fabric shop inspired her love of fashion and developed her flair for design. "In college," Marian wrote, "I plan to major in fine arts."

David B studied four languages in high school. Because of his bent toward languages and foreign cultures, he wants a career in international affairs as a businessman or diplomat, but he said, "A stint in the Peace Corps will come first."

Lisa C loves to read. "I can't imagine a career more suited to me than librarian in a school or a public library," she wrote.

Wendy W has wide and wandering interests. Last year it was dance, this year it is Greenpeace. Wendy thinks of college as a place for "accumulating more interests, for meeting people, for working hard, and ultimately, for finding a niche in life to fill."

Andy S has always taken the hardest courses. He doesn't know why, except that doing well in tough courses has made him feel good. "I hope to continue feeling good in college," he quipped.

Deena R admires one of her high school English teachers. Since he's told her wonderful stories of Williams College, she'd like to go there, too. "I plan to major in English," she wrote, "and find out if Mr. Stern's stories are true."

Karen S's "most joyful and gratifying high school experience" has been working with mentally retarded children. In college she'll major in special education.

Mark D lost his father and a brother last year. Yet he has retained his essential optimism. He wrote that "there is still a promise in life for me. There are so many things which I have not yet experienced, but inevitably must." That's why he wants to go to college.

Don E has met many people through playing guitar at festivals and nightspots. He thrives on people whose style of living differs from his. Don asked, "What better place than a giant university is there for finding a variety of people?"

Becky B is thinking of a career in acting. She expects a college education to help her become a more complete person. "My wish," she wrote, "is not only to be a good actor but also a good person, and my belief is that they might be the same thing."

Who Are You?

Colleges have heard what others think of you—teachers, counselors, interviewers. With self-assessment questions, they hope to learn what you think of yourself. Do you know who you are? Are you aware of how others react to you? Would you like to change in some way? Self-knowledge is often thought to be a prerequisite for understanding the world, and an essay that demonstrates that you know yourself well will give your application a big boost. To check the depth of your insight, colleges ask questions like these:

> What is important to you?
>
> How would you describe yourself as a human being?
>
> How might a freshman roommate describe you?
>
> Write your own recommendation to college.
>
> If you could strengthen one aspect of yourself, what would it be? Why?
>
> What quality do you like best in yourself? What quality do you like least?
>
> Imagine yourself as a book or other object. How would people react to you?
>
> What makes you different from other people?

In your response, readers hope to find clues to your personality. Unless you present yourself as a bizarre monster, they won't necessarily care whether you are soft-spoken or loud, a realist or a dreamer, a liberal or a rock-hard conservative. But they'll give you short shrift if they think you are a fake. Above all, then, in writing "who-are-you" essays, be truthful with yourself—as truthful as you've ever been before.

Telling the truth doesn't mean you must bare your soul and disclose your deepest secrets. Colleges don't need to know about your sex life, psychiatric treatment, or drug and drinking problems. On the other hand, you needn't portray yourself as a saint. Students have written successful essays about their cynicism, frustration, greed, and their favorite vices. In the end, let good taste govern your choice of material. If you have doubts, switch topics. Jenny G wrote an essay about a family drug problem, thought the better of it afterwards, and wrote another, highlighting her good judgment.

DO

■ Answer the question.

■ Be as honest as you can. Search for qualities you really have, not those you just wish for.

■ Emphasize specific, observable qualities that show your distinctive personality. Imagine that your reader will someday have to pick you out in a crowd.

- Illustrate your qualities with specific examples. Use telling anecdotes to support your opinions of yourself.

- Ask people who know you well whether they agree with your self-analysis.

DON'T

- Don't be evasive. Stand up for what you think about yourself.

- Don't be too cute or coy. Sincerity is preferable.

- Don't choose a characteristic merely to impress the college.

- Don't write everything you know about yourself. Focus on one or two of your outstanding qualities.

- Don't write an essay fit for *True Confessions*.

Remember that you can violate every rule and still write a compelling essay. Just be aware of the perils.

Answers That Worked

Suzannah R thinks of herself as a dynamo in danger of burning out by age 20. But she can't control her energy level. She's impatient and often intolerant of others' laid-back attitudes. But, she added, "As I have grown older, I feel I am learning to accept other people's shortcomings."

Betsy S wrote four paragraph-long sketches of important moments in her life. Each one—a sail with her father, her mother's remarriage, a breakfast at summer school, and a skiing trip in Vermont— has shaped her personality in some way.

Nancy S explained that "anxiety over taking tests has resulted in scores that reflect neither my academic achievement nor my enthusiasm for learning." Nancy has tried "every trick in the book" to overcome test anxiety, but none seems to work. She appealed to the college to be understanding.

David V said, "The most important fact to know about me is that I am a black person in a white society." David considers himself an outsider and expects to continue feeling alienated as long as racial prejudice exists.

Ellen E contrasted her goofing off early in high school ("personal problems and just plain stupidity") with her productive junior and senior years. In effect, she was reborn during the summer between 10th and 11th grade.

Allison R has fought shyness all her life. She recounted three moments in her life when shyness defeated her. In contrast, she told of three recent incidents that have helped to raise her self-esteem.

Steve M sees himself as a latter-day Clarence Darrow, always standing in defense of the little guy, often taking the minority point of view in class, just

to generate a little controversy. If others consider him obnoxious, he claimed, "it's a small price to pay for a life full of heated debates and discussions."

John K sees himself as a character in a movie. When he's alone he pretends he's Richard Dreyfuss, playing the role of a yuppie bachelor. He even hums background film music when he's driving or jogging.

Brendan B is a gourmet cook. He loves to eat. "You are what you eat," he believes, so he defined himself by the food he enjoys most. From meat and potatoes, for example, he has gained a strong will. From French sauces, he has derived a subtle sense of humor.

Nicole W is a perfectionist. From schoolwork to keeping her room in order, she cannot allow herself to do anything shabbily or incompletely. She is worried about "getting a slob for a college roommate."

Dena P, a gymnast since age eight, works like a demon to be number one. Ever striving for perfection, she wrote, "I know now that when it comes to making commitments, I can be ready to make them."

Doug W is an adopted Korean orphan. He sees himself as a child of two cultures. While a double identity causes confusion in others, he feels "more fortunate and richer" than his American classmates.

Jennifer B defines herself as a human computer. Instead of brains she has memory boards and micro-circuitry inside her head. Everything about computers comes so easily and naturally to her that she said, "I must have been conceived in an Atari factory."

Would You Tell Us a Story About Yourself?

Telling stories is a most natural thing to do. When you come home from school you tell what happened that day. You tell friends what Donna said to Fred and how Kathy felt afterwards.

The story you write for a college application isn't expected to be like a superbly crafted tale by Poe or O. Henry, but just an autobiographical account of an experience. It should tell about something that happened and what it meant to you. A good story both entertains and informs the reader. A story written for a college does even more. It suggests your values, clarifies your attitudes, and better yet, breathes life into your personality.

While storytelling possibilities are limitless, application questions usually direct you to identify and discuss a noteworthy time in your life:

> Write about a significant experience or event in your life and what it meant to you.

Write an original essay about a humorous personal experience.

What is it that you have done that best reflects your personality?

Describe a challenging situation and how you responded.

Comment on an experience that helped you discern or define a value you hold.

What is the most difficult thing you've ever done?

Write about a group endeavor in which you participated and describe your contribution.

In response to any of these topics, you can write a story about last night or pick an event from the time you wore diapers. The experience can have been instantaneous or long-lived, a once-in-a-lifetime occasion or a daily occurrence. It can have taken place in a schoolroom, a ballroom, a mountaintop—anywhere, in fact, including inside your head.

An event need not have been earth-shaking to inspire a story. Almost everything you do from the moment you wake up holds possibilities. If you haven't noticed how life is crammed with moments of drama, cast off those blurry lenses and start to look for the hidden realities behind the daily face of things: In a disagreement with your brother, in an encounter with a former girlfriend, or in a teacher's criticism you might find the ingredients for an insightful, dramatic essay. Simply by making a list of ten things that happened yesterday and another ten things that occurred last week, you might trigger more than one essay idea.

If you want to write about the time you made headlines, that's great. But most people lead ordinary lives. Taking a common experience and interpreting it as only you can is a perfectly acceptable way to handle the task of writing an application essay.

DO
- Answer the question.
- Choose an experience you remember well. Details will make or break your story.
- Pick an experience you can dramatize. Let the reader hear people speaking and see people acting.
- Focus on a specific incident or event.
- Make yourself the central character in the story.

DON'T
- Don't think that a commonplace event can't be turned into an uncommonly good story.
- Don't choose a complicated event unless you can explain it briefly. Fill in background, but focus on what happened.
- Don't lie. But if you must fabricate material for effect, be sure it has the ring of truth.

- Don't ramble. Rambling stories are boring.
- Don't explain your point with a lecture on what the reader is supposed to notice. Let the story make its own point.

Answers That Worked

Ted B collects things: match-box cars, license plates, matchbook covers, and rocks. From his hobby he has learned about design, geography, advertising, and geology. Interior decorating, too, for after five years of collecting, he literally wallpapered the foyer of his house with matchbook covers.

Pete S was riding in a car with his brother. At a stoplight a pretty girl in a neighboring car smiled at him. Pete looked away. Afterwards, he berated himself and resolved to become more outgoing and more responsive to others.

Colin V is Catholic. Last year on May 6 his Jewish godson was born. As a result, Colin's eyes have been opened to the world of Jewish customs. "I look at everything differently, now," Colin wrote.

Jenny B's hard-of-hearing grandfather lives with the family. Whenever Jenny tries to help the old man, he rebuffs her. A blow-up occurred after Jenny knocked too loudly on his door to summon him to the phone. The incident has caused her to reflect at length on the needs of the aged.

Mary G, from a middle-class family, works in a slum area soup kitchen with her church group. She'll never be a social reformer, but the work, she claims, has made her "more sensitive to the needs of the poor and homeless."

Roy O's summer at a lake with his father building a cabin gave him time to think about how lucky he was to have been born in the USA into a fairly well-to-do family. "I'll never take the blessings of life for granted again," he wrote.

Liz H and her twin sister Mary have rarely been apart. Lately, Liz has found it necessary to seek her own identity and has taken up running as a way to get away. Her hours of solitude on the road have helped to strengthen the bonds with her sister.

Sandy M says, "Sunday is always spent gathering the scattered fragments of my life." It's the day she uses to catch up on schoolwork, gain some perspective on her social life, make peace with her parents, and look in the mirror for a long time trying to figure out who she is.

Lauren S has always been plagued by insecurity. An off-hand remark by an art teacher ("Hey, you're good!") has helped her to build confidence and work that much harder in her courses. She's beginning to see signs of how good she really is.

Lisa R's parents were divorced. The complex legal negotiations that accompanied the split, while painful to her, so fascinated Lisa that she plans to become a lawyer.

Robert S thinks that he has been ostracized at his school because of his ragged appearance. Instead of wearing a jacket and tie to an honor society interview, he showed up in his jeans. The incident heightened his awareness that people are judged by superficialities, not by their character.

What Is Important to You?

Would you rather hear a Bach cantata or a Grateful Dead album? Would you prefer to go bowling or spend an afternoon in an art museum? Do you like fast foods or nouvelle cuisine? To a great extent, your preferences define you. Hoping for a glimpse of your taste and your biases, many colleges ask you to write a "choice" essay. But rather than give you a menu of choices, they tell you to come up with one of your own: your favorite quotation, an influential person in your life, a significant book you've read.

> What is your favorite quotation? Explain your choice.
>
> What have you read that has had special significance for you? Explain.
>
> Identify a person who has had a significant influence on you and describe that influence.
>
> Tell us about a personal, local, national, or international issue of particular concern to you.
>
> What is your favorite noun? What does it mean to you?
>
> If you could invent anything, what would you create? Discuss.
>
> If you could affect the outcome of human history by changing a particular event, what event would you choose? How would you change it, and why?
>
> If you could spend an evening with any prominent person—living, deceased, or fictional—whom would you choose, and why?

What you choose when responding to such questions is important. But the rationale for your choice is even more important and should make up the heart of your essay.

The key to writing a forceful response is that your choice has some direct, personal bearing on your life. A quotation from Shakespeare may sound impressive, but if you pick it only for effect, you'd be better off with a lyric from Rod McKuen or a maxim of your grandmother's. Before you select an important world issue like terrorism or over-population, be sure you've been personally touched by it. Instead of decrying the evils of apartheid, tell what you've done to support divestment. If you write on a book, don't limit yourself to school reading. What you've read on your own tells far more about you than any class assignment.

If you are wavering between two equally good choices, tip your scales toward less popular sub-

jects. Conversations with Columbus, Shakespeare, and Lincoln have already been written. So have numerous essays about cures for cancer and AIDS. Many students have already written about altering human history by eliminating war, preventing the birth of Hitler, and scrubbing the flight of the space shuttle *Challenger*. They have also expressed concerns about nuclear power, abortion, capital punishment, poor people, and women's rights. Countless others have been influenced by a grandparent, a sibling with a handicap, a teacher, or a virtuous public figure.

Nevertheless, the last word on all these subjects hasn't yet been written. Although admissions staffers may frown on still more essays about peace or pollution, they'll welcome any essay that's genuine, insightful and interesting.

DO

- Answer the question.
- Choose a subject that you care about.
- Let your head and heart be your source of material.
- Think of at least three very good personal reasons for your choice.
- Try out more than one answer. Submit the one that you like best.

DON'T

- Don't choose a topic merely to look good.
- Don't be self-conscious about your choice. Just tell the truth.
- Don't choose a subject that requires research. Let your experience guide you.

Answers That Worked

Lisa D, born in South Africa, came to the United States at age 11. Her anti-apartheid essay recalls her black nurse, who was forbidden to enter the park where Lisa and her friends played hopscotch and tag.

Amy B thinks that Hawkeye from TV's *M*A*S*H* would make an ideal dinner companion. She admires Hawkeye's humor, his understanding, and his impatience with hypocrisy. Amy, a feminist, would also like to "set Hawkeye straight on his sexist attitudes."

Jenny B has been fascinated with space flight ever since second grade, when the elementary school librarian introduced her to a sci-fi book, *Matthew Looney, the Boy from the Moon*. In college Jenny expects to major in physics or astronomy.

Luke J chose the word "family" as his favorite noun. To explain, he wrote a moving portrait of a close-knit family. Five times in the last ten years the family has moved. Luke's father works overseas for months at a time. Yet, Luke derives stability from his family, despite its fragmented life.

Robert B refuted the old adage, "You can't compare apples and oranges," by writing a tongue-in-cheek comparison of the two fruits. As a result, he wonders about the validity of other pieces of wisdom. He plans to research next "You can't tell a book by its cover" and "Absence makes the heart grow fonder."

Carl G, who has a deaf kid brother, wrote about *Dancing Without Music: Deafness in America*, a book that persuaded him and his parents to introduce young Danny to other deaf people as a way to help the boy find an identity as a hearing-impaired person.

Karen S would like to interview Margaret Mead. Being a young woman, Karen looks ahead to the problems of balancing a family and a career. Since reading Mead's autobiography, *Blackberry Winter*, Karen thinks that Mead would have some sound advice to give her.

Gary K wrote about Steven, his mentally retarded brother. All his life, Gary has been Steven's fun committee, psychiatrist-at-home, and teacher. Gary wept recently after he found Steven eating pineapple from a can. It had taken Gary six weeks to teach Steven how to use a can-opener.

Jordana S said that her favorite cartoon character, Linus from "Peanuts," has qualities that she envies: stability, self-confidence, and grace under pressure. As for his security blanket, "Linus carries it to show that he's secure enough not to worry what others think about his carrying it."

Joanna L named Miss B, her elementary school gym teacher, as a significant person in her life. Miss B so intimidated Joanna that "even today the smell of a gymnasium and the sight of orange mats stimulate feelings of terror and dread."

What Would You Like to Tell Us About Yourself?

Perhaps the toughest writing assignment is the one without a suggested topic. "Tell us anything you'd like, anything to help us know you better," says the application.

> We would welcome any comments you care to make about yourself.

> The essay is an important part of your application. It will help admissions officers gain a more complete picture of you. Use the essay to tell about yourself.

> If there is anything else you would like to tell us about you, please explain on an additional sheet.

> Please use this page to give us any information you think would be helpful to us as we consider your application.

> The purpose of this application is to help us learn about you. Is there additional information we should know which will help us to make an informed decision?

> To better understand you, what else should we know?

Without restrictions, you may literally send in anything. Starting from scratch, you can cook up a totally new piece of writing. Or you may submit a poem, a story, or a paper you've written for school or for yourself. Applicants who have written for publications often send samples of their writing. But if you include a previously written piece, don't just pull it from your files and throw it in the envelope. Carefully explain on a new cover page what it is and why you chose it.

DO

- Pick something important—something that matters to you.
- Consider explaining anything unusual that has influenced your school or home life.
- Use a style of writing that sounds like you.
- Write the sort of piece (e.g., essay, poem, internal monologue) you've written successfully in the past.

DON'T

- Don't turn down the college's invitation to write more about yourself.
- Don't put on airs or try to impress the college. Be yourself.
- Don't repeat what you've written elsewhere on your application.
- Don't try to use a form or style of writing for the first time unless you have a record of successful writing experiments.
- Don't write the essay—or any other part of your application—the night before it's due.

Another word of caution: Try to avoid submitting a reheated essay, one you've written for another application. A college which asks an open-ended question won't appreciate an essay entitled "My Most Significant Academic Experience" or "I'd like to spend an evening with . . . . " Naturally, you can use bits and pieces from your other college essays, but rework your material, disguise it, change its focus—do all you can to keep the college from suspecting that you're sending in a secondhand sample of your work. In a pinch you may, of course, need to send the same essay to two or more colleges. Or your essay may be so good you feel compelled to use it again. In either case, courteously tell the second or third college what you have done and why. Your decency will be appreciated.

Answers That Worked

Bonnie W asserted that writing the college essay helped her sort out her feelings about herself. She has finally accepted the fact that she is a non-conformist. "I used to run with the 'in' crowd," she wrote, "but now I don't give a damn. I can breathe."

Lillian S, a student of karate, wrote about how it feels to break a board with her bare hand. Writing about karate, she said, has heightened her concentration as she trains to earn a black belt.

Kevin B wrote a funny piece on being a New Yorker. On a recent trip to Massachusetts with the school band, his overnight host expected him to come equipped with a switchblade and chains. The folks in the Bay State seemed disappointed by his "normal" behavior and appearance.

Jenny J wrote a collection of fables, each concluding with a moral or maxim to illustrate a strongly held conviction. One story ended, "Be satisfied with who you are." Another, "Don't turn your back on anyone in pursuit of power."

Pitfalls to Avoid

Trying to Impress

Colleges ask for an essay largely because they want to get to know you. If you give them only what you think they want, you're being dishonest, posing as someone you are not. An imposter, for example, may try to pass himself or herself off as a seriously committed poet. But if the rest of the application makes no reference to writing poetry, working on publications, or taking poetry courses, admissions officials may question the validity of the applicant's claim. Therefore, it often makes sense to choose a subject that explains or amplifies something that appears elsewhere on the application.

On the other hand, don't hesitate to write on a personal subject that adds a new piece to your portrait. Just make it honest. Don't invent fiction that poses as fact. If you're not fascinated by politics, don't write on a political topic. If you don't thrive on art and music and books, don't try to pass yourself off as a humanist. Almost any topic will do, in fact, as long as it portrays the true you.

Trying to Include Everything

Don't expect to write an autobiography in 300 to 500 words. Yes, you can cover the highlights, but you won't reveal what lies below the surface—the facts that distinguish you from hundreds of other applicants. Besides, many of the highlights of your life already appear in other parts of the application—in your list of activities, travels, and interests. Therefore, don't use the "what-I-did-in-high-school-and-what-I-learned-from-it" approach. It's common and uninspired.

It's far better to focus on one topic, to show the depth of your feeling and thought in one very small area. Focusing on a single area may be tough when you've done a lot with your life. But by targeting one activity you can show how hard you've thrown yourself into it. You can also include specific details about yourself, details which make you more distinctive.

Boasting

Since most of us have been taught not to brag and boast, we usually don't puff ourselves up too much. We don't want to appear conceited. Yet, if you don't tell the college that you are a gourmet cook, a whiz at fixing stereos, or an ace rock-climber, who will? The problem, though, is that self-impressed people rarely impress others. So, if you're good at something, tell the college, of course, but don't shout. A champion with a touch of reserve or a sense of humor is always more endearing than a braggart.

One high school senior named Eliot, evidently dazzled by his own musical achievement, didn't realize how immodest he sounded when he declared, "My extraordinary talent and accomplishments in the field of music are sufficiently noteworthy to warrant my inclusion in the highly-exclusive all-county orchestra." Although Eliot may deserve respect for his musicianship, he could probably use a lesson in modesty.

Actually, modesty is rather easy to learn. Just say that you consider yourself lucky to have great talent. Or tell how you've struggled to attain success, then add that you're still trying to do better. For instance, Susan, another exceptional musician, wrote, "As a violinist, I have discovered wonderful feelings of accomplishment, surpassed only by the knowledge that this is only the beginning of a lifetime's experience."

The "Jock" Essay

Admissions personnel are rarely impressed by the so-called "jock" essay, the one which predictably tells the reader what you learned from being first-string left tackle or playing goalie on the field hockey team. Every reasonably successful athlete has learned self-discipline, courage, and sportsmanship on the field. If a sport has truly been a crucial part of your life, your essay will have to show how. But you'll have to do more than write the typical story of how you won the race or how losing it helped to build your character.

Raymond, an all-star high school baseball player, wrote an essay about his career on the diamond. But instead of summarizing his pitching and hitting records, he wrote a tongue-in-cheek analysis of his statistics. He said, for instance, that his 1.87 e.r.a. was close to 50% of his batting average (.400). "Does that make me only half as good a pitcher as I am a slugger?" he asked rhetorically. He went on to say that he registered ten strikeouts in one game. That same week he struck out with three different girls. "Am I a better pitcher or a better boyfriend?" he wondered.

In a more serious essay, Linda, a varsity tennis player, described the thoughts going through her head during a match. While she should have been concentrating on beating her opponent, she thought about doing her calculus homework, about the school carnival she helped to organize, about taking her driver's test, about an oil painting she was working on, and about attending a weekend retreat with her church youth group. Although Linda lost the tennis match, she wrote a winning essay that revealed not only her interests and concerns, but also told of her anxiety about trying to do too much and ending up doing nothing well.

The Travelogue

Travel is probably the most popular subject chosen for a college essay. Applicants seem extraordinarily fond of turning their travels into "significant experience" stories. But while travel has virtues galore, writing about it can be perilous. Colleges take a dim view of essays that are little more than personal narratives of "My Trip to Hawaii" or "What I Learned While Biking in Belgium." Even worse are those glorified itineraries, essays that list in order the national parks or countries you visited on that teen tour last summer.

But an admissions committee will welcome a well-written travel piece that reveals your personal and unique response to the experience. For instance, Barry, a tourist in Europe last year, wrote of awakening in the middle of the night in Switzerland and peering across the moonlit mountains to the Jungfrau. It was one of those memorable moments, he wrote, when "life's pieces come together"; he'd never been happier. He could not understand exactly why, but he preserved the experience in a sonnet (submitted with his essay) which he had completed as the sun came up the next morning.

Jodi, another European traveler, wrote of the irony she observed in a family trip. Her mother and father were on the verge of separation, but during the family's tour through Italy, France, and Spain, her parents seemed to make peace. How odd, Jodi thought, to leave home in order to preserve the home.

Barry and Jodi's travel pieces worked because they focused on a particular moment or idea. If all you can say, however, is that travel has broadened your life, made you more well-rounded or more tolerant of others, you'd be better off keeping the memories of your unforgettable trip in a scrapbook.

Straining to Be Funny

Although essays that contain gimmicks like puns, coined words, slang, and fractured English may attract attention among thousands of conventionally written essays, your cleverness could tarnish your otherwise sterling application. Like an ill-timed wisecrack, it could miss the funny bone of a weary admissions dean. That doesn't mean that humor is out of place in an application essay. On the contrary. Readers will relish something playful, satirical or whimsical. But don't overdo it. Tread lightly and cautiously with jokes and sarcasm. Humor is very difficult to write well. What you and your friends may think is uproarious in the school lunchroom could fall on its face in the admissions office.

Give your wit a workout in the application, but test your humor on an impartial adult before you send it to a college. If you're not usually a funny person, don't try to become one on your application. David Lettermans are not made overnight.

Being Too Creative

Some colleges, hoping to draw out the uniqueness in your personality, make unusual requests on their applications. Penn asks you to send page 217 of your autobiography, Stanford wants to know what you'd stow in a time capsule, and Dartmouth tells you to write your own question and answer it. Bates asks you to write your own recommendation, while Goucher instructs you to invent something and discuss it.

Such questions aren't meant to catch you. They don't have correct answers. It doesn't matter at Goucher whether you invent a cure for AIDS or a digital belt buckle. Colleges just want to get to know you better and see if you can think and write. When Swarthmore asks you to travel through time, choose a stopping place, and explain your choice, they're not interested in your mastery of history—your transcript contains that information. They'd rather hear why you picked the Jazz Age or the day Mt. Vesuvius exploded.

An off-beat question doesn't obligate you to write an off-beat answer. Just make your answer sound like you. If you are naturally creative, write a creative piece. But unusual creativity is not essential. You can bring out your best in a sober, sensitive, and sincere essay as well. You'll never be penalized for a clearly written, thoughtful essay that accurately reflects your beliefs and feelings.

Being Too Ordinary

While an odd-ball essay question may inspire quirky answers, an ordinary question shouldn't tempt you to write an ordinary response. A typical question—this one from Bates—might ask, "What personal or academic experiences were particularly rewarding for you (a project, teacher, piece of writing or research, a particular course of study)?" Although the question suggests that you write about school, you are free to pick any experience whatever. You may be better off, in fact, if you choose a unique personal experience. Finding you own topic demonstrates your initiative. You can also bet that most other people will play it safe and write about school. Don't run with the crowd. Take the less-travelled route, and choose a topic that is distinctively yours.

As you think about your essay, keep asking two key questions: What's unique about me? and What do I want my reader to think of me? You might begin, for example, by simply making a list of adjectives that describe what you like about yourself. Then make another list of what you dislike. Don't worry if the second list is longer than the first—most people are pretty hard on themselves. Study these lists for patterns, contradictions, and unusual combinations. How, for instance, might a person who "doesn't rest until a job is done" also consider himself "lazy"? Then rank the qualities in the order of importance. Which quality would you be most reluctant to give up? Which would you relinquish first? Which are you proudest of? Which would you most like to change? While you're answering such questions, you are beginning to define yourself and figure out what makes you unique. Think also of anecdotes or stories that illustrate each quality, as though you'd been asked for proof that you are "mysterious," "flirtatious" or "living in the past." Perhaps your best story could ultimately be developed into an essay that shows the true you.

You might also distinguish yourself from others by answering questions such as these:

What are you good at?

What are you trying to get better at?

What has been your greatest success? Your greatest failure?

What three words would you like engraved on your tombstone?

What is your strongest conviction?

What would you do with a million dollars?

If the world were to end one year from today, how would you spend your remaining time?

Generating thoughtful responses to often whimsical questions might trigger any number of possibilities for your essay.

Composing Your Essay

You probably won't get out of high school without writing some sort of essay on *Macbeth*—or if not *Macbeth*, then on the Great Depression or dissecting a frog. By this time in your life, in fact, you've probably written enough essays to fill a large book. When writing those essays, perhaps you sat down, spilled your thoughts onto the page and handed in your paper. Or maybe you wrote a rough draft and went back later to reorganize and rephrase your

ideas. Possibly, you thought out ahead of time what you wanted to say and prepared a list of ideas or an outline. Maybe you used a combination of methods, varying them from time to time according to the purpose and importance of the essay.

Everyone who writes uses a process of some kind. Some processes seem to work better than others. The variations are endless, and no one process is always better than another. The best one—the one you should use—is the process which helps you do your best writing.

Warming Up

The quality of your essay may depend in part on your warm-ups. Since writing forces you to do strenuous mental work, a warming-up period can help to prepare you. Once you know the question on your application, you're likely to start thinking about your response. Make lists. Toss ideas back and forth in your head. Tell someone what you're thinking. Keep a notebook in your pocket because a great thought may hit you at any time. Keep pen and pad by your bed to record a 4 A.M. inspiration. Do some free-writing. Think hard about what you want your readers to think of you. In short, do something to activate your writing muscles.

Some people call this part of the process "pre-writing." You might call it getting yourself "psyched." Whatever the name, it's the time you spend testing possible topics and tuning up to write. It may even include finding a quiet, uncluttered place to work, gathering together a pen, paper, a typewriter or word-processor and a dictionary. And it involves laying aside many hours of time for solitary, unhurried work.

Warm-up time should also include a search for the point, or focus, of your essay. Identifying a topic isn't enough. Now you must focus on what you'll say about it. The sharper your focus, the better. You can't expect to write everything in a 300- to 500-word essay.

Maybe the surest way to narrow your topic is to begin writing. If your essay seems dull and disappointing after a couple of paragraphs, you're probably being too vague, too impersonal, or both. But keep at it as long as you can, for you may discover the point of your essay at any time. Be prepared, however, to face the fact that you could write yourself into a dead end. Not every topic will work. If you're blocked on all sides, you have no choice but to grit your teeth, turn to another topic, and start over.

Writing the Essay

By the time some writers begin to compose their essays, they more or less know that they'll reach their destination using the famous five-paragraph essay formula. Other writers will start more tentatively, knowing their general direction, but not find-ing the specific route until they get there.

Neither method excels the other, for much depends on the subject matter and intent of the writer. The first method follows a simple, clear-cut formula, which may not win a prize for originality but can help to turn a muddle of ideas into a model of clar-ity. It has a beginning, a middle, and an end. You can call on it any time you need to set ideas in order. Each step has its place and purpose.

The Five-Paragraph Essay Formula

Title

Introduction

Body: Point 1

Point 2

Point 3

Conclusion

In reality, however, writers rarely follow "The For-mula." In fact, you may never see a formula essay in print. Yet a majority of college essays, even those which take circuitous paths between the beginning and end, adhere to some sort of three-step organi-zation. In the *introduction* writers tell readers what they plan to tell them. In the *body* they tell them. And in the *conclusion* they tell them what they told them. Since all writers differ, however, you find end-less variations within each step.

The Introduction: Grabbing the Reader's Interest

The best essays usually begin with something catchy, something to lure the readers into the piece. Basically, it's a hook—a phrase, sentence, or idea that will nab the readers' interest so completely that they'll keep on reading almost in spite of them-selves. Once you've hooked your readers, you can lead them anywhere.

1. Start with an incident, real or invented, that leads the readers gracefully to the point of your essay.

2. State a provocative idea in an ordinary way or an ordinary idea in a provocative way. Either will spark the readers' interest.

3. Use a quotation—not necessarily a famous one. Shakespeare's or your grandmother's will do, as long as the quote relates to the topic of your essay.

4. Knock down a commonly held assumption or define a word in a new and surprising way.

5. Ask an interesting question or two which you will answer in your essay.

In any collection of good essays you'd no doubt find other worthy techniques for writing a compelling opening. Even a direct statement that introduces your topic may be appropriate. Whatever your open-

ing, though, it must fit your writing style and per-sonality. Work hard at getting it right, but at the same time, not too hard. A forced opening may obscure the point of your essay, or worse, dim the reader's enthusiasm for finding out what you have to say. Furthermore, an opening that comprises, say, more than a quarter of your essay is probably too long.

The Body: Putting the Pieces Together

Order is important. What should come first? sec-ond? third? In most writing the best order is the clearest order, the arrangement your readers can follow with the least effort.

There is no single way to get from the beginning of a piece of writing to the end. The route you take will vary according to what you want to do to your read-ers. Whether you want to shock, sadden, inspire, move, or entertain them, each purpose will have its own best order. In story-telling, the events are often placed in the sequence they occur. But to explain a childhood memory or define who you are, to stand up for women's rights or describe a poignant moment—each may take some other kind of arrangement. No one plan is superior to another, provided you have a valid reason for using it.

The plan that fails is the aimless one, the one in which ideas are arranged solely on the basis of the order in which they popped into your head. To guard against aimlessness, rank your ideas in order of importance either before you start or while you're writing drafts. Although your first idea may turn out to be your best, you probably should save it for later in your essay. Giving it away at the start is self-defeating. To hold your readers' interest, it's better to work toward your best point, not away from it. If you have, say, three main points to make, save the strongest for last. Launch your essay with your sec-ond-best, and tuck your least favorite between the other two.

In a typical college essay, a body consisting of three sections will be just about right. Why three? Mainly because three is a number that works. When you can make three statements about a subject, you probably know what you're talking about. One is too simple, two is still pretty shallow, three is thought-ful. Psychologically, three creates a sense of whole-ness, like the beginning, middle, and end of a story. Each point doesn't necessarily receive equal treat-ment. You might manage one point with a single paragraph, while the others get more. But each point has to be distinctive. Your third point mustn't be a rerun of the first or second.

It shouldn't be difficult to break the main point of most essays into at least three secondary points, regardless of their topic or form. A narrative essay, for example, naturally breaks into a beginning, mid-dle, and end. A process is likely to have at least three steps, some of which may be broken into sub-steps. In an essay of comparison and contrast, you ought to be able to find at least three similarities and differences to write about. A similar division into thirds applies to essays of cause and effect, definition, description, and certainly to essays of argumentation.

The Conclusion: Giving a Farewell Gift

When you reach the end of your essay, you can lift your pen off the page and be done with it. Or you can present your readers with a little something to remember you by: a gift—an idea to think about, a line to chuckle over, a memorable phrase or quotation. Whatever you give, the farewell gift must fit the content, style, and mood of your essay. A tacked-on ending will puzzle, not delight, your readers.

Some writers think that endings are more important than beginnings. After all, by the time readers arrive at your conclusion, the memory of your introduction may have already begun to fade. A stylish ending, though, will stick with readers and influence their feelings not only about your essay, but also about its writer. Therefore, choose a farewell gift thoughtfully. Be particular. Send your reader off feeling good, laughing, weeping, angry, thoughtful or thankful, but above all, glad that they stayed with your essay to the end.

1. Have some fun with your ending. Readers may remember your sense of humor long after forgetting other details about you.

2. End with an apt quotation, drawn either from the essay itself or from elsewhere.

3. Create a sense of completeness by recalling something you said earlier in your essay.

4. Fill in what took place between the end of a story and the present time.

5. Tell the readers how an unresolved issue was settled.

6. Ask a rhetorical question that springs naturally from your essay.

7. Speculate on what might occur in the future.

Some essays don't need an extended conclusion. When they're over, they're over. But at the end of an essay the readers should feel that they've arrived somewhere. In a sense, your whole essay has prepared them to arrive at a certain destination. Your introduction should have told them approximately where you're taking them. En route you developed ideas that moved them toward the conclusion. And at the end they shouldn't be at all surprised to find that they are there. You don't want a reader to say, "Oh, now I see what you've been driving at."

When choosing an ending let your instinct guide you. A tacked-on ending is, well—tacky. Always ask whether your ending maintains the spirit and style of the whole essay. An ending to avoid, though, is

the summary. Trust your readers to know what you wrote in your two- or three-page essay. To say everything again is not only boring, it could be annoying. Your essay isn't a textbook. A chapter review isn't necessary. On the other hand, a quick general reiteration of the essay's theme and a memorable tag line could drive home your essay's main point. It's worth trying.

Presenting Your Essay
Appearance

Would you like to hear a sad but true story? It's about Robert, a high school senior, a good student likely to be accepted wherever he applied. He wrote his essay with care but sent it in looking as though he'd stored it in his jeans for a week. Robert was rejected. The admissions people concluded that Robert couldn't be seriously interested in their college if he submitted such a sloppy-looking piece of work.

Obviously, there's a lesson in Robert's tale: Don't send in an essay that looks anything less than gorgeous. Present your essay with pride. That is, make it neat, crisp, easy-to-read, accurately typed, in all respects as close to perfect as it can be. Its appearance speaks for you as clearly as its contents.

Unless the college asks for an essay written in your own hand, type it, preferably on an electric or electronic typewriter with a fresh ribbon. A word processor is fine, too, provided your printer is letter-quality or close to it. Dot-matrix prepared copy is often hard to read unless the ribbon is brand new. A handwritten essay needs to be as legible as you can make it. If your script is flawed, then print. Keep a bottle of white-out handy. In short, do all you can to make your essay easy on the eyes.

Use high-quality white paper, 8½ by 11 inches. Separate continuous computer paper into sheets and remove the perforated edges. Double-space for ease of reading. Center the text on the page, and leave at least a one-inch margin all around. Number your pages. If you're asked to write more than one essay, designate which is which with the question number or topic on the application.

Many colleges give you a word limit. They mean business, so stick to the number of words they ask for. It's permissible to go over or under by, say, ten percent, but more may count against you. Some applications provide a few inches of space for your answer. Rather than fill up every square millimeter with type or with miniscule writing, cut words from your piece. What you may lose in content, you'll make up in legibility. In a pinch, you can reduce the size of your type with a photocopying machine and glue the reduced version neatly onto the application.

It goes without saying that cross-outs and last-minute insertions using arrows, asterisks, paragraph markers or carets are not acceptable. Don't change anything on your final copy unless you are prepared to retype the whole page. Aim to make your essay letter-perfect. In all respects, neatness counts.

Proofreading

To proofread well, you need fresh eyes. Therefore, your best proofreading method is to let someone else do it. Xerox five copies of your essay and have five reliable readers scour your piece for flaws in grammar, punctuation, and spelling.

But if you're on your own, put your essay aside for a few days, if possible. Then read it slowly, once for the sense of it and once for mechanics. Read it a line at a time, keeping a hawklike watch on every letter, word, and mark of punctuation. You might even cut a narrow horizontal window out of a spare sheet of paper. Move the window over your essay a line at a time. Concentrate on that line only, reading it once forward and once back. On the backward reading you'll lose the sense of the meaning, allowing you to keep your mind on the spelling.

In Addition to Your Essay

Some colleges want more than an essay from you. They ask for paragraph-long responses to any number of questions—why you chose that particular college, which extracurricular activity you like the most, your favorite book, career plans, honors, and so on. Whatever your answers, write them with the same care as your essay. Start with drafts. Revise and edit. Use your most interesting writing style. Since you're usually limited to less than half a dozen lines, get to the point promptly and express yourself concisely. Be attentive to the sound and appearance of your responses.

Some questions invite you to reply with a list of some kind—travels, prizes, alumni connections. If you can, however, respond with a thoughtful, well-developed paragraph. Not only will your answer be more interesting to read, you'll have the opportunity to highlight the items that matter. Moreover, the reader will note that you took the trouble to write a coherent, lucid paragraph and that you have more than just a college essay in your writing repertoire.

When an application asks, "Is there additional information we should know?" try to reply with an emphatic "Yes!" Since your essay won't have told them everything, grab this chance to explain more of yourself or to show your interests and accomplishments. Applicants frequently send their creative work—a short story, a collection of poetry, articles written for the school paper, slides of artwork, photos—almost anything that fits into an envelope or small package. Don't overdo it, though. One carefully chosen term paper will suffice to reveal your love of history. One chapter of your novel is more than admissions people will have time to read, anyway. Quality, not quantity, counts.

Whatever you send, prepare it with the same high standards you used on your essay. Written material should be typed, photos and artwork should be attractively displayed and clearly explained or captioned. Before you mail a tape of your music or a video of your gymnastic performance, wind it to the starting spot. Make certain that it works and that it contains only what you want the college to hear or see. Also, submit only a few minutes' worth of material—not your whole concert or routine.

Your Friend, the Mailman

What a glorious feeling it will be to turn your application and essay over to the U.S. Postal Service. Before you do, however, make photocopies. Once in the mail, you'll never see them again. Then sit back and rejoice. Pat yourself on the back for a job well done. Relax and wait for the momentous day when the postman brings you the *fat* envelope—the one containing information about housing, courses, freshman orientation and, of course, the letter which begins, "It gives me great pleasure to tell you that you have been accepted in the class of . . . . "

If you would like more information and step-by-step guidance in writing your college application essay, see *Write Your Way into College: Writing a Successful College Application Essay.* It was written by George Ehrenhaft, who wrote this chapter, and is also published by Barron's Educational Series, Inc.

LOOKING FOR STUDY STRATEGIES THAT WORK? HAVE WE GOT SECRETS FOR YOU!

How to Beat Test Anxiety and Score Higher on Your Exams

$3.95, Can. $5.95

Every test taker should have this guide to better grades and more self-confidence. It shows how test-taking skills can be learned, and how memorization, familiarity with question types and basic preparation techniques can improve performance on tests.

Student Success Secrets

$6.95, Can. $9.95

From motivating forces to confidence boosters and basic academic skills, the secrets to being a success in school are revealed! Using the techniques of self-hypnosis, this book helps students achieve their educational pursuits.

Study Tactics *$6.95, Can. $9.95*

An easy-to-follow plan for sound study habits. Included are pointers for improving writing skills, increasing reading speed, reviewing for exams, and much more.

Better Grades in College With Less Effort *$5.95, Can. $8.95*

Super shortcuts to great grades! These legitimate methods for saving time and minimizing hassles make it easy to cope with college work loads.

Study Tips: How to Study Effectively and Get Better Grades *$4.95, Can. $6.95*

A guide to better skills for achieving higher grades. It helps organize study time; fosters quick memory recall; increases reading speed and comprehension; and much more!

Strategies for Taking Tests *$8.95, Can. $12.95*

Designed to boost test scores, this book shows how standardized exams can be mastered through analysis of question types. Each question type is covered in depth, and solid advice for the test taker is offered.

How to Succeed in High School: A Practical Guide to Better Grades

$4.50, Can. $6.95

Comprehensive and easy to follow, this self-help guide leads to success in everything from studying, note making and test taking to preparing for college and careers.

You Can Succeed! The Ultimate Study Guide for Students *$4.95, Can. $6.95*

Encourages students to make a personal pact with themselves for setting goals and achieving them. Topics covered range from Lack of Motivation and Success Habits to Word Power and How to Take Tests.

How to Find What You Want in the Library *$6.95, Can. $10.50*

A lively guide that takes the confusion out of all the library's resources. It presents the easy way to use the card catalogue, locate books and do research for term papers.

BARRON'S EDUCATIONAL SERIES
250 Wireless Boulevard
Hauppauge, New York 11788

In Canada: 195 Allstate Parkway
Markham, Ontario L3R 4T8

Prices subject to change without notice. Books may be purchased at your bookstore, or by mail from Barron's. Enclose check or money order for total amount plus sales tax where applicable and 10% for postage and handling (minimum charge $1.50). All books are paperback editions.